T0305301

DEBT MARKETS AND ANALYSIS

Since 1996, Bloomberg Press has published books for financial professionals on investing, economics, and policy affecting investors. Titles are written by leading practitioners and authorities, and have been translated into more than 20 languages.

The Bloomberg Financial Series provides both core reference knowledge and actionable information for financial professionals. The books are written by experts familiar with the work flows, challenges, and demands of investment professionals who trade the markets, manage money, and analyze investments in their capacity of growing and protecting wealth, hedging risk, and generating revenue.

For a list of available titles, please visit our website at www.wiley.com/go/bloombergpress.

DEBT MARKETS AND ANALYSIS

R. Stafford Johnson

BLOOMBERG PRESS
An Imprint of
WILEY

Cover image: background © Jamie Carroll/iStockphoto; chart courtesy of R. Stafford Johnson
Cover design: C. Wallace

Published by John Wiley & Sons, Inc., Hoboken, New Jersey.
Published simultaneously in Canada.

For general information on our other products and services or for technical support, please contact our Customer Care Department within the United States at (800) 762-2974, outside the United States at (317) 572-3993 or fax (317) 572-4002.

Wiley also publishes its books in a variety of electronic formats. Some content that appears in print may not be available in electronic books. For more information about Wiley products, visit our web site at www.wiley.com.

Library of Congress Cataloging-in-Publication Data:
Johnson, R. Stafford.
Debt markets and analysis / R. Stafford Johnson.
p. cm. -- (Bloomberg financial series)
Includes index.
ISBN 978-1-118-00000-7 (cloth); ISBN 978-1-118-22166-2 (ebk);
ISBN 978-1-118-26024-1 (ebk); ISBN 978-1-118-23543-0 (ebk)
1. Fixed-income securities. 2. Debt. 3. Bonds. 4. Securities. I. Title.
HG4650.J64 2013
332.63'2044--dc23

2012030691

P
10 9 8 7 6 5 4 3 2 1

To my wife, Jan.

Contents

PART III: DEBT DERIVATIVES

Preface

Over the past 20 years, the investment industry has seen stock market and real estate bubbles, the emergence of hedge funds and private equity companies, the globalization of financial markets, the proliferation of derivative securities, and the growth of securitized assets and structured financing. Mirroring these events have been the academic contributions to the investment discipline: the development of capital market theories, the derivation of option pricing models, and the explorations into efficient market theories. The financial events and the academic contributions together point out the challenges in mastering an understanding and developing a knowledge of investments and financial markets. In addition to the innovations in financial instruments, the investment and management of bonds and debt securities by financial and nonfinancial corporations has also experienced significant developments over the past two decades. Bond investors use strategies such as cash-flow matching, immunization, cell matching, contingent immunization, and bond selection based on forecasting yield curve shifts or the narrowing or widening of the quality yield spread. Many corporate borrowers, money managers, intermediaries, and bond portfolio managers have increased their use of futures, options, and swap contracts on debt securities as a hedge against interest rate and credit risk.

Today, managing fixed-income securities in this dynamic and innovative investment environment requires that professionals understand the debt markets and uses for an increasing number of securities, markets, strategies, and methodologies. In this increasingly complex environment, many practitioners manage their securities and portfolios using a Bloomberg terminal. Bloomberg is a computer information and retrieval system providing access to financial and economic data, news, and analytics. Bloomberg terminals are common on most trading floors and are becoming more common in universities where they are used for research, teaching, and managing student investment funds. Bloomberg is also the leader in data and information retrieval and analytical systems applicable to bond investment and management.

The purpose of this book is to provide finance students and professionals with a bond and debt management exposition that will take them from the basic bond investment theories and fundamentals that can be found in many investment books to a more detailed understanding of the markets and strategies. Given the widespread use of the Bloomberg system and its data and analytical systems that can be applied to bonds, this text also includes a detailed description of the Bloomberg system, a listing of many of the analytical functions that can be applied to fixed-income investment and management, and detailed explanations of how Bloomberg information and analytical functions can be applied to the fixed-income and debt market topics covered in the text. It is my hope that the synthesis of fundamental and advanced topics with Bloomberg information and analytics will provide professionals and students of finance with not only a better foundation in understanding the complexities and subtleties of the debt markets, but also with the ability to apply that understanding to real-world investment decisions—to grasp how it is done "on the street."

The book is written for professionals in the investment industry involved in bond and debt management and MBA, MS, and undergraduate finance students. For professionals, the text can be used as a training and instructional source and as a guide on how to apply Bloomberg to debt markets and analysis. As a debt markets text for students, the book is designed for a one-semester debt markets course. The Bloomberg material is presented in boxes in each chapter, and Chapter 2 provides an overview and guide to the Bloomberg system.

Content

All securities can be evaluated in terms of the characteristics common to all assets: value, return, risk, maturity, marketability, liquidity, and taxability. In Part One, debt securities are analyzed in terms of these characteristics. Chapter 1 presents an overview of the investment environment, examining the nature of financial assets, the types of securities that exist, the nature and types of markets that securities give rise to, and the general characteristics of assets. Chapter 2 presents an overview and guide to the Bloomberg system. With this background, the next four chapters examine bonds in terms of their characteristics, with exhibit boxes included in each chapter that identify how Bloomberg information and analytical screens can be used to evaluate bonds. Chapter 3 looks at how debt instruments are valued and how their rates of return are measured; Chapter 4 examines the level and structure of interest rates and shows how such factors as market expectations, economic conditions, and risk-return preferences are important in determining the level and structure of rates; Chapter 5 describes three types of bond risk—default, call, and market risk—and introduces two measures of bond volatility—duration and convexity. In Chapter 6, bond analysis is extended from evaluation to investment and management by examining a number of active and passive bond management strategies.

Part Two delineates the different debt securities and their markets in terms of the rules, participants, and forces that govern them, as well as investment strategies related to specific securities. Chapter 7 describes the debt claims of businesses; Chapter 8 looks at the types and markets for government securities—Treasury, federal agencies, municipals, and sovereigns; Chapters 9 examines intermediary securities and investment funds; Chapter 10 examines mortgage-backed and asset-backed securities. In each of these chapters, Bloomberg exhibit boxes are included to explain how Bloomberg screens can be used to access information. Part Three consists of four chapters covering bond derivatives. Chapters 11 and 12 provide overviews of the markets, uses, and pricing of bond and interest rate futures and option contracts. Chapter 13 examines embedded options using a binomial interest rate tree; Chapter 14 covers interest rate and credit default swaps.

The book covers most fixed-income security types and markets, the major theories and models, the practical applications of the models, and cases and empirical studies. The text stresses concepts, model construction, numerical examples, and Bloomberg applications and information sources. The text also includes Bloomberg exercises at the end of each of the chapters. These exercises are designed for practitioners who have access to such terminals at their jobs and for students who have access to Bloomberg terminals either at their universities or possibly through internships they may have at financial companies. It is my hope that the Bloomberg exercises will add depth to your understanding of debt markets and management, as well as an appreciation of the breadth of financial information and analytics provided by the Bloomberg system. On an accompanying website, there are end-of-chapter review questions and problems with accompanying solutions that are provided to reinforce concepts. The site also includes links to videos that explain how to work some of the Bloomberg exercises, Excel spreadsheet programs that can be used to solve a number of the problems, key terms, and chapter PowerPoints. The reader can access the text website by going to www.wiley.com/go/debtmarkets (password: johnson).

The book draws material directly from one of my earlier texts published by Wiley: *Bond Evaluation, Selection, and Management* (Wiley, 2010). The Bloomberg material presented here comes from knowledge picked up from using the terminal (or learned from my students who used Bloomberg) when I was the fund professor for the student equity investment fund and bond investment fund at Xavier University.

Acknowledgments

Many people have contributed to this text. First, I wish to thank Mary Beth Shagena, the O'Conor family, and my other colleagues at Xavier University, who have helped me in many different ways. My appreciation is extended to the editors and staff at John Wiley & Sons, Inc., particularly Bill Falloon, Executive Editor; Steven Kyritz, Senior Production Editor; Judy Howarth, Senior Development Editor; Meg Freeborn, Senior Development Editor; Mary Daniello, Production Manager; and Tiffany Charbonier, who oversaw the book's development and were a continued source of encouragement. My appreciation is also extended to Stephen Isaac, Bloomberg Press, for his support, help, and encouragement on this project.

I also wish to thank my wife Jan, my children, Wendi, Jamey, and Matt, and my grandchildren Bryce, Kendall, and Malin for their support, encouragement, and understanding. I also would like to recognize the pioneers in the development of fixed-income and debt management theory and strategy: Frank Fabozzi, Fischer Black, John Cox, Lawrence Fisher, John Hull, Robert Kolb, Martin Leibowitz, Frederick Macaulay, Robert Merton, Stephen Ross, Mark Rubinstein, and others cited in the pages that follow. Without their contributions, this text could not have been written. Finally, I extend my gratitude to the many people who make up the soul of the Bloomberg system—analysts, programmers, systems experts, reps, and journalists. It is truly a remarkable system.

I encourage you to send your comments and suggestions to me at johnsons@xavier .edu.

R. Stafford Johnson
Xavier University

PART I

Bond Evaluation and Selection

CHAPTER 1

Overview of the Financial System

Real and Financial Assets

Most new businesses begin when an individual or a group of individuals come up with an idea: manufacturing a new type of cell phone, developing land for a future housing subdivision, launching a new Internet company, or exploring for crude oil. To make the idea a commercial reality, though, requires funds that the individual or group generally lacks or personally does not want to commit. Consequently, the fledgling business sells *financial claims or instruments* to raise the funds necessary to buy the capital goods (equipment, land, etc.), as well as the human capital (architects, engineers, lawyers, etc.), needed to launch the project. Technically, such instruments are claims against the income of the business represented by a certificate, receipt, or other legal document. In this process of initiating and implementing the idea, both real and financial assets are therefore created. The *real assets* consist of both the tangible and intangible capital goods, as well as human capital, which are combined with labor to form the business. The business, in turn, transforms the idea into the production and sale of goods or services that will generate a future stream of earnings. The *financial assets,* however, consist of the financial claims on the earnings. Those individuals or institutions that provided the initial funds and resources hold these assets. Furthermore, if the idea is successful, then the new business may find it advantageous to initiate other new projects that it again may finance through the sale of financial claims. Thus, over time, more real and financial assets are created.

The creation of financial claims, of course, is not limited to the business sector. The federal government's expenditures on national defense, entitlements, and infrastructures, and state governments' expenditures on the construction of highways, for example, represent the creation of real assets that these units of government often finance through the sale of financial claims on either the revenue generated from a particular public sector project or from future tax revenues. Similarly, the purchase of a house or a car by a household often is financed by a loan from a savings and loan or commercial bank. The loan represents a claim by the financial institution on a portion of the borrower's future income, as well as a claim on the ownership of the real asset (house or car) in the event the household defaults on its promise.

Modern economies expend enormous amounts of money on real assets to maintain their standards of living. Such expenditures usually require funds that are beyond the levels a business, household, or unit of government has or wants to commit at a given point in time. As a result, to raise the requisite amounts, economic entities sell financial claims. Those buying the financial claims therefore supply funds to the economic entity in return for promises that the entity will provide them with a future flow of income. As such, financial claims can be described as financial assets.

All financial assets provide a promise of a future return to the owners. Unlike real assets, though, financial assets do not depreciate (since they are in the form of certificates or information in a computer file), and they are *fungible,* meaning they can be converted into cash or other assets. There are many different types of financial assets. All of them, though, can be divided into two general categories—equity and debt. Common stock is the most popular form of equity claims. It entitles the holder to dividends or shares in the business's residual profit and participation in the management of the firm, usually indirectly through voting rights. The stock market where existing stock shares are traded is the most widely followed market in the world, and it receives considerable focus in many investment and security analysis texts. The focus of this book, though, is on the other general type of financial asset—debt. Businesses finance more of their real assets and operations with debt than equity, whereas governments and households finance their entire real assets and operations with debt. This chapter provides an overview of the types of debt securities and markets, whereas Part Two provides more detailed analyses.

Types of Debt Claims

Debt claims are loans wherein the borrower agrees to pay a fixed income per period, defined as a coupon or interest, and to repay the borrowed funds, defined as the principal (also called redemption value, maturity value, par value, and face value). Within this broad description, debt instruments can take on many different forms. For example, debt can take the form of a loan by a financial institution. In this case, the terms of the agreement and the contract instrument generally are prepared by the lender/creditor, and the instrument often is nonnegotiable, meaning it cannot be sold to another party. A debt instrument also can take the form of a bond or note, whereby the borrower obtains her loan by selling (also referred to as issuing) contracts or IOUs to pay interest and principal to investors/lenders. Many of these claims, in turn, are negotiable, often being sold to other investors before they mature.

Debt instruments also can differ in terms of the features of the contract: the number of future interest payments, when and how the principal is to be paid (e.g., at maturity—the end of the contract) or spread out over the life of the contract (amortized), and the recourse the lender has should the borrower fail to meet her contractual commitments (i.e., collateral or security). For many debt instruments, standard features include the following:

Term to maturity is the number of years over which the issuer promises to meet the obligations. (Maturity refers to the date that the debt will cease to exist.) Generally, bonds with maturities between 1 and 5 years are considered short term; those with maturities between 5 and 12 years are considered intermediate term; and those with maturities greater than 12 years are considered long term.

Principal is the amount that the issuer/borrower agrees to repay the bondholder/lender.

Coupon rate (or nominal rate) is the rate the issuer/borrower agrees to pay each period. The dollar amount is called the coupon. There are, though, zero-coupon bonds in which the investor earns interest between the price paid and the principal, and floating-rate notes where the coupon rate is reset periodically based on a formula.

Amortization. The principal repayment of a bond can be either repaid at maturity or over the life of the bond. When principal is repaid over the life of the bond, there is a schedule of principal repayments. The schedule is called the amortization schedule. Securities with an amortization schedule are called amortizing securities, whereas securities without an amortized schedule (those paying total principal at maturity) are called nonamortizing securities.

Embedded options. Bonds often have embedded option features in their contracts, such as a call feature giving the issuer the right to buy back the bond from the bondholder before maturity at a specific price—*callable bond.*

Finally, the type of borrower or issuer—business, government, household, or financial institution—can differentiate the debt instruments. Businesses sell three general types of debt instruments, *corporate bonds, medium-term notes,* and *commercial paper,* and borrow from financial institutions, usually with a long-term or intermediate-term loan from commercial banks or insurance companies and with short-term *lines of credit* from banks. The corporate bonds they sell usually pay the buyer/lender coupon interest semiannually and a principal at maturity. For example, a manufacturing company building a \$100 million processing plant might finance the cost by selling 100,000 bonds at a price of \$1,000 per bond, with each bond promising to pay \$50 in interest every June 15 and January 15 for the next 10 years and a principal of \$1,000 at maturity. In general, corporate bonds are long-term securities when they are issued, sometimes secured by specific real assets that bondholders can claim in case the corporation fails to meet its contractual obligation (defaults). Corporate bonds also have a priority of claims over stockholders on the company's earnings and assets in the case of default. Medium-term notes (MTN) issued by a corporation are debt instruments sold through agents on a continuing basis to investors who are allowed to choose from a group of bonds from the same corporation, but with different maturities and features. Such instruments allow corporations flexibility in the way in which they can finance different capital projects. Commercial paper is a short-term claim (less than one year) that usually is unsecured. Typically, commercial paper is sold as a zero-discount note in which the buyer receives interest equal to the difference between the principal and the purchase price. For example, a company might sell paper promising to pay $1,000 at the end of 270 days for $970, yielding a dollar return of $30. Term loans to businesses have original maturities that are intermediate or long term, often with the principal amortized. Like all debt instruments, these loans have a priority of claims on income and assets over equity claims, and the financial institution providing the loan often requires collateral. Finally, lines of credit are short-term loans provided by banks and other financial institutions in which the business can borrow up to a maximum amount of funds from a checking account created for it by the institution.

The federal government sells a variety of financial instruments, ranging from short-term *Treasury bills* to intermediate-term and long-term *Treasury notes* and *Treasury bonds*. These instruments are sold by the Treasury to finance the federal deficit and to refinance current debt. In addition to Treasury securities, agencies of the federal government, such as the Tennessee Valley Authority, and government-sponsored corporations, such as the Federal National Mortgage Association and the Federal Farm Credit Banks, also issue securities, classified as *Federal Agency Securities,* to finance a variety of government programs ranging from the construction of dams to the purchase of mortgages to provide liquidity to mortgage lenders. The agency sector includes securities issued by federal agencies and also federally related institutions, referred to as *government-sponsored enterprises*. Similarly, state and local governments, agencies, and authorities also offer a wide variety of debt instruments, broadly classified as either *general obligation bonds* or *revenue bonds*. The former are bonds financed through general tax revenue, whereas the latter are instruments financed from the revenue from specific state and local government projects and programs.

Finally, there are financial intermediaries such as commercial banks, savings and loans, credit unions, savings banks, insurance companies, and investment funds that provide debt and equity claims. These intermediaries sell financial claims to investors and then use the proceeds to purchase debt and equity claims or to provide direct loans. In general, financial institutions, by acting as intermediaries, control a large number of funds and thus have a significant impact on financial markets. For borrowers, intermediaries are an important source of funds; they buy many of the securities issued by corporations and governments and provide many of the direct loans. For investors, intermediaries create a number of securities for them to include in their short-term and long-term portfolios. These include negotiable certificates of deposit (CDs), bankers' acceptances, mortgage-backed instruments, asset-backed securities, collateralized debt obligations, investment fund shares, annuities, and guaranteed investment contracts.

Financial Markets

Markets are conduits through which buyers and sellers exchange goods, services, and resources. In an economy there are three types of markets: a product market where goods and services are traded, a factor market where labor, capital, and land are exchanged, and a financial market where financial claims are traded. The financial market, in turn, channels the savings of households, businesses, and governments to those economic units needing to borrow.

The financial market can be described as a market for loanable funds. The supply of loanable funds comes from the savings of households, the retained earnings of businesses, and the surpluses of governments; the demand for loanable funds emanates from businesses that need to raise funds to finance their capital purchases of equipment, plants, and inventories; households that need to purchase houses, cars, and other consumer durables; and the Treasury, federal agencies, and municipal governments that need to finance the construction of public facilities, projects, and operations. The exchange of loanable funds from savers to borrowers is done either directly through the selling of financial claims (stock, bonds, commercial paper, etc.) or indirectly through financial institutions.

The financial market facilitates the transfer of funds from *surplus economic units* to *deficit economic units.* A surplus economic unit is an entity whose income from its current production exceeds its current expenditures; it is a saver or net lender. A deficit unit is an entity whose current expenditures exceed its income from its current production; it is a net borrower. Although businesses, households, and governments fluctuate from being deficit units in one period to surplus units in another period, on average, households tend to be surplus units, whereas businesses and government units tend to be deficit units. A young household usually starts as a deficit unit as it acquires homes and cars financed with mortgages and auto loans. In its midlife, the household's income usually is higher and its mortgage and other loans are often paid; at that time the household tends to become a surplus unit, purchasing financial claims. Finally, near the end of its life, the household lives off the income from its financial claims. In contrast, businesses tend to invest or acquire assets that cost more than the earnings they retain. As a result, businesses are almost always deficit units, borrowing or selling bonds and stocks; furthermore, they tend to remain that way throughout their entire life. Similarly, the federal government's expenditures on defense, education, and welfare have more often exceeded its revenues from taxes. Thus, the federal government, as well as most state and local governments, tend to be deficit units.

Types of Financial Markets

Financial markets can be classified in terms of whether the market is for new or existing claims (primary or secondary market); for short-term or long-term instruments (money or capital market); for direct or indirect trading between deficit and surplus units (direct or intermediary market); for domestic or foreign securities; and for immediate, future, or optional delivery (cash, futures, or options markets).

Primary and Secondary Markets

The *primary market* is the market where financial claims are created. It is the market in which new securities are sold for the first time. Thus, the sale of new government securities by the U.S. Treasury to finance a government deficit, or a $500 million bond issue by Duke Energy to finance the construction of electrical generating plant, is an example of a security transaction occurring in the primary market. The principal function of the primary market is to raise the funds needed to finance investments in new plants, equipment, inventories, homes, roads, and the like—it is where capital formation begins.

The *secondary market* is the market for the buying and selling of existing assets and financial claims. Its economic function is to provide marketability—ease or speed in trading a security. Given the accumulation of financial claims over time, the volume of trading on the secondary market far exceeds the volume in the primary market. The buying and selling of existing securities is done primarily through a network of brokers and dealers who operate through organized security exchanges, the over-the-counter market, and electronic communication networks. Brokers and dealers serve the function of bringing buyers and sellers together by finding opposite positions or by taking positions in a security. By definition, *brokers* are agents who bring security buyers and sellers together for a commission. *Dealers,* in turn, provide markets for investors to buy and sell securities by taking a temporary position in a security; they buy from investors who want to sell and sell to those who want to buy. Dealers receive compensation in terms of the spread between the *bid price* at which they buy securities and *asked price* at which they sell securities. Whereas brokers and dealers serve the function of bringing buyers and sellers together, exchanges serve the function of linking brokers and dealers together to buy and sell existing securities. In the United States, there is the New York Stock Exchange (NYSE) Euronext, as well as regional organized exchanges. Outside the United States, there are major exchanges in such cities as London, Tokyo, Hong Kong, Singapore, Sydney, and Paris. In addition to organized exchanges, a large number of existing securities and a large proportion of bonds are traded on the over-the-counter (OTC) market. In linking traders, exchanges and the OTC markets operate through humans, electronically, or both. Finally, there are *third markets,* in which exchange-listed securities are traded on the OTC market, and a *fourth market,* in which there is direct trading between financial institutions and not through the exchange and OTC markets.

New York Stock Exchange

The NYSE was formed in 1792 by a group of merchants who wanted to trade notes and bonds. Since then, it has grown to an exchange in which stocks and a limited number of bonds, exchange-traded funds (ETFs), and other securities are traded. The NYSE and a number of other organized exchanges provide a continuous market. A continuous market attempts to have constant trading in a security. This is accomplished by having *specialists* or *designated market makers* (DMMs). Specialists and

DMMs are dealers who are part of the exchange and who are required by the exchange to take opposite positions in a security if conditions dictate. Under a specialist system, the exchange board assigns a specific security to a specialist to deal. In this role, a specialist acts by buying the stock from sellers at low bid prices and selling to buyers at higher asked prices. Specialists and DMMs quote a bid price to investors when selling the security and an asked price to investors interested in buying. They hope to profit from the difference between the bid and asked prices; that is, *the bid-ask spread.*

In April 2007, the NYSE became part of *NYSE Euronext,* a holding company created by combining the NYSE Group, Inc. and Euronext N.V. NYSE Euronext can be described as a transatlantic exchange group that brings together six equities exchanges and six derivatives exchanges, providing physical and electronic trading in stocks, bonds, and derivatives. In the United States, NYSE Euronext includes the NYSE physical exchange and NYSE Arca. NYSE Arca is a fully electronic stock exchange, trading more than 8,000 exchange-listed equity securities. NYSE Arca's trading platform links traders to multiple U.S. market centers and provides customers with fast electronic execution and open, direct, and anonymous market access. NYSE Arca's functions are based on price-time priority system.[1]

Over-the-Counter Market

The OTC market is an informal exchange for the trading of stocks, corporate and municipal bonds, investment fund shares, asset-backed securities, and Treasury and federal agency securities. It can be described as a fragmented, noncentralized market of brokers and dealers linked to each other by a computer, telephone, and telex communications system. To trade, dealers must register with the Securities and Exchange Commission (SEC). As dealers, they can quote their own bid and asked prices on the securities they deal, and as brokers, they can execute a trade with a dealer providing a quote. The securities traded on the OTC market are those in which a dealer decides to take a position. Dealers on the OTC market range from regional brokerage houses making a market in a local corporation's stocks or bonds, to large financial companies, such as Merrill Lynch, making markets in Treasury securities, to investment bankers dealing in the securities they had previously underwritten, to dealers in federal agency securities and municipal bonds. Like the specialist on the organized exchanges, each dealer maintains an inventory in a security and quotes a bid and an asked price at which she is willing to buy and sell. Initially, the *National Association of Securities Dealers* (NASD) regulated OTC trading. In July 2007, the *Financial Industry Regulatory Authority* (FINRA), the largest independent regulator for all securities firms doing business in the United States, consolidated NASD and the member regulation, enforcement, and arbitration functions of the NYSE. Even though no physical exchange exists, communications among brokers and dealers takes place through a computer system known as the *National Association of Securities Dealers Automated Quotation System* (*Nasdaq*). Nasdaq is an information system in which current bid-ask quotes of dealers are offered, and also a system that sends brokers' quotes to dealers, enabling them to close trades.[2]

Electronic Trading Market

There are several other types of secondary market trading for stock. For example, the NYSE features both a physical auction convened by DMMs and a completely automated auction that includes algorithmic quotes from DMMs and other participants. As noted, NYSE Arca is an electronic stock exchange, trading more than 8,000 exchange-listed (Nasdaq included) equity securities. NYSE Euronext also has ArcaEdge, which is an all-electronic matching system to trade OTC stocks. The ArcaEdge platform offers best-price executions based on liquidity, transparency, speed, and anonymity. There are also other *electronic communication network* (ECN) systems provided by the OTC markets, regional exchanges, and exchanges in other countries. The crossing network systems allow institutional investors to cross order, matching buy and sell orders directly via computers.

Secondary Market for Bonds

The secondary market for bonds in the United States and throughout the world is not centralized, but rather is part of the OTC market. As noted, the OTC consists of a network of noncentralized or fragmented market makers who provide bid and offer quotes for each issue in which they participate. There are some corporate bonds that are listed on physical exchanges. Such bonds are sometimes said to be trading in the "Bond Room." Although they may be listed, they are more likely to be traded via dealers on the OTC market than on the exchange. There is also a transition to electronic trading. For example, NYSE Euronext recently began offering an all-electronic platform for trading NYSE bonds based on price-time priority system. There are also developing multidealer systems that allow customers to execute bond trades from multiple quotes. The systems display the best bid or offer prices of those posted by all dealers. The participating dealers usually act as the principal in the transaction. There are also developing single-dealer systems that allow investors to execute transactions directly with the specific dealers desired.

Direct and Intermediate Financial Markets

In addition to dividing the markets for financial instruments into primary and secondary, the markets can also be classified in terms of being either part of the direct financial market or the intermediary financial market.

Direct Financial Market

The *direct financial market* is where surplus units purchase claims issued by the ultimate deficit unit. This market includes the trading of stocks, corporate bonds, Treasury securities, federal agency securities, and municipal bonds. The claims traded in the direct financial market are referred to as *primary securities.*[3]

As is the case with many security markets, the direct financial market can be divided into primary and secondary markets. The secondary market for direct financial claims takes place in both the organized exchanges and the OTC market just discussed. In the primary market, new securities are sold either in a negotiated market or an open market. In a *negotiated market,* the securities are issued to one or just a few economic entities under a private contract. Such sales are referred to as a *private placement.* In an open market transaction, the securities are sold to the public at large. The key participant in an *open market trade* is the *investment banker.* The investment banker is a middleperson or matchmaker who, for a fee or share in the trading profit, finds surplus units who want to buy the security being offered by a deficit unit (see Exhibit 1.1). The major investment bankers include such firms as Merrill Lynch and Goldman Sachs. Investment bankers sell a security issue for the issuer for a commission (i.e., for a percentage of the total issue's value) using their *best effort, underwrite* the securities (i.e., buy the securities from the issuer and then sell them at hopefully a higher price), or form an *underwriting syndicate* whereby a group of investment bankers buys and sells the issue. Whatever the arrangements, the primary function of the investment banker is to match the needs of the surplus and deficit units. By performing this function the investment banker reduces the search and information costs to both the investors and the issuer, facilitating the efficient operation of the primary market.

Intermediary Financial Market

The intermediary financial market consists of financial institutions, such as commercial banks, savings and loans, credit unions, insurance companies, pension funds, trust funds, and mutual funds. In this market, the financial institution, as shown in Exhibit 1.2, sells financial claims (checking accounts, savings accounts, CDs, investment fund shares, payroll deduction plan, insurance plans, etc.) to surplus units, and uses the proceeds to purchase claims (stocks, bonds, etc.) issued by ultimate deficit units or to create financial claims in the form of term loans, lines of credit, and mortgages. Through their intermediary function, financial institutions in turn create intermediate securities, referred to as *secondary securities.*

Financial institutions making up the intermediary market can be divided into three categories: *depository institutions, contractual institutions,* and *investment companies.* Depository institutions include commercial banks, credit unions, savings and loans, and savings banks. These institutions obtain large amounts of their

EXHIBIT 1.1 Direct Financial Market

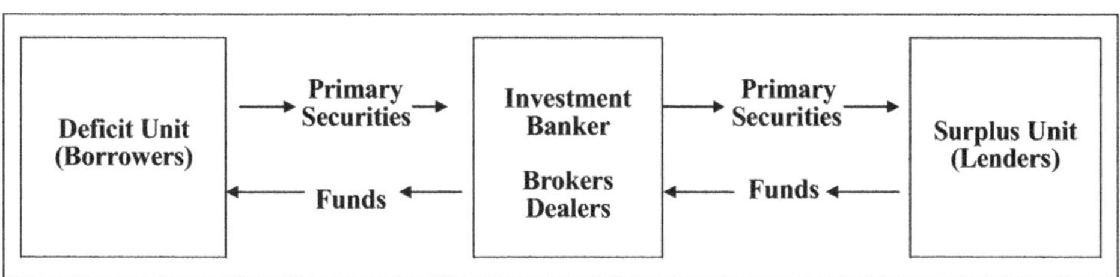

EXHIBIT 1.2 Intermediary Financial Market

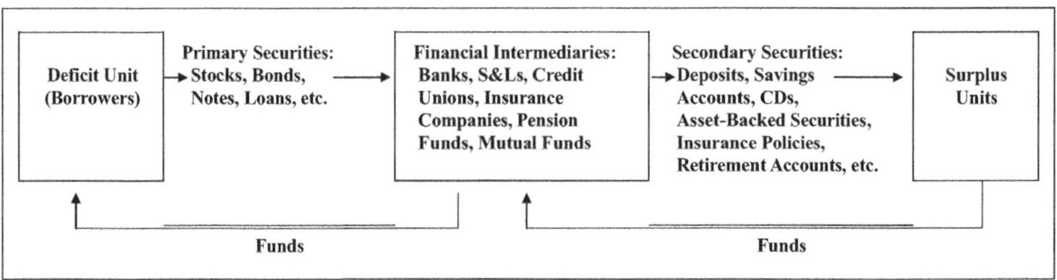

funds from deposits, which they use primarily to fund commercial and residential loans and to purchase Treasury, federal agency, and municipal securities. Contractual institutions include life insurance companies, property and casualty insurance companies, and pension funds. They obtain their funds from legal contracts to protect businesses and households from risk (premature death, accident. etc.), and from savings plans. Investment companies include mutual funds, money market funds, and real estate investment trusts. These institutions raise funds by selling equity or debt claims, and then use the proceeds to buy debt securities, stocks, real estate, and other assets. The claims they sell entitle the holder/buyer either to a fixed income each period or a pro rata share in the ownership and earnings generated from the asset fund. Also included with the securities of investment companies are *securitized assets.* Banks, insurance companies, and other financial intermediaries, as well as federal agencies, sell these financial assets. In creating a securitized asset, an intermediary will put together a package of loans of a certain type (mortgages, auto, credit cards, etc.). The institution then sells claims on the package to investors, with the claim being secured by the package of assets—securitized asset. The package of loans, in turn, generates interest and principal that is passed on to the investors who purchased the securitized asset.[4]

Some of the financial claims created in the intermediary financial market do not have a secondary market; that is, secondary markets where investors sell their bank saving accounts or insurance or pension plans to other investors are rare. However, there are secondary markets for many intermediary securities: negotiable CDs, investment fund shares, and securitized assets.

Money and Capital Markets

Financial markets can also be classified in terms of the maturity of the instrument traded. Specifically, the *money market* is defined as the market where short-term instruments (by convention defined as securities with original maturities of one year or less) are traded, and the *capital market* is defined as the market where long-term securities (original maturities over one year) are traded. The former would include such securities as CDs, commercial paper (CP), Treasury bills, savings accounts, and shares in money market investment funds, whereas the latter would include common and preferred stock, limited partnership shares, corporate bonds, municipal bonds, securitized assets, Treasury bonds, and investment fund shares. Investors with long-term liabilities or investment horizons buy securities in the capital markets. This includes many institutional investors, such as life insurance companies and pensions. The issuers of capital market securities include corporations and governments who use the market to finance their long-term capital formation projects or debt. Investors use the money market to earn interest on excess funds that they expect to have only temporarily. They also hold funds in money market securities as a store of value when they are waiting to take advantage of investment opportunities or when they fear precarious economic conditions are possible. The sellers of money market securities use the market to raise funds to finance their short-term assets (inventory or accounts receivable); to take care of cash needs resulting from the lack of synchronization between cash inflows and outflows from operations or, in the case of the U.S. Treasury, to finance the government's deficit or to refinance its maturing debt. It should be noted that the money market functions primarily as a *wholesale market,* in which many of the transactions are done by large banks and investment firms that buy and sell in large denominations. This feature helped to promote the popularity of money market funds. These funds pool the investments of small investors and invest them in money market securities, providing small investors an opportunity to obtain higher returns than they could obtain from individual bank savings accounts.

Foreign Security Markets

Over the past three decades, there has been substantial growth in the number of equity and fixed-income securities traded globally. This growth in the size of world equity and debt markets is reflected by the significant increase in global security investments among nonresidents. The popularity of global investments is generally attributed to the growing number of corporations, governments, and financial intermediaries issuing securities in foreign countries; to the emergence of currency futures, options, and swaps markets that have made it possible for investors to better manage exchange-rate risk; and to the potential diversification benefits investors can obtain by adding foreign stocks and bonds to their portfolios.

In general, an investor looking to internationally diversify his or her portfolio has several options. First, he or she might buy a stock or bond of a foreign government or foreign corporation that is issued in the foreign country or traded on that country's exchange. These securities are referred to as *domestic bonds.*[5] Second, the investor might be able to buy bonds or stocks issued in a number of countries through an international syndicate. Securities sold in this market are known as *Eurobonds* or *Euroequity.* Finally, an investor might be able to buy a bond of a foreign government or the bonds or corporation being issued or traded in his or her own country. Such bonds are called *foreign bonds.* Similarly, an investor may be able to buy a foreign stock in his or her own country that is listed on the local stock exchange. Many multinational corporations are listed not only on their national exchanges, but also on security exchanges in other countries, often where they have subsidiaries or conduct considerable business. If the foreign stock of interest is listed on a U.S. stock exchange, then a U.S. investor could easily purchase the stock there. Doing so would, in turn, help the investor avoid the risk of currency conversions and possibly foreign taxes.

If the investor were instead looking for short-term foreign investments, his choices could similarly include buying short-term domestic securities such as CP, CDs, and Treasuries issued in those countries; Eurocurrency CDs issued by Eurobanks; and foreign money market securities issued by foreign corporations and government in the local country. Similarly, a domestic financial institution or nonfinancial multinational corporation looking to raise funds may choose to do so by selling debt securities or borrowing in the company's own financial markets, the foreign markets, or the Eurobond or Eurocurrency markets. The markets where domestic, foreign, and Euro securities are issued and traded can be grouped into two categories—the *internal bond market* and the *external bond market.* The internal market, also called the *national market,* consists of the trading of both domestic bonds and foreign bonds; the external market, also called the *offshore market,* is where Eurobonds and Eurodeposits are bought and sold.

For foreign investments, one of the most important factors for an investor to consider is that their price, interest payments, and principal are denominated in a different currency. This currency component exposes them to *exchange-rate risk* and affects their returns and overall risk. Most of the currency trading takes place in the *Interbank Foreign Exchange Market.* This market consists primarily of major banks that act as currency dealers, maintaining inventories of foreign currencies to sell to or buy from their customers (corporations, governments, or regional banks). The price of foreign currency or the exchange rate is defined as the number of units of one currency that can be exchanged for one unit of another. It is determined by supply and demand conditions affecting the foreign currency market.

Spot, Futures, Options, and Swap Markets

A *spot market* (also called a *cash market*) is one in which securities are exchanged for cash immediately (usually within one or two business days). An investor's buying a stock or a Treasury bill, for example, is a transaction that takes place in the spot market. Not all security transactions, though, call for immediate delivery. A *futures or forward contract* calls for the delivery and purchase of an asset (either real or financial) at a future date, with the terms (price, amount, etc.) agreed upon in the present. For example, a contract calling for the delivery of a Treasury bill in 70 days at a price equal to 97 percent of the bill's principal would represent a futures contract on a Treasury bill. This agreement is distinct from buying a Treasury bill from a Treasury dealer in the spot market, where the transfer of cash for the security takes place almost immediately. Similar to a futures contract, an option is a security that gives the holder the right (but not the obligation) either to buy or to sell an asset at a specific price on or possibly before a specific date. Options include calls, puts, warrants, and rights. Both futures and options are traded on organized exchanges and through dealers on OTC market. In the United States, the major futures exchange is the Chicago Mercantile Exchange and the major option exchange is the Chicago Board Options Exchange. Options and futures are referred to as *derivative securities,* since their values are derived from the values of their underlying securities. In contrast, securities sold in the spot market are sometimes referred to as *primitive securities.* Derivatives have become important to both borrowers and investors in managing the risk associated with issuing and buying securities. Part Three of this book focuses on the markets and uses of derivative securities.

In addition to derivative securities, bonds often have *embedded option* features in their contracts. As noted earlier, many bonds have a call feature giving the issuer the right to buy back the bond from the bondholder before maturity at a specific price. In addition to these so-called callable bonds, there are putable bonds, giving the bondholder the right to sell the bond back to the issuer at a specified price, sinking fund clauses in which the issuer is required to orderly retire the bond by either buying bonds in the market or by calling them at a specified price, and convertible bonds that give the bondholder the right to convert the bond into a specified number of shares of stock. The inclusion of option features in a bond contract makes the valuation of such bonds more difficult.

Today, there is a large swap market. A swap is an exchange of cash flows. It is a legal arrangement between two parties to exchange specific payments. There are four types of swaps:

1. *Interest rate swaps.* Exchange of fixed-rate payments for floating-rate payments.
2. *Currency swaps.* Exchange of liabilities in different currencies.
3. *Cross-currency swaps.* Combination of interest rate and currency swap.
4. *Credit default swaps.* Exchange of premium payments for default protection.

The swap market consists primarily of financial institutions and corporations that use swap contracts to hedge more efficiently their liabilities and assets. For example, many institutions create synthetic fixed- or floating-rate assets or liabilities with better rates than the rates obtained on direct liabilities and assets or as a tool to change the rate on their existing debt. The markets and uses of swaps are also examined in Part Three of this book.[6]

Regulations

Prior to the enactment of federal security laws in 1933 and 1934, the regulation of security trading in the United States came under the auspices of state governments, which had passed a number of laws to prevent fraud and speculative schemes. The state security laws, known as the *blue-sky laws,* were often hard to enforce since many fraudulent promoters could operate outside a state's jurisdiction. With the passage of the *Securities Act of 1933* and the *Securities Exchange Act of 1934,* though, security regulations came more under the providence of the federal government. The 1933 act, known as the *truth-in-securities law,* requires registration of new issues, disclosure of pertinent information by issuers, and prohibits fraud and misrepresentation. The Securities Exchange Act (SEA) of 1934 established the *Securities and Exchange Commission,* extended the disclosure requirements of the 1933 act to include traders and participants in the secondary market, and outlawed fraud and misrepresentation in the trading of existing securities. Today, five commissioners appointed by the President and confirmed by the Senate for five-year terms run the SEC. The SEC is responsible for the administration of both the 1933 and 1934 acts, as well as the administration of a number of other security laws that have been enacted since then. The 1934 act gave the SEC authority over organized exchanges. Historically, the SEC has exercised its authority by setting only general guidelines for the bylaws and rules of an exchange, allowing the exchanges to regulate themselves. The SEC does have the power, though, to intervene and change bylaws, as well as close exchanges.

The 1933 and 1934 security acts were aimed at ensuring that information is disseminated efficiently to all investors and that fraud and misrepresentation are outlawed. Specifically, the acts outlawed price manipulation schemes such as wash sales, pools, churning, and corners. To comply with the disclosure provisions of the SEA (and its 1964 amendments), companies listed on the exchanges and those traded on the OTC market are required to file with the SEC *10-K reports,* which are audited financial statement forms; *10-Q reports,* which are quarterly unaudited financial statement forms; and *8-K forms,* which report significant developments by the company. Exhibit 1.3 summarizes the provisions in the security acts of 1933 and 1934, and Exhibit 1.4 describes some of the other important security laws in the United States.

There are also laws, regulations, and regulatory agencies that work to ensure the financial system is sound. Of particular note is the Federal Reserve System. Created in 1913, the Federal Reserve (Fed) is the most important central bank in the world. The Fed is responsible for managing the economy's money supply and the general level of interest rates. As we will discuss in more detail in later chapters, the Fed does this by open market operations, changing the reserve requirements banks maintain, and changing the discount rate they charge commercial banks on loans.

Identification

There are thousands of bond, stock, and investment fund shares outstanding. Publicly traded stocks can be identified by their *ticker* symbol. Most fixed-income securities can be identified by a nine-character *CUSIP* number. CUSIP stands for the Committee on Uniform Securities Identification Procedures. CUSIP is owned by the American Bankers Association and operated by Standard & Poor's (S&P). It is used to identify trades and for clearing. There is also a 12-character foreign security identification system known as the CUSIP International Numbering System (CINS).

EXHIBIT 1.3 Security Acts of 1933 and 1934: Price Manipulation

Price Manipulation	Description
Wash Sale	A wash sale is a sale and subsequent repurchase of a security or purchase of an identical security. It is done in order to establish a record to show, for example, a capital loss for tax purposes or to deceive investors into thinking there is large activity on the stock. The SEA of 1934 prohibits wash sales.
Pool	A pool is an association of people formed to manipulate the price of a security. For example, a pool might be formed with a group of brokers, specialists, corporate executives, and news reporters. Initially, the group could collude to bring a stock's price down through short sales and the dissemination of negative information; then, after the price has decreased to a certain level, they could buy the securities and use their connections and authority to increase the security's price to a level at which they could profit when they liquidate. The 1934 act forbids such pool activities, requires all pools to be reported, makes it illegal for members to be part of a pool, and requires corporate executives and other insiders to report their transactions in their own securities with the SEC.
Churning	Churning occurs when a broker manipulates his client to make frequent purchases and sales of a security in order to profit from increased commissions. While Section 10(b) of SEA of 1934 forbids churning, it is very difficult to prove in a court of law.
Corner	A corner occurs when someone buys up all of the security (or commodity) in order to have the monopolistic power to raise its price and to pressure short sellers to sell at higher prices. An investor or group of investors who try to corner the market could do so by forming pools to manipulate the security's price. Such manipulation is outlawed by the SEA of 1934.
Insider Activity	The SEA requires that all officers, directors, and owners of more than 10% file an *insider report* each month in which they trade their securities. This information is publicly reported in the financial press. The purpose of this requirement is to eliminate an insider from profiting from inside information.

Efficient Financial Markets

As defined earlier, an asset is any commodity, tangible or intangible good, or financial claim that generates future benefits. The value of an asset is equal to the current value of all of the asset's future expected cash flows; that is, the present value of the expected cash flow. Thus, if an investor requires a rate of return (R) of 10 percent per year on investments in a corporate bond that matures in one year, he would value (V_0) such a bond promising to pay \$100 interest and \$1,000 principal at the end of one year as worth \$1,000 today:

$$V_0 = \frac{Interest + Principal}{1+R} = \frac{\$100 + \$1,000}{1.10} = \$1,000$$

EXHIBIT 1.4 U.S. Federal Laws Related to Security Training

Legislation	Description
Glass-Steagall Act (enacted 1933; major provisions repealed 1999)	The Glass-Steagall Act, also known as the Banking Act of 1933, prohibited commercial banks from acting as investment bankers. Enacted after the 1929 stock market crash, the act also prohibited banks from paying interest on demand deposits (a prohibition that was later eliminated under the Monetary Control Act of 1980), and created the Federal Deposit Insurance Corporation. As a result of the Glass-Steagall Act, most commercial banks in the United States for years were not allowed to underwrite securities, act as brokers and dealers, and offer investment company shares. The Glass-Steagall Act also served to differentiate U.S. banking activities from those of many countries in which banks were allowed to provide investment banking and security services (merchant banking). Recognizing these differences, the U.S. Congress repealed many of the provisions of the Glass-Steagall Act.
Financial Services Modernization (Gramm-Leach-Bliley) Act (1999)	The act permitted finance companies and banks to form financial holding companies to offer banking, insurance, securities, and other financial services under one controlling corporation.
Federal Reserve Regulations T and U	Regulations T and U give the Board of Governors of the Federal Reserve the authority to set margin requirements for security loans made by banks, brokers, and dealers. Regulation T sets loan limits made by brokers and dealers, and Regulation U sets loan limits made by banks for securities transactions.
Maloney Act (1936)	This act requires associations such as NASD to register with the SEC and allows them to regulate themselves within general guidelines specified by the SEC.
Trust Indenture Act (1939)	This act gave the SEC the authority to ensure that there are no conflicts of interest between bondholders, trustees, and issuer. The act was in response to abuses in the 1930s that resulted from the issuer's having control over the trustee. Among its provisions, the act requires that the bond indenture clearly delineate the rights of the bondholders, that periodic financial reports be given to the trustee, and that the trustee act judiciously in bringing legal actions against the issuer when conditions dictate.
Investment Company Act (ICA) (1940)	This act extends the provisions of the security acts of 1933 and 1934 to investment companies. Like the security acts, it requires a prospectus to be approved and issued to investors with full disclosure of financial statements, and it outlaws fraud and misrepresentations. In addition, the act requires investment companies to state their goals (growth, balance, income, etc.), to have a management firm approved by the investment company's board, and to manage funds for the benefit of the shareholders. The 1940 act was amended in 1970 (Investment Company Amendment Act of 1970) with provisions calling for certain restrictions on management fees and contracts.
Investment Advisers Act (IAA) (1940)	This act requires individuals and firms providing investment advice for a fee to register with the SEC. The act does not, however, require certification of an adviser's qualifications. The act also outlaws fraud and misrepresentation.

Legislation	Description
Employee Retirement Income Security Act (ERISA) (1974)	This act requires that managers of pension funds adhere to the prudent man rule (a common-law principle) in managing retirement funds. When applied to investment management, this rule requires average portfolio returns and risk levels to be consistent with that of a prudent man. The probable interpretation (which is subject to legal testing) would be that pension managers be adequately diversified to minimize the risk of large losses.
Securities Investor Protection Corporation Act (SIPC) (1970)	This act provides investors with insurance coverage against losses resulting from the bankruptcy of brokerage firms. The act stipulates that all registered brokers, dealers, and exchange members be members of the SIPC.
Sarbanes-Oxley Act (2002)	This act mandated a number of reforms to enhance corporate responsibility, enhance financial disclosures, and combat corporate and accounting fraud, and created the Public Company Accounting Oversight Board (PCAOB) to oversee the activities of the auditing profession.

Similarly, an investor who expected ABC stock to pay a dividend of $10 and to sell at a price of $105 one year later would value the stock at $100 if she required a rate of return of 15 percent per year on such investments:

$$V_0 = \frac{Dividend + Expected\ Price}{1+R} = \frac{\$10+\$105}{1.15} = \$100$$

(See Appendix A for a primer on the time value of money.)

In the financial market, if stock investors expecting ABC stock to pay a $10 dividend and be worth $105 one year later required a 15 percent rate of return, then the equilibrium price of the stock in the market would be $100. Similarly, if one-year corporate bond investors required a 10 percent rate of return, then the equilibrium price of the corporate bond would be $1,000. The equilibrium price often is ensured by the activities of *speculators:* those who hope to obtain higher rates of return (greater than 15 percent in the case of the stock or 10 percent in the case of the bond) by gambling that security prices will move in certain directions. For example, if ABC stock sold below the $100 equilibrium value, then speculators would try to buy the underpriced stock. As they tried to do so, though, they would push the underpriced ABC stock toward its equilibrium price of $100. However, if ABC stock was above $100, investors and speculators would be reluctant to buy the stock, lowering its demand and the price. These actions might also be reinforced with some speculators selling the stock short. In a *short sale,* a speculator sells the stock first and buys it later, hoping to profit, as always, by buying at a low price and selling at a high one. For example, if ABC stock is selling at $105, a speculator could borrow a share of ABC stock from one of its owners (i.e., borrow the stock certificate, not money), and then sell the share in the market for $105. The short seller/speculator would now have $105 cash and would owe one share of stock to the share lender. Since the speculator believes the stock is overpriced, she is hoping to profit by the stock's decreasing in the near future. If she is right such that ABC stock decreases to its equilibrium value of $100, then the speculator could go into the market and buy the stock for $100 and return the borrowed share, leaving her with a profit of $5. However, if the stock goes up and the share lender wants his stock back, then the short seller would lose when she buys back the stock at a price higher than $105. In general, speculators help to move the market price of a security to its equilibrium value.

Theoretically, a market in which the price of the security is equal to its equilibrium value at all times is known as a *perfect market.* For a market to be perfect requires, among other things, that all the information on which investors and speculators base their estimates of expected cash flows be reflected in the security's price. Such a market is known as an *efficient market.* In a perfect market, speculators would not earn abnormal returns (above 15 percent in our stock example). However, if the information the market receives is *asymmetrical* in the sense that some speculators have information that others don't, or some receive information earlier than others, then the market price will not be equal to its equilibrium value at all times. In this inefficient market, there would be opportunities for speculators to earn abnormal returns.

Efficient markets would also preclude arbitrage returns. An *arbitrage* is a risk-free opportunity. Such opportunities come from price discrepancies among different markets. For example, if the same car sells for $10,000 in Boston but $15,000 in New York, an *arbitrageur* (one who exploits such opportunities) could earn a risk-free profit by buying the car in Boston and selling it in New York (assuming, of course, that the transportation costs are less than $5,000). In the financial markets, arbitrageurs tie markets together. For example, suppose there were two identical government bonds, each paying a guaranteed interest and principal of $1,100 at the end of one year, but with one selling for $1,000 and the other selling for $900. With such price discrepancies, an arbitrageur could sell short the higher-priced bond at $1,000 (borrow the bond and sell it for $1,000) and buy the underpriced one for $900. This would generate an initial cash flow for the arbitrageur of $100 with no liabilities. That is, at maturity the arbitrageur would receive $1,100 from the underpriced bond that he could use to pay the lender of the overpriced bond. Arbitrageurs, by exploiting this arbitrage opportunity, though, would push the price of the underpriced bond up and the price of the overpriced one down until they were equally priced and the arbitrage was gone. Thus, arbitrageurs would tie the markets for the two identical bonds together.

Characteristics of Assets

The preceding discussion on the types of financial claims and their markets suggest that there are considerable differences among assets. All assets, though, can be described in terms of a limited number of common characteristics or properties. These common properties make it possible to evaluate, select, and manage assets by defining and comparing them in terms of these properties. In fact, as an academic subject, the study of investments involves the evaluation and selection of assets. The evaluation of assets consists of describing assets in terms of their common characteristics, whereas selection involves selecting assets based on the trade-offs between those characteristics (e.g., higher return for higher risk). The characteristics common to all assets are value, rate of return, risk, maturity, divisibility, marketability, liquidity, and taxability.

Value

As defined earlier, the value of an asset is the present value of all of the asset's expected future benefits. Moreover, if markets were efficient, then, in equilibrium, the value of the asset would be equal to its market price.

Rate of Return

The rate of return on an asset is equal to the total dollar return received from the asset per period of time expressed as a proportion of the price paid for the asset. The total return on the security includes the income payments the security promises (interest on bonds, dividends on stock, etc.), the interest from reinvesting the coupon or dividend income during the life of the security, and any capital gains or losses realized when the investor sells the asset. Thus, if a corporate bond cost $P_0 = \$1{,}000$ and were expected to pay a coupon interest of $C = \$100$ and a principal of $F = \$1{,}000$ at the end of the year, then its annual rate of return would be 10 percent if all the expectations hold true:

$$R = \frac{C + (F - P_0)}{P_0} = \frac{\$100 + (\$1{,}000 - \$1{,}000)}{\$1{,}000} = .10$$

It should be noted that value (or price) and rate of return are necessarily related. If an investor knows the price he or she will pay for a security and the security's expected future benefits, then he or she can determine the security's rate of return. Alternatively, if the investor knows the rate of return he or she wants or requires and the security's expected future benefits, then he or she can determine the security's value or price.

Risk

The third property of an asset is its risk. Investment risk can be defined as the possibility that the rate of return an investor will obtain from holding an asset will be less than expected. For stock, realized returns can deviate from expected returns when there are changes in the underlying factors that determine a firm's earnings, dividends, growth rates, and required return. The total risk of stock is often explained in term of three general factors that influence a stock's return: factors related to the individual firm, the industry in which the firm competes, and the market in general.

For bonds, risk comes from concerns that a bond issuer might fail to meet his contractual obligations (default risk) or it could result from an expectation that conditions in the market will change, resulting in a lower price of the security than expected when the holder plans to sell the asset (market risk). Bond investors are exposed to one or more of the following risks:

- *Interest rate risk.* The risk that interest rates will change, causing the bond price to change (part of market risk).
- *Reinvestment risk.* The risk that the cash flows on the bond will be reinvested at lower rates (part of market risk).
- *Call risk.* The risk that the issuer will call the bond prior to maturity and the investor will have to reinvest in a market with lower rates.
- *Credit risk* or *default risk.* The risk that the issuer/borrower will fail to meet contractual obligations. Such risk is evaluated in terms of quality ratings by rating agencies (Moody's, S&P, and Fitch). Ratings range from triple A (high quality, low credit risk) to C.
- *Credit spread risk.* The risk that the bond's credit risk will increase, causing the bond's price to decrease relative to other bonds.
- *Liquidity risk.* The risk that the bond will be hard to sell at a price near its value.
- *Risk risk.* The risk of not being able to fully understand the risk of the security due to unexpected future events.

In the case of credit/default risk, investors often rely on bond rating companies to provide information about the default risk associated with a specific company, municipality, or government. The major rating companies in the United States are Moody's Investment Services, S&P, and Fitch Investors Service. Moody's and S&P have been rating bonds for almost 100 years. Today, they rate over 2,000 companies in addition to municipals, sovereigns, asset-backed securities, and other debt obligations. Moody's, S&P, and Fitch evaluate bonds by giving them a quality rating in the form of a letter grade (see Exhibit 1.5). The grades start at "A" with three groups: triple A bonds (Aaa for Moody's and AAA for S&P) for the highest-grade bonds, double A (Aa or AA) for bonds that are considered prime, single A for those considered high quality. Grade A bonds are followed by B-rated bonds, classified as either triple B (Baa or BBB), that have a medium grade, double B (Ba or BB), and single B. Finally, there are C-grade and lower-grade bonds. Moody's also breaks down bonds by using a 1, 2, or 3 designation, whereas S&P does the same with a plus or minus designation. In interpreting these ratings, triple A bonds are considered to have virtually no default risk, whereas low B-rated or C-rated bonds are considered speculative with some chance of default. In general, bonds with relatively low chance of default are referred to as *investment-grade bonds,* with quality rating of Baa (or BBB) or higher; bonds with relatively greater chance of default are referred to as *non-investment-grade, speculative-grade* or *junk bonds* and have a quality rating below Baa.

Risk, rate of return, and the value of an asset are necessarily related. In choosing between two securities with the same cash flows but with different risks, most investors will require a higher rate of return from the riskier of the two securities. For example, we would expect investors averse to risk to require a higher rate of return on a corporate bond issued by a fledgling company than on a U.S. government bond. If for some

EXHIBIT 1.5 Bond Ratings

	Very High Quality	High Quality	Speculative	Very Poor
Standard & Poor's	AAA AA	A BBB	BB B	CCC D
Moody	Aaa Aa	A Baa	Ba B	Caa C

Moody's	S&P	Description
Aaa	AAA	Bonds have the highest rating. Ability to pay interest and principal is very strong.
Aa	AA	Bonds have a very strong capacity to pay interest and repay principal. Together with the highest ratings, this group comprises the high-grade bond class.
A	A	Bonds have a strong capacity to pay interest and repay principal, although they are somewhat susceptible to the adverse effects of changes in economic conditions.
Baa	BBB	Bonds are regarded as having an adequate capacity to pay interest and repay principal. Adverse economic conditions or changing circumstances are more likely to lead to a weakened capacity to pay interest and repay principal for debt in this category than in higher-rated categories. These bonds are medium-grade obligations.
Ba B Caa Ca	BB B CCC CC	Bonds are regarded as predominantly speculative with respect to capacity to pay interest and repay principal in accordance with the terms of the obligation. BB and Ba indicate the lowest degree of speculations, and CC and Ca the highest degree of speculation.
C	C	This rating is reserved for income bonds on which no interest is being paid.
D	D	Bonds rated D are in default, and payment of interest and/or repayment of principal is in arrears.

Note: At times both Moody's and S&P have used adjustments to these ratings. S&P uses plus and minus signs: A+ is the strongest A rating and A– is the weakest. Moody's uses a 1, 2, or 3 designation, with 1 indicating the strongest.

reason both securities traded at prices that yielded the same expected rates, then we would expect that investors would want the government bond but not the corporate. If this were the case, the demand and price of the government bond would increase and its rate of return would decrease, whereas the demand and price of the corporate would fall and its rate of return would increase. Thus, if investors are risk averse, riskier securities must yield higher rates of return in the market or they will languish untraded.

Life

The fourth characteristic of an asset is its life. In the case of stock, the life of the stock is indefinite. For bonds, life is typically defined in term of the bond's maturity. Maturity is the length of time from the present until the last contractual payment is made. Maturity can vary anywhere from one day to indefinitely, as in the case of stock or a consul (a bond issued with no maturity). In defining a bond's life in terms of its maturity, though, one should always be aware of provisions such as a sinking fund or a call feature that modifies the maturity of a bond. For example, a 10-year callable bond issued when interest rates are relatively high may be more like a 5-year bond given that a likely interest rate decrease would lead the issuer to buy the bond back.

Divisibility

The fifth attribute, divisibility, refers to the smallest denomination in which an asset is traded. Thus, a bank savings deposit account, in which an investor can deposit as little as a penny, is a perfectly divisible security; a jumbo certificate of deposit, with a minimum denomination of $10 million, is a highly indivisible security. Moreover, one of the economic benefits that investment funds provide investors is divisibility. That is, an investment company, by offering shares in a diversified portfolio of stocks, makes it possible for small investors to obtain the returns and risk of a portfolio.

Marketability

The sixth characteristic is marketability. It can be defined as the speed at which an asset can be bought and sold. As a rule, for an asset to be highly marketable, its price should be independent of the time spent searching for buyers or sellers. Many tangible assets, such as houses, as well as a number of financial assets, require a certain length of time before they can be bought or sold at their fair market values. This does not mean that they can't be sold in a short period of time; but if they must be, they typically fetch a price substantially lower than what the market would yield if adequate time were allowed. In general, highly marketable securities tend to be very standardized items with a wide distribution of ownership. Thus, the stock of large corporations listed on the NYSE Euronext or Treasury issues are highly marketable securities that can be bought or sold on the exchanges electronically or through dealer in the OTC market in a matter of minutes. One way to measure the degree of marketability of a security is in terms of the size of the bid and ask spread that dealers in the OTC or a designated market maker on the exchanges offers. Dealers who make markets in less marketable securities necessarily set wider spreads than dealers who have securities that are bought and sold by many investors and therefore can be traded more quickly.

Liquidity

The seventh property, liquidity, is related to marketability. Liquidity can be defined as how cashlike or moneylike a security is. For an instrument to be liquid, it must be highly marketable and have little, if any, short-run risk. Thus, a Treasury security that can be sold easily and whose rate of return in the short-run is known with a high degree of certainty is said to be liquid. However, a security such as an exchange-listed stock is marketable, but given its day-to-day price fluctuations, is not considered liquid. Technically, the difference between marketability and liquidity is the latter's feature of low or zero risk that makes the security cashlike. It should be noted that although there is a difference between marketability and liquidity, the term *liquidity* is often used to describe a security's marketability.

Liquidity and marketability are often described in terms of price continuity and depth. *Price continuity* refers to a security's trading at its current level in the absence of any new information. A security with depth, or one with a *deep market,* is one in which there are a large number of buyers and sellers willing to trade at a price without a large change in price.

Taxability

The eighth characteristic of an asset is taxability. Taxability refers to the claims that the federal, state, and local governments have on the cash flows of an asset. Taxability varies in terms of the type of asset. For example, the coupon interest on a municipal bond is tax exempt, whereas the interest on a corporate bond is not. To the investor, the taxability of a security is important because it affects his after-tax rate of return.

Indexes

Security evaluation and selection is based on comparing the characteristics of different securities. In comparing securities, investors often compare their securities or portfolios to an index. They also constantly monitor trends in the market by following indexes. Indexes are constructed so as to provide an indication of how the market for a particular group of securities is performing. The index could be broad based, measuring the performance of the overall market; sector specific, measuring the performance of an particular industry or sector; or style specific, measuring the performance of certain type of investment (e.g., small-cap companies or investment-grade bonds). The oldest and still most frequently quoted index is the *Dow Jones Industrial Average (DJIA)*. Created in 1896, this broad-based stock index is computed as a price-weighted average of 30 large "blue-chip" stocks (not all of them being industrials). The other popular broad-base index is the *Standard & Poor's Composite 500 Index (S&P 500)*. In calculating this index, the price of each stock is multiplied by the market value of the company's outstanding shares, divided by the aggregate market value of the 500 stocks from a base year. The S&P 500 includes mostly mid- and large-cap stocks.

The proportional change in the index per time period gives the overall market's price appreciation or depreciation the index is representing:

$$\text{Proportional price change} = \frac{(\text{S\&P 500})_t - (\text{S\&P 500})_{t-1}}{(\text{S\&P 500})_{t-1}}$$

For example, from mid-2006 to September 2007, the S&P 500 increased from 1,200 to 1,565, a 30 percent price appreciation, whereas from September

2007 (the start of the financial crisis) to the beginning of 2008, the index decreased 57 percent from 1,565 to 676. A mutual fund manager looking at the proportional change in the index could compare his or her portfolio's price appreciation to that of the index to determine his or her portfolio's performance relative to the market.[7]

The most widely known bond indexes are those constructed by Barclay's and Merrill Lynch. These indexes cover different segments and parts of the bond market from investment-grade to lower-quality bonds, from governments to corporate, from short-term to long-term bonds. Ibbotson and Associates also has a set of indexes on T-bills, long-term and intermediate-term Treasuries, and long-term corporate. These indexes do not cover as many segments of the bond market as do the indexes of Barclay's and Merrill Lynch, but they do have a longer historical period, dating back to 1926. Finally, there are indexes for the major foreign stock exchanges and world indexes, such as the Nikkei 225 Index for the Tokyo Stock Exchange. Morgan Stanley, Dow Jones, and other financial service firms also calculate a number of indexes (in the local currency and in dollars), including national indexes, international industry indexes, a European index, an Asian index, and a world index.

Conclusion

In this chapter, we have given an overview of the financial system by examining the nature of financial assets, the types of markets that they give rise to, and their general characteristics. With this background, in the next chapter we will examine how information and news about securities and markets can be accessed and analyzed using the Bloomberg platform.

Website Information

- NYSE Euronext: www.nyse.com
- OTC market: www.finra.org/index.htm and www.nasdaq.com
- For financial information on securities, market trends, and analysis:
    - http://finance.yahoo.com
    - www.hoovers.com
    - www.bloomberg.com
    - www.businessweek.com
    - www.ici.org
    - http://seekingalpha.com
    - http://bigcharts.marketwatch.com
    - www.morningstar.com
    - http://free.stocksmart.com
    - http://online.wsj.com/public/us

- Data on most financial intermediaries is prepared by the Federal Reserve and is published in the *U.S. Flow of Funds* report. The report can be accessed from www.federalreserve.gov/releases (click the "Flow of Funds Account" tab).
- For information on investment funds, see the Investment Company Institute's website: www.ici.org.
- Information on derivatives:
  - CME Group: www.cmegroup.com
  - Chicago Board Options Exchange: www.cboe.com
- For information on the laws, regulations, and litigations of the SEC, go to www.sec.gov.
- For information on monetary policy, economic data, and research from the Federal Reserve, go to www.federalreserve.gov.
- For more on the efficient market hypothesis, go to www.investorhome.com/emh.htm.

Selected References

Mishkin, F. S., and S. G. Eakins. 2010. *Financial Markets and Institutions,* 6th edition. Boston: Addison-Wesley.

Revell, J. 1997. *The Recent Evolution of the Financial System*. New York: MacMillan.

Notes

1. In October 2008, the NYSE Euronext also acquired the American Stock Exchange and formed the NYSE Amex, which trades in small- and microcap listed companies. At the time of this writing, there is an offer by the Frankfurt Exchange to acquire NYSE Euronext.
2. For a security to qualify for the system, it must have at least two market makers, and its issuer must meet certain financial requirements. For a company to have its stock listed on the Nasdaq system, it must satisfy requirements related to its net worth and shares outstanding.
3. Some scholars refer to direct financial claims as those in which only the ultimate borrowers and lenders trade with each other and a *semidirect market* as one in which brokers and dealers bring borrowers and lenders together. The definition of direct financial market here includes both of these markets.
4. An occasional trend in the financial markets is towards disintermediation. *Disintermediation* refers to the shifting from intermediary financing to direct financing. This occurs when a surplus unit withdraws funds from a financial institution and invests the funds by buying primary claims from an ultimate borrower.
5. Security exchanges in different countries can be grouped into one of three categories: public bourse (exchange), private bourse, and banking bourse. A *public bourse* is a government security exchange in which listed securities (usually both bonds and stocks) are bought and sold through brokers who are appointed by the government. A *private bourse* is a security exchange owned by its member brokers and dealers. In countries where there

are private exchanges, a number of the exchanges will usually compete with each other; this is not the case in countries using a public bourse structure. A *banker bourse* is a formal or informal market in which securities are traded through bankers. This type of trading typically occurs in countries where historically commercial and investment banking have not separated.

6. In addition to domestic and foreign bonds and stocks, investment funds, and derivatives, many investors include gold and other precious metals such as silver as part of their portfolios. Since gold does not generate an income, its attraction as an international asset emanates from its tradition of being regarded as an international store of value. Gold is a precious metal that is unaffected by water, weather, and oxygen. Investors have often purchased it during periods of economic or political crisis.
7. It should be noted that the rate of return of the index needs to include the proportional price change and also the index's cash dividend income during the period:

$$R = \frac{[(S\&P\,500)_t - (S\&P\,500)_{t-1}] + Index's\ cash\ dividend\ during\ the\ period}{(S\&P\,500)_{t-1}}$$

$$R = \frac{[(S\&P\,500)_t - (S\&P\,500)_{t-1}]}{(S\&P\,500)_{t-1}} + \frac{Index's\ cash\ dividend\ during\ the\ period}{(S\&P\,500)_{t-1}}$$

$$R = Proportional\ change\ in\ price + dividend\ \ yield$$

From January 2010 to January 2011, the proportional price change in the S&P 500 was 25 percent and the dividend yield was 3 percent, yielding an overall market return of 28 percent.

CHAPTER 2

Overview and Guide to the Bloomberg System

Introduction

Bloomberg is a computer information and retrieval system providing access to financial and economic data, news, and analytics. Bloomberg terminals are common in most trading floors and are becoming more common in universities where they are used for research, teaching, and managing student investment funds. The Bloomberg system provides 24-hour, instant access to information on most U.S. and foreign securities: stocks, bonds, asset-backed securities, swaps, and derivatives; economic information by country; current and historical news and information on corporations and countries; and analytical packages for evaluating bonds, equity, derivatives, and portfolios. Moreover, many of the models used by financial economists to evaluate, select, and a manage fixed-income securities that are described in subsequent chapters are accessible on the Bloomberg system.

In this chapter, we present an overview and introductory guide to the Bloomberg system: how the systems works, its functionality, and some of the information that can be accessed from its monitors, screens, and search tools. As we examine the investment environment in future chapters, we will show many of the Bloomberg descriptive and analytical screens and explain how they can be used in the study of fixed-income investments. This chapter serves as a foundation for understanding how you can access such information and tools with a Bloomberg terminal, as well as a "show-and-tell" presentation of the Bloomberg screens.

Bloomberg System—Bloomberg Keyboard

The Bloomberg keyboard allows you to access information within the Bloomberg system. The keyboard consists of several specialized, color-coded function keys and yellow functional buttons:

- **Green action keys** send a specific request to the system with the system in turn responding:
  - **ENTER:** Press <Enter> to enter commands.
  - **NEWS:** Press <News> to access 24-hour, online global news service.
  - **HELP:** Press <Help> for terminology, formulas, and defaults. For specific information, type a name and then press <Help>; for help from a Bloomberg representative, press <Help> twice.
  - **MENU:** Press <Menu> to back up to the previous screen or menu.
  - **PRINT:** To send a document to the printer.
  - **PAGE FWD**
  - **PAGE BACK**
- **Yellow functional buttons** take the user to information and analytical functions for specific markets:
  - **GOVT:** Domestic and foreign securities.
  - **EQUITY:** Equity news, company information, company financial information, historical prices, equity indexes, mutual fund information, equity derivatives (a company's option, futures, warrants, convertibles, and swaps), and equity analytical functions.
  - **CMDTY:** Commodities by sector, futures, options, and OTC pricing contributors.
  - **CORP:** Corporate bonds and bond analytical functions.
  - **INDEX:** Indices for markets and countries, index composition, index derivatives, and other information and analytics.
  - **CRNCY:** Foreign exchange spot rates, forward rates, and cross rates, currency monitors, and currency indices.
  - **M-MKT:** Money market rates and indexes (e.g., London Interbank Offered Rate [LIBOR], commercial paper rates, and federal funds rates).
  - **MRTG:** Mortgage securities, agency pool reports, and prepayment statistics.
  - **MUNI:** Municipal bonds and municipal information.
  - **PFD:** Preferred stocks and related information.
  - **ALPHA/CLIENT:** General function for creating, customizing, and updating portfolios.
  - **LAW:** Law menu (BLAW).

Note: You can also type "Main" and hit <Enter> to bring up the Bloomberg "Main" menu, where you can access specific market screens.

The yellow functional buttons are a good way to get started on Bloomberg. You can simply enter the yellow key to bring up a menu screen providing access to information and analytical functions related to the category. For example, to access information on a company and its securities, press the "Equity" button, <Equity>, and then press the "Enter" button, <Enter>. A menu will appear that will identify where a function or information is located. You can then move your cursor to the subscreen of interest and click it, or you can type the screen's name (e.g., DES) (or its number) in the top left corner of the screen and hit <Enter>. For example, to find a company's stock ticker symbol from the Equity menu screen, you would:

- Press <Equity> and hit <Enter>.
- Click "Security Finder" to bring up the "SECF" screen Or just type SECF in the left corner and hit <Enter>.
- On the SECF screen, click the tab for the type of security (e.g., "Eqty" for equity) and then type the name of the company as accurately as possible to bring up a list of companies.
- Scroll down to find the name of the company.
- Click the name of the company or type the ticker symbol (in the left corner of the screen), press <Equity>, and hit <Enter> to access a menu of information and functions for that company: Company Information/Description, Historical Prices, News/Research.

Similar procedures can be followed using the SECF screen to find the menus for securities and to find tickers or identifiers (CUSIPS or ISN number) for bonds, corporate securities, countries, commodities, currencies, and indices: Type SECF in the left corner, click the tab for the type of security (e.g., "FI" for fixed income) and then type the name of the company . Note, if you know the ticker symbol or identifier, then you can access the stock, bond, index, or currency directly by typing the ticker/identifier and then pressing the relevant key; for example, to access IBM, enter: IBM <Equity> <Enter>.

Uploading Information on a Stock, Bond, Currency, or Index

In general, to upload a corporation's security (e.g., stock or bond), index, currency, or commodity in Bloomberg: (1) type in the ticker or identifier, (2) press the yellow key that represents the type of asset (e.g., <Equity> or <Corp>), and (3) hit <Enter>. Examples:

- To pull up IBM's stock screen: IBM <Equity> <Enter>.
- To pull up the screen for IBM's 6.5 percent coupon bond maturing 01/15/2028: IBM 6.5 01/15/2028 <Corp> <Enter> or CUSIP <Corp> <Enter>.
- To pull up the S&P 500 index screen: SPX <Index> <Enter>.
- To pull up the British Pound screen: GBP <Crncy> <Enter>.
- To pull up the screen for crude oil futures contracts traded on the New York Mercantile Exchange: Enter CLA <Cmdity> <Enter>.
- To pull up the screen for the U.S. Treasury note paying a 2 percent coupon and maturing 01/31/16: T 2 01/31/16 <Govt> <Enter>.

It should be noted that often, when you begin typing the name of the security, a dropdown will appear on the screen listing securities corresponding with the information being typed; clicking the security from the dropdown will bring up its menu. Once a security or index has been loaded, you are taken to a "homepage" menu that categorizes all the functions on the selected security and submenu screens. The functions can be accessed by either clicking the name on the menu option page or typing the name of the function in the left corner of the screen. Additional menu screens can be found on the homepage menu by clicking a topic heading (e.g., <Company Overview >).

There are two main types of screens in Bloomberg: descriptive and analytical. Descriptive screens provide information about the underlying security, such as trade information, expiration, and risk information. Descriptive screens pull data from Bloomberg and present it in an orderly fashion; they usually do not perform calculations. Analytical screens, on the other hand, determine prices, returns, variability, and other statistical and mathematical calculations based on customized inputs. In Bloomberg, many of the functions that are used for evaluating securities are common and as a result have a common command. For instance, the GP function is a price graph that can be used for each security type. Derivatives, indices, interest rates, currencies, commodities, and bond futures often use many of the same functions. If you know the name of the function (e.g., DES for description) and the security is already loaded, then you can access the function's screen directly by simply typing the name of the function (e.g., DES) in the top left corner; if the security is not loaded, then you can type the ticker, hit the yellow key, and type the function; for example: IBM <Equity> DES <Enter>. Also note that once you have accessed the function screen, you can always press the "Help" key to bring up a screen with information, defaults, and instructions related to that function or hit "Help" twice to access a message box to send questions to the Bloomberg helpdesk.

Accessing Some of the Information Discussed in Chapter 1

In Chapter 1, we examined the types and markets for equity and debt securities. A myriad of information and analytical function on many of these asset classes can be easily accessed using a Bloomberg terminal. Of note are the menus for stocks, corporate bonds, and government securities.

Bloomberg Menu for a Stock: Ticker <Equity> <Enter>

The Bloomberg menu for a stock (e.g., IBM: IBM <Equity> <Enter>) provides information on the stock and company: company information, historical prices, financials, derivatives, and news (Exhibit 2.1). Some of the functions and information on a stock's equity menu related to Chapter 1 include:

- **DES:** Provides details about the company. The description screen usually has a number of pages summarizing products, management, stock information, board members, financial summaries, and geographical distribution.

EXHIBIT 2.1 Bloomberg Description (DES), Event (EVT), Corporate Files (CF), Price Graph (GP), and Supply-Chain (SPLC) Screens for a Stock

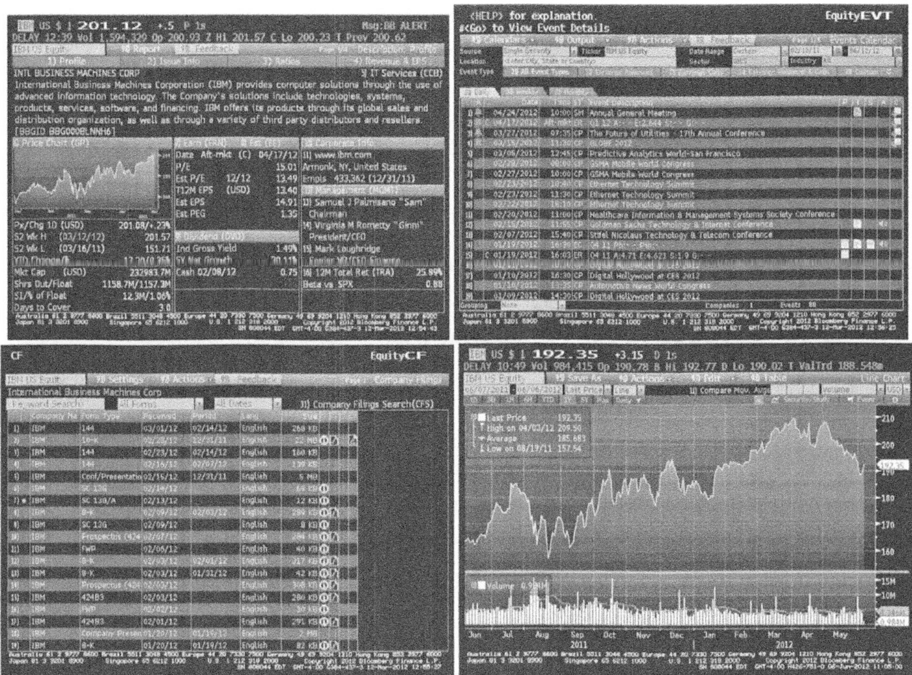

- **EVT:** Lists past and current events, such as earning announcements, stockholders' meeting, security issues, and the like.
- **CF:** Corporate filings and SEC filings (EDGAR [Electronic Data Gathering, Analysis, and Retrieval system]), 10-K reports, 10-Q reports, and other filings.
- **GP:** Price and volume graph.
- **SPLC**: Supply chain.

Bloomberg Corporate Bond Information and Functions: Ticker <Corp> <Enter>

To find a corporate bond for a company (IBM), first access the screen for all of the company's bonds (e.g., IBM <Corp> <Enter>). From this screen, you can bring up a menu screen for a specific bond by clicking the bonds of interest (see Exhibit 2.2). Some of functions and information on that menu that relate to Chapter 1:

- **DES:** Description.
- **HDS:** Shows the holders of the bond.
- **CSHF:** Shows the cash flows promised on the bond: semiannual interest and principal.
- **GP** graphs historical closing prices.

EXHIBIT 2.2 Bloomberg Menu, Description (DES), Holders (HDS), Cash Flows (CSHF), and Price Graph (GP) Screens for a Bond

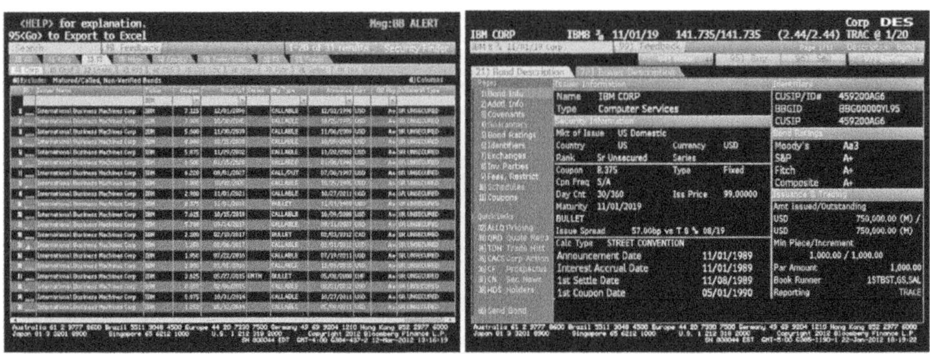

Note: The description screen shown for IBM is for an IBM credit paying 8 3/8 percent annual coupon and maturing on 11/01/19. *Note:* The par amount is $1,000 and the CUSIP is 459200AG6. On the right column of the screen, the user can find additional information, such as a covenant or current trading prices (TRACE), by clicking the entry.

<HELP> for explanation. dgp Corp HDS

IBM 8 ⅜ 11/01/19 - IBM CORP CUSIP 459200AG

	Holder Name	Portfolio Name	Source	Amt Held	% Out	Latest Chg	File Dt
1.	VANGUARD GROUP INC	Multiple Portfolios	MF-AGG	25,000	3.33	0	12/31/11
2.	WESTERN NATL LIFE INS C	WESTERN NATL LIFE	Sch-D	15,750	2.10	0	09/30/11
3.	PRUDENTIAL INSURANCE	PRUDENTIAL INSUR	Sch-D	14,000	1.87	0	09/30/11
4.	UNITED INSURANCE CO OF	UNITED INSURANCE	Sch-D	13,600	1.81	500	09/30/11
5.	BLACKROCK FUND ADVISOI	Multiple Portfolios	MF-AGG	11,125	1.48	0	03/08/12
6.	GLENMEDE ADVISORS INC	Multiple Portfolios	MF-AGG	11,000	1.47	0	10/31/11
7.	AMERICAN LIFE INSURANC	AMERICAN LIFE INS	Sch-D	10,750	1.43	0	09/30/11
8.	METROPOLITAN LIFE INSU	METROPOLITAN LIFE	Sch-D	10,450	1.39	0	09/30/11
9.	SOUTHERN FARM BUREAU	SOUTHERN FARM BU	Sch-D	10,000	1.33	0	09/30/11
10.	TRANSAMERICA FINANCIAL	TRANSAMERICA FIN	Sch-D	9,000	1.20	0	09/30/11
11.	ALLIANZ LIFE INS CO OF	ALLIANZ LIFE INSUR	Sch-D	8,750	1.17	0	09/30/11
12.	AMERICAN ECONOMY INSU	AMERICAN ECONOMY	Sch-D	8,000	1.07	0	09/30/11
13.	AVIVA LIFE & ANN CO	AVIVA LIFE & ANN C	Sch-D	6,670	0.89	0	09/30/11
14.	STANDARD INSURANCE CO	STANDARD INSURAN	Sch-D	6,335	0.84	0	09/30/11
15.	AUTO-OWNERS LIFE INSU	AUTO-OWNERS LIFE	Sch-D	6,300	0.84	0	09/30/11

% Out 39.03

Bloomberg Government Bond Information and Functions: Ticker GOVT <Enter>

To access a specific government bond, you first need to find a government bond's ticker. As noted, you can find a ticker by going to the GOVT menu page (<Govt> <Enter>) and then clicking the ticker lookup (TK), using SECF (FI tab and "Govt" tab), or directly find the ticker by entering <Govt> TK <Enter>. The direct approach will bring up a country screen in which you can click the country (e.g., U.S.A.) and then select the bond group of interest (e.g., T for "U.S. Treasury

EXHIBIT 2.3 Bloomberg Government Bond Ticker Symbols: <GOVT> TK <Enter>

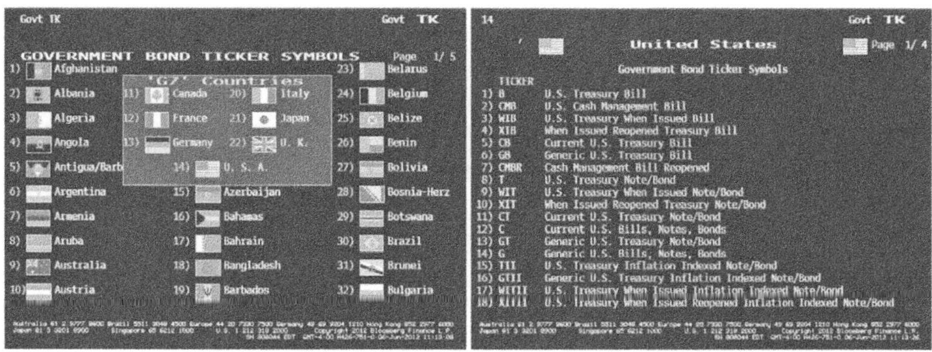

Notes and Bonds" or CT for "Current U.S. Treasury Notes and Bonds"), as shown in Exhibit 2.3.

Finally, you can click the bond of interest to bring up its menu (e.g., 5-year note) and then click DES to bring up the note's description page (Exhibit 2.4).

On the description page, you will find the bond's CUSIP number, which, as noted, can also be used to bring up the bond's menu screen: CUSIP <Govt> <Enter> (912828PC8 <Govt> <Enter>. As noted, one other way to bring up the menu page for a specific bond is to start typing the bond's coupon interest and maturity: T 2 5/8 11/15/20 (for Treasury, coupon, and maturity). This will bring up a dropdown list of bonds; clicking the bond of interest will bring up its menu (see Exhibit 2.5). Other information screens found on a specific government bond's menu include:

- **DES:** Issue and issuer information, access to the TRACE, prospectus, and other screens.
- **HDS:** Bondholders.
- **CSHF:** Shows the cash flows promised on the bond.

EXHIBIT 2.4

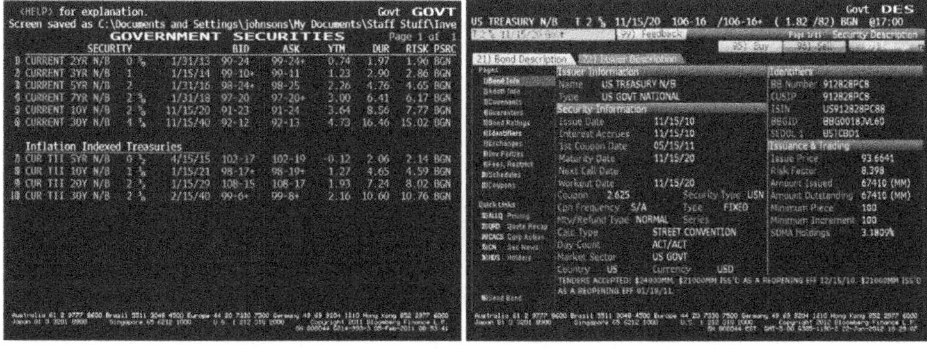

Note: The description is for U.S. Treasury, paying 2 5/8% coupon, maturing on 11/15/20.

EXHIBIT 2.5

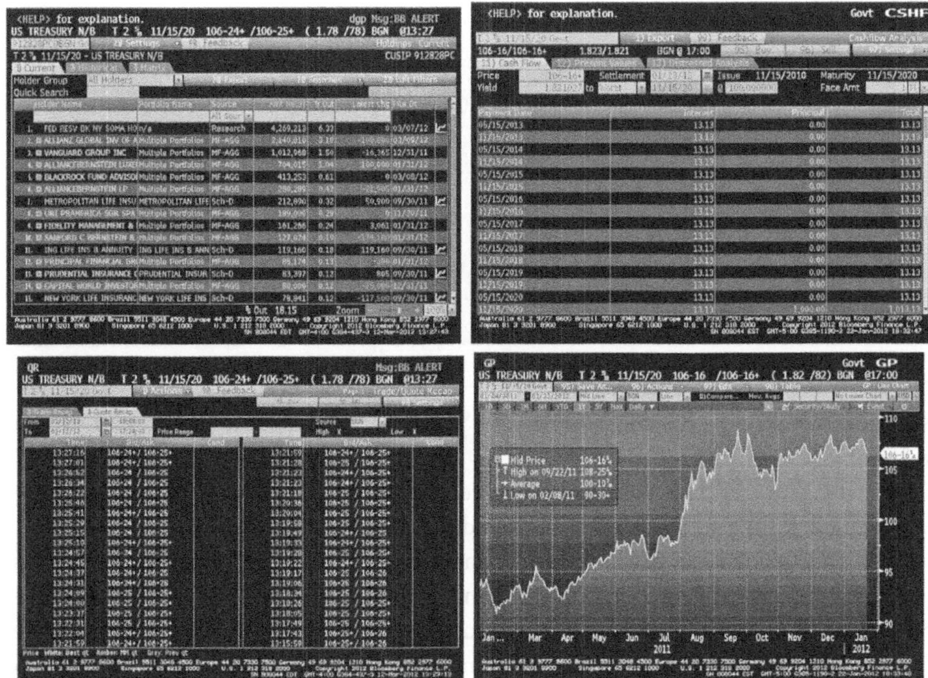

- **QR:** Trade recap: Tick-by-tick prices reported from TRACE.
- **GP:** Historical price graph.

Finding Securities: <Yellow Function Key> TK <Enter>

As noted, to directly find a government bond's ticker, enter <Govt> TK <Enter>. This will bring up a country screen in which you can click the country (e.g., U.S.A.) and then select the bond group of interest. This approach can be used to quickly search for other securities: foreign government securities (<Govt>), agencies (<Govt>), municipals (<Muni>), money market securities (<M-Mkt>), preferred securities (<Pfd>), and currency (<Curncy>).

Foreign Government Bonds

- <Govt> TK <Enter>.
- Example: Click U.K.
- Select type, such as UKT for all British gilts (bonds).
- Or enter: UKT <Govt> <Enter>.
- Click bond of interest to bring up its menu screen.
- Click function (e.g., description [DES] or price graph [GP]) on the bond's menu screen (see Exhibit 2.6).

EXHIBIT 2.6

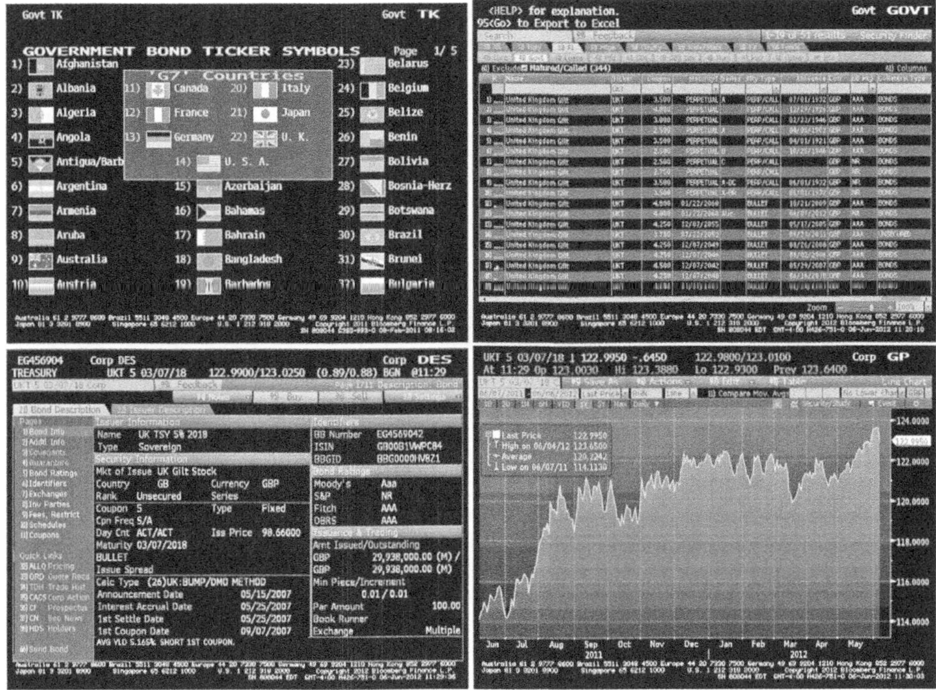

Municipal (Ohio State) Bonds

- <Muni> TK <Enter>.
- Enter State (e.g., Ohio).
- Select type (Ohio State) to bring up menu.
- On menu, click function (e.g., description [DES], filings [CF]), or price quotes [QP]) (See Exhibit 2.7).

EXHIBIT 2.7

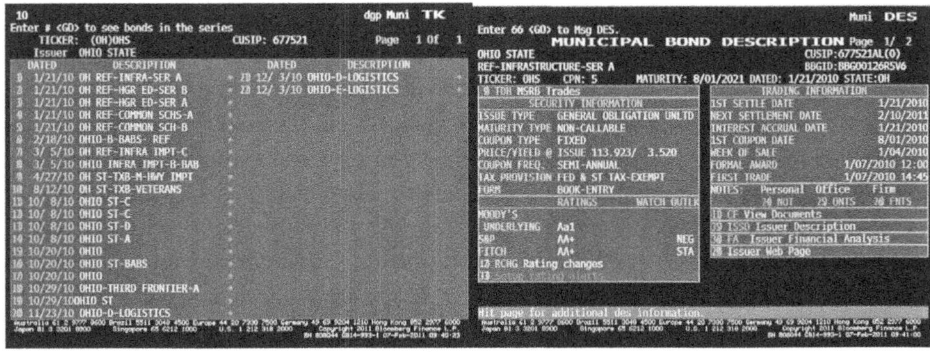

EXHIBIT 2.8

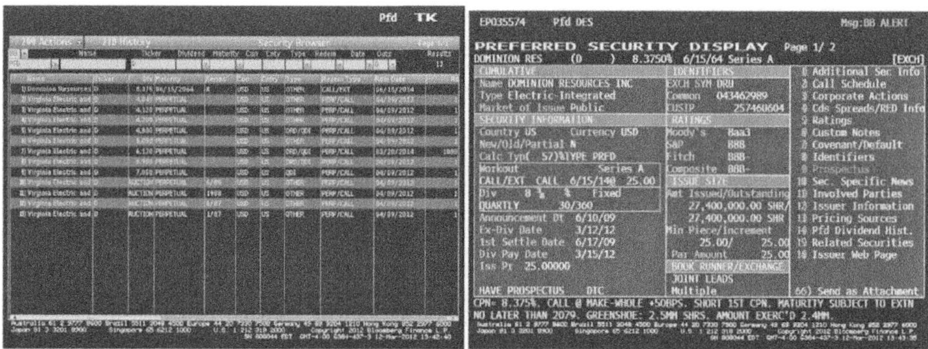

Preferred Stocks

- <Pfd> TK <Enter>.
- Enter company name or ticker in the yellow box (e.g., D or Dominican Resources) or ticker <Pfd>.
- On menu, click one of the functions (e.g., Description [DES]), as shown in Exhibit 2.8.

Currency

- <Curncy> TK <Enter>.
- Find country's menu (e.g., Swiss Franc [CHF] or ticker <Curncy> <Enter> (CHF <Curncy> <Enter>).
- On menu, click function (description [DES], price graph [QP], news [N] or other entries) (see Exhibit 2.9).

Indexes

The menu page for indexes provides information on different indexes by category, such as equity, world indexes, bonds, real estate, and municipals. One way to find the ticker for a specific index is to go to the WEI menu screen. On the WEI screen, you can click the dropdown "Display" tab and change the index listing from "names" to "tickers." Also on that screen, you can click the gray area above the geographical area (e.g., Americas) to bring up more indexes (Exhibit 2.10).

Two well-known indexes are the S&P 500 and the Dow Jones Industrial Average. Entering their tickers (SPX and INDU), pressing <Index> and hitting <Enter> brings up their menu screens showing descriptive and analytical functions: description (DES), stock holdings (in Description), index weighting (MEMB), price graph (GP), and stock movers in the index (MOV) (see Exhibit 2.11).

EXHIBIT 2.9

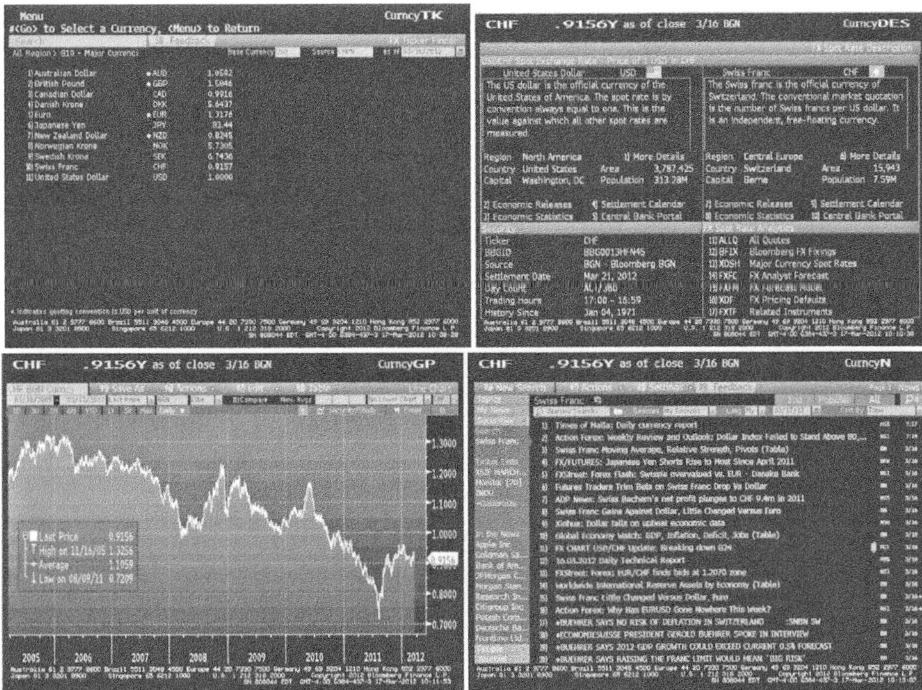

EXHIBIT 2.10

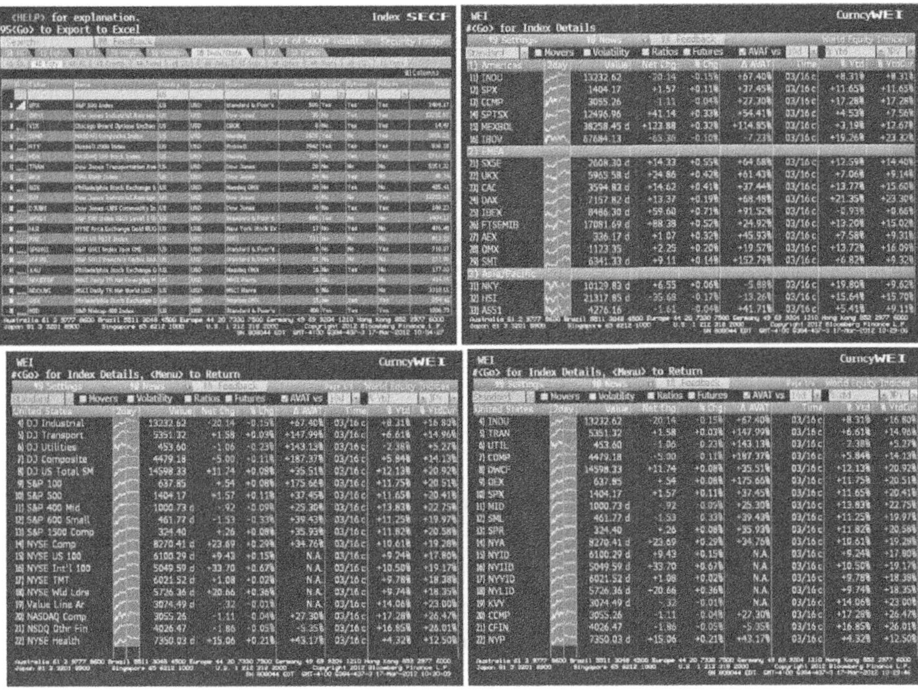

EXHIBIT 2.11

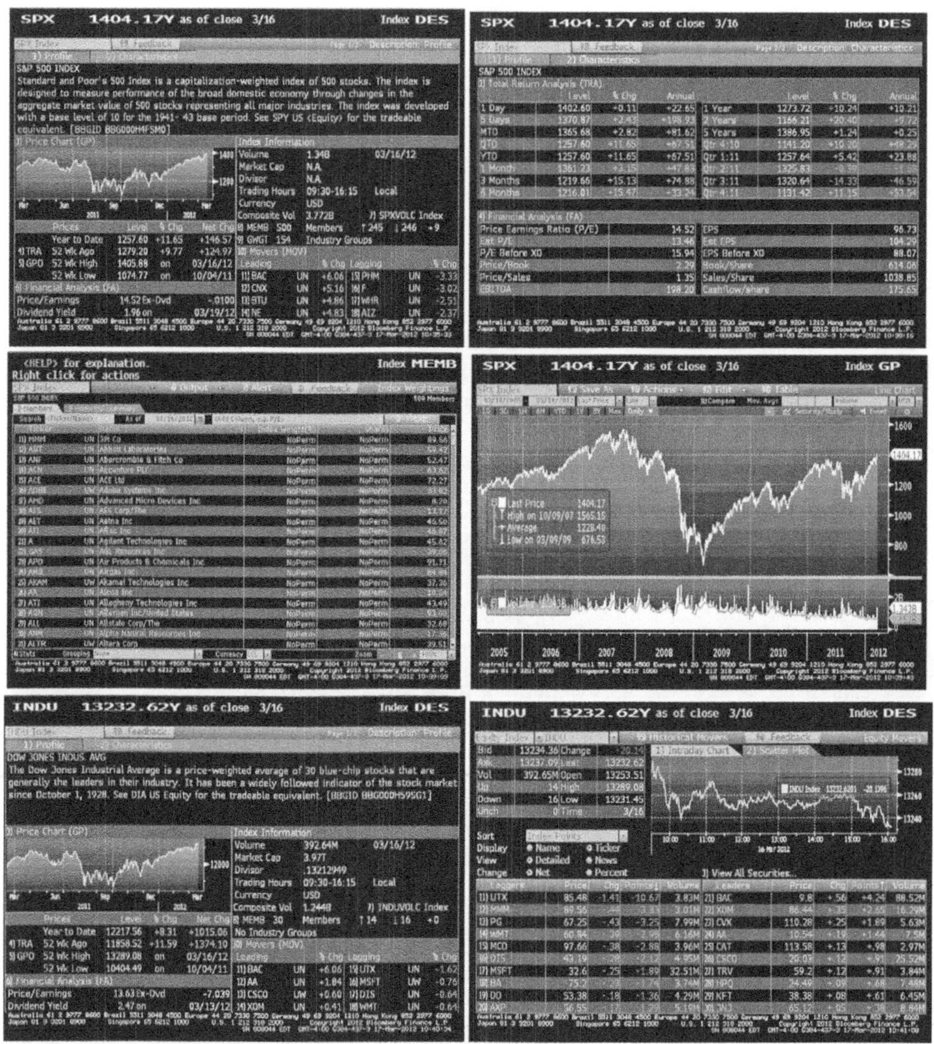

- S&P 500: SPX <Index> <Enter>.
- Dow Jones Industrial Average: INDU <Index> <Enter>.

From the WEI or MEMB screen, you can identify the tickers for different indexes constructed for style, industry, sector or area. Entering that index's ticker (ticker <Index> <Enter>) brings up the menu for that index. Another way to identify different indexes is to enter the general index name (e.g., SPX for S&P 500 or RUSS for the Russell index) and hit <Enter>. This will bring up a menu showing different indexes (Exhibit 2.12):

EXHIBIT 2.12

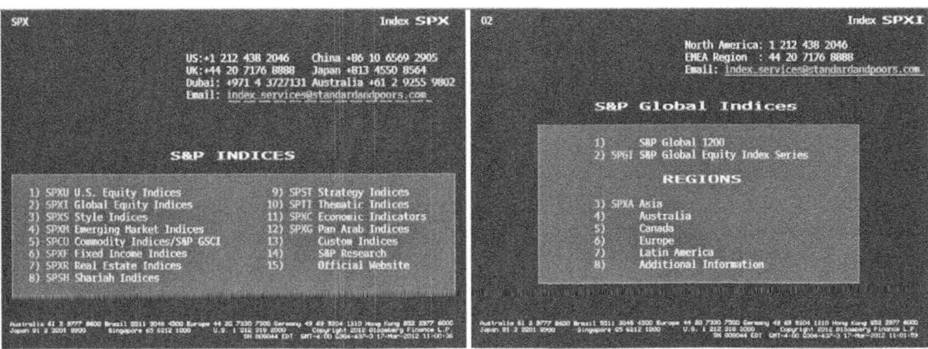

An index's menu has descriptive and analytical function similar to stock. Below are examples of the description (DES) and price graphs (GP) slides for the Nikkei 225 (NKY), the S&P Global 1200 index (SPGLOB), the Russell 3000 (RAY), and the S&P 500 Biotech indexes (see Exhibit 2.13):

EXHIBIT 2.13A

NKY <Index> <Enter>

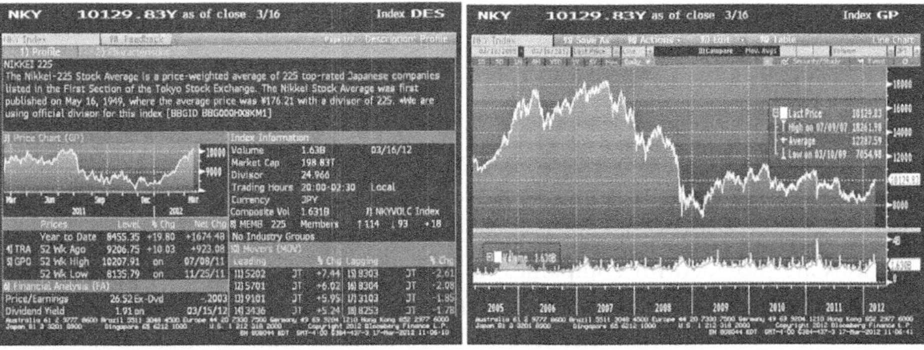

SPGLOB <Index> <Enter>

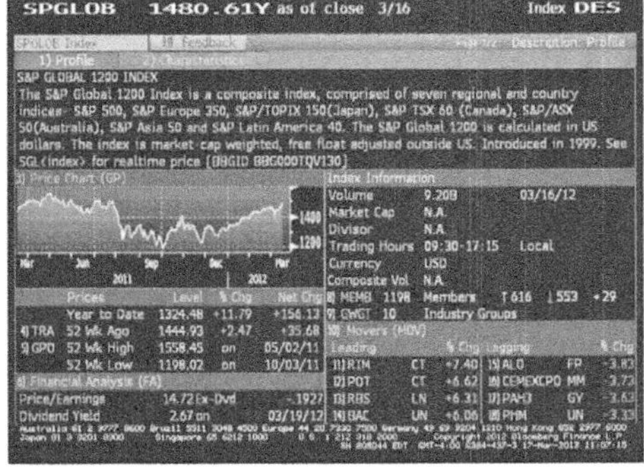

EXHIBIT 2.13B

Ray <Index> <Enter>

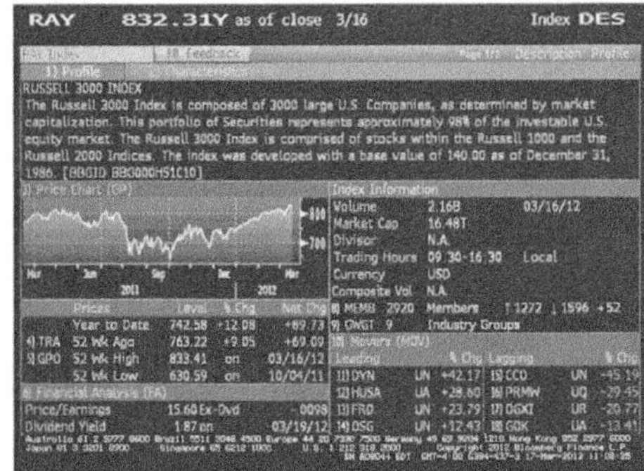

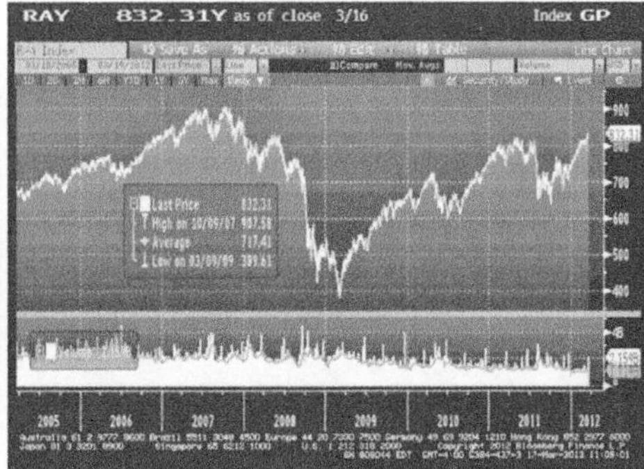

S5BIOT <Index> <Enter>

Functionality

Many Bloomberg screens provide functions and links that facilitate analysis of a company, security, market, fund, portfolio, or an economy. For example, the relative valuation (RV), financial analysis (FA), and fundamental graphs (GF) functions are provided for companies, indexes, portfolios, governments, and municipals. These functions allow the user to access key financial information for a company, index, or municipality (FA and GF) or for a group of peers (RV). For a company (e.g., Green Mountain Coffee Roasters [GMCR]), its FA, RV, and GF screens can be accessed from it equity menu screen or accessed directly: GMCR <Equity> RV <Enter>; GMCR <Equity> FA <Enter>; GMCR <Equity> GF <Enter>) (see Exhibit 2.14).

Financial Analysis: FA

The FA screen displays financial history for a specific company, equity index, or municipality (Exhibit 2.15). Using the FA screen, you can either select from a list of standard templates (e.g., income statements, ratio analysis, or detailed financial statements) or customize your own template. The data can be seen on a quarterly,

EXHIBIT 2.14

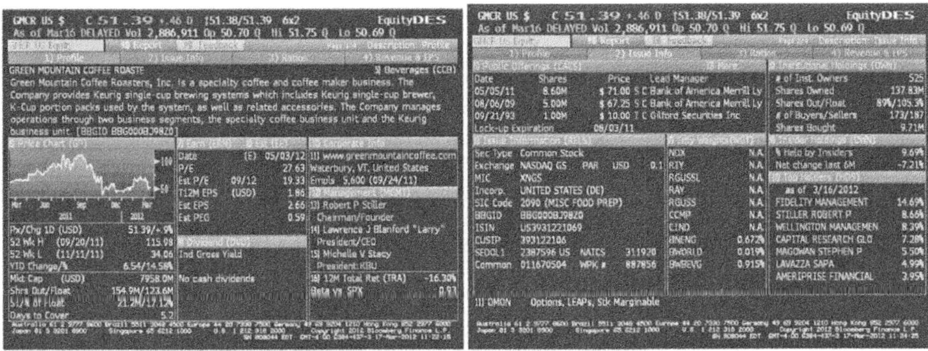

semiannual, annual, or trailing 12-month basis. On the FA screen, the template information can be viewed on the right panel and can be changed to chart form by clicking the chart icon in the left corner. Using the dropdown "Action" tab, you can create a PDF report of the table, graph, or table and graph, as well as send the data to Excel.

Relative Valuation: RV

The RV screen shows financial and market information of a company relative to its peers (Exhibit 2.16). On the screen, you can change the peer grouping by selecting a different peer group from the dropdown "Comp Source" menu tab. From the peers menu, you can then select a larger sector or subsector. In addition, you can also bring up a portfolio that you have constructed or a group of stocks identified from an equity screen/search that you have conducted and saved (portfolio construction and security searches are discussed later in this chapter). In addition to changing peers, the RV menu also allows you to change the template (gray tabs: Overview, Comp Sheets, Markets, EPS Preview, and Credit).

EXHIBIT 2.15

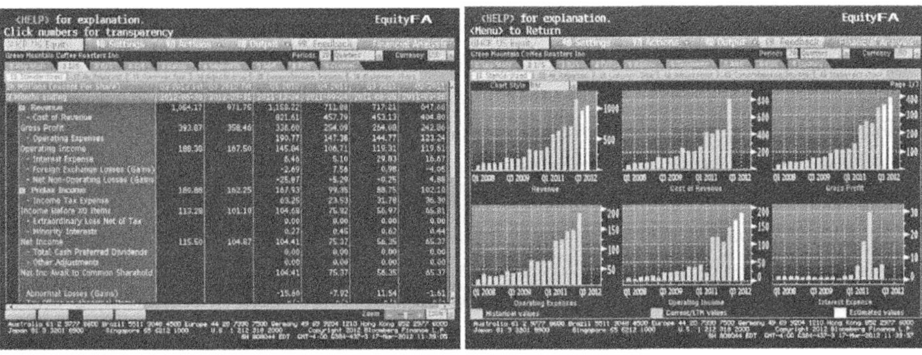

EXHIBIT 2.16

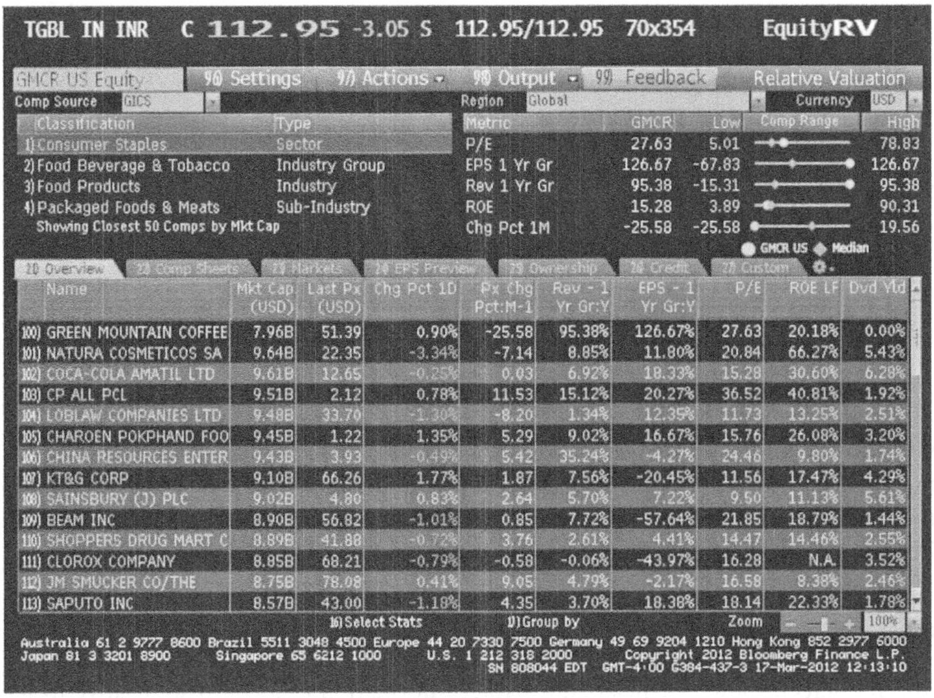

TGBL IN INR C 112.95 -3.05 S 112.95/112.95 70x354 EquityRV

GMCR US Equity | 96) Settings | 97) Actions | 98) Output | 99) Feedback | Relative Valuation

Comp Source GICS | Region Global | Currency USD

Classification	Type
1) Consumer Staples	Sector
2) Food Beverage & Tobacco	Industry Group
3) Food Products	Industry
4) Packaged Foods & Meats	Sub-Industry

Showing Closest 50 Comps by Mkt Cap

Metric	GMCR	Low	Comp Range	High
P/E	27.63	5.01		78.83
EPS 1 Yr Gr	126.67	-67.83		126.67
Rev 1 Yr Gr	95.38	-15.31		95.38
ROE	15.28	3.89		90.31
Chg Pct 1M	-25.58	-25.58		19.56

GMCR US ◆ Median

1) Overview | 2) Comp Sheets | 3) Markets | 4) EPS Preview | 5) Ownership | 6) Credit | 7) Custom

Name	Mkt Cap (USD)	Last Px (USD)	Chg Pct 1D	Px Chg Pct:M-1	Rev - 1 Yr Gr:Y	EPS - 1 Yr Gr:Y	P/E	ROE LF	Dvd Yld
100) GREEN MOUNTAIN COFFEE	7.96B	51.39	0.90%	-25.58	95.38%	126.67%	27.63	20.18%	0.00%
101) NATURA COSMETICOS SA	9.64B	22.35	-3.34%	-7.14	8.85%	11.80%	20.84	66.27%	5.43%
102) COCA-COLA AMATIL LTD	9.61B	12.65	-0.25%	0.03	6.92%	18.33%	15.28	30.60%	6.28%
103) CP ALL PCL	9.51B	2.12	0.78%	11.53	15.12%	20.27%	36.52	40.81%	1.92%
104) LOBLAW COMPANIES LTD	9.48B	33.70	-1.30%	-8.20	1.34%	12.35%	11.73	13.25%	2.51%
105) CHAROEN POKPHAND FOO	9.45B	1.22	1.35%	5.29	9.02%	16.67%	15.76	26.08%	3.20%
106) CHINA RESOURCES ENTER	9.43B	3.93	-0.49%	5.42	35.24%	-4.27%	24.46	9.80%	1.74%
107) KT&G CORP	9.10B	66.26	1.77%	1.87	7.56%	-20.45%	11.56	17.47%	4.29%
108) SAINSBURY (J) PLC	9.02B	4.80	0.83%	2.64	5.70%	7.22%	9.50	11.13%	5.61%
109) BEAM INC	8.90B	56.82	-1.01%	0.85	7.72%	-57.64%	21.85	18.79%	1.44%
110) SHOPPERS DRUG MART C	8.89B	41.88	-0.72%	3.76	2.61%	4.41%	14.47	14.46%	2.55%
111) CLOROX COMPANY	8.85B	68.21	-0.79%	-0.58	-0.06%	-43.97%	16.28	N.A.	3.52%
112) JM SMUCKER CO/THE	8.75B	78.08	0.41%	9.05	4.79%	-2.17%	16.58	8.38%	2.46%
113) SAPUTO INC	8.57B	43.00	-1.18%	4.35	3.70%	18.38%	18.14	22.33%	1.78%

16) Select Stats 1) Group by Zoom 100%

Australia 61 2 9777 8600 Brazil 5511 3048 4500 Europe 44 20 7330 7500 Germany 49 69 9204 1210 Hong Kong 852 2977 6000
Japan 81 3 3201 8900 Singapore 65 6212 1000 U.S. 1 212 318 2000 Copyright 2012 Bloomberg Finance L.P.
SN 808044 EDT GMT-4:00 G384-437-3 17-Mar-2012 12:13:10

The gray "Custom" tab on the right of the RV screen allows you to customize the table. The statistics settings box at the bottom of the screen (Select Stats) can be changed by clicking the averages, minimums, maximums, and standard deviations boxes. Alternatively, you can customize the screen by setting your cursor in the column heading area and holding the right clicker down on the mouse to access a menu. From the dropdown menu, you can bring up a description of the measure (DES) and how it is calculated; add a row displaying minimum, maximums, averages, and standard deviation (Show Statistics); delete the column, insert a new entry (Edit Column); and change the order for one of the measures (sort ascending or descending). New columns with new measures can also be added by clicking the gray button on the far right of the screen to bring up a menu and clicking "Add Column" from the menu to bring up an "Add Column" ribbon box area in the middle of the screen (this can also be done in the custom mode). In the box, you can type the name of the measure (e.g., market cap) and then hit <Enter> to activate. Doing this, the new entry will appear in the right column. Information on each of the companies can also be accessed by right clicking the company's name. This will bring up a menu that will allow you to access the company's description page (DES), its financials (FA), and other information. Finally, from the "Output" tab, you can send the screen data and information to Excel (see Exhibit 2.17).

EXHIBIT 2.17

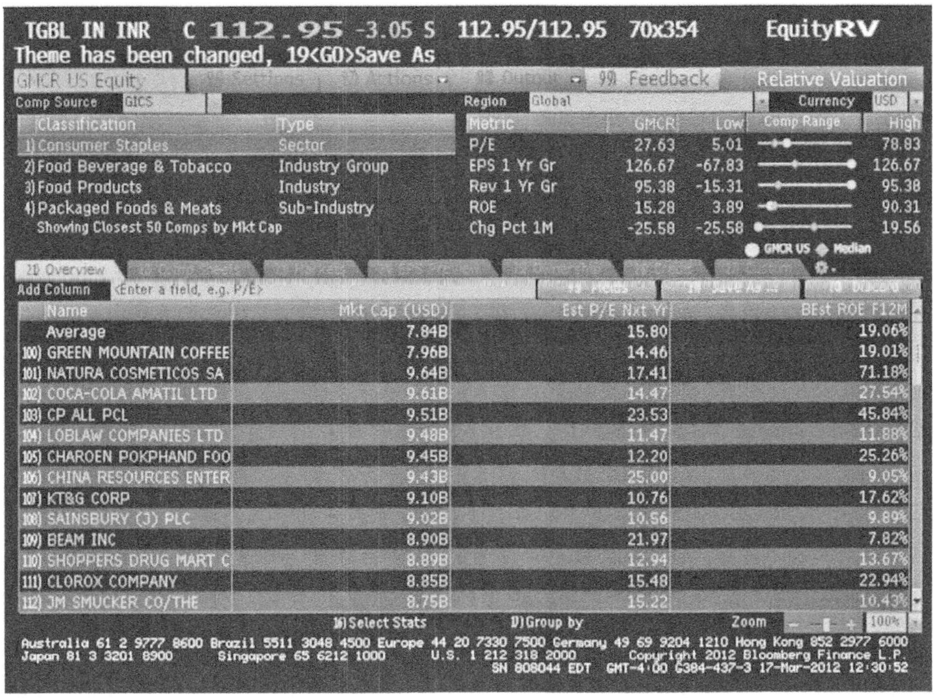

TGBL IN INR C 112.95 -3.05 S 112.95/112.95 70x354 EquityRV
Theme has been changed, 19<GO>Save As
GMCR US Equity 99) Feedback Relative Valuation
Comp Source GICS Region Global Currency USD

Classification	Type
1) Consumer Staples	Sector
2) Food Beverage & Tobacco	Industry Group
3) Food Products	Industry
4) Packaged Foods & Meats	Sub-Industry

Showing Closest 50 Comps by Mkt Cap

Metric	GMCR	Low	High
P/E	27.63	5.01	78.83
EPS 1 Yr Gr	126.67	-67.83	126.67
Rev 1 Yr Gr	95.38	-15.31	95.38
ROE	15.28	3.89	90.31
Chg Pct 1M	-25.58	-25.58	19.56

GMCR US Median

2) Overview
Add Column <Enter a field, e.g. P/E>

Name	Mkt Cap (USD)	Est P/E Nxt Yr	BEst ROE F12M
Average	7.84B	15.80	19.06%
100) GREEN MOUNTAIN COFFEE	7.96B	14.46	19.01%
101) NATURA COSMETICOS SA	9.64B	17.41	71.18%
102) COCA-COLA AMATIL LTD	9.61B	14.47	27.54%
103) CP ALL PCL	9.51B	23.53	45.84%
104) LOBLAW COMPANIES LTD	9.48B	11.47	11.88%
105) CHAROEN POKPHAND FOO	9.45B	12.20	25.26%
106) CHINA RESOURCES ENTER	9.43B	25.00	9.05%
107) KT&G CORP	9.10B	10.76	17.62%
108) SAINSBURY (J) PLC	9.02B	10.56	9.89%
109) BEAM INC	8.90B	21.97	7.82%
110) SHOPPERS DRUG MART C	8.89B	12.94	13.67%
111) CLOROX COMPANY	8.85B	15.48	22.94%
112) JM SMUCKER CO/THE	8.75B	15.22	10.43%

16) Select Stats 1) Group by Zoom 100%

Australia 61 2 9777 8600 Brazil 5511 3048 4500 Europe 44 20 7330 7500 Germany 49 69 9204 1210 Hong Kong 852 2977 6000
Japan 81 3 3201 8900 Singapore 65 6212 1000 U.S. 1 212 318 2000 Copyright 2012 Bloomberg Finance L.P.
SN 808044 EDT GMT-4:00 G384-437-3 17-Mar-2012 12:30:52

Name	EBITDA Mrgn	OPM T12M	ROIC	ROA	ROE
GREEN MOUNTAIN COFFEE ROASTERS	18.203199	13.9165	12.7726	8.7338	15.2789
SARA LEE CORP	13.1206	8.6741	11.3702	14.0127	75
GRUPO BIMBO SAB-SERIES A	10.5446	7.6115	7.6974	4.5422	11.5782
CONAGRA FOODS INC	14.3322	11.3988	10.792	7.0593	16.975901
CAMPBELL SOUP CO	20.857599	17.3857	23.3095	12.2545	79.0467
CHAROEN POKPHAND FOODS PUB	9.4333	7.1338	9.7624	11.075	26.0793
JM SMUCKER CO/THE	22.816999	18.9613	8.4395	5.8834	9.0309
SAPUTO INC	13.1133	11.3735	17.1313	13.0423	21.7185
NESTLE INDIA LTD	21.018801	18.9718	59.411598	27.6304	90.313004

EXHIBIT 2.18

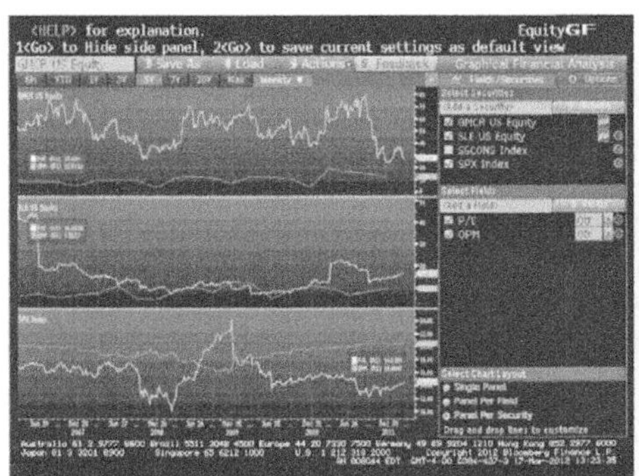

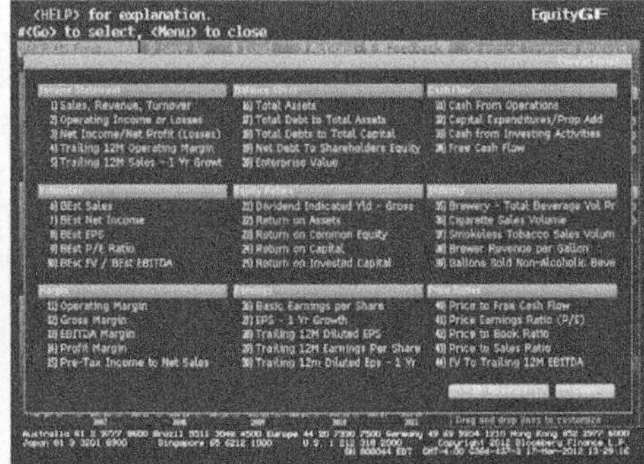

Fundamental Graphs: GF

The GF function (graphical financial analysis) allows you to graphically compare company fundamentals and ratios against other companies and indexes (see Exhibit 2.18). On the screen, select a fundamental measure or measures from a field (e.g., the price-to-earnings ratio [P/E] for Green Mountain, GMCR), and panels to display the measure over time, as well as other companies (e.g., Sara Lee, SLE), and indexes (e.g., S&P 500) for comparisons. Using the functions found in the tabs at the top of the GF screen, you can create a report (Actions) and save the settings (Templates) for future access. Similarly, the data or the graph images can be imported to a clipboard by clicking the function from the gray dropdown "Chart" tab in the graph panel.

Index FA, RV, and GF Functions

Note that there are GF, RV, and FA functions for indexes such as the S&P 500 (SPX). The RV screen for an index consists of the stocks making up the index. Like the stock RV screen, these screens also have considerable functionality (Exhibit 2.19). The screens can be accessed from the index's menu screen: Index ticker <Index> <Enter>.

Municipal FA, RV, and Other Functions

The municipal MIFA screen can be used to access financial information on state governments (MIFA <Enter>). The screen allows you to select a state and then access information on the state from a dropdown (Exhibit 2.20). On the dropdown, the state's identification number is also shown (e.g., California: stoca1 US). Using the identification number, you can access the state's menu directly: Stoca1 <Index> <Enter> or Stoca1 <Equity> <Enter>. Information on the dropdown or state screen that can be accessed includes description (DES), financials (FA), relative evaluations (RV), demographics, (DEMS), employment (BLS), and a municipal search (SMUN). The municipal FA and RV screen displays income statements, balance sheets, and other information useful for evaluating the government's financial strength. On the

EXHIBIT 2.19

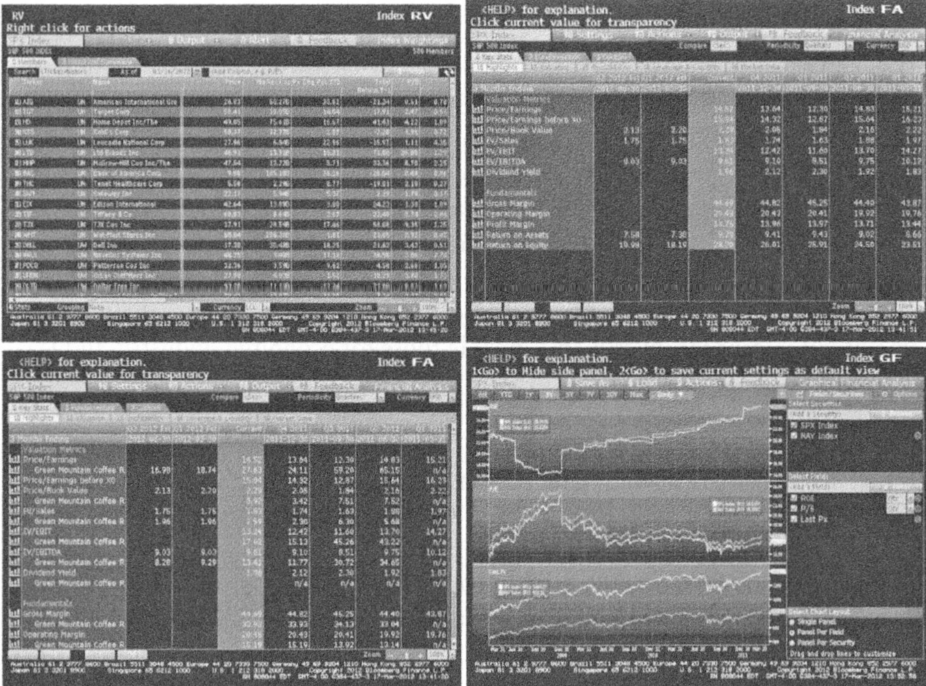

FA and RV screens, you can also change the fund category from general to pension to view the municipal pension position. Information on municipals securities of the state or municipalities in the state can be accessed by clicking the municipal screener (SMUN) from the dropdown MIFA menu screen for a state. Municipalities can also be accessed directly by entering SMUN <Enter>. Finally, municipals can be found using the SECF screen: SECF <Enter>, click FI tab and "Muni" tab, and type the name of the municipality (e.g., California) in the "Issuer Name" box.

EXHIBIT 2.20

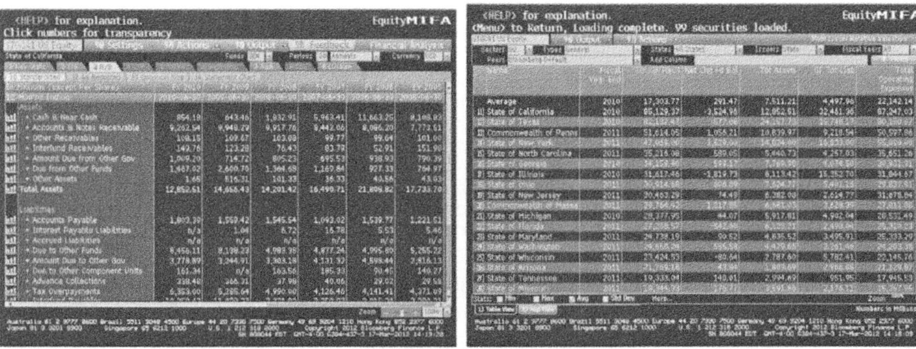

Screens

Many screens in Bloomberg can be accessed directly by typing in the name of the screen and hitting <Enter>. As noted, if a stock or security is loaded, typing in the name of the screen function, such as DES or GP, brings up that security's screen. Like the MIFA screen, there are also a number of screens that can be accessed by typing in the appropriate screen name. For example, typing EPR brings up a page showing the listing of exchanges with information on each exchange and its website; PRTU takes you to a screen for constructing portfolios; CIXB brings up a screen for inputting securities, indexes, or a portfolio in which historical prices and returns are calculated. This data can be later used in other functions to analyze the portfolio. Some useful screens for investments include those for economic, industry, and legal analysis.

Economic Information and Statistics: ECOF, ECO, and ECST

ECOF

Country and regional economic data on employment, business conditions, housing, balance of payments, prices, and other macroeconomic data can be accessed from the ECOF screen (Exhibit 2.21). Clicking an entry (e.g., nominal GDP) on the ECOF menu screen brings up a screen showing a graph of an economic measure (top left corner) and a listing of related measures whose graphs can be accessed by clicking the measure's entry. Using the dropdown "Chart" tab above the graph on the ECOF screen, you can copy the data or image to a clipboard, allowing you to move the data to Excel or Word. You can also find regional data by typing the name of a metropolitan city or state in the ribbon area above the graph. Finally, using the ticker for the economic series, you can upload a menu of screens for the series on the index screen: Ticker <Index> <Enter>.

EXHIBIT 2.21

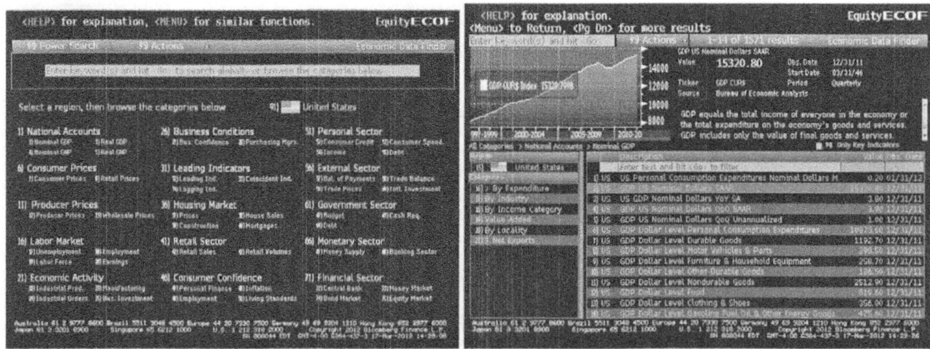

EXHIBIT 2.22

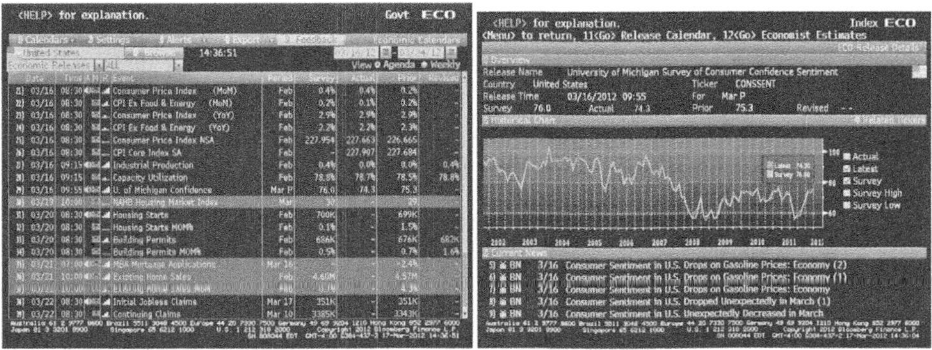

ECO

The ECO screen displays current, historical, and upcoming economic releases and events by region, country, and event type. Clicking an entry (e.g., U of Michigan Confidence index) brings up a screen showing a graph of the economic measure or indictor and a listing of news stories and commentaries related to the release or event. Using the dropdown tabs on the ECO screen, you can bring up ECO screens for different releases and events by country. Also, by moving your cursor to an entry and right clicking, you can access a menu of additional functions (e.g., description or graphs). On the ECO graphs, you can copy the data or image to a clipboard, allowing you to move the data to Excel or Word or bring up its menu screen: Ticker <Index> <Enter> (see Exhibit 2.22).

ECST, ECOW, and ECMX

The ECST, ECOW, and ECMX screens display current and historical economic statistics by country (Exhibit 2.23). The screens provide functions for changing the country and economic measure, converting the data to graphs, changing the time period, and exporting the information to Excel.

Sector and Industry Information: BI Platform

The BI platform (BI <Enter>) is Bloomberg's proprietary industry research portal (Exhibit 2.24). Information on the BI screen includes data, research, and analysts' insights about industries and companies in an industry. On the BI screen, you can click an industry (e.g., large pharmaceutical) to bring up its screen. On a selected industry's screen, you can then click entries under the gray "Monitor" tab for events, markets, comp sheets, and credit ratings. Historical financial data and information for the industry and the companies comprising it can be found by accessing the "Data Library" tab, and industry insights and analysis by sector analysis experts is found by accessing the "Analysis" tab.

EXHIBIT 2.23

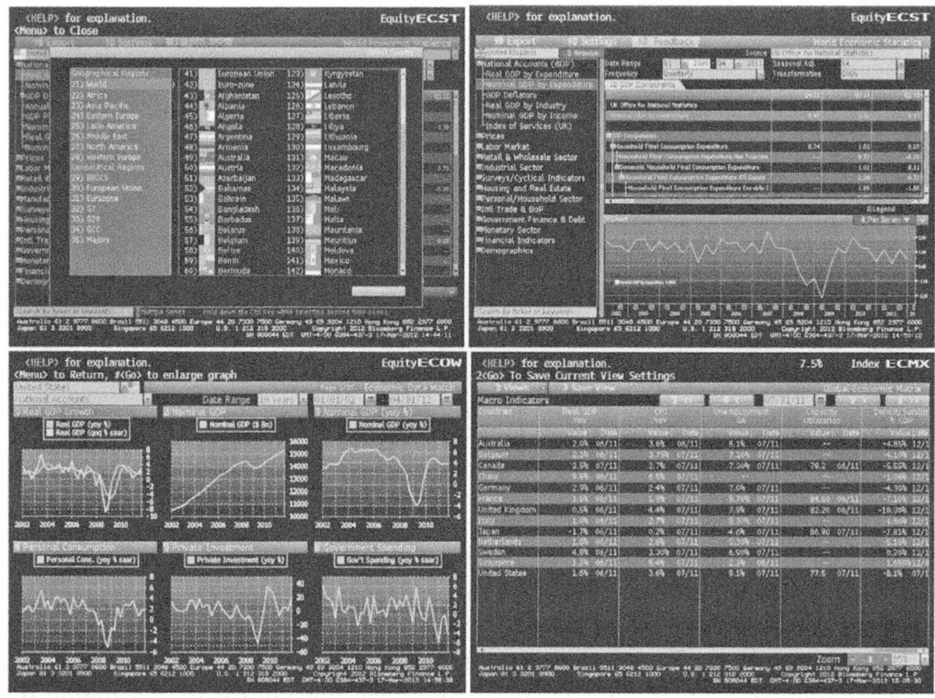

EXHIBIT 2.24

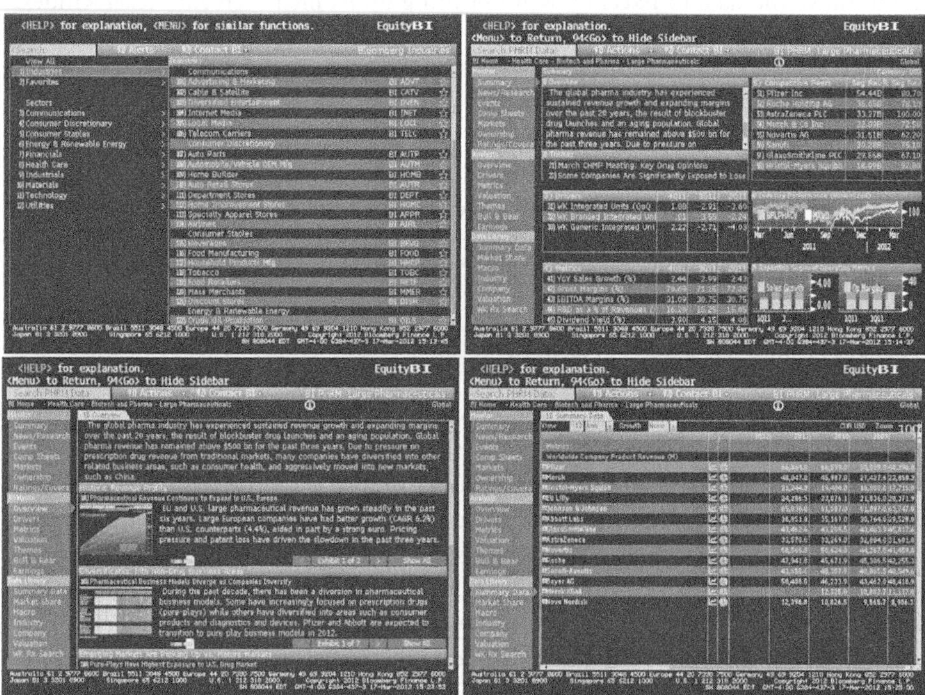

BLAW <Law>

The BLAW menu provides legal, regulatory, and compliance information and functions (Exhibit 2.25). The menu is useful for not only accessing laws as they relate to certain industries and regions, but also identifying judgments, rulings, and pending cases. For investment purposes, many companies' performances are impacted by laws and lawsuits brought against them. The BLAW menu is extensive. A good starting point is to use the search functions (BBLS) to look for laws, codes, filings, decisions, and other information. Such information can be found by country and region.

Monitor and Portal Screens

There are a number of screens that monitor current prices and events occurring in the various markets, as well as economic and financial events in different countries.

Bond Monitors: FIT, WB, RATT, RATC, CSDR, IM, and BTMM

Using the FIT screen, you can access U.S. Treasuries and other sovereign securities directly. For the United States FIT screen, you can select the types of Treasuries based on their maturities (bills, notes, bonds, TIPs, and strips) or those most recently issued and more actively traded (Actives). To access the menu screen for a particular bond, place your cursor on the bond of interest, right click to access the description (DES) screen to obtain a CUSIP or ISN number, and then enter: CUSIP <Govt> <Enter>.

Like the FIT screen, the WB monitor (WB <Enter>) displays and compares bonds by different global areas. From the monitor, you can compare bonds of different countries in terms of yields. From the screens (icons), you can also bring up historical yields and current yield curves (discussed in Chapter 4).

EXHIBIT 2.25

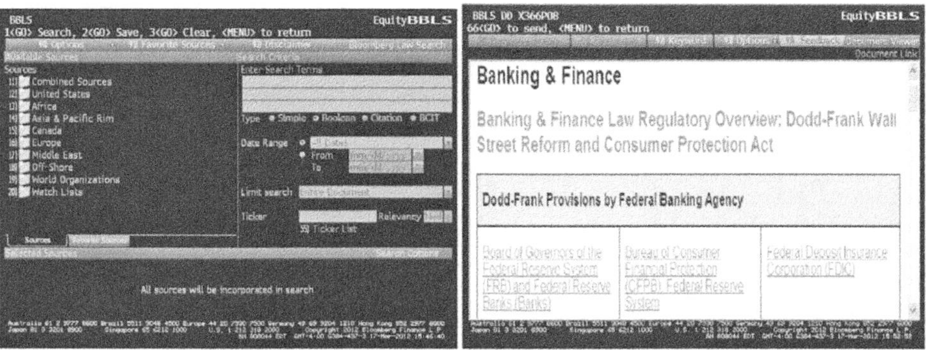

Three other bond monitors to note are RATC, RATT, and CSDR. RATC displays and searches for credit rating changes, RATT shows trends in quality ratings, and CSDR shows sovereign debt ratings. These screens will be described further in Chapter 5 when we examine bond risk.

The IM screen displays a directory of bond monitors for each country. Clicking the country, in turn, brings up a BTMM screen for that country. Alternatively, you can bring up the BTMM screen (BTMM <Enter>), which shows the U.S. bond monitor and then use the dropdown to "Change Country" tab to select a country (Exhibit 2.26).

EXHIBIT 2.26

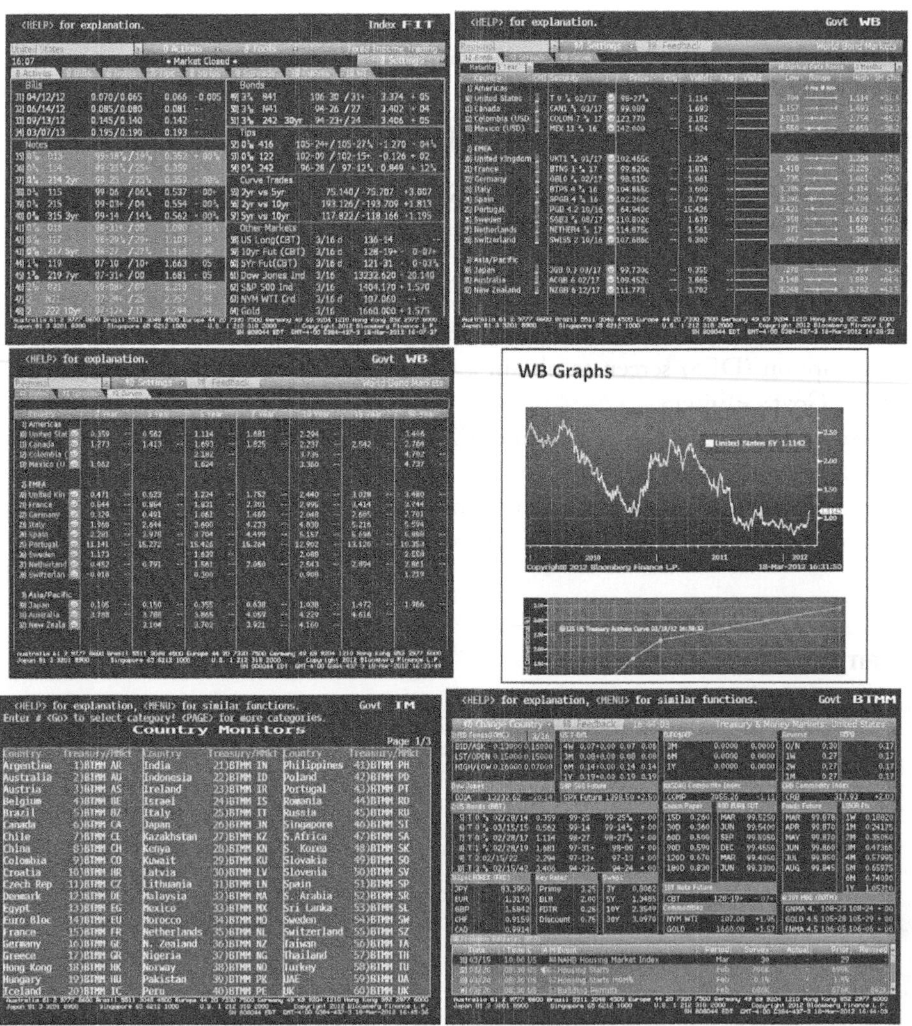

EXHIBIT 2.27

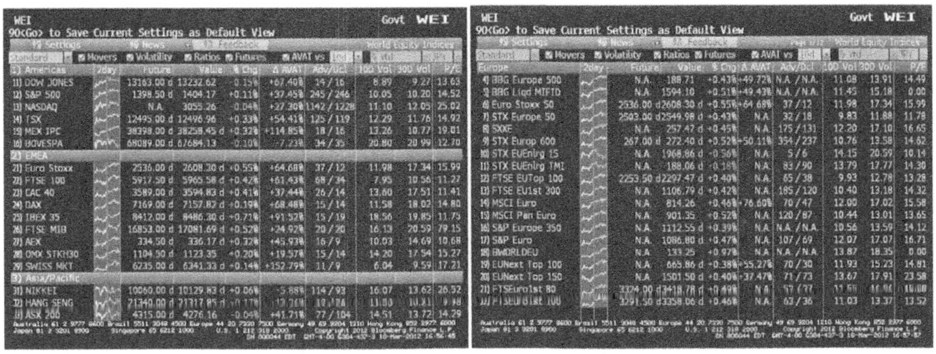

Stock Monitors: WEI, IMAP, MMAP, and MOST

WEI

The World Equity Indices (WEI) screen (WEI <Enter>) monitors world equity indexes. As noted previously, this index is a good way to find an index's ticker symbol. On the WEI screen (Exhibit 2.27), you can also select different information about the indexes, such as futures prices, movers (advance and declines), ratios (e.g., P/E ratio), and currency. On the screen, you can click the country area (e.g., EMEA) to bring up more indexes for that geographical area.

IMAP

The IMAP screen displays intraday price movements and news across industries, regions, and the companies (Exhibit 2.28). It includes a heat map showing the performances of stocks and sectors. Using the "Source" dropdown menu, you can select all securities, different indexes, constructed portfolios, and save searches. On the table menu listing stocks or areas, you can select sectors or regions, and on the table menu for stocks and areas, you can access both price information and news information.

MMAP

MMAP displays global market segments, and the companies that operate within those segments (Exhibit 2.29). The user can select investment parameters, (e.g., growth in earnings) for different global areas and sectors to do a comparative evaluation of stocks in a sector or a region.

MOST

MOST displays the day's most active stocks by volume, the leading advancers and decliners by percentage or net gain/loss, stocks with the most value traded on an

EXHIBIT 2.28

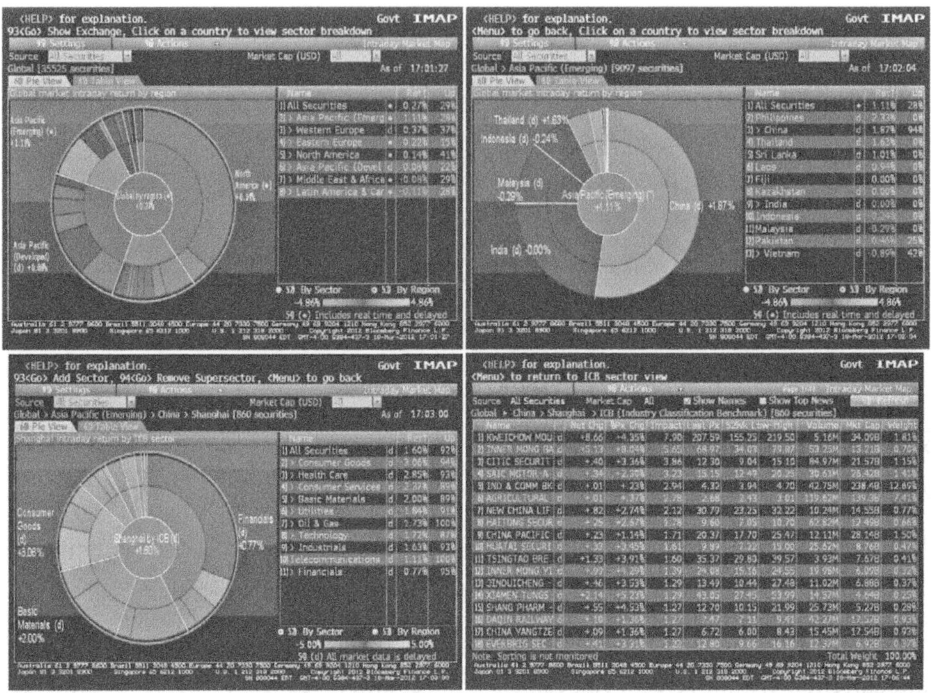

exchange, and stocks with the largest volume increase for the day (Exhibit 2.30). On the screen, you can change to different indexes, sectors, and time periods, as well as access portfolios and searches created by the user.

New Bond and Equity Offerings: NIM and IPO

The NIM screen monitors news headlines and security data for new stock and bond issues (Exhibit 2.31). Clicking a category on the NIM screen (e.g., U.S. Bond Market)

EXHIBIT 2.29

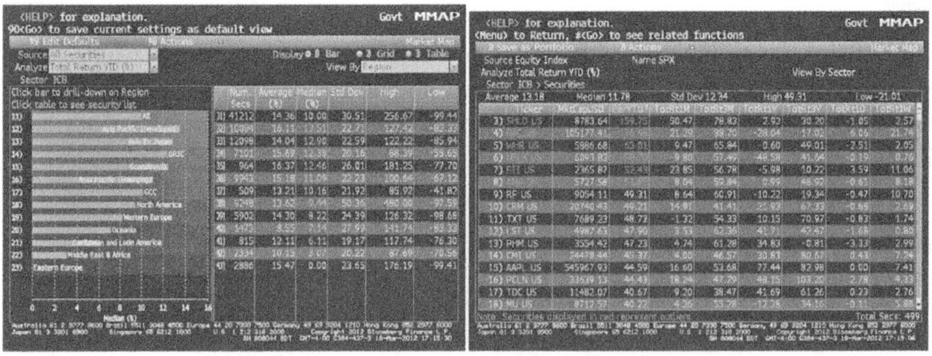

EXHIBIT 2.30

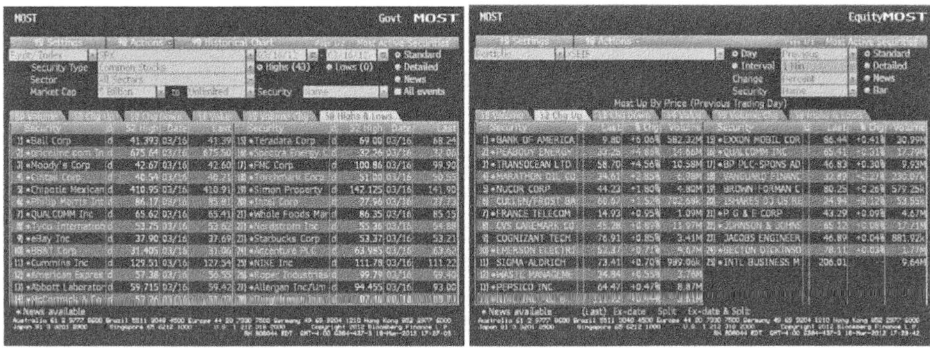

brings up a screen showing new or pending bond issues; clicking an issue brings up a description screen with details about the issue. Equity issues can also be accessed from the IPO screen: IPO <Enter>. On the IPO screen, you can search for issues in different stages of the issuance process.

COUN and BTMM: Country Information Indicators

Selecting a country on the COUN screen takes you to that country's screen, where there is summary information on the country's security markets, debt ratings, events,

EXHIBIT 2.31

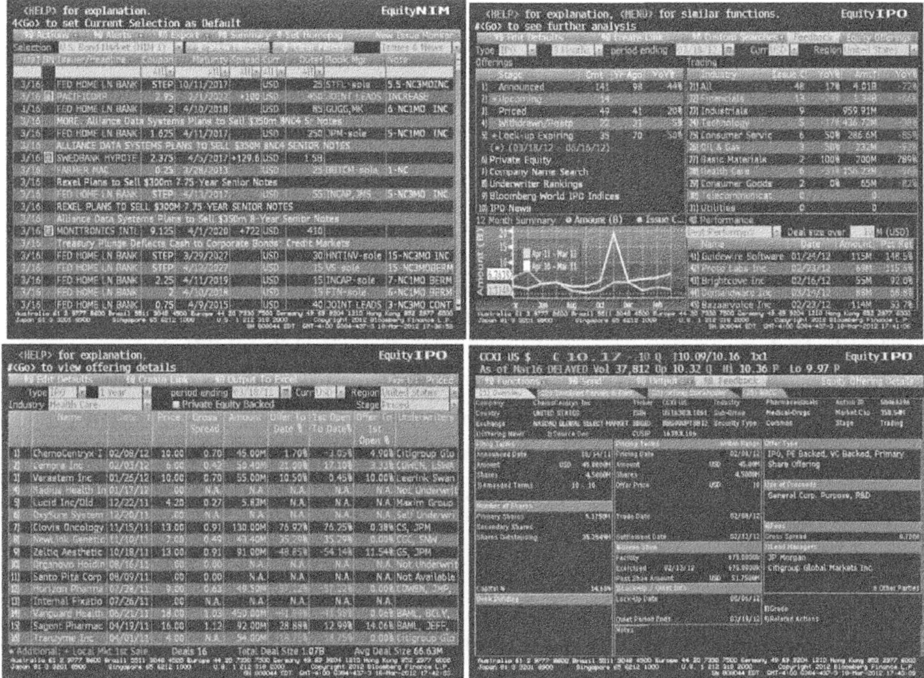

EXHIBIT 2.32

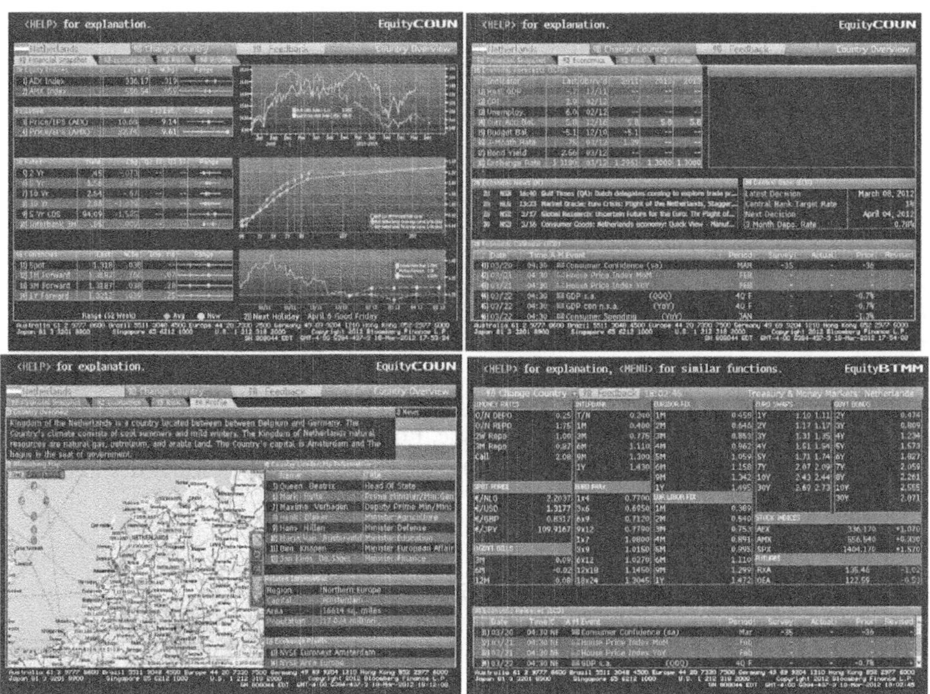

and most active stocks. On the country screen, you can also click summary areas to bring up screens with more detail information and other links. The BTMM screen (BTMM <Enter>) provides interest rate and security price information by country.

Calendar Screens

Bloomberg has several event calendar screens that allow users to monitor events, securities, and corporate actions. Two screens of note are EVTS and CACT.

EVTS

The EVTS calendar screen displays a calendar of corporate events and corresponding details, including transcripts and audio recordings (Exhibit 2.33). You can opt to display historical or upcoming events on a daily, weekly, or monthly basis. You can also select from the dropdown "Source" tab all securities, securities from an index, securities from a search, or securities from a portfolio created in Bloomberg. The user can also save the screen and set up alerts (click bell icon next to security) in which Bloomberg will notify the user by Bloomberg's message system.

CACT—Class Action and Corporate Action Filings

The CACT monitor screen displays a calendar of class actions and corporate action filings of corporations and municipalities, such as stock buybacks, capital changes,

EXHIBIT 2.33

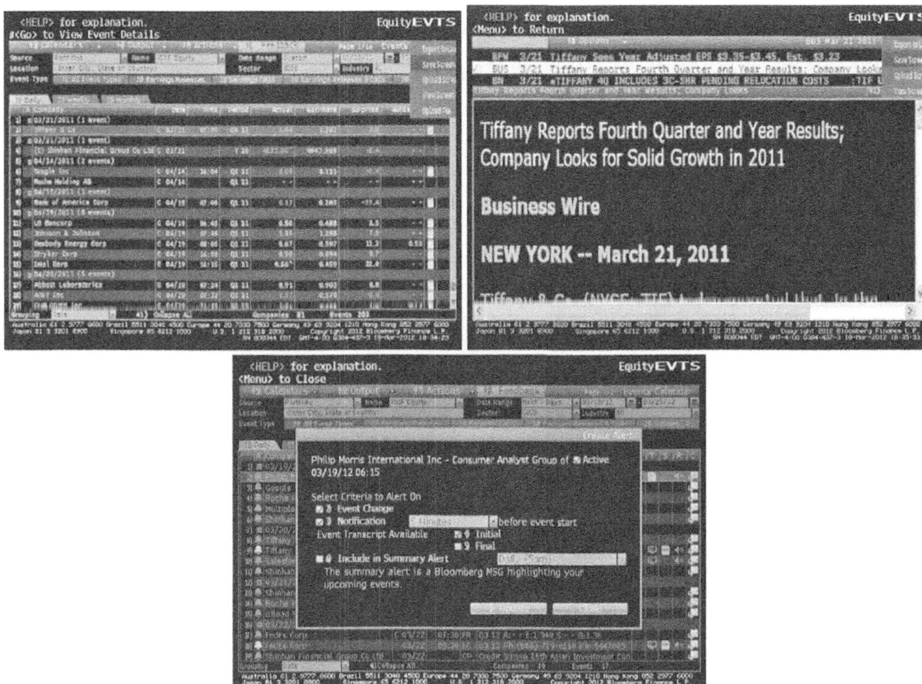

and mergers and acquisitions (Exhibit 2.34). At the top of the CACT screen, you can select time period, geographical area, and types of actions (e.g., merger and acquisition or stock splits). You can also customize the actions. (See Exhibit 2.35 for examples of some of the other monitors.)

Other Monitors and Portals

- MNSA Today's announced merger and acquisition deals
- PREL Pipeline of announced bonds

EXHIBIT 2.34

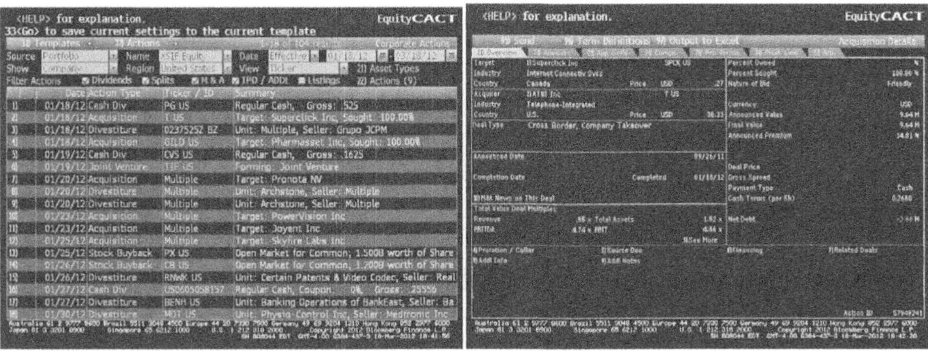

EXHIBIT 2.35

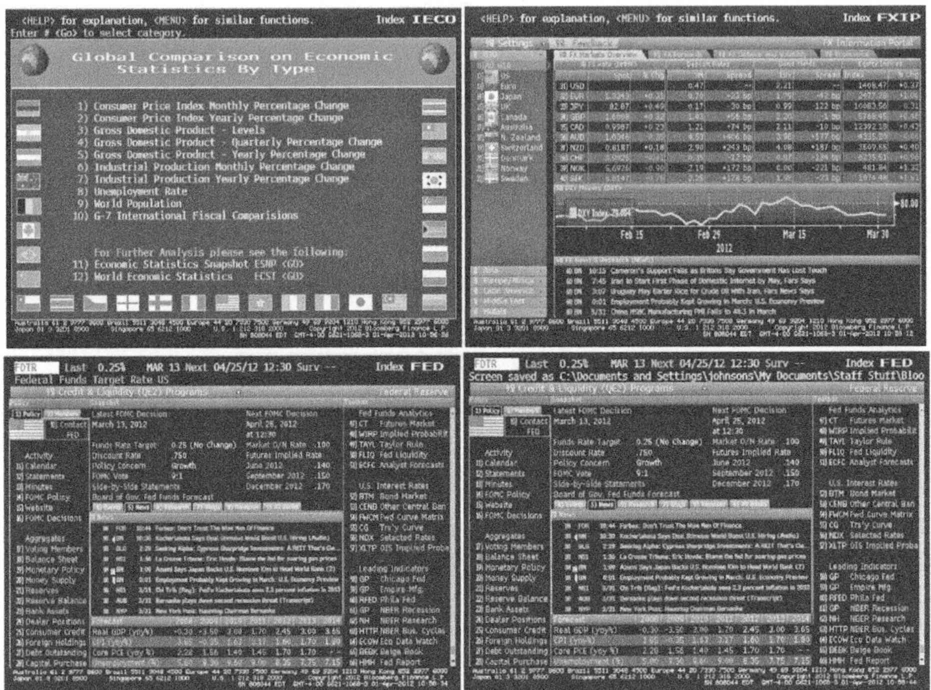

- DIS Distressed bonds
- BNKF Bankruptcy filings
- PE Private equity
- TACT Trade activity
- BRIEF Daily Economic Newsletter
- EIU Economist Intelligence Unit
- IECO Global Comparison of Economic Statistics
- FXIP Foreign Exchange Information Portal
- CENB Central Bank Menu: Use to access platforms of central banks
- FED Federal Reserve Bank portal
- ECB European Central Bank portal
- WWCC Portal for worldwide credit crunch
- LTOP Top underwriters
- FICM Fixed-income monitor
- PGM Money market lookup by program type

Portfolios and Baskets

Portfolio Construction and Analysis: PRTU and PMEN

A user can set up a stock or fixed-income portfolio on Bloomberg using PRTU and, once loaded, analyze and monitor the portfolio using the PMEN menu.

STEPS FOR CREATING PORTFOLIOS

STEP 1: PRTU

PRTU displays a list of portfolios. To create a portfolio using PRTU:

1. PRTU <Enter>.
2. On the PRTU screen, click the "Create" button. This will bring up a two-page screen for inputting information:
   a. Settings Page: Name of your portfolio, asset class (equity, fixed income, balanced), and benchmark (e.g., S&P 500).
   b. Securities Page: Screen for inputting securities by their identifiers. (*Note:* A help ful way to load a stock is to go to an RV or index screen and find the securities of interest; then drop and drag the security.)

Note: Searches and other portfolios that have been saved in Bloomberg can be imported. To import: Click the "Options" tab on the PRTU screen, click "Import," and then import and name the search.

3. Once the portfolio is loaded, hit "Save." The name given to the portfolio will then be displayed on the PRTU screen.

STEP 2: PMEN

With the portfolio loaded, click the "Portfolio Menu" tab on PRTU screen or type PMEN to access a menu of functions to apply to the portfolio.

The screens in Exhibit 2.36 show the PRTU Portfolio, PRTU Benchmark, PRTU Settings, and PRTU Create screens for loading a stock portfolio named XSIF Equity. This portfolio is evaluated relative to the S&P 500, and the portfolio prices are computed in dollars.

Note: Different Indexes for comparing portfolios can be added by accessing the Benchmark Screen (Click the Benchmark tab found on the right of the PRTU screen).

On the PMEN menu screen, there are number of useful screens for analyzing a portfolio's current and historical performances. To use these screens, click the "Enable History" and "Enable data acquisition" boxes for the portfolio on the PRTU page. See Exhibit 2.37 for steps needed to enable history.

Many of the screens found on the PMEN menu can be used for in depth portfolio analysis (see Exhibit 2.38). The "Portfolio Risk & Analytics" screen (PORT), for example, allows you to evaluate a portfolio in depth. By accessing the screen tabs (e.g., "Holdings," "Characteristics," "Performance," and "Attributions"), you can evaluate the features, drivers, and historical performances of the portfolio, securities in the portfolio, and the portfolio's index. (*Note:* Many of these same functions can be accessed directly: PORT HD to access holdings, PORT CH to access characteristics, and PORT PA to access performance attributes.) Other screens of note on the PMEN menu screen include the "Historical Performance" screen (PORT HP) that shows the historical total return of the portfolio, Portfolio Display (PDSP), Portfolio News (NPH), Events Calendar (EVTS), Equity Relative Valuation (RVP), Expected Cash Flow (PCF), PREP, Historical Fund Analysis (HFA), and Summary Reports (PRTS). Some of these screens can be found from the PMEN screen by clicking a

EXHIBIT 2.36

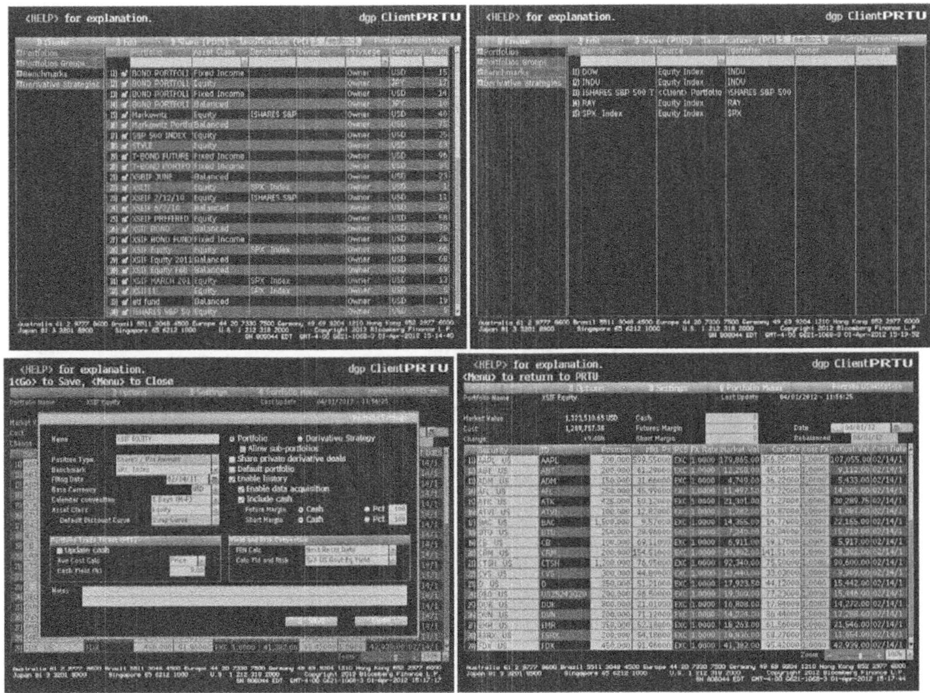

white heading (e.g., "Performance & Attributions"). Many of these screens have tabs for accessing different information, sending information to Excel, and downloading information to PDF and Excel reports.

Once a portfolio is created, it can be exported to other screens or imported from other screens. For example, if you wanted to analyze a portfolio created in PRTU using relative valuation, instead of using the RVP function in PMEN, you could select a stock in the portfolio (e.g., Apple [AAPL]), access the stock's menu (AAPL <Equity> <Enter>), and then bring up the stock's RV menu (Exhibit 2.39). On the RV menu of the stock, you can then import the portfolio by selecting "Portfolio" from the dropdown "Comp Source" tab and the name of the portfolio from the dropdown "Name" menu. Similarly, you can also import the portfolio from other screens, such as the CACT, MOST, IMAP, EVTS, and MMAP screens, and also from Excel using the Bloomberg Excel Add-In.

Creating Baskets: CIXB

Historical price and return data on stocks, bonds, commodities, and portfolios created from PRTU and securities found from searches and screens using the Bloomberg search/screen functions (discussed in the next section) can be imported from the CIXB screen and then evaluated as an index basket using the Index menu.

EXHIBIT 2.37

Enabling History

- On the PRTU settings screen, check "Enable history" and "Enable data acquisition" and click "Save" to bring up a blank menu screen.
- On the menu screen, the "Date" and "Rebalanced" tabs appear on the right above the list of securities. The "Rebalanced" tab will show today's date.
- On the "Date" tab select a date to begin the history (e.g. 6 years prior to today's date: 04/01/06).
- After selecting a past date, use the red "Option" tab to import a portfolio that you have created (e.g., XSIF Equity). On the import box, select "Portfolio" from the "Import" tab, name of portfolio (XSIF Equity), and then change the date to today's date, and click "Import."

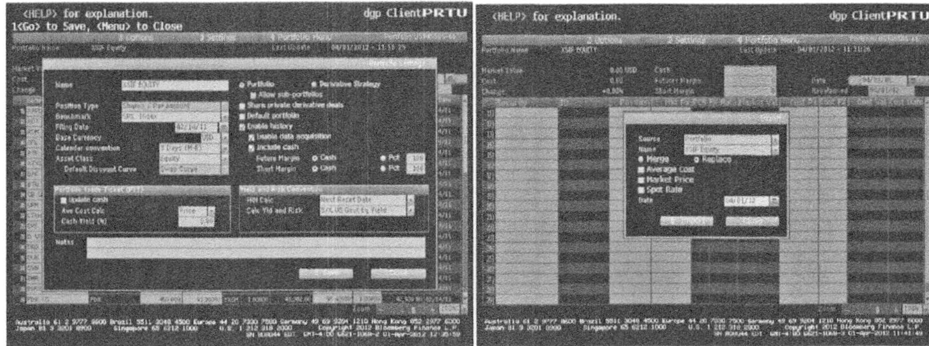

EXHIBIT 2.38

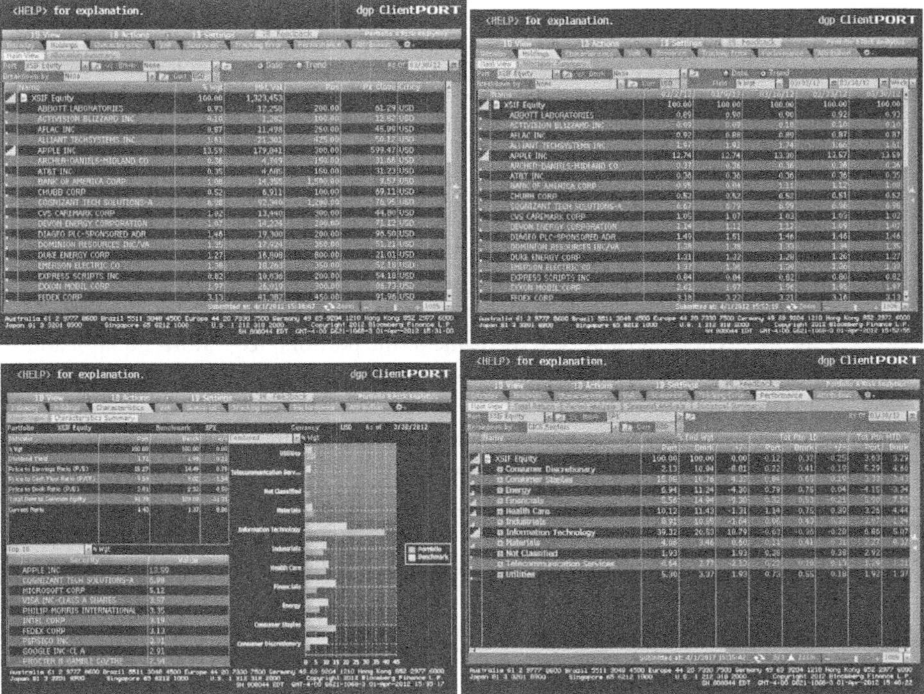

EXHIBIT 2.39

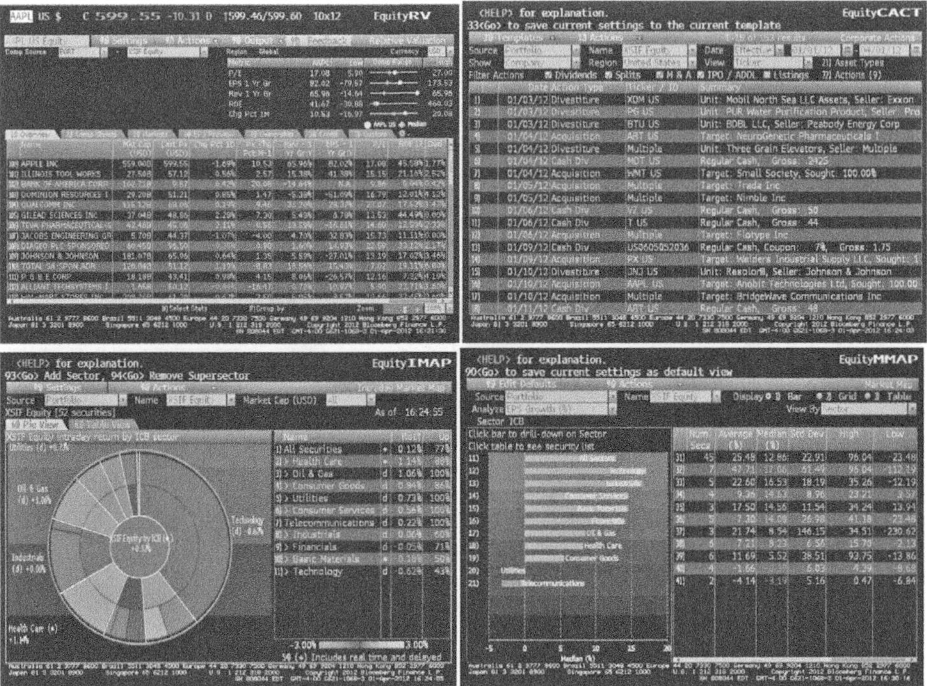

STEPS FOR CREATING AND ANALYZING A CIXB INDEX BASKET

1. To access: CIXB <Enter>.
2. On CIXB screen, type in securities ticker or import the securities from a portfolio or search. To import a portfolio from a list:

(1) Click "Actions" tab and click "Import" to bring up import screen.

(2) On import screen, click "Import from List" tab at bottom to bring up "Import from List" tab.

(3) On "Import from List" tab: (1) click dropdown "Source" tab and click "Portfolio"; (2) click "Name" tab and then the name of the portfolio (e.g., XSIF Equity); and (3) click "Import" tab. These steps will import the portfolio's stocks, shares, and price to the CIXB screen.

(4) On the CIXB screen, name the ticker and the portfolio in the "Ticker" and "Name" box and then click "Create" to bring up a data creation box.

(5) In the data creation box select the time period for price and return data. After selecting the time period, hit "Save." This will activate a Bloomberg program for calculating the portfolio's daily historical returns. The data will be sent to a report, RPT. To access this report, type "RPT" and hit <Enter>.

EXHIBIT 2.40

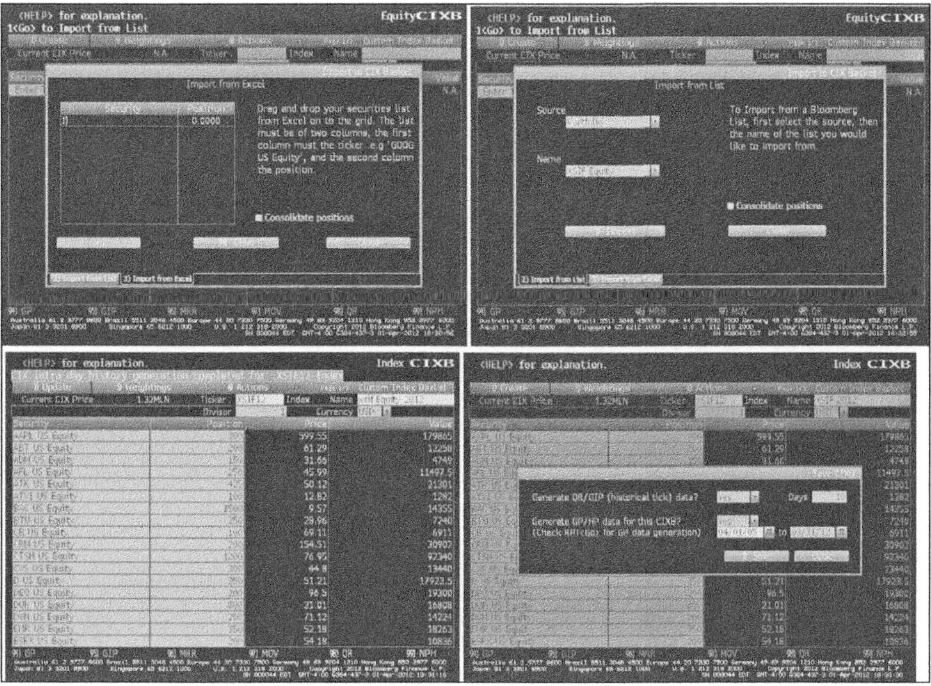

A portfolio created in CIXB can be identified on the PRTU screen where it can be analyzed using the functions on the PMEN screen. In addition, a CIXB portfolio can be treated as an index where it can be analyzed using the functions in the Index menu. To analyze a CIXB-generated portfolio as an index, type the ticker of the portfolio, such as .XSIF2012 (remember the period), strike the "Index" key, and hit <Enter>: .XSIF2012 <Index> <Enter>. From the index menu, the portfolio can be analyzed by accessing Description (DES), Price Graph (GP), Financial Graphs (GF), Market Heat Map (MMAP), Intraday Market Map, Comparative Total Return (COMP), Historical Regression, and other functions applicable to indexes (Exhibit 2.41).

Screening and Search Functions

Given the thousands of securities and funds that exist globally, investment analysis requires being able to search and screen for securities. Bloomberg provides screening and search functions for most security types and funds.

Equity Screener Analysis: EQS

Equity Screener Analysis, EQS, searches for equity securities. Using this screen, you can screen by general categories, such as countries, exchanges, indices, security types, and security attributes, by security lists, and by data categories, such as fundamentals,

EXHIBIT 2.41

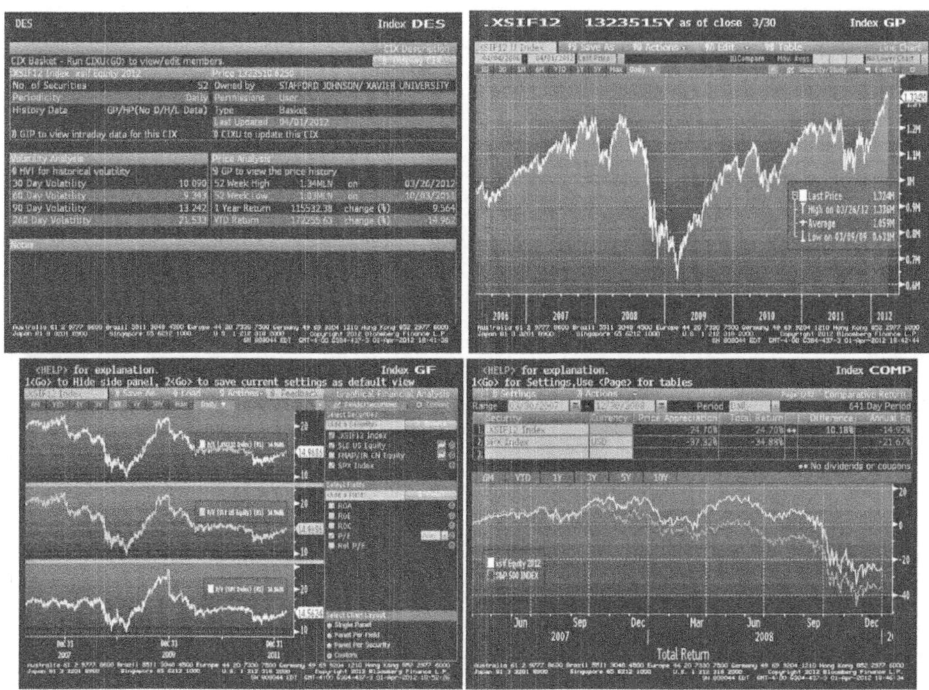

estimates, financial and price ratios, and technical fields. You can also save the screening criteria so that the identified securities can be analyzed using other functions or inputted to form a portfolio in PRTU.

EQS SEARCH EXAMPLE STEPS

- Bring up EQS screen: EQS <Enter>.
- Select a category such as "Indices."
- Scroll down the list of indexes and identify a specific index (e.g., S&P 1200 global index).
- On the ribbon, type in screening features, such as market cap greater than $15 billion, price-to-earnings ratio greater than 10, debt to total capital greater than 20 percent and less than 50 percent.
- Save the search by clicking the "Save As" from the action tab dropdown and then name the search (e.g., Equity SP 500 Style). *Note:* By clicking the "My Search" tab at the bottom of the EQS screen, you can find the stocks found from the search. Also, other Bloomberg functions such as relative valuation analysis (RV) can import stocks from your search for analysis.
- Click the "Output" tab at the bottom right corner to see the stocks found from the search.
- On the "Output" screen, you can export the screen information to Excel by clicking the "Output" tab and then clicking Excel.
- On the "Output" screen, you can click a stock on the output screen to access information on the stock (e.g., DES) or its menu.

EXHIBIT 2.42

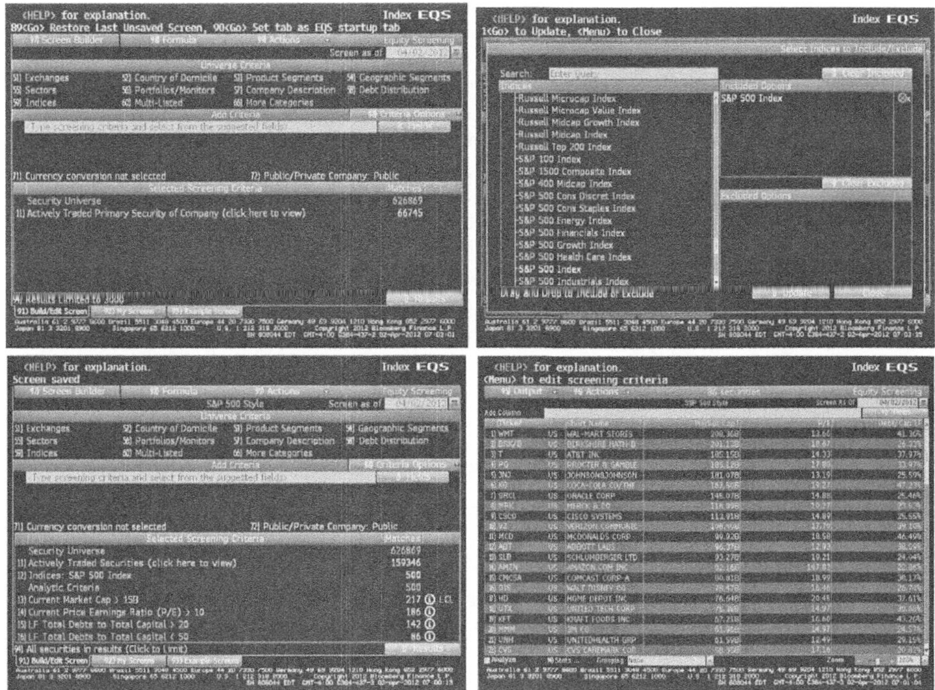

Custom Bond Searches (SRCH), and Municipal Bond Searches (MSRC)

From the SRCH screen, you can search for bonds that fit specified criteria based on coupon, maturity, country, currency, and structure type for government, corporate, structured notes and private securities. Using the MSRC screen, you can search and screen the universe of municipal bonds. Information on municipal securities and other information of a state or municipality in the state can also be accessed from the municipal screener (SMUN): SMUN <Enter>.

SRCH SEARCH EXAMPLE STEPS

- Bring up SRCH screen: SRCH <Enter>.
- Select features: currency, country, coupon, maturity, and the like.
- Save the search by clicking the "Save" tab, clicking "Save As," and then naming the search (e.g., "Investment Grade Select Sectors"). By clicking the "Saved Search" tab at the top of the SRCH screen, you can find the identified search.
- Click "Search" tab to see output.

EXHIBIT 2.43

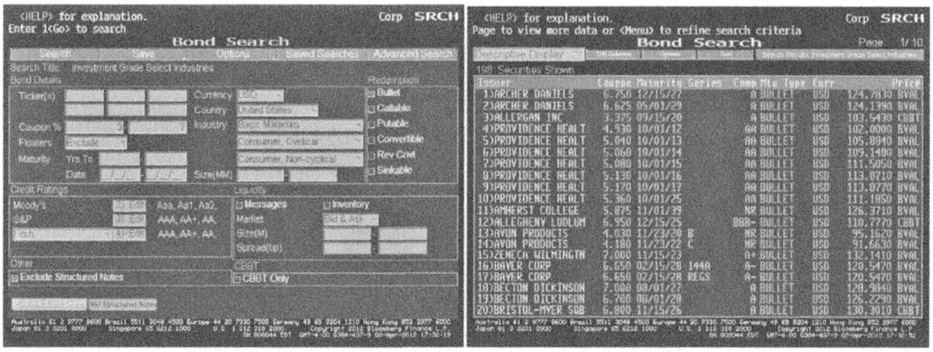

MRSC SEARCH EXAMPLE STEPS

- Bring up MSRC screen: MSRC <Enter>.
- Select features.
- Save the search by clicking the "Actions" tab, clicking "Save As," and then naming the search: "Ohio Municipals." Clicking the "My Searches" tab at the bottom of the MSRC screen, you can find the identified search. Also, other Bloomberg functions can import bonds from your search for analysis.
- Click the gray "Results" tab at the bottom right corner to see output.
- On the results screen, you can click the "Output" tab to export the screen's information to Excel.
- Place cursor on a bond on the output screen and left click to see a menu of information (e.g., description, DES).
- Use the CUSIP number (found on the Results screen) to access the bond's menu: Cusip # <Muni> <Enter>.

EXHIBIT 2.44

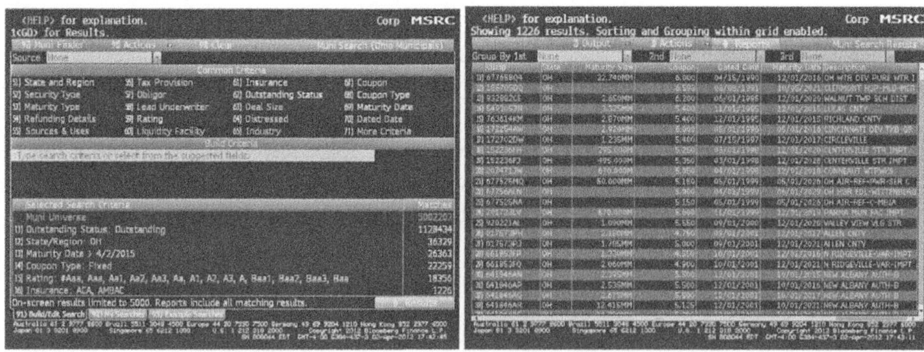

Fund Searches: FSRC

From the FRSC screen, you can search and screen investment funds by general investment criteria, such as asset class (stock, bond) balance, or type (open, closed, unit investment trust, or exchange-traded product); by country; by asset holding criteria (industry, market cap, maturity, or ratings); and by adding fields. The user can save the search. The screen menus of any of the funds listed from the search can be accessed by clicking the name of the fund. On the fund menu, the fund can be evaluated. Some of the uses of the FSRC screen are presented in our examination of investment funds in Chapter 8.

News Searches

The menu screens for each stock, bond, government security, and commodity provide a news function in which news and information on a selected company, country, or commodity can be accessed. The Bloomberg system also has news platforms that you can use to select areas for news or to conduct new searches. Two of note are "News, by Category" (NI or N) and "News Search" (TNI). NI can be used to search and screen the universe of news by category. TNI can be used to conduct advanced news searches. Using TNI, the selected news search criteria can be saved and a corresponding custom news alert can be set so that you can receive message from Bloomberg.

> **NI SEARCH EXAMPLE STEPS**
>
> - N <Enter>.
> - Select type of news from menu (e.g., Business News).
> - Select type of selected news, such as Economic News, Countries, and Economies (e.g., China).
> - Click a specific news story to bring up a PDF of that story.
> - On the dropdown tabs above the news stories, screen the news by sources, language, type, and time period.

EXHIBIT 2.45

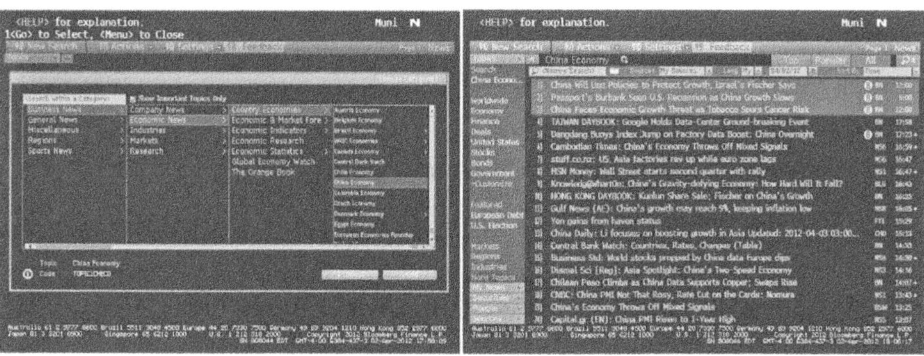

EXHIBIT 2.46

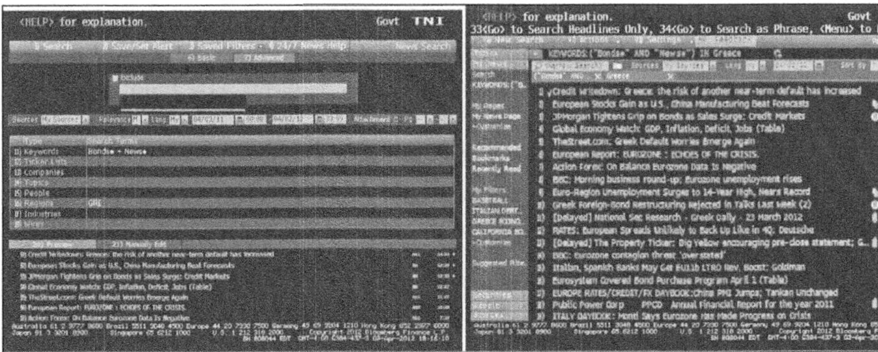

TNI SEARCH EXAMPLE STEPS

- TNI <Enter>.
- Select type of selected news, such as Topics, Economic News, Countries, and Economies (e.g., Greece); time period (past year); keywords (Bonds).
- Click the "Save and Set Alerts" tab to save the search: Greek Bonds.
- Click the Search tab to find stories.
- Click a specific news story to bring up a PDF of that story.
- On the dropdown tabs above the news stories, screen the news by sources, language, type, and time period.

Other Bloomberg Searches and Screeners

- GENL General news search by category
- MA Merger and acquisition searches
- RATC Search for credit rating changes
- PSCH Preferred stock search
- MSCH Money market search
- CTM Search commodities exchanges
- RSE Research search
- AV Bloomberg's media links
- LIVE Bloomberg's live links
- BBLS Search for legal documents
- ETF Exchange-traded products
- BMAP World energy and commodity map and platform

The Bloomberg Excel Add-In: Importing Bloomberg into Excel

In Bloomberg, many screens showing information can be exported to Excel by accessing an "Action" tab or output tab (Exhibit 2.47). The data behind many graphs also can be sent to a clipboard where it can be moved to Excel. Instead of exporting Bloomberg data, you can alternatively import Bloomberg information from Excel

EXHIBIT 2.47

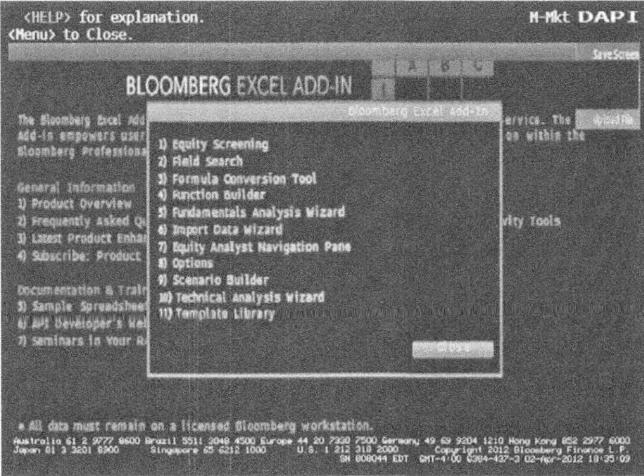

using the Bloomberg Excel Add-In. Using Excel to import Bloomberg data and information enables you to develop customized programs for analyzing securities and portfolios.

STEPS TO LOAD BLOOMBERG ADD-IN IN EXCEL

1. On computer, click Start.
2. Click "All Programs."
3. Click Bloomberg.
4. Click Excel Add-In
5. Click Install.

In addition, on the Bloomberg Add-In, there are a number of templates, data wizards, screeners, and other functions. The DAPI screen in Bloomberg provides a list of Bloomberg Add-In functions and how to use them. From the list, the "Import Data Wizard," "Fundamental Analysis Wizard," and "Template Library" are good ways to get started using the Bloomberg Add-In functions (Exhibit 2.48).

Import Data Wizard

Using the Import Data Wizard, you can import Bloomberg data into an Excel spreadsheet and customize the data using a variety of functions and formulas. The Import Data Wizard generates tables for various data types corresponding to that security. Using the "Market, Reference, Analytical, Data Sets," you can import current snapshot data. This Wizard function is good for compiling cross-sectional information. The "Historical End of Day" wizard can be used to pull data for a specified time period in increments; it is useful for time-series analysis. In each wizard, you move sequentially,

EXHIBIT 2.48

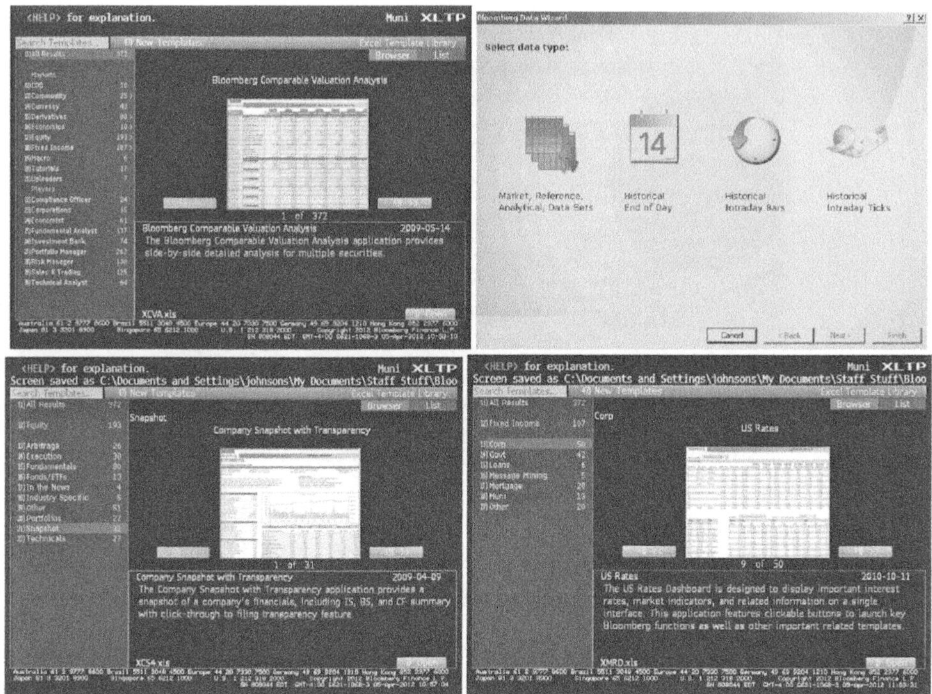

starting from a window where securities, portfolios, searches, and indexes are selected; to a fields window where data can be selected from an extensive list of financial, economics, and market information; next to a time period window for selecting the number of periods (for historical wizard); and finally to a window for selecting the Excel table layout.

Fundamental Analysis Wizard

Using the Fundamentals Analysis Wizard (accessed from the Financial/Estimates tab on the Bloomberg Excel Add-in), you can import customized data such as income statements, balance sheets, and cash flow statements on a company, index, or portfolio of stocks. The information can be viewed for selected single or multiple periods. The Excel table in Exhibit 2.49 shows an income statement for Duke Energy generated from the Fundamental Analysis Wizard.

Template Library

The Template Library enables you to locate and download a preconstructed Bloomberg spreadsheet from an extensive list of available spreadsheets. You can then save the spreadsheet to use as a template for future analysis. The sheets are grouped by

EXHIBIT 2.49 Excel Output from Bloomberg Excel Wizard: Fundamental Analysis

Ticker	DUK Equity
Currency	USD
Name	DUKE ENERGY CORP
Periodicity	Calendar Annually
Display Order	Chronological
Data Type	Bloomberg Fundamentals
Reported Status	Most Recent

Date:	CY1 2000	CY1 2001	CY1 2002	CY1 2003	CY1 2004	CY1 2005	CY1 2006	CY1 2007	CY1 2008	CY1 2009	CY1 2010	CY1 2011
Sales/Rev/Turnover	15,342.00	17,946.00	15,860.00	22,080.00	20,549.00	16,297.00	10,607.00	12,720.00	13,207.00	12,731.00	14,272.00	14,529.00
COGS/F E & P P &G	7,199.00	8,931.00	7,551.00	13,494.00	11,732.00	7,437.00	3,711.00	4,503.00	5,020.00	4,444.00	4,925.00	5,145.00
SG&A/Oth Op/Dep Op & Maint	5,054.00	5,400.00	5,343.00	6,114.00	5,580.00	5,839.00	5,499.00	5,719.00	5,660.00	5,654.00	6,313.00	6,280.00
Op Income (Loss)	3,089.00	3,615.00	2,966.00	2,472.00	3,237.00	3,021.00	1,397.00	2,498.00	2,527.00	2,633.00	3,034.00	3,104.00
Net Non-Oper Loss(Gains)	-925	-619	-153	2,815.00	-4	-2,394.00	-778	-423	-105	51	-16	-220
EBIT(Earn Bef Int & Tax)	3,089.00	3,615.00	2,966.00	2,472.00	3,237.00	3,021.00	1,397.00	2,498.00	2,527.00	2,633.00	3,034.00	3,104.00
Interest expense	911	760	1,097.00	1,380.00	1,281.00	1,066.00	632	685	741	751	840	859
Pretax income	3,103.00	3,474.00	2,022.00	-1,649.00	1,985.00	4,349.00	1,543.00	2,236.00	1,891.00	1,831.00	2,210.00	2,465.00
Income Tax Exp (Credits)	1,020.00	1,149.00	611	-707	533	1,282.00	450	712	516	758	890	752
Inc(Loss) Bef XO Items	2,083.00	2,325.00	1,411.00	-942	1,452.00	3,067.00	1,093.00	1,524.00	1,275.00	1,073.00	1,320.00	1,713.00
XO (G)L net of tax	0	101	261	320	-238	705	-783	22	-83	-12	-3	-1
Net Inc/Net Profit (Loss)	1,776.00	1,898.00	1,034.00	-1,323.00	1,490.00	1,824.00	1,863.00	1,500.00	1,362.00	1,075.00	1,320.00	1,706.00
Tot Cash Preferred Dvds	19	14	13	15	9	12	0	0	0	0	0	0
Net Inc Avail/Com Sharehldr	1,757.00	1,884.00	1,021.00	-1,338.00	1,481.00	1,812.00	1,863.00	1,500.00	1,362.00	1,075.00	1,320.00	1,706.00
Tot Cash Com Dvds	809.27	857	920	993	1,018.00	1,093.00	1,488.00	1,089.00	1,143.00	1,215.42	1,278.46	1,318.68
Reinvested earnings	947.73	1,027.00	101	-2,331.00	463	719	375	411	219	-140.42	41.54	387.32

EXHIBIT 2.50

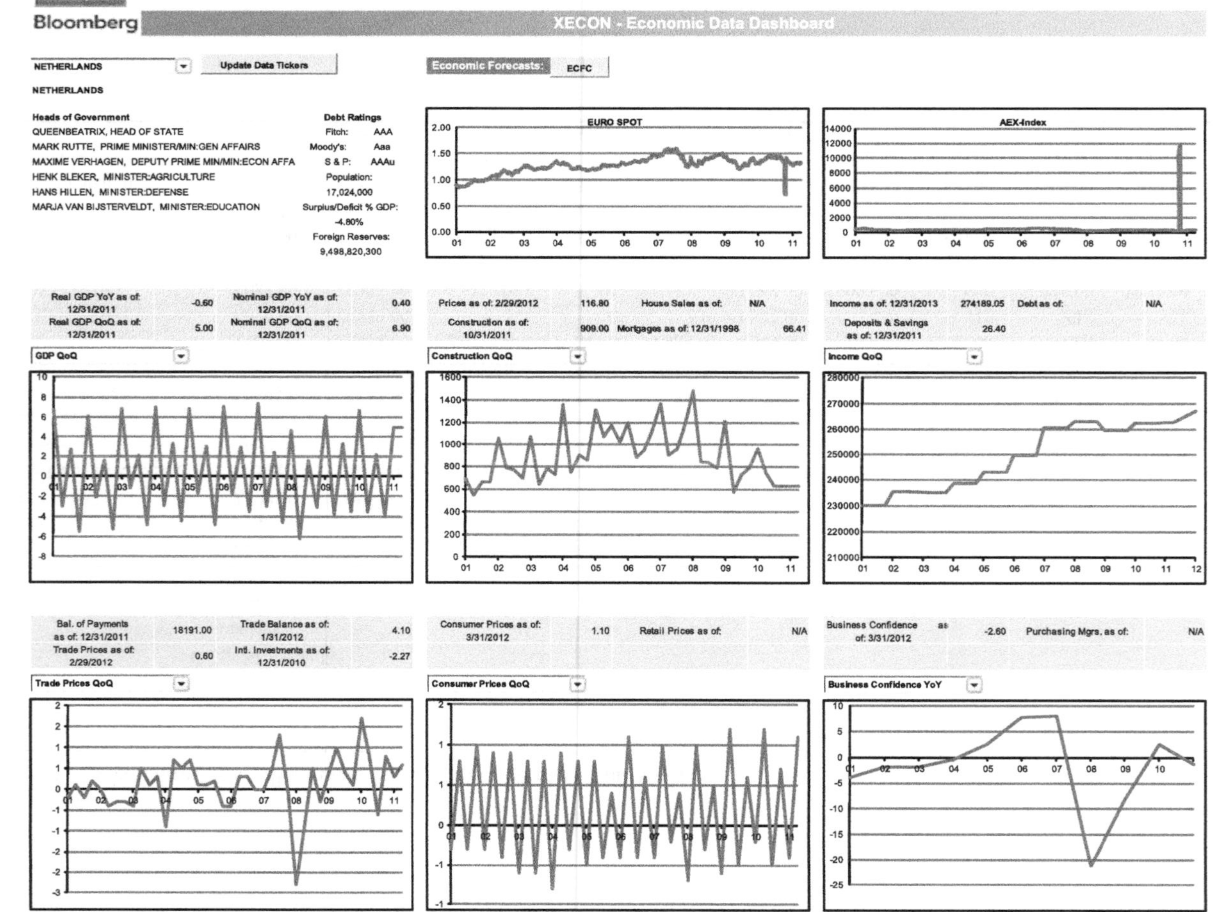
Help
Bloomberg
XECON - Economic Data Dashboard
NETHERLANDS
Update Data Tickers
Economic Forecasts:
ECFC
NETHERLANDS
Heads of Government
QUEENBEATRIX, HEAD OF STATE
MARK RUTTE, PRIME MINISTER/MIN:GEN AFFAIRS
MAXIME VERHAGEN, DEPUTY PRIME MIN/MIN:ECON AFFA
HENK BLEKER, MINISTER:AGRICULTURE
HANS HILLEN, MINISTER:DEFENSE
MARJA VAN BIJSTERVELDT, MINISTER:EDUCATION
Debt Ratings
Fitch: AAA
Moody's: Aaa
S & P: AAAu
Population: 17,024,000
Surplus/Deficit % GDP: -4.80%
Foreign Reserves: 9,498,820,300
EURO SPOT
AEX-Index
Real GDP YoY as of: 12/31/2011 -0.60
Nominal GDP YoY as of: 12/31/2011 0.40
Real GDP QoQ as of: 12/31/2011 5.00
Nominal GDP QoQ as of: 12/31/2011 6.90
Prices as of: 2/29/2012 116.80
House Sales as of: N/A
Construction as of: 10/31/2011 909.00
Mortgages as of: 12/31/1998 66.41
Income as of: 12/31/2013 274189.05
Debt as of: N/A
Deposits & Savings as of: 12/31/2011 26.40
GDP QoQ
Construction QoQ
Income QoQ
Bal. of Payments as of: 12/31/2011 18191.00
Trade Balance as of: 1/31/2012 4.10
Trade Prices as of: 2/29/2012 0.60
Intl. Investments as of: 12/31/2010 -2.27
Consumer Prices as of: 3/31/2012 1.10
Retail Prices as of: N/A
Business Confidence as of: 3/31/2012 -2.60
Purchasing Mgrs. as of: N/A
Trade Prices QoQ
Consumer Prices QoQ
Business Confidence YoY

categories: Equity, Fixed-Income, Industry, Currency, In-the-News, Markets, and New Templates. The templates can be accessed directly from the Bloomberg Add-In in Excel or by clicking "Sample Spreadsheets" from the DAPI screen in Bloomberg, selecting the template, and then clicking "Open" to open the customized workshop in Excel. Several template examples are shown in Exhibits 2.50 and 2.51.

Launchpad

The type of financial analysis analysts do can vary from managing a portfolio, analyzing stocks in a particular industry, identifying new security offerings, monitoring markets, or identifying relevant economic news and events. Each of these different types of analysis requires accessing specific types of information. Given the myriad Bloomberg screens, Bloomberg's Launchpad function enable you to customize a Window-esque interface, allowing you to easily access the information you need to conduct a specific type of analysis.

Other Bloomberg Functions

In subsequent chapters, we will identify many of the screens discussed in this chapter and how to access them, as well as use the information in them to explain the financial market and fixed-income investment concepts and analysis. A directory listing of many of screens by functions can be found in Appendix C. A cursory look at these functions shows the breadth and depth of the Bloomberg system and its value in the study of financial markets and investments. For detailed applications of the system, you should view the Bloomberg video tutorials and training documents. The tutorials training documents (with topical cheat sheets) can be accessed directly from the Bloomberg system by typing BU to bring up the Bloomberg information menu and then clicking "View Training Videos" or "Access Training Documents." Bloomberg is also constantly adding and improving its platforms. Bloomberg's NEXT screen (NEXT <Enter>) provides brochures, fact sheets, and videos about Bloomberg NEXT enhancements (Exhibit 2.52).

Conclusion

In this chapter, we have given an overview of the Bloomberg system and a starting guide on to how to access financial and economic news, information, and analytics from the system. In subsequent chapters we will use this powerful system as a guide to the study of investments. Given the overview of the financial system explained in Chapter 1 and the Bloomberg news, data, analytical retrieval system in this chapter, we now take up the study of debt markets and fixed-income analysis.

EXHIBIT 2.51

Help | Peers | Indices | Financials | Ratings | EST Brokers | EST Detail | VAL Graphs | Owners

Bloomberg

Ticker:	AAPL US	APPLE INC
Language:	English	
Currency:	Local	NASDAQ GS: AAPL, Currency: USD

Benchmark:
S&P 500 INDEX (SPX)

Apple Inc. designs, manufactures, and markets personal computers and related personal computing and mobile communication devices along with a variety of related software, services, peripherals, and networking solutions. The Company sells its products worldwide through its online stores, its retail stores, its direct sales force, third-party wholesalers, and resellers.

Sector: Information Technology   Industry: Computers & Peripherals

Year: 2011

Telephone	1-408-996-1010	Revenue (M)	108,249
Website	www.apple.com	No of Employees	60,400
Address	1 InfiniteLoop Cupertino, CA95014 United States		

Share Price Performance in USD

Price	631.37	1M Return	18.4%
52 Week High	634.66	6M Return	66.9%
52 Week Low	310.50	52 Wk Return	86.3%
52 Wk Beta	0.75	YTD Return	55.9%

Credit Ratings

Bloomberg	IG1				
S&P	NR	Date	4/16/2004	Outlook	-
Moody's	WR	Date	3/31/2004	Outlook	-
Fitch	-	Date	-	Outlook	-

Valuation Ratios Fiscal Year

	9/08	9/09	9/10	9/11	9/12E	9/13E	9/14E
P/E	18.9x	20.1x	19.3x	14.6x	14.3x	12.5x	10.7x
EV/EBIT	10.7x	11.1x	11.8x	8.7x	-	-	-
EV/EBITDA	10.1x	10.4x	11.2x	8.3x	8.5x	7.3x	6.3x
P/S	3.0x	3.8x	4.1x	3.5x	3.7x	3.1x	2.7x
P/B	5.1x	5.2x	5.6x	4.9x	5.2x	3.9x	2.6x
Div Yield	0.0%	0.0%	0.0%	0.0%	0.2%	0.9%	0.0%

Profitability Ratios %

	9/08	9/09	9/10	9/11	9/12E	9/13E	9/14E
Gross Margin	35.2	40.1	39.4	40.5	43.0	42.1	41.1
EBITDA Margin	23.5	29.1	29.8	32.9	36.2	35.7	35.9
Operating Margin	22.2	27.4	28.2	31.2	34.5	33.5	34.9
Profit Margin	16.3	19.2	21.5	23.9	26.0	25.4	26.9
Return on Assets	20.0	19.7	22.8	27.1	26.7	24.5	21.5
Return on Equity	33.2	30.5	35.3	41.7	40.1	34.7	27.6

Leverage and Coverage Ratios

	9/ 08	9/ 09	9/ 10	9/ 11
Current Ratio	2.6	2.7	2.0	1.6
Quick Ratio	2.2	2.3	1.5	1.1
EBIT/Interest	-	-	-	-
Tot Debt/Capital	0.0	0.0	0.0	0.0
Tot Debt/Equity	0.0	0.0	0.0	0.0
Eff Tax Rate %	31.6	31.8	24.4	24.2

Business Segments in USD	Sales (M)
iPhone	47057
Macintosh	21783
iPad and related products and services	20358
iPod	7453
Other music related products and service s	6314
Software, service, and other sales	2954
Peripherals and other hardware	2330

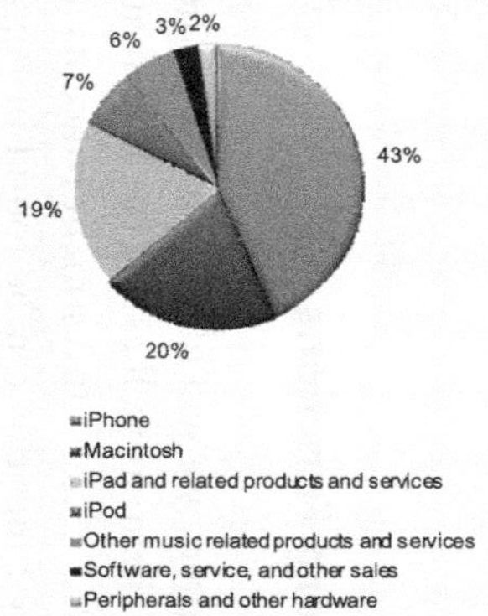

GeographicSegments in USD	Sales (M)
Americas	38315
Europe	27778
Asia-Pacific (Australia & Asia)	22592
Retail (U.S., Canada, Japan, U.K.)	14127
Japan	5437

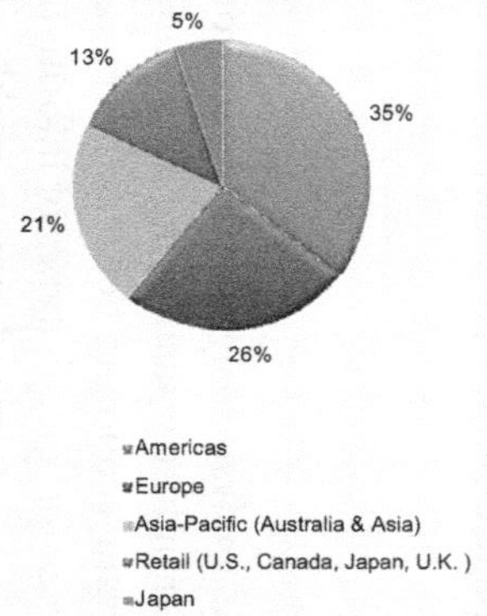

Current Capitalization in USD	
Common Shares Outstanding (M)	929.3
Market Capitalization (M)	588672.3
Cash and ST Investments (M)	97601.0
Total Debt (M)	0.0
Preferred Equity (M)	0.0
LT Investments in Affiliate Companies (M)	0.0
Investments (M)	0.0
Enterprise Value (M)	491071.3

EXHIBIT 2.52

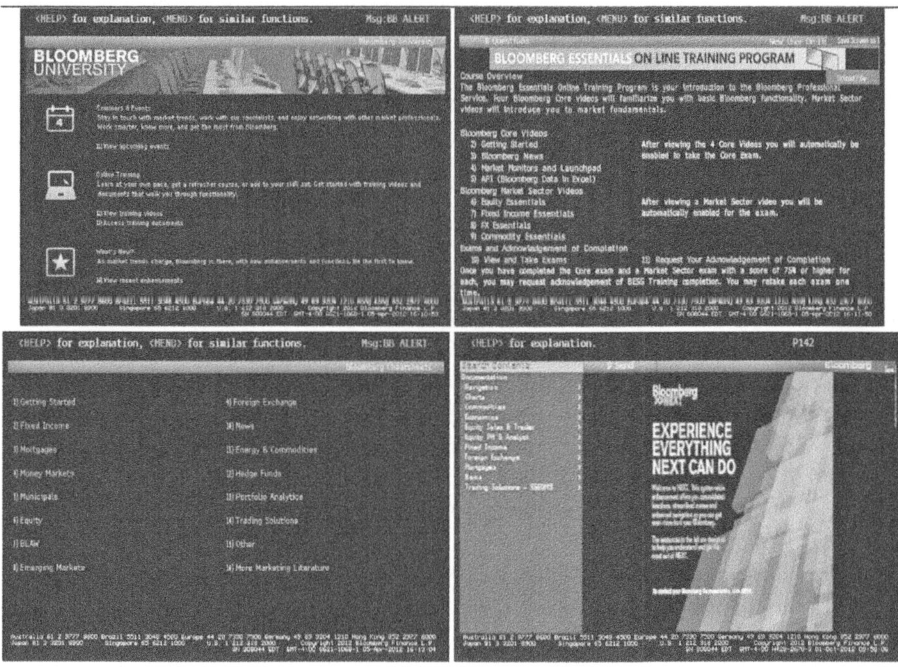

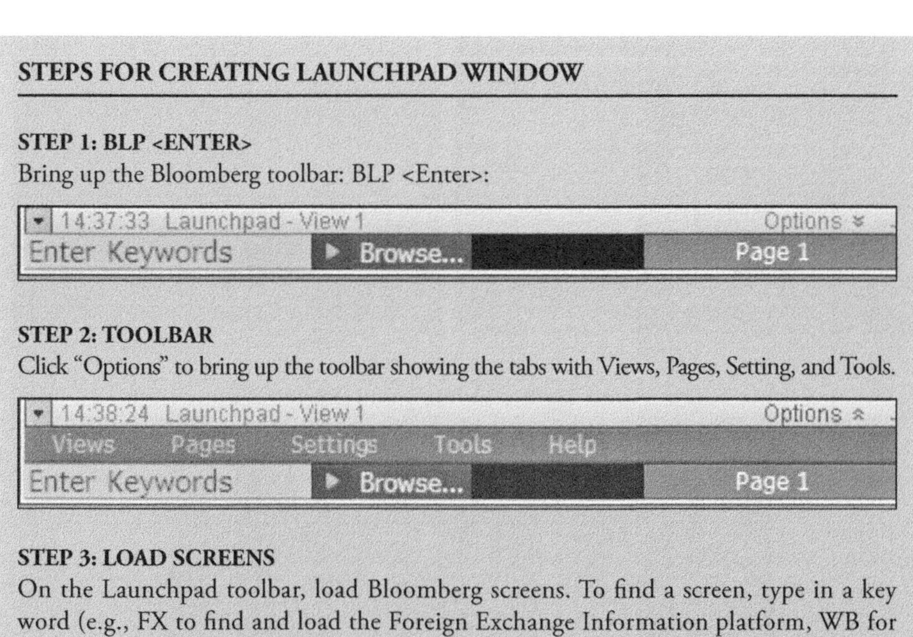

STEPS FOR CREATING LAUNCHPAD WINDOW

STEP 1: BLP <ENTER>
Bring up the Bloomberg toolbar: BLP <Enter>:

STEP 2: TOOLBAR
Click "Options" to bring up the toolbar showing the tabs with Views, Pages, Setting, and Tools.

STEP 3: LOAD SCREENS
On the Launchpad toolbar, load Bloomberg screens. To find a screen, type in a key word (e.g., FX to find and load the Foreign Exchange Information platform, WB for the World Bond Monitor, MOST for the most active stocks monitor, and IMAP for stock index heat maps). In the Views dropdown tab on the toolbar, save the screen

(Continued)

being created by clicking "Save As" and then name the screen (e.g., Monitors). To create new screens or access previously created screens, use the "New" and "Open" tabs in the View tab.

On the Launchpad toolbar, the Views, Pages, Settings, and Tools tabs can be used to manage and customize screens:

- In the Pages dropdown, you can create, delete, share, and send pages in the view.
- In the "Setting" tab, you can set the default option for your Launchpad View, such as "XSIF Equity."
- The Tools tab allows you to create groups of functions.

STEP 4: LOADING SCREENS FROM BROWSER

One quick and efficient way to load screens is to click the "Browse" tab. The Browser option tab lists common categories to load or allows you to type in a name in the amber search field box (e.g., MOST) to find and load a screen. For example, to load securities, currencies, or portfolios, a frequently used panel is the "Monitor" panel. Clicking "Monitor" and the "Launch Component" brings up a stock monitor screen similar to PRTU. From that screen, you can load securities by entering their tickers in the "Ticker" boxes. If you want to import a portfolio that has been created in PRTU or from a search, or if you want to load an index, you can click the "Monitor" tab and then "Import Securities." This will bring up a box where you can select from a source type: portfolios (PRTU), equity searches (EQS), equity indexes, fund screens (FSCR), Bloomberg peers, and other sources. After selecting the type, select the portfolio, index, or search, and then click imports. For example, to download one of Xavier's Student funds, the author selected Portfolio and then "XSIF Equity."

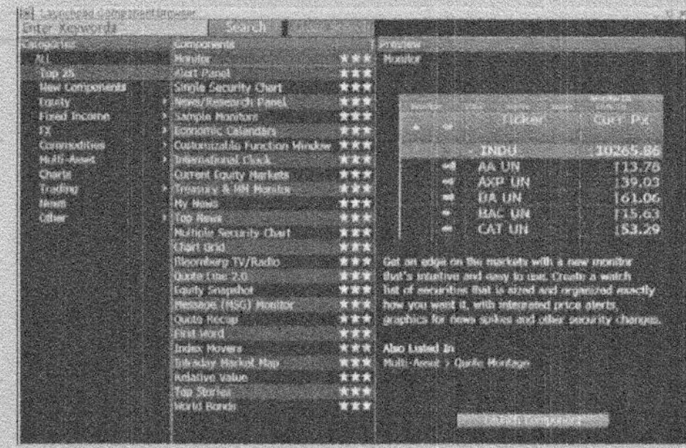

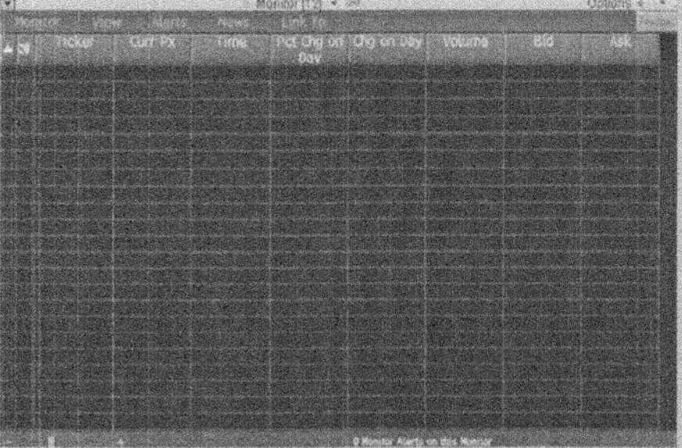

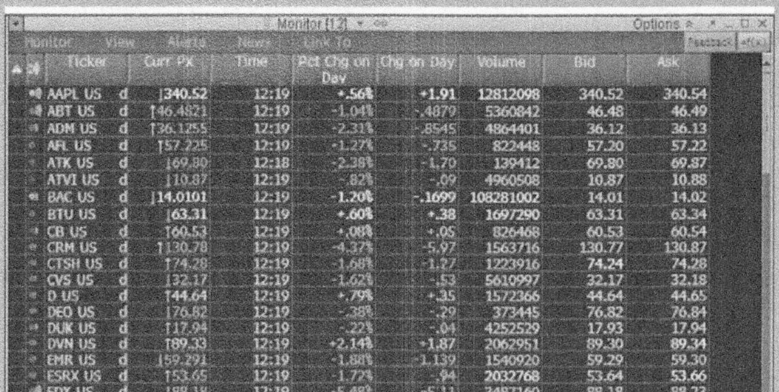

Monitor [1 2]

Ticker		Curr Px	Time	Pct Chg on Day	Chg on Day	Volume	Bid	Ask
AAPL US	d	340.52	12:19	+.56%	+1.91	12812098	340.52	340.54
ABT US	d	46.4821	12:19	-1.04%	-.4879	5360842	46.48	46.49
ADM US	d	36.1255	12:19	-2.31%	-.8545	4864401	36.12	36.13
AFL US	d	57.225	12:19	-1.27%	-.735	822448	57.20	57.22
ATK US	d	69.80	12:18	-2.38%	-1.70	139412	69.80	69.87
ATVI US	d	10.87	12:19	-.82%	-.09	4960508	10.87	10.88
BAC US	d	14.0101	12:19	-1.20%	-.1699	108281002	14.01	14.02
BTU US	d	63.31	12:19	+.60%	+.38	1697290	63.31	63.34
CB US	d	60.53	12:19	+.08%	+.05	826468	60.53	60.54
CRM US	d	130.78	12:19	-4.37%	-5.97	1563716	130.77	130.87
CTSH US	d	74.28	12:19	-1.68%	-1.27	1223916	74.24	74.28
CVS US	d	32.17	12:19	-1.62%	-.53	5610997	32.17	32.18
D US	d	44.64	12:19	+.79%	+.35	1572366	44.64	44.65
DEO US	d	76.82	12:19	-.38%	-.29	373445	76.82	76.84
DUK US	d	17.94	12:19	-.22%	-.04	4252529	17.93	17.94
DVN US	d	89.33	12:19	+2.14%	+1.87	2062951	89.30	89.34
EMR US	d	59.291	12:19	-1.88%	-1.139	1540920	59.29	59.30
ESRX US	d	53.65	12:19	-1.72%	-.94	2032768	53.64	53.66
FDX US	d	88.18	12:19	-5.48%	-5.11	3487160	88.18	88.23
GILD US	d	38.272	12:19	-.62%	-.238	2909621	38.27	38.28
GOOG US	d	604.61	12:19	-.92%	-5.60	1467912	604.60	604.86
INTC US	d	21.09	12:19	-3.30%	-.72	38883087	21.09	21.10

0 Monitor Alerts on this Monitor

The loaded monitor screen can be further customized using tab functions on the screen: Monitor, View, Alerts, News, and Link to:

- Using the "View" tab, you can change the view to show securities grouped by industries or sectors (Group by), different panels (Panel), size (Zoom), and add or delete columns (Manage Columns).
- Using the "Alert" tab, you can set alerts, such as security prices changing by a specified percentage or volume changes.
- Using the "News Alerts," you can enable the "News Alert" to create a column to click on news for each security.
- Using the "link to" tab, you can bring up the portfolio or index's heat map.

STEP 5: LOADING OTHER SCREENS

- Going back to the Launchpad toolbar, you can use the Browser option to find other screens to load or use the amber keyword box to search for other items. For example, type in ECO to find the ECO screen to load or "Live" to bring up the menu showing live news events to monitor (or type in "Sports" to find and bring up a sports monitor).

STEP 6: SAVING SCREEN

- Once the screens are loaded on the View screen (or as they are being loaded), the view can be saved by clicking "Save As" in the "View" tab of the toolbar.

STEP 7: CREATING ADDITIONAL PAGES

- Additional pages in the saved view can be created by clicking the + icon next to the "Pages" tab. For example, pages for each sector in the portfolio and stocks in each sector, other funds, and stock index and economic calendars. Pages in a view can be deleted by going to the page tab.

STEP 8: CREATING NEW VIEWS

- New views focusing on a different topics can also be created by clicking the "View" tab and then "New."

STEP 9: EXITING BLOOMBERG

- You can exit Launchpad and return to a general Bloomberg screen by clicking x on the Launchpad toolbar (or by clicking "Exit Launchpad" from the Views tab). To access Launchpad again, you can type in BLP and hit <Enter>.
- See Exhibit 2.53 for example of a Launchpad for the Xavier Student Funds.

(Continued)

EXHIBIT 2.53

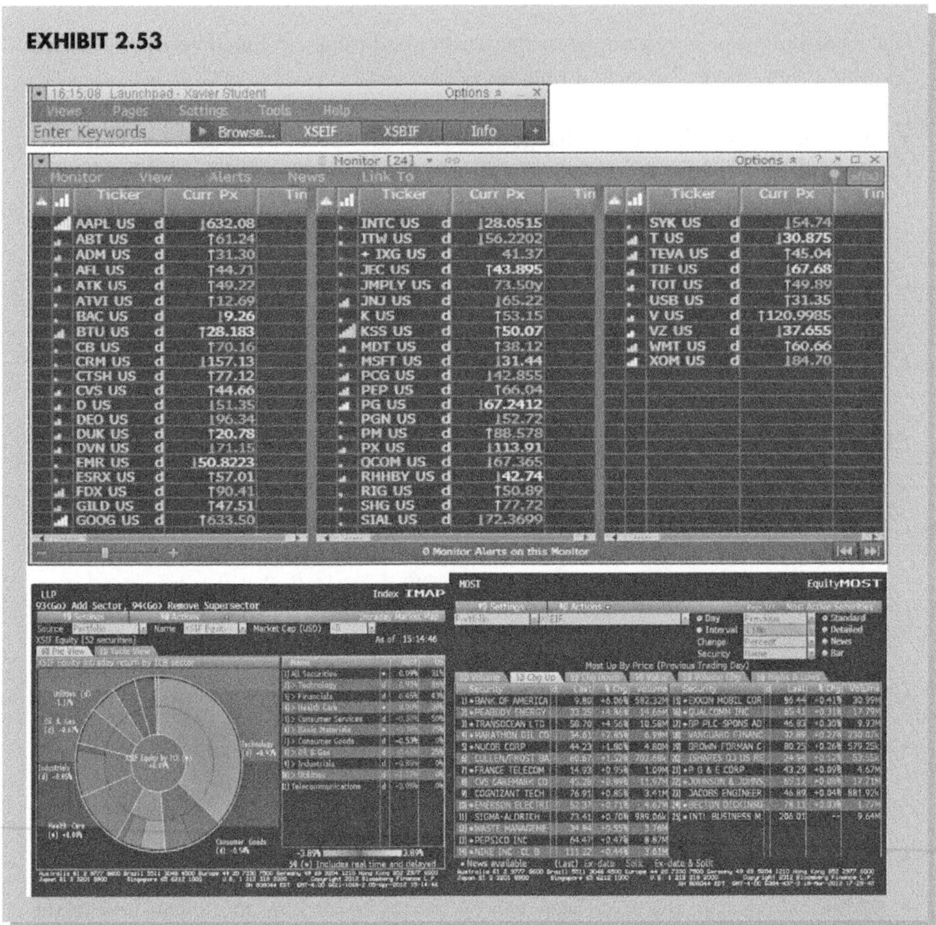

Bloomberg Exercises

1. Select a stock of interest and study it by going to its equity menu and accessing the following screens:
   - DES Description
   - CF Corporate filings (view or download the company's 10-K)
   - SPLC Supply chain
   - RELS Related securities (e.g., debt, preferred stocks)
   - HDS Major holders of the stocks
   - CN Company news
   - GP Stock price graph (vary time period and activate events and volume)
   - GIP Intraday price graph
2. Study some of the market trends by using MOST: MOST <Enter>. Using the MOST screen examine the S&P 500 stocks by selecting "Equity Indexes" and "SPX" from the dropdowns. Use the bottom tabs to identify the high stocks, low stocks, stocks with the greatest volume, and so on.

3. Using the WEI screen, identify a broad-based index such as the S&P 500 and a sector index. Find the index's ticker by going to the WEI "display" window and clicking "Ticker." Access the following information about the indexes from their menus (Index ticker <Index> <Enter>):
   - DES Description of index
   - IMOV Index movers
   - MRR Member returns
   - IMAP Industry market heat map
   - GP Price graph (vary time period and activate events and volume)

Using the index's RV screen compare the features of the stocks that comprise the Index.

Using the index's FA screen, examine the index's summary statement and then select a stock that is a member of the index to compare its financials with the index: type stock's ticker and hit <Equity> in "Compare vs." box.

4. Select a corporation of interest and examine one of its bonds: Ticker <Corp> <Enter> and then select a bond. Possible screens to examine for the selected bond:
   - DES Description of the bond (see prospectus)
   - HDS Bondholders
   - AGGD Largest creditors
   - DDIS Debt distribution
   - GP Price graph
   - GRBI Guarantors of the bond
   - CRPR Credit rating
   - CSHF Bond payment schedule
   - QR Trade recap
5. Select and examine a U.S. Treasury note that was recently issued: <Govt> TK <Enter> and then select U.S.A. and CT. Possible screens to examine:
   - DES Description of the bond
   - HDS Bondholders
   - DDIS Debt distribution
   - GP Price graph
   - GIP Intraday
   - CSHF Bond payment schedule
   - QR Trade recap
6. Search, select, and examine a state municipal bond: MSRC <Enter> or SECF <Enter>; FI tab; "Muni" tab; type in municipal's name in "Issuer Name" box. To access the bond's screen: Identifier <Muni> <Enter>. Possible screens to examine:
   - DES Description of the bond
   - GY Yield graph
   - CF Filings
7. Search and find the municipal bonds of a state of interest by using SMUN: SMUN <Enter>.
8. Search, select, and examine a new stock offering: IPO <Enter>. On the screen, (a) click "All" from the "Types" dropdown, (b) click for stage (e.g., "Look-Up

Expiring") or click a sector and then select stage from the stage dropdown (e.g., Trading), and (c) click an offering to bring up the offering's description. On the description screen, download the reports to get more details. See if the prospectus has been released by accessing the company's equity menu (ticker <Equity> <Enter>) and then clicking CF.

9. Explore different sources of economic information using some of the following screens:
   a. Examine the economic statistics of the United States and other countries by going to ECST:
      - GDP
      - Population
      - Housing
      - International Trade
   b. Examine the economic statistics of the United States and other countries by going to ECOF:
      - National accounts
      - Business conditions
      - Prices
      - Labor conditions
      - Housing conditions
      - Leading economic indicators
      - Government sector
      - Balance of payments
      - Monetary sector
      - Financial sector
   c. Get an economic snapshot of several countries by going to ECOW (ECOW <Enter>) and clicking country of interest from the country dropdown (or ECST <Enter>, click "3") Economic Snapshot, and then click country of interest).
   d. Review some recent economic releases for the United States by going to ECO: ECO <Enter>.
   e. Review some recent economic releases for a country or area by going to WECO: WECO <Enter>.
   f. Study economic trends and analysis by going to BRIEF and downloading the "Economics" PDF.
   g. Study the economy or a market by going to AV. On the AV screen, select a topic from AV Categories dropdown. To connect to a live broadcast, click "Live" tab; to connect to Bloomberg's radio and TV broadcast, click the "TV/Radio" tab.
   h. Go to EIU to access news information and analysis from the *Economist* by topical areas (suggestion: economic information on countries can be found in "Economic Structure" and "Economic Indicators").
   i. Go to research search (RSE) to access research on a country: (1) RSE <Enter>; (2) click "Topics," "Business Topics," "Economic News," "Country Economies"; (3) select country; and (4) download story.

10. Using the BI screen, select an industry sector (e.g., Biotechnology) and evaluate the sector using the following screens:
    - Drivers/metrics
    - Comp sheets
    - News/research
    - Events
    - Data library
    - Analysis
11. Analyze an industry by examining the sector's index on the Index menu. The index ticker can be found from the BI screen (e.g., BRMATBIO for Biotechnology) or by identifying the index from the WEI screen: Index ticker <Index> <Enter>. Possible screens to examine:
    - DES Description
    - IMAP Heat map
    - GP Price graph (vary time period and activate events and volume)
    - FA Financials
    - GF Fundamental graphs
12. Select research, news stories, and videos on a sector using the following screens:
    - TNI Advanced News Search (click "Industries")
    - RSE Research search (click "Industry Overview Search")
    - AV Videos (in AV Categories dropdown, click "Company Teleconferences")
13. Compare financials of state governments: SMUN <Enter>. From the SMUN screen, click a state of interest and then examine its financials and demographics (e.g., FA SS) or access the governments screen directly by entering state identifier (e.g., stocal US) <Equity> <Enter>). Possible screens to examine:
    - FA SS Financial summary
    - FA BS Balance sheet (select "Pension" in Funds dropdown)
    - DEMS State demographics
    - CF Issuer filings (state's annual report)
14. Get more information about the state from the following sources:
    - BRIEF BRIEF <Enter> and click "Municipal Markets"
    - TNI Advanced news search (e.g., Region: California; Topic: Bonds); Save the Search
15. Conduct a simple screen and stocks search using EQS. Suggestion: Limit search to S&P 500 stocks (search for the S&P 500 stocks using the "Index" dropdown) and a market cap greater than $20 billion (in the ribbon box, type in "Market Cap" to bring down dropdown and follow input instructions). Be sure to save your search (go to "Actions" tab to find "Save As").
16. Select one of the stocks from the search you did in Exercise 15 and bring up its RV screen, and then import your search to the RV screen: Company ticker <Equity> <Enter>; click RV; in "Comp Source" dropdown tab, click "Equity Screen" (EQS), and in "Name" tab, click the name of your search and hit <Enter> to activate. On the RV screen, evaluate your stocks by selecting different template (gray tabs).

17. Create a basket consisting of the stocks from your search in Exercise 15 using the CIXB screen. See "Creating Baskets: CIXB" for steps to import a search or portfolio to create a CIXB basket. After creating the basket, evaluate your portfolio of stocks from the search using the index menu (Basket ticker name [e.g., Name] <Index> <Enter>). Possible screens to consider on the index screen:
    - DES Description
    - GP Price graph
    - IMAP Intraday market map
    - COMB Total return
    - HRA Historical regression analysis
18. Create a portfolio of stocks of interest using PRTU:
    - PRTU <Enter>.
    - Click "Create" tab to bring up "Settings" screen
    - On the "Settings" screen, name the portfolio, set index (INDU for DJA) and currency (USD), click "Enable," and click the "Save" tab to bring up the security input page.
    - On the security input page, input stocks by entering the stock's ticker, the number of shares, and the cost of each stock (you can input the current stock's price).
    - *Note:* Instead of inputting stocks, you can import the stocks from your search done in Exercise 15: Click the "Options" tab and "Import" to bring up a box; in the box, click "Equity Screen" in the "Source" dropdown and the name of your search in the "Name" dropdown. Once stocks are loaded, input number of shares and the cost of each stock.
    - Create historical data for your portfolio: On the menu screen, select a date on the "Date" tab to begin the history. After selecting a past date, use the "Option" tab to import the portfolio you have created. On the import box, select "Portfolio" from the "Import" tab and select the name of the portfolio, then change the date to today's date, and click "Import."
        - After inputting your stocks, click "Save" on the security input screen. Your created portfolio can now be accessed from PRTU.
        - Click "Portfolio Menu" on the security setting screen to bring up the portfolio menu screen (PMEN).
19. Using the PMEN screen, analyze the portfolio you created in Exercise 18. Possible screens to consider on the PMEN screen:
    - PORT Portfolio Risk and Analytics (select some of the grey tabs)
    - PDSP Portfolio Display
    - NPH Portfolio News
    - RVP Equity Relative Value
20. Select one of the stocks from the portfolio you created in Exercise 18 and bring up its RV screen and then import your portfolio to the RV screen: Company ticker <Equity> <Enter>; click RV; in the "Comp Source" dropdown tab, click "Portfolio", and in the "Name" tab, click the name of your portfolio, and hit <Enter> to activate. On the RV screen, evaluate your portfolio by selecting different tabs.

21. Using the EVTS screen, load the portfolio you created in Exercise 18 on that screen: EVTS <Enter>, on the "Source" dropdown tab click "Portfolio," and on the "Name" dropdown tab click the name of your portfolio. Once your portfolio is loaded, click the news announcement you want to monitor (e.g., All Event Types, Earnings Releases, etc.). Next, set the stock alerts by clicking the bell icon next to the stock's name and setting the timing of the alert (this will send Bloomberg messages to you). This is the type of screen that you might want to send to a Launchpad page that you have created.
22. Two important security laws are the Securities Act of 1933 and the Securities Exchange Act of 1934. Learn more about these acts and others (e.g., Sarbanes-Oxley Act of 2002) by going to the BLAW screen: BLAW <Enter> and clicking PRAC (Practice Areas), "Securities Law," and "Securities Act of 1933", "Exchange Act of 1934," and "Sarbanes-Oxley of 2002.
23. Explore the following Wizards in Bloomberg's Excel Add-Ins:
    - "Real Time/Historical" and "Market, Reference, Analytical, and Data Sets"
    - "Real Time/Historical" and "Historical End of the Day"
    - "Financial/Estimates" and "Fundamental Data"
24. Explore the Template Library found in the Bloomberg Excel Add-In from Excel or by going to the DAPI screen: DAPI <Enter> and click "Sample Spreadsheets."
25. Learn about the NYSE Euronext and other exchanges in the United States and throughout the world by going to their websites. To find general information about exchanges and their websites, go to Bloomberg's EPR screen.
26. Underwriters play an important role in issuing securities in the primary market. Examine the top equity underwriters and their recent deals by going to LTOP.
27. Review the current economic climate in the United States. Limit your review to key bullet points, screen savers of graphs, and tables. Use the following:
    - BRIEF Bullet the economic report.
    - ECOF Show key economic graphs; including leading economic indicators.
    - Fed Bullet key recent remarks from Fed.
    - Fed Find Beige report and bullet key points.
    - IECO Compare U.S. key statistics with other countries (screen saver).
    - COUN Country
    - WB Compare U.S. rates with other countries; screen saver; bullet major differences.
    - EIU Go to EIU to find a forecast of U.S. rates.
28. Conduct a research and advanced news search to find stories related to a financial crisis (e.g., sovereign debt crisis): TNI <Enter>.
29. Create a Launchpad view with pages for one or more categories described in the chapter. Some possible views:
    - Stock portfolio monitor of the portfolio or search you created in Exercise 15 or 18.
    - Economic monitor that includes screens such as ECO, IECO, WECO, and AV.

CHAPTER 3

Bond Value and Return

Introduction

All securities can be evaluated in terms of the characteristics common to all assets: value, return, risk, maturity, marketability, liquidity, and taxability. In this and the next two chapters, we will analyze debt securities in terms of these characteristics. In this chapter, we look at how debt instruments (which we will usually refer to here as bonds) are valued and how their rates of return are measured. It should be noted that this chapter is very technical, entailing a number of definitions. Understanding how bonds are valued and their rates determined, though, is fundamental to being able to evaluate and select bonds.

Bond Valuation

Pricing Bonds

An investor who has purchased a bond can expect to earn a possible return from the bond's periodic coupon payments, from capital gains (or losses) when the bond is sold, called, or matures, and from interest earned from reinvesting coupon payments. Given the market price of the bond, the bond's yield is the interest rate that makes the present value of the bond's cash flow equal to the bond price. This yield takes into account these three sources of return. Later in this chapter, we will discuss how to solve for the bond's yield given its price. Alternatively, if we know the rate we require to buy the bond, then we can determine its value.

Like the value of any asset, the value of a bond is equal to the sum of the present values of its future cash flows:

$$V_0^b = \sum_{t=1}^{M} \frac{CF_t}{(1+R)^t} = \frac{CF_1}{(1+R)^1} + \frac{CF_2}{(1+R)^2} + \cdots + \frac{CF_M}{(1+R)^N} \tag{3.1}$$

where V_0^b is the value or price of the bond, CF_t is the bond's expected cash flow in period *t*, including both coupon income and repayment of principal, *R* is the discount rate; and *N* is the term to maturity on the bond. The discount rate is the required rate; that is, the rate investors require to buy the bond. This rate is typically estimated by determining the rate on a security with comparable features: same risk, liquidity, taxability, and maturity.

Many bonds pay a fixed-coupon interest each period, with the principal repaid at maturity. The coupon payment, *C*, is often quoted in terms of the bond's coupon rate, C^R. The coupon rate is the contractual rate the issuer agrees to pay on the bond. This rate is often expressed as a proportion of the bond's face value (or par) and is usually stated on an annual basis. Thus, a bond with a face value (*F*) of $1,000 and a 10 percent coupon rate would pay an annual coupon of $100 each year for the life of the bond: $C = C^R F = (.10)(\$1{,}000) = \$100$.

The value of a bond paying a fixed coupon interest each year (annual coupon payment) and the principal at maturity, in turn, would be:

$$V_0^b = \sum_{t=1}^{M} \frac{C}{(1+R)^t} + \frac{F}{(1+R)^M}$$

$$V_0^b = \frac{C}{(1+R)^1} + \frac{C}{(1+R)^2} + \cdots + \frac{C}{(1+R)^M} + \frac{F}{(1+R)^M} \tag{3.2}$$

where M = number of years to maturity.

With the coupon payment fixed each period, the *C* term in Equation (3.2) can be factored out and the bond value can be expressed as:

$$V_0^b = C \sum_{t=1}^{M} \frac{1}{(1+R)^t} + \frac{F}{(1+R)^M}$$

The term $\Sigma 1/(1 + R)^t$ is the present value of $1 received each period for *N* periods (*M* years in the above case). It is defined as the present value interest factor (PVIF). The PVIF for different terms and discount rates can be found using PVIF tables found in many finance text books. It also can be calculated using the following formula:

$$\text{PVIF}(R,N) = \frac{1-[1/(1+R)^N]}{R}$$

Thus, if investors require a 10 percent annual rate of return on a 10-year, investment-grade corporate bond paying a coupon equal to 9 percent of par each year and a principal of $1,000 at maturity ($M$ = 10 years), then they would price the bond at $938.55:

$$V_0^b = \sum_{t=1}^{M} \frac{C}{(1+R)^t} + \frac{F}{(1+R)^M}$$

$$V_0^b = \sum_{t=1}^{10} \frac{\$90}{(1.10)^t} + \frac{\$1,000}{(1.10)^{10}}$$

$$V_0^b = \$90 \sum_{t=1}^{M} \frac{1}{(1.10)^t} + \frac{\$1,000}{(1.10)^{10}}$$

$$V_0^b = \$90[\text{PVIF}(10\%, 10\text{yrs}] + \frac{\$1,000}{(1.10)^{10}}$$

$$V_0^b = \$90 \left[\frac{1 - [1/1.10]^{10}}{.10} \right] + \frac{\$1,000}{(1.10)^{10}}$$

$$V_0^b = \$938.55$$

Bond Price Relations

Relation between Coupon Rate, Required Rate, Value, and Par Value

The value of the bond in the above example is not equal to its par value. This can be explained by the fact that the discount rate and coupon rate are different. Specifically, for investors in the above case to obtain the 10 percent rate per year from a bond promising to pay an annual rate of C^R = 9 percent of par, they would have to buy the bond at a value, or price, below par: the bond would have to be purchased at a discount from its par, $V_0^b < F$. In contrast, if the coupon rate is equal to the discount rate (i.e., R = 9 percent), then the bond's value would be equal to its par value, $V_0^b = F$. In this case, investors would be willing to pay $1,000 for this bond, with each investor receiving $90 each year in coupons. Finally, if the required rate is lower than the coupon rate, then investors would be willing to pay a premium over par for the bond, $V_0^b > F$. This might occur if bonds with comparable features were trading at rates below 9 percent. In this case, investors would be willing to pay a price above $1,000 for a bond with a coupon rate of 9 percent. Thus, the first relationship to note is that a bond's value (or price) will be equal, greater than, or less than its face value depending on whether the coupon rate is equal, less than, or greater than the required rate:

BOND-PRICE RELATION 1

If $C^R = R \Rightarrow V^b = F$: Bond valued at par
If $C^R < R \Rightarrow V^b < F$: Bond valued at discount
If $C^R > R \Rightarrow V^b > F$: Bond valued at premium

In addition to the above relations, the relation between the coupon rate and required rate also explains how the bond's value changes over time. If the required rate is constant over time, and if the coupon rate is equal to it (i.e., the bond is priced at par), then the value of the bond will always be equal to its face value throughout the life of the bond. This is illustrated in Exhibit 3.1 by the horizontal line that shows the value of the 9 percent coupon bond is always equal to the par value. Here, investors would pay $1,000 regardless of the terms to maturity. On the other hand, if the required rate is constant over time and the coupon rate is less (i.e., the bond is priced at a discount), then the value of the bond will increase as it approaches maturity; if the required rate is constant and the coupon rate is greater (i.e., the bond is priced at a premium), then the value of the bond will decrease as it approaches maturity. These relationships are also illustrated in Exhibit 3.1.

Relation Between Value and Rate of Return

Given known coupon and principal payments, the only way an investor can obtain a higher rate of return on a bond is for its price (value) to be lower. In contrast, the

EXHIBIT 3.1 The Value Over Time of an Original 10-Year, 9 Percent Annual Coupon Bond Selling at Par, Discount, and Premium

Year	Discount Bond Price of Bond Selling to Yield 11%	Par Bond Price of Bond Selling to Yield 9%	Premium Bond Price of Bond Selling to Yield 7%
10	$882.22	$1,000.00	$1,140.47
9	$889.26	$1,000.00	$1,130.30
8	$897.08	$1,000.00	$1,119.43
7	$905.76	$1,000.00	$1,107.49
6	$915.39	$1,000.00	$1,095.33
5	$926.08	$1,000.00	$1,082.00
4	$937.95	$1,000.00	$1,067.74
3	$951.13	$1,000.00	$1,052.49
2	$965.75	$1,000.00	$1,036.16
1	$981.98	$1,000.00	$1,018.69
0	$1,000.00	$1,000.00	$1,000.00

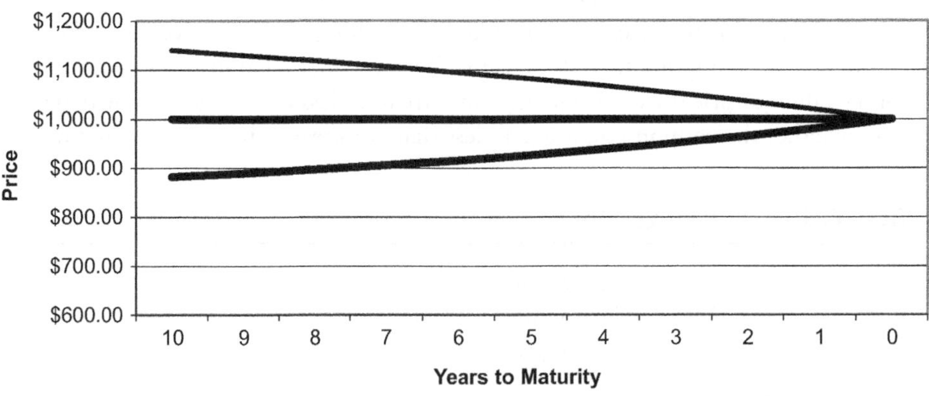

only way for a bond to yield a lower rate is for its price to be higher. Thus, an inverse relationship exists between the price of a bond and its rate of return. This, of course, is consistent with Equation (3.1), in which an increase in *R* increases the denominator and lowers V_0^b. Thus, the second bond relationship to note is that there is an inverse relationship between the price and rate of return on a bond:

BOND-PRICE RELATION 2

If $R\uparrow \Rightarrow V_0^b \downarrow$

If $R\downarrow \Rightarrow V_0^b \uparrow$

The inverse relation between a bond's price and rate of return is illustrated by the negatively sloped *price-yield curve* shown in Exhibits 3.2 and 3.3. The curve shown in Exhibit 3.2 shows the different values of a 10-year, 9 percent annual coupon bond given different rates. As shown, the 10-year bond has a value of \$938.55 when $R = 10$ percent and \$1,000 when $R = 9$ percent. Exhibit 3.3 shows the price and yields for the 5 3/8 percent, 2020 Kraft bond accessed from the Bloomberg PT screen. In addition to showing a negative relation between price and yield, the price-yield curve is also convex from below (bowed shape). This convexity implies that for equal increases in yields, the value of the bond decreases at a decreasing rate (for equal decreases in yields, the bond's price increases at an increasing rate). The bow-shapedness of a bond's price-yield curve is referred to as the bond's *convexity.* It has important implications related to bond investment and management that we will examine in more detail later.

The Relation between a Bond's Price Sensitivity to Interest Rate Changes and Term to Maturity

The third bond relationship to note is the relation between a bond's price sensitivity to interest rate changes and its maturity. This relationship can be seen by comparing the price sensitivity to interest rate changes of the 10-year, 9 percent coupon bond

EXHIBIT 3.2 Price-Yield Relation, 10-Year, 9 Percent Annual Coupon Bond

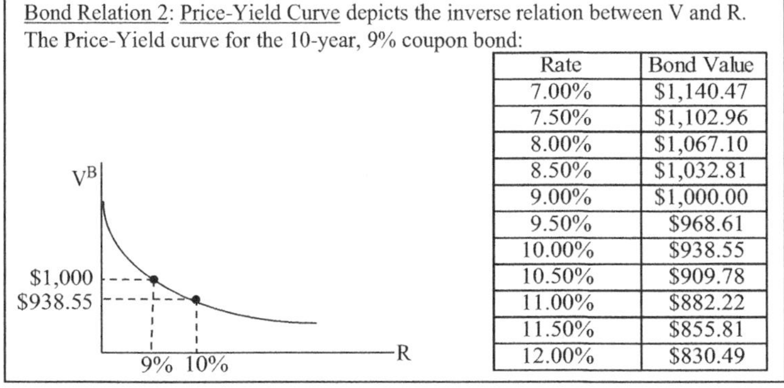

Bond Relation 2: Price-Yield Curve depicts the inverse relation between V and R.
The Price-Yield curve for the 10-year, 9% coupon bond:

Rate	Bond Value
7.00%	\$1,140.47
7.50%	\$1,102.96
8.00%	\$1,067.10
8.50%	\$1,032.81
9.00%	\$1,000.00
9.50%	\$968.61
10.00%	\$938.55
10.50%	\$909.78
11.00%	\$882.22
11.50%	\$855.81
12.00%	\$830.49

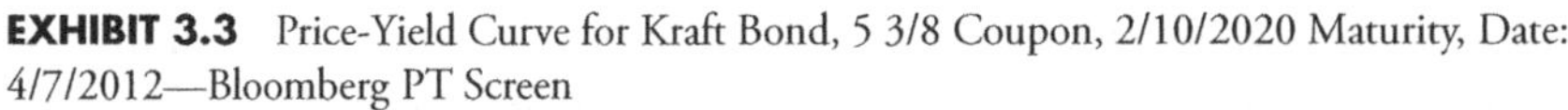

EXHIBIT 3.3 Price-Yield Curve for Kraft Bond, 5 3/8 Coupon, 2/10/2020 Maturity, Date: 4/7/2012—Bloomberg PT Screen

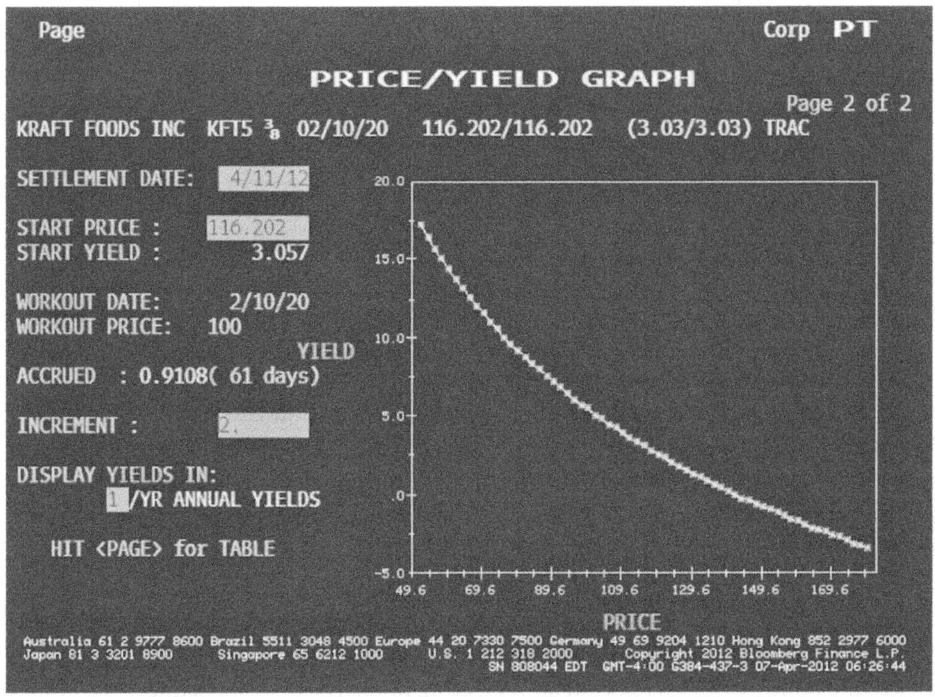

in our above example with a 1-year, 9 percent coupon bond. If the required rate is 10 percent, then the 10-year bond would trade at $938.55, whereas the 1-year bond would trade at $990.91 ($1,000 / 1.10). If the interest rate decreases to 9 percent for each bond (a 10 percent change in rates), both bonds would increase in price to $1,000. For the 10-year bond, the percentage increase in price would be 6.55 percent (($1,000 – $938.55) / $938.55), whereas the percentage increase for the 1-year bond would be only 0.9 percent. Thus, the 10-year bond's price is more sensitive to the interest rate change than the 1-year bond. In addition, the greater price sensitivity of longer maturity bonds also implies that their price-yield curves are more convex than the price-yield curves for smaller maturity bonds.

BOND RELATION 3

The greater the bond's maturity, the greater its price sensitivity to a change in interest rates.

- 10-year, 9 percent annual coupon bond

$$R = 10\% \Rightarrow V_0^b = \$938.55$$

$$R = 9\% \Rightarrow V_0^b = \$1{,}000$$

$$\%\,\Delta\,R = -10\% \Rightarrow \%\Delta\,V_0^b = 5.53 \text{ percent}$$

- 1-year, 9 percent annual coupon bond

$$R = 10\% \Rightarrow V_0^b = \$990.91$$

$$R = 9\% \Rightarrow V_0^b = \$1{,}000$$

$$\%\Delta\,R = -10\% \Rightarrow \%\Delta\,V_0^b = 0.9 \text{ percent}$$

The Relation between a Bond's Price Sensitivity to Interest Rate Changes and Coupon Payments

The fourth bond relationship to note is the relation between a bond's price sensitivity to interest rate changes and its coupon rate. Consider two 10-year bonds, each priced at discount rate of 10 percent and paying annual coupons and a $1,000 principal at maturity, but with one bond having a coupon rate of 10 percent and priced at $1,000, and the other having a coupon rate of 2 percent and priced at $508.43. If the rate required on each bond were to decrease to a new level of 9 percent, the price on the 10 percent coupon bond would increase by 6.4 percent to equal $1,064.18, whereas the price on the 2 percent coupon bond would increase by 8.3 percent to $550.76. In this case, the lower coupon bond's price is more responsive to a given interest rate change than the price of the higher coupon bond. Thus, the lower a bond's coupon rate, the greater its price sensitivity to changes in discount rates.

BOND RELATION 4

The lower a bond's coupon rate, the greater its price sensitivity to a change in interest rates.

- 10-year, 10 percent annual coupon bond: Rate change from 10 percent to 9 percent causes 6.4 percent price increase
- 10-year, 2 percent annual coupon bond: Rate change from 10 percent to 9 percent causes 8.3 percent price increase.

Pricing Bonds with Different Cash

Flows and Compounding Frequencies

Equation (3.2) defines the value of a bond that pays coupons on an annual basis and a principal at maturity. Bonds, of course, differ in the frequency in which they pay coupons each year, and many bonds have maturities less than one year. Also, when investors buy bonds they often do so at noncoupon dates. Equation (3.2), therefore, needs to be adjusted to take these practical factors into account.

Semiannual Coupon Payments

Many bonds pay coupon interest semiannually. When bonds make semiannual payments, three adjustments to Equation (3.2) are necessary: (1) The number of periods is doubled; (2) the annual coupon rate is halved; (3) the annual discount rate is halved. Thus, if our illustrative 10-year, 9 percent coupon bond trading at a quoted annual rate of 10 percent paid interest semiannually instead of annually, it would be worth \$937.69:

$$V_0^b = \sum_{t=1}^{20} \frac{\$45}{(1.05)^t} + \frac{\$1,000}{(1.05)^{20}} = \$937.69$$

$$V_0^b = \$45\left[\frac{1-[1/(1.05)]^{20}}{.05}\right] + \frac{\$1,000}{(1.05)^{20}} = \$937.69$$

$$V_0^b = \sum_{t=1}^{20} \frac{\$45}{(1.05)^t} + \frac{\$1,000}{(1.05)^{20}} = \$937.69$$

$$V_0^b = \$45\left[\frac{1-[1/(1.05)]^{20}}{.05}\right] + \frac{\$1,000}{(1.05)^{20}} = \$937.69 \qquad (3.2)$$

Note that the rule for valuing semiannual bonds is easily extended to valuing bonds paying interest even more frequently. For example, to determine the value of a bond paying interest four times a year, we would quadruple the periods and quarter the annual coupon payment and discount rate. In general, if we let n be equal to the number of payments per year (i.e., the compoundings per year), M be equal to the maturity in years, R^A be the discount rate quoted on an annual basis (simple annual rate), and R be equal to the periodic rate, then we can express the general formula for valuing a bond as follows:

$$V_0^b = \sum_{t=1}^{N} \frac{C^A/n}{(1+(R^A/n))^t} + \frac{F}{(1+(R^A/n))^{Mn}} \qquad (3.3)$$

MC^A = annual coupon = $(C^R)(F)$

n = number of payments per year

Periodic coupon = annual coupon / n

M = term to maturity in years

N = number of periods to maturity = $(n)(M)$

Required periodic rate = R = annual rate / n = R^A / n

Thus, the value of a 20-year, 6 percent coupon bond, with semiannual payments, a par value of $1,000, and a required return of 8 percent would be 802.78:

$$V_0 = \sum_{t=1}^{N} \frac{C}{(1+R)^t} + \frac{F}{(1+R)^N}$$

$$V_0 = \sum_{t=1}^{40} \frac{\$30}{(1.04)^t} + \frac{\$1,000}{(1.04)^{40}}$$

$$V_0 = \$30\left[\frac{1-1/(1.04)^{40}}{.04}\right] + \frac{\$1,000}{(1.04)^{40}}$$

$$V_0 = \$593.78 + \$208.92 = \$802.78$$

N = number of periods = 40 (= (20 years)(2))
F = $1,000
C = semiannual coupon = (.06/2)($1,000) = $30
R = required semiannual rate = .08/2 = .04

Compounding Frequency

The 10 percent annual rate in the first example and 8 percent in the second are simple annual rates: The rate with one annualized compounding. With one annualized compounding and a 10 percent annual rate, we earn 10 percent every year and a $100 investment would grow to equal $110 after one years: $100(1.10) = $110. If the simple annual rate were expressed with semiannual compounding, then we would earn 5 percent every six months with the interest being reinvested; in this case, $100 would grow to equal $110.25 after one year: $\$100(1.05)^2 = \$110.25$. If the rate were expressed with monthly compounding, then we would earn 0.8333 percent (10 percent/12) every month with the interest being reinvested; in this case, $100 would grow to equal $110.47 after one year: $\$100(1 + (.10/12))^{12} = \$110.47$. If we extend the compounding frequency to daily, then we would earn 0.0274 percent (10 percent/365) daily, and with the reinvestment of interest, a $100 investment would grow to equal $110.52 after one year: $\$100(1 + (.10/365))^{365} = \$110.52$. Note that the rate of 10 percent is the simple annual rate, whereas the actual rate earned for the year is $(1 + (R^A/n))^n - 1$. This rate that includes the reinvestment of interest (or compounding) is known as the *effective rate.*

When the compounding becomes large, such as daily compounding, then we are approaching continuous compounding with the n term in Equation (3.3) becoming very large. For cases in which there is continuous compounding, the future value (FV) for an investment of A dollars M years from now is equal to:

$$FV = Ae^{RM}$$

where e is the natural exponent (equal to the irrational number 2.71828). Thus, if the 10 percent simple rate were expressed with continuous compounding, then $100 ($A$)

would grow to equal \$110.52 after one year: $\$100e^{(.10)(1)} = \$110.52$. (After allowing for some slight rounding differences, this is the value obtained with daily compounding.) After two years, the \$100 investment would be worth \$122.14: $\$100e^{(.10)(2)} = \$122.14$.

Note that from the FV expression, the present value (A) of a future receipt (FV) is

$$A = PV = \frac{FV}{e^{RM}} = FVe^{-RM}$$

If $R = .10$, a security paying \$100 two years from now would be worth \$81.87, given continuous compounding: $PV = \$100e^{-(.10)(2)} = \$81.87$. Similarly, a security paying \$100 each year for two years would be currently worth \$172.36:

$$PV = \sum_{t=1}^{2} \$100e^{-(.10)(t)} = \$100e^{-(.10)(1)} + \$100e^{-(.10)(2)} = \$172.36$$

Thus, if we assume continuous compounding and a discount rate of 10 percent, then the value of our 10-year, 9 percent bond would be \$908.82:

$$V_0^b = \sum_{t=1}^{M} C^A e^{-Rt} + Fe^{-RM}$$

$$V_0^b = \sum_{t=1}^{10} \$90e^{-(.10)(t)} + \$1{,}000e^{-(.10)(10)} = \$908.82$$

It should be noted that most practitioners use interest rates with annual or semi-annual compounding. Most of our examples in this book, in turn, will follow that convention. However, continuous compounding is often used in mathematical derivations, and we will make some use of it when it is helpful.

Valuing Bonds with Maturities Less than One Year

Some bonds do not make any periodic coupon payments. Instead the investor realizes interest as the difference between the maturity value and the purchase price. These bonds are called *zero-coupon bonds* (also called *zeros* and *pure discount bonds* [PDB]). The value of a zero-coupon bond is

$$V_0^b = \frac{R}{(1+R)^N}$$

For example, a zero-coupon bond maturing in 10 years and paying a maturing value of \$1,000 would be valued at \$385.54 if the required rate is 10 percent and annual compound is assumed:

$$V_0^b = \frac{1{,}000}{(1.10)^{10}} = \$385.54$$

If the convention is to double the number of years and halve the annual discount rate, then the bond would be valued at \$376.89 to yield a semiannual rate of 5 percent, simple annual rate of 10 percent, and effective annual rate of 10.25 percent $(= (1.05)^2 - 1)$:

$$V_0^b = \frac{1{,}000}{(1.05)^{20}} = \$376.89$$

Many zero-coupon bonds have maturities less than a year. In valuing such bonds, the convention is to discount by using an annual rate and to express the bond's maturity as a proportion of a year. Thus, on March 1, a zero-coupon bond promising to pay \$100 on September 1 (184 days) and trading at an annual discount rate of 8 percent would be worth \$96.19:

$$V_0^b = \frac{\$100}{(1.08)^{184/365}} = \$96.19$$

The \$96.19 bond value reflects a maturity measured in terms of the actual number of days between March 1 and September 1 (184) and 365 days in the year. If we had instead assumed 30-day months and a 360-day year, then the maturity expressed as a proportion of year would be 0.5 and the value of the bond would be \$96.225 $(= \$100/(1.08)^{.5})$. The choice of time measurement used in valuing bonds and computing accrued interest is known as the *day count convention*. The day count convention is defined as the way in which the ratio of the number of days to maturity (or days between dates) to the number of days in the reference period (e.g., year) is calculated. The bond value of \$96.19 is based on a day count convention of actual days to maturity to actual days in the year (actual/actual), whereas the value of \$96.225 is based on a day count convention of 180 days to maturity (30 days × 6) to 360 days in the year (30/360). For short-term U.S. Treasury bills and other money market securities, for example, the convention is to use actual number of days based on a 360-day year (actual/360).

Valuing Bonds at Noncoupon Dates

Equations (3.2) and (3.3) can be used to value bonds at dates in which the coupons are to be paid in exactly one period. However, most bonds purchased are not bought on coupon dates, but rather at dates in between coupon dates. An investor who purchases a bond between coupon payments must compensate the seller for the coupon interest earned from the time of the last coupon payment to the settlement date of the bond. (An exception to this rule would be when a bond is in default. Such a bond is said to be quoted flat, that is, without accrued interest.) This amount is known as *accrued interest* (*AI*). The formula for determining accrued interest is:

$$AI = \text{Coupon}\left[\frac{\text{Number of days from last coupon to settlement date}}{\text{Number of days in the coupon period}}\right]$$

For U.S. Treasury coupon securities, the convention is to use the actual number of days since the last coupon date and the actual number of days between coupon payments: an actual/actual ratio. For example, consider a T-note whose last coupon payment was on March 1 and whose next coupon is six months later on September 1. Suppose the note is purchased with a settlement date of July 20. The actual number of days in the coupon period (sometimes referred to as the basis) is 184 days, and the actual number of days between coupons is 43:

- July 20 to July 31 = 11 days
- August = 31 days
- September 1 = 1 day
- Total = 43 days

For corporate, agency, and municipal bonds, the practice is to use 30-day months and a 360-day year: 30/360 ratio; each month is assumed to have 30 days and each year is assumed to have 360 days. If the preceding T-note were a corporate credit with a 30/360 day count convention, then the number of days in the coupon period would be 180 and the days between coupons would be 41:

- Remainder of July = 10 days
- August = 30 days
- September 1 = 1 day
- Total = 41 days

In trading bonds on a noncoupon date, the amount the buyer pays to the seller is the agreed-upon price plus the accrued interest. This amount is often called the *full-price* or *dirty price.* The price of a bond without accrued interest is called the *clean price:*

$$\text{Full price} = \text{Clean price} + \text{Accrued interest}$$

The full price of the bond can be founds by:

1. Determining the number of days between the settlement date and the next coupon date.
2. Determining the number of days in the coupon period.
3. Computing the following:

$$v = \frac{\text{Number of days between settlement and the next coupon}}{\text{Number of days in the coupon period}}$$

4. Computing the value.

For a bond with N semiannual coupon payments of C remaining, the full-price value would be:

$$V_0 = \sum_{t=1}^{N} \frac{C}{(1+R)^{t+1}} + \frac{F}{(1+R)^{N-1+v}}$$

$$V_0 = \frac{C}{(1+R)^{v}} + \frac{C}{(1+R)^{1+v}} + \frac{C}{(1+R)^{2+v}} + \cdots + \frac{C}{(1+R)^{N-1+v}} + \frac{F}{(1+R)^{N-1+v}}$$

As an example, suppose a corporate bond with an annual coupon rate of 8 percent, semiannual payments, face value of $100, and maturing in 2016 is purchased with a settlement date of July 20, 2010. If the required yield is 10 percent (semiannual rate of 5 percent), the price of the bond would be $94.636:

Period *t*	***t* − 1**	**Period**	**Cash Flow per $100 Par**	**PV of CF at 5%**
1	**0**	**0.227778**	**$4.00**	**$3.955793**
2	1	1.227778	$4.00	$3.767422
3	2	2.227778	$4.00	$3.588021
4	3	3.227778	$4.00	$3.417163
5	4	4.227778	$4.00	$3.254441
6	5	5.227778	$4.00	$3.099467
7	6	6.227778	$4.00	$2.951873
8	7	7.227778	$4.00	$2.811308
9	8	8.227778	$4.00	$2.677436
10	9	9.227778	$4.00	$2.549939
11	10	10.227778	$4.00	$2.428514
12	11	11.227778	$104.00	$60.134623
	$v = 41/180 = 0.227778$			$94.636

Alternatively, the full price can also be found by:

1. Moving to the next coupon date and determining the value of the bond at that date based on the future coupons.
2. Adding the coupon at the next coupon date to the value of bond.
3. Discounting the bond value plus coupon back to the current date.

Thus, the 8 percent corporate bond maturing in 2016, purchased with a settlement date of July 20, 2010, at a required yield of 10 percent would have a value of 91.693586 per $100 face at the next coupon date. Discounting the sum of that value and the $4 coupon back to the settlement date (v = .227778 years) yields the full-bond price of $94.636:

- Value of the bond at next coupon date in 41 days or 41/180 = .227778 year.

$$V^B = \sum_{t=1}^{11} \frac{\$4}{(1.05)^t} + \frac{\$100}{(1.05)^{11}} = \$91.693586$$

- Value of the bond at the next coupon date plus coupon paid at that date.

$$\$91.693586 + \$4 = \$95.693586$$

- Current value of the bond—full price:

$$V^B = \frac{\$95.693586}{(1.05)^{.227778}} = \$94.636$$

The full or dirty price of $94.636 includes the portion of the coupon interest the buyer will receive but the seller has earned. Even though the price the buyer pays the seller is the full price, in the United States, the convention is to quote a bond's clean price. In this example, given that there are 41 days to the next coupon and 180 days in the coupon period, the number of days from the last coupon is 139 (180 – 41). The accrued interest (AI) per $100 par is $3.0222 and the clean price or flat price is $91.547 (full price minus the AI):

$$AI = \$4(139/180) = \$3.089$$

$$\text{Clean Price} = 94.636 - \$3.089 = \$91.547$$

Exhibit 3.4 shows Bloomberg Description, Trace, and Yield Analysis (YA) screens for a Kraft bond that pays an annual coupon of 5.375 percent, principal of $1,000, and matures on 2/10/2020. On 4/5/2012, the bond was trading at 116.202 per $100 face value (clean price). As shown on the YA screen, the bond has settlement date of 4/11/2012, 61 days of accrued interest on that date of $9.11 (for $1,000 face), and an invoice price of $1,171.13. Finally, the bond yields a rate of return of 3.034167 percent; that is, 3.034167 percent is the discount rate that equates the price of the bond to the present value of its semiannual coupon payments and principal payment at 2/10/2020.

Price Quotes, Fractions, and Basis Points

Whereas many corporate bonds pay principals of $1,000, this is not the case for many noncorporate bonds and other fixed-income securities. As a result, many traders quote bond prices as a percentage of their par value. For example, if a bond is selling at par, it would be quoted at 100 (100 percent of par); thus, a bond with a face value of $10,000 and quoted at 80 1/8 would be selling at (.80125)($10,000) = $8,012.50. When a bond's price is quoted as a percentage of its par, the quote is usually expressed in points and fractions of a point, with each point equal to $1. Thus, a quote of 97 points means that the bond is selling for $97 for each $100 of par. The fractions of points differ among bonds. Fractions are either in thirds, eighths, quarters, halves, or 64ths. On a $100 basis, a 1/2 point is $0.50 and a 1/32 point is $0.03125. A price quote of 97 4/32 (97 – 4) is 97.125 for a bond with a 100 face value. It should also be noted that when the yield on a bond or other security changes over a short period, such as a day, the yield and subsequent price changes are usually quite small. As a result, fractions on yields are often quoted in

EXHIBIT 3.4 Kraft Bond 4/5/2012, Bloomberg Screens: DES, QR, and YA (Custom Tab)

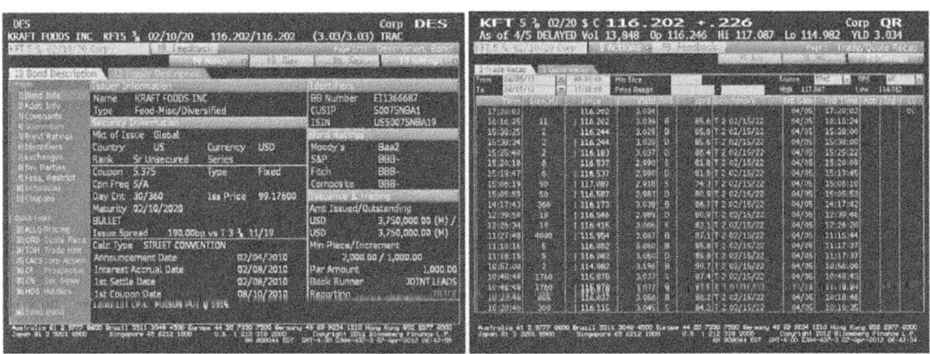

terms of basis points (bps). A bp is equal to 1/100 of a percentage point, or phrased differently, 100 bps = 1 percent. Thus, 6.5 percent may be quoted as 6 percent plus 50 bps, or 650 bps, and an increase in yield from 6.5 percent to 6.55 percent would represent an increase of 5 bps.

Exhibit 3.5 shows the Bloomberg FIT screen showing the prices and yields of U.S. Treasury bonds, Treasury notes, and Treasury bills that were recently issued and actively traded. As shown on the screen, there is a 10-year T-note paying a coupon of 2 percent. The Bloomberg description screen (DES) for the Treasury provides more details; specifically, the bond was issued on 2/15/12, matures on 2/15/22, pays a 2 percent coupon semiannually, its quoted bid and ask prices from one dealer (BVAL) (ALLQ screen) are 99-15 1/4 and 99-18 3/4. The Bloomberg yield analysis (YA) screen shows, for an investment period from the settlement date of 4/19/12 to 2/15/22, the yield or total return on the bond (with semiannual compounding) is 2.054441 percent.

EXHIBIT 3.5 Bloomberg Price Quotes and Descriptions of U.S., Treasury Securities: Bloomberg FIT, DES, YA (Custom Tab), Cash Flows (CSHF), Composite Quotes (AllQ), and Trade Recap (QR), 4/5/12

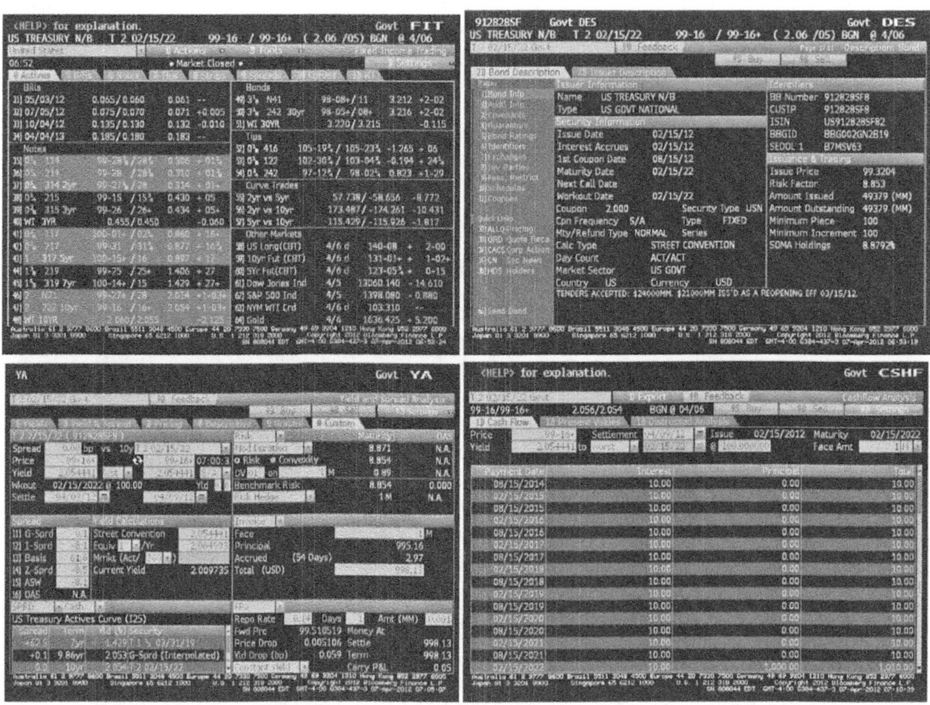

Exhibit 3.6 shows the Bloomberg description screen (DES) and yield analysis screen (YA) for a Disney bond paying a coupon of 5.875 percent semiannually, issued (first settled) on 12/19/02, and maturing on 12/15/17. On 4/5/12, the bond was trading at 122.3720 (clean price) per $100 par and had 116 days of accrued interest of 18.93 and an invoice price (dirty) of $1,242.65 (per $1,000 face value). For the investment period of approximately six years, the yield or total return (with semiannual

EXHIBIT 3.6 Bloomberg Descriptions of Disney Bond, Bloomberg Screens: DES and YA Screens, 5/15/12

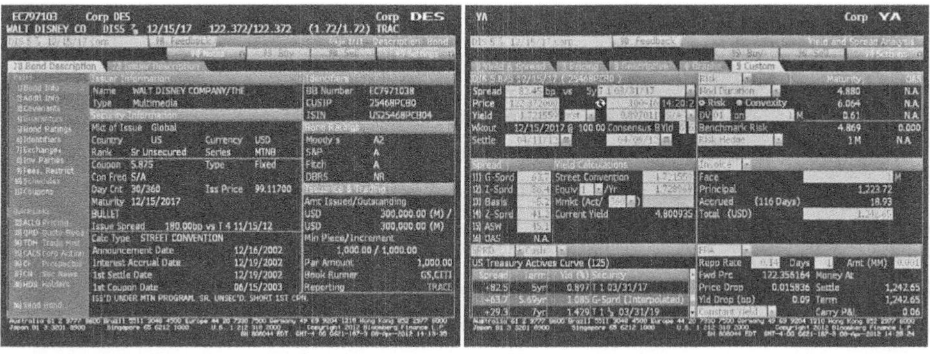

compounding) on the bond is 1.721559 percent (the return calculations for the Treasury note and Disney bonds are explained in the next section).

The Yield to Maturity and Other Rates of Return Measures

The financial markets serve as conduits through which funds are distributed from borrowers to lenders. The allocation of funds is determined by the relative rates paid on bonds, loans, and other financial securities, with the differences in rates among claims being determined by risk, maturity, and other factors that serve to differentiate the claims. There are a number of different measures of the rates of return on bonds and loans. Some measures, for example, determine annual rates based on cash flows received over 365 days, whereas others use 360 days; some measures determine rates that include the compounding of cash flows, whereas some do not; and some measures include capital gains and losses, whereas others exclude price changes. In this section, we examine some of the measures of rates of return, including the most common measure—the yield to maturity—and in subsequent sections we look at three other important rate measures: the spot rate, the total return, and the geometric mean.

Common Measures of Rates of Return

When the term rate of return is used it can mean a number of different rates, including the interest rate, coupon rate, current yield, or discount yield. The term *interest rate* is sometimes referred to the price a borrower pays a lender for a loan. Unlike other prices, this price of credit is expressed as the ratio of the cost or fee for borrowing and the amount borrowed. This price is typically expressed as an annual percentage of the loan (even if the loan is for less than one year). Today, financial economists often refer to the yield to maturity on a bond as the interest rate. In this book, the term interest rate will mean yield to maturity.

Another measure of rate of return is a bond's *coupon rate*. As noted in the last section, the coupon rate, C^R, is the contractual rate the issuer agrees to pay each period. It is usually expressed as a proportion of the annual coupon payment to the bond's face value:

$$C^R = \frac{\text{Annual Coupon}}{F}$$

Unless the bond is purchased at par, the coupon rate is not a good measure of the bond's rate of return because it fails to take into account the price paid for the bond.

In examining corporate bond quotes, the *current yield* on a bond is often provided. As noted, this rate is computed as the ratio of the bond's annual coupon to its current price. This measure provides a quick estimate of a bond's rate of return, but in many cases not an accurate one because it does not capture price changes. The current yield is a good approximation to the bond's yield, if the bond's price is selling at or near its face value or if it has a long maturity. That is, we noted earlier that if a bond is selling at par, its coupon rate is equal to the discount rate. In this case, the current yield is equal to the bond's yield to maturity. Thus, the closer the bond's price is to its face value, the closer the current yield is to the bond's yield to maturity. As for maturity, note that a coupon bond with no maturity or repayment of principal, known as a *perpetuity* or *consul,* pays a fixed amount of coupons forever. As shown in Exhibit 3.7, the value of such a bond is

$$V_0^B = \sum_{t=1}^{\infty} \frac{C}{(1+R)^t} \rightarrow \frac{C}{R}$$

If the bond is priced in the market to equal V_0^B, then the rate on the bond would be equal to the current yield: $R = C/V_0^B$. Thus, when a coupon bond has a long-term maturity (e.g., 20 years), then it is similar to a perpetuity, making its current yield a good approximation of its rate of return.

EXHIBIT 3.7 Value of Perpetuity: Proof

$$V_0^B = \sum_{t=1}^{\infty} \frac{C}{(1+R)^t} = \frac{C}{(1+R)^1} + \frac{C}{(1+R)^2} + \frac{C}{(1+R)^3} + \cdots$$

Factor out C·

$$V_0^B = C\left[\frac{1}{(1+R)^1} + \frac{1}{(1+R)^2} + \frac{1}{(1+R)^3} + \cdots\right]$$

Multiply through by $(1+R)$

$$V_0^B(1+R) = C\left[1 + \frac{1}{(1+R)^1} + \frac{1}{(1+R)^2} + \frac{1}{(1+R)^3} + \cdots\right]$$

Subtract V_0^B from both sides

$$V_0^B(1+R) - V_0^B = C\left[1 + \frac{1}{(1+R)^1} + \frac{1}{(1+R)^2} + \frac{1}{(1+R)^3} + \cdots\right] - V_0^B$$

$$\text{Note}: V_0^B = C\left[\frac{1}{(1+R)^1} + \frac{1}{(1+R)^2} + \frac{1}{(1+R)^3} + \cdots\right]. \text{ Thus}$$

$$V_0^B(1+R) - V_0^B = C\left[1 + \frac{1}{(1+R)^1} + \frac{1}{(1+R)^2} + \frac{1}{(1+R)^3} + \cdots\right] - C\left[\frac{1}{(1+R)^1} + \frac{1}{(1+R)^2} + \frac{1}{(1+R)^3} + \cdots\right]$$

$$V_0^B(1+R) - V_0^B = C$$

$$V_0^B\,[(1+R) - 1] = C$$

$$V_0^B\,R = C$$

$$V_0^B = \frac{C}{R}$$

Finally, the *discount yield* is the bond's return expressed as a proportion of its face value. For example, a one-year zero-coupon bond costing \$900 and paying a par value of \$1,000 yields \$100 in interest and a discount yield of 10 percent:

$$\text{Discount Yield} = \frac{F - P_0}{F} = \frac{\$100}{\$1{,}000} = .10$$

The discount yield used to be the rate frequently quoted by financial institutions on their loans (because the discount rate is lower than a rate quoted on the borrowed amount). The difficulty with this rate measure is that it does not capture the conceptual notion of the rate of return being the rate at which the investment grows. In this example, the \$900 bond investment grew at a rate of over 11 percent, not 10 percent:

$$\frac{F - P_0}{P_0} = \frac{\$100}{\$900} = .111$$

Because of tradition, the rates on Treasury bills are quoted by dealers in terms of the bills' discount yield. Whereas Treasury bills have maturities less than one year, the discount yields are quoted on an annualized basis. Dealers quoting the annualized rates use a day count convention of actual days to maturity but with a 360-day year:

$$\text{Annual Discount Yield} = \frac{F - P_0}{F}\,\frac{360}{\text{Days to Maturity}}$$

Given the dealer's discount yield, the bid or ask price can be obtained by solving the yield equation for the bond's price, P_0. Doing this yields:

$$P_0 = F\left[(1 - R_D(\text{Days to Maturity}/360)\right]$$

Yield to Maturity

The most widely used measure of a bond's rate of return is the *yield to maturity* (YTM). As noted earlier, the YTM, or simply the yield, is the rate that equates the purchase price of the bond, P_0^b, with the present value of its future cash flows. Mathematically, the YTM (y) is found by solving the following equation for y (YTM):

$$P_0^b = \sum_{t=1}^{M} \frac{CF_t}{(1+y)^t} \tag{3.4}$$

The YTM is analogous to the internal rate of return used in capital budgeting. It is a measure of the rate at which the investment grows. From our first example, if the 10-year, 9 percent annual coupon bond were actually trading in the market for \$938.55, then the YTM on the bond would be 10 percent. The 5.375 percent Kraft bond with a maturity of 2/10/2020 shown in Exhibit 3.4, in turn, is priced at 116.202 (per \$100 face value). At the 4/11/12 settlement date, the cost of the bond (per \$1,000 face value) is \$1,171.127 (equal to the clean price of \$1,162.02 plus \$9.1076 of 61 days of accrued interest). Based on this cost and using semiannual compounding the annualized yield of the Kraft bond is 3.03 percent. Unlike the current yield, the YTM incorporates all of the bonds cash flows (CFs). It also assumes the bond is held to maturity and that all CFs from the bond are reinvested to maturity at the calculated YTM.

Estimating YTM: Average Rate to Maturity

If the cash flows on the bond (coupons and principal) are not equal, then Equation (3.4) cannot be solved directly for the YTM. Alternatively, one must use an iterative (trial and error) procedure: substituting different y values into Equation (3.4), until that y is found that equates the present value of the bond's cash flows to the market price. An estimate of the YTM, however, can be found using the bond's *average rate to maturity* (ARTM; also referred to as the *yield approximation formula*). This measure determines the rate as the average return per year as a proportion of the average price of the bond per year. For a coupon bond with a principal paid at maturity, the average return per year on the bond is its annual coupon plus its average annual capital gain. For a bond with an M-year maturity, its average gain is calculated as the total capital gain realized at maturity divided by the number of years to maturity: $(F - P_0^b)/M$. The average price of the bond is computed as the average of two known prices, the current price and the price at maturity (F): $(F + P_0{}^b)/2$. Thus, the ARTM is:

$$\text{ARTM} = \frac{C+[(F-P_0^b)/M]}{(F+P_0^b)/2} \tag{3.5}$$

The ARTM for the 10-year, 9 percent annual coupon bond trading at \$938.55 is 0.0992:

$$\text{ARTM} = \frac{\$90+[(\$1{,}000-\$938.55)/10]}{(\$1{,}000+\$938.55)/2} = .0992$$

Bond Equivalent Yields

The YTM calculated above represents the yield for the period (in the above example this was an annual rate, given annual coupons). If a bond's CFs were semiannual, then solving Equation (3.4) for y would yield a six-month rate; if the CFs were monthly, then solving (3.4) for y would yield a monthly rate. To obtain a *simple annualized rate* (with no compounding), y^A, one needs to multiply the periodic rate, y, by the number of periods in the year. Thus, if a 10-year bond paying \$45 every six months and

\$1,000 at maturity were selling for \$937.69, its six-month yield would be .05 and its simple annualized rate, y^A, would be 10 percent:

$$\$937.69 = \sum_{t=1}^{20} \frac{\$45}{(1+y)^t} + \frac{\$1{,}000}{(1+y)^{20}} \Rightarrow y = .05$$

$$y^A = \text{Simple Annualized Rate} = (n)(y) = (2)(.05) = .10$$

In this example, the simple annualized rate is obtained by determining the periodic rate on a bond paying coupons semiannually and then multiplying by two. Because Treasury bonds and many corporate bonds pay coupons semiannually, the rate obtained by multiplying the semiannual periodic rate by two is called the *bond-equivalent yield.* Bonds with different payment frequencies often have their rates expressed in terms of their bond-equivalent yields so that their rates can be compared to each other on a common basis. This bond-equivalent yield, though, does not take into account the reinvestment of the bond's cash flows during the year. Therefore, it underestimates the actual rate of return earned. Thus, an investor earning 5 percent semiannually would have \$1.05 after six months from a \$1 investment that he or she can reinvest for the next six months. If he or she reinvests at 5 percent, then the investor's annual rate would be 10.25 percent (= (1.05)(1.05) – 1 = $(1.05)^2 - 1$), not 10 percent. As noted earlier, the 10.25 percent annual rate, which takes into account compounding, is known as the effective rate.

Cash Flow Yield

Fixed-income securities whose CF's include schedule principal payments prior to maturity are *amortized securities.* Their CFs include principal and interest payments. If the CFs are constant, then the yields can be found by solving for the yield that equates the present value of the CF to the current price:

$$P_0^B = \sum_{t=1}^{N} \frac{CF}{(1+YTM)^t}$$

For example, a 10-year, fully amortized bond that pays interest of 8 percent on a semiannual basis and has a principal of \$100, would make semiannual payments of \$7.358175 per \$100 par:

$$P_0^B = \sum_{t=1}^{N} \frac{CF}{(1+YTM)^t}$$

$$P_0^B = CF \sum_{t=1}^{N} \frac{1}{(1+YTM)^t}$$

$$100 = CF\left[\frac{1-1/(1+R)^N}{R}\right]$$

$$CF = \frac{100}{\left[\frac{1-1/(1+R)^N}{R}\right]}$$

$$CF = \frac{100}{\left[\frac{1-1/(1+(.08/2))^{20}}{.08/2}\right]} = 7.358175$$

If the bond were priced at 95, its semiannual yield would be 4.586656 percent and its simple annualized yield would be 9.1733 percent:

$$\$95 = \sum_{t=1}^{20}\frac{\$7.358175}{(1+YTM)^t} \Rightarrow \text{YTM} = .04586656$$

$$\text{Simple Annualized YTM} = (2)(.04586656) = .091733$$

Examples of amortized securities include many securitized securities, such as mortgage-backed securities and asset-backed securities. As we will see in Chapter 10, many of these securities have prepayment options, and as a result, their CFs are not fixed over the life of the securities.

Yield to Call, Yield to Put, and Yield to Worst

Yield to Call

Many bonds have a call feature that allows the issuer to buy back the bond at a specific price known as the call price. (Call features and other option features will be discussed in some detail in Chapters 5 and 13.) Given a bond with a call option, the *yield to call* (YTC) is the rate obtained by assuming the bond is called on the call date. Like the YTM, the YTC is found by solving for the rate that equates the present value of the CFs to the market price:

$$P_0^b = \sum_{t=1}^{N_{CD}}\frac{CF_t}{(1+y)^t} + \frac{CP}{(1+y)^{N_{CD}}}$$

where:

CP = Call Price

N_{CD} = Number of periods to the call date

Thus, a 10-year, 9 percent coupon bond callable in 5 years at a call price of $1,100, paying interest semiannually, and trading at $937.69, would have a YTM of 10 percent and an annualized YTC of 12.2115 percent:

$$\$937.69 = \sum_{t=1}^{10} \frac{\$45}{(1+y)^t} + \frac{\$1,100}{(1+y)^{10}} \Rightarrow \text{YTC} = .0610575$$
$$\text{Simple Annualized YTC} = (2)(.0610575) = .122115$$

The indenture specifies when the bond may be called and at what price. For some issues, the call price is the same. For other callable bonds, the call price depends on when the bond is called. There is a call schedule that specifies the call price for each call date. The convention is to calculate the YTC for each date and call price.

Yield to Put

An issue can be putable, allowing the bondholder the right to sell the bond back to the issuer at a specified price, the put price (PP). As with callable bonds, putable bonds can have a constant put price or a put schedule. When a bond is putable, the convention is to calculate the yield to put (YTP). Like the YTM and YTC, the YTP is found by solving for the rate that equates the present value of the CFs to the market price:

$$P_0^B = \sum_{t=1}^{N_{PD}} \frac{CF_t}{(1+YTP)^t} + \frac{PP}{(1+YTP)^{N_{PD}}}$$

where:

PP = put price
N_{PD} = number of periods to the put date

A 10-year, 9 percent coupon bond, first putable in 5 years at a put price of $950, paying interest semiannually and trading at $937.69 would have an annualized YTP of 9.807741 percent:

$$\$937.69 = \sum_{t=1}^{10} \frac{\$45}{(1+\text{YTP})^t} + \frac{\$950}{(1+\text{YTP})^{10}} \Rightarrow \text{YTP} = .04903870$$
$$\text{Simple Annualized YTP} = (2)(.04903870) = .09807741$$

Yield to Worst

Many investors calculate the YTC for all possible call dates and the YTP for all possible put dates, as well as the YTM. They then select the lowest of the yields as their yield return measure. The lowest yield is sometimes referred to as the ***yield to worst.*** Exhibit 3.8 shows the Bloomberg call schedule for a 7.5 percent Ford bond with a maturity of 8/20/2032, the Bloomberg's YTC screen showing the bond's YTC calculations for the

EXHIBIT 3.8 Call Schedule and Yield-to-Call Calculations, Bloomberg YA Screen (Custom Tab), DES Screen (Schedule Tab), YA Screen (Yield to Call Tab), and YTC Screen Ford Bond, Coupon = 7.5 Percent, Maturity = 1/13/12

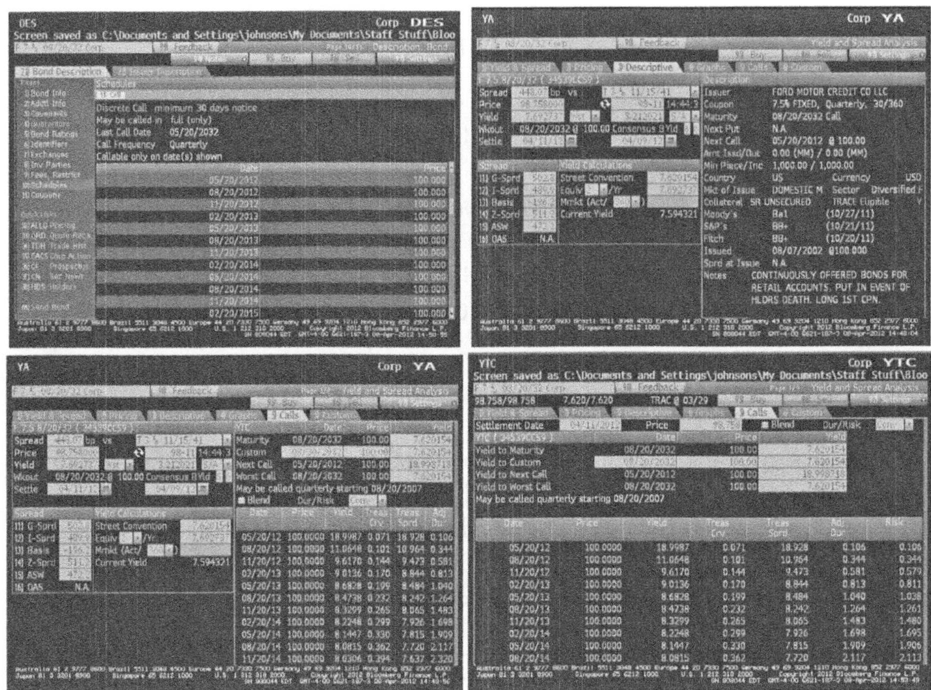

G-sprd = selected bond's yield minus the interpolated government bond yield
I-Sprd = selected bond's yield minus the interpolated swap rate
Z-Sprd = selected bond's spread over the benchmark zero coupon swap curve
OAS = the incremental return of the security compared to a benchmark interest rate curve adjusted for embedded options.
Basis = credit default swap (CDS) spread minus the selected bond's z-spread
ASW, asset swap spread, is the difference between the coupon cash flow of the security and the fixed coupon of an offsetting swap in basis points.
Note: Swap spreads referred to the price (in basis points) of a credit default swap (cost of insurance against default) on the bond or bonds of the creditor. It is used as an indicator of a bond's credit spread.
Features: Benchmark rates can be changed by inputting ticker. Panels appearing on the right show related information on the bond. To change panel, click bottom tabs.

call dates, and the Bloomberg YA screen showing the yield calculations, including the yield to worst. The Ford bond has a YTM of 7.620154 percent, yield to the next call of 18.99877 percent, and a yield to worst of 7.692737 percent.

Bond Portfolio Yields

The yield for a portfolio of bonds is found by solving the rate that will make the present value of the portfolio's cash flow equal to the market value of the portfolio. For example, a portfolio consisting of a two-year, 5 percent annual coupon bond priced at par (100) and a three-year, 10 percent annual coupon bond priced at 107.87 to yield 7 percent (YTM) would generate a three-year cash flow of \$15, \$115, and \$110 and would have a portfolio market value of \$207.87. The rate that equates this portfolio's cash flow to its portfolio value is 6.2 percent:

$$\$207.87 = \frac{\$15}{(1+y)^1} + \frac{\$115}{(1+y)^2}\frac{\$110}{(1+y)^3} \Rightarrow y = .062$$

Note that this yield is not the weighted average of the YTMs of the bonds comprising the portfolio. In this example, the weighted average (R_P) is 6.04%:

$$R_P = w_1(\text{YTM}_1) + w_2(\text{YTM}_2)$$

$$R_P = \left[\frac{\$100}{\$207.87}\right](.05) + \left[\frac{\$107.87}{\$207.87}\right](.07) = .0604$$

Thus, the yield for a portfolio of bonds is not the average of the YTMs of the bonds making up the portfolio.

Rates on Zero-Coupon Bonds

Formula for the Rate on Zero-Coupon Bond

Whereas no algebraic solution for the YTM exists when a bond pays coupons and principal that are not equal, a solution does exists in the case of a zero-coupon bond or pure discount bonds (PDBs) in which there is only one cash flow (F). That is

$$P_0^b = \frac{F}{(1+\text{YTM}_M)^M}$$

$$(1+\text{YTM}_M)^M = \frac{F}{P_0^b}$$

$$\text{YTM}_M = \left[\frac{F}{P_0^b}\right]^{1/M} - 1 \qquad (3.6)$$

where: M = maturity in years. Thus, a zero-coupon bond with a par value of \$1,000, a maturity of three years, and trading for \$800 would have an annualized YTM of 7.72 percent:

$$\text{YTM}_3 = \left[\frac{\$1{,}000}{\$800}\right]^{1/3} - 1 = .0772$$

If the convention is to assume semiannual compounding, then the semiannual YTM would be 3.789 percent and the simple annual rate or bond-equivalent yield would be 7.578 percent:

$$M = 3\,\text{years}$$

$$n = \text{compound frequency} = 2$$

$$N = nM = (2)(3) = 6$$

$$\text{Semiannual YTM} = \left[\frac{\$1{,}000}{\$800}\right]^{1/6} - 1 = .03789$$

$$\text{Bond} - \text{Equivalent Yield} = (2)(.03789) = .075782$$

Similarly, a pure discount bond paying $100 at the end of 182 days and trading at $96 would yield an annual rate using a 365-day year of 8.53 percent:

$$\text{YTM} = \left[\frac{\$100}{\$96}\right]^{365/182} - 1 = .0853$$

Rate on Zero-Coupon Bond with Continuous Compounding

Using the properties of logarithms (see Appendix B at the end of the book for a primer on logarithms), the rate on a zero-coupon bond with continuous compounding is:

$$P_0^b e^{Rt} = F$$

$$e^{Rt} = \frac{F}{P_0^b}$$

$$\ln(e^{Rt}) = \ln\left[\frac{F}{P_0^b}\right]$$

$$Rt = \ln\left[\frac{F}{P_0^b}\right]$$

$$R \frac{\ln[F/P_0^b]}{t}$$

A zero-coupon bond selling for $96 and paying $100 at the end of 182 days would yield an annual rate of 8.1868 percent with continuous compounding:

$$S = \frac{\ln[\$100/\$96]}{182/365} = .081868$$

When the rate of return on a security is expressed as the natural log of the ratio of its end of the period value to its current value, the rate is referred to as the *logarithmic return*. Thus, a bond currently priced at \$96 and expected to be worth \$100 at the end of the period would have an expected logarithmic return of 4.082 percent: $R = ln(\$100 / 96) = .04082$.

It should be noted that the rate on a zero-coupon bond is called the *spot rate*. As discussed later in this chapter, spot rates are important in determining a bond's equilibrium price.

Total Return

Equation (3.6) provides the formula for finding the YTM for a zero-discount bond. A useful extension of Equation (3.6) is the *total return* (TR), also called the *realized return* and *average realized return* (ARR). The total return is the yield obtained by assuming the cash flows are reinvested to the investor's horizon at an assumed reinvestment rate and at the horizon the bond is sold at an assumed rate given the horizon is not maturity or pays its principal if the horizon is maturity. The TR is computed by first determining the investor's horizon, HD; next, finding the HD value, defined as the total funds the investor would have at HD; and third, solving for the TR using a formula for the zero-coupon bond (Equation (3.6)).

To illustrate, suppose an investor buys a four-year, 10 percent coupon bond, paying coupons annually, and selling at its par value of \$1,000. Assume the investor needs cash at the end of year three (HD = 3), is certain he can reinvest the coupons during the period in securities yielding 10 percent, and expects to sell the bond at his HD at a rate of 10 percent. To determine the investor's TR, we first need to find the HD value. This value is equal to the price the investor obtains from selling the bond at HD and the value of the coupons at the HD. In this case, the investor, at his HD, will be able to sell a one-year bond paying a \$100 coupon and a \$1,000 par at maturity for \$1,000, given the assumed discount rate of 10 percent:

$$P_0^b = \frac{\$100 + \$1,000}{(1.10)^1} = \$1,000$$

Also at the HD, the \$100 coupon paid at the end of the first year will be worth \$121, given the assumption it can be reinvested at 10 percent for two years and there is annual compounding, $\$100(1.10)^2 = \$121$, and the \$100 received at the end of year two will, in turn, be worth \$110 in cash at the HD, $\$100(1.10) = \$110$. Finally, at the HD the investor would receive his third coupon of \$100. Combined, the investor would have \$1,331 in cash at the HD: HD value = \$1,331. The horizon value of \$1,330 consists of a bond valued at \$1,000, coupons of \$300, and interest earned from reinvesting coupons of \$31 (HD coupon value – total coupon received = \$331 – \$300 – \$31) see Exhibit 3.9). Note that if the rates at which coupons can be reinvested

EXHIBIT 3.9 Total Realized Return

- Example: You buy 4–year, 10% annual coupon bond at par (F = 1,000). *Assuming* you can reinvest CFs at 10%, your TR would be 10%:

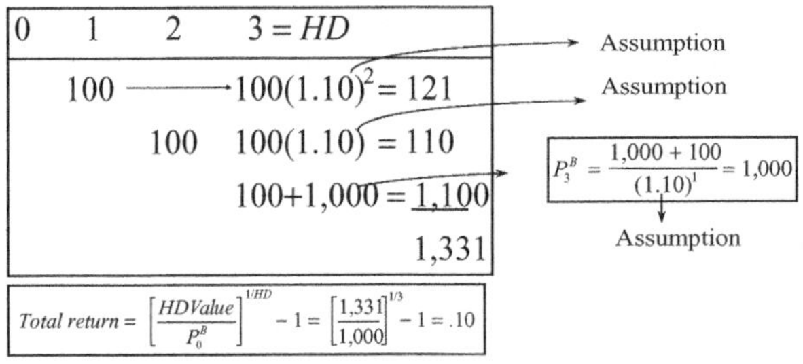

0	1	2	3 = *HD*
	100		100(1.10)^2 = 121
		100	100(1.10) = 110
			100+1,000 = 1,100
			1,331

Assumption

Assumption

$$P_3^B = \frac{1{,}000 + 100}{(1.10)^1} = 1{,}000$$

Assumption

$$\text{Total return} = \left[\frac{HD\,Value}{P_0^B}\right]^{1/HD} - 1 = \left[\frac{1{,}331}{1{,}000}\right]^{1/3} - 1 = .10$$

$$\text{Coupon Value} = \sum_{t=0}^{HD-1} C(1+R)^t = \$100\left[\frac{(1.10)^3 - 1}{.10}\right] = \$331$$

$$\text{Interest-on-Interest} = \$331 - \$300 = \$30$$

$$P_{HD}^b = \frac{\$1{,}000n\$100}{1.10} = \$1{,}000$$

$$\text{Horizon Value} = \text{Coupon Value} + P_{HD}^b = \$331 + \$1{,}000 = \$1{,}331$$

$$\$1{,}000 = \frac{\$1{,}331}{(1 + \text{Total return})^3}$$

$$\text{Total return} = \left[\frac{\$1{,}331}{\$1{,}000}\right]^{1/3} - 1 = .10$$

(reinvestment rates) are the same (as assumed in this example), then the coupon value at the horizon would be equal to the period coupon times the future value of an annuity of ($FVIF_a$):

$$\text{Coupon Value at HD} = \sum_{t=0}^{HD-1} C(1+R)^t$$

$$\text{Coupon Value at HD} = C\sum_{t=0}^{HD-1} (1+R)^t$$

$$\text{Coupon Value at HD} = C\,FVIF_a$$

$$\text{Coupon Value at HD} = C\left[\frac{(1+R)^{HD} - 1}{R}\right]$$

$$\text{Coupon Value at HD} = \$100\left[\frac{(1.10)^3 - 1}{.10}\right] = \$331$$

The reinvestment income or interest earned from reinvesting coupons (interest on interest), in turn, is equal to the coupon value at HD minus the total coupons received, $(N)(C)$:

$$\text{Reinvestment Income} = \text{Coupon Value at HD} - \text{Total Coupons}$$

$$\text{Reinvestment Income} = \sum_{t=0}^{HD-1} C(1+R)^t - NC$$

$$\text{Reinvestment Income} = \$100\left[\frac{(1.10)^3 - 1}{.10}\right] - (3)(\$100)$$

$$\text{Reinvestment Income} = \$331 - \$300 - \$31$$

Given the HD value of \$1,331, the TR is found in the same way as the YTM for a zero-coupon bond. In this case, a \$1,000 investment in a bond returning \$1,331 at the end of three years yields a total return of 10 percent:

$$P_0^b = \frac{\text{HD Value}}{(1+TR)^{HD}}$$

$$(1+TR)^{HD} = \frac{\text{HD Value}}{P_0^b}$$

$$TR = \left[\frac{\text{HD Value}}{P_0^b}\right]^{1/HD} - 1$$

$$TR = \left[\frac{\$1{,}331}{\$1{,}000}\right]^{1/3} - 1 = .10$$

Note that the total return is the rate that makes the initial investment grow to equal the horizon value. That is, \$1,000 grows at an annual rate of 10 percent to equal the horizon value of \$1,331 at the end of year three:

$$\$1{,}000 = (1.10)^3 = \$1{,}331$$

The total return can be applied to any period length. For example, if the four-year bond purchased by the investor made semiannual payments and the six-month yield were at 5 percent (a simple annual yield of 10 percent and an effective annual yield of 10.25 percent (= $(1.05)^2 - 1$)), then the investor's coupon value, reinvestment income, price at HD, and HD value at his HD would respectively be \$340.10, \$40.10, \$1,000, and \$1,340.10 (see Exhibit 3.10):

$$\text{Coupon Value} = \sum_{t=0}^{6-1} \$50(1.05)^t = \$50\left[\frac{(1.05)^6 - 1}{.05}\right] = \$340.10$$

$$\text{Reinvestment Income} = \$340.10 - (6)(\$50) = \$40.10$$

$$\text{HD Price} = \sum_{t=1}^{2} \frac{\$50}{(1.05)^t} + \frac{\$1{,}000}{(1.05)^2} = \$50\left[\frac{1-(1/(1.05)^2)}{.05}\right] + \frac{\$1{,}000}{(1.05)^2} = \$1{,}000$$

$$\text{HD Value} = \$340.10 + \$1{,}000 = \$1{,}340.10$$

EXHIBIT 3.10 Total Realized Return with Semiannual Cash Flows

Maturity = 4-years; Annual coupon rate = 10%; Interest paid semiannually, par = $1,000; Reinvestment rate = 5% semiannually; Purchase price = $1,000, Horizon = 3 years, Bond expected to sell at the HD at a 5% semiannual rate.

Horizon Value = $1,340, Semiannual Total Return = 5%, Simple Total Return = 10%, and Effective Total Rate = 10.25%:

Year	0.0	0.5	1.0	1.5	2.0	2.5	3.0		Values
		$50.00						$50(1.05)^5$	$63.81
			$50.00					$50(1.05)^4$	$60.78
				$50.00				$50(1.05)^3$	$57.88
					$50.00			$50(1.05)^2$	$55.13
						$50.00		$50(1.05)^1$	$52.50
							$50.00	$50	$50.00
							$1,000.00	$50/1.05+($1,050/(1.05)^2$	$1,000.00
								Horizon Value	$1,340.10

The investor's semiannual total return would be 5 percent, the simple annual rate would be 10 percent, and the effective annual rate would be 10.25 percent:

$$\text{Semiannual Total Return} = \left[\frac{\$1,340.10}{\$1,000}\right]^{1/6} - 1 = .05$$

$$\text{Simple Annual Rate} = 2\left[\left[\frac{\$1,340.10}{\$1,000}\right]^{1/6} - 1\right] = .10$$

$$\text{Effective Annual Rate} = (1.05)^2 - 1 = .1025$$

In this example, the semiannual TR of 5 percent is the same rate at which the bond was purchased; that is, a 10 percent coupon bond, paying interest twice a year, and selling at par, yields a semiannual YTM of 5 percent and bond-equivalent yield of 10 percent. In this case, obtaining a total return equal to the initial YTM should not be surprising because the coupons are assumed to be reinvested at the same semiannual rate as the initial YTM (5 percent) and the bond is also assumed to be sold at that rate as well (recall, the YTM measure assumes that all coupons are reinvested at the calculated YTM).

It should be noted that the yield on the Kraft bond shown on the YA screen in Exhibit 3.4 is obtained by using a total return calculation and assuming the coupons are reinvest at the YTM. Specifically, the yield of 3.034167 percent on the Kraft bond is based on the cost of purchasing the bond on the settlement date of 4/11/12 for \$1,171.13 (bond clean price of \$1,161.02 plus 61 days of accrued interest of \$9.11), and the dollar return at maturity of \$1,483: \$1,000 in principal, \$430 in coupons (= (\$26.875)(16)), and interest of \$53 earned from investing coupons at 3.034 percent. For an investment period of approximately 8 years, the yield or to tal return (with semiannual compounding) on the bond is 3.0 percent (allow for rounding differences):

$$\text{Semiannual Total Return} = [\$1{,}483.00 / \$1{,}171.13]^{1/(2)(8)} - 1 = .015$$
$$\text{Annual Rate} = (2)(.015) = .03$$

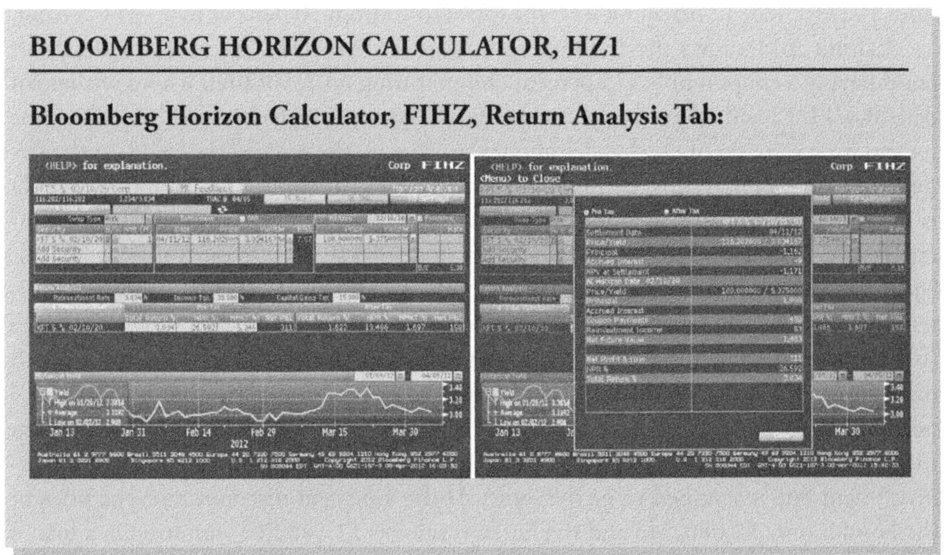

BLOOMBERG HORIZON CALCULATOR, HZ1

Bloomberg Horizon Calculator, FIHZ, Return Analysis Tab:

Market Risk and Horizon Analysis

If the coupons in our above total return examples were expected to be reinvested at different rates or the bonds sold at a different YTM, then a total return equal to the initial YTM would not have been realized. For example, if the rates on all maturities were to increase from 10 percent to 12 percent (simple annual rate), just after the four-year, 10 percent bond was purchased at par, then the total semiannual total return would decrease to 4.8735 percent and the simple annual rate would be 9.7471 percent:

$$\text{Coupon Value at HD} = \sum_{t=0}^{HD-1} \$50(1+R)^t = \$50\left[\frac{(1.06)^6 - 1}{.06}\right] = \$348.77$$

$$\text{Reinvestment Income} = \$348.77 - (6)(\$50) = \$48.77$$

$$\text{HD Price: } P_{HD}^b = \frac{\$50}{(1.06)} + \frac{\$1{,}000 + \$50}{(1.06)^2} = \$981.67$$

$$\text{Horizon Value} = \text{Total Dollar Return} + P_{HD}^B = \$348.77 + \$981.67 = \$1{,}330.44$$

$$\text{Total Return} = \left[\frac{\$1{,}330.44}{\$1{,}000}\right]^{1/6} - 1 = .048735$$

$$\text{Simple Annualized Total Return} = (2)(.048735) = .097471$$

In this case, the rate increase has augmented the reinvestment income by \$0.67 from to \$48.10 to \$48.77, but it has also lowered the horizon price by \$18.33 from \$1,000 to \$981.67. As a result, the price decrease has reduced the total return more than the interest-on-interest increase has increased the realized return. Thus, the increase in rates from 10 percent to 12 percent lowers the total return from 10 percent to 9.7471 percent.

Exhibit 3.11 shows the Bloomberg horizon analysis (HZ1) screen for the Kraft bond paying a coupon of 5.375 percent and maturing on 2/10/2020 with a settlement date of 4/11/12 and selected one-year horizon. The top screens in the exhibit show the returns for a scenario of no changes in rates. As shown, the price of the bond on the settlement date is \$1,171,128 (per \$1 million face value). The price of the bond at the HD is \$1,141,805 given the discount rate of 3.034 percent, and the selected reinvestment rate is 3.034 percent. The investor's horizon value of \$1,209,958 on April 11, 2013 is equal to the sum of the clean price (redemption value) of \$1,141,805, the accrued interest of \$13,587, the coupon income of \$57,750, and the interest on interest of \$816 (based on reinvestment rate of 3.034 percent). This difference in the horizon value and payment cost (profit) is \$38,830 and the one-year total return is approximately 3.3 percent (= [\$1,209,958/\$1,171,128] – 1). The lower left screen in the exhibit shows the case in which the discount yield at the HD is assumed to be 4 percent and the reinvestment rate is assumed to be the same. At the 4 percent discount rate, the price of the bond is only \$1,080,543 and the horizon value is \$1,148,701, resulting in a loss of \$22,427 and a total return of approximately –1.9 percent (= [\$1,209,958/\$1,171,128] – 1). Finally, the lower right screen in the exhibit shows the case in which the discount yield at the HD is assumed to be 2 percent and the reinvestment rate is assumed to be the same. At the 2 percent discount rate, the price of the bond is \$1,212,000 and the horizon value is \$1,280,159, resulting in a gain of \$109,031 and a total return of approximately 9.3 percent (= [\$1,280,159/\$1,171,128] – 1).

The possibility of the actual return on a bond deviating from the expected return because of a change in interest rates is known as *market risk.* As illustrated in the above total return example, a change in interest rates has two effects on a bond's return. First,

EXHIBIT 3.11 Total Return/Horizon Analysis, Kraft Bond: 5 3/8 Coupon Maturity, Date = 2/10/2020—Bloomberg HZ1 Screen

The BLOOMBERG HZ1 Screen calculates the total return on a selected bond. The user can select the horizon period, the discount yield at the HD, and the reinvestment rate. Page two of the screen shows the payment of the bond (price plus accrued interest), redemption value of the security at HD, accrued interest, coupon interest, and interest on interest. The total HD value (redemption value) is equal to the sum of the redemption value, coupon, accrued interest, and interest on interest.

Kraft bond horizon analysis: One-year horizon, scenarios of no change in rates, increase in bond's discount yield to 5 percent, and decrease in yields to 2 percent.

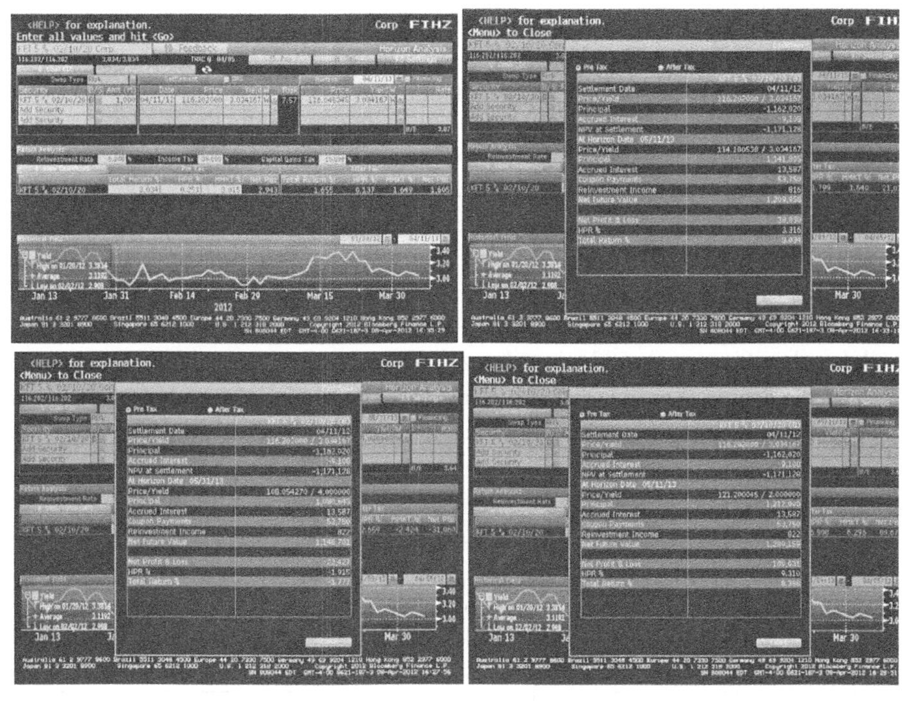

interest rate changes affect the price of a bond; this is referred to as *price risk*. If the investor's horizon is different from the bond's maturity date, then the investor will be uncertain about the price he will receive from selling the bond (if HD < *M*), or the price he will have to pay for a new bond (if HD > *M*). Also, as we noted earlier in discussing the properties of bonds, the price of a bond is inversely related to interest rates and is more price responsive to a change in interest rates if it has a longer term to maturity and its coupon rates are less. Thus, if interest rates change, the price effect on the total return will be negative (i.e., lower rates increase the horizon price and therefore the total return), with the effect being greater for bonds with greater terms to maturity and lower coupon rates. Secondly, interest rate changes affect the return the investor expects from reinvesting the coupon—*reinvestment risk.* If an investor buys a coupon bond, he automatically is subject to market risk. Thus, if interest rates change, the interest-on-interest effect on the total return will be direct (i.e., greater rates increase the reinvestment return and therefore the total return), with the effect being greater for bonds with greater coupon rates.

One way to evaluate market risk for a bond is to estimate the bond's total returns given different interest rate scenarios. Such analysis is known at *horizon analysis.* Moreover, by conducting horizon analysis on one or more bonds or bond portfolios, an investor or portfolio manager can project the performance of the bonds or portfolios and can compare different bonds or bond portfolios based on a planned investment horizon and expectations concerning the market. Exhibit 3.12 shows the total returns for a three-year horizon for four bonds with different coupons and maturities under three interest rate scenarios: yields stay at 7.5 percent, yields decrease to 5 percent, and yields increase to 10 percent. For each scenario, it is assumed the reinvestment rate and the rate for determining the horizon price of the bond are equal to the scenario yield. In terms of market risk, Bond A has the smallest deviations in total returns, with the lowest rate being 7.23 percent and the highest being 7.77 percent. Bond A's total return also decreases when rates decrease and increases when rates increase, suggesting Bond A's interest-on-interest effect dominates its price effect. In contrast, longer-term Bond D has the greatest market risk, with the range in total returns being 2.01 percent to 13.8 percent, and with its total return increasing when rates decrease and decreasing when rates increase, implying its price effect dominates its interest-on-interest effect. Ultimately, which bond an investor should select depends on her expectations about future interest rates and the degree of market risk she wants to assume. Horizon analysis, though, is a useful tool for analyzing market risk and facilitating bond investment decisions.

EXHIBIT 3.12 Horizon Analysis

Total returns for a 3-year horizon for four bonds under three interest rate scenarios: yields stay at 7.5%, yields decrease to 7.5%, and yields increase to 10%. For each scenario it is assumed the reinvestment rate and the rate for determining the horizon price of the bond are equal to the scenario yield.

				Total Return	Total Return	Total Return
Bond	**Annual Coupon Rate**	**Maturity**	**Price at 7.5%**	**5.00%**	**7.50%**	**10.00%**
A	10.00%	3 yrs	106.61	7.23%	7.50%	7.77%
B	7.50%	5 yrs	100.00	8.59%	7.50%	6.48%
C	10.00%	10 yrs	117.37	10.85%	7.50%	4.47%
D	5.00%	15 yrs	77.71	13.80%	7.50%	2.01%

Horizon = 3 years

Semi-annual payments

Yield same on all matuirites

BLOOMBERG YIELD AND RETURN ANALYSIS SCREENS

BOND VALUATION AND YIELD: YA

YA calculates the yield on the bond given the bond's prices using different market conventions:

Current yield = Coupon / Price; Street convention = yield based on the convention the bond is calculated in the market; corporate bond equivalent, and after-tax yield (see Exhibits 3.4 and 3.5).

YIELD TO CALL SCREEN: YTC

YTC calculates yields to predetermined call dates (see Exhibit 3.8).

YIELD-TO-PUT SCREEN: YTP

BOND PAYMENT SCHEDULE SCREEN: CSHF

The CSHF screen shows the bond's cash flow schedule. On the CSHF screen, the user can select either the cash flow or its present value (see Exhibit 3.5).

FIXED INCOME HORIZON ANALYSIS: FIHZ

The Bloomberg FIHZ screen calculates the total return on a selected bond. The user can select the horizon period, the discount yield at the HD, and the reinvestment rate. The "View Cashflow" tab shows the payment of the bond (price plus accrued interest), redemption value of the security at HD, accrued interest, coupon interest, and interest on interest. The total HD value (redemption value) is equal to the sum of the redemption value, coupon, accrued interest, and interest on interest (see Exhibit 3.11).

HISTORICAL COMPARATIVE RETURN SCREEN: COMP

COMP compares bond's historical total returns with a comparable bond index and other selected bonds.

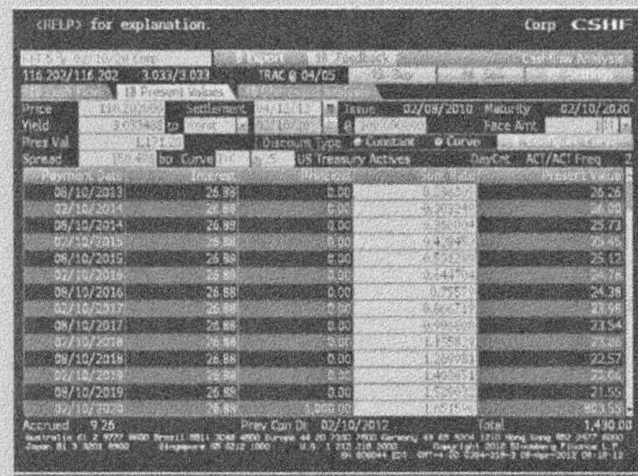

TOTAL RETURN SCREEN: TRA

The TRA screen calculates total returns given different interest rate cases. The user can select different horizons, reinvestment rates (semiannual rate, S/A Reinv), and yield shifts

(Continued)

(YLD SHFT). The yield shifts are projected basis point shifts in the baseline yield curve (e.g., Treasury) between the settlement date and horizon date. The screen shows the price of the calculated price of the bond at the horizon at the yield reflecting the shift and the annualized total return based on the price, coupon, and interest on interest at the horizon and the current price. *Note:* By setting the horizon date equal to the settlement date, one can do a shock analysis to determine the total return for immediate change in rates.

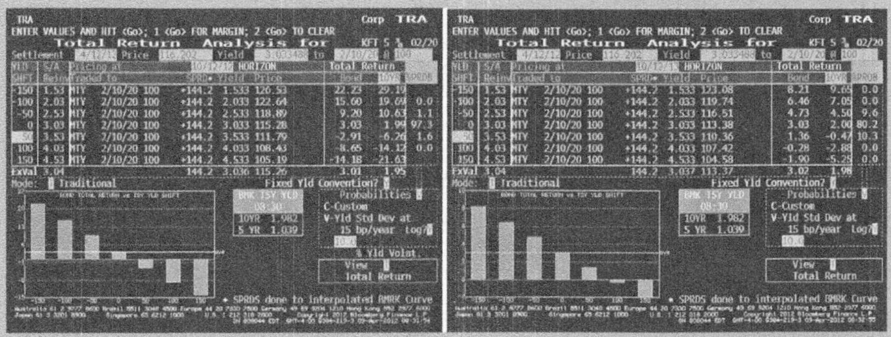

FIXED INCOME SCENARIO ANALYSIS: FISA

FISA allows one to compare and analyze the profit/loss and percentage return of a selected bond under different scenarios based on changes in specific yields, dates, reinvestment rates, or specified yield curve shifts (yield curved are examine in Chapter 4).

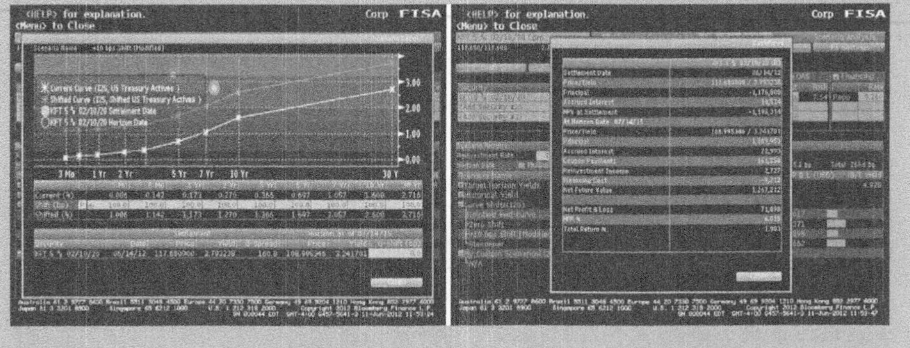

Spot Rates and Equilibrium Prices

The rate on a zero-coupon bond is called the *spot rate*. We previously examined how bonds are valued by discounting their cash flows at a common discount rate. Given different spot rates on similar bonds with different maturities, the correct approach to valuing a bond, though, is to price it by discounting each of the bond's CFs by the appropriate spot rates for that period (S_t). Theoretically, if the market does not price a bond with spot rates, arbitrageurs would be able to realize a free lunch by buying the bond and stripping it into a number of zero-coupon bonds (Chapter 8 discusses strip securities), or by buying strip bonds and bundling them into a coupon bond to sell. Thus, in the absence of arbitrage, the *equilibrium price* of a bond is determined by discounting each of its CFs by their appropriate spot rates.

To illustrate this relationship, suppose there are three risk-free zero-coupon bonds, each with principals of $100 and trading at annualized spot rates of S_1 = 7 percent, S_2 = 8 percent, and S_3 = 9 percent, respectively. If we discount the CF of a three-year, 8 percent coupon bond, paying an $8 coupon annually and a principal of $100 at maturity at these spot rates, its equilibrium price, P_0^*, would be $97.73:

$$P_0^* = \frac{C_1}{(1+S_1)^1} + \frac{C_2}{(1+S_2)^2} + \frac{C_3+F}{(1+S_3)^3}$$

$$P_0^* = \frac{\$8}{(1.07)^1} + \frac{\$8}{(1.08)^2} + \frac{\$108}{(1.09)^3} = \$97.73$$

Suppose this coupon bond is trading in the market at a price ($\mathrm{P}_0^{\mathrm{M}}$) of $95.03 to yield 10 percent:

$$\mathrm{P}_0^{\mathrm{M}} = \sum_{t=1}^{3} \frac{\$8}{(1.10)^t} + \frac{\$100}{(1.10)^3} = \$95.03$$

At the price of $95.03, an arbitrageur could buy the bond, then strip it into three risk-free zero-coupon bonds: a one-year zero paying $8 at maturity, a two-year zero paying $8 at maturity, and a three-year zero bond paying $108 at maturity. If the arbitrageur could sell the bonds at their appropriate spot rates, she would be able to realize an initial cash flow (CF_0) from the sale of 97.73 and a risk-free profit of $2.70 (see Exhibit 3.13). Given this risk-free opportunity, this arbitrageur, as well as others, would exploit this strategy of buying and stripping the bond until the price of the coupon bond was bid up to equal its equilibrium price of $97.73.

However, if the 8 percent coupon bond were trading above its equilibrium price of $97.73, then arbitrageurs could profit by reversing the above strategy. For example, if the coupon bond were trading at $100, then arbitrageurs would be able to go into the market and buy proportions (assuming perfect divisibility) of the three pure discount bonds (8 percent of Bond 1, 8 percent of Bond 2, and 108 percent of Bond 3) at a cost of $97.73, and bundle them into one three-year, 8 percent coupon bonds to be sold at $100. As shown in Exhibit 3.14, this strategy would result in a risk-free cash flow of $2.27.

Estimating Spot Rates: Bootstrapping

Many investment companies use spot rates to value bonds, and there are a number of securities that have been created by arbitrageurs purchasing bonds valued at rates different than the spot rates, stripping the securities, and then selling them. One problem in valuing bonds with spot rates or in creating stripped securities is that there are not enough

EXHIBIT 3.13 Equilibrium Bond Price: Arbitrage when Bond Is Underpriced

Market price of 3-year, 8% coupon bond = 95

Arbitrage:

Buy the bond for 95

Sell three stripped zeros:

$$\text{1-year zero with } F = 8\text{: } P_0 = \frac{8}{1.07} = 7.4766$$

$$\text{2-year zero with } F = 8\text{: } \mathrm{m}_0 = \frac{8}{(1.08)^2} = 6.8587$$

$$\text{3-year zero with } F = 108\text{: } P_0 = \frac{108}{(1.09)^3} = 83.3958$$

Sale of stripped bonds = \$97.73

$$CF_0 = 97.73 - 95 = 2.73$$

longer-term zero-coupon bonds available to determine the spot rates on higher maturities. As a result, long-term spot rates have to be estimated. One estimating approach that can be used is a sequential process commonly referred to as *bootstrapping.* This approach requires having at least one zero-coupon bond, such as a Treasury bill. Given this bond's rate, a coupon bond with the next highest maturity is used to obtain an implied spot rate; then another coupon bond with the next highest maturity is used to find the next spot rates, and so on. As an example, consider the three risk-free bonds in Exhibit 3.15. Bond 1 is a one-year zero bond selling at \$100 and paying \$107 at maturity. The one-year spot rate using this bond is 7 percent: S_1 = (\$107/\$100) – 1. Bond 2 is an 8 percent annual coupon bond selling at par to yield 8 percent (YTM = 8 percent).

EXHIBIT 3.14 Equilibrium Bond Price Arbitrage when Bond Is Overpriced

Market price of 3-year, 8% coupon bond = 100.

Arbitrage:

Buy 3 Zeros:

$$\text{8\% of 1-year zero with } F = 100\text{: Cost} = (.08)\frac{100}{1.07} = 7.4766$$

$$\text{8\% of 2-year zero with } F = 100\text{: Cost} = (.08)\frac{100}{(1.08)^2} = 6.8587$$

$$\text{108\% of 3-year zero with } F = 100\text{: Cost} = (1.08)\frac{100}{(1.09)^3} = 83.3958$$

$$\text{Cost} = 7.4766 + 6.8587 + 83.3958 = 97.73$$

Bundle the bonds and sell them as 3-year, 9% coupon bond for 100

$$CF_0 = 100 - 97.73 = 2.27$$

Using bootstrapping, the spot rate on a two-year risk-free bond is found by setting this bond's price equal to the equation for its equilibrium price, P_0^*, and then solving the resulting equation for the two-year spot rate (S_2). Doing this yields a two-year spot rate of 8.042 percent (see Exhibit 3.15). Similarly, given one-year and two-year spot rates, the three-year spot rate can be found by setting the price of the three-year annual coupon bond equal to its equilibrium price, and then solving the resulting equation for S_3. Doing this yields a three-year spot rate of 9.12 percent (see Exhibit 3.15).

It should be noted that the equilibrium prices of other one-, two-, or three-year bonds can be obtained using these spot rates. For example, the equilibrium price of a risk-free, three-year, 10 percent annual coupon would be \$102.57:

$$P_0^* = \frac{\$10}{(1.07)^1} + \frac{\$10}{(1.08042)^2} + \frac{\$110}{(1.0912)^3} = \$102.57$$

EXHIBIT 3.15 Generating Spot Rates Using Bootstrapping

Maturity	Annual Coupon	F	P_0^b
1 year	7%	100	100
1 year	8%	100	100
1 year	9%	100	100

S_1

$$100 = \frac{107}{1+S_1} \Rightarrow S_1 = \left[\frac{107}{100}\right] - 1 = .07$$

S_2

$$P_0^b = \frac{CF_1}{(1+S_1)^1} + \frac{CF_2}{(1+S_2)^2}$$

$$100 = \frac{8}{1.07} + \frac{108}{(1+s_2)^2}$$

$$95.52 = \frac{108}{(1+S_2)^2} \Rightarrow S_2 = \left[\frac{108}{95.52}\right]^{1/2} - 1 = .08042$$

S_3

$$P_0^b = \frac{CF_1}{(1+S_1)^1} + \frac{CF_2}{(1+S_2)^2} + \frac{CF_3}{(1+S_3)^3}$$

$$100 = \frac{9}{1.07} + \frac{9}{(1.08042)^2} + \frac{109}{(1+s_3)^3}$$

$$83.88 = \frac{109}{(1+S_3)^3} \Rightarrow S_3 = \left[\frac{109}{83.88}\right]^{1/3} - 1 = .0912$$

BLOOMBERG: STRIP ANALYSIS SCREEN: SP

On the SP screen, one can analyze stripping a selected bond of its interest and principal payments. On the screen, the user can select yields to discount the stripped cash flow. Rates shown on the screen from the spot curve (X) are spot rates generated from the international yield curve; the curve reflects the yields of different maturities that a dealer stripping the securities might use to set the selling price. The screen also allows the user to change the yield (shifts) by adding or subtracting basis points from the selected maturities on the curve. The screen shows the value (*V*) of each stripped security and the profit from the strips (value of strips minus the cost of the bond).

Selected Security: U.S. Treasury and Kraft Bond, 4/8/12

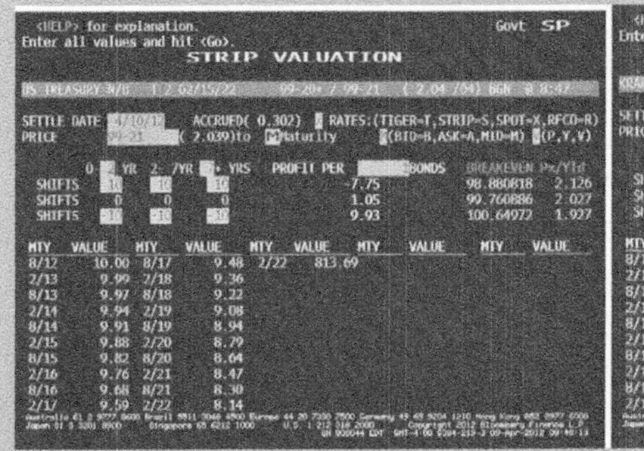

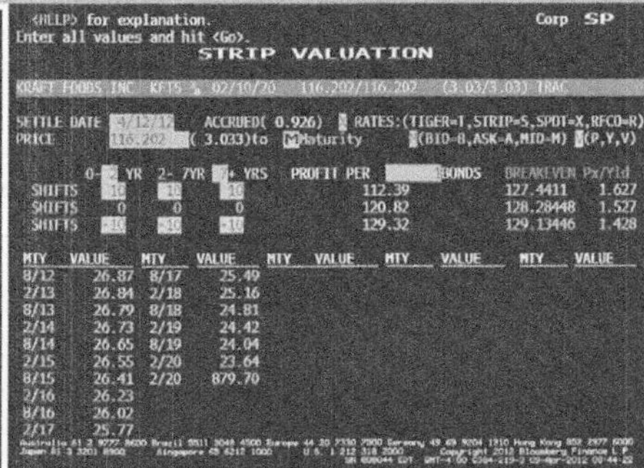

DES Screen for Stripped Treasury Security

U.S. Treasury Strip securities can be found from FIT/BBT screen.

DES Screen for Treasury Strip

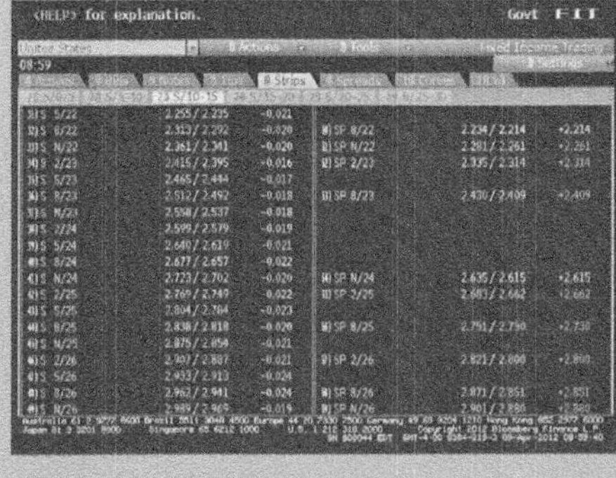

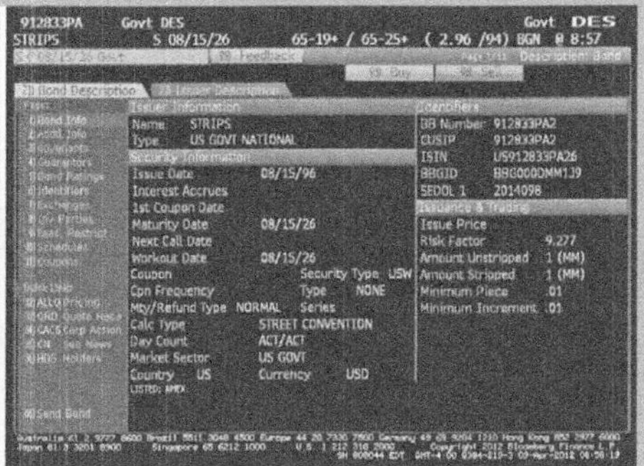

Geometric Mean

Another useful measure of the return on a bond is its *geometric mean*. Conceptually, the geometric mean can be viewed as an average of current and future rates. To see this, consider one of our previous examples in which we computed a YTM of

7.72 percent for a zero-discount bond selling for \$800 and paying \$1,000 at the end of year three. The rate of 7.72 percent represents the annual rate at which \$800 must grow to be worth \$1,000 at the end of three years assuming annual compounding. If we do not restrict ourselves to the same rate in each year, then there are other ways \$800 could grow to equal \$1,000 at the end of three years. For example, suppose one-year bonds are currently trading at a 10 percent rate, a one-year bond purchased one year from the present is expected to yield 8 percent ($R_{Mt} = R_{11} = 8$ percent), and a one-year bond to be purchased two years from the present is expected to be 5.219 percent ($R_{Mt} = R_{12} = 5.219$ percent). With these rates, \$800 would grow to \$1,000 at the end of year 3. Specifically, \$800 after the first year would be \$880 = \$800(1.10), after the second, \$950.40 = \$800(1.10)(1.08), and after the third, \$1,000 = \$800(1.10)(1.08)(1.05219). Thus, an investment of \$800 that yielded \$1,000 at the end of three years could be thought of as an investment that yielded 10 percent the first year, 8 percent the second, and 5.219 percent the third. Moreover, 7.72 percent can be viewed not only as the annual rate at which \$800 grows to equal \$1,000, but also as the average of three rates: one-year rates today ($R_{Mt} = R_{10}$), one-year rates available one year from the present ($R_{Mt} = R_{11}$), and one-year rates available two years from the present ($R_{Mt} = R_{12}$):

$$P_0^b(1+\text{YTM}_M)^M = F = P_0^b[(1+\text{YTM}_1)(1+R_{11})(1+R_{12})(1+R_{13})\cdots(1+R_{1,M-1})]$$

$$(1+\text{YTM}_M)^M = \frac{F}{P_0^b} = [(1+\text{YTM}_1)(1+R_{11})(1+R_{12})(1+R_{13})\cdots(1+R_{1,M-1})]$$

$$(1.0772)^3 = \frac{\$1,000}{\$800} = [(1.10)(1.08)(1.05219)]$$

Mathematically, the expression for the average rate on an M-year bond in terms of today's and future one-year rates (and assuming annual compounding) can be found by solving the above equation for YTM_M:

$$\text{YTM}_M = [(1+\text{YTM}_1)(1+R_{11})(1+R_{12})(1+R_{13})\cdots(1+R_{1,M-1})]^{1/M} - 1$$

$$\text{YTM}_3 = [(1.10)(1.08)(1.05219)]^{1/3} - 1 = .0772$$

This equation defines the rate of return on an M-year bond in terms of expected future rates. A more practical rate than an expected rate, though, is the implied forward rate.

Implied Forward Rate

An implied forward rate, f_{Mt}, is a future rate of return implied by the present interest rate structure. This rate can be attained by going long and short in current bonds. To see this, suppose the rate on a one-year, zero-coupon bond is 10 percent (i.e., spot rate is S_1 = 10 percent) and the rate on a similar two-year zero is S_2 = 9 percent. Knowing these current rates, we could solve for f_{11} in the equation below to determine the implied forward rate. That is:

$$S_2 = [(1+S_1)(1+f_{11})]^{1/2} - 1$$

$$f_{11} = \frac{(1+S_2)^2}{(1+S_1)} - 1$$

$$f_{11} = \frac{(1.09)^2}{(1.10)} - 1 = .08$$

With one-year and two-year zeros presently trading at 10 percent and 9 percent, respectively, the rate implied on 1-year bonds to be bought one year from the present is 8 percent. This 8 percent rate, though, is simply an algebraic result. This rate actually can be attained, however, by implementing the following locking-in strategy:

1. Sell the one-year zero-coupon bond short (or borrow an equivalent amount of funds at the one-year zero-coupon[spot] rate).
2. Use the cash funds from the short sale (or loan) to buy a multiple of the two-year zero.
3. Cover the short sale (or pay the loan principal and interest) at the end of the first year.
4. Collect on the maturing two-year bond at the end of the second year.

In terms of the above example, to obtain the 8 percent implied forward rate:

1. Execute a short sale by borrowing the one-year bond and selling it at its market price of $909.09 = $1,000/1.10 (or borrowing $909.09 at 10 percent).
2. With two-year bonds trading at $841.68 = $1,000/$(1.09)^2$, buy $909.09/$841.68 = 1.08 issues of the two-year bond.
3. At the end of the first year, cover the short sale by paying the holder of the one-year bond his principal of $1,000 (or repay loan).
4. At the end of the second year, receive the principal on the maturing two-year bond issues of (1.08)($1,000) = $1,080.

With this locking-in strategy the investor does not make an investment until the end of the first year when he covers the short sale; in the present, the investor simply initiates the strategy. Thus, the investment of $1,000 is made at the end of the first year. In turn, the return on the investment is the principal payment of $1,080 on the 1.08 holdings of the two-year bonds that comes one year after the investment is made. Moreover, the rate of return on this 1-year investment is 8 percent (($1,080 - $1,000) / $1,000). Hence, by using a locking-in strategy, an 8 percent rate of return on a one-year investment to be made one year in the future is attained, with the rate being the same rate obtained by solving algebraically for f_{11}.

Given the concept of implied forward rates, the geometric mean now can be formally defined as the geometric average of the current one-year spot rate and the implied forward rates. That is:

$$\text{YTM}_M = [(1+\text{YTM}_1)(1+f_{11})(1+f_{12})(1+f_{13})\cdots(1+\text{f}_{1,\text{M}-1})]^{1/\text{M}} - 1 \quad (3.7)$$

Two points regarding the geometric mean should be noted. First, the geometric mean is not limited to one-year rates. That is, just as 7.72 percent can be thought of as an average of three one-year rates of 10 percent, 8 percent and 5.219 percent, the implied rate on a two-year bond purchased at the end of one year, $f_{Mt} = f_{21}$, can be thought of as the average of one-year implied rates purchased one and two years, respectively, from now. Accordingly, the geometric mean could incorporate an implied two-year bond by substituting $(1 + f_{21})^2$ for $(1 + f_{11})(1 + f_{12})$ in Equation (3.7). Similarly, to incorporate a two-year bond purchased in the present period and yielding YTM_2, one would substitute $(1 + \text{YTM}_2)^2$ for $(1 + S_1)$ $(1 + f_{11})$. Thus:

$$\text{YTM}_3 = [(1+\text{YTM}_1)(1+f_{11})(1+f_{12})]^{1/3} - 1$$

$$\text{YTM}_3 = [(1+\text{YTM}_1)(1+f_{21})^2]^{1/3} - 1$$

$$\text{YTM}_3 = [(1+\text{YTM}_2)^2(1+f_{12})]^{1/3} - 1$$

Second, note that for bonds with maturities of less than one year, the same general formula for the geometric mean applies. For example, the annualized YTM on a zero-coupon maturing in 182 days (YTM_{182}) is equal to the geometric average of a current 91-day bond's annualized rate (YTM_{91}) and the annualized implied forward rate on a 91-day investment made 91 days from the present, $f_{91,91}$:

$$\text{YTM}_{182} = [(1+\text{YTM}_{91})^{91/365}(1+\text{f}_{91,91})^{91/365}]^{365/182} - 1$$

Thus, if a 182-day zero-coupon bond were trading at P_0^b (182) = \$97 per \$100 face value and a comparable 91-day bond were at P_0^b (91) = 98.35, then the implied forward rate on a 91-day bond purchased 91 days later would be 5.7 percent:

$$\text{YTM}_{182} = \left[\frac{100}{97}\right]^{365/182} - 1 = .063$$

$$\text{YTM}_{91} = \left[\frac{100}{98.35}\right]^{365/91} - 1 = .069$$

$$f_{91,91} = \left[\frac{(1+\text{YTM}_{182})^{182/365}}{(1+\text{YTM}_{91})^{91/365}}\right]^{365/91} - 1$$

$$f_{91,91} = \left[\frac{(1.063)^{182/365}}{(1.069)^{91/365}}\right]^{365/91} - 1 = .057$$

Usefulness of the Geometric Mean

One of the practical uses of the geometric mean is in comparing investments in bonds with different maturities. For example, if the present interest rate structure for zero-coupon bonds were such that two-year bonds were providing an average annual rate of 9 percent and one-year bonds were at 10 percent, then the implied forward rate on a 1-year bond, one year from now would be 8 percent. With these rates, an investor could equate an investment in the 2-year bond at 9 percent as being equivalent to an investment in a 1-year bond today at 10 percent and a one-year investment to be made one year later yielding 8 percent (possibly through a locking-in strategy). Accordingly, if the investor knew with certainty that one-year bonds at the end of one year would be trading at 9 percent (a rate higher than the implied forward rate), then he would prefer an investment in the series of one-year bonds over the two-year bond. That is, by investing in a one-year bond today and a one-year bond one year from now, the investor would obtain 10 percent and 9 percent, respectively, for an average annual rate on the two-year investment of 9.5 percent; specifically:

$$\text{Series Equivalent YTM}_2 = [(1+\text{YTM}_1)(1+\text{Expected Spot Rate})]^{1/2} - 1$$

$$\text{Series Equivalent YTM}_2 = [(1.10)(1.09)]^{1/2} - 1 = 0.95$$

This, of course, exceeds the 9 percent average annual rate the investor would obtain if he bought the two-year bond; thus in this case, the series of one-year bonds represents the better investment. In contrast, if the investor expected with certainty that, at the end of one year, one-year bonds would be trading at 6 percent (a rate below the implied forward rate), then a series of one-year bonds at 10 percent and 6 percent would yield a two-year average annual rate of only 8 percent (equivalent $\text{YTM}_2 = [(1.10)\ (1.06)]^{1/2} - 1 = .08$); a rate below the 9 percent average annual rate on the two-year bond. Thus, in this case, the investor would prefer the two-year bond to the series of one-year bonds. Finally, if the investor expects the rate in the future to equal the implied rate, then we can argue that he would be indifferent to an investment in a two-year bond and a series of one-year bonds (see Exhibit 3.16).

In general, whether the investor decides to invest in an *M*-year bond, a series of one-year bonds, or some combination with the equivalent maturity, depends on what the investor expects rates will be in the future relative to the forward rates implied by today's interest rate structure.

EXHIBIT 3.16 Geometric Mean

- With perfect expectations, an investor would:
  - –Prefer the 2-year bond over the series if $E(r_{11}) < f_{11}$
  - –Prefer the series over the 2-year bond if $E(r_{11}) > f_{11}$
  - –Indifferent if $E(r_{11}) = f_{11}$

$$YTM_2 = \sqrt[2]{(1.10)(1.08)} - 1 = .09$$

$$YTM_{2:series} = \sqrt[2]{(1.10)(1+E(r_{11})} - 1$$

.085 .09 .095   .07 .08 .09

BLOOMBERG FORWARD RATE CURVE MATRIX: FWCM

The FWCM screen can be used to find projected forward rates based on current interest rate.

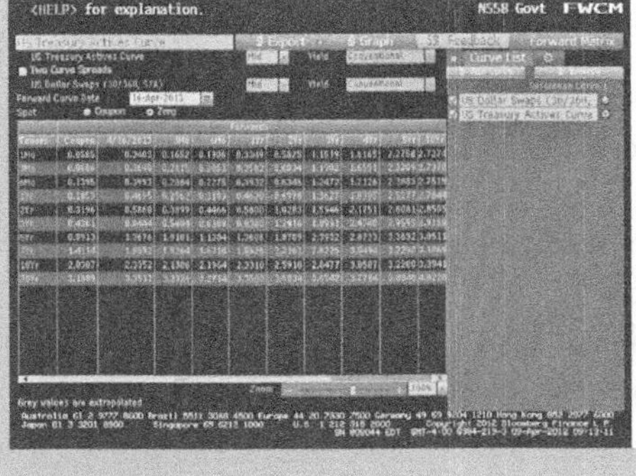

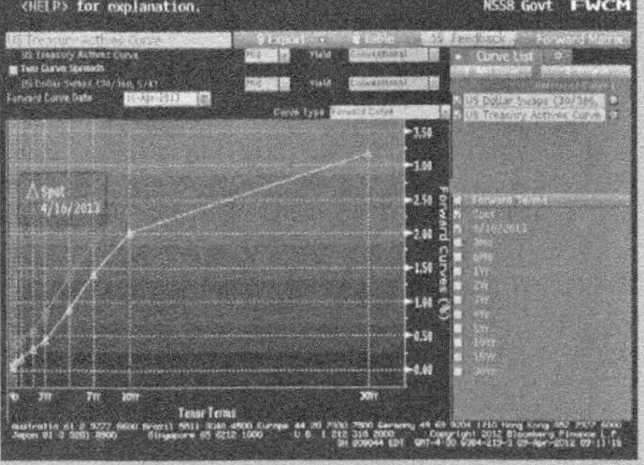

Conclusion

For most investors the most important characteristic of an asset is its rate of return. In this chapter we have examined how the rate of return on a bond and its related characteristic, value, can be measured. We are now in a position to take up the question of what determines the rate of return on a bond. Our preceding analysis suggests that the characteristics of bonds—taxability, liquidity, maturity, and risk—ultimately determine the yield on a bond. The two most important of these characteristics are the terms to maturity and risk—the subjects for the next two chapters.

Website Information

Treasury Information

Investinginbonds.com

1. Go to http://investinginbonds.com/.
2. Click "Government Market-at-a-Glance."
3. Treasury yields are based on price data for U.S. Treasury securities of different maturities. The yields are provided by GovPX, Inc. The issues listed here are "on-the-run" issues for the date, meaning they are the most recently issued in that maturity.
4. The Treasury yield data can be exported to Excel (right click and click "Export to Excel"). More detail information is obtained by clicking "See Data" at the bottom.

FINRA

1. Go to www.finra.org/index.htm, Sitemap, Market Data, and Bonds.
2. Click the "Treasury and Agency" tab and then click "Advanced Bond Search" to find Treasury and agency bonds with certain features.
3. Enter Treasury or agency symbol (e.g., FHLMC) and then click "Search."

Wall Street Journal

1. Go to http://online.wsj.com/public/us, Market Data, Bonds, Rates & Credit Markets, and Treasury Quotes.
2. The Treasury yield data can be exported to Excel (on data quote table, right click and then click "Export to Excel")
3. Go to http://online.wsj.com/public/us, Market Data; Bonds, Rates, and Credit Markets; and Treasury Strips.

Yahoo.com

1. Go to http://finance.yahoo.com/bonds, click "Advanced Bond Screener," and click "Treasury" or "Treasury Zero Coupon" (Treasury strips).

Corporate Bond Information

Investinginbonds.com

1. Go to http://investinginbonds.com/.

2. Click "Corporate Market at-a-Glance."
3. Search by Issuer.

FINRA

1. Go to www.finra.org/index.htm, Sitemap, Market Data, and Bonds.
2. For a bond search, click "Corporate" tab and then click "Advanced Bond Search" to find corporate bonds with certain features or issues of specific issuer (click "Search").

Wall Street Journal

1. Go to http://online.wsj.com/public/us, Market Data; Bonds, Rates, and Credit Markets; and Treasury Quotes.
2. The Treasury yield data can be exported to Excel (on data quote table, right click and then click "Export to Excel").
3. Go to http://online.wsj.com/public/us, Market Data; Bonds, Rates, and Credit Markets; and Corporate Bonds Most Active and Corporate Gainers and Losers.

Yahoo.com

1. Go to http://finance.yahoo.com/bonds, click "Advanced Bond Screener" and click the "Corporate" tab, and then provide information for search.
2. Go to http://finance.yahoo.com/bonds, enter "name of issuer" and click "Search."

Finance Calculator—FICALC

The online FICALC calculator (www.ficalc.com/calc.tips) computes a bond's price given its yield or its yield given its price, as well as other information, such as cash flows and total returns. The FICALC calculator is designed so it can either be used as a stand-alone fixed income calculator, or integrated into a website that has information on fixed income securities.

Selected References

Fabozzi, F. J. 1988. *Fixed Income Mathematics*. Chicago: Probus.

Rose, P. S. 2003. *Money and Capital Markets*. New York: McGraw-Hill/Irwin.

Bloomberg Exercises

1. Select an option-free (bullet) corporate bond of interest. You may want to use the Bloomberg search/screen function, SRCH, to find your bonds. Evaluate the bond in terms of its price, yield, yield spread, and price-yield curve. In your evaluations, you may want to consider the following screens on the bond's menu screen:
   a. CSHF screen to find the bond's cash flow.
   b. YA screen to determine price and yield.

   c. PT screen to view price-yield curve.
   d. TDH and ALLQ to determine the liquidity on the bond based on it trading activity and bid-ask spreads.
2. Select a callable corporate bond of interest. You may want to use the Bloomberg search/screen function, SRCH, to find your bonds or look at the corporate bonds offered by Ford (F <Corp> <Enter>). Using YA screen (click "Calls" tab), examine the call structure of the bond and determine its yield to next call, yield to maturity, and yield to worst.
3. Select a corporate bond that has a put features. You may want to use the Bloomberg search/screen function, SRCH, to find your bond (try to limit your search to fixed-rate putable bonds). Using the YTP screen, examine the put structure of the bond and determine its yield to next put, yield to maturity, and yield to worst.
4. Select a U.S. Treasury bond with a long-term maturity (15 to 20 years). You may want to use the FIT screen to find your bond.
   a. Conduct a total return analysis of the bond using the HZ1 screen for an instantaneous change in rates (set the horizon to the current settlement date) given different discount rates and reinvestment rates.
   b. Conduct a total return analysis of the bond using the HZ1 screen for a given horizon period (e.g., one year) given different discount rates and reinvestment rates.
   c. Conduct a total return analysis of the bond using the TRA screen. Select different horizon periods (current date, one-year horizon, etc.), yield curve shifts, and reinvestment rates.

Comment on the bond's sensitivity to interest rate changes.

5. Select a U.S. Treasury bond or note with an intermediate-term or long-term maturity (5 to 10 years). You may want to use the FIT screen to find your bond.
   a. Conduct a total return analysis of the bond using the HZ1 screen for an instantaneous change in rates (set the horizon to the current settlement date) given different discount rates and reinvestment rates.
   b. Conduct a total return analysis of the bond using the HZ1 screen for a given horizon period (e.g., one year) given different discount rates and reinvestment rates.
   c. Conduct a total return analysis of the bond using the TRA screen. Select different horizon periods (current date, one-year horizon, etc.), yield curve shifts, and reinvestment rates.

Comment on the bond's sensitivity to interest rate changes.

6. Select an intermediate-term to long-term investment grade corporate bond. Using the bond's GY or GP screen, examine its price, yield to maturity, yield to next call (if applicable), and spread over its benchmark over the past year. Click the "Event" checkbox and set the event settings to see if the spikes in spreads can be explained by certain events.
7. Select an intermediate-term to long-term speculative-grade corporate bond. Using the bond's GY or GP screen, examine its price, yield to maturity, yield to next call (if applicable), and spread over its benchmark over the past year. Click the "Event"

checkbox and set the event settings to see if the spikes in spreads can be explained by certain events.

8. Select a U.S. Treasury bond or note with an intermediate-term or long-term maturity (10 to 20 years). You may want to use the FIT screen to find your bond. Use the SP screen on the selected bond's menu screen (CUSIP <Govt> <Enter>) to evaluate the profitability of stripping the bond. What is the profit from buying the bond at its current price, stripping it, and selling the strips at the spot rate yields given on the screen? On the SP screen, look for the profit for no shift scenario. What is the profit from buying the bond at a lower price, stripping it, and selling the strips at the spot rate yields given on the screen? What is the profit from buying the bond at a higher price, stripping it, and selling the strips at the spot rate yields given on the screen?
9. Select a stripped U.S. Treasury bond with at least a 10-year maturity. You may want to use the FIT screen to find your bond.
   a. Using the bond's YA, GY, PT, and CSHF screens, find the strip bond's price, yield to maturity, price-yield curve, and cash flows.
   b. Using the TRA screen, conduct a one-year total return analysis of the bond. Comment on the interest-rate risk of the bond given a one-year horizon.
   c. Using the HZ1 screen, determine the selling price of the bond seven years from the settlement date if rates do not change. What would be the selling prices if rates changed by +300 bps, +200 bps, –300 bps, and –200 bps?
10. Select a municipal bond. You may want to use the MSRC search screen to find your bond and limit your search to one state, AAA ratings, and limited maturity range. Using the bond's menu screen (CUSIP <Muni> <Enter>), find the bond's price, yield, spread, and liquidity using the YA, GY, AllQ, and TDH screens. Using the HZ1 screen, calculate the before-tax and after-tax total return on the bond for different horizons and yields.
11. Select an option-free (bullet) corporate bond of interest. You may want to use the Bloomberg search/screen function, SRCH, to find your bonds. Evaluate the bond in terms of its yield spread, credit risk, liquidity, and interest rate risk. In your evaluations, you may want to consider the following screens on the bond's YA screen: the Yield and Spread tab to determine the bond's spread and the Graphs Tab to evaluate the bond's spread history. Do a comparative spread and credit risk analysis of the bond using the bond's COMB screen.

CHAPTER 4

The Level and Structure of Interest Rates

Introduction

Over the past three decades interest rates have often followed patterns of persistent increases or persistent decreases with fluctuations around those trends. This is illustrated in Exhibits 4.1 and 4.2 where 10-year Treasury rates and AAA and Baa corporate bond yields are shown from 1970 to 2012. As shown, in the late 1970s and early 1980s, interest rates increased dramatically, increasing from 7.38 percent in February 1977 to 15.75 percent in November 1981. This period was marked by high inflation and recession (stagflation) and by the implementation of a contractionary U.S. monetary policy in which the Federal Reserve pushed the rate up. This period of increasing rates was followed by a long period of declining rates from the early 1980s to 2012, with fluctuations around this declining trend.

In addition to the observed trends in interest rate levels, there have also been observed differences or spreads between the interest rates on bonds of different categories over this same period. The spreads can be seen in Exhibit 4.2, which shows the historical yields on AAA and Baa corporate bonds and the spread on Baa bonds over AAA from 1970 to 2012. From 1990 to 2002, the spreads in the rates were relatively small. More recently, the spreads have been wider, especially during the period around the 2008 financial crisis. In general, spreads are explained by differences in each bond's characteristics: risk, liquidity, and taxability. For example, the spread between yields on Baa and AAA are wider in the recessionary periods and tighter in periods of economic growth.

Finally, interest rate differences can be observed between similar bonds with different maturities. Exhibit 4.3 shows various plots of the YTM on Treasury securities with different maturities. The graph is known as a yield curve, and it illustrates what is referred to as the term structure of interest rates.

Understanding what determines both the overall level and structure of interest rates is an important subject in financial economics. In this chapter, we examine the factors that are important in explaining the level and differences in interest rates. We begin by examining the behavior of overall interest rates using basic supply-and-demand analysis and treating debt and bonds as one general type of security. With this foundation, we then look at how risk, liquidity, and taxes explain the differences in the rates on bonds of different categories. Finally, we complete our examination of the structure of interest rates by looking at four well-known theories that explain the term structure on interest rates.

Level of Interest Rates

In general, the overall level of interest rates in an economy is determined by economic and financial factors that affect the demand and supply of bonds (or loanable fund).

EXHIBIT 4.1 Historical 10-Year Treasury Yields, 1970–2012

USGG10YR <Index> <Enter>; Click GP

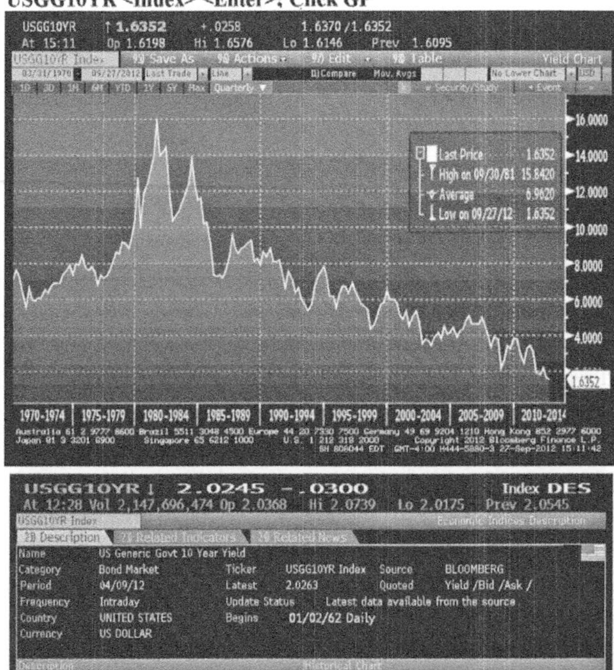

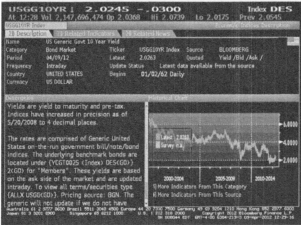

EXHIBIT 4.2 Historical Yields on Moody's AAA and BAA Industrials, 1970–2012

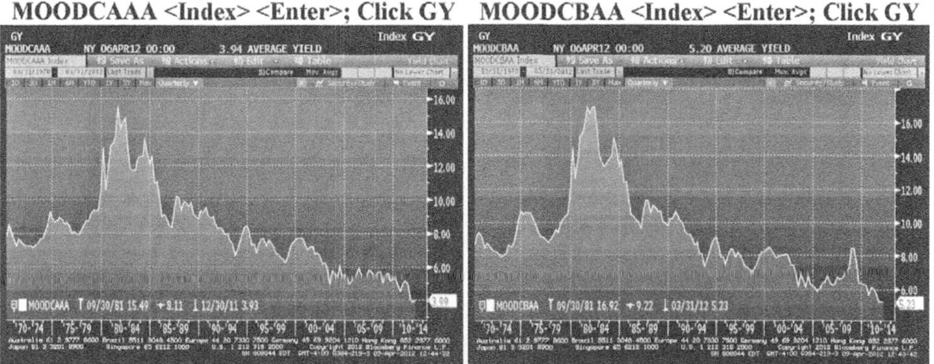

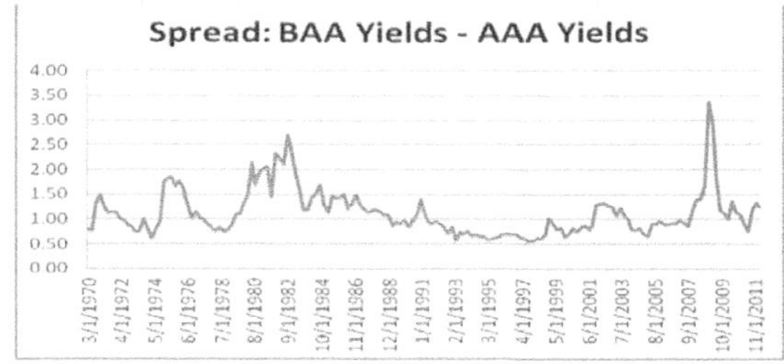

For example, if an economy is expanding and as a result corporations are selling more bonds, then the bond market will initially experience an excess supply of bonds at the current level of rates. In the financial markets, the excess supply will cause bond prices to fall and bond yields to increase. The general level of interest rates therefore depends on identifying the important factors determining the aggregate demand and supply of existing bonds. Among the determining factors are (1) the overall state of the economy; (2) government policies, such as monetary and fiscal policy; (3) international factors, such as foreign interest rates and exchange rates that influence the inflow and outflow of foreign capital; and (4) the current level of inflation and the expectation about future inflation. Some of these factors affect both the supply and

EXHIBIT 4.3 Treasury Yield Curves

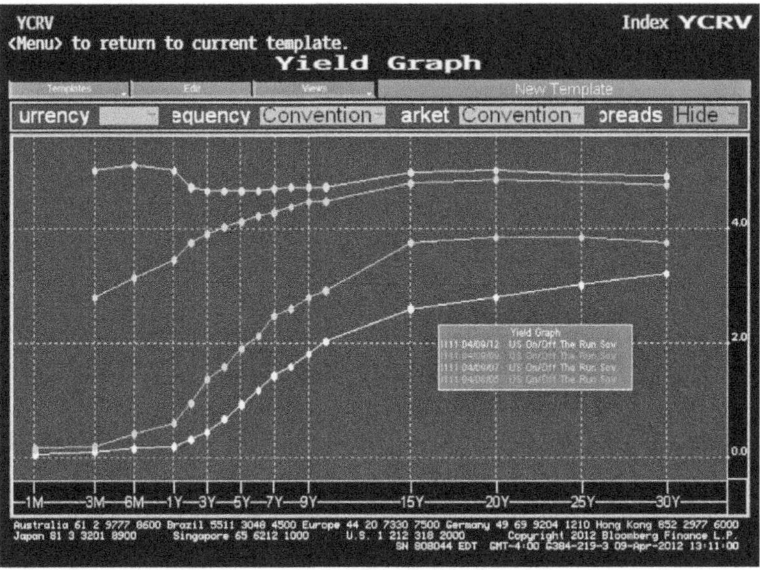

demand for bonds, such as the state of the economy (as measured by gross domestic product [GDP] or aggregate wealth) and expected inflation. Some factors are unique just to bond supply, such as Treasury financing; certain types of monetary policies, such as open market operations (OMO); international capital flows; and actual inflation. Some factors impact only bond demand, such as relative risk and certain types of monetary policies, such as changing the discount rate and changing reserve requirements.

Economic Conditions

When an economy is expanding, business demand for both short-term assets, such as inventories and accounts receivable, and long-term assets, such as plants and equipment, tend to increase. As a result, companies find themselves selling more bonds (demanding more loans) to finance the increases in their short-term and long-term capital formation. In addition to changes in corporate bond supply, aggregate economic growth is also likely to increase both the purchases of cars and homes by household and the number of public projects by municipal government (e.g., roads), augmenting the supply of bonds by financial intermediaries and state and local governments. Thus, the supply of bonds tends to increase in periods of economic growth, causing an excess supply that lowers bond prices and increases rates.[1] By contrast, in recessionary periods, there is less capital formation and fewer bonds being sold by corporations, governments, and intermediaries. This decrease in bond supply can cause rates to increase.

Government Monetary and Fiscal Policy

Government monetary and fiscal policies can indirectly impact interest rates by affecting the overall economy. Such policies can also have a direct impact on rates. Consider the actions of the Treasury in its financing of the federal government's budget. If the federal government has a deficit, then the Treasury will be raising funds in the financial market by selling more Treasury securities. At current interest rate levels, this would create an excess supply of bonds in the market, pushing bond prices down and rates up. In contrast, the bond supply would decrease if there were a government surplus and the Treasury decided to use the surplus to buy up existing Treasury securities in order to reduce the government's outstanding debt. In this case, the supply of bonds would decrease and the resulting excess demand would push bond prices up and rates down.

In addition to Treasury financing, bond supply is also affected by central bank policies. One important monetary tool central banks employ is an open market operation. In order to stimulate the economy, the central bank often uses an expansionary open market operation (OMO) to lower interest rates. In an expansionary OMO, the central bank buys existing securities (usually Treasuries), pushing bond prices up and yields down. In contrast, when the central bank is fighting inflation, it may try to slow the economy by increasing interest rates through a contractionary OMO. Here, the bank sells some of its security holdings, pushing prices down and rates up.

International Capital Flows

The globalization of financial markets over the past 25 years has led to significant increases in investment flows in and out of countries. These international capital flows also influence the supply of securities. For example, over the past 10 years, China has invested a significant amount of its international currency reserves (U.S. dollars) resulting from its balance of payment surpluses in intermediate-term U.S. Treasury securities. These investments have contributed to keeping U.S. intermediate rates low.

Actual and Expected Inflation

On the supply side, actual inflation increases borrowing and the supply of bonds as corporations and other economic entities are forced to borrow more funds to finance their inflated capital cost. In addition to actual inflation, the expectation of higher inflation can also lead to an increase in bond supply. That is, if inflation is expected to be higher in the future, then expected borrowing costs will be higher in the future and more funds (inflated funds) will be needed to finance capital formation. As a result, corporations will find it advantageous to borrow more funds now. Thus, both actual and expected inflation can increase current bond supply, lowering bond prices and increasing yields.

On the demand side, expected inflation is the important factor influencing bond demand. If investors expect the prices of consumer goods and services, as well as cars, houses, and other consumer durables, to be higher in the future, they will decrease their current purchases of bonds and other securities and buy more consumption goods and consumer durables. This decrease in demand will decrease bond prices and increase yields. Thus, actual inflation by increasing bond supply leads to a decrease in interest rates; and expected inflation by increasing bond supply and decreasing bond demand also leads to an increase in interest rates. It should be noted that in inflationary times, there is not only current inflation but often the expectation of higher inflation. Thus, in an inflationary climate characterized by actual and expected inflation, interest rates tend to increase.

In contrast, actual and expected deflation lowers bond supply as corporations find they need less funds (deflated funds) to finance capital formation and also as they find it advantageous to defer funding in expectation of lowering borrowing needs (deflated capital cost) in the future. On the demand side, expected deflation increases bond demand. That is, if investors expect the prices on goods and services, cars, houses, and other consumer durables to be lower in the future, they will increase their current purchases of bonds and other securities so that they can buy more consumption goods and consumer durables later after prices have fallen. Thus, actual deflation by decreasing bond supply leads to a decrease in interest rates; and expected deflation by decreasing bond supply and increasing bond demand also leads to a decrease in interest rates. Thus, in a deflationary climate in which there is actual and expected deflation, interest rates would be falling.

BLOOMBERG ECONOMIC AND FINANCIAL SCREENS

ECOF	Macroeconomic information (inflation, employment, economic indicators, housing prices) by country and region
ECO	Calendar of economic releases
WECO	World economic calendar and economic indicators
CBQ	Market summary benchmark information
FOMC	Information on policy changes of the Federal Open Market Committee
FED	Calendar of Federal Reserve releases
ECST	Key economic statistics by country
EIU	Economist Intelligence Unit
IECO	Global comparison of economic statistics
BRIEF	Daily Economic Newsletter
AV	Bloomberg's media links
CENB	Central Bank menu: Use to access platforms of Central Banks
ECB	European Central Bank portal
BOE	Bank of England portal
WWCC	Portal for worldwide credit crunch
IECO	Global comparison of economic statistics
GGR	Finds global summary of government bill and bond rates for countries

YCRV	Finds current and historical yield curves for government and corporate bond
IYC	Finds yield curves for different countries using IYC
CG	Curve graph: Find difference curves

BLOOMBERG ECONOMIC INDICATORS

The statistic series for many economic variables are identified in ECOF, ECST, and other economic screens. Many of the series can be analyzed further by going to the series menu page: Ticker <Index> <Enter>; clicking "Description," "GP," or other screens.

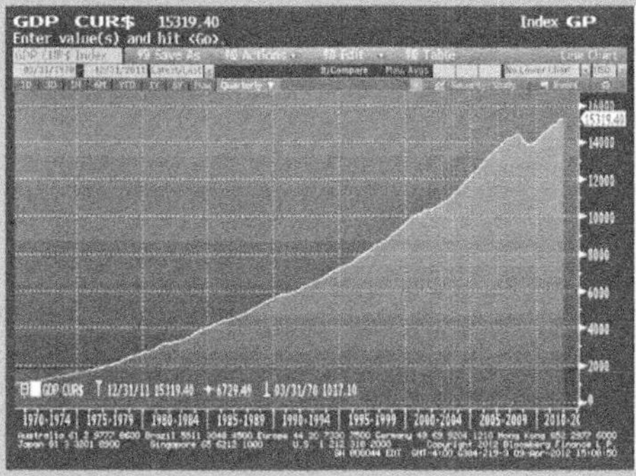

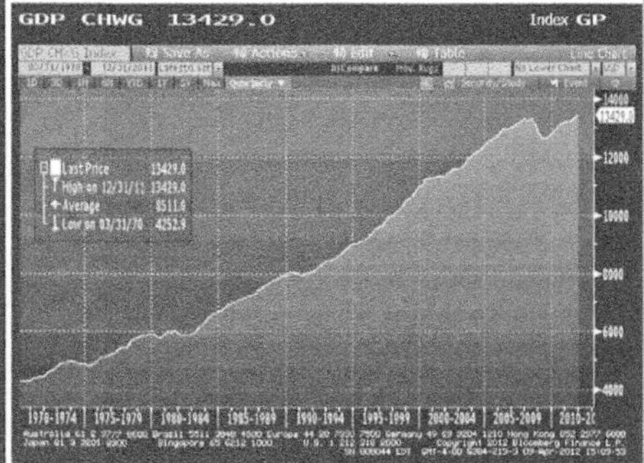

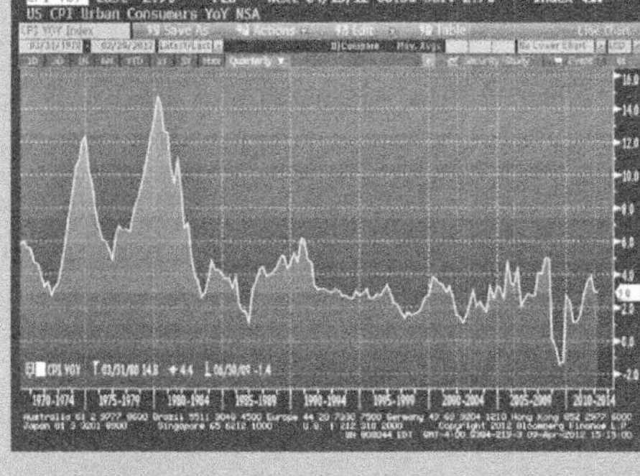

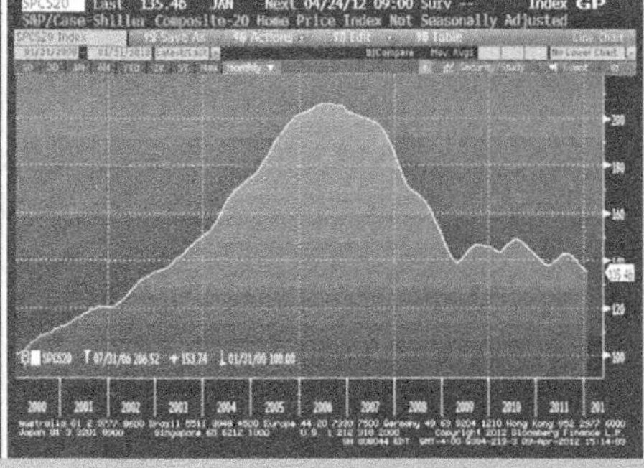

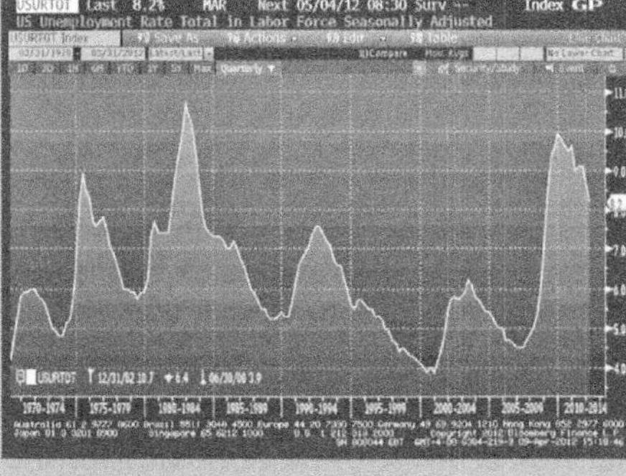

(*Continued*)

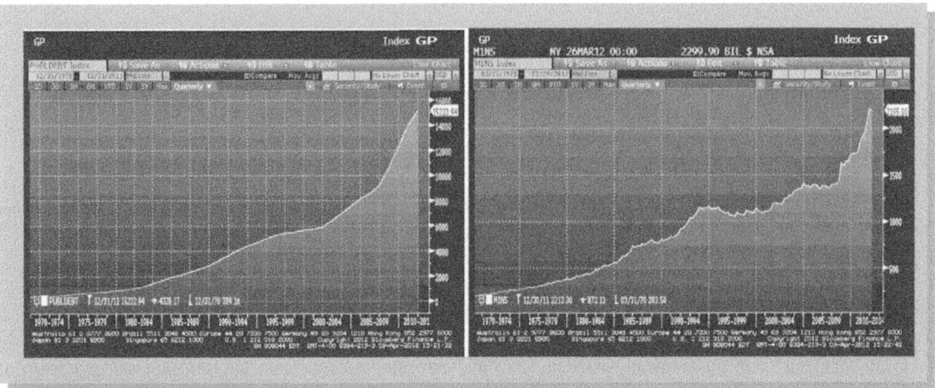

The Structure of Interest Rates

In addition to the level of interest rates, we also observe differences in rates among different types of bonds. The differences or spreads between rates, in turn, can be explained by differences in the fundamental features of bonds: risk, liquidity, taxability, and terms to maturity.

Risk Premium

In general, a riskier bond will trade in the market at a price that yields a greater YTM than a less risky bond. The difference in the YTM of a risky bond and the YTM of less risky bond is referred to as a *risk spread* or *risk premium.* The risk premium for bonds, RP, indicates how much additional return investors must earn to induce them to buy the riskier bond:

$$RP = \text{YTM on Risky Bond} - \text{YTM on Less Risky Bond}$$

In general, a risky bond will trade in the market with a positive risk premium, with the premium increasing the greater the bond's risk. For example, suppose economic conditions were to change such that there was now a greater chance of default on a corporate bond. The increased riskiness of the corporate bond would cause its demand and price to decrease and its yield and spread over the risk-free security to increase.[2]

In general, the sizes of the risk premiums for bonds with different quality ratings change as a result of changing economic conditions. In recessionary periods (or the expectation of recessions), the risk premium tends to widen as investors move their investment holdings from lower-quality, high-risk bonds to higher-quality corporate credits and Treasuries. By contrast, in periods of economic growth (or the expectations of growth), the risk premium tends to narrow as investors move their investment holdings to lower-quality, high-risk bonds from higher-quality corporate credits or Treasuries.

When the YTM on the less risky bond is the minimum rate, the rate is referred to as the *benchmark rate* or base rate, and the spread is referred to as a *benchmark spread*. Typically, the benchmark rate is the YTM on a Treasury that is comparable in maturity and is recently issued and therefore liquid.[3] Two factors that affect the risk premium or spread are credit risk and embedded option provisions in a bond. The spread between a Treasury security and a non-Treasury security that is identical except for credit risk is referred to as the *credit spread*. However, as discussed in Chapter 3, many bonds have embedded call or put options that give either the issuer or the bondholder the right to take some actions. In general, the market will require a bigger spread, with a call option that benefits the issuer and a smaller spread with a put option that benefits the holder. In analyzing a bond, analysts try to separate the portion of the benchmark spread that can be attributed to the embedded options. The analytical measure used to estimate this portion of the spread is called the option-adjusted spread (OAS).

Liquidity Premium

Liquid securities are those that can be easily traded and in the short run are absent of risk. Treasury securities, with their wide distribution of ownership, for example, are relatively easy to trade and are therefore more liquid than corporate bonds. In general, we can say that a less liquid bond will trade in the market at a price that yields a greater YTM than a more liquid one. The difference in the YTM of a less liquid bond and the YTM of a more liquid one is defined as the liquidity premium (LP):

$$LP = \text{YTM on Less Liquid Bond} - \text{YTM on More Liquid Bond}$$

One way to measure the degree of marketability of a security is in terms of the size of the bid and asked spread that dealers offer in the market. Dealers who make markets in less marketable securities necessarily set wider spreads than dealers who have securities that are bought and sold by many investors and therefore can be traded more quickly.

Similar to bond risk, liquidity risk can be influenced by the overall state of the economy. In slow economic periods, there is often a tightening of credit combined with a flight to safety to Treasury securities that can often slow the sale of new debt and loans. This can lead to illiquid markets for many non-Treasury securities, even those with good credit ratings. In such periods, corporate and municipal bonds that have relatively low default risk take longer to sell, leading to not only greater bid and asked spreads, but also lower prices and higher yields and spreads. The spread can be explained partly by the increase in risk due to the economy and partly to the illiquid market conditions—liquidity spread.

Taxability

Investors are more concerned with the after-tax yield on a security than its pretax yield. An investor in a 40 percent income tax bracket who purchased a fully taxable

10 percent corporate bond at par would earn an after-tax yield (ATY) of 6 percent: ATY = 10 percent (1 – .40). The ATY is found by solving for that yield, ATY, that equates the bond's price to the present value of its after-tax cash flows:

$$P_0 = \sum_{t=1}^{N} \frac{CF_t(1-\text{tax rate})}{(1+\text{ATY})^t}$$

Bonds that have different tax treatments but otherwise are identical will trade at different pre-tax yields. That is, the investor in the 40 percent tax bracket would be indifferent between the 10 percent fully-taxable corporate bond and a 6 percent tax-exempt municipal bond selling at par, if the two bonds were identical in all other respects. The two bonds would therefore trade at equivalent after-tax yields of 6 percent, but with a pre-tax yield spread of 4 percent: $y_0^C - y_0^M$ = 10 percent – 6 percent = 4 percent.

As we discussed in Chapter 1, taxability refers to the claims the government has on a security's cash flow. In general, securities whose cash flows are subject to less taxes trade at a lower YTM than those that are subject to more taxes. Historically, taxability explains why some municipal bonds whose coupon interest is exempt from federal income taxes, have at times traded at yields below default-free U.S. Treasury securities or AAA-quality corporate credits even though many municipals are subject to credit risk.

Example

Exhibit 4.4 shows the Bloomberg YA screen ("Yield & Spread" tab) and COMB screens for the 3.65 percent Teva bond with a maturity of November 10, 2021. As shown, the bond is priced at 100.779 per $100 face value to yield 3.5530674 percent on April 9, 2012 (yield to worse = YTM = yield to the next call). The YA screen shows a comparable Treasury that pays a 24 percent coupon and matures on February 15, 2022. Using this Treasury, the spread on the Teva bond over the Treasury is 1.5215 percent or 152.15 basis points. For analysts, the challenge is to determine how much of the spread is due to credit risk, liquidity risk, and embedded option risk. To facilitate that analysis, the YA screen shows various spread measures. For example, the Z-spread provides estimates of credit risk, whereas the options adjusted spread can be used to estimate a bond's call risk spread. OAS spread analysis is discussed in Chapter 5. The COMB screen shows the spreads of the Teva bond and other comparable bonds.

BLOOMBERG SPREAD SCREENS

YA: The YA screen displays for a selected bond pricing information, interpolated spreads to benchmark curves, and descriptive, fundamental, and ratings data and information. The screen can also be used to price a fixed income security using spreads to a benchmark issue/benchmark curve.

EXHIBIT 4.4 Bloomberg YA (Yield & Spread Tab) and COMB Screens: Teva Bond, Coupon = 3.65 Percent, Maturity = 4/9/12

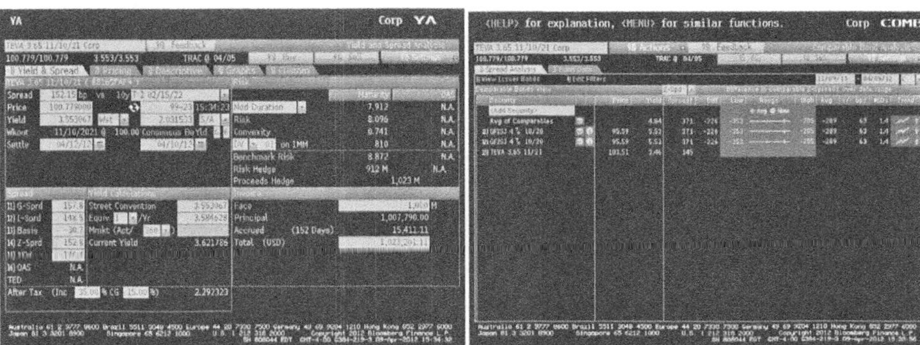

G-Sprd = selected bond's yield minus the interpolated government bond yield
I-Sprd = selected bond's yield minus the interpolated swap rate
Z-Sprd = selected bond's spread over the benchmark zero coupon swap curve
OAS = the incremental return of the security compared to a benchmark interest rate curve adjusted for embedded options.
Basis = credit default swap (CDS) spread minus the selected bond's Z-spread
ASW, asset swap spread, is the difference between the coupon cash flow of the security and the fixed coupon of an offsetting swap in basis points.
Note: Swap spreads referred to the price (in basis points) of a credit default swap (cost of insurance against default) on the bond or bonds of the creditor. It is used as an indicator of a bond's credit spread.
Features*:* Benchmark rates can be changed by inputting ticker. Panels appearing on the right show related information on the bond. To change panel, click bottom tabs.

Features:

- Benchmark rates can be changed by inputting ticker.
- Pricing a bond for a different spread can be found by changing the spread.
- Panels appearing at the top show related information on the bond. To change a panel, click tab.

See Exhibit 4.4 for examples of the YA screen for a corporate credit.

YAS for Municipal uses Municipal Market Advisor Index as the benchmark.

OAS1: The option-adjusted spread analysis screen can be used to calculate values for the early redemption features for the selected security. OAS analysis is a method for estimating the additional spread required to compensate investors for the call risk they are assuming. The methods are based on option pricing models. In general, models such as the Black-Derman-Toy and the Black Futures Swaption model, use an estimated volatility in interest rates to determine the likelihood of a bond's being called and the bond's value, yield, and OAS. The OAS screen allows the user to select an option model and volatility. The screen shows the calculated OAS and also the spread of the bond if there were no embedded options—the option-free spread. The spread due to embedded option can be estimated by subtracting the option-free spread from the total spread.

(Continued)

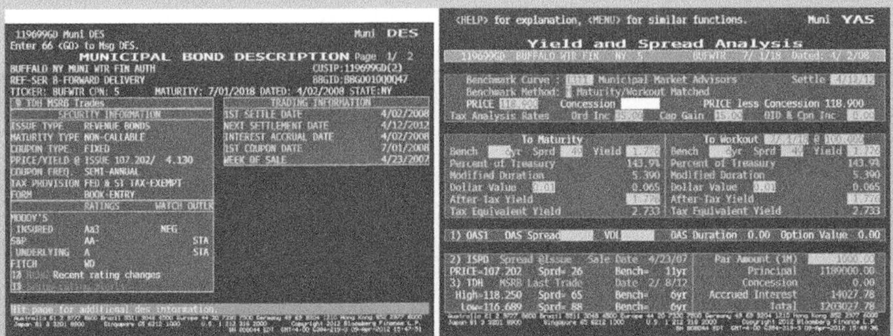

Credit default swap screen (CDSW): A credit default swap (CDS) is a contract in which the buyer purchases credit protection on a reference name in the event of default/credit loss on the part of the reference entity, in return for a stream of payments. The payments are referred to as spreads. In theory, the spread payments are equal to the credit spread on a bond. As such, they can be used as an estimate of a bond's credit spread. The Bloomberg CDSW screen shows the terms of the selected bond's issuer's CDS. The CDS spread is shown on the right side of the screen in basis points along with the implied probability of default.

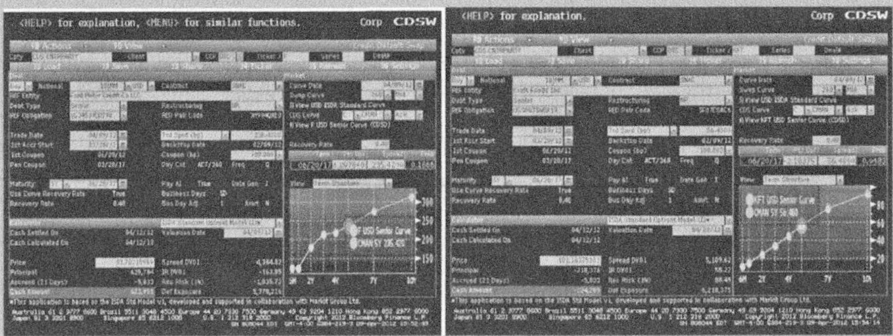

GOVI: The GOVI screen displays a matrix of yield spread information for sovereign debt of a selected tenor.

IYC: The IYC screen displays a menu of yield curves and analytics. One can view current and historical curves for different countries. Onc can select IYC8 and IYC9, which displays yield curve spreads for different sovereigns, sectors, and municipals.

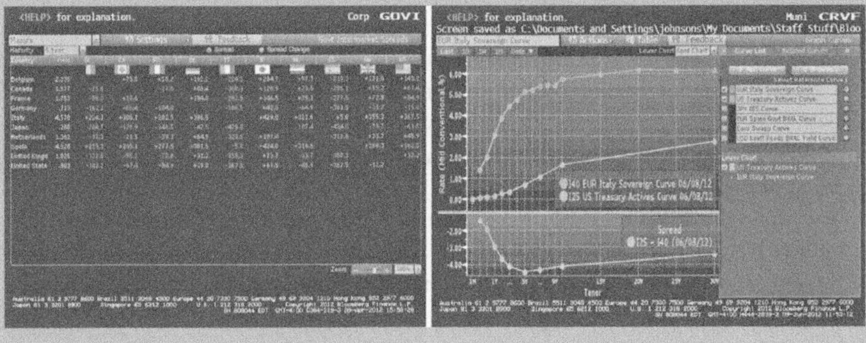

HISTORICAL SPREADS

GY and GP: The GY and GP screens show a selected bond's historical prices, YTM, spreads over the benchmark, CDS basis, and Z-spreads. Similar information is found from the GP screen.

HS: The HS screen can be used to compare the yields on multiple bonds.

GIP and GIY: The GIP and GIY screens show intraday prices and yields.

Note the large spreads on the Ford credit around the time of the 2008 financial crisis.

TDH: The TDH screen displays trade history of prices and spreads. One can adjust the time periods and the size of the trade.

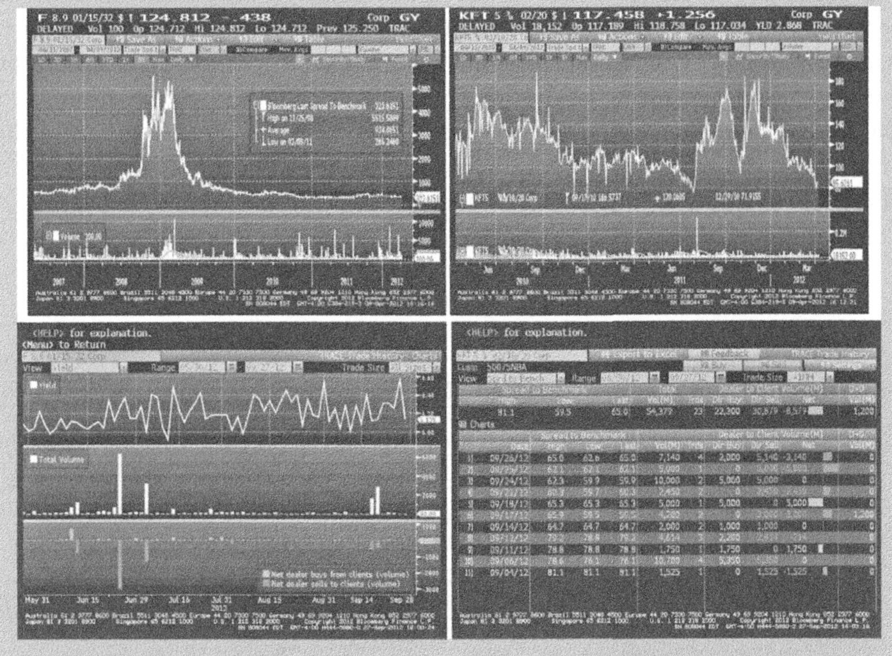

Term Structure and the Yield Curve

In the financial literature, the relationship between the yields on financial assets and their terms to maturity is referred to as the *term structure of interest rates.* As previously noted, the term structure is depicted graphically by a yield curve: a plot of the YTM against the terms to maturity for bonds that are otherwise alike. A yield curve constructed using Treasuries (see Exhibit 4.3) often serves as the benchmark yield curve for other sector yield curves. Yield curves have tended to take on one of three shapes. They can be positively sloped, with long-term rates being greater than short-term ones. Such yield curves are called *normal* or *upward sloping curves.* They are usually convex from below, with the YTM flattening out at higher maturities. Yield curves can also be negatively sloped, with short-term rates greater than long-term ones. These curves are known as *inverted* or *downward sloping yield curves.* Like normal curves, these curves also tend to be convex, with the yields flattening out at the higher maturities. Finally, yield curves can be relatively flat, with the YTM being invariant to maturity. Occasionally, a yield curve can take on a more complicated shape in which it can have both positively sloped and negatively sloped portions; these are often referred to as a *humped yield curve.*

The actual shape of the yield curve depends on the types of bonds under consideration (e.g., AAA bond versus B bond), economic conditions (e.g., economic growth or recession, tight monetary conditions, etc.), the maturity preferences of investors and borrowers, and the market's expectations about future rates, inflation, and the state of economy. Two theories encompassing many of these considerations have evolved over the years to try to explain the shapes of yield curves: Market Segmentation Theory (MST) and Pure Expectation Theory (PET). There are also two extensions of these theories that are also frequently used to explain the term structure: Preferred Habitat Theory (PHT) and the Liquidity Premium Theory (LPT).

BLOOMBERG YIELD CURVE SCREEN:

YCRV: The yield curve screen, YCRV, displays current and historical bond, money market, swap, and municipal market yield curves. YCRV provides a variety of yield curves for different security and market types from around the world, allowing one to analyze investment performance across multiple markets and currencies.

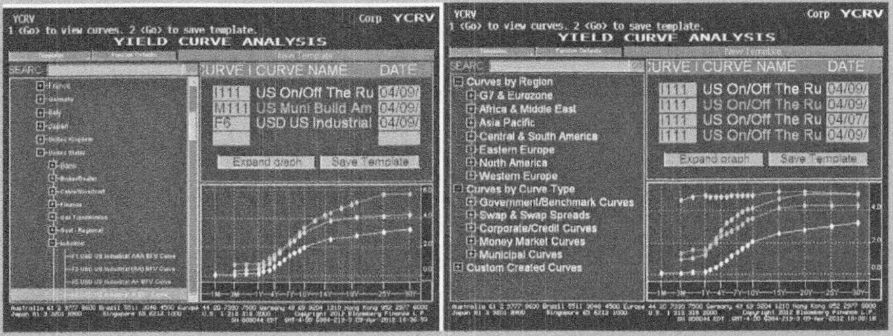

CRVF displays current and historical curves for different countries, sectors, and regions

CG screen displays yield curves for a loaded bond.

Municipal yield curves (MYC) displays current and historical municipal yield curves.

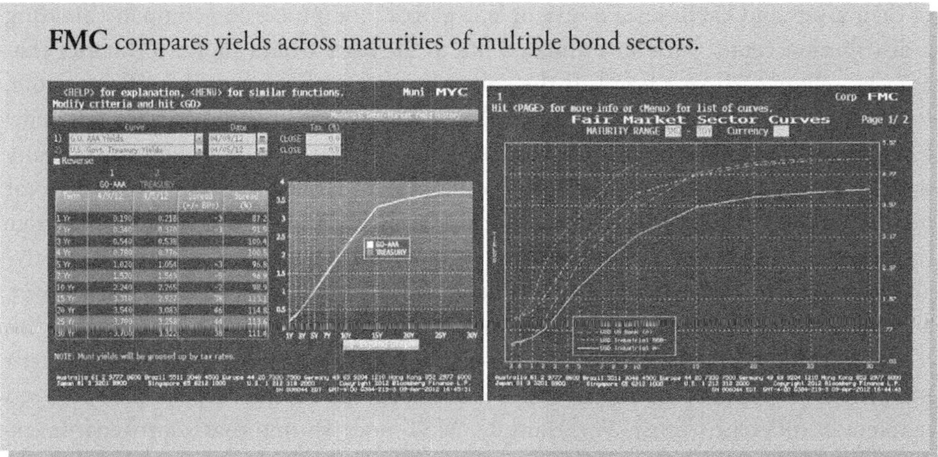

FMC compares yields across maturities of multiple bond sectors.

Market Segmentation Theory

Market Segmentation Theory (*MST*) is based on the assumption that investors and borrowers have strong maturity preferences that they try to attain when they invest in or issue fixed-income securities. As a result of these preferences, the financial markets are segmented by maturity into a number of smaller markets, with supply-and-demand forces unique to each segment determining the equilibrium yields for each segment. Thus, according to MST, the major factors that determine the interest rate for a maturity segment are supply-and-demand conditions unique to the maturity segment. For example, the yield curve for high-quality corporate bonds could be segmented into three markets: short-term, intermediate-term, and long-term. The supply of short-term corporate bonds, such as commercial paper, would depend on business demand for short-term assets such as inventories, accounts receivables, and the like, whereas the demand for short-term corporate bonds would emanate from investors looking to invest their excess cash for short periods. The demand for short-term bonds by investors and the supply of such bonds by corporations would ultimately determine the rate on short-term corporate bonds. Similarly, the supplies of intermediate-term and long-term bonds would come from corporations trying to finance their intermediate- and long-term assets (plant expansion, equipment purchases, acquisitions, etc.), whereas the demand for such bonds would come from investors, either directly or indirectly through institutions (e.g., pension funds, mutual funds, insurance companies, etc.), who have long-term liabilities. The supply and demand for intermediate funds would, in turn, determine the equilibrium rates on such bonds, whereas the supply and demand for long-term bonds would determine the equilibrium rates on long-term debt securities.

Important to MST is the idea of unique or segmented markets. According to MST, the short-term bond market is unaffected by rates determined in the intermediate- or long-term markets, and vice versa. This independence assumption is based on the premise that investors and borrowers have a strong need to match the maturities of their assets and liabilities. For example, a global food processing company building a distribution center with an estimated life of 20 years would prefer to finance that asset by selling a 20-year bond. If the company were to finance with a 10-year note, for example, it would be exposed to market risk in which it would have to raise new funds at an uncertain rate at the end of 10 years. Similarly, a life insurance company with an anticipated liability in 15 years would prefer to invest its premiums in 15-year bonds; a money market manager with excess funds for 90 days would prefer to hedge by investing in a money market security; a corporation financing its accounts receivable would prefer to finance the receivables by selling short-term securities. Moreover, according to MST, the desire by investors and borrowers to avoid interest rate risk leads to hedging practices that tend to segment the markets for bonds of different maturities. It should be noted that MST does recognize the interdependence between markets in different sectors. For example, MST does assume that short-term investors will substitute between short-term Treasuries and corporate commercial paper depending on their relative rates or that long-term investors will substitute between long-term Treasuries and long-term corporate depending on their relative rates.

In general, the positions and the shapes of yield curves depend on the factors that determine the supply and demand for short-term, intermediate-term, and long-term bonds: the economic state (GDP and wealth); expected inflation; credit risk; relative liquidity; and the sales and purchases of bonds by the Treasury, central bank, and foreign central bank.[4] Changes in these factors will cause a change in the structure of interest rates that will be reflected by different shifts and twists in the yield curves. For example, if the yield curve had been initially positively sloped, then an economic or financial change that increased short-term Treasury rates would caused the yield curve to become flatter. If the yield curve had been initially negatively sloped, then the rate change would have caused the curve to become even more negatively sloped. In general, we can describe such an impact as having a "tendency" to cause the yield curve to become negatively sloped. A change in an economic or financial factor can have not only a direct impact on one sector (e.g., open market operations affecting Treasury rates), but also an indirect impact on another sector (change in the Treasury rate resulting from an OMO affecting the demand for corporate bonds). Several cases of yield curve shifts and twists are discussed for the case of a simple two-sector (Treasury and corporate) and two-segment (short-term [ST] and long-term [LT]) economy.

Economic Conditions

Suppose the economy moved from an economic recession to a period of strong economic growth. When an economy is growing, business demand for short-term and long-term assets tends to increase. As a result, many companies find themselves selling more short-term bonds (or borrowing more from banks who in turn sell more bonds) given that they plan to increase inventories and expect to have more accounts receivables. They also find themselves selling more long-term bonds (or borrowing more from banks who in turn sell more bonds), given that they tend to augment planned investments in plants, equipment, and other long-term assets. In the bond markets, these actions cause the short-term and the long-term supplies of bonds to increase as the economy moves from slow growth or recession to expanded economic growth. At the initial interest rates, the increase in bonds creates an excess supply. This drives bond prices down and the yields up, until a new equilibrium rate is attained.

As the rates on short-term and long-term corporate bonds increase, short-term and long-term Treasury securities become relatively less attractive. As a result, the demands for short-term and long-term Treasuries decrease, creating an excess supply in both the short-term and long-term Treasury markets at their initial rates. Like the corporate bond markets, the excess supply in the Treasury security markets will cause their prices to decrease and their rates to increase until a new equilibrium is attained. Thus, economic growth has a tendency to increase both short-term and long-term rates for corporate bonds, and by a substitution effect, increase short-term and long-term Treasury rates. Thus, a period of economic expansion causes the yield curves for both sectors to shift up, as shown in Exhibit 4.5. In contrast, a recession would have the impact of shifting the yield curve down.

It should be noted that economic conditions can also affect the general demand for bonds, decreasing demand and pushing rates up in recessions, and increasing demand and pushing rates down in economic expansion. If economic conditions do impact the demand for bonds, then an economic expansion would cause interest rates to increase, provided that the supply impact on interest rate dominates the demand impact. If the demand impact dominates, then an economic expansion could push rates down. Economic conditions can also lead to changes in asset allocations. For example, in a recessionary period (or in anticipation of an economic recession), there is often a flight to safety from stocks to Treasury and high-quality bonds. Furthermore, this flight to safety is often accompanied by a tightening of credit by financial institutions.

Government Monetary and Fiscal Policy

Treasury Financing

Interest rates on government securities depend, in part, on the size and growth of the federal government debt. If federal deficits are increasing over time, then the Treasury will be constantly trying to raise funds in the financial market. If the Treasury were to finance a deficit by selling long-term Treasury securities, then there would be an increase in the supply of the long-term Treasuries. The increase in supply would push the price of the long-term government securities down, increasing their yield. In the corporate bond market, the higher rates on long-term government securities would lead to a "crowding out" effect, decreasing the demand for long-term corporate securities. The decrease in demand would lead to an excess supply in that market as long-term corporate bondholders try to sell their corporate bonds to buy the higher yielding Treasury securities. As bondholders try to sell their long-term corporate bonds, the prices on such bonds would decrease, causing the rates on long-term corporate bonds to rise until a new equilibrium is reached. Thus, the sale of the long-term Treasury securities increases both long-term government and long-term corporate rates. Moreover, if the corporate and Treasury yield curves are initially flat, as shown in Exhibit 4.6, the Treasury's sale of long-term securities would cause the yield curves to become positively sloped. By contrast, if the Treasury had financed the deficit with short-term securities, the impact would have been felt in the short-term bond market. In this case, the Treasury and corporate bond yield curves would have become negatively sloped.

In the opposite case of a budget surplus (such as the brief one that occurred in the United States in the late 1990s and early 2000), the yield curve could become negatively sloped if the Treasury used some of the surplus to buy up long-term Treasury securities. That is, the Treasury purchase of long-term securities would create an excess demand for long-term Treasury bonds, and by the substitution effect, an excess demand for long-term corporate bonds, leading to higher price and lower yields on long-term securities.

Open Market Operations

The yield curve can also be affected by the direction of monetary policy and how it is implemented. For example, if the central bank were engaged in an expansionary OMO in which it were buying Treasury securities, there would be a tendency for the yield curve to become positively sloped if the central bank were buying short-term securities, and a tendency for the yield curve to be become negatively sloped if it were purchasing long-term securities.[5] In a contractionary OMO, however, there would be

EXHIBIT 4.5 MST Model Economic Expansion Case

Outline:

Corporate Market:

Increase in capital formation (S-T and L-T) ⇒ Greater corporate bonds sold (S-T and L-T) ⇒ Excess supply for corporate bonds (S-T and L-T) ⇒ Corporate bond prices decrease and yields increase ⇒∴ Upward shift in Corporate YC

Treasury Market:

Substitution Effect: As corporate yields (S-T and L-T) increase ⇒ Demand for Treasury securities (S-T and L-T) decreases ⇒ Treasury bond prices decrease and yields increase ∴ Upward shift in Treasury YC

Corporate Bond
• Yield Curve

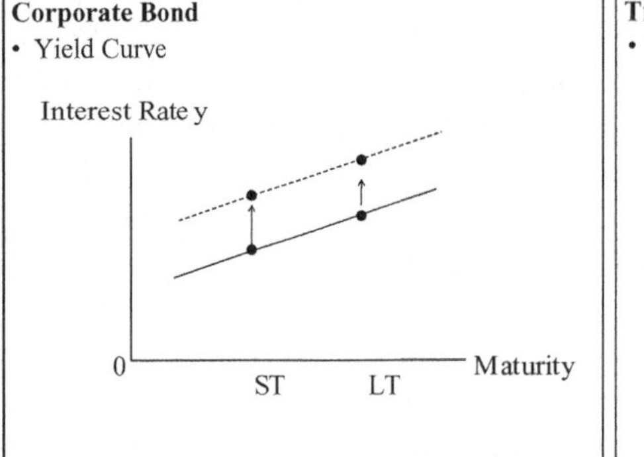

Treasury Bond
• Yield Curve

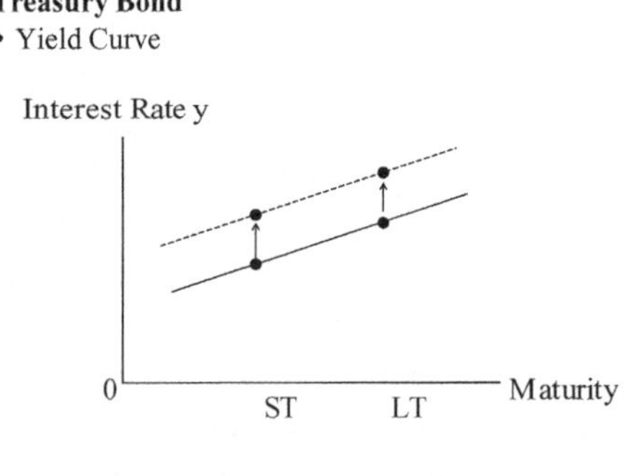

a tendency for the Treasury yield curve to become negatively sloped if the central bank were to sell some of its holdings of short-term bills and positively sloped if it were to sell some of its long-term security holdings.

In addition to affecting the Treasury yield curve, OMOs also change the yield curve for corporate securities through a substitution effect. For example, an expansionary OMO in which the Fed purchases short-term Treasury securities would tend to cause the yield curve for corporate securities to become positively sloped. That is, as the rate on short-term Treasury securities decreases as a result of the OMO, the demand for short-term corporate bonds would increase, causing higher prices and lower yields on the short-term corporate securities. Again, because the long-term market is assumed to be independent of short-term rates, the total adjustment to the central bank's purchases of short-term securities would occur only in the short-term corporate and Treasury market and not in the long-term markets. If both the Treasury and corporate yield curves were initially flat, as shown in Exhibit 4.7, then the expansionary OMO would result in new positively sloped yield curves.

International Capital Flows

The ability of other countries to invest heavily in liquid U.S. Treasuries gives them influence over U.S. rates similar to an exogenous central bank open market purchase. For example, when the China Central Bank buys long-term U.S. Treasury securities, there is an increase in the demand for long- term Treasuries. The increase

EXHIBIT 4.6 MST Model: Treasury Issue of Long-Term Securities Case

Outline:

Treasury Market

Treasury sells L-T Treasuries (T-Bonds) ⇒ T-Bond prices decrease and yields increase.
∴ Tendency for Treasury YC to become positively sloped.

Corporate Market

Substitution effect: As L-T Treasury yields increase, the demand for L-T corporate securities decreases ⇒ L-T Corporate bond prices decrease and their yields increase
∴ Tendency for Corporate YC to become positively sloped.

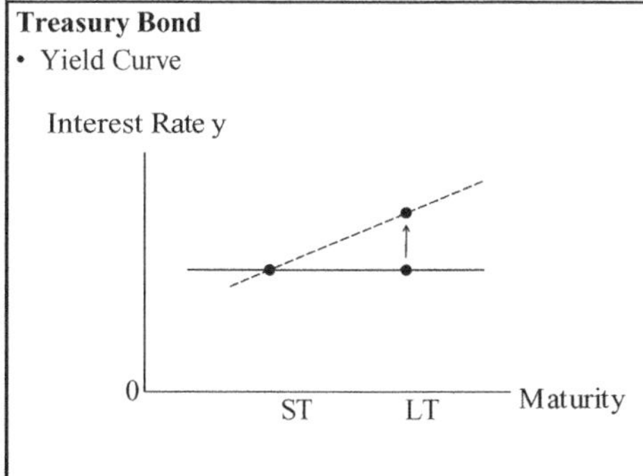

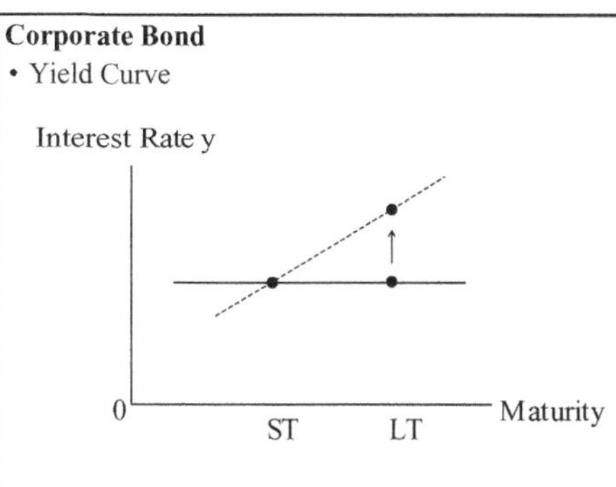

in demand pushes up the price of long-term government securities, resulting in a lower long-term Treasury yield. In the corporate bond market, the lower rates on long-term government securities leads to an increase in the demand for long-term corporate securities, which, in turn, leads to an excess demand in that market, causing the prices on long-term corporate bonds to rise and the yield to fall until a new equilibrium is reached. Because the short-term market is assumed to be independent of long-term rates, the market adjustment to the Chinese purchase of long-term securities would occur through the decrease in long-term corporate and Treasury rates. If the corporate and Treasury yield curves were initially flat, then China's purchase of U.S. long-term Treasuries would cause the yield curves to become negatively sloped.

Expected Inflation

As previously noted, when investors expect inflation to be greater in the future, then the demands for all bonds (short-term and long-term corporate and Treasury) has a tendency to decrease. This decrease leads to an overall decrease in bond prices, increasing rates on all securities and leading to upward shifts in the yield curves for both corporate and Treasury. In addition, corporations often sell more bonds in

EXHIBIT 4.7 MST Model: Central Bank Open Market Purchase of Short-Term Treasury Securities Case

Outline:

Treasury Market:

Central Bank buys S-T Treasuries (T-bills) ⇒ T-bill prices increase and yields decrease

∴ Tendency for Treasury YC to become positively sloped.

Corporate Market:

Substitution effect: As yields on S-T Treasury securities decrease, the demand for S-T corporate securities increases ⇒ prices of S-T corporate increase and their yields decrease.

∴ Tendency for Corporate YC to become positively sloped.

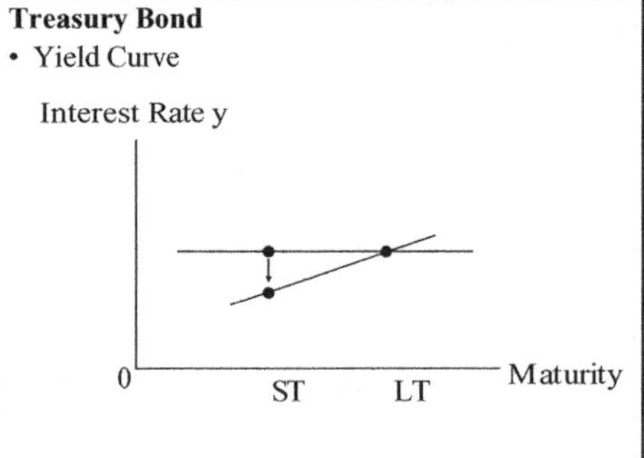

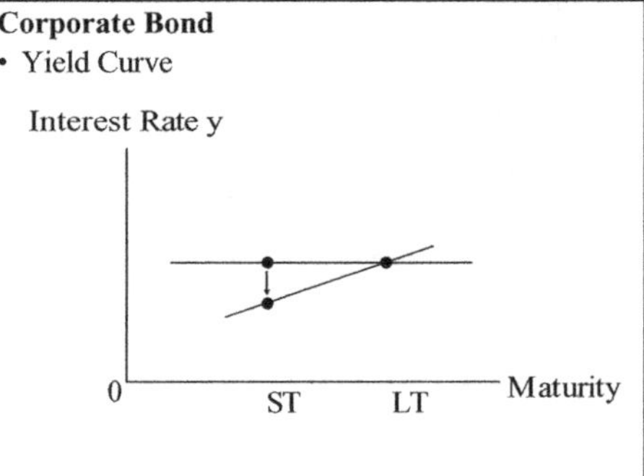

inflationary times to avoid the expected higher future borrowing costs. The resulting increased supply of corporate bonds lowers corporate bond prices further and increases rates more, leading to an ever greater upward shift in the corporate yield curve. Thus, expected inflation (deflation) affects the overall level of interest rates, shifting up (down) the yield curves for corporate and Treasury bonds.

Note that it may also be the case that inflation or deflation expectations impact the maturity segments differently. For example, an expectation of higher inflation may lead to a greater decrease in the demand for long-term bonds than short-term bonds. This, in turn, would lead to an increase in the demand for short-term bonds as more investors seek liquidity. If this were the case, then there would be a tendency for the yield curve to become steeper in inflationary time.

Summary of MST

The MST provides an economic foundation for explaining the shapes of yield curves in terms of fundamental supply-and-demand forces. As such, the model can be used to analyze the impacts of a number of economic activities on the term structure of interest rates. MST, though, has two shortcomings. First, by assuming independent markets, MST does not take into account cases in which bond yields in a particular maturity segment could increase to a level sufficient to induce investors and issuers/borrowers to move out of their preferred segment. Second, MST does not take into account the role of expectations in determining the structure of interest rates. An investor with a two-year horizon, for example, might prefer a series of one-year bonds (a one-year bond today rolled over into a one-year bond one year later) to a two-year bond if she expects relatively high yields on one-year bonds next year. If there are enough investors with such expectations, they could have an impact on the current demands for one- and two-year bonds. These limitations of MST are addressed in the other theories of term structures: Preferred Habitat Theory, Pure Expectations Theory, and Liquidity Preference Theory.

Preferred Habitat Theory

MST assumes that investors and borrowers have preferred maturity segments or habitats determined by the maturities of their securities that they want to maintain. The *Preferred Habitat Theory* (*PHT*) assumes that investors and borrowers may move away from their desired maturity segments if there are relatively better rates to compensate them. Furthermore, PHT argues that investors and borrowers will be induced to forego their perfect hedges and shift out of their preferred maturity segments when supply-and-demand conditions in different maturity markets do not match. For example, consider an economic world in which, on the demand side, investors in corporate securities, on average, prefer short-term to long-term instruments, whereas on the supply side, corporations have a greater need to finance long-term assets than short-term, and therefore prefer to issue more long-term bonds than short-term. Combined, these relative preferences would cause an excess demand for short-term bonds and an excess supply for long-term claims, and an equilibrium adjustment would have to occur. Specifically, the excess supply in the long-term market would force issuers to lower their bond prices, increasing long-term bond yields, and the excess demand in the short-term market would cause short-term bond prices to increase and their yields to fall. As long-term bond yields increase and short-term yields decrease, some investors would change their short-term investment demands or preference, increasing their demand for higher yielding long-term bonds and decreasing their demand for lower yielding short-term bonds. On the supply side, the decrease in short-term rates and the increase in long-term rates would induce some corporations to finance their long-term assets by selling short-term claims. This would lead to a substitution in which corporations would increase their sale of the lower-yielding short-term bonds, and decrease their sale on the higher-yielding long-term bonds. Ultimately, equilibriums in both markets would be reached, with long-term rates higher than short-term rates, a premium necessary to compensate investors and borrowers/issuers for the risk they've assumed.

As an explanation of term structure, the PHT would suggest that yield curves are positively sloped if investors, on the average, prefer short-term to long-term investments and borrowers/issuers prefer to finance their assets with long-term debt instead of short-term debt.[6] Of course, the opposite case in which investors want to invest more in long-term securities than short-term and issuers desire more short-term to long-term debt is possible. Under these conditions, the yield curve would tend to be negatively sloped.

Pure Expectation Theory

Expectation theories try to explain the impact of investors' and borrowers' expectations on the term structure of interest rates. A popular model is the *Pure Expectation Theory* (*PET*), also called the *Unbiased Expectations Theory* (*UET*). Developed by Fredrick Lutz, PET is based on the premise that the interest rates on bonds of different maturities can be determined in equilibrium where implied forward rates are equal to expected spot rates.

To illustrate PET, consider a market consisting of only two bonds: a risk-free one-year zero-coupon bond and a risk-free two-year zero-coupon bond, both with principals of $1,000. Suppose that supply-and-demand conditions are such that both the one-year and two-year bonds are trading at an 8 percent YTM. Second, suppose that the market expects the yield curve to shift up to 10 percent next year, but, as yet, has not factored that expectation into its current investment decisions (see Exhibit 4.8). Third, assume that one-year and two-year bond investors are willing to give up their preferred maturity habitats, assuming interest rate risk, but that issuers/borrowers have a strong maturity segmentation preference and are not willing to assume interest rate risk. This assumption suggests that those issuers financing one-year assets with one-year bonds and those issuers financing two-year assets with two-year bonds do not consider alternative segments (e.g., two-year borrowers financing with a series of one-year bonds). As a result, issuers' current financing decisions are not influenced by the

EXHIBIT 4.8 Pure Expectation Theory: Market Expectation of Higher Rates Investors-Only Response

(a)

- Expectations of rates increasing from 8% to 10%.
- Investors with HD of 2 years and those with HD of 1 year would prefer one-year bonds over two-year bonds.
- Market Response:

$B_2^D \downarrow \Rightarrow P_2^B \downarrow \Rightarrow \text{YTM}_2 \uparrow$ | $B_1^D \uparrow \Rightarrow P_1^B \uparrow \Rightarrow \text{YTM}_1 \downarrow$ | YC Becomes Positively Sloped

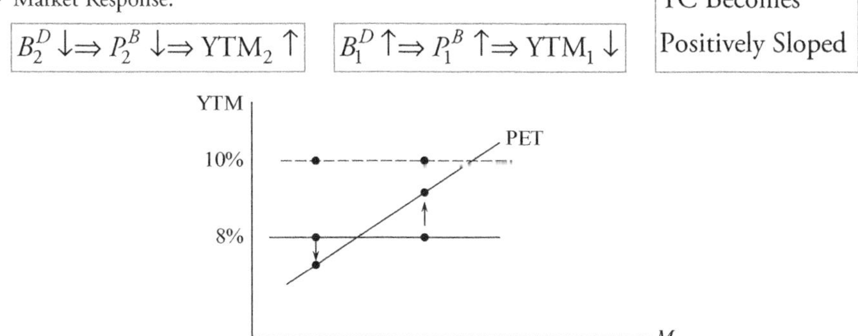

(b)

- If the market response to the expectation is only in terms of a change in the two-year bond, then then equilibrium yield on the two-year will be 9%.

$B_2^D \downarrow \Rightarrow P_2^B \downarrow \Rightarrow \text{YTM}_2 \uparrow$
$\text{YTM}_2 \uparrow$ until $\text{YTM}_2 = 9\%$

When $\text{YTM}_2 = 9\%$, $\text{YTM}_1 = 8\%$, then $f_{11} = E(R_{11}) = 10\%$.

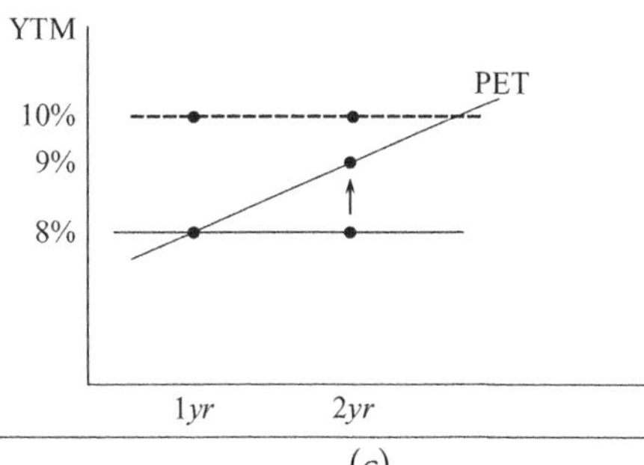

(c)

- If the market response to the expectation is only in terms of a change in the one-year bond, then then equilibrium yield on the one-year will be 6%.

$B_1^D \uparrow \Rightarrow P_1^B \uparrow \Rightarrow \text{YTM}_1 \downarrow$
$\text{YTM}_1 \downarrow$ until $\text{YTM}_1 = 6\%$

When $\text{YTM}_2 = 8\%$, $\text{YTM}_1 = 6\%$, then $f_{11} = E(R_{11}) = 10\%$.

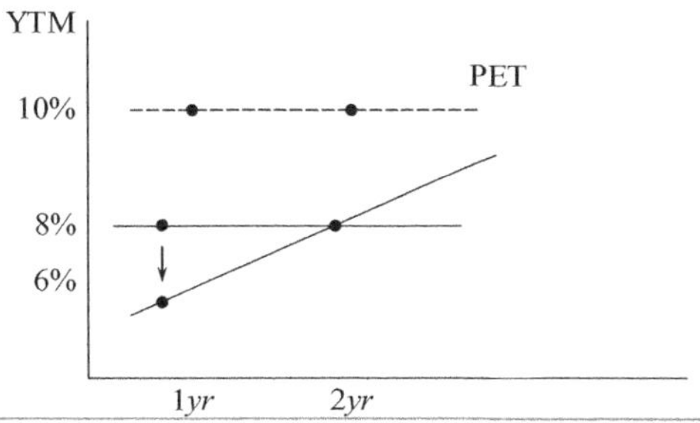

expected rates on one-year and two-year bonds. In contrast, investors with one-year and two-year horizons are willing to consider alternative segments. Finally, assume the market is risk neutral, such that investors do not require a risk premium for investing in risky securities (i.e., they will accept an expected rate on a risky investment that is equal to the risk-free rate).

To see the impacts of market expectations on the current structure of rates, consider first the case of investors with horizons of two years. These investors can buy the two-year bond with an annual rate of 8 percent, or they can buy the one-year bond yielding 8 percent, then reinvest the principal and interest one year later in another one-year bond expected to yield 10 percent. Given these alternatives, such investors would prefer the latter investment because it yields a higher expected average annual rate for the two years of 9 percent:

$$E(R) = [(1.08)(1.10)]^{1/2} - 1 = .09$$

Similarly, investors with one-year horizons would also find it advantageous to buy a one-year bond yielding 8 percent than a two-year bond (priced at \$857.34 = \$1,000/1.08^2) that they would sell one year later to earn an expected rate of only 6 percent:

$$P_{Mt} = P_{2,0} = \frac{\$1,000}{(1.08)^2} = \$857.34$$

$$E(P_{11}) = \frac{\$1,000}{(1.10)^1} = \$909.09$$

$$E(R) = \frac{\$909.09 - \$857.34}{\$857.34} = .06$$

Thus, in this market with an expectation of higher rates one year later, investors with both one-year and two-year horizons would prefer to purchase one-year bonds instead of two-year ones. If enough investors do this, an increase in the demand for one-year bonds and a decrease in the demand for two-year bonds would occur until the average annual rate on the two-year bond is equal to the equivalent annual rate from the series of one-year investments or where the one-year bond's rate is equal to the rate expected on the two-year bond held one year (see Exhibit 4.8a).

In the example, there are a number of possible one-year and two-year yields in which there is equilibrium. For example, suppose the equilibrium adjustment occurs only in the two-year market. In this case, if the price on the two-year bond fell such that it traded at a YTM of 9 percent, and the rate on a one-year bond stayed at 8 percent, then investors with two-year horizon dates would be indifferent between a two-year bond yielding a certain 9 percent and a series of one-year bonds yielding 8 percent and 10 percent, for an expected rate of 9 percent. Investors with one-year horizons would likewise be indifferent between a one-year bond yielding 8 percent and a two-year bond purchased at 9 percent and sold one year later at 10 percent, for an expected one-year rate of 8 percent. Thus, in this case, the impact of the market's expectation of higher rates would be to push the longer-term rates up to 9 percent (see Exhibit 4.8b). Another scenario would be for the adjustment to take place solely in the one-year market. In this case, if the price on the one-year bond increased such that it traded at a YTM of 6 percent, and the rate on the two-year bond stayed at 8 percent, then investors with one-year horizons would be indifferent between a one-year bond yielding a certain 6 percent and a two-year bond (priced at \$857.34 = \$1,000/1.08^2) that they would sell one year later at an expected one-year yield of 10 percent to earn an expected rate of 6 percent. At one-year and two-year yields of 6 percent and 8 percent, respectively, investors with two-year horizons would be indifferent between a two-year bond yielding a certain 8 percent and a series of one-year bonds yielding 6 percent and 10 percent, for an expected rate of 8 percent. Thus, in this adjustment scenario, the impact of the market's expectation of higher rates would be to push the shorter-term one-year rates down to 6 percent (see Exhibit 4.5c). In equilibrium, the one-year and two-year yields will be somewhere between 6 percent and 8 percent and 8 percent and 9 percent.

Recall that the implied forward rate is a future rate implied by today's rates. In this example, when the equilibrium YTM on the two-year bond is 9 percent and the equilibrium YTM on the one-year bond is 8 percent, the implied forward rate is 10 percent, the same as the expected rate on a one-year bond, one year from now. Similarly, when the equilibrium YTM on the two-year bond is 8 percent and the equilibrium YTM on the one-year bond is 6 percent, the implied forward rate is also 10 percent, the same as the expected rate on a one-year bond, one year from now. Thus, in equilibrium the yield curve will be governed by the condition that the implied forward rate is equal to the expected spot rate of 10 percent:

$$YTM_2 = [(1+YTM_1)(1+f_{11})]^{1/2} - 1$$

$$f_{11} = \frac{(1+YTM_2)^2}{(1+YTM_1)} - 1$$

$$f_{11} = \frac{(1.09)^2}{(1.08)} - 1 = .10$$

or

$$f_{11} = \frac{(1.08)^2}{(1.06)} - 1 = .10$$

Note that in this example, we assumed that bond issuers or borrowers had strong maturity segmentation preferences such that they were not influenced by expected rates. If we relax the assumption, positing that bond issuers and borrowers also consider expectation, we find that similar to investors, the response of issuers/borrowers to the expectation of higher rates also contributes to the steepening of the yield curves. The response of bond issuer is explained in more detail in Exhibit 4.9.

EXHIBIT 4.9 Pure Expectations Theory. Market Expectation of Higher Interest Rate—Investors and Issuers Response

A ***bond issuer*** financing a two-year asset—a two-year borrower—would consider issuing either a two-year bond at 8% or a series of one-year bonds: one-year today at 8% and a one-year bond one year later at 10% for an average rate of 9%. Given this choice, the two-year borrower would therefore prefer to issue two-year bonds at 8%. On the other hand, a bond issuer financing a one-year asset—a one-year borrower—could issue either one-year bonds at 8% or issue a two-year bond at 8% (for example, borrowing $857.3388 = 1{,}000/(1.08)^2$) and then buy the bond back in the market (or prepay) one year later when rates are at 10% and the price on bond is 909.09 (= \$1,000/1.10), paying a one-year borrowing rate of 6% (= (909.09 /857.3388) – 1). Thus, given this choice, a one-year borrower would also prefer to issue two-year bonds instead of one-year. In the two-year market, the expectation of higher rates would cause the supply of two-year bonds to increase, lowering their price and increasing the two-year yield. This would, in turn, reinforce the demand impact where the demand and price for two-year bonds are decreasing, causing two-year yields to increase. In the one-year market, the expectation of higher rates would cause the supply of one-year bonds to decrease, increasing their price and lowering the one-year yield. This would, in turn, reinforce the demand impact where the demand and price for one-year bonds are increasing, causing one-year yields to decrease.

In equilibrium, the increase in the supply of two-year bonds and the decrease in the supply for one-year bonds, combined with the demand adjustments of one-year bond demand increasing and two-year bond demand decreasing will continue until the average annual rate on the two-year bond is equal to the equivalent annual rate from the series of one-year loans (or the one-year bond's rate is equal to the rate expected on the two-year bond held one year). This is the same equilibrium condition governing bond investors. Thus, similar to investors, the response of issuers/borrowers to the expectation of higher rates contributes to the steepening of the yield curves.

- Expectations of rates increasing from 8% to 10%.
- Investors with HD of 2 years and those with HD of 1 year would prefer one-year bonds over two-year bonds.
- 2-year borrowers would prefer to finance with 2-year bonds and 1-year borrowers would prefer to finance with 2-year bonds.
- Market Response:

$B_2^D \downarrow \Rightarrow P_2^B \downarrow \Rightarrow YTM_2 \uparrow$	$B_1^D \uparrow \Rightarrow P_1^B \uparrow \Rightarrow YTM_1 \downarrow$	YC Becomes
$B_2^S \uparrow \Rightarrow P_2^B \downarrow \Rightarrow YTM_2 \uparrow$	$B_1^S \downarrow \Rightarrow P_1^B \uparrow \Rightarrow YTM_1 \downarrow$	Positively Sloped

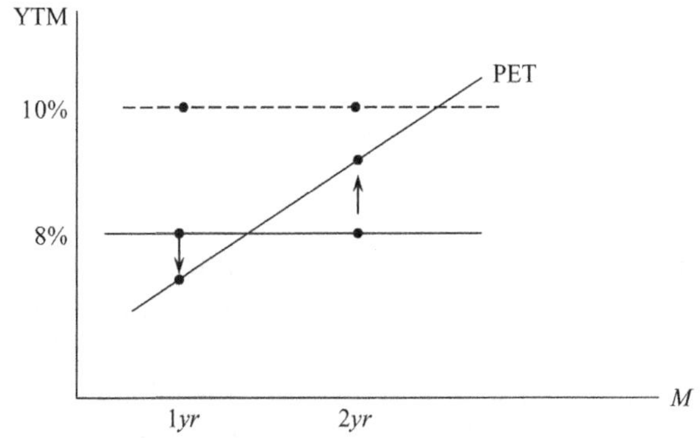

YTM
PET
10%
8%
M
1yr 2yr

Yield Curves that Incorporate Expectations

In the above example, the equilibrium yield curve is positively sloped, reflecting the market expectation of higher rates. By contrast, if the yield curve was currently flat at 10 percent and there was a market expectation that it would shift down to 8 percent next year, then the expectation of lower rates would cause the yield curve to become negatively sloped. In this case, an investor with a two-year horizon date would prefer the two-year bond at 10 percent to a series of one-year bonds yielding an expected rate of only 9 percent ($E(R) = [(1.10)(1.08)]^{1/2} - 1 = .09$). Similarly, an investor with a one-year horizon would also prefer buying a two-year bond that has an expected rate of return of 12 percent ($P_2 = 100/(1.10)^2 = 82.6446$; $E(P_{11}) = 100/1.08 = 92.5926$; $E(R) = [92.5926 - 82.6446]/82.6446 = .12$) to the one-year bond that yields only 10 percent. In the bond markets, the expectations of lower rates would cause the demand and price of the two-year bond to increase, lowering its rate, and the demand and price for the one-year bond to decrease, increasing its rate.[7]

One of the features of the Pure Expectations Theory is that in equilibrium, the yield curve reflects the market's expectations about future rates. From our PET examples, when the equilibrium yield curve was positively sloped, the market expected higher rates in the future; when the curve was negatively sloped, the market expected lower rates. Moreover, if PET strictly holds (i.e., we can accept all of the model's assumptions), then the expected future rates would be equal to the implied forward rates. As a result, one could forecast futures rates and future yield curves by simply calculating implied forward rates from current rates.

Exhibit 4.10 shows spot rates on bonds with terms to maturities ranging from one year to five years (column 2) and with assumed annual compounding. Using implied forward rates as estimates, expected spot rates (S_t) are generated for bonds one year from the present (column 3) and two years from the present (column 4) from the current spot rates. For example, the expected rate on a one-year bond one year from now ($E(S_{Mt}) = E(S_{11})$) is equal to the implied forward rate of $f_{Mt} = f_{11} = 11$ percent. This rate is obtained by using the geometric mean with the current two-year and one-year spot rates:

$$S_2 = [(1+S_1)(1+f_{11})]^{1/2} - 1$$

$$f_{11} = \frac{(1+S_2)^2}{(1+S_1)} - 1$$

$$f_{11} = \frac{(1.105)^2}{(1.10)} - 1 = .11$$

EXHIBIT 4.10 Forecasting Yield Curves Using Implied Forward Rates

(1)	(2)	(3)	(4)
Maturity	**Spot Rates**	**Expected Spot Rates One Year From Present**	**Expected Spot Rates Two Years from Present**
1	10.0%	f_{11} = 11%	f_{12} = 12%
2	10.5	f_{21} = 11.5%	f_{22} = 12.5%
3	11.0	f_{31} = 12.0%	f_{32} = 13%
4	11.5	f_{41} = 12.5%	
5	12.0		

Similarly, the expected two-year spot rate one year from now is equal to the implied forward rate on a two-year bond purchased one year from now of $f_{Mt} = f_{21}$ = 11.5 percent. This rate is obtained using three-year and one-year spot rates:

$$S_3 = [(1+S_1)(1+f_{11})(1+f_{12})]^{1/3} - 1$$

$$S_3 = [(1+S_1)(1+f_{21})^2]^{1/3} - 1$$

$$(1+S_3)^3 = [(1+S_1)(1+f_{21})^2]$$

$$f_{21} = \left[\frac{(1+S_3)^3}{(1+S_1)}\right]^{1/2} - 1$$

$$f_{21} = \left[\frac{(1.11)^3}{(1.10)}\right]^{1/2} - 1 = .115$$

The other expected spot rates for next year are found repeating this process. A similar approach also can be used to forecast the yield curve further out (t = 2 years out, t = 3 years out, and so on). All of these implied forward rates can be found using the following formula:

$$f_{Mt} = \left[\frac{(1+S_{M+t})^{M+t}}{(1+S_t)^t}\right]^{1/M} - 1$$

Using Forward Rates to Determine Expected Rates of Return

According to PET, the implied forward rate is equal to the expected spot rate, and in equilibrium, the expected rate of return for holding any bond for one year would be equal to the current spot rate on a one-year bond. Similarly, the rate expected to be earned for two years from investing in any bond or combination of bonds (e.g., such as a series of one-year bonds) would be equal to the rate on the two-year bond. This condition can be illustrated using the spot yield curve and expected yield curves (or forward rates) shown in Exhibit 4.10. For example, the expected rate of return from purchasing a two-year zero-coupon bond at the spot rate of 10.5 percent and selling it one year later at an expected one-year spot rate equal to the implied forward rate of f_{11} of 11 percent is 10 percent:

$$P_{20} = \frac{100}{(1.105)^2} = 81.8984$$

$$E(P_{11}) = \frac{100}{1.11} = 90.09$$

$$E(R) = \frac{90.09 - 81.8984}{81.8984} = .10$$

This is the same rate obtained from investing in a one-year bond. Similarly, the expected rate of return from holding a three-year bond for one year, then selling it at the implied forward rate of f_{21} is also 10 percent. Any of the bonds with spot rates shown in Exhibit 4.10 would have expected rates for one year of 10 percent if the implied forward rate were used as the estimated expected rate. Similar results hold for a two-year investment period. That is, any bond held for two years and sold at its forward rate would earn the two-year spot rate of 10.5 percent. For example, a four-year bond purchased at the spot rate of 11.5 percent and expected to be sold two years later at f_{22} = 12.5 percent, would have an expected rate of return of 10.5 percent—the same as the current two-year spot. Similarly, an investment in a series of one-year bonds at spot rates of S_1 = 10.0 percent and $E(S_{11}) = f_{11}$ = 11 percent yields a two-year rate of 10.5 percent (= $[(1.10)(1.11)]^{1/2} - 1$).

Hedgeable Rates

In practice, forward rates can be used as a spot predictor of future interest rates. Economic and financial conditions, though, do change, leading to new spot rates and therefore forward rates. Analysts often refer to forward rates as *hedgeable rates,* and most do not consider forward rates as the market's consensus on expected future rates. The most practical use of forward rates is that they provide *cutoff rates,* useful in evaluating investment decisions. For example, an investor with a one-year horizon date should only consider investing in the two-year bond in our above example, if she expected one-year rates one year later to be less than f_{11} = 11 percent; that is, assuming she is not risk-loving and wants an expected rate greater than 10 percent. Thus, forward rates serve as a good cutoff rate for evaluating investments. Such strategies of buying bonds with a given maturity and then selling them later when they have a shorter maturity and hopefully a rate less that forward rate are referred to as strategies of "trading down the yield curve."

Exhibit 4.11 shows a number of Bloomberg IYC9 (total return/yield curve screens). The IYC9 screen shows the total returns for different horizons and yield curve shift scenarios based on the U.S. on/off the run sovereign yield curve. The screen can be used in identifying strategies for trading down the yield curve given different interest rate forecasts. The top screen in the exhibit shows the total returns for each maturity from buying a Treasury and selling it one year later given no change in rates. As the total return graph shows, the largest returns occur from the intermediate-term and long-term maturities. The middle screen shows returns for a one-year horizon given a 100-bps upward shift in the yield curve and a 50-bps decrease in the yield curves. For the upward shift, the total returns are negative with the losses increasing with maturity. For the downward shift, total returns are positive and increasing with maturity. Finally, the lower screen shows an increasing and decreasing yield curve shifts for three-year horizon periods.

EXHIBIT 4.11 Total Returns Given Different Horizons and Yield Curve Shifts: Bloomberg IYC9 Screens, 4/9/2012

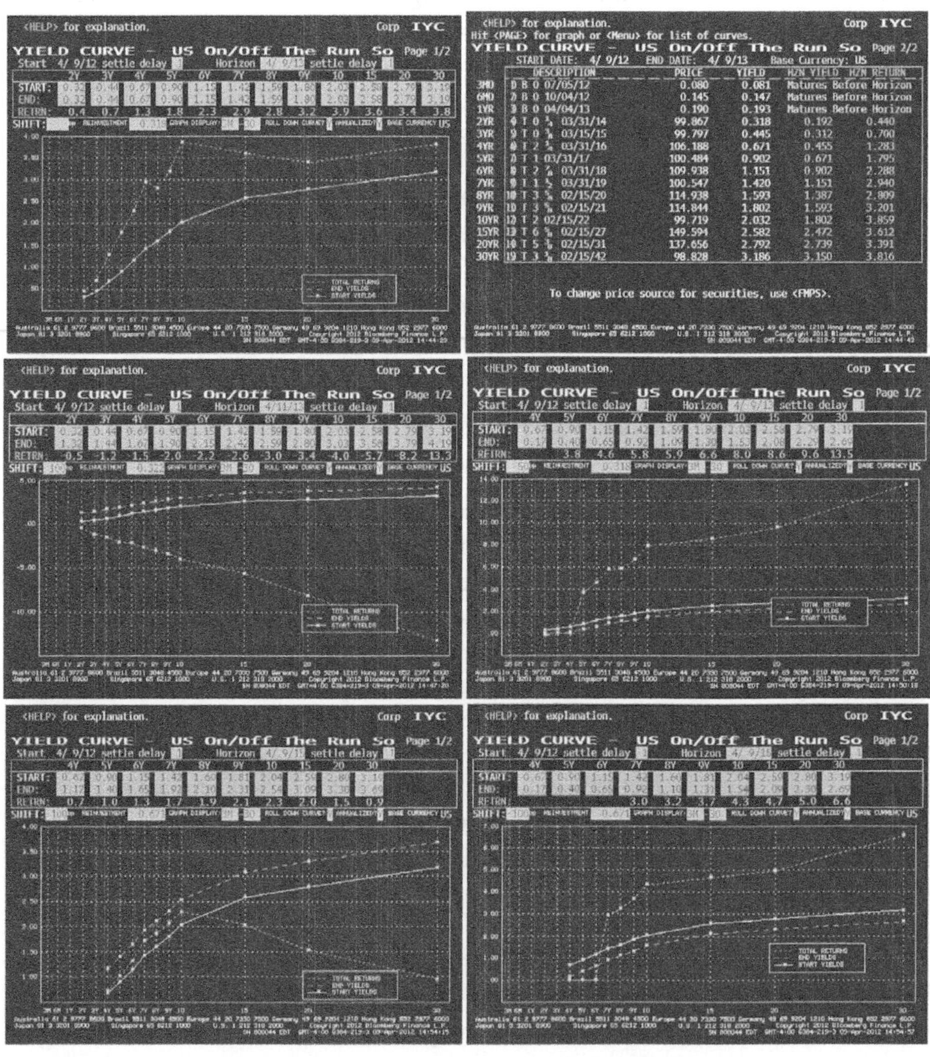

BLOOMBERG CRVF, IYC8, AND IYC9:

CRVF screen shows yield curves for different countries, sectors, and regions for selected periods

IYC8 shows yield curves for different periods and the total returns for that period that would be realized by buying bonds with different maturities.

IYC9 shows the current yield curve and allows the user to select different future rates in order to determine the total return for different maturities and different horizons.

Using the Bloomberg ICY8 (historical return analysis) and ICY9 (horizon return analysis), one can conduct an historical and future (horizon) total return analysis of buying bonds with different maturities and selling it a specified period later. The programs can be used to determine hedgeable rates and identifying strategies for trading down the yield curve.

See Exhibit 4.11 for IYC9 screens.

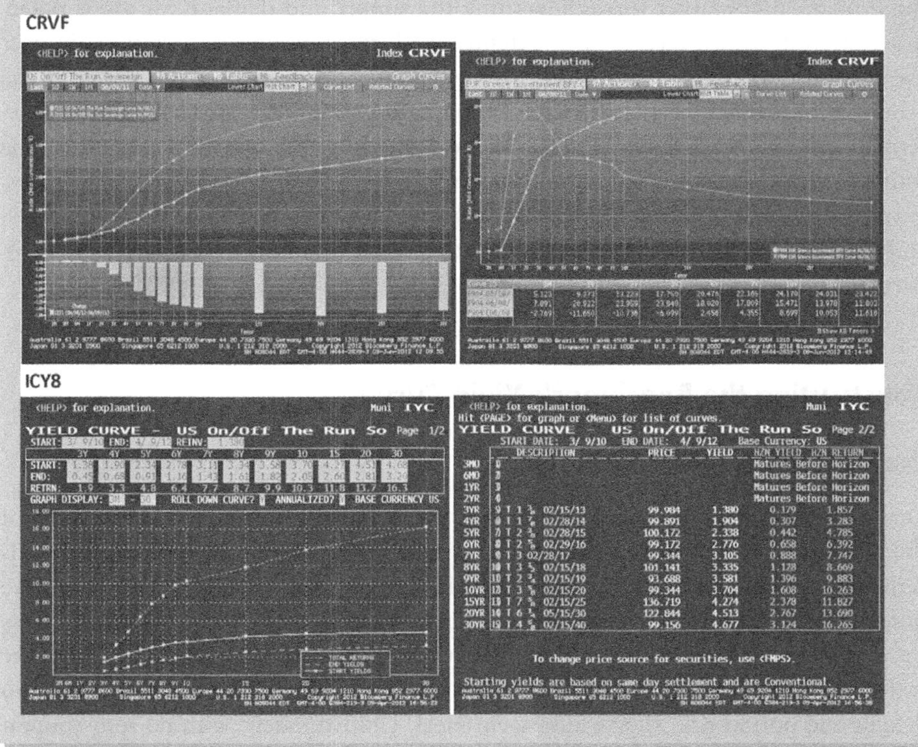

Liquidity Premium Theory

The fourth term structure theory is the *Liquidity Premium Theory* (*LPT*), also referred to as the *Risk Premium Theory* (*RPT*). LPT is based on the assumption that there is a liquidity premium for long-term bonds over short-term bonds. Recall how long-term bonds are more price sensitive to interest rate changes than short-term bonds. As a result, the prices of long-term securities tend to be more volatile and therefore more risky than short-term securities. According to LPT, if investors were risk averse, then they would require some additional return (liquidity/risk premium) in order to hold long-term bonds instead of short-term ones. Thus, if the yield curve were initially flat, but had no risk premium factored in to compensate investors for the additional volatility they assumed from buying long-term bonds, then the demand for long-term bonds would decrease and their rates increase until risk-averse investors were compensated. In this case, the yield curve would become positively sloped.[8]

Summary of Term Structure Theories

The term structure of interest rates cannot be explained in terms of any one theory; rather, it is best explained by a combination of theories. Of the four theories, the two major ones are MST and PET. MST is important because it establishes how the fundamental market forces governing the supply and demand for assets determine interest rates. PET, in turn, extends MST to show how expectations impact the structure of interest rates. PHT, by explaining how markets will adjust if the economy is poorly hedged, and LPT, by including a liquidity premium for longer-term bonds, both represent necessary extensions of MST and PET. Together, the four theories help us to understand how supply and demand, economic conditions, government deficits and surpluses, monetary policy, hedging, maturity preferences, and expectations all affect the bond market in general and the structure of rates in particular.

Constructing the Benchmark Yield Curve

Theoretical Spot Rate Curve

Treasury yield curves are the standard benchmark for yields on other sectors. One of the problems in constructing a benchmark yield curve from observed Treasury yields is that many Treasuries with the same maturity carry different yields because they have different coupon rates. To rectify this, the convention is to generate a *spot rate curve* showing the relation between spot rates and the terms to maturity. A spot Treasury rate is the rate on a zero-coupon Treasury. Because such bonds lack coupons and have no default and option risk, they would seem ideal. Unfortunately, with no zero-coupon Treasury debt issues with maturities greater than one year, it is not possible to construct such a curve from observed Treasury security yields.

In Chapter 3, we examined how spot rates are estimated using the bootstrapping technique. A spot yield curve in which the spot rates are estimated using bootstrapping, in turn, is referred to as a *theoretical spot rate curve.* Moreover, as examined Chapter 3, the equilibrium price of a bond is that price obtained by discounting its cash flows by spot rates. If the market prices a bond below its equilibrium value, then dealers/arbitrageurs can earn a risk-free profit by buying the bond and stripping it; if the market prices a bond above its equilibrium value, then dealers/arbitrageurs can realize a risk-free profit by buying stripped securities and then forming an identical coupon bond to sell. In practice, the process of stripping and rebundling causes the true yield curve for Treasury securities to approach the theoretical spot rate curve. As a result, the theoretical spot rate curve is often used by practitioners to price financial instruments and by dealers to identify arbitrage opportunities; as such, it represents a good estimate of the benchmark yield curve.

Estimating the Spot Rate Curve

In deriving a spot rate curve, possible Treasuries to include are either liquid on-the-run Treasury issues or on-the-run Treasury issues and select off-the-run issues (see Exhibit 4.12). On-the-run Treasuries are the most recently auctioned issues of a given maturity. They include 3-month, 6-month, 2-year, 5-year, 10-year, and 30-year issues. For on-the-run issues, the yield used is the one that makes the issue trade at par; that is, the coupon rate. The resulting yield curve is referred to as a *par coupon yield curve.*

In constructing the theoretical spot rate curve, 60 semiannual spot rates from 6-month rates to 30-year rates need to be estimated. For on-the-run issues there are

EXHIBIT 4.12 Benchmark Yield Curves: Current Treasury Yield Curve and On-the-Run and Off-the-Run Treasury Yield Curves, 4/9/12

Current On-the-Run Treasury Yield Curve

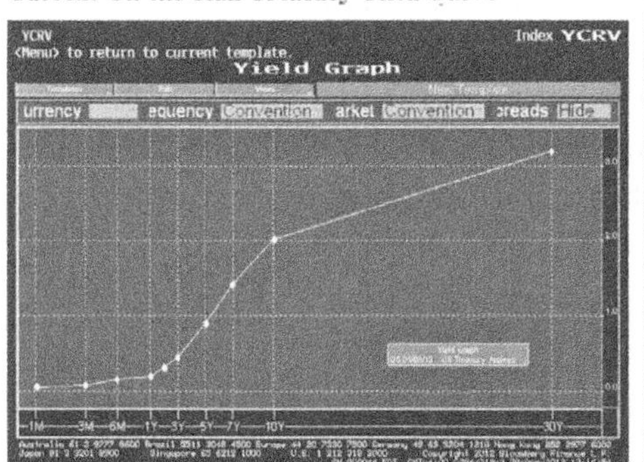

Current On-the-Run and Off-the-Run Yield Curve

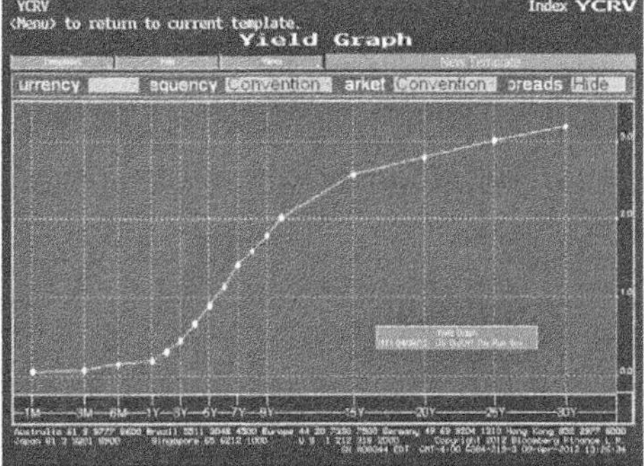

Treasury Strip Yield Curve

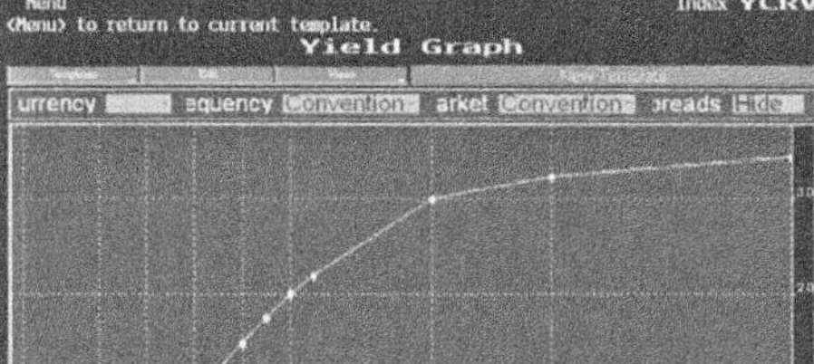

Benchmark Municipal

only six issues. The other maturity points for the par yield curve are estimated using linear extrapolation. One of the obvious problems with generating the theoretical spot rate curve from on-the-run issues is the significant proportion of yields that are generated from extrapolation. To minimize this problem and reduce the number of extrapolations, an on-the-run and off-the-run yield curve combines on-the-run issues with select off-the-run Treasury issues.

Given an on-the-run or on/off-the-run par coupon yield coupon curve, bootstrapping is then used to estimate the theoretical spot rate curve. The bootstrapping technique requires taking at least one zero-coupon bond and then sequentially generating other spot rates from the coupon bonds. Exhibit 4.13 shows spot rates generated from a hypothetical par yield curve using bootstrapping. In the exhibit there are two T-bills with maturities of six months (.5 years) and one year, trading at yields of S_5 = 5 percent and S_1 = 5.25 percent. The other bonds shown in the exhibit are coupon bonds assumed to be trading at par and therefore with yields equal to their coupon rates. Using bootstrapping, the annualized spot rate for these bonds are $S_{1.5}$ = 5.51 percent, S_2 = 5.577 percent, $S_{2.5}$ = 6.03 percent, and S_3 = 6.30 percent (see the last column of the Exhibit 4.13).

Note that if an arbitrageur prices the T-notes at par, then she could earn a risk-free profit by buying the note and stripping it. For example, consider the arbitrage from buying and stripping the three-year, 6.25 percent coupon bond. A dealer could buy the issue at par and strip the issue with the expectation of selling the strips at the yields corresponding to their maturities. As shown in Exhibit 4.14, the proceeds from selling the strips would be 100.1217, yielding the dealer a profit of $0.1217 per $100 face value. In contrast, if the dealer sells at the spot rates defining the theoretical spot rate curve, the profit is zero and the arbitrage disappears. Thus, the actions of arbitrageurs to exploit this opportunity would be to drive the prices and yields on Treasury securities to the theoretical spot rates where the arbitrage disappears.

Other Benchmark Yield Curves

An alternative approach to estimating the benchmark yield curve is to simply use stripped securities generated from Treasury coupon securities; in fact, this would seem to be the most promising approach. However, there are two problems using a *Treasury strip yield curve* as the benchmark yield curve. First, the liquidity of the stripped securities is less than that of Treasury securities.[9] As a result, the yields on strips reflect a liquidity premium. Second, the tax treatment (for U.S. residents) on strips differs from that of Treasury coupons in that the accrued interest on a strip is taxed even though no cash is received.

Another approach to estimating the benchmark yield curve is to use the rates on interest rate swaps. In a generic interest rate swap contract, fixed interest payments are swapped for floating rates. The fixed rate on the swap contract is called the swap rate and is equal to a T-note rate plus basis points. Dealers in the market, in turn, quote

EXHIBIT 4.13 Estimating Spot Rate Curve Using Bootstrapping

Security	Type	Maturity	Semi-Annual Coupon	Annualized	Face value	Current Price	Spot Rate
1	T-Bill	0.5 years	–	5%	100	97.561	5.00%
2	T-Bill	1.0 years	–	5.25%	100	94.9497	5.25%
3	T-Note	1.5 years	2.75	5.5%	100	100	5.51%
4	T-Note	2.0 years	2.875	5.75%	100	100	5.577%
5	T-Note	2.5 years	3	6.00%	100	100	6.03%
6	T-Note	3.0 years	3.125	6.25%	100	100	6.30%

Given the par coupon curve, bootstrapping is used to estimate the theoretical spot rate curve. The bootstrapping technique requires taking at least one zero-coupon bond and then sequentially generating other spot rates from the coupon bonds. In the table, there are two T-bills with maturities of six months (.5 years) and one year, trading at yields of 5% and 5.25%. Since T-bills are zero-coupon bonds, these rates can be used as spot rates (St) for maturities of .5 years ($S_{.5}$) and one year (S_1). The other bonds shown in the exhibit are coupon bonds assumed to be trading at par and therefore with yields equal to their coupon rates. Using bootstrapping, the spot rate for 1.5 years is found by:

- Taking the T-note with a maturity of 1.5 years and annual coupon rate of 5.5% (semiannual coupons of 2.75)
- Setting the par value of the 1.5-year bond equal to the present value of its cash flows discounted at known spot rates of $S_{.5}$ and S_1 and an unknown spot rate for 1.5 years, $S_{1.5}$
- Solving for the spot rate for 1.5 years.

This yields an annualized spot rate of $S_{1.5} = 5.51\%$:

$$P_{1.5} = \frac{CF_{.5}}{(1+(S_{.5}/2))^1} + \frac{CF_{1.0}}{(1+(S_1/2))^2} + \frac{CF_{1.5}}{(1+(S_{1.5}/2))^3}$$

$$100 = \frac{2.75}{(1+(.05/2))^1} + \frac{2.75}{(1+(.0525/2))^2} + \frac{102.75}{(1+(S_{1.5}/2))^3}$$

$$94.705956 = \frac{102.75}{(1+(S_{1.5}/2))^3}$$

$$S_{1.5} = 2\left[\left[\frac{102.75}{94.705956}\right]^{1/3} - 1\right] = .0551$$

To obtain the spot rate for a two-year bond (S_2), we repeat the process using the two-year bond paying semiannual coupons of 2.875 and selling at par. This yields a spot rate of $S_2 = 5.577\%$. Continuing the process with the other securities in the exhibit, we obtain spot rates for bonds with maturities of 2.5 years and 3 years: $S_{2.5} = 6.03\%$ and $S_3 = 6.30\%$ (see the last column of the table).

EXHIBIT 4.14 Valuing a Stripped Bond

Maturity Years	Semi-Annual Coupon	YTM	PV	Spot Rate	PV
0.5	3.125	0.0500	3.0488	0.0500	3.0488
1.0	3.125	0.0525	2.9672	0.0525	2.9672
1.5	3.125	0.0550	2.8807	0.0551	2.8804
2.0	3.125	0.0575	2.7900	0.0558	2.7994
2.5	3.125	0.0600	2.6957	0.0603	2.6936
3.0	103.125	0.0625	85.7394	0.0630	85.6210
			100.1217		100.01

Note: Allow for small rounding differences

swap rates for different maturities. The relation between the swap rate and maturity of a swap is called the *swap rate yield curve.*

Finally, it should be noted that for tax-exempt bonds, such as municipals, the benchmark yield curve is often a generic AAA general obligation municipal bond rather than a Treasury. The Municipal Market Advisors Inc. generates a municipal benchmark yield curve (see Exhibit 4.12).

Other Yield Curves

The spread between the interest rates offered in two sectors of the bond market with the same maturity (e.g., Treasury and non-Treasury) is referred to as the *intermarket sector spread,* whereas the spreads between two issues within the same sector is called the *intramarket sector spread.* Intermarket spreads can be examined by comparing the yield curve for different sectors to the benchmark yield curve and with each other. Exhibit 4.15 shows various yield curves for sectors, municipalities, and sovereign obtained from the Bloomberg YCRV and CG screens.

Forward Yield Curves

As discussed previously, a yield curve showing current rates, such as a spot rate curve, can also be used to estimate implied forward rates and to generate a forward yield curves. Exhibit 4.16 shows forward rates implied from the theoretical spot rate curve shown in Exhibit 4.13. As shown, using the semiannual spot rates, the implied forward rate on the six-month bill, six months from now is $f_{Mt} = f_{.5,.5}$ = 2.7502 percent (annualized rate of 5.5003 percent). This rate is obtained by defining the one-year spot rate as the geometric average of the current six-month spot rate and the implied

EXHIBIT 4.15 Yield Curves for Sovereigns, Municipals, and Corporate Credits

Bloomberg Yield Curve Screen: YCRV and CG Screens

YCRV: The yield curve screen, YCRV, displays current and historical bond, money market, swap, and municipal market yield curves. YCRV provides a variety of yield curves for different security and market types from around the world, allowing one to analyze investment performance across multiple markets and currencies.

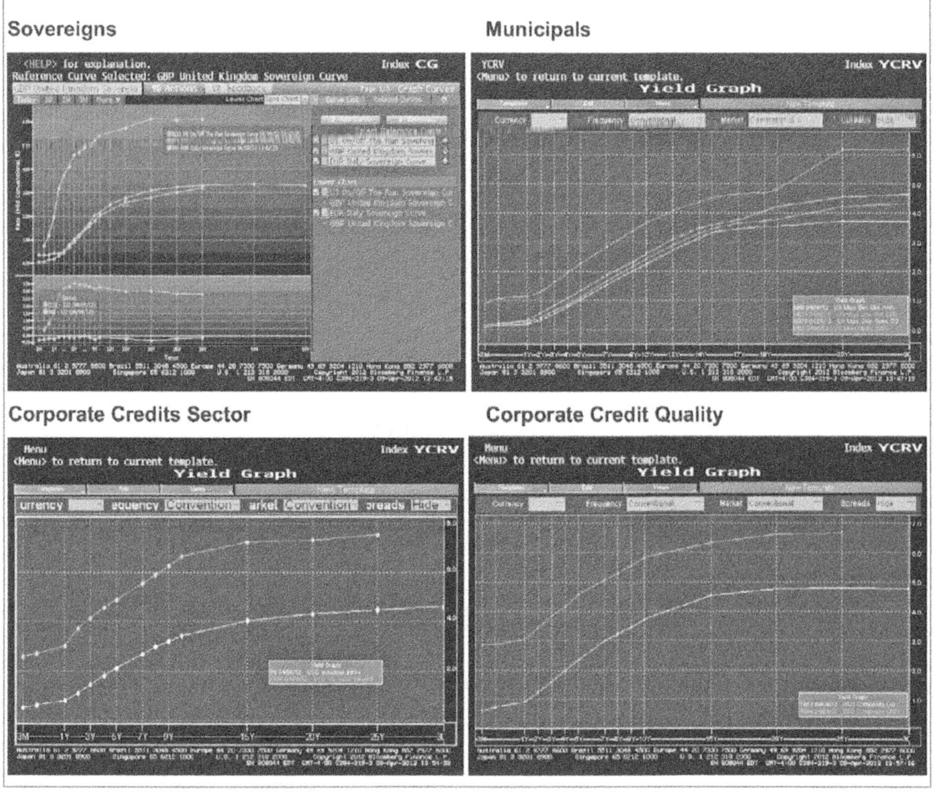

Sovereigns

Municipals

Corporate Credits Sector

Corporate Credit Quality

EXHIBIT 4.16 Forward Yield Curves

Security	Type	Maturity	Spot Rate	Semiannual	Forward Rate t = .5	Annual	$E(R_{M.5})$ Sold at Forward Rate	Forward Rate t = 1	Annual	$E(R_{M,1})$ Sold at Forward Rate
1	T-Bill	0.5 years	0.050000	0.025000	0.027502	0.055003	0.025000	0.030155	0.060310	
2	T-Bill	1.0 years	0.052500	0.026250	0.028827	0.057655	0.025000	0.029523	0.059045	0.026250
3	T-Note	1.5 years	0.055100	0.027550	0.028848	0.057697	0.025000	0.032758	0.065516	0.026250
4	T-Note	2.0 years	0.055770	0.027885	0.031442	0.062883	0.025000	0.034135	0.068270	0.026250
5	T-Note	2.5 years	0.060300	0.030150	0.032805	0.065610				
6	T-Note	3.0 years	0.063000	0.031500						

forward rate on a six-month rate, six months forward, and then solving the equation for the implied forward rate:

$$S_1 = [(1+S_{.5})(1+f_{.5,.5})]^{1/2} - 1$$

$$f_{.5,.5} = \frac{(1+S_1)^2}{(1+S_{.5})} - 1$$

$$f_{.5,.5} = \frac{(1.02625)^2}{(1.025)} - 1 = 0.027502$$

$$\text{Annualized } f_{.5,.5} = (2)(0.027502) = .055003$$

Similarly, the implied forward rate on a 1-year bond, purchased 6 months from now ($f_{Mt} = f_{1,.5} = 2.8827$ percent), is obtained by solving the 1.5-year geometric mean for $f_{1,.5}$. Similar approaches also can be used to generate forward yield curves one year, 1.5 years, and other years from the present. In general, semiannual forward rates on *M*-year bonds purchased *t* years from the present can be found using the following formula:

$$f_{Mt} = \left[\frac{(1+S_{M+t})^N}{(1+S_t)^i}\right]^{1/(N-i)} - 1$$

where:

S = Semiannual spot rate
M = time to maturity in years
t = time period from the present to the forward date in years
N = number of semiannual periods to $M + t$
i = number of semiannual periods to t

Note that in the illustration, if the implied forward rates six months from now are realized, then an investor with a six-month horizon, would earn the same semiannual rate of 2.5 percent obtained on the six-month bill by buying any maturity bond and selling it six months later at its implied forward rate. Similarly, if the implied forward rates one year from now are realized, then an investor with a one-year horizon would earn the same semiannual rate of 2.6255 percent obtained on the one-year by buying any maturity bond and selling it one year later at its implied forward rate. As discussed previously, one of the practical uses of the forward curve is that it can be used to identify the hedgable rates useful in determining alternative investments and evaluating strategies of trading down the yield curve.

Exhibit 4.17 shows one-, two-, and three-year forward curves generated from the Bloomberg FWCV screen based on the current yield curve (swap rate curve used as estimate of the benchmark curve). Note the current yield curve and the forward yield curves are positively sloped. According to expectations theory, this suggests higher future rates.

EXHIBIT 4.17 Bloomberg Forward Yield Curves: FWCV

FWCV

The FWCV screen can be used calculate forward rates for fair market curves based on yield curves (interest rate swap curves and government curves) for three future dates.

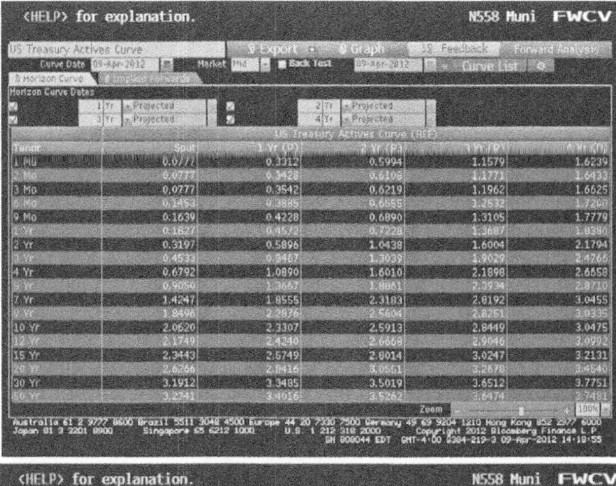

<HELP> for explanation. N558 Muni FWCV

US Treasury Actives Curve — Curve Date 09-Apr-2012 — Market Mid — Back Test 09-Apr-2012

Horizon Curve Dates: 1 Yr Projected; 2 Yr Projected; 3 Yr Projected; 4 Yr Projected

US Treasury Actives Curve (REF)

Tenor	Spot	1 Yr (P)	2 Yr (P)	3 Yr (P)	4 Yr (P)
1 Mo	0.0777	0.3312	0.5994	1.1579	1.6239
2 Mo	0.0777	0.3428	0.6106	1.1771	1.6433
3 Mo	0.0777	0.3542	0.6219	1.1962	1.6625
6 Mo	0.1453	0.3885	0.6555	1.2632	1.7200
9 Mo	0.1639	0.4228	0.6890	1.3105	1.7779
1 Yr	0.1827	0.4572	0.7228	1.3687	1.8380
2 Yr	0.3197	0.5896	1.0438	1.6004	2.1794
3 Yr	0.4533	0.8467	1.3039	1.9029	2.4766
4 Yr	0.6792	1.0890	1.6010	2.1898	2.6658
5 Yr	0.9050	1.3667	1.8861	2.3934	2.8710
7 Yr	1.4247	1.8555	2.3183	2.8192	3.0455
9 Yr	1.8496	2.2876	2.5604	2.8251	3.0335
10 Yr	2.0620	2.3307	2.5913	2.8449	3.0475
12 Yr	2.1749	2.4240	2.6668	2.9046	3.0992
15 Yr	2.3443	2.5749	2.8014	3.0247	3.2131
20 Yr	2.6266	2.8416	3.0561	3.2878	3.4540
30 Yr	3.1912	3.3485	3.5019	3.6512	3.7751
50 Yr	3.2741	3.4016	3.5262	3.6474	3.7481

Australia 61 2 9777 8600 Brazil 5511 3048 4500 Europe 44 20 7330 7500 Germany 49 69 9204 1210 Hong Kong 852 2977 6000 Japan 81 3 3201 8900 Singapore 65 6212 1000 U.S. 1 212 318 2000 Copyright 2012 Bloomberg Finance L.P. SN 808044 EDT GMT-4:00 G384-219-3 09-Apr-2012 14:19:55

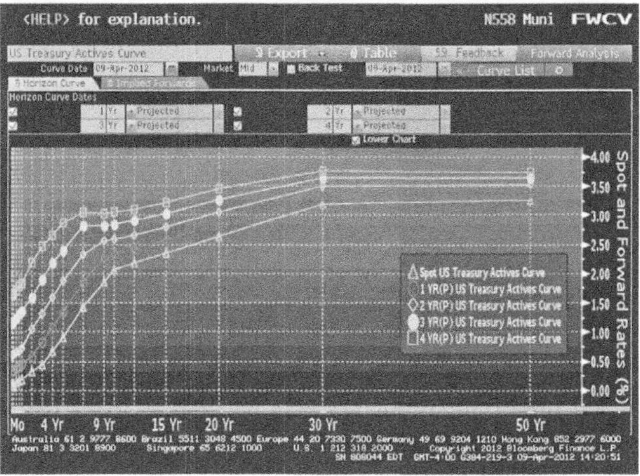

Conclusion

In this chapter, we have examined what determines the level and structure of interest rates. We started our analysis by first examining how economic factors such as economic growth, monetary and fiscal policy, international capital flows, and inflation affect the general level of interest rates. We next examined how differences in risk, liquidity, and tax features determine the spreads between interest rates on bonds of different categories. Finally, we completed our analysis of the structure of interest rates by examining the four theories of the term structure of interest rates. In discussing the level and structure of interest rates in this chapter, we have looked at the general relationship between risk and return. In the next chapter, we turn our attention to the specific types of risk associated with bonds.

Website Information

Economic Information

1. Federal Reserve sites:
   www.federalreserve.gov/releases/h15/data.htm
   FRED: www.research.stlouisfed.org/fred2
2. For information on Federal Reserve policies, go to www.federalreserve.gov/policy.htm.
3. For information on European Central Banks, go to www.ecb.int.
4. For information on rates on bonds and the current yield curve, go to www.bloomberg.com.
5. For information on the U.S. Treasury's debt, go to www.publicdebt.treas.gov.
6. For information on the distribution of U.S. debt, go to the Treasury Bulletin: http://www.fms.treas.gov/bulletin/.
7. For information on U.S. government's expenditures, revenues, deficits, and debt, go to: www.gpo.gov/fdsys/browse/collectionGPO.action?collectionCode=BUDGET.
8. For tables on U.S. government's expenditures, revenues, deficits, and debt to download, go to:
   www.gpo.gov/fdsys/search/pagedetails.action?granuleId=&packageId=BUDGET-2010-TAB.
9. For information on government information submitted by Congress, go to:
   www.gpo.gov/fdsys/search/home.action.
10. Information on the Federal Reserve System can be found by going to the Federal Reserve site: www.federalreserve.gov/pubs/Frseries/frseri.htm. The site has useful information on important monetary actions such as open market operations, changes in the discount rate, and reserve requirement changes.
11. For the Federal Reserve report on the state of the economy, go to the Federal Reserve "Beige Book": www.minneapolisfed.org/bb/. The book provides analysis of current and futures economic condition for the nation and regions.
12. For information on exchange rates and euro and yen bond yields, go to FXStreet.com: www.fxstreet.com.
13. Information on rates and other economic information can be found at www.economagic.com.
14. For information on U.S. security holding by foreigners, go to Treasury tic information: www.treas.gov/tic.
15. For information and report from the U.S. Treasury, go to www.treas.gov/.
16. For information on economic indicators and economic performance from the Council of Economic Advisors at the Federal Reserve Archival System for Economic Research (FRASER), go to http://fraser.stlouisfed.org/publications/ei/.

Yield Curves

1. For yield curves from Investinginbonds.com, go to http://investinginbonds.com/, click "Government Market-at-a-Glance."
2. For yield curves from Bloomberg, go to www.bloomberg.com, Click "Market Data" and "Rates and Bonds."
3. Go to FXstreet to find historical yields on U.S. dollar–denominated bonds, euro-denominated bonds, and yen-denominated bonds with 5-, 10-, and 30-year maturities. Go to www.fxstreet.com, Click "Rates and Charts" and "Bond Yields."

Selected References

Buser, S. A., and P. J. Hess. 1986. Empirical determinants of the relative yields on taxable and tax exempt securities. *Journal of Financial Economics* 17:335–355.

Campbell, J. Y. 1986. A defense of traditional hypotheses about the term structure of interest rates." *Journal of Finance* 41:183–93.

Carleton, W. R., and I. Cooper. 1976. Estimation and uses of the term structure of interest rates," *Journal of Finance* 31:1067–1083.

Cox, J. C., J. Ingersoll, and S. Ross. 1981. A re-examination of traditional hypotheses about the term structure of interest rates. *Journal of Finance* 36:769–799.

Cox, J. C., J. Ingersoll, and S. Ross. 1985. A theory of the term structure of interest rates. *Econometrica* 53:385–407.

Culbertson, J. M. 1957. The term structure of interest rates. *Quarterly Journal of Economics* 71:489–504.

Diament, P. 1993. Semi-empirical smooth fit to the treasury yield curve. *Journal of Fixed Income* 3:55–70.

Fama, E. F. 1976. Forward rates as predictors of future spot-rates. *Journal of Financial Economics* 3:361–377.

Fama, E. F. 1990. Term structure forecasts of interest rates, inflation and real returns. *Journal of Monetary Economics,* 25:59–76.

Fama, E. 1984. The information in the term structure. *Journal of Financial Economics* 13 :509–528.

Froot, R. A. 1989. New hope for expectations hypothesis of the term structure of interest rates. *Journal of Finance* 44:283–305.

Gibbons, M. R., and K. Ramaswamy. 1994). The term structure of interest Rates: Empirical Evidence. *Review of Financial Studies* 6:619–658.

Heath, D., R. Jarrow, and A. Morton. 1990. Bond pricing and the term structure of interest rates: A discrete time approximation. *Journal of Financial and Quantitative Analysis* 25:419–440.

Hicks, John R. *Value and Capital,* 2nd ed. London: Oxford University Press, 1946, pp. 141–145.

Ho, T. S. Y., and S. Lee, S. 1986. Term structure movements and pricing of interest rate contingent claims. *Journal of Finance* 41:1011–1029.

Johnson, R. S., R. Zuber, and J. Gandar. 2010. A re-examination of the Market Segmentation Theory as a pedagogical model. *Journal of Financial Education* 36:1–37.

Livingston, M. 1979. Bond taxation and the shape of the yield to maturity curve. *Journal of Finance* 34:189–196.

Lutz, F. A. 1940. The structure of interest rates. *Quarterly Journal of Economics* 55:36–63.

Malkiel, B. G. 1962. Expectations, bond prices and the term structure of interest rates. *Quarterly Journal of Economics* 76:197–218.

Mishkin, F. 1990. What does the term structure tell us about future inflation? *Journal of Monetary Economics* 25:77–95.

Modigliani, F., and R. Sutch. 1966. Innovations in interest rate policy. *American Economic Review* 56:178–197.

Mundell, R. 1963. Inflation and real interest. *Journal of Political Economy* 71:280–283.

Rose, P. S., 2003. *Money and Capital Markets.* New York: McGraw-Hill/Irwin.

Sargent, T. J. 1972. Rational expectations and the term structure of interest rates. *Journal of Money, Credit and Banking* 4:74–97.

Stambaugh, R. 1988. The information in forward rates: Implications for models of the term structure. *Journal of Financial Economics* 21:41–70.

Stojanovic, D., and M. D. Vaughn. 1997. Yielding clues about recessions: The yield curve as a forecasting tool. Economic Review, *Federal Reserve Bank of Boston,* pp. 10–21.

Ron, U. 2002. A practical guide to swap curve construction. In F. J. Fabozzi, ed., *Interest Rate, Term Structure, and Valuation Modeling.* New York: John Wiley & Sons.

Vasicek, O. A., and H. G. Fong. 1982. Term structure modeling using exponential splines. *Journal of Finance* 37:339–358.

Bloomberg Exercises

1. General economic conditions, inflation, the size of the government debt, monetary and fiscal policies, and international capital flows all have impacts on the general level of interest rates.
   a. Examine the historical trends in yields on Treasuries, AAA bond, and Baa bonds using the GP screen:
      - USGG10YR <Index> <Enter>, click "GP."
      - MOODCAAA <Index> <Enter>, click "GP."
      - MOODCBAA <Index> <Enter>, click "GP."

   On the GP graphs, check the "Events" box and set the events to study important economic events during the period.
   b. Examine some of the economic trends using the ECOF screen or by pulling up the economic indicator screen: Ticker <Index> <Enter>. Examples:
      - U.S. Nominal GDP: GDP CUR$ <Index>
      - U.S. Real GDP: GDP CHWG <Index>
      - U.S. Inflation: CPY YOY <Index>
      - S&P/Case-Shiller: SPCS20 <Index>
      - U.S. Unemployment Rate: USURTOT <Index>
      - U.S. Deficit: FDEBTY <Index>
      - Government Debt: PUBLDEBT <Index>
      - Money Supply (M2): M1NS <Index>
2. Using the Bloomberg YCRV screen, explore the yield curves on U.S. Treasuries (U.S. on/off-the-run sovereign, I111) over the past 10 years. Provide some economic and policy arguments that might explain the differences in yield curves you observe in different periods. Use information from the Federal Reserve sites (FED <Enter>; FOMC <Enter>) and some of the economic indicators from ECOF to find information to support your arguments. Possible indicators:
   - U.S. Nominal GDP: GDP CUR$ <Index>
   - U.S. Real GDP: GDP CHWG <Index>
   - U.S. Inflation: CPY YOY <Index>
   - S&P/Case-Shiller: SPCS20 <Index>
   - U.S. Unemployment Rate: USURTOT <Index>

- U.S. Deficit: FDEBTY <Index>
- Government Debt: PUBLDEBT <Index>
- Money Supply (M2): M1NS <Index>
- Balance of Payments: USCABAL <Ticker>
- Energy Prices: CPUPENER <Ticker>

3. Using the YCRV screen, compare current yield curves on Treasuries (I111) with different quality bonds, such as A– industrials (F7) and BBB Industrials (F9). Provide some economic and policy arguments that might explain the differences in yields.
4. Using the CRVF screen, select several countries and then compare each country's sovereign yield curve to the U.S. yield curve (denominate the yield curves in U.S. dollars).
5. Use the IYC9 screen to develop strategies for trading down the Treasury yield curve given the following scenarios and horizons:
   a. An upward yield curve shift of 100 bps and a horizon of one year.
   b. A downward yield curve shift of 100 bps and a horizon of one year.
   c. A flattening of the yield curve where short-term rates increase (e.g., 100 bps), intermediate-term and long-term rates remain the same and a one-year horizon.
   d. An upward yield curve shift of 100 bps and an horizon of three years.
   e. A downward yield curve shift of 100 bps and an horizon of three years.
   f. No change in the yield curve and an horizon of three years.
6. Suppose you are a bond portfolio manager who over the past year has focused your Treasury investments in intermediate bonds (8- to 10-year maturities). Further suppose you are preparing your annual report on your fund's performance and would like to explain how the changes in the yield curve over the past year affected the rates on your Treasury holdings.
   a. Use the CRVF screen to show the shift in the Treasury yield curve over the past year.
   b. Use the IYC8 screen to do your historical analysis of the total returns from your bond given the changes in yield curve.
7. Use the FWCV screen to determine forward rates one, two, and three years forward. Given your projected one-year forward rates determine your one year expected total return for different maturity investments using the IYC9 screens and inputting your forward rates.
8. Using the YCRV screen, compare municipal yield curves for different states: YCRV <Enter>; look for curves by "Curves Types," "Municipal Curves," and "State Specifics." Provide some economic arguments that might explain the differences in yields.
9. Using the CRVF screen (Muni & Regionals tab), compare municipal yield curves for different states.

Notes

1. On the demand side, investments in bonds and other securities also tend to increase in periods of economic growth. An increase demand for bonds would have the opposite impact on bond prices and rates than an increase in bond supply, causing bond demand

to increase and leading to an excess demand for bonds. The excess demand in the market would lead to higher prices and lower interest rates. In general, the net effect of economic growth or decline on interest rates depends on the relative impacts the economy has on the supply and demand for bonds. In growth periods, rates would increase (decrease) if the supply (demand) impact on interest rates dominates the demand (supply) impact.

2. Markets can be defined by whether they have risk premium that is positive, zero, or negative. A risk-neutral market is defined as having a risk premium that is zero, a risk-averse market as having a positive risk premium, and a risk-loving market as having a negative risk premium.
3. For tax-exempt bonds, such as municipals, the benchmark for calculating spreads is often a generic AAA general obligation municipal bond with a specified maturity rather than a Treasury. The spreads between the interest rates offered in two sectors of the bond market with the same maturity (e.g., Treasury and non-Treasury) is referred to as the *intermarket sector spread*, whereas the spreads between two issues within the same sector is called the *intramarket sector spread*.
4. One way to examine how market forces determine the shape of yield curves is to examine MST using supply and demand analysis. For such an analysis, see Johnson, Zuber, and Gandar (2010).
5. The open market operations of the U.S. Federal Reserve have historically been implemented through the purchase and sale of short-term Treasuries. In an effort to lower intermediate-term and long-term rates, the Fed in 2009 began purchasing intermediate and long-term Treasuries.
6. A priori, such preferences may be the case. That is, investors may prefer short-term investments given that longer maturity bonds tend to be more sensitive to interest rate changes or because there are more investors in the upper middle-age class (with shorter investment horizons) than in the young adult or middle-age class (with longer horizons). Borrowers also may have greater long-term than short-term financing needs and thus prefer to borrow long term. Hence, one could argue that the yield curve is positively sloped because investors' and borrowers' preferences make the economy poorly hedged.
7. If we assume that issuers/borrower also consider expectations in their current financing decision, then we find that both one-year and two-year borrowers would prefer to issue one-year bonds instead of two-year. In the market, this would cause the supply of two-year bonds to decrease, increasing their price and decreasing the two-year yield, and the supply of one-year bonds to increase, decreasing their price and increasing the one-year yield. These adjustments along with the demand adjustments of one-year bond demand decreasing and two-year bond demand increasing would continue until the rate on the two-year bond equaled the average rate from the series of one-year investments, or until the rate on the one-year bond equaled the expected rate from holding a two-year bond one year (or when the implied forward rate is equal to expected spot rates).
8. LPT can be thought of as an extension of the Pure Expectations Theory. That is, given that long-term bond are more responsive to interest rate changes, there is more risk holding a longer term bond for one period, with the risk increasing the greater the bond's maturity. As a result, LPT asserts that investors will hold longer maturity bonds if they offer higher yields than the expected future rate, with the risk premium increasing with the terms to maturity. See Cox, Ingersoll, and Ross (1981), pp. 774–775.
9. The Treasury strip security market is discussed in more detail in Chapter 8.

CHAPTER 5

Bond Risk

Introduction

Investment risk is the possibility that the actual rate of return realized from an investment will differ from the expected rate. For bond investors, there are three types of risk: (1) *default risk:* the possibility that the issuer/borrower will fail to meet the contractual obligations specified in the indenture; (2) *call risk:* the possibility that the issuer/borrower will buy back the bond, forcing the investor to reinvest in a market with lower interest rates; and (3) *interest rate risk* or *bond market risk:* the possibility that interest rates will change, changing the price of the bond and the return earned from reinvesting coupons. In this chapter, we examine these three types of risks and introduce two measures of bond volatility that are associated with bonds: duration and convexity.

Default and Credit Risks

Default risk (or credit risk) is the risk that the borrower/issuer—corporation, municipality, intermediary (e.g., bank), or sovereign government—will not meet all promises at the agreed-upon times. A failure to meet any of the interest payments, the principal obligation, or other terms specified in the bond contract (e.g., sinking fund arrangements, collateral requirements, or other protective covenants) places the borrower/issuer in default. If a bond issuer defaults, they can file for bankruptcy, their bondholders/creditors can sue for bankruptcy, or both parties can work out an agreement.

Many large institutional investors have their own credit analysis departments to evaluate bond issues to determine the abilities of companies to meet their contractual obligations. However, individual bond investors, as well as some institutional investors, usually do not make an independent evaluation of a bond's chance of default. Instead, they rely on bond rating companies.

As first discussed in Chapter 1, the major rating companies in the United States are Moody's Investment Services, Standard & Poor's, and Fitch Investors Service. Moody's and Standard & Poor's have been rating bonds for almost 100 years (see Exhibit 1.5). In general, bonds with relatively low chance of default are referred to as *investment-grade bonds,* with quality rating of Baa (or BBB) or higher; bonds with relatively greater chance of default are referred to as *non-investment-grade, speculative-grade,* or *junk bonds* and have quality rating below Baa.

Today, the rating agencies not only evaluate company credits, but also municipals, sovereigns, asset-backed securities, and other debt obligations. Moody's, Standard & Poor's, and Fitch all provide quality ratings on municipal securities similar to the ones they use for corporate bonds. In determining ratings, Moody's, Standard & Poor's, and Fitch consider such factors as the amount of outstanding debt, the economic conditions of the area, the revenue sources backing the issue, the provisions specified

EXHIBIT 5.1 Moody's Municipal Ratings Distributions by Sector and Ratings of Select GOs and Municipal Insurers—Bloomberg STGO, CTGO, and IMRS Screens

<HELP> for explanation, <MENU> for similar functions. Corp STGO

State General Obligation (G.O.) Bond Ratings
U.S. MUNICIPAL SECURITIES
(See MTAX for Individual State Income Tax Rates)

State	Moody's	S&P	State	Moody's	S&P	State	Moody's	S&P
ALABAMA	Aa1	AA	KENTUCKY			OHIO	Aa1	AA+
ALASKA	Aaa	AAA	LOUISIANA	Aa2	AA	OKLAHOMA	Aa2	AA+
ARIZONA			MAINE	Aa2	AA	OREGON	Aa1	AA+
ARKANSAS	Aa1	AA	MARYLAND	Aaa	AAA	PENNSYLVANIA	Aa1	AA
CALIFORNIA	A1	A-	MASSACHUSETTS	Aa1	AA+	PUERTO RICO	Baa1	BBB
COLORADO			MICHIGAN	Aa2	AA-	RHODE ISLAND	Aa2	AA
CONNECTICUT	Aa3	AA	MINNESOTA	Aa1	AA+	SOUTH CAROLINA	Aaa	AA+
D OF COLUMBIA	Aa2	A+	MISSISSIPPI	Aa2	AA	SOUTH DAKOTA		
DELAWARE	Aaa	AAA	MISSOURI	Aaa	AAA	TENNESSEE	Aaa	AA+
FLORIDA	Aa1	AAA	MONTANA	Aa1	AA	TEXAS	Aaa	AA+
GEORGIA	Aaa	AAA	NEBRASKA			UTAH	Aaa	AAA
GUAM		B+	NEVADA	Aa2	AA	VERMONT	Aaa	AA+
HAWAII	Aa2	AA	NEW HAMPSHIRE	Aa1	AA	VIRGIN ISLANDS		
IDAHO			NEW JERSEY	Aa3	AA-	VIRGINIA	Aaa	AAA
ILLINOIS	A2	A+	NEW MEXICO	Aaa	AA+	WASHINGTON	Aa1	AA+
INDIANA			NEW YORK	Aa2	AA	WEST VIRGINIA	Aa1	AA
IOWA			NORTH CAROLINA	Aaa	AAA	WISCONSIN	Aa2	AA
KANSAS			NORTH DAKOTA			WYOMING		

<HELP> for explanation, <MENU> for similar functions. N131 Corp CTGO

State, County and City Municipal Ratings

State	Issuer	Moody's	S&P	Fitch
AK	ALASKA ST	Aaa	AAA	AA+
AK	ANCHORAGE ALASKA	Aa2	AA	AA+
AL	ALABAMA ST	Aa1	AA	
AL	ATHENS ALA	Aa2	AA-	
AL	AUBURN	Aa2	AA+	
AL	BALDWIN CNTY ALA	Aa1	AA+	
AL	BIRMINGHAM AL	Aa2	AA	AA
AL	DECATUR ALA	Aa2	AA	
AL	JEFFERSON CNTY ALA	Caa3	D	WD
AL	MADISON ALA	Aa2	AA	
AL	MOBILE AL	Aa2	AA-	
AL	MONTGOMERY	Aa2	AA+	WD
AL	ST CLAIR CNTY	Aa2		WD
AR	ARKANSAS ST	Aa1	AA	
AZ	PHOENIX ARIZ	Aa1	AAA	
AZ	SCOTTSDALE ARIZ	Aaa	AAA	AAA
AZ	TUCSON ARIZ	Aa2	AA-	AA
CA	CALIFORNIA ST	A1	A-	A-
CA	LANCASTER CALIF SCH	A1	A+	WD
CA	LOS ANGELES CALIF	Aa3	AA-	AA-

Page 1/11

<HELP> for explanation. N131 Corp CTGO

State, County and City Municipal Ratings

State	Issuer	Moody's	S&P	Fitch
NJ	MORRIS PLAINS	Aa1	NR	
NJ	NEW JERSEY ST	Aa3	AA-	AA-
NJ	NEWARK N J	A3		WD
NJ	PASSAIC CNTY N J	Aa3		
NM	NEW MEXICO ST	Aaa	AA+	
NV	LAS VEGAS NEV	Aa2	AA	AA
NV	NEVADA ST	Aa2	AA	AA+
NY	BUFFALO N Y	A2	A	A+
NY	CORTLAND CNTY N Y		A+	
NY	HEMPSTEAD VLG N Y	A2	A	
NY	ITHACA CITY NY	Aa2		
NY	NASSAU CNTY N Y	A1	A+	A+
NY	NEW YORK CITY	Aa2	AA	AA
NY	NEW YORK ST	Aa2	AA	AA
NY	ROCHESTER N Y	Aa3	A	
NY	SYRACUSE N Y	A1	A-	A
NY	WESTCHESTER CNTY N Y	Aaa	AAA	AAA
OH	CINCINNATI OHIO	Aa1	AA+	
OH	CLEVELAND OHIO	A1	AA	A+
OH	COLUMBUS OHIO	Aaa	AAA	AAA

Page 7/11

IMRS Equity IMRS

Insured Municipal Ratings

Insurer	Moody's	S&P	Fitch
1)ACA	Not Rated	NR	Not Rated
2)Ambac	WR	NR	WD
3)Assured Gty.	Aa3 (Neg Watch)	AA- (Sta Outlook)	WD
4)BHAC	Aa1 (Sta Outlook)	AA+ (Neg Outlook)	Not Rated
5)CIFG	WR	NR	WD
6)FGIC	WR	NR	WD
7)AGM (f. FSA)	Aa3 (Neg Watch)	AA- (Sta Outlook)	WD
8)NATL (f. MBIA)	Baa2 (Neg Outlook)	BBB (Dev Oulook)	Not Rated
9)Radian	Ba1 (Neg Watch)	B+ (Neg Outlook)	WD
10)XLCA (Syncora)	Ca (Dev Outlook)	NR	WD

**PLEASE NOTE: All ratings data has been supplied to Bloomberg by Moody's, S&P and Fitch. Bloomberg does not modify this data from the ratings agencies nor form an opinion regarding their ratings policies.

**Please use RATD <GO> for rating scales and definitions.

**Click on insurer's name for credit profile and rating history.

As of 03/20/2012

in the indenture, and the legal opinion. If the bond is insured, Moody's & Standard Poor's also look at the credit quality of the insurer.[1] Approximately 50 percent of municipal bonds have an A rating, with 10 percent having a triple-A rating. Included in this group are many of the insured bonds and refunded issues. Exhibit 5.1 shows Moody's rating distribution by select sectors and the Bloomberg screens showing the ratings for state and city general obligations and municipal bond insurers.

Moody's, Standard & Poor's, and Fitch also assign quality ratings to sovereign debt. In evaluating a sovereign government bond issue, these rating agencies consider not only economic risk, but also and cross-border risk: risk due to changes in political, social, and economic conditions in countries where the bonds are issued or where the company is incorporated. They also include exchange-rate risk for foreign currency-defaulted bonds (e.g., dollar-denominated or euro-denominated bond). The latter risk relates to the ability of a foreign government to purchase the foreign currency to meet its debt obligations. Exhibit 5.2 shows several select ratings of countries grouped by regions. The ratings are pulled from the Bloomberg CSDR screen.

Probability Intensities from Historical Default Rates

Historical default rates provide bond investors with a perspective for evaluating the default risk of a bond; they are also used as an estimate of a bond's probability of default. Exhibit 5.3 shows three different probabilities for corporate bonds with quality ratings of AAA, AA, A, BBB, BB, B, and CCC: cumulative default rates, unconditional probability rates, and conditional probability rates. Exhibit 5.4 shows similar Moody's cumulative default rates from 1970 to 2005 for municipals, and Exhibit 5.5 shows cumulative default rates for sovereigns. The cumulative probabilities show the default chance through time. The cumulative probabilities shown in the Exhibit 5.3 are the average historical cumulative default rates from 1977 to 2006 as compiled by Moody's. Based on past frequencies, the BBB corporate bonds shown in the table have a 0.18 percent chance of defaulting after 1 year, 0.51 percent chance after 2 years, 1.94 percent chance after 5 years, and 4.64 percent chance after 10 years. The unconditional probabilities are the probabilities of default in a given year as viewed from time zero. The unconditional probability of a bond's defaulting during year t is equal to the difference in the cumulative probability in year t minus the cumulative probability of default in year $t-1$. As shown in the exhibit, the probability of a CCC bond default during year 4 is equal to 7.18 percent (= 46.90 percent - 39.72 percent). Finally, the conditional probability is the probability of default in a given year conditional on no prior defaults. Conditional probabilities of default are known as *probability intensities.* This probability is equal to the unconditional probability of default in time t as a proportion of the bond's probability of survival at the beginning of the period. The probability of survival is equal to 100 minus the cumulative probability. For example, the probability that a CCC bond will survive until the end of year three is 60.28 percent (100 minus its cumulative probability 39.72 percent), and the probability that the CCC bond will default during year 4 conditional on no prior defaults is 11.91 percent (= 7.18 percent/60.28 percent).

EXHIBIT 5.2 Sovereign Ratings as of 4/13/2012—Bloomberg CSDR Screen

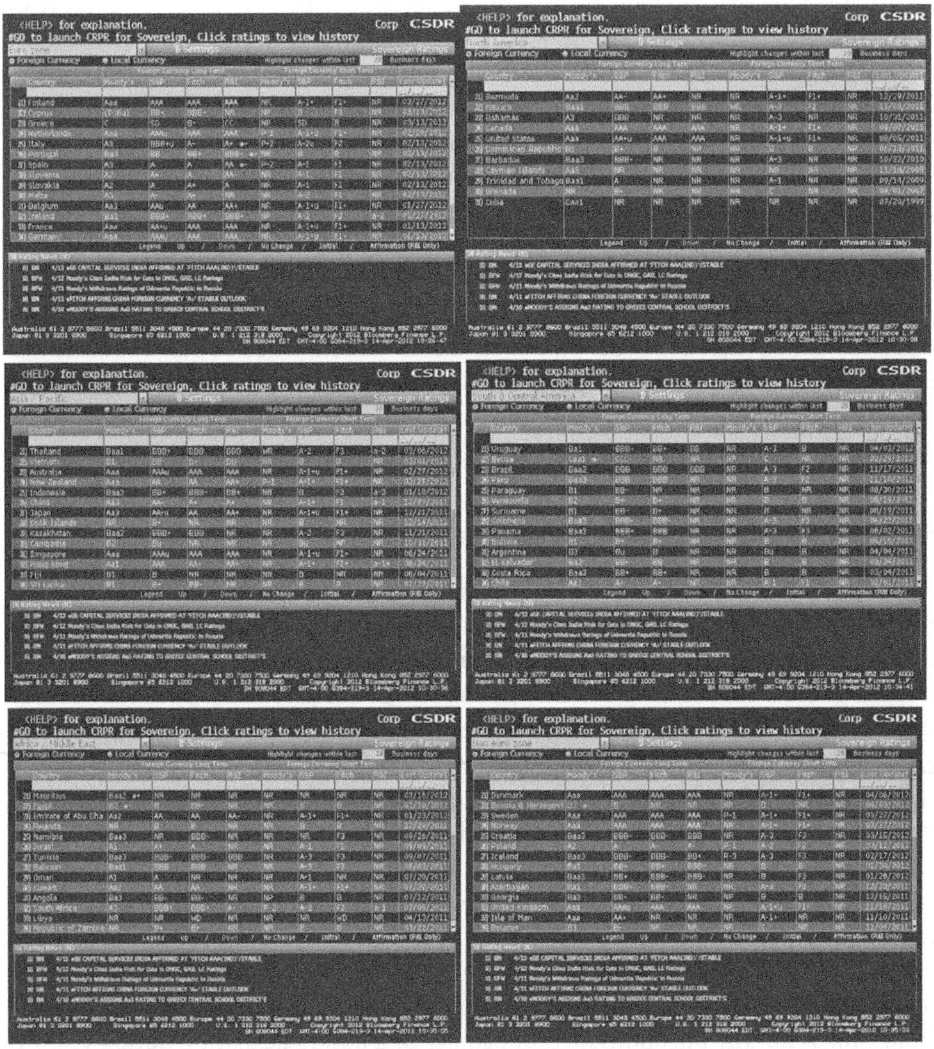

The historical default rates in Exhibit 5.3 show the 10-year cumulative default rate for AAA bonds is only .52 percent, and the average conditional probability of default is .0579 percent. The default rates, in turn, increase the lower the quality rating:

- For BBB-rated bonds, their historical 10-year cumulative probability is 4.64 percent, and their average probability intensity is .50656 percent.
- For B-rated bonds, their 10-year cumulative probability is 43.4 percent, and their average probability intensity is 5.551 percent.
- For CCC-rated bonds, their 10-year cumulative default rate is 69.18 percent, and their average conditional probability of default is 10.093 percent.

EXHIBIT 5.3 Historical Default Rates: 1977 to 2006 Moody's

Year	1	2	3	4	5	6	7	8	9	10
Aaa										
Cumulative Probability (%)	0.00000	0.00000	0.00000	0.03000	0.10000	0.17000	0.25000	0.34000	0.42000	0.52000
Unconditional Probability (%)		0.00000	0.00000	0.03000	0.07000	0.07000	0.08000	0.09000	0.08000	0.10000
Conditional Probability p (%)		0.00000	0.00000	0.03000	0.07002	0.07007	0.08014	0.09023	0.08027	0.10042
AA										
Cumulative Probability (%)	0.01000	0.02000	0.04000	0.11000	0.18000	0.26000	0.34000	0.42000	0.46000	0.52000
Unconditional Probability (%)		0.01000	0.02000	0.07000	0.07000	0.08000	0.08000	0.08000	0.04000	0.06000
Conditional Probability p (%)		0.01000	0.02000	0.07003	0.07008	0.08014	0.08021	0.08027	0.04017	0.06028
A										
Cumulative Probability (%)	0.02000	0.10000	0.22000	0.34000	0.47000	0.61000	0.76000	0.93000	1.11000	1.29000
Unconditional Probability (%)		0.08000	0.12000	0.12000	0.13000	0.14000	0.15000	0.17000	0.18000	0.18000
Conditional Probability p (%)		0.08002	0.12012	0.12026	0.13044	0.14066	0.15092	0.17130	0.18169	0.18202
BBB										
Cumulative Probability (%)	0.18000	0.51000	0.93000	1.43000	1.94000	2.45000	2.96000	3.45000	4.02000	4.64000
Unconditional Probability (%)		0.33000	0.42000	0.50000	0.51000	0.51000	0.51000	0.49000	0.57000	0.62000
Conditional Probability p (%)		0.33060	0.42215	0.50469	0.51740	0.52009	0.52281	0.50495	0.59037	0.64597
BB										
Cumulative Probability (%)	1.21000	3.22000	5.57000	7.96000	10.22000	12.24000	14.01000	15.71000	17.39000	19.12000
Unconditional Probability (%)		2.01000	2.35000	2.39000	2.26000	2.02000	1.77000	1.70000	1.68000	1.73000
Conditional Probability p (%)		2.03462	2.42819	2.53098	2.45545	2.24994	2.01686	1.97597	1.99312	2.09418
B										
Cumulative Probability (%)	5.24000	11.30000	17.04000	22.05000	26.79000	30.98000	34.77000	37.98000	40.92000	43.34000
Unconditional Probability (%)		6.06000	5.74000	5.01000	4.74000	4.19000	3.79000	3.21000	2.94000	2.42000
Conditional Probability p (%)		6.39510	6.47125	6.03905	6.08082	5.72326	5.49116	4.92105	4.74041	4.09614
Caa										
Cumulative Probability (%)	19.48000	30.49000	39.72000	46.90000	52.62000	56.81000	59.94000	63.27000	66.28000	69.18000
Unconditional Probability (%)		11.01000	9.23000	7.18000	5.72000	4.19000	3.13000	3.33000	3.01000	2.90000
Conditional Probability p (%)		13.67362	13.27866	11.91108	10.77213	8.84339	7.24705	8.31253	8.19494	8.60024

EXHIBIT 5.4 Municipal Cumulative Default Rates: 1970 to 2005

Years	1	2	3	4	5	6	7	8	9	10
Aaa	0.00%	0.00%	0.00%	0.00%	0.00%	0.00%	0.00%	0.00%	0.00%	0.00%
Aa	0.03%	0.03%	0.04%	0.04%	0.04%	0.05%	0.05%	0.05%	0.06%	0.06%
A	0.01%	0.01%	0.02%	0.02%	0.02%	0.03%	0.03%	0.03%	0.03%	0.03%
Baa	0.06%	0.07%	0.08%	0.09%	0.10%	0.10%	0.11%	0.12%	0.13%	0.13%
Ba	1.42%	1.56%	1.62%	1.70%	1.78%	1.98%	2.21%	2.41%	2.56%	2.65%
B	5.86%	7.71%	9.32%	10.64%	11.60%	11.86%	11.86%	11.86%	11.86%	11.86%
Caa-C	15.84%	16.58%	16.58%	16.58%	16.58%	16.58%	16.58%	16.58%	16.58%	16.58%
Investment-Grade	0.03%	0.03%	0.04%	0.04%	0.05%	0.05%	0.05%	0.06%	0.06%	0.07%
Speculative-Grade	2.42%	2.80%	3.08%	3.33%	3.54%	3.74%	3.93%	4.09%	4.22%	4.29%
All Municipals	0.05%	0.06%	0.06%	0.07%	0.08%	0.08%	0.09%	0.10%	0.10%	0.10%

Source: Moody's, www.moodys.com

A comparison of these default rates shows there is a high degree of default risk associated with lower-quality bonds.

The most current conditional probabilities can be found on the Bloomberg RATD screen. Bloomberg estimates of conditional probabilities as of January 16, 2012, are shown in Exhibit 5.6.

Default and Recovery Rates

Holders of defaulted bonds usually recover a percentage of their investment—the recovery rate. As a result, the default loss rate from an investment is lower than the default rate:

$$\text{Default Loss Rate} = \text{Default Rate}\,(1 - \text{Recovery Rate})$$

EXHIBIT 5.5 Sovereign Default Rates: Moody's Historical Cumulative Default Rate, 1983 to 2007

Year	1	2	3	4	5	6	7	8	9	10
Aaa	0.00%	0.00%	0.00%	0.00%	0.00%	0.00%	0.00%	0.00%	0.00%	0.00%
Aa	0.00%	0.00%	0.00%	0.00%	0.00%	0.00%	0.00%	0.00%	0.00%	0.00%
A	0.00%	0.52%	1.09%	1.73%	2.44%	3.20%	3.20%	3.20%	3.20%	3.20%
Baa	0.00%	0.52%	1.09%	1.73%	2.44%	3.20%	3.20%	3.20%	3.20%	3.20%
Ba	0.89%	1.95%	3.78%	5.86%	8.13%	9.80%	12.01%	14.49%	16.49%	18.42%
B	2.80%	5.77%	6.90%	8.72%	10.51%	12.68%	14.50%	16.07%	18.08%	20.83%
Caa-C	22.54%	26.79%	32.42%	32.42%	32.42%	32.42%	32.42%	32.42%	32.42%	32.42%
Investment	0.00%	0.11%	0.22%	0.34%	0.48%	0.62%	0.62%	0.62%	0.62%	0.62%
Speculative	2.65%	4.64%	6.36%	8.25%	10.23%	12.01%	13.99%	16.06%	17.97%	20.05%
All	0.78%	1.43%	2.01%	2.63%	3.28%	3.86%	4.39%	4.91%	5.37%	5.82%

Source: Moody's, www.moodys.com

EXHIBIT 5.6 Bloomberg Conditional Probabilities

<HELP> for explanation. N842 EquityBRAV
<Menu> to return
Back Forward Stop Refresh Edit Done: http://bbportal.bloomberg.com/PROMO/docs/Bloc Save Screen as

	Default Likelihood		Default Likelihood			
IG-1	0.0000%	-	0.0005%	HY-1	0.300% -	0.800%
IG-2	0.0005%	-	0.0037%	HY-2	0.800% -	1.200%
IG-3	0.0037%	-	0.0068%	HY-3	1.200% -	1.800%
IG-4	0.0068%	-	0.0100%	HY-4	1.800% -	2.500%
IG-5	0.0100%	-	0.0333%	HY-5	2.500% -	6.000%
IG-6	0.0333%	-	0.0567%	HY-6	6.000% -	12.000%
IG-7	0.0567%	-	0.0800%	DS-1	12.000% -	18.000%
IG-8	0.0800%	-	0.1533%	DS-2	18.000% -	24.000%
IG-9	0.1533%	-	0.2267%	DS-3	24.000% -	30.000%
IG-10	0.2267%	-	0.3000%	DS-4	30.000% -	50.000%
				DS-5	50.000% -	100.000%

Australia 61 2 9777 8600 Brazil 5511 3048 4500 Europe 44 20 7330 7500 Germany 49 69 9204 1210 Hong Kong 852 2977 6000
Japan 81 3 3201 8900 Singapore 65 6212 1000 U.S. 1 212 318 2000 Copyright 2012 Bloomberg Finance L.P.
SN 808044 EDT GMT-4:00 G384-219-2 14-Apr-2012 11:32:26

For example, if the recovery rate from a defaulted bond is estimated to be 30 percent and the bond's default rate is 6 percent, then the default loss rate would be 4.2 percent:

$$\text{Default Loss Rate} = 6 \text{ percent } (1 - .30) = 4.2 \text{ percent}$$

Focusing on just the default rate highlights the worst possible scenario. Moody's, Fitch, and Standard & Poor's have developed *recovery rating scale systems* for secured corporate bonds. These ratings scale system estimate historical recovery rates based on collateral, subordination, debt in the capital structure, and expected value of the issue in distress. The recovery rating scale systems of Standard & Poor's and Fitch are shown in Exhibit 5.7.

Downgrades and Upgrades

Credit risk includes not only the concern over default but also the chance of a bond's rating being downgraded. The downgrade of a bond or the market expectation of a downgrade leads to an increase sale of the bond by its holders and a lower demand by investors, both of which lower the bond's price and increases its credit spread. Exhibit 5.8 shows the recent history of ratings changes for Ford and Kraft.

EXHIBIT 5.7 Recovery Ratings

Standard & Poor's Rating	Prospect	Recovery
1	Highest expectation of full recovery	100% of principal
2	Substantial recovery of principal	80% to 100%
3	Meaningful	50% to 80%
4	Marginal	25% to 50%
5	Negligible	0 to 25%

Fitch Rank	Prospect	Recovery
R1	Outstanding	91% to 100%
R2	Superior	71% to 90%
R3	Good	51% to 70%
R4	Average	31% to 50%
R5	Below average	11% to 30%
R6	Poor recovery	0 to 10%

EXHIBIT 5.8 Ford and Kraft Credit Ratings History—Bloomberg CRPR Screens

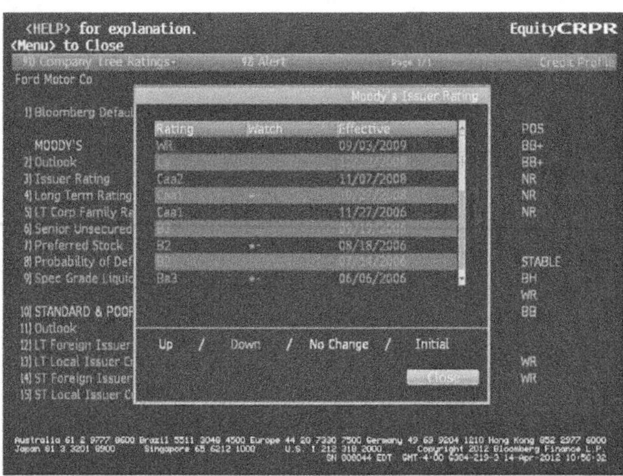

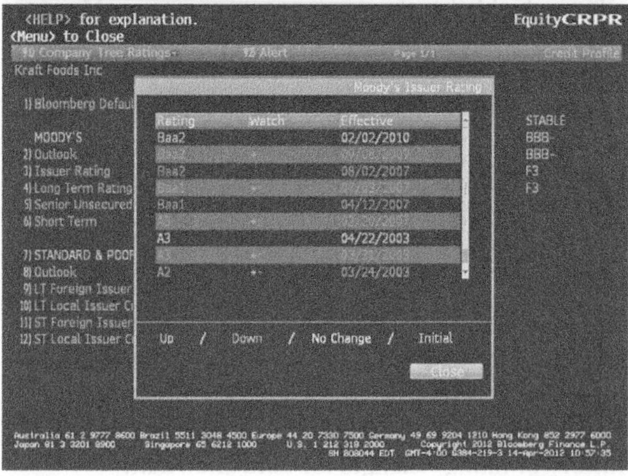

The number of bond downgrades tends to increase (decrease) and the number of upgrades tends to decrease (increase) in slow (expanding) economic periods. This can be seen in Exhibit 5.9, which shows the Bloomberg RATT screens. The screens display the current and historical number of upgrades and downgrades by Moody's and Standard & Poor's. As shown, the ratio of the number of upgrades to downgrades in 2006 and 2007 (prior to the 2008 financial crisis and recession) were near one for Standard & Poor's and exceeding one for Moody's, in 2008 and 2009 the ratios were significantly less, and in 2011 and 2012 were higher.

Credit Risk and Credit Spreads

Because of the default risk on corporate, municipal, and other non-U.S. Treasury bonds, such bonds trade with a default risk premium or credit spread. For corporate bonds, this premium is often measured as the spread between the rates on the credit and a U.S. Treasury security that is the same in all respects except for their default risk—the benchmark spread.

EXHIBIT 5.9 Upgrades and Downgrades, 4/13/2012—Bloomberg RATT Screens

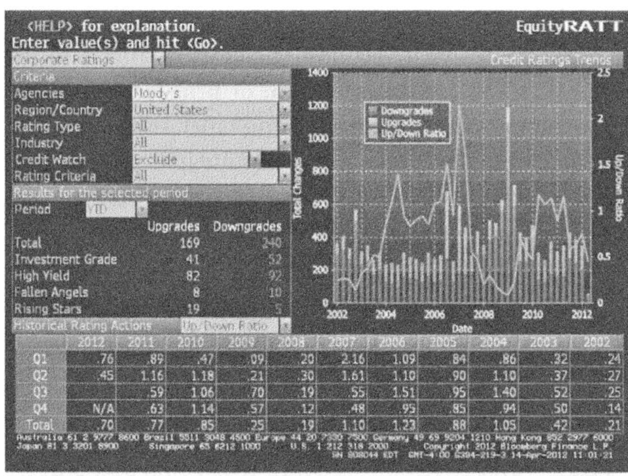

	2012	2011	2010	2009	2008	2007	2006	2005	2004	2003	2002
Q1	.76	.89	.47	.09	.20	2.16	1.09	.84	.86	.32	.24
Q2	.45	1.16	1.18	.21	.30	1.61	1.10	.90	1.10	.37	.27
Q3		.59	1.06	.70	.19	.55	1.51	.95	1.40	.52	.25
Q4	N/A	.63	1.14	.57	.12	.48	.95	.85	.94	.50	.14
Total	.70	.77	.85	.25	.19	1.10	1.23	.88	1.05	.42	.21

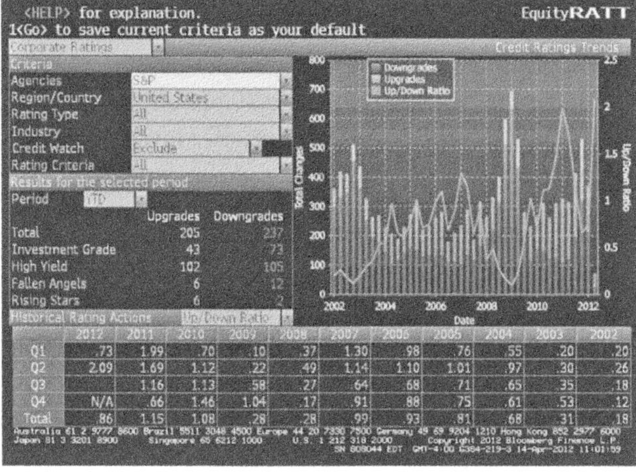

	2012	2011	2010	2009	2008	2007	2006	2005	2004	2003	2002
Q1	.73	1.99	.70	.10	.37	1.30	.98	.76	.55	.20	.20
Q2	2.09	1.69	1.12	.22	.49	1.14	1.10	1.01	.97	.30	.26
Q3		1.16	1.13	.58	.27	.64	.68	.71	.65	.35	.18
Q4	N/A	.66	1.46	1.04	.17	.91	.88	.75	.61	.53	.12
Total	.86	1.15	1.08	.28	.28	.99	.93	.81	.68	.31	.18

For tax-exempt bonds, the benchmark for calculating spreads is not Treasuries, but instead a generic AAA general obligation bond with a comparable maturity.

A credit spread on a bond can be thought of as bond investors' expected loss from the principal resulting from default. To see this, consider a portfolio of five-year BBB bonds trading at a 2 percent credit spread. The 2 percent premium that investors receive from the bond portfolio represents their compensation for an implied expected loss of 2 percent per year of the principal from the defaulted bonds. If the spread were 2 percent and bond investors believed that the expected loss from default on such bonds would be only 1 percent per year of the principal, then bond investors would want more BBB bonds, driving BBB bond prices up and the yields down until the premium reflected a 1 percent spread. However, if the spread were 2 percent and bond investors believed the default loss on a portfolio of BBB bonds would be 3 percent per year, then the demand and price for such bonds would decrease, increasing the yield to reflect a credit spread of 3 percent. Thus, in an efficient market, the credit spreads on bonds represent the market's implied expectation of their expected loss per year from the principal from default.

Over a period of time, probabilities of default and associated spreads will change, increasing or decreasing depending on the quality of the credit. Usually, adverse economic conditions result in greater default probabilities and credit spreads. For corporate issues, such developments could be aggregate economic factors such as a recession, industry factors like declining sales due to competition, or firm factors related to a company's investment or financing decisions.[2] For municipal issues, adverse economic developments include declining property values, municipal government deficits, increasing regional unemployment, or increased use of debt reserves. Like corporate bonds, the spreads between municipals with different quality ratings tend to narrow during economic upturns and widen during economic downturns, reflecting a flight to quality. In addition to quality spreads, there are also geographical spreads, reflecting differences in state income taxes and perhaps some parochialism. The yields on in-state issues from states with high income taxes tend to be lower than the yields from those states with low or no state income taxes.

Over the past two decades, the spread between high-yield, non-investment-grade bonds and Treasuries has ranged from 150 basis points (bps) to over 1,000 bps, reflecting economic conditions and default probabilities (see Exhibit 5.10). More recently, during the economic growth period from 2002 to 2006, credit spreads were narrow, with many high-quality (AAA or AA) bonds trading only 20 to 30 bps off the Treasury yields and with many BBB bonds trading only 150 to 200 bps off. However, during the 2008 financial crisis, spreads widened significantly. Many of the corporate credits experiencing significant widening were financials. Moreover, with the uncertainty regarding the financial bailout policies of the Treasury and the Federal Reserve, many financial credits experienced significant fluctuations in their spreads. For example, in September 2008, just after the collapse of Washington Mutual and before the announcement by the Treasury of its takeover by Wells Fargo, Wachovia Bank, which was deep in subprime mortgage holdings, had it bonds trading with 15 percent to 25 percent spreads. After Wachovia was acquired, their bonds were trading with a 6 percent to 8 percent spread as a Wells Fargo bond.

A Note on Liquidity Risk and Credit Risk

Liquidity risk is the possibility that market trading conditions will change, making a security harder to trade and, in turn, causing the security's price to decrease and its yield to increase. Occasionally in recessionary periods when credit is tight, some higher-quality bonds can become more difficult to trade if the overall demand for bonds decreases or if investors begin holding such bonds longer. This decrease in liquidity will cause a widening in the bond's spread over Treasury yields. It is important for bond investors to be able to differentiate between bonds whose spreads increase due to credit conditions and those that increase due to liquidity conditions, that is, to differentiate between liquidity risk and credit risk.

EXHIBIT 5.10 High-Yield Spreads

Year	High-Yield YTM (%)	Treasury YTM (%)	Spread
2005	7.98	3.94	4.04
2004	7.35	4.21	3.14
2003	8.00	4.26	3.74
2002	12.38	3.82	8.56
2001	12.31	5.04	7.27
2000	14.56	5.12	9.44
1999	11.41	6.44	4.97
1998	10.04	4.65	5.39
1997	9.20	5.75	3.45
1996	9.58	6.42	3.16
1995	9.76	5.58	4.18
1994	11.50	7.83	3.67
1993	9.08	5.80	3.28
1992	10.44	6.69	3.75
1991	12.56	6.70	5.86
1990	18.57	8.07	10.50
1989	15.17	7.93	7.24
1988	13.70	9.15	4.55
1987	13.89	8.83	5.06
1986	12.67	7.21	5.46
1985	13.50	8.99	4.51
Average	11.60	6.31	5.30
Standard Deviation	2.78	1.70	2.14

Source: Edward Altman, et al. "High Yield Bond and Distressed Debt Default and Returns." NYU, Stern School of Business.

BLOOMBERG CREDIT RISK AND SPREAD SCREENS

RATD: The Bloomberg RATD screen displays links to Moody's, Standard & Poor's, Fitch, and other rating agency portals. Clicking RATD on the screen bring up Bloomberg's estimated probability intensities (see Exhibit 5.6).

BRAV: The Bloomberg BRAV screen describes the methodologies used in the Bloomberg Default Risk (DRSK) and Company Equity Valuation (CVAL) functions. From the BRAV screen, you can access Bloomberg's proprietary default risk rating scale. The scale shows default probabilities ranging for investment grades ranging from IG-1 to IG-10 and for non-investment grades from HY-1 to HY-6: BRAV <Enter>, Click: "Proprietary Default Risk Scale." See Exhibit 5.6.

CRPR: The CRPR screen displays ratings and history of ratings changes by ratings companies (see Exhibit 5.8).

RATT: The RATT screen displays current and historical numbers of upgrades and downgrades by ratings companies (see Exhibit 5.9).

DRSK: The DRSK screen analyzes the credit of a company

DRAM: The DRAM screen allows one to analyze a group of securities or portfolios in terms of their default risk, CDS spread, and a Bloomberg credit risk score.

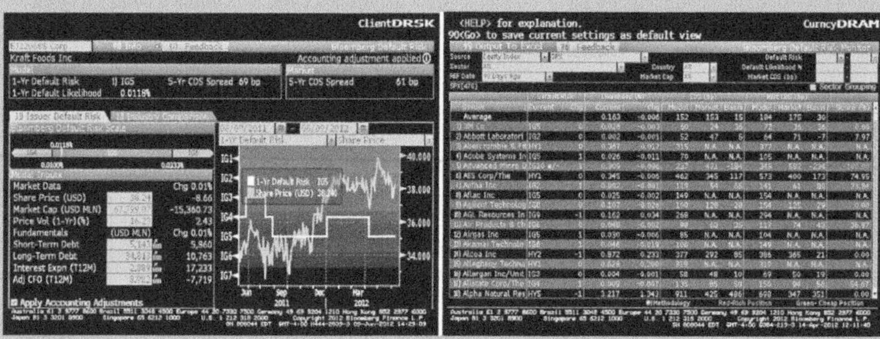

COMB: The comparative bond analysis (COMB) screen displays a list of the selected bond's comparable bonds and their features, including spreads to benchmark, Z-spread, and credit default swap (CDS) spread.

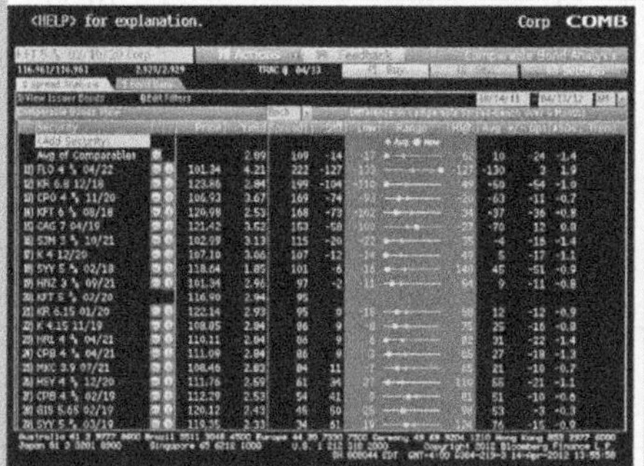

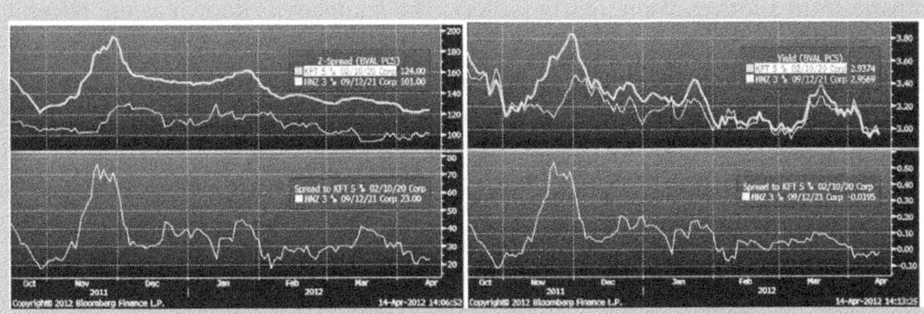

SGY and HSN screens show differences in the yields of two selected bonds.
RATC: The RATC screen shows ratings revisions.

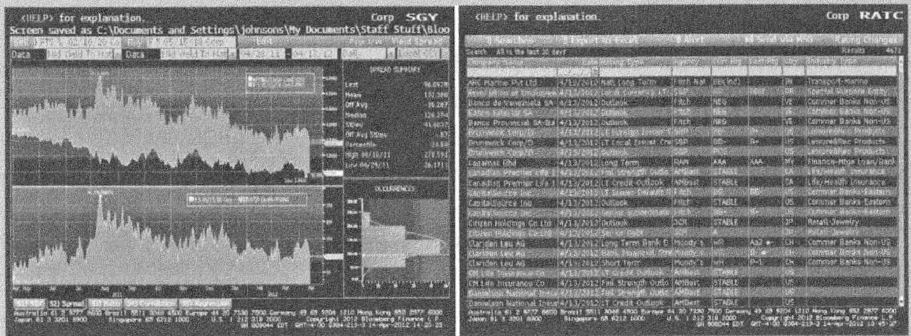

YA (Yield & Spread tab) or YAS screen displays for a selected bond its market data, pricing information, interpolated spreads to benchmark curves, and descriptive, fundamental, and ratings data and information. The screen can also be used to price a fixed income security using spreads to a benchmark issue/benchmark curve.
GOVI: The GOVI screen displays a matrix of yield spread information for sovereign debt of a selected tenor.
CRVF: The CRVF screen displays yield curve spreads for different sovereigns, sectors, and regions
GY: The GY screen shows the selected bond's historical prices, YTM, spreads over the benchmark, CDS basis, and Z-spreads. Similar information is found from the GP screen.
GIP and GIY: The GIP and GIY screens show intraday prices and yields.
TDH: The TDH screen displays trade history of prices and spreads. You can adjust the time periods and size of trade.

Credit Default Swaps and Spreads

The relationship between credit risk, credit spreads, and the probability of default are also related to the price of credit default swaps. In a standard *credit default swap* (*CDS*), a counterparty such as a bank buys protection against default by a particular company from another counterparty (seller). The company is known as the reference entity, and a default by that company is known as a credit event. The buyer of the CDS makes periodic payments or a premium to the seller until the end of the life of the CDS or until the credit event occurs. If the credit event occurs, the buyer, depending on the contract, has either the right to sell a particular bond (or loan) issued by the company for its par value (physical delivery) or receive a cash settlement based on the difference between the par value and the defaulted bond's market price times a notional principal equal to the bond's total par value.

To illustrate, suppose two parties enter into a five-year CDS with a notional principal (NP) of $100 million. The buyer agrees to pay 100 bps annually for protection against default by the reference entity. If the reference entity does not default, the buyer does not receive a payoff and ends up paying $1 million each year for five years. If a credit event does occur, the buyer will receive the default payment and pay a final accrual payment on the unpaid premium; for example, if the event occurs halfway through the year, then the buyer pays the seller $500,000. If the swap contract calls for physical delivery, the buyer will sell $100 million par value of the defaulted bonds for $100 million. If there is a cash settlement, then an agent will poll dealers to determine a mid-market value. If that value were $30 per $100 face value, then the buyer would receive $70 million minus the $500,000 accrued interest payment.

In the standard CDS, payments are usually made in arrears either on a quarter, semiannual, or annual basis. The par value of the bond or debt is the notional principal used for determining the payments of the buyer. In many CDS contracts, a number of bonds or credits can be delivered in the case of a default. A company like Kraft, for example, might have five bonds with similar maturities, coupons, and embedded option and protection features that a buyer of a CDS can select in the event of a default. In the event of a default, the payoff from the CDS is equal to the face value of the bond (or NP) minus the value of the bond just after the default. The payments on a CDS are quoted as an annual percentage of the NP. The payment is referred to as the *CDS spread.*

CDSs are primarily used to manage the credit risk on debt and fixed-income positions. For example, a bond fund manager who just purchased a five-year BBB corporate bond at a price yielding 8 percent and wanted to eliminate the credit risk on the bond might buy a five-year CDS on the bond. If the payments or spread on the CDS were equal to 3 percent of the bond's principal, then the purchase of the CDS would have the effect of making the 8 percent BBB bond a default risk-free bond yielding approximately 5 percent.

In equilibrium, the payment or spread on a CDS should be approximately equal to the credit spread on the CDS's underlying bond or credit. In terms of the above example, if the only risk on a five-year BBB corporate bond yielding 8 percent were credit risk (i.e., there is no option risk associated with embedded call options and the like and no interest rate risk), and the risk-free rate on five-year investments were 5 percent, then the BBB bond would be trading in the market with a 3 percent credit spread. If the spread on a five-year CDS on a BBB quality bond or credit were 3 percent, then an investor could obtain a five-year risk-free investment yielding 5 percent by either buying a five-year Treasury or by buying the five-year BBB corporate yielding 8 percent and purchasing the CDS on the underlying credit at a 3 percent spread. If the spread on a CDS is not equal to the credit spread on the underlying bond, then an arbitrage opportunity would exist by taking positions in the bond, risk-free security, and the CDS. For example, suppose a swap bank were offering the above CDS for 2 percent instead of 3 percent. In this case, an investor looking for a five-year risk-free investment would find it advantageous to create the synthetic risk-free investment with the BBB bond and the CDS. That is, the investor could earn 1 percent more than the yield on the Treasury by buying the five-year BBB corporate yielding 8 percent and purchasing the CDS on the underlying credit at 2 percent. In addition to the investor gaining, an arbitrageur could also realize a free lunch equivalent to a five-year cash flow of 1 percent of the par value of the bond by shorting the Treasury at 5 percent and then using the proceeds to buy the BBB corporate and the CDS. Such arbitrage strategies might take the form of a collateral debt obligation (CDO; discussed in Chapter 9), where a financial company issues a high-quality CDO with the proceeds used to purchase lower quality bonds and CDS. The actions by investors and arbitrageurs, in turn, would have the impact of pushing the spread on the CDS towards 3 percent—the underlying bond's credit risk spread.[3]

In equilibrium, arbitrageurs and investors should ensure that the spreads on CDS are approximately equal to spreads on the underlying bond or credit. This spread can be defined as the equilibrium spread or the *arbitrage-free spread.* The arbitrage-free spread, Z, on a bond or CDS can also be thought of as the bond investor's or CDS buyer's expected loss from the principal from default. That is, the 3 percent premium on the CDS on the five-year BBB bonds should not only be equal to the 3 percent credit spread on the bond, but also a probability of loss principal of 3 percent from a default. Thus, in an efficient market, the credit spread on bonds and the equilibrium spreads on CDS represent the market's implied expectation of the expected loss per year from the principal from default. In the case of a CDS, the equilibrium spread can therefore be defined as the implied probability of default loss of the principal on the contract. Given an equilibrium spread of .02 and a recovery rate of 30 percent, the implied probability density for our illustrative CDS would be .02857. This implied probability is obtained by solving for the probability, $\bar{p}$, that makes the present value of the expected payout equal to present value of the payments:

$$
\begin{aligned}
PV(\text{Expected Payout}) &= PV(\text{Payments}) \\
\sum_{t=1}^{M} \frac{\bar{p}\, NP(1-RR)}{(1+R)^t} &= \sum_{t=1}^{M} \frac{Z\, NP}{(1+R)^t} \\
\bar{p} &= \frac{Z}{(1-RR)} \\
\bar{p} &= \frac{.02}{(1-.30)} = .02857
\end{aligned}
$$

EXHIBIT 5.11 CDS Spreads—DRSK and SOVR

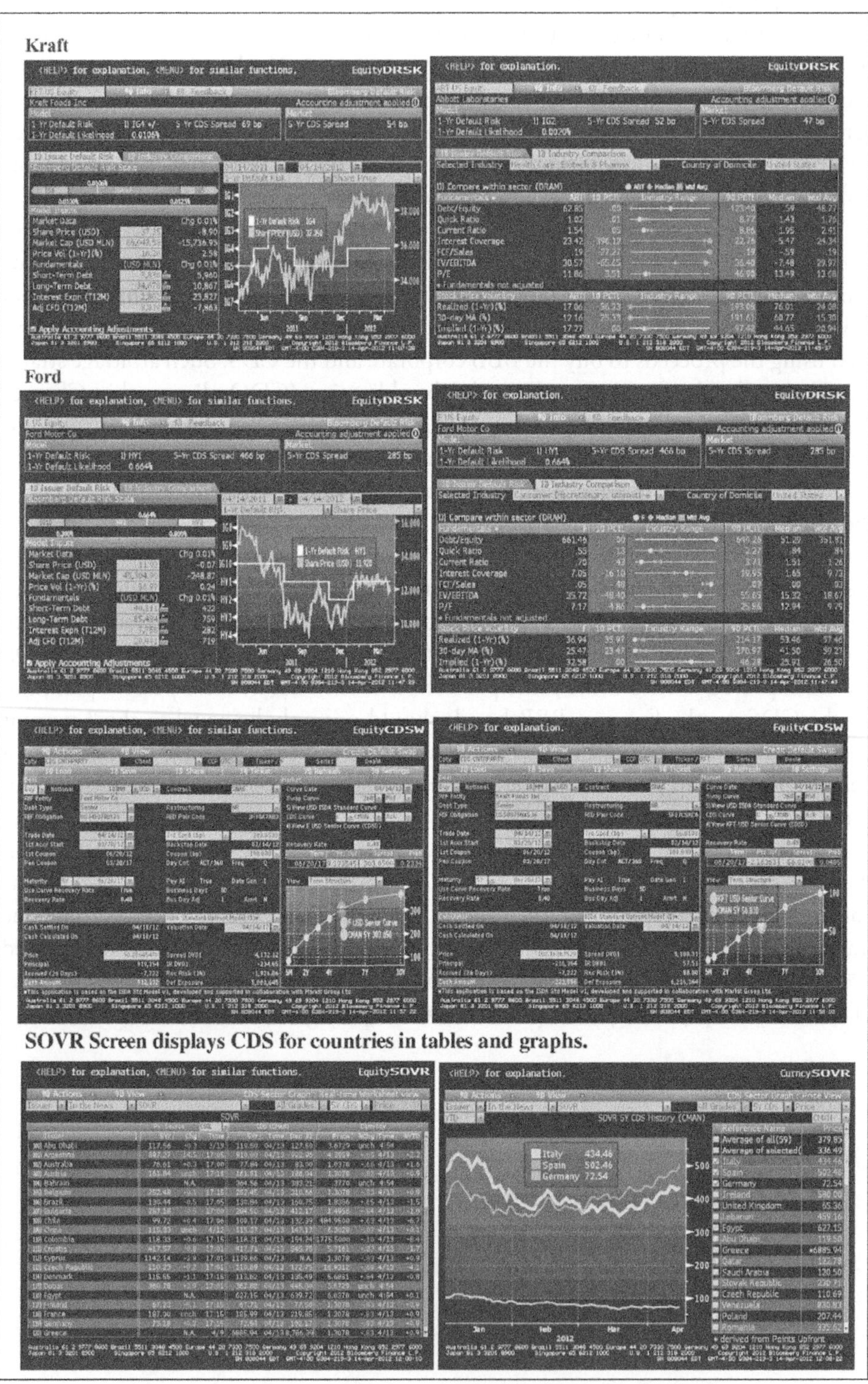
Kraft
Ford
SOVR Screen displays CDS for countries in tables and graphs.

In theory, the spread payments on a CDS are equal to the credit spread on a bond and the probability of default. As such, many analysts use CDS to assess the credit risk of a company and as an estimate of a bond's credit spread. Exhibit 5.11 shows the Bloomberg DRSK screens for Ford and Kraft showing their five-year CDS and implied probabilities and the Bloomberg SOVR screen showing CDS for select countries.

Call Risk

Call risk relates to the possibility that the issuer will call the bond. A call feature on a bond gives the issuer the right to buy back the bond before maturity at a stated price, known as the call price. As discussed in Chapter 3, the call price is sometimes set a certain percentage above the bond's par value, say 110 ($1,100, given a par value of $1,000); for some bonds the call price may decrease over time (e.g., a 20-year bond's call price decreasing each year by 5 percent). Some callable bonds can be called at any time, whereas for others the call is deferred for a certain period, giving the investor protection during the deferment period. Also, some bonds, as part of their sinking fund arrangements, are retired over the life of the bond, usually with the issuer having the choice of purchasing the bonds directly at market prices or calling the bonds at a specified call price.

A call provision is advantageous to the issuer. If interest rates in the market decline, an issuer can lower his interest costs by selling a new issue at a lower interest rate, then use the loan proceeds to call the outstanding issue. What is to the advantage of the issuer, though, is to the disadvantage of the investor. When a bond is called, the investor's realized rate of return is affected in two ways. First, since the call price is typically above the bond's face value, the actual rate of return the investor earns for the period from the purchase of the bond to its call generally is greater than the yield on the bond at the time it was purchased. However, if an investor originally bought the bond because its maturity matched her horizon date, then she will be faced with the disadvantage of reinvesting the call proceeds at lower market rates. Moreover, this second effect, known as reinvestment risk, often dominates the first effect, resulting in a rate of return over the investor's horizon period that is lower than the promised YTM when the bond was bought.

Example

To illustrate the nature of call risk, consider the case of an investor with a 10-year horizon who purchases a 10-year, 10 percent coupon bond at its par value of $1,000, with coupon payments paid annually and with the bond callable at a call price (CP) of $1,100. In addition, suppose the reinvestment rate is 10 percent and that it remains that way for the first three years the investor holds the bond. At the end of year three, however, assume interest rates decrease across all maturities to 8 percent and the issuer calls the bond. The investor's total return (TR) for the three-year period would be 12.69 percent. Specifically, at the end of year three the investor's cash value would be \$1,431. This would include the \$1,100 call price, \$300 in coupons, and \$31 in interest earned from investing the coupons, yielding a total return of 12.69 percent:

Year	1	2	3	CF	Values
	\$100			$\$100(1.10)^2$	\$121
		\$100		\$100(1.10)	\$110
			\$100	\$100	\$100
			\$1,100	\$1,100	\$1,100
				Call Date Value	\$1,431

$$TR_3 = \left[\frac{\$1,431}{\$1,000}\right]^{1/3} - 1 = .1269$$

Thus, for the call period, the investor earns a rate of return greater than the initial YTM. However, with a 10-year horizon, the investor must reinvest the \$1,431 cash for seven more years at the lower market rate. If we assume she reinvests all coupons to the horizon date at 8 percent, then the \$1,431 will grow at an 8 percent annual rate to equal \$2,452.48 (= $\$1,431(1.08)^7$) at the end of the tenth year, yielding a total return for the 10-year period of 9.386 percent:

$$TR_{10} = \left[\frac{\$2,452.48}{\$1,000}\right]^{1/10} - 1 = .09386$$

Note that the 9.386 percent rate is also equal to the geometric average of the 12.69 percent annual rate earned for the three years and the 8 percent annual rate earned for seven years:

$$TR_{10} = \left[(1.1269)^3(1.08)^7\right]^{1/10} - 1 = .09386$$

With the total return of 9.386 percent less than the initial YTM of 10 percent, the second effect of reinvesting in a market with lower rates dominates the first effect of a call price greater than the bond's face value.

Call Risk Spread

The example shows that bonds that are callable are subject to the possibility that the actual rate will be less than the investor's expected YTM. Because of this call risk, there is usually a lower market demand and price for callable bonds than noncallable bonds, resulting in a higher rate of return or interest premium on callable over option-free bonds. The size of this call risk spread, in turn, depends on investors' and borrowers' expectations concerning interest rates. When interest rates are high and expected to fall, bonds are more likely to be called; thus, in a period of high interest rates, a relatively lower demand and higher rate on callable over option-free bonds would occur. In contrast, when interest rates are low and expected to rise, we expect the effect of call provisions on interest rates to be negligible.

When valuing a callable bond or trying to estimate its spread, one needs to take into account the possibility that interest rates could decrease, leading to the bond being called. If called, the bond's cash flow patterns would be different than if rates increased and the bond was not called. Given the uncertainty of the bond's cash flows, valuing callable bonds and other bonds with embedded option features or determining their option spread is more difficult than valuing option-free bonds. One approach to valuing bonds with embedded options and estimating their spreads is to incorporate interest rate volatility by using a binomial interest rate tree, such as the Black-Derman-Toy model. This model is one of the models that can be selected on the Bloomberg OAS1 screen to estimate a bond's call, sinking fund call, or puts option spreads; the model is presented in Chapter 13.

Another approach is to estimate the value of the call, sinking fund call, or put feature using an option-pricing model. Conceptually, when an investor buys a callable bond, she implicitly sells a call option to the bond issuer, giving the issuer the right to buy the bond from the bondholder at a specified price before maturity. Theoretically, the price of a callable bond should therefore be equal to the price of an identical, option-free bond minus the value of the call feature or call premium. In contrast, when an investor buys a putable bond, she implicitly buys a put option from the bond issuer, giving the investor the right to sell the bond back to the issuer at a specified price before maturity. Theoretically, the price of a putable bond should be equal to the price of an identical option-free bond plus the value of the put feature or put premium. The values of call and put features can be estimated using the option-pricing model developed by Black and Scholes. The Black Futures model, a model similar to the Black-Scholes model, is another model that can be selected on the Bloomberg OAS1 screen to estimate a bond's call, sinking fund call, or put option spreads.

Option-Adjusted Spread Analysis

Option-adjusted spread (OAS) analysis is a method for estimating the additional spread required to compensate investors or issuers for the call risk or put risk they are assuming. The aforementioned Black-Derman-Toy model and the Black-Scholes and Black Futures models can be used to determine the likelihood of a bond being called and the bond's value, yield, and OAS given an estimated volatility in interest rates. The Bloomberg OAS1 screen allows the user to select the option model and volatility. The screen then shows the calculated OAS and also the spread of the bond if there were no embedded options—the *option-free spread.* The spread due to embedded options can be estimated by subtracting the option-free spread from the total spread.

Example

Exhibit 5.12 shows the Bloomberg YA screen for the 7.5 percent callable Ford bond with a maturity of 8/20/2032 analyzed in Chapter 3. As shown in the exhibit, on April 13, 2012 the bond was priced at 98.758 per $100 face value to yield 7.692811 percent. The YA screen also shows a comparable Treasury that pays a 3.125 percent coupon, matures on November 15, 2032 , and is priced to yield 3.123284 percent. Using this Treasury as the benchmark, the spread on the Ford bond over the Treasury is 456.95 basis points. For analysts, the challenge is to determine how much of the spread is due to credit risk, liquidity risk, and embedded option risk. The second screen in Exhibit 5.12 is the Bloomberg OAS1 screen.

EXHIBIT 5.12 Bloomberg YAS Screen and OAS1 Screens for Ford Credit Bond: Coupon = 7.5 percent, Maturity = 8/20/2032; Date = 4/13/2012

As noted, this screen allows the user to select an option model and volatility. The screen then shows the calculated OAS and also the spread of the bond if there were no embedded options—the option-free spread. The spread due to the embedded option can be estimated by subtracting the option-free spread from the total spread. The OAS1 screen for the Ford bond on April 13, 2012 shows an option-free spread of 406.3 basis points using the Black-Derman-Toy model. Given the total spread of 459.95 bps, Ford's estimated call spread is 50.65 bps. Thus, the total spread of 456.95 bps consists of a call risk spread of 50.65 bps and a credit and liquidity risk spread of 406.30 bps.

Interest Rate Risk

Interest rate risk or bond market risk is the possibility that interest rates in the market will change, causing the actual rate of return earned on the bond to differ from the expected return. A change in interest rates has two effects on a bond's return. First, interest rate changes affect the price of a bond. If the investor's horizon date (HD) is different from the bond's maturity date, then the investor will be uncertain about the price he will receive from selling the bond (if HD < M), or the price he will have to pay for a new bond (if HD > M). Second, interest rate changes affect the return the investor expects from reinvesting the coupon.

Interest Rate Risk Example 1

To illustrate market risk, consider the case of an investor with a horizon of 3.5 years who buys a 10-year, 10 percent annual coupon bond at its par value of $1,000 to yield 10 percent. If the yield curve were initially flat at 10 percent and if there were no changes in the yield curve in the ensuing years, then the investor would realize a rate of return (as measured by her TR) of 10 percent (see Exhibit 5.13). That is, with no change in the flat yield curve, the investor would be able to reinvest each of her coupons at a rate of 10 percent, yielding a coupon value of $347.16 at year 3.5. The $347.16 coupon value consists of $300 in coupons and $47.16 in interest earned from reinvesting the coupon; that is, interest on interest of $47.16:

$$\text{Coupon Value} = \$100(1.10)^{2.5} + \$100(1.10)^{1.5} + \$100(1.10)^{.5} = \$347.16$$

$$\text{Interest on Interest} = \text{Coupon Value} - \text{Coupon} = \$347.16 - \$300 = \$47.16$$

In addition, with no change in the flat yield curve, the investor would be able to sell the original 10-year bond (now with a maturity of 6.5 years) for $1,048.81 at the end of 3.5 years.[4] Note, since this bond is being sold at a non-coupon date, its price is determined by discounting the value of the bond at the next coupon date (year 4) when the bond has six years left to maturity (P_4) plus the $100 coupon received on that date back .5 years to the HD. That is:

$$P_4 = \sum_{t=1}^{6} \frac{\$100}{(1.10)^t} + \frac{\$1{,}000}{(1.10)^{10}} = \$1{,}000$$

$$P_{3.5} = \frac{\$1{,}000 \ + \ \$100}{(1.10)^{.5}} = \$1{,}048.81$$

Combined, the selling price of $1,048.81 and the coupon value of $347.16 yield an HD value of $1,395.97, which equates to a total return of 10 percent for the 3.5 years. This is the same rate as the initial YTM:

$$\$1{,}000 = \frac{\$1{,}395.97}{(1+TR)^{3.5}}$$

$$TR = \left[\frac{\$1{,}395.97}{\$1{,}000}\right]^{1/3.5} - 1 = .10$$

As we first discussed in Chapter 3, the TR will equal the initial YTM if the yield curve is flat and remains that way to the horizon. However, suppose that shortly after the investor purchased the bond the flat 10 percent yield curve shifted up to 12 percent and then remained there for the 3.5 years. As shown in Exhibit 5.13, at her HD the investor would be able to sell the bond for only $961.70, resulting in a capital loss of $38.30. This loss would be partly offset, though, by the gains realized from reinvesting the coupons at 12 percent. Combined, the investor's HD value would be $1,318.81— $77.16 less than the HD value of $1,395.97 realized if rates had remained constant at 10 percent. As shown in the exhibit, the TR would be only 8.23 percent. In contrast, if the yield curve had shifted down from 10 percent to 8 percent and remained there, then the investor would have gained on the sale of the bond (selling it at a price of $1,147.44) but would have earned less interest from reinvesting the coupons. In this case, the HD value increases to $1,484.82 to yield a TR of 11.96 percent (see Exhibit 5.13).

In these examples, note that interest rate changes have two opposite effects on the total return. First, there is a direct interest-on-interest effect in which an interest rate increase (decrease) causes the interest earned from reinvesting coupons to be greater (less), augmenting (decreasing) the TR. Second, there is a negative price effect, in which an interest rate increase (decrease) lowers (increases) the price of the bond, causing the TR to decrease (increase). Whether the TR varies directly or inversely with interest rate changes depends on which effect dominates. If the price effect dominates, as in this example, then the TR will vary inversely with interest rates. If the interest-

EXHIBIT 5.13 Total Returns for 10-Year, 10 Percent Coupon Bond: HD 3.5 Years, Evaluated at Rates of 10 Percent, 12 Percent, and 8 Percent

Yr	0	1	2	3	3.5	CF at 10%	CF at 12%	CF at 8%
		$100				$\$100(1.10)^{2.5}$	$\$100(1.12)^{2.5}$	$\$100(1.08)^{2.5}$
			$100			$\$100(1.10)^{1.5}$	$\$100(1.12)^{1.5}$	$\$100(1.08)^{1.5}$
				$100		$\$100(1.10)^{.5}$	$\$100(1.12)^{.5}$	$\$100(1.08)^{.5}$
					$P_{3.5}$	$1,048.81	$961.70	$1,147.44
P = $1,000					HD Value	$1,395.97	$1,318.81	$1,484.82
					TR 3.5 yrs	.10	.0823	.1196

$$P_{3.5}^B = \frac{1,000+100}{(1.10)^{.5}} = 1,048.81$$

$$P_4^B = \sum_{t=1}^{6} \frac{100}{(1.10)^t} + \frac{1,000}{(1.10)^6} = 1,000$$

$$TR_{3.5} = \left[\frac{1,395.97}{1,000}\right]^{1/3.5} - 1 = .10$$

$$P_{3.5}^B = \frac{917.77+100}{(1.12)^{.5}} = 961.70$$

$$P_4^B = \sum_{t=1}^{6} \frac{100}{(1.12)^t} + \frac{1,000}{(1.12)^6} = 917.77$$

$$TR_{3.5} = \left[\frac{1,318.81}{1,000}\right]^{1/3.5} - 1 = .0823$$

$$P_{3.5}^B = \frac{1,092.46-100}{(1.08)^{.5}} = 1,147.44$$

$$P_4^B = \sum_{t=1}^{6} \frac{100}{(1.08)^t} + \frac{1,000}{(1.08)^6} = 1,092.46$$

$$TR_{3.5} = \left[\frac{1,484.82}{1,000}\right]^{1/3.5} - 1 = .1196$$

on-interest effect dominates, though, the TR will vary directly with the interest rate changes. For example, suppose our investor had purchased a four-year, 20 percent annual coupon bond when the yield curve was flat at 10 percent (price of \$1,317). As shown in Exhibit 5.14, when the yield curve shifts up to 12 percent shortly after the purchase and remains there, then the investor realizes a TR of 10.16 percent. In this case, the additional interest earned from reinvesting coupons slightly offsets the capital loss. When the yield curve shifts down to 8 percent, though, the investor realizes a lower TR of 9.845 percent (see Exhibit 5.14). With an HD of 3.5 years, the 4-year, 20 percent bond has an interest-on-interest effect that slightly dominates the price effect, resulting in the direct relationship between the TR and interest rate changes.

Finally, it is possible to select a bond in which the two effects exactly offset each other. When this occurs, the TR will not change as rates change, and the investor will not be subject to interest rate risk. For example, suppose our investor had purchased a four-year, 9 percent annual coupon for \$968.30 to yield 10 percent. As shown in Exhibit 5.15, when the flat yield curve shifts to 12 percent, 8 percent, or any other rate, the TR remains at 10 percent. To reiterate, what is occurring in this case is that we have a bond with price and interest-on-interest effects that are of the same magnitude in absolute value; thus, when rates change the two effects cancel each other out.

Duration and Bond Immunization

The last example illustrates how an investor with an HD = 3.5 years can apparently eliminate market risk by buying a 4-year, 9 percent annual coupon bond. Note, the investor can do this by buying a bond that pays a coupon and has a maturity different than her HD (i.e., it is not a zero-coupon bond with a maturity equal to her HD). What is distinctive about this 4-year, 9 percent coupon bond is that it has a duration equal to 3.5 years—the same as the HD. A bond's *duration* (*D*) can be defined as the weighted average of the bond's time periods, with the weights being each time period's relative present value of its cash flow:

$$D = \sum_{t=1}^{N} t \frac{PV(CF_t)}{P_0^b} \tag{5.1}$$

In our example, the duration of a 4-year, 9 percent annual coupon bond is 3.5 years, given a flat yield curve at 10 percent (see Exhibit 5.16). It should be noted that duration also extends to a portfolio of bonds. The duration of a bond portfolio, D_p, is simply the weighted average of each of the bond's durations (D_i), with the weights being the proportion of investment funds allocated to each bond (w_i):

$$D_p = \sum_{i=1} w_i D_i \tag{5.2}$$

Thus, instead of selecting a specific bond with a desired duration, an investor could determine the allocations (w_i) for each bond in his portfolio that would yield the desired portfolio duration.

EXHIBIT 5.14 Total Returns for 4-Year, 20 percent Coupon Bond: HD 3.5 Years, Evaluated at Rates of 12 percent and 8 percent

Yr	0	1	2	3	3.5	CF at 12%	CF at 8%
		$200				$200(1.12)^{2.5}$	$200(1.08)^{2.5}$
			$200			$200(1.12)^{1.5}$	$200(1.08)^{1.5}$
				$200		$200(1.12)^{.5}$	$200(1.08)^{.5}$
					$P_{3.5}$	$1,133.89	$1,154.70
P = $1,317					HD Value	$1,848.12	$1,829.45
					TR 3.5 yrs	.1016	.09845

$$P_0^b = \sum_{t=1}^{4} \frac{200}{(1.10)^t} + \frac{1,000}{(1.10)^4} = 1,317$$

$$P_{3.5}^B = \frac{1,000+200}{(1.12)^{.5}} = 1,133.89$$

$$TR_{3.5} = \left[\frac{1,848.12}{1,317}\right]^{1/3.5} - 1 = .1016$$

$$P_{3.5}^b = \frac{1,000+200}{(1.08)^{.5}} = 1,154.70$$

$$TR_{3.5} = \left[\frac{1,829.45}{1,317}\right]^{1/3.5} - 1 = .09845$$

EXHIBIT 5.15 Total Returns for 4-Year, 9 percent Coupon Bond: HD 3.5 Years, Evaluated at Rates of 12 percent and 8 percent

Yr	0	1	2	3	3.5	CF at 12%	CF at 8%
		$90				$\$90 \times 6(1.12)^{2.5}$	$\$90 \times 6(1.08)^{2.5}$
			$90			$\$90 \times 6(1.12)^{1.5}$	$\$90 \times 6(1.08)^{1.5}$
				$90		$\$90 \times 6(1.12)^{.5}$	$\$90 \times 6(1.08)^{.5}$
					$P_{3.5}$	$1,029.95	$1,048.85
P = $968.30					HD Value	$1,351.35	$1,352.49
					TR 3.5 yrs	.10	.10

$$P_0^B = \sum_{t=1}^{4} \frac{90}{(1.10)^t} + \frac{1,000}{(1.10)^4} = 968.30$$

$$P_{3.5}^B = \frac{1,000+90}{(1.12)^{.5}} = 1,029.95$$

$$TR_{3.5} = \left[\frac{1,351.35}{968.30}\right]^{1/3.5} - 1 = .10$$

$$P_{3.5}^B = \frac{1,000+90}{(1.08)^{.5}} = 1,048.85$$

$$TR_{3.5} = \left[\frac{1,352.49}{968.30}\right]^{1/3.5} - 1 = .10$$

EXHIBIT 5.16 Duration 4-Year, 9 Percent Coupon Bond with Annual Coupon Payments and YTM of 10 Percent

t	CF_t	$CF_t/(1.10)^1$	$PV(CF_t)/P^B$	$t[PV(CF_t)/P^B]$
1	90	81.818	.084496	.084496
2	90	74.380	.076815	.153630
3	90	67.618	.069832	.209496
4	1090	744.485	.768857	3.075428
		$P^B = 968.30$		$D = 3.52$

$$D = \sum_{t=1}^{N} t\left[\frac{PV(CF_t)}{P_0^B}\right]$$

Duration is an important measure in setting up *bond immunization strategies.* The objective of bond immunization is to minimize market risk. As our discussion here indicates, one way to achieve this goal is to select a bond or portfolio of bonds with a duration matching the investor's horizon date. Duration and a related characteristic known as convexity are also important parameters in describing a bond or bond portfolio's volatility in terms of its price sensitivity to interest rate changes.

Interest Rate Risk Example 2

Suppose an investor with a horizon of five years bought a five-year, 9 percent coupon bond paying interest semiannually when the yield curve was flat at 9 percent (bond-equivalent yield). If the investor could invest the semiannual coupons at a reinvestment rate of 4.5 percent for the five-year horizon, her horizon value would be \$1,552.97, her total dollar return (HD value – Investment) would be \$552.97, and her annualized TR would be 9 percent:

$$\text{Investment: } P_5 = \sum_{t=1}^{10} \frac{\$45}{(1.045)^t} + \frac{\$1,000}{(1.045)^{10}} = \$1,000$$

$$\text{Coupon Value} = \sum_{t=0}^{10-1} \$45\,(1.045)^t = \$45\left[\frac{(1.045)^{10} - 1}{.045}\right] = \$552.97$$

$$\text{Interest on Interest} = \$552.97 - (\$45)(10) = \$102.97$$

$$\text{Horizon Price} = F = \$1,000$$

$$\text{HD Value} = \$1,000 + \$552.97 = \$1,552.97$$

$$\text{Total Dollar Return} = \text{HD Value} - \text{Investment} = \$1,552.97 - \$1,000 = \$552.97$$

$$\text{Semiannual total return} = \left[\frac{\$1,552.97}{\$1,000}\right]^{1/10} - 1 = .045$$

$$\text{Simple Annualized Rate} = 2\ (.045) = .09$$

$$\text{Effective Annual Rate} = (1.045)^2 - 1 = .092025$$

With the maturity of the bond matching the investor's horizon, the investor would have no price risk, but she would be subject to reinvestment risk. Of the total dollar return of \$552.97, 18.62 percent comes from the interest-on-interest (\$102.97/\$552.91), 81.38 percent from coupons (\$450/\$552.97), and zero from capital gains. If the flat yield curve were to shift down to 8 percent and remain there for the next five years, then the investor's HD value would decrease to \$1,540.27, with interest-on-interest decreasing \$12.70 from \$102.97 to \$90.27, reducing the annualized total return by 1.94 percent to 8.8285 percent.

In this case, the bond's maturity matches the investor's horizon, and in the absence of a default or a call, the investor knows she will receive the face value of \$1,000 at her horizon. As a result, the investor's interest rate risk consists only of reinvestment risk. Note that the five-year, 9 percent coupon bond has a duration lower than 5 (D = 3.9546). If the investor wanted to minimize market risk, she would need to find a bond that has a duration closer to her horizon of five years. Such a bond would have a maturity greater than five years given that it pays coupons. Thus, at the horizon, if interest rates were lower, the resulting lower interest-on-interest would be offset by a higher selling price on the bond. As shown in Exhibit 5.17, a 9 percent bond with a maturity of 6.5 years (13 semiannual periods), has an annualized duration of 5.0593 (a duration equal to 10.1186 in semiannual periods). At the investor's horizon, this bond would have a maturity of 1.5 years. If the yield curve had shifted down to 8 percent, the \$12.70 decrease in interest-on-interest from \$102.97 to \$90.27 would have been offset by a \$13.88 increase in price to \$1,013.88. The total return from the investment would therefore stay at approximately 9 percent:

$$\text{Investment: } P_{6.5} = \sum_{t=1}^{13} \frac{\$45}{(1.045)^t} + \frac{\$1{,}000}{(1.045)^{13}} = \$1{,}000$$

$$\text{Coupon Value} = \sum_{t=0}^{10-1} \$45\,(1.04)^t = \$45\left[\frac{(1.04)^{10}-1}{.04}\right] = \$540.27$$

$$\text{Interest on Interest} = \$540.27 - (\$45)(10) = \$90.27$$

$$\text{Horizon Price} = P_{1.5} = \sum_{t=1}^{3} \frac{\$45}{(1.04)^t} + \frac{\$1{,}000}{(1.04)^3} = \$1{,}013.88$$

$$\text{HD Value} = \$1{,}013.88 + \$540.27 = \$1{,}554.15$$

$$\text{Semiannual Total Return} = \left[\frac{\$1{,}554.15}{\$1{,}000}\right]^{1/10} - 1 = .045$$

$$\text{Simple Annualized Rate} = 2(.045) = .09$$

$$\text{Effective Annual Rate} = (1.045)^2 - 1 = .092025$$

EXHIBIT 5.17 Duration: 6.5-Year, 9 Percent Coupon bond with Semiannual Payment and YTM of 9 Percent

t	CF_t	$CF_t/(1.045)^t$	$PV(CF_t)/P^B$	$t[PV(CF_t)/P^B]$
1	$45.00	$43.06	0.0431	0.0431
2	$45.00	$41.21	0.0412	0.0824
3	$45.00	$39.43	0.0394	0.1183
4	$45.00	$37.74	0.0377	0.1509
5	$45.00	$36.11	0.0361	0.1806
6	$45.00	$34.56	0.0346	0.2073
7	$45.00	$33.07	0.0331	0.2315
8	$45.00	$31.64	0.0316	0.2531
9	$45.00	$30.28	0.0303	0.2725
10	$45.00	$28.98	0.0290	0.2898
11	$45.00	$27.73	0.0277	0.3050
12	$45.00	$26.53	0.0265	0.3184
13	$1,045.00	$589.66	0.5897	7.6656
		$1,000.00		10.1186
Annualized Duration = 10.1186/2 = 5.0593				

$$D = \sum_{t=1}^{N} t\left[\frac{PV(CF_t)}{P_0^B}\right]$$

It should be noted that the greater the maturity and coupon on a bond, the more dependent its total return is on interest-on-interest to realize its YTM. Longer-term, higher-coupon bonds are therefore subject to more reinvestment risk. For example, if the investor's horizon were 10 years and she had bought a 10-year, 9 percent coupon bond at par, her total dollar return would be $1,411.71, with 36.25 percent coming from the interest-on-interest ($511.71/$1,411.71). The 10-year, 9 percent bond has a duration of 6.7966 when yields are at 9 percent. To offset the large interest-on-interest effect would require buying a bond with a duration of 10 years. For a 9 percent coupon, the investor would have to buy a bond with a maturity of 25 years to obtain a duration of 10 years.

Interest Rate Example 3: Kraft Bond

The Bloomberg HZ1 screen calculates the total return on a selected bond for a selected horizon period, discount yield at the HD, and reinvestment rate. Exhibit 5.18 shows the total return calculations for Kraft bond with a 5.375 percent coupon and a maturity date = February 10, 2020. On April 13, 2012, the bond was

EXHIBIT 5.18 Total Return/Horizon Analysis—Bloomberg HZ1 Screen Kraft Bond: 5 3/8 Coupon, Maturity Date = 2/10/2020, Duration = 6.6, Horizon = 6.5 years

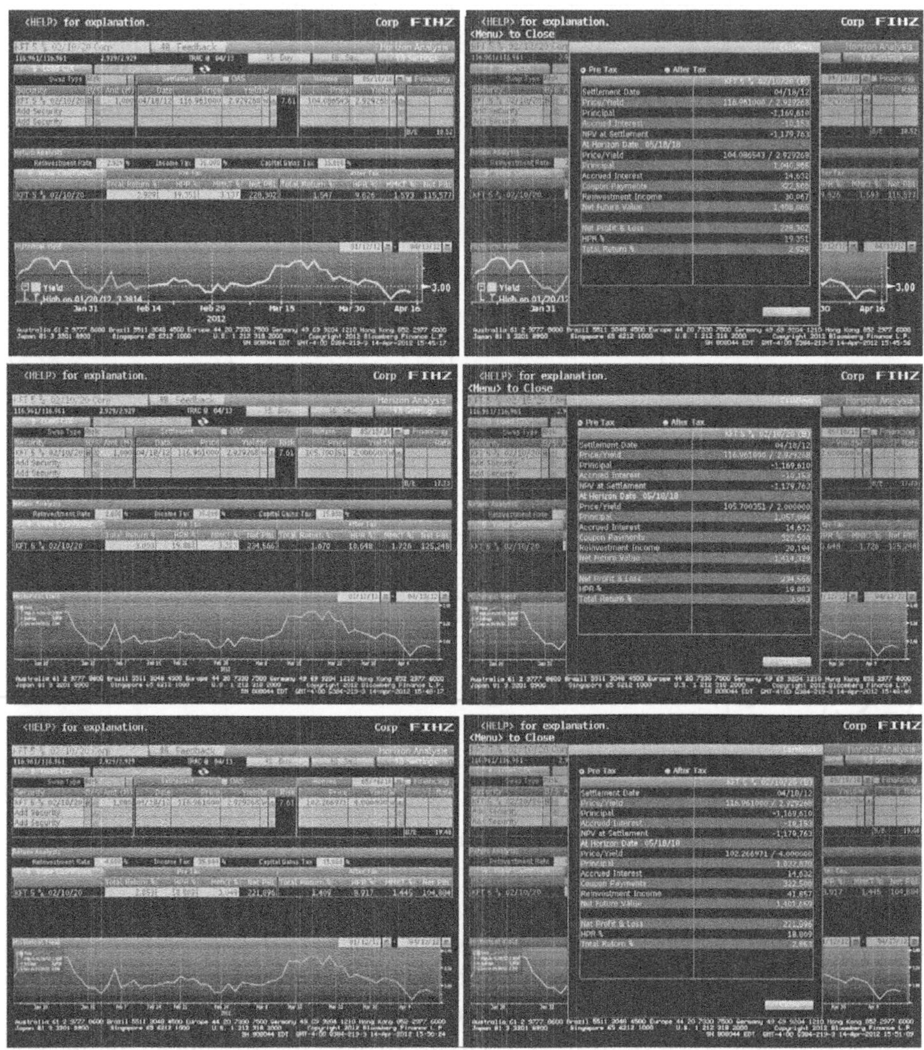

trading at 116.961 to yield 2.929268 percent and had a duration of 6.63 (duration can be found on the Bloomberg YA screen). The HZ1 screens shown in the exhibit show a horizon date set at May 18, 2018, which is a 6.5-year period that closely matches the Kraft bond's duration. The top screen shows a scenario of no change in rates with the discount rate and reinvestment rate both set at the current YTM of 2.929268 percent. The middle screen shows a lower rate scenario with the bond's discount rate set at 2 percent on the HD and with the reinvestment rate set at 2 percent. The bottom screen shows a higher rate scenario with the bond's discount rate set at 4 percent on the HD and with the reinvestment rate set at 4 percent.

The total returns for each case are approximately 3.1 percent: 2.929 percent (no change), 3.003 percent (2 percent scenario), and 2.853 percent (4 percent scenario) for the 6.5-year period.

With a duration of approximately 6.5 years, an investor with an horizon of 6.5 years would find this Kraft bond would minimize her interest rate risk. In contrast, an investor with a 1-year horizon would find this Kraft bond subjecting her to interest rate risk. As shown in Chapter 3 (Exhibit 3.11), with a 1-year horizon the total returns are 3.1 percent, –1.9 percent, and 9.30 percent for discount rates of 3.101 percent, 4 percent, and 2 percent, respectively.

A similar total return/horizon analysis for the Kraft bond is shown in Exhibit 5.19. The exhibit shows Bloomberg Total Return Analysis (TRA) screens for the Kraft bond for the horizon scenarios of 6.5 years and one year. The scenarios vary from three parallel yield curve shifts from –300 bps to +300 bps for both discount rate and reinvestment rates. For the 6.5-year horizon the total returns for all the scenarios are approximately 3 percent (range between 2.94 percent and 2.98 percent), whereas for the 1-year scenario the total returns vary from –6.70 percent to 13.5 percent.

EXHIBIT 5.19 Total Return/Horizon Analysis—Bloomberg TRA Screen Kraft Bond: 5 3/8 Coupon Maturity, Date = 2/10/2020, Duration = 6.6, Horizon = 6.5 years and 1 year

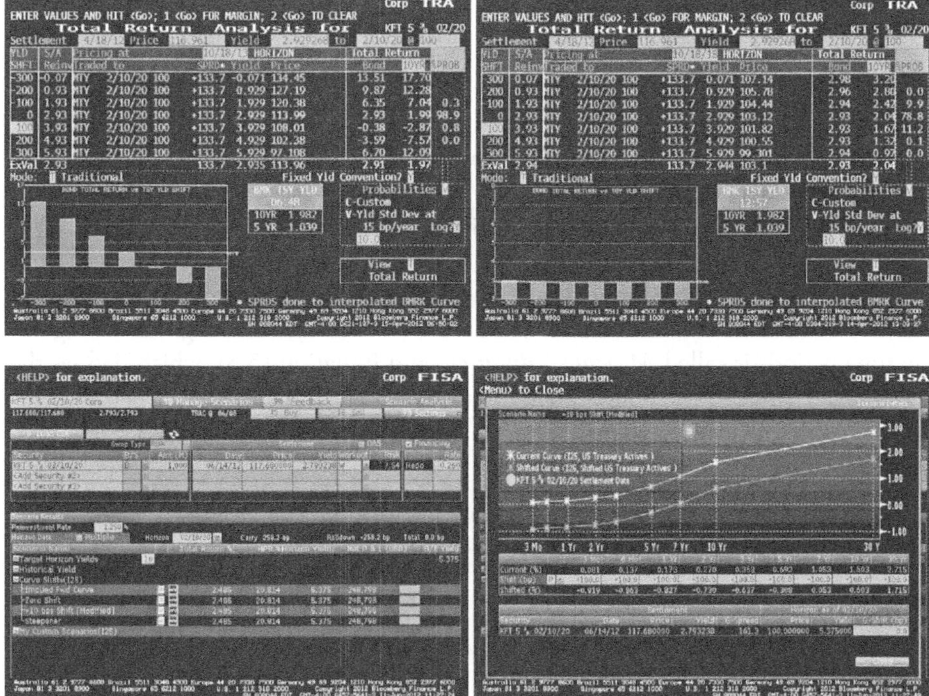

Duration and Convexity

Duration Measures

Duration was introduced in finance in 1938 when Frederick Macaulay suggested using the weighted average of a bond's time periods as a better measure of the life of a bond than maturity. J. R. Hicks in 1939, Paul Samuelson in 1945, and F. M. Redington in 1952 also came up with duration measures, each somewhat different, to explain the relationship between price and the life of a bond. In 1971, duration attracted widespread attention when Fisher and Weil published their work on the use of duration as a way of minimizing market risk.

Though duration is defined as the weighted average of a bond's time periods, it is also an important measure of volatility and of a bond's price responsiveness to a change in interest rates. Just as the beta of stock measures the responsiveness of stock's return to changes in the market rate, and as such measures a stock's market risk, the duration of a bond measures the proportional change in a bond's price to changes in interest rates, and as such is a measure of a bond's or bond portfolio's market or interest rate risk. Mathematically, duration is obtained by taking the derivative of the equation for the price of a bond with respect to the yield, dividing by the bond's price, and expressing the resulting equation in absolute value (this derivation is presented in Exhibits 5.20 and 5.21). Doing this we obtain the following formula for duration:

$$\text{Duration} = \frac{dP/P}{dy} = -\frac{1}{(1+y)}\left(\sum_{t=1}^{N} t\,\frac{PV(CF_t)}{P_0^B}\right) \tag{5.3}$$

where:

dP/P_0 = percentage change in the bond's price
dy = small change in yield
N = number of periods to maturity

The bracketed expression in Equation (5.3) is the weighted average of the time periods, defined in the last section as duration. Formally, the weighted average of the time periods is called *Macaulay's duration,* and Equation (5.3), which defines the percentage change in the bond's price for a small change in yield (expressed in absolute value) is called the *modified duration.*[5] Thus, the modified duration is equal to Macaulay's duration divided by 1 + *y:*

$$\text{Modified Duration} = -\frac{1}{(1+y)}\left[\text{Macaulay's Duration}\right]$$

$$\text{Macaulay's Duration} = \left(\sum_{t=1}^{N} t\,\frac{PV(CF_t)}{P_0^B}\right)$$

EXHIBIT 5.20 Derivation of Duration and Convexity

Duration:

$$P_0^B = \sum_{t=1}^{M} \frac{CF_t}{(1+y)^t} = \sum_{t=1}^{M} CF_t \ (1+y)^{-t}$$

$$P_0^B = CF_1(1+y)^{-1} + CF_2(1+y)^{-2} + \cdots + CF_M(1+y)^{-M}$$

Take the derivative with respect to *y*:

$$\frac{dP^B}{dy} = (-1)CF_1(1+y)^{-2} + (-2)CF_2(1+y)^{-3} + \cdots + (-M)CF_M(1+y)^{-(M+1)}$$

$$\text{Factor out } -\ (1+y)^{-1} = -\frac{1}{(1+y)^1}$$

$$\frac{dP^B}{dy} = -\frac{1}{(1+y)}((1)CF_1(1+y)^{-1} + (2)CF_2(1+y)^{-2} + \cdots + (M)CF_M(1+y)^{-M})$$

$$\frac{dP^B}{dy} = -\frac{1}{(1+y)}\left((1)\frac{CF_1}{(1+y)^1} + (2)\frac{CF_2}{(1+y)^2} + \cdots + (M)\frac{CF_M}{(1+y)^M}\right)$$

$$\frac{dP^B}{dy} = -\frac{1}{(1+y)}\big((1)\ PV(CF_1) + (2)\ PV(CF_2) + \cdots + (M)\ PV(CF_M)\big)$$

Divide through by *P*:

$$\frac{dP^B}{dy}\frac{1}{P} = \frac{dP/P}{dy} = -\frac{1}{(1+y)}\left((1)\frac{PV(CF_1)}{P_0^B} + (2)\frac{PV(CF_2)}{P_0^B} + \cdots + (M)\frac{PV(CF_M)}{P_0^B}\right)$$

$$\frac{dP/P}{dy} = -\frac{1}{(1+y)}\left(\sum_{t=1}^{M} t\ \frac{PV(CF_t)}{P_0^B}\right)$$

Modified duration is *dP/P/dy* expressed in absolute value:

$$\text{Modified Duration} = \left|\frac{dP/P}{dy}\right| = \frac{1}{(1+y)}\left(\sum_{t=1}^{M} t\ \frac{PV(CF_t)}{P_0^B}\right)$$

EXHIBIT 5.21 Derivation of Duration and Convexity (continued)

Convexity:
Take the derivative of

$$\frac{dP^B}{dy} = (-1)CF_1(1+y)^{-2} + (-2)CF_2(1+y)^{-3} + \cdots + (-M)CF_M(1+y)^{-(M+1)}$$

$$\frac{d^2P^B}{dy^2} = 2CF_1(1+y)^{-3} + 6CF_2(1+y)^{-4} + \cdots + M(M+1)CF_M(1+y)^{-(M+2)}$$

Divide through by P_0^B and express as a summation:

$$\frac{d^2P^B}{dy^2}\frac{1}{P_0^B} = \frac{d\Delta/P_0^B}{dy} = \text{Convexity} = \frac{1}{P_0^B}\left(\sum_{t=1}^{M}\frac{t(t+1)(CF_t)}{(1+y)^t}\right)$$

The 4-year, 9 percent annual coupon bond (used in the first example in the last section), has a Macaulay's duration of 3.5 years, and given the initial yield of 10 percent, a modified duration of 3.18[6]:

$$\text{Modified Duration} = \frac{1}{(1+y)}\left[\text{Macaulay's Duration}\right]$$

$$\text{Modified Duration} = \frac{1}{(1.10)}[3.5] = 3.18$$

The Kraft bond has a Macaulay's duration of 6.63 and a modified duration of 6.529 on January 16, 2012 (both durations can be found on the Bloomberg YA screen).

Mathematically, *dP/dy* is the slope of the price-yield curve. Thus, the modified duration is also the slope of price-yield curve divided by *dy* and then expressed in absolute value. Also note that the price of bond that pays a coupon each period and its principal at maturity is

$$P_0^B = C\left[\frac{1-(1/(1+y))^N}{y}\right] + \frac{F}{(1+y)^N}$$

Taking the first derivative of this equation, dividing through by P_0^b and expressing the resulting equation in absolute value provides a measure of duration for a bond that pays its principal at maturity[7]:

$$\text{Modified Duration} = \frac{\dfrac{C}{y^2}\left[1-\dfrac{1}{(1+y)^N}\right]+\dfrac{N[F-(C/y)]}{(1+y)^{N+1}}}{P_0^b} \tag{5.4}$$

Note that the above measures of duration are defined in terms of the length of the period between payments. Thus, if the cash flow is distributed semiannually, then duration reflects half years. The convention, though, is to express duration as an annual measure. Annualized duration is obtained by dividing duration by the number of payments per year (n):

$$\text{Annualized Duration} = \frac{\text{Duration for bond with } n-\text{payments per year}}{n}$$

For example, the modified duration measured in half-years for a 10-year, 9 percent coupon bond selling at par (F = 100) and with coupon payments made semi-annually is 13 and its annualized duration is 6.5:

$$\text{Duration in Half Years} = \frac{\dfrac{4.5}{.045^2}\left[1-\dfrac{1}{(1.045)^{20}}\right]+\dfrac{20[100-(4.5/.045)]}{(1.045)^{21}}}{100} = 13$$

$$\text{Annualized Duration} = \frac{13}{2} = 6.5$$

Properties of Duration

In Chapter 3, we described the relationship between a bond's price sensitivity to interest rate changes and its maturity and coupon rate. These relationships also can be defined in terms of duration. Specifically, the greater the maturity, the greater a bond's duration, and therefore the greater its price sensitivity to interest rates changes; the smaller the coupon rate, the greater a bond's duration, and therefore the greater its price sensitivity to interest rate changes. Thus, in addition to identifying bonds for immunization strategies, duration is also an important descriptive parameter, defining a bond's volatility as measured by its price sensitivity to interest rate changes. To summarize, the following properties apply to duration:

- The lower the coupon rate, the greater the duration.
- The longer the term to maturity, the greater the duration.
- For zero-coupon bonds, Macaulay's duration is equal to the bond's term to maturity (N) and modified duration is equal to $N/(1 + y)$.
- The higher the yield to maturity, the lower the duration.

Knowing a bond or bond portfolio's duration is important in formulating bond strategies. For example, a bond speculator who is anticipating a decrease in interest rates across all maturities (downward parallel shift in the yield curve) could realize a potentially greater expected return, but also greater risk, by purchasing a bond with a relatively large duration (longer maturity and lower coupon). In contrast, a bond portfolio manager expecting a parallel upward shift in the yield curve could take defensive actions against possible capital losses by reallocating his portfolio such that it would have a lower portfolio duration.[8]

Portfolio Duration

As noted, the duration of a portfolio is the weight average of the durations of the bonds comprising the portfolio:

$$D_p = \sum w_i D_i$$

A bond portfolio formed with five investment-grade, option-free bonds is shown in Exhibit 5.22. The portfolio consists of 1,000 issues of each bond. On 5/6/2011 the portfolio was worth \$5,673,340, and it had a modified duration of 6.8022. If the yields on each of the bonds change by 100 bp, the portfolio value on that date would change by approximately 6.8022 percent. Note that each bond's weighted duration, $w_i D_i$, measures that bond's contribution to the overall portfolio's duration.

Convexity

Duration is a measure of the slope of the price-yield curve at a given point (*dP/dy*). As we noted in Chapter 3, the price-yield curve is not linear, but convex from below (bowed-shaped). Convexity means that the slope of the price-yield curve ($\Delta = dP/dy$) gets smaller as you move down the curve or as the YTM increases (see Exhibit 5.23). This, in turn, implies that for a given absolute change in yields, the percentage increase in price will be greater in absolute value for the yield decrease than the percentage decrease in price in absolute value for the yield increase. For an investor who is long in a bond, its convexity suggests that the capital gain resulting from a decrease in rates will be greater than the capital loss resulting from an increase in rates of the same absolute magnitude. That is, bonds or bond portfolios with greater convexity have a greater asymmetrical gain-loss relation. Thus, all other things equal, the greater a bond convexity the more valuable the bond (see Exhibit 5.24).

Mathematically, convexity is the change in the slope of the price-yield curve for a small change in yield; it is the second-order derivative. It is derived by taking the derivative of the equation for *dP/dy* with respect to a change in yield and dividing the resulting equation by the current price. (This derivation is presented in Exhibit 5.21.) Doing this we obtain the following formula:

$$\text{Convexity} = \frac{1}{P_0^b}\left[\sum_{t=1}^{N} \frac{t(t+1)(CF_t)}{(1+y)^{t+2}}\right]$$

EXHIBIT 5.22 Portfolio Duration and Convexity—5/6/2011

Bond	Coupon	Maturity	Price	Number of Issues	Market Value = (Price× 10) × Issues
IBM	0.075	41,440	113.206	1,000	$1,132,060
Wal-Mart	0.028	42,475	102.011	1,000	$1,020,110
Kraft	0.05375	43,871	109.094	1,000	$1,090,940
P&G	0.0645	46,037	125.023	1,000	$1,250,230
Ford	0.0896	11,703	118.000	1,000	$1,180,000
Total					$5,673,340

Bond	Allocation	Modified Duration	Weighted Duration	Convexity	Weighted Convexity
IBM	0.1995	1.921	0.3833	0.049	0.0098
Wal-Mart	0.1798	4.576	0.8228	0.24	0.0432
Kraft	0.1923	6.943	1.3351	0.585	0.1125
P&G	0.2204	9.902	2.1821	1.281	0.2823
Ford	0.2080	9.995	2.0789	1.624	0.3378
Total	**1.00**		**6.8022**		**0.7855**

EXHIBIT 5.23 Convexity

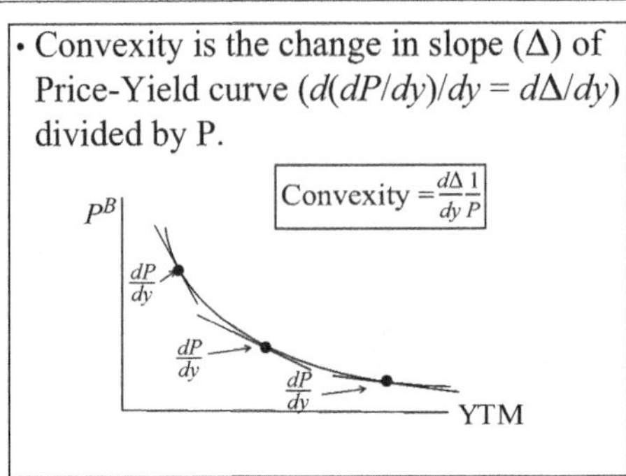

Properties of Convexity

1. As the yield increases (decreases), the convexity of the bond decreases (increases). This is referred to as positive convexity.
2. For a given yield and maturity, the lower the coupon, the greater the convexity.
3. For a given yield and modified duration, the lower the coupon, the smaller the convexity.

The convexity of a bond that pays a fixed coupon each period and the principal at maturity is obtained by taking the derivative of Equation (5.4):

$$\text{Convexity} = \frac{\dfrac{2C}{y^3}\left[1 - \dfrac{1}{(1+y)^N}\right] - \dfrac{2CN}{y^2(1+y)^{N+1}} + \dfrac{N(N+1)[F-(C/y)]}{(1+y)^{N+2}}}{P_0^b} \quad (5.5)$$

Like duration, convexity reflects the length of periods between cash flows. The annualized convexity is found by dividing convexity, measured in terms of n-payments per year, by n^2:

$$\text{Annualized Convexity} = \frac{\text{Convexity for bond with } n-\text{payments per year}}{n^2}$$

Thus, the convexity is half-years for the 10-year, 9 percent coupon bond with semiannual payments is 225.43, and its annual convexity is 56.36:

$$\text{Convexity (1/2 yrs)} = \frac{\dfrac{2(4.5)}{.045^3}\left[1 - \dfrac{1}{(1.045)^{20}}\right] - \dfrac{2(4.5)(20)}{(.045)^2(1.045)^{21}} + \dfrac{(20)(21)[100-(4.5/.045)]}{(1.045)^{22}}}{100}$$

$$\text{Convexity (1/2 yrs)} = 225.43$$

$$\text{Annualized Convexity} = \frac{225.43}{2^2} = 56.36$$

EXHIBIT 5.24 Value of Convexity

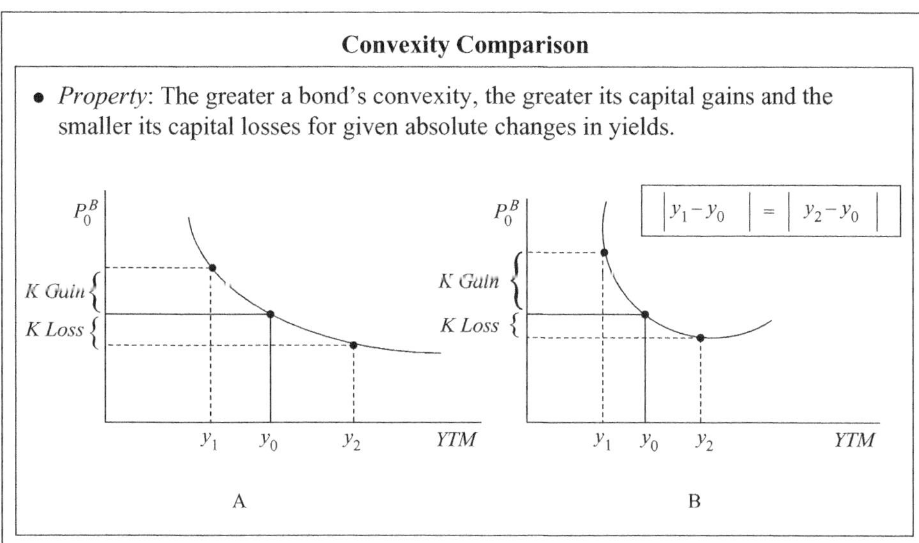

Value of Convexity

Consider two similar bonds—X and Y—that are trading at the same yield (y_0) and have the same duration, but with Bond X having a greater convexity than Bond Y. Investors would take the greater convexity of X into account, pricing it higher than Y and accepting a lower yield. The question is how much would the market pay for the convexity? The answer depends on how much the market expects rates to change. If investors expect yields to change very little—market with low interest rate volatility—then the advantage of X over Y is small. Thus, in this market, investor would pay little for convexity. On the other hand, if investors expect yields to change significantly—a market with high interest rate volatility—then the advantage of X over Y is more important. Thus, in this market, investor would pay more for convexity.

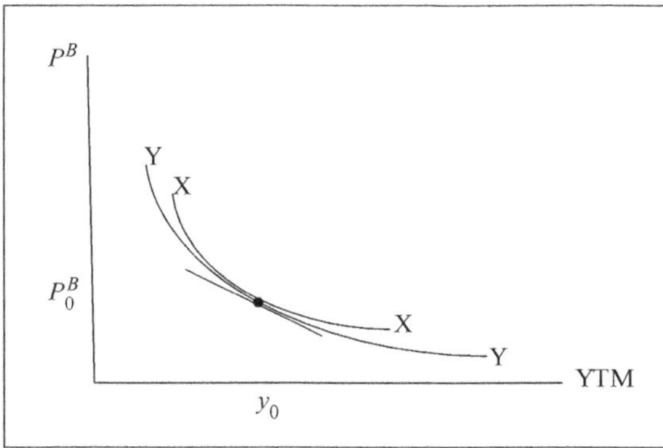

Alternative Formulas for Duration and Convexity

Duration and convexity can also be estimated by determining the price of the bond when the yield increases by a small number of basis points (e.g., 10 basis points), P_+, and when the yield decreases by the same number of basis points, P_-. These measures are referred to as *approximate duration* and *convexity* and can be estimated using the following formulas:

$$\text{Approximate Duration} = \frac{P_- - P_+}{2(P_0)(\Delta y)} \tag{5.6}$$

$$\text{Approximate Convexity} = \frac{P_+ + P_- - 2P_0}{P_0(\Delta y)^2} \tag{5.7}$$

Caveats

Duration and convexity are important characteristics that can be used to determine a bond's price sensitivity to interest rates and the asymmetry of its capital gains to capital losses for given absolute changes in yields. However, there are two problems with the measures we have defined here for determining a bond's duration and convexity. First, in deriving duration and convexity, we assumed the cash flows were discounted at the same rate. This implies that we are assuming the yield curve is flat and all shifts in the curve are parallel. These assumptions create problem when we use the modified portfolio duration to estimate the impact of a change in interest rates on the portfolio value. That is, if the portfolio has bonds with different maturities, then the duration measure will not give good estimates if there is a nonparallel shift in the yield curve in which there are unequal changes in the yields on different maturities. There are several techniques that can be used to estimate a bond or bond portfolio's value to changes in rates resulting from a nonparallel shift in the yield curve. The most popular technique is called *key rate determination.*[9] The Bloomberg BSA and PSA screens for conducting total return analysis on bond portfolios allow the user to simulate nonparallel shifts.

A second and more serious problem with our measures is that they apply only to option-free bonds. Call, put, and sinking fund arrangements alter a bond's cash flow patterns and can dramatically change a bond's duration and convexity. Moreover, since many bonds have option features, adjusting their cash flow patterns to account for such features is important in measuring a bond's duration and convexity. In Chapter 13, we will present valuation approaches for bonds with embedded option features using a binomial interest rate tree. With this valuation model, you can estimate the prices of bonds with call and put option features, then substitute these prices into Equations (5.6) and (5.7) to estimate the duration and convexity of bonds with embedded options. The duration and convexity measures using this approach are referred to as *effective duration* and *effective convexity.* Effective durations (OAD) and convexity (OAC) are estimated on the Bloomberg PREP and BSA screen for evaluating portfolios. Information on how to use Bloomberg screens for bond portfolios created in PRTU is presented in Chapter 6.

Conclusion

In a world of certainty, bonds with similar features—risk, liquidity, taxability, and maturity—would, in equilibrium, trade at the same rates. If this were not the case, then investors would try to buy bonds with higher rates and sell or short bonds with lower rates, causing their prices and rates to change until they were all equal. We, of course, live in a world of uncertainty. Issuers can default on their obligations, borrowers can redeem their bonds early, and interest rates can change. This is why we have differences in the relative demands, prices, and yields on bonds. Thus, an important factor explaining different rates among debt instruments is uncertainty. In addition, bonds also have different liquidity, maturity, taxability, duration, and convexity features, which cause bonds to trade at different prices and yields. In this chapter, we have examined the nature and impact of uncertainty by examining the nature of default, call, and interest rate risk and their corresponding spreads. In the next chapter, we examine how investment and portfolio managers select and analyze these various fixed-income securities.

Website Information

1. Rating Agencies
   - www.moodys.com
   - www.standardandpoors.com
2. FINRA
   - Go to www.finra.org/index.htm, Sitemap, Market Data, and Bonds.
   - For a bond search, click the "Corporate" tab, and then click "Advanced Bond Search" to find corporate bonds with certain features.
   - For bonds of a specific issuer, enter issuer's symbol and then click "Search."
3. *Wall Street Journal:* http://online.wsj.com/public/us
4. Yahoo.com
   - Go to http://finance.yahoo.com/bonds, click "Advanced Bond Screener" and click the "Corporate" tab, and then provide information for search.
   - Go to http://finance.yahoo.com/bonds, enter "name of issuer" and click "Search."
5. Investinginbonds.com: http://investinginbonds.com/
6. Online Finance Calculator: www.ficalc.com/calc.tips; use to calculate duration and convexity.
7. Federal Reserve: Historical interest rate data on different bonds can be found at the Federal Reserve site. www.federalreserve.gov/releases/h15/data.htm and www.research.stlouisfed.org/fred2.

Selected References

Altman, E. 1992. Revisiting the high-yield bond market. *Financial Management* 21:78–92.
Altman, E. I. 1993. *Corporate Financial Distress and Bankruptcy*, 2nd ed. New York: John Wiley & Sons.

Altman, E. I. 1989. Measuring corporate bond mortality and performance. *Journal of Finance* 44: 909–922.

Altman, E. I. 1990. Setting the record straight on junk bonds: A review of the research on default rates and returns." *Journal of Applied Corporate Finance* 3:82–95.

Altman, E. I., and S. A. Nammacher. 1987. *Investing in Junk Bonds*. New York: John Wiley & Sons.

Bierwag, G. 1977. Immunization, duration and the term structure of interest rates. *Journal of Financial and Quantitative Analysis* 12:725–743.

Bierwag, G. O., G. G. Kaufman, and A. Toevs. 1983. Duration: Its development and use in bond portfolio management. *Financial Analysts Journal* (July–August):15–35.

Bierwag, G. O., G. G. Kaufman, and A. Toevs, eds. 1983. *Innovations in Bond Portfolio Management: Duration Analysis and Immunization*. Greenwich, CT: JAI Press.

Black, F., E. Derman, and W. Toy. 1990. A one-factor model of interest rates and its application to Treasury bond options. *Financial Analysts Journal* (January/February):33–39.

Black, F., and P. Karasinski. 1991. Bond and option pricing when short rates are lognormal. *Financial Analysts Journal* 47:52–59.

Chamber, D., and W. Carleston. 1988. A generalized approach to duration. *Research in Finance* 7: 163–181.

Chance, D. M. 1990. Default, risk and the duration of the zero coupon bonds. *Journal of Finance* 55:265–274.

Cox, J., J. Ingersoll, and S. Ross. 1979. Duration and the measurement of basis risk. *Journal of Business* 52:51–61.

Fisher, I. 1930. *The Theory of Interest*. New York: Macmillan.

Fisher, L. 1959. Determinants of risk premiums on corporate bonds. *Journal of Political Economy* (June):217–237.

Fons, J. 1994. Using default rates to model the term structure of credit risk. *Financial Analysts Journal* 50:25–32.

Hickman, W. B. 1958. *Corporate Bond Quality and Investor Experience*. New York: National Bureau of Economic Research.

Hicks, J. R. 1946. *Value and Capital*, 2nd ed. London: Oxford University Press.

Ho, T. S. Y. 1992. Key rate determination: Measure of interest rate risk. *Journal of Fixed Income* 2 :29–44.

Howe, J. T. 2001. Credit analysis for corporate bonds. In F. Fabozzi, ed., *The Handbook of Fixed Income Securities*, 6th ed. New York: McGraw-Hill, 2001.

Hull, J. C. 2005. *Options, Futures, and Other Derivatives*, 6th ed. Upper Saddle River, NJ: Prentice Hall, Chapters 20–21.

Hull, J., M. Predescu, and A. White. 2004. Relationship between credit default swap spreads, bond yields, and credit rating announcements. *Journal of Banking and Finance* 28:2789–2811.

Hull, J. C., and A. White. 2004. Valuation of a CDO and *n*th-to-default swap without Monte Carlo simulation. *Journal of Derivatives* 12:8–23.

Ilmanwen, A. 1996. Market's rate expectations and forward rates, *Journal of Fixed Income* (September):8–22.

Ilmanwen, A. 1996. Does duration extension enhance long-term expected return? *Journal of Fixed Income* (September):23–36.

Ilmanwen, A. 2000. Convexity bias in the yield curve. In *Advanced Fixed-Income Valuation Tools*. New York: John Wiley & Sons, Chapter 3.

Ingersoll, J. E., J. Skelton, and R. L. Weil. 1978. Duration forty years later. *Journal of Financial and Quantitative Analysis* 13:627–650.

Johnson, R. E. 1967. Term structures of corporate bond yields as a function of risk of default. *Journal of Finance* 22:313–345.

Johnson, R. S. 2009. *Introduction to Derivatives: Options, Futures, and Swaps*. Oxford University Press, Chapter 20.

Johnson, R. S., J. E. Pawlukiewicz, and J. M. Mehta. 1997. Binomial option pricing with skewed asset returns. *Review of Quantitative Finance and Accounting* 9:89–101.

Klaffky, T. E., Y. Y. Ma, and A. Nozari 1992. Managing yield curve exposure: Introducing reshaping durations. *Journal of Fixed Income* (December):5–15.

Macaulay, F. R. 1938. *The Movement of Interest Rates, Bond Yields, and Stock Prices in the United States Since 1856.* New York: National Bureau of Economic Research.

Reitana, R. 1990. Non-parallel yield curve shifts and duration leverages. *Journal of Portfolio Management* (Summer):62–67.

Weil, R. L. 1973. Macaulay's duration: An appreciation. *Journal of Business* 46:589–592.

Bloomberg Exercises

1. Select an option-free (bullet) corporate bond of interest. Evaluate the bond in terms of its yield spread, credit risk, liquidity, and interest rate risk. In your evaluations, you may want to consider the following screens on the bond's menu screen or it company's equity menu screen.
   - YA ("Yield & Spread" tab) to determine the bond's spread.
   - YA ("Graph" tab) to compare its market spread with other spreads (e.g., CDS spreads).
   - GY to evaluate the bond's spread history.
   - RSKC to see it credit risk profile.
   - LITI to see if the company is subject to any major litigation.
   - DRSK to see graphs of bond's CDS and default probability (set graph screen to see those measures).
2. Use the Bloomberg RATC screen to identify bonds that have had recent ratings changes. On the RATC screen, you may want to limit your search to bonds in a particular industry (select industry from the "Search" tab). Examine one of the bonds with ratings changes using the RSKC, CRPR, and DRSK screens. Comment on the ratings changes and information you find from the screens, such as Altman Z-score, probability of default, changes in financials, CDS spreads, and litigation.
3. Select a callable investment-grade corporate bond of interest. Evaluate the bond in terms of its YTM, yield to first call, and yield to worst. Use the OAS1 screen to determine the option-free spread on the bond, and the YA screen to determine its total spread. What is the bond's credit and liquidity spread? What is its callable spread?
4. Select a U.S. Treasury bond or note with an intermediate-term or long-term maturity (10 to 20 years). You may want to use the FIT screen to find your bond.
   - Using the YA screen on the selected bond's menu screen (CUSIP <Govt> <Enter>), determine the bond's Macaulay and modified duration.
   - Conduct a total return analysis of the bond using the TRA screen. Select different horizon periods, yield curve shifts, and reinvestment rates.
   - Conduct a total return analysis of the bond using the FIHZ screen using different horizon periods, discount rates, and reinvestment rates.

5. Suppose you have a horizon that matches the duration of the bond you selected in Exercise 4. Evaluate the interest rate risk on the bond using FIHZ and TRA screens:
   - Using the FIHZ screen for the selected bond, evaluate its interest rate risk by setting the screen to the horizon matching the bond's duration and then selecting a discount rate and reinvestment rate showing a low interest rate scenario and then rates reflecting a high interest rate scenario.
   - Using the TRA screen for the selected bond, evaluate interest rate risk by setting the screen to the horizon matching the bond's duration and then selecting a reinvestment rate.
6. Select five investment-grade, option-free bonds with different maturities (e.g., 3, 7, 10, 15, and 20 years). Using the YA and DES screens find each one's maturity, coupon rate, quality rating, YTM, spread, modified duration, Macaulay duration, and convexity. Summarize your information in a table. Comment on the properties of duration and convexity in terms of the bonds you selected. If your horizon were three years, which bond would you select if you expected interest rates to decreases? Which bond would you select if you expected rates to increase?

Notes

1. It should be noted that each ratings company can rate an issue differently. When a bond is rated differently, it reflects a different emphasis that each ratings company places on certain parameters or differences in methodologies.
2. In a widely cited study by Lawrence Fisher, yield premiums for corporate securities were found to be directly related to a company's volatility in earnings and inversely related to the company's equity-to-debt ratio, number of outstanding bonds, and how long the company had been solvent.
3. However, if the swap bank were offering the CDS at a 4 percent spread, then an investor looking for a five-year risk-free investment would obviously prefer a Treasury yielding 5 percent to a synthetic risk-free investment formed with the five-year BBB corporate yielding 8 percent and a CDS on the credit requiring a payment of 4 percent. A more aggressive investor looking to invest in the higher yielding five-year BBB bonds, though, could earn 1 percent more than the 8 percent on the BBB bond by creating a synthetic five-year BBB bond by purchasing the five-year Treasury at 5 percent and selling the CDS at 4 percent. Similarly, a bond portfolio manager holding five-year BBB bonds yielding 8 percent could pick up an additional 1 percent yield with the same credit risk exposure by selling the bonds along with the CDS at 4 percent and then using the proceeds from the bond sale to buy the five-year Treasuries yielding 5 percent.
4. Note that for this example, we are assuming annual coupon payments.
5. The proportional change in the bond price to a change in yield ($dP/P/dy$) is negative (inverse relationship between price and yield). The convention, though, is to express modified duration in absolute value.
6. The modified duration is the most commonly used measure of duration. Some applications of duration use the *dollar duration*. The dollar duration is the change in the bond price given a small change in yield (dP/dy). The dollar duration is obtained by multiplying both sides of Equation (5.3) by P_0: Dollar Duration = (Modified Duration) P_0.

7. For a zero-coupon bond, Macaulay's duration would be equal to the bond's maturity, whereas the modified duration would be less than the maturity.
8. A second application of duration is its use as an estimate of the percentage change in a bond's price for a small change in rates. In the case of the 10-year, 9 percent coupon bond selling at 100 to yield 9 percent, if the yield were to increase by 10 basis points (from 9 percent to 9.10 percent), then using the duration formula, the bond would decrease by approximately 0.65 percent. It should be noted that duration as an estimator is only good for measuring small changes in yields. For example, if the yield had increased by 200 basis points to 11 percent, instead of only 10 basis points, the approximate percentage change using the duration measure would be -13 percent. This contrasts with the actual percentage change of -11.95 percent.
9. See Chamber and Carleston (1988); Reitana (1990); and Ho (1992).

CHAPTER 6

Bond Investment Strategies

Introduction

Bond investment strategies can be classified as active, passive, or hybrid. *Active strategies* involve taking speculative positions in which the primary objective is to obtain greater returns. This might include taking a long position in longer duration bonds in anticipation of a decrease in long-term rates, investing in Treasury securities based on the expectation of the Fed's implementing an expansionary monetary policy, or investing in lower-quality bonds in hopes of future economic growth. Active strategies also include defensive strategies in which the objective is to protect the value of a bond investment. For example, to minimize the potential decrease in a bond fund's value from an expected increase in interest rates, a fund manager might reallocate more of the fund's holdings toward lower-duration bonds and away from higher-duration ones. Institutional investors, hedge funds, and individual investors all use active strategies. In the case of a hedge fund, the fund itself might be defined by the strategy. For example, Long-Term Capital Management was a hedge fund that could be defined by one of its active strategies of trying to profit from a narrowing of a yield spread. However, an institutional investor such as a pension or a life insurance company might use an active approach only in the initial investment of its funds, and then afterwards follow a passive or hybrid investment-style approach. Finally, institutional fund managers might use an active approach to change the allocation of their exiting funds from one bond group to another in order to increase the expected return or as a defensive strategy to protect the value of the fund. This latter active strategy involves liquidating one bond group and simultaneously purchasing another. Such strategies are referred to as *bond swaps.*

A *passive strategy* is one in which no change in holdings is necessary once the bonds are selected, or in the case of investing new funds, the investment strategy is not changed once it is set up. Prudence and practicality, though, usually dictate at least minimal monitoring and change. Life insurance companies, deposit institutions, and pensions that have a primary objective of ensuring that there are sufficient funds to meet future liabilities typically use passive strategies. Some investment companies that manage bond portfolios and some fixed-income mutual funds try to construct bond portfolios whose returns over time replicate those of some specified bond index. Such a strategy is known as *indexing*.

Hybrid active-passive strategies consist primarily of immunization positions. Recall that in Chapter 5 we defined immunization as a strategy of minimizing market risk by selecting a bond or bond portfolio with a duration that matched the investor's horizon date. Fund managers of pensions and insurance companies that have future liabilities whose amounts and times of payments are known often employ immunization. The discussion of bond immunization in Chapter 5 suggested that such a strategy is a passive one of simply matching duration to the horizon date. In practice, though, immunization requires frequent changing or rebalancing of the bond portfolio, and as such can be characterized as having both passive and active management styles. In addition to immunization, other hybrid strategies are contingent immunization and combination matching, both of which have active and passive elements.

In this chapter, we extend our analysis from the evaluation of bond securities to the selection of bonds by examining the various active, passive, and hybrid investment strategies. We begin by first examining some of the popular active selection strategies, including trading strategies based on anticipated interest rate changes, credit strategies, and fundamental valuation approaches. This is followed by an analysis of two passive strategies: cash flow matching and indexing. Finally, we conclude the chapter by examining bond immunization strategies.

Active Investment Strategies

In our evaluation of bond characteristics, we identified a number of fundamental relationships. For example, in our discussion of bond price relationships in Chapter 3, we noted that the greater a bond's maturity or the lower its coupon rate, the greater its price sensitivity to interest rate changes (or equivalently the greater its duration). In Chapter 5, we discussed how the spread between the yields on low- and high-quality bonds widens in periods of economic downturn and narrows in periods of economic growth. We also noted in Chapter 5 that the spread between yields on callable and noncallable bonds tended to widen in high interest rate periods and narrow in low-rate period. Many active bond strategies are, in turn, predicated on these fundamental bond relations. Some of the more popular ones are interest rate expectation strategies based on anticipated changes in interest rates or yield curve shifts, credit strategies based on credit analysis and economic forecast, and valuation strategies based on determining the fundamental values of bonds in order to identify mispriced ones.

Each of these strategies can be applied as an approach for investing initial funds or as a bond swap in which two or more bond positions are simultaneously changed in order to change the allocation of a bond portfolio.

Interest Rate Anticipation Strategies

If a bond investor expects interest rates to decrease across all maturities by the same number of basis points (i.e., a parallel shift in the yield curve), he could attain a greater expected return by purchasing bonds with larger durations or, if he is managing a bond fund by reallocating his portfolio, by selling shorter-duration bonds and buying longer-duration ones. In contrast, if the bond manager expected the yield curve to shift up, he could minimize his exposure to interest rate risk by changing his investments or portfolio to include more bonds with shorter durations. One way to shorten the fund's duration is for the manager to buy *cushion bonds*. A cushion bond is a callable bond with a coupon that is significantly above the current market rate. The bond has the features of a high-coupon yield and, with its embedded call option, a market price that is lower than a comparable noncallable bond. (See Exhibit 6.1 for an example of using a cushion bond when rates are expected to increase.)

Active strategies of selecting bonds or bond portfolios with specific durations based on interest rate expectations are referred to as *rate anticipation strategies,* and when they involve simultaneously selling and buying bonds with different durations, they are referred to as a *rate anticipation swap.*[1]

Rate Anticipation Strategies and Horizon Analysis

Rate anticipation strategies are often formed using *total return analysis* or *horizon analysis*. In this approach, potential returns from several strategies with different durations

EXHIBIT 6.1 Cushion Bond

One way to shorten the fund's duration is for the manager to buy ***cushion bonds***. A cushion bond is a callable bond with a coupon that is significantly above the current market rate. The bond has the features of a high coupon yield and with its embedded call option a market price that is lower than a comparable noncallable bond. For example, suppose a bond manager had a fund consisting of 10-year, 10% option-free bonds valued at 113.42 per $100 par to yield 8%. Also suppose that there were comparable 10-year, 12% coupon bonds callable at 110 that were trading in the market at a price close to their call price (note: callable bonds cannot trade at prices higher than their call prices). If the manager expected rates to increase, he could cushion the negative price impact on the fund's value by selling some of his option-free bonds and buying the higher coupon, callable bonds—the cushion bonds. The swap of his existing bonds (priced at 113.42) for the cushion bonds (priced at 110) would, in turn, provide him an immediate gain in income plus he would receive higher coupon income in the future. Thus, the interest rate swap of option-free bonds for cushion bonds provides some value preservation. Note: A callable bond has a lower duration than a noncallable one with the same maturity. The 10-year cushion bond with it call feature and higher coupon rate has a relatively lower duration than the 10-year option-free bond; thus, the swap of cushion bonds for option-free bonds in this example represents a switch of longer duration bonds for shorter ones.

are evaluated for a number of possible interest rate changes over different horizon periods to identify the best strategy. By conducting horizon analysis on one or more bonds or bond portfolios, an investor or portfolio manager can project the performance of the bonds or portfolios and can compare different bonds or bond portfolios based on a planned investment horizon and expectations concerning the market. Exhibit 6.2 shows horizon analysis conducted on the Xavier Student Investment Fund (XSIF) bond portfolio on April 13, 2012, using the Bloomberg Bond Scenario Analysis (BSA) screen. The XSIF fund consists of Treasuries, federal agencies, and investment-grade corporate credits and is managed against the Barclay's Government Credit Index (an index consisting of approximately 5,000 Treasuries, agencies, and investment-grade corporate bonds). On April 13, the portfolio consisted of 30 bonds, and had a duration of 4.48 and a market value of $1,003,654 (see Slice and Dice [PSD] screens in Exhibit 6.2; the Slice and Dice screen is now found on the Bloomberg PORT screen on the Characteristics tab). As shown on the BSA screens, for a two-year horizon

EXHIBIT 6.2 Horizon Analysis—Bloomberg BSA Screen

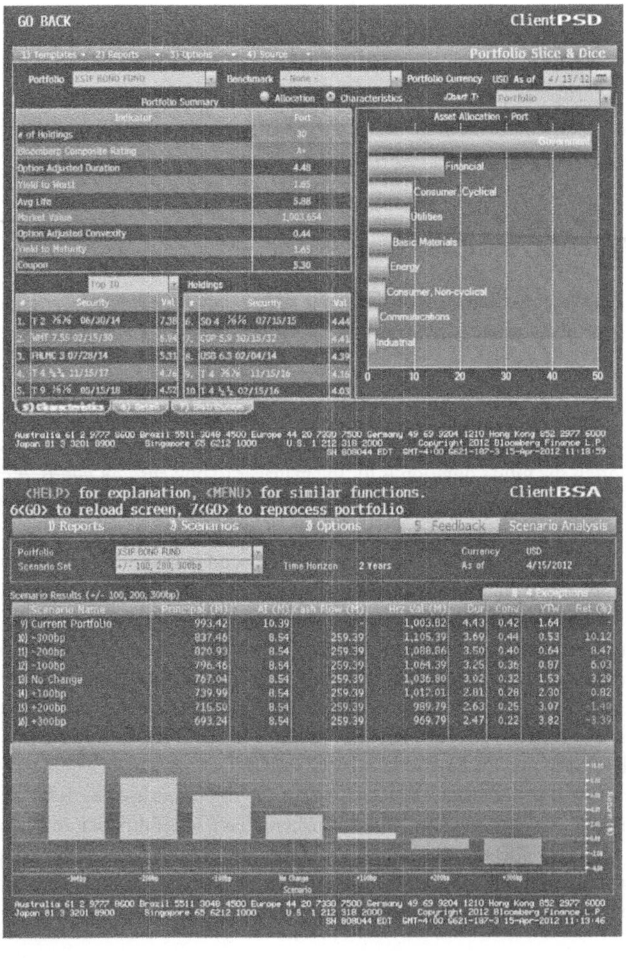

Indicator	Port
# of Holdings	30
Bloomberg Composite Rating	A+
Option Adjusted Duration	4.48
Yield to Worst	1.65
Avg Life	5.88
Market Value	1,003,654
Option Adjusted Convexity	0.44
Yield to Maturity	1.65
Coupon	5.30

Scenario Name	Principal (M)	AI (M)	Cash Flow (M)	Hrz Val (M)	Dur	Conv	YTW	Ret (%)
9) Current Portfolio	993.42	10.39	-	1,003.82	4.43	0.42	1.64	-
10) -300bp	837.46	8.54	259.39	1,105.39	3.69	0.44	0.53	10.12
11) -200bp	820.93	8.54	259.39	1,088.86	3.50	0.40	0.64	8.47
12) -100bp	796.46	8.54	259.39	1,064.39	3.25	0.36	0.87	6.03
13) No Change	767.04	8.54	259.39	1,036.80	3.02	0.32	1.53	3.29
14) +100bp	739.99	8.54	259.39	1,012.01	2.81	0.28	2.30	0.82
15) +200bp	716.50	8.54	259.39	989.79	2.63	0.25	3.07	-1.40
16) +300bp	693.24	8.54	259.39	969.79	2.47	0.22	3.82	-3.39

the total return on the portfolio ranges from 10.12 percent with a –300-basis point (bps) parallel yield curve shift to –3.39 percent for a +300-bps parallel shift. For a two-year horizon, this portfolio would be attractive if one expected rates to decrease but perhaps too risky if one expected rates to increase. An alternative portfolio would be to swap some of the longer-term bonds for shorter-term ones and then analyze that portfolio again using horizon analysis.

Yield Curve Shifts and Strategies

Interest rate anticipation strategies require not only forecasting general interest rate movements, but also changes in the term structure of rates. Some rate anticipation strategies are based on estimating the type of yield curve shift. Three types of yield curve shifts occur with some regularity: parallel shifts, shifts with twists, and shifts with humpedness. In a *parallel shift,* yields on all maturities change by the same magnitude (see Exhibit 6.3a). A *twist* is a nonparallel shift. It implies either a flattening or steepening of the yield curve. As shown in Exhibit 6.3b, if there is a flattening, the spread between long-term and short-term rates decreases; if there is a steepening, the spread increases. A shift with *humpedness* is also a nonparallel shift in which short-term and long-term rates change by different magnitudes than intermediate rates. An increase in both short-term and long-term rates relative to intermediate rates is referred to as a *positive butterfly,* and a decrease is known as a *negative butterfly* (see Exhibit 6.3c).

Given the different types of yield curve shifts, investors actively managing bond portfolios will pursue different strategies based on their yield curve forecast. There are three general types of yield curve strategies used by active bond investors: bullet, barbell, and ladder. The *bullet strategy* is implemented by constructing a portfolio concentrated in one maturity area. For example, a bullet strategy consisting of a portfolio of long-term bonds could be formed if there were an expectation of a downward shift in the yield curve with a twist such that long-term rates were expected to decrease more than short-term.[2]

Similarly, if investors expected a simple downward parallel shift in the yield curve, a bullet strategy with longer duration bonds would also yield greater returns than an investment strategy in intermediate-term or short-term bonds if the expectation turns out to be correct. The *barbell strategy* is one in which investments are concentrated in both the short-term and long-term bonds. This strategy could be profitable for an investor who is forecasting a negative butterfly yield curve shift. Finally, the *ladder strategy* is constructed with equal allocations in each maturity group.

In implementing an active strategy based on a forecasted shift in the yield curve, horizon analysis is again useful for identifying the appropriate strategy to evaluate potential returns from several yield curve strategies for a number of possible interest rate changes over different horizon periods to identify the best strategy. Exhibit 6.4 shows horizon analysis conducted on the Xavier Student Investment Fund using the Bloomberg BSA screen for the followings scenarios: yield curve flattening, with long-term yield decreasing 100 bps and 50 bps, yield curve not changing, and yield curve steepening, with long-term rates increasing 50 bps and 100 bps. As shown, the total returns

EXHIBIT 6.3 Yield Curve Shifts

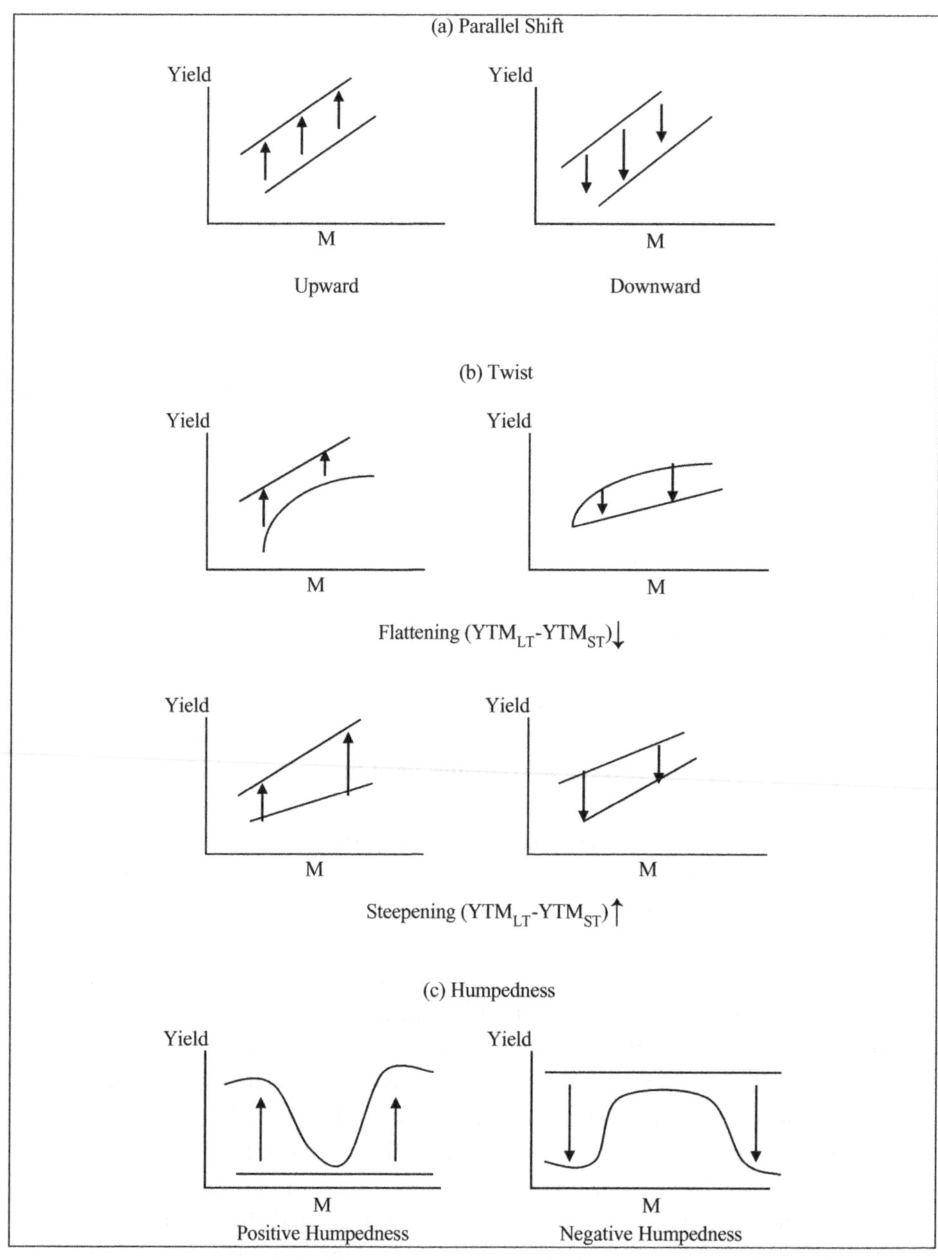

for a two-year horizon range from 5.55 percent to 1.24 percent. The relatively small range in total returns is explained by the portfolio having a relatively small proportion of bonds with durations exceeding 10. This can be seen by examining the Bloomberg PREP screen that shows the portfolio's duration distribution. The portfolio has approximately 58 percent of its holding concentrated in bonds with durations between

EXHIBIT 6.4 Horizon Analysis for Nonparallel Yield Curve Shifts—Bloomberg BSA Screen

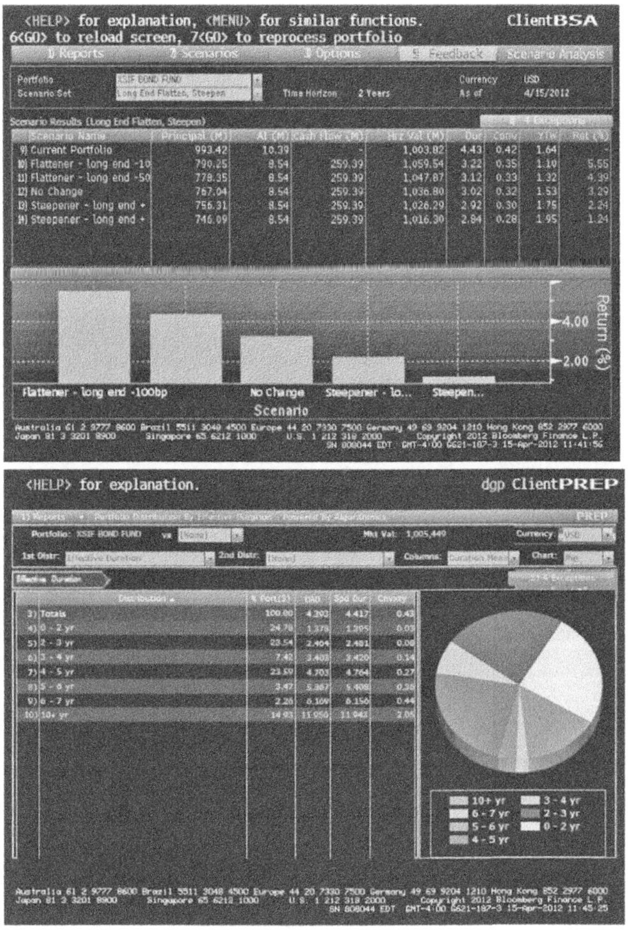

<HELP> for explanation, <MENU> for similar functions. ClientBSA
6<GO> to reload screen, 7<GO> to reprocess portfolio

Portfolio: XSIF BOND FUND | Currency: USD
Scenario Set: Long End Flatten, Steepen | Time Horizon: 2 Years | As of: 4/15/2012

Scenario Results (Long End Flatten, Steepen)

Scenario Name	Principal (M)	AI (M)	Cash Flow (M)	Hrz Val (M)	Dur	Conv	Ytw	Rot (%)
9) Current Portfolio	993.42	10.39	-	1,003.82	4.43	0.42	1.64	-
10) Flattener - long end -10	790.25	8.54	259.39	1,059.54	3.22	0.35	1.10	5.55
11) Flattener - long end -50	778.35	8.54	259.39	1,047.87	3.12	0.33	1.32	4.39
12) No Change	767.04	8.54	259.39	1,036.80	3.02	0.32	1.53	3.29
13) Steepener - long end +	756.31	8.54	259.39	1,026.29	2.92	0.30	1.75	2.24
14) Steepener - long end +	746.09	8.54	259.39	1,016.30	2.84	0.28	1.95	1.24

Flattener - long end -100bp | No Change | Steepener - lo... | Steepen...
Scenario | Return (%) | 4.00 | 2.00

<HELP> for explanation. dgp ClientPREP

Portfolio: XSIF BOND FUND | Mkt Val: 1,005,449 | Currency: USD
1st Distr: Effective Duration | 2nd Distr: [None]

Effective Duration

Distribution	% Port($)	OAD	Spd Dur	Cnvxty
3) Totals	100.00	4.393	4.417	0.43
4) 0 - 2 yr	24.70	1.378	1.395	0.03
5) 2 - 3 yr	23.54	2.404	2.481	0.08
6) 3 - 4 yr	7.42	3.403	3.420	0.14
7) 4 - 5 yr	23.59	4.703	4.764	0.27
8) 5 - 6 yr	3.47	5.367	5.408	0.38
9) 6 - 7 yr	2.26	6.109	6.150	0.44
10) 10+ yr	14.93	11.950	11.942	2.05

10+ yr | 6 - 7 yr | 5 - 6 yr | 4 - 5 yr | 3 - 4 yr | 2 - 3 yr | 0 - 2 yr

two and six years and only 15 percent in durations exceeding 10. The Xavier portfolio can, in turn, be described as being closer to a bullet portfolio with a duration distribution focused more on intermediate bonds than long-term one. As a result, the fund is less sensitive to yield curve shifts that affect the long-end of the curve.

CONSTRUCTING AND ANALYZING BOND PORTFOLIOS WITH THE BLOOMBERG PRTU AND PMEN SCREENS

PRTU, PORT, PREP, PCF, BSA, PSA, AND EVTS

Using the PRTU screen, one can construct bond portfolios (see Chapter 2 for Bloomberg portfolio construction boxes).

From the PMEN menu, some useful screens for analyzing fixed-income portfolios include: PORT: Portfolio & Risk Analytics; BSA: Scenario Analysis; PDSP: Portfolio

(*Continued*)

Display; NPH: Portfolio News; CACT: Corporate Action Calendar; EVTS: Events Calendar; BSA: Scenario Analysis; PSH: Proposed Trade/Hedge Analysis; PCF: Expected Cash Flow; PREP.

The historical total return performance of the portfolio can be evaluated by using the CIXB screen to create a basket of the portfolio's daily returns (see Chapter 2) and then evaluating the basket as an index on the index screen using the COMP and GP functions.

The PORT, PCF, PREP, PSA, BSA, EVTS, and DRAM screens that are shown here are for the Xavier Student Investment Fund (XSIF) bond portfolio as of September 29, 2012; the GP and COMP screens are for the fund as of April 15, 2012. BSA and PREP screens for the fund as of April 15, 2012 are also shown in Exhibits 6.2 and 6.4.

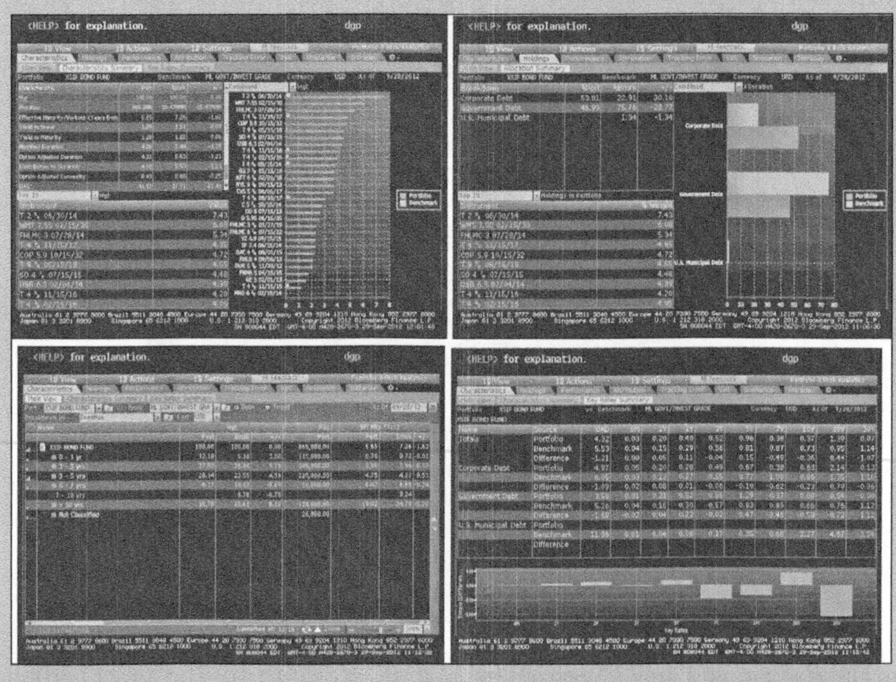

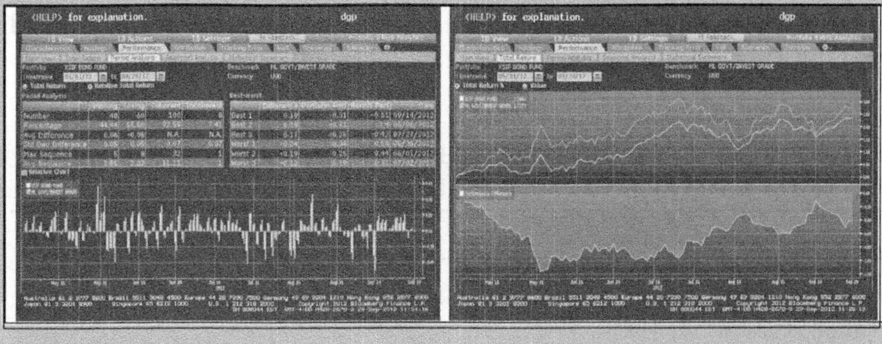

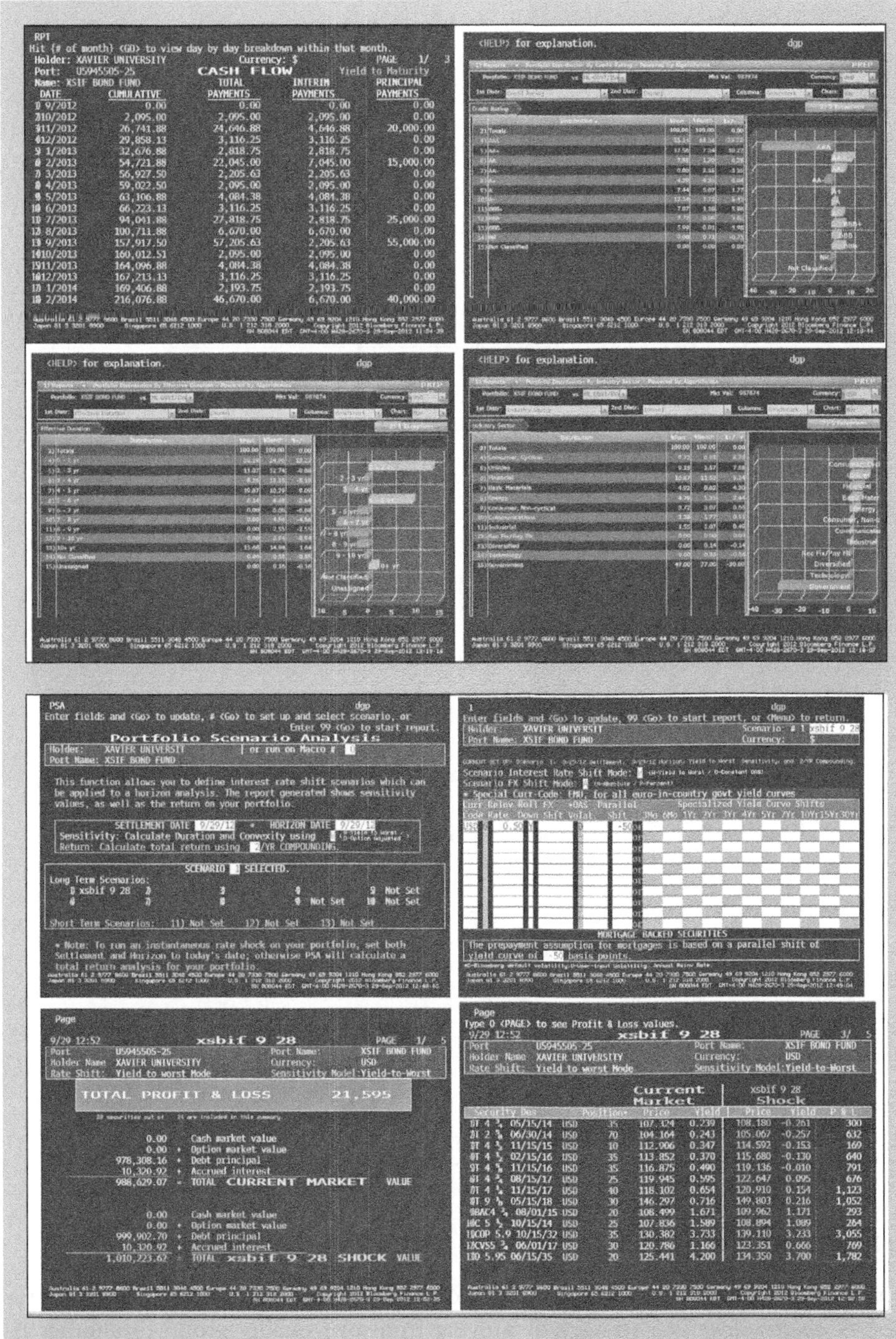
Hit (# of month) <GO> to view day by day breakdown within that month.
Holder: XAVIER UNIVERSITY
CASH FLOW
<HELP> for explanation.
Portfolio Scenario Analysis
Holder: XAVIER UNIVERSITY
Port Name: XSIF BOND FUND
TOTAL PROFIT & LOSS 21,595
TOTAL CURRENT MARKET VALUE
TOTAL xsbif 9 28 SHOCK VALUE
Current Market
xsbif 9 28 Shock
MORTGAGE BACKED SECURITIES

(Continued)

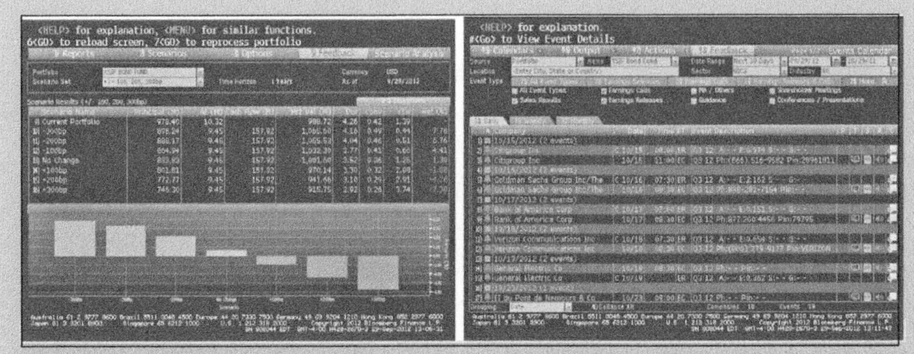

Note: OAD is effective duration; OAC is effective convexity.
Note: Values in different screens differ due to the screens' being saved at different times. BSA ExcAnalysis (to access: click "Excel" from "Reports" tab). The report shows total returns for each shift for the portfolio, individual bonds, and sectors.

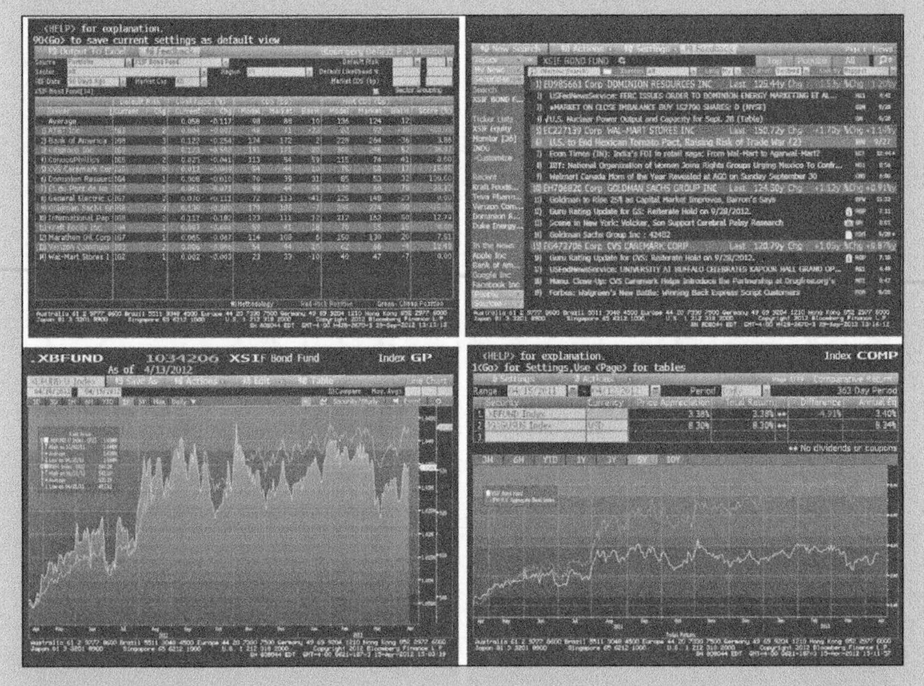

Credit Strategies

Active credit investment strategies consist of quality swaps and credit analysis strategies. A *quality swap* is a strategy of moving from one quality group to another in anticipation of a change in economic conditions. A credit analysis strategy, in turn, involves a credit analysis of corporate, municipal, or foreign bonds in order to identify potential changes in credit risk. This information is then used to identify bonds to include or exclude in a bond portfolio or bond investment strategy.

Quality Swap

In a *quality swap,* investors try to profit from expected changes in yield spreads between different quality sectors. Quality swaps often involve a *sector rotation* in which more funds are allocated to a specific quality sector in anticipation of a price change. For example, suppose a bond fund manager expected a recession accompanied by a flight to safety in which the demand for higher-quality bonds would increase and the demand for lower-quality ones would decrease. To profit from this expectation, the manager could change the allocation of her bond fund by selling some of her low-quality ones and buying more high-quality bonds. In contrast, suppose the economy were in a recession, but the bond manager believed that it was near its trough and that economic growth would follow. To capitalize from this expectation, the manager could tilt her bond portfolio toward lower-quality bonds by selling some of her higher-quality bonds and buying lower-quality ones.

In addition to sector rotations, quality swaps can also be constructed to profit from anticipated changes in yield spreads between quality sectors. Quality yield spreads have tended to widen during periods of economic recession and narrow during periods of economic expansion. If the economy were at the trough of a recession and were expected to grow in the future, speculators or a hedge fund might anticipate a narrowing in the spread between lower- and higher-quality bonds. To exploit this, they could form a quality swap by taking a long position in lower-quality bonds and a short position in higher-quality bonds with similar durations. Whether rates increase or decrease, speculators would still profit from these positions, provided the quality spread narrows. For example, if rates increase but the quality spread narrows because of economic growth, then the percentage decrease in the price of lower-quality bonds would be less than the percentage decrease in the price of higher-quality bonds. As a result, the capital gain from the short position in the higher-quality bonds would dominate the capital loss from the long position in the lower-quality bonds. Similarly, if rates decrease but the quality spread narrows, then the percentage increase in the price for the lower-quality bonds would be greater than the percentage increase for the higher-quality bonds. In this case, the capital gain from the long position in lower-quality bonds would dominate the capital loss from the short position in the higher-quality bonds.[3]

Credit Analysis—The Evaluation of Credit Risk

A credit analysis strategy, in turn, involves evaluating a corporate, municipal, or foreign bond in order to identify potential changes in credit risk. This information is then used to identify bonds to include or exclude in a bond portfolio or bond investment strategy.

The objective of a credit analysis strategy is to determine expected changes in credit risk. If changes in quality ratings of a bond can be projected prior to an upgrade or downgrade announcement by Moody's, Standard & Poor's, or Fitch (if the market is efficient, it may be necessary to project the change before the announcement), bond investors can realize gains by buying bonds they project will be upgraded, and they can avoid losses by selling or not buying bonds they project will be downgraded. With astute credit analysis there are significant gains possible by being able to forecast upgrades and significant losses that can be avoided by projecting downgrades. In fact, the strategy of many managers of high-yield bond funds or funds that have some of their investments allocated to high-yield bonds is to develop effective credit analysis models so that they can identify bonds with high yields and high probabilities of upgrades to include in their portfolios, as well as identify bonds with high probabilities of downgrades to exclude from their fund. Credit analysis can be done through basic fundamental analysis of the bond issuer and the indenture and with statistical-based models, such as a multiple discriminate model.

Fundamental Credit Analysis

Many large institutional investors and banks have their own credit analysis departments to evaluate bond issues in order to determine the abilities of companies, municipalities, and foreign issuers to meet their contractual obligations, as well as to determine the possibility of changes in a bond's quality ratings and therefore a change in its price.

The credit analysis for corporate bonds often includes the following types of examination:

- *Industrial analysis.* Assessment of the growth rate of the industry, stage of industrial development, cyclicality of the industry, degree of competition, industry and company trends, government regulations, and labor costs and issues.
- *Fundamental analysis.* Comparison of the company's financial ratios with other firms in the industry and with the averages for bonds based on their quality ratings. Ratios often used for analysis include: (1) interest coverage (earnings before interest and taxes [EBIT]/interest), (2) leverage (long-term debt/total assets), (3) cash flow (net income + depreciation + amortization + depletion + deferred taxes) as a proportion of total debt (cash flow/debt), and (4) return on equity.
- *Asset and liability analysis.* Determination of the market values of assets and liabilities, age and condition of plants, working capital (current assets minus current liabilities), intangible assets and liabilities (e.g., unfunded pension liabilities), and foreign currency exposure.
- *Indenture analysis.* Analysis of protective covenants, including a comparison of covenants with the industry norms.[4]

The two most important areas of examination in the credit analysis for municipals (general obligations [GOs] and revenue bonds) are indenture analysis and economic analysis. The important areas of inquiry in economic analysis relate to debt burden, fiscal soundness, overall economic climate, and red flags.[5] Some of the negative indicators suggesting greater credit risk are decreases in population, unemployment increases, decreases in the number of building permits, actual revenue levels consistently falling below projections, declines in property values, loss of large employers, use of debt reserves, and declines in debt coverage ratios. For revenue bonds, additional red flags could include cost overruns on projects, schedule delays, and frequent rate or rental increases.

The credit analysis for foreign bonds issued by corporations takes into account the same issues of any corporate bond (fundamental ratio analysis, financial soundness, industry analysis, and indenture examination). In addition, the analysis also needs to consider cross-border risk: risk due to changes in political, social, and economic conditions in countries where the bonds are issued or where the company is incorporated. In the case of sovereign foreign debt, especially the debt of emerging markets, analysis needs to include an examination of sovereign risk: The risk that the government is unable or unwilling (due to political changes) to service its debt.

Multiple Discriminate Models and the Altman Z-Score

Multiple discriminate models are statistical models that some analysts use to forecast default or changes in credit ratings. When applied to credit analysis, the models estimate a bond's credit score or index, S_i, to determine its overall credit quality. The score is based on a set of explanatory variables, X_i, and estimated weights or coefficients measuring the variables relative impact on the bond's overall credit quality. One of the more popular models using multiple discriminate analysis is the Altman Z-Score Model. Developed by Edward Altman in 1968, the scores predict the probability of business failure leading to bankruptcy. The Altman Z-score is a linear function calculated as follows:

$$Z = 1.2X_1 + 1.4X_2 + 3.3X_3 + 0.6X_4 + 1.0X_5 \quad (6.1)$$

where:

X_1 = Ratio of working capital to total assets
X_2 = Ratio of retained earnings to total assets
X_3 = Ratio of earnings before interest and taxes to total assets
X_4 = Market value of equity to total liabilities ratio
X_5 = Ratio of sales to total assets

Altman Z-scores can range from –5.0 to +20.0. Z-scores above 3.0 indicate that bankruptcy is unlikely, scores between 1.8 and 3.0 are inconclusive, and scores below 1.8 indicate an increased risk of business failure. The Z-scores are ordinal and not proportional. That is, a score of 4.0 is better than a score of 2.0, but not necessarily twice as good. A Z-score below zero indicates an extremely risky situation. Z-scores should also be viewed over time, with consistently low scores over time being more of a concern than a one-time low score.

In 2002, Altman extended his 1968 work with the "Double Prime" Model for nonmanufacturing industrial companies:

$$Z'' = 6.56\,X_1 + 3.26\,X_2 + 6.72\,X_3 + 1.05\,X_4$$

where:

X_1, X_2, and X_3 are identical to variable in Equation (6.1)
X_4 = shareholder value as measured by book value instead of market value

The cutoff scores are somewhat lower for the double prime Z″-score, with the cutoff scores being between 1.1 and 2.6.

Finally, there is the *Hillegeist Z-score.* This is an updated estimate of the Altman Z-score:

$$\text{Hillegeist Z-Score} = 3.835 + 1.13\,X_1 + 0.005\,X_2 + 0.269\,X_3 + 0.399\,X_4 - 0.033\,X_5$$

The Hillegeist Z-score (HS) is equal to $-\log(p/[1-p])$, where p is the one-year probability of default. The one-year probability of default, in turn, is equal to $1/(exp(\text{HS}) + 1)$. Like the Altman score, the higher the value, the lower the probability of bankruptcy.

Exhibit 6.5 shows the Bloomberg Altman Z-score model applied to Kraft and Ford on April 15, 2012. As shown, Kraft has a score of 3.20, placing it in the unlikely default category, and a relatively stable Z-score history. In contrast, Ford has a Z-score of 0.87, placing it in the increased risk of failure category. However, it has a Z-score

BLOOMBERG CREDIT AND BOND RISK ANALYSIS SCREENS: DRSK, RVRD, AND RSKC

The Bloomberg RVRD, RSKC, and DRSK screens are useful in conducting credit analysis.

RVRD

The RVRD screen shows fundamental debt and credit ratios of the company of a selected bond against the relative index of the company.

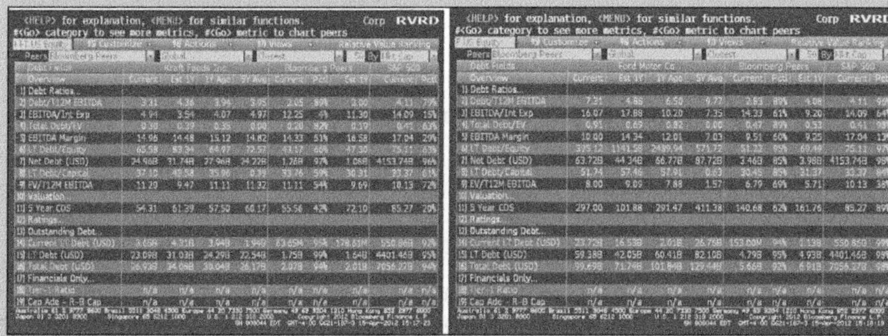

RSKC: CREDIT PROFILE

The RSKC screen provides a risk profile of the company, a peer comparison (by clicking bottom "Peer Comparison" tab) and historical analysis of ratios (by clicking "Historical Trend" tab).

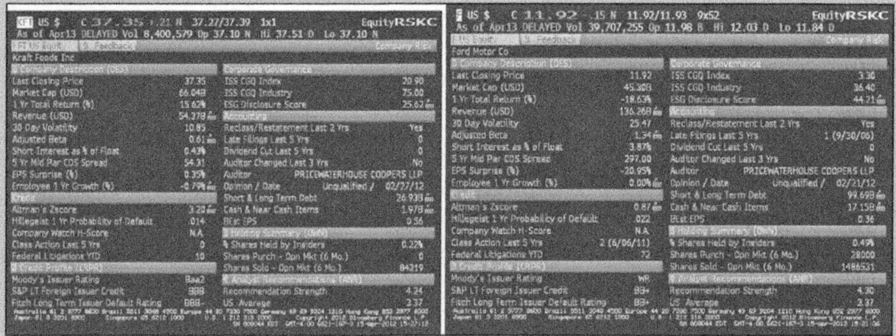

CREDIT RISK MEASURES ON RSKS

Altman's Z-score: The probability of a company's entering bankruptcy within the next two years. The higher the value, the lower the probability of bankruptcy. A score above 3 indicates bankruptcy is unlikely; below 1.8, bankruptcy is possible.

Hillegeist Z-score: The Hillegeist Z-score is equal to $-\log(p/[1 - p])$, where p is the one-year probability of default. The higher the value, the lower the probability of bankruptcy.

Class Action Last 5 Yrs: The number of class action lawsuits brought against the company in the past five years and the date of the most recent class action lawsuit filing, if applicable.

Federal Litigations YTD: The number of federal litigation cases year-to-date to which the company corresponding to the security is a party.

DRSK

The DRSK screen provides estimates of the default probability, credit rating, and the five-year CDS spread for a selected company and its peers.

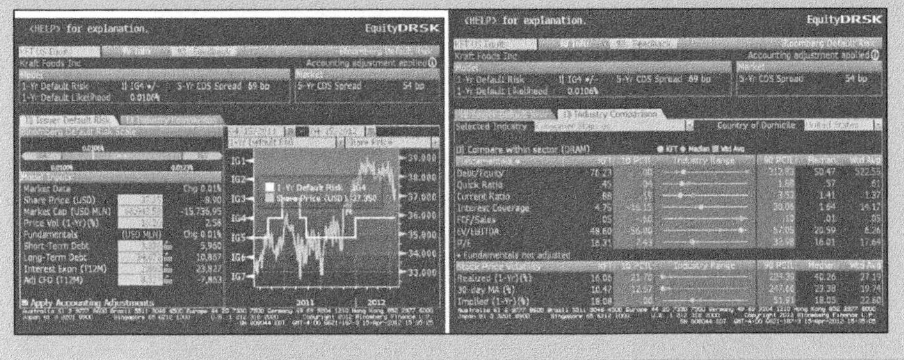

history in which its score has increased from a low of –0.0384 in 3/31/09 to 0.87 on April 15, 2012, indicating a significant improvement in credit quality.

High-Yield Bond Funds

Credit analysis is an important tool for managing high-yield funds. Successful funds have fund managers that are able to identify those low-quality bonds that have the potential for being upgraded and therefore should be included in the fund and those bonds that are in jeopardy of being downgraded and therefore should be excluded. It should be noted that today the management of high-yield bond funds has become quite challenging, given the many types of high-yield bonds. In the 1980s, many high-yield funds consisted only of privately placed junk bonds of corporations that issued them to finance their mergers. Today, many lower-quality corporate bonds are sold with special provisions. As we will discuss in Chapter 7, these bonds include income bonds, reset notes, payment-in-kind bonds, convertibles, putable notes, extendable bonds, bonds with warrants, and credit-sensitive bonds. The successful performance of today's high-yield funds therefore requires not only effective credit analysis of the company, government, or country issuer, but also a careful analysis of the bond's indenture and its special security provisions.

A special type of high-yield fund is the *Chapter 11 Fund:* A fund consisting of the bonds of bankrupt or distressed companies. Such funds are comprised of the issues of

EXHIBIT 6.5 Altman Z-Score Model—Bloomberg AZS Screen

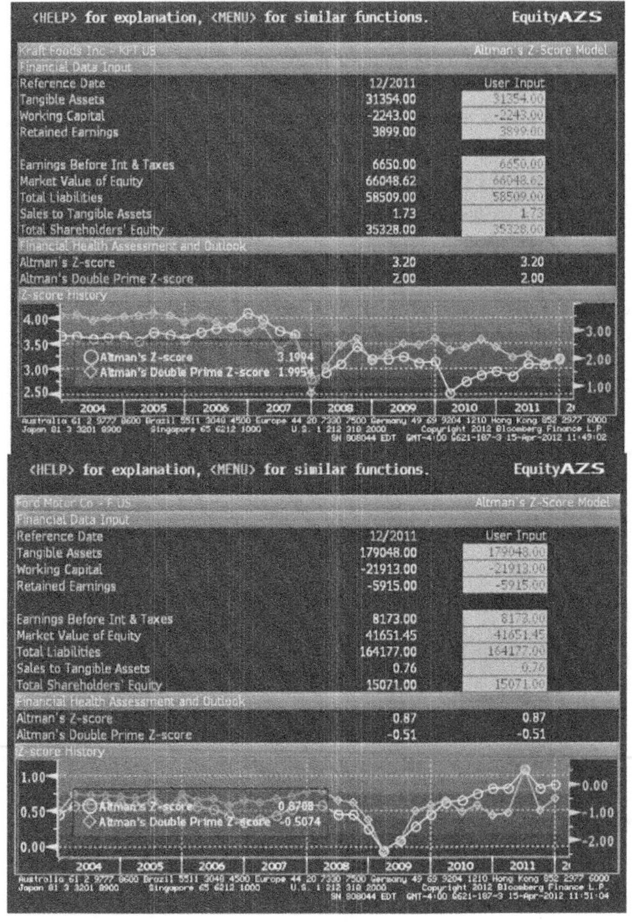

AZS forecasts the probability of a selected company entering bankruptcy within the next two years. One can use AZS to evaluate the general financial condition of a company and the associated risk of investing in the selected security. One can input forecasted values of the variable defining the model to predict changes in the Z-Score. *Note:* AZS does not calculate a score for financial institutions. Explanatory variables:

Tangible Assets: The total assets minus the intangible assets.

Working Capital: The amount of capital available to a corporation to fund its short-term operations. It is calculated by taking the difference between current assets and current liabilities.

Retained Earnings: The amount of earnings a company does not pay out to stockholders, but instead retains to reinvest into the firm's operations.

Earnings Before Interest and Taxes: The company's profit/loss after paying all expenses, but before subtracting interest expenses or taxes. Calculated on a trailing 12-month basis.

Market Value of Equity: The company's shares outstanding multiplied by its last closing price.

Total Liabilities: The total of all current and noncurrent liabilities.

Sales to Tangible Assets: The ratio of sales to tangible assets. Sales are calculated on a trailing 12-month basis.

Total Shareholders' Equity: The total of preferred equity, minority interest, and total common equity.

corporations who are going through a bankruptcy process or those that are in distress, but have not yet filed. The general strategy is to buy bonds whose prices have plummeted as a result of a filing (or on information that indicates a filing is imminent) but where there is a good expectation that there will be a successful reorganization or possible asset sale that will lead in the future to an increase in the debt's value or to the replacement of the debt with a more valuable claim. Chapter 11 funds are sometimes set up as a hedge fund in which large investors buy, through the fund, a significant block of debt of a specific bankrupt company, giving them some control in the reorganization. The funds are also set up as so-called *vulture funds* that invest in the securities of a number of bankrupt firms. Just like any high-yield fund, the success of Chapter 11 funds depends on the ability of the fund managers to conduct an effective credit-type analysis. In this case, though, the analysis often involves studying the feasibility of the reorganization plan submitted out of the bankruptcy process or trying to project the type of plan that will be submitted.[6]

Fundamental Valuation Strategies

A common approach to stock selection is fundamental analysis. The objective of fundamental stock analysis is to determine a stock's equilibrium price or intrinsic value. By doing this, fundamentalists hope to profit by purchasing stocks they estimate to be underpriced (a stock whose market price is below the intrinsic value) and selling or shorting stocks they determine to be overpriced. The objective of fundamental bond analysis is the same as that of fundamental stock analysis. It involves determining a bond's intrinsic value and then comparing that value with the bond's market price.

The intrinsic value of a bond is estimated by discounting its cash flows by its required rate. The bond's required rate, k_d, depends on the current level of interest rates as measured by the risk-free rate on a Treasury with the same maturity as the bond in question, R_f, and the bond's characteristics (maturity, option features, and quality risk) and the risk premiums or spreads associated with the bond's characteristic: default risk premium (DRP), liquidity premium (LP), and option-adjusted spread (OAS):

$$k_d = R_f + \text{DRP} + \text{LP} + \text{OAS}$$

The active management of a bond portfolio using a fundamental strategy, in turn, involves buying bonds that are determined to be underpriced and selling or avoiding those determined to be overpriced. Fundamentalists conduct detailed credit analysis and use various models, such as multiple discriminate analysis or CDS analysis to estimate or forecast a change in the probability of default or to estimate a credit spread or a change in the spread. They also use option pricing models such as the Black-Derman-Toy model to estimate spreads due to embedded options or to forecast changes in those spreads.

Yield Pickup Strategy

A variation of fundamental bond strategies is a *yield pickup swap.* In a yield pickup swap, investors try to find bonds that are identical, but for some reason are temporarily mispriced, trading at different yields. When two identical bonds trade at different yields, abnormal returns can be realized by portfolio managers by buying underpriced (higher yield) bonds and selling overpriced (lower yield) bond. It is important to note that to profit from a yield pickup swap, the bonds must be identical. It could be the case that two bonds appear to be identical, but are not. For example, two bonds with the same durations, default ratings, and call features may appear to be identical, when in fact, they have different marketability characteristics that explain the observed differences in their yields.

Other Active Strategies

In the preceding discussion of active strategies, we identified three bond swaps: rate anticipation swaps, quality swaps, and yield pickup swaps. In addition to these swaps, two other swaps that should be noted are tax swaps and swaps of callable and noncallable bonds.

Tax Swap

In a *tax swap,* an investor sells one bond and purchases another in order to take advantage of the tax laws. For example, suppose a bond investor purchased $10,000 worth of a particular bond and then sold it after rates decreased for $15,000, realizing a capital gain of $5,000 and also a capital gains tax liability. One way for the investor to negate the tax liability would be to offset the capital gain with a capital loss. If the investor were holding bonds with current capital losses of say $5,000, he could sell those to incur a capital loss to offset his gain. Except for the offset feature, though, the investor may not otherwise want to sell the bond; for example, he might want to hold the bond because he expects an upgrade in the bond's quality rating. If this were the case, then the investor could execute a bond swap in which he sells the bond needed for creating a capital loss and then uses the proceeds to purchase a similar, though not identical, bond. Thus, the tax swap allows the investor to effectively hold the bond he wants, while still reducing his tax liability. It should be noted that for the capital loss to be tax deductible, the bond purchased in the tax swap cannot be identical to the bond sold; if it were, then the swap would represent a wash sale that would result in the IRS's disallowing the deduction.[7] In contrast to the IRS's wash sales criterion on stocks, though, the wash sale criterion used for bonds does permit the purchase of comparable bonds that have only minor differences.

Callable/Noncallable Bond Swaps

During periods of high interest rates, the spread between the yields on callable and noncallable bonds is greater than during periods of relatively low interest rates. Accordingly, if investors expect the spread between callable and noncallable bonds to narrow, they could capitalize by forming a *callable/noncallable bond swap:* long in the callable bond and short in the noncallable one. To effectively apply this bond swap requires investors to forecast changes in the spread. Similar swaps can also be extended to bonds with and without other option features, such as putable and nonputable bonds.

Passive Bond Management Strategies

The objectives underlying passive management strategies vary from a simple buy-and-hold approach of investing in bonds with specific features with the intent of holding the bonds to maturity, to forming portfolios with returns that mirror the returns on a bond index, to constructing portfolios that ensure there are sufficient funds to meet future liabilities. Here, we look at two passive strategies: indexing and cash flow matching.[8] Indexing strategies involve constructing bond portfolios that are highly correlated with a specified bond index. These strategies are applicable for investment funds whose performances are evaluated on a period-by-period basis or total return funds. Cash flow matching strategies involve constructing bond portfolios with cash flows that will meet future liabilities. They are liability management strategies applicable to insurance companies, deposit institutions, and pension funds that have cash outlays that must be made at specific times.

Indexing

Bond indexing involves constructing a bond portfolio whose returns over time replicate the returns of a bond index. Indexing is a passive strategy, often used by investment fund managers who believe that actively managed bond strategies do not outperform bond market indexes.

The first step in constructing a bond index fund is to select the appropriate index. Bond indexes can be either general, such as the Barclays Aggregate Composite Index, or specialized, such as Barclays Global Government Bond Index. Also, some investment companies offer their own customized index specifically designed to meet certain investment objectives. After selecting the index, the next step is to determine how to replicate the index's performance. One approach is to simply purchase all of the bonds comprising the index in the same proportion that they appear in the index. This is known as pure bond indexing or the full-replication approach. This approach would result in a perfect correlation between the bond fund and the index. However, with some indexes consisting of as many as 5,000 bonds, the transaction costs involved in acquiring all of the bonds is very high. An alternative to selecting all bonds is to use only a sample. By using a smaller-size portfolio, the transaction costs incurred in constructing the index fund would be smaller. However with fewer bonds, there may be less than perfect positive correlation between the index and the index fund. The difference between the returns on the index and the index fund are referred to as tracking errors. Using a sample is subject to tracking errors.

When a sample approach is used, the index fund can be set up using an optimization approach to determine the allocation of each bond in the fund such that it minimizes the tracking error. Another approach is to use a *cell matching* strategy. With this approach, the index is decomposed into cells, with each cell defining a different mix of features of the index (duration, credit rating, sector, etc.). For example, a bond index might be described as having two durations ($D > 5$ years and $D < 5$ years), two sectors (Corporate and Treasury), and two quality ratings (AAA, AA). These features can be broken into eight unique types of cells, C_i ($2 \times 2 \times 2 = 8$):

$$
\begin{aligned}
C_1 &= D < 5, \text{AAA, Corp}\\
C_2 &= D < 5, \text{AAA, Treasury}\\
C_3 &= D < 5, \text{AA, Corp}\\
C_4 &= D < 5, \text{AA, Treasury}\\
C_5 &= D > 5, \text{AAA, Corp}\\
C_6 &= D > 5, \text{AAA, Treasury}\\
C_7 &= D > 5, \text{AA, Corp}\\
C_8 &= D > 5, \text{AA, Treasury}
\end{aligned}
$$

Given the cells, the index fund is constructed by selecting bonds to match each cell and then allocating funds to each type of bond based on each cell's allocation.

Given the number of possible attributes describing an index, cell matching can be quite complex. For example, three duration classes, three sectors, and three quality ratings give rise to 27 cells. To minimize the number of constraints, one approach is to base the cell identification on just two features such as the durations and sectors or the durations and quality ratings. A duration/sector index is formed by matching the amounts of the index's durations that make up each of the various sectors. This requires estimating the duration for each sector comprising the index (e.g., Treasury, federal agency, corporate industry, corporate utility, corporate foreign, sovereign, and asset-backed) and determining each sector's percentage of value to the index. If 20 percent of an index's value consists of Treasury securities with the Treasuries having an estimated portfolio duration of 4.5, then the index portfolio being constructed would consist of 20 percent Treasuries with an average duration of 4.5 (see top of Exhibit 6.6). Instead of sectors, duration matching could be done with quality sectors. This would require determining the percentages of value and average durations of each quality-rating group making up the index (see bottom of Exhibit 6.6).

Whether the index fund is formed with the population of all bonds encompassing the specified index or a sample, the objective of indexing is still to replicate the performance of the index. A variation of straight indexing is *enhanced bond indexing*. This approach allows for minor deviations of certain features and some active management in order to attain a return better than the index. For example, a fund indexed primarily to the Barclays index but with more weight given to lower-quality bonds based on an expectation of an improving economy would be an enhanced index fund combining indexing and sector rotation.

Cash Flow Matching—Dedicated Portfolios

Liabilities of financial institutions can vary. Some liability amounts and timing are known with certainty (for example, a CD obligation of a bank); for others the amount is predictable, but not the timing (e.g., life insurance policy); and in others both the amount and the time are unknown (e.g., property insurance or pension obligations).

EXHIBIT 6.6 Duration/Sector and Duration/Quality Cell Matching

Sector	Percentage of Value	Duration
Treasury	20%	4.50
Federal Agency	10%	3.25
Municipals	15%	5.25
Corporate Industry	15%	6.00
Corporate Utility	10%	6.25
Corporate Foreign	10%	5.55
Sovereign	10%	5.75
Asset-Backed	10%	6.25
	100%	Weighted Average = 5.29
Quality Sector	**Percentage of Value**	**Duration**
AAA	60%	5.25
AA	15%	5.35
A	10%	5.25
BBB	5%	5.65
BB	5%	5.25
B	5%	5.30
	100%	Weighted Average = 5.29

In the latter two cases, the law of large numbers makes it possible for actuaries to make reasonably accurate forecasts of the future cash outlays. Given projected cash outlays, the objective of the investment manager is to obtain a sufficient return from investing the premiums, deposits, or pension contributions, while still meeting the projected liabilities. Among the most popular approaches used in liability management strategies are cash flow matching and bond immunization.

A *cash flow matching strategy*, also referred to as a *dedicated portfolio strategy*, involves constructing a bond portfolio with cash flows that match the outlays of the liabilities. For example, a pension fund forming a cash flow matching strategy to meet projected liabilities of $1 billion, $3 billion, and $4 billion for each of the next three years, would need to construct a bond portfolio with the same, or approximately the same, cash flows.

One method that can be used for cash flow matching is to start with the final liability for time T and work backwards. For the last period, one would select a bond with a principal (F_T) and coupon (C_T) that matches the amount of that final liability (L_T):

$$L_T = F_T + C_T$$

$$L_T = F_T\,(1 + C_{R0})$$

where C^{R0} is the coupon rate (C_T/F_T). To meet this liability, one could buy $L_T/(1+C^{R0})$ of par value of bonds maturing in T periods. Since these bonds' coupons will also be paid in earlier periods, they can be used to reduce the liabilities in each of the earlier periods. Thus, to match the liability in period $T-1$, one would need to select bonds with a principal of F_{T-1} and coupon C_{T-1} (or coupon rate of $C^{R1} = C_{T-1}/F_{T-1}$) that is equal to the projected liability in period $T-1$ (L_{T-1}) less the coupon amount of C_T from the T-period bonds selected:

$$L_{T-1} - C_T = F_{T-1} + C_{T-1}$$

$$L_{T-1} - C_T = F_{T-1}\,(1+ C^{R1})$$

To meet this liability, one could buy $(L_{T-1} - C_T)/(1 + C^{R1})$ worth of bonds maturing in $T-1$ periods. The C_{T-1} coupons paid on these bonds, as well as the first bonds (C_T) would likewise be used to reduce liabilities in all earlier periods. Thus, to meet the liability in period $T-2$, the next bonds to be selected would have a principal and coupon in which

$$L_{T-2} - C_T - C_{T-1} = F_{T-2} + C_{T-2}$$

$$L_{T-2} - C_T - C_{T-1} = F_{T-2}\,(1+ C^{R2})$$

For this liability, one could buy $(L_{T-2} - C_T - C_{T-1})/(1+ C^{R2})$ worth of par value of bonds maturing in $T-2$ periods. A simple cash-flow matching case is presented in Exhibit 6.7.

With cash flow matching, the basic goal is to simply build a portfolio that will provide a stream of payments from coupons, sinking funds, and maturing principals that will match the liability payments. A dedicated portfolio strategy is subject to some minor market risk given that some cash flows may need to be reinvested forward. It also can be subject to default risk if lower quality bonds are purchased. The biggest risk with cash flow matching strategies, though, is that the bonds selected to match forecasted liabilities may be called, forcing the investment manager to purchase new bonds yielding lower rates. To minimize such risk, one can look for noncallable bonds, deep discount bonds, or zero-coupon stripped securities. There are also option and hedging strategies that can be implemented to hedge the risk of embedded call options.

Bond Immunization Strategies

Classical Immunization

An alternative to cash flow matching strategies for pensions, insurance companies, and thrifts is to apply immunization strategies to liability management. In Chapter 5, we defined immunization as a strategy of minimizing market risk by selecting a bond or

EXHIBIT 6.7 Cash Flow Matching Case

Bonds	Coupon Rate	Par	Yield	Market Value	Liability	Year
3-Year	5%	100	5%	100	$4,000,000	3
2-year	5%	100	5%	100	$3,000,000	2
1-year	5%	100	5%	100	$1,000,000	1

Match Strategy:

The $4,000,000 liability at the end of Year 3 is matched by buying $3,809,524 worth of three-year bonds: $3,809,524 = $4,000,000/1.05.
The $3,000,000 liability at the end of Year 2 is matched by buying $2,675,737 of 2-year bonds: $2,675,737 = ($3,000,000 – (.05)($3,809,524))/1.05.
The $1,000,000 liability at the end of Year 1 is matched by buying $643,559 of 1-year bonds: $643,559 = ($1,000,000 – (.05)($3,809,524) – (.05)($2,675,737))/1.05

1	2	3	4	5	6
Year	Total Bond Values	Coupon Income	Maturing Principal	Liability	Ending Balance (3) + (4) – (5)
1	$7,128,820	$356,441	$643,559	$1,000,000	0
2	$6,485,261	$324,263	$2,675,737	$3,000,000	0
3	$3,809,524	$190,476	$3,809,524	$4,000,000	0

The exhibit shows the matching of liabilities of $4 million, $3 million, and $1 million in years 3, 2, and 1 with 3-year, 2-year, and 1-year bonds each paying 5% annual coupons and selling at par.

- The $4 million liability at the end of Year 3 is matched by buying $3,809,524 worth of three-year, 5% annual coupon bonds trading at par: $3,809,524 = ($L_3$ /(1+ C^{R0}) = $4,000,000/1.05).
- At the end of Year 3, the bonds will pay a principal of $3,809,524 and interest of $190,476 ((.05) ($3,809,524)) that match the $4 million liability.
- The $3 million liability at the end of Year 2 is matched by buying $2,675,737 of 2-year, 5% annual coupon bonds trading at par: $2,675,737 = ($L_2$ - C_3)/(1+ C^{R1}) = ($3,000,000 - $190,476)/1.05. At the end of Year 2, these 2-year bonds will pay a principal of $2,675,737 and coupon interest of $133,787; this amount combined with the interest of $190,476 from the original 3-year bond will meet the $3 million liability of Year 2.
- Finally, the $1million liability at the end of Year 1 is matched by buying $643,559 of a 1-year, 5% annual coupon bonds trading at par: $643,559 = ($L_1$– C_3 – C_2)/(1+ C^{R2}) = ($1,000,000 - $190,476 - $133,787)/1.05. At the end of Year 1, these 1-year bonds will pay principal of $643,559 and coupon interest of $32,178; this principal and interest plus the interest of $190,476 and $133,787 from the original 3-year and 2-year bonds will meet the $1 million liability of Year 2.

bond portfolio with a duration equal to the horizon date. For liability management cases, the liability payment date is the liability's duration. Thus, immunization can be described as a duration-matching strategy of equating the duration of the bond to the duration of the liability. As we examined in Chapter 5, when a bond's duration is equal to the liability's duration, the direct reinvestment effect, in which the interest earned from reinvesting the bond's cash flows changes directly with interest rate changes, and the inverse price effect, in which the bond's price changes inversely to interest rate changes, exactly offset each other. As a result, the total return from the investment (TR) or the value of the investment at the horizon or liability date does not change because of an interest rate change.

The foundation for bond immunization strategies comes from a 1952 article by F. M. Redington.[9] He argued that a bond investment position could be immunized against interest rate changes by matching durations of the bond and the liability. To illustrate, consider a pension fund with a single liability of $1,352 due in 3.5 years. Assuming a flat yield curve at 10 percent, the pension fund could immunize its investment against market risk by purchasing a bond with a duration of 3.5 years (using Macaulay's measure), priced at $968.50 ($\$1{,}352/(1.10)^{3.5}$). This could be done by buying a four-year, 9 percent annual coupon bond with a principal of $1,000.[10] This bond has both a duration of 3.5 years and is worth $968.50, given a yield curve at 10 percent. If the pension fund buys this bond, then any parallel shift in the yield curve in the very near future would have price and interest rate effects that exactly offset each other. As a result, the cash flow or ending wealth at year 3.5, referred to as the *accumulation value* or *target value,* would be $1,352 (see Exhibit 6.8, upper panel).

Note that in addition to matching duration, immunization also requires that the initial investment of assets purchased be equal to or greater than the present value of the liability using the current YTM as a discount factor. In this example, the present value of the $1,352 liability is $968.50 ($= \$1{,}352/(1.10)^{3.5}$), which equals the current value of the bond and implies a 10 percent rate of return.

Redington's duration-matching strategy is sometimes referred to as *classical immunization.* Again, it works by having offsetting price and reinvestment effects. In contrast, a maturity-matching strategy in which a bond is selected with a maturity equal to the horizon date has no price effect and therefore no way to offset the reinvestment effect. This can be seen in Exhibit 6.8 (lower panel) where unlike the duration-matched bond, a 10 percent annual coupon bond with maturity of 3.5 years and initially priced at $1,000 has different ending values given different interest rates.

Exhibit 6.9 displays a Bloomberg BSA screen showing a total return analysis for a bond portfolio given a six-year horizon. The total returns for the six-year period ranges from 16.78 percent (annual rate = $(1.1678)^{1/6} - 1 = 2.62$ percent) for a –300-bps shift to 11.67 percent (annual rate = $(1.1167)^{1/6} - 1 = 1.86$ percent) for a +300-bps shift. The relatively small variability is explained by the portfolio's duration of 5.518 being closer to the six-year horizon. Thus, a pension or insurance company who wanted to minimize market risk in meeting a liability with a duration of six years might consider investing in this portfolio with its 5.5 duration.

Rebalancing

In a 1971 study, Fisher and Weil compared duration-matched immunization positions with maturity-matched ones under a number of interest rate scenarios. They found

EXHIBIT 6.8 Duration Matching and Maturity Matching

Ending Values at 3.5 Years Given Different Interest Rates for 4 Year, 9% Annual Coupon Bond with Duration of 3.5 and 10% Annual Coupon Bond with Maturity of 3.5 Years

Duration = 3.5 years Time (yr)	6%		10%		11%	
1	$ $90(1.06)^{2.5}$ =	$ 98.22	$ $90(1.10)^{2.5}$ =	$114.21	$ $90(1.11)^{2.5}$ =	$116.83
2	$90(1.06)^{1.5}$ =	$104.11	$90(1.10)^{1.5}$ =	$103.83	$90(1.11)^{1.5}$ =	$105.25
3	$90(1.06)^{.5}$ =	$ 92.66	$90(1.10)^{.5}$ =	$ 94.39	$90(1.11)^{.5}$ =	$ 94.82
3.5	$1{,}090/(1.06)^{.5}$ =	$1,058.70	$1{,}090/(1.10)^{.5}$ =	$1,039.27	$1{,}090/(1.11)^{.5}$ =	$1,034.58
Target Value		$1,352		$1,352		$1,352
Total Return from $968.50	10%		10%		10%	
Maturity = 3.5 years Time (yr)	**6%**		**10%**		**11%**	
1	$100(1.06)^{2.5}$ =	$109.13	$100(1.10)^{2.5}$ =	$126.91	$100(1.11)^{2.5}$ =	$129.81
2	$100(1.06)^{1.5}$ =	$115.68	$100(1.10)^{1.5}$ =	$115.37	$100(1.11)^{1.5}$ =	$116.95
3	$100(1.06)^{.5}$ =	$102.96	$100(1.10)^{.5}$ =	$104.88	$100(1.11)^{.5}$ =	$105.36
3.5	1,050 =	$1,050	1,050 =	$1,050	1,050 =	$1,050
		$1,378		$1,397		$1,402
Total Return from $1,000	9.59%		10%		10.135	

Note: The 4-year, 9% bond with duration of 3.5 is initially priced at $968.50 and has a total return of 10% for each scenario: Total Return = $[\$1{,}352/\$968.50]^{1/3.5} - 1]$

The 3.5-year, 10% bond is priced at $1,000 and has a target value and total return that varies with each scenario: Total Return = $[\text{Target Value}/\$1{,}000]^{1/3.5} - 1]$

that even though the duration-matched positions were closer to their initial YTM than the maturity-matched strategies, they were not absent of market risk. Two reasons they offered for the presence of market risk with classical immunization were that the shifts in yield curves were not parallel and that immunization only works when the duration of assets and liabilities are equal at all times. To achieve immunization, Fisher and Weil pointed out that the duration of the bond or portfolio must be equal to the remaining time in the horizon period.

EXHIBIT 6.9 Total Returns for Portfolio with Duration of 5.5 and Horizon of 6—Bloomberg PSD (PORT), PREP, and BSA Screens

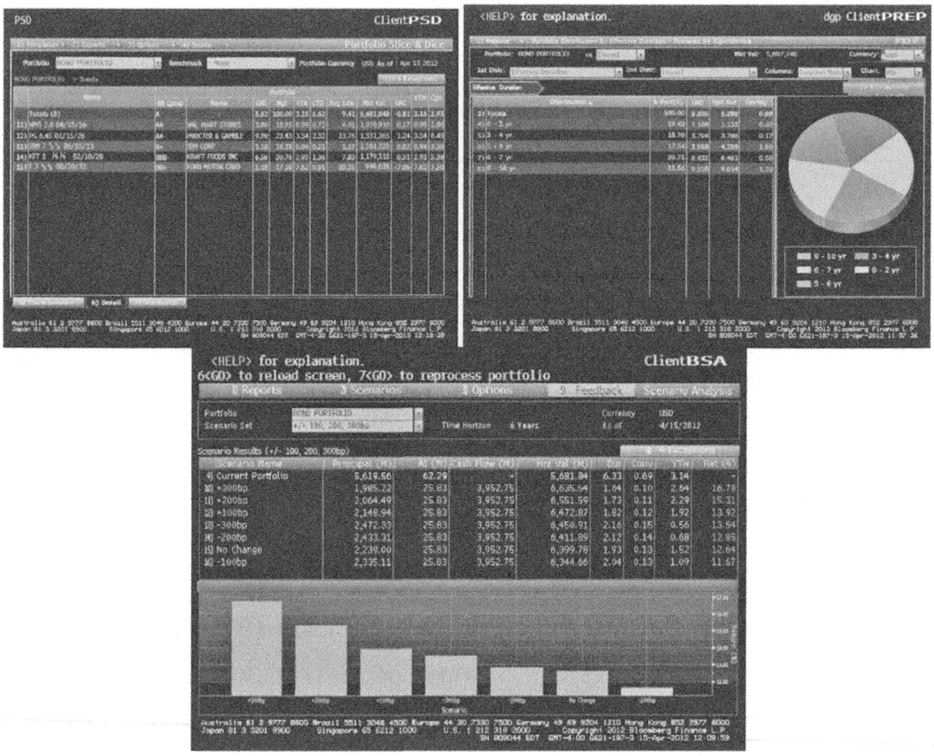

Since the durations of assets and liabilities change with both time and yield changes, immunized positions require active management, called *rebalancing,* to ensure that the duration of the portfolio is always equal to the remaining time to horizon. Thus, a bond and liability that currently have the same durations will not necessarily be equal as time passes and rates change. For one, the duration of a coupon bond declines more slowly than the terms to maturity. In our earlier example, our four-year, 9 percent bond with a Macaulay duration of 3.5 years (modified duration of 3.2) when rates were 10 percent, one year later would have duration of 2.77 years (modified of 2.5) with no change in rates. Secondly, duration changes with interest rate changes. Specifically, there is an inverse relation between interest rates and duration: duration increasing as rates decrease and increasing with interest rate increases.

Maintaining an immunized position when the bond's duration is no longer equal to the duration of the liability or remaining horizon period requires resetting the bond position such that the durations are again matched. This rebalancing could be done by selling the bond and buying a new one with the correct match, adding a bond to form a portfolio that will have the correct portfolio duration, investing the bond's cash flows differently, or perhaps taking a futures, options, or swap positions. In practice, an important consideration for a bond manager immunizing a position is how frequently the position must be rebalanced. Greater transaction costs incurred from frequent rebalancing must be weighed against having a position exposed to less market risk.

In addition to rebalancing the asset position over time and in response to interest rate changes, bond managers also have to decide whether to immunize with a bond or a portfolio of bonds. For a single liability, immunization can be attained with a focus strategy or a barbell strategy. In a *focus strategy*, a bond is selected with a duration that matches the duration of the liability, or a bullet approach is applied where a portfolio of bonds are selected with all the bonds close to the desired duration. For example, if the duration of the liability is four years, one could select a bond with four-year duration or form a portfolio of bonds with durations of four and five years. In a barbell strategy, the duration of the liability is matched with a bond portfolio with durations more at the extremes. Thus, for a duration liability of four years, an investor might invest half of his funds in a bond with two-year duration and half in a bond with six-year duration. The problem with the barbell strategy is that it may not immunize the position if the shift in the yield curve is not parallel.

Immunizing Multiple-Period Liabilities

For multiple-period liabilities, bond immunization strategies can be done either by matching the duration of each liability with the appropriate bond or bullet bond portfolio or by constructing a portfolio with its duration equal to the weighted average of the durations of the liabilities (D_L^P). For example, if a pension fund had multiple liabilities of $100 million each in years 2, 6, and 10, it could either invest in three bonds, each with respective durations of 2 years, 6 years, and 10 years, or it could invest in a bond portfolio with duration equal to 6 years:

$$D_L^P = \frac{\$100\text{m}}{\$300\text{m}}\,2\,\text{yrs} + \frac{\$100\text{m}}{\$300\text{m}}\,6\,\text{yrs} + \frac{\$100\text{m}}{\$300\text{m}}\,10\,\text{yrs} = 6\,\text{yrs}$$

The latter approach is relatively simple to construct, as well as to manage. However, studies have shown that matching the portfolio's duration of assets with the duration of the liabilities does not always immunize the positions.[11] Thus, for multiple-period liabilities, the best approach is generally considered to be one of immunizing each liability. As with single liabilities, this also requires rebalancing each immunized position.

The costs of setting up and managing a matching immunization strategy with rebalancing applied to multiple liabilities must be weighed against having a position exposed to market risk. In some cases, a bond manager may find that a cash flow matching strategy with little or no rebalancing is preferable to an immunization strategy that requires frequent rebalancing.[12] In fact, some managers combine cash flow matching and immunization strategies. Known as *combination matching* or *horizon matching*, these strategies consist of using cash flow matching strategies for early liabilities and an immunization strategy for longer-term liabilities.

Surplus Management and Duration Gap Analysis

Institutions that make use of immunization strategies include pensions, insurance companies, and commercial banks. Pensions and life insurance companies use multiple-period immunization to determine the investments that will match a schedule of forecasted payouts. Insurance companies, banks, and other financial institutions also use immunization concepts for *surplus management.* Surplus management refers to managing the surplus value of assets over liabilities. This surplus can be measured as *economic surplus,* defined as the difference between the market value of the assets and the present value of the liabilities. Thus, a pension with a bond portfolio currently valued at $200 million and liabilities with a present value of $180 million would have an economic surplus of $20 million. Whether the $20 million surplus is adequate depends, in part, on the *duration gap:* the difference in the duration of assets and the duration of the liabilities. If the duration of the assets exceeds the duration of the liabilities, then the economic surplus will vary inversely to interest rates: increasing if rates fall and decreasing if rates rise. For example, if the duration of the bond portfolio is 7 and the duration of the liabilities is 5, a decrease in rates by 100 bps would augment the value of bond portfolio from $200 million to approximately $214 million (= $200 million (1.07)) and increase the present value of the liabilities from $180 million to approximately $189 million (= $180 million (1.05)), causing the economic surplus to increase from $20 million to $25 million. However, if rates were to increase by 100 bps, then the surplus would decrease from $20 million to approximately $15 million:

$$\text{Economic Surplus} = \$200 \text{ million } (1 - .07) - \$180 \text{ million } (1 - .05)$$

$$\text{Economic Surplus} = \$15 \text{ million}$$

However, if the duration of the bond portfolio is less than the duration of the liabilities, then the surplus value will vary directly with interest rates. Finally, if the durations of assets and liabilities are equal (an immunized position), then the surplus will be invariant to rate changes.

In addition to its use by pensions and insurance companies, duration gap analysis is also used by banks to determine changes in the market value of the institution's net worth to changes in interest rates.

Contingent Immunization

Developed by Leibowitz and Weinberger, *contingent immunization* is an enhanced immunization strategy that combines active management to achieve higher returns and immunization strategies to ensure a floor.[13] In a contingent immunization strategy, a client of an investment management fund agrees to accept a potential return below an immunized market return. The lower potential return is referred to as the *target rate* and the difference between the immunized market rate and the target rate is called the *cushion spread.* The acceptance of a lower target rate means that the client is willing to take an end-of-the period investment value, known as the *minimum target value,* which is lower than the fully immunized value. This acceptance, in turn, gives the management fund some flexibility to pursue an active strategy.

As an example, suppose an investment management fund sets up a contingent immunization position for a client who has just placed $1 million with them and who has an investment horizon of 3.5 years. Furthermore, suppose that the yield curve is currently flat at 10 percent and that even though the investment fund can obtain an immunized rate of 10 percent (for example, it could buy a 4-year, 9 percent annual coupon bond trading at 10 percent), the client agrees to a lower immunization rate of 8 percent in return for allowing the fund to try to attain a higher rate using some active strategy. By accepting a target rate of 8 percent, the client is willing to accept a minimum target value of $1,309,131 at the 3.5-year horizon date:

$$\text{Minimum Target Value} = \$1{,}000{,}000(1.08)^{3.5} = \$1{,}309{,}131$$

The difference between the client's investment value (currently $1 million) and the present value of the minimum target value is the management fund's *safety margin* or cushion. The initial safety margin in this example is $62,203:

$$\text{Safety Margin} = \text{Investment Value} - \text{PV (Minimum Target Value)}$$

$$\text{Safety Margin} = \$1{,}000{,}000 - \$1{,}309{,}131/(1.10)^{3.5} = \$62{,}203$$

As long as the safety margin is positive, the management fund will have a cushion and can therefore pursue an active strategy. For example, suppose the fund expected long-term rates to decrease in the future and invested the client's funds in 10-year, 10 percent annual coupon bonds trading at par (YTM = 10 percent). If rates in the future decreased as expected, then the value of the investment and the safety margin would increase; if rates increased, though, the value of the investment and safety margin would decrease. Moreover, if rates increased to the point that the investment value was equal to the present value of the minimum target value (i.e., where the safety margin is zero), then the management fund would be required to immunize the investment position. For example, suppose one year later the yield curve shifted down as the management fund was hoping to 8 percent (continue to assume a flat yield curve). The value of the investment (value of the original 10-year bonds plus coupons) would now be $1,224,938:

$$\text{Bond Value} = \sum_{t=1}^{9}\frac{10}{(1.08)^t} + \frac{100}{(1.08)^9} = 112.4938$$

$$\text{Investment Value} = \frac{112.4938}{100}(\$1{,}000{,}000) + (.10)(\$1{,}000{,}000) = \$1{,}224{,}938$$

The present value of the minimum target value (MTV) would be $1.08 million:

$$PV(MTV) = \frac{\$1{,}309{,}131}{(1.08)^{2.5}} = \$1{,}080{,}000$$

and the safety margin would be $144,938:

$$\text{Safety Margin} = \$1{,}224{,}938 - \$1{,}080{,}000 = \$144{,}938$$

Thus, the downward shift in the yield curve has led to an increase in the safety margin from $62,203 to $144,938. At this point, the investment management fund could maintain its position in the original 10-year bond or take some other active position. Note that if the management fund immunized the client's position when rates were at 8 percent and the safety margin was positive, it would be able provide the client with a rate of return for the 3.5-year period that exceeded the initial immunization rate of 10 percent. For example, if the fund sold the bonds and reinvested the proceeds and coupons in bonds with durations of 2.5 years and a yield of 8 percent, it would be able to lock in a total return of 11.96 percent for the 3.5-year period:

$$TR_{3.5} = \left[\frac{\$1{,}224{,}938(1.08)^{2.5}}{\$1{,}000{,}000}\right]^{1/3.5} - 1 = .1196$$

Suppose after one year, though, the yield curve shifted up to 12.25 percent instead of down to 8 percent. At 12.25 percent, the value of investment would be only $981,245 and the present value of the minimum target value would be $980,657, leaving the fund with a safety margin that is close to zero ($588):

$$\text{Bond Value} = \sum_{t=1}^{9}\frac{10}{(1.1225)^t} + \frac{100}{(1.1225)^9} = 88.1245$$

$$\text{Investment Value} = \frac{88.1245}{100}(\$1{,}000{,}000) + (.10)(\$1{,}000{,}000) = \$981{,}245$$

$$\text{PV(MTV)} = \frac{\$1{,}309{,}131}{(1.1225)^{2.5}} = \$980{,}657$$

$$\text{Safety Margin} = \$981{,}245 - \$980{,}657 = \$588$$

The investment management fund now would be required to immunize the portfolio. This could be done by selling the bond and reinvesting the proceeds plus the coupon (total investment of $981,245) in bonds with durations of 2.5 years and yielding the current rate of 12.25 percent. Doing this would yield a value of $1,309,916, which is approximately equal to the minimum target value of $1,309,131 at the end of the period, and the target rate of 8 percent:

$$TR_{3.5} = \left[\frac{\$981{,}245(1.1225)^{2.5}}{\$1{,}000{,}000}\right]^{1/3.5} - 1 = .08$$

Exhibit 6.10 summarizes the investment values, present values of the minimum target value, safety margins, and total return for various interest rates. As shown in the table in Exhibit 6.10, for rates below 12.25 percent, safety margins are positive and the total returns for the 3.5-year period are above the 8 percent target rate if the position were immunized; for rates above 12.25 percent, though, safety margins are negative and the total returns are less than 8 percent. Thus, 12.25 percent is the trigger rate for immunizing the position when there are 2.5 years left. The relation between the investment values and the present values of the minimum target value given different rates is also shown graphically in the figure in Exhibit 6.10. The difference between the two graphs in the figure shows the safety margins and the point of intersection of the graphs defines the trigger rate at 12.25 percent.

In general, the contingent immunization strategy provides investors with a return-risk opportunity that is somewhere between those provided by active and fully immunized strategies. In practice, setting up and managing contingent immunization strategies are more complex than this example suggests. Safety margin positions must be constantly monitored to ensure that if the investment value decreases to the trigger point it will be detected and the immunization position implemented. In addition, active positions are more detailed, nonparallel shifts in the yield curve need to be addressed, and if the immunization position is implemented, it will need to be rebalanced.

Conclusion

In this chapter, we extended our analysis of bonds from evaluation to selection and management. As with all investment strategies, the method of selecting bonds or portfolios depends on the objective of the investor. Active strategies can be pursued to obtain better expected returns. These include trying to profit from forecasting yield curve shifts, taking positions in different quality bonds in anticipation of a narrowing or a widening of the credit spread, identifying mispriced bonds, or taking positions in identical bonds that are not equally priced. Active strategies can also be used to set up defensive positions in order to protect the value of a portfolio. For example, moving to lower-duration bonds when rates are expected to increase or tilting a bond portfolio more toward higher-quality bonds when economic slowdowns are anticipated. For investors who must meet future liability requirements or obtain maximum returns subject to risk constraints, passive strategies such as cash flow matching or indexing, or hybrid strategies such as immunization or contingent immunization strategies can be used.

EXHIBIT 6.10 Contingent Immunization: Investment Value, Present Value of the Minimum Target Value, and Safety Margin after One Year Given Different Rates

Interest Rate	Investment Value	PV(Minimum Target Value)	Safety Margin	Total Return
0.0800	$1,224,937.76	$1,079,999.91	$144,937.85	0.1196
0.0850	$1,191,785.94	$1,067,600.48	$124,185.46	0.1145
0.0900	$1,159,952.47	$1,055,399.45	$104,553.02	0.1095
0.0950	$1,129,376.42	$1,043,392.74	$85,983.68	0.1047
0.1000	$1,100,000.00	$1,031,576.39	$68,423.61	0.1000
0.1050	$1,071,768.38	$1,019,946.55	$51,821.83	0.0954
0.1100	$1,044,629.52	$1,008,499.44	$36,130.09	0.0909
0.1150	$1,018,534.03	$997,231.39	$21,302.65	0.0865
0.1200	$993,435.00	$986,138.81	$7,296.20	0.0823
0.1225	$981,245.15	$980,657.23	$587.93	0.0802
0.1250	$969,287.88	$975,218.21	-$5,930.32	0.0781
0.1275	$957,557.98	$969,821.33	-$12,263.35	0.0761
0.1300	$946,050.35	$964,466.17	-$18,415.82	0.0741
0.1350	$923,682.17	$953,879.36	-$30,197.19	0.0701
0.1400	$902,145.13	$943,454.54	-$41,309.41	0.0663

Investment Value = Value of 9-year, 10% bond with face value of $1M plus $100,000 coupon interest

PV(Minumum Target Value) = $\$1,309,131/(1+\text{Rate})^{2.5}$

Safety Margin = Investment Value - PV(Minimum Target Value)

Trigger Rate = 12.25%

TR = $(\text{Investment Value}(1+\text{Rate})^{2.5}/\$1,000,000)^{1/3.5}$

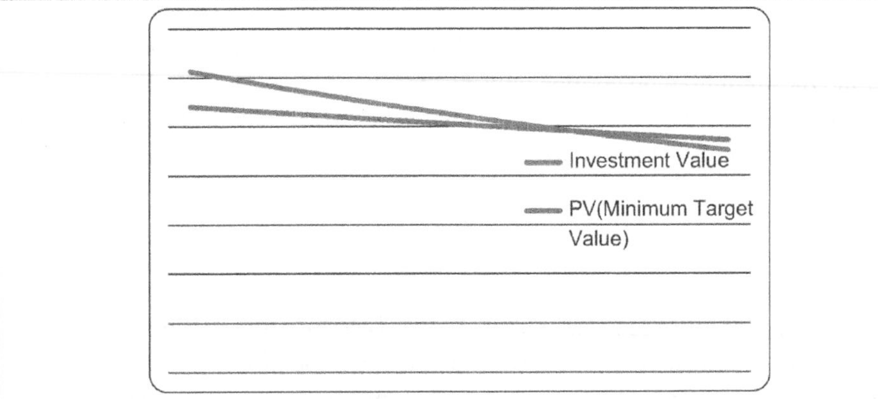

Website Information

For Information on Bond Funds

- *Wall Street Journal* site: http://online.wsj.com/public/us. Click "Market Data" tab, Mutual Funds. Click "Mutual Fund" tab. Use screener.
- FINRA
    - www.finra.org/index.htm. Sitemap, Mutual Funds, and Fixed Income
- Yahoo!
    - http://screen.yahoo.com/funds.html. Fund Screener

Selected References

Altman, E. 1992. Revisiting the high-yield bond market. *Financial Management* 21:78–92.

Altman, E. I. 1993. *Corporate Financial Distress and Bankruptcy*, 2nd ed. New York: John Wiley & Sons.

Altman, E. I. 1989. Measuring corporate bond mortality and performance. *Journal of Finance* 44: 909–922.

Altman, E. I. 1990. Setting the record straight on junk bonds: A review of the research on default rates and returns. *Journal of Applied Corporate Finance* 3:82–95.

Altman, E. I., and S. A. Nammacher. 1987. *Investing in Junk Bonds*. New York: John Wiley & Sons.

Barr, P. G. 1994. Strong market boosts immunized portfolios. *Pensions & Investments* (May 16):16, 96.

Bierwag, G. 1977. Immunization, duration and the term structure of interest rates. *Journal of Financial and Quantitative Analysis* 12:725–743.

Bierwag, G. O., G. G. Kaufman, and A. Toevs, eds. 1983. *Innovations in Bond Portfolio Management: Duration Analysis and Immunization*. Greenwich, CT: JAI Press.

Choie, K. S. 1990. A simplified approach to bond portfolio management: DDS. *Journal of Portfolio Management* 16:40–45.

Cox, J., J. Ingersoll, and S. Ross. 1979. Duration and the measurement of basis risk. *Journal of Business* 52:51–61.

Dattatreya, R. E., and F. J. Fabozzi. 1995. *Active Total Return Management of Fixed Income Portfolios*, rev. ed. Burr Ridge, IL: Irwin Professional.

Douglas, K. S. and D. J. Lucas. 1989. *Historical Default Rates of Corporate Bond Issuers, 1970–1988*. New York: Moody's Investors Services.

Elton, E. J., M. J. Gruber, S. Brown, and W. N. Goetzman. 2003. *Modern Portfolio Theory and Investment Analysis*, 6th edition. New York: John Wiley & Sons, Inc., 525-546.

Fabozzi, F. J. 2008. Credit analysis for corporate bonds. In F. J. Fabozzi, ed., *The Handbook of Fixed Income Securities*, 7th ed. New York: McGraw-Hill, 733–777.

Fabozzi, F. J., and P. F. Christensen. 2008. Bond immunization: An asset/liability optimization strategy. In F. J. Fabozzi, ed., *The Handbook of Fixed Income Securities*, 7th ed. New York: McGraw-Hill.

Fabozzi, F. J., and P. F. Christensen. 2001. Dedicated bond portfolios. In F. J. Fabozzi, ed., *The Handbook of Fixed Income Securities*, 6th ed. New York: McGraw-Hill.

Feldstein, S. G., F. J. Fabozzi, and P. M. Kennedy. 2001. Municipal bonds. In F. J. Fabozzi, ed., *The Handbook of Fixed Income Securities*, 6th ed. New York: McGraw-Hill.

Feldstein, S. G. 2009. Guidelines in the credit analysis of general obligation and revenue municipal bonds. In F. J. Fabozzi, ed., *The Handbook of Fixed Income Securities*, 7th ed. New York: McGraw-Hill.

Fisher, L., and R. Weil. 1971. Coping with the risk of interest rate fluctuations: Returns to bondholders from naive and optimal strategies. *Journal of Business* 44:408–431.

Fong, G., and V. Oldrich. 1984. A risk minimizing strategy for multiple liability immunization. *Journal of Finance* 39:1541–1546.

Fong, H. G.. 1983. Active strategies for managing bond portfolios. In Donald Tuttle, ed., *The Revolution in Techniques for Managing Bond Portfolios*. Charlottesville, VA: Institute of Chartered Financial Analysts, 21–38.

Garbade, K. 1985. Dedicated bond portfolios: Construction, rebalancing, and swapping. *Topics in Money and Securities Markets*. New York: Bankers Trust Company.

Granito, M. 1987. The problem with bond index funds. *Journal of Portfolio Management* 13:41–48.

Homer, S., and M. L. Leibowitz. 1972. *Inside the Yield Book*. Englewood Cliffs, NJ: Prentice Hall, Chapter 5.

Howe, J. T. 2001. Credit analysis for corporate bonds. In F. J. Fabozzi, ed., *The Handbook of Fixed Income Securities*, 6th ed. New York: McGraw-Hill.

Howe, J. T. 2001. Credit considerations in evaluating high-yield bonds. In F. J. Fabozzi, ed., *The Handbook of Fixed Income Securities*, 6th ed. New York: McGraw-Hill.

Howe, J. T. 2001. Investing in Chapter 11 and other distressed companies. In F. J. Fabozzi, ed., *The Handbook of Fixed Income Securities*, 6th ed. New York: McGraw-Hill.

Ingersoll, J. E. 1983. Is immunization feasible? Evidence from CRSP data. In G. Kaufman, C. Bierwag, and A. Toevs, eds. *Innovations in Bond Portfolio Management: Duration analysis and immunization.* Greenwich, CT: JAI Press.

Ingersoll, J. E., J. Skelton, and R. L. Weil. 1978. Duration forty years later. *Journal of Financial and Quantitative Analysis* 13:627–650.

Leibowitz, M. 1987. *Matched-Funding Techniques: The Dedicated Bond Portfolio in Pension Funds.* New York: Salomon Brothers Inc., Mortgage Research.

Leibowitz, M., and A. Weinberger. 1982. Contingent immunization—Part I: Risk control procedures. *Financial Analysts Journal* 38:17–32.

Leibowitz, M., and A. Weinberger. 1983. Contingent immunization—Part II: Problem areas. *Financial Analysts Journal* 39:35–50.

Leibowitz, M. L. 1986. The dedicated bond portfolio in pension funds—Part I: Motivations and basics. *Financial Analysts Journal* 42:68–75.

Leibowitz, M. L. 1986. The dedicated bond portfolio in pension funds—Part II: Immunization, horizon matching, and contingent procedures. *Financial Analysts Journal* 42:47–57.

Merton, R. C. 1974. On the pricing of corporate debt: The risk structure of interest rates. *Journal of Finance* 29:449–470.

Redington, F. M. 1952. Review of the principles of life—Office foundation. *Journal of the Institute of Actuaries* 78:286–340.

Reilly, F., and R. Sidhu. 1980. The many uses of bond duration. *Financial Analysts Journal* (July–August):58–72.

Reilly, F. K., and K. Brown. *Investment Analysis and Portfolio Management,* 6th ed. Fort Worth, TX: Dryden Press.

Reilly, F. K., and D. J. Wright. 2001. Bond market indexes. In F. J. Fabozzi, ed., *The Handbook of Fixed Income Securities*, 6th ed. New York: McGraw-Hill.

Reilly, F. K., D. J. Wright, and E. I. Altman. 1998. Including defaulted bonds in the capital markets spectrum. *Journal of Fixed Income* 8:33–48.

Seix, C., and R. Akhoury. 1986. Bond indexation: The optimal quantitative approach. *Journal of Portfolio Management* 12:50–53.

Ward, D. J., and G. L. Griepentrog. 1993. Risk and return in defaulted bonds. *Financial Analysts Journal* 49:61–65.

Weil, R. L. 1973. Macaulay's duration: An appreciation. *Journal of Business* 46:589–592.

Bloomberg Exercises

1. Select an option-free (bullet) corporate bond of interest. Evaluate the bond in terms of its credit risk, liquidity, and interest rate risk. In your evaluations, you may want to consider the following screens on the bond's menu screen or it company's equity menu screen.
   - YA (Yield & Spread tab) to determine the bond's spread.
   - YA (Graphs tab) to compare its market spread with other spreads (e.g., CDS spreads).
   - GY to evaluate the bond's spread history.
   - TDH to evaluate the bond's spreads over different periods (98 Charts).
   - RSKC to see it credit risk profile.

- RSKC ("Historical Trends" tab) to see it risk profile historically.
- LITI to see if the company is subject to any major litigation.
- DRSK (Issuer Default Risk Profile tab) to evaluate credit risk parameter graphically.
- DRSK (Industry Comparison tab) to evaluate the company relative to its peers.
- DRSK to see graphs of bond's CDS and default probability (set graph screen to see those measures).
- CRPR to see the bond's credit history.

2. Do a comparative spread and credit risk analysis of the bond you selected in Exercise 1 using the following screens:
   - RSKC ("Peer" tab) to see its credit risk profile relative to its peers.
   - RVRD to see the company's financials relative to its peers and the S&P 500.
   - DRSK screen for an industry comparison, click "Industry Comparison" tab.
   - COMB to compare the bond's spread and risk with similar bonds.
3. Select a speculative-grade bond and determine its Altman Z-score and probability of default using the AZS screen. Using the AZS screen, examine the sensitivity of Altman's Z-score and probability of default by changing some of the financials parameters defining the model.
4. Study the economic and financial climate by examining the number of bond upgrades and downgrades found on the RATT screen. What does the recent trend say about economic conditions?
5. Using the GOVI screen, do a comparison of different countries spreads. Identify countries in which the United States has a relatively small spread and those in which she has a relatively large spread. Using the SOVR screen, see if the spreads of the countries you identify are consistent with their CDS spreads.
6. Compare the U.S. Treasury yield curve with the yield curves of Greece, Ireland, Spain, and Portugal using the IYC2 screen: IYC2 <Enter>, select United States and other countries.
7. Use the STGO screen to identify states that do not have AAA ratings on their general obligation bonds. Using the MIFA screen (MIFA <Enter>), study the financial conditions of one of the states you have identified. On the MIFA screen you can select a state and then access information on the state from a dropdown. On the dropdown, the state's identification number is also shown (e.g., California: stoca1 US). Using the identification number, you can access the state's menu directly: Stoca1 US <Equity> <Enter>. Information on the dropdown or state screen that can be accessed include description (DES), financials (FA), relative evaluations (RV), demographics, (DEMS), employment (BLS), and a municipal search (SMUN). The municipal FA and RV screens display income statements, balance sheets, and other information useful for evaluating the government's financial strength. On the FA and RV screens, you can also change the fund category from general to pension to view the municipal's pension position.

Bloomberg Exercises 8 through 14 require forming a bond portfolio in PRTU. The following boxes describe the steps for constructing portfolios in PRTU and creating a basket of historical returns in CIXB.

STEPS FOR CREATING A BOND PORTFOLIO

Step 1: PRTU: PRTU displays a list of portfolios. To create a portfolio using PRTU:

1. To access: PRTU <Enter>.
2. On the PRTU screen, click the "Create" button. This will bring up a screen pages for inputting information:
   a. Settings Page: Name of your portfolio, asset class (equity, fixed income, balanced), and benchmark (e.g., S&P 500).
   b. Securities: Screen for inputting securities by their identifiers. (*Note:* A helpful way to load stock is to go to an RV or index screen and find the securities of interest; then drop and drag the security.)

Note: Searches and other portfolios that have been saved in Bloomberg can be imported. To import: Click the "Options" tab on the PRTU screen, click "Import from List," and then the name of the search.

3. Once the portfolio is loaded, hit "Save." The name you have given to the portfolio will then be displayed on the PRTU screen.
4. On the PRTU settings screen, you may want to create history. To do this, click "Enable History" and hit "1 Save" to bring up a securities screen. On the securities screen, the "Date" and "Rebalanced" tabs appear on the right above the list of securities. The "Rebalanced" tab will show today's date. On the "Date" tab use the calendar to select a date (or change it in the date box) to begin the history (e.g., two years prior to today's date). After selecting a past date, use the "Option" tab to import the portfolio that you have created. On the import box, select Portfolio from import tab, name of portfolio, and change the date to today's date, and then click "Import." On the PRTU screen, click "Saved."

Step 2: PMEN: With the portfolio loaded, click the "Analysis" tab on PRTU screen or type PMEN to access a menu of functions to apply to the portfolio. From the PMEN menu, some useful screens for analyzing fixed-income portfolios include: PORT, PDSP: Portfolio Display; NPH: Portfolio News; CACT: Corporate Action Calendar; EVTS: Events Calendar; BSA: Scenario Analysis; PSH: Proposed Trade/Hedge Analysis; PCF: Expected Cash Flow; PREP: For portfolio features.

CIXB

Steps for Creating and Analyzing a CIXB Index Basket

1. To access: CIXB <Enter>.
2. On the CIXB screen, one can type in security tickers or import the securities from a portfolio or search. To import a portfolio from a list:
   a. Click "Import" in the Actions tab to bring up import box.
   b. In the import box, click "Import from List" tab at bottom to bring up "Import from List" box.

c. On "Import from List" box: (1) click dropdown "Source" tab and click "Portfolio"; (2) click "Name" tab and then the name of the portfolio; and (3) click "Import" tab. These steps will import the portfolio's securities, issues, and prices to the CIXB screen.
d. On the CIXB screen, name the ticker and the portfolio in the "Ticker" and "Name" box and hit <Enter> to update.
e. After naming the ticker and portfolio, click the "Create" tab. This will bring up a box for selecting the time period for price and return data. After selected the time period, hit "Save." This will activate a Bloomberg program for calculating the portfolio's daily historical returns. The data will be sent to a report, RPT. To access this report, type "RPT" and hit <Enter>.

8. Conduct a horizon/total return analysis on five Treasury notes and bonds with different maturities (e.g., 3, 7, 10, 15, and 20). Use FIT to help you select the bonds. To conduct the analysis, construct a portfolio of the bonds using PRTU (enter the bond's CUSIP on the PRTU screen). Once you have constructed the portfolio, use the BSA screen to conduct the scenario analysis. To evaluate each bond in terms of its sensitivity, download the BSA scenario to Excel report (click "Excel" from "Reports" tab). This report shows total returns for each shift for the portfolio and the individual bonds.
9. Construct a portfolio of investment-grade corporate bonds and U.S. Treasuries using the PRTU screen. You may want to use the Bloomberg search/screen function, SRCH, to identify the bonds for your portfolio. After constructing the bond fund, evaluate the portfolio. Possible evaluations you may want to consider:
   a. Evaluate the portfolio's features using the PORT, PREP, and PCF screens.
   b. Using the BSA and/or PSA screens, evaluate the portfolio's duration and it sensitivity to different interest rate changes for different horizon periods.
   c. Using the BSA and/or PSA screens, evaluate the portfolio's total return for rate changes in which the yield curve steepens and for changes in which it flattens.
   d. Using the PORT screen, evaluate the duration distribution of your portfolio. From the "Characteristics tab," click "Main View" tab and then select "Duration" from the "Breakdown by" dropdown.
   e. Using the PREP screen, evaluate the bonds in your portfolio in terms of their "ratings and YTMs" and "ratings and duration." For ratings analysis, select (on the PREP screen) "Credit Ratings" from the "1st Distr" dropdown, ; for duration, select "Effective Duration" from the "1st Distr" dropdown.
   f. Using the corporate actions calendar, CACT, and events calendar, EVTS, identify past and future events that merit consideration. Use "Source" tab to import your portfolio. You may want to consider setting up alerts from the "Actions" tab on the EVTS screen.

10. Examine the performance of the portfolio you constructed in Exercise 9 over the past year relative to one or both of the following bond indexes:
    - J. P. Morgan Global Aggregate Bond Index: JGAGUSUS <Index> <Enter>.
    - One of the Bloomberg bond government indexes, such as All Bond Government Index: USGATR <Index> <Enter>.

    In examining the past performance, create a basket of historical returns of the bonds from the portfolio you formed in Exercise 9 using the CIXB screen. See CIXB Explanation Box for steps to import a search or portfolio in order to create a CIXB basket. After creating the basket, evaluate your portfolio of bonds relative to the indexes using the total return screen, COMP, on the index menu (Basket ticker name (e.g., .BOND <Index> <Enter>).
11. Suppose you are a bond portfolio manager for an insurance company and you are looking at investing premiums to meet expected liabilities in seven years. Construct a portfolio of investment grade corporate bonds and U.S. Treasuries with a portfolio duration of approximately seven years using the PRTU screen. You may want to limit you search to bonds with maturities between 10 and 15 years. After constructing the bond fund, evaluate the portfolio's duration features using the PREP and PORT screens (on the PORT Characteristics tab, click "Main View" tab and then select "Duration" from the "Breakdown by" dropdown). Using the BSA screen, evaluate the portfolio's interest rate risk given different interest rate changes for a horizon of seven years.
12. Suppose you are a bond portfolio manager constructing a high-yield fund. Use the Bloomberg search/screen function, SRCH, to help you identify possible bonds to include in your portfolio. After identifying your bonds, construct a portfolio using the PRTU screen and evaluate the portfolio. Possible evaluations:
    - Evaluate the portfolio's features using the PORT, PREP, DRAM, and PCF screens.
    - Using the PREP screen, evaluate the bonds in your portfolio in terms of their ratings and spreads: Select "Credit Ratings" from the "1st Distr" dropdown, "YTM" from the "2nd Distr" dropdown, and "Analysis" from the "Columns" dropdown.
    - Evaluate the ratings histories and risks of some of the bonds in your portfolio using the DRSK and CRPR screens for the bonds.
    - Use the corporate actions calendar, CACT, and events calendar, EVTS, to identify past and future events that merit consideration. Use "Source" tab to import your portfolio. You may want to consider setting up alerts from the "Actions" tab on the EVTS screen.
13. Examine the performance of the high yield portfolio you constructed in Exercise 12 over the past year relative to the J. P. Morgan Global Aggregate Bond Index (ticker: JGAGUSUS; JGAGUSUS <Index> <Enter>). In examining the past performance, create a basket consisting of the bonds from the portfolio you formed in Exercise 12 using the CIXB screen. See the CIXB Box for steps to import a search or a portfolio in order to create a CIXB basket. After creating the basket, evaluate your portfolio of bonds relative to the indexes using the total return screen, COMP, on the index menu (Basket ticker name; e.g., .HYBOND <Index> <Enter>).

14. Set up an RV screen for evaluating and monitoring the companies comprising the high-yield portfolio you constructed in Exercise 12. To set up the screen, you may want to use PRTU to form an equity portfolio of the companies whose credits you hold in your high-yield bond portfolio. Once you have constructed the portfolio, bring up the RV screen. Use the equity screen for one on the companies in your portfolio and then import your equity portfolio (select "Portfolio" from the "Comp source" tab and select your equity portfolio from "Name" tab). Customize your columns by selecting financial parameters that will help you evaluate credit risk. Parameters to consider: Debt/EBDIT, EBIT/Interest Expenses, Debt/Equity, liquidity ratios, operating performance measures, Altman Z-Score, and five-year CDS. Be sure to save your screen.

Notes

1. In Chapter 11, we will describe how rate anticipation swaps can be implemented using futures contracts.
2. Concentrating in one maturity group does not mean constructing a portfolio with a portfolio duration corresponding to that maturity. For example, if an investor expected five-year bond rates to decrease, but not short-term or long-term rates, she could profit by investing in a bond with duration of five years, but she could incur losses from a portfolio of short and long-term bonds with portfolio duration of five years.
3. Note that instead of taking positions in different quality bonds, speculators alternatively can form a quality swap by taking positions in futures contracts on bonds with different quality ratings (e.g., opposite positions in a Treasury bond futures contract and a municipal bond index contract). Constructing bond swaps with futures is examined Chapter 11.
4. For a more detailed analysis covering the guideline in the credit analysis of corporate credits, see Fabozzi (2008).
5. For a more detailed analysis covering the guideline in the credit analysis of municipals, see Feldstein (2009).
6. For more discussion on investing in the debt securities of bankrupt firms, see Jane Howe, "Investing in Chapter 11 and Other Distressed Companies," pp. 469–489.
7. Another type of tax swap involves switching between high and low coupon bonds to take advantage of different tax treatments applied to capital gains and income. This swap can be used if the tax rate on capital gains differs from the tax rate on income. If it does, then an investor might find it advantageous to swap a low coupon bond for a high-coupon bond with the same duration.
8. One of the most well-known approaches to portfolio construction is the use of the Markowitz portfolio model. Although most of the applications of the Markowitz model are to stocks, it can be used for constructing bond portfolios. For a discussion of the use of the Markowitz model, see Elton, Gruber, Brown, and Goetzman (2003).
9. See Redington (1952).
10. This example is similar to the one presented in Chapter 5.
11. See Bierwag, Kaufman, and Tuevs (1983).
12. For an analysis of the cost and benefits of cash flow matching and immunization, see Fong (1983).
13. See Leibowitz and Weinberger (1982, 1983).

PART II

Debt Markets and Securities

CHAPTER 7

Corporate Debt Securities

Introduction

Major corporations can be viewed as perpetual investment machines: constantly developing new products and technologies, regularly expanding their markets, and from time-to-time acquiring other companies. To finance these investments, corporations obtain funds both internally and externally. With *internal financing*, companies retain part of their earnings that otherwise would go to existing shareholders in the form of dividends, whereas with *external financing*, companies generate funds from outside by selling new shares of stock, selling debt instruments, or borrowing from financial institutions. From the corporation's perspective, decisions on internal versus external financing depend on the dividend policy it wants to maintain and the cost of raising funds from the outside.

The company's choice of financing with debt or equity, in turn, depends on the return-risk opportunities management wants to provide its shareholders. Because debt instruments have provisions that give creditors legal protection in the case of default, the rate corporations are required to pay creditors for their investments is typically smaller than the rate their shareholders require. As a result, a firm that tends to finance its projects with relatively more debt than equity (i.e., a *leveraged firm*) benefits its shareholders with the relatively lower rates it pays to creditors. In addition, debt financing also has a major tax advantage to corporations: the interest payments on debt are treated as an expense by the Internal Revenue Service (IRS), and are therefore tax deductible, whereas the dividends a corporation pays its shareholders are not tax deductible. The relatively lower rates required by creditors and the tax advantage of debt make debt financing cheaper than equity financing for a corporation, all other things being equal. The lower rates on debt, though, are not without costs. Unlike equity financing in which funds are paid to shareholders only if they are earned, the obligations of debt instruments are required to be made. Thus, if a company has a period with poor sales or unexpected high costs, it still has to make payments to the bondholders, leaving fewer earnings available for shareholders. Moreover, very low sales or very high costs could lead to the company being unable to meet its interest and/or principal payments. In this case, the creditors can sue the company, forcing them to sell company assets to meet their obligations or the company can petition the courts to reorganize.

When firms need capital to grow and acquire additional assets, they usually finance their capital formation with the following equity and debt sources or instruments:

- Retained earnings
- Common stock
- Preferred stock
- Straight debt
- Medium-term notes
- Commercial paper
- Leases
- Direct financing
- Limited partnerships
- Debt and stock with options

At a given point in time, a company's core operations and its past investments are reflected in its current balance sheet. Exhibit 7.1 provides a financial snapshot of Kraft Foods Inc. from several Bloomberg screens accessed on March 21, 2012: description (DES) screen, 10-K corporate filing (CF), key financials (FA), supply chain (SPLC), debt and equity breakdowns (ISSD screen), outstanding equity holders (HDS) and bond holders (AGGD), and corporate actions (CACS). From these compiled screens, we find that in 2011, Kraft Foods was the world's second-largest food company, with revenues of over $14.688 billion and operating income of $1.628 billion (CF and 10-K and FA screens). Of its $14.688 billion in revenue in 2011, 46.3 percent came from North America and 25.3 percent from Europe (FA, Segment tab, By Geography tab), and by product, 29.5 percent came from confectionary, 21.8 percent from biscuits, 17.52 percent from beverage, and 15.09 percent from cheese and dairy (FA, Segment tab, By Measure tab), with Wal-Mart and Kroger being its biggest customers (SPLC). The company had 126,000 employees, sold products in 170 countries, and operated in 75 countries, with 220 manufacturing and processing plants (10-K). Kraft's gross assets were $93.8 billion, with $58.5 billion of its assets financed with debt (FA, B/S tab), consisting in part of $24.8 billion in outstanding bonds and $8.5 in loans (ISSD, Debt Summary page). As a corporation, Kraft is structured as a holding company—Kraft Foods Inc.—with 665 subsidiaries (RELS). On April 21, 2012, Kraft had 1,772 million shares outstanding and a market cap of $68.395 billion (DES), with its principal equity holders being Capital Research (5.56 percent), State Street (5 percent), and Berkshire Hathaway (4.91 percent) (HDS) and its principal bond holders being Vanguard (2.84 percent) and Pimco (1.83 percent) (AGGD). Like many large multinational companies, Kraft is an investment machine. For example, on March 8, 2010, Kraft acquired Cadbury PLD for 13.5 billion British pounds (CACS). To finance part of that acquisition and to meet antitrust compliance, Kraft was active in divesting some of its other holding (information on the Cadbury deal can be found on Kraft's "Company Research" screen [BRC]).

When a corporation like Kraft decides to finance its investments with equity, it may do so internally by retaining earnings, using its cash position, or selling a division,

EXHIBIT 7.1 Kraft: Bloomberg Screens: Kft<Equity> DES, CF, RELS, ISSD, and HDS

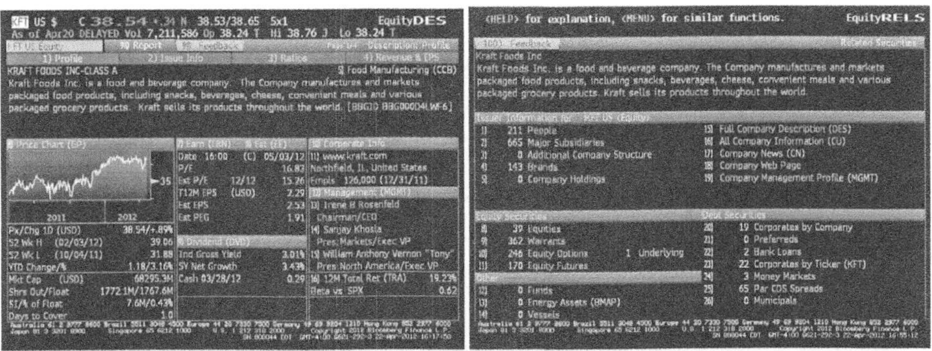

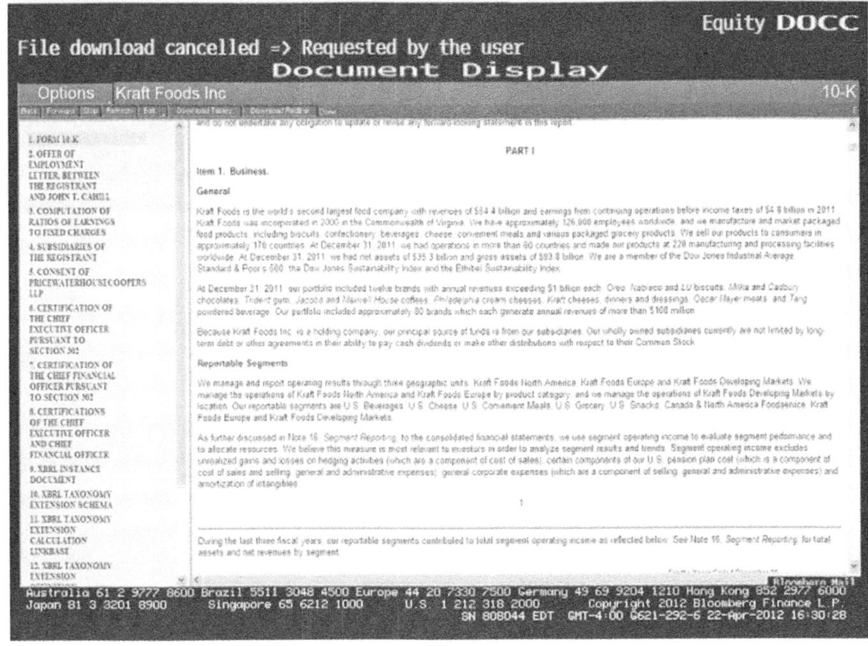

(*Continued*)

EXHIBIT 7.1 *(continued)*

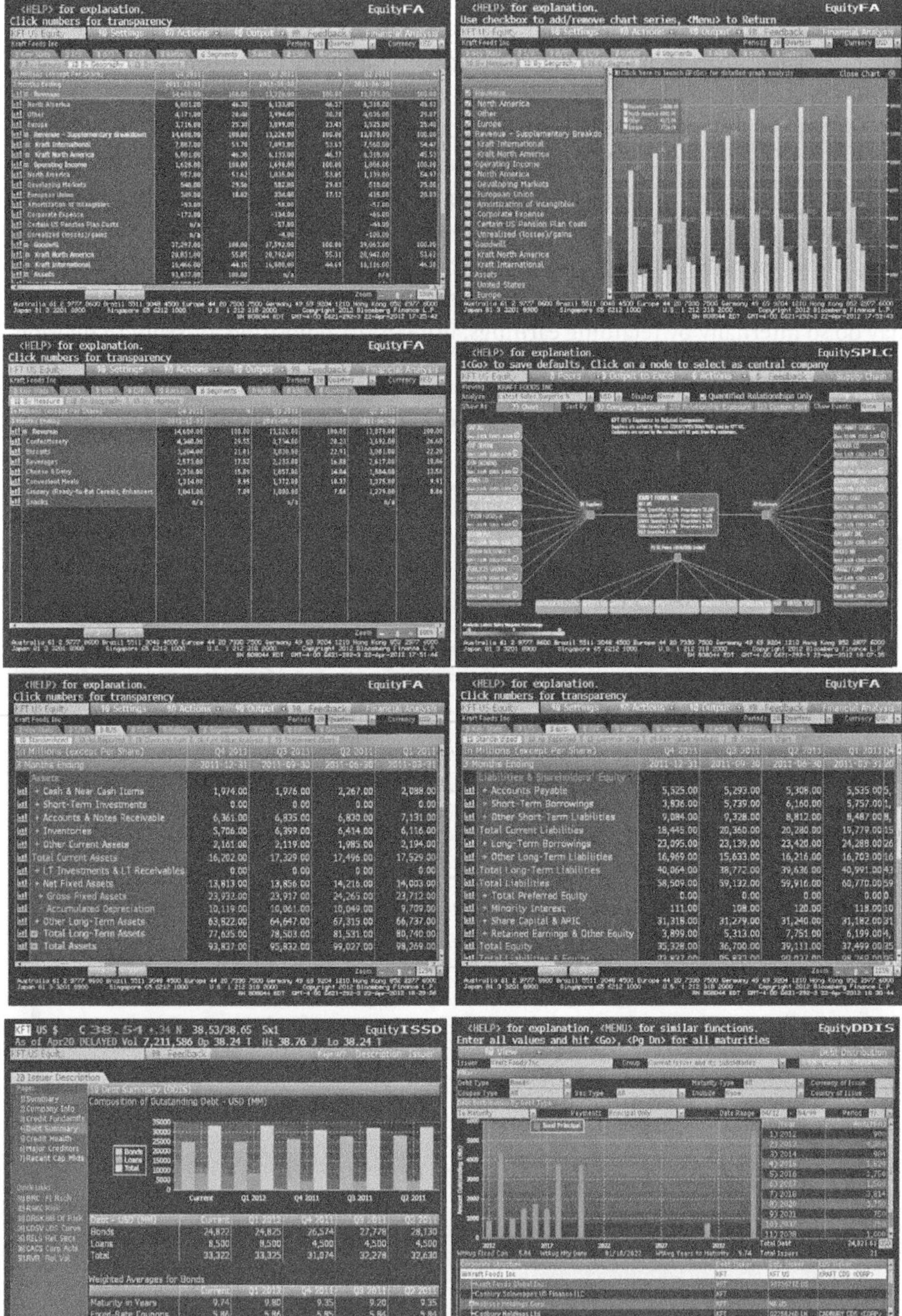

EXHIBIT 7.1 *(continued)*

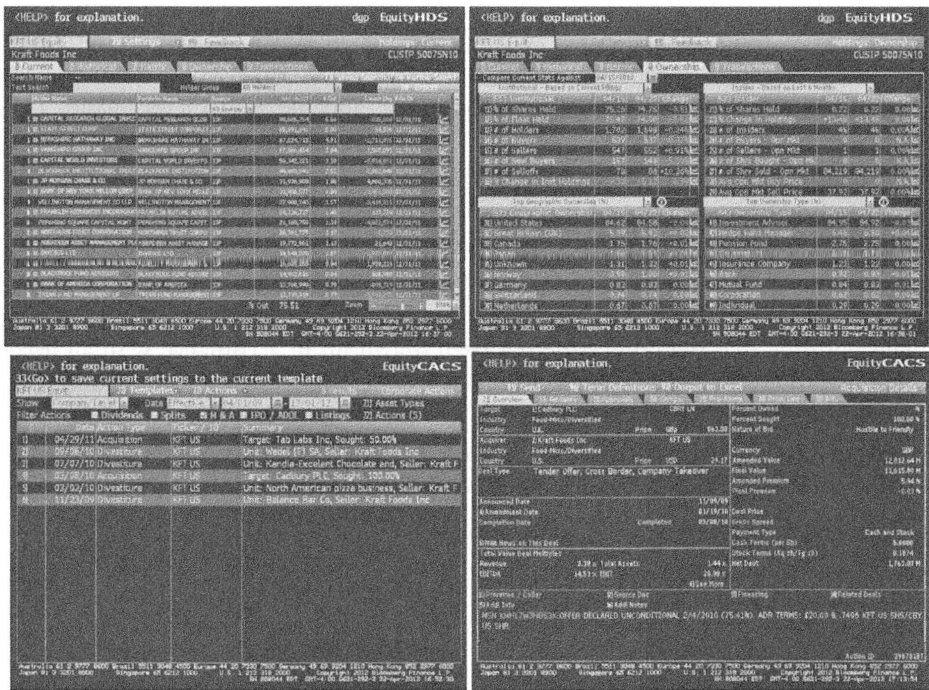

or externally by issuing common stock or preferred stock, forming a limited partnership, or borrowing directly from a financial institution or issuing bonds. In this chapter, we examine the types of debt securities issued by businesses like Kraft and the primary and secondary markets in which investors buy and sell such securities.

Corporate Bonds

When a corporation decides to finance its investments with debt, it will do so either by selling corporate bonds or notes or by securing a loan from a financial institution. Larger corporations, whose credit standings are often strong, prefer to finance their long-term and intermediate-term assets by selling corporate bonds and notes or by issuing, though an agent, medium term notes and to finance their short-term assets by selling commercial paper. These securities, in turn, offer different investment features to investors.

A corporate bond is a debt obligation with an original maturity of over five years, whereas a corporate note is an obligation with an original maturity of less than five years. Since bonds and notes are similar we will follow the custom of referring to both as corporate bonds. Corporate bondholders have a legal claim over common and preferred shareholders as to the income and assets of the corporation. Their contractual claim is specified in the bond's *indenture.* An indenture is the contract between the borrower and the lender (all the bondholders). The document is very extensive, detailing all the characteristics of the bond issue, including the time, amounts, manners in which interest and principal are to be paid, the type of collateral, and all restrictive covenants or clauses aimed at protecting the bondholders. In addition to the indenture, a corporation issuing a bonds or stock must also file with the Securities and Exchange Commission a prospectus. For bonds, this smaller document is a summary of the main provisions included in the indenture.

By federal law, all corporations offering bonds in excess of $5 million and sold interstate must have a *trustee.* A trustee is a third party, often a commercial or investment bank or the trust department of a bank, who is selected to represent the bondholders. The trustee has three major responsibilities: (1) bond certification, which entails ensuring that the bond issue has been drawn up in accordance with all legal requirements; (2) overseeing the issue, which requires ensuring the bondholders that the issuer is meeting all of the prescribed functions specified in the indenture; and (3) taking legal action against the corporation if it fails to meet its interest and principal payments or satisfy other terms specified in the indenture.

General Features of Corporate Bonds

The characteristics of many security issues often are determined by the underlying real assets they are financing. For example, to finance the construction of a $1 billion nuclear generating plant with an estimated economic life of 50 years, a utility company might sell one million corporate bonds priced at $1,000 par, with each bond promising to pay $100 each year for 50 years plus a principal of $1,000 at maturity. Given the wide variety of assets and bonds financing them, the differences in corporate bonds can best be explained by examining their general characteristics. These include how they pay interest (fixed-, zero-, or floating-coupon rates) and principal, and their maturities, call features, protective covenants, and collateral.

Coupon Bonds

In the United States, many corporate bonds are coupon bonds paying interest semiannually. For U.S. bonds, the coupon interest is typically based on a 360-day year and 30-day month. Thus, the Kraft 6.125 coupon with a $1,000 principal and maturing 2/1/2018 shown below pays $61.25 per year and $30.63 semiannually. The first coupon payment on the bond was 8/1/08, with the $30.63 semiannual payments made on 8/1 and 2/1 until 2/1/2018. Technically, a coupon bond is one that has a series of coupons attached to the bond certificate, which the holder cuts out at specified times and sends to a designated party (e.g., trustee) for collection. At one time, most bonds were sold with attached coupons. Such bonds were called *bearer bonds* since their coupon payment was made to whoever had physical possession of the bond. Bearer bonds have been replaced by *registered bonds.* The interest on registered bonds is paid by the issuer or a third party (usually the trustee) to all bondholders who are registered with the issuer or the trustee. If the bond is sold, the issuer or trustee must cancel the name of the old holder and register the new one. In addition, issuers of U.S. bonds are required by law to report to the IRS all bondholders receiving interest. A variation of a registered bond is a bond sold in *book-entry form.* Such bonds have one master certificate with all bondholder names. A depository holds the certificate and issues ownership receipts to each bondholder.

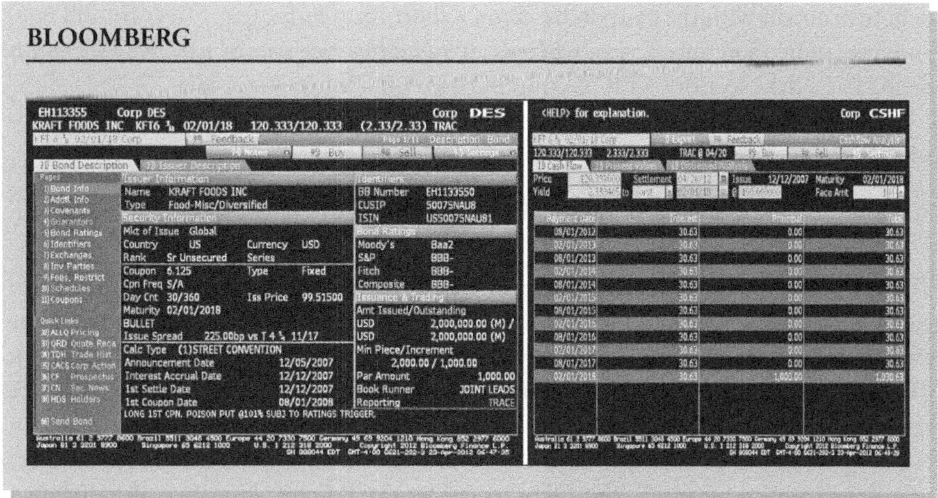

Zero-Coupon Bonds

As discussed in Chapter 3, bonds that pay no coupon interest are referred to as zero-discount bonds or as pure discount bonds. For zeros, the difference between the bond's face value and the offering price when the bond is issued is called the *original-issue discount* (*OID*). Zero-coupon bonds were first issued in the U.S. corporate market during the high interest rate period of the early 1980s. In 1982, for example, Beatrice Foods (later acquired by ConAgra) sold a 10-year, $250 million zero-coupon bond priced at $255 per $1,000 face value. In addition to zeros, many firms also issued *deep-discount bonds* that paid low coupon interest and sell at a price below par. With little or no reinvestment risk, some fund managers find zero-coupon and deep-discount bonds attractive investments for matching their future liabilities.

Floating-Rate Notes

During the high—and often volatile—interest-rate periods of the late 1970s and early 1980s, a number of companies began selling floating-rate notes (FRNs). Similar to variable rate loans offered by financial institutions, FRNs pay a coupon rate that can vary in relation to another bond, benchmark rate, or formula. Floating-rate securities originated in Europe and were introduced in the United States in 1974 when Citigroup issued a $650 million FRN. Citigroup's note was reset semiannually to be one percent above the rate on a three-month Treasury-bill rate. Subsequently, Standard Oil, Georgia Pacific, and other corporations issued FRNs. By 1990, there were approximately 500 floating-rate offerings, with two-thirds being offered by banks and financial service companies. Today, floating-rate securities are issued primarily by financial institutions.

The term floating-rate note or *floater* is often used to define any bonds with an interest rate that is adjusted periodically. Technically, though, a FRN is defined as a debt instrument with the coupon based on a short-term index (e.g., Treasury-bill rate) and reset more than once a year, whereas an *adjustable-rate note* or *variable-rate note* is defined as a debt security with its coupon based on a longer-term rate.

The rate on a floater is reset based on a reference rate plus a quoted margin or spread:

$$\text{Reset Rate} = \text{Reference Rate} + \text{Margin}$$

The reference rate is based on different benchmarks—Treasury rates, commercial paper rate, prime rate, and London Interbank Offered Rate (*LIBOR;* this is the average bank rate paid by London Eurocurrency bank; discussed in Chapter 9). The quoted margin is the additional rate the issuer agrees to pay above the reference rate (typically related to credit risk). Floaters might also have restrictions place on the coupon rate. For example, a floater could have a cap (maximum coupon rate) or a floor (minimum rate). The FRN issued by the Ralcorp Holdings, Inc. (shown below) pays quarterly interests tied to the LIBOR plus a margin of 2.54 percent, a principal of $1,000 and it matures on 8/15/2018. (*Note:* Most of this issue is held by Metropolitan Life.)

BLOOMBERG

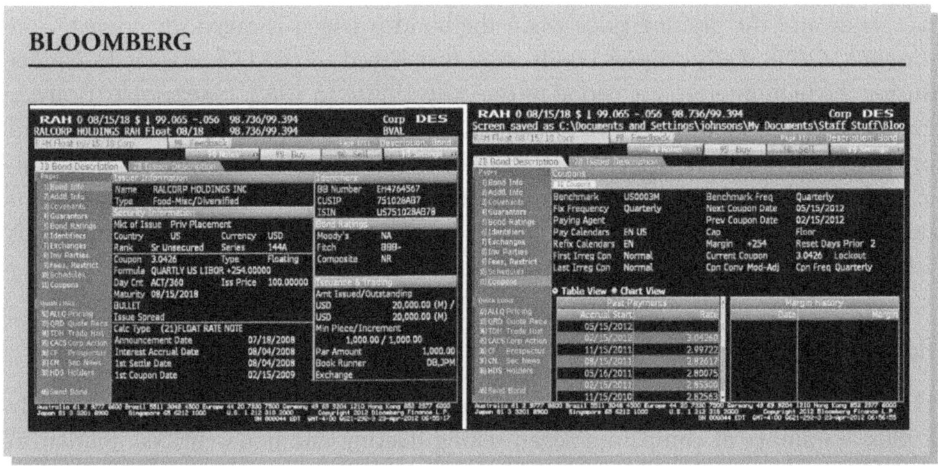

Some FRN issues are sometimes sold with sweeteners, such as convertibility to stock, a put option giving the holder the right to sell the bond back, or a drop-lock rate (i.e., a rate that will be fixed if it is hit). A number of FRNs are also inversely related to the reference rate. An *inverse FRN* or *inverse floater* is often constructed from a fixed-income security (the collateral) and sold along with a floater. The two notes are created such that the interests paid on both are equal or less than the interest paid on the collateral. The coupon rate on the floater is usually set equal to a reference rate such as LIBOR, whereas the rate on the inverse floater is determined by a formula that is inversely related to the reference rate. See Exhibit 7.2 for an example of how the rates on floaters and inverse floated are related to a fixed rate on the collateral.

Maturity

The maturities of corporate bonds vary from intermediate-term bonds with original maturities of five years or less to long-term bonds with original maturities of over five years. Today, the rapid change in technology has led to more corporate bonds being issued with original maturities averaging 15 years.[1] This contrasts with the 1950s and 1960s, when the original maturities on corporate bonds ranged from 20 years to 30 years.

EXHIBIT 7.2 Rates on Floaters, Inverse Floater, and Collateral

- Example:
  - Collateral is \$30 million, 7.5% coupon bond rate.
  - \$22.5 million floater is issued.
  - \$7.5 million inverse floater is issued.
- The rate on the floater, R_{FR}, is set to the LIBOR plus 50 basis points, with the maximum rate permitted being 9.5%.
- The rate on the inverse floater, RI_{FR}, is determined by the following formula:

$$R_{IFR} = 28.5 - 3\text{ LIBOR}$$

- This formula ensures that the weighted average coupon rate (WAC) of the floater and inverse floater will be equal to the coupon rate on the collateral of 7.5%, provided the LIBOR is less than 9.5%.
- For example, if the LIBOR is 8%, then the rate on the floater is 8.5%, the inverse floater's rate is 4.5%, and the WAC of the floater and inverse floater is 7.5%.

$$\begin{aligned} \text{LIBOR} &= 8\% \\ R_{FR} &= \text{LIBOR} + 50\text{BP} = 8.5\% \\ R_{IFR} &= 28.5 - 3\text{LIBOR} = 4.5\% \\ \text{WAC} &= .75R_{FR} + .25R_{IFR} = 7.5\% \end{aligned}$$

- Note: If the LIBOR is greater than 9.5%, then the rate on the inverse floater will be negative. To prevent this from occurring, the inverse floater would have to have a floor equal to zero. Moreover, a floor of zero on the inverse floater would require that a cap of 10% be set on the floater.

Call and Redemption Features

A call provision or option redemption provision in an indenture gives the issuer the right to redeem some or all of the issue for a specific amount (call price) before maturity. Bonds issued without a call or other embedded options are referred to as *bullet bonds.* Callable bonds are often issued when interest rates are relatively high. Many callable bonds can be called at par, often on specific dates. For example, the Ford callable bond paying a 5 percent coupon and maturing on 11/20/2021 was callable at par (100) on the dates 1/20 and 5/20 each year to the bond's maturity.

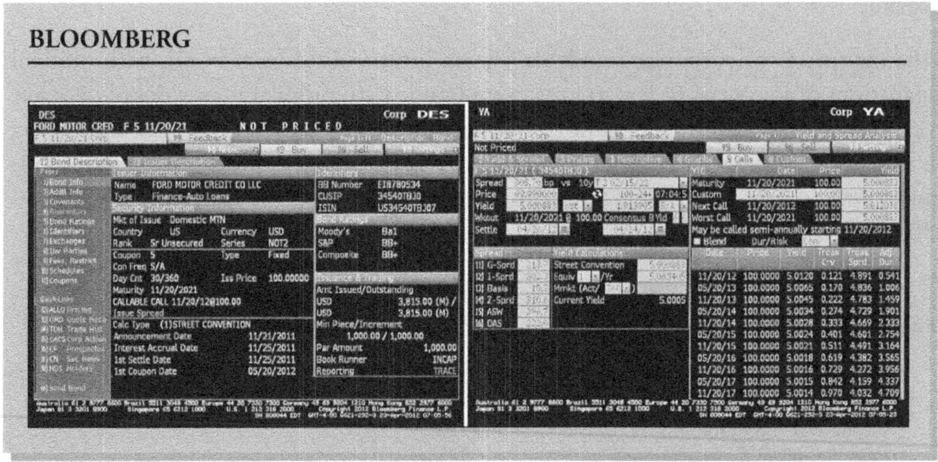

The call provision may often require that the company redeem the bonds at a price greater than the par value. The additional amount is defined as the *call premium.* For some issues, the call price (CP) is the same, for other callable bonds, the call price depends on the time the bond is called. Such issues will have a call schedule indicating the call price for each call date. For example, some companies set the premium equal to one year's interest for the first year if the bond is called, with the premium declining thereafter. For instance, a 10-year, 10 percent, $1,000 par value bond might be called the first year at a call price of $1,100 ($100 premium = (.10)($1,000)), the second year for $1,090 ($90 premium = (9/10)(.10)[$1,000)), and so on, with the premium rate declining by 1/10 each year. Finally, instead of a specified call price or call schedule, some callable bonds have a *make-whole premium provision* (also called a *yield maintenance provision*). This provision specifies that the amount of the premium be such that when it is added to the principal and reinvested at the redemption date in U.S. Treasury securities with the same remaining life as the bond, the yield would equal the bond's original yield. For example, the Ford callable bond shown below pays a 7.7 percent coupon rate and matures on 5/15/2097, and can be called with the premium based on a make-whole premium provision determined by the Treasury rate.

BLOOMBERG

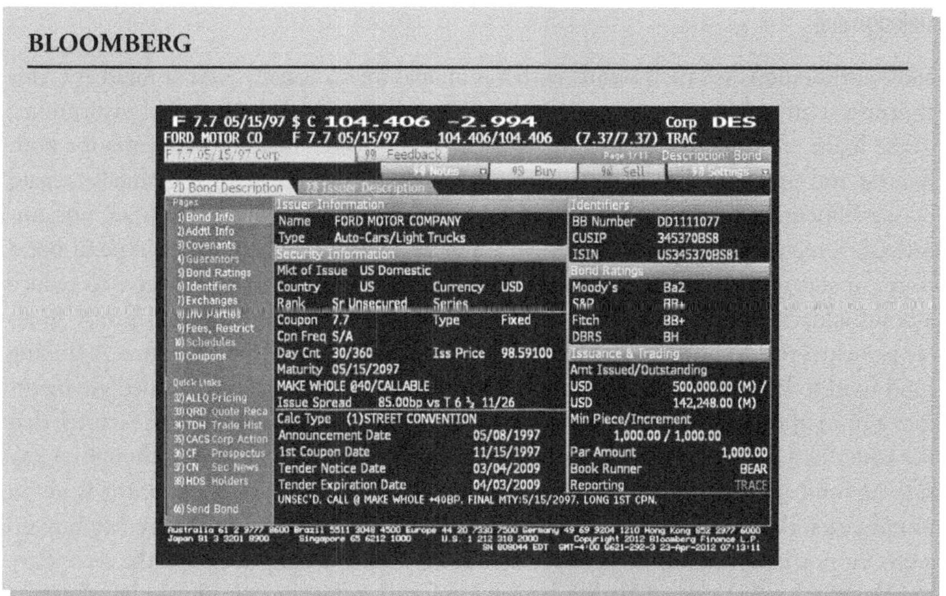

As discussed in Chapter 5, a call option is to the advantage of the issuer. For example, during a period of high interest rates, a corporation might sell a 20-year callable bond, with a 10 percent coupon rate at its par value of $1,000. Suppose two years later, though, interest rates on all bonds dropped and bonds similar to this corporation's were selling at 8 percent. Accordingly, the company might find it advantageous to sell a new 18-year, 8 percent callable bond with the funds of the new issue used to redeem the 10 percent issue. If a company decides to call its bond issue, it would send a *notice of redemption* to each holder and then at a specified time a check equaling the call price.

To the investor, a bond being called provides a benefit, to the extent that the call price exceeds the par value. However, as examined in Chapter 5, if a bond is called, the investor is forced to reinvest her proceeds in a market in which rates are generally lower. Consequently, on balance call provisions tend to work against the investor. As a result, the issuer, in addition to the call premium, might provide the investor with some call protection. For example, provisions could be included in the indenture in which only a certain proportion of the bonds issued could be called for a specified period. Investor protection could also be provided with a *deferred call* feature that prohibits the issuer from calling the bond before a certain period of time has expired. The investor would therefore have call protection for the period. However, a more common practice is to prohibit the issuer from buying back the bonds during a specified period (e.g., five years) from proceeds from a debt issue that ranks senior or par with the bond. Under this type of provision, the issuer has the right to redeem the bonds from excess cash or from the proceeds from the sale of equity, property, or higher interest rate debt. This type of redemption is called *refunding:* the replacement of an old issue with a new one at a lower cost.

Sinking Fund

Most corporations sell their bonds with a principal that is usually paid at maturity. This contrasts with real estate mortgages and consumer loans made by financial institutions. These loans are usually *fully amortized* with the borrower making payments for both interest and principal during the life of the loan such that the loan is gradually repaid by installments before maturity arrives. Given that many corporate bonds are not amortized, some corporations do sell their bonds as a *serial bond* issue. This type of bond issue consists of a series of bonds with different maturities. Such bonds serve to reduce a bondholder's concern over the payment of principal. A more common feature to allay principal risk is the inclusion of a *sinking fund* provision in the indenture. A sinking fund used to be simply a provision requiring that the issuer make scheduled payments into a fund often maintained by the trustee, or in some cases to certify to the trustee that the issuer had added value to its property and plant investments. Today, though, many sinking fund agreements have provisions requiring an orderly retirement of the issue. In recent years, this has been commonly handled by the issuer's being required to buy up a certain portion of bonds each year either at a stipulated call price or in the secondary market at its market price. Usually, the sinking fund's call is the par value unless the issue is originally sold above par; then the call price is typically the issuance price.

This sinking fund call provision benefits the issuer and is a disadvantage to the bondholder. If interest rates are relatively high, then the issuer will be able to buy back the requisite amount at a relatively low market price, and if rates are low and bond prices are high, the issuer will be able to buy back the bonds at the sinking fund call price. A sinking fund with a call option is therefore valuable to the issuer and should trade at a lower price in the market than an otherwise identical non-sinking-fund bond.[2]

It should be noted that since many sinking fund provisions require the repayment of the debt in installments, they effectively reduce the life of the bond. As such, a better measure of a sinking fund bond's life than its maturity is its *average life*. The average life is the average amount of time the debt will be outstanding. It is equal to the weighted average of the time periods, with the weights being relative principal payments:

$$\text{Average Life} = \frac{\sum_{t=1}^{M} t(A_t)}{F}$$

where A_t is the sinking fund due at time t. Thus, a bond that matures in 10 years and requires equal sinking fund payments each year would have an average life of 5.5 years (average life = .1(1) + .1(2) + . . . + .1(10)).

Protective Covenants

The board of directors hires the managers and officers of a corporation. Since the board represents the shareholders, this arrangement can create a moral hazard problem in which the managers may engage in activities that could be detrimental to the bondholders. For example, the managers might use the funds provided by creditors to finance projects different and riskier than bondholders were expecting. Since bondholders cannot necessarily seek redress from managers after they have made decisions that could harm them, they need to include rules and restriction on the company in the bond indenture. Such provisions are known as ***protective*** or ***restrictive covenants.***

The covenants often specify the financial criterion that must be met before borrowers can incur additional debt (debt limitation) or pay dividends (dividend limitations). For example, a debt limitation covenant would be one that prohibits a company from incurring any new long-term debt if it causes the company's interest-coverage ratio (earnings before interest and taxes/interest) to fall below a specified level. In addition to limits on debt and dividends, other possible covenants include limitations on liens, borrowing from subsidiaries, asset sales, mergers and acquisitions, and leasing.

PROTECTIVE COVENANTS

1. Limitations on debt.
2. Limitations on dividends.
3. Limitations on share repurchases.
4. Limitations that prohibit issuing long-term debt if certain ratios (e.g., interest coverage ratio) are lowered.
5. Limitations on liens.
6. Limitations on borrowing from subsidiaries.
7. Limitations on mergers, acquisitions, and asset sales.
8. Limitations on selling assets and leasing them.

Exhibit 7.3 displays several Bloomberg screens describing some of the protective covenants governing the Kraft bond paying an annual coupon rate of 5.375 percent and maturing in 2/10/2020. The covenants include restrictions on mergers and changes of control, downgrades, and certain asset sales.

Over the past two decades, there has been an increase in the number of mergers, corporate restructurings, and stock and bond repurchases. Often, these events benefit the shareholders at the expense of the bondholders, resulting in a downgrade in a bond's

EXHIBIT 7.3 Protective Covenants on Kraft Bond

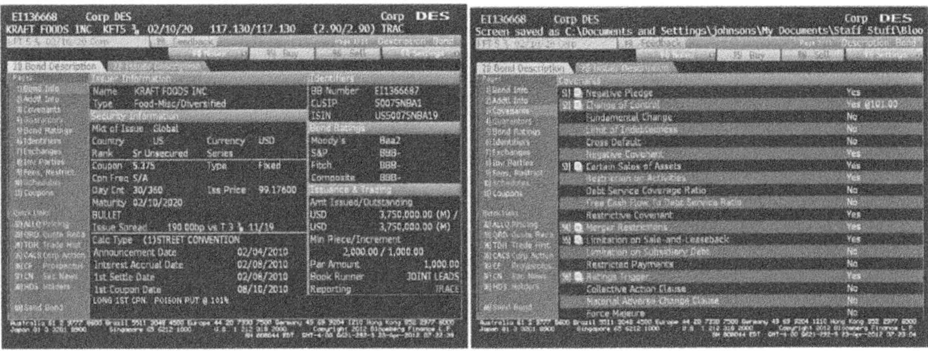

quality ratings and a lowering of its price. Bond risk resulting from such actions is known as *event risk.*[3] Certain protective covenants such as poison puts and net worth maintenance clauses have been used to minimize event risk. A *poison put* clause in the indenture gives the bondholders the right to sell the bonds back to the issuer at a specified price under certain conditions arising from a specific event such as a takeover, change in control, or an investment ratings downgrade. A *net worth maintenance clause,* in turn, requires that the issuer redeem all or part of the debt or to give bondholders the right to sell (*offer-to-redeem clause*) their bonds back to the issuer if the company's net worth falls below a stipulated level.

Secured Bonds, Debentures, and Guaranteed Bond

In the case of corporate bonds, the bonds can be either *secured bonds,* backed by a specific asset, or *unsecured bonds,* backed by a general creditor's claim but not by a specified asset. The latter are called *debentures.* A secured bond is defined as one that has a lien giving the bondholder, via the trustee, the right to sell the pledged asset to pay the bondholders if the company defaults. Secured bonds can be differentiated in terms of the types of collateral pledged and the priority of the lien.

Assets that can be used as security are real, financial, or personal. A mortgage bond and an equipment-trust bond are bonds secured by real assets. A *mortgage bond* has a lien on real property or buildings whereas an *equipment-trust bond* has a lien on specific equipment, such as airplanes, trucks, or computers (see Exhibit 7.4). A *collateral-trust bond,* in turn, is secured by a lien on equity shares of a company's subsidiary, holdings of other company's stocks and bonds, government securities, and other financial claims. Finally, a company might secure its debt with personal property, such as the corporation's cash or liquid assets, accounts receivables, or inventory. Since these assets are short term in nature, they are usually used as collateral for short-term debt obligations.

Mortgage Bonds

In the case of a mortgage bond, if the issuer defaults and the assets are liquidated, then the mortgage bondholders can claim the underlying asset and sell it to pay off their

EXHIBIT 7.4 Collateral on CSX Bond—Equipment Trust Bond

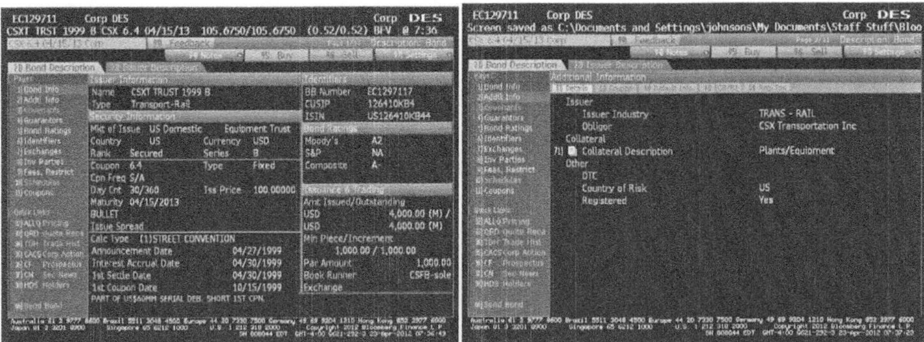

obligation, or if the issuer defaults and the company is reorganized, then the bondholders' mortgage lien will give them a stronger bargaining position relative to other creditors on any new securities created. Often, in a mortgage bond, there are provisions in the indenture that allow the mortgaged asset to be sold provided it is replaced with a suitable substitute; some mortgage bonds also have a *release and substitution provision* that allows for the asset to be sold with the proceeds used to retire the bonds. Mortgage bonds are sometimes sold in a series, similar to a serial bond issue, with the bonds of each series secured by the same mortgage. Generally, it is more efficient for a company to issue a series of bonds under one mortgage and one indenture than it is to arrange collateral and draw up a new indenture for each new bond issue.

Equipment-Trust Bonds

Usually equipment trust bonds are secured by one piece of property and often are named after the security. Equipment-trust bonds are sometimes formed through a lease-and-buy-back agreement involving a third party or trustee. Under this type of agreement, a trustee (e.g., bank, leasing company, or the manufacturer) might purchase the equipment (plane, machine, etc.) and lease it to a company who would agree to take title to the equipment at the termination date of the lease. Alternatively, the company could buy the equipment and sell it the trustee who would then lease it to them. The trustee would finance the equipment purchase from the company or the manufacturer by selling equipment trust bonds (sometime called equipment trust certificates). Such bonds often have a maturity that reflects the life of the equipment and the terms of the lease, and often the principal is amortized. Each period the trustee would then collect rent from the company and pay the interest and principal on the certificates. At maturity, the certificates would be paid off, the trustee would transfer the title of the equipment to the company, and the lease would be terminated. This arrangement (sometimes referred to as the *Philadelphia Plan* and *rolling stock*) and other variations work well when the underlying equipment is relatively standard (e.g., plane, railroad car, or computer) and therefore can be easily sold in the event the company defaults on the lease. Airlines and railroad companies are big users of this type of financing.

Collateral-Trust Bonds

A collateral-trust bond is secured by a lien on the company's holdings of other company's stocks and bonds, other securities and financial claims, or the issuer's subsidiaries. The legal arrangements governing collateral-trust bonds generally require the issuer to deliver to the trustee the pledged securities (if the securities are stock or the stock of a subsidiary, the company still retains its voting rights). The company is usually required to maintain the value of the securities, positing addition collateral (e.g., cash or more securities) if the collateral decreases in value. There are also provisions in the indenture allowing for the withdrawal of the collateral provided there is an acceptable substitute. Finally, some collateral trust bonds are sold as a series like some mortgage bonds, with the same indenture and financial collateral defining each series.

Priority of Claims

In designating an asset as collateral, it is possible for a company to have more than one bond issue or debt obligation secured by that asset. When this occurs, debt obligations must be differentiated in terms of the priorities of their claims. A *senior lien,* or first lien, has priority over a *junior lien* (second or third lien). Thus, if a company defaults and the real property pledged is sold, then the senior bondholders would be paid first, with the second or third lien holders being paid only after the senior holders have been paid in full.[4] It should be noted that such bonds are typically not defined in their title as second or third lien bonds (e.g., second mortgage bond) because of the insinuation of weakness (see Exhibit 7.5).

Closely associated with priorities in claims are clauses in the indenture that specify the issuer's right to incur additional debt secured by the assets already encumbered. At one extreme, there are *closed-end bonds* (usually mortgage bonds) that prohibit the company from incurring any additional debt secured by a first lien on the assets already being used as security. For example, a company with a processing plant and land valued at $20 million might use those assets as security for a $14 million bond issue. If the issue were closed-ended, then no other debt obligation with first liens could be obtained. In contrast, an issue silent on this point is an *open-end bond;* it allows for more debt to be secured by the same collateral. Thus, in the case of the company with a $14 million secured bond, if the company were to later sell a new $6 million bond issue, it could

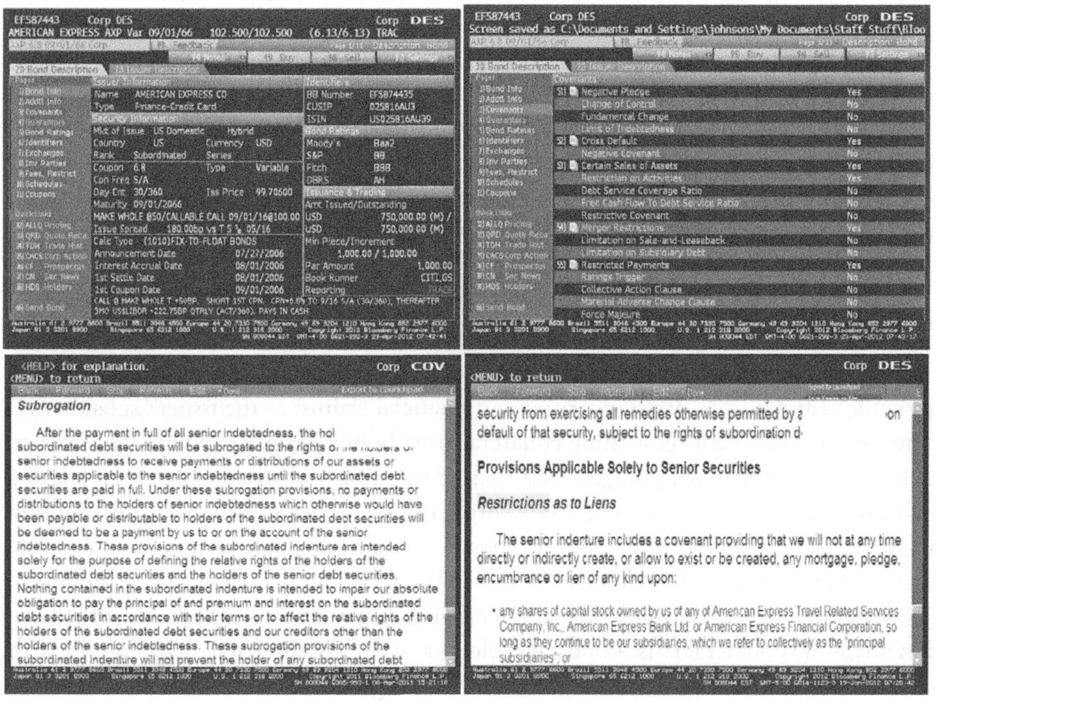

EXHIBIT 7.5 Subordination, Priority of Claims, and Other Covenants

secure the new debt with the $20 million plant and land assets, provided the earlier issue was open ended. In turn, if the company defaulted and the assets were sold for only $14 million, then the first bondholders would receive only 70 cents on each dollar of their loan, compared to a dollar on a dollar if their issue had been closed-end.

Because of the adverse effects to investors, most open-end bonds include certain covenants that limit the amount of additional indebtedness the company can incur. A typical case is an open-end bond accompanied with an *after-acquired property clause.* This clause dictates that all property or assets acquired after the issue be added to the property already pledged. Finally, within the extremes of open- and closed-end bonds are bonds with limited open-end clauses that allow the company to incur additional debt secured by assets up to a certain percent of the pledged asset's value.

Debenture

The majority of all corporate bonds are unsecured. As noted, such bonds are defined as *debentures.* Even though such instruments lack asset-specific collateral, they still make the holder a general creditor. As such, debenture holders are protected by assets that are not already pledged, and they also have a claim on pledged assets to the extent that those assets have values in excess of the secured debt. For investors, it is important to distinguish between strong companies that sell debentures and have no bonds secured with pledged assets and companies that sell debentures and have bond secured with pledged assets—the latter needs closer scrutiny.

Debentures can be issued with a number of protective covenants. For example, the indenture might include a restriction on additional debt that can be incurred or specifications that new debt can be incurred only if earnings grow at a certain level or if certain financial ratios are met. The Kraft bond described in Exhibit 7.3 is an example of unsecured bond with a number of protective covenants. Debentures can also be classified as either *subordinate* or *unsubordinate.* In the case of liquidation, subordinated debt (junior security) has a claim only after an unsubordinated claim (senior claim) has been met. Accordingly, a debenture can be made subordinate to other claims such as bank loans or accounts payable. Subordination may be the result of the terms agreed to by the firm in its other debt obligations. For example, a bank might require that all future debts of a company be made subordinate to its loans. Since subordinated debenture bondholders are last in line among creditors if the issuer defaults, they are sometimes sold with a sweetener or inducement such as an option to convert to shares of the company's stock or a put option giving the holders the right to sell the bond back to the issuer at a specific price (see Exhibit 7.6).

Guaranteed Bonds

Bonds issued by one company and guaranteed by another economic entity are defined as *guaranteed bonds.* The guarantee ensures that the bondholders will be paid interest and principal in the event the issuer defaults. With the guarantee, the default risk of the bond shifts from the borrower to the financial capacity of the insurer.

EXHIBIT 7.6 Subordinate Bonds with Embedded Conversions, Call, or Put Options Found from Bloomberg Search: SRCH

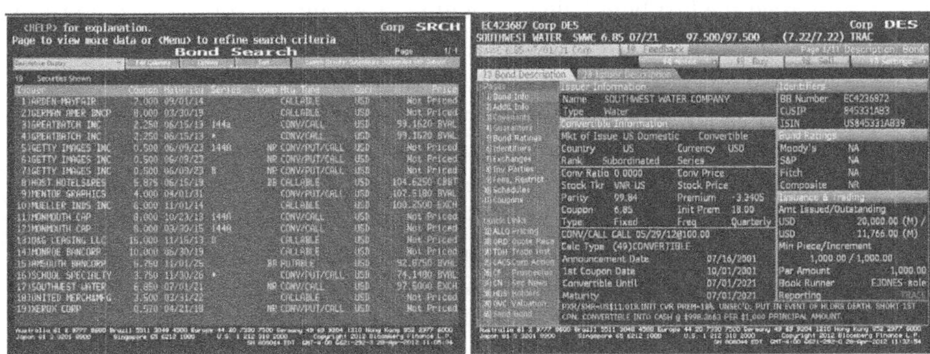

The guarantor could be the parent company or another company securing the issue in return for an option on an equity interest in the project the bond is financing. There may also be multiple guarantors. In a joint venture, for example, a limited partnership may be formed with several companies who jointly agree to guarantee the bond issue of the venture. For some corporate issues, a financial institution may provide the guarantee. For example, banks for a fee provide corporations with *credit enhancements* in the form of *letters of credit* that guarantee the interest and principal payment on the corporation's debt obligation. Similarly, insurance companies have expanded their insurance coverage of municipal bonds that they began providing in the 1970s to the coverage of corporate bonds. Often, the insurance is provided in the form of a *surety bond;* this is an insurance policy written by an insurance company to protect a party against loss or the violation of a contract. Finally, municipal governments and governmental agencies sometimes offer guarantees.

BLOOMBERG

Click "Guarantors" tab on the bond's description page or GRBI on a bond's menu screen to determine if the bond is insured or guaranteed and who is the insurer.

Example: PPL 4.80436 percent bond maturing in 12/21/37:

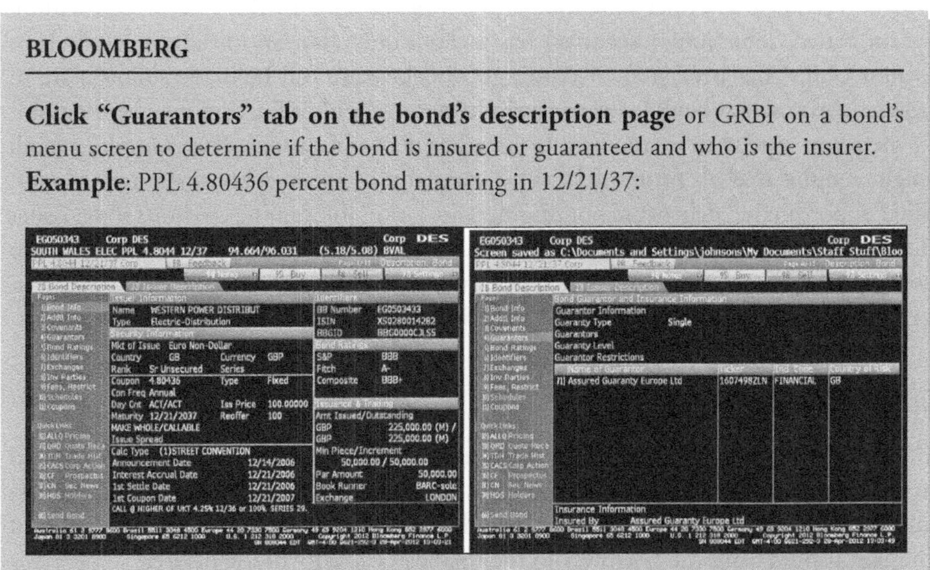

Corporate Bonds with Special Features

In addition to the general characteristics of corporate bonds, many corporate bonds also have special features included in their covenants that make them more identifiable with stocks, options, or other securities. Bonds with special features may be created out of Chapter 7 corporate reorganization or they may be features of low-quality, high-yield bonds that are added to make the bonds more attractive. High-yield bonds used to have a conventional structure. In the 1980s, though, many companies that were active in leveraged buyout acquisitions or in debt-for-equity recapitalization faced cash flow constraints. To minimize their cash flow problems or to try to maintain quality ratings, they often issued bonds with special features.

Income Bonds

Income bonds are instruments that pay interest only if the earnings of the firm are sufficient to meet the interest obligations; principal payments, however, are required. Thus, a failure by the issuer to pay interest does not constitute a default. Because income bonds are rare, companies who have been reorganized because of financial distress sometimes issue them. In general, because the interest payments are not required unless earnings hit a certain level, income bonds are similar to preferred stock. In fact, some income bonds have the cumulative dividend feature of preferred stock: if interest is not met, it accumulates. Similarly, some income bonds permit voting or limited voting rights (usually if interest is not paid). Unlike preferred stock, though, income bonds do provide corporations with the tax advantage of interest deductibility. Finally, income bonds often include such features as sinking fund arrangements and convertibility to the company's stock.

Participating Bonds

Participating bonds provide a guaranteed minimum rate, as well as additional interest up to a certain point if the company achieves a certain earnings level. Like income bonds, participating bonds are similar to preferred stock, except for the interest deductibility benefit. However, for obvious reasons, participating bonds are not very popular to shareholders. As a result, such bonds are very rare.

Deferred Coupon Bonds

Some corporations sell bonds with a deferred coupon structure that allows the issuer to defer coupon interest for a specified period. Included in the group of deferred coupon bonds are *deferred-interest bonds, reset bonds, extendable reset bonds,* and *payment-in-kind bonds.* Many of these debt securities with special features were created during the merger period of the 1980s. For example, in 1989, the RJR leveraged buyout created convertible and exchangeable debentures that had both payment-in-kind and reset features.

A deferred-interest bond (DIB) has its coupon interest deferred for a specified period. They are often structured so that they do not pay coupons for specified number of years (e.g., five years). At the end of the deferred-interest period, they begin to pay interest, usually semiannually, until they mature or are called. Such bonds sell originally like deep discount bonds. A reset bond or step coupon bond is similar in structure to a DIB except that it starts with a low coupon interest, which is later increased. A reset bond may have a call option that is likely to be exercises as the coupon level increases. An extendable reset bond has a rate that is reset to reflect the current level of interest and credit spread (usually determined by an independent investment firm or firms). Extendable reset bonds are like FRNs. Finally, A payment-in-kind bond (PIK) gives the issuer the option on the interest-payment date to pay the coupon interest either in cash or in-kind, usually by issuing the bondholder a new bond. In essence, a PIK allows coupons to be paid in units of the security (baby bonds). If the issuer pays in kind, then at maturity the investor would own a number of bonds and the cash flow from her PIK would be similar to that of a zero-coupon bond.

Tax-Exempt Corporate Bonds

To promote investments in projects that are in the public interest, Congress grants tax-exempt status for bonds used for specified purposes. When a project qualifies for tax exemption, the holders of the bond do not have to pay federal income tax on the interest they receive. As a result, investors in tax-exempt bonds will accept a lower interest rate, lowering the interest cost to the issuing corporation. Prior to 1986, a number of activities qualified for tax-exempt status. The Tax Reform Act of 1986, though, significantly reduced the number of eligible activities. Examples of eligible tax-exempt activities would be the construction of solid and hazardous waste disposal facilities.

Bonds with Warrants

A *warrant* is a security or a provision in a security that gives the holder the right to buy a specified number of shares of stock or another designated security at a specified price. It is a call option issued by the corporation. As a sweetener, some corporate bonds, such as a subordinated debenture, are sold with warrants. A warrant that is attached to the bond can be exercised only by the bondholder. Often, the warrant can be detached from the bond as of a particular date and sold separately.

Convertible Bonds

A *convertible bond* is one that has a conversion provision that grants the bondholder the right to exchange the bond for a specified number of shares of the issuer's stock. A convertible bond is similar to a bond with a nondetachable warrant. Like a regular bond, it pays interest and principal, and like a warrant, it can be exchanged for a specified number of shares of stock. Convertible bonds are often sold as a subordinate debenture (convertible debentures). The conversion feature of the bond, in turn, serves as a sweetener to the bond issue. *Note:* Some convertibles can be converted into other securities. For example, a company owning a significant proportion of another company could issue a convertible bond giving the convertible bondholders the right to convert the bond into shares the issuer owns of the other company. Similarly, a gold-mining company could issue a bond convertible into gold claims.

To issuers, convertibles tend to lower the interest costs on their debt. The conversion feature may also make it possible for issuers to reduce the number of protective covenants they normally would include in their debt obligations. In general, convertibles give issuers the opportunity to sell stock at a better price via the convertible than the stock price they currently would receive it they were sold directly. This advantage could be negated later if the stock were sold on the convertible at a price below the market. However, most convertibles have a call option that the issuer can use to force the conversion to a price that in some cases would be higher than the price realized in the market. Exhibit 7.7 describes a convertible bond issued by American Equity Investment Life. As a bond, the convertible pays an annual coupon of 5.25 percent and matures on 12/6/2024. The bond can be converted to 71.2758 shares of American Equity common stock. The bond also has put option, allowing the bondholder to sell the bond back to American at its

EXHIBIT 7.7 American Equity Investment Life Convertible Bond: Bloomberg DES Screen

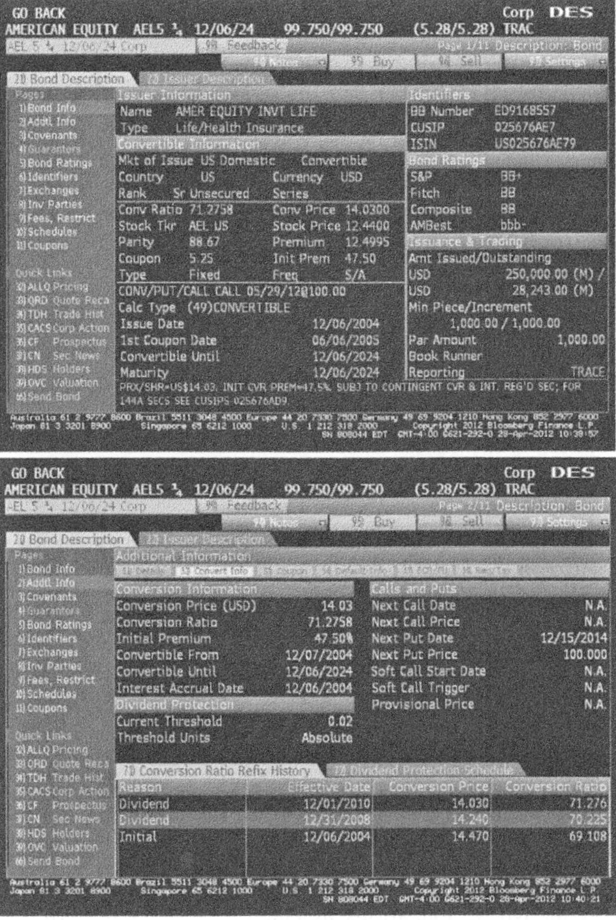

par value. For investors, convertible bonds provide a floor against a stock price decrease. That is, if the stock price decreases, the value of the convertible will only drop to its value as a straight bond. However, if the stock price increases, then the convertible bond's price will also increase, providing upside potential. The disadvantage of a convertible to investors is that the yield on the bond is less than the yield on a comparable nonconvertible and the issuer can call the convertible forcing the conversion.

Putable Bonds

As noted in Chapter 3, a *putable bond* or *put bond* gives the holder the right to sell the bond back to the issuer at a specified price. In contrast to callable bonds, putable bonds benefit the holder: if interest rates increase and as a result the price of the bond decreases below the specified price, then the bondholder can sell the bond back to the issuer and reinvest in a market with higher rates. As we noted earlier, a bond with a put option may also be used to protect the bondholder against a decrease in the price of the bond due to a downgrade in its quality rating.

Extendable Bonds

Extendable bonds have an option to extend the maturity of the bond. Typically, the bond issuer holds the option. Some extendable bonds give the holder the right to extend and some give both the issuer and the investor the extension option.

Credit-Sensitive Bonds

Credit-sensitive bonds are bonds with coupons that are tied to the issuer's credit ratings. For example, the coupon rate may be 10 percent if the bond has a quality rating of A or better, 10.25 percent if rating is BBB, 10.5 percent if the rating is BB, and so on. Such bonds provide bondholders some protection against management pursuing risky investments or diluting the quality of current bonds by management's increase use of debt financing. However, such clauses also increase the company's interest costs at a time when it may not need higher rates.

Commodity-Linked Bonds

A *commodity-linked bond* is one that has its coupons and possibly principal tied to the price of a particular commodity. The bonds are designed to provide a company a hedge against adverse changes in the price of a commodity. For example, an oil-producing company might sell an oil-index bond in which the interest is tied to the price of crude oil.

Voting Bonds

As the name indicates, *voting bonds* give voting privileges to the holders. The vote is usually limited to specific corporate decisions under certain conditions.

Assumed Bonds

An *assumed bond* is one whose obligations are taken over or assumed by another company or economic entity. In many cases, such bonds are the result of a merger. That is, when one firm takes over or buys a second firm, the second firm usually loses its identity (legally and in name). As a result, the first company takes over the liabilities of the second. Accordingly, the bonds of the second are assumed by the first firm's promise to pay, often with additional security pledged by the first company in order to allay any fears of the creditors.

BLOOMBERG'S SECF AND ADVANCED BOND SEARCH

SRCH <ENTER>; CLICK "ADVANCED SEARCH"

Given the many type of corporate bonds, Bloomberg's bond "Advanced Search" screen (accessible on the SRCH screen) can be used to find bonds with certain features. The slides in this exhibit show a bond search for U.S., dollar-denominated, investment-grade corporate bonds in the energy sector.

SECF: The SECF screen is also a good way to screen for bonds with certain features. The slides show screenings for equipment-trust bonds and subordinate debentures.

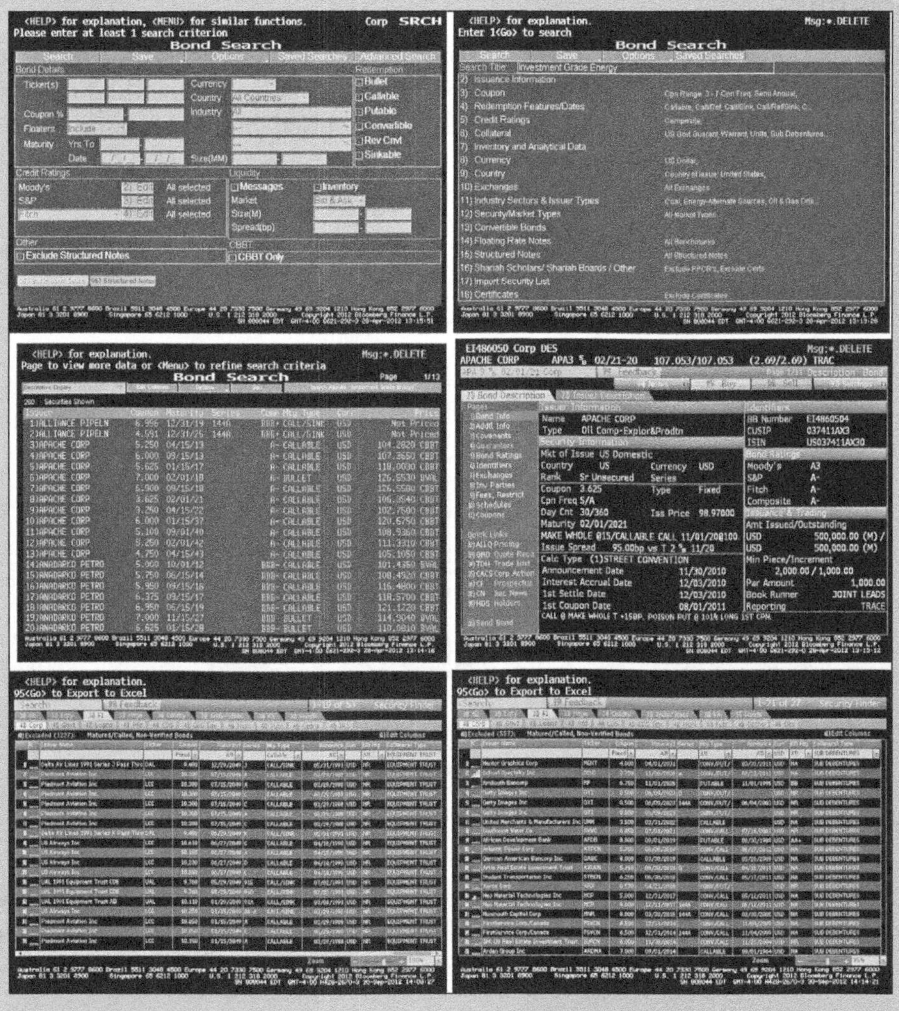

Medium-Term Notes

A *medium-term note* (*MTN*) is a debt instrument sold on a continuing basis to investors who are allowed to choose from a group of bonds from the same corporation, but with different maturities—serial corporate bond issue. MTNs were first introduced in the 1970s when General Motors Acceptance Corporation (GMAC) sold such instruments to finance its automobile loans. However, the market for MTNs did not take off until the early 1980s when Merrill Lynch began acting as an agent in issuing MTNs and also as a dealer by making a secondary market for the notes. Since then, the MTN market has grown significantly. The market's growth can be attributed to the flexibility MTN issues provide corporations in the types of securities they can offer. MTN also take advantage of SEC Rule 415. This rule allows issuers to sell several issues over different periods without having to go through SEC registration procedures each time.

Issuing Process

MTNs are often sold through investment banking firms who act as agents. The agents will often post the maturity range for the possible notes in the program and their offering rates. For example, Duke Power has several outstanding MTN issues shown below. One of the notes from one of its issues pays an 8.24 percent coupon and matures on 8/22/2022. This bond was part of MTN series issued in 1993.

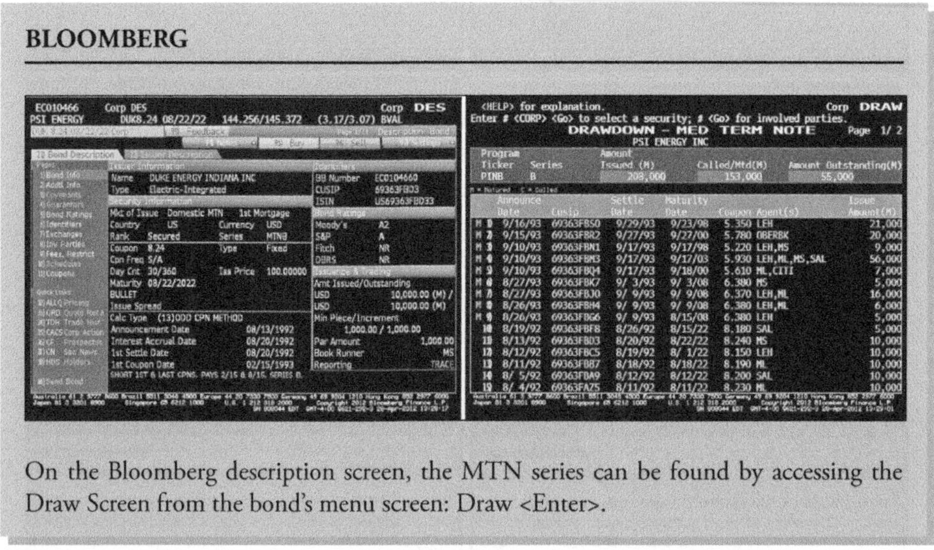

On the Bloomberg description screen, the MTN series can be found by accessing the Draw Screen from the bond's menu screen: Draw <Enter>.

When a new MTN issue is announced, an investor interested in one of the note offerings will notify the agent who, in turn, contacts the issuing corporation for a confirmation. Once a MTN issue is sold, then the company can file a new registration to sell a new MTN issue—an action known as reloading. In addition to providing issuing corporations with flexibility in their capital budget, a MTN program also gives institutional investors the opportunity to choose notes whose maturities best fit their liabilities, thereby minimizing their market risk. In many instances, the market for MTNs starts with institutional investors indicating to agents the type a maturity they want; this is known as *reverse inquiry.* On a reverse inquiry, the agent will inform the corporation of the investor's request; the corporation could then agree to sell the notes with that maturity from its MTN program, even if they are not posted.

Special Features

Today, MTNs are issued not only by corporations, but also by bank holding companies, government agencies, supranational institutions, and sovereign countries. MTNs vary in terms of their features. Some, for example, are offered with fixed rates, where others pay a floating rate; some are unsecured whereas others are secured (e.g., equipment trust MTN). Floaters and inverse floater are also created from MTN and some MTN have currency clauses. It is also common for MTN to be offered with derivatives (swaps, caps, floors, futures and forward contracts). MTNs that are combined with other instruments are referred to as a *structured MTN.* The most common derivative used is a swap. A corporation, for example, might issue MTNs with floating rates and then take a position in an interest rate swap contract to form a synthetic fixed-rate debt.

FINDING MTNs USING THE BLOOMBERG PGM AND SECF SCREENS

The Bloomberg PGM screen displays debt market programs such as MTN issues by issuer. To find MTNs: PGM <Enter>, click "Medium Term Notes" and then search for issuer and click for issue. From the MTN's menus screen, you can access the "Draw" screen (showing the MTN issue): Draw <Enter>.

SECF: On the SECF screen (FI tab), MTNs can be found by typing MTN in the "Series" box.

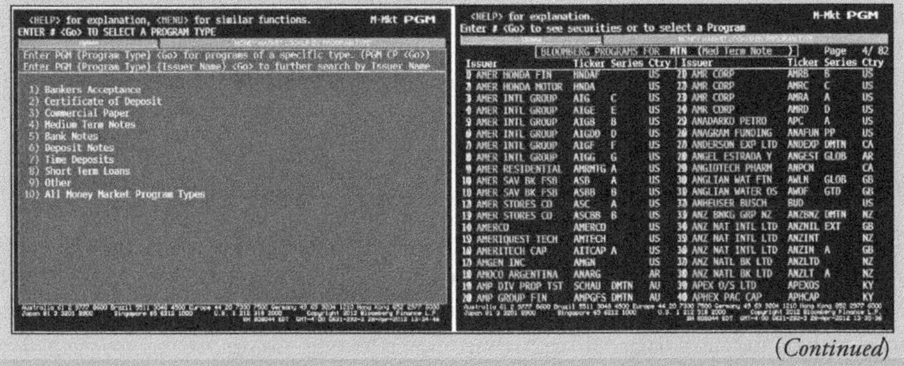

(*Continued*)

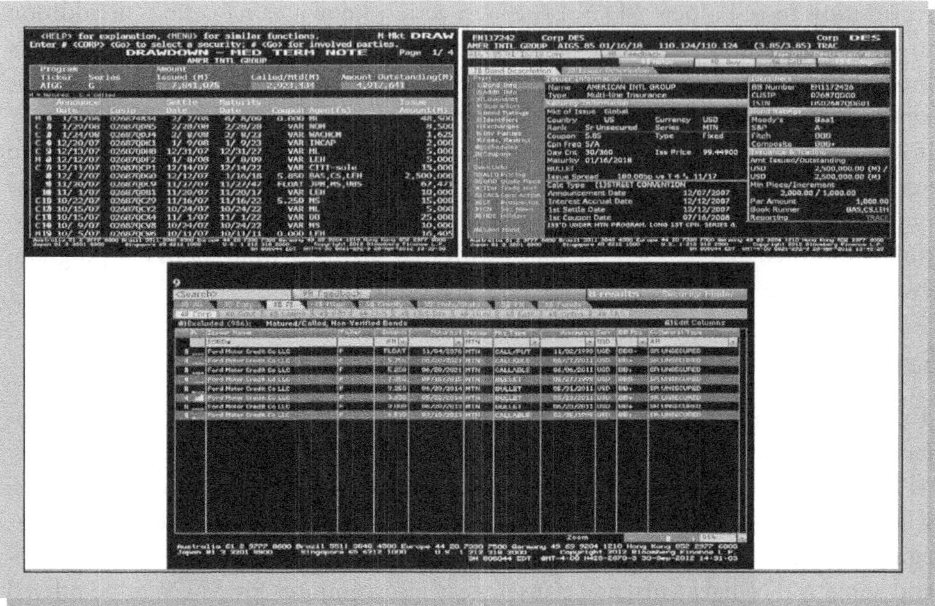

Commercial Paper

Commercial paper (CP) is a short-term debt obligation usually issued by large, well-known corporations. As a source of corporate funds, CP is a substitute for a bank's line of credit and other short-term loans provided by a financial institution. Some companies use the proceeds from CP sales to finance their cash flow needs between the time when they pay workers, resource suppliers, and the like, and the time when they sell their products. Other companies use CP to provide their customer with financing for the purchase of their products, and some companies use CP as bridge financing for their long-term investments, including corporate takeovers.

CP investors include money market funds, pensions, insurance companies, bank trust departments, other corporations, and governments. Many of the institutional investors purchase CP as part of their liquidity investments. Other corporations and state and local governments usually buy CP when they have temporary excess cash balances that they want to invest for a short period before they are needed to pay workers, accounts payable, accrued expenses, and other short-term liabilities. Finally, money market funds include CP in their portfolios with other money market securities. Money market funds are one of the largest investors in CP.

Direct Paper

CP issuers can be divided into finance companies and nonfinance companies, with the paper being either direct paper or dealer paper. As the name suggests, *direct paper* is sold by the issuing company directly to investors, instead of through dealers. The issuing companies include the subsidiaries of large companies, referred to as *captive finance companies,* bank holding companies, independent finance companies, and nonfinancial corporations.

Frequently, these companies employ sales forces to place their CP with large institutional investors. The major captive finance companies selling direct paper are General Motors Acceptance Corporation (GMAC), Ford Credit Corporation, and GE Capital. These companies use the proceeds from their CP sales to finance installment loans and other credit loans extended to customers buying the products of their parent companies. GE Capital, for example, has had between \$50 billion and \$70 billion CP outstanding over the last several years and has been issuing CP for 50 years. Bank holding companies use CP sales to finance equipment purchases they lease to businesses, working capital loans, and installment loans.

Dealer Paper

Dealer paper, also called *industrial paper*, is the CP of corporations sold through CP dealers. Historically, the dealer's market for CP has been dominated by the major investment banking firms. In 1987, though, the Federal Reserve gave the subsidiaries of bank holding companies permission to underwrite CP. This action served to increase the competition among CP dealers. Some of the major CP dealers include Bank of America, Goldman Sachs, Credit Suisse First Boston, Citicorp, and Banker's Trust. These dealers usually buy the CP from the issuer, mark it up (usually about 1 percent), and then resell it. Exhibit 7.8 summarizes the key features of commercial paper.

BLOOMBERG INFORMATION ON COMMERCIAL PAPER

- PGM: The PGM screen displays CP programs: PGM <Enter>, click "Commercial Paper":
- FDCP shows CP outstanding.
- CPPR displays direct CP issuer.
- DOCP finds and trades CP offerings.

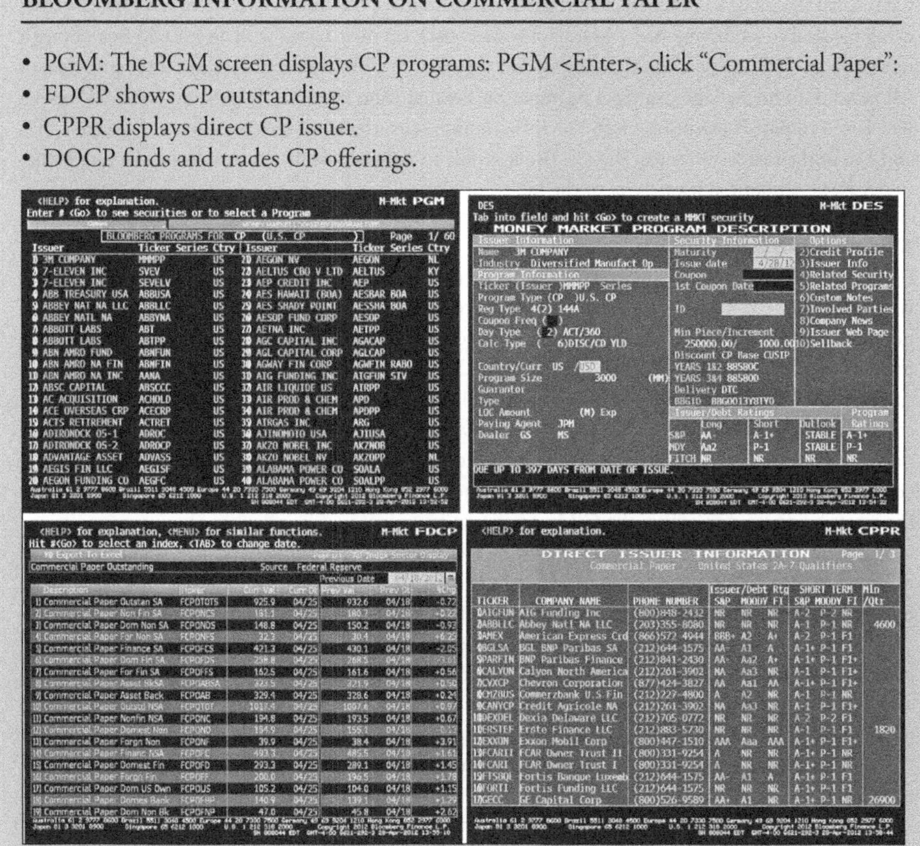

EXHIBIT 7.8 Features of Commercial Paper

Zero-Coupon

Most CP issues are sold on a pure discount basis, although there are some that are sold with coupon interest. CP is quoted on a discount basis like T-bills with a year being 360 days. The yields on CP are higher than the yields on T-bills, reflecting the credit and liquidity risk associated with CP.

Maturity

The original maturities of CP range from three days (weekend paper) to 270 days, with the average original maturity being 60 days. The Securities Act of 1933 exempts companies issuing CP from registering with the SEC if the issue is less than 270 days. As a result of this provision, many CP issues have original maturities of less than 270 days; this reflects the desire by issuers to avoid the time consuming SEC registration. CP can also be used as collateral for a bank that wants to borrow from the Fed discount window provided the CP's maturity does not exceed 90 days. As a result, many CP issues have maturities of less than 90 days.

Denominations

CP issues are usually sold in denominations from $100,000, although some are sold in $25,000 denominations. CP Investors tend to hold their paper to maturity. As a result, the secondary market of CP is small.

Security and Line of Credit

CP is often described as unsecured. The unsecured feature of CP means that there is no specific asset being pledged to secure the issue. Many CP issuers back up their paper with an unused line of credit from a bank. The line of credit is a safeguard in the event the CP issuer cannot pay off the principal or sell new CP to finance the principal payment on the maturing issue. CP issuers often roll CP, selling new issues to payoff maturing ones. For this commitment, the bank charges a fee of between 0.5% and 1% of the issue. In return, the CP issuer is able to reduce default risk and lower the rate he has to pay by an amount at least equal to the fee.

Credit Enhancements

Issuers of CP tend to have high credit ratings. Some smaller and less well-known companies also issue CP. These companies often issue CP with credit supports—credit-supported CP. Credit-supported CP include issues backed by letters of credit. Paper sold with this type of credit enhancement is called *LOC paper* or *documented paper.* Credit enhancements can also take the form of a surety bond from an insurance company. Finally, instead of a credit enhancement, some companies collateralize their issue with other assets—***asset-backed CP***. Included in this group of asset-based paper is securitized CP, often issued by a bank holding company. In these cases, a bank holding company sells CP to finance a pool of credit card receivables, leases, or other short-term assets, with the assets being used to secure the CP issue.

In recent years, there has been a decline in the market for medium- and low-quality CP. This decline is partly due to the reluctance of banks to provide backup line of credit facilities and partly due to SEC Rule 2a-7 of the Investment Company Act of 1970 that governs the quality standards of CP held by money-market funds. This rule constrains money market funds to investments in *eligible paper* as defined by Tier-1 (eligible paper that is rated "1" by at least two of the rating agencies) and Tier-2 (eligible paper that is not Tier-1). SEC Rule 2a-7 specifies that money market funds may hold no more than 5% of their assets in Tier-1 paper in any industrial user and no more than 1% of their assets in Tier-2 paper of any industrial issuer, and that Tier-2 paper may not represent more than 5% of the fund's assets.

Bankruptcy

A number of factors can lead to the financial distress and deterioration of a company: poor investments, competition, excessive debt, litigation, and poor management. One of the main risks that an investor assumes when she buys a bond is the chance the company will become financially distressed and the issuer will default. If a corporation defaults, the amount the investor receives depends, in part, on the security pledged and the priority of the claim; however, equally important is how the bankruptcy is handled.

A company is considered bankrupt if the value of its liabilities exceeds the value of its assets; it is considered in default if it cannot meet its obligations. Technically, default and bankruptcy are dependent. A company with liabilities exceeding assets (bankrupt) will inevitably be in default when the future income from its assets is insufficient to cover future obligations on its liabilities. It should be noted that bankruptcy is not limited to size. There have been many large corporations that have declared bankruptcy: GM, Enron, Texaco, Federated Department Stores, Continental Airlines, Penn Central, Eastern Airlines, Southland Corporation, and Pan Am, to name a few. Also, there are occasions when a company is currently solvent but files for bankruptcy in order to obtain protection against future claimants. This was the motivation for the bankruptcy petition filed by the Manville Corporation in the 1980s, in which the company was solvent but had legal claims against it due to asbestos-related diseases.

In the United States, when a company defaults on its obligations to bondholders and other creditors, the company can voluntarily file for bankruptcy with the courts; the bondholders (via their trustee) and other creditors can sue for bankruptcy; or both parties can try to work out an agreement. In the first two cases, the court will decide whether the assets should be liquidated or whether the company should be reorganized. In the third case, the parties can settle by extending or changing the composition of the debt with minimum court involvement. In the United States, the Bankruptcy Reform Act of 1994 governs bankruptcies. The act is composed of 15 chapters. Chapter 7 deals with liquidation of a corporation and Chapter 11 deals with reorganization. Technically, liquidation means that all of the assets will be distributed to the holders of claims and the corporate entity will not survive. In contrast, when there is reorganization a new entity emerges, with claim holders getting new securities in the new corporation or cash and new securities. The Bankruptcy Act, in turn, provides the framework under which liquidation and reorganization are considered (see Exhibit 7.9 for a summary of the bankruptcy process). In addition, the law also provides stay protection for the distressed company from its creditors.

If the court decides on asset liquidation, creditors with security pledged will receive, to the extent possible, the par value of their debt from the sale of the secured assets. Next the sale of unsecured assets and any excesses from the secured assets' sale will be used to satisfy priority creditors. Finally, what is left will be used to pay

EXHIBIT 7.9 U.S. Bankruptcy Process for Reorganization

Filings:

(a) A bankruptcy filing by creditors or the debtor (distressed company) is done in the appropriate circuit and district court. Appropriate can mean the court with jurisdiction over the company's headquarters or its principal place of business.
(b) The filing requires the best estimate of the value of the company's assets and liabilities and a listing of its 20 largest creditors.
(c) The company files a petition for protection, creditors are contacted, and a meeting is set up.

Debtor-in-Possession:

(a) When a company files for protection it becomes a debtor-in-possession. As a debtor-in-possession, the company continues to operate, but under the supervision of the court.
(b) Court supervision includes the court's approval on major transactions, the appointment of a trustee to oversee, and the possible appointment of an examiner. In certain cases, the court may appoint a trustee to take over control of the business.
(c) The bankruptcy judge issues an automatic stay.
(d) All debt is frozen: Creditors are precluded from trying to enforce collection.
(e) Lawsuits are suspended.

Formulation of a Plan:

(a) A committee consisting of officers and representatives for creditors and possibly shareholders is formed to formulate a plan of reorganization.
(b) The debtor must file the plan in 120 days, although the length can be extended.
(c) No other plans can be filed during this period. Thereafter any interested party can submit a plan.
(d) Plans usually consider reorganization, the creation of new financial securities, elimination or changing expensive contracts (e.g., leases or union contracts), and substantial consolidation.
(e) Under substantial consolidation, all assets and liabilities of all of the company's subsidiaries are pooled and used; this can have important ramification for security holders.

Disclosure Statement:

(a) Once the committee approves the plan for reorganization, the debtor produces and files for approval a disclosure statement.
(b) The disclosure statement summarizes the plan. It also includes pro formas and a liquidation analysis supporting the claim that the creditors will receive more under the reorganization plan than liquidation.
(c) If the court approves the disclosure statement, then it is sent to all impaired parties for approval.
(d) Parties are given 30 days to vote.
(e) To be accepted, at least two-thirds of the impaired parties and half of the claimants must accept the plan.
(f) If approved, the court sets a date for the reorganization.
(g) If the required number of creditors do not approve, the plan may be approved under a cramdown provision. Approval under this provision requires meeting several specified criteria.

unsecured creditors, followed by shareholders. Thus, when a company is liquidated, senior creditors are paid in full before junior are paid, and secured creditors and unsecured creditors have senior claim over equity holders. This distribution of assets to creditors is referred to as the *absolute priority rule.* In the case of liquidation, the bankruptcy courts have generally upheld this rule in their decisions.

Alternatively, if a court decides that the value of the company's operation is worth more if it continues as a business than if it is liquidated, then the court may order reorganization. For reorganization to be feasible (or preferable to liquidation) the causes of the firm's insolvency must be rectified and the prospects of a profitable future must be defended. Moreover, to achieve profitability, reorganization often requires a restructuring of the debt. When this occurs, creditors are usually given new claims on the reorganized firm that are at least equal in value to an amount estimated to be received if liquidation had occurred. This could take the form of debenture holders receiving long-term income bonds, stock, or convertible bonds, and short-term creditors receiving long-term claims. In contrast to liquidations, there have been numerous cases in which the absolute priority rule (APR) has been violated in Chapter 11 reorganizations; that is, where the actual distribution of assets was different from what the terms called for in the debt agreement.[5] Such violations can occur as a result of efforts to reach an agreement during the bankruptcy process among all impaired parties, including equity holders. In such cases, unsecured creditors may end up bearing a disproportionate cost of the reorganization, with possibly equity holders benefiting.

In summary, the amount of funds the bondholder will ultimately receive when an issuer defaults depends on whether the bankruptcy is handled through liquidation, reorganization, or voluntary settlement. Current U.S. law generally favors reorganization. Since bankruptcy proceedings can take some time, some speculators specialize in buying defaulted issues. They, in turn, can profit from such investments if the present value of the cash received at liquidation or the value of the new instrument (replacing the defaulted bond) from reorganization exceeds the price they paid for the defaulted bonds.

BLOOMBERG BANKRUPTCY SCREENS

- BNKF: bankruptcy filings (brings up CACT screen set for Bankruptcy filings).

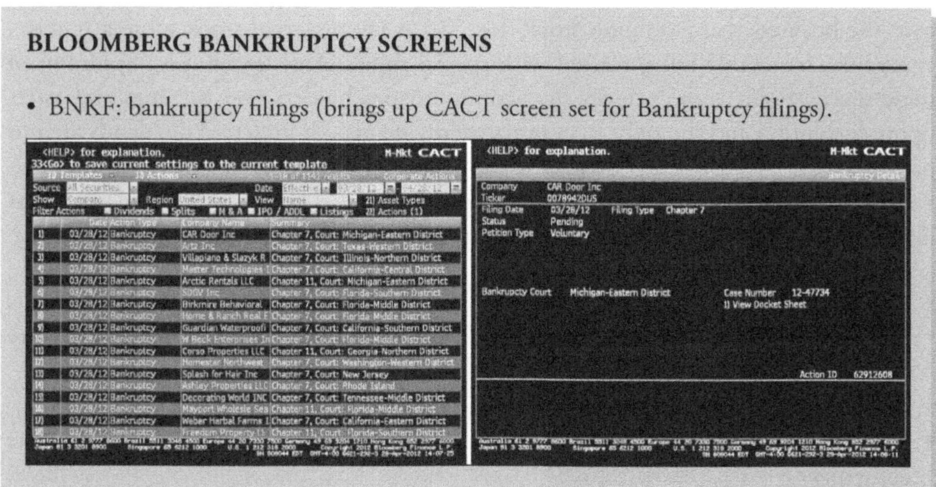

DISTRESSED BONDS: DIS <ENTER>

BONDS WITH RATINGS CHANGES: RATC <ENTER>

The DIS screen displays a list of all bonds that traded at a yield of at least 10 percent over the Treasury benchmark rate the past five business days.

The RATC screen displays a list of current and historical credit ratings for various issuers. RATC allows you to evaluate the financial security of the issuer based on their ability to meet debt obligations. You can use the historical ratings to analyze the issuer's creditworthiness and to track upgrades, downgrades, and other moves that reflect the issuer's fiscal strength and degree of risk.

The DIS list and RATC search on 4/27/2012:

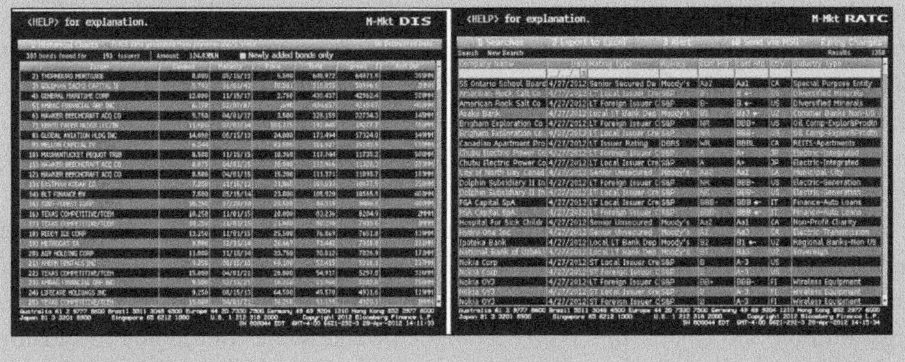

Preferred Stock

As noted in Chapter 1, preferred stock can be thought of as a limited ownership share. It provides its owners with only limited income potential in the form of a stipulated dividend (*preferred dividend*), which is usually expressed as a percentage of a stipulated par value. Preferred stock also gives its holders fewer voting privileges and less control over the business than common stock does. To make preferred stock more attractive, companies frequently sell preferred with special rights. Among the most common of these special rights is the priority over common stockholders over earnings and assets upon dissolution and the right to cumulative dividends—if preferred dividends are not paid, then all past dividends must be paid before any common dividends are paid. A variation of a preferred stock is a *preference stock*. Preference stock is a preferred stock that is subordinate in claims to preferred. Other possible rights and features of preferred are:

- The right to vote on new stock issues.
- The right to vote on the levels of retained earning the company can maintain before dividends are declared.
- The election of directors under certain circumstances.
- The conversion of the preferred stock to common stock or another security of the company.

- The payment of a variable dividend rate in which the dividend is tied to the rate on another security.
- A call feature or optional redemption provision giving the company the right to buy the preferred stock from the holder.
- A sinking fund clause used by the issuer to buy back the issue.

To the investor, preferred stock is similar to a bond in its priority of claims and its fixed-income feature, and it is similar to common stock in that there is often no maturity and there is no corporate default if preferred dividends are not paid by the company. Hence, preferred is commonly referred to as a *hybrid security.* Exhibit 7.10 shows a description, dividend, and price graph screens of a preferred stock issue of Con Edison of New York. The preferred pays a fixed dividend of 4.65 percent per $100 par, is callable at any time, and from 4/30/2010 to 4/30/2012 was trading between $82.21 and $101.05. Like common stock, one of the disadvantages of preferred is that it has the double taxation feature. For corporate investors, this feature is

EXHIBIT 7.10 Con Edison Preferred Stock: Bloomberg Screens CUSIP (209111301) <Pfd>, DES, DVD, and GP

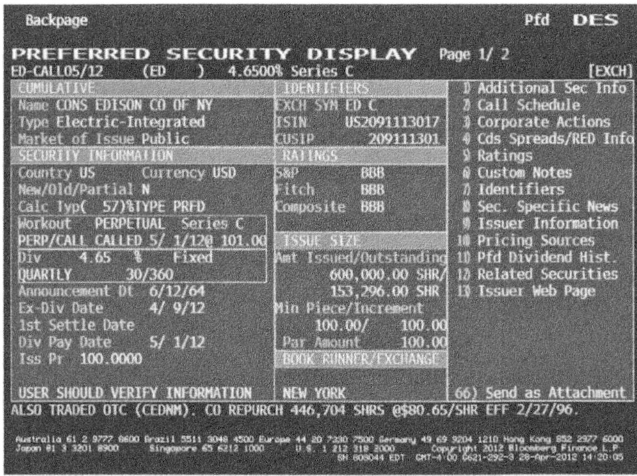

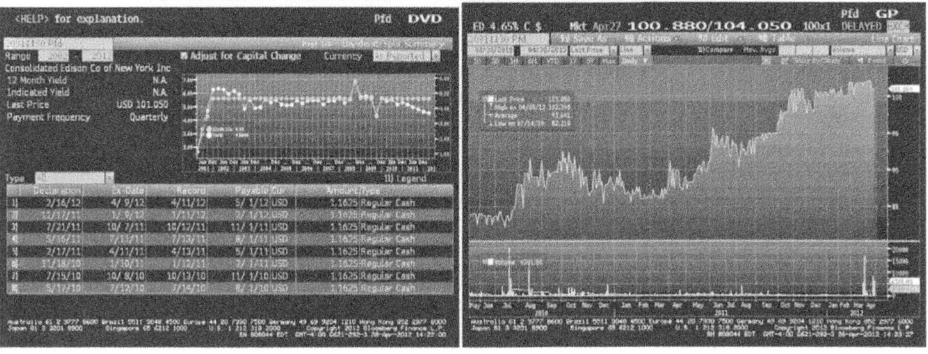

minimized to some extent by the *70 percent dividend exclusion rule.* Based on federal tax laws, other corporations who buy the equity of domestic companies can exclude 70 percent of the dividends they receive from corporate taxes. From a corporate perspective, if a firm does not have taxable income to take advantage of debt financing, it may consider preferred as an alternative to debt financing. Preferred stock tends to be offered by financial institutions and utilities.

The Markets for Corporate Bonds

Primary Market

Billions of dollars of new corporate bonds and stock are sold each year in the primary market. New corporate bonds are sold either in the open market or privately placed to a limited number of investors.

Open-Market Sales

Many new bonds issued in the open market (*open market sales*) are handled through investment banks such as Morgan Stanley, J.P. Morgan, Bank of America, Merrill Lynch, Goldman Sachs, and Barclays. Investment bankers may underwrite the issue themselves or with other investment banks as a syndicate, or they may use their best effort: selling the security on commission at the best prevailing price. The way a company chooses to offer an issue to the public depends, in part, on the size of the issue and the risk of a price decrease during the time the issue is being sold. For relatively strong companies, the investment banker often underwrites the issue: buying the issue at an agreed-upon price and then selling it in the market at hopefully a higher price. Such an agreement is referred to as a *firm commitment.* The issuer may choose the investment banker or syndicate, either individually or by a bid process, selecting the underwriting group with the highest price. With an underwriting arrangement, the selected investment banker will try to profit from the spread between the selling price (retail) and the price paid to the issuer. The spread represents the *flotation cost* to the issuer.

When a new issue is underwritten, the investment banker underwriting the issue bears the risk that the price of the issue could decrease during the time the stocks or bonds are being sold. One way investment banks tries to minimize such risk is to solicit offers (often from the regional offices of the investment bank) to buy the security prior to its sale. A successful solicitation occurs when the issue is *fully subscribed:* all securities being offered are met prior to the issue date. However, it may be that the issue is *undersubscribed* or *oversubscribed.* An undersubscribed issue may be the result of the underwriter setting the price of the security too high, whereas an oversubscribed issue may be the result of the underwriter setting the price too low. Alternatively, the investment banker may elect to sell the issue on a best-effort basis or use a combination of underwriting and best effort by using a *standby underwriting agreement.* In this latter agreement, the investment banker sells the issue on a commission, but agrees to buy all unsold securities at a specified price.

Before the issue is sold to the public, the issuer must comply with the Securities Act of 1933 and the Securities Exchange Act of 1934 governing disclosure by filing registration statements with the SEC. All open market issues of $1.5 million or more and with maturities greater than 270 days must file registration statements. These statements include the relevant business and financial information of the firm, information about the use of the funds, and a risk assessment. Once the company has registered, it must then wait until the SEC verifies the information before it can sell the security issue (usually 20 days). Typically, the investment banker uses this period to advertise the offering and to distribute to potential buyers a preliminary prospectus called a *red herring* that details all the pertinent information the official *prospectus* will have, except the price. Finally, after the SEC confirms the registration statements or 20 days have passed, the indenture and prospectus become official and the investment banker offers the issue for sale. The SEC requires that most primary issues be accompanied by a prospectus (see Exhibit 7.11 for a listing of disclosure information required by the SEC). For bond issues, the investment baker must also obtain a credit rating from Standard & Poor's, Moody's, or Fitch, and select a bond trustee for the bondholder to ensure the issuer meets the obligations specified in the indenture. For an equity issue, the investment banker may have to arrange for the security to be listed on an exchange or for a market maker to deal the security in the over-the-counter market.

In selling the issue, the investment banker often forms a selling group. This group consists of the investment banker who, as an underwriter, acts as a wholesaler (or initial distributor if best-effort is being used) by selling the issue to a number of dealers who, in turn, sell to their clients. The arrangements between the investment banker and the selling group are specified in a *selling group agreement* (described in the prospectus). The agreement defines the period of time

EXHIBIT 7.11 Disclosure Information Required By SEC For New Issues

1. Articles of Incorporation
2. Use of proceeds
3. Offering price to the public
4. Offering price to special groups
5. Underwriter's fee
6. Information on the issuer: business, history, and location
7. Indentures associated with the offerings
8. Officers
9. Detailed statement of capitalization
10. Detailed balance sheet
11. Detailed income and expense statements
12. Identification of anyone owning more than 10 percent
13. Copy of underwriting agreement
14. Copy of the legal opinions on matters related to the issue

the members of the group have to sell their portion of the issue, commissions that they can charge, and restrictions such as prohibiting members from selling below a certain price.

In summary, the floating of bond issue can be quite complex, involving the preparation of registration documents, the selection of an underwriter, and the formation of a selling group. Since 1983 some corporations have been able to shorten this process, as well as reduce the floatation costs of issuing stocks or bonds, by taking advantage of the SEC's *Rule 415*. Known as the *shelf registration rule,* Rule 415 as noted previously allows a firm to register an inventory of bonds of a particular type for up to two years. The firm can then sell the securities whenever it wishes during that time—the securities remain on the shelf. To minimize costs, a company planning to finance a number of projects over a period of time could register a large issue, and then sell parts of the issue at different times.

BLOOMBERG LTOP SCREEN

The LTOP screen displays top underwriters for the major fixed income, equity, equity-linked securities, and syndicated loan securities markets. To access: LTOP <Enter>. On the LTOP screen, right click to access a menu showing descriptions and the underwriter's deals for that period.

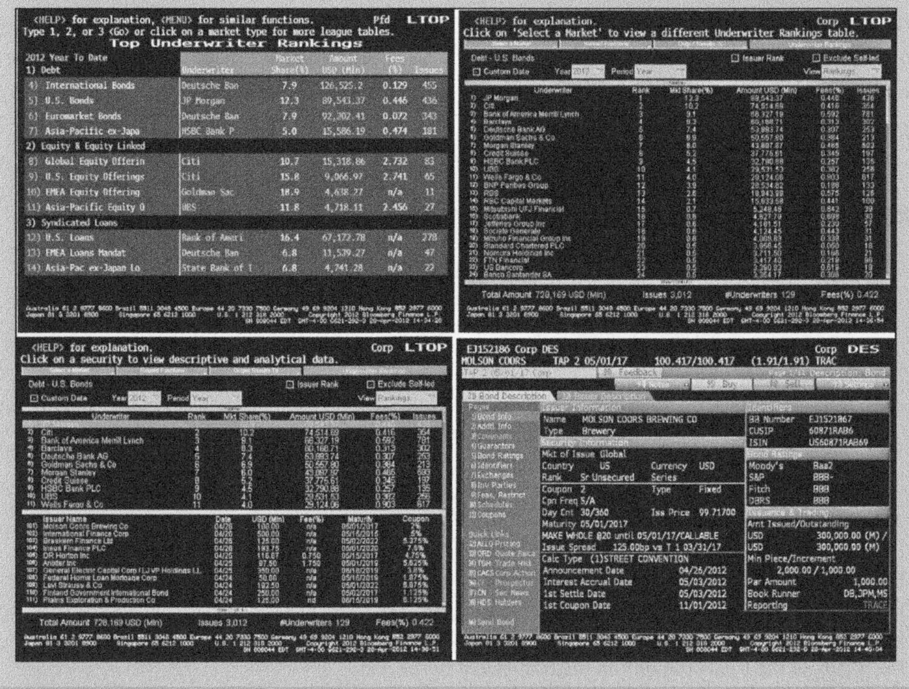

BLOOMBERG NIM AND SECF SCREENS

The Bloomberg NIM screen identifies new security offerings by security type, period, and region. The screen can be customized to identify certain types of bonds and securities and news about announced offerings. Using the screen, one can set alerts for when new issues are announced.

SECF: The SECF screen is also a good way to screen for bonds that have just been recently issued. SECF <Enter>; On the SECF screen (FI tab), click "Announced Today" or "Announced in the Last Week" from the "Announced" dropdown box.

Private Placement

An alternative to selling securities to the public is to sell them directly to institutional investors through a private placement. One of the attractions of privately placed bonds is that they are exempt from SEC registration because they do not involve a public offering. During the 1980s, an increasing proportion of new corporate bonds were sold through *private placement.* Because they are sold through direct negotiation with the buyer, privately placed bonds usually have fewer restrictive covenants than publicly issued ones, and they are more tailor-made to both the buyer's and seller's particular needs.[6] Historically, one of the disadvantages of privately placed bonds was their lack of marketability due to the absence of an active secondary market. Under the Securities Act of 1933, firms could only offer securities privately (which did not require SEC registration) to investors deemed sophisticated—insurance companies, pension funds, banks, and endowments. In 1991, the SEC adopted Rule 144A under Securities Act 1933. Under this rule, issuer could sell unregistered securities to one or more investment bankers who could resell the securities to *qualified investment buyers* (*QIBs*). QIBs could then sell freely with each other in securities that have not been registered. The adoption of *SEC Rule 144A* eliminated some of the restrictions on the secondary trading of privately placed bonds by institutional investors. As such, it opened up the secondary market for privately placed bonds.

Another reason for the growth in privately placed bonds during the 1980s was their use in financing many of the corporate mergers and takeovers. During this period, many corporations and investment groups sold bonds and borrowed from financial institutions to finance their corporate acquisitions. Because privately placed bonds had less restrictive covenants, they were frequently used to finance these leveraged buyout acquisitions. Moreover, many of these bonds were non-investment-grade bonds. By the late 1980s, these bonds accounted for approximately one-third of the new corporate bonds offered, with two-thirds of those bonds being used to finance mergers or corporate restructurings aimed at stopping a corporate takeover. The economic recession of the late 1980s and early 1990s, however, depressed the earning of many leveraged companies to levels that were not sufficient to pay their high interest obligations. Over 250 companies defaulted between 1989 and 1991.

The junk bond market did eventually recover from its near collapse in the early 1990s. Today, the market for privately placed issues consists of medium-sized, less-well-known companies, who see private placement as an alternative to the corporate bank loan market. For these companies, not all their private placements are Rule 144A placements. The market does have some large issuers whose placements make use of Rule 144A. Many of these issues are underwritten similar to publicly issued bonds.

Secondary Market

Although a substantial number of new stocks and bonds are issued each year to finance corporate investments, most of the trading of these securities still consists of buying and selling existing shares. As noted in Chapter 1, the trading of existing stock in the United States takes place on the organized exchanges (New York Stock Exchange Euronext and regional exchanges), the over-the-counter (OTC) market, or through an electronic communications network (ECN) or electronic exchange.

Much of the trading of existing corporate bonds takes place on the OTC market, where the trading is handled by brokers and dealers specializing in certain types of issues. In the OTC market, a core of large dealers dominates the corporate bond market. These dealers buy and sell existing corporate bonds to and from life insurance companies, pension funds, and other institutional investors. They also provide an important wholesale market in which they trade with other dealers and brokers who are executing buy and sell orders from the customers. Although the number of corporate bonds outstanding is large, the secondary market activity of corporate bonds is less than the activity in the secondary markets for stocks. This is due to the passive investment practices of some large institutions that tend to buy and hold their corporate bonds to maturity. It is important to remember that the degree of trading activity determines a bond's degree of marketability and the spread between a dealer's bid and asked prices. In the corporate bond markets, the spreads range from a low of one-fourth to one-half of a point (good marketability) to as high as 2 percent (poor marketability). For an investor who plans to buy a bond at its initial offering and hold it to its maturity a thin market is not a concern; it as a major concern, though, to a bond speculator or a fund manager who needs marketability or whose profit margins could be negated by a large spread.

BLOOMBERG BOND PRICES, TRACE: TRADE RECAP, QR

In 2002, the National Association of Security Dealers (NASD) established mandatory reporting requirement of OTC market transactions to make the secondary market for bonds more transparent. The reporting system that was established was the Trading Reporting and Compliance Engine (TRACE). By 2005 TRACE included all corporate bonds publicly traded (29,000). On most bond screens, TRACE can be accessed by entering QR (also found on the description page). Dealer bid and ask quotes and spreads can be accessed from ALLQ and trade history from TDH (also found on the description page).

KFT 5 ⅜ 02/20 $ C 117.680 -.331 Corp QR
As of 6/8 DELAYED Vol 9,769 Op 119.220 Hi 119.220 Lo 117.680 YLD 2.794

Page 1 Trade/Quote Recap

From 05/08/12 00:00:00 Min Size Source TRAC RPS All
To 06/08/12 17:30:00 Price Range High 119.220 Low 117.680

Date	Time	Size(M)	Price	Yield	RPS	Sprd	Benchmark	Trd Dat	Trd Time	Act	Ind	CC
06/08	17:20:05		117.680	2.794				06/08	17:20:05			OC
06/08	16:11:56	2	117.680	2.794	B	116.0	T1 ¾ 05/15/22	06/08	16:11:26			
06/08	16:11:27	2	117.680	2.794	D	116.0	T1 ¾ 05/15/22	06/08	16:11:26			
06/08	15:45:31	5	117.938	2.760	B	113.2	T1 ¾ 05/15/22	06/08	15:44:51			
06/08	14:58:49	4880	119.200	2.594	D	96.0	T1 ¾ 05/15/22	06/08	14:56:48			
06/08	10:50:29	4880	119.220	2.591	S	100.1	T1 ¾ 05/15/22	06/08	10:46:00			
06/07	17:20:03		118.011	2.751				06/07	17:20:03			OC
06/07	16:26:44	1	118.011	2.751	B	110.5	T1 ¾ 05/15/22	06/07	16:26:44			
06/07	16:18:08	1	118.011	2.751	D	110.6	T1 ¾ 05/15/22	06/07	16:16:00			
06/07	15:33:00	4810	118.079	2.742	S	109.4	T1 ¾ 05/15/22	06/07	15:28:00			
06/07	15:12:07	30	118.464	2.691	S	103.6	T1 ¾ 05/15/22	06/07	15:10:03			
06/07	15:10:26	30	118.364	2.704	D	104.9	T1 ¾ 05/15/22	06/07	15:10:03			
06/07	15:00:08	5	118.612	2.672	S	102.2	T1 ¾ 05/15/22	06/07	14:59:05			
06/07	14:59:37	5	118.612	2.672	D	102.0	T1 ¾ 05/15/22	06/07	14:59:25			
06/07	14:59:04	1500	117.988	2.754	B	110.4	T1 ¾ 05/15/22	06/07	14:58:53			
06/07	14:59:03	1500	117.988	2.754	S	110.4	T1 ¾ 05/15/22	06/07	14:58:54			
06/07	14:54:30	275	118.011	2.751	S	109.8	T1 ¾ 05/15/22	06/07	14:54:25			
06/07	14:50:57	2	117.595	2.806	B	115.6	T1 ¾ 05/15/22	06/07	14:50:52			
06/07	14:42:48	11	117.822	2.776	B	112.3	T1 ¾ 05/15/22	06/07	14:42:34			
06/07	13:10:22	9	117.887	2.767	D	112.1	T1 ¾ 05/15/22	06/07	13:10:12			

BLOOMBERG DES (EXCHANGES TAB), EPR, EIS, AND MMTK SCREENS

Bloomberg Description: (DES, Exchanges tab) shows where the bond is traded.
EPR: The EPR screen can be used to find information on exchanges, including web sites.
EIS: EIS displays exchange products and menus.
MMTK: MMTK displays a list of market makers and their corresponding codes. You can use MMTK to search for market makers by their name, code, or alternate code. You can also search for a market maker by their registered exchange.

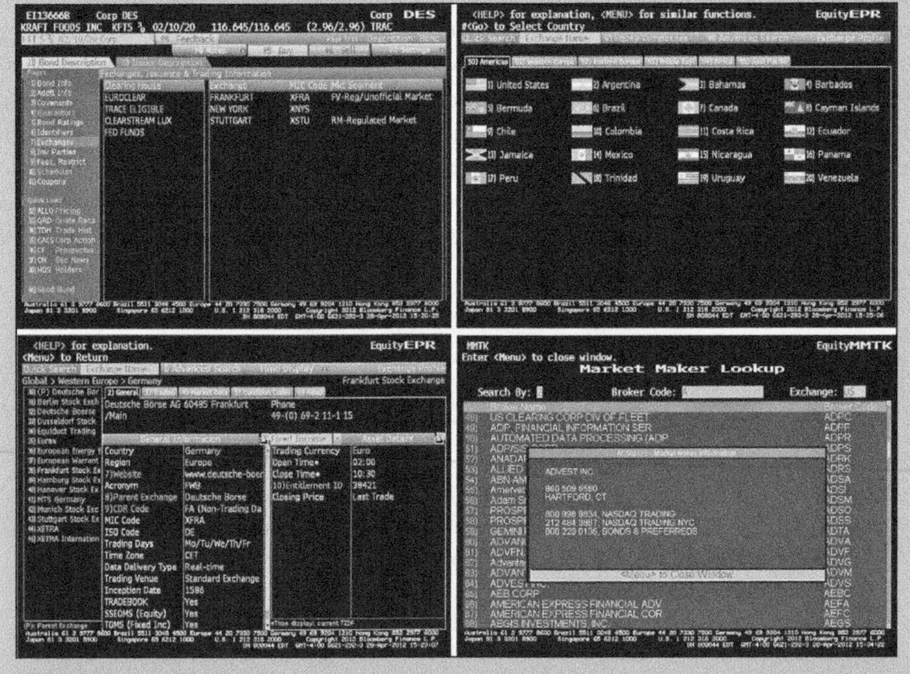

Global Bond Investments

A fixed-income investor looking to globally diversify his bond portfolio has several options. First, he might buy a bond of a foreign government or foreign corporation that is issued in the foreign country or traded on that country's exchange. These bonds are referred to as *domestic bonds.* Second, the investor might be able to buy bonds issued in a number of countries through an international syndicate. Such bonds are known as *Eurobonds.* Finally, the investor might be able to buy a bond of a foreign government or corporation being issued or traded in his own country. These bonds are called *foreign bonds.* If the investor were instead looking for short-term foreign investments, his choices would similarly include buying short-term domestic securities such CP, CDs, and Treasuries issued in those countries, Eurocurrency CDs issued by Eurobanks, and foreign money market securities issued by foreign corporations and governments in their local countries. Similarly, a domestic financial institution or nonfinancial multinational corporation looking to raise funds may choose to do so by selling debt securities.

Foreign Bonds

A foreign bond market refers to that market in which the bonds of issuers not domiciled in that country are sold and traded. For example, the bonds of a German company issued in the United States or traded in the U.S. secondary markets would be part of the U.S. foreign bond market. Foreign bonds are sold in the currency of the local economy. They are also subject to the regulations governing all securities traded in the national market and sometimes to special regulations and disclosure requirements governing foreign borrowers.[7] Foreign bonds have been issued and traded on national markets for centuries. For example, U.S. bonds sold in London in the nineteenth century financed a large proportion of the U.S. railroad system. In the United States, foreign bonds are referred to as *Yankee bonds;* in Japan, they are called *samurai bonds;* in Spain, they are called *matador bonds;* in the United Kingdom, they are nicknamed *bulldog bonds;* and in the Netherlands, they are called *Rembrandt bonds.* In the United States, Yankee bonds are registered with the SEC, and like other U.S. bonds, they typically pay interest semiannually.

Eurobond

The Eurobond market is handled through a multinational syndicate consisting of international banks, brokers, and dealers.[8] A corporation or government wanting to issue a Eurobond will usually contact a multinational bank that will form a syndicate of other banks, dealers, and brokers from different countries. The members of the syndicate usually agree to underwrite a portion of the issue, which they usually sell to other banks, brokers, and dealers. The multinational makeup of the syndicate allows the issue to be sold in many countries.[9] The major investors in the market are institutional investors and corporations.

Market makers handle the secondary market for Eurobonds. Many of them are the same dealers that are part of syndicate that helped underwrite the issue. An investor who wants to buy or sell an existing Eurobond can usually contact several market makers in the international OTC market to get several bid/ask quotes before selecting the best one. Although most secondary trading of Eurobonds occurs in the OTC market, many Eurobonds are listed on organized exchanges in Luxembourg, London, and Zurich. These listings are done primarily to accommodate investors from countries that prohibit (or at one time did prohibit) institutional investors from acquiring securities that are not listed.

The generic Eurobond is a straight bond paying an annual fixed interest and having an intermediate-term or long-term maturity. There are several different currencies in which Eurobonds are sold with the major currency denominations being the U.S. dollar, yen, and the euro. Dollar-denominated Eurobonds are the largest currency segment, currently comprising about 50 percent of the market. Some Eurobonds are also valued in terms of a portfolio of currencies, sometime referred to as a currency cocktail.

One feature of Eurobonds that has served to differentiate them from U.S. bonds is that many are issued as bearer bonds.[10] Although this feature of Eurobonds provides confidentiality, it has created some problems in countries such as the United States, where regulations require that security owners be registered on the books of issuers. However, to accommodate U.S. investors, the SEC allows U.S. investors to purchase these bonds after they are "seasoned" (sold for a period of time). Thus, U.S. investors are locked out of initial offerings of Eurobonds, but are active in acquiring them in the secondary market. The fact that U.S. investors are locked out of the primary market does not affect U.S. borrowers from issuing Eurobonds. In 1984, U.S. corporations were allowed to issue bearer bonds directly to non-U.S. investors; another factor that contributed to the growth of this market.

Like many securities issued today, Eurobonds often are sold with many innovative features. There are *dual-currency Eurobonds,* for example, that pay the coupon interest in one currency and the principal in another, and *option-currency Eurobonds* that offer investors a choice of currency. A sterling/Canadian dollar bond, for instance, gives the holder the right to receive interest and principal in either currency. A number of Eurobonds have special conversion features or warrants attached to them. One type of convertible is a dual-currency bond that allows the holder to convert the bond into stock or another bond that is denominated in another currency. For example, the Toshiba Corporation sold a bond denominated in Swiss francs that could be converted into shares of Toshiba stock at a set yen/Swiss franc exchange rate.

Euro Medium-Term Notes and Global Bonds

There is a growing market for *Euro medium-term notes* (Euro-MTNs). Like regular MTN, they are offered to investors as a series of notes with different maturities. In addition, Euro-MTN programs also offer different currencies. They are sold through international syndicates and also through offshore trusts (offshore centers are discussed later) set up by banks, investment banks, and banking groups.

A global bond is both a foreign bond and a Eurobond. Specifically, it is issued and traded as a foreign bond (being registered in a country) and also it is sold through a Eurobond syndicate as a Eurobond. The first global bond issued was a 10-year, $1.5 billion bond sold by the World Bank in 1989. This bond was registered and sold in the U.S. (Yankee bond) and also in the Eurobond market. Currently, U.S. borrowers dominate the global bond market, with an increasing number of these borrowers being U.S. federal agencies.

NIM SCREEN

Newly issued Eurobonds can be found on the NIM screen: NIM <Enter> and select "Eurobonds" from the dropdown.

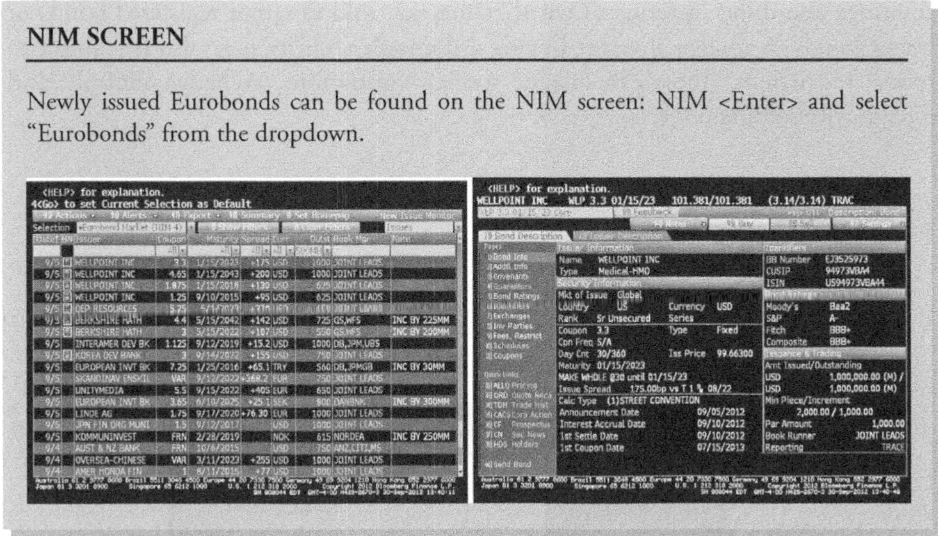

EURO-DENOMINATED BONDS OF U.S. MULTINATIONALS

SECF: On the SECF screen, bonds denominated in different currencies can be screen by typing in the currency in the "Curr" box.

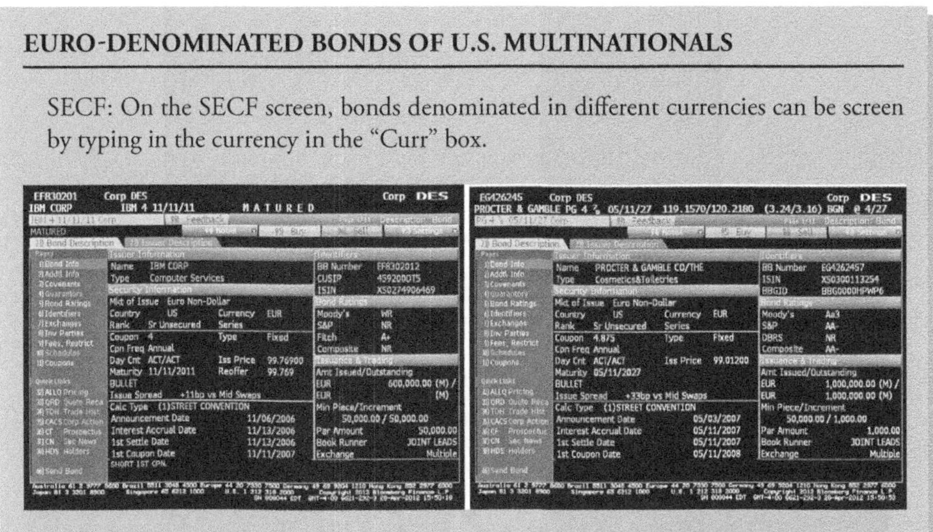

Non-U.S. Domestic Bonds

Bonds sold in a national market by companies, agencies, or intermediaries domiciled in that country are referred to as domestic bonds. Like the United States, there are many countries whose corporations, governments, and financial institutions offer bonds that are attractive to global investors. For foreign investors, usually the most important factor for them to consider is that their price, interest payments, and principal are denominated in a different currency. This currency component exposes them to exchange-rate risk and affects their returns and overall risk. Bonds sold in different countries also differ in terms of whether they are sold as either registered bonds or bearer bonds. A foreign investor buying a domestic security may also be subject to special restrictions. These can include special registrations, exchange controls, and foreign withholding taxes.

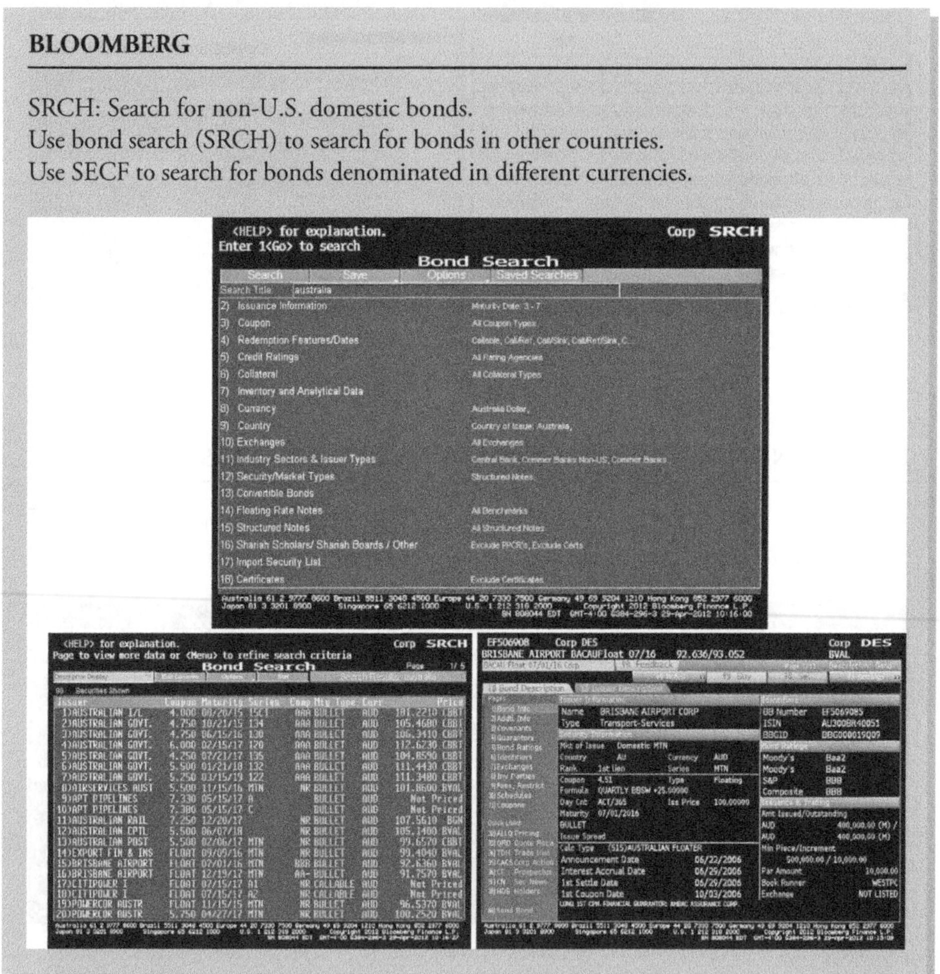

BLOOMBERG

SRCH: Search for non-U.S. domestic bonds.
Use bond search (SRCH) to search for bonds in other countries.
Use SECF to search for bonds denominated in different currencies.

Note on Exchange-Rate Risk

Investors buying foreign securities in national or offshore markets denominated in foreign currency are subject to changes in exchange rates that, in turn, affect the rates of return they can obtain from their investments. For example, suppose a U.S. investor bought a one-year French zero-coupon bond for €900 paying a principal of €1,000 when the $/€ spot exchange rate was at $1.4717/€. The U.S. investor's total dollar investment would, therefore, be $1,324.53:

$$\text{Dollar Investment} = (\$1.4717/€)(€900) = \$1{,}324.53$$

Suppose a year later the \$/€ spot exchange rate decreased (a dollar appreciation) by 15 percent from \$1.4717/€ to \$1.250945/€. If the U.S. investor had to liquidate his investment at that time, he would lose 5.5 percent in dollars:

$$\text{Rate} = \frac{(\$1.250945/€)\ (1{,}000€)}{\$1{,}324.53} - 1 = -.055$$

The example illustrates that when investors purchase foreign securities they must take into account not only the risk germane to the security, but also the risk that exchange rates will move to an unfavorable level. It should be noted that the forward exchange market makes it possible for investors to hedge their investments against exchange-rate risk. In the preceding case, for example, suppose that when he purchased the French bond, the U.S. investor had entered into a forward contract to sell 1,000 euros one year later at the forward rate of \$1.4717/€. At the end of the year, the investor would be sure of converting €1,000 into \$1,471.70. Thus, even if the \$/€ spot rate fell by 15 percent, the investor would still be able to earn 11.11 percent (= \$1,471.70/\$1,324.53) – 1) from his dollar investment. Thus, by entering a forward contract to sell foreign currency, the investor is able to profit from his bond investment. As we will examine in Part Three, there are other ways investors, as well as borrowers, can hedge against exchange risk (future, options, and swaps). Using these tools, in turn, allows investors and borrowers to focus on the choice of securities and the type of funding.

BLOOMBERG: SPOT AND FORWARD EXCHANGE RATES

- FXIP <Enter>.
- Currency Ticker <CRNCY>; Screens: ALLQ, Composite Quotes; CQ, Competing Quotes; GP, Price Graph.
- FXFR: Forward and spot quotes.
- FXDV: Foreign Exchange Derivative menu.

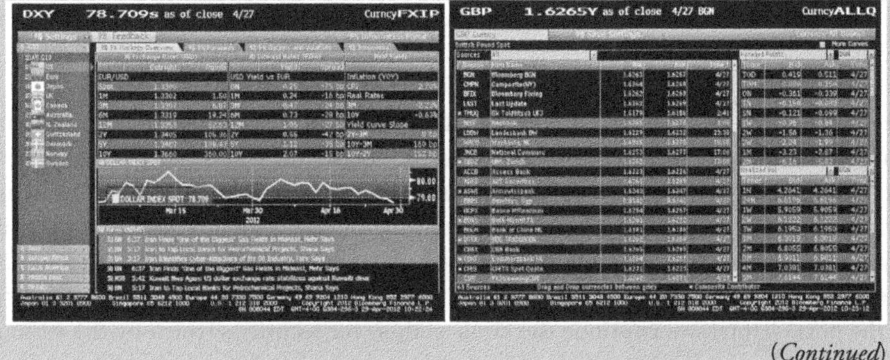

(*Continued*)

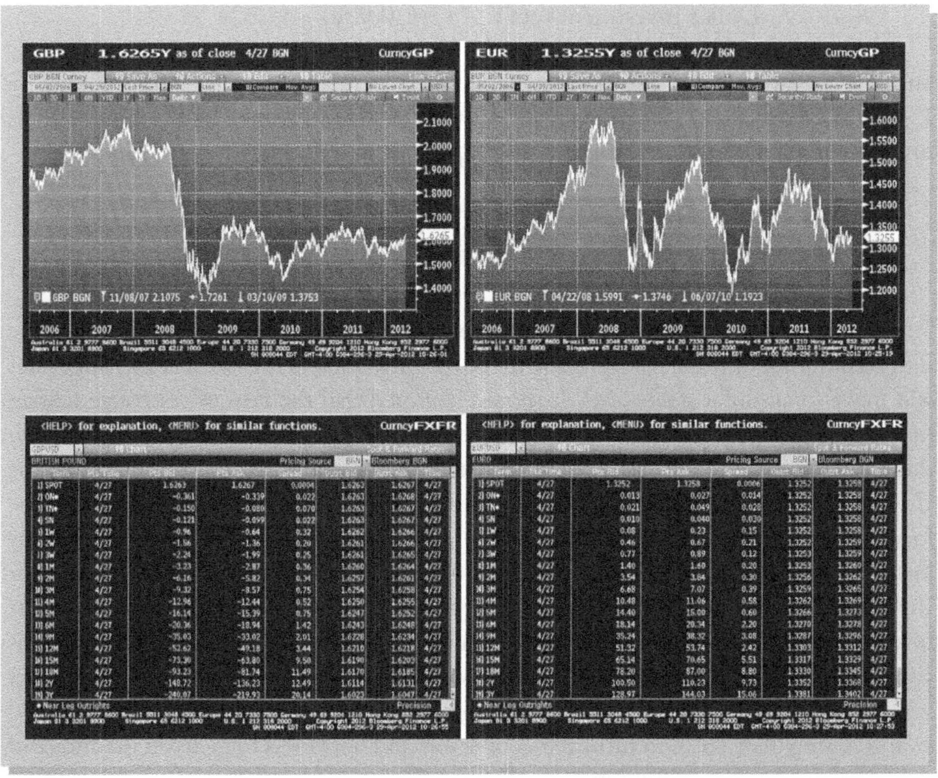

Conclusion

In the early 1980s, Chrysler Corporation issued a variable-rate subordinated debenture with a maturity of 10 years and exchangeable at Chrysler's option into a 10-year, fixed-rate note with the rate to be set at 124 percent above the 10-year rate on Treasury notes. The variable rate paid on the subordinated security made the note relatively attractive to investors given this period of high interest rates, whereas the option to exchange to a fixed-rate note was potentially beneficial to Chrysler. This security is only one example of the different ways in which corporations structure debt instruments. Given the types of assets being financed and the conditions and risk-return preferences of the financial markets, there are many different types of corporate debt securities extant in the market. The differences that we observe among bonds, in turn, are reflected in different interest rates payments (fixed, floating, or discount), original maturities (CP, medium-term notes, corporate notes, and corporate bonds), option features (callable bonds, redemption features, and putable bonds), sinking fund arrangements, security (collateral, credit enhancements, and guarantees), and protective covenants. In this chapter, we have delineated many of these features that serve to differentiate the many types of corporate debt securities offered in the financial markets. In the next chapter, we continue the same analysis for securities issued by the various government bodies: Treasury, federal agencies, and municipalities.

Website Information

Corporate Bond Price Information

FINRA

- Go to www.finra.org/index.htm, Sitemap, Market Data, and Bonds.
- For a bond search, click the "Municipal" tab and then click "Advanced Bond Search" to find corporate bonds with certain features.

Wall Street Journal

- Go to http://online.wsj.com/public/us, Market Data and Bonds, Rates, and Credit Markets.

Yahoo.com

- Go to http://finance.yahoo.com/bonds, click "Advanced Bond Screener" and click the "Corporate Bond" tab, and then provide information for search.

Investinginbonds.com

- Go to http://investinginbonds.com/; click "Corporate Market-at-a-Glance."

Selected References

Asquith, P., R. Gertner, and D. Scharfstein. 1994. Anatomy of financial distress: An examination of junk-bond issues. *Quarterly Journal of Economics* 109:625–658.

Baird, D. G., and T. H. Jackson. 1988. Bargaining after the fall and the contours of the absolute priority rule. *University of Chicago Law Review* 55:738–789.

Bebchuk, L. A. 1988. A new approach to corporate reorganizations. *Harvard Law Review* 101:775–804.

Blume, M. E., D. B. Keim, and S. A. Patel. 1991. "Returns and volatility of low-grade bonds 1977–1989. *Journal of Finance* 46:49–74.

Bulow, J. I., and J. B. Shoven, 1978. The bankruptcy decision. *Bell Journal of Economics* 9(2):437–456.

Cheung, R., J. C. Bencivenga, and F. J. Fabozzi. 1992. Original issue high-yield bonds: Historical return and default experiences 1977–1989. *Journal of Fixed Income* 2:58–76.

Cornell, B., and K. Green. 1991. The investment performance of low-grade bond funds. *Journal of Finance* 46:29–48.

Franks, J. R., and W. N. Torous. 1989. An empirical investigation of U.S. firms in reorganization. *Journal of Finance* 44:747–769.

Jackson, T. H. 1986. Of liquidation, continuation, and delay: An analysis of bankruptcy policy and nonbankruptcy rules. *American Bankruptcy Law Journal* 60:399–428.

Jensen, M. C. 1989. Eclipse of the public corporation. *Harvard Business Review* 89:61–62.

John, K. 1993. Managing financial distress and valuing distressed securities: A survey and a research agenda. *Financial Management* (special issue on financial distress)22:31–42.

Kim, I. J., K. Ramaswamy, and S. M. Sundaresan. 1993. Valuation of corporate fixed-income securities. *Financial Management* (special issue on financial distress), 22:60–78.

Leland, H. 1994. Risky debt, bond covenants and optimal capital structure. *Journal of Finance* 49:1213–1252.

Meckling, W. H. 1977. Financial markets, default, and bankruptcy. *Law and Contemporary Problems* 41:124–177.

Miller, M. H. 1977. The wealth transfers of bankruptcy: Some illustrative examples. *Law and Contemporary Problems* 41:39–46.

Moody's Investor Service. 1994. *Corporate bond defaults and default rates, 1970–1993.* Moody's Investor Service, Global Credit Research.

Nayar, N., and Rozeff, M. S. 1994. Ratings, commercial paper and equity returns. *Journal of Finance* 49:1431–1449.

Warner, J. B. 1977. Bankruptcy, absolute priority, and the pricing of risky debt claims. *Journal of Financial Economics* 4:239–276.

Weiss, L. A. 1990. Bankruptcy resolution: Direct costs and violation of priority of claims. *Journal of Financial Economics* 27:285–314.

Wruck, K. H. 1990. Financial distress, reorganization, and organizational efficiency. *Journal of Financial Economics* 27:419–444.

Bloomberg Exercises

1. Select a company of interest and study its size, capital structure (debt/equity ratio), the geographical distribution of its products, outstanding bonds, and major equity holders. Screens to examine from its equity menu:
   - DES Description
   - RELS Related securities (e.g., debt, preferred stocks)
   - CF Company filings (10-K)
   - HDS Majors holders of the stock
   - OWN Equity ownership
   - SPLC Supply chain
   - FA Tabs: Segments/By Geography, Segments/By Measures, and B/S
   - ISSD Issuer description
   - DDIS Debt distribution
   - AGGD Debt holders
   - BRC Research on company
   - RSKC Risk
   - DRSK Credit risk
   - LITI Litigation
2. Select a company of interest or the one that you selected in Exercise 1 and use its CACS screen to find if it has taken any of the following actions in the past few years:
   - Acquisitions
   - Divestures
   - New stock offerings
3. Bloomberg information on corporate actions such as acquisitions and limited partnership deals can be accessed on the CACS screen found on the company's equity menu. Select a company of interest that you know has been active in acquisitions and divestures and use CACS to search for its previous activities.
4. Given the many types of corporate bonds with their different features (callable, option-free bonds, putable, higher-quality, investment-grade, lower-quality, non-investment-grade, debentures, and secured bonds), use Bloomberg's "Advanced Search" screen to search for bonds with certain features. Possible searches: U.S., dollar-denominated, investment-grade (BBB and up) corporate bonds for a specific sector; bonds in a certain sector that are callable and either investment-grade or non-investment-grade. To access: SRCH <Enter> and click "Advanced Search." On the Advanced Search screen customize your search by using the

settings: coupon, redemption features, credit ratings, collateral, and industry sectors.

5. Using Bloomberg's "Advanced Search" (SRCH <Enter> and click "Advanced Search"), search for callable bonds that do not have a make-whole premium provision for determining the call. On the screen setting for redemption features, click "Callable" and "Not Make Whole Call." Take one of the callable bonds from your search and study its call provisions. Call schedules can be accessed from the bond's description page.
6. Using Bloomberg's search functions (SRCH <Enter> or SECF <Enter>, click FI tab, Corp tab, and "Floating" in the "Coupon" dropdown box), search for floating-rate notes. To keep the search manageable on the SRCH screen, you may want to limit your search to certain sectors. On the screen setting, click "Include Only" in the dropdown "floater" tab. Take one of the floating-rate notes from your search and study its features using the bond's menu: reference rate, margin, cap, floor, and call features. Most of this information can be found on the bond's description page.
7. Using Bloomberg's regular or advanced search function (SRCH <Enter> and click "Advance Search"), search for a zero-coupon corporate bond. To keep the search manageable, you may want to limit your search to nonfinancial sectors. Take one of the zeros from your search and study its features. You may also want to search for zeros by using the SECF screen: SECF <Enter>, click FI tab, Corp tab, and "Zero" in the "Coupon" dropdown box.
8. The protective covenants, collateral, and priority of claims (subordination) for a bond issue can be found in a bond's prospectus. Select a bond of interest, identify its covenants and collateral, and determine whether there is any subordination. The covenants can be found on the bond's description page (DES, "Covenants" tab).
9. Many subordinate debenture bonds have embedded options such as call options, put options, and convertibility to stock. Conduct a bond search for such bonds using Bloomberg's "Advanced Search" (SRCH <Enter> and click "Advanced Search"). On the Advanced Search screen, customize the setting for redemption feature by selecting callable, putable, and convertible and for collateral feature by selecting "Sub debenture." You may also want to search for the bonds by using the SECF screen: SECF <Enter>, click FI tab, Corp tab, and "Callable," "Putable," or "Convertible" in the "Mty Type" dropdown box.
10. The PGM screen displays MTN program by issuer. Search for a past or current MTN issue of a company using this screen: PGM <Enter>, click "Medium Term Notes," and then search for issuer and click for series. On the menu page, access the Draw screen: Draw <Enter>. You may also want to search for MTN by using the SECF screen: SECF <Enter>, click FI tab, Corp tab, and type MTN in the "Series" box.
11. Study the CP market by examining the following screen:
    - PGM: The PGM screen displays CP programs: PGM <Enter>, click "Commercial Paper."

- FDCP: Shows CP outstanding.
- CPPR: Displays direct CP issuer.

12. The BNKF/CACT screen lists recent bankruptcy filings (BNKF <Enter>). Use the screen to identify one of more companies that have filed for bankruptcy and then evaluate the current state of the company by going to its equity menu and reviewing some of the screens.
13. The DIS screen displays a list bonds that have traded at a yield of at least 10 percent over the Treasury benchmark rate the past five business days. Use the screen to identify one or more companies with distressed debt and then evaluate the current state of the company by going to its equity menu and reviewing some of the screens.
14. The LTOP screen displays top underwriters for the major fixed income, equity, equity-linked securities, and syndicated loan securities markets. Using the screen, identify the top underwriters over the past year for global fixed-income issues. Using the dropdown menu, study some of the recent deals for several of the bond underwriters. To access: LTOP <Enter>. On the LTOP screen, right click an investment banker to access the underwriter's deals for that period (right click and hold to access menu and then click "Securities").
15. Using Bloomberg's search function (SRCH <Enter>), search for bonds issued or traded outside the United States and in currencies other than the U.S. dollar: SRCH <Enter>, on Advance screen select and screen by type of bond and country. You may also want to search for different denominated bonds by using the SECF screen: SECF <Enter>, click FI tab, Corp tab, and type the currency in the "Curr" box.

Notes

1. An exception to this trend was the $150 million bond issue of Coca-Cola in 1993 that had a maturity of 100 years.
2. Sinking funds are usually applied to a particular bond issue. There are, though, nonspecific sinking funds (sometimes referred to as *tunnel, funnel,* or *blanket sinking funds*) that are applied to a company's total outstanding bonds. For most bonds, the periodic sinking fund payments are the same each period. Some indentures do allow the sinking fund to increase over time or to be determined by the level of earnings, and some bonds have accelerated sinking fund provisions giving the issuer the option to redeem more than the stipulated amount.
3. Event risk is default risk resulting from dramatic and unexpected changes. As such, it includes not only takeovers and corporate restructuring, but also natural or industrial accidents or government regulatory changes.
4. It should be noted that in terms of priorities it could be the case that a default could lead to the company being acquired by another company. The new company, in turn, may be able to get the bondholders to agree to subordinate their debt to a new issue; this is quite possible if the bondholders determined that the sale of the pledged assets would be inadequate.

5. See Franks and Torous (1989); Weiss (1990); Fabozzi et. al. (1993); Baird and Jackson (1988); Wruck (1990); and Jensen (1989).
6. Investment banking firms often assist firms in privately placing securities, often using best effort.
7. Possible restrictions imposed by regulatory authorities on foreign bonds relate to disclosure of information and reporting, the bond's structure, and minimum and maximum issue sizes. With the growth of the foreign bond market, many of these restrictions have been eliminated or relaxed.
8. Eurobonds issued with only one underwriter are becoming more common. Such issues are referred to as "bought deals."
9. The underwriting of Eurobonds is subject to some underwriting risk. Often, the lead or managing underwriter has to handle any issues not sold by second-tier and third-tier underwriters. The underwriting agreement specifies the terms of the issue, including price, before the issue is sold; this is referred to as a bought deal. The increased underwriting risk is often reflected by a bigger spread
10. Some Eurobonds, such as those issued by sovereign countries, are sold as registered bonds.

CHAPTER 8

Government Securities and Markets: Treasury, Agencies, Municipals, and Sovereign Debt Securities

Introduction

The U.S. Treasury security market began over 230 years ago when the U.S. Treasury sold government securities to finance the new country's debt. The U.S. debt in 1790 consisted of $54 million in national debt and $25 million in assumed state debt, with most of the debt incurred as a result of the Revolutionary War. Today, the U.S. Treasury is the largest debt issuer in the world. Its size, as well as its wide distribution of ownership and low default feature, makes the rates on Treasury securities the benchmark for all other securities.

In addition to U.S. Treasury securities, there are also debt instruments issued by U.S. federal agencies, and a large market for the securities of municipal governments. In the United States, it is estimated that there are as many as 80,000 state, county, and municipal governments and government authorities (agencies created by the government with the authority to float bonds).[1] Over the last 30 years, there has been a significant increase in borrowing by these governments and authorities, with the debt being financed primarily through the sale of municipal securities. In this chapter, we extend our analysis of securities by examining the types and markets for securities issued by the U.S. Treasury, U.S. agencies, and municipal governments, as well as government securities issued by other sovereign countries.

Treasury Securities and Markets

The U.S. Treasury is responsible for implementing the fiscal policy of the federal government and managing the federal government's enormous debt. In 2010, the federal government raised over \$2.3326 trillion in revenue from income, social insurance, and corporate taxes, and it spent over \$3.5911 trillion on welfare and individual security programs (Social Security, health care, and income security programs), national defense, interest on the federal government debt, physical resources (energy, commerce and housing, transportation, and regional development) and other expenditures. The government's excess of expenditures over revenue in 2010 equated to a deficit of \$1.2584 trillion. Since 1930, the U.S. federal government has operated with a deficit in almost every year, with the deficits growing dramatically over the past two decades, especially since 2008 (see Exhibit 8.1). The accumulation of deficits over the years has, in turn, contributed to a total government indebtedness of over \$14.5603 trillion as of 2010 (see Exhibit 8.2).

EXHIBIT 8.1 U.S. Treasury Receipts, Outlays, Deficits, and Surplus

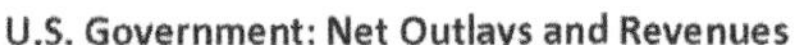

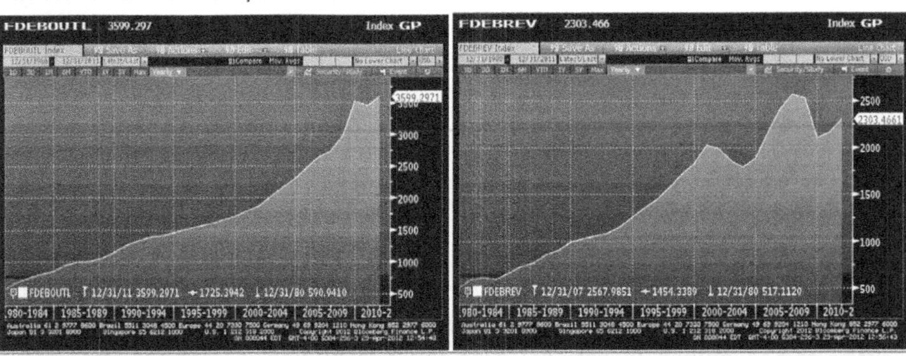

Surplus/Deficits: Level and as Percentage of GDP:

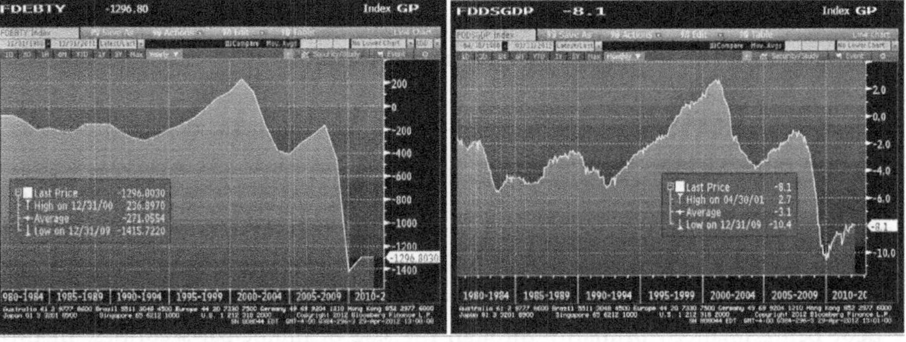

This statement summarizes the financial activities of the federal government and off-budget federal entities conducted in accordance with the budget of the U.S. government, that is, receipts and outlays of funds, surplus or deficit, and the means of financing the deficit or disposing of the surplus. Bloomberg: ECOF Screen.

EXHIBIT 8.2 U.S. Government Debt and Debt as a Percentage of GDP

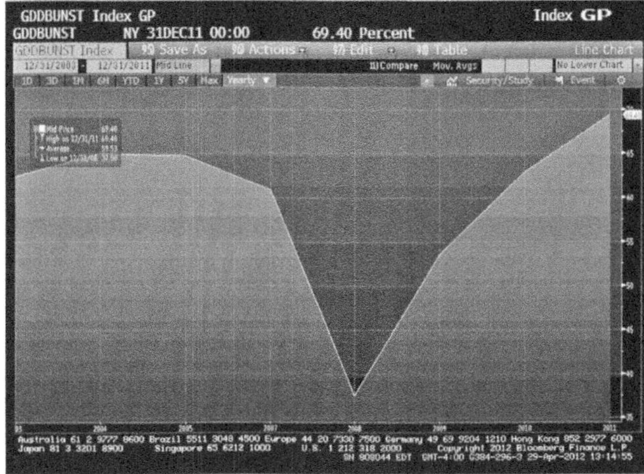

The U.S. government debt held by the public is all federal debt held by individuals, corporations, state or local governments, foreign governments, and other entities outside the U.S. government less federal financing bank securities. Types of securities held by the public include Treasury bills, notes, bonds, Treasury inflation-protected securities (TIPS), U.S. savings bonds, and state and local government series securities. Intragovernmental holdings are government account series securities held by government trust funds, revolving funds, and special funds; and federal financing bank securities. A small number of marketable securities are held in government accounts.

To finance the government's deficit each year and to manage its debt (refinancing maturing issues), the Treasury sells a number of securities. All of the securities sold by the Treasury are backed by the full faith and credit of the U.S. government. As such, they are considered default free.[2] The Treasury's securities can be broken into marketable and nonmarketable securities. Of the total government debt of $14.5603 trillion in 2010, investors held approximately $9.048 trillion in marketable securities and $5.146 trillion in nonmarketable securities

EXHIBIT 8.3 Public Debt: Marketable Securities and Nonmarketable Debt, Bloomberg: ECOF Screen, United States, Debt

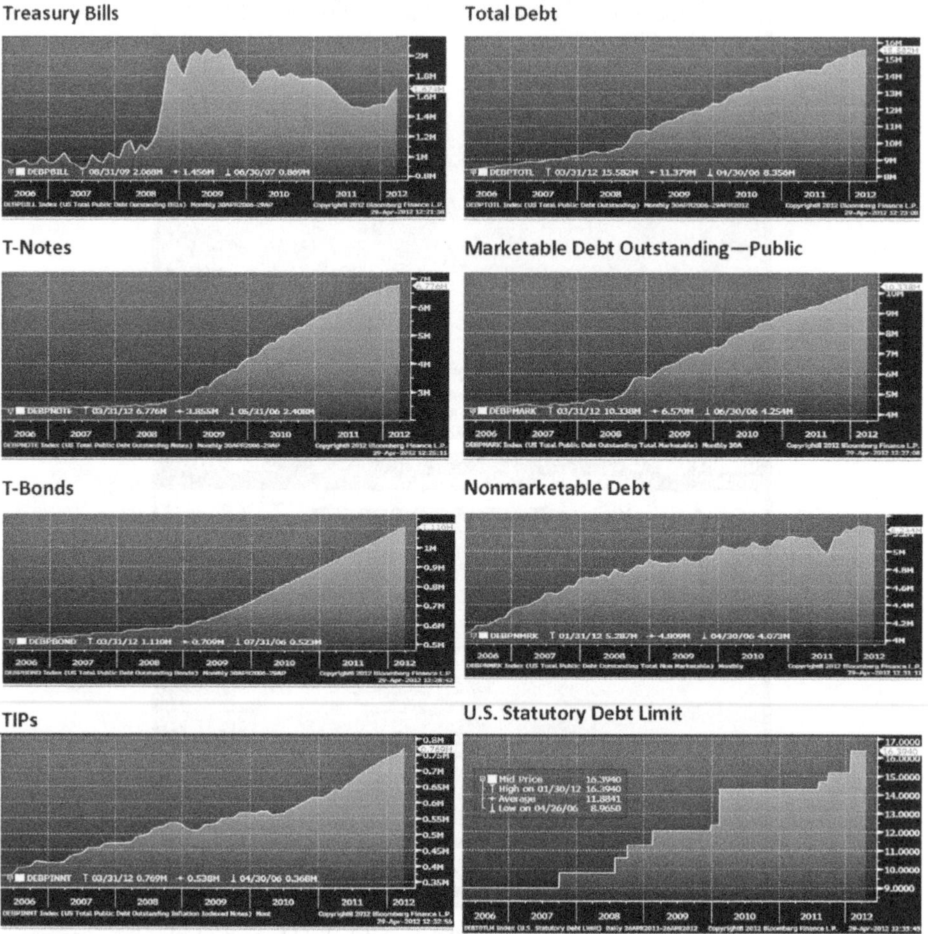

(see Exhibit 8.3). Marketable securities include Treasury bills (T-bills), T-notes, T-bonds, and Treasury inflation-protected securities (TIPS).[3] The Treasury sells these securities using an auction method, and there is an active secondary market trading the existing marketable Treasury securities. Nonmarketable Treasury debt, in turn, includes the state and local government series (SLGS), the government account series, U.S. savings bonds, and nonmarketable securities sold to foreign governments. Original investors hold these securities until they mature or are redeemed. The government account series is one of the largest portions of the nonmarketable securities sold. These series include Treasury securities sold to government agencies such as Social Security. These agencies use their excess funds to purchase Treasury securities.

BLOOMBERG: TREASURY SECURITY SCREENS: FIT AND GOVT SCREENS

Recently issued or active T-bills, notes, bonds, strips, and tips, as well as seasoned Treasury securities can be found from the FIT screen: FIT <Enter>, click "Actives, Bills, Notes, Tips, or Strips." To access the menu screen, enter CUSIP (or coupon rate and maturity) <Govt>. On the menu, one can access description (DES), dealer bid-ask quotes (ALLQ), calculation of the yield (YA), and other information.

Treasuries can also be found by entering <Govt> TK <Enter>, selecting U.S., and then selecting type of Treasury.

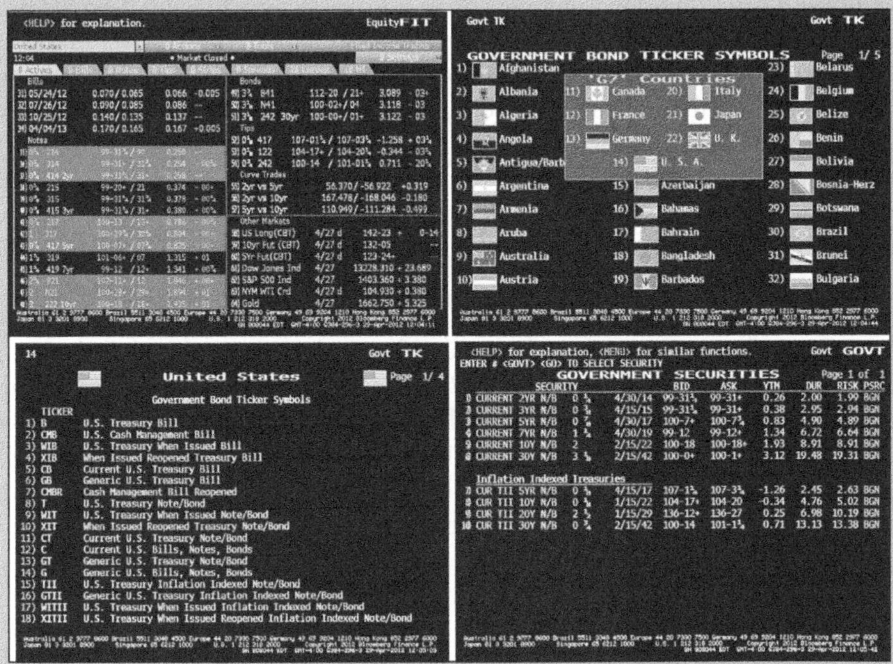

BLOOMBERG SCREENS RELATED TO 2008 FINANCIAL CRISIS

The 2008 financial crisis led to the American Recovery and Reinvestment Act and the Emergency Economic Stabilization Act, Troubled Asset Relief Program (TARP), and Term Asset-Backed Securities Loan Facility (TALF). Bloomberg screens related to the financial crisis:

- TARP: <Enter> TARP Program
- TALF: <Enter> TALF Program
- STRS: <Enter> Stress Test Overviews
- GGRP: <Enter> Government Relief Programs
- NI TARP: <Enter> TARP News
- RESQ: <Enter> Bailout and Rescue Menu

Treasury Bills

Treasury bills are short-term instruments sold as zero-coupon bonds in multiples of \$1,000 (par), with the minimum denomination being \$1,000. The interest on a T-bill is the difference between the face value and the price paid. This interest, in turn, is subject to federal income taxes, but not state and local taxes. T-bills with original maturities of 13 weeks (91 days) and 26 weeks (182 days) are sold weekly on a regular basis. The Treasury also sells special types of T-bills on an irregular basis. Included with this irregular series are *strip bills*. This is a package of T-bills with different maturities in which the buyer agrees to buy bills at their bid price for several weeks. The Treasury also issues additional amounts of an existing security (T-bills, T-bonds, and T-notes). Such offerings are known as *reopenings*. For example, the Treasury may offer 13-week T-bills as a reopening of a previously issued 26-week T-bill. All T-bills are issued and registered in a book-entry form, with the computerized record of ownership maintained by the Federal Reserve at their offices in Washington. At maturity, the Treasury sends a check to the investor of record, unless the holder has requested payment in terms of new T-bills.[4] In an effort to make the securities more attractive, the Fed has set up a direct purchase option, allowing investors to purchase T-bills over the Internet.

Exhibit 8.4 shows the Bloomberg screen for active and recently issued T-bills (FIT) and the description and price quotes of one of the issues. The bill shown in the exhibit was issued on February 2, 2012, matures on August 2, 2012, and on date May 2, 2012 there were 92 days to the bill's maturity. T-bill yields are often quoted by dealers as an annualized discount yield (R_D) (also called the *banker's discount yield*); this is the annualized return (principal [F] minus price [P_0)] specified as a proportion of the bill's principal, with the principal being \$100 (this makes the actual price a percentage of the actual face value (e.g., \$1 million)[5]:

$$R_D = \frac{F - P_0}{F} \frac{360}{\text{Days to Maturity}}$$

For example, if the bill is offered by a dealer at 99.977 (see YA screen in Exhibit 8.4), it would be quoted at a discount rate of .09 percent:

$$R_D = \frac{100 - 99.977}{100} \frac{360}{92} = .0009$$

Solving the equation for the discount yield for P_0 gives us the formula for the bid or ask price given the dealer's discount yield:

$$P_0 = F[1 - (R_D)(\text{Days to Maturity}/360)]$$
$$P_0 = 100[1 - (.0009)(92/360)] = 99.977$$

EXHIBIT 8.4 Select Treasury Bills: Bloomberg Screens

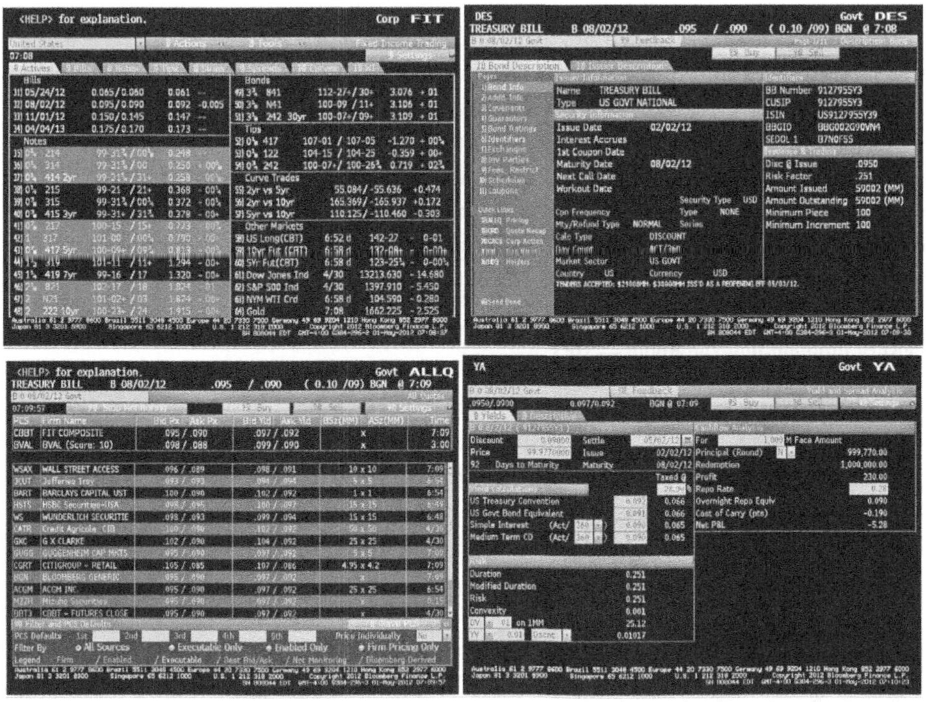

Treasury Bonds and Notes

Treasury bonds and notes are the Treasury's coupon issues. Both are identical except for maturity: T-notes have original maturities up to 10 years, whereas T-bonds have original maturities ranging between 10 and 30 years. Both are sold in denominations of $1,000 or greater, and both pay semiannual coupon interest. Like all Treasury securities, interest income from T-bonds and T-notes is subject to federal taxes, but not state and local. Since 1984, the Treasury has not issued callable bonds.

All Treasury coupon securities are issued by the Treasury at prices approximately equal to par.[6] Like T-bills, notes and bonds are issued in a book-entry form, with the investor's name and amount maintained in a computerized account. The Treasury currently issues new notes with 2-, 5-, and 10-year maturities. They also resumed issuing the 30-year T-bond in February 2006. New 2-year T-notes are sold every month, whereas 5-year and 10-year notes are sold quarterly, and T-bonds are sold semiannually (see FIT screen in Exhibit 8.5). Sometimes when bonds or notes are sold in order to refund an earlier issue, they are offered only to the holders of the bond being replaced. This special type of issue takes the form of an advanced refunding in which the Treasury sets the maturity of the new issue equal to the remaining life of the bond being replaced to ensure the holder his original maturity. In addition, the Treasury established in 2000 a debt buyback program in which it buys back outstanding issues by purchasing them in the secondary market.

Exhibit 8.5 shows the Bloomberg screen for active and recently issued T-notes and bonds (FIT) and the description and price quotes of one the issues. The note shown in the exhibit was issued on April 30, 2012, matures on April 30, 2019, and pays a 1.25 percent coupon. The information on Bloomberg's ALLQ screen shows the dealer's bid and asked prices, expressed as a percentage of the face value, or equivalently, as the price of a note with a $100 par value. The numbers to the right of the decimals on the bid and ask prices are in 32nd and not the usual 100s (e.g., 99-08 or $98^{8/32}$ or 99.25). A plus sign next to the decimal mean that one half of one thirty-second is added to the price (99-08+ or $99^{8.5/32}$ = 99.265625). As shown on the YA screen, the note is priced at 99-12 (= 99.9782778) on May 2, 2012, to yield 1.343917 percent.

Treasury Inflation-Indexed Bonds—TIPS

Although Treasury securities are considered default free, they are subject to market risk when rates change in the market causing the prices of Treasuries to change. Treasuries and other fixed-income bonds are also subject to *purchasing-power risk.* Purchasing-power risk is the uncertainty that the rate of return earned from an investment is

EXHIBIT 8.5 Treasury Notes and Bonds: Bloomberg Screens

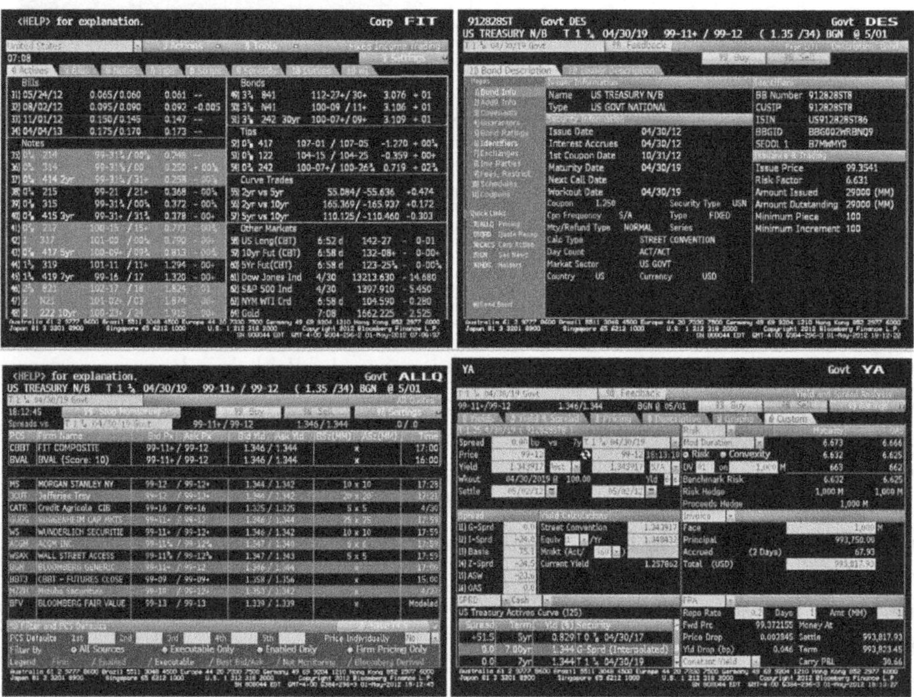

Bloomberg: Recently issued or active T-bonds and T-notes, as well as seasoned issues, can be found from the FIT screen: FIT <Enter>, click "T/ACT." To access the menu screen, enter CUSIP (or coupon rate and maturity) <Govt>. On the menu, one can access description (DES), dealer bid-ask quotes (ALLQ), and calculation of the yield on the note or bond (YA). T-notes and bonds can also be found on BTMM or entering <Govt> TK <Enter> and selecting U.S.

less than the inflation rate. Equivalently, it is the risk of a negative real interest rate, where the *real interest rate* is the actual or nominal rate minus the inflation rate: Real Interest = Nominal Interest – Inflation.

To address purchasing-power risk, the Treasury began offering Treasury inflation-indexed bonds in 1997, called *Treasury inflation-protected securities* or simply *TIPS*. Inflation-adjusted securities, though, are not new or unique. Many countries have offered such securities for a number of years, and a number of corporations, agencies, and municipalities offer or have offered inflation-adjusted bonds. The U.S. Treasury's TIPS are patterned after the successful inflation-adjusted bonds introduced in Great Britain. They are structured so that each period's coupon payment is equal to a specified fixed rate times an inflation-adjusted principal, and at maturity, the bond pays the larger of the inflation-adjusted principal or the original par value. For example, suppose the Treasury issues a three-year TIPS with a nominal principal of $1,000 and semiannual coupon rate of 2 percent. If there is no inflation in the ensuing three years, then the TIPS will pay bondholders $20 semiannually for three years and $1,000 at maturity. If there is inflation, as measured by the consumer price index for all urban consumers (CPI-U), then the Treasury will adjust the nominal principal.[7] For example, suppose the U.S. experiences an annual inflation rate of 3 percent or a 1.5 percent semiannual rate for the first semiannual period of the bond. In this case, the inflation-adjusted principal would be $1,015 and a bondholder would receive a semiannual coupon of $20.30 (= ($1,015)(.02)). If the 1.5 percent semiannual inflation continues for each period of the bond, then the bondholder would receive inflation-adjusted coupon interests in each of the next five semiannual periods and a principal at maturity of $1,195.62 (see Exhibit 8.6).

EXHIBIT 8.6 Cash Flow from Six-Year TIPS with an Annual Inflation Rate of 3 Percent

Year	Annual Inflation	Semi-Annual Inflation	Inflation-Adjusted Principal	TIP Cash Flow
0.5	3%	1.50%	$1,015.00	$20.30
1.0	3%	1.50%	$1,030.23	$20.60
1.5	3%	1.50%	$1,045.68	$20.91
2.0	3%	1.50%	$1,061.36	$21.23
2.5	3%	1.50%	$1,077.28	$21.55
3.0	3%	1.50%	$1,093.44	$21.87
3.5	3%	1.50%	$1,109.84	$22.20
4.0	3%	1.50%	$1,126.49	$22.53
4.5	3%	1.50%	$1,143.39	$22.87
5.0	3%	1.50%	$1,160.54	$23.21
5.5	3%	1.50%	$1,177.95	$23.56
6.0	3%	1.50%	$1,195.62	$23.91+$1,195.62

The inflation-adjusted returns from TIPS offset the loss in purchasing power resulting from the inflation. Thus, even though the principal and interest fluctuate with the CPI, the purchasing power of each payment and the real rate of return are fixed. Because the real rate of return is fixed, Treasury inflation-indexed bonds are attractive to retirees who have their retirement funds invested in fixed-income securities. Inflation-index bonds also have relatively low correlations with other bonds, and as such provide some diversification benefits when included in a fixed-income portfolio.

Exhibit 8.7 shows the Bloomberg screen for TIPS and the description and price quotes of one the issues. The strip shown in the exhibit was issued on January 15, 2009, matures on January 15, 2019, and pays a 2.125 percent coupon. On the YA screen, observe the yield without an assumed inflation adjustment is –0.938845 based on a price of 121-08 and the yield adjusted for an assumed inflation of 2.8639 percent is 1.971674 percent.

EXHIBIT 8.7 Treasury Inflation-Protected Securities—TIPS

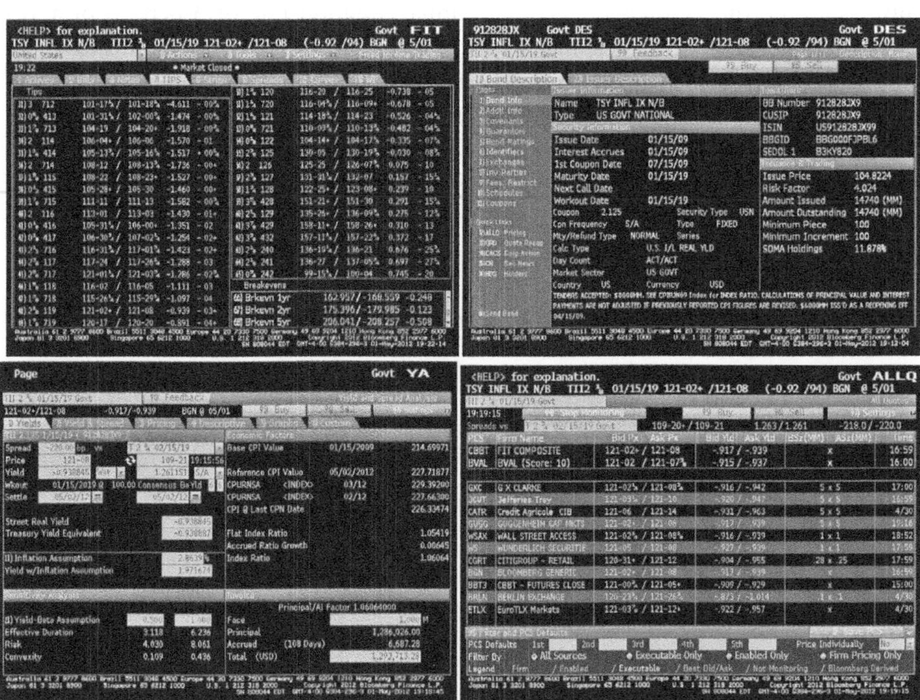

Bloomberg: Recently issued or active TIPS, as well as seasoned issues, can be found on the FIT screen: FIT <Enter>, click T/ACT. To access the menu screen enter CUSIP (or coupon rate and maturity) <Govt>. On the menu, one can access description (DES), dealer bid-ask quotes (ALLQ), and calculation of the yield on the TIPS (YA). On the YA screen and cash flow screen (CSHF), one can change the inflation assumption and determine the yield based on the assumed inflation rate. YA screen also shows the yield based on nominal coupons without inflation adjustments. TIPS can also be found by entering <Govt> TK <Enter> and selecting U.S. and TIPS

Treasury Strips

In the 1980s, one of the more innovative instruments was introduced—the Treasury stripped security, or *Treasury strip*. A Treasury strip is formed by a dealer who purchases a T-bond or T-note and then creates two general types of zero-coupon securities to sell to investors: a *principal-only security* (*PO*) (also called the *corpus* and denoted by *n* or *np* when quoted) and an *interest-only security* (*IO*, denoted by *i* when quoted). As the name suggests, the PO security is a zero discount bond that pays the T-bond's principal at its maturity; the IO securities are zero discount instruments, with each paying a principal equal to the T-bond's coupon and with a maturity coinciding with the bond's coupon date. To create Treasury strips, a dealer could take a five-year U.S. Treasury note and strip it into 11 discount bonds, one maturing in five years and paying the T-bond's principal, the others paying principals equal to the bond's coupon interest and maturing on the coupon dates. For example, suppose a dealer purchased $500 million of five-year, 6 percent notes. The cash flow from the securities would be 10 semiannual payments of $15 million and a repayment of principal of $500 million at maturity. From this, the dealer could create 10 IO strips, with each one representing a single-payment claim on each interest payments and with a maturity date matching the coupon payment dates and a PO strip paying the principal and maturing at the end of five years.

Merrill Lynch and Salomon Brothers were the first to create and market stripped securities. Both investment-banking firms introduced their securities in 1982. Merrill Lynch called its stripped securities *Treasury Income Growth Receipts* (*TIGRs*), and Salomon Brothers referred to theirs as *Certificates of Accrual on Treasury Securities* (*CATS*). To create these strips, the companies would purchase a Treasury-coupon security and deposit it in a bank custodial account. They would then sell to investors separate IO receipts representing ownership of a coupon and a PO receipt representing ownership of the principal. Following the lead of Merrill Lynch and Salomon Brothers, other investment firms, such as Lehman Brothers, E. F. Hutton, and Dean Witter Reynolds, introduced their own stripped securities, with colorful names such as LIONS, GATORS, COUGARS, and DOGS. Collectively, these receipts were called *trademarks*. One of the problems with trademarks was that dealers only made markets in their own strip securities. In an effort to expand the market, a group of dealers introduced Treasury receipts. Different from trademarks, which represented ownership in a custodial account, Treasury receipts represented ownership in the Treasury security. The U.S. Treasury facilitated the market for these generic stripped securities when in 1985 it initiated the Separate Trading of Registered Interest and Principal of Securities (STRIPS) program to aid dealers in stripping Treasury securities.[8] The securities created under the STRIPS program were, in turn, deemed direct obligations of the government. Furthermore, for clearing and payment purposes, the names of the buyers of these securities were included in the book entries of the Treasury and cleared through the Federal Reserve's book-entry system, thus eliminating the need to set up custodial accounts and therefore trademarks.

Stripped securities are attractive investments for institutional investors who buy the strips with maturities that match the maturities of their liabilities, thereby eliminating reinvestment risk. In addition to Treasuries, dealers also strip mortgage-backed, agency and municipal securities. There is also a secondary market for existing stripped securities. Like all Treasuries, strips are subject to federal taxes. However, with strips the accrued interest is taxed each year even though the interest is not paid (i.e., taxes are paid on interest earned, not on interest received). Thus, for taxable entities, strips generate a negative cash flow until maturity. It should be noted that the tax codes in some countries treat the return from PO strip as capital gains instead of ordinary income. With the capital gain tax rate lower, investors from these countries find PO strips relatively attractive.

Exhibit 8.8 shows the Bloomberg FIT screen for strips and the description and price quotes of one strip. The strip shown was issued on February 15, 2001, pays a zero coupon, and a principal on February 15, 2030. The information on the YA screen, shows the strip yields a return of 3.041014 percent based on price of 58-14⅜.

EXHIBIT 8.8 Treasury Strips

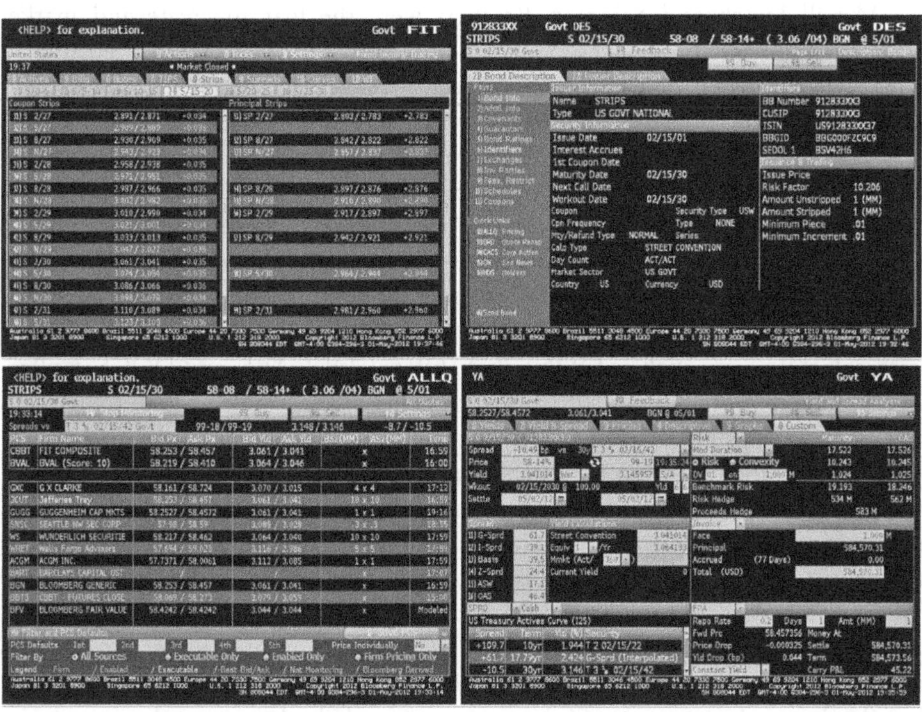

Bloomberg: Strips can be found from the FIT screen: FIT <Enter>, click "STRIPS." To access the menu screen, enter CUSIP (or coupon rate and maturity) <Govt>. On the menu, one can access description (DES), dealer bid-ask quotes (ALLQ), and yield calculations screen for the STRIP (YA). Strips can also be found by entering <Govt> TK <Enter> and selecting U.S. and Strips.

The Primary and Secondary Markets for Treasury Securities

New issues of Treasury securities are sold through a sealed-bid auction process in which the Treasury announces an issue and dealers and investors submit either a competitive or a noncompetitive bid (see Exhibit 8.9 for the Bloomberg auction screens). With a competitive bid, an investor specifies the yield (annualized discount yield for T-bills and annualized YTM for Treasury coupon issues) and the quantity he wants, whereas with a noncompetitive bid an investor specifies only the amount he wants and accepts the weighted average price. Bidders must file tender forms with one of the Federal Reserve banks or its branches or with the Treasury Bureau of Public Debt. The

EXHIBIT 8.9 Treasury Auction Information

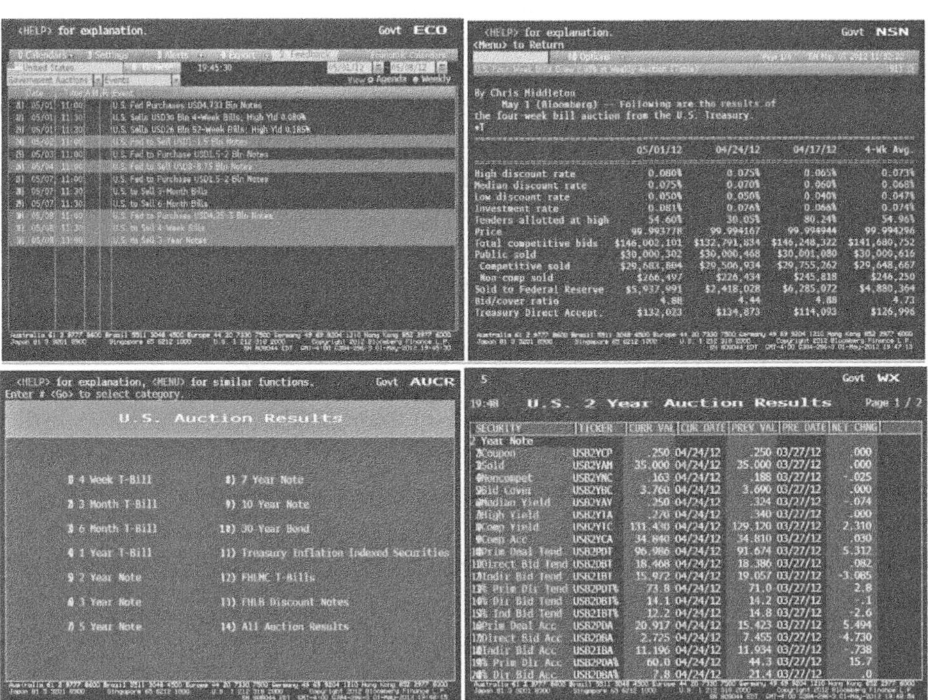

Issue	Frequency
13-week T-bill	*Weekly*
26-week T-bill	*Weekly*
2-year T-note	*Monthly*
5-year T-note	*Quarterly*
10-year T-note	*Quarterly*
30-year T-bond	*Semiannual*

Bloomberg Treasury Auction Information: Information on current and recent Treasury auctions can be found from:

AUCR <Enter>

ECO20

distribution is determined by first subtracting the noncompetitive bids and nonpublic purchases (such as those from the Federal Reserve) from the total bids; the remainder represents the amount that is awarded to competitive bidders. The distribution to competitive bidders is then determined by arraying the bids from lowest yield (highest price) to highest yield (lowest price). The lowest price at which at least some bills are awarded is called the *stop price* or *stop-out price.* Those bidding above the stop price are awarded the quantity they requested, whereas those with bids below the stop price do not receive any bills. The bids at the stop price are awarded a proportion of the remaining bids. At the completion of the auction, the Treasury will adjust the coupon rate on the issue to reflect the stop-out yield, selecting that rate that will bring the price closest to par without exceeding it.

This auction process used by the Treasury is known as an *English auction* or *first-price sealed-bid auction.* For bidders, an English auction may lead them to either overbid and pay too much for the securities, or underbid and be shut out of the auction. Those shut out, though, can buy them as a secondary market transaction from one of the successful bidders. This English system also may encourage collusion and a cornering of the market.[9] An alternative to the English auction is the *Dutch auction system* in which securities are ranked, but all are sold at just one price. Finally, there is a *when-issued market* or *wi market* for Treasuries. When-issued securities are those that have been announced for auction but have not yet been issued. In this market, Treasuries are traded to the time they are issued and settle on the issue date.

The secondary market for Treasury securities is very large. This market is part of the over-the-counter (OTC) market and is handled by Treasury security dealers. It is a 24-hour market with major dealers in New York, London, and Tokyo. The OTC market consists of investors who prefer to buy from dealers instead of through the auctions; investors buying and selling outstanding securities; and the Federal Reserve, which buys T-bills and other Treasury securities as part of their open markets operations. In the secondary market, the recently issued *on-the-run* Treasuries securities are the most liquid securities with a very narrow bid-ask spread; approximately 70 percent of the total secondary market trading involves on-the-run issues. In contrast, *off-the-run* Treasury securities issued earlier are not quite as liquid and can have slightly wider spreads.

Government Security Dealers

Because of the difficulty in determining the best price to bid, individual investors, regional banks, fund managers, and corporations often prefer to buy new Treasury securities from dealers who specialize in the Treasury auction market rather than buy them directly at the auction. Although any firm can deal in government securities, the Treasury auction is principally carried out with *primary dealers.* Primary dealers are those firms that trade with the Federal Reserve Bank of New York as part of their open market operations. For a firm to be on the primary dealer's list, it must have adequate capital and be willing to trade securities at any time. As of 2012, there were 21 primary dealers participating in the market (see Exhibit 8.10 for a list of these dealers).

EXHIBIT 8.10 Primary Government Security Dealers, 2012

Bank of Nova Scotia, New York Agency	Jefferies & Company, Inc.
BMO Capital Markets Corp.	J.P. Morgan Securities LLC
BNP Paribas Securities Corp.	Merrill Lynch, Pierce, Fenner & Smith Incorporated
Barclays Capital Inc.	Mizuho Securities USA Inc.
Cantor Fitzgerald & Co.	Morgan Stanley & Co. LLC
Citigroup Global Markets Inc.	Nomura Securities International, Inc.
Credit Suisse Securities (USA) LLC	RBC Capital Markets, LLC
Daiwa Capital Markets America Inc.	RBS Securities Inc.
Deutsche Bank Securities Inc.	SG Americas Securities, LLC
Goldman, Sachs & Co.	UBS Securities LLC
HSBC Securities (USA) Inc.	

Source: Federal Reserve Bank of New York: www.newyorkfed.org/markets/pridealers_current.html

The dealers include many of the major investment banking firms, such as UBS, Barclays Capital, Jefferies, J. P. Morgan, Merrill Lynch, and Goldman Sachs. For new issues, primary dealers distribute new Treasury securities to nonprimary dealers and institutional investors. They also maintain large dealer positions in the secondary market.

In addition to the primary and secondary market for Treasury securities, there is also an *interdealer market* in which primary and nonprimary dealers trade billions of dollars each day among themselves. This interdealer market functions through government security brokers that for a commission match dealers and other investors who want to sell with those wanting to buy.[10] The government brokers include such firms as BrokerTec, Cantor Fitzgerald, Garban-Inter Capital, Hilliard Farber and Company, and Tullett Libert.

By taking temporary positions, dealers hope to profit from two sources: carry income and position profit. *Carry income* is the difference between the interest dealers earn from holding the securities and the interest they pay on the funds they borrow to purchase the securities. When dealers acquire securities, they often finance the purchase by borrowing from banks, other dealers, and other institutions. One major source of funds for them is demand loans from banks. Demand loans are short-term loans to dealers (one or two days), secured by the dealer's securities. These loans are usually renewable and often can be called at any time by the bank. Another important source of dealer funding is repurchase agreements; these are discussed in the next section. When dealers sell their securities, the invoice price is equal to the agreed-upon price plus the accrued interest. Generally, dealers profit with a positive carry income by earning higher accrued interest than the interest they pay on their loans.

The *position profit* of dealers comes from long positions, as well as short positions. In a long position, a dealer purchases the securities and then holds them until a customer comes along. The dealer will realize a position profit if rates decrease and prices increase during the time she holds the securities. In contrast, in a short position, the dealer borrows securities and sells them hoping that rates will subsequently increase and prices will fall by the time he purchases the securities to close the short position. To minimize their exposure to position risk, dealers do make use of futures and other derivative contracts to hedge against interest rate changes.

Repurchase Agreements

As noted earlier, many dealers finance their temporary holdings of securities with *repurchase agreements,* also called *repos* (*RPs*). Under a repurchase agreement, the dealer sells securities to a lender, such as an investment or commercial bank, with an agreement that he will buy the securities back at a later date and price. To the dealer, the RP represents a collateralized loan, with the Treasury securities serving as the collateral. Government security dealers often use overnight repos to finance their positions, agreeing to buy back the securities the next day or two. To the lender, the RP position, defined as a *reverse repo,* represents a secured short-term investment. Banks, investment banking firms, dealers, corporations, state and local governments, and other institutions find reverse RPs attractive securities for investing their excess cash (see Exhibit 8.11 for an example of a repo used to finance a dealer's position).

The RP market is not limited to overnight repos or those arranged just with Treasury securities. Repos can have maturities that range from one day (overnight) to one year. An RP that is not overnight is called a *term repo.* The repo market consists of investors with excess cash who find reverse repos as an attractive investment alternative to other money market securities and dealers and holders of securities who want to borrow short-term funds and find repurchase agreements as an efficient and less

EXHIBIT 8.11 Repurchase Agreement Example

As an example, suppose a Treasury dealer plans to buy \$20 million of T-notes on the Treasury auction day and anticipates holding them for one day before selling the securities to her customers for \$20 million plus a premium. To finance the purchase, the dealer could buy the notes and simultaneously enter a repurchase agreement with an investor/lender. Per the agreement, the dealer would agree to deliver the notes for \$20 million minus interest to be paid to the lender. In this market, dealers and lenders state the interest in terms of an annualized repo rate based on a 360-day year. If this rate were 6%, then the interest would be \$3,333 and the price the dealer would sell the notes for on the repo agreement would be for \$19,996,667:

$$\text{Interest} = (\text{Principal})\ (\text{Repo Rate})\ (\text{Length of Loan}/360)$$
$$\text{Interest} = (\$20{,}000{,}000)\ (0.06)\ (1/360)$$
$$\text{Interest} = \$3{,}333$$
$$\text{Price Sold} = \$20{,}000{,}000 - \$3{,}333 = \$19{,}996{,}667$$
$$\text{Repurchase Price} = \$20{,}000{,}000$$

One day later, the dealer would buy back the T-notes on the repurchase agreement for \$20 million and then sell them to her customers for hopefully \$20 million or more plus the one day accrued interest.

expensive financing alternative. Many financial and nonfinancial companies take both repo and reverse repo positions. A bank, for example, might loan funds to a dealer with an open reverse repo while financing part of its short-term loan portfolio with term repos (collateral seller).[11]

Agency Securities and Markets

The U.S. Treasury is responsible for financing and managing the government's debt. In addition to the Treasury, there are also federal agencies and quasi-government corporations that issue securities. Many of these agencies were established to ensure that sufficient credit or liquidity was provided to certain segments of the economy having difficulties raising funds. Among those entities are farmers, students, homeowners, small businesses, and international businesses. These federal agencies raise funds by issuing short-, intermediate-, and long-term debt securities. They, in turn, use the proceeds to directly provide loans to farmers, students, and businesses or to provide loan guarantees and liquidity to private lenders who make loans to those entities. The securities they sell are part of the *federal agency security market*. In addition, some of the entities, such as the Federal National Mortgage Association (FNMA or "Fannie Mae") and the Government National Mortgage Association (GNMA or "Ginnie Mae"), are major players in the mortgage-back securities market. In that market, they buy mortgages to securitize and market as mortgage-back securities or they insure the mortgage-backed securities.

The federal credit agencies can be divided into two groups: *government-sponsored enterprises* (*GSEs*) and *non-GSE federal agencies*. GSEs can, in turn, be divided into publicly owned corporations and federally chartered bank lending institutions. The former includes Fannie Mae, Federal Agriculture Mortgage Corporation (FAMC or Farmer Mac), the Federal Home Loan Mortgage Corporation (FHLMC or "Freddie Mac"), and the Student Loan Marketing Association (SLMA or "Sallie Mae"). The federally chartered bank lending institutions include the federal home loan banks and the federal farm credit banks. GSEs sell securities and use the proceeds to provide loans and liquidity to support the housing industry, banking system, agriculture sector, and college loan programs.

Non-GSE federal agencies are true federal agencies created by the U.S. government. Included in this group are the Export-Import Bank, the Private Export Funding Corporation, Tennessee Valley Authority (TVA), Federal Housing Administration (FHA), and Small Business Administration (SBA). Some of the non-GSEs, like the TVA, issue their own securities. Those agencies that do not issue their own debt use the Federal Financing Bank to raise their funds. Finally, there are some outstanding issues of one-time GSE issuers. These include the Resolution Trust Corporation, the Farm Credit Assistance Program, and the Financing Corporation.

Collectively, the debt claims sold by GSEs and federal agencies are referred to as agency securities. For investors, these claims have been considered virtually default free because of the agency's or company's affiliation with the federal government (some federal agency issues are backed by Treasury bonds and many agencies have lines of credit with the Treasury). Following the bailout of savings and loans institutions and banks in the 1980s and early 1990, the General Accounting Office and the Treasury began requiring that all federally sponsored agencies maintain a triple-A credit rating or lose their government support. Following the 2008 financial crisis, the securities of Fannie Mae and Freddie Mac received backing by the U.S. Treasury as part of the Treasury's bailout program. The yields on agency securities are highly correlated with the yields on Treasuries, with the yield spread of federal over Treasury being positive.

Federal agency issues vary from short to long term in maturity, ranging from overnight issues to bonds with original 30-year terms to maturity. Agency money market securities are sold as zero-discount bonds, whereas intermediate and long-term notes and bonds are sold as coupon bonds; agencies also sell floating-rate bonds. The denominations on the bonds vary from $1,000 to $50,000 and up. Fannie Mae, Freddie Mac, the Federal Home Loan Bank system, and several other agencies also offer *agency benchmark programs* similar to corporate medium-term note issues. These programs provide for the regular issuance of coupon securities covering a range of maturities. In general, there are a variety of different types of agencies with different features: callable and noncallable, fixed and floating, coupon and zero coupon, and agencies denominated in different currencies. Unlike Treasury securities, which are exempt from state and local taxes, and municipal bonds, which are exempt from federal taxes, some agency securities are fully taxable. Because of their tax status, as well as their maturities and relatively low risk, agency claims are attractive investments for pension and trust funds, state and local governments, banks, and corporations. The Federal Reserve System also trades in some federal agency securities.

The primary market for many federal agency securities is handled through a network of federal security fiscal agents, brokers, and dealers. Depending on the type of security, a new issue can be sold through dealers, by auction, or by direct sales. Short-term securities are sold on a continuous basis, whereas intermediate issues are sold on a monthly basis, and long-term bonds are offered several times a year. Similar to the primary market for Treasuries, there is also an interdealer market that helps to improve the efficiency of the market. Intermediate- and long-term issues are usually sold through a *solicitation method.* Under this method, a fiscal agent puts the selling group together. The selling group then provides potential investors with information on the issues. Given that information, the potential investor indicates the amount of the issue they plan to buy and the price they believe the issue should be. The fiscal agent then sets the price based on the inputs of the potential investors. The secondary market for agency securities is handled through dealers on the OTC market.

Exhibit 8.12 shows the Bloomberg FIT screen for agency securities and description, price quotes, and closing prices of one of the issues. The issue shown is a note issued by Freddie Mac maturing on 9/10/2015 and paying a coupon of 1.75 percent. Exhibit 8.13 shows Bloomberg bond menu screens and descriptions for selected notes for the Federal Home Loan Mortgage Corporation. Using the SECF screen (Exhibit 8.13), other agency bonds can also be found, such as Federal National Mortgage Association, Federal Home Loan Bank System, Federal Agriculture Mortgage Association, Federal Farm Credit Bank, Tennessee Valley Authority, International Bank for Reconstruction and Development, and Student Loan Marketing Association.

EXHIBIT 8.12 Select GSE and Agency Price Information from FIT

Recently issued, active and seasoned Agencies can be found from the FIT screen: FIT <Enter> and click "Agency" in the amber dropdown box. To access the menu screen, enter CUSIP (or coupon rate and maturity) <Corp>. On the menu, one can access description (DES), dealer bid-ask quotes (ALLQ), TRACE, and calculation of the yield on the (YA).

Other Screens:

Enter <Govt> TK <Enter> and select U.S. and agency.

SECF: SECF <Enter>; FI tab, Corp tab, and type ticker (e.g., FNMA, FHLMC, SLMA) or type name in issuer name box (e.g., Export Import Bank or Bank for Reconstruction).

For new or active issues: Enter PXAM.

Although different agency securities have many similar characteristics, the purpose for which each agency and government-sponsored company uses its funds varies considerably. As noted, the major areas of financing for federal agencies are housing, agriculture, savings and loans and bank funding and reorganizing, student loans, and international business. Exhibit 8.14 summarizes the activities of some of agencies.

Housing and Real Estate Financing

Of particular note is the role agencies have played in the housing market. The Federal National Mortgage Association, the Government National Mortgage Association, the Federal Home Loan Mortgage Corporation, and the Federal Agriculture Mortgage Corporation are all GSEs or agencies involved with providing funding and liquidity

EXHIBIT 8.13 Select GSE and Agency Bonds Menus and Descriptions

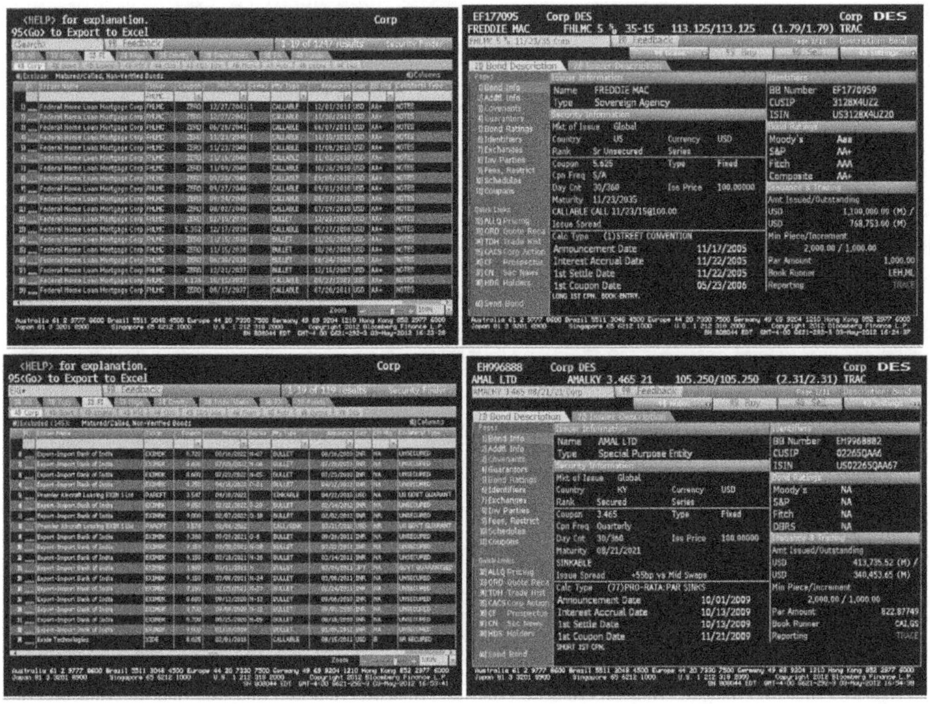

SECF*:* SECF <Enter>; FI tab, Corp tab, and type ticker (e.g., FNMA, FHLMC, SLMA) or type name in issuer name box (e.g., Export Import Bank or Bank for Reconstruction).

for the mortgage industry. Until the introduction of mortgage-backed securities, the primary function of Fannie Mae, Ginnie Mae, and Freddie Mac was to provide a secondary market for mortgages. They did this by issuing their own securities and then using the proceeds to buy mortgages from savings and loans, mortgage banks, and commercial banks. In the 1980s, Fannie Mae, Ginnie Mae, and Freddie Mac began offering *pass-through securities* or *participation certificates* (*PCs*). These instruments are securitized assets formed by pooling a group of mortgages and then selling a security representing interest in the pool and entitling the holder to the income generated from the pool of mortgages. In 2000, Fannie Mae and Freddie Mac activities in the subprime mortgage market led to their near collapse and precipitated the 2008 financial crisis. In September 2008, Fannie Mae and Freddie Mac were taken over by the U.S. government.

In addition to mortgage-backed securities, Fannie Mae issues a variety of short-, intermediate-, and long-term debt securities: benchmark bills, notes, and bonds, callable benchmark notes, subordinated benchmark notes, callable securities, and bullet and callable medium-term notes. Similarly, Freddie Mac issues its own bullet and callable benchmarks, called *reference* bills, notes, and bonds; they also issue euro-denominated notes, medium-term notes, and global bonds. Many of the debt securities of Freddie

EXHIBIT 8.14 Federal Agencies Functions and Securities Issued

Agriculture Credit Financing
The Federal Farm Credit Bank System (FFCBS) originally consisted of 12 Federal Land Banks (FLB), 12 Federal Intermediate Credit Banks (FICB), and 12 Banks for Cooperatives. The Federal Land Banks (created by an act of Congress in 1916) made mortgage loans and provided financial funds to farmers and ranchers for purchasing or improving their farms and ranches; the Federal Intermediate Credit Banks (created in 1923) provided short-term loans for farmers; the Banks for Cooperatives (created in 1933) provided seasonal loans to farm cooperatives. Prior to 1979, these banks sold their own securities. In 1979, though, they consolidated their financing and sold separate and joint obligations of the Federal Farm Credit Bank System. In 1987, the FFCBS was reorganized under the Agriculture Credit Act. This reorganization led to the merger of the regional FLBs, FICBs, and Banks for Cooperatives into four regional Farm Credit Banks (FCBs), the Agriculture Credit Bank, and approximately 100 Production Credit Associations, Federal Land Credit Associations, and Agriculture Credit Association. The Federal Farm Credit Bank System (FFCBS) issues a variety of debt securities, ranging from short-term money markets securities with maturities ranging from 5 days to 270 days, to short-term bonds with maturities from three to nine months, and to intermediate bonds with maturities ranging from one year to 10. All of the FFCBS obligations are handled by the Federal Farm Credit Bank Funding Corporation, which sells new issues through a selling group of brokers and dealers.

Savings and Loans and Bank Financing
The savings and loan and banking crises of the 1980s led to the passage of the Federal Institutional Reform, Recovery, and Enforcement Act (FIRREA) of 1990. This act restructured some existing agencies and created several new programs involved in regulating and insuring commercial banks, savings and loans, and savings banks. Prior to the act, the Federal Home Loan Bank Board (FHLBB) was responsible for regulating federally chartered savings and loans and federally insured state-chartered savings and loans. The passage of FIRREA significantly curtailed these responsibilities, shifting the FHLBB regulatory authority to the Office of Thrift Supervision and dismantling the board but keeping the system of 12 federally chartered, privately owned Federal Home Loan Banks (FHL Bank System). These 12 privately owned banks provide loans to over 8,000 member bank institutions for the financing of their residential mortgage, small business, rural, and agricultures loans. FHL Bank issues a number of securities, including benchmark securities, notes, and medium-term notes.

Tennessee Valley Authority
The Tennessee Valley Association (TVA) was created by an act of Congress in 1933 to create and promote electrification and the development of the Tennessee Valley. Like the U.S. Postal Service, TVA is defined as *government-owned corporation* or a wholly owned corporate agency. It is the largest public power system in the U.S. Similar to stockholder-owned power companies, TVA issues a number of debt obligations to finance its power programs and development projects. The debt obligations it issues are not guaranteed by the government, but are rated triple A. The TVA offers a variety of debt securities, many with interesting features and structures.

Global Financing
In addition to federal agencies, international organizations such as the International Bank for Reconstruction and Development (World Bank) and various development banks also raise funds through the sale of bonds to finance development and guarantee programs. The World Bank provides loans to private and government sectors in various countries (generally when such loans are not available from private sources) to finance public and quasi-public projects such as educational establishments, power plants, transportation systems, dams, harbors, and other infrastructures. The loans made by the World Bank usually have maturities between 10 and 30 years and often the principal is amortized. Loans are typically made to governments or to firms with guarantees from the government, with an emphasis on building a country's infrastructure. To finance these projects the World Bank borrows directly from the U.S. and other developed countries as well as issuing short-term and intermediate-term World Bank bonds. Similar in structure to the World Bank are various regional development banks such as the Inter-American Development Bank (IDB), Asian Development Bank (ADB), and the African Development Bank. These institutions provide financing to support private and infrastructure developments in their specific regions.

Mac's are purchased by agents and dealers and then stripped. In 2001, both Fannie Mae and Freddie Mac began issuing subordinate securities—Fannie Mae subordinated benchmark notes and the Freddie Mac subs.

The Federal Agriculture Mortgage Corporation (Farmer Mac) was established in 1988 to provide a secondary market for agriculture real estate loans and for rural homeowner and business loans and to improve agriculture and rural credit and liquidity. Similar to Fannie Mae, Ginnie Mae, and Freddie Mac, Farmer Mac buys loans, pools them, and sells claims on the pool. These securitized assets are called *agriculture mortgage-backed securities* (*AMBS*). Farmer Mac also finances its purchase of loans by selling discount notes and medium-term notes.

BLOOMBERG AGENCY SECURITY INFORMATION: FIT AND TK<CORP> SCREENS:

Recently issued, active, and seasoned Agencies can be found on the FIT screen: FIT <Enter>, and click "Agency" from the amber dropdown tab. To access the menu screen, enter CUSIP (or coupon rate and maturity) <Corp>. On the menu, one can access description (DES), dealer bid-ask quotes (ALLQ), TRACE, and calculation of the yield (YA). Agency bonds and their menus can also be found by entering Agency ticker <Corp>:

- Federal Home Loan Mortgage Corporation: FHLMC <Corp> <Enter>
- Federal National Mortgage Association: FNMA <Corp> <Enter>
- Federal Home Loan Bank System: FHLB <Corp> <Enter>
- Federal Agriculture Mortgage Association: FAMCA <Corp> <Enter>
- Federal Farm Credit Bank: FFCB <Corp> <Enter>
- Tennessee Valley Authority: TVA <Corp> <Enter>
- World Bank (International Bank for Reconstruction and Development): IBRD <Corp> <Enter>
- Student Loan Marketing Association: SLMA <Corp> <Enter>
- EXI <Enter> Bonds with export-import bank guarantee

OTHER SCREENS:

SECF: SECF <Enter>; FI tab, Corp tab, and type ticker (e.g., FNMA, FHLMC, SLMA) or type name in issuer name box (e.g., Export Import Bank or Bank for Reconstruction). For new or active issues: Enter PXAM (active agencies), and ADN (agency offerings). See Exhibits 8.12 and 8.13)

Municipal Securities and Markets

Like corporations, state and local governments undertake many long-term capital projects such as the construction of school buildings, highways, water treatment facilities, airports, hospitals, inner-city housing, and infrastructures that facilitate economic growth and job creation. To finance these long-term capital investments, they sell two types of notes and bonds: *general obligation bonds* and *revenue bonds*. In addition to their long-term investments, state and local governments also have short-term cash flow needs created from differences in their expenditure and revenue patterns and the time gaps between when projects begin and when the permanent financing supporting the projects is received. To finance their short-term cash needs, they sell short-term anticipation notes. Security traders collectively refer to short-term anticipation notes, general obligations bonds, and revenue bonds as municipals or munis.[12]

Although there are a number of different types of municipal debt securities, one feature most of them have in common is their tax-exempt status. Specifically, the interest on municipals (but not the capital gain) is exempt from federal income taxes (both personal and corporate). In addition, most states also exempt the coupon interest earned on in-state issues from state income taxes and personal property taxes where it is applicable. This tax-exempt feature makes municipals very attractive to individuals and corporations in the higher income tax brackets and investment funds whose clients are in the higher brackets. An investor in the 35 percent tax bracket would be indifferent, with all other factors being equal, to a fully taxed bond yielding 10 percent and a tax-exempt bond yielding 6.5 percent.[13]

Anticipation Notes

To finance short-term to intermediate-term cash needs municipal governments issue several types of securities. These securities are sold to obtain funds in lieu of anticipated revenues. They include *tax-anticipation notes* (*TANs*), *revenue-anticipation notes* (*RANs*), *grant-anticipation notes* (*GANs*), *bond-anticipation notes* (*BANs*), and *municipal tax-exempt commercial paper.* These obligations are usually secured by the issuer's taxing power and sell at yield spreads over short-term Treasuries that reflect their tax-exempt status and credit ratings. Most are sold as zero discount bonds with face values ranging from $5,000 to $1 million and maturities ranging from one month to three years. There is also municipal tax-exempt commercial paper (CP) sold primarily to finance recurring expenses. Like CP sold by corporations, tax-exempt CP has a maturity ranging from 30 days to 270 days and is often secured with a bank letter of credit, line of credit, or a purchase agreement in which the bank agrees to buy the bond if the issuer fails. Some municipal governments also finance their cash needs with a tax-exempt *floating-rate obligation.* These obligations have a coupon reset periodically.

General Obligation Bonds

General obligation bonds (*GOs*) are originally intermediate-term and long-term debt obligations that are secured by the issuing government's general taxing power and that can pay interest and principal from any revenue source. The GOs issued by states and large municipal governments that have a number of tax revenue sources and unlimited tax power are referred to as *unlimited tax GOs.* They are considered backed by the *full faith and credit of the issuer.* The GOs issued by smaller municipalities or authorities whose revenues are limited to only one or two sources (e.g., property tax), or who have statutory limits on the tax rate that the issuer may levy to finance the debt are known as *limited-tax*

GO bonds. Like corporate bonds, the contract between the issuer and the investor is specified in the GO's trust indenture. With municipals, this document is usually accompanied by an official statement and a legal opinion. The *official statement* is a document, similar to the prospectus for a stock or corporate bond that details the return, risk, and other characteristics of the issue and provides information on the issuer (see Exhibit 8.15). The *legal opinion* is a document that interprets legal issues related to the bond's collateral, priority of claims, and the like. Municipal bond attorneys with Wall Street–based law firms, as well as local firms, prepare legal opinions. In addition, many bank and investment-banking firms have their own counsel to review and prepare such documents.

The municipal defaults that have occurred over the past 20 years and the subsequent problems related to legally defining the security, revenue sources, and priorities have made the legal opinion an important information source for assessing a municipal bond's credit risk. In evaluating the creditworthiness of a GO bond, municipals investors often review the legal opinion to determine the state or local government's unlimited taxing authority. The legal opinion identifies if there are any statutory or constitutional limitations on the jurisdiction's taxing power, as well as any priority of claims on general funds. The legal opinion may also specify what the bondholders' redress is in the case of a default and whether there are any statutory or constitutional questions involved. Municipal defaults are usually handled through a restructuring, which makes the security and priorities as defined in the indenture and explained in the legal opinion important in establishing the types of new debt the municipal bondholders might receive.

Exhibit 8.16 shows the Bloomberg screens for a GO bond issued by the City of Charlotte, North Carolina. The bond was issued on 6/5/2008, matures on 8/1/2016, pays a 4 percent annual coupon, and in November of 2011 traded around 112. The bond was also issued as part of a series, with bonds in the series ranging in maturity from 8/1/2009 to 8/1/2023.

Revenue Bonds

Revenue bonds are municipal securities paid by the revenues generated from specific public or quasi-public projects, by the proceeds from a specific tax, or by a special

EXHIBIT 8.15 Information in Official Statement

- Amount of the Issue
- Credit Rating
- Information on Issuer
- The Names of the Underwriters
- Selling Group
- Sources of Payments
- Sources and Uses of Fund Statement
- Financial Statements
- Debt Service Required
- Notice of any Pending Legislation
- Bond Insurance (if any)

EXHIBIT 8.16 General Obligation Bonds

Charlotte, N.C. GO: CUSIP <Muni>

assessment on an existing tax. Occasionally, revenue bonds are issued with some general obligation backing and thus have characteristics of both GOs and revenue bonds. For example, some revenue bonds are secured by user charges as well as a GO pledge. Such bonds are referred to being *double barreled*. Similarly, some revenue bonds are secured by and paid from more than one revenue source. For example, some school districts issue bonds to finance certain capital projects that are paid for by property taxes earmarked for the project and are also secured by special funds of the state such that, in the event of a default, the investors can go to the state. Finally, there are *dedicated tax-backed revenue bonds* that are paid from dedicated revenues such as a tobacco settlement, lottery, or special fee.

To the issuer, revenue bonds are an important source of funding for a number of public projects. They are used to finance major capital projects such as roads, bridges, tunnels, airports, hospitals, power-generating facilities, water treatment plants, and municipal and university buildings; they also support educational programs, inner-city housing development, and student loan programs. The revenues used to pay the interest and principal payments on these bonds are usually project specific and include tolls, rents, user charges, earmarked revenues from fees, and specific taxes. It should be noted that many revenue bonds are used to support not just public projects, but also those projects that benefit both public and private interests. Exhibit 8.17 shows the Bloomberg screens for a revenue bond issued by the Water District of the city of Buffalo, New York.

EXHIBIT 8.17 Revenue Bonds

Buffalo N.Y: Municipal Water Financing Authority Bond: CUSIP <Muni>

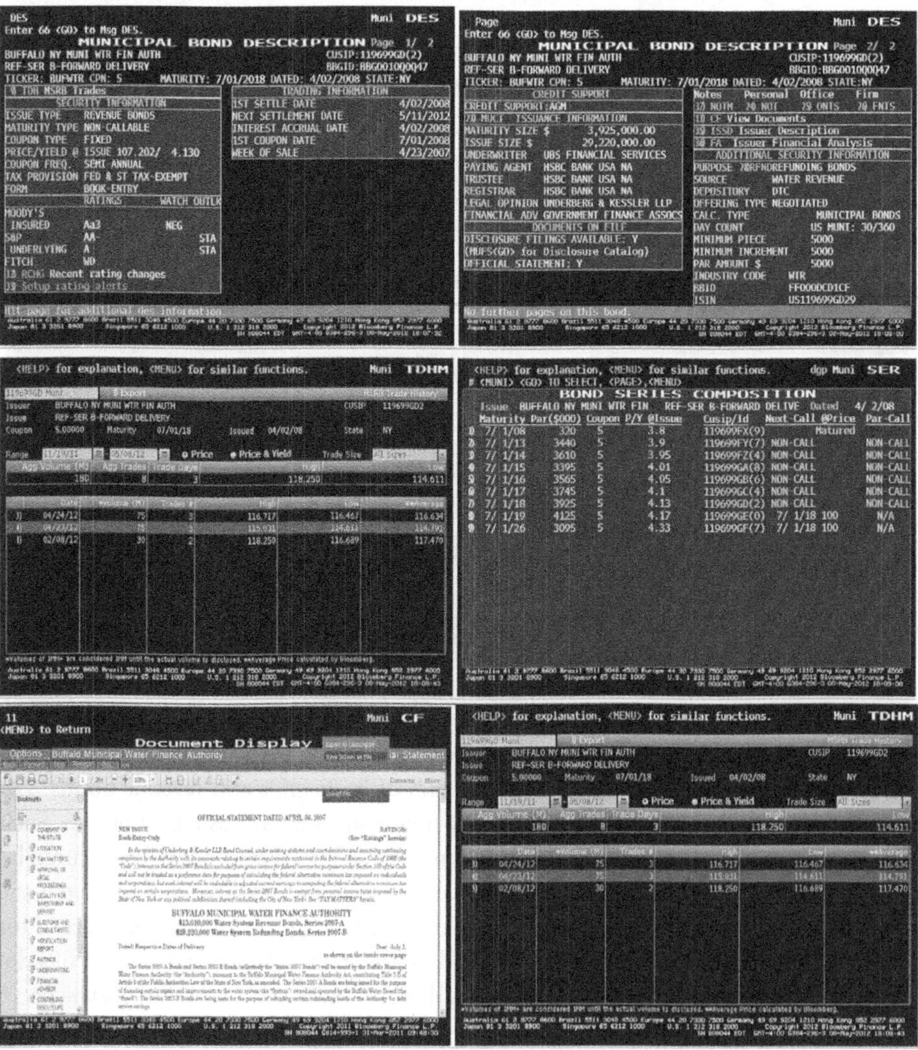

In the 1980s, many private-sector companies began to use tax-exempt revenue bonds to finance industrial parks, electric-generating plants, and other capital projects. One popular revenue bond used to support private-/public-sector projects is the industrial development bond (IDB), also called an industrial revenue bond (IRB) and development bond. Today, many state and local governments or authorities sell IDBs to finance the expansion of an area's industrial base or to attract new industries. Typically, the government or authority floats a bond issue and then uses the proceeds to build a plant or an industrial facility; it then leases the facility to a company or provides a low-interest loan for the company to acquire the asset. Because of the tax-exempt status of municipal bonds, this type of financial arrangement benefits all parties: investors receive a higher after-tax yield, corporations received lower interest rates on loans or lower rental rates, and the area benefits from a new or expanding industry.[14]

As with GOs, revenue bonds have an indenture, legal opinion, and an official statement. Some of the important provisions delineated in the indenture and legal opinion include (1) whether the issuer can increase the tax or user's fee underlying the revenue source; (2) whether the issuer can incur additional debt secured by the revenue of the project (referred to as minimum revenue clauses) or under what conditions new debt can be incurred; (3) how the revenues of the project are to be directed—if they are to be paid to bondholders after operating expenses but before other expenses (this is called a net revenue–structured revenue bond) or to bondholders first (this is called a gross revenue structured bond); and (4) whether there is any additional collateral or guarantees.

Taxable Municipals

The tax-exempt feature of many municipals makes them an attractive investment for many investors. However, there are a number of *taxable municipal bonds,* in which the interest is subject to federal income taxes. Like corporate credits, taxable municipals like Build America Bonds, sell at a lower price and higher yield than comparable tax-exempt municipals. The types of taxable municipals include those used to finance projects (e.g., sports facilities or private investors' housing initiatives) in which there are federal restrictions that limit or prohibit financing with tax-exempt municipal bonds (many of these are specified in Tax Reform Act of 1986). Taxable municipals are attractive investments to tax-exempt investors (e.g., private trust) or foreign investors who cannot benefit from the tax benefits of tax-exempt municipals. Exhibit 8.18 shows the Bloomberg description screen for Taxable Municipal bonds issued by the state of Ohio as part of the Build America Bonds program.

Special Features of Municipals

Two features that are more common among municipal bonds than corporate debt securities are serialization and default insurance. Serialization refers to the breaking up of a bond issue into different maturities. For example, to finance a $20 million convention center, a county might sell a serial issue with four types of securities, each with a face

EXHIBIT 8.18 Taxable Municipals

Ohio Taxable Municipal—Build America Bond: CUSIP <Muni>

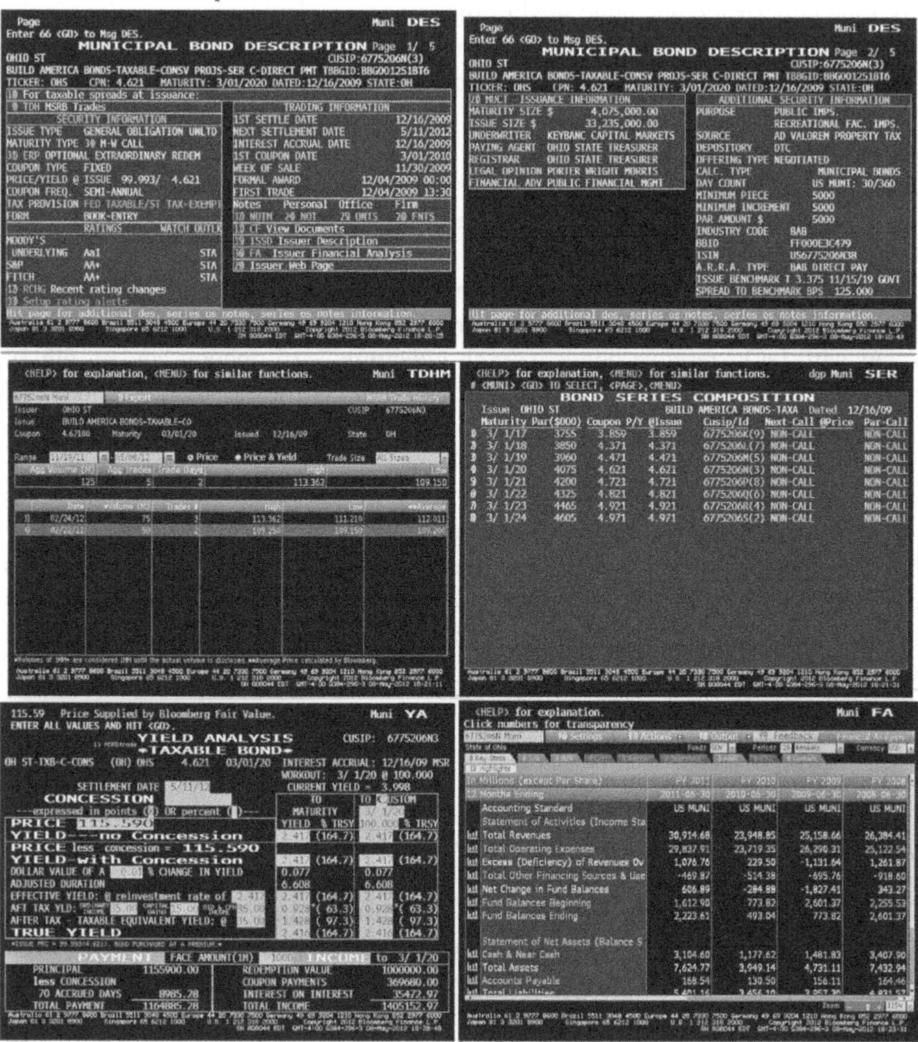

value of $5 million, but with one maturing in year 5, one in year 10, one in year 15, and one in year 20 (see the Bloomberg SER screens in Exhibits 8.17 and 8.18). Instead of a serial issue, some municipals are sold with a serial maturity structure that requires a portion of the debt to be repaid each year. Like many corporate bonds, a number of municipals are sold with the principal paid at maturity. Many of these term bonds, though, often include sinking fund arrangements. There are also several GOs and revenue bonds sold as zero-discount bonds. Municipal governments and authorities also sell a variation of a zero-coupon bond known as a municipal multiplier, accretion, or compound interest bond. This bond pays coupon interest, which is not distributed, but rather is reinvested to the bond's maturity, making the bond similar to a zero-coupon bond.

Insured municipal bonds are ones secured by an insurance company. Insurance is provided by single-line/monoline insurance companies whose primary business is providing municipal bond insurance. There are also multiline property and casualty insurance companies who provide municipal bond insurance along with their other types of insurance products. Major monoline insurers include AMBAC Indemnity Corporation (AMBAC), Municipal Bond Investors Assurance Company (MBIA), and Financial Guaranty Insurance Company (FGIC). The insurers write insurance policies in which they agree to pay interest and principal to bondholders in the event the issuer fails to do so (see Exhibit 8.19 for a description of a municipal bond insured by AMBAC). The municipal issuer and not the bond investor usually pays the insurance premium. Once the insurance is issued, the insurance company has a contractual commitment to pay the bondholders if they do not receive interest or principal payments from the issuer. Municipal insurance can also be obtained from the bondholder or issuer after it is issued. This is referred to as secondary-market insurance.

Prior to 2007, about 50 percent of all new municipal bond issues were insured, with many trading with AAA quality ratings. After the downgrades of several monoline insurers resulting from their subprime mortgage losses in 2007 and 2008, many insured municipal bonds were downgraded.

EXHIBIT 8.19 Insured Municipals

Louisville & Jefferson County Insured Municipal: Insurer: AMBAC
CUSIP <Muni>

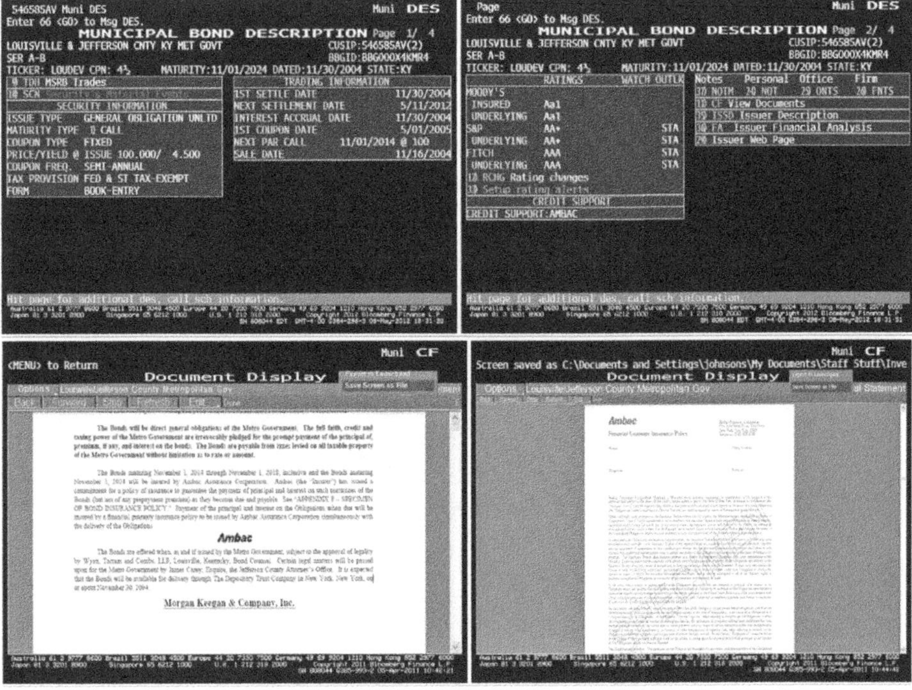

In addition to insured bonds, two other types of municipal bonds with external protection are letter-of-credit (LOC) bonds and refunded bonds. Letter-of-credit-backed municipal bonds are secured by a letter of credit from a commercial bank. In some cases, the municipality must maintain a certain investment quality rating to maintain the guarantee. Refunded bonds are municipal bonds secured by an escrow fund consisting of high-quality securities, such as Treasuries and federal agencies. There are also refunded municipals backed by an escrow fund consisting of a mix of Treasuries and non-Treasuries such as municipals. Because of their backing, insured municipal bonds, LOC-backed municipals, and refunded bonds all sell at yields lower than they would without such protection. Exhibit 8.20 shows a Bloomberg description screen (DES) for a refunded California bond and several sections from the bond's escrow report (CF) describing the refunding provision in the escrow report. The refunded bond was found from Bloomberg municipal search (MSRC).

In contrast to bonds insured or backed by a bank or collateral, Mello-Roos and moral obligation bonds are securities that are not fully backed. Mello-Roos bonds are municipal securities issued by local governments in California that are not backed by the full faith and credit of the government. These bonds were the result of Proposition 13. This law, approved in 1978, set maximum property tax rates, prohibited statewide property taxes, and required a two-thirds vote of the legislature for approval of any increase in state taxes. With such constraints on

EXHIBIT 8.20 Refunded Municipals

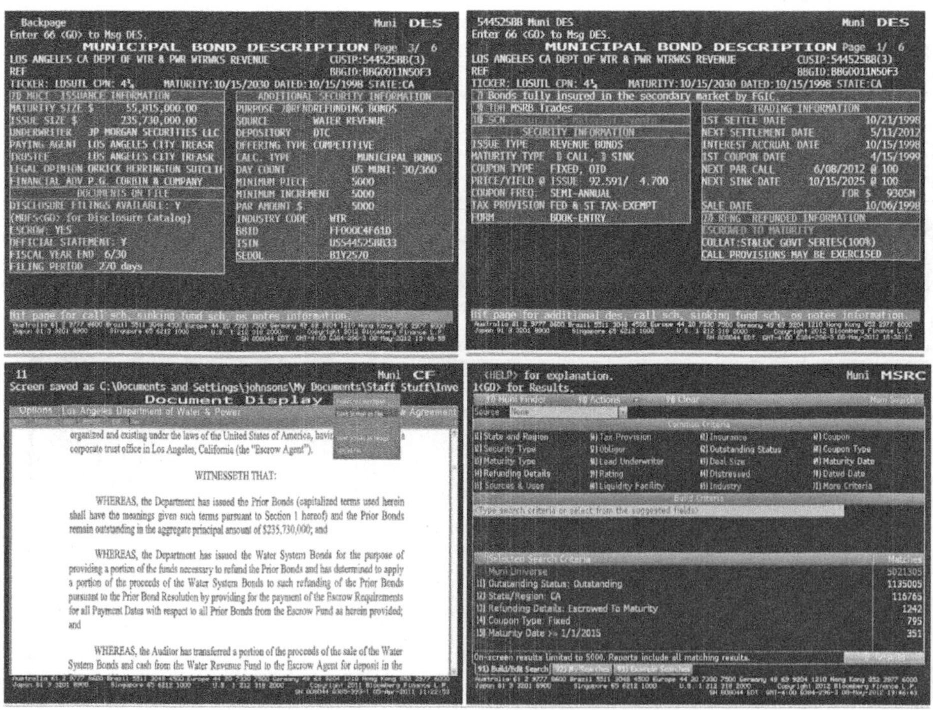

revenue, some local governments in California were forced to issue municipal bonds without full backing. Moral-obligation bonds, in turn, are bonds issued without the legislature's approving appropriation. The bonds are therefore considered backed by the permissive authority of the legislature to raise funds, but not the mandatory authority.[15]

In addition to serial municipal bonds and insured bonds, there are also GOs and revenue bonds introduced over the past two decades with elaborate security structures and features. For example, there are municipal put bonds (bonds that can be cashed in at a specific value before maturity), municipals with warrants that allow the holder to buy additional bonds at set prices, municipal floaters (municipal bonds with floating rate tied to a reference rates such as T-bill rates, London Interbank Offered Rate [LIBOR], or municipal bond index), and minibonds (low denomination issues [$100, $500, and $1,000 par]) that are sold directly to the public without an investment banker. Like Treasury stripped securities, the municipal bond market has developed interest-only and principal-only stripped municipals and floating-rate and inverse floating-rate stripped securities. Many of these municipal derivatives are created by investment-banking firms, such as Goldman Sachs, who buy municipals, place them in a trust, and then create derivative securities.

Credit Risk

In 1975, the Urban Development Corporation of the state of New York defaulted on a $100 million New York City obligation. Three years after that default, Cleveland became the first major U.S. city since the Depression to default on its debt obligations. Although both cities were able to work out arrangements with local banks to pay their creditors, these events nevertheless raised immediate concern among investors over the quality of municipal bonds—bonds that up until then had been considered second in security to Treasury and federal agency securities. Unfortunately, these concerns did not abate. For example, in 1983, the Washington Public Power Supply System (WPPSS) defaulted on a $2 billion municipal government bond issue, with the court ruling that bondholders did not have claims to certain revenues identified in the indenture. In 1994, Orange County, California, defaulted after some ill-conceived investment strategies by the county treasurer. Although aggregate economic growth and prosperity experienced for most of the decade of the 1990s served to increase the revenues of many state and local governments, the financial problems faced by many governments in the 1980s and early 1990s, pointed to the credit risk associated with municipals. More recently, the financial crisis and recession of 2008 and 2009 has again put many municipalities in precarious financial states, leading to defaults, downgrades, federal government assistance, and the issuance of IOUs. To assist investors in determining the creditworthiness of municipals, Moody's, Standard and Poor's, and Fitch provide quality ratings on municipal securities similar to the ones they use for corporate bonds.

Municipal Bond Markets

In the primary market, the sale of GOs and some revenue bonds is handled by investment bankers or a syndicate of commercial banks and dealers who underwrite the issue and then resell them in the open market. Traditionally, the selection of an underwriter or syndicate was done on a competitive bid basis, with many states requiring GOs to be marketed with competing bids. Because of the complexities with municipal bonds, more underwriters are being selected through negotiation. Many revenue bonds and some GOs are also sold through private placements with commercial banks, investment funds, insurance companies, and the like, and since 2000, some brokers and dealers have auctioned some municipals, as well as dealt in existing issues, over the Internet.[16] Information on upcoming municipal bond sales can be found using the Bloomberg PICK screen. The screen can be customized with an alert to notify the user of news on new releases.[17]

In the secondary market, municipal bonds are primarily traded in the OTC market through municipal bond dealers specializing in particular issues. Local banks and regional brokerage firms often handle the issues of smaller municipalities (referred to as *local credits*), whereas larger investment companies and the municipal bond departments of larger banks handle the issues of larger governments (referred to as *general names*). Many dealers in the secondary market make bid and ask quotes in terms of the yield to maturity or yield to call. With the wide variety of municipal bonds, the spreads on municipals can range from ¼ to 1 point.

Regulations

From 1930 to 1970, the municipal bond market was relatively free of federal regulations. Municipal securities were exempted from the disclosure and reporting requirements defined under the security acts of 1933 and 1934. However, following some of the municipal defaults and state and local government budgetary problems of the 1970s, Congress passed the Security Act Amendment of 1975 that expanded federal regulations to the municipal bond market. Although the act did not require compliance to registration requirements under the 1933 act, it did put municipal bond dealers, brokers, and bankers under the Securities and Exchange Commission (SEC) regulatory system. The amendment also mandated that the SEC establish the *Municipal Securities Rule Board* (*MSRB*), a self-regulatory board responsible for establishing rules for brokers, dealers, and banks operating in the municipal bond market. As a result of this board, the SEC amended Rule 15c2-12 to prohibit dealers from marketing new municipal issues if issuers did not agree to provide annual financial reports and disclose relevant events such as credit rating changes, property sales, and the like. The SEC also approved a rule limiting the campaign contributions that municipal security dealers, brokers, and bankers could make to government officials that they did business with who were running for office.

BLOOMBERG MUNICIPAL INFORMATION

SMUN

Information on municipal securities and other information of a state or on municipalities in the state can be accessed from the municipal screener, SMUN: SMUN <Enter>. The SMUN menu displays: a "States" dropdown tab from which one can select either all states, specific states, or multistates; a dropdown "Sector" tab to select either all bonds, general obligations, school revenue bonds, and revenue bonds; and an "Issuer" dropdown to select all, state, county, or city. In addition, from the "Types" dropdown, the user can select bond issues, pensions, and government. After selecting the choices (e.g., general obligations, General, California, "All" Issuers [state, country, and city]), a menu list of all municipalities will appear. On that menu, one can select one of the entries (e.g., State of California or the county of Los Angeles); this will bring up its menu screen that includes the municipal's identifier (California: Stocal US; Los Angeles County: 8784Z US), DES, FA, RV, News, and demographics. The municipal's menu can also be accessed by entering the municipal identifier and hitting <Equity> (e.g., Stocal <Equity> Enter). By clicking RV for a municipal (from the municipal's menu page or from the dropdown menu on the SMUN screen), you can compare states or municipalities in the state in terms of their financials.

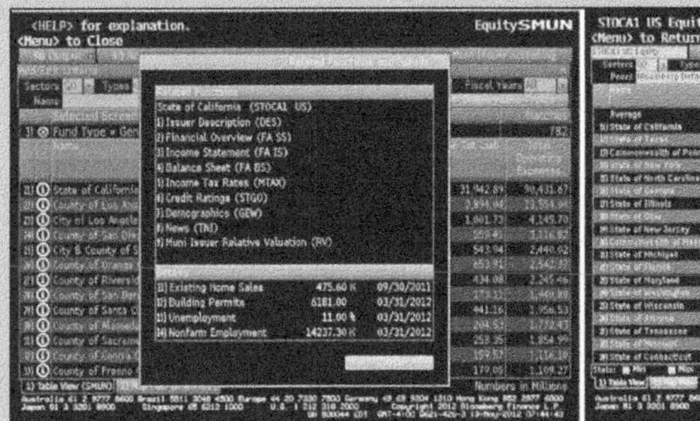

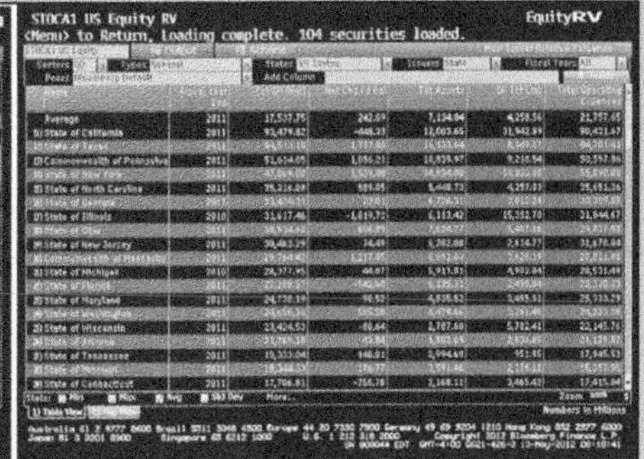

MUNI AND SECF: MUNI <MUNI> <ENTER>:

From the MUNI screen, you can screen and search for specific municipal bond (state, city, fixed, floating rate, callable, etc.). Selecting one of the bonds on the MUNI screen bring up that bond's menu screen for accessing information and analytics. A similar screen can be accesses from SECF: SECF <Enter>, FI tab, Muni tab.

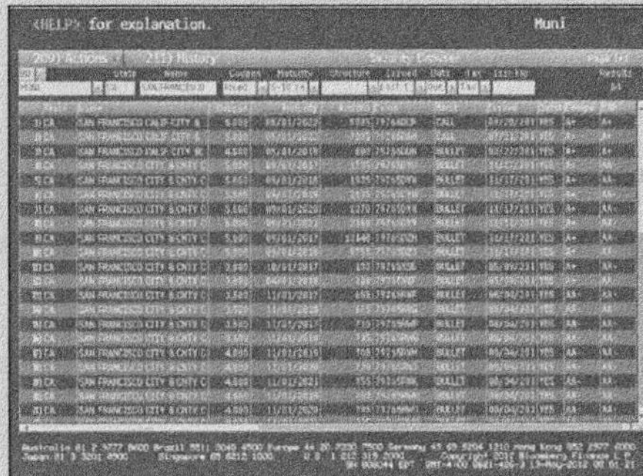

(*Continued*)

MSRC

Using the MSRC screen, one can search and screen the universe of municipal bonds.

1. MSRC <Enter>.
2. Select features.
3. Save the search by clicking the "Actions" tab, clicking "Save As," and then naming the search: "Ohio Muni." Clicking the "My Search" tab at the bottom of the MSRC screen, one can find the identified search. Also, other Bloomberg functions can import the bonds found from search for analysis.
4. Click the "Results" tab at the bottom right corner to see output.
5. On the results screen, one can click the "Output" tab to export the screen's information to Excel.
6. Place cursor on a bond on the output screen and left click and hold to see a menu of information (e.g., DES).

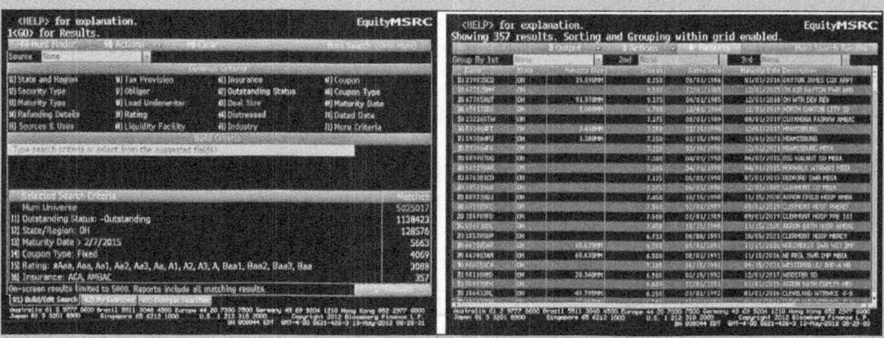

IMGR

Recently issued, actives, and seasoned municipals can be found from the IMGR screen: IMGR. On the IMGR screen, one can screen for municipals by state using the dropdown on the "State" column. To access the menu screen for a particular issue, enter CUSIP (or coupon rate and maturity) <Muni>. Recent issues can also be accessed from SECF by clicking "Last Month" in the "Dated Date" dropdown: SECF <Enter>, FI tab, Muni tab.

PICK

PICK posts and monitors primary and secondary municipal bond offerings and trades. It can be customized to monitor specific types of municipals.

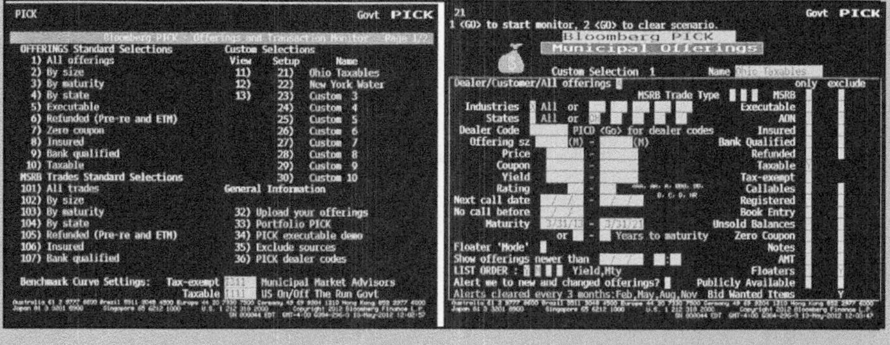

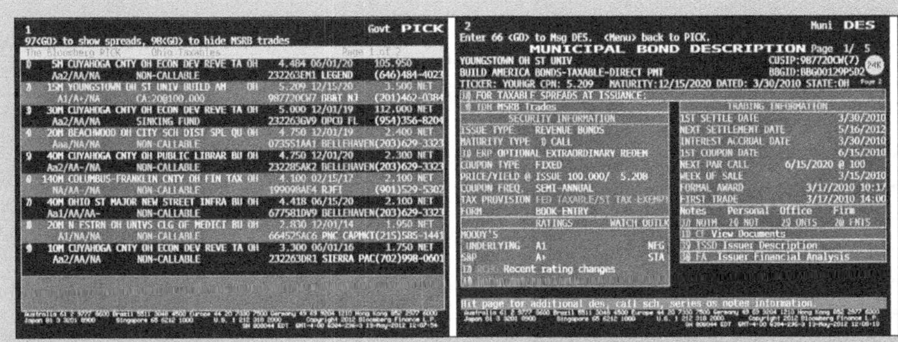

PICK SCREEN BY MUNICIPAL TYPE

On the customize screen, you can select municipals by revenue type or GO using Industry codes:

Industry Codes: APT: Airport; BBK: Bond Bank; DEV: Development; EDU: Education; ENV: Environment; EQP: Equipment; FAC: Facilities; GEN: General; GOB: General Obligation; HGR Higher Education; MED: Medical; MEL: Mello-Roos; MFH: Multi-Family Housing; MUD: Municipal Utility District; NHA: New Public Housing; NTS: Notes; NUR: Nursing Home; OBL: Special Obligation; POL: Pollution; PWR: Power; SCD: School District; SFH: Single Family Housing; STD: Student Loan; TRN: Transportation; UTL: Utilities; VET: Veteran; WTR: Water

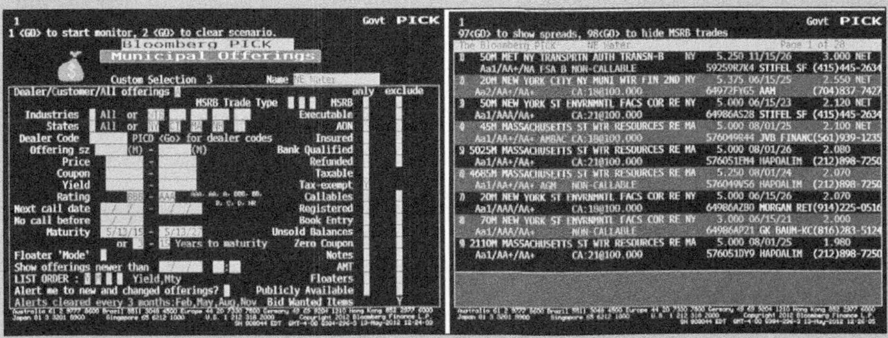

BUILD AMERICAN BONDS: BAB <ENTER>

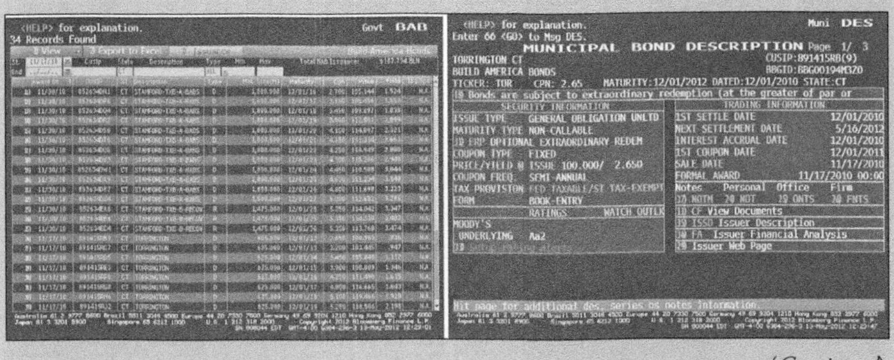

(Continued)

<MUNI>

Sample of functions for municipal bonds on the municipal menu screen:
Ticker <Muni> <Enter> OR <Muni> <Enter>

- RCHG: Ratings History
- YAS: Yield/Spread Analysis
- HP: Historical Analysis
- ISSD: Issuer Description
- TDH: MSRC Reported
- YA: Yield Analysis
- CF: Municipal Filings
- SER: Series

BLOOMBERG MIFA SCREEN: MUNICIPAL FA, RV, AND OTHER FUNCTIONS

The municipal MIFA screen can be used to access financial information on state governments (MIFA <Enter>). The screen allows one to select a state and then access information on the state from a dropdown. On the dropdown, the state's identification number is also shown (e.g., California: Stocal US). Using the identification number, one can access the state's menu directly: Stocal stocal<Equity> <Enter>. Information on the dropdown or the state screen that can be accessed include description (DES), financials (FA), relative evaluations (RV), demographics, (DEMS), employment (BLS), and a municipal search (SMUN). The municipal FA and RV screens display income statements, balance sheets, and other information useful for evaluating the government's financial strength. On the FA and RV screens, one can also change the fund category from general to pension to view the municipal's pension position. Furthermore, from the MIFA menu, one can click the "Table View" to access a screen comparing governments in terms of revenues, expenses, assets, and liabilities. Information on municipals securities of the state or municipality in the state can be accessed by clicking the municipal screener (SMUN) from the dropdown MIFA menu screen for a state. Municipalities can also be accessed directly by entering SMUN <Enter>.

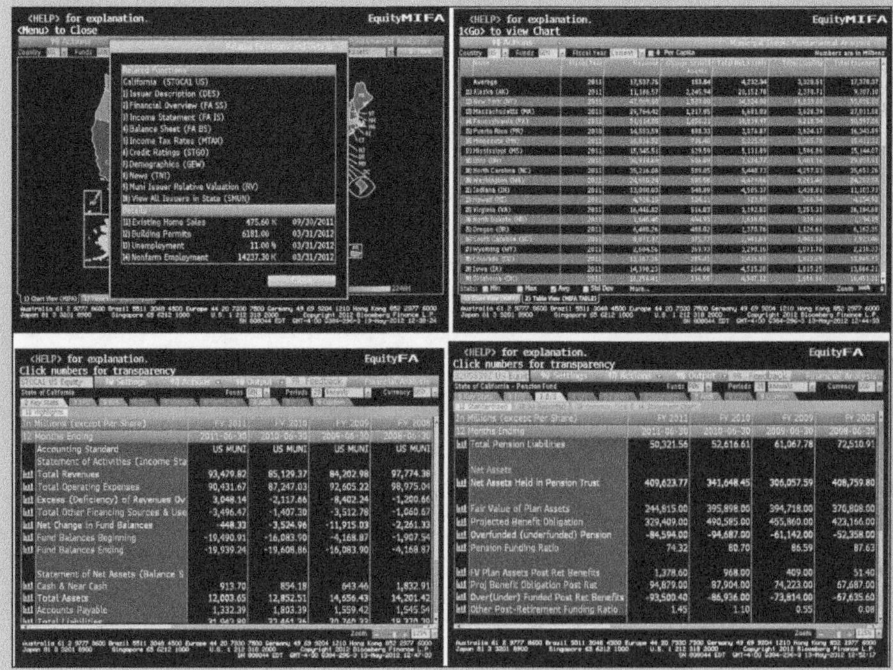

Sovereign Government Debt

Non-U.S. Government Bonds

The largest government bond markets after the United States are the markets in the United Kingdom and Japan, followed by Germany, France, and Italy:

- The British government issues a variety of bonds, also referred to as *gilts,* from short-term bonds to perpetuity.
- Japanese government bonds (JGBs) include intermediate-term and long-term bonds
- German government bonds (*Bunds*) have original maturities from 8 to 30 years, and their notes (*Bolbs*) have original maturities of 5 years.
- French government long-term bonds (*OATS*) have original maturities of 30 years and their notes (*BTAN*) have original maturities of between 2 and 5 years.
- Italian government issues include a variety of securities: 5-, 10-, and 30-year fixed-rate and 7-year floating-rates, and 2-year zero coupon issues.

Like the U.S. government's TIPS, sovereign governments also issue inflation-linked bonds, referred to as *linkers.* See Exhibit 8.21 for Bloomberg descriptions and price quotes of 10-year bond issues of the United Kingdom, Japan, and Italy.

Emerging Market Debt—Brady Bonds

Emerging markets include Latin America, Eastern Europe, Russia, and a number of Asian countries, and their sovereign debt includes Eurobonds, bonds they offer and trade domestically, performing loans that are tradable, and Brady bonds (sovereign bonds issued in exchange for rescheduled banks loans). For investors, emerging market public and private debt securities provide relatively high expected returns, but they are also subject to considerable risk. Much of the risk germane to emerging market securities comes from concerns over changes in political, social, and economic conditions (referred to as *cross-border risk*), and *sovereign risk* in which the government is unable, or in some cases unwilling, to service its debt. Some of the recent sovereign debt crises of note occurred in Latin America in the 1980s, Venezuela in 1994, East Asia in 1994, Mexico in 1995, and Russia in 1998. In 2012, the concern was over default by Greece, Italy, Spain, Ireland, and Portugal.

One of the more popular emerging debt securities is the *Brady bond.* Named after U.S. Treasury Secretary Nicholas Brady, these bonds were issued by a number of emerging countries in exchange for rescheduled bank loans. The bonds were part of a U.S. government program started in 1989 to address the Latin American debt crisis of the 1980s. The plan allowed debtor countries to exchange their defaulted bank debt for Brady bonds or restructured loans at lower rates. In return for this debt relief, the countries agreed to accept economic reforms proposed by the International Monetary Fund. The principal on a Brady bond was secured by U.S. Treasury securities, and the interest was backed by investment-grade bonds.[18]

EXHIBIT 8.21 Sovereign Government Bonds

U.K. Gilt:

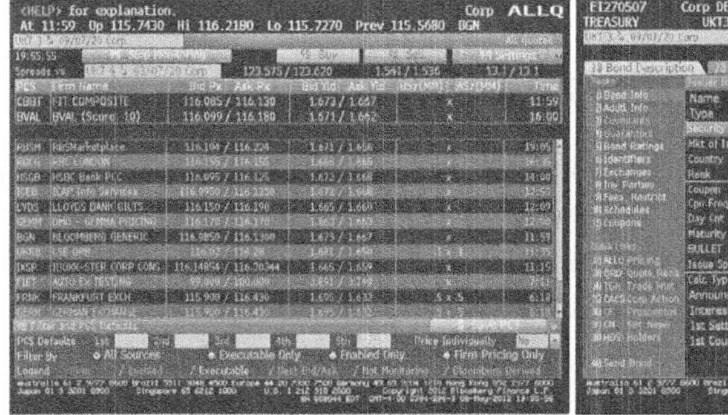

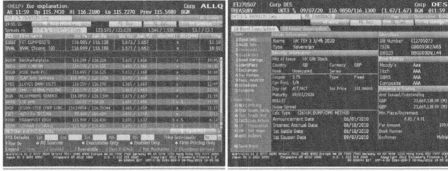

Japan Government Bonds

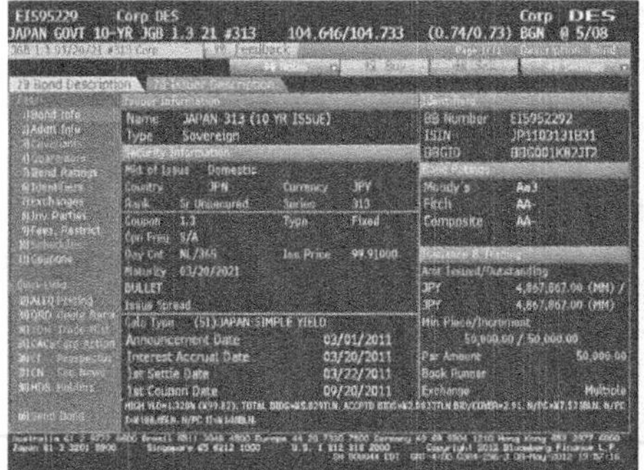

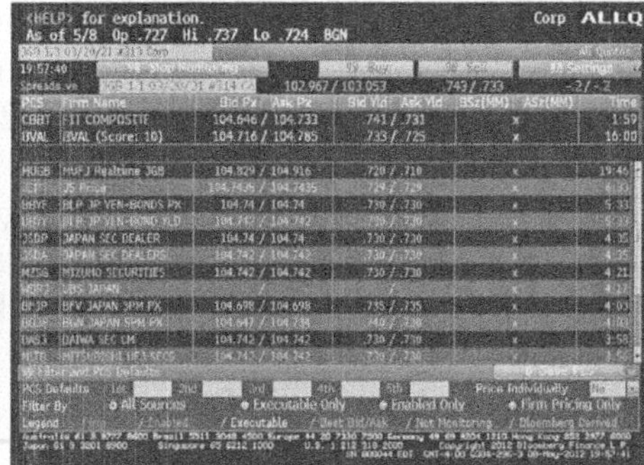

Italian Government Bond

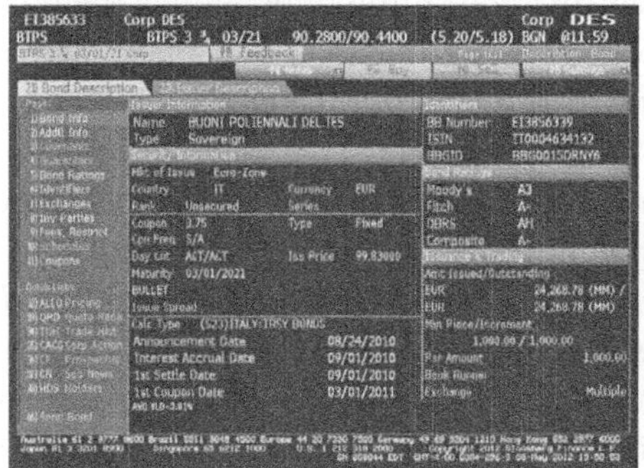

The first country to accept a Brady plan was Mexico, who used it in 1989 to restructure its approximate $50 billion in foreign debt to commercial banks.[19] Seventeen countries with significant debt repayment problems took advantage of the Brady plan with Brazil, Mexico, Venezuela, and Argentina accounting for approximately 73 percent of the debt. When they were introduced, the initial holders of Brady bonds were the creditor banks. With the principal and interest guarantees and the potentially

EXHIBIT 8.22 Emerging Market and Brady Bonds

China Government Bond

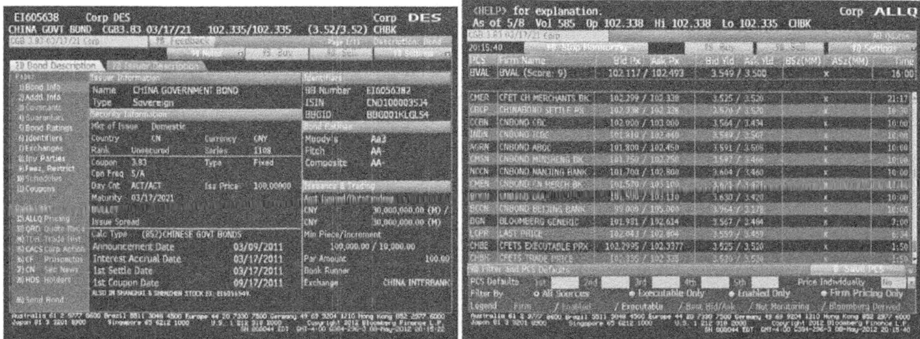

India Government Bond

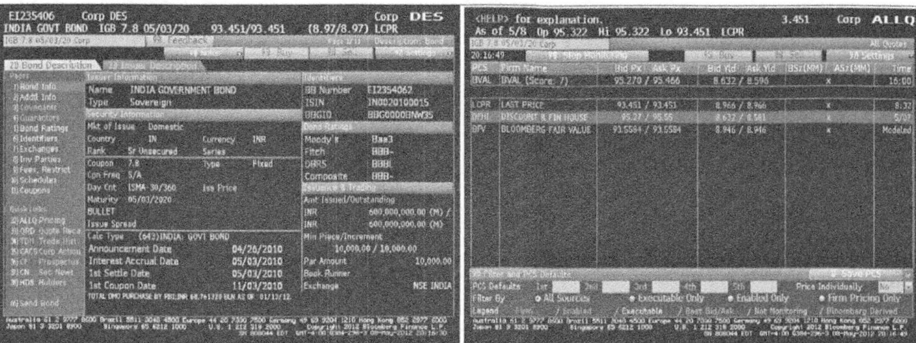

Brady Bond: Argentina

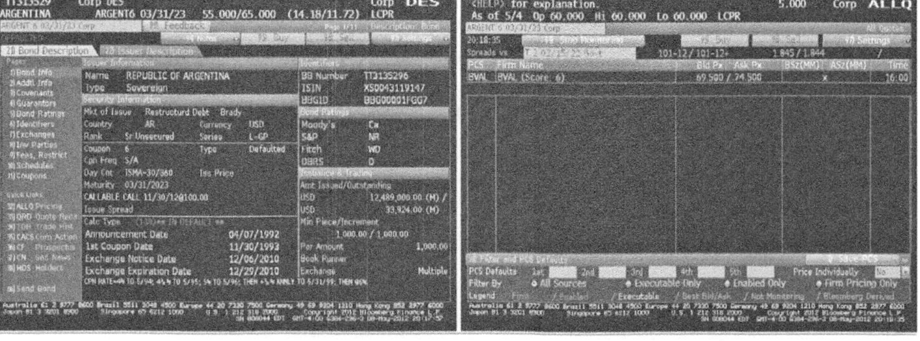

high returns, the bonds were attractive investments to hedge funds, global bond funds, growth funds, and emerging market funds. As a result, many banks sold their Brady bonds to nonbank institutional investors who, in turn, became one of the primary holders. See Exhibit 8.22 for Bloomberg descriptions and price quotes of government bonds of China and India and a Brady bond issued by Argentina.

BLOOMBERG SOVEREIGN GOVERNMENT BOND INFORMATION

BLOOMBERG: FOREIGN GOVERNMENT BONDS

- <Govt> TK <Enter>
- Example: Click "U.K."
- Select type such as UKT for all British gilts (bonds)
- Or enter: UKT <Govt> <Enter>
- Click bond of interest to bring up its menu screen
- Or Enter CUSIP <Govt> <Enter>

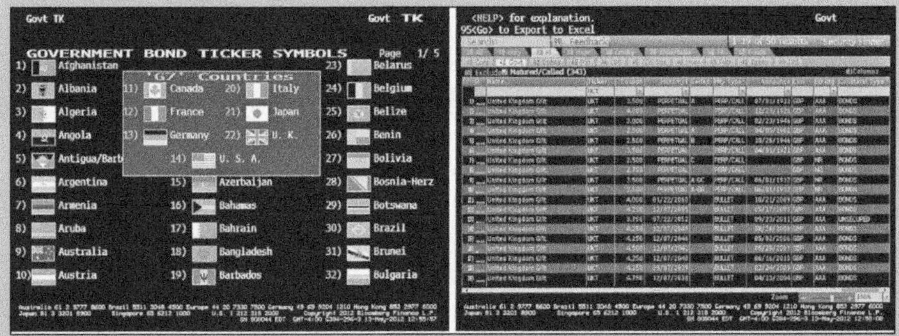

FIT <ENTER>

From the FIT screen, one can access sovereigns and other securities directly. On the dropdown tab of FIT, select country.

WB: WB <ENTER>

The WB monitor displays and compares bonds by different global areas. From the monitor, one can click a bond to bring up a menu of functions: descriptions, price graph, and the like. Also one can access a listing of actively traded bonds of a given maturity class by region by selecting a region and maturity from the dropdown box (e.g., Eurozone and 5 years) and then clicking the bar over the geographic area to bring up the country's SOVM screen.

SOVM: SOVM <ENTER>

The SOVM screen monitors bonds of country.

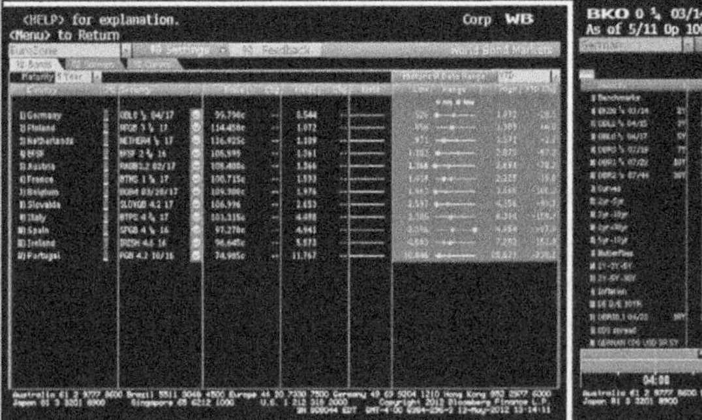

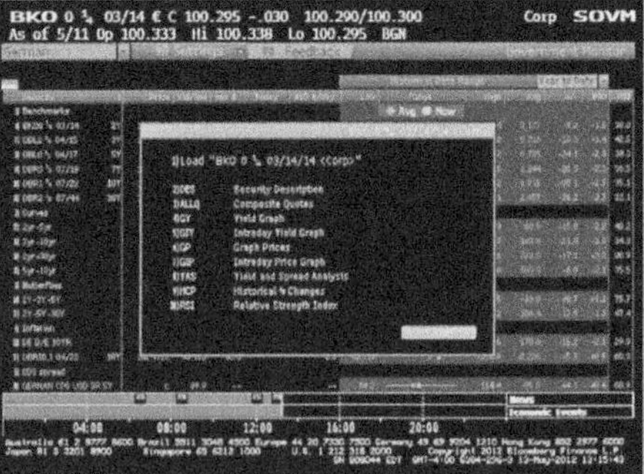

BOND MONITORS BY COUNTRY: IM AND BTMM

The IM screen displays a directory of bond monitors for each country. Clicking the country, in turn, brings up a BTMM screen for that country. Alternatively, one can bring up the BTMM screen (BTMM <Enter>), which typically shows the U.S. bond monitor. One can then use the dropdown to "Change Country" tab to select a country.

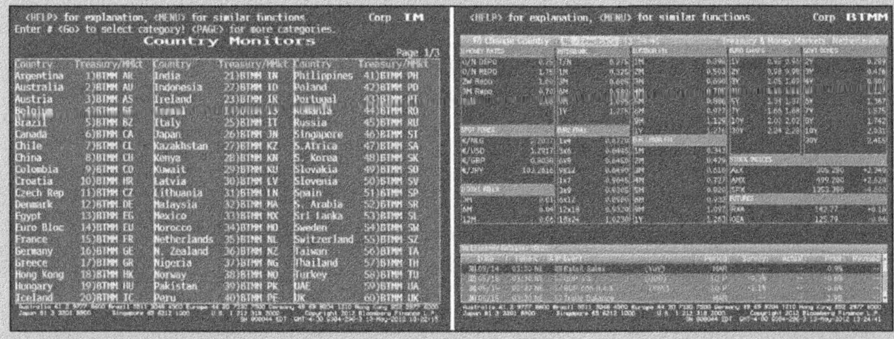

DEVELOPED MARKETS MONITOR: DMMV <ENTER>

MOST ACTIVE EXCHANGE TRADED BONDS: MOSB <ENTER>

EMERGING MARKETS: EMERGING MARKET MONITOR: EMMV <ENTER>

ACTIVE BRADY BONDS: PXBR <ENTER>

SOVEREIGN DEBT RATINGS: CSDR <ENTER>

Conclusion

In this chapter, we have examined the markets for Treasury, agency, municipal, and sovereign government securities. Treasury and agency securities are used to finance not only the U.S. government's debt, but also a number programs and operations of the federal government. For investors, the securities offered by the U.S. governments vary from short-term to long-term, from zero-coupon to fixed-income securities, and from generic fixed-income to inflation-adjusted coupon issues. There is also an extensive market for government securities with special features such as stripped Treasury securities. Municipal securities are used to finance a myriad of capital projects, programs, and operations of state and local governments. The list of issuers of government securities is extensive: states, state agencies, cities, counties, and municipal authorities. For investors, municipals offer many types of instruments, from short-term municipal anticipation notes to long-term municipal GOs and revenue bonds. Finally, there is an extensive amount of government debt securities issued by developed and emerging nations.

In the next chapter, we will complete our analysis of securities and financial market by examining intermediary securities. As we will see, the number and different types of these securities, like corporate and government securities, is also extensive.

Website Information

Treasury

1. The Wall Street Journal and other sites provide price information on existing Treasury issues: http://online.wsj.com/public/us.
2. Prices on T-notes and T-bonds can be found at various websites (e.g., Wall Street Journal site, http://online.wsj.com/public/us; FINRA, www.finra.org/index.htm; Investinginbonds.com, http://investinginbonds.com/).
3. U.S. Treasury's debt: www.publicdebt.treas.gov
4. Reports from the U.S. Treasury: www.treas.gov/
5. Treasury auctions:
   - www.treasurydirect.gov/indiv/products/prod_auctions_glance.htm
   - Recent bills auction: www.treasurydirect.gov/RI/OFBills
   - Recent bonds, notes, and TIPS auctions: www.treasurydirect.gov/RI/OFNtebnd
6. For the distribution of U.S. debt, go to the Treasury Bulletin: www.fms.treas.gov/bulletin/.
7. U.S. government's expenditures, revenues, deficits and debt: www.gpo.gov/fdsys/browse/collectionGPO.action?collectionCode=BUDGET
8. For tables on U.S. government's expenditures, revenues, deficits, and debt to download, go to: www.gpo.gov/fdsys/search/pagedetails.action?granuleId=&packageId=BUDGET- 2010-TAB.
9. Government fiscal information submitted by Congress: www.gpo.gov/fdsys/search/home.action
10. Marketable Treasury securities issued and outstanding: www.treasurydirect.gov/govt/reports/pd/pd_electreas.htm
11. Primary security dealers: www.newyorkfed.org/markets/pridealers_current.html
12. Treasury debt market, securities, prices, and other U.S. Treasury market information: http://investinginbonds.com/
13. FINRA:
    - Go to www.finra.org/index.htm, Sitemap, Market Data, and Bonds.
    - Click the "Treasury and Agency" tab, and then click "Advanced Bond Search" to find Treasury and Agency bonds with certain features.
14. Yahoo.com:
    - Go to http://finance.yahoo.com/bonds, click "Advanced Bond Screener," and Click "Treasury" or "Treasury Zero Coupon" (Treasury strips).
15. For U.S. security holding by foreigners, go to Treasury tic information: www.treas.gov/tic.
16. Historical interest rate data on Treasuries from the Federal Reserve:
    - www.federalreserve.gov/releases/h15/data.htm
    - FRED: www.research.stlouisfed.org/fred2

Agency

1. Federal National Mortgage Association (FNMA, Fannie Mae)
   - Home page: www.fanniemae.com/
   - Investments: www.fanniemae.com/investors/index.html
2. Federal Home Loan Mortgage Corporation (FHLMC, Freddie Mac)
   - Home page: www.freddiemac.com/
   - Debt securities: www.freddiemac.com/debt/
3. Federal Agriculture Mortgage Corporation (FAMC, Farmer Mac)
   - Home page: www.farmermac.com/
   - Debt securities: www.farmermac.com/investors/debtsecurities/index.aspx
4. Federal Home Loan Bank (FHLB)
   - Home page: www.fhlbanks.com/
   - Financial information: www.fhlb-of.com/specialinterest/financialframe2.html
5. Federal Farm Credit Bank System
   - Home page: www.farmcredit-ffcb.com/farmcredit/fcsystem/overview.jsp
6. Federal Farm Credit Funding Corporation
   - www.farmcredit-ffcb.com/farmcredit/index.jsp
7. Export-Import Bank
   - www.exim.gov/
8. Private Export Funding Corporation
   - www.nndb.com/company/895/000127514/
9. Small Business Administration
   - www.sba.gov/
10. Federal Housing Administration (FHA)
    - www.hud.gov/offices/hsg/fhahistory.cfm
11. Tennessee Valley Authority (TVA)
    - www.tva.gov/
12. Government National Mortgage Association (GNMA, Ginnie Mae)
    - Home page: www.ginniemae.gov/
    - Investors: www.ginniemae.gov/investors/investors.asp?Section=Investors
13. Federal Financing Bank
    - www.treas.gov/ffb/
14. Student Loan Marketing Association (SLMA, Sallie Mae)
    - Home page: www.salliemae.com/
    - Investors: www.salliemae.com/about/investors/
    - Debt securities: www.salliemae.com/about/investors/debtasset/default.htm
15. International Bank for Reconstruction and Development—World Bank
    - Home page: www.worldbank.org/
    - Debt securities: http://treasury.worldbank.org/cmd/htm/index.html

Municipals

1. Rating agencies
   - www.moodys.com

- www.standardandpoors.com
- http://reports.fitchratings.com

2. FINRA
   - Go to www.finra.org/index.htm, Sitemap, Market Data, and Bonds.
   - For a bond search, click the "Municipal" tab, and then click "Advanced Bond Search" to find municipal bonds with certain features.
3. *Wall Street Journal:* Go to http://online.wsj.com/public/us, Market Data, Bonds, Rates, and Credit Markets, and Tax-Exempt Bonds.
4. Yahoo.com: Go to http://finance.yahoo.com/bonds, click "Advanced Bond Screener" and Click Municipal tab, and then provide information for search
5. Investinginbonds.com: Go to http://investinginbonds.com/
6. Municipal Securities Rule Board (MSRB): www.msrb.org/msrb1
7. Electronic Municipal Market Access: http://emma.msrb.org/
8. For news and information links on municipals go to Muni Net Guide: www.muninetguide.com/categories/municipal-bond-documents-nrmsirs.php.
9. For information on state and local government fiscal conditions, go to Bureau of Economic Analysis go to www.bea.gov.
10. For information on state and local government finances, go to www.census.gov/govs/estimate/index.html or www.census.gov/govs/www/financegen.html.
8. Monoline insurers:
   - MBIA: www.mbia.com/
   - AMBAC: www.ambac.com/
   - FGIC: www.fgic.com/aboutfgic/

Sovereign Government Bonds

1. Global bonds: http://online.wsj.com/public/us
   - Click "Market Data" tab.
   - Click "Bond Rates" and "Credit Market."
   - Click "Global Government Bonds."
2. Brady debt and bonds: www.bradynet.com
3. Emerging markets: www.securities.com

Selected References

Bikchandani, S., and C. Huang. 1993. Auction with resale markets: An exploratory model of Treasury bill markets. *Review of Financial Studies* 2:311–339.

Cammack, E. 1991. "Evidence of bidding strategies and the information in Treasury-bill auctions. *Journal of Political Economy* 99:100–130.

Feldstein, S. G, F. J. Fabozzi, A. M. Grant, and P. M. Kennedy, 2005. *Handbook of Fixed Income Securities.* Editor: F. J. Fabozzi. New York: McGraw-Hill, 251-280.

Jegadeesh, N. 1993. Treasury auction bids and the Salomon squeeze. *Journal of Finance* 18:1403–1419.

Mishkin, F. S., and S. G. Eakins. 2002. *Financial markets and institutions*, 4th ed. Boston: Addison-Wesley.

Rose, P. S. 2003. *Money and capital markets.* New York: McGraw-Hill/Irwin.

Sorensen, B. E., and O. Yosha. 2001. Is state fiscal policy asymmetric over the business cycle? *Economic Review*, Federal Reserve Bank of Kansas City (Third Quarter):43–64.

Sundaresan, S. 1994. An empirical analysis of U.S. Treasury auctions: Implications for auction and term structure theories. *Journal of Fixed Income* 4:35–50.

Bloomberg Exercises

1. Find the features on T-bills, T-notes, and T-bonds recently issued at a Treasury auctions by going to the Bloomberg FIT screen: FIT <Enter>, click "T/ACT." To access the menu screen, enter CUSIP (or coupon rate and maturity) <Govt>. Screens on the menu you may want to consider include description (DES), dealer bid-ask quotes (ALLQ), and calculation of the yield on the security (YA).
2. Select a TIPS from the FIT screen and study its features: FIT <Enter>, click "TIPS." To access the menu screen, enter CUSIP (or coupon rate and maturity) <Govt>. Screens on the menu you may want to consider include description (DES), dealer bid-ask quotes (ALLQ), and calculation of the yield on the bill (YA). On the YA screen, change the inflation assumption and determine the yield based on the assumed inflation rate.
3. Select a Treasury STRIP from the FIT screen and study its features: FIT <Enter>, click "STRIP." To access the menu screen, enter CUSIP (or coupon rate and maturity) <Govt>. Screens on the menu you may want to consider include description (DES), dealer bid-ask quotes (ALLQ), and calculation of the yield on the strip (YA).
4. Using the SECF or FIT screen, select and evaluate several types of Treasury and agency securities using the functions on the security's menu screen (DES, ALLQ, YA, HDS, and CSHF [payment schedule]). Types of securities to possibly select: U.S. currents, U.S. STRIPS, U.S. bonds, active agencies, and foreign government bonds (e.g., Greece—Government Bonds).
5. Select a recently issued T-note (e.g., 5-year to 10-year) from the SECF or FIT screen. On the menu screen for the selected note, use the SP function (strip analysis) to see how the bond could be stripped into interest-only and principal-only strips.
6. Study the features from the description screens (DES) of some of the following GSEs:
   - Federal Home Loan Mortgage Corporation: FHLMC <Corp> <Enter>
   - Federal National Mortgage Association: FNMA <Corp> <Enter>
   - Federal Home Loan Bank System: FHLB <Corp> <Enter>
   - Federal Agriculture Mortgage Association: FAMCA <Corp> <Enter>
   - Federal Farm Credit Bank: FFCB <Corp> <Enter>
   - Tennessee Valley Authority: TVA <Corp> <Enter>
   - World Bank (International Bank for Reconstruction and Development): IBRD <Corp> <Enter>
   - Student Loan Marketing Association: SLMA <Corp> <Enter>
7. The 2008 financial crisis led to the American Recovery and Reinvestment Act and the Emergency Economic Stabilization Act, Troubled Asset Relief Program (TARP), and Total Asset-Backed Security Asset Loan Facility (TALF). Review these and other programs by going to the following Bloomberg screens:
   a. TARP: <Enter> TARP Program
   b. TALF: <Enter> TALF Program

c. STRS: <Enter> Stress Test Overviews
d. GGRP: <Enter> Government Relief Programs
e. RESQ: <Enter> Bailout and Rescue Menu

8. Changes in U.S. government debt depend on the federal government expenditures and revenues. Information on the U.S. government's expenditures, revenues, and deficits can be found on the ECOF screen ("Budget" tab). Examine and comment on the number of budget deficits that have occurred over the past 20 years. Comment on the deficit increases after 2008. Data series to consider: U.S. Treasury federal budget yearly summary deficit or surplus, net outlays, revenues, types of revenues, types of expenditures, and deficits as a percentage of GDP.
9. Determine the growth in the government's debt over the past 20 years by going to the ECOF screen ("Debt" tab). Data series to consider: U.S. total public debt outstanding, U.S. debt as a percentage of GDP, and U.S. total public debt outstanding total nonmarketable.
10. Information on current and recent Treasury auctions can be found on ECO20. <Enter>. Use ECO 20 to find details about purchases and sales of recent or proposed issues.
11. Find municipals for a particular state by going to MUNI: MUNI <Enter>. Using the tabs, select municipals with certain features (coupon, maturity, structure, and issued). Study several of the bonds using the functions on the bond's menu screen.
12. Use MSRC to search for bonds for the following types of bonds:
    a. Insured general obligations (select from "Industry" tab) in a state or particular region (e.g., Northeast). You may want to narrow the search by limiting the search by maturity and coupon type.
    b. Specific revenue bond (select from "Industry" tab: Airport, assisted living, Community Development, etc., or select from "Sources & Uses" tab) in a particular region (e.g., Northeast). You may want to narrow the search by limiting the search by maturity and coupon type.

    Study several of the bonds from each search using the functions on the bond's menus screen (CUSIP <MUNI>. Functions to include: DES, CF (official statement or annual report), TDH (trades), SER (bond serial information), and FA (financial analysis).
13. Use PICK to post and monitor new or secondary municipal bonds. Create a custom bulletin board of offerings/trades that match your investment strategies (e.g., municipal water authorities in a given state or region). Select one of the bonds from the PICK search and study it using the functions on the bond's menu screen (CUSIP <MUNI>. Functions to include: DES, CF (official statement or annual report), FA, and TDH (trades).
14. Do a relative comparison of states using SMUN and DEMS screen:
    - SMUN <Enter>: Compare financial conditions by using SMUN. On SMUN select "All States" from "States" tab and several templates from the "Types" tab (e.g., General, Pension, Government, or All Types). Comment on any state whose financials or changes in financial are significantly different, indicating a red flag.

- DEMS <Enter>: Do a relative analysis of state demographics.

15. On the SMUN screen, click a state of interest to bring up a menu and state identification number (e.g., STOCA1 for California). Study the economic and financial conditions of the state by going to its menu page (e.g., Stoca1 <Equity>). Screens to consider: BLS (Employment), FA SS (financial overview), and FA (on "Funds" tab you can look at pensions, general, and government financials).
16. Use the BAB screen to search for Taxable Build America Bonds issued in a particular state. Select one of the bonds from the BAB search and study it using the functions on the bond's menus screen (CUSIP <MUNI>). Functions to include: DES, CF (official statement or annual report), TDH, FA, and SER.
17. Official statements are important sources of information on a municipal issue. Review the "official statement" on a municipal bond.
18. Taxable municipals are attractive investments for tax-exempt investors. Search for some of these issues by going to MSRC. On the MSRC search screen, select "Federally Taxable" in the "Tax Provision" tab. You may want to narrow the search by limiting the search by maturity and coupon type. Use the PICK screen to customize a search for new and existing taxable municipals to possibly monitor.
19. Bloomberg provides a review of conditions and trends in the municipal bond market in their "Municipal Market" newsletter. Review recent trends in the municipal market reported in the newsletter. To access: BRIEF <Enter>.
20. Use the Advanced News Search TNI to customize a news search for the following:
    - Municipals in a certain area
    - Sovereign in a distress country
21. Compare the yields on bonds of different maturities (e.g., 5 years and 10 years) for an advanced country using the DMMV screen.
22. Click one of the foreign government bonds of interest from the DMMV screen to find its identification number. Evaluate that bond by using the functions (DES, ALLQ, HDS, and CRVD) on its menu screen: Identification Number <Govt>. Study the country's economic and financial conditions using information from the ECOF and ECST screens.
23. Compare the yields on the bonds of different maturities (e.g., 5 years and 10 years) for a developing country using the EMMV screen.
24. Click one of the foreign government bonds of interest from the EMMV screen to find its identification number. Evaluate that bond by using the functions (DES, ALLQ, HDS, and CRVD) on its menu screen: Identification Number <Govt>. Study the country's economic and financial conditions using information from the ECOF and ECST screens.
25. Study the credit ratings of different countries using the CSDR screen: CSDR <Enter>.

Notes

1. The actual number varies depending on how funding authorities are counted and how long they exist. Bloomberg, for example, estimates the total number to be closer to 60,000. Whether 60,000 or 80,000, the number is still impressive.
2. There was a threat of default in 1996 due to a political debate over the budget between President Clinton and the U.S. Congress. The debate led to a temporary impasse in which Congress refused to approve a spending program. In 2011 and 2012, there were similar debates between President Obama and the Congress over the budget.
3. Marketable securities are sometimes classified as fixed-principal securities (T-bills, T-notes, and T-bonds) and inflation-indexed securities (TIPS).
4. The Treasury also sells *tax-anticipation bills* to corporations four times a year. The bills mature one week after a corporate tax payment is due. They are used to pay corporate taxes.
5. In the secondary market, T-bills are typically quoted two decimal places and three decimal places for more active issues.
6. When auctioned, Treasury bids are quotes on a yield basis. The coupon rate, though, is not set until the auction is completed.
7. The inflation index used is the nonseasonally adjusted all items consumer price index for all urban consumers (CPI-U).
8. At one point, the U.S. Treasury was not a supporter of strips because of their lower tax liability.
9. In 1991, Salomon Brothers was charged with trying to corner the Treasury note market. In cornering the Treasury market, Salomon Smith-Barney would purchase the permitted 35 percent maximum of an issue in its own name by submitting a high bid. They would then buy additional securities in the name of its customers without their knowledge and subsequently would buy them from the customers. From these acquisitions Salomon Smith-Barney was able to successfully corner the market, enabling them to sell their holdings at a monopoly premium. In one of the February 1991 auctions, they were awarded 57 percent of the issue, and in a May 1991 auction, they were able to attain 94 percent of the market. Following this scandal, the Treasury enacted new rules to ensure competitiveness in the Treasury auction market. For more information, see the *Joint Report on the Government Securities Market,* Department of Treasury and the Board of Governors of the Federal Reserve System, January 1992.
10. Dealers give government security brokers their bid or offer price. The brokers then display the highest bid and lowest offer through a computer network tied to trading desks of dealers.
11. Another important use of repurchase agreements is by depository institutions as a way to finance their federal funds position. Federal funds are deposits of banks and deposit institutions with the Federal Reserve that are used to maintain the bank's reserve position required to support their deposits. Banks maintain federal funds desks where they manage their federal funds positions: borrowing funds when they are deficient and lending funds when they have an excess amount of reserves. Two common ways depository institutions finance a deficient reserve positions are through the federal funds market and the repo market. The federal funds market is a market in which depository institutions with excess reserves lend to institutions that are deficient. Federal funds market loans over typically overnight to one week, unsecured, and traded directly between the lending bank (usually a small regional bank) and the borrowing bank (often a money center bank). This contrasts with the repo loan that is secured and often offered by dealers making a market.

The repo market also includes the Federal Reserve as one of its participants. In addition to its open market operations, the Federal Reserve uses the repo market to influence interest rates. To lower rates, they will buy Treasuries in the repo market (a reverse repo agreement) to inject money into the financial markets; this action is called a system repo. To increase rates, the Federal Reserve will sell Treasuries (enter repo agreements) via the repo market to contract money from the financial markets; this action is called a customer repo.

12. In 2009, the total expenditure for all state and local governments was approximately $3 trillion. The major expenditures were allocated to education (29 percent) and social services (14 percent), with the remainder being spread among a variety of state and local government expenditures: transportation, correction facilities, police and fire protection, public safety, environmental cleanup, interest on debt, and public employee pension. The total revenue generated in 2009 by all state and local governments to support these expenditures was approximately $3 trillion. The major sources for this revenue came from taxes on sales, property, individual income, corporations, and other sources such as user fees and lotteries and federal government transfers (see U.S. Census Bureau: www2.census.gov/govs/estimate/0700ussl_1.txt).
13. It should be noted that the tax code governing tax-exempt securities is quite complex. For example, consider a municipal bond purchased at a discount from its par at the initial offering, referred to as an *original-issue discount bond* (OID). An investor, who buys an OID and holds it to maturity, can treat the difference between the issue price and the par value as tax-exempt interest. If the bondholder subsequently sells the OIB before maturity, any increase in its price up to its par value is generally considered interest income and is tax exempt, whereas any increase above the par value is considered a capital gain and is taxable. For an investor who buys an OIB in the secondary market, though, the tax treatment depends on the purchase price relative to what the IRS defines as the market discount cutoff price (the price defining the allowable discount) and the revised issue price (price reflecting the price change over time that must be accreting). Another factor investors need to consider in determining tax liabilities is whether they leveraged the investment. In general, the interest expense on funds borrowed to purchase securities is tax deductible, except when the funds are used to purchase or carry tax-exempt securities. At one point, banks were exempt from this rule and were allowed to deduct all interest expense; later they were allowed to deduct 85 percent of the interest expense; finally, in 1986, their interest deductibility for financing tax-exempt bonds was eliminated unless the issue was a bank-qualified issue (generally this is tax-exempt bonds by small issuers and purchased for an investment portfolio). In addition to defining tax-exempt interest and deductibility of interest expenses, there are other tax considerations individual and institutional investors need to consider, such as the adjustments for specified tax preferences that some taxpayers are allowed. Finally, there are different state and local tax treatments that can also be complex. For a discussion of the tax provisions affecting municipals, see Feldstein et. al., (2005).
14. The Deficit Reduction Act of 1984 places a limit of $40 million on small IDB issues, prohibits certain capital projects from IDB funding, and restricted the total amount of IDBs that can be issued by a state based on its population.
15. A moral obligation bond is classified as an appropriation-backed bond. It represents a nonbinding pledge to approve appropriations and is considered a credit enhancement. In contrast, municipalities do issue credit-enhanced bonds that are legally binding. Such bonds often take the form of an obligation to withhold and/or provide government aid

to pay any defaulted debt issue. For example, a state might provide this type of public credit enhance to debt securities issued by one of the state's school systems, with the state standing ready to cover shortfalls in the case of default. Often, with this type of guarantee, there is a provision that the state would withhold some state aid earmarked to the school system's municipality.

16. I-Deal and Ipreo are companies offering platforms for negotiating bond sales and providing a muni auction platform.
17. Information on upcoming bonds can also be found in the *Bond Buyer*. The *Bond Buyer* is the trade publication of the municipal bond industry. The book or online subscription to its web site provides information on futures bond sales and the results from recent sales. Trade information and recent issues can also be found from *Muni Net Guide:* www.muninetguide.com/categories/municipal-bond-documents-nrmsirs.php.

    In 2007, the SEC designated four firms as Nationally Recognized Municipal Securities Information Repositories (NRMSIRs) to improve the disclosure of municipal bond information. Through NRMSIRs, these firms provide "official statements" and other information from municipal issuers (see Electronic Municipal Market Access: http://emma.msrb.org/).
18. Although there was some variation, the basic Brady plan offered creditor banks two choices for the nonperforming loans of emerging countries they were carrying: (1) a discount bond issued below par (e.g., 50 percent or 65 percent of par) in exchange for the original loan or a discount bond paying a floating rate tied to the LIBOR in exchange for fewer bonds than the original loan; (2) a bond issued at par and paying a below-market coupon in exchange for the original face value of the loan. All Brady bonds were callable and some gave bondholders a "value recovery" option, giving them the right to recover some of the debt if certain events occurred such as an increase in gross domestic product or energy prices.
19. *Aztec bonds* preceded the Mexican Brady bonds. These bonds were created in 1988 to redress J. P. Morgan's nonperforming loans to Mexico. J. P. Morgan accepted 30 percent reduction in the face value amount of its loan in return for a floating rate tied to LIBOR + 1.625 percent. The bonds were paid off eight years after they were issued.

CHAPTER 9

Intermediary Debt Securities, Investment Funds, and Markets

Introduction

The intermediary financial market consists of commercial banks, savings and loans, insurance companies, investment funds, and other financial intermediaries. These intermediaries sell financial claims to investors, and then use the proceeds to purchase debt and equity claims or to provide direct loans. Commercial banks, for example, obtain funds from investors by providing deposits and money market accounts, selling securities, and borrowing and then using these funds to provide loans and make investments. Life insurance companies, pensions, trust funds, and investment funds offer financial instruments in the form of insurance policies, retirement plans, and shares in stock or bond portfolios. The proceeds from their premiums, savings plans, and fund shares are used by these institutions to buy stocks, corporate bonds, Treasury securities, and other debt instruments, as well as provide corporate, residential, and commercial loans. A major segment of the intermediary market is the market for the intermediary shares created by investment funds. These funds offer financial instruments in the form of shares in portfolios. The proceeds from their fund shares are used by these institutions to buy the stocks, corporate bonds, Treasury securities, and other debt instruments that comprise the portfolios.

In general, financial institutions, by acting as intermediaries, control a large share of the economy's savings and investments and thus have a significant impact on financial markets. For borrowers, intermediaries are an important source of funds; they buy many of the securities issued by corporations and governments and provide many of the direct loans. For investors, intermediaries create a number of securities for them to include in their portfolios. These include negotiable certificates of deposit, bankers' acceptances, mortgage- and asset-backed instruments, investment fund shares, annuities, and guaranteed investment contracts. In this chapter, we examine the types and markets for investment funds and intermediary securities.

Commercial Banks: Intermediary Securities

Commercial banks obtain funds from investors by providing demand deposits and money market accounts, selling certificates of deposit, and bank bonds, and borrowing from other banks. They, in turn, use their funds to satisfy legal reserve requirements, to make loans, and to purchase financial securities. They also are major players in securitization, creating and acting as conduits on MBS and asset-backed security issues. They also issue equipment-trust bonds to finance equipment they lease, act as commercial paper dealers, create large syndicated loans, manage pensions, create retirement securities, buy and sell currency, and maintain active trading desk where they take positions in repurchase agreements, borrow or lend federal funds, and maintain short-term money market position. For investors, there are a number of securities that banks offer: certificate of deposit, bank notes, leverage loans, syndicated loans, and bankers' acceptances. Banks also provides securities and loans through their foreign subsidiary banks that are part of the Eurocurrency market.

Negotiable Certificates of Deposit

A certificate of deposit (CD) is a certificate issued by a financial institution certifying that a specified sum of funds has been deposited at the issuing depository's institution. Banks and thrift institutions offer CDs to finance their loans and investments. The CD has a specified maturity date and interest rate, and it can be either nonnegotiable or negotiable. Nonnegotiable CDs are deposits that cannot be transferable and typically must be held to maturity, with often a penalty applied for early withdrawal. They can be issued in any denomination. Negotiable CDs are higher denomination certificates typically issued to institutions. Unlike nonnegotiable CDs, negotiable CDs can be sold to other investors in the secondary CD market (see Exhibit 9.1 for a brief history of the secondary CD market and its significance).

Negotiable CDs are one of the more popular money market instruments for institutional investors. The maturities on negotiable CDs generally range from 3 to 18 months, although most have original maturities of 6 months or less. CDs issued with maturities greater than one year are called *term CDs*. CDs are interest-bearing notes, usually sold at their face value, with the principal and interest paid at maturity if the CD is less than one year and semiannually if it is a term CD. The minimum denomination on negotiable CDs is \$100,000, with the average denomination being

EXHIBIT 9.1 History of the Secondary CD Market

Prior to 1961, commercial banks lacked an effective instrument to compete for the temporary excess cash funds of corporations and state and local governments. At that time, there was no interest paid on demand deposits, and corporations were reluctant to tie their funds up in nonnegotiable CDs. Also with the rates paid on time deposits fixed by the Federal Reserve's Regulation Q, sometimes at a level below T-bill rates, banks had no security to offer corporations. Consequently, corporations tended to opt for T-bills instead of bank deposits when they invested their excess funds.

The solution to the problem for banks came in 1961 when First Bank of New York (now Citigroup) issued a negotiable CD, accompanied by an announcement by First Boston Corporation and Salomon Brothers that they would stand ready to buy and sell the CDs. Thus, the first secondary market for CDs was born. Moreover, what the secondary market provided was a way for banks to circumvent Regulation Q and offer investors rates competitive with T-bills and CP. To do this, the yield curve needed to be positively sloped and remain that way for the foreseeable future. With Regulation Q setting higher maximum rates on longer term CDs and the Fed rarely changing the maximum rate these conditions were met. The existence of a secondary market meant that an investor could earn a rate higher than both the shorter or longer term CD, by buying the longer term CD and selling it later in the secondary market at a higher price associated with the short-term maturity. For example, if six-month CDs yielded 5% ($P = 100/(1.05)^{.5} = 97.59$) and a 1-year CD yielded 6% ($P = 100/1.06 = 94.3396$), then an investor could buy the 1-year CD for 94.3396, hold it for six months, and sell it for 97.59 (given the yield curve did not change) to realized an annualized yield of 7% (= $(97.59/94.3396)^{1/.5} - 1$). Thus, to recapitulate, the significance of the secondary market for CDs was that it provided a way for banks to increase their CD yields to customers without violating Regulation Q.

Following First Bank of New York, Salomon Brothers, and First Boston's lead, other banks, brokers, and dealers quickly entered into the market for negotiable CDs.

$1 million; there are also *jumbo CDs* with face values of $10 million or more. Like other bank and savings and loan deposits, the Federal Deposit Insurance Corporation (FDIC) insures CDs up to $100,000 against default. Most negotiable CDs, though, have denominations exceeding $100,000 and are therefore subject to default risk. The yields on CDs generally reflect the risk of the issuing financial institution and the maturity of the CD. CD yields tend to exceed the rates on Treasury and short-term federal agency instruments. Also, the yields for the CDs of larger (supposedly more secured) banks (called *prime CDs*) tend to be lower than those of smaller banks (called *nonprime CDs*).

Today, dealers and brokers form the core of the primary and secondary markets for negotiable CDs, selling new CDs and trading and maintaining inventories in existing ones. Money-market funds, banks, bank trust departments, state and local governments, foreign governments, central banks, and corporations are the major investors in CDs. Since many of these investors hold their CDs until maturity, the secondary market for these instruments is not as active as the secondary T-bill market. There are three types of CDs: domestic, foreign, and Eurodollar. From a U.S. investor's perspective, domestic CDs are those issued by U.S. banks, whereas foreign CDs are dollar-denominated CD issued by foreign banks through their U.S. branches; they are often referred to as *Yankee CDs*. Eurodollar CDs, in turn, are dollar-denominated

CDs issued by foreign branches of banks from the United States, Europe, and Japan that are incorporated in countries with favorable banking laws. The yields on dollar-denominated Eurodollar CDs are higher than the yields on domestic CDs. This is because foreign subsidiary banks issuing the CDs are incorporated in countries with favorable banking laws such as low- or zero-reserve requirements.[1]

Bank Notes

In addition to CDs, commercial banks also issue *bank notes*. Bank notes are similar to medium-term notes (MTNs). They are sold as a program consisting of a number of notes with different maturities, typically ranging from one to five years, and offered either continuously or intermittently. Bank notes are usually sold to institutions in high denominations ranging from $5 million to $25 million, with the total offering ranging from $50 million to $1 billion. Different from corporate MTNs discussed in Chapter 7, bank notes are not registered with the Securities and Exchange Commission (SEC) unless it is the bank's holding company (and not the individual bank) issuing the MTN. Banks also sell banker notes and MTNs through international syndicates as part of the Eurocapital market (see Exhibit 9.2 for Bloomberg descriptions of bank securities such as bank notes and MTNs).

EXHIBIT 9.2 Examples of Bank Securities

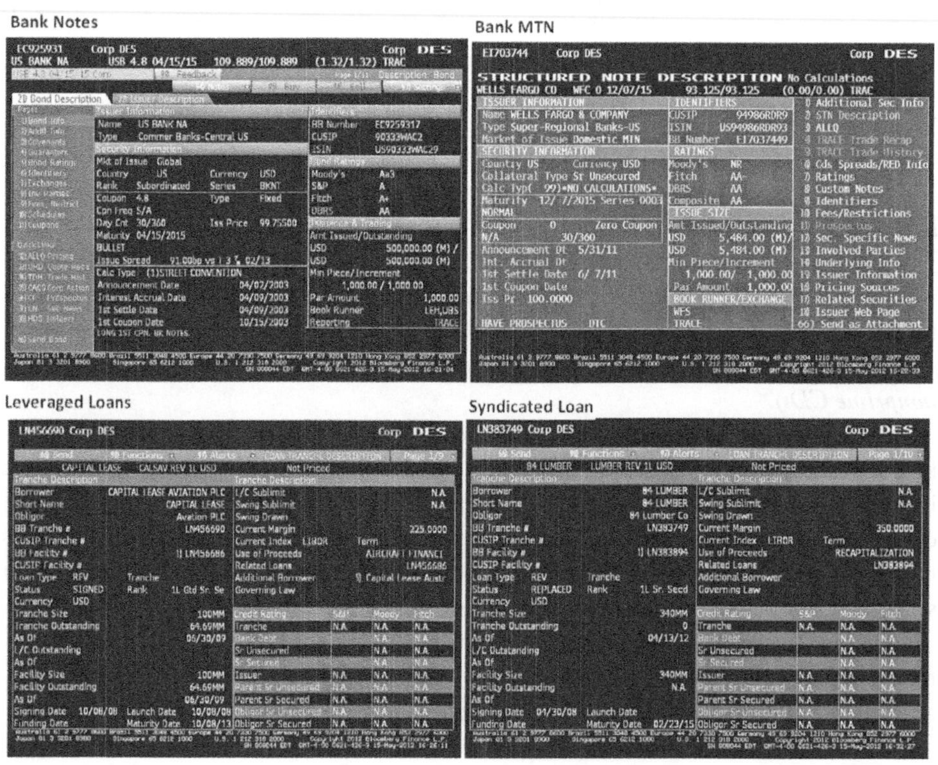

Leveraged Loans

Commercial bank loans can be classified as investment-grade loans and leveraged loans. *Investment-grade loans* are loans to borrowers with investment-grade ratings. They usually take the form of a revolving line of credit, with no maturity and with the bank setting a maximum amount that the company can borrow. Investment-grade loans set up as a line of credit are generally held by the originating bank and not sold. *Leveraged loans* are loans to corporations with below investment-grade ratings. These loans usually have a maturity and a floating rate, and in contrast to investment-grade bonds, they are often sold to institutional investors. Some of these loans are packaged and securitized as collateralized debt obligations (discussed later in this chapter).

Today, leveraged bank loans and some investment-grade loans with specific maturities are traded in the secondary markets or securitized to create a collateralized loan obligation. To institutional investors, leverage loans represent an alternative to high-yield bonds. In contrast to high-yield bonds, leveraged loans are typically characterized by a floating-rate structure, shorter original maturities (5 years on average compared to 10 years on high-yield bonds), no call provisions, a senior claim within the corporation's capital structure, more loan covenants, and higher recovery rates (see Exhibit 9.2).

Syndicated Loans

Banks often form a syndicate to provide loans to borrowers who seek large amounts of funds. The resulting syndicated loan serves to spread the credit risk among the participating banks. The loans created usually have a senior claim with a priority position over subordinated lenders and bondholders, the terms to maturity are usually fixed, the loans often pays a floating rate, and depending on the use of the funds, the syndicated loan can be either an amortized or a bullet loan. Like leveraged loans, there is also a secondary market for syndicated loans. This market is usually characterized by loan sales by the banks in the syndicate. Often, banks in the group have the right to sell their parts of the loan to other banks by either assignment or participation. With assignment, the seller transfers all right to the new holder, whereas with participation, the new holder does not become a party to the loan agreement but instead has a relation with the seller (see Exhibit 9.2).[2]

Bankers' Acceptances

Bankers' acceptances (*BAs*) are time drafts (postdated checks) guaranteed by a bank—guaranteed postdated checks. The guarantee of the bank improves the credit quality of the draft, making it marketable. BAs are used to finance the purchase of goods that have to be transferred from a seller to the buyer. They are often created in international business transactions where finished goods or commodities have to be shipped (see Exhibit 9.3 for an example of how BAs are created).

EXHIBIT 9.3 The Creation of Bankers' Acceptances—Example

To see how BAs originate, consider the case of a U.S. oil refinery that wants to import 50,000 barrels of crude oil at $100 per barrel ($5 million) from an oil producer in South America. Suppose the South American oil exporter wants to be paid before shipping, while the U.S. importer wants the crude oil before payment. To facilitate the transaction, suppose they agree to finance the sale with a BA in which the U.S. importer's banks will guarantee a $5 million payment 60 days from the shipment date. With this understanding, the U.S. oil importer would obtain a letter of credit (LOC) from his bank. The LOC would say that the bank would pay the exporter $5 million if the U.S. importer failed to do so. The LOC would then be sent by the U.S. bank to the South American bank of the exporter. Upon receipt of the LOC, the South American bank would notify the oil exporter who would then ship the 50,000 barrels of crude oil. The oil exporter would then present the shipping documents to the South American bank and receive the present value of $5 million in local currency from the bank. The South American bank would then present a time draft to the U.S. bank who would stamp 'accepted' on it, thus creating the BA. The U.S. importer would sign the note and receive the shipping documents. At this point, the South American bank is the holder of the BA. The bank can hold the BA as an investment or sell it to the American bank at a price equal to the present value of $5 million. If the South American bank opts for the latter, then the U.S. bank holds the BA and can either retain it or sell it to an investor such as a money market fund or to a bankers' acceptance dealer. If all goes well, at maturity the oil importer will present the shipping documents to the shipping company to obtain his 50,000 barrels of crude oil, as well as deposit the $5 million funds in his bank; whoever is holding the BA on the due date will present it to the U.S. importer's bank to be paid.

The use of BAs to finance transactions is known as *acceptance financing* and banks that create BAs are referred to as *accepting banks*. In the United States, the major accepting banks are the money center banks such as Citicorp and Bank of America, as well as some large regional banks. Many of the large Japanese banks have also been active in creating BAs. In the secondary market, BAs are traded as zero-coupon bonds, with the face value equal to the payment order and with the maturity between 30 and 270 days. With the bank guarantee, they are considered prime-quality instruments with relatively low yields. The secondary market trading of BAs takes place principally among banks and dealers. There are approximately 20 dealers who facilitate trading in the secondary market. The major dealers include the major investment banking firms and money center banks. Money market funds, banks, institutional investors, nonfinancial corporations, and municipal governments are the primary purchasers of BAs. The Federal Reserve also buys and sells BAs as part of their open market operations, and commercial banks use BAs as collateral for Federal Reserve loans.[3]

Eurocurrency Market

The *Eurocurrency market* is the money market equivalent of the Eurobond market. It is a market in which funds are intermediated (deposited or loaned) outside the country of the currency in which the funds are denominated. For example, a certificate of deposit denominated in dollars offered by a subsidiary of a U.S. bank incorporated in the Bahamas is a Eurodollar CD. Similarly, a loan made in yens from a bank located in the United States would be an American-yen loan. In both cases, the Eurodollar deposit and the American-yen loan represent intermediation occurring in the Eurocurrency market. Even though the intermediation occurs in many cases outside Europe, the Euro prefix usually remains. An exception is the Asian dollar market. This market includes banks in Asia that accept deposits and make loans in foreign currency; this market is sometimes referred to separately as the Asian dollar market.

Today the total amount of Eurocurrency deposits is estimated to be in excess of $3 trillion. The actual size of the market, though, is difficult to determine because of the lack of regulation and disclosure. By most accounts, though, it is one of the largest financial markets. The underlying reason for this is that Eurocurrency loan and deposit rates are often better than the rates on similar domestic loans and deposits because of the differences that exist in banking and security laws among countries. Foreign lending or borrowing, regardless of what currency it is denominated in and what country the lender or borrower is from, is subject to the rules, laws, and customs of the foreign country where the deposits or loans are made. Thus, a U.S. bank offering a CD through its foreign subsidiary located in the Bahamas (maybe in the form of a P.O. box) would be subject to the Bahamian laws with respect to reserve requirements, taxes on deposits, anonymity of the depositor, and the like. Accordingly, if a country's banking laws are less restrictive, then it is possible for a foreign bank or a foreign subsidiary of a bank to offer more favorable rates on its loans and deposits than it could in its own country by simply intermediating the deposits and loans in that country.[4] Thus, the absence of reserve requirements or regulations on rates paid on deposits in the Bahamas, for example, makes it possible for the rates on Bahamian Eurodollar loans to be lower than U.S. bank loans and the rates on their deposits to be higher.

Currently, the Eurocurrency market consists of a number of large banks (referred to as Eurobanks), corporations, and governments. For large investors, the market offers two types of instruments: Eurocurrency CDs and primary deposits. As noted previously, because of favorable regulations in the offshore centers, the rates on the CDs are usually higher than comparable domestic CDs. The maturities on Eurocurrency CDs range from one day to several years, with the most common maturities being 1, 3, 6, and 12 months. For longer-term CDs, the rates can be either fixed or variable. Eurocurrency CDs can also take the form of *tap CDs;* these are CDs issued in single amounts to finance a specific Eurodollar loan. Also there exist the *tranche CDs,* which are of a smaller denomination ($10,000), often offered to the public through a broker or an underwriter.

Primary deposits are time deposits with negotiated rates and short-term maturities. Once deposited, these deposits, in turn, are often sold and bought as part of the Eurocurrency's interbank deposit network. In the interbank market, many deposits are bought by large Eurobanks who use the proceeds to make large short-term loans (see Exhibit 9.4 for an example of the Eurocurrency interbank market). The rates paid on funds purchased by large London Eurobanks in the interbank market is called the *London Interbank Bid Rate* (LIBID), whereas the rate on funds offered for sale by London Eurobanks is the *London Interbank Offered Rate* (LIBOR). The average LIBOR among London Eurobanks is a rate commonly used to set the rate on bank loans, deposits, and floating-rate notes and loans. The LIBOR can vary from overnight rates to 30-day ones. There are also similar rates

EXHIBIT 9.4 The Eurocurrency Interbank Market

Suppose the ABC Company of Cincinnati wanted to invest $20 million excess cash from its operations for 30 days in the Nassau branch of the Midwest Bank of Cincinnati. To initiate this, the treasurer of ABC would call Midwest Bank's Eurocurrency trader in Cincinnati to get a quote on its Nassau bank's 30-day deposit rate. (Note, the Nassau branch of the Midwest bank is likely to be staffed in Cincinnati, with its physical presence in Nassau being nothing more than the Nassau incorporation papers and other documents in a lawyer's office.) The treasurer would give ABC a quote based on similar Eurocurrency rates. If acceptable, a 30-day Eurocurrency deposit would be created with ABC transferring its cash account to Midwest Bank who would set up the Nassau account by recording it in its Nassau books in Cincinnati. Now unless the bank has an immediate need for the $2 million, the trader would invest the funds through the interbank market. This might involve selling the deposit to a London Eurobank who might be arranging a 30-day, $100 million loan to a Japanese company to finance its inventory of computer equipment purchased in New York. If Midwest and the Eurobank agree, then Midwest would transfer the $20 million Eurodollar deposit to the London Eurobank.

for other currencies (e.g., Sterling LIBOR) and areas (e.g., Paris Interbank Offered Rate, PIBOR, or the Singapore Interbank Offered Rate, SIBOR).

In addition to being an important source of funds for banks, the Eurocurrency market is also an important funding source for corporations and governments. The loans to corporations and governments can be either short or intermediate term, ranging in maturity from overnight to 10 years. The loans with maturities of over one year are sometimes called Eurocredit loans. Since euro deposits are short term, Eurobanks often offer Eurocredits with a floating rate tied to the LIBOR. Eurocurrency loans also vary in terms of some of their other features: many take the form of lines of credit (LOCs); some require an LOC, instead of detailed covenants; loans can be either fixed or floating; loans can be in different currencies and have different currency clauses; many of the larger loans are provided by a syndicate of Eurobanks.

BLOOMBERG BANK SECURITY INFORMATION

MMR <Enter>: Money Market Rates

PGM <Enter>, Money Market Lookup Program: PGM <Enter>: Click security type (e.g., Bank Note); select bank.

Bank Ticker <Corp> <Enter>: List of bank notes, CDs, and MTNs.

MSCH <Enter>, Money Market Search: Search can be used to find bank and money market programs: CDs, BAs, Bank Notes, and the like.

LSRC <Enter>: Search for loans, including leveraged loans.

SECF <Enter>, FI tab and Loans Tab**:** Loans look-up and screener.

LOAN: Screen provides search and analysis of syndicated loans.

PREL <Enter>: Loan pipeline.

LONZ <Enter>: Loan homepage.

SRCH <Enter>, Custom Bond Search: Use search to find leveraged loans, syndicated loans, and bank notes.

LTOP <Enter>, Click "Syndicated Loans," click "U.S. Loans" and "U.S. Leveraged Loans": provides rankings and information on deals:

BBAM <Enter>: Information on LIBOR

BTMM <Enter>: Money market rate, including LIBOR

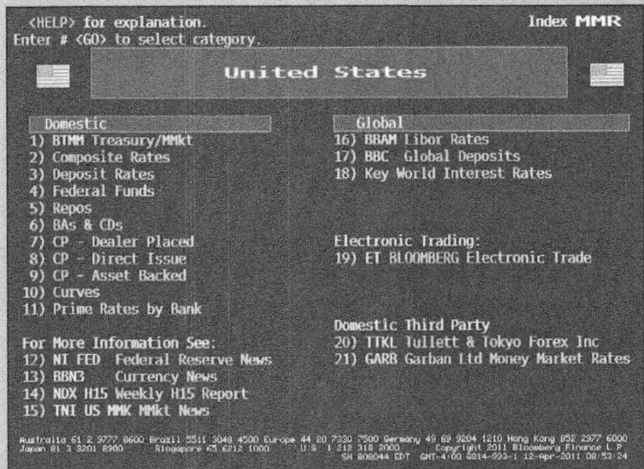

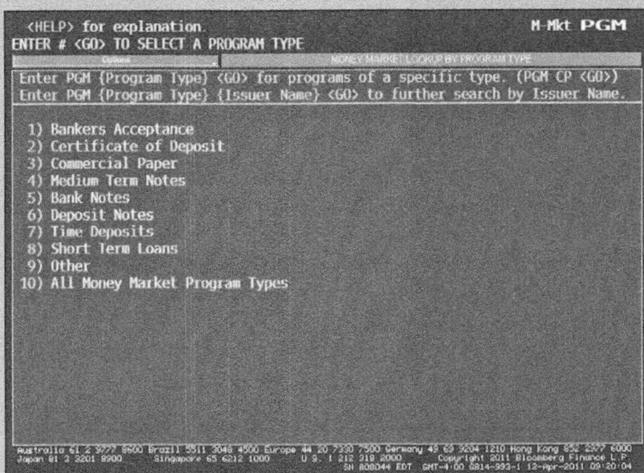

<HELP> for explanation.
1<GO> for results.
Corp LSRC
Source
Common Criteria
51) Type 52) Rank 53) Borrower 54) Currency 55) Tranche Size
56) Use of Proceeds 57) Industry 58) Agent/Participant 59) Leveraged 60) Amended
61) Country of Domicil 62) Country of Risk 63) Maturity Date 64) Signing Date 65) Current Margin
66) Price 67) Yield
71) Currency Conversion not selected
Loan Universe 177754
11) Issue Status: Live 80216
12) Agent (Syndication Agent Include, Most Recent): Wells Fargo Bank NA, US 528
91) Build/Edit Search

(*Continued*)

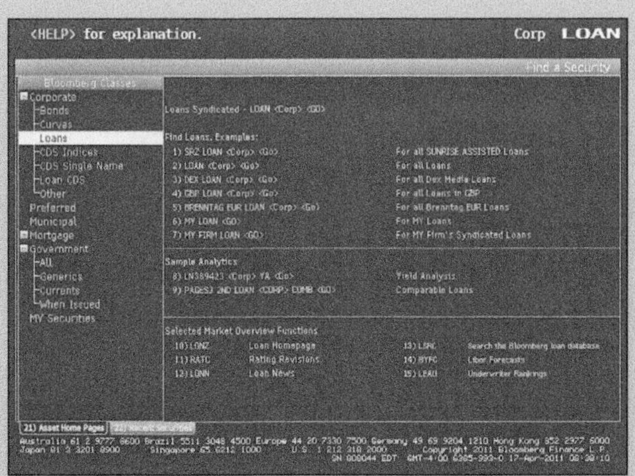
<HELP> for explanation.
Corp LOAN
Find a Security
Corporate
Bonds
Curves
Loans
CDS Indices
CDS Single Name
Loan CDS
Other
Preferred
Municipal
Mortgage
Government
All
Generics
Currents
When Issued
MY Securities
Loans Syndicated - LOAN <Corp> <GO>
Find Loans. Examples:
2) LOAN <Corp> <Go>
For all Loans
Sample Analytics
Yield Analysis
Comparable Loans
Selected Market Overview Functions
Loan Homepage
Rating Revisions
Loan News
21) Asset Home Pages

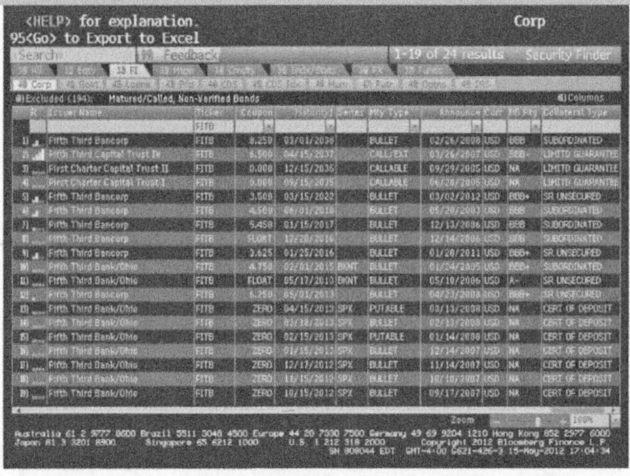
<HELP> for explanation.
95<Go> to Export to Excel
Corp
Feedback
1-19 of 24 results
Security Finder
Matured/Called, Non-Verified Bonds
Columns
Fifth Third Bancorp
Fifth Third Capital Trust IV
First Charter Capital Trust II
Fifth Third Bank/Ohio
SUBORDINATED
LIMITD GUARANTEE
SR UNSECURED
CERT OF DEPOSIT
BULLET
CALLABLE
PUTABLE

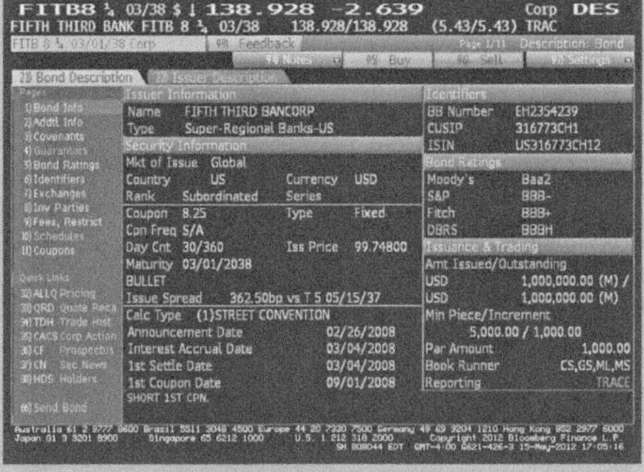
FITB8 ¼ 03/38 $ ↓ 138.928 -2.639 Corp DES
FIFTH THIRD BANK FITB 8 ¼ 03/38 138.928/138.928 (5.43/5.43) TRAC
Feedback
Description: Bond
Notes
Buy
Sell
Settings
1) Bond Description
2) Issuer Description
1) Bond Info
2) Addtl Info
3) Covenants
4) Guarantors
5) Bond Ratings
6) Identifiers
7) Exchanges
8) Inv Parties
9) Fees, Restrict
10) Schedules
11) Coupons
Quick Links
32) ALLQ Pricing
33) QRD Quote Recap
34) TDH Trade Hist
35) CACS Corp Action
36) CF Prospectus
37) CN Sec News
38) HDS Holders
66) Send Bond
Issuer Information
Name FIFTH THIRD BANCORP
Type Super-Regional Banks-US
Security Information
Mkt of Issue Global
Country US
Currency USD
Rank Subordinated
Series
Coupon 8.25
Type Fixed
Cpn Freq S/A
Day Cnt 30/360
Iss Price 99.74800
Maturity 03/01/2038
BULLET
Issue Spread 362.50bp vs T 5 05/15/37
Calc Type (1)STREET CONVENTION
Announcement Date 02/26/2008
Interest Accrual Date 03/04/2008
1st Settle Date 03/04/2008
1st Coupon Date 09/01/2008
SHORT 1ST CPN.
Identifiers
BB Number EH2354239
CUSIP 316773CH1
ISIN US316773CH12
Bond Ratings
Moody's Baa2
S&P BBB-
Fitch BBB+
DBRS BBBH
Issuance & Trading
Amt Issued/Outstanding
USD 1,000,000.00 (M) /
USD 1,000,000.00 (M)
Min Piece/Increment
5,000.00 / 1,000.00
Par Amount 1,000.00
Book Runner CS,GS,ML,MS
Reporting TRACE

Investment Funds

Major investment firms and investment banks offer a wide variety of investment funds. For many investors, shares in these funds are an alternative to directly buying stocks and bonds. Fund investment provides several advantages over directly purchasing securities. First, investment funds provide divisibility. An investment company offering shares in a portfolio of negotiable, high-denomination CDs, for example, makes it possible for small investors to obtain a higher rate than they could obtain by investing in a lower yielding, small-denomination CD. Second, an investment in a fund consisting of a portfolio of securities often provides an investor more liquidity than forming his own portfolio; that is, it is easier for an individual investor to buy and sell a share in an investment fund than it is to try to buy and sell a number of securities. Third, the investment companies managing funds provide professional management. They have a team of security analysts and managers who know the markets and the securities available. They buy and sell securities for the fund, reinvest dividends and interest, and maintain records. Finally, since investment companies often buy large blocks of securities, they can obtain lower brokerage fees and commission costs for their investors. In summary, funds provide investors the benefits of divisibility, diversification, and lower transaction costs.

The Market for Funds

From the end of World War II to the late 1960s, investments in funds grew substantially, boasting as many as 40 million investors in the 1960s. Most of the investment funds consisted of stocks, with their popularity attributed primarily to the general rise in stock prices during that period. In the 1970s, investments in funds declined as stock prices fell due to rising energy prices, inflation, and economic recessions. During this period, a number of funds specializing in debt securities were introduced. In the mid-1980s and in the 1990s, though, the popularity of equity fund investments rebounded. This more recent growth can be attributed to not only the bull market of the 1990s, but also to financial innovations. In addition to the traditional stock funds, investment companies today offer shares in bond funds (municipal bonds, corporate, high-yield bonds, and foreign bonds), *money market funds* (consisting of CDs, commercial paper, Treasury securities, etc.), *index funds* (funds whose values are highly correlated with a stock or bond index), funds with options and futures, *global funds* (funds with stocks and bonds from different countries), and even *vulture funds* (funds consisting of debt securities of companies that are in financial trouble or in Chapter 11 bankruptcy). Exhibit 9.5 display the Bloomberg Fund Heat Maps (FMAP <Enter>) for the United States and world as it appeared on May 17, 2012. The maps break down the total funds and show their total returns for the past year by type: equity, debt (bond), asset allocation (balanced), money market, and others.

EXHIBIT 9.5 Fund Heat Map, 5/17/2012

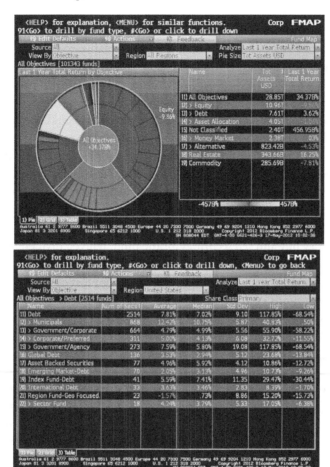

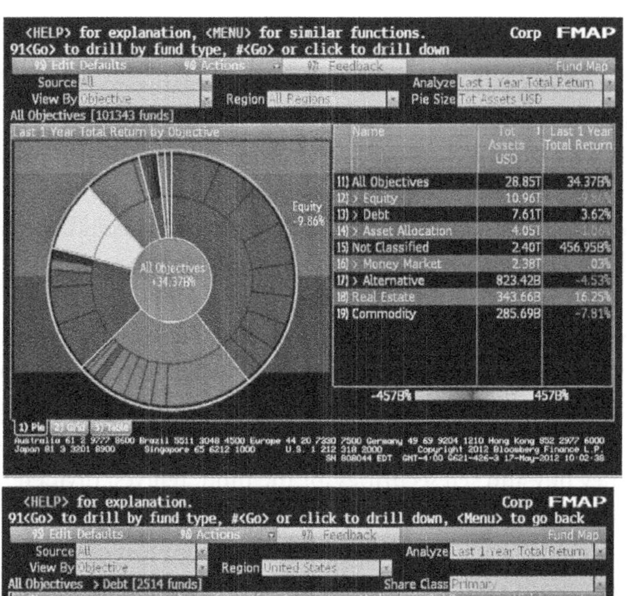

<HELP> for explanation. Corp FMAP

91<Go> to drill by fund type, #<Go> or click to drill down, <Menu> to go back

Source All | View By Objective | Region United States | Analyze Last 1 Year Total Return | Share Class Primary

All Objectives > Debt [2514 funds]

Name	Num of Secs	Average	Median	Std Dev	High	Low
11) Debt	2514	7.81%	7.02%	9.10	117.85%	-68.54%
12) > Municipals	868	12.42%	10.75%	5.87	40.83%	.50%
13) > Government/Corporate	664	4.79%	4.99%	5.56	55.90%	-58.22%
14) > Corporate/Preferred	311	5.00%	4.13%	6.08	32.72%	-11.55%
15) > Government/Agency	273	7.59%	5.80%	19.08	117.85%	-68.54%
16) Global Debt	136	3.53%	2.94%	5.12	23.68%	-13.84%
17) Asset Backed Securities	77	4.96%	5.92%	4.12	10.86%	-12.72%
18) Emerging Market-Debt	70	2.05%	3.13%	4.96	10.73%	-9.26%
19) Index Fund-Debt	41	5.59%	7.41%	11.35	29.47%	-30.44%
20) International Debt	33	3.63%	3.46%	2.83	8.39%	-1.70%
21) Region Fund-Geo Focused	23	-1.57%	.73%	8.86	15.20%	-15.73%
22) > Sector Fund	18	4.24%	3.79%	5.33	17.05%	-6.38%

A number of investment companies, such as Fidelity and Vanguard, manage a family of funds. From this family (sometimes referred to as a complex) these investment companies are able to offer investors different funds based on the investor's risk-return preferences. Currently there are over 8,500 funds in the United States—a number that exceeds the number of stocks listed on the major exchanges. Contributing to this large number is the increased percentage of fund investment coming from retirement investments such as individual retirement accounts (IRAs) and 401(k) accounts.

Structure of Funds

There are three types of investment fund structures: open-end funds (also called mutual funds), closed-end funds, and unit investment trusts (UITs). The first two can be

EXHIBIT 9.6 Investment Company Assets by Types: Billions of Dollars, Year-End, 1995–2010

Investment Company Total Net Assets by Type
Billions of dollas, year-end, 1995–2010

	Mutual funds	Closed-end funds	ETFs	UITs	Total
1995	$2,811	$143	$1	$73	$3,028
1996	3,526	147	2	72	3,747
1997	4,468	152	7	85	4,712
1998	5,525	156	16	94	5,791
1999	6,846	147	34	92	7,119
2000	6,965	143	66	74	7,248
2001	6,975	141	83	49	7,248
2002	6,390	159	102	36	6,687
2003	7,414	214	151	36	7,815
2004	8,107	254	228	37	8,626
2005	8,905	277	301	41	9,524
2006	10,397	298	423	50	11,167
2007	12,000	313	608	53	12,974
2008	9,601	188	531	29	10,349
2009	11,121	228	777	38	12,164
2010	11,821	241	992	51	13,104

Source: Investment Company Fact Book, www.icifactbook.org

Bloomberg Fund Heat Map by Type for U.S. Funds, 5/17/2012:

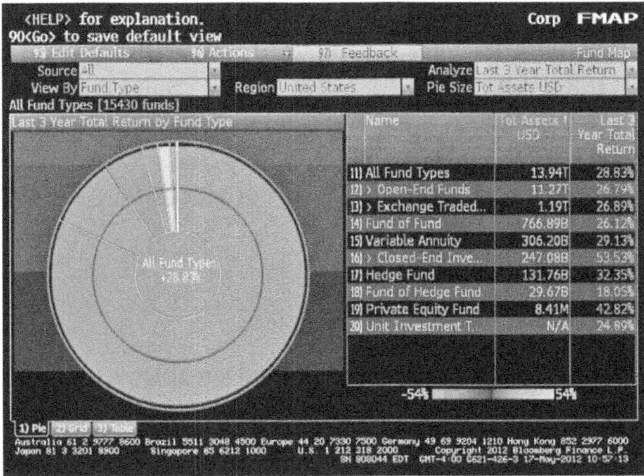

defined as managed funds, whereas the third is an unmanaged one. Exhibit 9.6 shows the distribution of assets among investment companies by type (including exchange-traded funds [ETFs]); discussed later) from 1995 to 2010 and the Bloomberg Fund Heat Map screen for U.S. funds by type as of May 17, 2012.

Open-End Fund

Open-end funds (*mutual funds*) stand ready to buy back shares of the fund at any time the fund's shareholders want to sell, and they stand ready to sell new shares any time an investor wants to buy into the fund. Technically, a mutual fund is an open-end fund. The term *mutual fund,* though, is often used to refer to both open- and closed-end funds. With an open-end fund, the number of shares can change frequently. The price an investor pays for a share of an open-end fund is equal to the fund's *net asset values* (*NAV*). At a given point in time, the NAV of the fund is equal to the difference between the value of the fund's assets (V_t^A) and its liabilities (V_t^L) divided by the number of shares outstanding (N_t): $NAV_t = (V_t^A - V_t^L)/N_t$. For example, suppose a balanced stock and bond fund consists of a stock portfolio with a current market value \$100 million, a corporate bond portfolio with current market value of \$100 million, liquid securities of \$8 million, and liabilities of \$8 million. The current net worth of this fund would be \$200 million. If the fund, in turn, has 4 million shares outstanding, its current NAV would be \$50 per share: NAV = (\$208 million – \$8 million)/4 million = \$50. This value, though, can change if the number of shares, the asset values, or the liability values change.

Open-end funds can be classified as either *load funds* or *no-load funds.* Load funds are sold through brokers or other intermediates; as such, the shares in load funds sell at their NAV plus a commission. The fees are usually charged up-front when investors buy new shares. Some funds charge a redemption fee (also called an exit fee or back-end load) when investors sell their shares back to the fund at their NAV. No-load funds, however, are sold directly by the fund and therefore sell at just their NAV. The fund does charge fees for management and for transferring individual investments from one fund to another. Exhibit 9.7 shows the Bloomberg descriptions screens, price graph (QP), and holdings of the Putnam Global Equity Fund. As shown on the description screen, the fund is an open-end fund that focuses on global equity investment in mid- to high-cap companies. The fund charges a 5 percent back load fee, a 0.73 percent management fee, and on May 17, 2012 the fund's NAV was at \$7.60 per share.

Closed-End Fund

A *closed-end fund* has a fixed number of nonredeemable shares sold at its initial offering. Unlike an open-end fund, the closed-end fund does not stand ready to buy existing shares or sell new shares. The number of shares of a closed-end fund is therefore fixed. An investor who wants to buy shares in an existing closed-end fund

EXHIBIT 9.7 Open-End Fund: Putnam Global Equity Fund, 5/17/2012

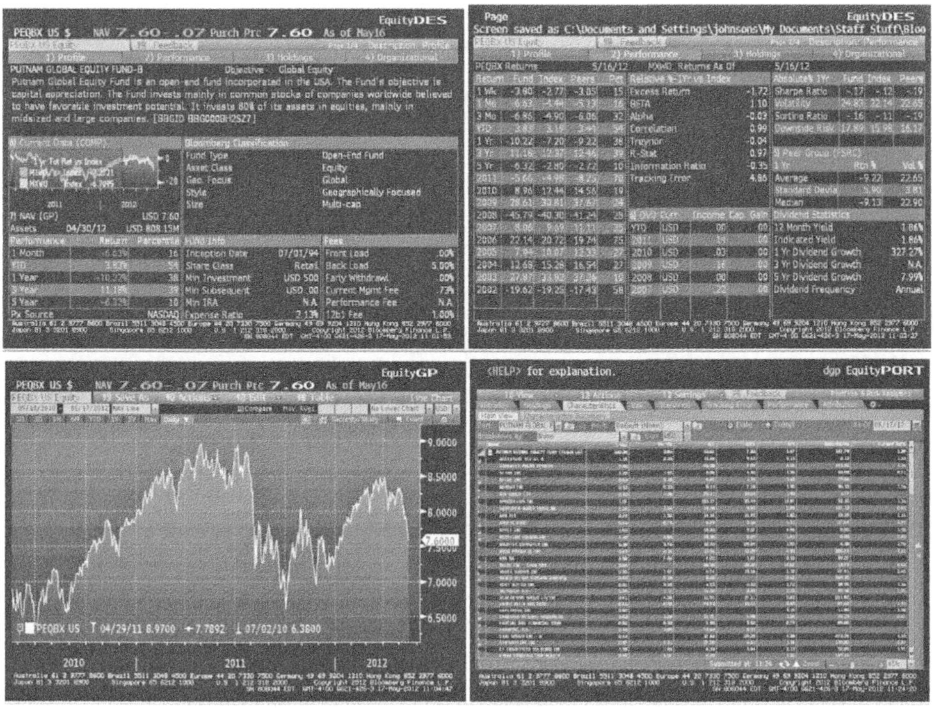

can do so only by buying them in the secondary market from an existing holder. Shares in existing funds are traded on the exchanges and the over-the-counter market. Interestingly, the prices of many closed-end funds often sell at a discount from their NAVs.[5] Exhibit 9.8 shows the Bloomberg descriptions screens, price graph (QP), and holdings of the Dividend and Income Fund. The fund is a closed-end fund that focuses on high current income, with 50 percent of its holdings in stock and the balance in corporate bonds. On May 17, 2012, the fund's shares were trading at $3.40 per share.

Unit Investment Trust

Although the composition of open- and closed-end fund investments can change as managers buy and sell securities, the funds themselves usually have unlimited lives. In contrast, a *unit investment trust* has a specified number of securities that are rarely changed, and the fund usually has a fixed life. A unit investment trust is formed by a sponsor, such as an investment bank, who buys a specified number of securities, deposits them with a trustee, and then sells claims on the security, known as *redeemable trust certificates,* at their NAV plus a commission fee. These trust certificates entitle the holder to proportional shares in the income from the deposited securities. For example, an investment company might purchase $20 million worth of corporate bonds at an

EXHIBIT 9.8 Closed-End Fund: Dividend and Income Fund, 5/17/2012; Unit Investment Trust: First Trust Corporate Investment Grade, 5/17/2012

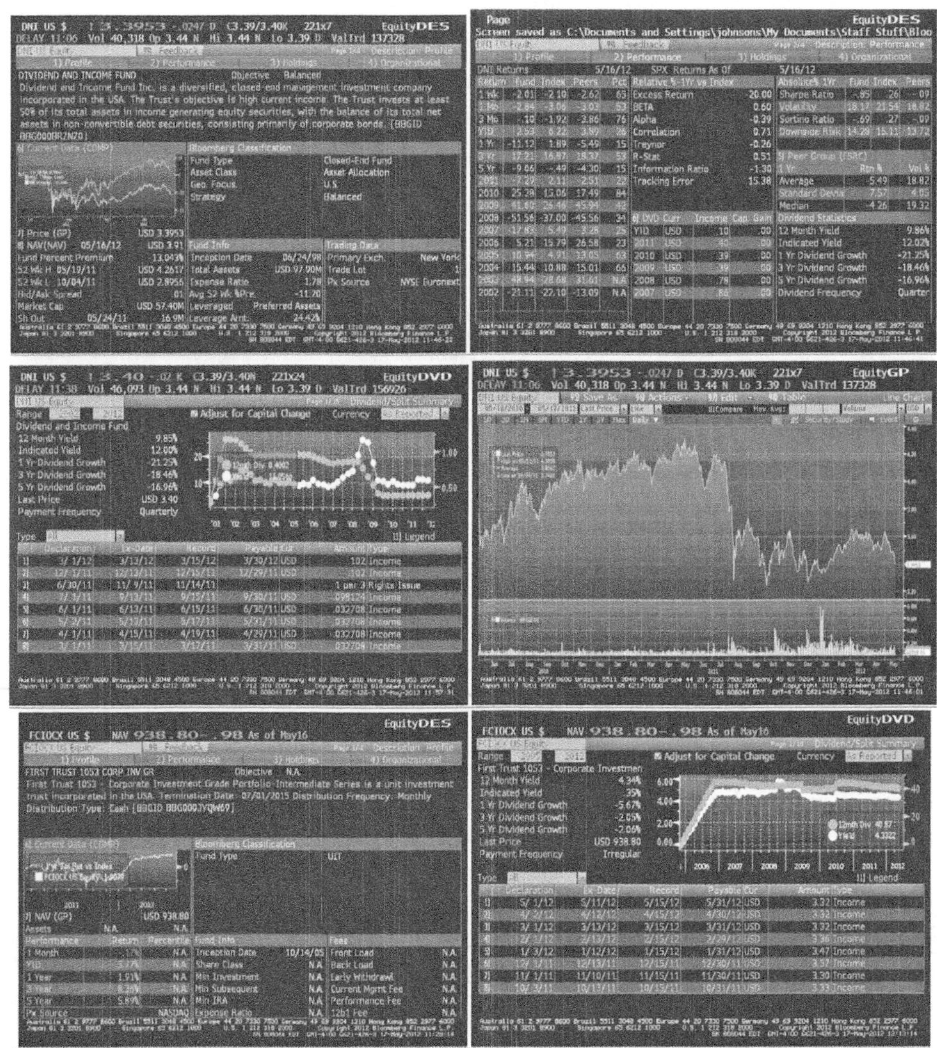

average price of \$1,000 per bond, place them in a trust, and then issue 20,000 redeemable trust certificates at \$1,025 per share: NAV + Commission = (\$20 million/2,000) + \$25 = \$1,025. If the investment company can sell all of the shares, it will be able to finance the \$20 million bond purchase and earn a 2.5 percent commission of \$500,000.

Unit investment trusts are formed with government securities, corporate bonds, municipal bonds, preferred stock, and common stock (often of the firms in a particular sector). The trustee pays all the interest and principal generated from the bonds or dividends from the stock to the certificate holders. Unlike open- and closed-end funds, the fund has a termination date when the investment trust ceases and the fund is liquidated with the holders receiving a liquidation dividend. Depending on the types of securities, the maturity on a unit investment trust can vary from 6 months to 20 years. The holders of the securities, though, usually can sell their shares back to the trustee prior to maturity at their NAV plus a load. To finance the purchase of the certificate, the trustee often sells a requisite amount of securities making up the trust. The description screen and cash flow screen for the First Trust Unit Investment Trust (UIT) is shown at the bottom of Exhibit 9.8. The UIT consists of corporate investment-grade bonds, has a termination date of July 1, 2015, a NAV of $938.80 on May 17, 2012, and has paid monthly dividends ranging between $3.32 and $3.57 over the past year.

Types of Investment Funds

A board of directors elected by the fund's shareholders determines the general investment policies of open- and closed-end investment funds. Typically, a management or investment advisory firm, often consisting of those who originally set up the fund, does the actual implementation and management of the policies. Some funds are actively managed, with fund managers aggressively buying stocks and bonds, whereas others follow a more passive buy-and-hold investment strategy.

One way of grouping the many types of funds is according to the classifications defined by Weisenberger's *Annual Investment Companies Manual* for growth funds, income funds, and balanced funds. *Growth funds* are those whose primary goal is in long-term capital gains. Such funds tend to consist primarily of those common stocks offering growth potential. Many of these are diversified stock funds, although there are some that specialize in certain sectors. *Income funds* are those whose primary goal is providing income. These funds are made up mainly of stocks paying relatively high dividends or bonds with high coupon yields. Finally, *balanced funds* are those with goals somewhere between those of growth and income funds. Balance funds are constructed with bonds, common stocks, and preferred stocks that are expected to generate moderate income with the potential for some capital gains. Similar to balanced funds are *asset allocation* funds (or *flexible funds*). These funds consist of both stocks and bonds, but are more actively managed, changing the bond and equity allocation over time in anticipation of changes in the market or interest rate conditions.

A second way of classifying funds is in terms of their specialization. There are four general classifications: equity funds, bond funds, hybrid funds (stocks and bonds), and money market funds. As shown in Exhibit 9.9, each of these fund types can be broken down further by their specified investment objectives. Equity funds consist of index fund, sector funds, and funds based on style. An index fund tries to match the performance of an index (indexes are discussed in the next section). For example, the Vanguard 500 Index Fund is an open-end fund that tries to replicate the performance of the Standard & Poor's (S&P 500). Sector funds, in turn, focus on a particular sector, such as telecommunications or energy. Finally, style funds form portfolios that reflect a certain type of investment such as investments in growth stocks or value stocks or investment based on size, such as large-cap, mid-cap, or small-cap stocks. Bond funds can be classified as corporate, municipal, government, high-yield, global, mortgage-backed securities, and tax free. Each category reflects a different investment objective. Municipal bond funds, for example, specialize in providing investors with tax-exempt municipal securities; corporate bond

EXHIBIT 9.9 Categories of Investment Funds

Equity Funds
Value Funds
Growth Funds
Sector Funds
World Equity Funds
Emerging Market Funds
Regional Equity Funds
Small-Cap, Mid-Cap, and Large-Cap Funds

Taxable Bond Funds (short-, intermediate-, and long-term)
Corporate Bond Funds
High Yield Funds
Global Bond Funds
Government Bond Funds
Mortgage-Backed Securities

Tax-Free Bond Funds (short-, intermediate-, and long-term)
State Municipal Bond Funds
National Municipal Bond Funds

Hybrid Funds
Asset Allocation Funds
Balanced Funds
Income-Mixed Funds

Money Market Funds
Taxable Money Market Funds
Tax-Exempt Money Market Funds

funds are constructed to replicate the overall performance of a certain type of corporate bond, with a number of them formed to be highly correlated with a specific index; money market funds are constructed with money market securities in order to provide investors with liquid investments. Exhibit 9.10 shows examples of the policy statements of several types of funds accessed from the Bloomberg description screens.

International Mutual Funds

Instead of buying foreign stocks or bonds, an investor looking for an internationally diversified portfolio, may find a more practical alternative is to buy shares in one of many international mutual funds or to invest in a commingled international portfolio offered by a bank trust department or insurance company. Most of these funds provide expertise in foreign security selection and management, and many use currency-hedging tools to minimize exchange-rate risk. The funds differ in terms of the degree of their diversification. Some, for example, offer investments only in certain countries or areas (e.g., Latin American funds), whereas others provide worldwide diversification. See Exhibit 9.10 for an example of a global investment funds.

EXHIBIT 9.10 Examples of Investment Funds, May 17, 2012—Bloomberg Description Files

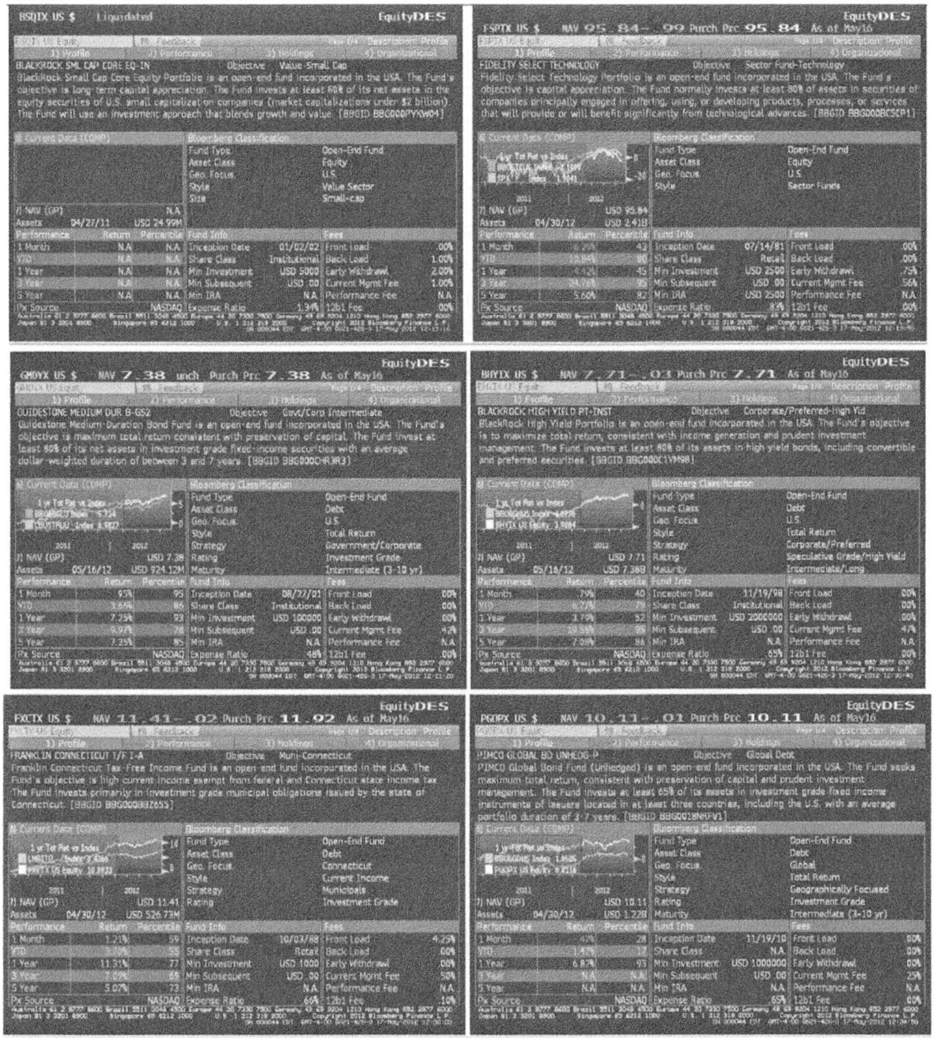

Accumulation Plans

Typically, most fund investors buy shares and receive cash from the fund when it is distributed. For investors looking for different cash flow patterns, investment funds also provide voluntary and contractual accumulation plans with different types of contributions and withdrawal plans. Included here are automatic reinvestment plans in which the net income and capital gains of the fund are reinvested, with the shareholders accumulating additional shares, and fixed contribution plans in which investors contribute (either contractually or voluntarily) a fixed amount on a regular basis for a set period.

Taxes and Regulations

Most mutual funds make two types of payments to their shareholders: a net income payment from dividends and interest and a realized capital gain payment. If an investment fund complies with certain rules, it does not have to pay corporate income taxes. To qualify for this favorable tax treatment, the company must have a diversified portfolio and it must pay out at least 90 percent of the fund's net income to shareholders. As a result, most investment companies distribute all of the net income from the fund to their shareholders. Investment companies can either distribute or retain their realized capital gains. Most investment companies distribute capital gains. If they retain the gain, they are required to pay a tax equal to the maximum personal income tax rate; the shareholders, in turn, receive a credit for the taxes paid.

Investment funds are regulated under a number of federal laws: The security acts of 1933 and 1934 require disclosure of funds and specifies antifraud rules; the Security Act of 1940 requires that all funds be registered; the Investment Advisers Act of 1940 regulates fund advisers. In addition, the SEC rules require that funds publish detailed information on directors and that there be independence of the directors.[6]

BLOOMBERG INVESTMENT FUND SCREENS

FMAP <Enter>, Fund Map: FMAP displays and analyzes mutual fund performance by objective, fund type, and region (see Exhibits 9.5 and 9.6)
FUND <Enter>: Funds and Holding Menu.
FL <Enter>: Fund Lookup.
Fund Ticker <Equity> <Enter>: Fund menu page.
SECF <Enter>, Funds Tab: Funds look-up and screener.
NI FND <Enter>: Fund News.
FSRC <Enter>, Fund Searches: The FRSC screen searches and screens investment funds by general investment criteria, such as asset class (stock, bonds, or balance) by type (open, closed, unit investment trust, or exchange-traded product), by country, by asset holding criteria (industry, market cap, maturity, or ratings) and by adding fields.
WMF <Enter>: Best mutual fund players snapshot.

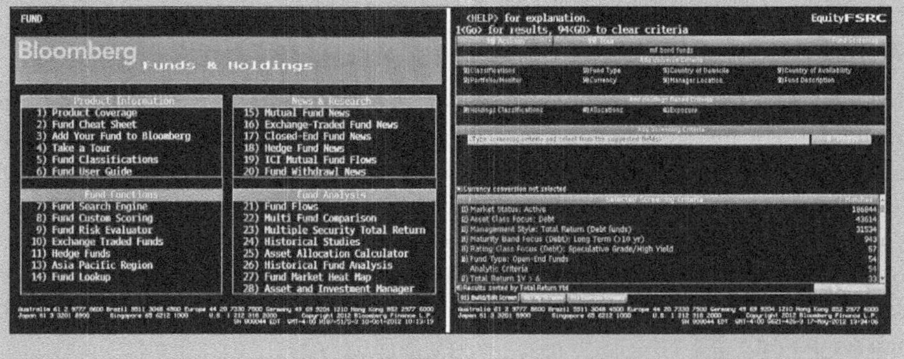

Note on Indexes

Equity investment funds are often classified by their investment style: S&P 500 index fund, large-cap stock fund, small-cap stock funds, emerging market funds, and the like. Similarly, bond funds can be classified as corporate, municipal, government, high-yield, global, mortgage-backed securities, and tax free. Each category reflects a different investment objective. Managers of these various funds, as well as the managers of pension, insurance, and other fixed-income funds, often evaluate the performance of their funds by comparing their fund's return with those of an appropriate index. In addition, as we discussed in Chapter 6, many bond funds are constructed so that their returns replicate those of a specified index.

A number of stock and bond indexes have been developed in recent years on which funds can be constructed or benchmarked. A number of investment companies also publish a variety of indexes; these include Barclays and Merrill Lynch. As noted in Chapter 1, stock indexes can be: broad based, measuring the performance of the overall market; sector specific, measuring the performance of a particular industry or sector; or style specific, measuring the performance of certain type of investment (e.g., investments in small-cap companies or high-yield bond fund). The Dow Jones Industrial Average (DJIA), S&P 500, and Russell 3000 stock index, for example, are broad-based indexes measuring the performance of the overall stock market. Stock market indexes are also calculated for a number of stock markets. From these broad-based indexes, there are subindexes for the S&P, Russell, or Dow based on size (e.g., small-cap or large-cap) or style (value stocks or growth stocks).

The most cited indexes of the major foreign stock exchanges and world indexes are the Nikkei 225 Index for the Tokyo Stock Exchange and the Financial Times-Stock Exchange Index for the London Stock Exchange, called the "footsie." Some other widely used indexes are the Morgan Stanley and the Dow Jones indexes. Both calculate a number of indexes (in the local currency and in dollars), including national indexes, international industry indexes, a European index, an Asian index, and a world index. Morgan Stanley International computes indexes for more than 20 countries, different geographical areas, and an Aggregate World Index. Finally, a number of bond indexes have been developed by investment companies in recent years on which bond funds can be constructed or benchmarked. The indexes can be grouped into three categories: U.S. investment-grade bonds indexes (including Treasuries), U.S. high-yield bond indexes, and global government bond indexes. Within each category, subindexes are constructed based on sector, quality ratings, or country.[7] Exhibit 9.11 shows the Bloomberg descriptions screens for a number of indexes.

Exchange-Traded Funds

In 1993, the American Stock Exchange created an S&P 500 index fund called an exchange-traded fund (ETF) that could be traded continuously like a stock. This first ETF received exemptions from the SEC from various provisions of the Investment

EXHIBIT 9.11 Stock and Bond Indexes

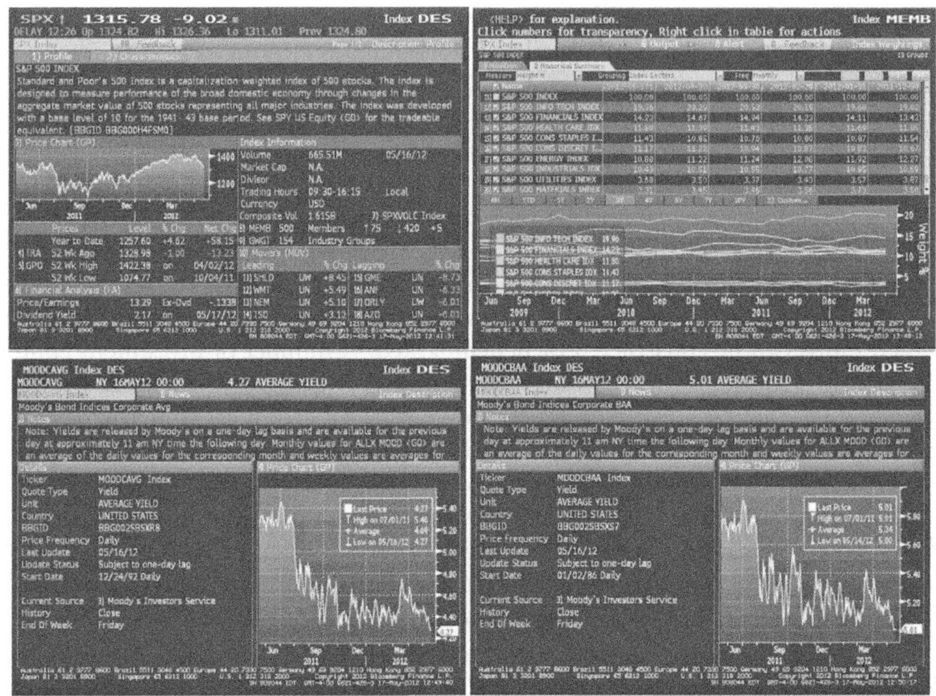

BLOOMBERG INDEX INFORMATION

WEI

The World Equity Indices (WEI) screen (to access: WEI <Enter>) monitors world equity indexes. On the WEI screen, one can also select different information about the indexes, such as premarket (futures prices), movers (advance and declines), ratios (e.g., price-to-earnings ratio), and currency. On the screen, one can click the country area (e.g., EMEA) to bring up more indexes for that geographical area.

Index Ticker <Index>: Index menu screen.

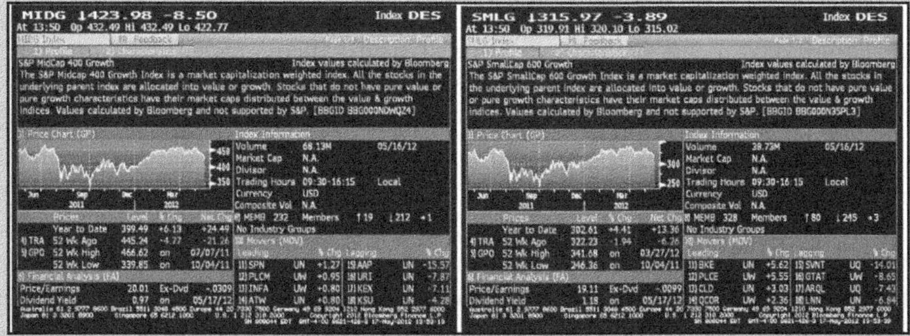

BI <Enter>: BI has comprehensive list of Bloomberg sectors and industries and provides detailed financials and analysis for each.

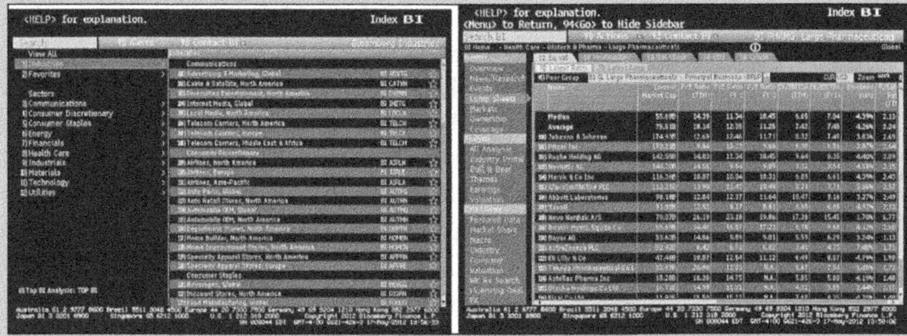

EQS <Enter>: Select Index from "Indices" tab.

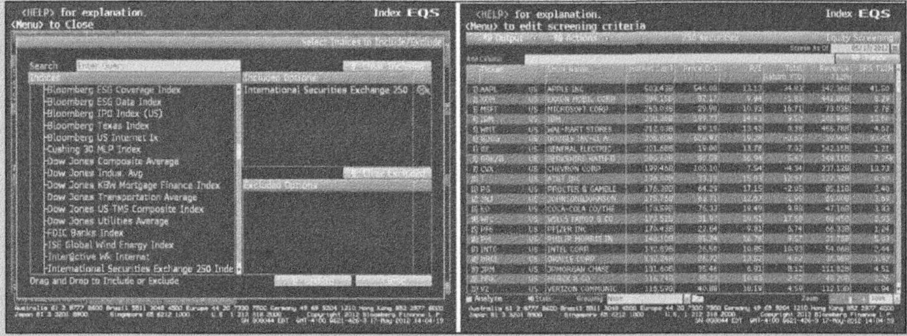

SECF <Enter>, All tab and Index/Stats tab: Index search and screener.
SPX <Enter>: S&P 500 Index menu.
Russ <Enter>: Russell Index menu.

Company Act of 1940. The exemptions made it possible for the ETF to be structured so that it could be listed and traded continuously. By 2008, there were over 400 separate ETFs, many with esoteric names such as Spiders (ETF that replicates the S&P 500), Qubes (an ETF indexed to the Nasdaq), Diamonds (an ETF that replicates the DJIA), and Vipers (name for Vanguard ETFs). In 2008, most of the ETFs were designed to track the performance of a specified index or, in some cases, a multiple of or an inverse of their indexes. Today, ETFs include most sectors, commodities, and investment styles. In early 2008, the SEC granted exemptive relief to several fund sponsors to offer actively managed ETFs that met certain requirements. These actively managed ETFs, in turn, have led to new exchange-traded products (ETPs) defined by a particular investment objective and policy. By 2010, the total number of index-based and actively managed ETFs had grown to over 728, with total net assets of over $530 billion.

Most ETFs originate with a sponsor, who defines the investment objective of the ETF and the method for tracking the performance. The sponsor of an index-based ETF, for example, defines the index (e.g., large U.S. Bank Sector), and the method of tracking it (e.g., a total replication index method that holds every security in the target index or a sample index-based method that holds a representative sample of securities in the index). Given the fund's objective and tracking method, a *creation basket* is identified that specifies the names and quantities of securities and other assets designed to track the performance of the index portfolio. ETF shares are created after an *authorized participant* (typically an institutional investor) deposits the creation basket and/or cash into the fund—the ETF. In return for the creation basket and/or cash, the authorized participant received the block of ETF shares, referred to as a *creation unit.* The authorized participant can then either keep the ETF shares that make up the creation unit or sell all or part of them on a stock exchange (see Exhibit 9.12).

ETFs are like mutual funds in that their value is derived from the underlying portfolio of securities. Different from mutual funds, ETFs trade like stocks: investors

EXHIBIT 9.12 Creation Process of Exchange-Traded Funds

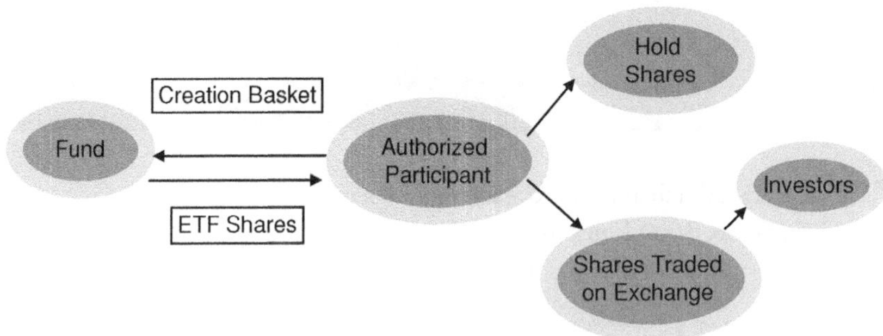

Source: 2009 Investment Company Fact Book: www.icifactbook.org/index.html.

can buy and sell them on a continuous basis and can execute trades with market or limit orders; they can also buy ETFs on margin and sell short. Also different from mutual funds, the price of an ETF is based on market supply and demand conditions. However, because of the disclosure requirements that call for the composition of the ETF's basket to be made public, arbitrageurs are in a position to ensure that the price of an ETF trades close to the underlying net asset value of the securities held in the index basket.[8]

Not surprising, the demand for ETFs has accelerated in recent years with institutional investors increasing using them to take positions on broad movements in the financial markets. Retail investors and households have also started to add ETFs to their portfolio holdings. According to the Investment Company Institute, an estimated 3 million households owned ETFs in 2009. Although many ETFs are equity based, there are an increasing number of fixed-income ETFs and ETPs being offered. These fixed-income ETPs vary from ETFs that are tied to bond indexes, to those linked to Treasury yields, to ETFs that are tied to a multiple of the Treasury yield. There is also an increasing number of equity, commodity, and fixed-income ETFs and ETPs being offered outside the United States. The ETPs vary from ETFs that are tied to foreign equity and bond indexes to those linked to emerging markets. Exhibit 9.13 shows the Bloomberg descriptions screens for several different types of equity and fixed-income ETFs.

EXHIBIT 9.13 Examples of ETFs—Bloomberg Description Files

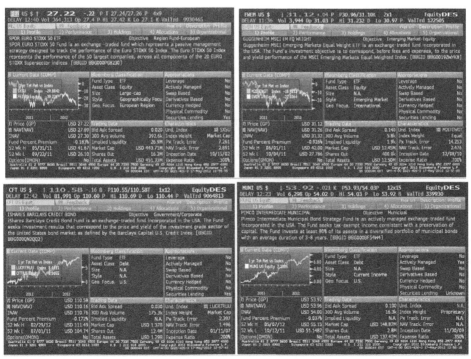

BLOOMBERG ETF INFORMATION

ETF <Enter>
SECF <Enter>, Funds tab and ETFs tab: ETF search and screener.
FSRC <Enter>: Screen by "Fund Type" and "Exchange-Traded Products."

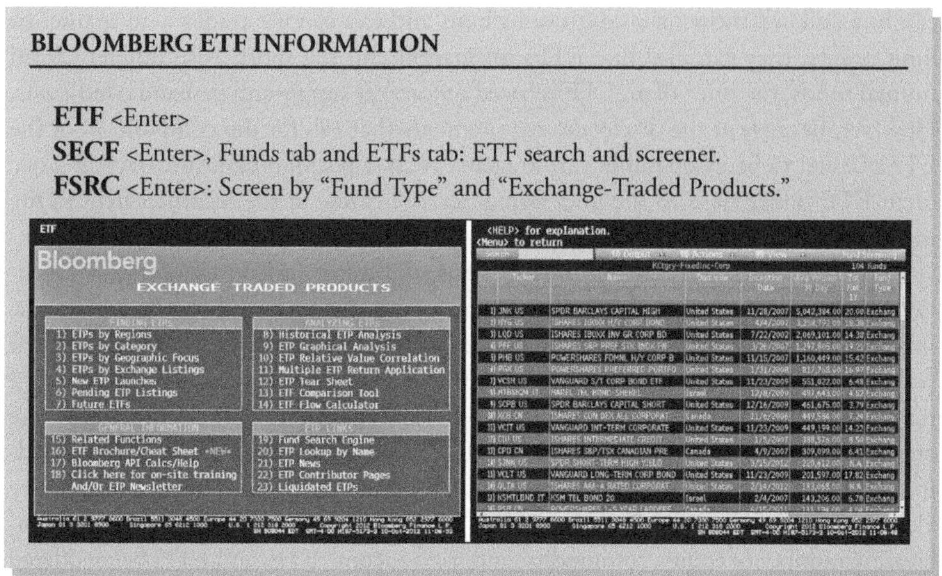

Other Investment-Type Funds and Securities

In addition to open-end and closed-end investment funds, unit investment trusts, and ETFs, several other investment funds of note are hedge funds, real estate investment trusts (REITs), mortgage-backed and asset-backed securities, and collateral debt obligations (CDOs).

Hedge Funds

Hedge funds can be defined as special types of mutual funds. There are estimated to be as many as 4,000 such funds. They are structured so that they can be largely unregulated. To achieve this, they are often set up as limited partnerships. By federal law, as limited partnerships, hedge funds are limited to no more than 99 limited partners each with annual incomes of at least \$200,000 or a net worth of at least \$1 million (excluding home), or to no more than 499 limited partners each with a net worth of at least \$5 million. Many funds or partners are also domiciled offshore to circumvent regulations. Hedge funds acquire funds from many different individual and institutional sources; the minimum investments range from \$100,000 to \$20 million, with the average investment being \$1 million. Because they are lightly regulated, hedge funds often set up investment strategies that use derivatives, short sales, and leveraging, with debt-to-equity ratio in some cases as high as 20 to 1—strategies not open to mutual funds. Some hedge funds use their funds to invest or set up investment strategies reflecting pricing aberrations. One of the most famous is that of Long-Term Capital, which in 1998 set up a fund to profit from an expected narrowing of the default spread on bonds that instead widened. Other notable hedge fund collapses

EXHIBIT 9.14 Examples of Hedge Funds

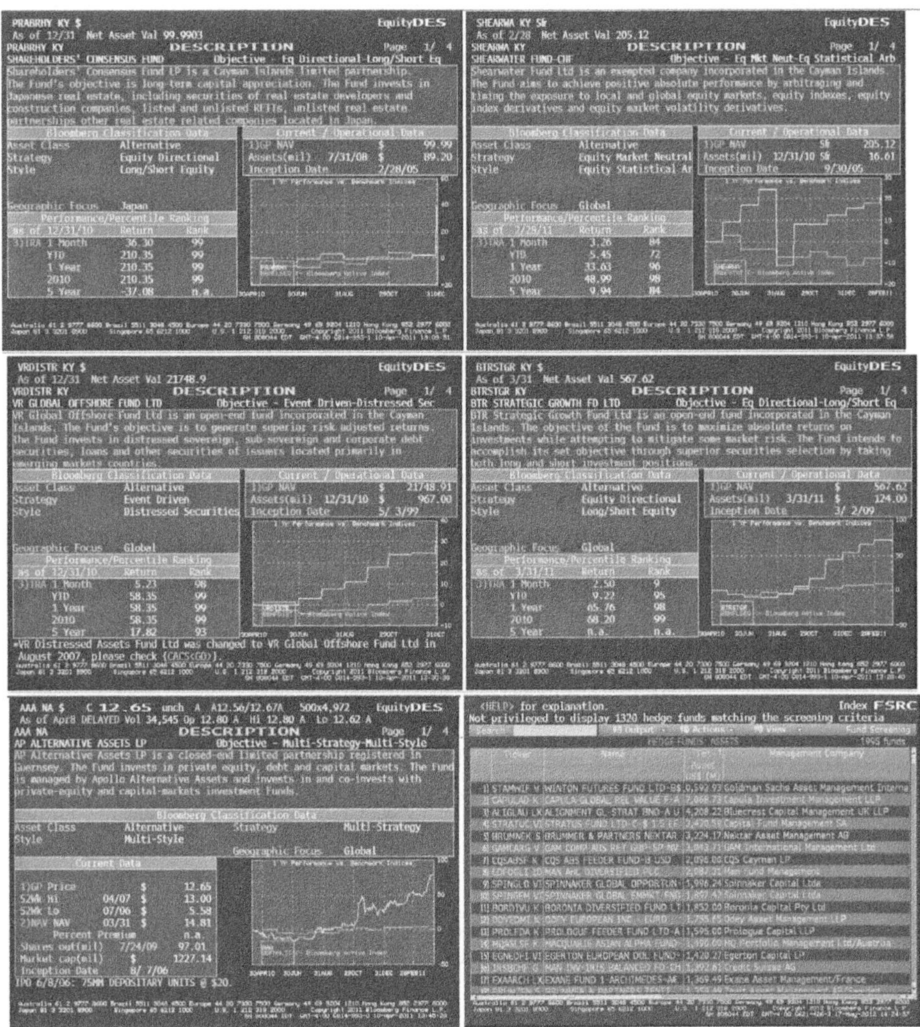

include Amaranth Advisors, Advanced Investment Management, Bayou Management, and Lipper Convertibles.

One of the fastest-growing sectors in the hedge fund industry is hedge funds that invest in one or more other hedge funds. Such funds are referred to as funds of funds or feeder funds. These funds also receive considerable attention when it was learned in December 2008 that many large feeder funds were large clients of Bernard Madoff and were hurt by his large Ponzi scheme. Exhibit 9.14 shows Bloomberg description screens for a number of different types of hedge funds.

BLOOMBERG HEDGE FUNDS INFORMATION:

Hedge Fund Menus Page: HFND <Enter>
FMAP <Enter>, Click "Fund Type" on "View" tab, Click "Hedge Fund."
HFR <Enter>: Hedge Fund Research
Hedge Fund News: HEDN <Enter>.
Hedge Fund News: BRIEF <Enter> and click "Hedge Fund Newsletter."
Best Hedge Fund Player Snapshot: WHF <Enter>.

Real Estate Investment Trusts

A real estate investment trust (REIT) is a fund that specializes in investing in real estate or real estate mortgages. The trust acts as an intermediary, selling stocks and warrants and issuing debt instruments (bonds, commercial paper, or loans from banks), then using the funds to invest in commercial and residential mortgage loans and other real estate securities. REITs can take the form of an equity trust that invests directly in real estate, a mortgage trust that invests in mortgage loans or mortgage-backed securities, or a hybrid trust that invests in both. Many REITs are highly leveraged, making them more subject to default risks. Most REITs are tax-exempt corporations. To qualify for tax exemptions, the company must receive approximately 75 percent of its income from real estate, rents, mortgage interest, and property sales, and distribute 95 percent of its income to its shareholders. The stocks of many existing shares in REITs are listed on the organized exchanges and the OTC market. Exhibit 9.15 shows Bloomberg description screens for a number of different types of REITS.

BLOOMBERG REIT INFORMATION

REIT <Enter>: REIT menu screen; REIT Ticker <Equity> <Enter>; NI REIT <Enter>: REIT News; RMEN <Enter>: Real Estate Indices of the World; HOIN <Enter>: Housing and Construction.

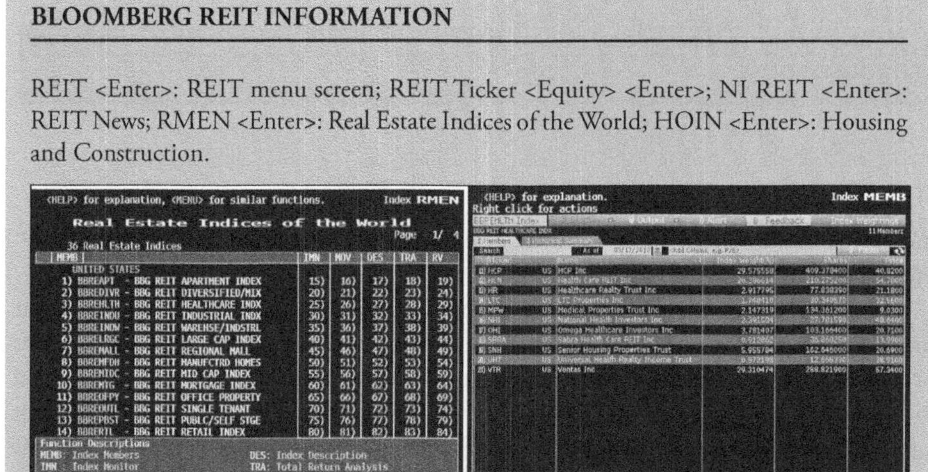

EXHIBIT 9.15 Examples of REITs

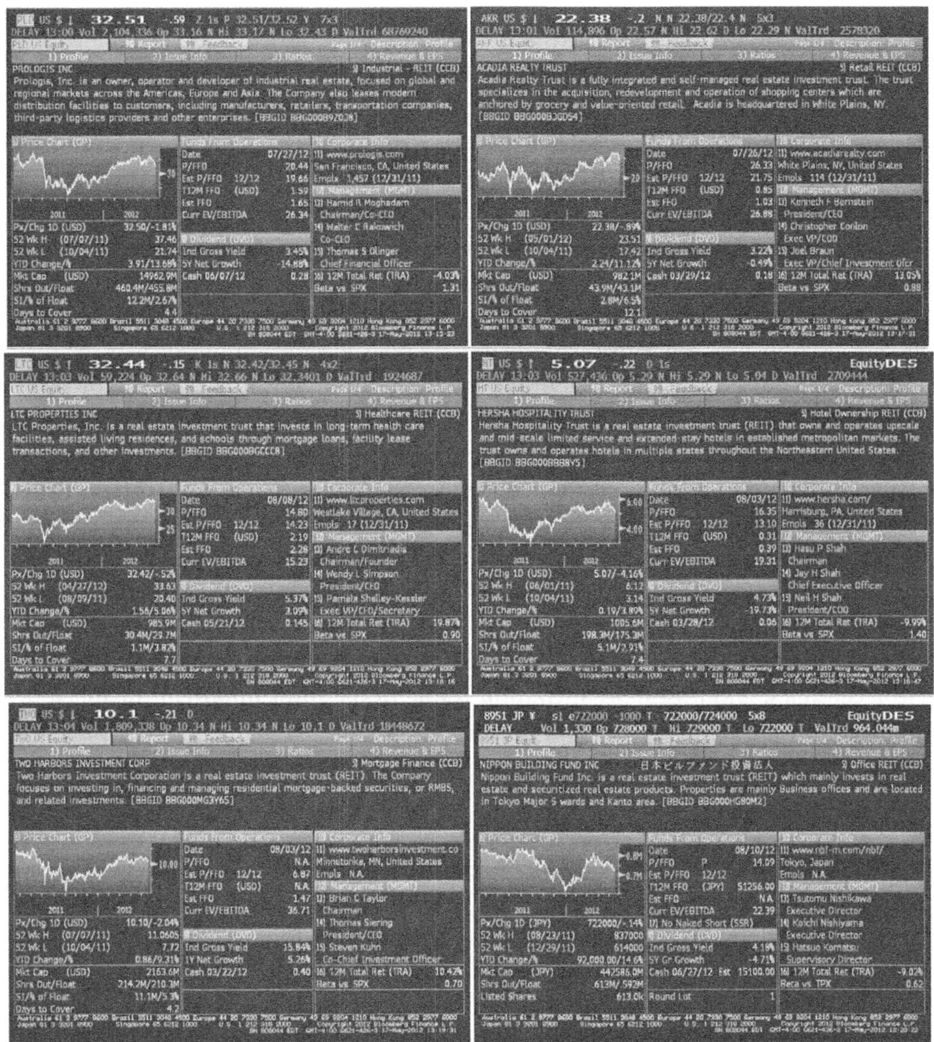

Mortgage-Backed and Asset-Backed Securities

Up until the mid-1970s, most home mortgages originated when saving and loans, commercial banks, and other thrift institutions borrowed funds or used their deposits to provide loans to home purchasers, possibly later selling the resulting instruments in the secondary market to Fannie Mae or Ginnie Mae. To a large degree, individual deposits financed real estate, with little financing coming from corporations or institutions. In an effort to attract institutional funds away from corporate bonds and other capital market securities, as well as to minimize their poor hedge (short-term deposit liabilities and long-term mortgage assets), financial institutions began to sell mortgage-backed securities in the 1970s. These securities provided them with an instrument that could compete more closely with corporate bonds for inclusion in the portfolios of institutional investors, and it provided the mortgage industry with more liquidity.

By definition, mortgage-backed securities (MBSs) are instruments that are backed by a pool of mortgage loans. Typically, a financial institution, agency, or mortgage banker buys a pool of mortgages of a certain type from mortgage originators (e.g., Federal Housing Administration–insured mortgages or mortgages with a certain minimum loan-to-value ratio or a specified payment-to-income ratio). This mortgage portfolio is financed through the sale of the MBSs, which has a claim on the portfolio. The mortgage originators usually agree to continue to service the loans, passing the payments on to the MBS holders. An MBS investor has a claim on the cash flows from the mortgage portfolio. This includes interest on the mortgages, scheduled payment of principal, and any prepaid principal. Since many mortgages are prepaid early as homeowners sell their homes or refinance their current mortgages, the cash flows from a portfolio of mortgages, and therefore the return on the MBS, can be quite uncertain. To address this type of risk, a number of derivative MBSs were created in the 1980s. For example, in the late 1980s, Freddie Mac introduced the *collateralized mortgage obligations* (*CMOs*). These securities had different maturity claims and different levels of prepayment risk.

An MBS is an asset-backed security created through a method known as *securitization.* As noted in Chapter 1, securitization is the process of transforming illiquid financial assets into marketable capital market instruments. Today, it is applied not only to mortgages but also home equity loans, automobile loans, lines of credit, credit card receivables, and leases. Securitization is one of the most important financial innovations introduced in the last two decades; it is examined in detail in Chapter 10.

Collateralized Debt Obligations

Collateralized debt obligations (*CDOs*) are securities backed by a diversified pool of one or more fixed-income assets or derivatives. The portfolio of debt obligations underlying the CDO are referred to as the collateral, with the funds to purchase the collateral assets being obtained by the issuance of debt obligations. Assets from which CDOs are formed include: investment-grade corporate bonds, high-yield corporate bonds, asset-backed securities, real estate MBSs, commercial loans, commercial MBSs, REITs, municipal bonds, and emerging market bonds. CDOs have a collateral manager who is responsible for managing the portfolio of debt obligations. Restrictions are, in turn, imposed on what the collateral manager can do. The issuance of CDOs grew from the 1990s to 2007, but stopped in 2008 in the aftermath of the 2008 financial crisis. There are still, though, a number of issues outstanding.

Insurance Companies, Pension Funds, and Investment Banks

Insurance companies, pension funds, and investment banks are important financial intermediaries. Insurance companies and pension funds, on the one hand, use the premiums paid on various insurance policies and the investment funds from retirement and savings plans to invest in bonds, stocks, mortgages, and other assets. On the other hand, many individuals use insurance policies and pension plans as their primary investment conduit. Like commercial banks, large investment banks are multifunctional, serving as an important intermediary.

Insurance Companies' Role in the Financial Market

Insurance companies invest billions of dollars into the financial markets each year from the inflows they received from insurance premiums, savings and investment product they offer, and the funds from pension and endowment funds they managed. In 2010, life insurance companies held approximately $6.08 trillion in assets. Since their liabilities tend to be more predictable and long term, life insurance companies tend to invest in long-term assets.[9] In 2010, about 40 percent of their assets were in corporate bonds, followed by equity (22 percent), government securities (11 percent), mortgages (7 percent), and various other assets. In contrast to life insurance companies, property and casualty insurance companies insure against many different types of events, with the amount of potential losses on many of the events they insure more difficult to predict. As a result, property and casualty companies tend to invest in more liquid assets than life insurance companies.

Life insurance companies provide basic life insurance: protection in the form of income to benefactors in the event of the death of the insurer. They also provide disability insurance, health insurance, annuities, and guaranteed investment contracts. Annuities and guaranteed investment contracts are investment-type instruments. A life insurance company annuity pays the holder a periodic fixed income for as long as the policyholder lives in return for an initial lump-sum investment (coming, for example, from a retirement benefit or insurance cash value). Annuities provide policyholders protection against the risk of outliving their retirement income.[10] They are constructed based on the rates of return insurance companies can obtain from investing an individual's payment for a period equal to the individual's life expectancy (fixed-life annuity), or for a prespecified period (fixed-period annuity).

A guaranteed investment contract (GIC) is an obligation of an insurance company to pay a guaranteed principal and rate on an invested premium. For a lump-sum payment, the insurance company guarantees a specified dollar amount will be paid to the policyholder at a specified future date. For example, a life insurance company for a premium of $1 million, guarantees the holder a five-year GIC paying 8 percent interest compounded annually. The GIC, in turn, obligates the insurance company to pay the GIC holder $1,469,328 (= $1million$(1.08)^5$) in five years. Pension funds are one of the primary investors in GICs. The GICs provide them not only an investment with a known payment but also an investment that always has a positive value to report; this contrast with bond investments whose values may decrease if interest rates increase.[11]

BLOOMBERG INSURANCE INFORMATION

FLNG <Enter>, select Insurance Company in "Institutions" tab.

Pension Funds

Pension funds are financial intermediaries that invest the savings of employees in financial assets over their working years, providing them with a pool of funds at their retirements. Pension funds are one of the fastest-growing intermediaries in the United States. The total assets of pension funds (private and state and local government) have grown from $700 billion in 1980 to approximately $10 trillion in 2010. Part of this growth reflects a workforce of Baby Boomers making contributions to their pensions. As this generation enters retirement over the next decade and begins to draw from its investments, there is expected to be a marked decline in such growth.

Pension fund can be grouped as public or private plans. The largest public plan is the Federal Old Age and Disability Insurance Program (Social Security). It is a pay-as-you-go system in which current workers' contributions pay for the benefits to the current recipients.[12] The other public pension funds are those sponsored by state and local governments. Private pension plans are those sponsored by employers, groups, and individuals.

There are two general types of pension plans: a defined-benefit plan and a defined-contribution plan. A *defined-benefit plan* promises the employee a specified benefit when they retire. The benefit is usually determined by a formula. Financial problems can arise when pension funds are underfunded and the company goes bankrupt. As a result, over the past two decades most new plans are structured as *defined-contribution plans.* These plans specify what the employee will contribute to the plan, instead of what the plan will pay. At retirement, the benefits are equal to the contributions the employee has made and the returns earned from investing them. The employee's contributions to the fund are usually a proportion of his income, often with a proportion of that contribution made by the employer. An insurance company, bank trust department, or investment company often acts as the trustee and investment manager of the fund's assets. In many defined-contribution plans, the employee is allowed to determine the general allocation between equity, bonds, and money market securities in his individual accounts.

To pension contributors, pension funds represent long-term investments through intermediaries. As of 2010, private funds sponsored by employers, groups, and individuals were one of the largest institutional investors in equity, with about 70 percent of their total equity investments going to equity (stock and mutual fund shares). In 2008, public funds sponsored by state and local governments had invested assets valued at over $3 trillion, with 38 percent in equity, 6 percent in mutual funds, 9 percent in corporate bonds, 10 percent in federal agency and Treasury securities, and 26 percent in credit market instruments (see Federal Reserve Flow of Fund Accounts, Table L118; www.federalreserve.gov/releases/z1/Current/).

Pension members are not taxed on their contributions, but they do pay taxes on benefits when they are paid out. Pension funds in the United States are governed by the 1974 *Employee Retirement Income Security Act* (*ERISA*). ERISA requires prudent management of the fund's investments and requires that all private plans be fully funded; that is, that the assets and income cover all promised benefits. The act also ensures transferability of plans when employees change jobs, specifies disclosure requirements, and defines the minimum vesting requirements for determining eligibility. In 1974, Congress also created the *Pension Benefit Guaranty Corporation* (*PBGC* or *Penny Benny*) to provide insurance for employee benefits. Similar to the FDIC, Penny Benny is a government agency that insures pension benefit up to a limit if a company goes bankrupt and has an underfunded pension plan. It operates by charging pension plans a premium and it can borrow fund from the Treasury. In 2008, Penny Benny paid benefits to over 700,000 retirees of failed pension plans.[13]

In addition to employee and institutional pension plans, retirement plans for U.S. individuals can also be set up through *Keogh plans* and *individual retirement accounts* (*IRAs*). In accordance with the Self-Employed Individual Tax Retirement Act of 1962, self-employed people can contribute up to 20 percent of their net earnings to a Keogh plan (retirement account) with the contribution being tax deductible from gross income. The Pension Reform Act of 1978 updated the 1962 act to permit individual retirement accounts (IRAs). Subsequent legislation in 1981 and 1982, in turn, expanded the eligibility for creating tax-deferred accounts to include most individuals. The Small Business Protection Act of 1996 created a simplified retirement plans for businesses with 100 or fewer workers. In addition to company-sponsored and group-sponsored pensions, bank trust departments, insurance companies, and investment companies offer and manage individual retirement accounts and Keogh plans. For small accounts, these institutions often combine the accounts in a *commingled fund,* instead of managing each account separately. A commingled fund is similar to a mutual fund. For accounting purposes, individuals setting up accounts are essentially buying shares in the fund at their NAV and when they withdraw funds they are selling essential shares at their NAV. Like mutual funds, insurance companies and banks offer a number of commingled funds, such as, money market funds, stock funds, and bond funds

BLOOMBERG PENSION INFORMATION

FLNG <Enter>, select Pensions in "Institutions" tab.

Investment Banks

As discussed in Chapter 7, investment banks are active in the primary market where they underwrite or privately place stock and bond issues, and in the secondary market where they provide brokerage services through their electronic systems or directly through customer relation offices. Investment banks are also important intermediaries. They act as dealers on the OTC market and as position traders on block trades, and many have specialist and market makers where they keep the market continuous. Furthermore, as discussed in this chapter, investment banks are active participants in setting up investment funds, structuring and managing collateralized debt obligations and hedge funds. Two additional areas of note in which investment banks are quite active are mergers, consolidations, and acquisitions and corporate equity sales.

Mergers, consolidations, and acquisitions are complicated undertakings. Investment banks are active in serving both the acquirers and the target firms. Acquiring firms use investment bankers to help them identify attractive firms to pursue, to solicit shareholders who might sell, to structure tender offers, to raise financial capital, and to structure the deal. Targeted firms may use investment banks to indicate their interest and commitment or possibly their disinterest and protection, especially when there is a hostile takeover effort.

Investment banks are also active in the sale of not just companies in a merger and acquisition, but also in a division of a company, sometime referred to as an *equity sale.* When a company decides to sell a division or some of its assets, it may come from interest expressed by another company or from a change in the company's strategic plan. The decision to sell a division may also be necessitated by the need to raise funds to finance the acquisition of another company or an investment, or it may be to raise funds to pay off its debt obligations to avoid bankruptcy. Investment banks help in equity sales by providing expertise in determining the value of the business as an ongoing concern and the value of the synergy of a division with other firms. They also help in moving the equity sale forward by initially setting up a bidding process that discretely identifies potential buyers, later procuring letters of intent, and finally obtaining a final contract.

BLOOMBERG UNDERWRITER SCREENS

LTOP <Enter>: The LTOP screen displays top underwriters for the major fixed-income, equity, equity-linked securities, and syndicated loan securities markets. To access: LTOP <Enter>. On the LTOP screen, right click to access a dropdown menu showing descriptions and the underwriter's deals for that period.

Underwriter's Ticker (e.g., GS) <Equity> <Enter>: See DES and CF.

LEAG <Enter>: Underwriter/Legal Advisor rankings.

LMX <Enter>: Underwriter/Legal Advisor rankings.

CACT <Enter>: CACT screen tracts major corporate moves including mergers and division sales.

MA <Enter>: Merger Advisor search engine.

<HELP> for explanation, <MENU> for similar functions. EquityLTOP
Type 1, 2, or 3 <Go> or click on a market type for more league tables.

Top Underwriter Rankings

	Underwriter	Market Share(%)	Amount USD (Mln)	Fees (%)	Issues
1) Debt					
4) International Bonds	Deutsche Ba	8.0	139,867.	0.14	517
5) U.S. Bonds	JP Morgan	12.0	100,908.	0.44	510
6) Euromarket Bonds	Deutsche Ba	7.9	97,166.8	0.07	378
7) Asia-Pacific ex-Japa	HSBC Bank	5.0	17,477.8	0.47	200
2) Equity & Equity Linked					
8) Global Equity Offeri	Citi	10.4	17,304.2	2.80	100
9) U.S. Equity Offering	Citi	15.1	10,770.0	2.83	81
10) EMEA Equity Offeri	Goldman Sac	12.4	3,234.97	n/a	8
11) Asia-Pacific Equity	UBS	10.6	4,849.51	2.53	29
3) Syndicated Loans					
12) U.S. Loans	Bank of Amer	16.3	78,758.5	n/a	320
13) EMEA Loans Manda	RBS	7.1	14,624.4	n/a	77
14) Asia-Pac ex-Japan	ANZ Banking	7.4	6,249.77	n/a	51

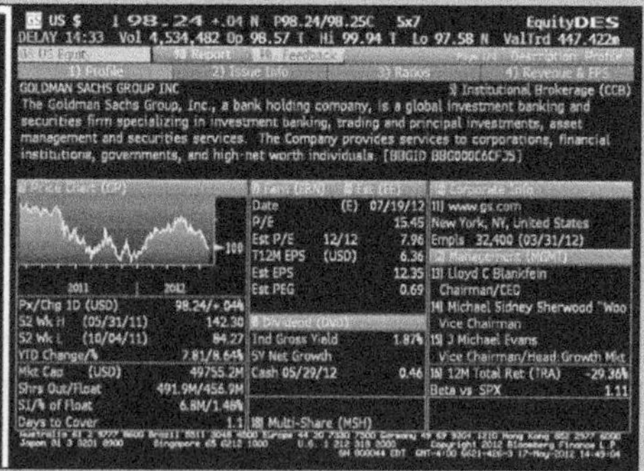

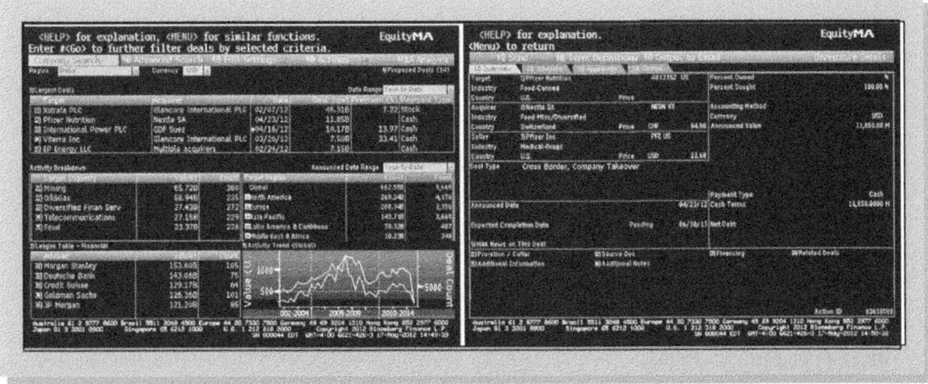

Financial Service Industry, the 2008 Financial Crisis, and Regulations

Investment banking firms, commercial banks, insurance companies, and pensions are the key participants in the financial service industry. Prior to the Great Depression, many commercial banks acted as investment bankers by underwriting securities and buying and selling securities for their customer. With over 10,000 commercial banks collapsing during the depression, Congress passed the Glass-Steagall Act in 1932, which separated investment banking from commercial banking. Starting in the 1980s and later with the passage of the Gramm-Leach-Bliley Act, though, the legal barriers between commercial and investment banking began to diminish. As a result, the financial industry saw many commercial bank holding companies acquiring investment banks, and later investment banks expanding their scope into insurance, real estate and other financial areas. During this period, Merrill-Lynch became an even larger multifunctional financial firm acquiring insurance and real estate companies to combine with its extensive investment banking and brokerage operations. However, large commercial banks such as Citicorp and UBS (formally United Bank of Switzerland) added investment banking to their commercial banking operation. Finally, the industry saw firms such as Goldman Sachs and Lehman Brother expand the scope of activities in investment banking and developing specializations in stocks, bonds, and derivatives.

2008 Financial Crisis

In June 2008, the subprime mortgage meltdown that began in August 2007 developed into a global credit crisis. This crisis gained steam throughout the first half of 2008 with the substantial asset value write downs by many global financial institutions, and a subsequent panic by these firms to raise billions of dollars in new capital from a variety of sources to repair their balance sheets. In an effort to stabilize financial markets, the Federal Reserve pumped billions of dollars into the banking system via new lending programs like the Term Auction Facility (TAF), Primary Dealer Credit

BLOOMBERG CREDIT CRISIS SCREENS

RESQ <Enter>: Bailout and Rescue Program.
SBPR <Enter>: Subprime News.
STNI Rumor <Enter>: Rumors and Speculation.
LEAD <Enter>: Economic Activity Trends.
HSST <Enter>: U.S. Housing and Construction Statistics.
DQRP <Enter>: Rank Deals by Collateral Performance.
DQSP <Enter>: Delinquent Loan Data by Servicer.
DELQ <Enter>: Credit Card Delinquency Rate.
BBMD <Enter>: Mortgage Delinquency Monitor.
REDQ <Enter>: Commercial Real Estate Delinquencies.
DQLO <Enter>: Delinquency Rates by Loan Originators.

Facility (PDCF), and the Term Securities Lending Facility (TSLF). By September 2008, the subprime mortgage meltdown had developed into a global credit crisis, culminating in a dramatic 10-day period from September 7 to September 17: the trillion-dollar mortgage giants Fannie Mae and Freddie Mac were placed into conservatorship by the Treasury; Merrill Lynch was hastily acquired by Bank of America; Lehman Brothers filed for the largest bankruptcy in American history; American International Group (AIG) received an emergency $85 billion lifeline from the Federal Reserve as it teetered on the brink of insolvency; Washington Mutual was seized by the FDIC and its deposits were sold to JPMorgan Chase; the $700 billion Emergency Economic Stabilization Act (EESA) was passed by Congress and signed by the President Bush. During this period, the U.S. Federal Reserve took extraordinary emergency steps by guaranteeing money market funds, backstopping commercial paper programs, coordinating a global interest rate cut with other central banks, making loans to institutions collateralized by mortgage-backed and asset-backed securities, and purchasing such securities as part of their open market operations. Similarly, the Treasury structured the Troubled Asset Relief Program (TARP) to shore up U.S. bank balance sheets with capital injections. The impact of these unprecedented liquidity measures undertaken by the Fed was to increase the Fed's balance sheet from $850 billion in August to $2.2 trillion in November and led to lower rates from there already existing low levels. In fact, short-term Treasury rates were at one point at negative levels!

Dodd-Frank Wall Street Reform and Consumer Protection Act

As for the financial industry, the events leading up to the 2008 crisis led to passage of the Dodd-Frank Wall Street Reform and Consumer Protection Act, aimed at preventing another financial crisis. Some of the key tenets of the act include those aimed at protecting consumers, constraining large Wall Street bonuses, and ending bailouts to financial institutions in distress (i.e., ending the "Too Big to Fail" bailouts). See Exhibit 9.16 for a summary of some of the provisions related to the investment industry.

EXHIBIT 9.16 Dodd-Frank Wall Street Reform and Consumer Protection Act—Select Provisions Related to Investment Banks

Constraints on Size: The Financial Stability Oversight Council can make recommendations to the Federal Reserve for increasingly strict rules for capital, leverage, liquidity, risk management, and other requirements as companies grow in size and complexity, with significant requirements on companies that pose risks to the financial system.

Fed Regulation of Nonbank Financial Companies: With a 2/3 vote of the Financial Stability Oversight Council and vote of the chair, gives the Federal Reserve the authority to regulate a nonbank financial company if the council believe there would be negative effects on the financial system if the company failed or its activities would pose a risk to the financial stability of the US.

Break Up Large, Complex Companies: Able to approve, with a 2/3 vote of The Financial Stability Oversight Council and vote of the chair, a Federal Reserve decision to require a large, complex company, to divest some of its holdings if it poses a grave threat to the financial stability of the United States .

Technical Expertise: Creates a new Office of Financial Research within Treasury to be staffed with a highly sophisticated staff of economists, accountants, lawyers, former supervisors, and other specialists to support the council's work by collecting financial data and conducting economic analysis.

Bankruptcy: Most large financial companies that fail are expected to have their reorganization or liquidation resolved through the bankruptcy process.

Limits on Debt Guarantees: To prevent bank runs, the FDIC can guarantee debt of solvent insured banks, but only after meeting serious requirements: 2/3 majority of the Board and the FDIC board must determine there is a threat to financial stability; the Treasury Secretary approves terms and conditions and sets a cap on overall guarantee amounts; the President activates an expedited process for Congressional approval.

Raising Standards and Regulating Hedge Funds: Requires that hedge funds and private equity firms have their advisors register with the SEC as investment advisers and provide information about their trades and portfolios necessary to assess systemic risk. This data will be shared with the systemic risk regulator and the SEC will report to Congress annually on how it uses this data to protect investors and market integrity.

Oversight of Credit Rating Agencies: Creates an Office of Credit Ratings at the SEC with its own compliance staff and the authority to fine agencies. The SEC is required to examine Nationally Recognized Statistical Ratings Organizations at least once a year and make key findings public.

Disclosure: Requires Nationally Recognized Statistical Ratings Organizations to disclose their methodologies, their use of third parties for due diligence efforts, and their ratings track record.

SEC: (1) Gives SEC the authority to impose a fiduciary duty on brokers who give investment advice—the advice must be in the best interest of their customers; (2) Creates a program within the SEC to encourage people to report securities violations; (3) Gives the SEC authority to grant shareholders proxy access to nominate directors; (4) Directs the SEC to clarify disclosures relating to compensation, including requiring companies to provide charts that compare their executive compensation with stock performance over a five-year period; (5) Provides more resources to the chronically underfunded agency to carry out its new duties.

Source: "Brief Summary of the Dodd-Frank Wall Street Reform and Consumer Protection Act," http://banking.senate.gov/public/_files/070110_Dodd_Frank_Wall_Street_Reform_comprehensive_summary_Final.pdf.

Conclusion

Just like the direct markets for stocks and bonds, the intermediary financial markets offer investors a wide array of instruments for financing and investing: from short-term securities, such as CDs, BAs, and shares in money market funds, to intermediate- and long-term instruments, such as MBSs, mutual fund shares, ETFs, pension plans, annuities, and GICs. The investment and commercial banks, insurance companies, investment funds, and pension funds that make up the intermediary market are important players in the financial markets. They invest billions of dollars each year into equity and debt securities from the inflows they received from the premiums from their insurance policies, their savings and investment products, and the pension and endowment funds they managed. In the next chapter, we continue our analysis of intermediaries by examining in more detail mortgage-backed and asset-backed securities.

Website Information

1. *Wall Street Journal* site: http://online.wsj.com/public/us
   - Click "Market Data" tab.
   - Fixed-income ETFs:
     - Click "ETF" tab.
     - Click "ETF Screener."
     - Fixed-Income.
   - Mutual funds:
     - Click "Mutual Fund" tab.
     - Use Screener.
   - Money rates:
     - Click "Bond Rates" and "Credit Market."
     - Click "Money Rate."
2. FINRA: Go to www.finra.org/index.htm, Sitemap, Mutual Funds, and Fixed Income. Click "Taxable or Tax-Exempt Searches."
3. Yahoo: Go to http://screen.yahoo.com/funds.html, Fund Screener.
4. Real Estate Investment Trusts: www.nareit.com
   Price and other information on REITs can be found by going to Yahoo!, http://screen.yahoo.com/funds.html; use Stock Screener to find REITs.
5. Investment Company Institute: www.ici.org
6. Investment Company Institute Facts Book: www.icifactbook.org/index.html
7. Investment funds and ratings:
   - http://investing.quicken.com/investing/
   - www.morningstar.com
   - www.lipper.com
8. Money market funds: www.imoneynet.com
9. Hedge funds:
   - www.thehfa.org

- www.hedgefund.net
- Hedge fund Rankings: www.cta-online.com/hedgeland.asp (registration required)

10. Federal Reserve flow-of-fund accounts: www.federalreserve.gov/releases/z1/Current/
    - Go to PDF (Complete File) for Flow of Fund Tables by sector and security type.
    - See Table L109-L113 for banks.
    - See Table L122 for mutual funds.
    - See Table L123 for ETFs.
    - See Table L128 for REITs.
    - Go to "Data Download Program" to download series to Excel
11. British Bankers Association site: BBA, LIBOR, and other information: www.bba.org.uk
    - LIBOR rates: www.bbalibor.com
    - Information on how LIBOR used for benchmarking are determined: www.bbalibor.com/bba/jsp/polopoly.jsp?d=1627.
12. Insurance and Pension Funds:
    - Federal Reserve Flow of Fund Accounts: www.federalreserve.gov/releases/z1/Current/
    - Go to PDF for Flow of Fund Tables by sector and security type.
        - See Table L117 for life insurance assets.
        - See Table L116 for property and casualty insurance assets.
        - See Table L117-L119 for pension fund assets.
        - Go to "Data Download Program" to download series to Excel.
13. Pension fund information and updates: www.ifebp.org
14. Social Security Fund information: www.ssa.gov
15. Pension Benefit Guarantee Corporation: www.pbgc.gov

Selected References

Ambachtsbeer, K. P. 1998. How should pension funds manage risk? *Journal of Applied Corporate Finance* 11:122–127.

Friedberg, L., and M. T. Owyang. 2002. Not your father's pension plan: The rise of 401(k) and other defined contribution plans. *Review*, Federal Reserve Bank of St. Louis (January–February):23–34.

Mishkin, F. S., and S. G. Eakins. 2003. *Financial Markets and Institutions*, 4th ed. Boston: Addison-Wesley.

Zirky, E. A., and R. M. Mackey. 1993. Pension plan funding strategies: Defining terms. *Pension World* (August):40–41.

Bloomberg Exercises

1. Use the Bloomberg BTMM screen to find current money market rates.

2. Use the Bloomberg BBAM screen to find current and past LIBORs.
3. Select a commercial or investment bank (e.g., Bank of America [BAC], Well Fargo [WFC], U.S. Bank [USB], or Goldman Sachs) and study some of its debt offerings (e.g., commercial paper, bank notes, or MTNs) by going to the debt's menu screen: Ticker <Corp> <Enter>.
4. Bloomberg's LOAN, LONZ, and PREL screens can be used to search and analyze loans by categories. Study the functionality of the screens by searching for the following types of loans and information:
   - Syndicated loans: LOAN <Corp> <Enter>.
   - Corporate loan: Ticker (IBM) LOAN <Corp> <Enter>.
   - Loans in different countries: PREL <Enter>; select from the dropdown tabs: loans, country (e.g., North America), and currency (e.g., USD).
   - News on loans: TLOA <Enter>.
   - Newsletter on leveraged finance: BRIEF <Enter>, click "Leveraged Finance."
5. Learn more about the different types of funds and their classifications by going to the FUND screen and "Classification" link: FUND <Enter>; click "Fund Classification" and click type; or simply enter MFOD and click type: Equity, Debt, Money Market, Real Estate, Commodity, and Alternative.
6. The performances of funds by type (e.g., mutual, hedge fund, ETFs, and unit investment trust) can be found on Bloomberg's Fund Heat Map screen, FMAP. Use the screen to identify the top performers based on total return for several types: FMAP <Enter>, click "Fund Type" in "View By" dropdown.
7. The performances of funds by objective (e.g., equity, debt, asset allocation, money market, and alternative) can be found on Bloomberg's Fund Heat Map screen, FMAP. Use the screen to identify the top performers based on total return for several objectives: FMAP <Enter>, Click "Objective" in "View By" dropdown.
8. Bloomberg's WMF screen provides snapshots of the best mutual funds by category in terms of their total return. Using this screen, examine several funds in different categories. Select several of the funds and study them using the functions on the fund's menus screen (Fund Ticker <Equity> <Enter>). Functions to include: DES, historical fund analysis (HFA), fund holdings (MHD), relative valuation (RV), and price graph (GP).
9. Use the Bloomberg fund search screen, FSRC, to search for the following types of debt-type funds and ETFs:
   - Fund type: Open-End; Classification (Asset Class Focus): Debt; Management Style: Total Return; Analytic criterion: input total return for one year of greater than X percent (e.g., 10 percent or 20 percent).
   - Fund type: Open-End; Classification (Asset Class Focus): Debt; Management Style: Principal Preservation; Maturity band Focus: Long Term (> 10 years); Ratings Focus: Investment Grade; Analytic criterion: Input total return for one year of greater than X percent (e.g., 4 percent or 10 percent).
   - Fund Type: Exchange-Traded Product; Classification (Asset Class Focus): Debt; Ratings Focus: Speculative/High Yield.

- Fund type: Fund of Funds; classification (Asset Class Focus): Debt; Analytic criterion: input total return for one year of greater than X percent (e.g., 10 percent).
- Select one of the funds from each of your searches and study it using the functions on the fund's menus screen (Fund Ticker <Equity> <Enter>). Functions to include: DES, historical fund analysis (HFA), fund holdings (MHD), relative valuation (RV), and price graph (GP).

10. Bloomberg's HFND screen provides a menu for evaluating hedge funds. From the screen, you can access the WHF screen that ranks hedged funds by category (or you can simply access the screen directly (WHF <Enter>). Using the HFND or WHF screen, identify several hedge funds in different categories.
11. Use the Bloomberg fund search screen, FSRC, to search for different types of government, government/corporate, and global debt funds. That is: fund type: Open-end, Exchange-Traded Fund, or Closed-End Fund; classification, Bloomberg Objective, Debt: select type; analytic criterion: input total return for one year of greater than X percent (e.g., 10 percent). You can also use the SECF screen: SECF <Enter>, Funds tab and Open End tab, and enter debt in Focus box and type in objective (e.g., government) in the Objective box. Searches to consider:
    - Government/Agency—Long Term
    - Government/Agency—Intermediate Term
    - Government/Corporate
    - International Debt
    - Global Debt

    Select one of the funds from your searches and study it using the functions on the fund's menus screen (Fund Ticker <Equity> <Enter>. Functions to include: DES, historical fund analysis (HFA), relative valuation (RV), and price graph (GP).
12. Use the Bloomberg fund search screen, FSRC, to search for different types of money market funds. Money market funds can be screened by going to "Classifications" tab, selecting "Money Market" from "Bloomberg Objective" tab. You can also use the SECF screen: SECF <Enter>, Funds tab, and Open End tab, and enter money market in Focus box.

    Select some of the funds from your searches and study them using the functions on the fund's menus screen (Fund Ticker <Equity> <Enter>.
13. Use the Bloomberg fund search screen, FSRC, to search for different types of municipal mutual funds by state. Funds can be screened by state by going to "Classifications" tab, selecting "Debt" from "Bloomberg Objective" tab, and then selecting a state. That is: classification (Bloomberg Objective, Debt): select state. You can also use the SECF screen: SECF <Enter>, Funds tab and Open End tab, and enter debt in Focus box and type in objective (e.g., Muni-Florida) in the Objective box. Select some of the funds from your searches and study them using the functions on the fund's menus screen (Fund Ticker <Equity> <Enter>. Functions to include: DES, historical fund analysis (HFA), relative valuation (RV), and price graph (GP).

14. Bloomberg's REIT screen provides a menu for searching for real estate investment trusts by regions: U.S., Europe, Asia, Australia, Canada, and other. Using the screens, search and select some REITs from different regions. You can also use the SECF screen: SECF <Enter>, type "REIT" in the Search box. Study the REITs using the functions on the REIT's menus screen (Ticker <Equity> <Enter>). Functions to include: DES, total return (COMP), relative valuation (RV), holders (HDS), and price graph (GP).
15. Go to the FUND screen to find news and information on mutual funds, hedge funds, and ETFS: FUND <Enter>, use the "News and Research" links.
16. The hedge fund industry is a leader in creating new investment product. To keep current, go to the BRIEF screen to access the Bloomberg newsletter: "Hedge Fund."
17. Investment banks are an important financial intermediary. Study some of the activities and deals of investment banks by exploring Bloomberg's LTOP and LEAG screens.
18. Keep current on mergers by accessing the following screen:
    - BRIEF screen to access the Bloomberg newsletter: "Mergers."
    - MA to access merger adviser search.

Notes

1. The growth of the CD market over the past three decades has been accompanied by innovations. In the 1980s, a floating-rate CD (FRCD) was introduced. The maturity on a FRCD ranges from 18 months to 5 years, with the coupon rates reset periodically to equal the rate on a comparable CD rate or the London Interbank Offered Rate. Other CDs with unique features that have been introduced over the years are ones with rates tied to the stock market (bear and bull CDs), longer-term CDs with gradually increasing rates (rising-rates CDs), and contracts to buy CDs now and in the future (forward CDs and rollover or roly-poly CDs).
2. It should be noted that when bank loans are held in a portfolio they must be marked to market. This can be difficult if a market is not transparent. Reuters Loan Pricing Corporation's Loan Trade Data Base (Reuter's LPC) provides institutional investors with dealer quotes. S&P Leveraged Commentary and Data (LCD) also has developed a leveraged loan index that can be used as determine fair values of loans.
3. The market for BAs has existed for over 80 years in the United States, although its origin dates back to the twelfth century. In the United States, this market grew steadily in the 1960s and 1970s. The market accelerated from $7.6 billion in 1970 to almost $80 billion in 1985, reflecting the growth in world trade. Due to alternative financing, though, the BA market has declined marginally since 1985.
4. For example, if the United States' reserve requirement were 5 percent on time deposits for a certain size bank, while no requirements existed in the Bahamas, then a U.S. bank, by accepting a domestic deposit, could only loan out 95 percent of the deposit, earning 95 percent of the loan rate, in contrast to a Bahamian deposit in which 100 percent of the deposit could be loaned out to earn the full amount of the loan rate. In a competitive market for deposits and loans, the rates on the Bahamian loans and deposits would have to be made more favorable, since a depositor or borrower would prefer his own country.

5. Although it is generally true that the number of shares of a closed fund is fixed, such funds occasionally issue new shares either through a public offering or through a share dividend, which is sometimes offered to shareholders who are given an option of receiving either cash or new shares based on the NAV of the fund if the dividend or interest income is reinvested. Also, some funds occasionally go into the market and purchase their own shares.
6. Section 13(f) of the 1934 Securities Exchange Act requires institutional investment managers with investment discretion on over $100 million or more of certain equity securities to file quarterly reports disclosing their equity holdings. An institutional investment manager is an entity that either invests in, or buys and sells, securities for its own account. For example, banks, insurance companies, broker/dealers, and corporations and pension funds that manage their own investment portfolios. An institutional investment manager is also a natural person or an entity that exercises investment discretion over the account of any other natural person or entity. Form 13F must be filed within 45 days of the end of each calendar quarter. The Bloomberg's FLNG Screen: FLNG <Go>, screen displays 13F Filings. From the 13F Filings screen, one can search through a list of companies with 13F Filings status. One can also display aggregated 13F Filings and break down the filings by type: All, Pensions, Banks, Mutual Funds, Venture Capital, and Private Equity.
7. The Barclays, J. P. Morgan, and Merrill Lynch indexes require a subscription to access. The subscription can be made through Bloomberg. With the subscription, one is able to access the indexes from the Bloomberg terminal.
8. Managers of ETFs contract with third parties to calculate a real-time estimate of an ETF's current value, called the *intraday indicative value* (*IIV*). The IIVs are disseminated at regular intervals during the trading day. Investors, in turn, can observe any discrepancies between the ETF's share price and its IIV during the trading day. When a gap exists between the ETF share price and its IIV, investors may decide to trade in either the ETF share or the underlying securities that the ETF holds in its portfolio in order to attempt to capture a profit. This trading helps to narrow the discrepancy between the price of the ETF share and IIV. For more information on ETF, see *Investment Company Fact Book*, www.icifactbook.org/fb_sec3.html#what.
9. Using actuarial tables, life insurance companies can predict with a relatively high degree of accuracy when death benefits would have to be paid.
10. There are three general types of annuities: A *life annuity*, which pays a fixed amount regularly until the investor's death; a *last survivor's annuity*, which pays regular fixed amounts until both the investor and spouse die; and a *fixed-period annuity*, which makes regular fixed payments for a specified period (e.g., 5, 10, or 20 years), with payments made to a beneficiary if the investor dies. These annuities are referred to as fixed annuities. In addition to fixed annuities, insurance companies also offer a *variable annuity* in which regular payments are not fixed, but rather depend on the returns from the investments made by the insurance company (the insurance company sometimes invests in a mutual fund that they also manage). Finally, insurance companies offer *deferred annuities* (variable or fixed) that allow an investor to make a series of payments instead of a single payment.
11. The growth in GICs started in the 1980s with the increased investment in 401(k) plans. In addition to insurance companies, banks have also become an active participant in this market offering *bank investment contracts* (*BICs*). BICs are deposit obligations with a guaranteed rate and fixed maturity. BICs and GICs are sometimes referred to as *stable value investments*.
12. With the large Baby Boom generation starting to reach retirement, the government forecast that the Social Security Trust Fund (built from excess payroll taxes) will be depleted by 2040 (some economist predict this will happened as early as 2020). After that, social

security taxes would cover only 75 percent of the benefits. Compounding the problem is that the investments of the Social Security Trust Fund are in government securities (financing the deficit) that would have to be redeemed. For information on the Social Security Fund Assets, go to www.ssab.gov; www.ssab.gov/oact/stats.

13. Penny Benny is facing a severe funding crisis. Currently, there are many defined-benefit plans facing problems with funding obligations as a result of longer life spans, higher medical costs, and weaker economic conditions. Many firms with defined-benefit plans are also at a competitive disadvantage to other companies. Before their bankruptcy, General Motors' profit margin per car was estimated to be 0.5 percent; without pension and retiree health cost, there margins would have been 5.5 percent. For a further analysis of the pension fund crisis facing some U.S. companies, see Mishkin and Eakins (2003), pp. 585–587. For information on the funding crisis facing Penny Benny, go to www.pbgc.gov and www.pbgc.gov/media/key-resources-for-the-press/content/page15247.html#qi1.

CHAPTER 10

Mortgage-Backed and Asset-Backed Securities and Securitization

Introduction

One of the most innovative developments to occur in the security markets over the last three decades has been the securitization of assets. Securitization involves creating a new security backed by a large number of assets (e.g., mortgages or accounts receivable) that have been grouped into a pool. A trustee, such as a financial institution or government agency, often holds the pool of assets that serve as the collateral for the new securities. The new securities are then sold to investors as asset-backed securities. The most common type of asset-backed security is a *pass-through*: a security that has the cash flows from the pool of assets pass through the trustee before being disbursed to the asset-backed security holders.

The securitization process starts when an *originator,* who owns the assets, sells them to *conduit* (e.g., government agency or bank) that assembles the pool of assets. The conduit/issuer then creates a security backed by the assets; the asset-backed security or pass-through is then sold to investors. As noted, the securitization process often involves a third-party trustee, who not only holds the securities but also ensures that the issuer complies with the terms underlying the asset-backed security. Further, many securitized assets are backed by credit enhancements, such as a guarantee from the conduit or a third-party against the default on the underlying assets.

The most common types of asset-backed securities are those secured by mortgages, automobile loans, credit card receivables, and home equity loans. The largest type and the one in which the process of securitization has been most extensively applied is mortgages. Asset-backed securities formed with mortgages are called *mortgage-backed securities* (*MBSs*), or *mortgage pass-throughs.* These securities entitle the holder to the cash flow from a pool of mortgages. Typically, the issuer of a MBS buys a portfolio or pool of mortgages of a certain type from mortgage originators, such as a commercial banks, savings and loans, or mortgage bankers. The issuer finances the purchases of the mortgages through the sale of the mortgage pass-throughs, which have a claim on the mortgage portfolio's cash flow. The mortgage originators usually agree to continue to service the loans, passing the payments on to the MBS holders.

In this chapter, we examine the construction and characteristics of agency residential MBSs, nonagency residential MBSs, commercial MBSs and other asset-backed securities. As we will see, the characteristics and value of such securities ultimately depends on the characteristics of the underlying asset. We begin our analysis with an overview of residential mortgage loans.

Residential Mortgage Loans

A mortgage is a loan secured by a specific real estate property, typically the one being acquired by the borrower. Real estate property can be either residential or nonresidential. Residential includes houses, condominiums, and apartments; it is classified as either single family or multiple family. Nonresidential includes commercial and agricultural property. In a standard mortgage, the lender will place a lien against the property. A *lien* is a public record attached to the title of the property that specifies the lender has the right to sell the property if the owner defaults.

Most mortgages originate from commercial banks, savings and loans, other thrifts, or mortgage bankers.[1] The mortgage originator underwrites the loan, processes the necessary documents, conducts credit checks, evaluates the property, sets up the loan contracts and terms, and provides the funds. Mortgages differ in terms of their maturity, interest rate (fixed or adjustable), security, credit quality, and prepayment.

Maturity

Many residential mortgages have original maturities of 30 years, with shorter maturities of 10, 15, or 20 years also popular. The majority of mortgages are fully amortized, meaning each month the mortgage payment includes both a payment of interest on the mortgage balance and a payment of principal, with the total number of monthly payments being such that the loan is retired at maturity. There are some mortgages structured as *balloon loans.* With a balloon loan, the borrower makes payments based on an amortized schedule, such as 30 years (or just interest-only payments), for a specified period (e.g., three to five years), at which time the total loan balance becomes due. If the borrower's credit profile has not deteriorated, then the lender will typically refinance the debt.[2]

Fixed-Rate and Adjustable-Rate Mortgages

Mortgage loans are either fixed rate (FRM), with the rate fixed for the life of the mortgage, or adjustable rate, in which the rate is reset periodically based on some prespecified rate or index. For an *adjustable-rate mortgage* (ARM), the monthly payments are recalculated at each specified reset date. At each reset date, the rate is set equal to a reference rate plus a margin (spread over the reference rate or index). The reference rate could be a market-determined rate, such as the average T-bill rate, London Interbank Offered Rate (LIBOR), the Constant Maturity Treasury (CMT) rate, or a 12-month Moving Treasury Average (MTA), or the reference rate could be an index, such as the National or Federal Home Loan Calculated Cost of Fund Index (COFI). Some ARMs also place a periodic cap on the reset rate, limiting the amount the rate can increase or decrease each period and some have a lifetime cap, specifying the maximum and minimum rates on the mortgage over its term to maturity. Both FRMs and ARMs can include *discount points* (or *points*). Points are interest payments made at the beginning of the loan. For example, the borrower might agree to pay 1 percent (one point) of the loan at the beginning in return for a reduced interest rate.

Other Mortgage Types

Since the late 1970s, other types of mortgage loans have been introduced. These include *graduated payment mortgages* (*GPMs*), which start with low monthly payments in earlier years and then gradually increase. One type of GPM is the *2/28 ARM,* often referred to as the *teaser loan.* These loans fix the rate for two years and then increase them significantly. There are also *reset mortgages,* which allows the borrower to renegotiate the terms of the mortgage at specified future dates and *interest-only mortgages* (IOs), in which only the interest is paid for a specified period (*lockout period*), after which the loan is fully amortized for the remaining life of the loan. Between FRMs and ARMs, there are also *hybrid ARMs* in which the rate is fixed for the early years of the mortgages (e.g., five years) and then reset to an ARM. Exhibit 10.1 summarizes the different types of mortgage loans.

Mortgage Payment

The monthly payment on a mortgage, p, is found by solving for the p that makes the present value of all scheduled payments equal to the mortgage balance, F_0. That is:

$$F_0 = \sum_{t=1}^{M} \frac{p}{(1+(R^A/12))^t}$$

$$F_0 = p\left[\frac{1-1/(1+(R^A/12))^M}{R^A/12}\right] \tag{10.1}$$

$$p = \frac{F_0}{\left[\frac{1-1/(1+(R^A/12))^M}{R^A/12}\right]}$$

where:

F_0 = face value of the loan $\quad$ p = monthly payment

R^A = annualized interest rate $\quad$ M = maturity in months

EXHIBIT 10.1 Mortgage Types and Terms

1. **Conventional Mortgage:** Mortgage loan not guaranteed by the government or federal agency.
2. **Insured Mortgage**: Mortgage guaranteed by the Federal Housing Administration or Veterans Administration.
3. **Private Mortgage Insurance** (PMI) **Mortgage:** Conventional mortgage insured by a private mortgage insurer.
4. **Adjustable-Rate Mortgage** (ARM): Mortgage whose rates are tied to the rates on another security or index and adjusted periodically.
5. **Graduated Payment Mortgage** (GPM): Mortgage that starts with low monthly payments in earlier years and then gradually increases.
6. **Reset Mortgage**: Mortgage that allows the borrower to renegotiate the terms of the mortgage at specified future dates.
7. **Interest-only Mortgage** (IO): Mortgage in which only the interest is paid for a specified period (lockout period), after which the loan is fully amortized for the remaining life of the loan.
8. **Hybrid Adjustable-Rate Mortgage**: Mortgage in which the rate is fixed for the early years of the mortgage (e.g., five years) and then reset to an ARM.
9. **Shared-Appreciation Mortgage:** Mortgage in which the lender provides a low interest rate in exchange for a share in the appreciation of the real estate.
10. **Equity Participation Mortgage**: Mortgage in which the lender accepts a lower down payment or lower monthly payments in exchange for a share in the appreciation of the property.
11. **Second Mortgage:** Loan secured by a second lien against the property.
12. **Reverse Annuity Mortgage**: Mortgage that has an increasing balance in which the lender advances periodic funds (usually on a monthly basis) to the owner/borrower. The loan comes due when the property is sold.
13. **2/28 ARM or Teaser Loan:** An ARM that starts at a very low rate for first two years and then is reset at a significantly higher rate.
14. **Stretch Loan**: Loan that allows borrowers to commit more than 50% of their gross monthly income to the monthly mortgage payment.
15. **Stated-Income Loan:** Mortgage loan that allows borrowers to state their incomes without verification.
16. **Piggyback Loan:** Two loans consisting of a first mortgage and a second loan (usually a second mortgage) that starts at origination. The second loan is used to finance the down payment.
17. **Conforming Limit Loan:** Mortgages guaranteed by Fannie Mae and Freddie Mac have limits on the loan balance, referred to as conforming limits. As of January 2008, the maximum for one-family homes in the lower 48 was $417,000 and $801,950 for four-family homes. (The 2008 Economic Stimulus Act gave Fannie Mae and Freddie Mac temporary authority to purchase mortgages with loan balances that exceed the conforming limits.)
18. **Jumbo Loan:** Loan greater than the conforming limits set by Fannie Mae and Freddie Mac.

Thus, the monthly payment on a $100,000, 30-year, 9 percent FRM would be $804.62:

$$p = \frac{\$100{,}000}{\left[\dfrac{1 - 1/(1 + (.09/12))^{360}}{.09/12}\right]} = \$804.62$$

The \$804.62 payment applies toward both the interest and principal. After the monthly payment (p) has been made, the principal balance at the end of month t is

$$F_t = F_{t-1} + \left[(R^A/12)F_{t-1}\right] - p \tag{10.2}$$

and the interest payment for month t is

$$\text{Interest Payment} = (R^A/12)(F_{t-1}) \tag{10.3}$$

Exhibit 10.2 shows the schedule of interest and principal payments on the \$100,000, 30-year, 9 percent mortgage for selected months, and the figure in the exhibit shows the payments of scheduled interest and principal payments over the life of mortgage. The figure highlights the pattern that in the early life of the mortgage most of the monthly payments go toward paying interest, whereas in the later life of the mortgage, the payments are applied more towards the payment of the principal.

Suppose the \$100,000, 30-year mortgage were an ARM with an annual reset. For an ARM, the monthly payments are adjusted at the reset dates, with the new payment, p, calculated based on the balance, the remaining term, and the new reset rate. This process of resetting payments is known as *recasting*. For example, at the beginning of month 13, the balance is \$99,316.80 and there are 29 years or 348 months remaining on the mortgage. If the reset rate were 10 percent, then the monthly payment would increase from \$804.62 to \$876.45:

$$p = \frac{\$99{,}316.80}{\left[\dfrac{1 - 1/(1 + (.10/12))^{348}}{.10/12}\right]} = \$876.45$$

Next, suppose the \$100,000, 30-year, 9 percent mortgage were an interest-only mortgage for five years and then was set at the 9 percent note rate for the remaining 25 years. For the first five years (the lockout period), the monthly mortgage payments would be \$750 (= (.09 / 12)(\$100,000). Starting in year five, the mortgage payment would be set to equal the payment on a fully amortized loan for 25 years at 9 percent. This would result in the monthly payment's increasing 11.89 percent from \$750 to \$839.20:

$$p = \frac{\$100{,}000}{\left[\dfrac{1 - 1/(1 + (.09/12))^{300}}{.09/12}\right]} = \$839.20$$

Finally, suppose the \$100,000, 9 percent mortgage were a balloon loan with payments based on a 30-year amortization schedule and with the loan balance due at the end of five years (or the beginning of year 6). As shown in Exhibit 10.2, the borrower in this case would pay \$804.62 each month and would owe \$95,965.02 at the balloon date.

EXHIBIT 10.2 Cash Flow from Fixed-Rate Mortgage: Maturity = 30 Years (360 months), Rate = 9 percent

Period	Balance	Interest	Principal	Payment
1	$100,000.00	$750.00	$54.62	$804.62
2	$99,945.38	$749.59	$55.03	$804.62
3	$99,890.35	$749.18	$55.45	$804.62
4	$99,834.90	$748.76	$55.86	$804.62
5	$99,779.04	$748.34	$56.28	$804.62
60	$95,965.02	$719.74	$84.88	$804.62
263	$55,698.95	$417.74	$386.88	$804.62
264	$55,312.07	$414.84	$389.78	$804.62
265	$54,922.28	$411.92	$392.71	$804.62
266	$54,529.58	$408.97	$395.65	$804.62
267	$54,133.93	$406.00	$398.62	$804.62
268	$53,735.31	$403.01	$401.61	$804.62
269	$53,333.70	$400.00	$404.62	$804.62
270	$52,929.08	$396.97	$407.65	$804.62
360	$798.63	$5.99	$798.63	$804.62

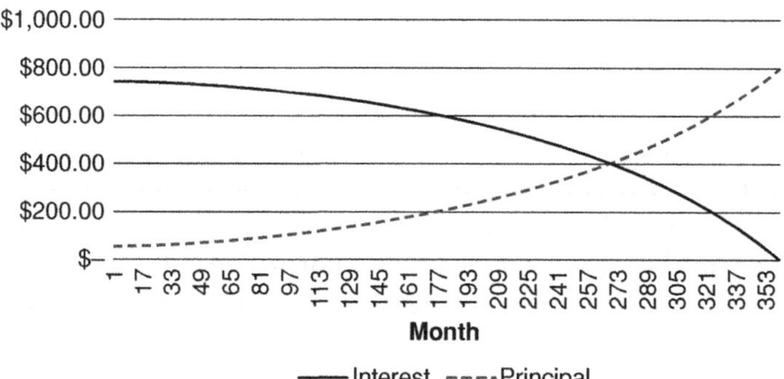

Mortgage Guarantees

In addition to the property securing the mortgage, many mortgages are also insured against default by the borrower. Two federal agencies, the *Federal Housing Administration (FHA)* and the *Veteran's Administration (VA)* provide mortgage insurance to qualified borrowers.[3] FHA and VA mortgages typically require smaller down payments than conventional mortgages. The FHA is under the Department of Housing and Urban Development (HUD). HUD also administers the VA loan guarantee program that comes under the auspices of the U.S. Department of Veterans Affairs. FHA- and VA-insured mortgages are referred to as *insured mortgages*. Mortgage loans not guaranteed by these agencies are called *conventional loans*. Many conventional loans, though, are insured by *private mortgage insurance* companies (PMIs), such as the Mortgage Guarantee Investment Corporation (MGIV) or the PMI Group Inc. In addition to PMI-insured mortgages there are also many conventional loans that are not initially insured, but later receive insurance when they are pooled with other mortgages to back a MBS issue. Conventional loans that are packaged by Fannie Mae and Freddie Mac are ones that meet the underwriting guidelines of Fannie Mae and Freddie Mac (per type of property, loan-to-value ratios, credit score, and documentation). These loans are referred to *conforming loans*.

Credit Quality

Mortgage loans can be classified as prime, subprime, or alternative-A loans. A *prime* loan is considered a high-quality loan in which the borrower is deemed to have a strong income and credit history sufficient to make the loan payments, as well as a sufficient equity-to-property value such that the lender would be able to recover the mortgage balance in case there was a default and the lender was forced to sell the property. A *subprime loan,* however, is considered low quality, where the borrower is of higher risk of default and where the equity-to-property value is low, or where the mortgage has a secondary claim (e.g., a second mortgage). *Alternative-A loans* (or an *Alt-A-loans*) are mortgage loans somewhere between prime and subprime. They are considered to have almost prime quality, but have some factors that tend to increase their credit risk.

In assessing credit quality, lenders consider measures such as the payment-to-income (PTI) and *loan-to-value* (LTV) ratios. A *front PTI* ratio is the monthly payments (including property taxes and insurance) to the borrower's monthly gross income, whereas a *back PTI* is the ratio of monthly payments of the mortgage plus other monthly debt obligations (e.g., car loans and credit cards payments) to the borrower's monthly income. Front and back PTI ratios measure the ability of the borrower to make monthly payments. For a mortgage loan to be considered prime, it typically has to have a front ratio of 28 percent or less and a back ratio of 36 percent or less. The LTV, in turn, is the ratio of the amount of the loan to the market or appraised value of the property. The lower the LTV ratio, the greater the protection the lender has to recover the loan if the borrower defaults and the lender has to sell the repossessed property. In addition to PTI and LTV ratios, lenders also look at credit ratings and credit scores computed from statistically based models. Most of these ratings models are patterned after the one developed by Fair, Isaac, and Company (FICO). The models calculate a credit risk index or score for most borrowers based on such factors as the borrower's payment history, current debt, types of credit held, and number of credit inquiries. The borrower's credit score is commonly referred to as the *FICO score*. Today, the FICO score is one of the important inputs used to classify prime and subprime loans. Prime loans tend to have a FICO score of 600 or higher, with the average being 742, front and back PTIs of 28 percent and 26 percent, respectively, and LTV ratios of less than 95 percent. In contrast, a subprime loan typically has a FICO score below 660, with the average being 624, and higher PTIs and LTV ratios. An Alt-A-Loan, in turn, could have scores and ratios between the prime and subprime; for example, high FICO scores, but low PTI and LTV ratios.

Before securitization, most potential homebuyers who did not meet strict qualification standards were denied loans. As a result, most mortgages were considered prime. In 2000, the Mortgage Bankers Association estimated that 70 percent of all loans were prime conventional, 20 percent were FHA, 8 percent were VA, and 2 percent were subprime. With the combination of the growth in MBSs, the push by Congress to increase home ownership, and the introduction of innovative mortgage loans such as teasers, stretch loans, piggyback loans, and stated income loans (see Exhibit 10.1), subprime mortgages accelerated from 2000 to 2006. In 2006, the Mortgage Bankers Association estimated that 70 percent of all mortgage loans were conventional, with 17 percent of those being subprime. As a rule, if property values increase, subprime borrowers are in a position to sell their properties and payoff their loans. Unfortunately, the real estate market, which had been accelerating since 2001, cooled in 2006 when a number of the innovative loans were reset at higher rates that many borrowers could not make. This led to defaults, bankruptcies, the decline in property values, and ultimately the collapse of the subprime market and the beginning of financial crisis of 2008.

Prepayment

Prepayment is the amount of payment made in excess of the monthly mortgage payment. Total prepayment occurs when the entire balance is paid off before maturity. This can be the result of the borrower refinancing the loan or selling the property. Most mortgages have a *due-on-sale* requirement in which the mortgage balance must be paid when the property is sold. Prepayment can also be for only part of the balance. This is known as a *curtailment.* The borrower's right to prepay a loan in total or partially is an option that benefits the borrower. Some mortgages impose a prepayment penalty to minimize prepayment or to lower the prepayment cost to the lender for originating new loans at lower interest rates.

Mortgage Portfolio

After creating a number of mortgages, the mortgage originator ends up with a mortgage loan portfolio, which he may hold or sell to an agency or financial institution. The holder of the mortgage portfolio is subject to credit risk if the mortgages are not insured, liquidity risk, given that the portfolio is large and lacking divisibility, and *prepayment risk.*

Prepayment Risk

For the holder of a mortgage portfolio, prepayment creates an uncertainty concerning the portfolio's cash flows. For example, if a bank has a pool of mortgages with a weighted-average mortgage rate of 9 percent and mortgage rates, in turn, decrease in the market from 9 percent to 7 percent, then the bank's mortgage portfolio is likely to experience significant prepayment as borrowers refinance their loans. The option borrowers have to prepay makes it difficult for the lender to predict future cash flows or to determine the value of the portfolio. A number of prepayment models have been developed to try to predict the cash flows from a portfolio of mortgages. Most of these models estimate the prepayment rate, referred to as the *prepayment speed* or simply *speed,* in terms of four factors: refinancing incentive, seasoning (the age of the mortgage), monthly factors, and prepayment burnout.

The refinancing incentive is the most important factor influencing prepayment. If mortgage rates decrease below the mortgage loan rate, borrowers have a strong incentive to refinance. This incentive increases during periods of falling interest rates, with the greatest increases occurring when borrowers determine that rates have bottomed out. The refinancing incentive can be measured by the difference between the mortgage portfolio's weighted average rate, referred to as the *weighted-average coupon rate* (*WAC*) or *weighted average loan rate* (*WALT*) and the refinancing rate (R^{ref}). A study by Goldman, Sachs, and Company found that the annualized prepayment speed, referred to as the *conditional prepayment rate* (*CPR*), is greater the larger the positive difference between the WAC and R^{ref}. The study reported that when WAC – R^{ref} = 0 (known as the current coupon), FHA and VA mortgages prepay at a rate of approximately 6 percent, and conventional mortgages prepay at approximately 9 percent. The study also found that prepayment rates decrease slightly when mortgage rates are at a discount (WAC < R^{ref}) and the refinancing rate is increasing relative to the mortgage rate. In such cases, prepayment is primarily due to new home purchases and defaults. In contrast, Goldman, Sachs, and Company found that prepayment rates increase significantly when mortgage rates are at a premium (WAC > R^{ref}) and the refinancing rate is decreasing relative to the mortgage rate. For example, when the difference between the WAC and R^{ref} is between 3 percent and 4 percent, the prepayment rate for conventional mortgages equals approximately 50 percent of the outstanding pool, and for FHA/VA mortgages the rate equals 40 percent.

A second factor determining prepayment is the age of the mortgage, referred to as *seasoning.* Prepayment tends to be greater during the early part of the loan, and then stabilize after about three years. Exhibit 10.3 depicts a commonly referenced seasoning pattern known as the *PSA model* (Public Securities Association). In the standard PSA model, known as 100 PSA, the CPR starts at .2 percent for the first month and then increases at a constant rate of .2 percent per month to equal 6 percent at the 30th month; then after the 30th month the CPR stays at a constant 6 percent. Thus, for any month *t,* the CPR is

$$\begin{aligned} CPR &= .06\left(\frac{t}{30}\right), \text{ if } t \le 30, \\ CPR &= .06, \text{ if } t > 30 \end{aligned} \tag{10.4}$$

Note that the CPR is quoted on an annual basis. The monthly prepayment rate, referred to as the *single monthly mortality rate* (*SMM*), can be obtained given the annual CPR by using the following formula:

$$\text{SMM} = 1 - \left[1 - \text{CPR}\right]^{1/12} \tag{10.5}$$

The 100 PSA model is often used as a benchmark. The actual aging pattern will differ depending on whether the mortgage pool is current (WAC = R^{ref}), at a discount (WAC < R^{ref}), or at premium (WAC > R^{ref}). Analysts often refer to the applicable pattern as being a certain percentage of the PSA. For example, if the pattern is described as being 200 PSA, then the prepayment speeds are twice the 100 PSA rates, and if the pattern is described as 50 PSA, then the CPRs are half of the 100 PSA rates (see Exhibit 10.3). Thus, a current mortgage pool described by a 100 PSA would have an annual prepayment rate of 2 percent after 10 months (or a monthly prepayment rate of SMM = .00168), and a premium pool described as a 150 PSA would have a 3 percent CPR (or SMM = .002535) after 10 months.

In addition to the effect of seasoning, mortgage prepayment rates are also influenced by the month of the year, with prepayment tending to be higher during the summer months. *Monthly factors* can be taken into account by multiplying the CPR by the estimated monthly multiplier to obtain a monthly-adjusted CPR. PSA provides estimates of the monthly multipliers. Finally, many prepayment models also try to capture what is known as the *burnout factor*. The burnout factor refers to the tendency for premium mortgages to hit some maximum CPR and then level off. For example, in response to a 2 percent decrease in refinancing rates, a pool of premium mortgages might peak at a 40 percent prepayment rate after one year, then level off at approximately 25 percent.

In addition to the refinancing incentives, seasoning, monthly adjustments, and burnout factors, there are other factors that can influence the pool of mortgages:

EXHIBIT 10.3 PSA Prepayment Model

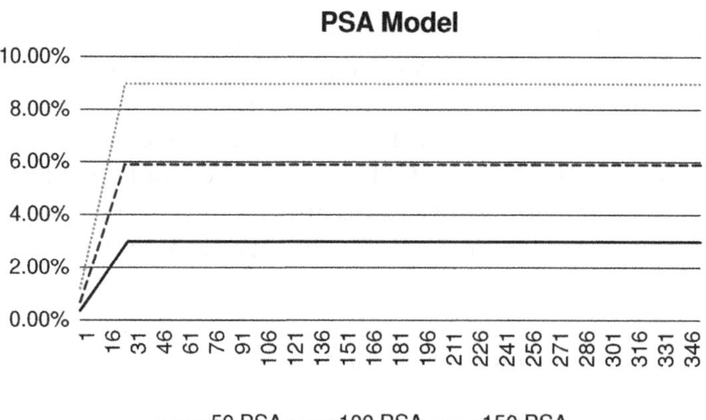

secular variations (variations due to different locations such as California or New York mortgages), types of mortgages (e.g., FRM or ARM, single-family or multiple-family, residential or commercial, etc.), and the original terms of the mortgage (30 years or 15 years). With these myriad factors influencing prepayment, analysts have found that estimating the cash flows from a pool of mortgages is significantly more difficult than estimating the cash flows of other fixed income securities.

Estimating a Mortgage Pool's Cash Flow with Prepayment

The cash flow from a portfolio of insured mortgages consists of the interest payments, scheduled principal, and prepaid principal. Consider a bank that has a pool of current fixed rate insured mortgages that are worth \$100 million, yield a WAC of 8 percent, and have a weighted average maturity of 360 months. For the first month, the portfolio would generate an aggregate mortgage payment of \$733,765:

$$p = \frac{\$100{,}000{,}000}{\left[\dfrac{1 - 1/(1 + (.08/12))^{360}}{.08/12}\right]} = \$733{,}765$$

From the \$733,765 payment, \$666,667 would go toward interest and \$67,098 would go toward the scheduled principal payment:

$$\text{Interest} = \left(\frac{R^A}{12}\right)F_0 = \left(\frac{.08}{12}\right)\$100{,}000{,}000 = \$666{,}667$$

$$\text{Scheduled Principal Payment} = p - \text{Interest} = \$733{,}765 - \$666{,}667 = \$67{,}098$$

The projected first month prepaid principal can be estimated with a prepayment model. Using the 100 PSA model, the monthly prepayment rate (SMM) for the first month ($t = 1$) is equal to 0.0001668:

$$CPR = \left(\frac{1}{30}\right).06 = .002$$

$$SMM = 1 - [1 - .002]^{1/12} = .00016682$$

Given the prepayment rate, the projected prepaid principal in the first month is found by multiplying the balance at the beginning of the month minus the scheduled principal by the SMM. Doing this yields a projected prepaid principal of \$16,671 in the first month:

$$\text{Prepaid Principal} = SMM\,[F_0 - \text{Scheduled Principal}]$$

$$\text{Prepaid Principal} = .00016682[\$100{,}000{,}000 - \$67{,}098] = \$16{,}671$$

Thus, for the first month, the mortgage portfolio would generate an estimated cash flow of \$750,435 and a balance at the beginning of the next month of \$99,916,231:

CF = Interest + Scheduled Principal + Prepaid Principal

CF = \$666,666 + \$67,098 + \$16,671 = \$750,435

Beginning Balance for Month 2 = F_0 − Scheduled Principal − Prepaid Principal

Beginning Balance for Month 2 = \$100,000,000 − \$67,098 − \$16,671 = \$99,916,231

In the second month (t = 2), the projected payment would be \$733,642 with \$666,108 going to interest and \$67,534 to scheduled principal:

$$p = \frac{\$99{,}916{,}231}{\left[\dfrac{1 - 1/(1 + (.08/12))^{359}}{.08/12}\right]} = \$733{,}642$$

$$\text{Interest} = \left(\frac{.08}{12}\right)(\$99{,}916{,}231) = \$666{,}108$$

$$\text{Scheduled Principal} = \$733{,}642 - \$666{,}108 = \$67{,}534.$$

Using the 100 PSA model, the estimated monthly prepayment rate is 0.000333946, yielding a projected prepaid principal in Month 2 of \$33,344:

$$CPR = \left(\frac{2}{30}\right).06 = .004$$

$$SMM = 1 - [1 - .004]^{1/12} = .000333946$$

$$\text{Prepaid Principal} = .000333946[\$99{,}916{,}231 - \$67{,}534] = 33{,}344$$

Thus, for the second month, the mortgage portfolio would generate an estimated cash flow of \$766,986 and have a balance at the beginning of month three of \$99,815,353:

$$CF = \$666{,}108 + \$67{,}534 + \$33{,}344 = \$766{,}986$$

$$\text{Beginning Balance for Month 3} = \$99{,}916{,}231 - \$67{,}534 - \$33{,}344 = \$99{,}815{,}353$$

Exhibit 10.4 summarizes the mortgage portfolio's cash flow for the first two months and other selected months. In examining the exhibit, two points should be noted: First, starting in month 30 the SMM remains constant at 0.005143; this reflects the 100 PSA model's assumption of a constant CPR of 6 percent starting in month 30; second, the projected cash flows are based on a static analysis in which rates are assumed fixed over the time period. A more realistic model would incorporate interest rate changes and corresponding different prepayment speeds.

EXHIBIT 10.4 Projected Cash Flows: Mortgage Portfolio = $100,000,000; WAC = 8 percent; WAM = 360 Months; Prepayment: 100 PSA

Period	Balance	Interest	*p*	Scheduled Principal	SMM	Prepaid Principal	Cash Flow
1	$100,000,000	$666,667	$733,765	$67,098	0.0001668	$16,671	$750,435
2	$99,916,231	$666,108	$733,642	$67,534	0.0003339	$33,344	$766,986
3	$99,815,353	$665,436	$733,397	$67,961	0.0005014	$50,011	$783,409
4	$99,697,380	$664,649	$733,029	$68,380	0.0006691	$66,664	$799,694
5	$99,562,336	$663,749	$732,539	$68,790	0.0008372	$83,294	$815,833
6	$99,410,252	$662,735	$731,926	$69,191	0.0010055	$99,892	$831,817
7	$99,241,170	$661,608	$731,190	$69,582	0.0011742	$116,449	$847,639
23	$94,291,147	$628,608	$703,012	$74,405	0.0039166	$369,010	$1,072,023
24	$93,847,732	$625,652	$700,259	$74,607	0.0040908	$383,607	$1,083,866
25	$93,389,518	$622,597	$697,394	$74,798	0.0042653	$398,017	$1,095,411
26	$92,916,704	$619,445	$694,420	$74,975	0.0044402	$412,234	$1,106,653
27	$92,429,495	$616,197	$691,336	$75,140	0.0046154	$426,250	$1,117,586
28	$91,928,105	$612,854	$688,146	$75,292	0.0047909	$440,059	$1,128,204
29	$91,412,755	$609,418	$684,849	$75,430	0.0049668	$453,653	$1,138,502
30	$90,883,671	$605,891	$681,447	$75,556	0.0051430	$467,027	$1,148,475
31	$90,341,088	$602,274	$677,943	$75,669	0.0051430	$464,236	$1,142,179
32	$89,801,183	$598,675	$674,456	$75,781	0.0051430	$461,459	$1,135,915
110	$54,900,442	$366,003	$451,112	$85,109	0.0051430	$281,916	$733,028
111	$54,533,417	$363,556	$448,792	$85,236	0.0051430	$280,028	$728,820
112	$54,168,153	$361,121	$446,484	$85,363	0.0051430	$278,148	$724,632
113	$53,804,641	$358,698	$444,188	$85,490	0.0051430	$276,278	$720,466
114	$53,442,873	$356,286	$441,903	$85,617	0.0051430	$274,417	$716,320
115	$53,082,839	$353,886	$439,631	$85,745	0.0051430	$272,565	$712,195
357	$496,620	$3,311	$126,231	$122,920	0.0051430	$1,922	$128,153
358	$371,778	$2,479	$125,582	$123,103	0.0051430	$1,279	$126,861
359	$247,395	$1,649	$124,936	$123,287	0.0051430	$638	$125,574
360	$123,470	$823	$124,293	$123,470	0.0051430	$0	$124,293

$$p = \frac{\text{Balance}}{\left[\dfrac{1-[1/(1+(.08/12))]^{\text{Remaining Periods}}}{(.08/12)}\right]}$$

$$\text{Interest} = (.08/12)(\text{Balance})$$

$$\text{Scheduled Principal} = p - (.08)\text{Balance}$$

$$\text{Prepaid Principal} = \text{SMM}[\text{Beginning Balance} - \text{Scheduled Principal}]$$

BLOOMBERG

Mortgages, MBS and Cash Flows: <Mtge> TK and CFT

<Mtge> TK <Enter>:

- To find generic agency mortgage-backed securities, enter <Mtge> TK <Enter>.
- From the "Mtge TK" screen one can select FNMA, GNMA, and FHLMC generic mortgages by type (e.g., 30-year, 15-year, etc.) to analyze as a generic mortgage or mortgage-back security by entering the generic mortgage's ticker.
- For example, to analyze the 30-year FNMA, enter: FNCL <Mtge> <Enter>. This will bring up a menu of FNMA mortgage-backed securities showing different coupon rates. Clicking a mortgage type (e.g., 8 percent) brings up a menu page for analyzing the security.

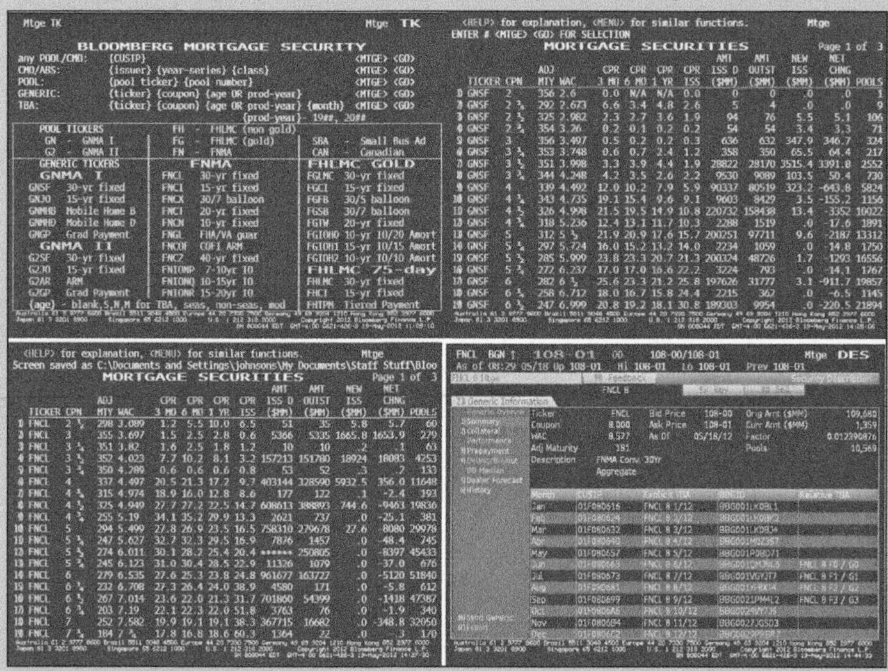

CFT: The Cash Flow Table (CFT) can be used to analyze the mortgage collateral's cash flows given different prepayment assumptions. On the CFT screen, one can change the coupon rate, WAM, and prepayment model (CPR and PSA). The CFT screen below shows the table and graph of $100 million, 30-year mortgage with 8 percent coupon rates and 100 PSA (example in text).

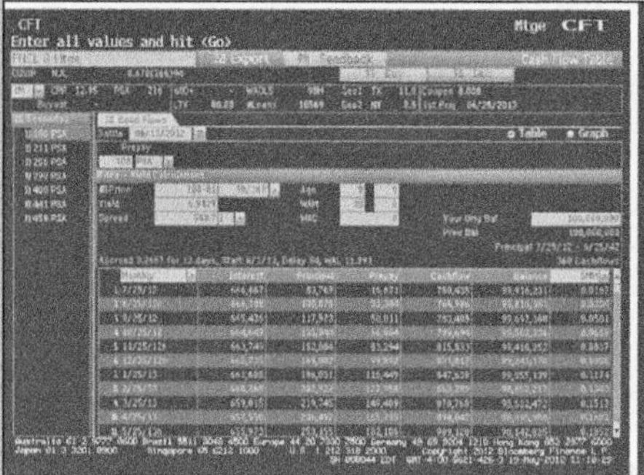

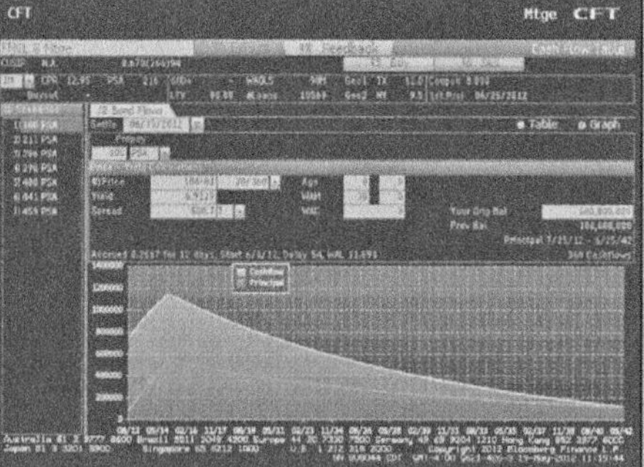

MBSS: The MBSS screen can be used to identify MBSs and their underlying collateral: MBSS <Enter>. On the MBSS screen, click the "Select" tab for an agency (e.g., FNMA) to bring up a menu of mortgage types and their prefix.

SECF: Security finder screen searches for mortgage pools by types of mortgages: SECF <Enter>. To find agency MBSs on the SECF screen, click "Mtge" tab, "Pool" tab, and then enter the prefix for type of mortgage you want to evaluate. To find non-agency MBS on the SECF screen, click "Mtge" tab, "All Structures" tab, and then enter an institution's ticker or name (e.g. WF or Wells Fargo) and select (e.g., Wells Fargo Mortgage Loan Trust, WFMLT). From the search, select an MBS: Right click an issue of interest to obtain the issue's menu or enter the security's identification number: Number <Mtge> <enter> (WFMLT <Mtge> <Enter>).

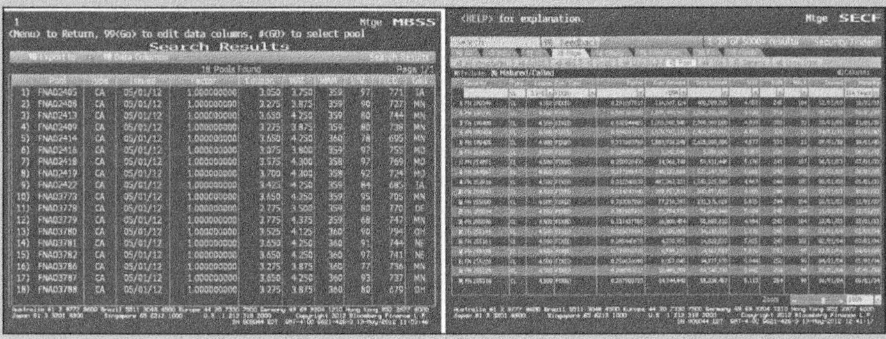

The screens below show the description pages of a FNMA conventional mortgage pool originating in 2009 and serviced by Bank of America and Wells Fargo. The menu for the issue can be accessed by entering the security's ticker or identification number (found on the SECF screen). The description page provides information on the issues, collateral, and other information.

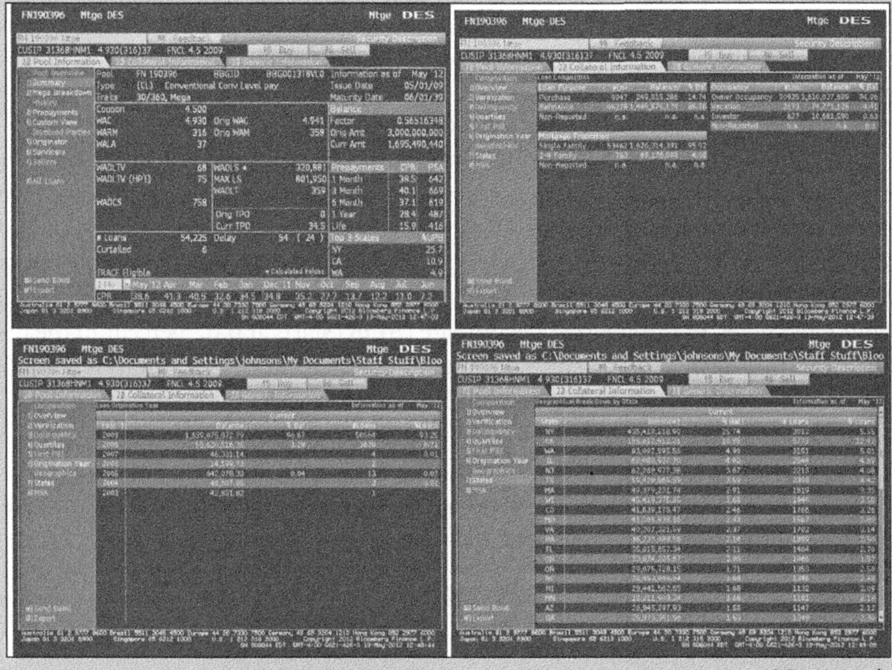

(*Continued*)

Default Risk

A portfolio of residential mortgages insured by FHA or VA, or as a mortgage pool by Ginnie Mae, is subject to prepayment risk but not default risk. Such mortgages are referred to as *agency mortgages.* In contrast, conventional prime and subprime residential mortgages are subject to default risk, as well as mortgages insured by private insurer where the risk has simply been transferred. A portfolio of these *nonagency mortgages* is therefore subject to both prepayment and default risk.

In estimating the cash flows from a portfolio of nonagency mortgages, the expected default losses need to be taken into account. In addition to its prepayment models, the Public Service Association also provides models for estimating standardized default rates for different mortgages. Exhibit 10.5 shows the PSA's *standardized default assumption* (*SDA*) model for 30-year mortgage—the *100 SDA* model. In this default rate model, the annualized default rate (ADR) starts at 0.02 percent in the first month and then increases at a constant rate of 0.02 percent per month to reach 0.60 percent at the 30th month; from month 30 to month 60, the ADR remains constant at 0.60 percent; from month 61 to month 120, the ADR declines from 0.60 percent to .03 percent; from month 120 on, the ADR remains constant at 0.03 percent.

In calculating monthly cash flows, monthly default rates (MDRs) can be obtained given the annual default rates by using the following formula:

$$MDR = 1 - \left[1 - ADR\right]^{1/12} \tag{10.6}$$

EXHIBIT 10.5 PSA Default Loss Model

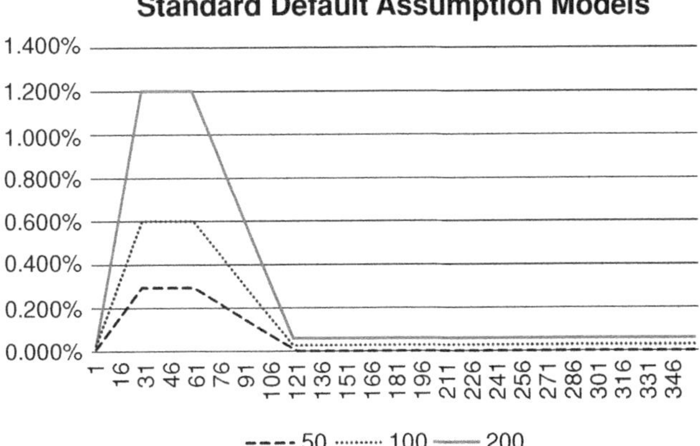

The estimated monthly loss due to default is equal to the MDR times the balance minus the monthly scheduled principal payments:

Monthly Default Loss = MDR (Beginning Balance – Monthly Scheduled Principal Payment)

The 100 SDA model is used like the PSA prepayment model as a benchmark in evaluating different types of prime and subprime mortgages. To reflect greater or lower default risk, analysts will adjust the baseline SDA model to be equal to a certain percentage of the 100 SDA model. For example, if the pattern is described as being 200 SDA, then ADRs will be twice the 100 SDA rates, and if the pattern is described as 50 SDA, then the ADRs will be set equal to half of the 100 PSA rates (see Exhibit 10.5). Thus, a current mortgage pool described by a 200 SDA would start with an annualized default rate of 0.04 percent in the first month and then would increase at a constant rate of 0.04 percent per month to reach 1.20 percent at the 30th month; from month 30 to month 60, the ADR would remain constant at 1.20 percent; from month 61 to month 120, the ADR would declines from 1.20 percent to 0.06 percent; from month 120 on, the ADR would remain constant at 0.06 percent.

To see the applicability of the SDA model, consider again the bank with a pool of current FRMs worth \$100 million, with a WAC of 8 percent and WAM of 360 months. If there were no default or prepayment, the portfolio would generate an aggregate mortgage payment of \$733,765, with \$666,667 going toward interest and \$67,098 toward the scheduled principal payment:

$$P = \frac{\$100{,}000{,}000}{\left[\dfrac{1-1(1+(.08/12))^{360}}{.08/12}\right]} = \$733{,}765$$

$$\text{Interest} = \left(\frac{R^A}{12}\right)F_0 = \left(\frac{.08}{12}\right)\$100{,}000{,}000 = \$666{,}667$$

$$\text{Scheduled Principal Payment} = p - \text{Interest} = \$733{,}765 - \$666{,}667 = \$67{,}098$$

If the portfolio, though, consisted of mortgages that were characterized by the 100 SDA model, then in the first month the monthly loss due to default would be \$1,665.70 and the balance at the beginning of the next month would be \$99,916,236:

$$\text{Annual Default Rate} = ADR = .0002$$

$$MDR = 1 - [1 - .0002]^{1/12} = .00001666819$$

$$\text{Monthly Default Loss} = MDR[\text{Beginning Balance} - \text{Sch Principal}]$$
$$\text{Monthly Default Loss} = (.00001666819)(\$100{,}000{,}000 - \$67{,}097.91)$$
$$\text{Monthly Default Loss} = \$1{,}665.70$$

$$\text{Beginning Balance for Month 2} = F_0 - \text{Scheduled Principal} - \text{Default Loss}$$
$$\text{Beginning Balance for Month 2} = \$100{,}000{,}000 - \$67{,}098 - \$1{,}665.70$$
$$\text{Beginning Balance for Month 2} = \$99{,}931{,}236$$

As expected, the losses are miniscule in the beginning. By month 30, though, the monthly default loss is \$48,670 and the balance is \$97,152,847; if there were no default loss, the principal would have been \$97,861,164.

Exhibit 10.6 summarizes the mortgage portfolio's cash flow for the first month and other selected months. In examining the exhibit, several points should be noted. First, starting in month 30 and going to month 60, the MDR remains constant at 0.00050138; this reflects the 100 SDA model's assumption of a constant ADR of 0.6 percent from month 30 to month 60. During this period, the monthly default losses decrease slightly from the \$48,671 in month 30 to \$46,615 in month 60. Second, from month 60 to month 120, the monthly default rates decrease at a greater rate, causing the monthly default losses to fall from \$46,614 in month 60 to \$2,210 in month 120. From month 120 on, though, there is slight decrease in rates, causing the monthly losses to decrease from \$2,210 in month 120 to only \$21.79 in month 359.

The total default loss for the 30-year, 8 percent mortgage portfolio with a total principal of \$100 million is \$3,904,890 using the 100 SDA model; this equates to a cumulative loss rate for the period of 3.9 percent (cumulative default losses / \$100,000,000). Columns 7, 8, and 9 in Exhibit 10.6 show the monthly default and cumulative default losses and rates, and Exhibit 10.7 shows the cumulative default rates and losses for the mortgage portfolio given different SDAs of 100, 200, and 300. As shown, the cumulative default rates for the 100 SDA model are 0.76 percent after 30 months, 2.19 percent after 60 months, 3.59 percent after 120 months, and 3.9 percent after 360 months. For the riskier mortgage portfolio characterized by the 200 SDA, the total loss for the period is \$7,668,089 and the cumulative default rates are 1.52 percent after 30 months, 4.34 percent after 60, 7.06 percent after 120, and 7.67 percent after 360 months. Finally, the riskier 300 SDA model has total losses of \$11,294,229, with cumulative default rates after 30, 60, 120, and 360 months of 2.28 percent, 6.64 percent, 10.42 percent, and 11.29 percent—the 300 SDA model might be an example of a mortgage portfolio of subprime mortgages.

EXHIBIT 10.6 Projected Cash Flows with Default Loss: Mortgage Portfolio = \$100,000,000; WAC = 8 percent; WAM = 360 Months; 100 SDA Model

1	2	3	4	5	6	7	8	9
Period	Balance	p	Interest	Scheduled Principal	Monthly Default Rate	Default Loss	Cumulative Loss	Cumulative Default Rates
1	\$100,000,000	\$733,765	\$666,667	\$67,098	0.00001667	\$1,666	\$1,666	0.0017%
2	\$99,931,236	\$733,752	\$666,208	\$67,544	0.00003334	\$3,329	\$4,995	0.0050%
3	\$99,860,363	\$733,728	\$665,736	\$67,992	0.00005001	\$4,991	\$9,986	0.0100%
4	\$99,787,380	\$733,691	\$665,249	\$68,442	0.00006669	\$6,650	\$16,636	0.0166%
5	\$99,712,287	\$733,642	\$664,749	\$68,894	0.00008337	\$8,307	\$24,944	0.0249%
6	\$99,635,086	\$733,581	\$664,234	\$69,347	0.00010006	\$9,962	\$34,906	0.0349%
7	\$99,555,777	\$733,508	\$663,705	\$69,803	0.00011674	\$11,614	\$46,520	0.0465%
23	\$98,001,040	\$730,672	\$653,340	\$77,332	0.00038414	\$37,617	\$454,554	0.4546%
24	\$97,886,091	\$730,392	\$652,574	\$77,818	0.00040088	\$39,210	\$493,764	0.4938%
25	\$97,769,063	\$730,099	\$651,794	\$78,305	0.00041762	\$40,798	\$534,562	0.5346%
26	\$97,649,960	\$729,794	\$651,000	\$78,794	0.00043437	\$42,382	\$576,944	0.5769%
27	\$97,528,784	\$729,477	\$650,192	\$79,285	0.00045112	\$43,961	\$620,905	0.6209%
28	\$97,405,538	\$729,148	\$649,370	\$79,778	0.00046787	\$45,536	\$666,441	0.6664%
29	\$97,280,224	\$728,807	\$648,535	\$80,272	0.00048462	\$47,105	\$713,546	0.7135%
30	\$97,152,847	\$728,454	\$647,686	\$80,768	0.00050138	\$48,670	\$762,216	0.7622%
31	\$97,023,409	\$728,088	\$646,823	\$81,266	0.00050138	\$48,605	\$810,821	0.8108%
32	\$96,893,538	\$727,723	\$645,957	\$81,766	0.00050138	\$48,540	\$859,360	0.8594%
60	\$93,069,494	\$717,576	\$620,463	\$97,113	0.00050138	\$46,615	\$2,190,995	2.1910%
61	\$92,925,767	\$717,216	\$619,505	\$97,711	0.00049342	\$45,803	\$2,236,798	2.2368%
62	\$92,782,253	\$716,862	\$618,548	\$98,314	0.00048546	\$44,994	\$2,281,793	2.2818%
63	\$92,638,944	\$716,514	\$617,593	\$98,921	0.00047750	\$44,188	\$2,325,981	2.3260%
120	\$84,568,276	\$706,172	\$563,789	\$142,383	0.00002500	\$2,111	\$3,588,684	3.5887%
121	\$84,423,782	\$706,154	\$562,825	\$143,329	0.00002500	\$2,107	\$3,590,791	3.5908%
358	\$2,589,160	\$874,586	\$17,261	\$857,325	0.00002500	\$43	\$3,904,869	3.9049%
359	\$1,731,791	\$874,564	\$11,545	\$863,019	0.00002500	\$22	\$3,904,891	3.9049%
360	\$868,751	\$874,542	\$5,792	\$868,751	0.00002500	\$0	\$3,904,891	3.9049%

EXHIBIT 10.7 Cumulative Default Rates for 100, 200, and 300 SDA Models: Mortgage Portfolio = \$100,000,000; WAC = 8 percent; WAM = 360 Months

SDA/Month	30	60	120	360	Total Loss
100	0.76%	2.19%	3.59%	3.90%	\$3,904,891
200	1.52%	4.34%	7.06%	7.67%	\$7,668,089
300	2.28%	6.46%	10.42%	11.29%	\$11,294,229

(Continued)

EXHIBIT 10.7 *(continued)*

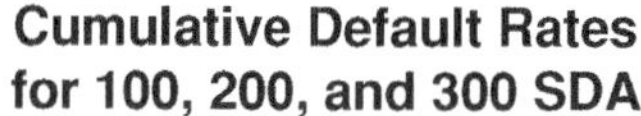

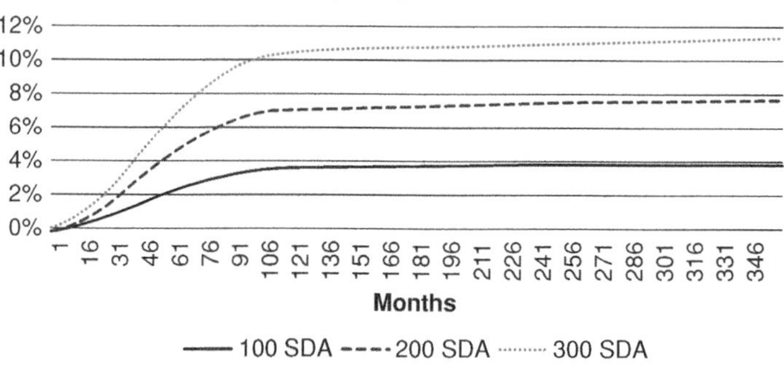

MORTGAGES AND MBS COLLATERAL RISK ANALYSIS: CLP, CFT, VAC, AND SPA

The screens show the description page for a Chase Mortgage Company Mortgage-Backed Security. The menu for the issue can be accessed by entering the security's CUSIP or identification number.

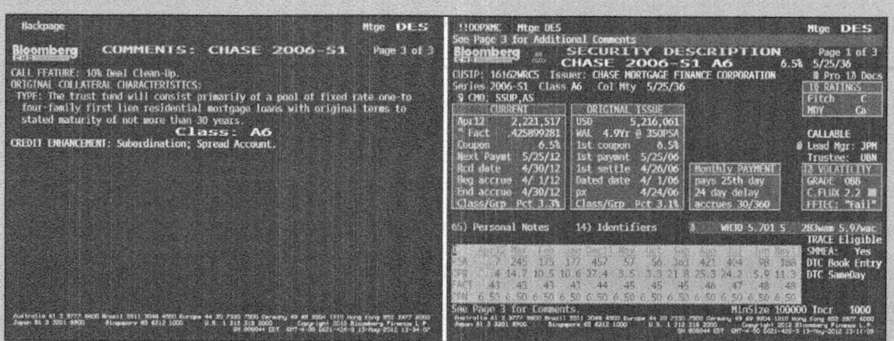

CFT: The CFT screen displays the cash flow table and the CFG screen shows the graph for a selected pool and generic mortgage-backed security, collateralized mortgage obligation (CMO), asset-backed securities (ABSs), and commercial mortgage-backed securities (CMBSs). CFT can be used to analyze the collateral cash flows for a structured security (CMO/ABS/CMBS). Depending on the security you choose, the projected cash flows can be based upon prepayments (CPRs) and defaults (CDRs).

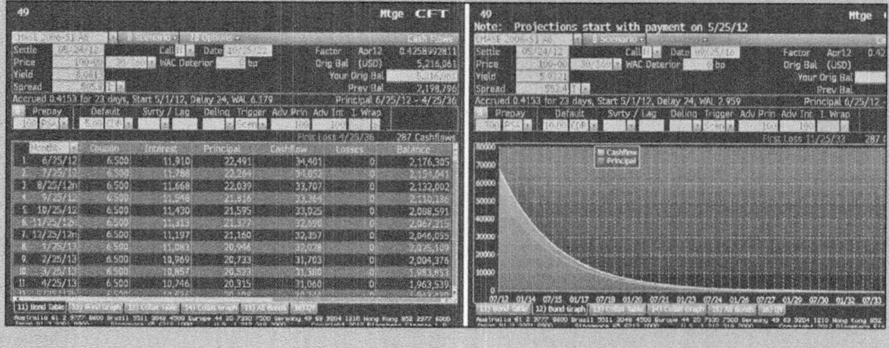

CLP: The CLP screen shows the historical performance of the collateral underlying the MBS issues. From the CLP table screen, one can click "Graph" from the "Options" tab to see historical information (e.g., foreclosures, delinquencies, credit scores, cumulative losses, and loan-to-value ratios) on the collateral.

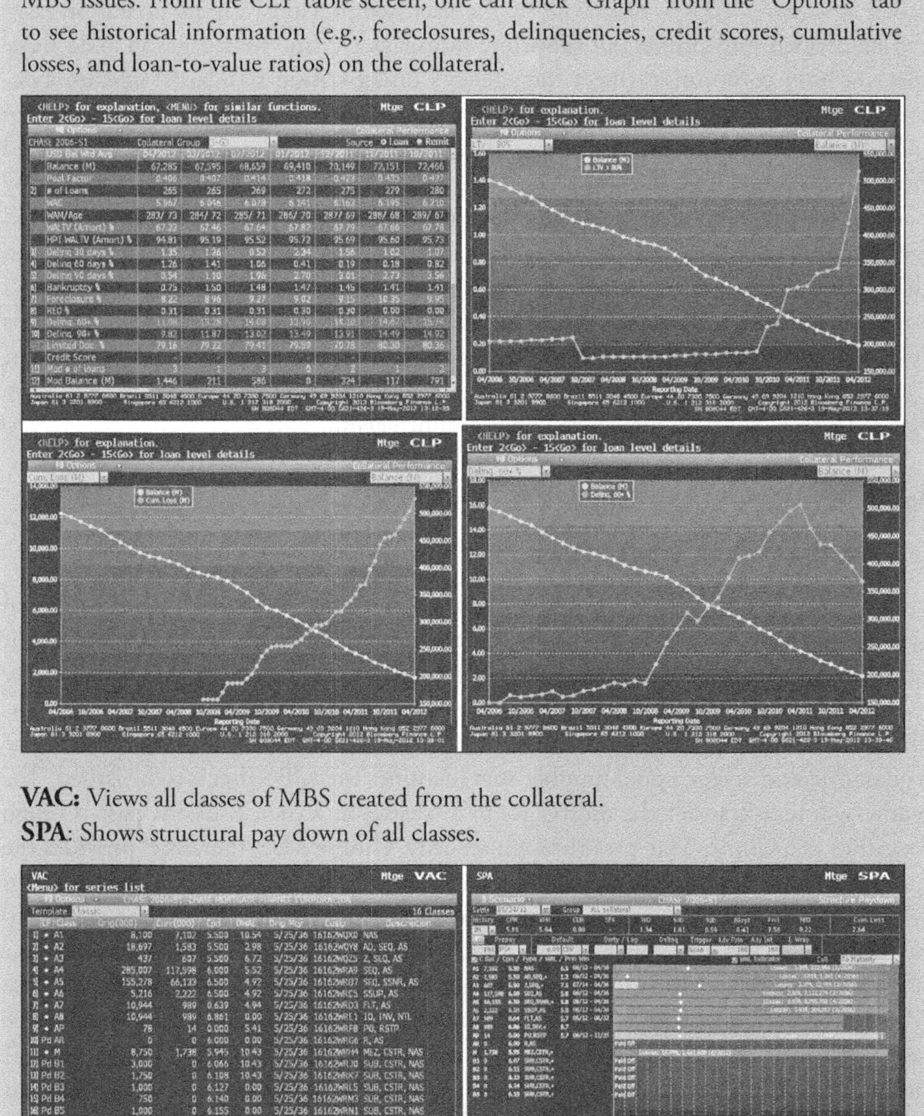

VAC: Views all classes of MBS created from the collateral.

SPA: Shows structural pay down of all classes.

Mortgage-Backed Securities

A mortgage originator with a pool of mortgages has the option of holding the portfolio, selling it, or selling it to be used to securitize a MBS issue or deal. Depending on the types of mortgages, the originator who sells mortgages to become a securitized asset can sell them to one of the three agencies (Fannie Mae, Ginnie Mae, or Freddie

Mac) or to a private-sector conduit.[4] Residential MBSs created by one of the agencies are collectively referred to as *agency MBSs,* and those created by private conduits are called *nonagency MBSs or private labels.* As discussed previously, residential mortgages can be divided into prime and subprime mortgages. Prime mortgages include those that are both conforming (meet the agency's underwriting standards) and nonconforming but still meeting credit quality standards. In contrast, subprime mortgages include those with low credit ratings. Typically, agency residential MBSs are created from conforming loans. In more recent periods, though, agency MBS issues backed by pools of lower-quality mortgages were issued. All other mortgages that are securitized are nonagency MBS. After the mortgages are sold to an agency or private conduit, the originator typically continues to service the loan for a service fee (that is, collect payments, maintain records, forward tax information, and the like). The service fee is typically a fixed percentage (25 to 100 bps) of the outstanding balance. The originator can also sell the servicing to another party. Investors who buy the MBSs receive a pro rata share from the cash flow of the pool of mortgages.

Agency MBS

Ginnie Mae Mortgage-Backed Securities

Ginnie Mae (Government National Mortgage Association [GNMA]) is a true federal agency. As such, the MBSs that it guarantees are backed by the full faith and credit of the U.S. government. Ginnie Mae MBSs are put together by a lender/originator (bank, thrift, or mortgage banker), who presents a block of mortgages that meets Ginnie Mae's underwriting standards. If Ginnie Mae finds them in order, it will issue a guarantee and assign a pool number that identifies the MBS that is to be issued. The lender will then transfer the mortgages to a trustee, and then issue the pass-through securities as a Ginnie Mae pass-through security. Ginnie Mae, therefore, provides the guarantee, but does not issue the Ginnie Mae MBS. Thus, different from the standard MBS that is issued by the other agencies or a conduit, Ginnie Mae MBSs are issued by the lenders. The mortgages underlying Ginnie Mae MBSs can be grouped into one of two Ginnie Mae MBS programs: Ginnie Mae I and Ginnie Mae II. The Ginnie Mae I program consists of MBSs backed by single-family and multifamily mortgage loans that have a fixed note rate and are sold by only one issuer. The Ginnie Mae II program consists of just single-family mortgage loans that can have either fixed or adjustable rates and have multiple issuers. The minimum denomination on a Ginnie Mae pass-through is $25,000 and the minimum pool is $1 million.

Fannie Mae and Freddie Mac Mortgage-Backed Securities

As we examined in Chapter 8, Fannie Mae and Freddie Mac are government-sponsored enterprises (GSEs) initially created to provide a secondary market for mortgages. Today, their activities include not only the buying and selling of mortgages but also creating and guaranteeing mortgage-backed pass-through securities, as well as buying MBSs. Both GSEs are regulated by the Office of Federal Housing Enterprise

Oversight (OFHEO), and both were placed in conservatorship in September 2008. Prior to being placed in conservatorship, the Fannie Mae and Freddie Mac MBSs were guarantee by each of the companies, but not the government. As part of the banking bailout in 2008, though, government backing was provided to their MBSs.

Freddie Mac issues MBSs that it refers to as participation certificates (PCs). Freddie Mac and Fannie Mae have regular MBSs (also called cash PCs), which are backed by a pool of conforming mortgages that they have purchased from mortgage originators. They also offer a pass-through formed through their Guarantor/Swap Program. In this program, mortgage originators can swap mortgages for a FMLMC pass-through. Unlike Ginnie Mae, Fannie Mae's and Freddie Mac's MBSs are formed with more heterogeneous mortgages. The minimum denomination on a Freddie Mac and Fannie Mae pass-through is $100,000, and their mortgage pools range up to several hundred million dollars.

Nonagency MBS

Nonagency pass-throughs or private labels are sold by commercial banks, investment banks, other thrifts, and mortgage bankers. As noted, nonagency pass-throughs are often formed with prime or subprime nonconforming mortgages. As such, Nonagency residential MBSs can be classified as either *prime MBSs,* in where the underlying mortgages are all prime, or *subprime MBSs,* where the underlying mortgage pool consists of subprime mortgages. In grouping the different types of securitized assets (residential mortgages, commercial mortgages, and other assets) nonagency subprime MBSs are typically grouped with asset-backed securities and not mortgage-backed securities. Larger issuers of nonagency MBSs include Citigroup, Bank of America, and GE Capital Mortgage. Their pass-throughs are often guaranteed against default through external credit enhancements, such as the guarantee of a corporation or a bank letter of credit or by private insurance from a monoline insurer. Many are also guaranteed internally through the creation of senior and subordinate classes of bonds with different priority claims on the pool's cash flows in case some of the mortgages in the pool default. The more subordinate claims sold relative to the senior claims, the more secure the senior claims. Some private labels also provide internal protection by providing an excess spreads or by being overcollateralization. Because of their credit risk, nonagency MBSs are rated by Moody's and Standard and Poor's, and, unlike agency pass-throughs, they must be registered with the SEC when they are issued. Finally, most financial entities that issue private-labeled MBSs or derivatives of MBSs are legally set up so that they do not have to pay taxes on the interest and principal that passes through them to their MBS investors. The requirements that MBS issuers must meet to ensure tax-exempt status are specified in the Tax Reform Act of 1983 in the section on trusts referred to as *real estate mortgage investment conduits* (*REMICs*). Private-labeled MBS issuers who comply with these provisions are sometimes referred to as REMICs.

Nonagency residential MBSs differ fundamentally from agency MBSs in that their cash flows are subject to default risk, whereas agency MBSs with their government and agency guarantees are considered default free.

Features of Mortgage-Backed Securities

Cash Flows

Cash flows from MBSs are generated from the cash flows from the underlying pool of mortgages, minus servicing and other fees. Typically, fees for constructing, managing, and servicing the underlying mortgages (also referred to as the mortgage collateral) and the MBSs are equal to the difference between the WAC associated with the mortgage pool and the MBS *pass-through (PT) rate* (also called *pass-through coupon rate*). Exhibit 10.8 shows the monthly cash flows for an agency MBS issue constructed from a mortgage pool with a current balance of $100 million, a WAC of 8 percent, a WAM of 355 months, and a PT rate of 7.5 percent. The monthly fees implied on the MBS issue are equal to .04167 percent = (8 percent – 7.5 percent) / 12 of the monthly balance.[5]

The cash flow for the MBS issue shown in Exhibit 10.8 differs in several respects from the cash flow for the $100 million mortgage pool shown in Exhibit 10.4. First, the MBS issue has a WAM of 355 months and an assumed prepayment speed equal to 150 percent of the standard PSA model, compared to 360 months and an assumption of 100 percent PSA for the pool.[6] As a result, the first month's CPR for the MBS issue reflects a five-month seasoning in which $t = 6$, and a speed that is 1.5 times greater than the 100 PSA. For the MBS issue, this yields a first month SMM of .0015125 and a constant SMM of .0078284 starting in month 25. Secondly, for the mortgage pool, a WAC of 8 percent is used to determine the mortgage payment, scheduled principal, and interest; on the MBS issue, though, the WAC of 8 percent is used only to determine the mortgage payment and scheduled principal, while the PT rate of 7.5 percent is used to determine the interest. Finally, the MBS is an agency issue and therefore has cash flows that have no default losses, which is similar to the cash flows shown in Exhibit 10.4, but not Exhibit 10.6 that shows default losses.

Price Quotes

Investors can acquire newly issued MBSs from the agencies, originators, or dealers specializing in specific pass-throughs. There is also a secondary MBS market consisting of dealers who operate in the OTC market as part of the *Mortgage-Backed Security Dealers Association.* These dealers form the core of the secondary market for the trading of existing pass-throughs. The Mortgage-Backed Securities Clearing Corporation (MBSCC) automates the trading of these MBSs.

Mortgage pass-throughs are normally sold in denominations ranging from $25,000 to $250,000, although some privately placed issues are sold with denominations as high as $1 million. There are mortgage-backed mutual funds and ETFs, which provide individual investors with an opportunity to invest in a lower-denominated MBS fund share. The prices of MBSs are quoted as a percentage of the underlying mortgages' balance. The mortgage balance at time t, F_t, is usually calculated by the

EXHIBIT 10.8 Projected Cash Flows from an Agency MBS Issue: Mortgage Portfolio = $100,000,000; WAC = 8 percent; WAM = 355 Months; PT Rate = 7.5 percent; Prepayment: 150 PSA

Period	Balance	Interest	*p*	Scheduled Principal	SMM	Prepaid Principal	Principal	Cash Flow
1	$100,000,000	$625,000	$736,268	$69,601	0.0015125	$151,147	$220,748	$845,748
2	$99,779,252	$623,620	$735,154	$69,959	0.0017671	$176,194	$246,153	$869,773
3	$99,533,099	$622,082	$733,855	$70,301	0.0020223	$201,148	$271,449	$893,531
4	$99,261,650	$620,385	$732,371	$70,627	0.0022783	$225,990	$296,617	$917,002
5	$98,965,033	$618,531	$730,702	$70,936	0.0025350	$250,701	$321,637	$940,168
6	$98,643,396	$616,521	$728,850	$71,227	0.0027925	$275,262	$346,489	$963,011
20	$91,641,550	$572,760	$684,341	$73,398	0.0064757	$592,971	$666,369	$1,239,128
21	$90,975,181	$568,595	$679,910	$73,408	0.0067447	$613,101	$686,510	$1,255,105
22	$90,288,672	$564,304	$675,324	$73,399	0.0070144	$632,804	$706,204	$1,270,508
23	$89,582,468	$559,890	$670,587	$73,370	0.0072849	$652,066	$725,436	$1,285,327
24	$88,857,032	$555,356	$665,702	$73,321	0.0075563	$670,873	$744,194	$1,299,550
25	$88,112,838	$550,705	$660,671	$73,253	0.0078284	$689,211	$762,463	$1,313,169
26	$87,350,375	$545,940	$655,499	$73,164	0.0078284	$683,243	$756,406	$1,302,346
27	$86,593,968	$541,212	$650,368	$73,075	0.0078284	$677,322	$750,397	$1,291,609
28	$85,843,572	$536,522	$645,277	$72,986	0.0078284	$671,448	$744,434	$1,280,957
29	$85,099,137	$531,870	$640,225	$72,897	0.0078284	$665,621	$738,519	$1,270,388
30	$84,360,619	$527,254	$635,213	$72,809	0.0078284	$659,840	$732,649	$1,259,903
31	$83,627,969	$522,675	$630,240	$72,721	0.0078284	$654,106	$726,826	$1,249,501
32	$82,901,143	$518,132	$625,307	$72,632	0.0078284	$648,416	$721,049	$1,239,181
33	$82,180,094	$513,626	$620,411	$72,544	0.0078284	$642,772	$715,317	$1,228,942
100	$44,933,791	$280,836	$366,433	$66,874	0.0078284	$351,237	$418,111	$698,947
101	$44,515,680	$278,223	$363,564	$66,793	0.0078284	$347,965	$414,758	$692,981
102	$44,100,923	$275,631	$360,718	$66,712	0.0078284	$344,718	$411,430	$687,061
103	$43,689,493	$273,059	$357,894	$66,631	0.0078284	$341,498	$408,129	$681,188
200	$16,163,713	$101,023	$166,983	$59,225	0.0078284	$126,073	$185,298	$286,321
201	$15,978,416	$99,865	$165,676	$59,153	0.0078284	$124,623	$183,776	$283,641
353	$148,527	$928	$50,171	$49,181	0.0078284	$778	$49,958	$50,887
354	$98,569	$616	$49,778	$49,121	0.0078284	$387	$49,508	$50,124
355	$49,061	$307	$49,388	$49,061	0.0078284	$0	$49,061	$49,368

$$\text{Monthly Payment} = p = \frac{\text{Balance}}{\left[\dfrac{1-[1/(1+(.08/12))]^{\text{Remaining Periods}}}{(.08/12)}\right]}$$

Interest = (.075/12)(Balance)

Scheduled Principal = *p* − (.08 Balance)

Prepaid Principal = SMM[Beginning Balance − Scheduled Principal]

servicing institution and is quoted as a proportion of the original balance, F_0. This proportion is referred to as the *pool factor* (*pf*):

$$pf_t = \frac{F_t}{F_0} \tag{10.7}$$

For example, suppose a Fannie Mae MBS, backed by a mortgage pool with an original par value of $100 million, is currently priced at 95-16 (the fractions on MBSs are quoted like Treasury bonds and notes in terms of 32nds), with a pool factor of .92. An institutional investor who purchased $10 million of the MBS when it was first issued (and had a pool fact of *pf* = 1) would now have securities valued at $8.786 million that are backed by mortgages that are worth $9.2 million:

Par Value Remaining = ($10,000,000) (.92) = $9,200,000

Market Value = ($9,200,000) (.9550) = $8,786,000

The market value of $8.786 million represents a clean or flat price that does not include accrued interest. If the institutional investor were to sell the MBS, the accrued interest (ai) would need to be added to the flat price to determine the invoice price. The normal practice is to determine accrued interest based on the time period between the settlement date (SD) (usually two days after the trade date) and the first day of the month, M_0. If the coupon rate on the Fannie Mae MBS held by the institutional investor were 5 percent and the time period between SD and M_0 were 20 days, then the accrued interest would be $25,556.

$$ai_t = \frac{SD - M_0}{30} \frac{WAC}{12} F_t$$

$$ai_t = \left(\frac{20}{30}\right)\left(\frac{.05}{12}\right)\$9,200,000 = \$25,556$$

Extension Risk, Prepayment Risk, and Average Life

Like other fixed-income securities, the value of a MBS is determined by the MBS's future cash flow, maturity, credit risk, liquidity, and other features germane to fixed-income securities. In contrast to other bonds, though, MBSs are also subject to prepayment risk. As discussed earlier, the mortgage borrower's option to prepay makes it difficult to estimate the cash flow from the MBS. The prepayment risk associated with a MBS is primarily a function of interest rates. If interest rates decrease, then the prices of MBSs, like the prices of all bonds, increase as a result of lower discount rates. However, the decrease in rates will also augment prepayment speed, causing the earlier cash flow of the mortgages to be larger which, depending on the level of rates and the maturity remaining, could also contribute to increasing a MBS's price. In contrast, if interest rates increase, then the prices of MBSs will decrease as a result of higher discount rates and possibly the smaller earlier cash flow resulting from lower prepayment speeds.

The effect of an interest rate increase in lowering the price of the bond by decreasing the value of its cash flow is known as *extension risk*. Extension risk can be described in terms of the relationship between interest rates and the MBS's *average life*. The average life of a MBS is the weighted average of the security's time periods, with the weights being the periodic principal payments (scheduled and prepaid principal) divided by the total principal:

$$\text{Average Life} = \frac{1}{12}\sum_{t=1}^{T} t\left(\frac{\text{Principal Received at } t}{\text{Total Principal}}\right)$$

For example, the average life for the MBS issue described in Exhibit 10.8 is 9.18 years:

$$\text{Average Life} = \frac{1}{2}\left(\frac{1(\$220{,}748) + 2(\$246{,}153) + \ldots + 355(\$49{,}061)}{\$100{,}000{,}000}\right) = 9.18 \text{ Years}$$

The average life of a MBS depends on prepayment speed. For example, if the PSA speed of the $100 million MBS issue were to increase from 150 to 200, the MBS's average life would decrease from 9.18 to 7.55, reflecting greater principal payments in the earlier years; in contrast, if the PSA speed were to decrease from 150 to 100, then the average life of the MBS would increase to 11.51. For MBSs, *prepayment risk* can be evaluated in terms of how responsive a MBS's average life is to changes in prepayment speeds:

$$\text{Prepayment Risk} = \frac{\Delta \text{Average Life}}{\Delta \text{PSA}}$$

Thus, a MBS with an average life that did not change with PSA speeds, in turn, would have stable principal payments over time and would be absent of prepayment risk. Moreover, one of the more creative developments in the security market industry over the past two decades has been the creation of derivative securities formed from MBSs that have different prepayment risk characteristics, including some that are formed that have average lives that are invariant to changes in prepayment rates. The most popular of these derivatives are collateralized mortgage obligations and stripped MBS.

Collateralized Mortgage Obligations and Strips

To address the problems of prepayment risk, many MBS issuers began to offer *collateralized mortgage obligations* (*CMOs*). Introduced in the mid-1980s, these securities are formed by dividing the cash flow of an underlying pool of mortgages or a MBS issue into several classes, with each class having a different claim on the mortgage collateral and with each sold separately to different types of investors. The different classes making up a CMO are called *tranches* or bond classes. There are two general types of CMO tranches: sequential-pay tranches and planned amortization class tranches.

Sequential-Pay Tranches

A CMO with sequential-pay tranches, called a *sequential-pay CMO,* is divided into classes with different priority claims on the collateral's principal. The tranche with the first-priority claim has its principal paid entirely before the next priority class, which has its principal paid before the third class, and so on. Interest payments on most CMO tranches are made until the tranche's principal is retired.

An example of a sequential-pay CMO is shown in Exhibit 10.9. This CMO consists of three tranches, A, B, and C, formed from the collateral making up the $100 million agency MBS described in Exhibit 10.8. In terms of the priority disbursement rules, tranche A receives all principal payment from the collateral until its principal of $50 million is retired. No other tranche's principal payments are disbursed until the principal on A is paid. After tranche A's principal is retired, all principal payments from the collateral are then made to tranche B until its principal of $30 million is retired. Finally, tranche C receives the remaining principal that is equal to its par value of $20 million. Even though the principal is paid sequentially, each tranche does receive interest each period equal to its stated pass-through rate (7.5 percent) times its outstanding balance at the beginning of each month.

Given the different possible prepayment speeds, the actual amount of principal paid each month and the time it will take to pay the principal on each tranche is uncertain. Exhibit 10.9 shows the cash flow patterns on the three tranches based on a 150 percent PSA prepayment assumption. As shown, the first month cash flow for tranche A consist of a principal payment (scheduled and prepaid) of $220,748 and an interest payment of $312,500 [= (.075/12)($50 million) = $312,500]. In Month 2, tranche A receives an interest payment of $311,120 based on the balance of $49,779,252 and a principal payment of $246,153. Based on the assumption of a 150 percent PSA speed, it takes 88 months before A's principal of $50 million is retired. During the first 88 months, the cash flows for tranches B and C consist of just the interest on their balances, with no principal payments made to them. Starting in month 88, tranche B begins to receive the principal payment. Tranche B is paid off in month 180, at which time principal payments begin to be paid to tranche C. Finally, in month 355 tranche C's principal is retired.

Features of Sequential-Pay CMOs

By creating sequential-pay tranches, issuers of CMOs are able to offer investors maturities, principal payment periods, and average lives different from those defined by the underlying mortgage collateral. For example, tranche A in our example has a maturity of 88 months (7.33 years) compared to the collateral's maturity of 355 months; tranche B's maturity is 180 months (15 years); tranche C's maturity is 355 months (29.58 years). Each tranche also has a larger cash flow during the

EXHIBIT 10.9 Cash Flows from Sequential-Pay CMO Collateral: Balance = $100 million, WAM = 355 Months, WAC = 8 percent, PT Rate = 7.5 percent, Prepayment: 150 PSA, Tranches: A: $50 million, B = $30 million, C = $20 million

	Par = $100m	Rate = 7.5%		A: Par = $50m	Rate = 7.5%		B: Par = $30m	Rate = 7.5%		C: Par = $20m	Rate = 7.5%	
Period	Collateral	Collateral	Collateral	Tranche A	A	A	Tranche B	B	B	Tranche C	C	C
Month	Balance	Interest	Principal	Balance	Interest	Principal	Balance	Principal	Interest	Balance	Principal	Interest
	$100,000,000			$50,000,000			$30,000,000			$20,000,000	0	
1	$100,000,000	$625,000	$220,748	$50,000,000	$312,500	$220,748	$30,000,000	0	$187,500	$20,000,000	0	$125,000
2	$99,779,252	$623,620	$246,153	$49,779,252	$311,120	$246,153	$30,000,000	0	$187,500	$20,000,000	0	$125,000
3	$99,533,099	$622,082	$271,449	$49,533,099	$309,582	$271,449	$30,000,000	0	$187,500	$20,000,000	0	$125,000
4	$99,261,650	$620,385	$296,617	$49,261,650	$307,885	$296,617	$30,000,000	0	$187,500	$20,000,000	0	$125,000
5	$98,965,033	$618,531	$321,637	$48,965,033	$306,031	$321,637	$30,000,000	0	$187,500	$20,000,000	0	$125,000
85	$51,626,473	$322,665	$471,724	$1,626,473	$10,165	$471,724	$30,000,000	0	$187,500	$20,000,000	0	$125,000
86	$51,154,749	$319,717	$467,949	$1,154,749	$7,217	$467,949	$30,000,000	0	$187,500	$20,000,000	0	$125,000
87	$50,686,799	$316,792	$464,204	$686,799	$4,292	$464,204	$30,000,000	0	$187,500	$20,000,000	0	$125,000
88	$50,222,595	$313,891	$460,488	$222,595	$1,391	$222,595	$30,000,000	$237,893	$187,500	$20,000,000	0	$125,000
89	$49,762,107	$311,013	$456,802	0	0	0	$29,762,107	$456,802	$186,013	$20,000,000	0	$125,000
90	$49,305,305	$308,158	$453,144	0	0	0	$29,305,305	$453,144	$183,158	$20,000,000	0	$125,000
91	$48,852,161	$305326	$449,515	0	0	0	$28,852,161	$449,515	$180,326	$20,000,000	0	$125,000
92	$48,402,646	$302,517	$445,915	0	0	0	$28,402,646	$445,915	$177,517	$20,000,000	0	$125,000
178	$20,650,839	$129,068	$222,016	0	0	0	$650,839	$222,016	$4,068	$20,000,000	0	$125,000
181	$19,990,210	$124,939	$216,625	0	0	0	0	0	0	$19,990,210	$216,625	$124,939

(Continued)

EXHIBIT 10.9 *(continued)*

	Par = $100m	Rate = 7.5%		A: Par = $50m	Rate = 7.5%		B: Par = $30m	Rate = 7.5%		C: Par = $20m	Rate = 7.5%	
Period	Collateral	Collateral	Collateral	Tranche A	A	A	Tranche B	B	B	Tranche C	C	C
Month	Balance	Interest	Principal	Balance	Interest	Principal	Balance	Principal	Interest	Balance	Principal	Interest
182	$19,773,585	$123,585	$214,856	0	0	0	0	0	0	$19,773,585	$214,856	$123,585
183	$19,558,729	$122,242	$213,101	0	0	0	0	0	0	$19,558,729	$213,101	$122,242
184	$19,345,627	$120,910	$211360	0	0	0	0	0	0	$19345,627	$211,360	$120,910
353	$148,527	$928	$49,958	0	0	0	0	0	0	$148,527	$49,958	$928
354	$98,569	$616	$49,508	0	0	0	0	0	0	$98,569	$49,508	$616
355	$49,061	$307	$49,061	0	0	0	0	0	0	$49,061	$49,061	$307

Tranche	Maturity	Window	Average Life	PSA	Collateral	Tranche A	Tranche B	Tranche C
A	88 Months	87 Months	3.69 years	50	14.95	7.53	19.4	26.81
B	179 Months	92 Months	10.71 years	100	11.51	4.92	14.18	23.99
C	355 Months	176 Months	20.59 years	150	9.18	3.69	10.71	20.59
Collateral	355 Months	355 Months	9.18 years	200	7.55	3.01	8.51	17.46
				300	5.5	2.26	6.03	12.82

periods when their principal is being retired. The period between the beginning and ending principal payment is referred to as the ***principal pay-down window.*** Tranche A has a window of 87 months, B's window is 92 months, and C's window is 176 months (see table at the bottom of Exhibit 10.9). CMOs with certain size windows and maturities often are attractive investments for investors who are using cash flow matching strategies. Moreover, issuers of CMOs are able to offer a number of CMO tranches with different maturities and windows by simply creating more tranches.

Finally, each of the tranches has an average life that is either shorter or longer than the collateral's average life of 9.18 years. With a 150 PSA model, tranche A has an average life of 3.69 years, B has an average life of 10.71 years, and C has a life of 20.59 years. In general, a CMO tranche with a lower average life is less susceptible to prepayment risk. Such risk, though, is not eliminated. As noted earlier, if prepayment speed decreases, a MBS's average life will increase, resulting in lower than projected early cash flow and therefore lower returns. In the table at the bottom of Exhibit 10.9, the average lives for the collateral and the three tranches are shown for different PSA models. Note that the average life of each of the tranches still varies as prepayment speed changes.

Accrual Tranche

Many sequential-pay CMOs have an *accrual bond class.* Such a tranche, also referred to as the *Z bond,* does not receive current interest but has it deferred. For example, suppose in our illustrative sequential-pay CMO example we make tranche C an accrual tranche in which its interest of 7.5 percent accrues with its principal of $20 million and its accrued interest is to be paid after tranche B's principal has been retired (see Exhibit 10.10).

Floating-Rate Tranches

In order to attract investors who prefer floating-rate securities, CMO issuers often create floating-rate and inverse floating-rate tranches. The monthly coupon rate on the floating-rate tranche is usually set equal to a reference rate such as the LIBOR, whereas the rate on the inverse floating-rate tranche is determined by a formula that is inversely related to the reference rate. An example of a sequential-pay CMO with a floating and inverse floating tranches is shown in Exhibit 10.11. The CMO is identical to our preceding CMO, except that tranche B has been replaced with a floating-rate tranche, FR, and an inverse floating-rate tranche, IFR. The par values of the FR and IFR tranches are equal to the par value of tranche B, with the FR tranche's par value of $22.5 million representing 75 percent of B's par value of $30 million, and the IFR's par value of $7.5 million representing 25 percent of B's par value. The rate on the FR tranche (R_{FR}) is set to the LIBOR plus 50 basis points, with the maximum rate permitted being 9.5 percent; the rate on the IFR tranche (R_{IFR}) is determined by the following formula:

$$R_{IFR} = 28.5 - 3 \text{ LIBOR}$$

EXHIBIT 10.10 Cash Flows from Sequential-Pay CMO with Z Tranche Collateral: Balance = $100 million, WAM = 355 Months, WAC = 8 percent, PT Rate = 7.5 percent, Prepayment: 150 PSA, Tranches: A: $50m, B = $30m, C = $20m

	Par = $100m Rate = 7.5%			A: Par = $50m Rate = 7.5%			B: Par = $30m Rate = 7.5%			Z: Par = $20m Rate = 7.5%		
Period	Collateral	Collateral	Collateral	A	A	A	B	B	B	Z	Z	Z
Month	Balance	Interest	Principal	Balance	Interest	Principal	Balance	Principal	Interest	Bal.+Cum Int	Principal	Interest
1	$100,000,000	$625,000	$220,748	$50,000,000	$312,500	$345,748	$30,000,000	0	$187,500	$20,000,000	0	0
2	$99,779,252	$623,620	$246,153	$49,654,252	$310,339	$371,153	$30,000,000	0	$187,500	$20,125,000	0	0
3	$99,533,099	$622,082	$271,449	$49,283,099	$308,019	$396,449	$30,000,000	0	$187,500	$20,250,000	0	0
4	$99,261,650	$620,385	$296,617	$48,886,650	$305,542	$421,617	$30,000,000	0	$187,500	$20,375,000	0	0
5	$98,965,033	$618,531	$321,637	$48,465,033	$302,906	$446,637	$30,000,000	0	$187,500	$20,500,000	0	0
68	$60,253,239	$376,583	$540,668	$1,878,239	$11,739	$665,668	$30,000,000	0	$187,500	$28,375,000	0	0
69	$59,712,571	$373,204	$536,352	$1,212,571	$7,579	$661,352	$30,000,000	0	$187,500	$28,500,000	0	0
70	$59,176,219	$369,851	$532,069	$551,219	$3,445	$551,219	$30,000,000	$105,850	$187,500	$28,625,000	0	0
71	$58,644,150	$366,526	$527,821	0	0	0	$29,894,150	$652,821	$186,838	$28,750,000	0	0
72	$58,116,329	$363,227	$523,605	0	0	0	$29,241,329	$648,605	$182,758	$28,875,000	0	0
122	$36,470,935	$227,943	$350,111	0	0	0	$1,345,935	$475,111	$8,412	$35,125,000	0	0
123	$36,120,824	$225,755	$347,292	0	0	0	$870,824	$472,292	$5,443	$35,250,000	0	0
125	$35,429,038	$221,431	$341,719	0	0	0	0	0	0	$35,429,038	$341,719	$221,431
126	$35,087,319	$219,296	$338,966	0	0	0	0	0	0	$35,087,319	$338,966	$219,296
354	$98,569	$616	$49,508	0	0	0	0	0	0	$98,569	$49,508	$616
355	$49,061	$307	$49,061	0	0	0	0	0	0	$49,061	$49,061	$307

Tranche	Window	Average Life
A	69 Months	3.06 Years
B	54 Months	8.23 Years

This formula ensures that the WAC of the two tranches will be equal to the coupon rate on tranche B of 7.5 percent, provided the LIBOR is less than 9.5 percent. For example, if the LIBOR is 8 percent, then the rate on the FR tranche is 8.5 percent, the IFR tranche's rate is 4.5 percent, and the weighted-average PT rate (WPTR) of the two tranches is 7.5 percent:

$$\begin{aligned} LIBOR &= 8\% \\ R_{FR} &= LIBOR + 50\,bps = 8.5\% \\ R_{IFR} &= 28.5 - 3LIBOR = 4.5\% \\ WPTR &= .75R_{FR} + .25R_{IFR} = 7.5\% \end{aligned}$$

Notional Interest-Only Class

Each of the fixed-rate tranches in the previous CMOs has the same coupon rate as the collateral PT rate of 7.5 percent. Many CMOs, though, are structured with tranches that have different rates. When CMOs are formed this way, an additional tranche, known as a *notional interest-only (IO) class,* is often created. This tranche receives the excess interest on the other tranches' principals, with the excess rate being equal to the difference in the collateral's PT rate minus the tranches' PT rates. To illustrate, a sequential-pay CMO with a Z bond and notional IO tranche is shown in Exhibit 10.12. This CMO is identical to our previous CMO with a Z bond, except that each of the tranches has a coupon rate lower than the collateral rate of 7.5 percent and there is a notional IO class. The notional IO class receives the excess interest on each tranche's remaining balance, with the excess rate based on the collateral rate of 7.5 percent. In the first month, for example, the IO class would receive interest of $87,500:

$$\text{Interest} = \left(\frac{.075 - .06}{12}\right)\$50{,}000{,}000 + \left(\frac{.075 - .065}{12}\right)\$30{,}000{,}000$$
$$\text{Interest} = \$62{,}500 + \$25{,}000 = \$87{,}500$$

In the exhibit, the IO class is described as paying 7.5 percent interest on a notional principal of $15,333,333. This notional principal is determined by summing

EXHIBIT 10.11 Sequential-Pay CMO with Floaters

Tranche	Par Value	PT Rate
A	$50,000,000	7.5%
FR	$22,500,000	LIBOR + 50 bps
IFR	$7,500,000	28.3 – 3 LIBOR
Z	$20,000,000	7.5%
Total	$100,000,000	7.5%

EXHIBIT 10.12 Sequential-Pay CMO with Notional IO Tranche Collateral: Balance = $100 million, WAM = 355 Months, WAC = 8 percent, PT Rate = 7.5 percent, Prepayment: 150 PSA, Tranches: A: $50m, B = $30m, Z = $20m, Notional IO = $15.333333m

	Collateral:	Par = $100m	Rate = 7.5%	Tranche A:	Par = $50m	Rate = 6%		Tranche B:	Par = $30m	Rate = 6.5%		Tranche Z:	Par = $20m	Rate = 7%		Notional Par = $15.333m
Period	Collateral	Collateral	Collateral	A	A	A	Notional	B	B	B	Notional	Z	Z	Z	Notional	Notional
Month	Balance	Interest	Principal	Balance	Interest	Principal	Interest	Balance	Principal	Interest	Interest	Balance	Principal	Interest	Interest	Total CF
	$100,000,000			$50,000,000	0.06		0.015	$30,000,000		0.065	0.01	20,000,000	0	0.07	0.005	
1	$100,000,000	$625,000	$220,748	$50,000,000	$250,000	$345,748	$62,500	$30,000,000	0	$162,500	$25,000	$20,000,000	0	0	0	$87,500
2	$99,779,252	$623,620	$246,153	$49,654,252	$248,271	$371,153	$62,068	$30,000,000	0	$162,500	$25,000	$20,125,000	0	0	0	$87,068
3	$99,533,099	$622,082	$271,449	$49,283,099	$246,415	$396,449	$61,604	$30,000,000	0	$162,500	$25,000	$20,250,000	0	0	0	$86,604
4	$99,261,650	$620385	$296,617	$48,886,650	$244,433	$421,617	$61,108	$30,000,000	0	$162,500	$25,000	$20,375,000	0	0	0	$86,108
5	$98,965,033	$618,531	$321,637	$48,465,033	$242,325	$446,637	$60,581	$30,000,000	0	$162,500	$25,000	$20,500,000	0	0	0	$85,581
70	$59,176,219	$369,851	$532,069	$551,219	$2,756	$551,219	$689	$30,000,000	$105,850	$162,500	$25,000	$28,625,000	0	0	0	$25,689
71	$58,644,150	$366,526	$527,821	0	0	0	0	$29,894,150	$652,821	$161,927	$24,912	$28,750,000	0	0	0	$24,912
72	$58,116,329	$363,227	$523,605	0	0	0	0	$29,241,329	$648,605	$158,391	$24,368	$28,875,000	0	0	0	$24,368
122	$36,470,935	$227,943	$350,111	0	0	0	0	$1,345,935	$475,111	$7,290	$1,122	$35,125,000	0	0	0	$1,122
123	$36,120,824	$225,755	$347,292	0	0	0	0	$870,824	$472,292	$4,717	$726	$35,250,000	0	0	0	$726
124	$35,773,533	$223,585	$344,494	0	0	0	0	$398,533	$398,533	$2,159	$332	$35,375,000	-$54,038	$206,354	$14,740	$15,072
125	$35,429,038	$221,431	$341,719	0	0	0	0	0	0	0	0	$35,429,038	$341,719	$206,669	$14,762	$14,762
126	$35,087,319	$219,296	$338,966	0	0	0	0	0	0	0	0	$35,087,319	$338,966	$204,676	$14,620	$14,620
127	$34,748,353	$217,177	$336,235	0	0	0	0	0	0	0	0	$34,748,353	$336,235	$202,699	$14,478	$14,478
353	$148,527	$928	$49,958	0	0	0	0	0	0	0	0	$148,527	$49,958	$866	$62	$62
354	$98,569	$616	$49,508	0	0	0	0	0	0	0	0	$98,569	$49,508	$575	$41	$41
355	$49,061	$307	$49,061	0	0	0	0	0	0	0	0	$49,061	$49,061	$286	$20	$20

each tranche's notional principal. A tranche's notional principal is the number of dollars that makes the return on the tranche's principal equal to 7.5 percent. Thus, the notional principal for tranche A is $10 million, for B, $4 million, and for Z, $1,333,333, yielding a total notional principal of $15,333,333:

$$\text{A's Notional Principal} = \frac{(\$50{,}000{,}000)(.075-.06)}{.075} = \$10{,}000{,}000$$

$$\text{B's Notional Principal} = \frac{(\$30{,}000{,}000)(.75-.065)}{.075} = \$4{,}000{,}000$$

$$\text{Z's Notional Principal} = \frac{(\$20{,}000{,}000)(.075-.07)}{.075} = \$1{,}333{,}333$$

$$\text{Total Notional Principal} = \$15{,}333{,}333$$

Planned Amortization Class

Sequential-pay-structured CMOs provide investors with different maturities and average lives. As noted earlier, though, they are still subject to prepayment risk. A CMO with a *planned amortization class* (*PAC*), though, is structured such that there is virtually no prepayment risk. In a PAC-structured CMO, the underlying mortgages or MBSs (i.e., the collateral) is divided into two general tranches: the PAC (also called the PAC bond) and the *support class* (also called the *support bond* or the *companion bond*). The two tranches are formed by generating two monthly principal payment schedules from the collateral; one schedule is based on assuming a relatively low PSA speed, whereas the other is obtained by assuming a relatively high PSA speed. The PAC bond is then set up so that it will receive a monthly principal payment schedule based on the minimum principal from the two principal payments. Thus, the PAC bond is designed to have no prepayment risk provided the actual prepayment falls within the minimum and maximum assumed PSA speeds. The support bond, however, receives the remaining principal balance and is therefore subject to prepayment risk.

To illustrate, suppose we form PAC and support bonds from the $100 million collateral that we used to construct our sequential-pay tranches (underlying MBS = $100 million, WAC = 8 percent, WAM = 355 months, and PT rate = 7.5 percent). To generate the minimum monthly principal payments for the PAC, assume a minimum speed of 100 PSA, referred to as the *lower collar*, and a maximum speed of 300 PSA, called the *upper collar*. Exhibit 10.13 shows the principal payments (scheduled and prepaid) for select months for each collar. The fourth column in the exhibit shows the minimum of the two payments. For example, in the first month the principal payment is $170,085 for the 100 PSA and $374,456 for the 300 PSA; thus, the principal payment for the PAC would be $170,085. In examining the exhibit, note that for the first 98 months the minimum principal payments come from the 100 PSA model, and from months 99 on the minimum principal payment come from the 300 PSA model. Based on the 100-300 PSA range, a PAC bond can be formed that would promise to pay the principal based on the minimum principal payment schedule shown in Exhibit 10.13. The support bond would receive any excess monthly principal payment. The sum of the PAC's principal payments is $63,777,030. Thus, the PAC can be described as having a par value of $63,777,030, a coupon rate of 7.5 percent, a lower collar of 100 PSA, and an upper collar of 300 PSA. The support bond, in turn, would have a par value of $36,222, 970 ($100 million – $63,777,030) and pay a coupon of 7.5 percent (see Exhibit 10.13).

As noted, the objective in creating a PAC bond is to eliminate prepayment risk. In this example, the PAC bond has no prepayment risk as long as the actual prepayment speed is between 100 and 300. This can be seen by calculating the PAC's average life, given different prepayment rates. The table at the bottom of Exhibit 10.13 shows the average lives for the collateral, PAC bond, and support bond for various prepayment speeds ranging from 50 PSA to 350 PSA. As shown, the PAC bond has an average life of 6.98 years between 100 PSA and 300 PSA; its average life does change, though, when prepayments speeds are outside the 100-300 PSA range. In contrast, the support bond's average life changes as prepayment speed changes. In fact, changes in the support bond's average life due to changes in speed are greater than the underlying collateral's responsiveness.

Other PAC-Structured CMOs

The PAC and support bond underlying a CMO can be divided into different classes. Often the PAC bond is divided into several sequential-pay tranches, with each PAC having a different priority in principal payments over the other tranches. Each sequential-pay PAC, in turn, will have a constant average life if the prepayment speed is within the lower and upper collars. In addition, it is possible that some PACs will have ranges of stability that will increase beyond the actual collar range, expanding their effective collars.

In addition to a sequential structure, a PAC-structured CMO can also be formed with PAC classes having different collars; in fact, some PACs are formed with just one PSA rate. These PACs are referred to as *targeted amortization class* (*TAC*) *bonds.* Finally, different types of tranches can be formed out of the support bond class. These include sequential-pay, floating and inverse-floating rate, and accrual bond classes.

Given the different ways in which CMO tranches can be formed, as well as the different objectives of investors, perhaps it is not surprising to find PAC-structured CMOs with as many as 50 tranches. In the mid-1990s, the average number of tranches making up a CMO was 23.[7]

Stripped Mortgage-Backed Securities

In the mid-1980s, FNMA introduced *stripped mortgage-backed securities.* Similar to Treasury stripped securities, stripped MBSs consist of two classes: a *principal-only* (*PO*) class and an *interest-only* (*IO*) class. As the names imply, the PO class receives only the principal from the underlying mortgages, whereas the IO class receives just the interest.

EXHIBIT 10.13 PAC and Support Bonds: PAC formed with 100 and 300 PSA Collars Collateral: Balance = \$100 million, WAM = 355 Months, WAC = 8 percent, PT Rate = 7.5 percent, Prepayment: 150 PSA

	Pac	Pac	Pac	Pac	Pac	Collateral	Collateral	Collateral	Collateral	Support	Support	Support	Support
Period	Low PSA Pr	High PSA Pr	Min. Principal	Int	CF	Balance	Interest	Prncipal	CF	Principal	Balance	Interest	CF
Month	100	300		0.075		$100,000,000.00				Col Pr – PAC Pr		0.075	
1	$170,085	$374,456	$170,085	$398,606	$568,692	$100,000,000	$625,000	$220,748	$845,748	$50,662	$36,222,970	$226,394	$277,056
2	$187,135	$425,190	$187,135	$397,543	$584,678	$99,779,252	$623,620	$246,153	$869,773	$59,018	$36,172,308	$226,077	$285,095
3	$204,125	$475,588	$204,125	$396,374	$600,499	$99,533,099	$622,082	$271,449	$893,531	$67,324	$36,113,290	$225,708	$293,032
4	$221,048	$525,572	$221,048	$395,098	$616,147	$99,261,650	$620,385	$296,617	$917,002	$75,568	$36,045,966	$225,287	$300,856
5	$237,895	$575,064	$237,895	$393,716	$631,612	$98,965,033	$618,531	$321,637	$940,168	$83,742	$35,970,398	$224,815	$308,557
98	$381,871	$386,139	$381,871	$135,237	$517,108	$45,780,181	$286,126	$424,898	$711,025	$43,028	$24,142,190	$150,889	$193,916
99	$380,032	$379,499	$379,499	$132,851	$512,349	$45,355,283	$283,471	$421,491	$704,962	$41,993	$24,099,163	$150,620	$192,613
100	$378,204	$372,970	$372,970	$130,479	$503,449	$44,933,791	$280,836	$418,111	$698,947	$45,141	$24,057,170	$150,357	$195,498
101	$376,384	$366,552	$366,552	$128,148	$494,700	$44,515,680	$278,223	$414,758	$692,981	$48,205	$24,012,029	$150,075	$198,281
102	$374,575	$360,242	$360,242	$125,857	$486,099	$44,100,923	$275,631	$411,430	$687,061	$51,188	$23,963,824	$149,774	$200,962
201	$235,460	$61,932	$61,932	$19,312	$81,245	$15,978,416	$99,865	$183,776	$283,641	$121,844	$12,888,435	$80,553	$202,396
202	$234,395	$60,806	$60,806	$18,925	$79,731	$15,794,640	$98,716	$182,266	$280,982	$121,460	$12,766,592	$79,791	$201,251
203	$233,336	$59,699	$59,699	$18,545	$78,244	$15,612,374	$97,577	$180,768	$278,345	$121,069	$12,645,131	$79,032	$200,101
204	$232,283	$58,611	$58,611	$18,172	$76,783	$15,431,606	$96,448	$179,282	$275,729	$120,671	$12,524,062	$78,275	$198,946
205	$231,235	$57,542	$57,542	$17,806	$75,348	$15,252,325	$95,327	$177,807	$273,134	$120,265	$12,403,392	$77,521	$197,786
206	$230,193	$56,492	$56,492	$17,446	$73,938	$15,074,517	$94,216	$176,344	$270,560	$119,852	$12,283,127	$76,770	$196,622
354	$124,660	$2,559	$2,559	$32	$2,591	$98,569	$616	$49,508	$50,124	$46,948	$93,517	$584	$47,533
355	$124,203	$2,493	$2,493	$16	$2,509	$49,061	$307	$49,061	$49,368	$46,568	$46,568	$291	$46,859
			Par = $63,777,030							Par = $36,222,970			

(*Continued*)

EXHIBIT 10.13 *(continued)*

	Pac	Pac	Pac	Pac	Pac	Collateral	Collateral	Collateral	Collateral	Support	Support	Support	Support
Period	Low PSA Pr	High PSA Pr	Min. Principal	Int	CF	Balance	Interest	Prncipal	CF	Principal	Balance	Interest	CF
Month	100	300		0.075		$100,000,000.00				Col Pr – PAC Pr		0.075	

	Average Life		
PSA	Collateral	PAC	Support
50	14.95	7.90	21.50
100	11.51	6.98	19.49
150	9.18	6.98	13.05
200	7.55	6.98	8.55
250	6.37	6.98	5.31
300	5.50	6.98	2.91
350	4.84	6.34	2.71

In general, the return on a PO MBS is greater with greater prepayment speed. For example, a PO class formed with $100 million of mortgages (principal) and priced at $75 million would yield an immediate return of $25 million if the mortgage borrowers prepaid immediately. Since investors can reinvest the $25 million, this early return will have a greater return per period than a $25 million return that is spread out over a longer period. Because of prepayment, the price of a PO MBS tends to be more responsive to interest rate changes than an option-free bond. That is, if interest rates are decreasing, then like the price of most bonds, the price of a PO MBS will increase. In addition, the price of a PO MBS is also likely to increase further because of the expectation of greater earlier principal payments as a result of an increase in prepayment caused by the lower rates. In contrast, if rates are increasing, the price of a PO MBS will decrease as a result of both lower discount rates and lower returns from slower principal payments. Thus, like most bonds, the prices of PO MBSs are inversely related to interest rates, and, like other MBSs with embedded principal prepayment options, their prices tend to be more responsive to interest rate changes.

Cash flows from an IO MBS come from the interest paid on the mortgages portfolio's principal balance. In contrast to a PO MBS, the cash flows and the returns on an IO MBS will be greater, the slower the prepayment rate. For example, if the mortgages underlying a $100 million, 7.5 percent MBS with PO and IO classes were paid off in the first year, then the IO MBS holders would receive a one-time cash flow of $7.5 million (= (.075)($100 million)). If $50 million of the mortgages were prepaid in the first year and the remaining $50 million in the second year, then the IO MBS investors would receive an annualized cash flow over two years totaling $11.25 million (= (.075) ($100 million) + (.075)($100 million – $50 million)); if the mortgage principal is paid down $25 million per year, then the cash flow over four years would total $18.75 million (= (.075)($100 million) + (.075)($100 million – $25 million) + (.075)($75 million – $25 million) + (.075)($50 million – $25 million)). Thus, IO MBSs are characterized by an inverse relationship between prepayment speed and returns: the slower the prepayment rate, the greater the total cash flow on an IO MBS. Interestingly, if this relationship dominates the price and discount rate relation, then the price of an IO MBS will vary directly with interest rates.

Examples of a PO MBS and an IO MBS are shown in Exhibit 10.14. The stripped MBSs are formed from the collateral described in Exhibit 10.4 (Mortgage = $100 million, WAC = 8 percent, PT Rate = 8 percent, WAM = 360, and PSA = 100). The table at the bottom of Exhibit 10.14, in turn, shows the values of the collateral, PO MBS, and IO MBS for different discount rate and PSA combinations of 8 percent and 150, 8.5 percent and 125, and 9 percent and 100. As shown in the exhibit, the IO MBS is characterized by a direct relation between its value and rate of return.

Note that issuers can form IO and PO classes not only with MBSs, but also with CMOs. For example, one of the tranches of the PAC-structured CMOs or sequential-structured CMOs discussed in the preceding sections could be divided into

EXHIBIT 10.14 Projected Cash Flows for Stripped PO and IO Collateral: Mortgage Portfolio = $100 million, WAC = 8 percent, WAM = 360 Months, Prepayment: 100 percent PSA

Period	Collateral						Stripped	Stripped
Month	Balance	Interest	Scheduled Principal	Prepaid Principal	Total Principal	CF	PO	IO
1	$100,000,000	$666,667	$67,098	$16,671	$83,769	$750,435	$83,769	$666,667
2	$99,916,231	$666,108	$67,534	$33,344	$100,878	$766,986	$100,878	$666,108
3	$99,815,353	$665,436	$67,961	$50,011	$117,973	$783,409	$117,973	$665,436
4	$99,697,380	$664,649	$68,380	$66,664	$135,044	$799,694	$135,044	$664,649
5	$99,562,336	$663,749	$68,790	$83,294	$152,084	$815,833	$152,084	$663,749
100	$58,669,646	$391,131	$83,852	$301,307	$385,159	$776,290	$385,159	$391,131
101	$58,284,486	$388,563	$83,977	$299,326	$383,303	$771,866	$383,303	$388,563
200	$27,947,479	$186,317	$97,308	$143,234	$240,542	$426,858	$240,542	$186,317
201	$27,706,937	$184,713	$97,453	$141,996	$239,449	$424,162	$239,449	$184,713
358	$371,778	$2,479	$123,103	$1,279	$124,382	$126,861	$124,382	$2,479
359	$247,395	$1,649	$123,287	$638	$123,925	$125,574	$123,925	$1,649
360	$123,470	$823	$123,470	0	$123,470	$124,293	$123,470	$823

	Price Sensitivity			
Discount Rate	PSA	Value of PO	Value of IO	Value of Collateral
8.00%	150	$54,228,764	$47,426,196	$101,654,960
8.50%	125	$49,336,738	$49,513,363	$98,850,101
9.00%	100	$44,044,300	$51,795,188	$95,799,488

an IO class and a PO class. Such tranches are referred to as *CMO strips*. CMOs can also be formed from PO MBSs. These CMOs are called *PO-collateralized CMOs*.

Default Loss and Credit Tranches

In addition to prepayment risk, nonagency MBSs or nonagency CMOs are subject to default losses. As shown in Exhibit 10.7, a portfolio of 30-year, 8 percent mortgages with a 100 standard default assumption (SDA) has a cumulative default rate after 120 months of 3.59 percent and one with a 300 SDA has a cumulative default rate of 10.42 percent. MBS conduits address credit risk on nonagency MBSs by providing credit enhancements designed to absorb the expected losses from the underlying mortgage pool resulting from defaults. For nonagency MBSs or CMOs, credit enhancements include senior-subordinate structures, excess spreads, overcollateralization, and monoline insurance.

Senior-Subordinate Structures

A MBS issue with a senior-subordinate structure is formed with two general bond classes: a senior bond class and a subordinated bond class, with each class consisting of one or more tranches. The following table shows a $500 million senior-subordinate structured MBS with one senior bond class with a principal of $400 million and six subordinate or junior classes with a total principal of $100 million.

Senior-Subordinated Structured MBS

Bond Class	Tranche	Principal	Credit Ratings
Senior	1	$400 million	AAA
Subordinate	2	$30 million	AA
Subordinate	3	$20 million	A
Subordinate	4	$10 million	BBB
Subordinate	5	$10 million	BB
Subordinate	6	$10 million	B
Subordinate	7	$10 million	Not Rated

For this MBS issue, the default losses are absorbed first by tranche 7 (starting at the bottom and ascending up). Thus, if losses on the collateral are less than $10 million, then only tranche 7 will experience a loss; if losses are $30 million, then tranches 7, 6, and 5 will realize losses. The senior-subordinated structured MBS spreads the credit risk amongst the bond classes. This is referred to as *credit traunching.* The rules for the distribution of the cash flows that include the distribution of losses are referred to as the *cash flow waterfalls* or simply *waterfalls.* Because of the different levels of default risk, each of the subordinate tranches created in a senior-subordinate structured MBS are separately rated by Moody's or Standard and Poor's, with the lower tranches receiving lower ratings.

In evaluating the credit risk of the bond classes of a senior-subordinated structured MBS, the more subordinate claims that are issued relative to the senior claims, the more secured the senior claims. The proportion of the mortgage balance of the senior bond class to the total mortgage deal is referred to as *senior interest* (initial senior interest = $400 million / $500 million = .80), whereas the proportion of the mortgage balance of the subordinated bond classes to the total mortgage deal is referred to as *subordinate interest* (initial subordinate interest = $100 million / $500 million = .20). The greater the subordinate interest, the greater the level of credit protection for the senior bond.

Over the life of the MBS deal, the level of credit protection will change as principal is prepaid. In general, with prepayment, senior interest will increase and the subordinate interest will decrease over time. Because of this, most senior-subordinate structured MBS deals have a *shifting interest schedule* designed to maintain the credit protection for the senior bond class. The schedule is used to determine the allocation of prepayment that goes to the senior and subordinate tranches. An example of a shifting interest schedule might be:

Shifting Interest Schedule

Years after Issuance	Shifting Interest Percentage
1–5	100%
6	70%
7	60%
8	40%
9	20%
10	10%
After 10	0

In determining the allocation to the senior holders, their percentage of prepayment is equal to their initial senior interest (for example, 80 percent = $400 million / $500 million) plus the shifting interest (based on the schedule) times the subordinate interest (20 percent = ($100 million / $500 million):

Senior Prepayment Percentage = Initial Senior Interest Percent + (Shifting Interest Proportion) (Initial Subordinate Interest)

Based on the above schedule, 100 percent of the prepayment would go to the senior class for the first five years (= 80 percent + (1)(20 percent) = 100 percent); 94 percent in year 6, (= 80 percent + (.70)(20 percent), and 92 percent in year 7, and so on. After year 10, the allocation of principal between senior and subordinate classes would match their initial senior and subordinate interest proportions of 80 percent and 20 percent. The shifting-interest schedule from 100 percent to 70 percent in year 6, to 60 percent in year 7, to finally 0 percent after year 10 is known as a *step-down provision;* such a provision allows for reductions in the credit support over time.

In many senior-subordinated structured MBS deals, provisions are included that allow for changes in the shifting interest schedule if credit conditions related to the underlying collateral deteriorate. Typically, the provisions prohibit the step-down provision in the shifting interest schedule from occurring if certain performance measures are not met. For example, if the cumulative default losses exceed a certain limit of the original balance or if the 60-day delinquency rate exceeds a specified proportion of the current balance, then step downs would not be allowed.

Other Credit Enhancements

Two other internal credit enhancements that can be found on nonagency MBS are excess interest and overcollateralization. *Excess interest* (or *excess spread*) is the interest from the collateral that is not being used to pay MBS investors and fees (mortgage servicing and administrative services). The excess spread can be used to offset any losses.

If the excess interest is retained, it can be accumulated in an account and used to offset futures default losses. When this is done, the excess interest can be set up similar to a notional IO class, with the proceeds going to a reserve account and paid out to IO holders at some future date if there is an excess. *Overcollateralization* is having the par value of the collateral exceed the value of the MBS issue. For example, if the MBS issue of $500 million had $550 million in collateral, the $50 million excess would then be used to absorb default losses.

Senior-subordinate structures, excess interest, and overcollateralization are internal credit enhancement tools. Some nonagency MBSs also have external credit enhancements in the form of insurance provided by Monoline insurance companies such as the Finance Guarantee Insurance Corporation, the Capital Markets Insurance Corporation, or the Financial Security Assurance Company. The guarantees provided by monocline insurers, in turn, shifts the default risk to the insurer.

MBS

CLASS: THE BLOOMBERG CLASS SCREEN PROVIDES LISTINGS, DESCRIPTIONS, AND TERMS FOR DIFFERENT MBS AND ABS SECURITIES

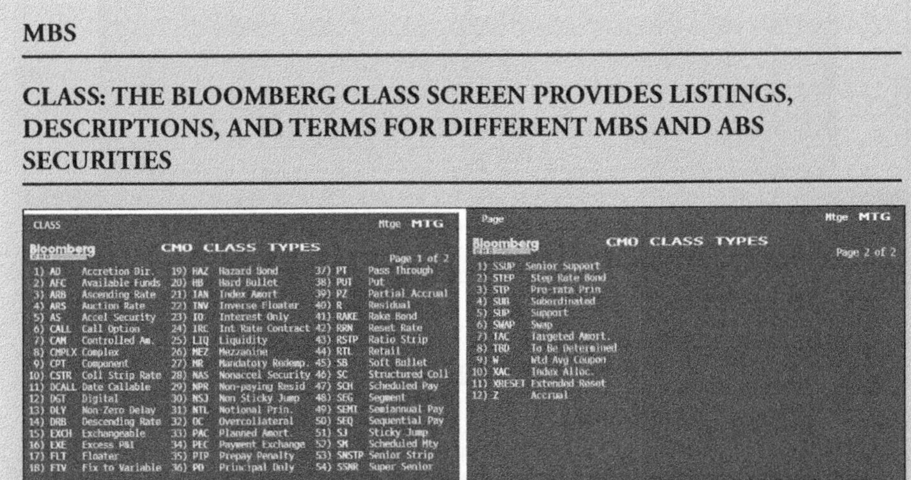

SECF: SECF <Enter>: The SECF screen can be used to screen and search for MBSs. To find mortgage-backed security issuers and tickers, use the "All" tab on the SECF screen and then select mortgages in the "Category" dropdown and residential mortgage-backed securities" in the "Sub-Category" dropdown. On the screen for residential MBS, you will see tickers for Fannie Mae (FNR), Freddie Mac (FHR), Ginnie Mae (GNR), Well Fargo MBS Trust (WFMBS), Bank of America (BAFC), Chase Mortgages (Chase), and other agency and private label MBSs. Clicking the issuer will bring up a menu showing their series.

Given an RMBS ticker, you can also screen for different types of MBS from the "Mtge" tab and "RMBS" tab on the SECF screen: SECF <Enter>, click "Mtge" tab and "RMBS" tab. In the "Ticker" box, type the MBS ticker (e.g., FNR, FHR, GNR, FHG (GNMC and FHLMC), WFMBS, BAFC, or Chase). To find special types of CMO tranches, type in the code in the "Type" box (the codes can be found on the Class Menu screen): for a sequential-pay tranche, type Seq; for an interest-only, type IO; for a PAC, type PAC. This

(*Continued*)

will bring up a menu of the CMOs. From the screen, you can click the CMO of interest to bring up its menu page or enter CUSIP <Mtge> <Enter>.

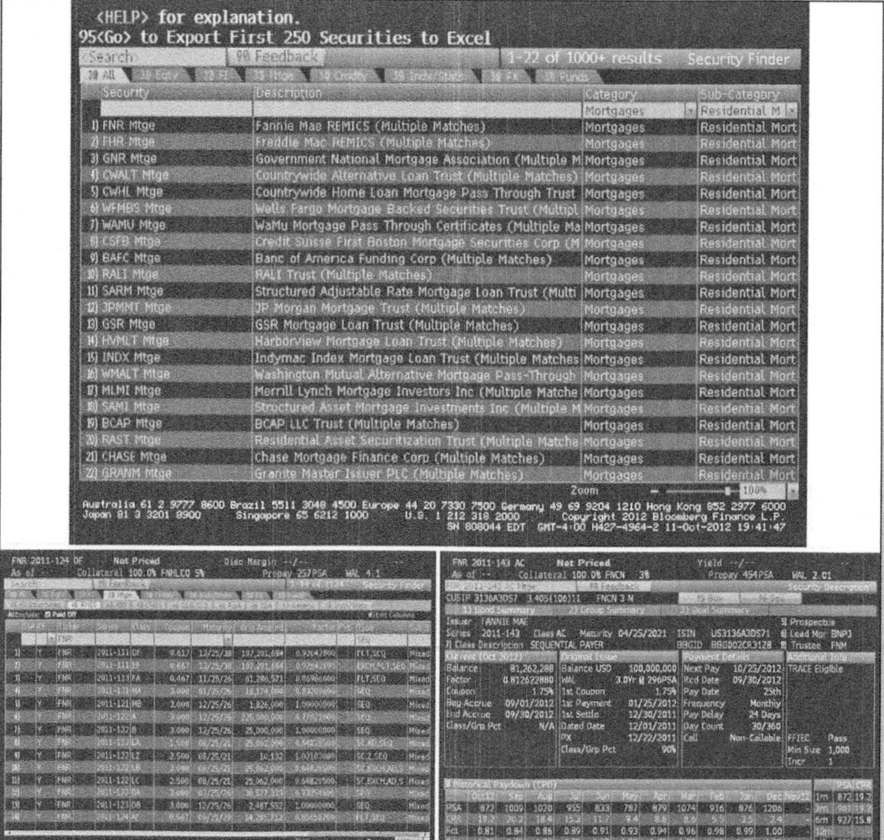

PAC

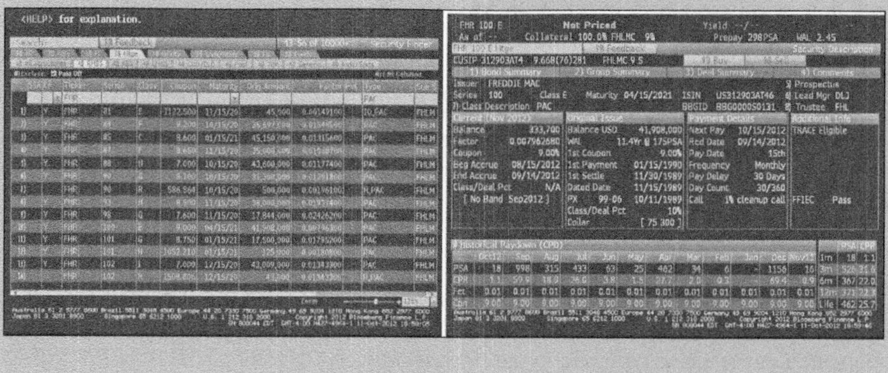

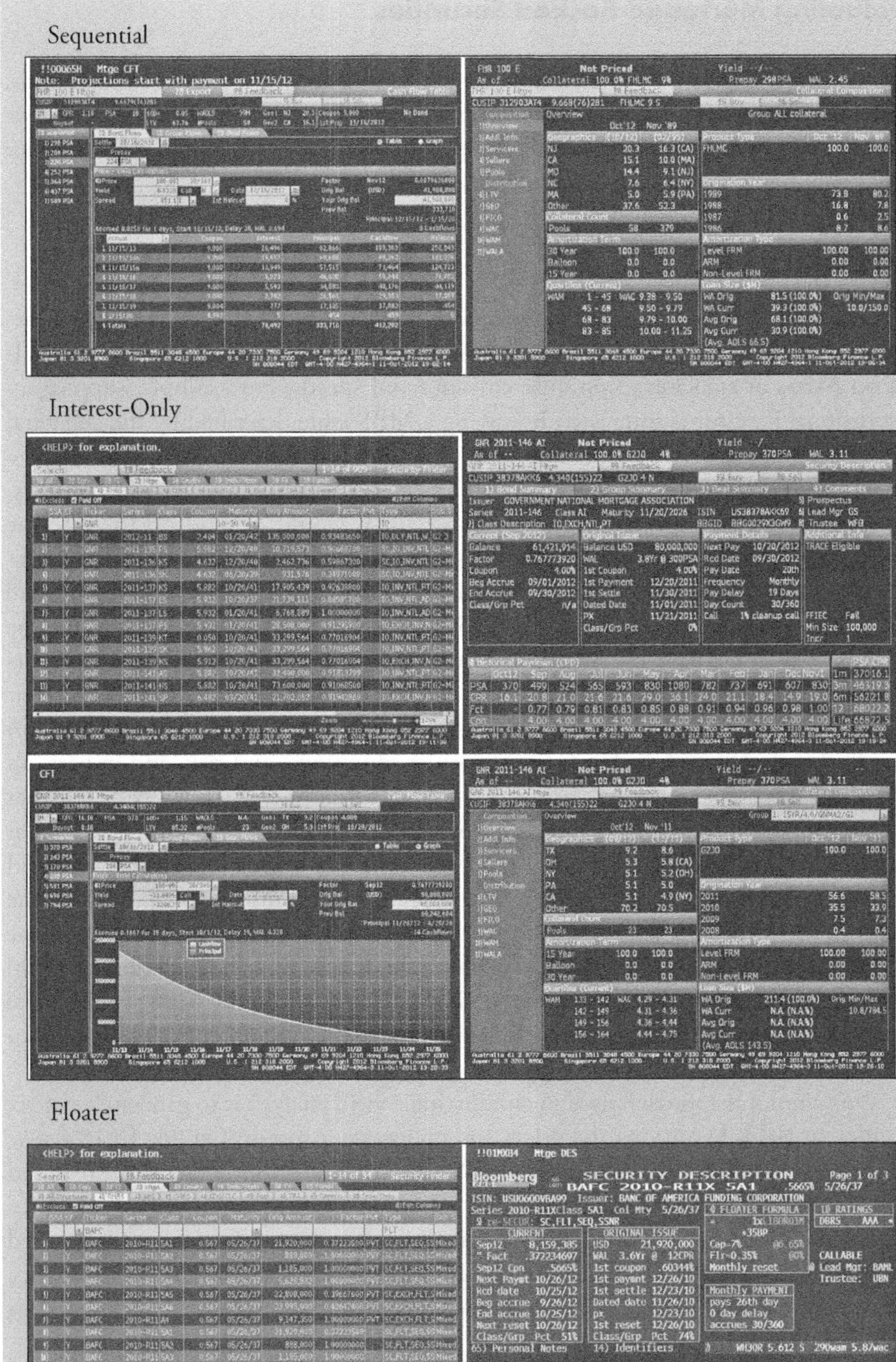
Sequential
Interest-Only
Floater

Evaluating Mortgage-Backed Securities

Like all securities, MBSs can be evaluated in terms of their characteristics. With MBSs, such an evaluation is more complex because of the difficulty in estimating cash flows due to prepayment. Two approaches are used to evaluate MBS and CMO tranches: yield analysis and Monte Carlo simulation.

Yield Analysis

Yield analysis involves calculating the yields on MBSs or CMO tranches given different prices and prepayment speed assumptions or alternatively calculating the values on MBSs or tranches given different rates and speeds. For example, suppose an institutional investor is interested in buying a MBS issue described by the collateral in Exhibit 10.8. This MBS issue has a par value of $100 million, WAC = 8, WAM = 355 months, and a PT rate of 7.5 percent. The value, as well as average life, maturity, duration, and other characteristics of this security, would depend on the rate the investor requires on the MBS and the prepayment speed she estimates. If the investor's required return on the MBS is 9 percent (which would include the appropriate risk premiums) and her estimate of the PSA speed is 150, then she would value the MBS issue at $93,702,142. At that rate and speed, the MBS would have an average life of 9.18 years (see Exhibit 10.15). Whether a purchase of the MBS issue at $93,702,142 to yield 9 percent represents a good investment depends, in part, on rates for other securities with similar maturities, durations, and risk, and in part, on how good the prepayment rate assumption is. For example, if the investor felt that the prepayment rate should be the 100 PSA and her required rate with that level of prepayment is 9 percent, then she would price the MBS issue at $92,732,145 and the average life would be 11.51 years. In general, for many institutional investors the decision on whether or not to invest in a particular MBS or tranche depends on the price the institution can command. For example, based on an expectation of a 100 PSA, our investor might conclude that a yield of 9 percent on the MBS would make it a good investment. In this case, the investor would be willing to offer no more than $92,732,145 for the MBS issue.

One common approach used in conducting a yield analysis is to generate a matrix of different yields by varying the prices and prepayment speeds. Exhibit 10.15 shows the different values for our illustrative MBS given different combinations of required rates and prepayment speeds. Using this matrix, an investor could determine, for a given price and assumed speed, the estimated yield, or determine, for a given speed and yield, the price. Using this approach, an investor can also evaluate for each price the average yield and standard deviation over a range of PSA speeds.

Vector Analysis

One of the limitations of the above yield analysis is the assumption that the PSA speed used to estimate the yield is constant during the life of the MBS; in fact,

EXHIBIT 10.15 Cash Flow Analysis Mortgage Portfolio = $100 million, WAC = 8 percent, WAM = 355 Months, PT Rate = 7.5

Rate/PSA	50	100	150
	Value	*Value*	*Value*
7%	$106,039,631	$105,043,489	$104,309,207
8%	$98,251,269	$98,526,830	$98,732,083
9%	$91,442,890	$92,732,145	$93,702,142
10%	$85,457,483	$87,554,145	$89,146,871
Average Life	14.95	11.51	9.18
	Vector	*Vector*	*Vector*
	Month Range: PSA	*Month Range: PSA*	*Month Range: PSA*
	1–50: 200	1–50: 200	1–50: 200
	51–150: 250	51–150: 300	51–150: 150
	151–250: 150	151–250: 350	151–250: 100
	251–355: 200	251–355: 400	251–355: 50
Rate	*Value*	*Value*	*Value*
7%	$103,729,227	$103,473,139	$104,229,758
8%	$98,893,974	$98,964,637	$98,756,370
9%	$94,465,328	$94,794,856	$93,826,053
10%	$90,395,704	$90,929,474	$89,364,229

such an analysis is sometimes referred to as *static yield analysis*. In practice, prepayment speeds change over the life of a MBS as interest rates change in the market. To address this, a more dynamic yield analysis, known as *vector analysis,* can be used. In applying vector analysis, PSA speeds are assumed to change over time. In the above case, a matrix of values for different rates can be obtained for different PSA vectors formed by dividing the total period into a number of periods with different PSA speeds assumed for each period. A vector analysis example is also shown in Exhibit 10.15.

YA SCREEN

The YA screen can be used to evaluate a MBS in terms of their value, yield, and PSA. It creates a matrix showing prices for different yields and PSA speeds (PT), yields for different prices and PSA speeds.

(*Continued*)

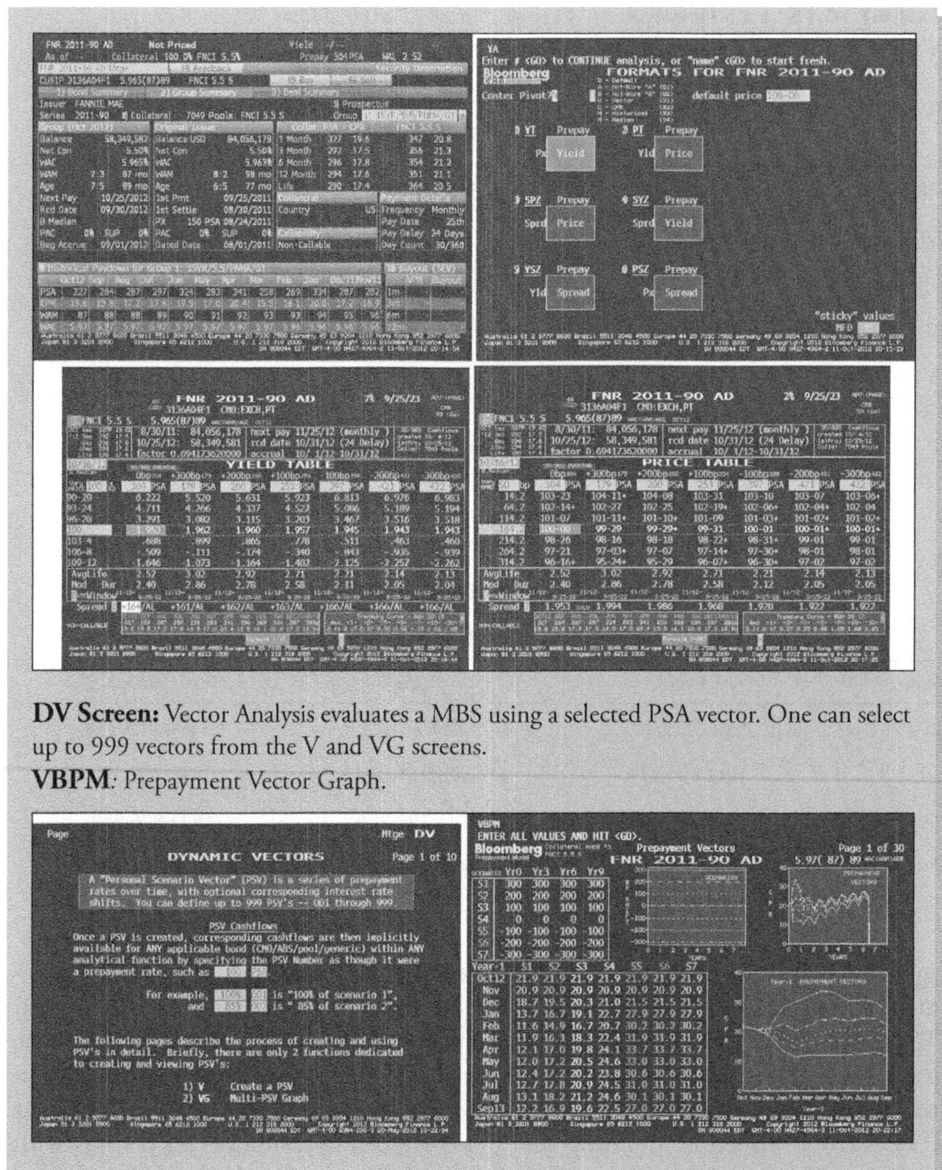

DV Screen: Vector Analysis evaluates a MBS using a selected PSA vector. One can select up to 999 vectors from the V and VG screens.

VBPM: Prepayment Vector Graph.

Commercial Mortgage-Backed Securities

Commercial Mortgage Loans

Real estate property can be either residential or nonresidential. Residential includes houses, condominiums, and apartments; it is classified as either single family or multiple family. Nonresidential includes commercial and agricultural property. Commercial real estate loans are for income-producing properties. They are used to finance the purchase of the property or to refinance an existing one. Commercial property can include:

- Shopping centers
- Shopping strips
- Multifamily apartment buildings
- Industrial properties
- Warehouses
- Hotels
- Health care facilities

In contrast to residential mortgages where the interest and principal payments come from borrowers' income-generating ability or wealth, commercial mortgage loans come from income produced from the property. As such, commercial mortgage loans are referred to as *nonrecourse* loans. Lenders in assessing the credit quality of commercial loans look at the *debt-to-service ratio* (= Rental Income – Operating Expenses) / Interest Payments) and the *loan-to-value ratios,* where value is equal to the present value of expected cash flows or the appraised value.

Commercial mortgage loans also differ from residential mortgage loans in that they typically have prepayment protection. Such protection can take the form of prepayment penalties, provisions prohibiting prepayment for a specified period, and defeasance. The latter is an agreement whereby the borrower agrees to invest funds in risk-free securities in an amount that would match the cash flows of a prepayment schedule. Finally, unlike residential mortgage loans in which the principal is amortized over the life of the loan, commercial mortgage loans are typically balloon loans. At the balloon date, the borrower is therefore obligated to pay the remaining balance. This is typically done by refinancing. As a result, the lender is subject to *balloon risk:* The risk that the borrower will not be able to make the balloon payment because they either cannot refinance or sell the property at a price that will cover the loan. With many commercial property loans, there is a *special servicer* who takes over the loan when default is imminent. These servicers have the responsibility to try to modify the loan terms to avert default.

Commercial Mortgage-Backed Securities

A commercial mortgage-backed security (CMBS) is a security backed by one or more commercial mortgage loans. Some CMBSs are backed by Fannie Mae, Freddie Mac, and Ginnie Mae. These agency CMBSs are limited to multifamily mortgages and healthcare facilities. Most CMBSs are private labels formed by either a single borrower with many properties or by a conduit with multiple borrowers. Similar to nonagency residential MBSs, many CMBSs have credit tranches (senior-subordinated structures), credit enhancements (overcollaterialization, excess interests, and monocline insurance) and prepayment tranches (sequential-pay, PACs, NIO, floaters, etc.).

One feature common to residential and commercial mortgage-backed securities is *cross-collateralization:* property used to secure one loan is also used to secure the other loans in the pool. Cross-collateralization prevents the MBS investors/lenders from calling the loan if there is a default, provided there is sufficient cash flows from the other loans to cover the loan's default loss. Such protection is called *cross-default protection.* Unlike residential MBSs that tend to be formed with a larger number of homogeneous mortgages, commercial MBS can be formed with a fewer number of loans and with some loans being more important to the pool than others. As a result, commercial MBSs often have less cross-default protection. To redress this, some commercial MBSs include a *property release provision* that requires the borrower of a commercial loan to pay a premium (e.g. 105 percent of par) if the property is removed from the pool. The provision is aimed at averting potential deterioration in the overall credit quality of the collateral when the best property in the pool is prepaid.

As noted, CMBSs can be formed from a single borrower with multiple properties. These deals are often set up by large real estate developers who use commercial MBSs as a way to finance or refinance their numerous projects: shopping malls, office buildings, hotels, apartment complexes, and the like. The other type of commercial MBS deal is one in which there are multiple borrowers or originators with the MBS set up through a conduit—a *conduit deal.* When the deal has one large borrower or property combined with a number of smaller borrowers, the deal is referred to as a *fusion conduit deal.* Conduit deals are often structured by large banks such as Bank of America, Wells Fargo, or J. P. Morgan. Moreover, it is not uncommon for the conduit deal to be used to finance properties totaling as much as $1 billion, with as many as 200 property loans, varying in type (office, multi, warehouses, etc.), geographical distributions, and credit enhancements. With such large deals, there are different servicing levels. For example, there may be subservicing by the local originators who are required to collect payments and maintain records, a master servicer responsible for overseeing the commercial MBS deal, and a special servicer responsible for taking action if a loan becomes past due.

Commercial MBS investors include institutional investors. These investors, in turn, evaluate a commercial MBS issue not only in terms of issue's general sensitivity to economic conditions and interest rates, but also assess each income-producing property on an ongoing basis.

COMMERCIAL MBS

LLKU <Enter>: Screens for CMBS.

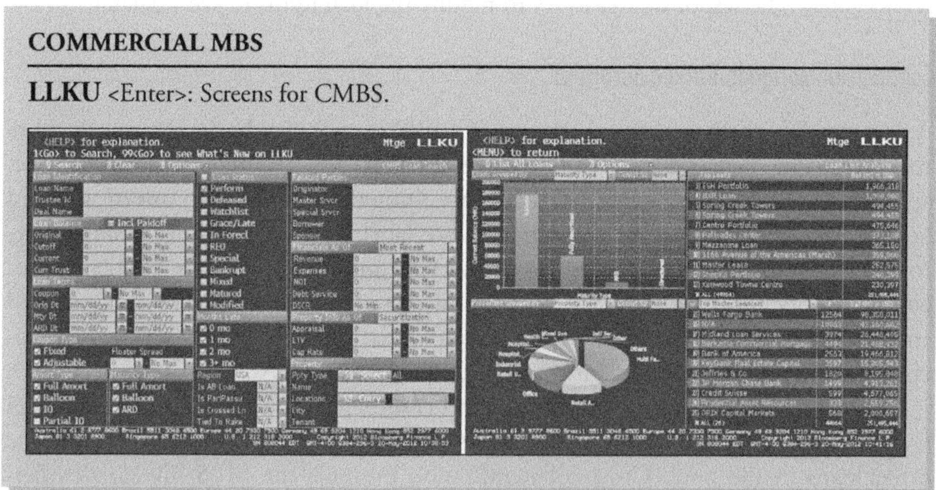

SECF: SECF <Enter>: The SECF screen can be used to search for CMBS. To find CMBS issuers and tickers, use the "All" tab on the SECF screen and then select mortgages in the "Category" dropdown and commercial mortgage-backed securities" in the "Sub-Category" dropdown. On the screen for CMBS, you will see tickers for J.P. Morgan Chase (JPMCC), Wells Fargo (WFCM), Bank of America (BACM), and other institutions. Clicking the issuer will bring up a menu showing their series.

Given a CMBS ticker, you can also screen for different types of CMBS from the "Mtge" tab and "CMBS" tab on the SECF screen: SECF <Enter>, click "Mtge" tab and "CMBS" tab. In the "Ticker" box type the CMBS ticker (e.g., JPMCC, BACM, or WFCM). To find special types of CMO tranches, type in the code (e.g., PAC, Seq, or IO) in the "Type" box. This will bring up a menu of that type of CMOs. From the screen, you can click the CMO of interest to bring up its menu page or enter CUSIP <Mtge> <Enter>.

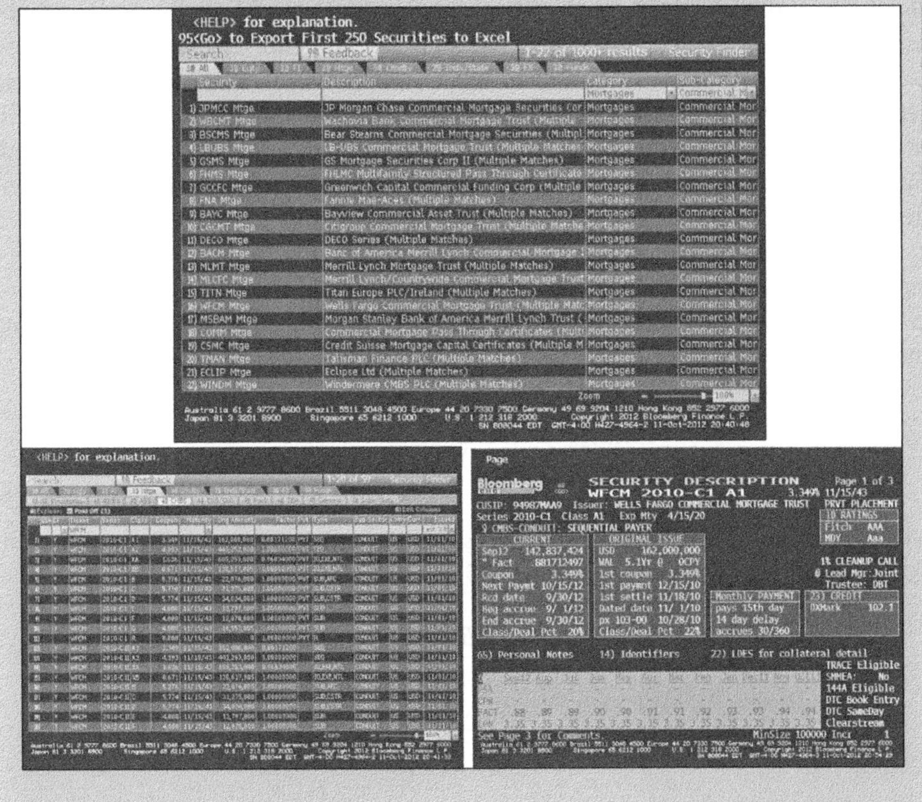

Asset-Backed Securities

Asset-backed securities (ABSs) are securities created from securitizing pools of loans other than residential prime mortgage loans and commercial loans; as noted, residential subprime MBS are included in the ABS category. Loans used to create ABSs include home equity loans, credit card receivables, student loans, home improvement loans, trade receivables, franchise loans, small business loans, equipment leases, operating assets, and subprime mortgages. Like most securitized assets, ABSs can be structured with different prepayment and credit tranches and can include different credit enhancements. The three most common types of ABSs are those backed by automobile loans, credit card receivables, and home equity loans.

Automobile Loan–Backed Securities

Automobile loan-backed securities are often referred to as *CARs* (*certificates for automobile receivables*). They are issued by the financial subsidiaries of auto manufacturing companies, commercial banks, and finance companies specializing in auto loans. The automobile loans underlying these securities are similar to mortgages in that borrowers make regular monthly payments that include interest and a scheduled principal. Also like mortgages, automobile loans are characterized by prepayment. For such loans, prepayment can occur as a result of car sales, trade-ins, repossessions, wrecks, and refinancing when rates are low. CARs differ from MBSs in that they have shorter maturities, their prepayment rates are less influenced by interest rates than mortgage prepayment rates, and they are subject to greater default risk.

The prepayment for auto loans is typically measured in terms of the *absolute prepayment speed* (*APS*). APS measures prepayment as a percentage of the original collateral amount, instead of the prior period's balance. The relation between APS and the monthly prepayment rate (single monthly mortality rate maturity, SMM) is

$$SMM = \frac{ABS}{1-(ABS)(M-1)}$$

where M = month. For example, if the absolute prepayment speed is 2 percent, then the monthly prepayment rate in month 25 is 3.8462 percent

$$SMM = \frac{ABS}{1-(ABS)(M-1)}$$

$$SMM = \frac{.02}{1-(.02)(25-1)} = .038462$$

A large part of auto manufacturers' sales are sold from installment sales contracts, with the company's credit department (often a financial subsidiary) making administrative decisions on extending credit, setting underwriting standards, originating loans, and then later servicing the loans. Automobile loan-backed securities are often created from these loans and typically issued by *special-purpose vehicles* (*SPVs*) created by the manufacturer or its financial subsidiary; the financial subsidiary may also be set up as a special purpose vehicle. For example, a car manufacturer might have $500 million of installment loans resulting from monthly car sales. The manufacturer could set up (or may already have set up) an SPV to sell the installment loans for $500 million cash. The SPV would then sell the $500 million in securities backed by the loans as ABSs.

Instead of securitizing the installment loans as ABS through an SPV, the auto manufacturer could have alternatively raised $500 million by issuing corporate notes, either as a debenture or collateralized by the installment loans. If the manufacturer were to default, though, all of its creditors would be able to go after all of its assets. If the manufacturer sells the installment loans to its SPV, though, the SPV owns the loans/assets and not the manufacturer. Thus, if the manufacturer were forced into bankruptcy, its creditors would not be able to recover the installment loans of the SPV. Thus, when the SPV issues ABS, investors only look at the credit risk associated with the installment loans and not the manufacturer. As a result, by financing with securitization via an SPV, the ABS issue often has a better credit rating and a lower rate than the manufacturer's notes.[8]

In addition to the use of SPVs, ABSs also are characterized by having a number of features: credit tranches, overcollateralization, excess interest, sequential-pay tranches, and derivative positions. Exhibit 10.16 shows an example of an ABS deal of a representative U.S. auto manufacturer's financial subsidiary in which car loans are securitized.[9] The key features of the deal include:

- Car loans totaling $1.1 billion purchased from the car manufacturer's financial subsidiary by an SPV.
- $1 billion of CARs (auto-loan-backed securities) issued (overcollateralization).
- A senior-subordinated structure consisting of $800 million senior class bond (A) and $200 million subordinate class bonds (B, C, and D).
- Bond classes Aa (A1a, 2a, A3a) are fixed rate.
- Bond classes Ab (A1b and A2b) are floating rate.
- Senior bond classes A are sequential pay: 1, 2, and 3.
- Principal amount for senior fixed-rate is $600 million:
  - A1a = $300 million
  - A2a = $200 million
  - A3a = $100 million
- Principal amount for senior floating-rate is $200 million:
  - A1b = $100 million
  - A2b = $100 million
- Principal amount for subordinate fixed-rate is $200 million:
  - B = $100 million
  - C = $50 million
  - D = $50 million
- The SPV entered into an interest rate swap with a financial institution for each of the floating rate bonds to fix the rate (swaps are discussed in Chapter 14).
- Each month the cash flows from the collateral are used to pay the service fee and the payments to the swap.
- Bank A is the Trustee.

EXHIBIT 10.16 Auto-Loan-Backed Security Deal

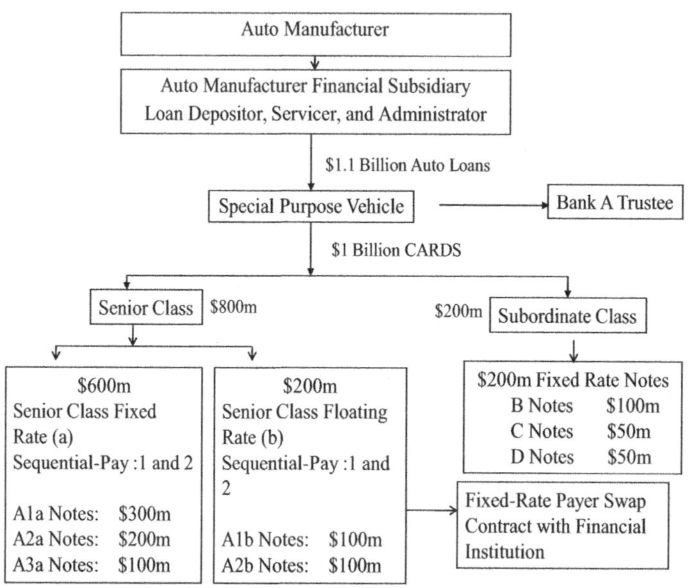

CAR LOANS

AUTO <Enter>: list of auto loan issuers; Ticker <Mtge> <Enter>; Cusip <Mtge> Enter.

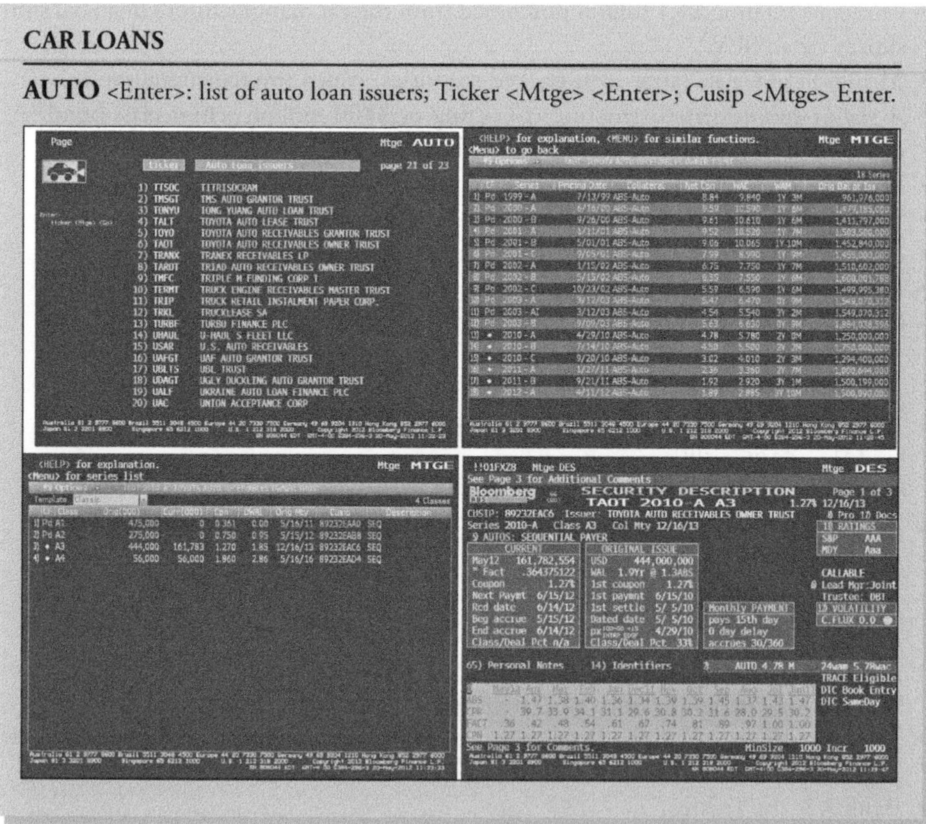

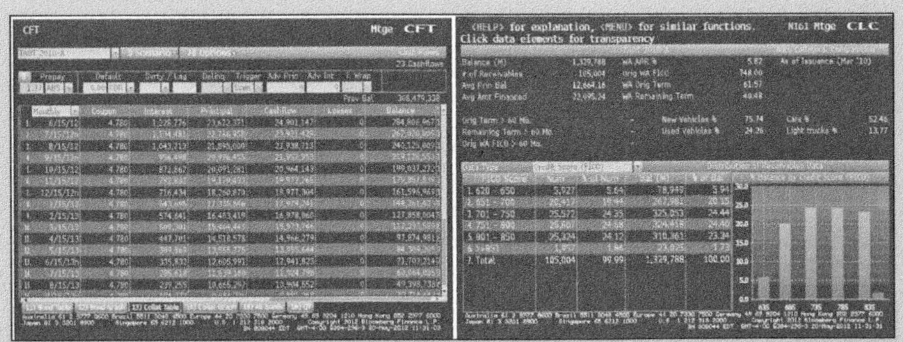

SECF: SECF <Enter>: The SECF screen can be used to search for ABSs. To find ABS issuers and tickers securitized by auto loans, use the "All" tab on the SECF screen, select mortgages in the "Category" dropdown and asset-backed securities" in the "Sub-Category" dropdown, and then type auto in the description box. On the screen for ABSs, you will see tickers, such as Fordo (Ford), Valet (Volkswagen), Harot (Honda), and BAAT (Bank of America). Clicking the issuer will bring up a menu showing their series.
Given an ABS ticker, you can also screen for different types of ABSs from the "Mtge" tab and "ABS" tab on the SECF screen: SECF <Enter>, click "Mtge" tab and "ABS" tab. In the "Ticker" box, type the ABS ticker (e.g., Fordo, Harot, BAAT, or Valet). To find special types of ABS tranches, type in the code (e.g., PAC or IO) in the "Type" box. From the screen, you can click the CMO of interest to bring up its menu page or enter CUSIP <Mtge> <Enter>.

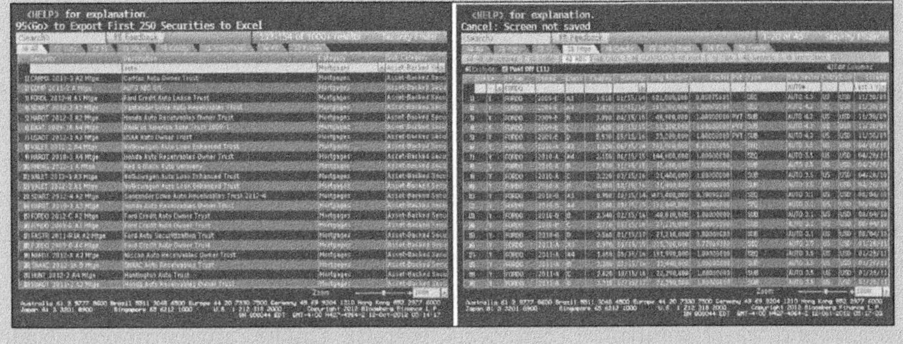

Home Equity Loan–Backed Securities

Home equity loan–backed securities are referred to as *HELS*. They are similar to MBSs in that they pay a monthly cash flow consisting of interest, scheduled principal, and prepaid principal. In contrast to mortgages, the home equity loans securing HELS tend to have shorter maturities and different factors influencing their prepayment rates. The home equity loans forming the pool backing a HEL issue are also subject to default. Like nonagency MBS, commercial MBS, and CARDS, HEL deals are often structured with different prepayment tranches, credit tranches, and credit enhancements.

HOME EQUITY LOANS

HEQ <Enter>: list of home equity loans by issuer; Ticker <Mtge> <Enter>; Cusip <Mtge>.

SECF: SECF <Enter>: Given an ABS ticker, you can also screen for different types of ABSs from the "Mtge" tab and "ABS" tab on the SECF screen: SECF <Enter>, click "Mtge" tab and "ABS" tab. In the "Ticker" box, type the ABS ticker (e.g., ARSI (Argent Securities Inc.). Use the HEQ screen to find tickers. From the SECF screen, you can click the CMO of interest to bring up its menu page or enter CUSIP <Mtge> <Enter>

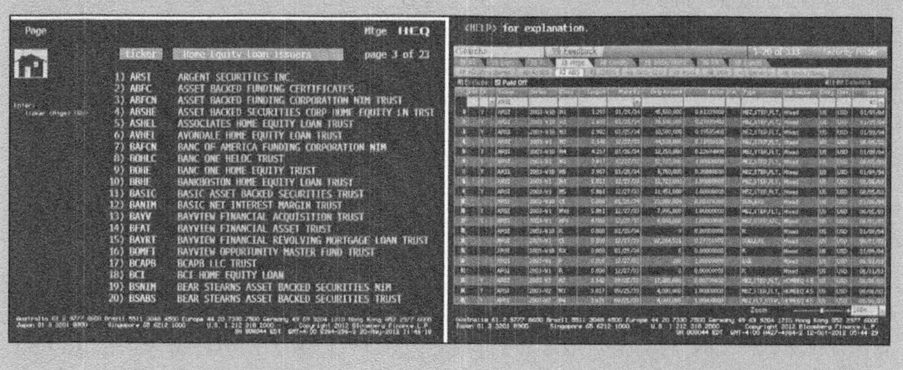

Credit-Card Receivable–Backed Securities

Credit-card receivable–backed securities are commonly referred to as *CARDs* (*certificates for amortizing revolving debts*). Securitized assets formed with home equity loans, residential mortgages, and auto loans are backed by loans that are amortized. ABSs with amortizing assets are sometime referred to as *self-liquidating structures.* In contrast, CARD investors do not receive an amortorized principal payment as part of their monthly cash flow. That is, the credit card receivables backing a CARD are nonamortizing loans where there is not a schedule of periodic principal payments. As such, prepayment does not apply for a pool of credit card receivable loans.

Credit cards are issued by banks (VISA and MasterCard), retailers, and global payment and travel companies (American Express). Credit card borrowers usually make a minimum principal payment, in which if the payment is less than the interest on the debt, the shortfall is added to the principal balance, and if it greater, it is used to reduce the balance. The cash flow from a pool of card receivables comes from finance charges (interest charges based on unpaid balance), principal collected, and fees. The CARDs formed from a pool of credit card receivables are often structured with two periods. In one period, known as the *lockout period* (or *revolving period*) all principal payments made on the receivables are retained and either reinvested in other receivables or invested in other securities. When new assets are added to an ABS deal, the structure is called a *revolving structure.* In the other period, known as the *principal-amortization period* (or *amortizing period*), all current and accumulated principal payments are distributed to the CARD holders.

In structuring an ABS secured by credit card receivable, the issuer often sets up a *master trust* where the credit card accounts meeting certain eligibility requirement are pledged. The master trust is very large, including millions of credit card accounts, totaling billions of dollars. Numerous credit card deals or series are then issued from the master trust. Each series is, in turn, identified by a year and a number:

2007-1	2008-1	2009-1
2007-2	2008-2	2009-2
2007-3	2008-3	2009-3
2007-4	2008-4	
2007-5		

Each series has a lockout period where, as noted, the principal payments made by the credit card borrowers are retained by the trustee and reinvested in additional receivables or securities. During the lockout period, the cash flow to CARD investors comes from finance charges and fees. This period can last a number of years. The lockout period is followed by the principal amortizing period when principal received by the trustee is paid to CARD investors. There can also be an early amortizing provision in some series that requires early amortization of principal if certain events occur.

In evaluating a CARD series, investors often monitor the *monthly payment rate* (*MPR*): the monthly payment of finance charges, fees, and principal repayment from the credit card receivable portfolio (e.g., $50 million) as a percentage of the credit card debt outstanding (e.g., $500 million; MPR = 10 percent). For a CARD series with low or declining MPRs, there is a chance there may not be sufficient cash to pay off the principal. If there is an early amortization provision, an MPR falling below a threshold MPR would be the trigger for early amortization. Other important rate measures for evaluating CARDs include:

- *Gross portfolio yield:* Finance charges collected and fees as a proportion of credit card debt outstanding.
- *Charge-offs:* The accounts charged off as uncollectable as a proportion of credit card debt outstanding.
- *Net portfolio yield:* Gross profit yield minus charge-offs as a proportion of credit card debt outstanding; this is the return CARD holders receive.
- *Delinquency rate:* Proportion of receivables that are past due—30, 60, or 90 days.

Like many ABSs, CARDs are characterized by having a number of features. Exhibit 10.17 shows an example of a CARD deal of a representative credit card issuer. Key features of the series include:

- The issuing entity is the credit card issuer's master trust
  - The depositor is the card issuer's finance corporation.
  - The sponsors and originators are the credit card issuer's bank.
  - The service is the credit card company.
  - The CARD is identified as 2008 Series 1.

- Total CARDS issue is $600 million.
- There is a senior-subordinate structure with $550 million issued to the Senior A Class and $50 million to Subordinate B Class.
- Interest payment to each class is equal to the monthly LIBOR + spread.
- The final payment date of the series is anticipated to be 2015.
- Principal collected during the lockout period is to be used to invest in additional receivables. Principal is to be accumulated in a "principal funding account."
- In January 2012, the Trust will begin accumulating collection of receivables for principal repayment and begin distributing principal to Bond Class A and Bond Class B.
- Early amortization is triggered if MPR for any three consecutive months is less than a specified base level.
- If the collection of receivables is less than expected, principal may be delayed.

EXHIBIT 10.17 Credit Card–Backed Security Deal

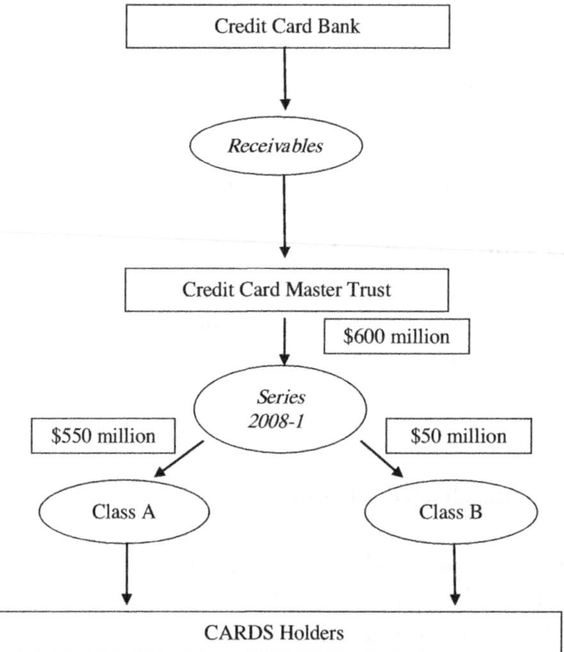

Provisions:

1. Interest payment to each class is equal to the monthly LIBOR + spread.
2. The final payment date of the series is anticipated to be 2015.
3. Principal collected during the lockout period is to be used to invest in additional receivables. Principal is to be accumulated in a "principal funding account."
4. In January 2012, the Trust will begin accumulating collection of receivables for principal repayment and begin distributing principal to Bond Class A and Bond Class B.
5. Early amortization is triggered if MPR for any three consecutive months is less than 10%.
6. If the collection of receivables is less than expected, principal may be delayed.

CREDIT CARD RECEIVABLES

CARD <Enter>: list of credit card receivables by issuer; Ticker <Mtge> <Enter>; Cusip <Mtge>.

SECF: SECF <Enter>: The SECF screen can be used to search for CARD ABSs. To find ABS issuers and tickers securitized by receivables, use the "All" tab on the SECF screen, select mortgages in the "Category" dropdown and asset-backed securities" in the "Sub-Category" dropdown, and then type CARD in the description box. On the screen for ABSs, you will see tickers, such as CCCIT (Citibank). Clicking the issuer will bring up a menu showing their series. Given an ABS ticker, you can also screen for different types of ABSs from the "Mtge" tab and "ABS" tab on the SECF screen: SECF <Enter>, click "Mtge" tab and "ABS" tab. In the "Ticker" box, type the ABS ticker (e.g., CCCIT).

Conclusion

Until the mid-1970s, most mortgages originated when savings and loans, commercial banks, and other thrifts borrowed funds or used their deposits to provide mortgage loans, possibly later selling the resulting instruments in the secondary market to Fannie Mae, Freddie Mae, or Ginnie Mae. To a large degree, residential real estate until then was financed by individual deposits, with little financing coming from institutional investors. In an effort to attract institutional investors' funds away from corporate bonds and other securities, as well as to minimize their poor hedge, financial institutions began to sell mortgage-backed securities. Over time, these securities were structured in different ways (as PACs, POs, IOs, etc.) to make them more attractive to different types of investors. Today, MBS have becoming one of the most popular securities held by institutional investors, competing with a number of different types of bonds for inclusion in the portfolio of institutional investors. More significantly, they have revolutionized the way in which real estate is financed.

The securitization process, the creation of prepayment tranches like PACs, the use of credit tranches such as senior-subordinate structures, the structuring of ABSs for credit cards, home equity loans, receivable, and other assets, all point to the innovativeness that has characterized the financial community over the last 20 years. These innovations, in turn, have revolutionized the way real estate property, account receivable, car loans, and other assets are financed. Moreover, like securitized assets, all of the fixed-income securities that we have examined over the last five chapters demonstrate how well the financial system is able to create securities needed to finance the myriad investments of corporations, governments, intermediaries, and consumers.

Website Information

MBS Price Information

1. *Wall Street Journal:* Go to http://online.wsj.com/public/us, "Market Data" and "Bonds" and "Mortgage-Backed Securities, CMO."
2. For information on the mortgage industry, statistics, trends, and rates go to www.mbaa.org.
3. For information on mortgage rates in different geographical go to www.interest.com.
4. For historical 30-year mortgage rates go to http://research.stlouisfed.org/fred2 and click on "Interest Rates."
5. Agency information:
   Fannie Mae: www.fanniemae.com
   Ginnie Mae: www.ginniemae.gov
   Freddie Mac: www.freddiemac.com
6. Fannie Mae Information and Prospectus:
   - Use Advance Search to find a MBS and its pool number:
   - Go to Fannie Mae: www.fanniemae.com; Site Map; Mortgage-Backed Securities; "More Search Options."
   - Or go to http://sls.fanniemae.com/slsSearch/Home.do. Use pool number to find information on Fannie Mae MBS. Information includes prospectus and common pool information.
7. Ginnie Mae Information and Prospectus:
   - Go to Ginnie Mae: www.ginniemae.gov.
   - To find pool number, go to "Multiple Issue Pool Number" found under "Issuer."
   - To find prospectus on MBS, go to "REMIC Offering Circulars" under "Investors."
   - Or go to www.ginniemae.gov/investors/prospectus.asp?Section=Investors.

8. Freddie Mae Information on types of MBSs: www.freddiemac.com Go to "Mortgage Securities"

Selected References

Anderson, G. A., J. R. Barber, and C. H. Chang, 1989. Prepayment risk and the duration of default-free mortgage-backed securities. *Journal of Financial Research* 16:1–9.

Bartlett, W. W. 1989. *Mortgage Backed Securities: Products, Analysis, Trading.* New York: New York Institute of Finance.

Bhattacharya, A., and H. Chin. 1992. Synthetic mortgage backed securities. *Journal of Portfolio Management* 18:44–55.

Carron, A. S. 1992. Understanding CMOs, REMICs and other mortgage derivatives. *Journal of Fixed Income* 2:25–43.

Dunn, K., and J. McConnell. 1981. Valuation of GNMA mortgage-backed securities. *Journal of Finance* 36:599–616.

Fabozzi, F. J., ed. *The Handbook of Mortgage-Backed Securities.* Chicago: Probus.

Fabozzi, F. J., A. K. Bhattacharya, and W. S. Berliner. 2007. *Mortgage-Backed Securities: Products, Structuring, and Analytical Techniques,* Hoboken, NJ: John Wiley & Sons.

Fabozzi, F. J. 2009. *Bond Markets, Analysis and Strategies,* 5th ed. Upper Saddle River, NJ: Prentice-Hall, 214–321.

Goldman, Sachs and Company. 1990. *Understanding Securitized Investments and their use in Portfolio Management.* Charlottesville, VA: Association of Investment Management and Research.

Hayre, L., C. Mohebbi, and T. A. Zimmerman. 2001. Mortgage pass-throughs. In F. Fabozzi, ed., *The Handbook of Fixed Income Securities,* 6th ed. New York: McGraw-Hill.

Hurst, R. R. 2001. Securities backed by closed-end home equity loans. In F. Fabozzi, ed., *The Handbook of Fixed Income Securities,* 6th ed. NewYork: McGraw-Hill.

Jacob, D., and A. Toevs. 1988. An analysis of the new valuation, duration and convexity models for mortgage-backed securities. In F. Fabozzi, ed., *The Handbook of Mortgage-Backed Securities,* rev. ed. Chicago: Probus.

McElravey, J. N. 2001. Securities backed by credit card receivables. In F. Fabozzi, ed., *The Handbook of Fixed Income Securities,* 6th ed. New York: McGraw-Hill.

Public Securities Association. 2008. *Uniform Practices for the Clearance and Settlement of Mortgage-Backed Securities.* New York: SIFMA.

Roever, W. A., J. N. McElravey, and G. M. Schultz. 2001. Securities backed by automobile loans. In F. Fabozzi, ed., *The Handbook of Fixed Income Securities,* 6th ed. New York: McGraw-Hill.

Schwartz, B., and W. Torous. 1992. Prepayment and the valuation of mortgage pass-through securities. *Journal of Business* 15:221–240.

Bloomberg Exercises

1. Use the Bloomberg mortgage ticker screen to identify and load a generic agency mortgage (example: FNCL <Mtge> <Enter>; click mortgage type to bring up the menu page). Analyze the mortgages cash flows given different PSA speeds using the CFT screen.
2. Use the SECF screen to identify an agency MBS and its collateral: SECF <Enter>. On the SECF screen, use the "Mtge" tab and "RMBS" tab, and then type the

MBS ticker in the ticker box (e.g., FNR, FHR, GNR, or FHG (GNMC and FHLMC)), Right click an issue of interest to obtain the issue's menu and CUSIP or enter the security's identification number: Number <Mtge> <Enter>. Analyze the MBS using the following screens: DES, CFT, YA, CLP (collateral composition), MTST (structure analysis), SPA (structure paydown), TRA (total return analysis), and HTR (historical total return).

3. The SECF screen can be used to find different CMOs tranches: SECF <Enter>, click "Mtge" tab and "RMBS" tab; in the "Ticker" box, type the MBS ticker (e.g., FNR, FHR, GNR, FHG, WFMBS, BAFC, or Chase); in the "Type" box, type in the code. Using the SECF screen, select and analyze (CUSIP <Mtge> <Enter>) the following agency MBS tranches:
   a. Sequential-Pay (Class code: Seq)
   b. PAC (PAC)
   c. Interest-Only (IO)
   d. Principal-Only (PO)
   e. Accrual Bond (Z)
   f. Floater (Flt)
   g. Inverse Floater (Inv)

   Bloomberg screens you may want to use in your analysis: DES, CLC, CFT, SPA, CLP, MTST, TRA HTR, and YA.

4. Use the SECF screen to identify different types of CMBS. To find CMBS issuers and tickers, use the "All" tab on the SECF screen and then select mortgages in the "Category" dropdown and commercial mortgage-backed securities in the "Sub-Category" dropdown. On the screen for CMBSs, you will see tickers for J.P. Morgan Chase (JPMCC), Wells Fargo (WFCM), Bank of America (BACM), and other institutions. Clicking the issuer will bring up a menu showing their series. Given a CMBS ticker, you can also screen for different types of CMBS from the "Mtge" tab and "CMBS" tab on the SECF screen: SECF <Enter>, click "Mtge" tab and "CMBS" tab. In the "Ticker" box, type the CMBS ticker (e.g., JPMCC, BACM, or WFCM). To find special types of CMO tranches, type in the code (e.g., PAC or IO) in the"Type" box. Select several CMBSs and analyze them on their CMBS screens using CFT, LDES, TRA, and YA.
5. Use the AUTO screen (AUTO <Enter>) to select a CAR issuer and one of its series. You can also find CARs using SECF. To find CAR ABS issuers and tickers, use the "All" tab on the SECF screen, select mortgages in the "Category" dropdown and "asset-backed securities" in the "Sub-Category" dropdown, and then type auto in the description box. On the screen for ABSs, you will see tickers, such as Fordo (Ford), Valet (Volkswagen), Harot (Honda), BAAT (Bank of America), and other institutions. Clicking the issuer will bring up a menu showing their series. Given an ABS ticker, you can also screen for different types of ABSs from the "Mtge" tab and "ABS" tab on the SECF screen: SECF <Enter>, click "Mtge" tab and "ABS" tab. In the "Ticker" box, type the ABS

ticker (e.g., Fordo). To find special types of ABS tranches, type in the code (e.g., PAC or IO) in the "Type" box. From the screen, you can click the CMO of interest to bring up its menu page or enter CUSIP <Mtge> <Enter>. From the issue's menu page, analyze the issue using the following screens: DES, CFT, CLC, SPA, TRA, and YA.

6. Use the HEQ screen (HEQ <Enter>) to select a home equity loan issuer and one of its series. From the issue's menu page (Ticker <Mtge> <Enter>), analyze the issue using the following screens: DES, CFT, CLC, CFT, SPA, TRA, and YA.
7. Use the CARD screen (CARD <Enter>) to select a credit card issuer and one of its series. You can also find CARDs using SECF. To find ABS issuers and tickers securitized by receivables, use the "All" tab on the SECF screen, select mortgages in the "Category" dropdown and "asset-backed securities" in the "Sub-Category" dropdown, and then type CARD in the description box. On the screen for ABSs, you will see tickers, such as CCCIT (Citibank). Clicking the issuer will bring up a menu showing their series. Given an ABS ticker, you can also screen for different types of ABSs from the "Mtge" tab and "ABS" tab on the SECF screen: SECF <Enter>, click "Mtge" tab and "ABS" tab. In the "Ticker" box type the ABS ticker (e.g., CCCIT). From the issue's menu page, analyze the issue using the following screens: DES, CFT, CLC, SPA, TRA, and YA.

Notes

1. *Mortgage bankers* are dealers, not bankers, who either provide mortgage loans or purchase them, holding them for a short period before selling them to a financial institution.
2. Many mortgages in the 1930s were balloon loans that the lender would not renew or the borrower defaulted. To redress the mortgage collapse of the 1930s, the government implemented a recovery program in which it assumed delinquent balloon loans and allowed the borrower to repay the loans over a longer period.
3. The Farmer's Home Administration (FmHA) also provides mortgage insurance to qualified borrowers for agricultural-related real estate.
4. As noted in Chapter 8, Fannie Mae and Freddie Mac are Government-sponsored enterprises (GSE), whereas Ginnie Mae is a federal agency. In our discussion of MBSs, we will refer to all three as being agencies.
5. For nonagency MBSs, a prepayment benchmark profile is provided by the issuer in the prospectus. It is called the *prospectus prepayment schedule*.
6. After a MBS is issued, the WAM of the underlying pool will change. The remaining number of months to maturity of the mortgage collateral is sometimes referred to as the *weighted-average remaining maturity* (WARM).
7. PAC-structured CMOs, as well as sequential-pay CMOs, are issued by agencies and financial institutions. By definition, CMOs issued by Fannie Mae, Ginnie Mae, and Freddie Mac are called *agency CMOs*. CMOs issued by nonagencies in which the collateral consists of mortgage-backed securities that are guaranteed by one of the federal agencies are called *private-labeled CMOs*. Finally, CMOs formed with a pool of unsecured mortgages or MBSs are called *whole-loan CMOs*.

8. It should be noted that, in practice, the manufacturer often uses a *two-step securitization* process whereby it first sells the loans to its financial subsidiary (an intermediate SPV) who then sells the loans to the SPV who creates the ABS. This two-step securitization process is done to ensure that the transaction is considered a true sale for tax purposes. If the manufacturer's financial subsidiary is considered a wholly owned subsidiary, then it may only be allowed to engage in purchasing, owning, and selling receivables.
9. This example is based on the ABS deal issued by DaimlerChrysler Auto Trust 2007. The deal is described in detail in Fabozzi (2009).

PART III

Debt Derivatives

CHAPTER 11

Bond and Interest Rate Futures Contracts

Introduction

In the 1840s, Chicago emerged as a transportation and distribution center for agriculture products. Midwestern farmers transported and sold their products to wholesalers and merchants in Chicago, who often would store and later transport the products by either rail or the Great Lakes to population centers in the East. Partly because of the seasonal nature of grains and other agriculture products and partly because of the lack of adequate storage facilities, farmers and merchants began to use *forward contracts* as a way of circumventing storage costs and pricing risk. These contracts were agreements in which two parties agreed to exchange commodities for cash at a future date, but with the terms and the price agreed upon in the present. For example, an Ohio farmer in June might agree to sell his expected wheat harvest to a Chicago grain dealer in September at an agreed-upon price. This forward contract enabled both the farmer and the dealer to lock in the September wheat price in June. In 1848, the Chicago Board of Trade (CBOT) was formed by a group of Chicago merchants to facilitate the trading of grain. This organization subsequently introduced the first standardized forward contract, called a "to-arrive" contract. Later, it established rules for trading the contracts and developed a system in which traders ensured their performance by depositing good-faith money to a third party. These actions made it possible for speculators as well as farmers and dealers who were hedging their positions to trade their forward contracts. By definition, *futures* are marketable forward contracts. Thus, the CBOT evolved from a board offering forward contracts to the first organized exchange listing futures contracts—a futures exchange.

Beginning in the 1840s, as new exchanges were formed in Chicago, New York, London, Singapore, and other large cities throughout the world, the types of futures contracts grew from grains and agricultural products to commodities and metals and finally to financial futures: futures on foreign currency, debt securities, and security indices. Because of their use as a hedging tool by financial managers and investment bankers, the introduction of financial futures in the early 1970s led to a dramatic growth in futures trading, with the users' list reading as a who's who of major investment houses, banks, and corporations. The financial futures market formally began in 1972 when the Chicago Mercantile Exchange (CME) created the International Monetary Market (IMM) division, to trade futures contracts on foreign currency. In 1976, the CME extended its listings to include a futures contract on a Treasury bill. The CBOT introduced its first futures contract in October 1975 with a contract on the Government National Mortgage Association (GNMA) pass-through, and in 1977 they introduced the Treasury bond futures contract. The first cash-settled futures contract was introduced by the CME in 1981 with its contract on a three-month Eurodollar deposit. The Kansas City Board of Trade was the first exchange to offer trading on a futures contract on a stock index, when it introduced the Value Line Composite Index (VLCI) contract in 1983. This was followed by the introduction of the Standard & Poor's (S&P) 500 futures contract by the CME and the New York Stock Exchange (NYSE) index futures contract by the New York Futures Exchange (NYFE).

Whereas the 1970s marked the advent of financial futures, the 1980s saw the globalization of futures markets, with the openings of the London International Financial Futures Exchange (LIFFE) in 1982, Singapore International Monetary Market in 1986, Toronto Futures Exchange in 1984, New Zealand Futures Exchange in 1985, and Tokyo Financial Futures Exchange in 1985. Exhibit 11.1 shows the Bloomberg CTM screen that lists the major exchanges trading futures and derivatives. The increase in the number of futures exchanges internationally led to a number of trading innovations: electronic trading systems, 24-hour worldwide trading, and alliances between exchanges. Concomitant with the growth in future trading on organized exchanges has been the growth in futures contracts offered and traded on the over-the-counter (OTC) market. In this market, dealers offer and make markets in more tailor-made forward contracts in currencies, indexes, and various interest rate products. Today, the total volume of forward contracts created on the OTC market exceeds the volume of exchange-traded futures contracts. The combined growth in the futures and forward contracts has also created a need for more governmental oversight to ensure market efficiency and to guard against abuses. In 1974, the Commodity Futures Trading Commission (CFTC) was created by Congress to monitor and regulate futures trading and in 1982 the National Futures Association (NFA), an organization of futures market participants, was established to oversee futures trading. Finally, the growth in futures markets led to the consolidation of exchanges. In 2006, the CME and the CBOT approved a deal in which the CME acquired the CBOT, forming the CME Group, Inc.

EXHIBIT 11.1 Major Futures and Derivative Exchanges

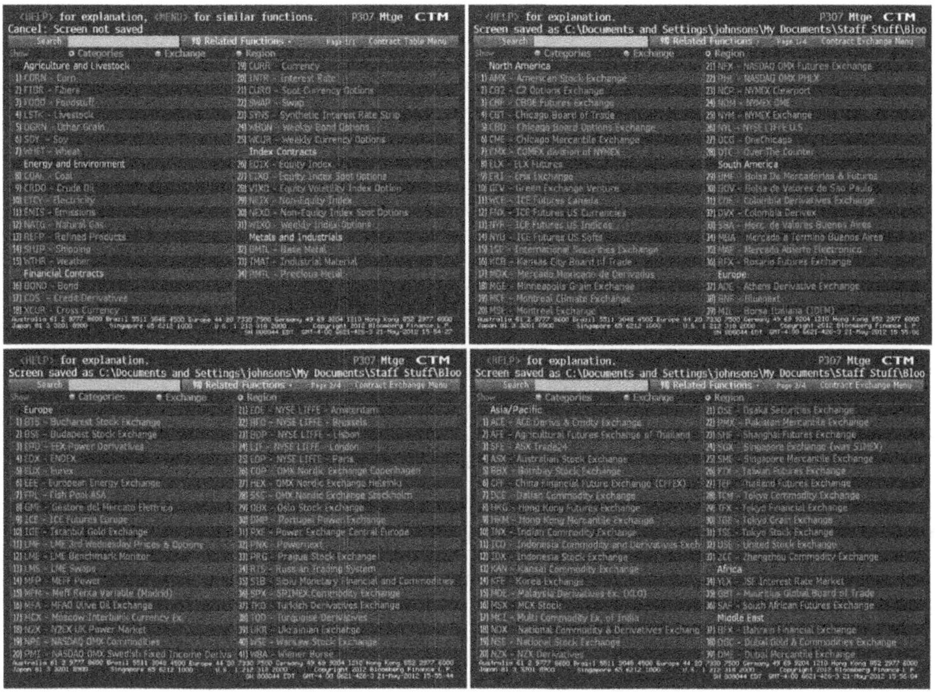

Definition

Formally, a *forward contract* is an agreement between two parties to trade a specific asset at a future date, with the terms and price agreed upon today. A futures contract, in turn, is a "marketable" forward contract, with marketability provided through futures exchanges that list hundreds of standardized contracts, establish trading rules, and provide for clearinghouses to guarantee and intermediate contracts. In contrast, forward contracts are provided by financial institutions and dealers, are less standardized and more tailor-made, are usually held to maturity, and unlike futures, they often do not require initial or maintenance margins. Both forward and futures contracts are similar to option contracts in that the underlying asset's price on the contract is determined in the present with the delivery and payment occurring at a future date. The major difference between these derivative securities is that the holder of an option has the right, but not the responsibility, to execute the contract (i.e., it is a contingent-claim security), whereas the holder of a futures or forward contract has an obligation to fulfill the terms of the contract. In this chapter, we examine the markets and fundamental uses of interest rate futures and forward contracts, and in Chapter 12 we examine the markets and fundamental uses of options.

The Market and Characteristics of Futures on Debt Securities

Microstructure

For many years, the mode of trading on futures exchanges in the United States, London (LIFFE), Paris (MATIF), Sydney (SFE), Singapore (SIMEX), and other locations was that of brokers and dealers going to a pit and using the *open outcry* method to trade. In this system, orders were relayed to the floor by runners or by hand signals to a specified trading pit. The order was then offered in open outcry to all participants (e.g., commission brokers or locals [those trading for their own accounts]) in the pit, with the trade being done with the first person to respond.

Although the open-outcry system is still used, electronic trading systems are today the primarily mode used by the organized exchanges to trade derivatives. The CME and CBOT developed, with Reuters (the electronic information service company), the *GLOBEX* trading system. This is a computerized order-matching system with an international network linking member traders. Since 1985 all new derivative exchanges have been organized as electronic exchanges. Most of these electronic trading systems are order-driven systems in which customer orders (bid and ask prices and size) are collected and matched by a computerized matching system. In addition to linking futures traders, the futures exchanges also make contracts more marketable by standardizing contracts, providing continuous trading, establishing delivery procedures, and providing 24-hour trading through exchange alliances.

Standardization

The futures exchanges provide standardization by specifying the grade or type of each assets and the size of the underlying asset. Exchanges also specify how contract prices are quoted. For example, the contract prices on Eurodollar futures are quoted in terms of an index equal to one hundred minus a discount yield, and a T-bond futures contract is quoted in terms of dollars and 1/32s of a T-bond with a face value of $100.

Continuous Trading

Many physical exchanges use market makers or specialists to ensure a continuous market. On many futures exchanges, continuous trading also is provided, but not with market makers or specialists assigned by the exchange to deal in a specific contract. Instead, futures exchanges provide continuous trading through locals who are willing to take temporary positions in one or more futures. These exchange members fall into one of three categories: *scalpers*, who offer to buy and sell simultaneously, holding their positions for only a few minutes and profiting from a bid-ask spread; *day traders*, who hold positions for less than a day; *position traders*, who hold positions for as long as a week before they close. Collectively, these exchange members make it possible for the futures markets to provide continuous trading.

Price and Position Limits

Without market makers and specialists to provide an orderly market, futures exchanges are allowed to impose price limits as a tool to stopping possible destabilizing price trends from occurring. When done, the exchanges specify the maximum price change that can occur from the previous day's settlement price. The price of a contract must be within its daily price limits, unless the exchange intervenes and changes the limit. When the contract price hits its maximum or minimum limit, it is referred to as being limited up or limited down. In addition to price limits, futures exchanges also can set position limits on many of their futures contracts. This is done as a safety measure both to ensure sufficient liquidity and to minimize the chances of a trader trying to corner a particular asset.

Delivery Procedures

Only a small number of contracts lead to actual delivery. As we will discuss later, most futures contracts are closed prior to expiration. Nevertheless, detailed delivery procedures are important to ensure that the contract prices on futures are determined by the spot price on the underlying asset and that the futures price converges to the spot price at expiration. The exchanges have various rules and procedures governing the deliveries of contracts and delivery dates. The date or period in which delivery can take place is determined by the exchange. When there is a delivery period, the party agreeing to sell has the right to determine when the asset will be delivered during that period.

Alliances and 24-Hour Trading

In addition to providing off-hour trading via electronic trading systems, 24-hour trading is also possible by using futures exchanges that offer trading on the same contract. A number of exchanges offer identical contracts. This makes it possible to trade the contract in the United States, Europe, and the Far East. Moreover, these exchanges have alliance agreements making it possible for traders to open a position in one market and close it in another.

Types of Interest Rate Futures

Exhibit 11.2 describes the features of various interest rates futures contracts traded on the CBOT, CME, NYSE LIFFE, and Euroex. One of the first financial futures contracts listed on the CME was the T-bill contract. Today, the three most popular interest rate futures contracts are T-bonds, T-notes, and Eurodollar deposits.

T-Bill Futures

A generic T-bill futures contract calls for the delivery (short position) or purchase (long position) of a T-bill with a maturity of 91days and a face value of $1 million.

Futures prices on T-bill contracts are quoted in terms of an index. This index, I, is equal to 100 minus the annual percentage discount rate, R_D, for a 90-day T-bill:

$$I = 100 - R_D(\%)$$

Given a quoted index value or discount yield, the actual contract price on the T-bill futures contract is:

$$f_0 = \frac{100 - R_D\%(90/360)}{100} \$1{,}000{,}000 \tag{11.1}$$

EXHIBIT 11.2 Select Interest Rate Futures Contracts: Bloomberg Screens

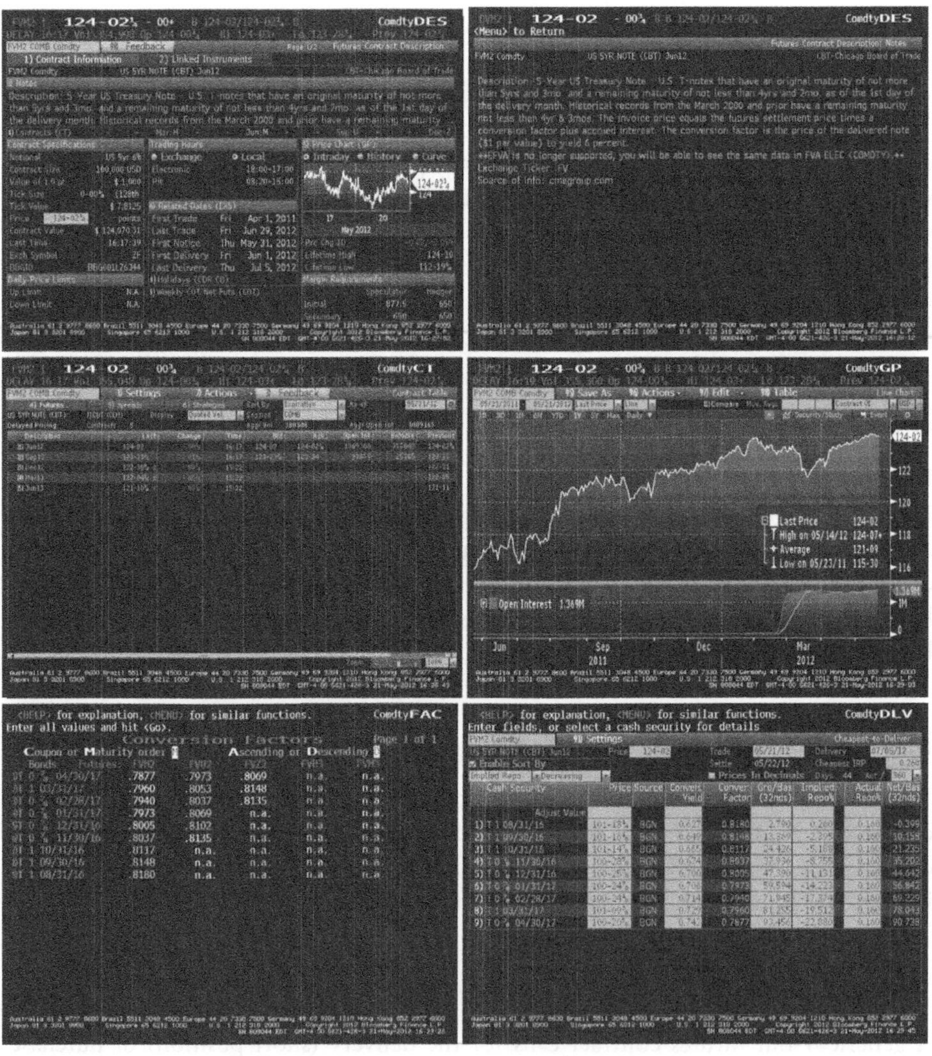

EXHIBIT 11.2 *(Continued)*

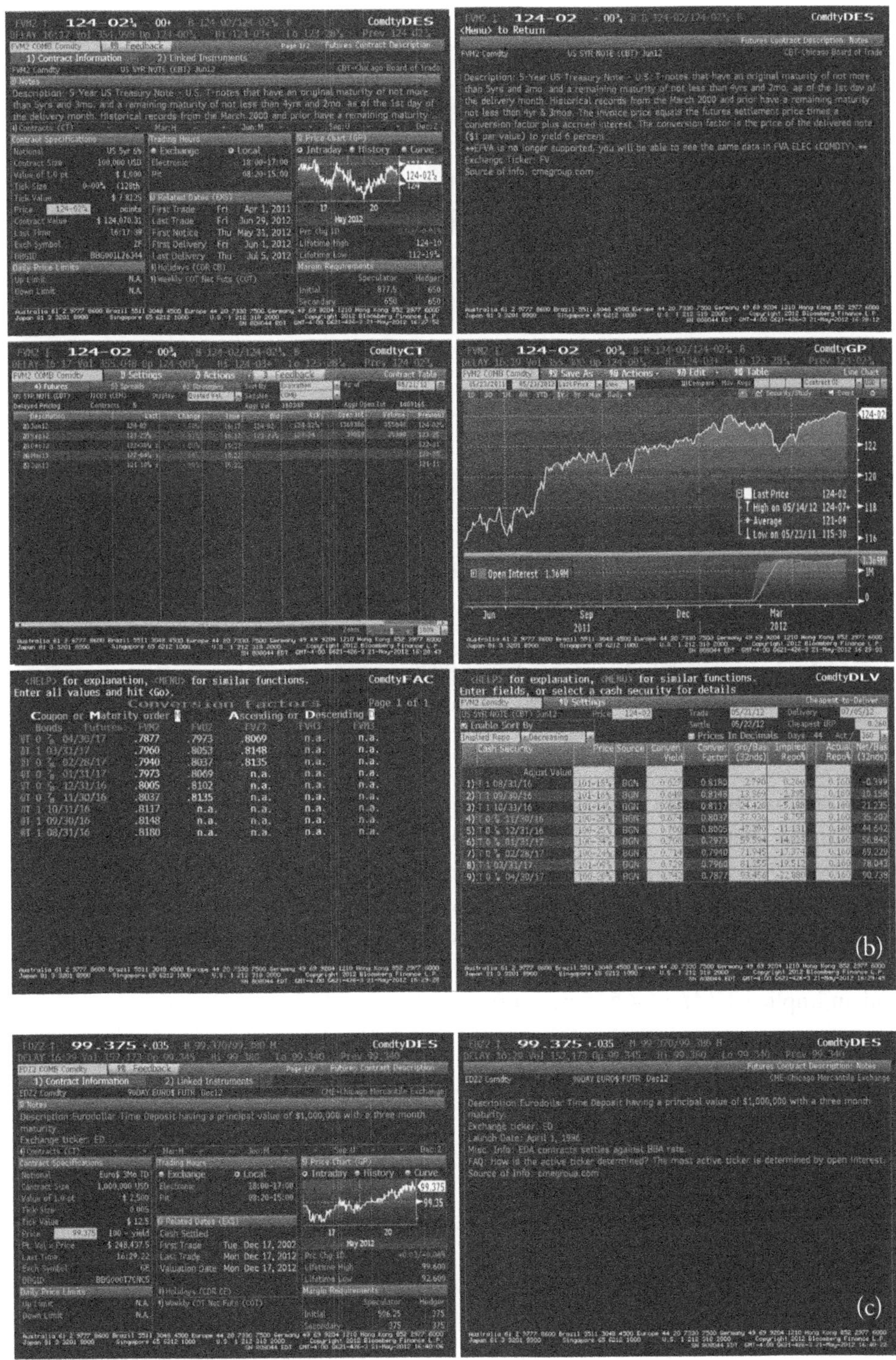

(Continued)

EXHIBIT 11.2 *(Continued)*

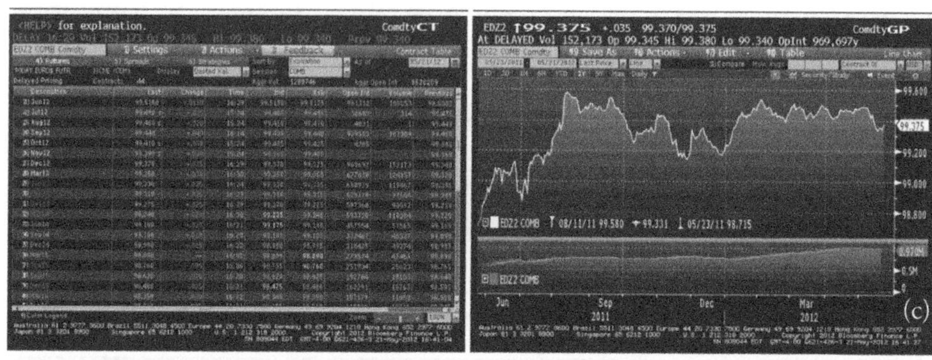

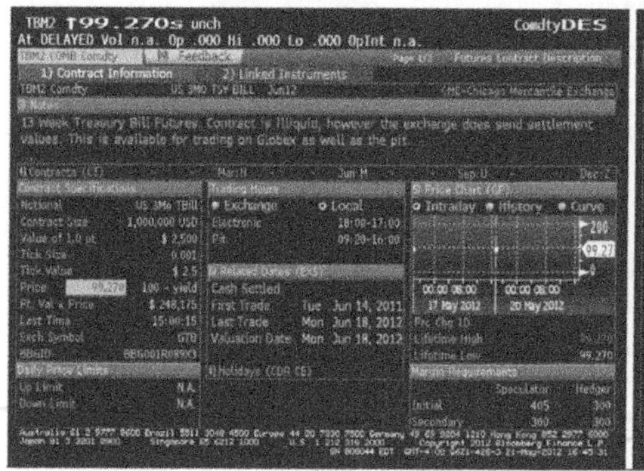

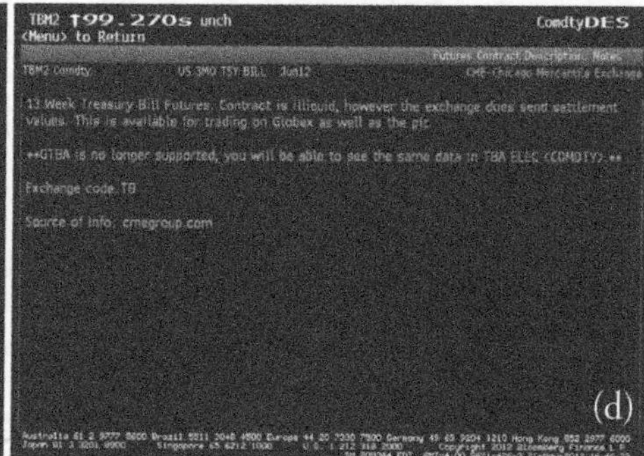

Note that the index is quoted on the basis of a 90-day T-bill with a 360-day year. This implies that a one-point move in the index would equate to a $2,500 change in the futures price. The implied yield to maturity (YTM_f) on a T-bill that is delivered on the contract is often found using 365 days and the actual maturity on the delivered bill of 91 days. For example, a T-bill futures contract quoted at a settlement index value of 95.62 (R_D = 4.38 percent) would have a futures contract price (f_0) of $989,050 and an implied YTM_f of 4.515 percent:

$$f_0 = \frac{100 - 4.38(90/360)}{100}\$1{,}000{,}000 = \$989{,}050$$

and

$$YTM_f = \left[\frac{F}{f_0}\right]^{365/91} - 1$$

$$YTM_f = \left[\frac{\$1{,}000{,}000}{\$989{,}050}\right]^{365/91} - 1 = .04515$$

Eurodollar Futures Contract

As noted in Chapter 9, a Eurodollar deposit is a time deposit in a bank located or incorporated outside the United States. A Eurodollar interest rate is the rate that one large international bank is willing to lend to another large international bank. The average rate paid by a sample of London Eurobanks is known as the London Interbank Offered Rate (LIBOR). The LIBOR is frequently used as a benchmark rate on bank loans and deposits.

The CME's futures contract on the Eurodollar deposit calls for the delivery or purchase of a Eurodollar deposit with a face value of $1 million and a maturity of 90 days. Like T-bill futures contracts, Eurodollar futures are quoted in terms of an index equal to 100 minus the annual discount rate, with the actual contract price found by using Equation (11.1). For example, given a settlement index value of 95.09 on a Eurodollar contract, the actual futures price would be $987,725:

$$f_0 = \frac{100 - 4.91(90/360)}{100}\ \$1{,}000{,}000 = \$987{,}725 \qquad (11.1)$$

The major difference between the Eurodollar and T-bill contracts is that Eurodollar contracts have cash settlements at delivery, whereas T-bill contracts call for the actual delivery of the instrument. When a Eurodollar futures contract expires, the cash settlement is determined by the futures price and the settlement price. The settlement price or expiration futures index price is 100 minus the average three-month LIBOR offered by a sample of designated Eurobanks on the expiration date:

$$\text{Expiration Futures Price} = 100 - \text{LIBOR}$$

In addition to the CME's Eurodollar futures, there are also a number of other contracts traded on interest rates in other countries. For example, there are Euroyen, Euroswiss, and Euribor contracts (three-month LIBOR contract for the euro).

T-Bond Futures Contracts

The most heavily traded long-term interest rate futures contract is the CBOT's T-bond contract. The contract calls for the delivery or purchase of a T-bond with a maturity of at least 15 years. The CBOT has a conversion factor to determine the actual price received by the seller. The futures contract is based on the delivery of a T-bond with a face value of $100,000. To ensure liquidity, any T-bond with a maturity of at least 15 years is eligible for delivery, with a conversion factor used to determine the actual price of the deliverable bond. Since T-bonds futures contracts allow for the delivery of a number of T-bonds at any time during the delivery month, the CBOT's delivery procedure on such contracts is more complicated than the procedures on other futures contracts. The T-bond futures contract delivery procedure is described in many derivative books.

T-bond futures prices are quoted in dollars and 32nds for T-bonds with a face value of $100. Thus, if the quoted price on a T-bond futures were 106-14 (i.e., 106 14/32, or 106.437), the price would be $106,437 for a face value of $100,000.

The actual price paid on the T-bond or revenue received by the seller in delivering the bond on the contract is equal to the quoted futures price times the conversion factor, CFA, on the delivered bond plus any accrued interest:

$$\text{Seller's Revenue} = (\text{Quoted Futures Price})(\text{CFA}) + \text{Accrued Interest}$$

Thus, at the time of delivery, if the delivered bond has a CFA of 1.3 and accrued interest of $2 and the quoted futures price is 94-16, then the cash received by the seller of the bond and paid by the futures purchaser would be $124.85 per $100 face value:

$$\text{Seller's Revenue} = (94.5)(1.3) + 2 = 124.85$$

T-Note Futures Contracts

T-note contracts are similar to T-bond contracts, except that they call for the delivery of any T-note with maturities between 6 1/2 and 10 years; the five-year T-note contracts are also similar to T-bond and T-note contracts except that they require delivery of the most recently auctioned five-year T-note. Both contracts, though, have delivery procedures similar to T-bond contracts.

Forward Contracts—Forward Rate Agreements (FRA)

Forward contracts for interest rate products are private, customized contracts between two financial institutions or between a financial institutions and one of its clients. Interest rate forward contracts predate the establishment of interest rate futures markets. A good example of an interest rate forward product is a *forward rate agreement*, FRA.[1] This contract requires a cash payment or provides a cash receipt based on the difference between a realized spot rate such as the LIBOR and a pre-specified rate. For example, the contract could be based on a specified rate of R_k = 6 percent (annual) and the three-month LIBOR (annual) in five months and a notional principal, NP (principal used only for calculation purposes) of $10 million. In five months, the payoff would be

$$\text{Payoff} = (\$10{,}000{,}000)\frac{[\text{LIBOR} - .06](91/365)}{1 + \text{LIBOR}(91/365)}$$

If the LIBOR at the end of five months exceeds the specified rate of 6 percent, the buyer of the FRA (or long position holder) receives the payoff from the seller; if the LIBOR is less than 6 percent, the seller (or short position holder) receives the payoff from the buyer. Thus, if the LIBOR were at 6.5 percent, the buyer would be entitled to a payoff of $12,267 from the seller; if the LIBOR were at 5.5 percent, the buyer would be required to pay the seller $12,297. Note that the terminology is the opposite of futures. In a Eurodollar or T-bill futures, the party with the long position hopes rates will decrease and prices will go up, whereas the short position holder hopes that rates will increase and prices will go down.

BLOOMBERG COMMODITY SCREENS

CTM: Exchange-listed commodities can be found by accessing the CTM screen: CTM <Enter>.

Contracts can be found by category, exchange, and region. For example, to find bond or interest rate contracts offered by the CBOT, use the CTM "Exchange" screen and click "Bond" or "Interest Rates" from the dropdown menu in the "Category" column.

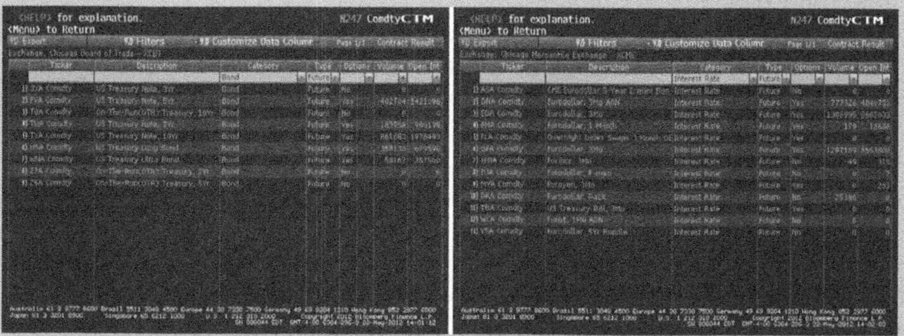

The menu screen for a commodity is accessed by entering the commodity's ticker, pressing the "Comdty" key, and hitting <Enter>: Ticker <Comdty> <Enter>. The menu includes:

- **CT:** Contract Table (see Exhibit 11.2)
- **GIP:** Intraday Graph
- **EXS:** Expiration Schedule
- **GP:** Price Graph (see Exhibit 11.2)
- **DLV:** Cheapest-to-deliver bond (see Exhibit 11.2)
- **FAC:** Conversion Factor (see Exhibit 11.2)
- **Option Analytics, OMON, OMST, etc.:** Information on the option futures contract

FRAZ: Forward Rate Agreements

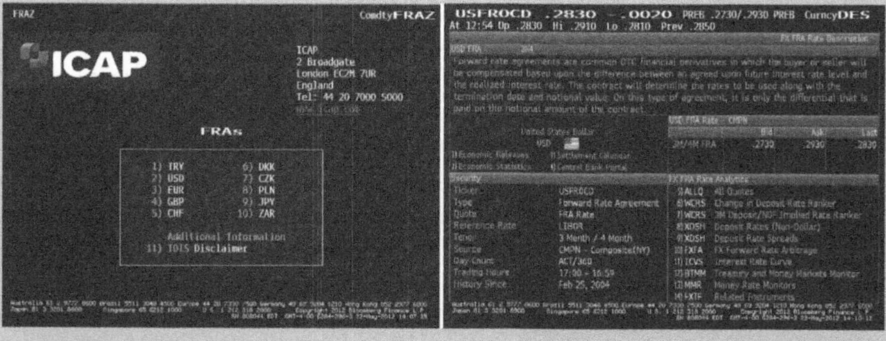

IRDD list interest rate derivatives

SWPM: BLOOMBERG SWAPS AND INTEREST RATE DERIVATIVES SCREEN

SWPM analyzes, creates, and values swaps and interest rate derivative contracts. The Forward Rate Agreement screen in SWPM can be used to set up and evaluate a forward rate agreement.

To access the screen: go to the "Swaps & Options" tab and click "Vanilla," "FRA," and "Regular." This will bring up the main screen that can be used to create the FRA. You can then change the settings on the main screen:

Options: Notional principal, rate, and effective period.

Forward Graph Options: SWPM determines future cash flows at the effective dates based on the forward rate at that date. The user can select which yield curve the forward rates are to be determined. On the "Curve" screen ("Curve" tab), one can view the forward graph and make shift adjustment.

See Bloomberg Information box in Chapter 12 for more information on SWPM.

The Nature of Futures Trading and the Role of the Clearinghouse and Margins

Futures Positions

A futures holder can take one of two positions on a futures contract: a *long position* (or futures purchase) or a *short position* (futures sale). In a long futures position, the holder agrees to buy the contract's underlying asset at a specified price, with the payment and delivery to occur on the expiration date (also referred to as the delivery date); in a short position, the holder agrees to sell an asset at a specific price, with delivery and payment occurring at expiration.

To illustrate how positions are taken, suppose in September, Speculator A believes that a slow economic growth will lead to lower long-term rates and higher prices on T-bonds. With hopes of profiting from this expectation, suppose Speculator A decides to take a long position in the T-bond futures contract and instructs her broker to buy one December futures contract listed on the CBOT. To fulfill this order, suppose A's broker finds through the exchanges' electronic matching system a broker representing Speculator B, who believes that there will be an improved economic climate pushing long-term rates up and prices down and as such is wanting to take a short position in the December T-Bond contract. After matching offers, suppose the price on the December contract for the speculators is 145 per \$100 face value or f_0 = \$145,000 per \$100,000 face. In terms of futures positions, Speculator A would have a long position in which she agrees to buy a notional T-bond with a 20-year maturity, 6 percent coupon, and face value of \$100,000 for \$145,000 from Speculator B during the December delivery month, and Speculator B would have a short position in which he agrees to sell the T-bond to Speculator A during the delivery month by delivering an eligible T-bond bond at 145 times a CFA (needed to convert the value of the delivered bond to a 20-year, 6 percent coupon bond) plus accrued interest.

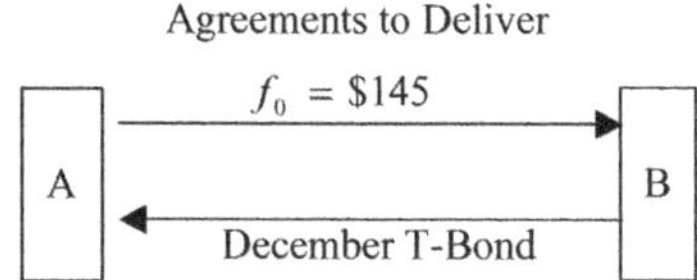

If both parties hold their contracts to the delivery month, their profits or losses would be determined by the price of the T-bond on the spot market. For example, suppose during the delivery month the yield on spot T bonds fell such that a 6 percent, 20-year T-bond (the bond underlying the futures contract or its equivalent adjusted by the CFA) were trading at 147 with a conversion factor of one. If Speculator B bought that bond on a coupon payment date at 147 and delivered it to Speculator A on the contract at 145, he would lose \$2 per \$100 face value or \$2,000 per \$100,000 face value. Speculator A, on the other hand, would be buying the 6 percent, 20-year T-bond for 145, which she could sell in the market for 147, realizing a \$2,000 profit.

Clearinghouse

To provide contracts with marketability, futures exchanges use clearinghouses. The exchange clearinghouse is an adjunct of the exchange. It consists of clearinghouse members who guarantee the performance of each party of the transaction and act as intermediaries by breaking up each contract after the trade has taken place. Thus, in the above example, the clearinghouse (CH) would come in after Speculators A and B have reached an agreement on the price of a December T-bond, becoming the effective seller on A's long position and the effective buyer on B's short position:

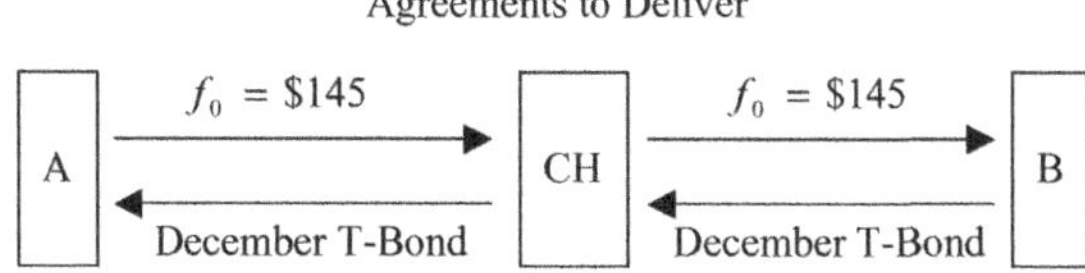

Once the clearinghouse has broken up the contract, then A's and B's contracts would be with the clearinghouse. The clearinghouse, in turn, would record the following entries in its computers:

Clearinghouse Record:

1. Speculator A agrees to buy December T-bond at \$145 from the clearinghouse.
2. Speculator B agrees to sell December T-bond at \$145 to the clearinghouse.

The intermediary role of the clearinghouse makes it easier for futures traders to close their positions before expiration. To see this, suppose that in October, long-term interest rates drop, leading speculators such as C to want to take a long position in the December T-bond contract. Seeing a profit potential from the increased demand for long positions in the December contract, suppose Speculator A agrees to sell a December T-bond futures contract to Speculator C for \$146. Upon doing this, Speculator A now would be short in the new December T-bond contract, with Speculator C having a long position, and there now would be two contracts on December T-bond. Without the clearinghouse intermediating, the two contracts can be described as follows:

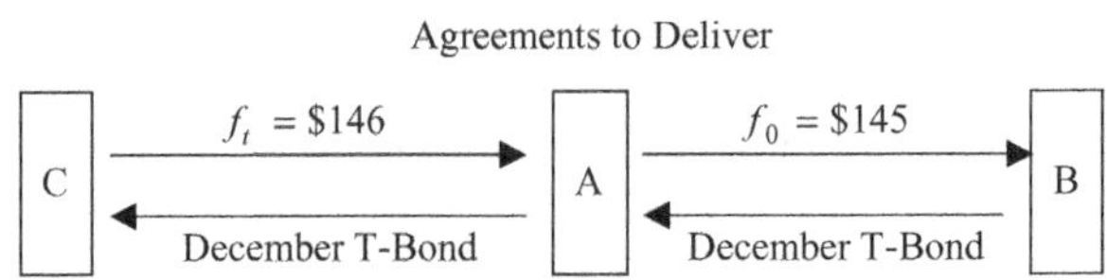

After the new contract between A and C has been established, the clearinghouse would step in and break it up. For Speculator A, the clearinghouse's records would now show the following:

Clearinghouse Records for Speculator A:

1. Speculator A agrees to BUY December T-bond from the clearinghouse for \$145.
2. Speculator A agrees to SELL December T-bond to the clearinghouse for \$146.

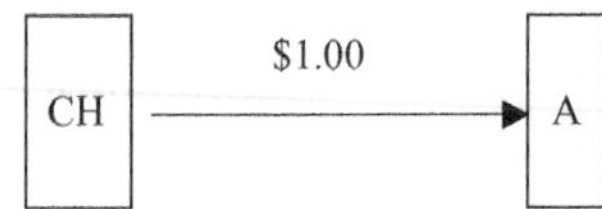

Accordingly, the clearinghouse would close Speculator A's positions by paying her \$1 per \$100 face value or \$1,000 per \$100,000 face at expiration. Since Speculator A's short position effectively closes her position, it is variously referred to *as a closing, reversing out, or offsetting position* or simply as an offset. Thus, the clearinghouse makes it easier for futures contracts to be closed prior to expiration.

The expense and inconvenience of delivery causes most futures traders to close their positions instead of taking delivery. As the delivery date approaches, the number of outstanding contracts, referred to as *open interest,* declines, with only a relatively few contracts still outstanding at delivery (see Bloomberg's CT screens in Exhibit 11.2). Moreover, at expiration (T), the contract prices on futures contracts established on that date (f_T) should be equal (or approximately equal for some contracts) to the prevailing spot price on the underlying asset (S_T). That is, at expiration: $f_T = S_T$. If f_T does not equal S_T at expiration, an arbitrage opportunity would exist. Arbitrageurs could take a position in the futures contract and an opposite position in the spot market. For example, if the December T-bond futures contracts were trading at \$146 during the delivery period and the spot price on T-bonds were trading at \$147 (i.e., 6 percent, 20-year bond with CFA = 1), an arbitrageur could go long in the December contract, take delivery by buying the T-bond at \$146 on the futures contract, then sell the bond on the spot at \$147 to earn a risk-free profit of $1 per $100 face value (assume no accrued interest for this example). The arbitrageur's efforts to take a long position, though, would drive the contract price up to $147. On the other hand, if f_T exceeds $147, then an arbitrageur would reverse their strategy, pushing f_T down to $147. Thus, at delivery, arbitrageurs will ensure that the price on an expiring contract is equal to the spot price. As a result, closing a futures contract with an offsetting position at expiration will yield the same profits or losses as purchasing (selling) the asset on the spot and selling (buying) it on the futures contract.

Returning to our example, suppose near the delivery date on the September contract the spot T-bond price and the price on the expiring December futures contracts are $147. To close his existing short contract, Speculator B would need to take a long position in the December contract, while to offset her existing long contract, Speculator C would need to take a short position. Suppose Speculators B and C take their offsetting positions with each other on the expiring December T-bond contract priced at $f_T = S_T =$ $147. After the clearinghouse breaks up the new contract, Speculator B would owe the clearinghouse $2 and Speculator C would receive $1 from the clearinghouse:

Clearinghouse Records for Speculator B:

1. Speculator B agrees to SELL December T-bond to CH for $145.
2. Speculator B agrees to BUY December T-bond from CH at $147.

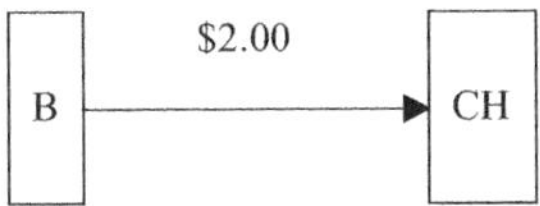

And,

Clearinghouse Records for Speculator C:

1. Speculator C agrees to BUY December T-bond at $146.
2. Speculator C agrees to SELL December T-bond for $147.

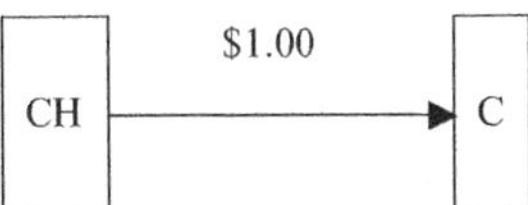

To recapitulate, in this example, the contract prices on the December T-bond contracts went from $145 on the A and B contract to $146 on the A and C contract, to $147 on the B and C contract at expiration. Speculators A and C each received $1.00 from the clearinghouse, whereas Speculator B paid $2.00 to the clearinghouse, the clearinghouse with a perfect hedge on each contract received nothing (other than clearinghouse fees attached to the commission charges), and no T-bond was actually purchased or delivered.

Margin Requirements

Since a futures contract is an agreement, it has no initial value. Futures traders, however, are required to post some security or good faith money with their brokers. Depending on the brokerage firm, the customer's margin requirement can be satisfied either in the form of cash or cash-equivalents.

Futures contracts have both initial and maintenance margin requirements. The *initial (or performance) margin* is the amount of cash or cash equivalents that must be deposited by the investor on the day the futures position is established. The futures trader does this by setting up a margin (or commodity) account with the broker and depositing the required cash or cash equivalents. The amount of the margin is determined by the margin requirement, defined as a proportion (m) of the contract value (usually 3 percent to 5 percent). For example, if the initial margin requirement is 5 percent, then Speculators A and B in our example would be required to deposit $7,250 in cash or cash equivalents in their commodity accounts as good faith money on their September futures contracts:

$$m[\text{Contract Value}] = .05[\$145{,}000] = \$7{,}250$$

At the end of each trading day, the futures trader's account is adjusted to reflect any gains or losses based on the settlement price on new contracts.

In our example, suppose the day after Speculators A and B established their respective long and short positions, the price on the December T-bond was 146. The values of A's and B's margin accounts would therefore be:

$$\text{A: Account Value} = \$7{,}250 + (\$146{,}000 - \$145{,}000) = \$8{,}250$$
$$\text{B: Account Value} = \$7{,}250 + (\$145{,}000 - \$146{,}000) = \$6{,}250$$

With a higher futures price, A's long position has increase in value by $1,000 and B's short position has decreased by $1,000. When there is a decrease in the account value, the futures trader's broker has to exchange money through the clearing firm equal to the loss on the position to the broker and clearinghouse with the gain. This process is known as *marking to market.* Thus in our case, B's broker and clearing firm would pass on $1,000 to A's broker and clearing firm.

To ensure that the balance in the trader's account does not become negative, brokerage firms require that a *maintenance (or variation) margin* be maintained by the trader. The maintenance margin is the amount of additional cash or cash equivalents that futures traders must deposit to keep the equity in their commodity account equal to a certain percentage (e.g., 75 percent) of the initial margin value. If the maintenance margin requirement were set equal to 100 percent of the initial margin, then Speculators A and B would need to keep the equity values of their accounts equal to $7,250. If Speculator B did not deposit the required margin immediately, then he would receive a *margin call* from the broker instructing him to post the required amount of funds. If Speculator B did not comply with the margin call, the broker would close the position.

Maintaining margin accounts can be viewed as part of the cost of trading futures. In addition to margin requirements, transaction costs are also involved in establishing futures positions. Such costs include broker commissions, clearinghouse fees, and the bid-ask spread. On futures contracts, commission fees usually are charged on a per contract basis and for a round lot (i.e., the fee includes both opening and closing the position), and the fees are negotiable. The clearinghouse fee is relatively small and is collected along with the commission fee by the broker. The bid-ask spreads are set by locals and represent an indirect cost of trading futures.

It should be noted that the margin requirements and clearinghouse mechanism that characterize futures exchanges also serve to differentiate them from customized forward contracts and OTC debt and interest rate contracts written by banks and investment companies. OTC contacts are more tailor-made contracts, usually do not require margins, and the underlying asset is typically delivered at maturity instead of closed; they are, though, less marketable than exchange-traded futures.

Futures Hedging

Futures markets provide corporations, financial institutions, and others with a tool for hedging their particular spot positions against adverse price movements, for speculating on expected spot price changes, and for creating synthetic debt and investment positions with better rates than direct positions. Of these uses, the most extensive one is hedging.

Two hedging positions exist: *long hedge* and short hedge. In a long hedge (or hedge purchase), a hedger takes a long position in a futures contract to protect against an increase in the price of the underlying asset or commodity. Long hedge positions on debt securities are used by money-market managers, fixed-income managers, and dealers to lock in their costs on future security purchases. In a *short hedge*, a hedger takes a short futures position to protect against a decrease in the price of the underlying asset. In contrast to long hedging, short hedge positions are used by bond and money market managers, investment bankers, and dealers who are planning to sell securities in the future, by banks and other intermediaries to lock in the rates they pay on future deposits, and by corporate treasurers and other borrowers who want to lock in the future rates on their loans or who want to fix the rates on floating-rate loans.

Long Hedge

A long position in an interest rate futures contract can be used by money market and fixed-income managers to lock in the purchase price on a future investment. As illustrated in Exhibit 11.3, if interest rates at the future investment date are lower, then the price on the fixed-income securities will be higher, and as a result, the cost of buying the securities will be higher. With a long futures position, though, the manager would be able to profit when he closes his long futures position. With the profit from the futures, the manager would be able to defray the additional cost of purchasing the higher priced fixed-income securities. In contrast, if rates are higher, the cost of securities will be lower,

EXHIBIT 11.3 Long Hedge: Hedging Bond Purchase with Long Position in Interest Rate Futures

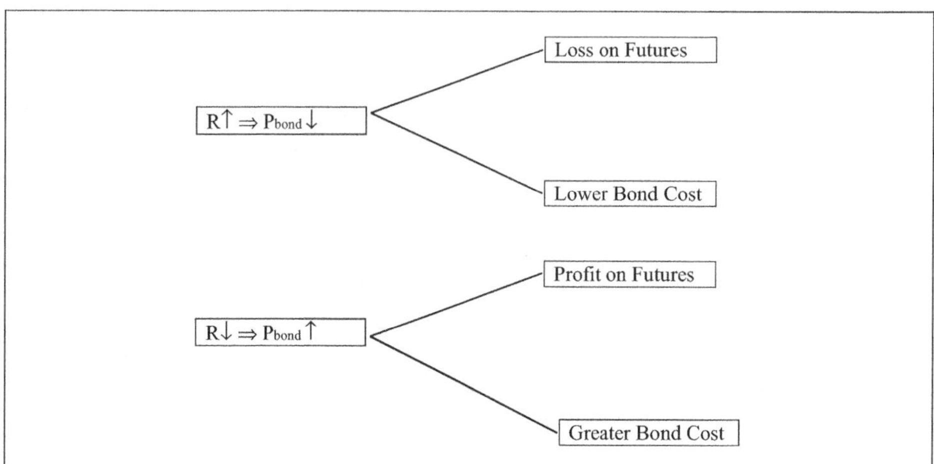

but the manager would have to use part of investment cash inflow to cover losses on his futures position. In either interest rate scenario, though, the manager would find he can purchase approximately the same number of securities given his hedged position.

Long Hedge Example: Future Eurodollar Investment

To illustrate a long hedge position, consider the case of a money market manager who is expecting a cash inflow of $9,875,000 in September that he plans to invest in 90-day jumbo certificates of deposit (CDs) with a face value of $10 million. Fearing that short-term rates could decrease (causing CD prices to increase), suppose the manager goes long in ten September Eurodollar futures trading at R_D = 5 percent or f_0 = $987,500. Given equal spot and expiring futures prices at expiration, the manager will find that any additional costs of buying the jumbo CD above the $9,875,000 price on the spot market will be offset by a profit from his futures position, while any benefits from the costs of the CD being less than the $9,875,000 price would be negated by losses on the Eurodollar futures position. As a result, the manager's costs of buying CDs on the spot and closing his futures position would be $9,875,000.

The money market manager's long hedge position is shown in Exhibit 11.4. In the exhibit, the third row shows three possible costs of buying the $10 million face value CD at the September delivery date of $9,850,000, $9,875,000 and $9,900,000 given settlement LIBORs of 6 percent, 5 percent, and 4 percent. The fourth row shows the profits and losses from the long futures position in which the offset position has a contract or cash settlement price (f_T) equal to the spot price (S_T). The last row shows the net costs of $9,875,000 resulting from purchasing the CDs and closing the futures position. Thus, if the spot Eurodollar discount rate is at 6 percent at the September delivery date, the manager would pay $9,850,000 for the jumbo CD and $25,000 to the clearinghouse to close his futures positions (i.e., the agreement to buy 10 contracts at $987,500 per contract and the offsetting agreement to sell at $985,000 means the

EXHIBIT 11.4 Long Hedge Example

Initial Position: Long in 10 September Eurodollar futures contracts at $R_D = 5$ (Index = 95, f_0 = \$987,500) to hedge \$9,875,000 CD investment in September.			
Positions			
(1) September Spot R_D	6%	5%	4%
(2) September Spot and futures Price	\$985,000	\$987,500	\$990,000
(3) Cost of \$10M face value 90-day CD	\$9,850,000	\$9,875,000	\$9,900,000
(4) Profit on Futures	(\$25,000)	0	\$25,000
Net Costs: Row (3) – Row (4)	\$9,875,000	\$9,875,000	\$9,875,000
Profit on futures = 10 (Spot Price – \$987,500)			

manager must pay the clearinghouse \$25,000); if the spot Eurodollar rate is 4 percent, then the manager will have to pay \$9,900,000 for the CD, but will be able to finance part of that expenditure with the \$25,000 received from the clearinghouse from closing (i.e., agreement to buy 10 contracts at \$987,500 and the offsetting agreement to sell at \$990,000 means the clearinghouse will pay the manager \$25,000).

Short Hedge

Short hedges are used when corporations, governments, financial institutions, dealers, and underwriters are planning to sell bonds or borrow funds at some future date and want to lock in the rate. As illustrated in Exhibit 11.5, if interest rate have increased at the time the fixed income securities are sold (or the loan starts), then the price on the fixed-income securities will be lower, and as a result, the revenue from selling the fixed-income securities will be less (or the rate on the loan is higher). With a short futures-hedged position, though, the security seller (or borrower) would be able to profit when he closes his short position by going long in a lower priced expiring futures contract. With the profit from the futures, the seller would be able to offset the lower revenue from selling the securities (or defray the additional interest cost of the loan). In contrast, if rates decrease, the revenue from selling the securities at higher prices will be greater (or loan interest cost lower), but the security seller will have to use part of investment cash inflow (interest savings) to cover losses on his futures position. In either interest rate scenario, though, the manager will find less revenue variation from selling securities and closing his futures given his hedged position.

Short Hedge Example: Future T-Bond Sale

To illustrate how a short hedge works, consider the case of a fixed-income manager who in July anticipates needing cash in September that she plans to obtain by selling ten 6 percent T-bonds, each with face values of \$100,000 and currently trading at

EXHIBIT 11.5 Short Hedge: Hedging Bond Sale with Short Position in Interest Rate Futures

$R\uparrow \Rightarrow P_{bond}\downarrow$	Profit on Futures
	Lower Revenue from Bond Sale
$R\downarrow \Rightarrow P_{bond}\uparrow$	Loss on Futures
	Greater Revenue from Bond Sale

par. Suppose that the September T-bond futures contract is trading at 100, and at the time of the anticipated September sale, the T-bonds will be at a coupon date with a maturity of exactly 20 years and no accrued interest at that date. If the manager wants to lock in a September selling price on her T-bonds of $100,000 per bond, she could go short in 10 September T-bond futures contracts. At the September expiration, if the cheapest-to-deliver bond is the 20-year, 6 percent coupon bond with a conversion factor of 1, then the treasurer would receive $1 million in revenue at delivery from selling her T-bonds on the spot market and closing the futures contract by going long in the expiring September contract trading at price equal to the spot price on the 20-year, 6 percent T-bond. This can be seen in Exhibit 11.6. In the exhibit, the second row shows three revenue amounts from selling the ten T-bonds at three possible spot T-bond prices of 95, 100, 105; the third row shows the profits and losses from the futures position, and the last row shows the hedged revenue from aggregating both positions. For example, at 95, the manager receives only $950,000 from selling her 10 bonds. This lower revenue, though, is offset by $50,000 profit from her futures position; that is, the agreement to sell September 10 T-bonds for $100,000 per bond is closed with an agreement to buy 10 expiring September T-bonds futures for $95,000 per bond, resulting in a $50,000 receipt from the clearinghouse. However, if the manager is able to sell her 10 bonds for $105,000 per bond, she also will have to pay the clearinghouse $50,000 to close the futures position. Thus, regardless of the spot price, the manager receives $1,000,000 from selling the bonds and closing the futures positions.

Hedging with a Short Eurodollar Futures Contract—Managing the Maturity Gap

An important use of short hedges is in minimizing the interest rate risk that financial institutions are exposed to when the maturity of their assets does not equal the

EXHIBIT 11.6 Short Hedge Example

Initial Position: Short in 10 September T-bond futures contracts at f_0 = 100 to hedge a September sale of 10 T-bonds.
At the delivery expiration date the 10 T-bonds each have a maturity of 15 years, no accrued interest, and can be delivered on the futures contracts with a conversion factor of 1.

Positions	95	100	105
(1) September spot and futures Price	$95,000	$100,000	$105,000
(2) Revenue from sale of 10 T-bonds	$950,000	$1,000,000	$1,050,000
(3) Profit on futures	$50,000	0	($50,000)
Net Revenue: Row (2) + Row (3)	$1,000,000	$1,000,000	$1,000,000

Profit on futures = 10 ($100,000 – Spot Price)

maturity of their liabilities—*maturity gap*. As an example, consider the case of a small bank with a maturity gap problem in which its short-term loan portfolio has an average maturity greater than the maturity of the CDs that it is using to finance its loans. Specifically, suppose in June, the bank makes loans of $100 million, all with maturities of 180 days. To finance the loans, though, suppose the bank's customers prefer 90-day CDs to 180-day CDs, and as a result, the bank sells $100 million worth of 90-day CDs at a rate equal to the current LIBOR of 5 percent. Ninety days later (in September) the bank would owe $101,210,311 = $100 million $(1.05)^{90/365}$; to finance this debt, the bank would have to sell $101,210,311 worth of 90-day CDs at the LIBOR at that time. In the absence of a hedge, the bank would be subject to interest rate risk. If short-term rates increase, the bank would have to pay higher interest on its planned September CD sale, lowering its interest spread; if rates decrease, the bank's spread would increase.

Suppose the bank is fearful of higher rates in September and decides to minimize its exposure to market risk by hedging its $101,210,311 CD sale in September with a September Eurodollar futures contract trading at an index value of 95. To hedge the liability, the bank would need to go short in 102.491454 September Eurodollar futures (assume perfect divisibility):

$$f_0(\text{Sept}) = \frac{100-(5)(90/360)}{100}(\$1{,}000{,}000) = \$987{,}500$$

$$n_f = \frac{\$101{,}210{,}311}{\$987{,}500} = 102.491454 \text{ Short Eurodollar Contracts}$$

At a futures price of $987,500, the bank would be able to lock in a rate on its September CDs of 5.23376 percent. With this rate and the 5 percent rate it pays on its first CDs, the bank would pay 5.117 percent on its CDs over the 180-day period:

$$YTM_f(\text{Sept}) = \left[\frac{\$1{,}000{,}000}{\$987{,}500}\right]^{365/90} - 1 = .0523376$$

$$YTM_{180} = \left[(1.05)^{90/365}\,(1.0523376)^{90/365}\right]^{365/180} - 1 = .05117$$

That is, when the first CDs mature in September, the bank will issue new 90-day CDs at the prevailing LIBOR to finance the $101,210,311 first CD debt plus (minus) any loss (profit) from closing its September Eurodollar futures position. If the LIBOR in September has increased, the bank will have to pay a greater interest on the new CD, but it will realize a profit from its futures contracts, decreasing the amount of funds it needs to finance at the higher rate. However, if the LIBOR is lower, the bank will have lower interest payments on its new CDs, but it will also incur a loss on its futures position and therefore will have more funds that need to be financed at the lower rates. The impact that rates have on the amount of funds needed to be financed and the rate paid on them will exactly offset each other, leaving the bank with a fixed debt amount when the September CDs mature in December. This can be seen in Exhibit 11.7, where the bank's December liability (the liability at end of the 180-day period) is shown to be approximately $102.4914 million given September LIBOR scenarios of 4.5 percent and 5.5 percent (this will be true at any rate). Note that the debt at the end of 180 days of $102.4914 million equates to a 180-day rate for the period of 5.117 percent:

EXHIBIT 11.7 Hedging Maturity Gap

(1) September LIBOR	R	.045	.055
(2) September spot and expiring futures price	$S_T = f_T = \$1{,}000{,}000/(1+R)^{90/365}$	$989,205	$986,885
(3) Profit on futures	$\pi_f = 102.491454[\$987{,}500 - f_T]$	–$174,748	$63,032
(4) Debt on June CD	$\$100{,}000{,}000(1.05)^{90/365}$	$101,210,311	$101,210,311
(5) Total funds to finance	Row (4) – Row (3)	$101,385,059	$101,147,279
(6) Debt at end of period	$[\text{Row (5)}](1+R)^{90/365}$	102,491,433	102,491,462
(7) Rate paid for 180-day period	$[(\text{Row (6)})/\$100{,}000{,}000]^{365/180}$	5.117%	5.117%
	(Allow for slight rounding differences)		

$$R = \left[\frac{\$102.4914 \text{ million}}{\$100 \text{ million}}\right]^{365/180} - 1 = .05117$$

Hedging Risk

The above examples represent perfect hedging cases in which certain revenues or costs can be locked in at a future date. In practice, perfect hedges are the exception and not the rule. There are three types of hedging risk that preclude one from obtaining a zero risk position: *quality risk*, *timing risk*, and *quantity risk*.

Quality risk exists when the commodity or asset being hedged is not identical to the one underlying the futures contract. The manager in our long hedge example, for instance, may be planning to invest in commercial paper instead of a Euro-dollar CD. In such hedging cases, futures contracts written on a different underlying asset are often used to hedge the spot asset. In this case, the manager could use a Eurodollar futures contract to hedge the CP purchase. Similarly, a portfolio manager planning to buy corporate bonds in the future might hedge the acquisition by going long in T-bond futures. These types of hedges are known as *cross hedges*. Unlike *direct hedges*, in which the future's underlying assets are the same as the assets being hedged, cross-hedges minimize price risk, but do not eliminate it.[2]

Timing risk occurs when the delivery date on the futures contract does not coincide with the date the hedged asset needs to be purchased or sold. For example, timing risk would exist in our long hedging example if the manager needed to invest in Eurodollar CDs on the first of September instead of at the futures' expiration at the end of the September. If the spot asset is purchased or sold at a date that differs from the expiration date on the futures contract, then the price on the futures (f_t) and the spot price (S_t) will not necessarily be equal. The difference between the futures and spot price is called the *basis* (B_t). The basis tends to narrow as expiration nears, converging to zero at expiration ($B_T = 0$). Prior to expiration, the basis can vary, with greater variability usually observed the longer the time is to expiration. Given this *basis risk*, the greater the time difference between buying or selling the hedged asset and the futures' expiration date, the less perfect the hedge. To minimize timing risk or basis risk, hedgers often select futures contracts that mature before the hedged asset is to be bought or sold but as close as possible to that date. For very distant horizon dates, though, hedgers sometimes follow a strategy known as *rolling the hedge forward*. This hedging strategy involves taking a futures position, then at expiration closing the position and taking a new one. Finally, because of the standardization of futures contracts, a futures hedge is subject to quantity risk.

The presence of quality, timing, and quantity risk means that pricing risk cannot be eliminated totally by hedging with futures contracts. As a result, the objective in hedging is to try to minimize risk. Several hedging models try to achieve this objective: naïve-hedge, price-sensitivity, minimum variance, and utility-based hedging models. Two commonly used models for cross hedging are the regression model and the price-sensitivity model. In the *regression model*, the estimated slope coefficient of the regression equation is used to determine the hedge ratio. The coefficient, in turn, is found by regressing the spot price on the bond to be hedged against the futures price. The second hedging approach is to use the *price-sensitivity model* developed by Kolb and Chiang (1981) and Toevs and Jacobs (1986). This model has been shown to be relatively effective in reducing the variability of debt positions. The model determines the number of futures contracts that will make the value of a portfolio consisting of a fixed-income security and an interest rate futures contract invariant to small changes in interest rates. The optimum number of futures contracts that achieves this objective is:

$$n_f = \frac{Dur_S}{Dur_f}\frac{V_0}{f_0}\frac{(1+YTM_f)^T}{(1+YTM_S)^T} \tag{11.2}$$

where:

Dur_S = duration of the bond being hedged
Dur_f = duration of the bond underlying the futures contract (for T-bond futures this would be the cheapest-to-deliver bond)
V_0 = current value of bond to be hedged
YTM_S = yield to maturity on the bond being hedged
YTM_f = yield to maturity implied on the futures contract

BLOOMBERG HEDGING SCREENS: FIHR

FIHR calculates the number of bond futures contracts needed to hedge the interest rate risk of a position in a bond you specify. To use, load a fixed-income security and then type FIHR.

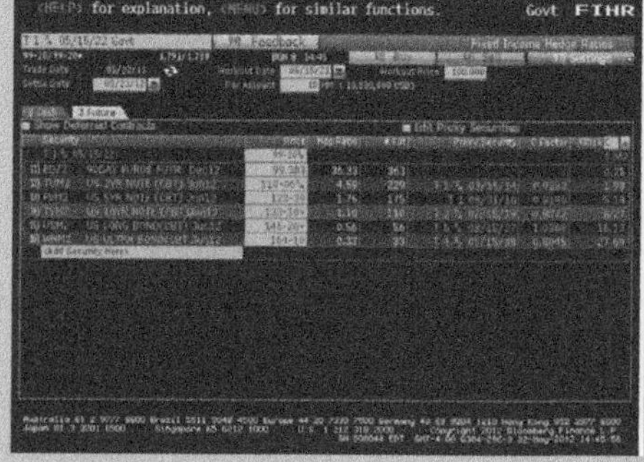

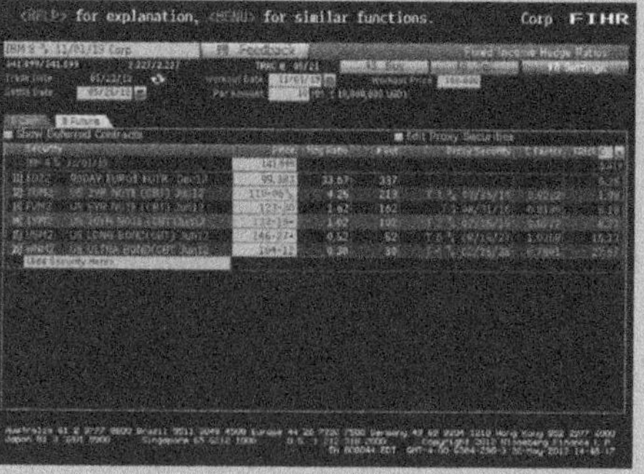

Speculating with Interest Rate Derivatives

Although interest rate derivatives are extensively used for hedging, they are also frequently used to speculate on expected interest rate changes. A long futures position can be taken when interest rates are expected to fall and a short futures position can be taken when rates are expected to rise. In the case of futures, speculating on interest rate changes by taking an outright or naked futures positions represents an alternative to buying or short selling a bond on the spot market. Because of the risk inherent in such outright futures positions, though, some speculators form spreads instead of taking a naked position. A futures spread is formed by taking long and short positions on different futures contracts simultaneously. Two general types of spreads exist: intracommodity and intercommodity. An *intracommodity spread* is formed with futures contracts on the same asset but with different expiration dates; an *intercommodity spread* is formed with two futures contracts with the same expiration but on different assets.

Intracommodity Spread

An intracommodity spread is often used to reduce the risk associated with a pure outright position. The prices on more distant futures contracts (T_2) are more price sensitive to changes in the spot price, S, than near-term futures (T_1):

$$\frac{\%\Delta f_{T_2}}{\%\Delta S} > \frac{\%\Delta f_{T_1}}{\%\Delta S}$$

Thus, a speculator who expects the interest rate on long-term bonds to decrease in the future could form an intracommodity spread by going long in a longer-term T-bond futures contract and short in a shorter-term one. This type of intracommodity spread will be profitable if the expectation of long-term rates decreasing occurs. That is, the increase in the T-bond price resulting from a decrease in long-term rates will cause the price on the longer-term T-bond futures to increase more than the shorter-term one. As a result, a speculator's gains from his long position in the longer-term futures will exceed his losses from his short position. If rates rise, though, losses will occur on the long position; these losses will be offset partially by profits realized from the short position on the shorter-term contract. In contrast, if a bond speculator believes rates would increase but did not want to assume the risk inherent in an outright short position, she could form a spread with a short position in a longer-term contract and a long position in the shorter-term one. Note that in forming a spread, the speculator does not have to keep the ratio of long-to-short positions one-to-one, but instead could use any ratio (2-to-1, 3-to-2, etc.) to obtain his desired return-risk combination.

Intercommodity Spread

Intercommodity spreads consist of long and short positions on futures contracts with the same expirations, but with different underlying assets. Recall that in Chapter 6 we defined two active bond strategies: the rate-anticipation swap and the quality swap. These swap strategies can be set up as intercommodity spreads formed with different debt security futures.

Consider the case of a speculator who is forecasting a general decline in interest rates across all maturities (i.e., a downward parallel shift in the yield curve). Since bonds with greater maturities are more price sensitive to interest rate changes than those with shorter maturities, the speculator could set up a rate-anticipation swap by going long in a longer-term bond with the position partially hedged by going short in a shorter-term one. Instead of using spot securities, the speculator alternatively could form an intercommodity spread by going long in a T-bond futures contract that is partially hedge by a short position in a T-note (or T-bill) futures contract. On the other hand, if an investor were forecasting an increase in rates across all maturities, instead of forming a rate-anticipation swap with spot positions, she could go short in the T-bond futures contract and long in the T-note (or T-bill). Forming spreads with T-note and T-bond futures is sometimes referred to as the *NOB strategy* (Notes over Bonds). It should be noted that instead of forming a spread, investors can also take a position in a futures spread contract offered on the CBOT, NYSE LIFFE, or other exchange (see Exhibit 11.8).

Another type of intercommodity spread is a quality swap formed with different futures contracts on bonds with different default risk characteristics. For example, a spread formed with futures contracts on a dollar-denominated Brazilian bond and a U.S. T-bond. A speculator forecasting an economic expansion in Brazil could, in turn, profit from an anticipated narrowing in the risk premium by forming an intercommodity spread consisting of a long position in dollar-denominated Brazilian bond (e.g., a contract on a 2018 Brazilian sovereign debt bond listed on the BMF—Bolsa de Mercadorias e Futuros; see Bloomberg: MIF <Comdty>) and a short position in a T-bond futures contract. Alternatively, the speculator could take a position in a spread contract (see Exhibit 11.8).

Managing Asset and Liability Positions

Interest rate derivatives can also be used by financial and non-financial corporations to alter the exposure of their balance sheets to interest rate changes. The change can be done for speculative purposes (increasing the firm's exposure to interest rate changes) or for hedging purposes (reducing exposure). As an example, consider the case of a bond fund that manages its bond portfolio against Barclays' aggregate government-corporate index. Suppose the fund expects interest rates to decrease in the coming year across all maturities. To outperform the index, suppose the fund would like to lengthen the duration of its bond fund relative to the index's duration. The fund could do this by swapping some of its shorter-term Treasuries in its portfolio for longer-term ones. Given that longer-term (higher duration) bonds are more price sensitive to interest rate changes, the bond fund would find an interest rate decrease across all maturities would cause the value of its bond portfolio to increase proportionally more than the index if it made the swap. However, instead of increasing the duration of its bond portfolio by changing the fund's allocation from long-term to short-term Treasuries, the fund alternatively could take a long position in T-bond futures contracts.

EXHIBIT 11.8 Futures Spread, 5/22/2012

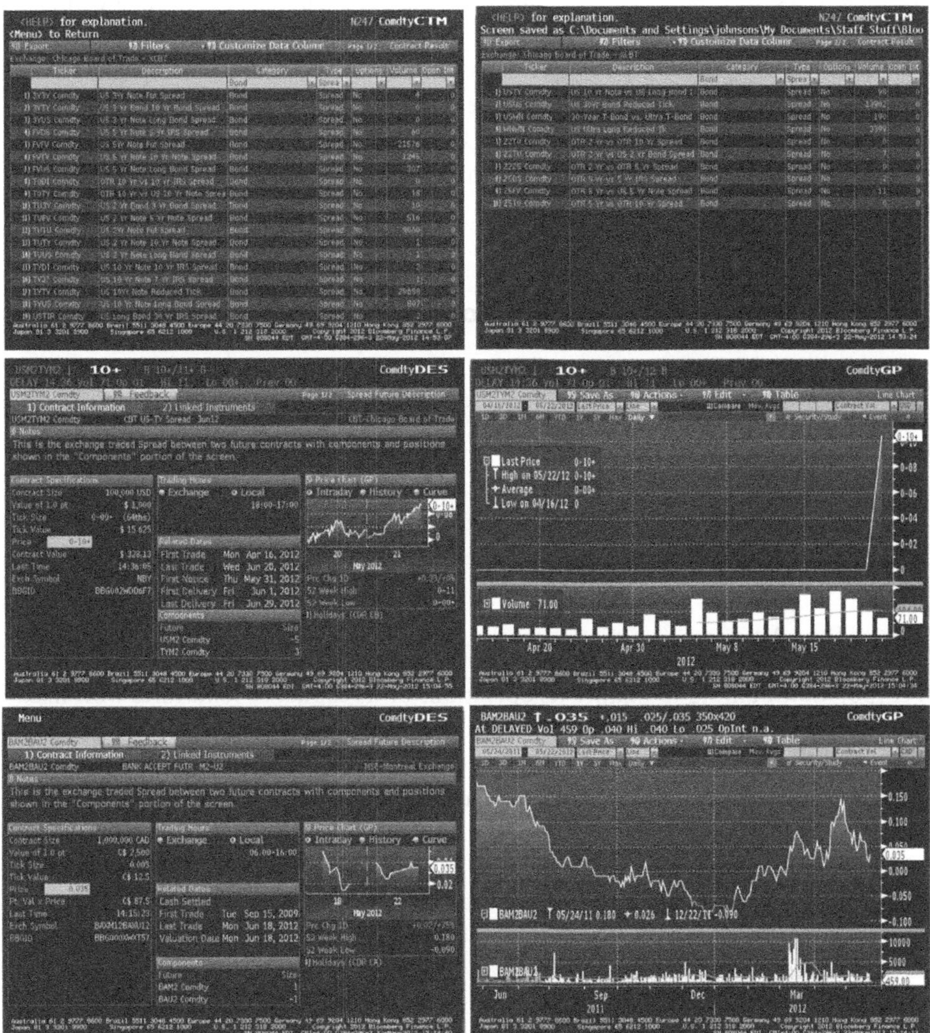

If rates, in turn, were to decrease across all maturities as expected, then the fund would realize not only an increase in the value of its bond portfolio, but also a profit from its long futures position; on the other hand, if rates were to increase, then the fund would see not only a decrease in the value of its bond portfolio but also losses on it futures position. Thus, by adding futures to its fund, the fund would be changing its bond portfolio's exposure to interest rates by effectively increasing its duration.

Instead of increasing its balance sheet's exposure to interest rate changes, a company may choose to reduce it. For example, if the above bond fund expected interest rates to increase, it could reduce its bond portfolio's duration by taking a short position in an interest rate futures contract.

Using derivatives to change the exposure of an asset or liability to interest rates, exchange rates, or other market parameters without changing the original composition of the assets and liabilities is referred to as *off-balance sheet restructuring*. It should be noted that companies need to guard against unplanned actions that might change their hedging positions to speculative ones. Many companies have traders hired to manage their risk exposure to interest rates. As time goes by, some traders take more speculative positions, often causing a transformation of the company's treasury department into a de facto profit center.

Synthetic Debt and Investment Positions

There are some cases in which the rate on debt and investment positions can be improved by creating synthetic positions with futures and other derivative securities such as swaps. These cases involve creating a synthetic fixed-rate loan by combining a floating-rate loan with short positions in Eurodollar contracts and creating a synthetic floating-rate loan by combining a fixed-rate loan with long positions in Eurodollar contracts. Similar synthetic fixed-rate and floating-rate investment positions can also be formed.

Synthetic Fixed-Rate Loan

A corporation wanting to finance its operations or its capital expenditures with fixed-rate debt has a choice of either a direct fixed-rate loan or a synthetic fixed-rate loan formed with a floating-rate loan and short positions in Eurodollar futures contracts, whichever is cheaper. Consider the case of a corporation that can obtain a \$10 million fixed-rate loan from a bank at 9.5 percent or alternatively can obtain a one-year, floating-rate loan from a bank. In the floating-rate loan agreement, suppose the loan starts on date 9/20 at a rate of 9.5 percent and then is reset on 12/20, 3/20, and 6/20 to equal the spot LIBOR (annual) plus 250 basis points (bps) divided by four: (LIBOR + .025)/4.

To create a synthetic fixed-rate loan from this floating-rate loan, the corporation could go short in a series of Eurodollar futures contracts—*Eurodollar strip*. For this case, suppose the company goes short in a series of 10 contracts expiring at 12/20, 3/20, and 6/20 and trading at the following prices:

T	12/20	3/20	6/20
Index	93.5	93.75	94
f_0	\$983,750	\$984,375	\$985,000

The locked-in rates obtained using Eurodollar futures contracts are equal to 100 minus the index plus the basis points on the loan:

$$\text{Locked-in Rate} = [100 - \text{Index}] + \text{bps}/100$$

$$12/20\text{: } R_{12/20} = [100 - 93.5] + 2.5 = 9 \text{ percent}$$

$$3/20: R_{3/20} = [100 - 93.75] + 2.5 = 8.75 \text{ percent}$$

$$6/20: R_{6/20} = [100 - 94] + 2.5 = 8.5 \text{ percent}$$

For example, suppose on date 12/20, the settlement LIBOR is 7 percent, yielding a settlement index price of 93 and a closing futures price of $982,500. At that rate, the corporation would realize a profit of $12,500 (= (10)($1,250)) from its 10 short positions on the 12/20 futures contract:

$$f_0 = \frac{100 - (100 - 93)(90/360)}{100}(\$1{,}000{,}000) = \$982{,}500$$

$$\text{Profit on 12/20 contract} = (10)\ (\$983{,}750 - \$982{,}500) = \$12{,}500$$

At the 12/20 date, though, the new interest that the corporation would have to pay for the next quarter would be set at $237,500:

$$\text{12/20 Interest} = [(\text{LIBOR} + .025)/4](\$10{,}000{,}000)$$

$$\text{12/20 Interest} = [(.07 + .025)/4](\$10{,}000{,}000)$$

$$\text{12/20 Interest} = \$237{,}500$$

Subtracting the futures profit of $12,500 from the $237,500 interest payment (and ignoring the time value factor) the corporation's hedged interest payment for the next quarter is $225,000. On an annualized basis, this equates to a 9 percent interest on a $10 million loan, the same rate as the locked-in rate:

$$\text{Hedged Rate} = \frac{4(\$225{,}000)}{\$10{,}000{,}000} = .09$$

However, if the 12/20 LIBOR were 6 percent, then the quarterly interest payment would be only $212,500 (= ((.06 + .025) / 4)($10 million) = $212,500). This gain to the corporation, though, would be offset by a $12,500 loss on the futures contract (i.e., at 6 percent, f_T = $985,000, yielding a loss on the 12/20 contract of $12,500 (10($983,750 – $985,000) = –$12,500). As a result, the total quarterly debt of the company again would be $225,000 ($212,500 + $12,500). Ignoring the time value factor, the annualized hedged rate the company pays would again be 9 percent. Thus, the corporation's short position in the 12/20 Eurodollar futures contract at 93.5 enables it to lock in a quarterly debt obligation of $225,000 and a 9 percent annualized borrowing rate.

Given the other locked-in rates, the one-year fixed rate for the corporation on its floating-rate loan hedged with the Eurodollar futures contracts would be 8.9369 percent:

$$\text{Synthetic Fixed Rate} = \left[(1.095)^{.25}(1.09)^{.25}(1.0875)^{.25}(1.085)^{.25}\right]^{1} - 1 = .089369$$

Thus, the corporation would gain by financing with a synthetic fixed-rate loan at 8.9369 percent instead of a direct fixed-rate loan at 9.5 percent.

Synthetic Floating-Rate Loan

A synthetic floating-rate loan is formed by borrowing at a fixed rate and taking a long position in a Eurodollar or T-bill futures contract. For example, suppose the corporation in the preceding example had a floating-rate asset it wanted to finance and wanted a floating-rate loan instead of a fixed one. It could take the one offered by the bank of LIBOR plus 250 bps or it could form a synthetic floating-rate loan by borrowing at a fixed rate for one year and going long in a series of Eurodollar futures expiring at 12/20, 3/20, and 6/20. The synthetic loan will provide a lower rate than the direct floating-rate loan if the fixed rate is less than 9 percent. For example, suppose the corporation borrows at a fixed rate of 8.5 percent for one year with interest payments made quarterly at dates 12/20, 3/20, and 6/20 and then goes long in the series of Eurodollar futures to form a synthetic floating-rate loan. On date 12/20, if the settlement LIBOR were 7 percent (settlement index price of 93 and a closing futures price of $982,500), the corporation would lose $12,500 (= (10)($982,500 – $983,750)) from its 10 long positions on the 12/20 futures contracts and would pay $212,500 on its fixed-rate loan ((.085/4)($10,000,000) = $212,500). The company's effective annualize rate would be 9 percent ([4($212,500 + $12,500)]/$10 million = .09), which is .5 percent less than the rate paid on the floating-rate loan (LIBOR + 250 bps = 7 percent + 2.5 percent = 9.5 percent). If the settlement LIBOR were 6 percent, though (settlement index price of 94 and a closing futures price of $985,000), the corporation would realize a profit of $12,500 (= (10)($985,000 – $983,750)) from the 10 long positions on the 12/20 futures contracts and would pay $212,500 on its fixed-rate loan. Its effective annualize rate would be 8 percent ((4)($212,500 – $12,500))/$10,000,000 = .08), which again is .5 percent less than the rate on the floating-rate loan (LIBOR + 250 bps = 6 percent + 2.5 percent = 8.5 percent).

Synthetic Investments

Futures can also be used on the asset side to create synthetic fixed and floating rate investments. An investment company setting up a three-year unit investment trust offering a fixed rate could invest funds either in three-year fixed-rate securities or a synthetic one formed with a three-year floating-rate note tied to the LIBOR and long positions in a series of Eurodollar futures, which ever yields the higher rate. By contrast, an investor looking for a floating-rate security could alternatively consider a synthetic floating-rate investment consisting of a fixed-rate security and a short Eurodollar strip.

Futures Pricing

The underlying asset price on a futures contract is governed primarily by the spot price of the underlying asset. Theoretically, the relationship between the spot price and the futures or forward price can be explained by the *carrying-cost model* (or cost of carry model).

In this model, arbitrageurs ensure that the equilibrium forward price is equal to the net costs of carrying the underlying asset to expiration. The model is used to explain what determines the equilibrium price on a forward contract. However, if short-term interest rates are constant, the carrying-cost model can be extended to pricing futures contracts.

In terms of the carrying-cost model, the price difference between futures and spot prices can be explained by the costs and benefits of carrying the underlying asset to expiration. On debt securities, the carrying costs include the financing costs of holding the underlying asset to expiration, and the benefits include the coupon interest earned from holding the security.

Pricing a T-Bill Futures Contract

To illustrate the carrying-cost model consider the pricing of a T-bill futures contract.[3] With no coupon interest, the underlying T-bill does not generate any benefits during the holding period and the financing costs are the only carrying costs. In terms of the model, the equilibrium relationship between the futures and spot price on the T-bill is:

$$f_0 = S_0(1+R_f)^T \qquad (11.3)$$

where:

f_0 = contract price on the T-bill futures contract
T = time to expiration on the futures contract
S_0 = current spot price on a T-bill identical to the T-bill underlying the futures (maturity = M = 91 and F = \$1 million) except it has a maturity of 91 + T
R_f = risk-free rate or repo rate
$S_0(1 + R_f)^T$ = financing costs of holding a spot T-bill

If Equation (11.3) does not hold, an arbitrage opportunity occurs. The arbitrage strategy is referred to as a *cash-and-carry arbitrage* and involves taking opposite positions in the spot and futures contracts. For example, suppose in June there is a September T-bill futures contract expiring in 70 days and 161-day spot T-bills and the 70-day repo or risk-free rate are trading at the following price and yield:

- 161-day T-bill is priced at \$97.5844 per \$100 face to yield 5.7 percent.
- 70-day risk-free rate or repo rate is at 6.38 percent.

Using the carrying-cost model, the equilibrium price of the September T-bill futures contract is f_0 = 987,487 or \$98.74875 per \$100 par value:

$$f_0 = S_0(1+R_f)^T$$

$$f_0 = 97.5844(1.0638)^{70/365} = 98.74875$$

where:

$$S_0 = \frac{100}{(1.057)^{161/365}} = 97.5844$$

If the market price on the T-bill futures contract were not equal to 98.74875, then a cash-and-carry arbitrage opportunity would exist. For example, if the T-bill futures price is at $f_0^M = 99$, an arbitrageur could earn a risk-free profit of $2,512.50 per $1 million face value or 0.25125 per $100 face value (99 – 98.74875) at the expiration date by executing the following strategy:

1. Borrow $97.5844 at the repo (or borrowing) rate of 6.38 percent, and then buy a 161-day spot T-bill for $S_0(161) = 97.5844$
2. Take a short position in a T-bill futures contract expiring in 70 days at the futures price of $f_0^M = 99$

At expiration, the arbitrageur would earn $0.25125 per $100 face value ($2,512.50 per $1 million par) when she

1. Sells the T-bill on the spot futures contract at 99.
2. Repays the principal and interest on the loan of

$$97.5844(1.0638)^{70/365} = 98.74875$$

$$\pi_T = f_0^M - f_0^*$$

$$\pi_T = 99 - 97.5844(1.0638)^{70/365}$$

$$= 99 - 98.74875 = .25125$$

$$\pi_T = \frac{0.25125}{100}(\$1{,}000{,}000) = \$2{,}512.50$$

In addition to the arbitrage opportunity when the futures is overpriced at 99, a money market manager currently planning to invest for 70 days in a T-bill at 6.38 percent, also could benefit with a greater return by creating a synthetic 70-day investment by buying a 161-day bill and then going short at 99 in the T-bill futures contract expiring in 70 days. For example, using the above numbers, if a money market manager were planning to invest 97.5844 for 70 days, she could buy a 161-day bill for that amount and go short in the futures at 99. Her return would be 7.8 percent, compared to 6.38 percent from the 70-day spot T-bill:

$$R = \left[\frac{99}{97.5844}\right]^{365/70} - 1 = .078$$

Both the arbitrage and the investment strategies involve taking short positions in the T-bill futures. These actions would therefore serve to move the price on the futures down towards 98.74875.

If the market price on the T-bill futures contract is below the equilibrium value, then the cash-and-carry arbitrage strategy is reversed. In our example, suppose the futures were priced at 98. In this case, an arbitrageur would go long in the futures, agreeing to buy a 91-day T-bill seventy days later, and would go short in the spot T-bill, borrowing the 161-day bill, selling it for 97.5844, and investing the proceeds at 6.38 percent for 70 days. Seventy days later (expiration), the arbitrageur would buy a 91-day T-bill on the futures for 98 (f_0^M), use the bill to close her short position, and collect 98.74875 (f_0^*) from his investment, realizing a cash flow of \$7,487.50 or \$.74875 per \$100 par:

$$\pi_T = f_0^* - f_0^M$$

$$\pi_T = 97.5844(1.0638)^{70/365} - 98$$

$$= 98.74875 - 98 = .74875$$

$$\pi_T = \frac{.78475}{100}(\$1{,}000{,}000) = \$7{,}487.50$$

In addition to this cash-and carry arbitrage, if the futures price is below 98, a money manager currently holding 161-day T-bills also could obtain an arbitrage by selling the bills for 97.5844, investing the proceeds at 6.38 percent for 70 days, and then going long in the T-bill futures contract expiring in 70 days. Seventy days later, the manager would receive 98.74875 from the investment and would pay 98 on the futures to reacquire the bills for a cash flow of 0.74875 per \$100 par.

Other Equilibrium Conditions Implied by the Carrying-Costs Model

For T-bill futures and Eurodollar futures contracts, the equilibrium condition defined by the carrying-cost model in Equation (11.3) can be redefined in terms of the following equivalent conditions: (1) the rate on a spot T-bill (or actual repo rate) is equal to the rate on a synthetic T-bill (or implied repo rate); (2) the rate implied on the futures contract is equal to the implied forward rate.

Equivalent Spot and Synthetic T-Bill Rates

As illustrated in the above example, a money market manager planning to invest funds in a T-bill for a given short-term horizon either can invest in the spot T-bill or construct a synthetic T-bill by purchasing a longer-term T-bill, then locking in its selling price by going short in a T-bill futures contract. In the preceding example, the manager either could buy a 70-day spot T-bill yielding a 6.38 percent rate of return and trading at S_0 = 98.821 (= $100/(1.0638)^{70/365}$ = 98.821) or could create a long position in a synthetic 70-day T-bill by buying the 161-day T-bill trading at S_0 = 97.5844, and then locking in the selling price by going short in the T-bill futures contract expiring in 70 days. If the futures price in the market exceeds the equilibrium value as determined by the carrying-cost model ($f_0^M > f_0^*$), then the rate of return on the synthetic T-bill (R_{syn}) will exceed the rate on the spot; in this case, the manager should choose the synthetic T-bill.

As we saw, at a futures price of 99, the manager earned a rate of return of 7.8 percent on the synthetic, compared to only 6.38 percent from the spot. On the other hand, if the futures price is less than its equilibrium value ($f_0^M < f_0^*$), then R_{syn} will be less than the rate on the spot; in this case, the manager should purchase the spot T-bill. In an efficient market, money managers will drive the futures price to its equilibrium value as determined by the carrying-cost model. When this condition is realized, R_{syn} will be equal to the rate on the spot and the money manager would be indifferent to either investment. In our example, this occurs when the market price on the futures contract is equal to the equilibrium value of 98.74875. At that price, R_{syn} is equal to 6.38 percent.

$$R_{syn} = \left[\frac{98.74875}{97.5844}\right]^{365/70} - 1 = .0638$$

Thus, if the carrying-cost model holds, the rate earned from investing in a spot T-bill and the rate from investing in a synthetic will be equal. The rate earned from the synthetic T-bill is commonly referred to as the *implied repo rate*. Formally, the implied repo rate is defined as the rate where the arbitrage profit from implementing the cash and carry arbitrage strategy is zero:

$$\pi = f_0 - S_0(1+R_f)^T$$

$$0 = f_0 - S_0(1+R_f)^T$$

$$R = \left[\frac{f_0}{S_0}\right]^{1/T} - 1$$

The actual repo rate is the one we use in solving for the equilibrium futures price in the carrying-cost model; in our example, this was the rate on the 70-day T-bill (6.38 percent). Thus, the equilibrium condition that the synthetic and spot T-bill be equal can be stated equivalently as the equality between the actual and the implied repo rates.

Implied Forward and Futures Rates

The other condition implied by the carrying-cost model is the equality between the rate implied by the futures contract, YTM_f, and the implied forward rate, R_I, first explained in Chapter 3:

Implied Futures Rate = Implied Forward Rate

$$YTM_f = R_I$$

$$\left[\frac{F}{f_0}\right]^{365/91} - 1 = \left[\frac{S(T)}{S(T+91)}\right]^{365/91} - 1$$

where:

F = face value on the spot T-bill
$T + 91$ = maturity of the spot T-bill

The right-hand side of the above equation is the implied forward rate. This rate is determined by the current spot prices on T-bills maturing at T and at T + 91. In our illustrative example, the implied forward rate is 5.18 percent:

$$R_I = \left[\frac{S(70)}{S(161)}\right]^{365/91} - 1 = \left[\frac{98.821}{97.5844}\right]^{365/91} - 1 = .0518$$

The left-hand side of the equation is the rate implied on the futures contract. If an investor purchases a 91-day T-bill on the futures contract at the equilibrium price, then the implied futures rate will be equal to the implied forward rate. In terms of our example, if f_0 = 98.74875, then the implied futures rate will be 5.18 percent:

$$YTM_f = \left[\frac{F}{f_0^*}\right]^{365/91} - 1 = \left[\frac{100}{98.74875}\right]^{365/91} - 1 = .0518$$

Recall from Chapter 3, the implied forward rate is the interest rate attained at a future date that is implied by current rates. This rate can be attained by a locking-in strategy consisting of a short position in a shorter-term bond and a long position in a longer-term one. In terms of our example, the implied forward rate on a 91-day T-bill investment to be made 70 days from the present, $R_I(91,70)$, is obtained by

1. Selling short the 70-day T-bill at 98.821 (or equivalently borrowing 98.821 at 6.38 percent).
2. Buying $S_0(T) / S_0(T + 91) = S_0(70) / S_0(161)$ = 98.821/97.5844 = 1.01267 issues of the 161-day T-bill.
3. Paying 100 at the end of 70 days to cover the short position on the maturing bond (or the loan)
4. Collecting 1.01267(100) at the end of 161 days from the long position.

This locking-in strategy would earn an investor a return of \$101.267, 91 days after the investor expends \$100 to cover the short sale; thus, the implied forward rate on a 91-day investment made 70 days from the present is 1.267 percent, or annualized, 5.18 percent:

$$R_I(91,70) = \left[\frac{\$101.267}{\$100}\right]^{365/91} - 1 = .0518$$

If the futures price does not equal its equilibrium value, then the implied forward rate will not be equal to the implied futures rate, and an arbitrage opportunity will exist from the cash-and-carry arbitrage strategy.

In summary, we have three equivalent equilibrium conditions governing futures prices on T-bill and Eurodollar futures contracts: (1) the futures price is equal to the costs of carrying the underlying spot security; (2) the rate on the spot is equal to the rate on the synthetic security (or the implied repo rate is equal to the actual repo rate); (3) the implied rate of return on the futures contract is equal to the implied forward rate.

Equilibrium T-Bond Futures Price

Because of the uncertainty over the T-bond or T-note to be delivered and the time of the delivery created by the delivery procedure, the pricing of a T-bond and T-note futures contracts are more complex than the pricing of T-bill or Eurodollar futures contract. Pricing T-bond futures contracts are explained in many derivative texts.

Conclusion

During the 1980s, many countries experienced relatively sharp swings in interest rates. Because of their hedging uses, the market for interest rate futures grew dramatically during this period. Currently, the most popular interest rate futures are the T-bond contracts, T-note contracts, and the Eurodollar contracts, which have similar features to the T-bill contract. In this chapter, we have examined the characteristics and uses of these contracts. In the next chapter, we examine the markets and some of the uses of options on debt securities.

BLOOMBERG BOND FUTURES AND RELATED SCREENS:

- **TKA:** Monitors interest rates
- **WIR:** Monitors Eurodollar Packs
- **EDS:** Eurodollar markets versus futures
- **WBF:** Monitors world bond futures

Website Information

U.S. Exchanges

Chicago Mercantile Exchange (CME): www.cme.com

Chicago Board of Options Exchange (CBOE): www.cboe.com

Eurex (EUREX): www.eurexchange.com

Kansas City Board of Trade (KCBT): www.kcbt.com

New York Futures Exchange (NYFE): www.nyfe.com

Commodity Futures Trading Commission: www.cftc.gov

National Futures Association: www.nfa.futures.org

Current prices on futures contracts on Eurodollar and T-bill and other futures can be obtained by going to www.cme.com and clicking on "Quotes" in "Market Data" and then clicking on "Interest Rate Products." For T-bonds, T-notes, and other futures go to www.cme.com and click on "Quotes and Data."

Selected References

Carlton, D. 1984. Futures markets: Their purpose, their history, their growth, their successes and failures. *Journal of Futures Markets* 4:237–271.

Cox, J. C., J. E. Ingersoll, and S. A. Ross. 1981. The relation between forward prices and futures prices. *Journal of Financial Economics* 9:321–346.

Haley, C. W. 1994. Forward rate agreements (FRA). In J. C. Francis and A. S. Wolf, eds., *The handbook of interest rate risk management.* New York: Irwin Professional.

Hull, J. 2007. *Options, Futures and Other Derivative Securities.* Englewood Cliffs, NJ: Prentice Hall.

Jarrow, R., and G. Oldfield. 1981. Forward contracts and futures contracts. *Journal of Financial Economics* 9:373–382.

Johnson, R. S. 2009. *Introduction to Derivatives: Options, Futures, and Swaps.* New York: Oxford University Press, Chapter 15.

Livingston, M. 1984. The cheapest deliverable bond for the CBT Treasury bond futures contract. *Journal of Futures Markets* 4:161–172.

Klemkosky, R., and D. Lasser. 1985. An efficiency analysis of the T-bond futures market. *Journal of Futures Markets* 5:607–620.

Kolb, R. W., and R. Chiang. 1981. Improving hedging performance using interest rate futures. *Financial Management* 10:72–79.

McCable, G., and C. Franckle. 1983. The effectiveness of rolling the hedge forward in the Treasury bill futures market. *Financial Management* 12:21–29.

Park, H. Y., and A. H. Chen. 1985. Differences between futures and forward prices: A further investigation of marking to market effects. *Journal of Futures Markets* 5:77–88.

Petzel, T. E. 1994. Structure of the financial futures markets. In J. C. Francis and A. S. Wolf, eds., *The Handbook of Interest Rate Risk Management.* New York: Irwin Professional.

Rendleman, R., and C. Carabini. 1979. The efficiency of the Treasury bill futures market. *Journal of Finance* 34:895–914.

Rentzler, J. 1986. Trading Treasury bond spreads against Treasury bill futures: A model and empirical test of the turtle trade. *Journal of Futures Market* 6:41–61.

Resnick, B. 1984. The relationship between futures prices for U.S. Treasury bonds. *Review of Research in Futures Markets* 3:88–104.

Resnick, B., and E. Hennigar. 1983. The relation between futures and cash prices for U.S. Treasury bonds. *Review of Research in Futures Markets* 2:282–299.

Senchak, A., and J. Easterwood. 1983. Cross hedging CD's with Treasury bill futures. *Journal of Futures Markets* 3:429–438.

Siegel, D., and D. Siegel. 1990. *Futures Markets.* Chicago: Dryden Press, 203–342, 493–504.

Tamarkin, R. 1985. *The New Gatsbys: Fortunes and Misfortunes of Commodity Traders.* New York: William Morrow and Company.

Toevs, A., and D. Jacob. 1986. Futures and alternative hedge methodologies. *Journal of Portfolio Management* 12:60–70.

Viet, T., and W. Reiff. 1983. Commercial banks and interest rate futures: A hedging survey. *Journal of Futures Markets* 3:283–293.

Virnola, A., and C. Dale. 1980. The efficiency of the Treasury bill futures market: An analysis of alternative specifications. *Journal of Financial Research* 3:169–188.

Bloomberg Exercises

1. Find descriptions, recent prices, outstanding contracts, and other information on different types of exchange-traded financial futures contracts. Type CTM to bring up "Contract Table Menu," click "Bond," on the Bond screen, find the contract of interest, and bring up the contract's menu screen: Ticker <Comdty>.
2. Find descriptions, recent prices, outstanding contracts, and other information on exchange-traded interest rate futures contracts (e.g., three-month Eurodollar futures listed on the CME). Type CTM to bring up Contract Table menu, click "Interest Rates," on the Interest Rate screen, find the contract of interest, and bring up the contract's menu screen: Ticker <Comdty>.
3. Find the number of T-bonds or T-notes that can delivered on a selected T-bond or T-note futures contract and identify the cheapest-to-deliver. On the futures' menu page, click DLV (Cheapest to Deliver).
4. Access Bloomberg information on Eurodollar futures contracts and U.S. interest rates and then determine the equilibrium price on a Eurodollar futures contract using the carrying-cost model. Compare the equilibrium price to the market price. For example, to price a three-month Eurodollar futures listed on the CME, type CTM to bring up Contract Table menu, click "Interest Rates" on the Interest Rate screen, find the contract of interest, and bring up the contract's menu screen: Ticker <Comdty>. Alternatively, click "Exchange" on the CTM screen, select "Chicago Mercantile Exchange," and click "Interest Rate" in "Category" dropdown. For interest rate information (e.g., LIBOR), type BTMM.
5. Make a yield curve forecast for future intermediate-term or long-term interest rates and then form an intercommodity spread with a listed T-bond or T-note futures contract based on your forecast. Use Bloomberg for price quotes on futures.
6. Make a yield curve forecast and then form an intracommodity spread with a listed T-bond, T-note, or Eurodollar futures contract based on your forecast. Use Bloomberg for price quotes on futures.

Notes

1. To avoid exchanging principals, the FRA evolved from *forward-forward* contracts in which international banks would enter an agreement for a future loan at a specified rate.
2. Cross-hedging can occur when an entire group of assets or liabilities are hedged by one type of futures contract; this is referred to as macro-hedging. Micro-hedging, conversely, occurs when each individual asset or liability is hedged separately.
3. T-bill futures are often delisted. However, the more popular Eurodollar futures contracts are similar to T-bills, except for their cash settlement features.

CHAPTER 12

Bond and Interest Rate Option Contracts

Introduction

Like the futures market, the option market in the United States can be traced back to the 1840s when options on corn meal, flour, and other agriculture commodities were traded in New York. These option contracts gave the holders the right, but not the obligation, to purchase or to sell a commodity at a specific price on or possibly before a specified date. Like forward contracts, options made it possible for farmers or agriculture dealers to lock in future prices. In contrast to commodity futures trading, though, the early market for commodity option trading was relatively thin. The market did grow marginally when options on stocks began trading on the over-the-counter (OTC) market in the early 1900s. This market began when a group of investment firms formed the Put and Call Brokers and Dealers Association. Through this association, an investor who wanted to buy an option could do so through a member who either would find a seller through other members or would sell (write) the option himself.

The OTC option market was functional, but suffered because it failed to provide an adequate secondary market. In 1973, the Chicago Board of Trade (CBOT) formed the Chicago Board Options Exchange (CBOE). The CBOE was the first organized option exchange for the trading of options. Just as the CBOT had served to increase the popularity of futures, the CBOE helped to increase the trading of options by making the contracts more marketable. Since the creation of the CBOE, organized stock exchanges in the United States, most of the organized futures exchanges, and many security exchanges outside the United States also began offering markets for the trading of options. As the number of exchanges offering options increased, so did the number of securities and instruments with options written on them. Today, option contracts exist not only on stocks but also on foreign currencies, security indices, futures contracts, and of particular interest here, debt and interest rate-sensitive securities.

In addition to options listed on organized exchanges, there is also a large OTC market in debt and interest-sensitive securities and products in the United States and a growing OTC market outside the U.S. OTC derivatives are primarily used by financial institutions and nonfinancial corporations to manage their interest rate positions. The derivative contracts offered in the OTC market include spot options and forward contracts on Treasury securities, London Interbank Offered Rate (LIBOR)-related securities, and special types of interest rate products, such as interest rate calls and puts, caps, floors, and collars. OTC interest rate derivatives products are typically private, customized contracts between two financial institutions or between a financial institutions and one of its clients.

In this chapter, we define some of the common option terms, examine the fundamental option strategies and hedging uses of exchange-traded and OTC interest rate derivatives, and we identify some of the important factors that determine the price of an option. In Chapter 13, we extend our analysis of options to the valuation of debt options and bonds with embedded options using a binomial interest rate tree.

Option Terminology

Spot Options

By definition, an option is a security that gives the holder the right to buy or sell a particular asset at a specified price on, or possibly before, a specific date. Depending on the parties and types of assets involved, options can take on many different forms. Certain features, however, are common to all options. First, with every option contract there is a right, but not an obligation, to either buy or sell. Specifically, by definition a *call* is the right to buy a specific asset or security, whereas a *put* is the right to sell. Every option contract has a buyer who is referred to as the option *holder* (who has a *long* position in the option). The holder buys the right to *exercise* or evoke the terms of the option claim. An option also has a seller, often referred to as the option *writer* (and having a *short* position), who is responsible for fulfilling the obligations of the option if the holder exercises. For every option there is an option price, exercise price, and exercise date. The price paid by the buyer to the writer when an option is created is referred to as the *option premium* (call premium and put premium). The *exercise price* or *strike price* is the price specified in the option contract at which the asset or security can be purchased (call) or sold (put). Finally, the *exercise date* is the last day the holder can exercise. Associated with the exercise date are the definitions of European and American options. A *European option* is one that can be exercised only on the exercise date, whereas an *American option* can be exercised at any time on or before the exercise date.

Futures Options

Option contracts on stocks, debt securities, foreign currency, and indices are sometimes referred to as *spot options* or options on actuals. This reference is to distinguish them from *options on futures* contracts (also called options on futures, futures options, and commodity options). A futures option gives the holder the right to take a position in a futures contract. Specifically, a call option on a futures contract gives the holder the right to take a long position in the underlying futures contract when she exercises, and requires the writer to take the corresponding short position in the futures. Upon exercise, the holder of a futures call option in effect takes a long position in the futures contract at the current futures price and the writer takes the short position and pays the holder via the clearinghouse the difference between the current futures price and the exercise price. In contrast, a put option on a futures option entitles the holder to take a short futures position and the writer the long position. Thus, whenever the put holder exercises, he in effect takes a short futures position at the current futures price and the writer takes the long position and pays the holder via the clearinghouse the difference between the exercise price and the current futures price. Like all option positions, the futures option buyer pays an option premium for the right to exercise, and the writer, in turn, receives a credit when he sells the option and is subject to initial and maintenance margin requirements on the option position.

In practice, when the holder of a futures call option exercises, the futures clearinghouse will establish for the exercising option holder a long futures position at the futures price equal to the exercise price and a short futures position for the assigned writer. Once this is done, margins on both positions will be required and the position will be marked to market at the current settlement price on the futures. When the positions are marked to market, the exercising call holder's margin account on his long position will be equal to the difference between the futures price and the exercise price, $f_t - X$, whereas the assigned writer will have to deposit funds worth $f_t - X$ to satisfy her maintenance margin on her short futures position. Thus, when a futures call is exercised, the holder takes a long position at f_t with a margin account worth $f_t - X$; if he were to immediately close the futures he would receive cash worth $f_t - X$ from the clearinghouse. The assigned writer, in turn, is assigned a short position at f_t and must deposit $f_t - X$ to meet her margin. If the futures option is a put, the same procedure applies except that holder takes a short position at f_t (when the exercised position is marked to market), with a margin account worth $X - f_t$, and the writer is assigned a long position at f_t and must deposit $X - f_t$ to meet her margin.

The current U.S. market for futures options began in 1982 when the Commodity Futures Trading Commission (CFTC) initiated a pilot program in which it allowed each futures exchange to offer one option on one of its futures contracts. In 1987, the CFTC gave the exchanges permanent authority to offer futures options. Currently, the most popular futures options are the options on the financial futures on the Standard & Poor's (S&P) 500, T-bond, T-note, and Eurodollar deposit, and the major foreign currencies. In addition to options on financial futures contracts, futures options also are available on gold, precious metals, agriculture commodities, and energy products.[1]

It should be noted that spot options and futures options are equivalent if the options and the futures contracts expire at the same time, the carrying-costs model holds, and the options are European. There are, though, several factors that serve to differentiate the two contracts. First, since many futures contracts are relatively more liquid than their corresponding spot security, it is usually easier to form hedging or arbitrage strategies with futures options than with spot options. Second, futures options often are easier to exercise than their corresponding spot. For example, to exercise an option on a T-bond futures contract, one simply assumes the futures position, whereas exercising a spot T-bond option requires an actual purchase or delivery. Finally, most futures options are traded on the same exchange as their underlying futures contract, whereas most spot options are traded on exchanges different from their underlying securities. This, in turn, makes it easier for futures options traders to implement arbitrage and hedging strategies than spot options.

Markets and Types of Interest Rate Options

Many different types of interest rate options are available on both the OTC market and the organized futures and options exchanges. Exchange-traded interest rate options include both futures options and spot options. On the U.S. exchanges, the most heavily traded options are the CME's and CBOT's futures options on T-bonds, T-notes, and Eurodollar contracts. At one time, options on actual Treasury securities and Eurodollar deposits were offered on the CBOE, American Stock Exchange (AMEX), and Philadelphia Stock Exchange (PHLX). These spot options, however, proved to be less popular than futures options and were delisted. A number of non-U.S. exchanges, though, do list options on actual debt securities, typically government securities.

In addition to exchange-traded options, there is also a large OTC market in debt and interest-sensitive securities and products in the United States and a growing OTC market outside the United States. Currently, security regulations in the U.S. prohibit off-exchange trading in options on futures. All U.S. OTC options are therefore options on actuals. The OTC markets in and outside the United States consists primarily of dealers who make markets in the underlying spot security, investment banking firms, and commercial banks. OTC options are primarily used by financial institutions and nonfinancial corporations to hedge their interest rate positions. The options contract offered in the OTC market include spot options on Treasury securities, LIBOR-related securities, and special types of interest rate products, such as interest rate calls and puts, caps, floors, and collars.

Types of Interest Rate Options

As noted, on the organized exchanges the most heavily traded exchange-traded options are futures options on T-bonds, T-notes, and Eurodollar contracts. On the OTC market, the most popular interest rate options include options on spot Treasury securities and caps and floors (see Bloomberg's CTM screens shown in Exhibit 12.1).

EXHIBIT 12.1 CTM Screens: Futures Options on Bonds and Interest Rates

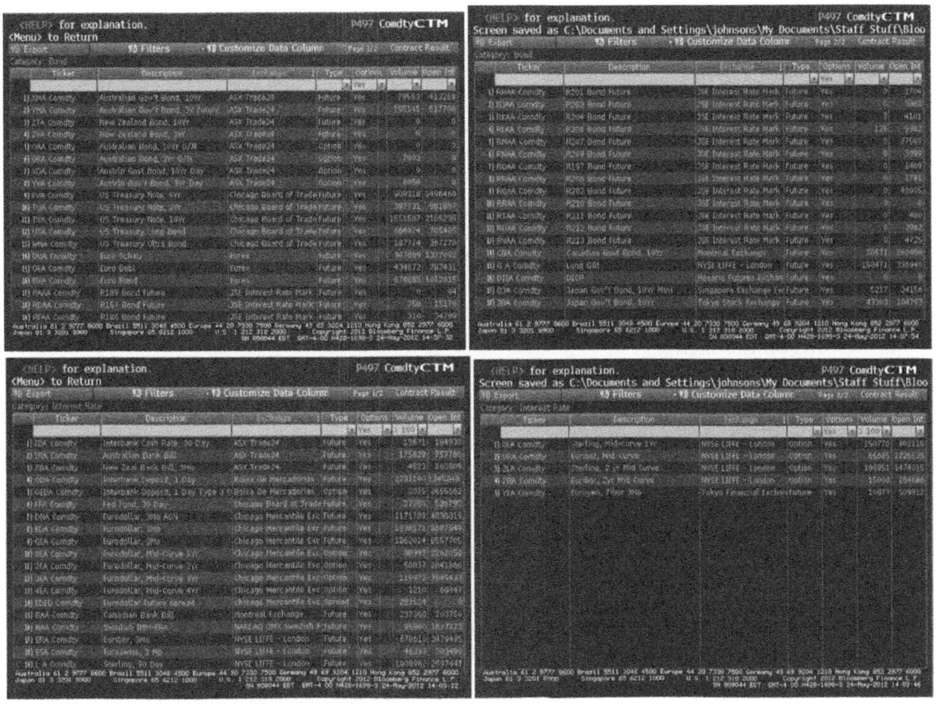

T-Bond Futures Options

The CBOT offers trading on futures options on T-bonds and T-notes with maturities of 10 years, 5 years, and 2 years, as well contracts on other financial futures. The premiums on the call and put option contracts on the T-bond and T-note futures are quoted as a percentage of the face value of the underlying bond or note. For example, a buyer of the May 109 T-bond futures call trading at 2 60/64 (= 2.9375) would pay \$2,937.50 for the option to take a long position in the May T-bond futures at an exercise price of \$109,000. If long-term rates were to subsequently drop, causing the May T-bond futures price to increase to $f_t = 113$, then the holder, upon exercising, would have a long position in the May T-bond futures contract and a margin account worth \$4,000. If she closed her futures contract at 113, she would have a profit of \$1,062.50:

$$\text{Value of Margin} = \frac{f_t - X}{100}(\$100{,}000) = \left[\frac{113 - 109}{100}\right]\$100{,}000 = \$4{,}000$$

$$\pi = \$4{,}000 - \$2{,}937.50 = \$1{,}062.50$$

By contrast, if long-term rates were to stay the same or increase, then the call would be worthless and the holder would simply allow it to expire, losing the \$2,937.50 premium.

BLOOMBERG FUTURES OPTION SCREENS: T-BONDS FUTURES OPTIONS

To Access information on T-Bond Futures Options Listed on CBOT:

1. CTM <Enter>; click "Exchange." Example: click "Chicago Board of Trade," from "Category" column, select "Bond"; from "Type" column, select futures; and from "Options" column, select yes.
2. Right click to bring up menu to select description (DES), contract table on futures (CT), or options on futures options (OMON)
3. Or Ticker <Comdty> to bring up menu; Example: USA <Comdty> will bring up the U.S. long-term Treasury Menu.
4. Screens on the menu:
   - DES: Description of Futures Contract
   - EXS: Futures Expirations Schedule
   - CT: Futures Contract Table
   - OTD: Description of Futures Option
   - OSL: Option Strike List
   - OMON: Option Monitor
   - OMST: Most Active Options

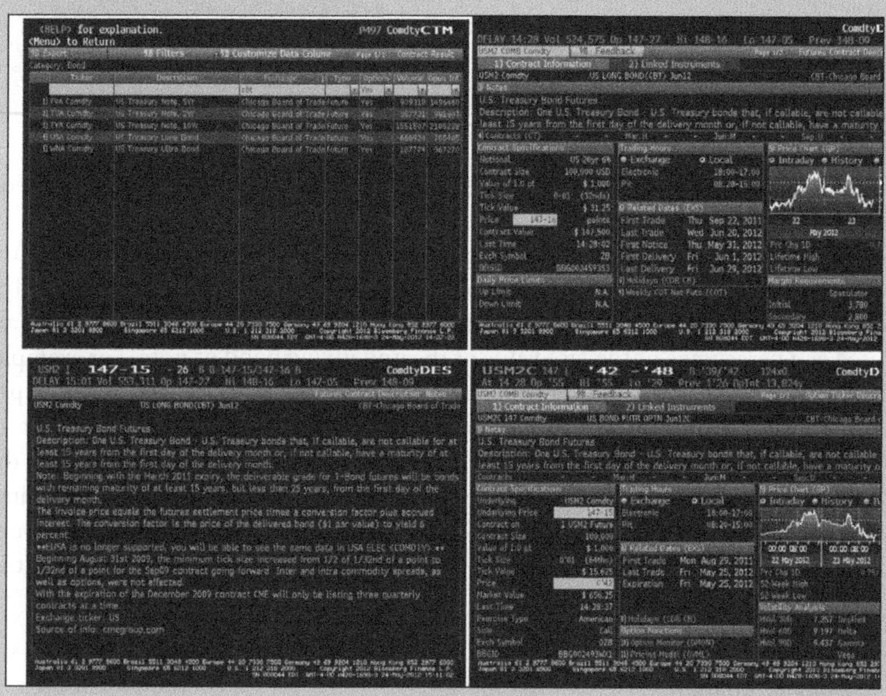

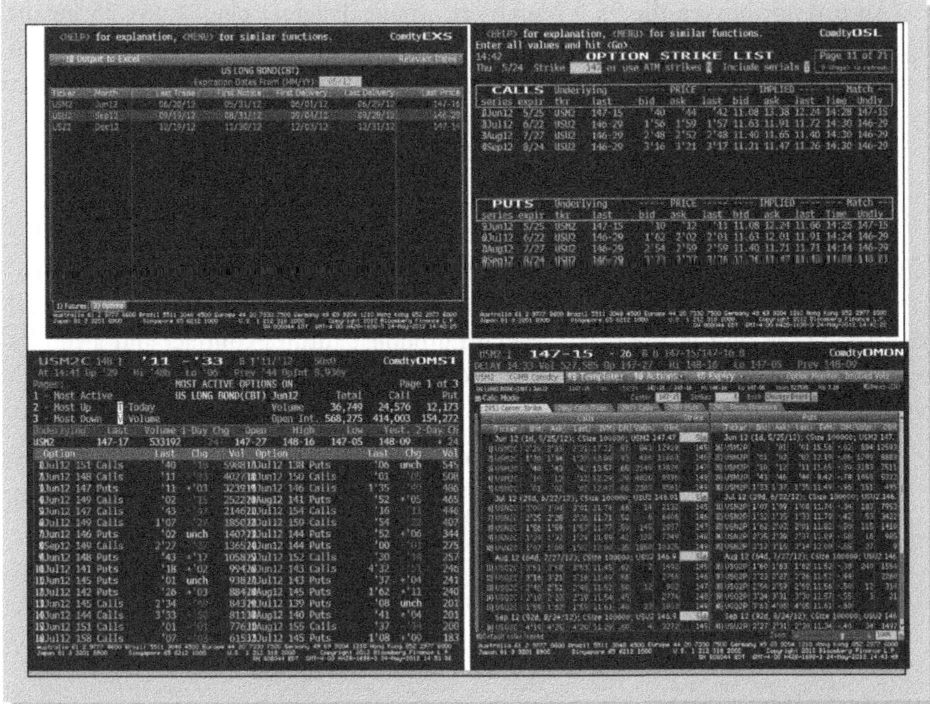

Eurodollar and T-Bill Futures Options

The CME offers trading on futures options on Eurodollar deposits, 30-day LIBOR contracts, and when listed T-bill futures. The maturities of the options correspond to the maturities on the underlying futures contracts, and the exercise quotes are based on the system used for quoting the futures contracts. Thus, the exercise prices on the Eurodollar and T-bill contracts are quoted in terms of an index (I) equal to 100 minus the annual discount yield: $I = 100 - R_D$. The option premiums are quoted in terms of an index point system. For T-bill and Eurodollars, the dollar value of an option quote is based on a \$25 value for each basis point underlying a \$1 million T-bill or Eurodollar. The actual quotes are in percentages; thus a 1.25 quote would imply a price of \$25 times 12.5 basis points: (\$25)(12.5) = \$312.50. In addition, for the closest maturing month, the options are quoted to the nearest quarter of a basis point; for other months, they are quoted to the nearest half of a basis point. For example, the actual price on a March Eurodollar call with an exercise price of 94.75 quoted at 5.92 is \$1,481.25. The price is obtained by rounding the 5.92 quoted price to 5.925, converting the quote to basis points (multiply by 10), and multiplying by \$25: (5.925)(10)(\$25) = \$1,481.25. More simply, multiply the quoted price by \$250: (5.925)(\$250).

An investor buying the 94.5 March call would therefore pay \$1,481.25 for the right to take a long position in the CME's \$1 million March Eurodollar futures contract at an exercise price of \$986,250:

$$X = \frac{100 - (100 - 94.5)(90/360)}{100}\$1,000,000 = \$986,250$$

If short-term rates were to subsequently drop, causing the March Eurodollar futures price to increase to an index price of 95.5 (R_D = 4.5 and f_t = [[100 – 4.5(90 / 360)] / 100](\$1 million) = \$988,750), the holder, upon exercising, would have a long position in the CME March Eurodollar futures contract and a futures margin account worth \$2,500. If she closed the position at 95.5, she would realize a profit of \$1,018.75:

$$\text{Margin Value } f_t - X = \$988,750 - \$986,250 = \$2,500$$

$$\text{Margin Value} = \$25(\text{Futures Index} - \text{Exercise Index})$$

$$= \$25[95.5 - 94.5](100) = \$2,500$$

$$\pi = \$2,500 - \$1,481.25 = \$1,018.75$$

BLOOMBERG FUTURES OPTIONS SCREENS: EURODOLLAR FUTURES OPTIONS

To Access information on Eurodollar Futures Options listed on the CME:

1. CTM <Enter>; click "Exchange." Example: click "Chicago Mercantile Exchange"; from "Category" column, select "Interest Rates"; from "Type" column, select futures; and from "Options" column, select yes.
2. Right click to bring up menu to select description (DES), contract table on futures (CT), or options on futures options (OMON).
3. Or enter Ticker <Comdty> to bring up menu. Example: EDA <Comdty> will bring up three-month Eurodollar futures menu.
4. Screens on the menu:
   - DES: Description of Futures Contract
   - EXS: Futures Expirations Schedule
   - CT: Futures Contract Table
   - OTD: Description of Futures Option
   - OSL: Option Strike List
   - OMON: Option Monitor
   - OMST: Most Active Options

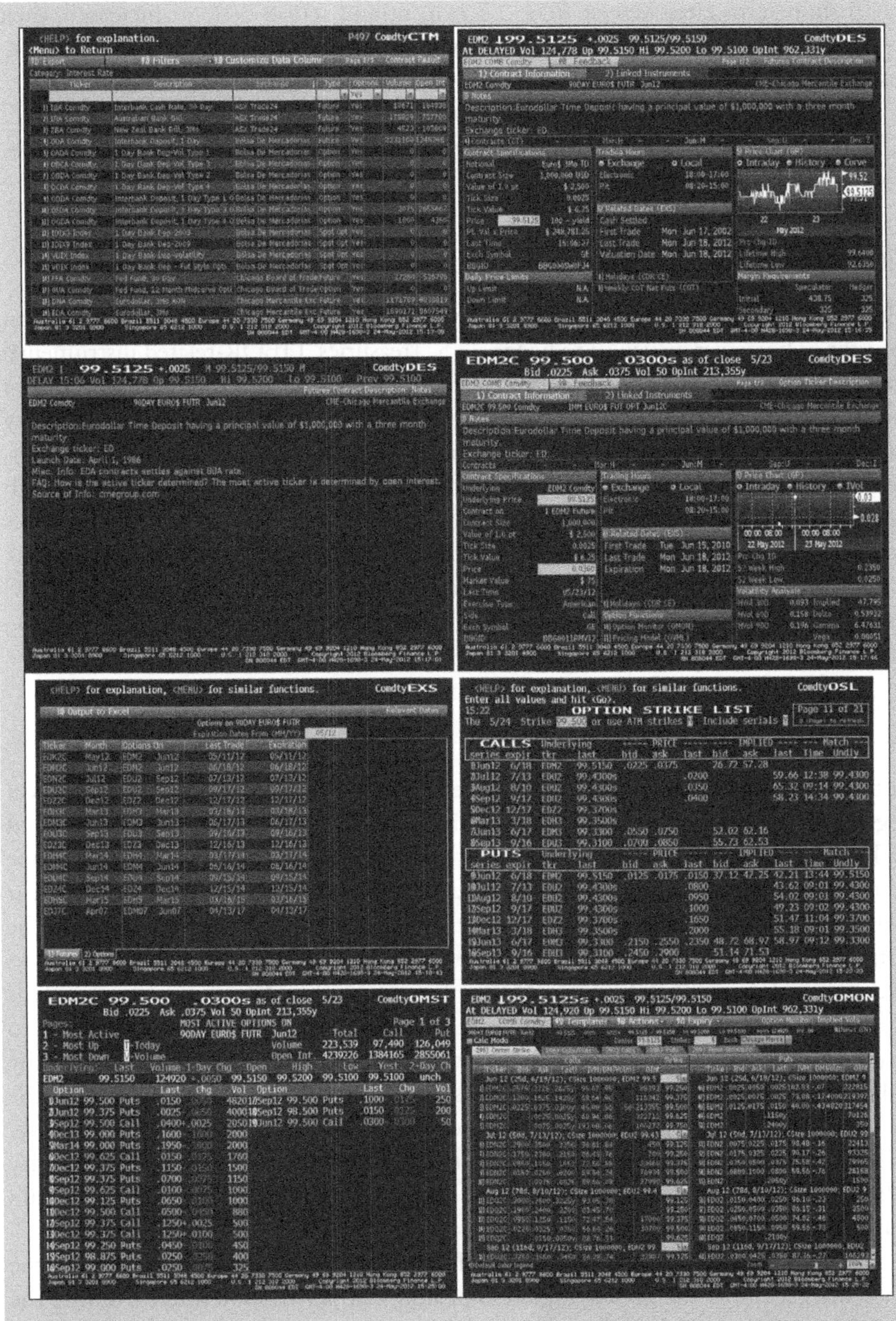

<HELP> for explanation.
<Menu> to Return
ComdtyCTM
EDM2 ↑99.5125 +.0025 99.5125/99.5150
At DELAYED Vol 124,778 Op 99.5150 Hi 99.5200 Lo 99.5100 OpInt 962,331y
ComdtyDES
EDM2C 99.500 .0300s as of close 5/23
Bid .0225 Ask .0375 Vol 50 OpInt 213,355y
ComdtyDES
<HELP> for explanation, <MENU> for similar functions.
ComdtyEXS
<HELP> for explanation, <MENU> for similar functions.
Enter all values and hit <GO>.
OPTION STRIKE LIST
ComdtyOSL
CALLS
PUTS
EDM2C 99.500 .0300s as of close 5/23
Bid .0225 Ask .0375 Vol 50 OpInt 213,355y
ComdtyOMST
MOST ACTIVE OPTIONS ON
90DAY EURO$ FUTR Jun12
EDM2 ↑99.5125s +.0025 99.5125/99.5150
At DELAYED Vol 124,920 Op 99.5150 Hi 99.5200 Lo 99.5100 OpInt 962,331y
ComdtyOMON

If short-term rates were at R_D = 5.5 percent and stayed there or increased, then the call would be worthless and the holder would simply allow the option to expire, losing her $1,481.25 premium.

In addition to futures options on Treasuries and Eurodollar contract, the CBT/CME and other organized exchanges offer other bond and interest rates derivatives. The CBT, for example, offers weekly bond options (see Exhibit 12.1).

OTC Options

Although OTC options can be structured on almost any interest-sensitive position an investor or borrower may wish to hedge, U.S. Treasuries, LIBOR-related instruments, and mortgage-backed securities are often the underlying security. When spot options are structured on securities, terms such as the specific underlying security, its maturity and size, the expiration, and the delivery are all negotiated. For Treasuries, the underlying security is often a recently auctioned Treasury (on-the-run bond), although some selected existing securities (off-the-run securities) are used. Although the prices on OTC options tend to conform to the basic option pricing relation, their bid-ask spreads tend to be larger than exchange-traded ones. The option maturities on OTC contracts can range from one day to several years, with a number of the options being European.

OTC T-Bond and T-Note Options

In the case of OTC spot T-bond or T-note options, OTC dealers often offer or will negotiate contracts giving the holder to right to purchase or sell a specific T-bond or T-note. For example, a dealer might offer a T-bond call option to a fixed income manager giving him the right to buy a specific T-bond, such as one maturing in year 2016 and paying a 6 percent coupon with a face value of $100,000. Because the option contract specifies a particular underlying bond, the maturity of the bond, as well as its value, will be changing during the option's life. For example, a one-year call option on the 15-year bond, if held to expiration, would be a call option to buy a 14-year bond. Note that in contrast, a spot T-bill option contract offered by a dealer on the OTC market usually calls for the delivery of a T-bill meeting the specified criteria (e.g., principal = $1 million, maturity = 91 days). With this clause, a T-bill option is referred to as a *fixed deliverable* bond, and unlike specific-security T-bond options, T-bill options can have expiration dates that exceed the T-bill's maturity.

A second feature of a spot T-bond or T-note option offered or contracted on the OTC market is that the underlying bond or note can pay coupon interest during the option period. As a result, if the option holder exercises on a non-coupon paying date, the accrued interest on the underlying bond must be accounted for. For a T-bond or T-note option, this is done by including the accrued interest as part of the exercise price. Like futures options, the exercise prices on a spot T-bond or T-note option is quoted as an index equal to a proportion of a bond with a face value of $100 (e.g.,

95). If the underlying bond or note has a face value of $100,000, then the exercise price would be:

$$X = \left[\frac{\text{Index}}{100}\right](\$100{,}000) + \text{Accrued Interest}$$

Other OTC Interest-Rate Option Products

In addition to option contracts on specific securities, the OTC market also offers a number of interest-rate option products. These products are usually offered by commercial or investment banks to their clients. Products of note are interest rate calls, interest rate puts, caps, and floors. The products and their use are examined later in this chapter.

Option Positions

Many types of option strategies, with esoteric names such as straddles, strips, spreads, combinations, and so forth, exist. The building blocks for these strategies are four fundamental option strategies: call and put purchases and call and put writes. The features of these fundamental strategies can be seen by examining the relationship between the price of the underlying security and the possible profits or losses that would result if the option either is exercised or expires worthless.[2]

Fundamental Spot Option Positions

Call Purchase

To see the major characteristics of a call purchase, suppose an investor buys a spot call option on a 6 percent T-bond with a face value of $100,000, a maturity at the option expiration of 15 year, no accrued interest at the option expiration date, and currently selling at par. Suppose the T-bond's exercise price (X) is $100,000 (quoted at 100) and the investor buys the option at a call premium of C_0 = $1,000 (quoted at 1). If the bond price reaches $105,000 at expiration, the holder would realize a profit of $4,000 by exercising the call to acquire the bond for $100,000, then selling the bond in the market for $105,000: a $5,000 capital gain minus the $1,000 premium. If the holder exercises at expiration when the bond is trading at $101,000, she will break even: The $1,000 premium will be offset exactly by the $1,000 gain realized by acquiring the bond from the option at $100,000 and selling in the market at $101,000. Finally, if the price of the bond is at the exercise price of $100,000 or below, the holder will not find it profitable to exercise, and as a result, she will let the option expire, realizing a loss equal to the call premium of $1,000. Thus, the maximum loss from the call purchase is $1,000.

The investor's possible profit/loss and bond price combinations can be seen graphically in Exhibit 12.2 and the accompanying table. In the graph, the profits/losses are shown on the vertical axis and the market prices of the spot T-bond, S, at expiration or when the option is exercised (signified as T: S_T) are shown along the horizontal axis.

EXHIBIT 12.2 Call Purchase

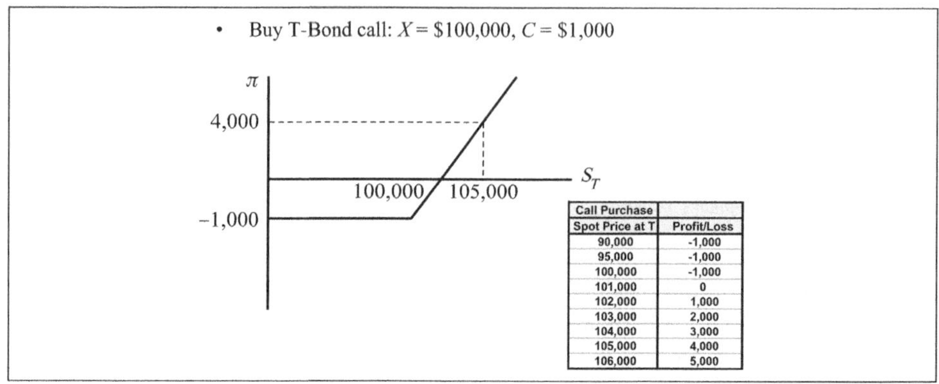

Call Purchase	
Spot Price at T	Profit/Loss
90,000	-1,000
95,000	-1,000
100,000	-1,000
101,000	0
102,000	1,000
103,000	2,000
104,000	3,000
105,000	4,000
106,000	5,000

This graph is known as a *profit graph.* The line from the ($100,000, −$1,000) coordinate to the ($105,000, $4,000) coordinate and beyond shows all the profit and losses per call associated with each bond price. The horizontal segment shows a loss of $1,000 that is equal to the premium paid when the option was purchased. Finally, the horizontal intercept is the break-even price ($101,000). The breakeven price can be found algebraically by solving for the bond price at the exercise date (S_T) in which the profit (π) from the position is zero. The profit graph in Exhibit 12.2 highlights two important features of call purchases. First, the position provides an investor with unlimited profit potential; second, losses are limited to an amount equal to the call premium.

Naked Call Write

The second fundamental strategy involves the sale of a call in which the seller does not own the underlying security. Such a position is known as a *naked call write.* To see the characteristics of this position, assume the same spot T-bond call option with an exercise price of $100,000 and premium of $1,000. The profits or losses associated with each bond price from selling the call are depicted in the figure in Exhibit 12.3. As shown, when the price of the bond is at $105,000 at expiration, the seller suffers a $4,000 loss when the holder exercises the right to buy the bond from the writer at $100,000. Since the writer does not own the bond, he would have to buy it in the market at its market price of $105,000, and then turn it over to the holder at $100,000. Thus, the call writer would realize a $5,000 capital loss, minus the $1,000 premium received for selling the call, for a net loss of $4,000. When the T-bond is at $101,000, the writer will realize a $1,000 loss if the holder exercises. This loss will offset the $1,000 premium received. Thus, the breakeven price for the writer is $101,000—the same as the holder's. Finally, at a bond price of $100,000 or less the holder will not exercise, and the writer will profit by the amount of the premium, $1,000.

As highlighted in the graph, the payoffs to a call write are just the opposite of the call purchase. Thus, in contrast to the call purchase, the naked call write position provides the investor with only a limited profit opportunity equal to the value of the premium, with unlimited loss possibilities. Although this limited profit and unlimited loss feature of a naked call write may seem unattractive, the motivation for an investor to write a call is

EXHIBIT 12.3 Naked Call Write

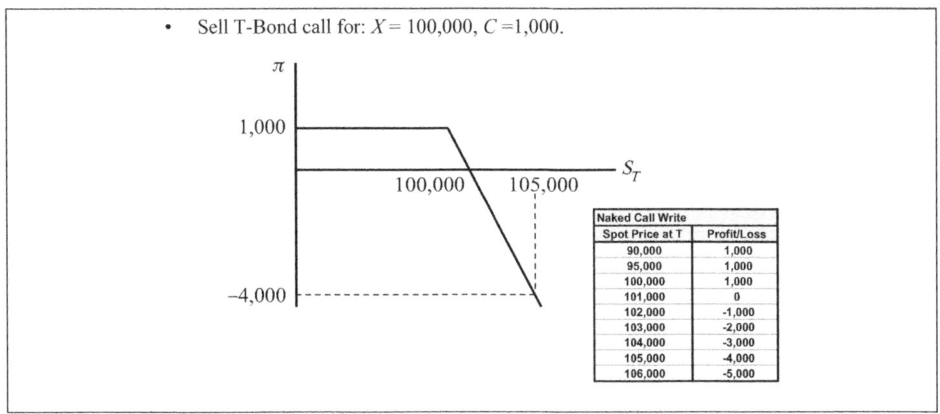

the cash or credit received and the expectation that the option will not be exercised. Like futures contracts, though, there are margin requirements on a naked write option position in which the writer is required to deposit cash or risk-free securities to secure the position.

Put Purchase

Since a put gives the holder the right to sell the underlying security, profit is realized when the security's price declines. With a decline, the put holder can buy the security at a low price in the market, and then sell it at the higher exercise price on the contract. To see the features related to the put purchase position, assume the exercise price on a put option on the 6 percent T-bond is again \$100,000 and the put premium (P) is \$1,000. If the T-bond is trading at \$95,000 at expiration, the put holder could purchase a 15-year, 6 percent T-bond at \$95,000, then use the put contract to sell the bond at the exercise price of \$100,000. Thus, as shown by the profit graph in Exhibit 12.4 and its accompanying table, at \$95,000 the put holder would realize a \$4,000 profit (the \$5,000 gain from buying the bond and exercising minus the \$1,000 premium). The breakeven price in this case would be \$99,000. Finally, if the T-bond is trading at \$100,000 or higher at

EXHIBIT 12.4 Put Purchase

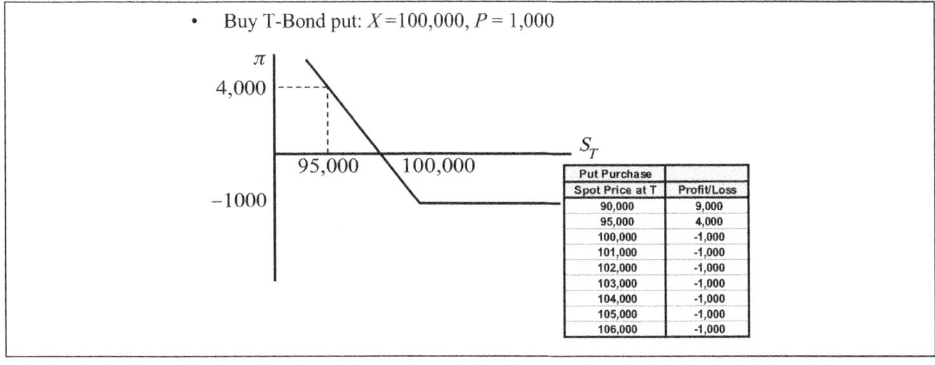

expiration, it will not be rational for the put holder to exercise. As a result, a maximum loss equal to the $1,000 premium will occur when the stock is trading at $100,000 or more (again assuming no accrued interest at expiration).

Thus, similar to a call purchase, a long put position provides the buyer with potentially large profit opportunities (not unlimited since the price of the security cannot be less than zero), while limiting the losses to the amount of the premium. Unlike the call purchase strategy, the put purchase position requires the security price to decline before profit is realized.

Naked Put Write

The exact opposite position to a put purchase (in terms of profit/loss and security price relations) is the sale of a put, defined as the naked put write. This position's profit graph is shown in Exhibit 12.5. Here, if the T-bond price is at $100,000 or more at expiration, the holder will not exercise and the writer will profit by the amount of the premium, $1,000. In contrast, if the T-bond decreases, a loss is incurred. For example, if the holder exercises at $95,000, the put writer must buy the bond at $100,000. An actual $5,000 loss will occur if the writer elects to sell the bond and a paper loss if he holds on to it. This loss, minus the $1,000 premium, yields a loss of $4,000 when the market price is $95,000. For this naked put write position, the breakeven price in which the profit from the position is zero is $99,000, the same as the put holder's.

Fundamental Futures Options Positions

The important characteristics of futures options can also be seen by examining the profit relationships for the fundamental call and put positions formed with these options. Exhibit 12.6 shows the profit and futures price relationship at expiration for a long call position on a Eurodollar futures contract. The call has an exercise price equal to 90 (index) or X = $975,000, is priced at $1,250 (quote of 5: (5)(10)($25) = $1,250),

EXHIBIT 12.5 Naked Put Write

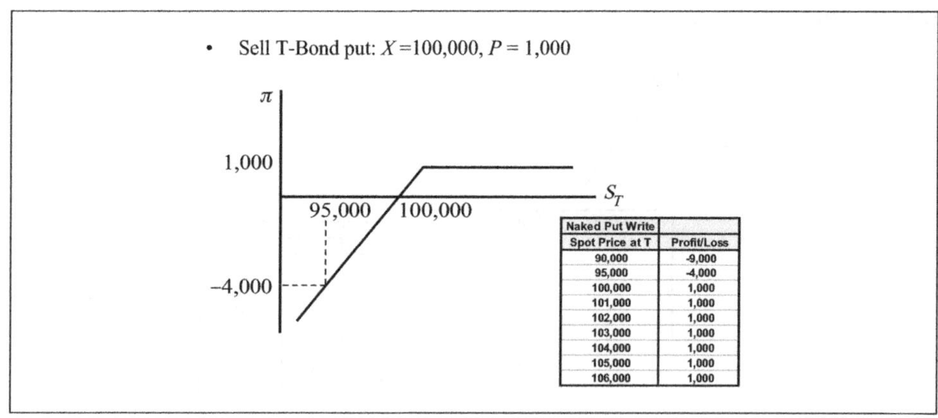

Naked Put Write	
Spot Price at T	Profit/Loss
90,000	-9,000
95,000	-4,000
100,000	1,000
101,000	1,000
102,000	1,000
103,000	1,000
104,000	1,000
105,000	1,000
106,000	1,000

EXHIBIT 12.6 Call Option on Eurodollar Futures

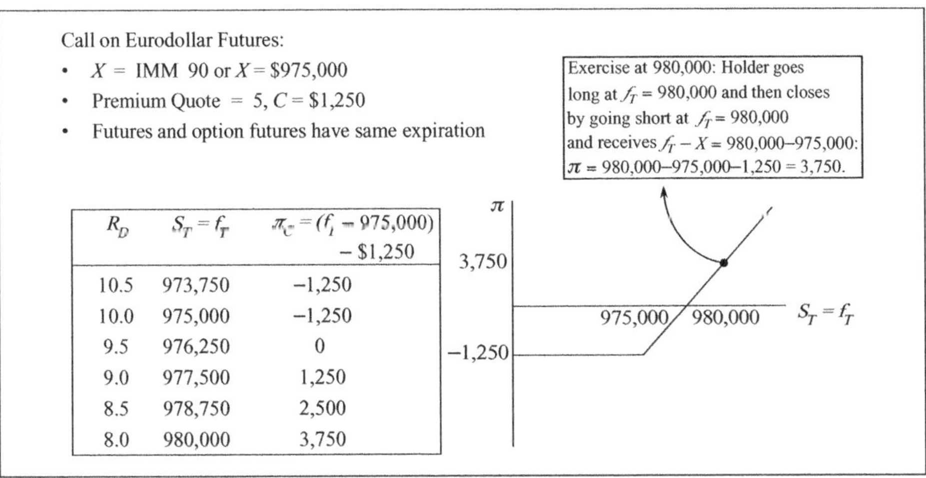

R_D	$S_T = f_T$	$\pi_C = (f_T - 975{,}000) - \$1{,}250$
10.5	973,750	−1,250
10.0	975,000	−1,250
9.5	976,250	0
9.0	977,500	1,250
8.5	978,750	2,500
8.0	980,000	3,750

and it is assumed the Eurodollar futures option expires at the same time as the underlying Eurodollar futures contract. The numbers shown in the exhibit reflect a case in which the holder exercises the call at expiration, if profitable, when the spot price is equal to the price on the expiring futures contract. For example, at $S_T = f_T =$ \$980,000, the holder of the 90 Eurodollar futures call would receive a cash flow of \$5,000 for a profit of \$3,750 (= \$5,000 - \$1,250). That is, upon exercising the holder would assume a long position in the expiring Eurodollar futures priced at \$980,000 and a futures margin account worth \$5,000 (($f_T - X$) = \$980,000 - \$975,000) = \$5,000). Given we are at expiration, the holder would therefore receive \$5,000 from the expired futures position, leaving her with a profit of \$3,750. The opposite profit and futures price relation is attained for a naked call write position. In this case, if the Eurodollar futures is at \$975,00 or less, the writer of the futures call would earn the premium of \$1,250, and if $f_T >$ \$975,000, he, upon the exercise by the holder, would assume a short position at f_T and would have to pay $f_T - X$ to bring the margin on his expiring short position into balance.

Exhibit 12.7 shows a long put position on the 90 Eurodollar futures purchased at \$1,250. In the case of a put purchase, if the holder exercises when f_T is less than X, then he will have a margin account worth $X - f_T$ on an expiring short futures position. For example, if $S_T = f_T =$ \$970,000 at expiration, then the put holder upon exercising would receive \$5,000 from the expiring short futures ($X - f_T =$ \$975,000 - \$970,000), yielding a profit from her futures option of \$3,750. The put writer's position, of course, would be the opposite.

It should be noted that even though the technicalities on exercising futures options are cumbersome, the profit from closing a futures option at expiration still are equal to the maximum of either zero or the difference in $f_T - X$ (for calls) or $X - f_T$ (for puts), minus the option premium. Moreover, if the futures option and the underlying futures contract expire at the same time, as we assumed above, then $f_T = S_T$, and the

EXHIBIT 12.7 Put Options on Eurodollar Futures

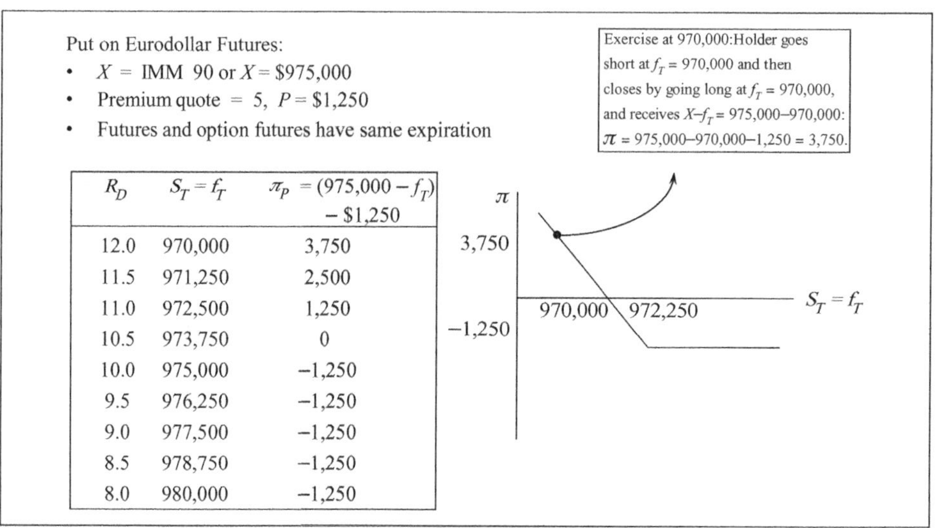
Put on Eurodollar Futures:
• X = IMM 90 or X = $975,000
• Premium quote = 5, P = $1,250
• Futures and option futures have same expiration
Exercise at 970,000:Holder goes short at f_T = 970,000 and then closes by going long at f_T = 970,000, and receives $X-f_T$ = 975,000–970,000: π = 975,000–970,000–1,250 = 3,750.
π
3,750
−1,250
970,000
972,250
$S_T = f_T$

R_D	$S_T = f_T$	$\pi_P = (975{,}000 - f_T) - \$1{,}250$
12.0	970,000	3,750
11.5	971,250	2,500
11.0	972,500	1,250
10.5	973,750	0
10.0	975,000	−1,250
9.5	976,250	−1,250
9.0	977,500	−1,250
8.5	978,750	−1,250
8.0	980,000	−1,250

futures option can be viewed simply as an option on the underlying spot security with the option having a cash settlement clause.

Other Option Strategies

One of the important features of an option is that it can be combined with positions in the underlying security and other options to generate a number of different investment strategies. Two well-known strategies formed by combining option positions are *straddles* and *spreads.*

Straddle

A straddle purchase is formed by buying both a call and put with the same terms—the same underlying security, exercise price, and expiration date. A straddle write, in contrast, is constructed by selling a call and a put with the same terms.

In Exhibit 12.8, the profit graphs are shown for spot T-bond call, put, and straddle purchases in which both the call and the put have exercise prices of $100,000 and premiums of $1,000 and there is no accrued interest at expiration.[3] The straddle purchase shown in the figure is geometrically generated by vertically summing the profits on the call purchase position and put purchase position at each bond price. The resulting straddle purchase position is characterized by a V-shaped profit and spot price relation. Thus, the motivation for buying a straddle comes from the expectation of a large price movement in either direction. Losses on the straddle occur if the price of the underlying security remains stable, with the maximum loss being equal to the costs of the straddle ($2,000) and occurring when the bond price is equal to the exercise price. Finally, the straddle is characterized by two breakeven prices ($98,000 and $102,000).

EXHIBIT 12.8 Straddle Purchase

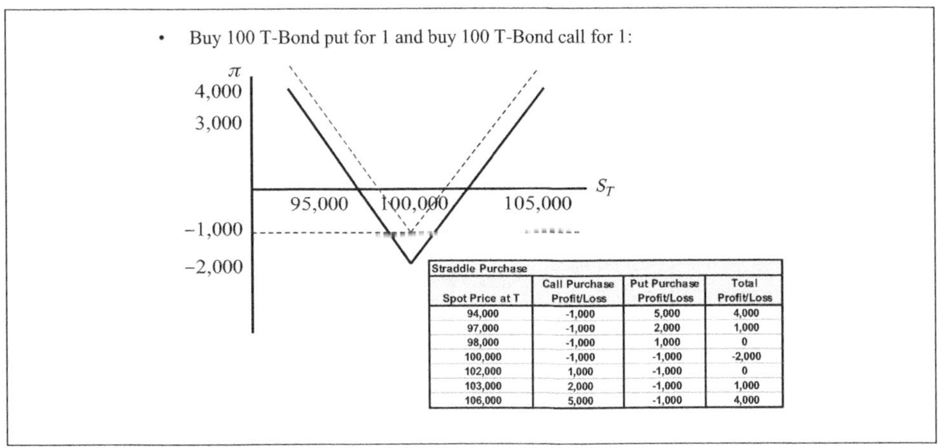

Straddle Purchase			
Spot Price at T	Call Purchase Profit/Loss	Put Purchase Profit/Loss	Total Profit/Loss
94,000	-1,000	5,000	4,000
97,000	-1,000	2,000	1,000
98,000	-1,000	1,000	0
100,000	-1,000	-1,000	-2,000
102,000	1,000	-1,000	0
103,000	2,000	-1,000	1,000
106,000	5,000	-1,000	4,000

In contrast to the straddle purchase, a straddle write yields an inverted V-shaped profit graph. The seller of a straddle is betting against large price movements. A maximum profit equal to the sum of the call and put premiums occurs when the bond price is equal to the exercise price; losses occur if the bond price moves significantly in either direction.

Spread

A spread is the purchase of one option and the sale of another on the same underlying security but with different terms: different exercise prices (*money spread*), different expirations (*time spread*), or both (*diagonal spread*). Two of the most popular time spread positions are the *bull spread* and the *bear spread.* A bull call spread is formed by buying a call with a certain exercise price and selling another call with a higher exercise price, but with the same expiration date. A bear call spread is the reversal of the bull spread; it consists of buying a call with a certain exercise price and selling another with a lower exercise price. (The same spreads also can be formed with puts.)

In Exhibit 12.9, the profit graph and table for a bull call spread strategy is shown. The spread is formed with the purchase of the 100 T-bond call (X = \$100,000) for 1 (C = \$1,000) and the sale of a 101 T-bond call (X = \$101,000) for 0.75 (C = \$750), with both options having the same underlying T-bond and expiration. The bull spread is characterized by losses limited to \$250 when the T-bond price is \$100,000 or less, limited profits of \$750 starting when the bond price hits \$101,000, and a breakeven price of \$100,250.

A bear call spread results in the opposite profit and security price relation as the bull spread: limited profits occur when the security price is equal or less than the lower exercise price and limited losses occur when the security price is equal or greater than the higher exercise price.

EXHIBIT 12.9 Bull Spread

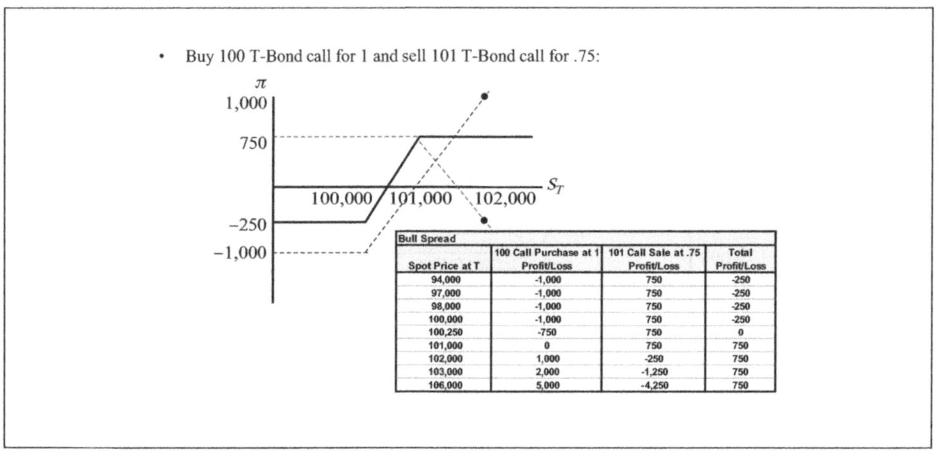

Bull Spread			
Spot Price at T	100 Call Purchase at 1 Profit/Loss	101 Call Sale at .75 Profit/Loss	Total Profit/Loss
94,000	-1,000	750	-250
97,000	-1,000	750	-250
98,000	-1,000	750	-250
100,000	-1,000	750	-250
100,250	-750	750	0
101,000	0	750	750
102,000	1,000	-250	750
103,000	2,000	-1,250	750
106,000	5,000	-4,250	750

OSA: BLOOMBERG'S OPTION SCENARIO SCREEN

Profit and value graphs for spot and futures options can be generated using the Bloomberg OSA screen. To access OSA for a security or futures, load the menu page of the security and type OSA (or click "OSA" from the menu). For example, for the T-bond futures:

1. Go to CTM, click "Exchange" and "Chicago Board of Trade."
2. Load Bond, Futures, and Options Categories.
3. From listings, select futures with a futures option (e.g., "USA" for long-term Treasury futures).
4. Type "OSA."
5. On the OSA screen, click the "Positions" tab and then click "Add Listed Options" to bring up options listed on the security. This brings up a screen showing the listed options from which to select (e.g., 1 call contract and 1 put contract on the September 2012 contract—straddle purchase).
6. After selecting the positions, type 1 <Enter> to load positions and bring up the OSA position screen.
7. On the position screen, click the "Scenario Chart" tab at the top of the screen to bring up the profit graph. The profit graph shows profits for the strategy at expiration where the option price is trading at its intrinsic value and also at time periods prior where the option price is determined by an option-pricing model. The profit graphs for different periods can be changed or deleted by using the select options at the top of the screen.
8. From the position screen (click "Position" tab), one can select different positions and then click "Scenario Chart" tab to view the profit graph.
9. The Scenario screen (grey "Scenario" tab) shows the profit table.

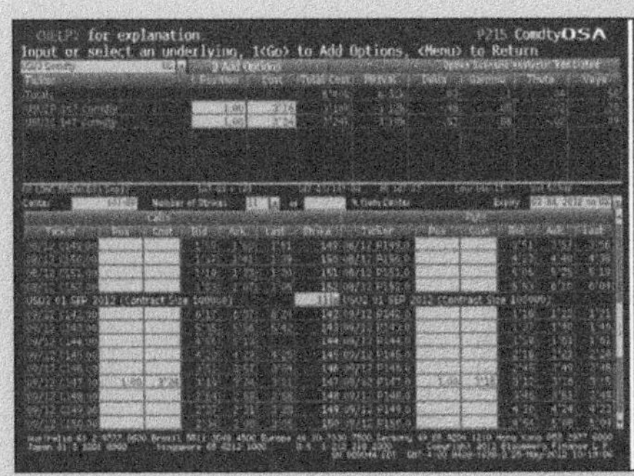

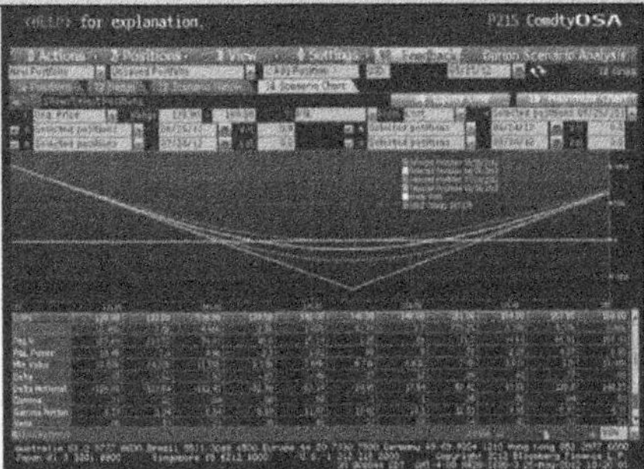

Futures Option Positions

Futures on U.S. T-Bond, September Expiration

Option on September T-Bond Futures

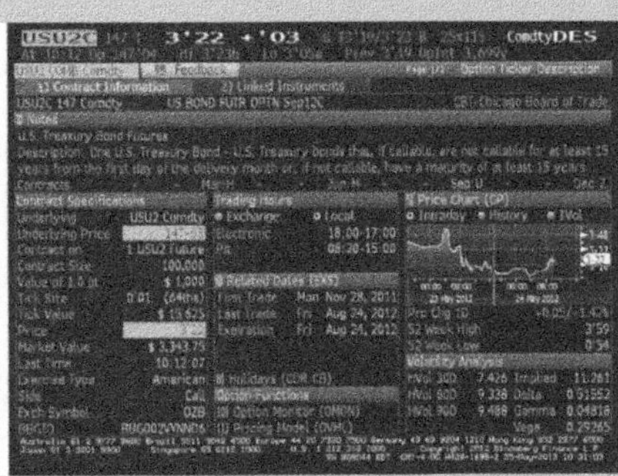

Call Purchase

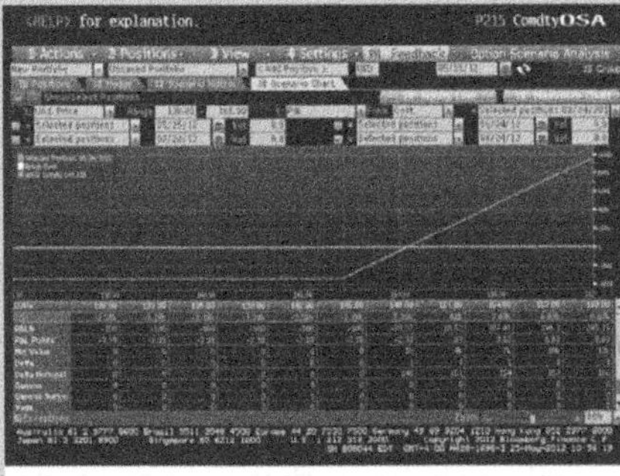

Call Sale—Naked Call Write

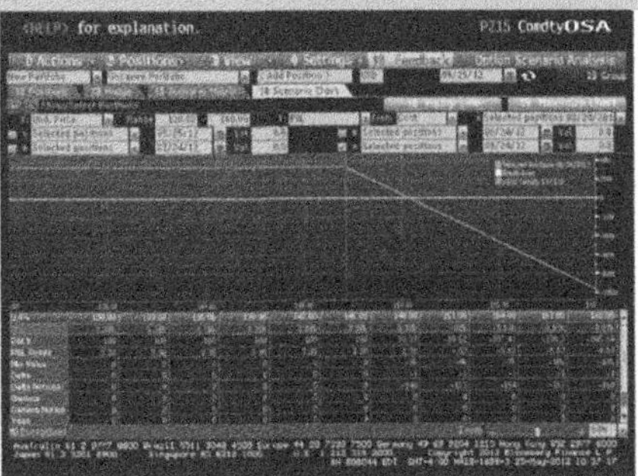

Put Purchase

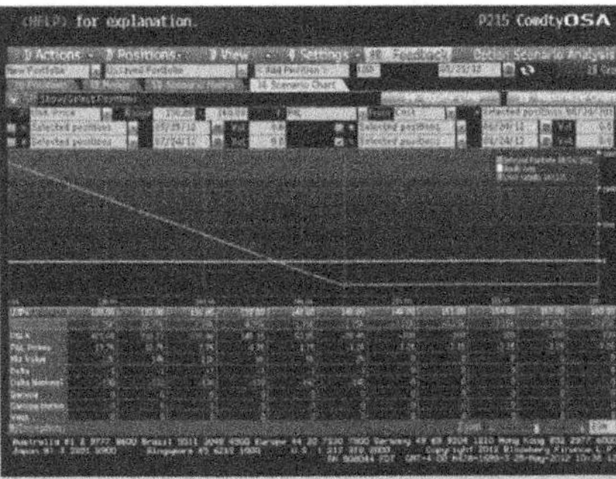

Put Sale—Naked Put Write

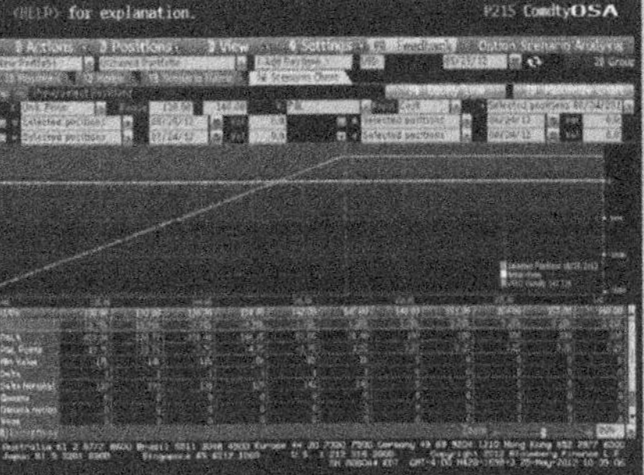

(Continued)

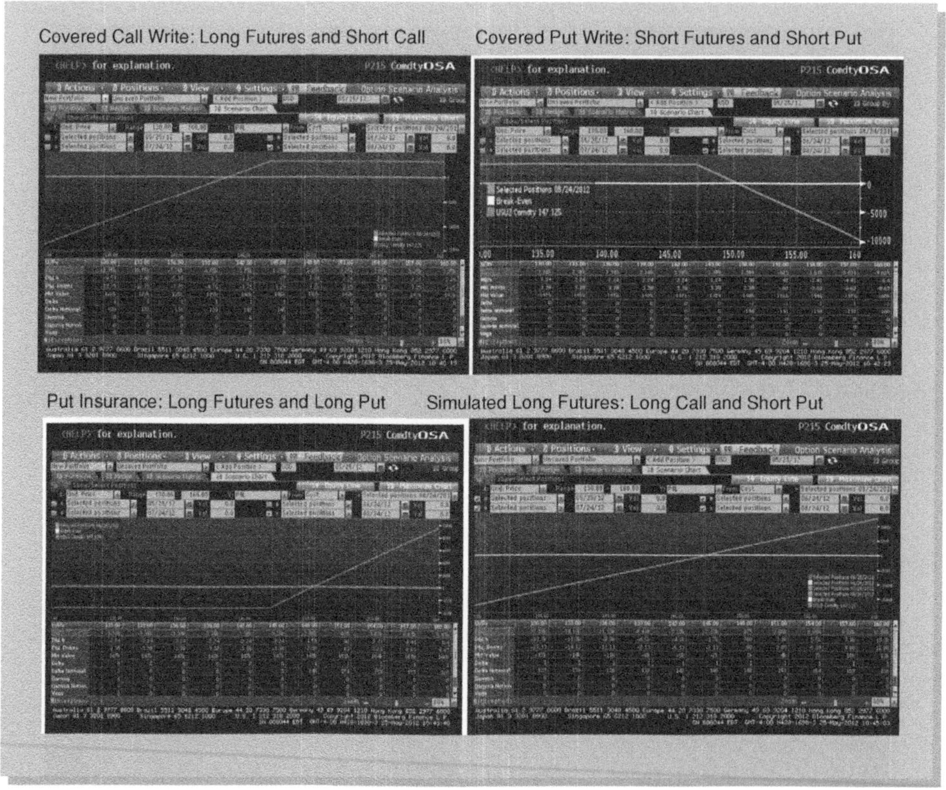

Speculation

The preceding profit graphs illustrate how interest rate options can be used to hedge, as well as speculate, on movements in interest rates. A speculator who believes long-term interest rates will be lower in the near future could profit (if her expectation is correct) by taking a long position in a T-bond futures call. As a speculative strategy, this long call position can be viewed as an alternative to a long position in a T-bond futures contract. When compared to the futures position, the call position provides a limited loss and unlimited profit, whereas the futures position provides an unlimited profit and loss profile. In contrast, if a speculator believes that long-term interest rates are going to increase in the near future, then she should take a long position in a T-bond futures put option. Similar positions could be taken in Eurodollar futures options by speculators who expect short-term rates to change.

Finally, between outright call and put positions, options can be combined in different ways to obtain various types of profit relations. Speculators who expect rates to increase in the future but don't want to assume the risk inherent in a put purchase position could form a bear call spread. In contrast, speculators who expect rates to be stable over the near term could, in turn, try to profit by forming a straddle write. Thus by combining different option positions, speculators can obtain positions that match their expectations and their desired risk-return preference. Exhibit 12.10 lists some of the other option positions. An exercise of generating profit tables and graphs to illustrate the features of different option positions is included as part of the end-of-the-chapter problems that can be found on the accompanying website for this text.

Hedging Fixed-Income Positions with Options

As examined in Chapter 11, a fixed-income manager planning to invest a future inflow of cash in high quality bonds could hedge the investment against possible higher bond prices and lower rates by going long in T-bond futures contracts. If long-term rates were to decrease, the higher costs of purchasing the bonds would then be offset by profits from his T-bond futures positions. If rates increased, however, the manager would benefit from lower bond prices, but he would also have to cover losses on his futures position. Thus, hedging future fixed-income investments with futures locks in a future price and return and therefore eliminates not only the costs of unfavorable price movements but also the benefits from favorable movements. However, by hedging with either exchange-traded futures call options on a Treasury note or bond or with an OTC spot call option on a debt security, a hedger can obtain protection against adverse price increases while still realizing lower costs if security prices decrease.

For cases in which bond or money market managers are planning to sell some of their securities in the future, hedging can be done by going short in a T-bond or Eurodollar futures contracts. If rates were higher at the time of the sale, the resulting lower bond prices and therefore revenue from the bond sale would be offset by profits from the futures positions (just the opposite would occur if rates were lower). The hedge also can be formed by purchasing an exchange-traded futures put options on Treasury or Eurodollar contracts or an OTC spot put option on a debt security. This hedge would provide downside protection if bond prices decrease while earning increasing revenues if security prices increase.

EXHIBIT 12.10 Different Option Positions

1. **Bull Call Spread**: Long in call with low *X* and short in call with high *X*
2. **Bull Put Spread**: Long in put with low *X* and short in put with high *X*
3. **Bear Call Spread**: Long in call with high *X* and short in call with low *X*
4. **Bear Put Spread**: Long in put with high *X* and short in put with low *X*
5. **Long Butterfly Spread**: Long in call with low *X*, short in 2 calls with middle *X*, and long in call with high *X* (similar position can be formed with puts)
6. **Short Butterfly Spread**: Short in call with low *X*, long in 2 calls with middle *X*, and short in call with high *X* (similar position can be formed with puts)
7. **Straddle Purchase**: Long call and put with similar terms
8. **Strip Purchase**: Straddle with additional puts (e.g., long call and long 2 puts)
9. **Strap Purchase**: Straddle with additional calls (e.g., long 2 calls and long put)
10. **Straddle Sale**: Short call and put with similar terms (strip and strap sales have additional calls and puts)
11. **Money Combination Purchase**: Long call and put with different exercise prices
12. **Money Combination Sale**: Short call and put with different exercise prices

Short hedging positions with futures and put options can be used not only by holders of fixed-income securities planning to sell their instruments before maturity, but also by bond issuers, borrowers, and debt security underwriters. A company planning to issue bonds or borrow funds from a financial institution at some future date, for example, could hedge the debt position against possible interest rate increases by going short in debt futures contracts or cap the loan rate by buying an OTC put or exchange-traded futures put. Similarly, a bank that finances its short-term loan portfolio of one-year loans by selling 90-day CDs could manage the resulting maturity gap (maturity of the assets (one-year loans) not equal to the maturity of liabilities (90-day CDs) by also taking short positions in Eurodollar futures or futures options. Finally, an underwriter or a dealer who is holding a debt security for a short period of time could hedge the position against interest rate increases by going short in an appropriate futures contract or by purchasing a futures put option.

Note that many debt and fixed-income positions involve securities and interest rate positions in which a futures contract on the underlying security does not exist. In such cases, an effective cross hedge needs to be determined to minimize the price risk in the underlying spot position. As noted in Chapter 11, one commonly used model for bond and debt positions is the *price-sensitivity model* developed by Kolb and Chiang (1981) and Toevs and Jacobs (1986). For option hedging, the number of options (call for long hedging positions and puts for short hedging positions) using the price-sensitivity model is:

$$n_{options} = \frac{Dur_s}{Dur_{option}} \frac{V_0}{X} \frac{(1+YTM_f)^T}{(1+YTM_S)^T}$$

where:

Dur_{option} = duration of the bond underlying the option contract
Dur_S = duration of the bond being hedged
V_0 = current value of bond to be hedged
YTM_S = yield to maturity on the bond being hedged
YTM_f = yield to maturity implied on the underlying futures contract

Example: Hedging a Bond Portfolio with T-Bond Futures Puts

Suppose a bond portfolio manager is planning to liquidate part of his portfolio in September. The portfolio he plans to sell consists of investment grade bonds with a weighted average maturity of 15.25 years, face value of \$10 million, weighted average yield of 8 percent, portfolio duration of 10, and current value of \$10 million. Suppose the manager would like to benefit from lower long-term rates that he expects to occur in the future but would also like to protect the portfolio sale against the possibility of a rate increase. To achieve this dual objective, the manager could buy an OTC spot or exchange-traded futures put on a T-bond. Suppose there is a September 95 (X =

$95,000) T-bond futures put option trading at $1,156 with the cheapest-to-deliver T-bond on the put's underlying futures being a bond with a current maturity of 15.25 years, duration of 9.818, and currently priced to yield 6.0 percent. Using the price-sensitivity model, the manager would need to buy 81 puts at a cost of $93,636 to hedge his bond portfolio:

$$n_p = \frac{\text{Dur}_s}{\text{Dur}_p} \frac{V_0}{X} \frac{(1+YTM_p)^T}{(1+YTM_S)^T}$$

$$n_p = \frac{10}{9.818} \frac{\$10\text{m}}{\$95{,}000} \frac{(1.06)^{15.25}}{(1.08)^{15.25}} \cong 81$$

$$\text{Cost} = (81)(\$1{,}156) = \$93{,}636$$

Suppose that in September, long-term rates were higher, causing the value of the bond portfolio to decrease from $10 million to $9.1 million and the price on September T-bond futures contracts to decrease from 95 to 86. In this case, the bond portfolio's $900,000 loss in value would be partially offset by a $635,364 profit on the T-bond futures puts: π = 81($95,000 – $86,000) – $93,636 = $635,364. The manager's hedged portfolio value would therefore be $9,735,364; a loss of 2.6 percent in value (this loss includes the cost of the puts) compared to a 9 percent loss in value if the portfolio were not hedged. However, if rates in September were lower, causing the value of the bond portfolio to increase from $10 million to $10.5 million and the prices on the September T-bond futures contracts to increase from 95 to 100, then the puts would be out of the money and the loss would be limited to the $93,636 costs of the put options. In this case, the hedged portfolio value would be $10,406,365—a 4.06 percent gain in value compared to the 5 percent gain for an unhedged position.

Note: If the manager were more certain that long-term rates would increase in the future, then he could minimize interest rate risk by alternatively going short in T-bond futures and using the price-sensitivity model to determine the number of contracts he needed to effectively hedge his position. Examples of a covered call write and put-insured bond hedging cases using Bloomberg's OSA screen is presented in Exhibit 12.11. The cases involved hedging a government bond ETF with a long position in a put contract on a 20-year T-bond futures contract and short position in call contract on the 20-year T-bond futures contract.

Using Options to Set a Cap or Floor on a Cash Flow

In Chapter 11, we examined how a series or strip of Eurodollar futures contracts could be used to create a fixed or floating rate on the cash flow of an asset or liability. When there is series of cash flows, such as a floating-rate loan or an investment in a floating-rate note, a strip of interest rate options can similarly be used to place a cap or a floor on the cash floors. For example, a company with a one-year floating-rate

EXHIBIT 12.11 Put Insured and Covered Call Write Position for Government Bond ETF Evaluated using Bloomberg OSA Screen, 5/27/2012

ETF: U.S. Government Bond Index Consisting of 20-year Treasuries

- Number of shares = 1,200
- Price = $123.38
- NAV = 123.44
- Value = $148,056
- Ticker: TLT US <Equity>

Futures Options on 20-year Treasury Futures: Futures = USZ2, Dec 148 Call = USZ2C; Dec 148 Put = USZ2P

- $X = 148$
- Contract Size = $100,000 Face Value
- Contract Value = $148,000
- Expiration = December 2012
- Number of Long Put Contracts to hedge:
- n = Mkt Value/X = $148,056/$148,000 1
- Number of Short Call Contracts to form Covered Call = 1

To load OSA Screen:

- USA <Comdty>
- Click OSA
- In "Positions" tab, add December 148 Treasury Futures Call and Put Options
- Add ETF: Type TLT US <Equity> in "Add Positions" box and input number of shares (1,200)

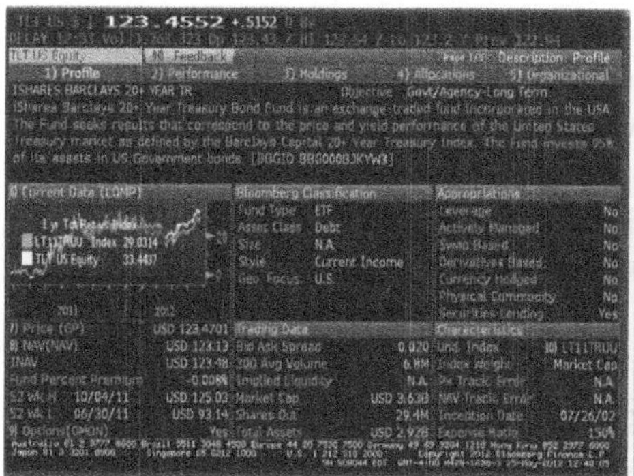

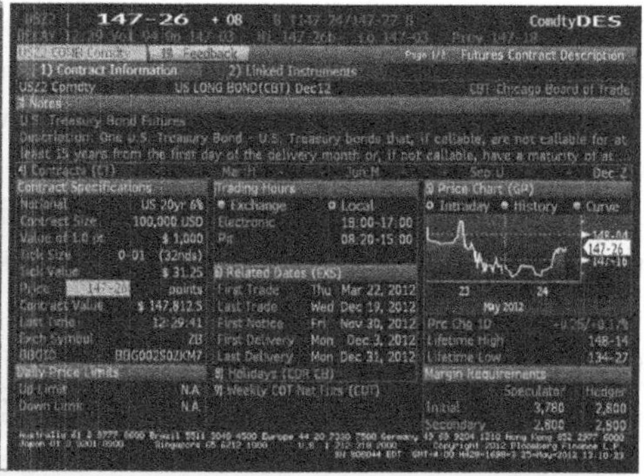

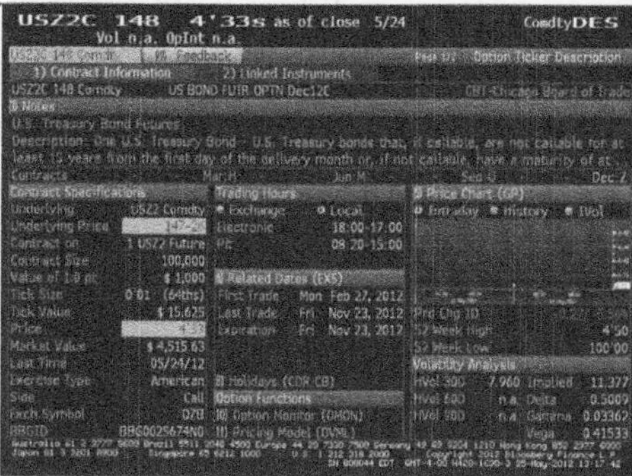

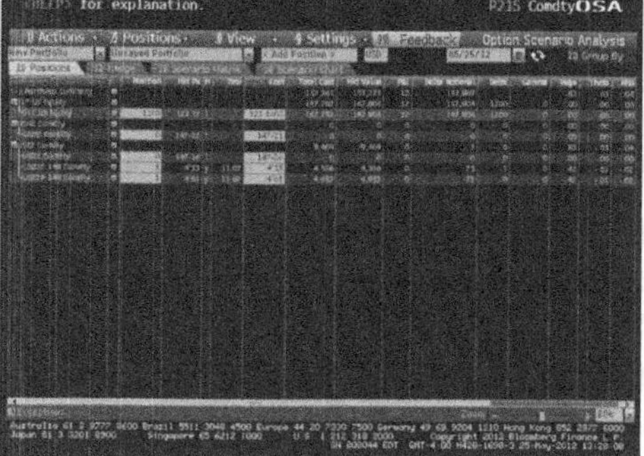

EXHIBIT 12.11 *(Continued)*

Profit Graph: No Hedge Position

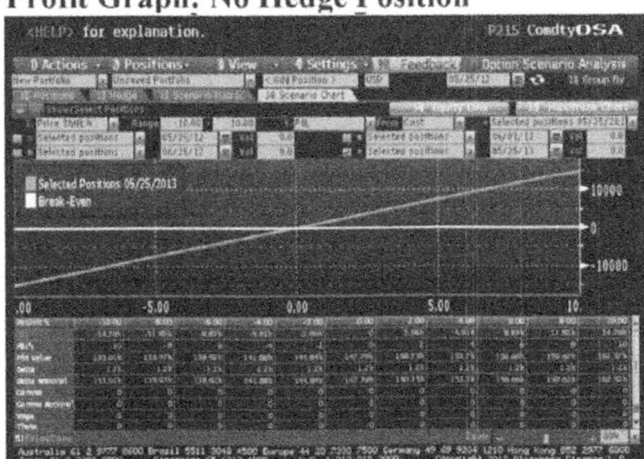

Profit Graph: Put-Insured Position

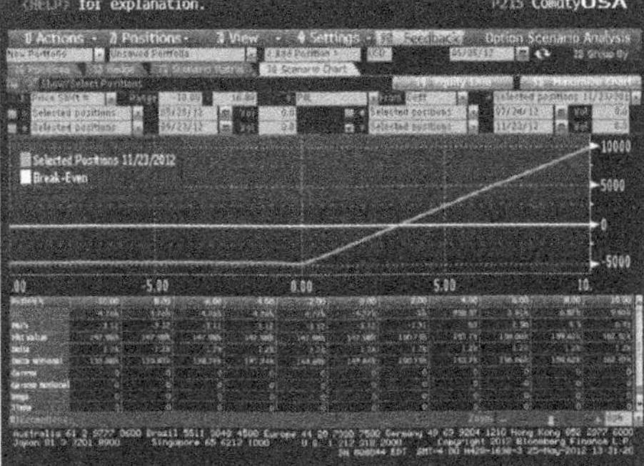

Value Graph: Put-Insured Position

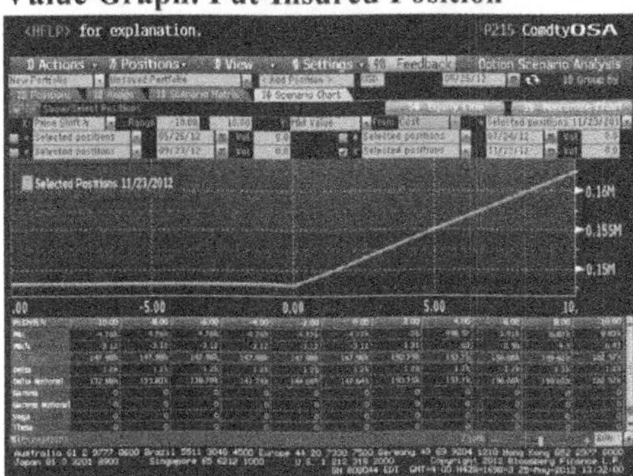

Profit Graph: Covered Call Write Position

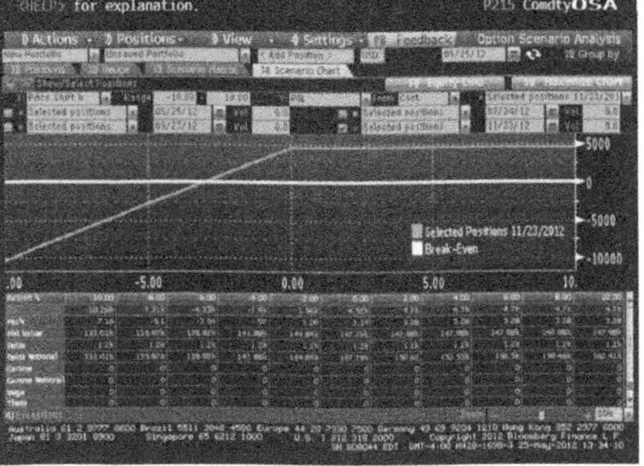

loan starting in September at a specified rate and then reset in December, March, and June to equal the spot LIBOR plus basis points, could obtain a cap on the loan by buying a series of Eurodollar futures puts expiring in December, March, and June. At each reset date, if the LIBOR exceeds the exercise discount yield on the put, the higher LIBOR applied to the loan will be offset by a profit on the nearest expiring put, with the profit increasing the greater the LIBOR; if the LIBOR is equal to or less than the discount yield on the put, the lower LIBOR applied to the loan will only be offset by the limited cost of the put. Thus, a strip of Eurodollar futures puts used to hedge a floating-rate loan places a ceiling on the effective rate paid on the loan.

In the case of a floating-rate investment, such as a floating-rate note tied to the LIBOR or a bank's floating rate loan portfolio, a minimum rate or floor can be obtained by buying a series of Eurodollar futures calls, with each call having an expiration near the reset date on the investment. If rates decrease, the lower investment return will be offset by profits on the calls; if rates increase, the only offset will be the limited cost of the calls.

BLOOMBERG HEDGING SCREENS: FIHR AND PDH1

FIHR calculates the number of bond futures contracts needed to hedge the interest rate risk of a position in a bond you specify. To use, load a fixed-income security and then type FIHR.

PDH1 calculates the position duration. To use, load a fixed-income security and then type FIHR.

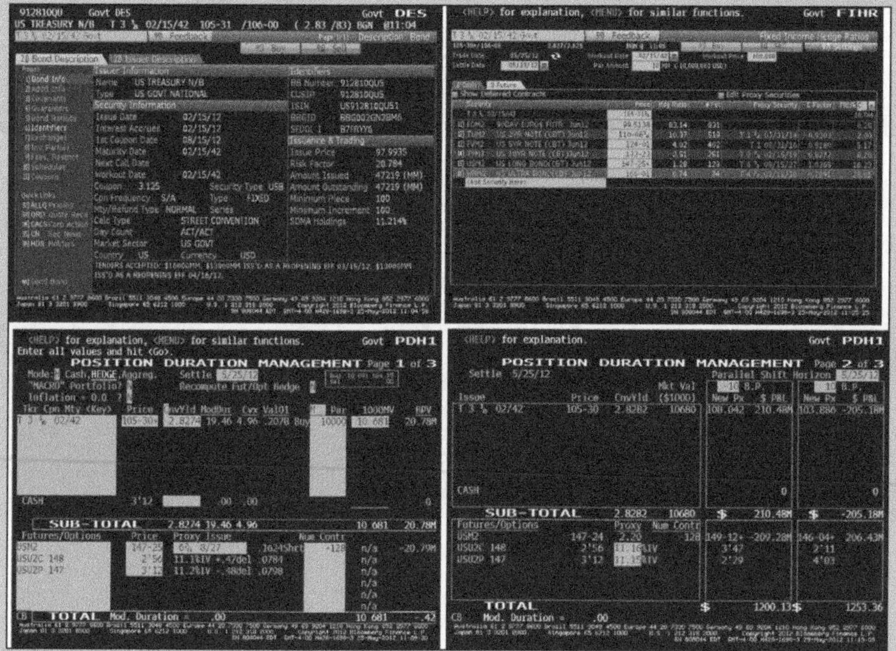

MARS (MULTI-ASSET RISK SYSTEM): MARS <ENTER>

Using the MARS screen, you can upload any fixed-income portfolio created in PRTU and then add futures options, caps, floors, and other derivatives ("Add Position" tab). Example: Hedging a bond portfolio with T-note futures puts:

1. On the MARS screen, import portfolio from PRTU (Portfolio (owned) tab).
2. Add futures options from the "Positions" tab (e.g., December 2012 put on a 10-year T-note futures contract with exercise price of 135).
3. Select positions on the MARS position screen (e.g., all bonds in the portfolio and 55 put options to hedge the portfolio).
4. Run scenarios on the Scenario screen (e.g., market value per percent price change, range plus or minus 20 percent, evaluation date of 12/13/2012 (near expiration), and scenario with puts and without puts).

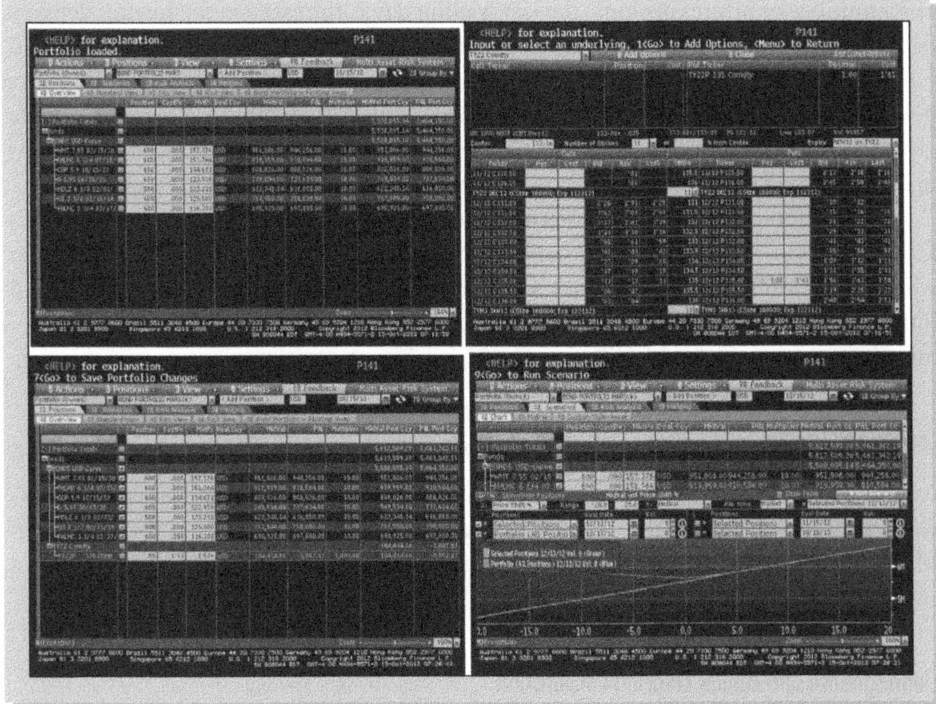

Option Trading—Microstructure

The primary objective of derivative exchanges offering options is to provide marketability to option contracts by linking brokers and dealers, standardizing contracts, establishing trading rules and procedures, guaranteeing and intermediating contracts through a clearinghouse, and providing continuous trading through electronic matching or with market makers, specialist, and locals.

Standardization

Similar to the futures exchanges, the option exchanges standardize contracts by setting expiration dates, exercise prices, and contract sizes on options. The expiration dates on options are defined in terms of an expiration cycle. For example, the March cycle has expiration months of March, June, September, and December. In a three-month option cycle, only the options with the three nearest expiration months trade at any time. Thus, as an option expires, the exchange introduces a new option. On many option contracts, the expiration day is the Saturday after the third Friday of the expiration month; the last day on which the expiring option trades, though, is Friday.

For a number of futures options, the last trading day is the same as the futures delivery date. For these options, exercising at expiration would be essentially a cash settlement. For other futures options, the expiration date on the option can be one to two weeks before the futures delivery period. Exercising such options at their expiration date gives the holder a futures position with a one- or two-week expiration and a current margin position equal to the difference between the futures and exercise prices.

In addition to setting the expiration, the exchanges also choose the exercise prices for each option, with as many as many as six strike prices associated with each option when an option cycle begins. Once an option with a specific exercise price has been introduced, it will remain listed until its expiration date. The exchange can, however, introduce new options with different exercise prices at any time.

Continuous Trading

As noted in Chapter 11, on the futures exchanges, continuous trading is typically provided through locals who are willing to take temporary positions to make a market. Many of the option exchanges, though, use market makers and specialist to ensure a continuous market.

Clearinghouse and Option Clearing Corporation

As we discussed in Chapter 11, to make derivative contracts more marketable, derivative exchanges provide a clearinghouse (CH) or Options Clearing Corporation (OCC), as it is referred to on the option exchange. In the case of options, the CH intermediates each transaction that takes place on the exchange and guarantees that all option writers fulfill the terms of their options if they are assigned. In addition, the CH also manages option exercises, receiving notices and assigning corresponding positions to clearing members.

As an intermediary, the CH functions by breaking up each option trade. After a buyer and seller complete an option trade, the CH steps in and becomes the effective buyer to the option seller and the effective seller to the option buyer. At that point, there is no longer any relationship between the original buyer and seller. If the buyer of a futures call option, for example, decides to later exercise, her broker will notify the exchange's CH (the brokerage firm may well be the clearing member). Overnight, the CH will select a writer from its pool of option sellers on the exercised futures call option and assign that writer the obligation of fulfilling the terms of the exercise request. Before trading commences on the following day, the CH will establish a long futures position at a futures price equal to the exercise price for the exercising option holder and a short futures position for the assigned writer. Once this is done, margins on both positions will be required and the positions will be marked to market at the current settlement price on the futures. As noted earlier, when the positions are marked to market, the exercising call holder's margin account on his long position will be equal to the difference between the futures price and the exercise price, $f_t - X$, while the assigned writer will have to deposit funds in a futures margin account equal to $f_t - X$ to satisfy his maintenance margin on his short futures position. At this point, the futures positions are indistinguishable from any other futures. If the futures option is a put, the same procedure applies except that holder takes a short position at f_t (when the exercised position is marked to market), with a margin account worth $X - f_t$, and the assigned writer is assigned a long position at f_t and must deposit $X - f_t$ to meet his margin.[4]

By breaking up each option contract, the CH makes it possible for option investors to close their positions before expiration. If a buyer of an option later becomes a seller of the same option, or vice versa, the CH computer will note the offsetting position in the option investor's account and will therefore cancel both entries. For example, suppose in January, Investor A buys a March 95 T-bill futures call for 10 (X = \$987,500, C = (10)(\$250) = \$2,500) from Investor B. When the CH breaks up the contract, it records Investor A's right to exercise with the CH (i.e., the right to take a long T-bill futures position at X) and Investor B's responsibility to take a short futures position at X if a party long on the contract decides to exercise and the CH subsequently assigns B the responsibility. The transaction between A and B would lead to the following entry in the clearing firms records:

January Clearinghouse Records for March 95 T-Bill Futures Call

1. Investor A has the *right* to exercise.
2. Investor B has *responsibility*.

Suppose that in late January, 60 days before the expirations on the T-bill futures and futures option, short-term rates have decreased resulting in the following prices:

- The price on the spot 151-day T-bill is at \$988,000.
- The price on the March T-bill futures is priced at its carrying cost value of \$995,956 ($f_t = S_0(1 + R_f)^T = f_t =$ \$988,000$(1.05)^{(60/365)}$ = \$995,956), where R_f = 60-day repo rate = .05).
- The price on the March 95 T-bill futures call is at \$9,000.

Seeing profit potential, suppose instead of exercising, Investor A decides to close her call position by selling a March 95 T-bill futures call at \$9,000 to Investor C. After the CH breaks up this contract, its records would have a new entry showing Investor A with the responsibility of taking a short position at X = \$987,500 if assigned. This entry, though, would cancel out Investor A's original entry giving her the right to take a long position at X = \$987,500:

February Clearinghouse Records for March 95 T-bill Futures Call

1. Investor A has the *right* to exercise.	Closed. (entries 1 and 4)
2. Investor B has *responsibility*.	
3. Investor C has the *right* to exercise.	
4. Investor A has *responsibility*.	

The CH would accordingly close Investor A's position. Thus, Investor A bought the call for $2,500 and then closed her position by simply selling the call for $9,000. Her call sale, in turn, represents an offsetting position and is referred to as an *offset* or *closing sale.*

If a writer also wanted to close his position at this date, he could do so by simply buying a March 95 T-bill futures call. For example, suppose Investor B feared that rates could go lower and therefore decided to close his short position by buying a March 95 T-bill futures call at $9,000 from Investor D. After this transaction, the CH would again step in, break up the contracts, and enter Investor B's and D's positions on its records. The CH's records would now show a new entry in which Investor B has the right to take a long position in the T-bill futures at $987,500. This entry, in turn, would cancel Investor B's previous entry in which he had a responsibility to take short position at $987,500 if assigned. The offsetting positions (the right to buy and the obligation to sell) cancel each other and the CH computer system simply erases both entries.

February Clearinghouse Records for March 95 T-bill Futures Call

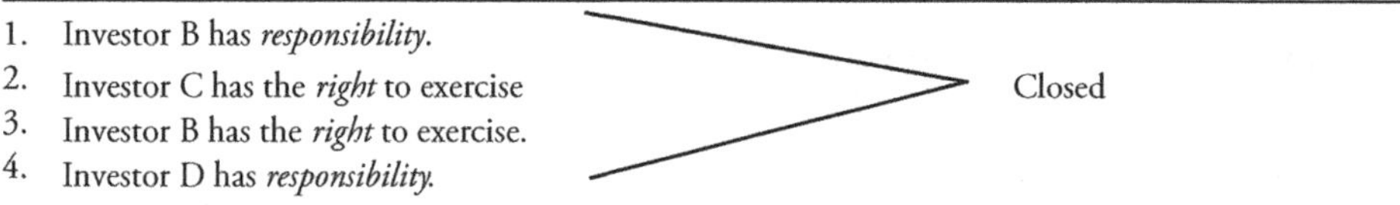

1. Investor B has *responsibility.*
2. Investor C has the *right* to exercise
3. Investor B has the *right* to exercise.
4. Investor D has *responsibility.*
Closed

Because Investor B's second transaction serves to close his opening position, it is referred to as a *closing purchase.* In this case, Investor B loses $6,500 by closing: selling the call for $2,500 and buying it back for $9,000.

Margin Requirements

To secure the CH's underlying positions, exchange-traded option contracts have initial and maintenance margin requirements. Different from the margin requirements on futures contracts, the margin requirements on options only apply to the option writer. On most exchanges, the initial margin is the amount of cash or cash equivalents that must be deposited by the writer. In addition to the initial margin, the writer also has a maintenance margin requirement with the brokerage firm in which he has to keep the value of his account equal to certain percentage of the initial margin value. Thus, if the value of option position moves against the writer, he is required to deposit addition cash or cash equivalents to satisfy his maintenance requirement.

In discussing margin requirements for futures options, one should remember that there are two sets of margins: a margin requirement for the option writer and a futures margin requirement that must be met if the futures option is exercised. If the futures option is exercised, both the holder and writer must establish and maintain the futures margin positions, with the writer's margin position on the option now being replaced by his new futures position.

Types of Option Transactions

The CH provides marketability by making it possible for option investors to close their positions instead of exercising. In general, there are four types of trades investors of an exchange-traded option can make: opening, expiring, exercising, and closing transactions. The *opening transaction* occurs when investors initially buy or sell an option. An *expiring transaction,* in turn, is allowing the option to expire: that is, doing nothing when the expiration date arrives because the option is worthless (out of the money). If it is profitable, a holder can exercise. Finally, holders or writers of options can close their positions with *offsetting* or *closing transactions* or orders.

As a general rule, option holders should close their positions rather than exercise. As we will discuss, if there is some time to expiration, an option holder who sells her option will receive a price that exceeds the exercise value. Because of this, many exchange-traded options are closed.

OTC Option Market Structure

In the OTC option market, interest rate option contracts are negotiable, with buyers and sellers entering directly into an agreement. Thus, the dealer's market provides option contracts that are tailor-made to meet the specific needs of the holder or writer. The market, though, does not have a clearinghouse to intermediate and guarantee the fulfillment of the terms of the option contract, nor market makers or specialists to ensure continuous markets; the options, therefore, lack marketability.

Since each OTC option has unique features, the secondary market is limited. Prior to expiration, holders of OTC options who want to close their position may be able to do so by selling their positions back to the original option writers or possibly to an OTC dealer who is making a market in the option. This type of closing is more likely to occur if the option writer is a dealer that can hedge option positions and also if the option is relatively standard (e.g., OTC option on a T-bond). Because of this inherent lack of marketability, the premiums on OTC options are higher than on exchange-traded options. For example, the bid-ask spread on an OTC T-bond is typically twice that of an exchange-traded T-bond futures option. Finally, since there is no CH to guarantee the option writer, OTC options also have different credit structures than exchange-traded options. Depending on who the option writer is, the contract may require initial and maintenance margins to be established.

Interest Rate Calls and Puts, Caps and Floors

Interest Rate Call

An *interest rate call,* also called a *caplet,* gives the buyer a payoff on a specified payoff date if a designated interest rate, such as the LIBOR, rises above a certain exercise rate, R_X. On the payoff date, if the rate is less than R_X, the interest rate call expires worthless; if the rate exceeds R_X, the call pays off the difference between the actual rate and R_X, times a notional principal, NP, times the fraction of the year specified in the contract. For example, given an interest rate call with a designated rate of LIBOR, $R_X = 6$ percent, $NP = \$1$ million, time period of 180 days, and day count convention of 180/360, the buyer would receive a \$5,000 payoff on the payoff date if the LIBOR were 7 percent: (.07 - .06)(180/360)(\$1,000,000) = \$5,000.

Interest rate call options are often written by commercial banks in conjunction with future loans they plan to provide to their customers. The exercise rate on the option usually is set near the current spot rate, with that rate often being tied to the LIBOR. For example, a company planning to finance a future \$10 million inventory 60 days from the present by borrowing from a bank at a rate equal to the LIBOR + 100 basis points at the start of the loan could buy from the bank an interest rate call option with an exercise rate equal to say 8 percent, expiration of 60 days, and notional principal of \$10 million. At expiation (60 days later) the company would be entitled to a payoff if rates were higher than 8 percent. Thus, if the rate on the loan were higher than 8 percent, the company would receive a payoff that would offset the higher interest on the loan.

Interest Rate Put

An *interest rate put,* also called a *floorlet,* gives the buyer a payoff on a specified payoff date if a designated interest rate is below the exercise rate, R_X. On the payoff date, if the rate is more than R_X, the interest rate put expires worthless; if the rate is less than R_X, the put pays off the difference between R_X and the actual rate times a notional principal, *NP,* times the fraction of the year specified in the contract. For example, given an interest rate put with a designated rate of LIBOR, $R_X = 6$ percent, NP = \$1 million, time period of 180 days, and day-count of 180/360, the buyer would receive a \$5,000 payoff on the payoff date if the LIBOR were 5 percent: (.06 – .05)(180/360)(\$1 million) = \$5,000.

A financial or nonfinancial corporation that is planning to make an investment at some future date could hedge that investment against interest rate decreases by purchasing an interest rate put from a commercial bank, investment banking firm, or dealer. For example, suppose that instead of needing to borrow \$10 million, the previous company was expecting a net cash inflow of \$10 million in 60 days from its operations and was planning to invest the funds in a 90-day bank CD paying the LIBOR. To hedge against any interest rate decreases, the company could purchase an interest rate put (corresponding to the bank's CD it plans to buy) from the bank with the put having an exercise rate of say 7 percent, expiration of 60 days, and notional principal of \$10 million. The interest rate put would provide a payoff for the company if the LIBOR were less than 7 percent, giving the company a hedge against interest rate decreases.

Fundamental Interest Rate Call and Put Positions

The profit graphs for interest rate calls and puts can be defined in terms of the profit and interest rate relations for the option. Exhibit 12.12 shows the profit graph and table for an interest rate call with the following terms: Exercise rate = 6 percent,

EXHIBIT 12.12 Interest Rate Call Option Exercise Rate = 6 Percent, Reference Rate = LIBOR, NP = \$10 Million, Period = .25 Year, Option Cost + \$12,500

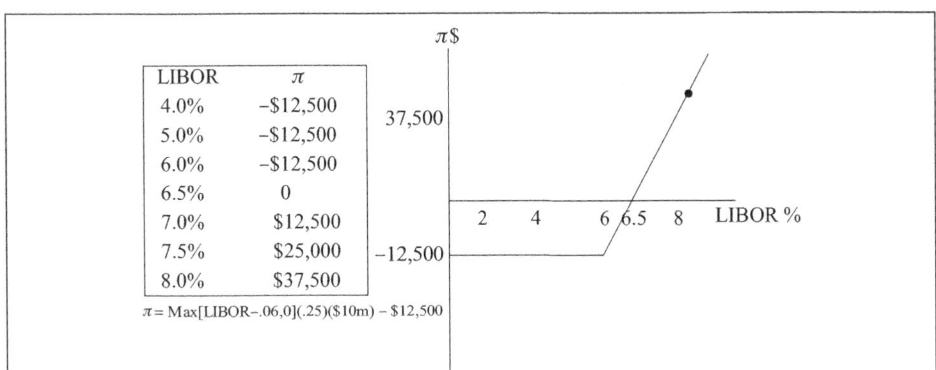

LIBOR	π
4.0%	-\$12,500
5.0%	-\$12,500
6.0%	-\$12,500
6.5%	0
7.0%	\$12,500
7.5%	\$25,000
8.0%	\$37,500

reference rate = LIBOR, NP = \$10 million, time period as proportion of a year = .25, and the cost of the option = \$12,500. As shown in the exhibit, if the LIBOR reaches 7.5 percent at expiration, the holder would realize a payoff of (.075 – .06)(\$10 million)(.25) = \$37,500 and a profit of \$25,000; if the LIBOR is 6.5 percent, the holder would breakeven with the \$12,500 payoff equal to the option's cost; if the LIBOR is 6 percent or less, there would be no payoff and the holder would incur a loss equal to the call premium of \$12,500. Just the opposite relationship between profits and rates exist for an interest rate put. Exhibit 12.13 shows the profit graph and table for an interest rate put with terms similar to those of the interest rate call.

Cap

A popular option offered by financial institutions in the OTC market is the *cap*. A plain-vanilla cap is a series of European interest rate call options—a portfolio of

EXHIBIT 12.13 Interest Rate Put Option Exercise Rate = 6 Percent, Reference Rate = LIBOR, NP = \$10 Million, Period = .25 Year, Option Cost = \$12,500

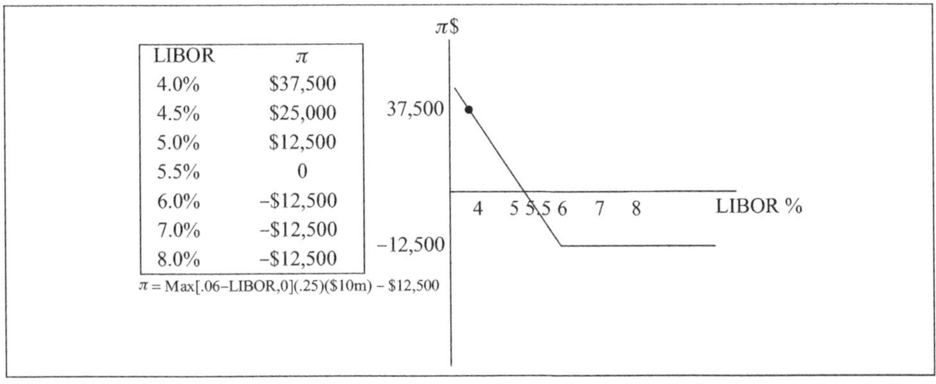

LIBOR	π
4.0%	\$37,500
4.5%	\$25,000
5.0%	\$12,500
5.5%	0
6.0%	-\$12,500
7.0%	-\$12,500
8.0%	-\$12,500

caplets. For example, a 7 percent, two-year cap on a three-month LIBOR, with a NP of $100 million, provides, for the next two years, a payoff every three months of (LIBOR – .07)(.25)($100 million) if the LIBOR on the reset date exceeds 7 percent and nothing if the LIBOR equals or is less than 7 percent. (Typically, the payment is not on the reset date, but rather on the next reset date three months later.) Caps are often written by financial institutions in conjunction with a floating-rate loan and are used by buyers as a hedge against interest rate risk. For example, a company with a floating-rate loan tied to the LIBOR could lock in a maximum rate on the loan by buying a cap corresponding to its loan. At each reset date, the company would receive a payoff from the caplet if the LIBOR exceeded the cap rate, offsetting the higher interest paid on the floating-rate loan; however, if rates decrease, the company would pay a lower rate on its loan while its losses on the caplet would be limited to the cost of the option. Thus, with a cap, the company would be able to lock in a maximum rate each quarter and still benefit with lower interest costs if rates decrease.

As an example, suppose the Zuber Development Company borrows $100 million from Commerce Bank to finance a two-year construction project. Suppose the loan is for two years, starting on March 1 at a known rate of 8 percent, then resets every three months—6/1, 9/1, 12/1, and 3/1—at the prevailing LIBOR plus 150 basis points. In entering this loan agreement, suppose the Zuber company is uncertain of future interest rates and therefore would like to lock in a maximum rate, while still benefiting from lower rates if the LIBOR decreases. To achieve this, suppose the Zuber company buys a cap corresponding to its loan from Commerce Bank for $300,000, with the following terms:

- The cap consist of seven caplets with the first expiring on 6/1/Y1 and the others coinciding with the loan's reset dates.
- Exercise rate on each caplet = 8 percent.
- NP on each caplet = $100 million.
- Reference rate = LIBOR.
- Time period to apply to the payoff on each caplet = 90/360 (Typically the day count convention is defined by actual number of days between reset dates.)
- Payment date on each caplet is at the loan's interest payment date, 90 days after the reset date
- The cost of the cap = $300,000; it is paid at beginning of the loan, 3/1/Y1.

On each reset date, the payoff on the corresponding caplet would be

$$\text{Payoff} = (\$100{,}000{,}000)\,(\text{Max}[\text{LIBOR} - .08,\ 0])(90/360)$$

With the 8 percent exercise rate (sometimes called the *cap rate*), the Zuber company would be able to lock in a maximum rate each quarter equal to the cap rate plus the basis points on the loan (9.5 percent), while still benefiting with lower interest costs if rates decrease. This can be seen in Exhibit 12.14, where the quarterly interests on the loan, the cap payoffs, and the hedged and unhedged rates are shown for different assumed

EXHIBIT 12.14 Hedging a Floating-Rate Loan with a Cap

Loan: Floating Rate Loan; Term = 2 years; Reset dates: 3/1, 6/1, 9/1, 12/1; Time frequency = .25; Rate = LIBOR + 150bps; Payment Date = 90 days after reset date

Cap: Cost of cap =$300,000; Cap Rate = 8%; Reference Rate = LIBOR; Time frequency = .25; Caplets' Expiration: On loan reset dates, starting at 6/1/Y1; Payoff made 90 days after reset date.

1 Reset Date	2 Assumed LIBOR	3 Loan Interest on Payment Date (LIBOR + 150bps) (.25)($100m)	4 Cap Payoff on Payment Date (Max[LIBOR-.08,0]) (.25)($100m)	5 Hedged Interest Payment Col. (3) - Col. (4)	6 Hedged Rate 4[Col (5)/$100m]	7 Unhedged Rate LIBOR + 150bps
3/1/Y1[n]	0.065					
6/1/Y1	0.070	$2,000,000	$0	$2,000,000	0.080	0.080
9/1/Y1	0.075	$2,125,000	$0	$2,125,000	0.085	0.085
12/1/Y1	0.080	$2,250,000	$0	$2,250,000	0.090	0.090
3/1/Y2	0.085	$2,375,000	$0	$2,375,000	0.095	0.095
6/1/Y2	0.090	$2,500,000	$125,000	$2,375,000	0.095	0.100
9/1/Y2	0.095	$2,625,000	$250,000	$2,375,000	0.095	0.105
12/1/Y2	0.100	$2,750,000	$375,000	$2,375,000	0.095	0.110
3/1/Y3		$2,875,000	$500,000	$2,375,000	0.095	0.115

[n] There is no cap on this date

LIBORs at each reset date on the loan. For the four reset dates from 3/1/Y2 to the end of the loan, the LIBOR exceeds 8 percent. In each of these cases, the higher interest on the loan is offset by the payoff on the cap yielding a hedged rate on the loan of 9.5 percent (the 9.5 percent rate excludes the $300,000 cost of the cap). For the first two reset dates on the loan, 6/1/Y1 and 9/1/Y1, the LIBOR is less than the cap rate. At these rates, there is no payoff on the cap, but the rates on the loan are lower with the lower LIBORs.

Floor

A plain-vanilla *floor* is a series of European interest rate put options—a portfolio of floorlets. For example, a 7 percent, two-year floor on a three-month LIBOR, with an NP of $100 million, provides, for the next two years, a payoff every three months of (.07 – LIBOR)(.25)($100 million) if the LIBOR on the reset date is less than 7 percent and nothing if the LIBOR equals or exceeds 7 percent. Floors are often purchased by investors as a tool to hedge their floating-rate investments against interest rate declines. Thus, with a floor, an investor with a floating-rate security is able to lock in a minimum rate each period, while still benefiting with higher yields if rates increase.

As an example, suppose Commerce Bank in the above example wanted to establish a minimum rate on the rates it was to receive on the two-year floating-rate loan it made to the Zuber Development Company. To this end, suppose the bank purchased from another financial institution a floor for $200,000 with the following terms corresponding to its floating-rate asset:

- The floor consist of seven floorlets with the first expiring on 6/1/Y1 and the others coinciding with the reset dates on the bank's floating-rate loan to the Zuber Company.
- Exercise rate on each floorlet = 8 percent.
- NP on each floorlet = $100 million.
- Reference rate = LIBOR.
- Time period to apply to the payoff on each floorlet = 90/360. Payment date on each floorlet is at the loan's interest payment date, 90 days after the reset date.
- The cost of the floor = $200,000; it is paid at beginning of the loan, 3/1/Y1.

On each reset date, the payoff on the corresponding floorlet would be

$$\text{Payoff} = (\$100{,}000{,}000)\ (\text{Max}[.08 - \text{LIBOR}, 0])(90/360)$$

With the 8 percent exercise rate, Commerce Bank would be able to lock in a minimum rate each quarter equal to the floor rate plus the basis points on the floating-rate asset (9.5 percent), while still benefiting with higher returns if rates increase. In Exhibit 12.15, Commerce Bank's quarterly interests received on its loan to Zuber, its floor payoffs, and its hedged and unhedged yields on its loan asset are shown for different assumed LIBORs at each reset date. For the first two reset dates on the loan, 6/1/Y1 and 9/1/Y1, the LIBOR is less than the floor rate of 8 percent. At these rates, there

EXHIBIT 12.15 Hedging a Floating-Rate Asset with a Floor

Asset: Floating rate loan made by bank; Term = 2 years; Reset dates: 3/1, 6/1, 9/1, 12/1; Time frequency = .25; Rate = LIBOR + 150bps; Payment Date = 90 days after reset date

Floor: Cost of floor =$200,000; Floor Rate = 8%; Reference Rate = LIBOR; Time frequency = .25; Floorlets' expirations: On loan reset dates, starting at 6/1/Y1; Payoff made 90 days after reset date.

1 Reset Date	2 Assumed LIBOR	3 Interest Received on Payment Date (LIBOR + 150bps) (.25)($100m)	4 Floor Payoff on Payment Date (Max[.08-LIBOR,0})(.25) ($100m)	5 Hedged Interest Income Col. (3) + Col. (4)	6 Hedged Rate 4[Col (5)/$100m]	7 Unhedged Rate LIBOR + 150bps
3/1/Y1[n]	0.065					
6/1/Y1	0.070	$2,000,000	$0	$2,000,000	0.080	0.080
9/1/Y1	0.075	$2,125,000	$250,000	$2,375,000	0.095	0.085
12/1/Y1	0.080	$2,250,000	$125,000	$2,375,000	0.095	0.090
3/1/Y2	0.085	$2,375,000	$0	$2,375,000	0.095	0.095
6/1/Y2	0.090	$2,500,000	$0	$2,500,000	0.100	0.100
9/1/Y2	0.095	$2,625,000	$0	$2,625,000	0.105	0.105
12/1/Y2	0.100	$2,750,000	$0	$2,750,000	0.110	0.110
3/1/Y3		$2,875,000	$0	$2,875,000	0.115	0.115

[n] There is no floor on this date

is a payoff on the floor that compensates the Commerce Bank for the lower interest it receives on the loan; this results in a hedged rate of return on the bank's loan asset of 9.5 percent (the cost of the floor excluded). For the five reset dates from 12/1/Y1 to the end of the loan, the LIBOR equals or exceeds the floor rate. At these rates, there is no payoff on the floor, but the rates the bank earns on its loan are greater, given the greater LIBORs.

Collars and Corridors

A *collar* is a combination of a long position in a cap and a short position in a floor with a different exercise rate. The sale of the floor is used to defray the cost of the cap. For example, the Zuber Development Company in our previous case could reduce the cost of the cap it purchased to hedge its floating-rate rate loan by selling a floor. By forming a collar to hedge its floating-rate debt, the Zuber company, for a lower net hedging cost, would still have protection against a rate movement against the cap rate, but it would have to give up potential interest savings from rate decreases below the floor rate. For example, suppose the Zuber company decided to defray the $300,000 cost of its 8 percent cap by selling a 7 percent floor for $200,000, with the floor having similar terms to the cap (effective dates on floorlet = reset dates, reference rate = LIBOR, NP on floorlets = $100 million, and time period for rates = .25). By using the collar instead of the cap, the Zuber company reduces its hedging cost from $300,000 to $100,000, and the company can still lock in a maximum rate on its loan of 9.5 percent. However, when the LIBOR is less than 7 percent, the company has to pay on the 7 percent floor, offsetting the lower interest costs it would pay on its loan.

An alternative financial structure to a collar is a corridor. A *corridor* is a long position in a cap and a short position in a similar cap with a higher exercise rate. The sale of the higher exercise-rate cap is used to partially offset the cost of purchasing the cap with the lower strike rate. For example, the Zuber company, instead of selling a 7 percent floor for $200,000 to partially finance the $300,000 cost of its 8 percent cap, could sell a 9 percent cap for say $200,000. If cap purchasers, however, believe there was a greater chance of rates increasing than decreasing, they would prefer the collar to the corridor as a tool for financing the cap. In practice, collars are more frequently used than corridors.

A *reverse collar* is combination of a long position in a floor and a short position in a cap with different exercise rates. The sale of the cap is used to defray the cost of the floor. For example, the Commerce Bank in our above floor example could reduce the $200,000 cost of the 8 percent floor it purchased to hedge the floating-rate loan it made to the Zuber company by selling a cap. Finally, instead of financing a floor with a cap, an investor could form a *reverse corridor* by selling another floor with a lower exercise rate.

Other Interest Rate Products

Caps and floors are one of the more popular interest rate products offered by the OTC derivative market. In addition to these derivatives, a number of other interest rate products have been created over the last decade to meet the many different interest rate hedging needs. Many of these products are variations of the generic OTC caps and floors; two of these to note are barrier options and path-dependent options.

Barrier options are options in which the payoff depends on whether an underlying security price or reference rate reaches a certain level. Barrier options can be classified as either knock-out or knock-in options: A ***knock-out option*** is one that ceases to exist once the specified barrier rate or price is reached; a ***knock-in option*** is one that comes into existence when the reference rate or price hits the barrier level.

Some caps and floors are structured so that their payoff is dependent on the path of the reference rate. An *average cap,* for example, is one in which the payoff depends on the average reference rate for each caplet. If the average is above the exercise rate, then all the caplets will provide a payoff; if the average is equal or below, the whole cap expires out of the money. Another type of path-dependent interest rate option is a *cumulative cap (Q-cap).* In a Q-cap, the cap seller pays the holder when the periodic interest on the accompanying floating-rate loan hits or exceeds a specified level. Q-caps, average caps, knock-in options, and knock-out options are sometimes referred to as exotic options. Exotic option products are nongeneric products that are created by financial engineers to meet specific hedging needs and return-risk profiles.

IRDD LIST INTEREST RATE DERIVATIVES

SWPM: Bloomberg Swaps and Interest Rate Derivatives screen.

SWPM analyzes, creates and values swaps and interest rate derivative contracts. The Caps/Floors Screen in SWPM can be used to set up caps, floors, and collars and to value them.

To access the screen: go to the "Products" tab, click "Cap" under the "Options" drop-down. This will bring up the main screen that can be used to create the cap. You can then change the settings on the main screen. For a floor, click "Floor" from the "Products" tab.

1. Options: Notional Principal, Payment Frequency, Cap Strike Rate, Spread (the amount of basis points to add or subtract from the floating rate, LIBOR).
2. Forward Graph Options: SWPM determines future cash flows at each reset date based on the forward rate at that date. The user can select which yield curve the forward rates are to be determined. On the "Curve" screen ("Curve" tab), one can view the forward graph and make shift adjustment.
3. Discount Rate Option: SWPM also discounts cash flows to determine the market value (shown at the bottom of main screen; the user can also select which yield curve to be used for discounting).

Tab Screens

1. "Details" tab shows the detail of the swap.
2. "Resets" tab shows the reset rate at each effective date (forward LIBOR plus basis point you added to spread). One can change the rates from this tab.
3. "Cashflow" tab shows cash flows for each counterparty.
4. "Scenario" tab allows one to make scenario changes.

The cap is valued by using a forward rate curve and the Black futures option model (discussed in Chapter 13); each caplet is valued in the cash flow table.

(*Continued*)

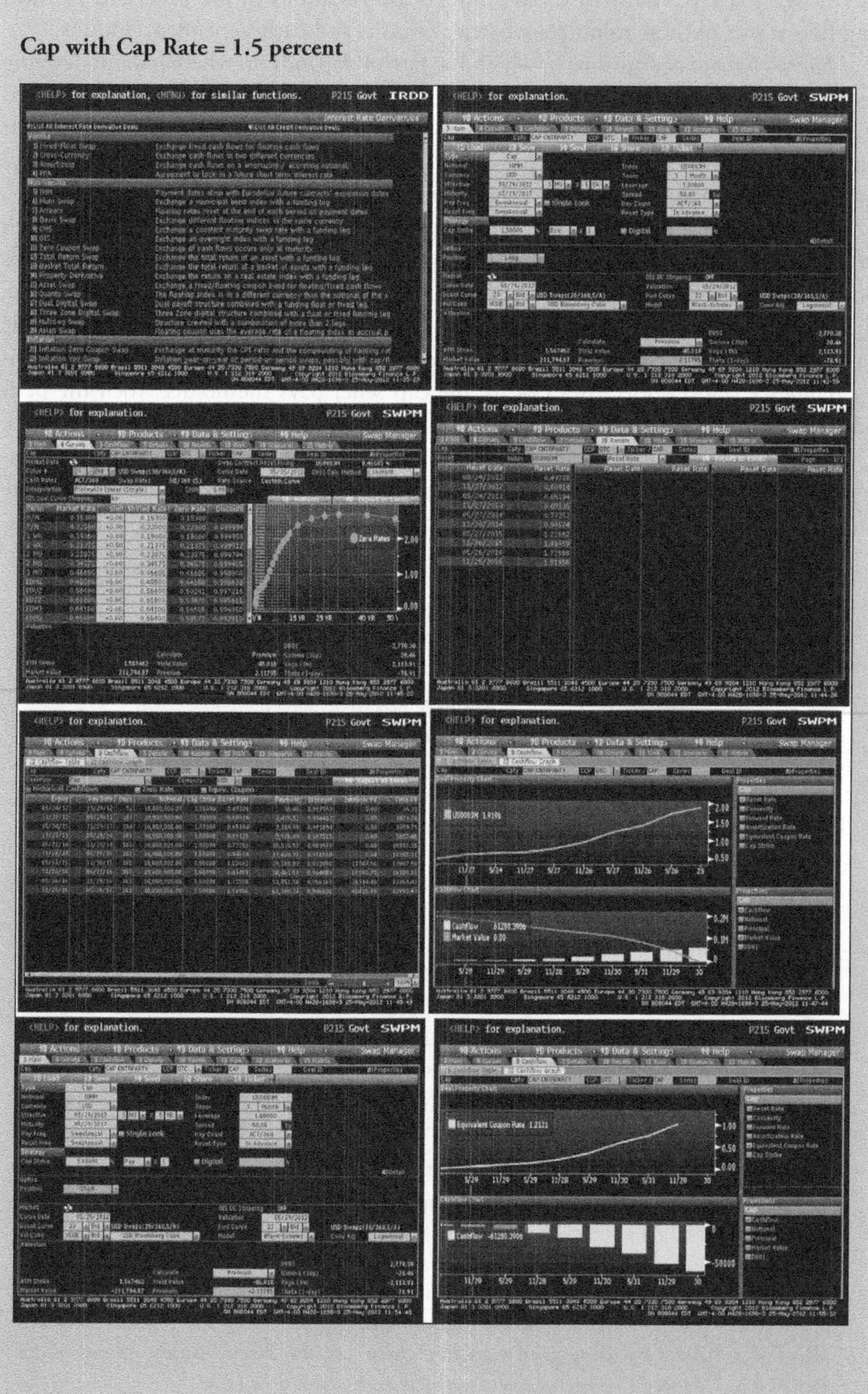
Cap with Cap Rate = 1.5 percent

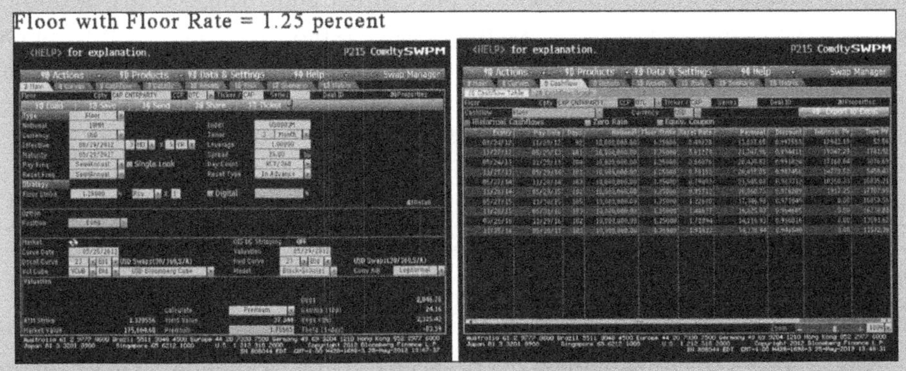

Floor with Floor Rate = 1.25 percent

SAVING AND LOADING A SWAP TO A PORTFOLIO

To save and load the cap position created in SWPM, go to the "Action" tab and click "Save." This will bring up an input box. In the box, name the interest rate derivative position (Custom ID), click "Add to Portfolio" box, and then click "Save." Saved derivative position can be identified by clicking "Load" in the "Actions" tab, analyzed using MARS, and combined with portfolios created in PRTU.

MARS (MULTIASSET RISK SYSTEM): MARS <ENTER>

Using the MARS screen, one can upload any fixed-income portfolio created and then add futures options, caps, floors, and other derivatives ("Add Position" tab). MARS can also add swap positions, FRAs, caps, floors, and other interest rate products created and saved in SWPM.

See previous Bloomberg Box and Chapter 14 Bloomberg Boxes for examples.

Option Price Relationships

The price of an option is a function of the time to expiration, the strike price, the security price, and the volatility of the underlying security. These factors and how the option price is determined is the basis of the option pricing model. The pricing of interest rate options using the binomial interest rate model and the Black futures option model is examined in Chapter 13. Here, we identify some of the factors that determine the prices of spot and futures interest rate options.

Call Price Relationships

Boundary Conditions and Time Value Premium

The price of any option is constrained by certain boundary conditions. One of those boundary conditions is the intrinsic value. By definition, the *intrinsic value* (*IV*) of a call at a time prior to expiration (let t signify any time prior to expiration), or at expiration (T again signifies expiration date) is the maximum of the difference between the price of the underlying security or futures (S_t or f_t) and the exercise price or zero: IV = Max[f_t – X, 0] or Max[S_t – X, 0]. The intrinsic value can be used as a reference to define *in-the-money*, *on-the-money*, and *out-of-the-money* calls. Specifically, an in-the-money call is one in which the price of the underlying security or futures contract exceeds the exercise price; as a result, its IV is positive. When the price of the security or futures is equal to the exercise price, the call's IV is zero and the call is said to be on the money. Finally, if the exercise price exceeds the security or futures price, the call would be out of the money and the IV would be zero:

Type	Spot Call	Futures Call
In-the-Money	$S_t > X \geq \text{IV} > 0$	$f_t > X \geq \text{IV} > 0$
On-the-Money	$S_t = X \geq \text{IV} = 0$	$f_t = X \geq \text{IV} = 0$
Out-of-the-Money	$S_t < X \geq \text{IV} = 0$	$f_t < X \geq \text{IV} = 0$

For an American futures option, the IV defines a boundary condition in which the price of a call has to trade at a value at least equal to its IV: $C_t \geq \text{Max}[f_t - X, 0]$. If this condition does not hold ($C_t < \text{Max}[f_t - X, 0]$), an arbitrageur could buy the call, exercise, and close the futures position. For example, suppose a T-bill futures contract expiring in 182 days were trading at $987,862 (index = 95.1448) and a 95 T-bill futures call expiring in 182 days (X = $987,500) were trading at $100, below its IV of $362. Arbitrageurs could realize risk-free profits by (1) buying the call at $100, (2) exercising the call to obtain a margin account worth $f_t - X$ = $987,862 − $987,500 = $362 plus a long position in the T-bill futures contract priced $987,862, and (3) immediately closing the long futures position by taking an offsetting short position at $987,862. Doing this, arbitrageurs would realize a risk-free profit of $262. By pursuing this strategy, though, arbitrageurs would push the call premium up until it is at least equal to its IV of $f_t - X$ = $362 and the arbitrage profit is zero. Note that this arbitrage strategy requires that the option be exercised immediately. Thus, the condition applies only to an American futures option. The boundary conditions for European futures, American spot, and European spot interest rate options are explained in many derivative texts.

The other component of the value of an option is the *time value premium* (*TVP*). By definition, the TVP of a call is the difference between the call's price and IV: TVP = $C_t - IV$. For example, if the 95 T-bill futures call expiring in 182 days (X = $987,500) was trading at $562 when the T-bill futures contract expiring in 182 days was trading at $987,862 (index = 95.1448), the IV would be $362 and the TVP would be $200. It should be noted that the TVP decreases as the time remaining to expiration decreases.

Call Price Curve

Graphically, the relationship between C_t, TVP, and IV is depicted in Exhibit 12.16. In the figure, graphs plotting the call price and the IV (on the vertical axis) against the futures price (on the horizontal axis) are shown for the American 95 T-bill futures call option. The IV line shows the linear relationship between the IV and the futures price. The line emanates from a horizontal intercept equal to the exercise price. When the price of the futures is equal or less than the exercise price, the IV is equal to zero; when the futures price exceeds the exercise price, the IV is positive and increases as the futures price increases. The IV line, in turn, serves as a reference for the call price curve (CC). The noted arbitrage condition dictates that the price of the call cannot trade (for long) at a value below its IV. Graphically, this means that the call price curve cannot go

EXHIBIT 12.16 Call and Futures Price Relation

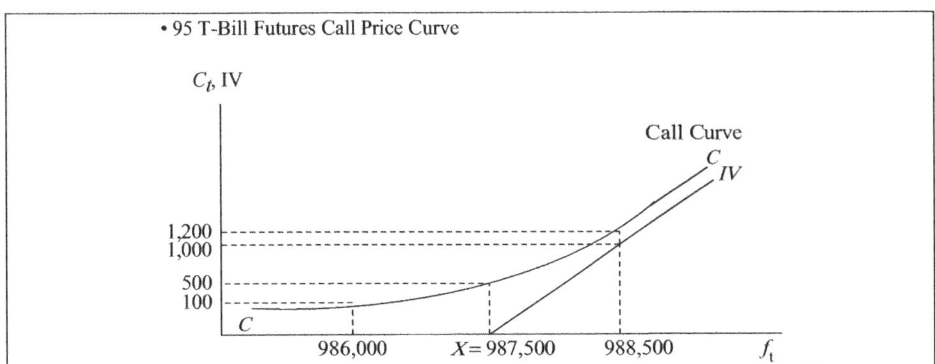

below the IV line. Furthermore, the IV line would be the call price curve if we are at expiration since the TVP = 0 and thus C_T = IV. The call price curve (CC) in Exhibit 12.16 shows the positive relationship between C_t and f_t. The vertical distance between the CC curve and the IV line, in turn, measures the TVP. The CC curve for a comparable call with a greater time to expiration would be above the CC curve, reflecting the fact that the call premium increases as the time to expiration increases. It should be noted that the slopes of the CC curves approach the slope of the IV line when the security price is relatively high (known as a *deep in-the-money-call*), and it approaches zero (flat) when the price of the futures is relatively low (a *deep out-of-the-money call*).

Variability

The call price curve illustrates the positive relation between a call price and the underlying security or futures price and the time to expiration. An option's price also depends on the volatility of the underlying security or futures contract. Since a long call position is characterized by unlimited profits if the security or futures increases but limited losses if it decreases, a call holder would prefer more volatility rather than less. Specifically, greater variability suggests, on the one hand, a given likelihood that the security will increase substantially in price, causing the call to be more valuable. However, greater volatility also suggests a given likelihood of the security price decreasing substantially. However, given that a call's losses are limited to just the premium when the security price is equal to the exercise price or less, the extent of the price decrease would be inconsequential to the call holder. Thus, the market will value a call option on a volatile security or contract more than a call on one with lower variability.

Put Price Relationships

Boundary Conditions

Analogous to calls, the price of a put at a given point in time prior to expiration (P_t) also can be explained by reference to its IV, boundary conditions, and TVP. In the case of puts, the IV is defined as the maximum of the difference between the exercise price and the security or futures price or zero: IV = Max[$X - f_t$, 0] or Max[$X - S_t$, 0]. Similar to calls, in-the-money, on-the-money, and out-of-the-money puts are defined as:

Type	Spot Put	Futures Put
In-the-Money:	$X > S_t \geq \text{IV} > 0$	$X > f_t \geq \text{IV} > 0$
On-the-Money:	$X = S_t \geq \text{IV} = 0$	$X = f_t \geq \text{IV} = 0$
Out-of-the-Money	$X < S_t \geq \text{IV} = 0$	$X < f_t \geq \text{IV} = 0$

For an American futures option, the IV defines a boundary condition in which the price of the put has to trade at a price at least equal to its IV: $P_t \geq \text{Max}[X - f_t, 0]$. If this condition does not hold, an arbitrageur could buy the put, exercise, and close the futures position. For example, suppose a T-bill futures contract expiring in 182 days were trading at \$987,200 and a 95 T-bill futures put expiring in 182 days (X = \$987,500) were trading at \$100, below its IV of \$300. Arbitrageurs could realize risk-free profits by (1) buying the put at \$100, (2) exercising the put to obtain a margin account worth $X - f_t$ = \$987,500 – \$987,200 = \$300 plus a short position in the T-bill futures contract priced \$987,200, and (3) immediately closing the short futures position by taking an offsetting short position at \$987,200. Doing this, the arbitrageur would realize a risk-free profit of \$200. By pursuing this strategy, though, arbitrageurs would push the put premium up until it is at least equal to its IV of $X - f_t$ = \$300 and the arbitrage profit is zero.

Put Price Curve

Similar to calls, the TVP for a put is: TVP = P_t – IV. The relation between the price of a put and the IV to the underlying futures price is shown in Exhibit 12.17. The figure shows a negatively sloped put-price curve (PP) and a negatively sloped IV line going from the horizontal intercept (where $f_t = X$) to the vertical intercept where the IV is equal to the exercise price when the futures is trading at zero (i.e., IV = X, when $f_t = 0$). The slope of the PP curve approaches the slope of the IV line for relatively low futures prices (*deep in-the-money puts*) and approaches zero for relatively large futures prices (*deep out-of-the money puts*).

Variability

Like calls, the price of a put option depends not only on the underlying security or futures price and time to expiration, but also on the volatility of the underlying security

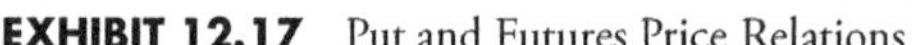

EXHIBIT 12.17 Put and Futures Price Relations

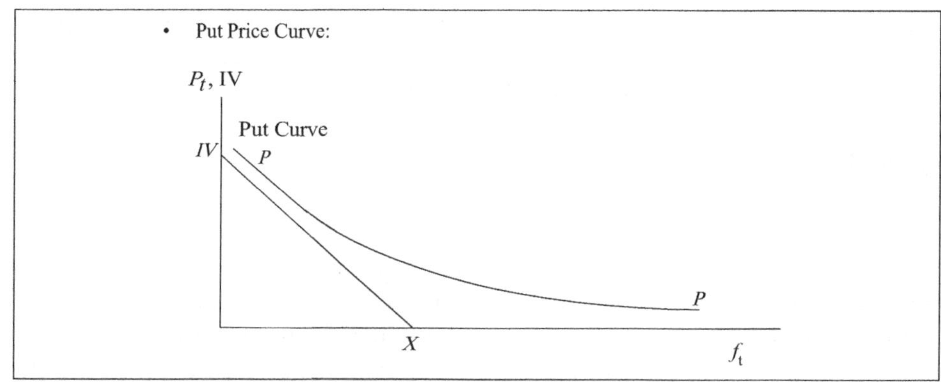

or futures contract. Since put losses are limited to the premium when the price of the underlying security or futures is greater than or equal to the exercise price, put buyers, like call buyers, will value puts on securities or futures with greater variability more than those with lower variability.

VOLATILITY: BLOOMBERG HVG AND GV SCREENS

The volatility of the underlying futures and spot contracts are shown on the HVG and GV screens. These screens can be accessed from the futures menu screen.

For futures on long-term Treasuries (USA) <Comdty>:

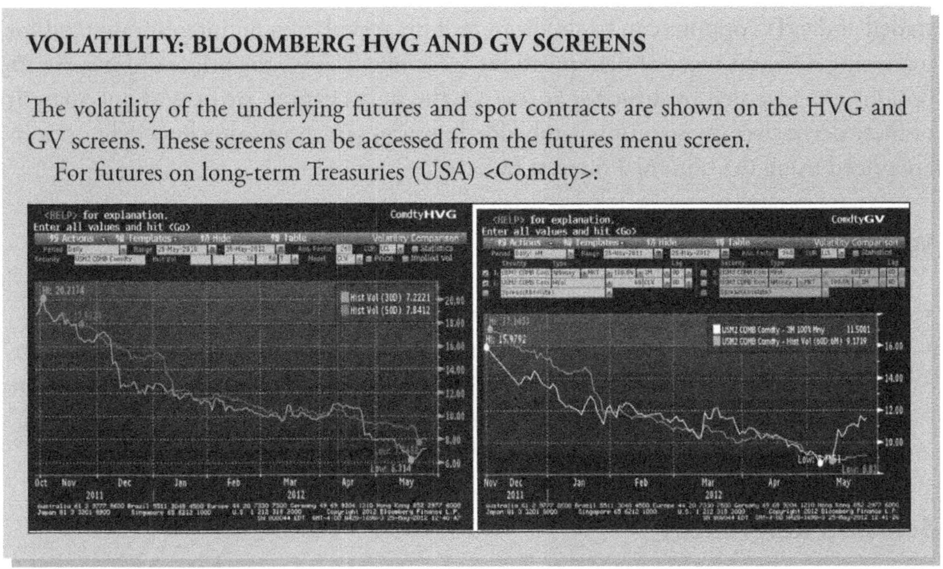

Closing Instead of Exercising

As noted earlier, if there is some time to expiration, an option holder who sells her option will receive a price that exceeds the exercise value; that is, she will receive a price equal to the IV plus a TVP. If she exercises, though, her exercise value is only equal to the IV. As a result, by exercising instead of closing, she loses the TVP. Thus, an option holder in most cases should close her position instead of exercising. There are some exceptions to the general rule of closing instead of exercising. For example, if an American option on a security that was to pay a high coupon that exceeded the TVP on the option, then it would be advantageous to exercise.

Put-Call Parity

Since the prices of options on the same security are derived from that security's price, it follows that the put and call prices are related. The relationship governing the prices of spot put and call option and futures call and put options is known as *put-call parity:*

$$\text{Spot Options: } P_0 - C_0 + S_0 = \frac{X}{(1+R_f)^T}$$

$$\text{Futures Options: } P_0 - C_0 = \frac{X - f_0}{(1+R_f)^T}$$

Put-call parity is explained in many derivative and investment books.

Conclusion

In this chapter, we have provided an overview of bond and interest rate options by defining option terms and markets, examining the fundamental option strategies, and describing the basic option pricing relations. Like interest rate futures, exchange-traded and OTC options can be used as a tool for speculating on interest rates and for managing different types of debt positions. Also like futures, the prices of interest rate options are governed by arbitrage forces. In the next chapter, we extend our analysis of these derivatives by examining embedded options and examining how debt options are priced using the binomial interest rate tree.

Website Information

- Information on the CBOE: www.cboe.com.
- For market information and prices on futures options, go to CME: www.cme.com.
- Current prices on futures option contracts on Eurodollar and other futures can be obtained by going to www.cme.com and clicking on "Quotes" in "Market Data" and then clicking on "Interest Rate Products."

Selected References

Abken, P. 1989. Interest rate caps, collars, and floors. *Federal Reserve Bank of Atlanta Economic Review* 74:2–24.

Abken, P. A. 1994. Introduction to over-the-counter (OTC) options. In J. C. Francis and A. S. Wolf, eds., *The Handbook of Interest Rate Risk Management*. New York: Irwin Professional, 1994, Chapter 25.

Bhattacharya, A. K. 2001. Interest-rate caps and floors and compound options. In F. Fabozzi, ed., *The Handbook of Fixed Income Securities*, 6th ed. New York: McGraw-Hill.

Black, F., and M. Scholes. 1973. The pricing of options and corporate liabilities. *Journal of Political Economy* 81:637–659.

Dehnad, K. 1994. Characteristics of OTC options. In J. C. Francis and A. S. Wolf, eds., *The Handbook of Interest Rate Risk Management*. New York: Irwin Professional.

Johnson, H. 1987. Options on the maximum and minimum of several assets. *Journal of Financial and Quantitative Analysis* 22:277–283.

Johnson, R. S. 2009. *Introduction to Derivatives: Options, Futures, and Swaps*. New York: Oxford University Press.

Kolb, R. W., and R. Chiang. 1981. Improving hedging performance using interest rate futures. *Financial Management* 10:72–79.

Rendleman, R., and B. Bartter. 1980. The pricing of options on debt securities. *Journal of Financial and Quantitative Analysis* 15:11–24.

Toevs, A., and D. Jacob. 1986. Futures and alternative hedge methodologies. *Journal of Portfolio Management* 12:60–70.

Bloomberg Exercises

1. Find descriptions, recent prices, and other information on different types of exchange-traded futures options contracts. Type CTM to bring up "Contract

Table" menu, click "Bond" on the CTM Screen, find the contract of interest, and bring up the contract's menu screen: Ticker <Comdty>. Screens to consider: DES, OTD, OMON, and OMST.

2. Find descriptions, recent prices, outstanding contracts, and other information on exchange-traded interest rate futures options contracts (e.g., three-month Eurodollar futures listed on the CME). Type CTM to bring up "Contract Table" menu, click "Interest Rates," on the CTM screen, find the contract of interest, and bring up the contract's menu screen: Ticker <Comdty>. Screens to consider: DES, OTD, OMON, and OMST.
3. Select an exchange-listed futures option on a T-Bond or T-Note (use CTM). Using the Bloomberg OSA screen, evaluate the following strategies with a profit graph:
   a. Call purchase
   b. Call sale
   c. Put purchase
   d. Put sale
   e. Covered call write
   f. Covered put write
   g. Straddle purchase
   h. Straddle sale
4. Select an exchange-listed option on a Eurodollar futures (use CTM to find the futures option). Using the Bloomberg OSA screen, evaluate the following strategies with a profit graph:
   a. Call purchase
   b. Call sale
   c. Put purchase
   d. Put sale
   e. Covered call write
   f. Covered put write
   g. Straddle purchase
   h. Straddle sale
5. Identify several option strategies that you would consider if you expected intermediate or long-term yields to decrease in the next three months. Select a T-note or T-bond futures options and analyze your strategies using Bloomberg's OSA screen.
6. Identify several option strategies that you would consider if you expected intermediate or long-term yields to increase in the next three months. Select a T-note or T-bond futures options and analyze your strategies using Bloomberg's OSA screen.
7. Identify several option strategies that you would consider if you expected intermediate or long-term yields to be stable over the next three months. Select a T-note or T-bond futures options and analyze your strategies using Bloomberg's OSA screen.
8. Select a fixed-income ETF (e.g., government bond ETF, investment-grade corporate, or combination of government and corporate): ETF <Enter>. Select a put futures option on a government bond that could be used to provide downside

protection (e.g., option on 20-year T-bond futures, USA <Comdty>). Using the OSA screen for the futures contract, analyze your hedging strategy using a profit or value graph.

9. Select a fixed-income ETF (e.g., Government bond ETF, investment-grade corporate, or combination of government and corporate): ETF <Enter>. Select a call futures option on a government bond that could be used to set up a covered call write strategy (e.g., option on 20-year Tbond futures, USA <Comdty>). Using the OSA screen for the futures contract, analyze your hedging strategy using a profit or value graph.
10. Select a fixed-income portfolio that you have constructed from a previous chapter exercise (or construct a new bond portfolio in PRTU). Using the MARS screen, import your portfolio from PRTU to MARS and then add futures put options to hedge the portfolio. Run scenarios of your portfolio (e.g., market value per percent price change, range plus or minus 20 percent, and evaluation date near expiration) with and without the puts.
11. Use the Bloomberg SWPM screen to create and analyze a cap. Tabs to include in your analysis: Details, Resets, Cashflows, and Curves. Save the cap position you created in SWPM: go to the "Action" tab and click "Save"; in the box, name the swap position (Custom ID), and click "Save." Go to IRDL to identify your cap.
12. Use the Bloomberg SWPM screen to create and analyze a floor. Tabs to include in your analysis: Details, Resets, Cashflows, and Curves. Save the floor position you created in SWPM: go to the "Action" tab and click "Save"; in the box, name the swap position (Custom ID), click "Save." Go to IRDL to identify your floor.
13. Use the Bloomberg SWPM screen to create and analyze a collar. Tabs to include in your analysis: Details, Resets, Cashflows, and Curves. Save the collar position you created in SWPM: go to the "Action" tab and click "Save"; in the box, name the swap position (Custom ID), click "Save." Go to IRDL to identify your collar.

Notes

1. Before 1936, the U.S. futures exchanges offered futures options for a number of years. In 1936, though, the instruments were banned when U.S. security regulations were tightened following the 1929 stock market crash. Futures options have been available on foreign exchanges for a number of years.
2. Although many OTC options are exercised, most exchange-traded options are not exercised, but instead are closed by holders selling contracts and writers buying contracts. As a starting point in developing a fundamental understanding of options, though, it is helpful to first examine what happens if the option is exercised.
3. In many of our examples we assume calls and puts with the same terms are priced the same. We do this for simplicity. In most cases, though, calls and puts with the same terms are not priced equally.
4. On some exchanges, assignment of exercise is random; on other exchanges it is based on first in and first out: the clearing member with the oldest written position will be assigned first.

CHAPTER 13

The Valuation of Bonds with Embedded Options and Debt Options—The Binomial Interest Rate Tree

Introduction

Many bonds have a call feature giving the issuer the right to buy back the bond from the bondholder. In addition to callable bonds, there are also putable bonds, giving the bondholder the right to sell the bond back to the issuer, sinking fund bonds in which the issuer has the right to call the bond or buy it back in the market, mortgage- and asset-backed securities with prepayment options on the underlying collateral, and convertible bonds that give the bondholder the right to convert the bond into specified number of shares of stock.

The inclusion of option features in a bond contract makes the evaluation of such bonds more difficult. A 10-year, 10 percent callable bond issued when interest rate are relatively high may be similar to a 3-year bond given that a likely interest rate decrease would lead the issuer to buy the bond back. Determining the value of such a bond requires taking into account not only the value of the bond's cash flow, but also the value of the call option embedded in the bond. One way to capture the impact of a bond's option feature on its value is to construct a model that incorporates the random paths that interest rates follow over time. Such a model allows one to value a bond's option at different interest rate levels. One such model is the *binomial interest rate tree.* Patterned after the binomial option pricing model, this model assumes that interest rates follow a binomial process in which in each period the rate is either higher or lower. In this chapter, we examine how to evaluate bonds with option features using a binomial interest rate tree approach. We begin by defining a binomial tree for spot rates and then showing how the tree can be used to value a callable bond. After examining the valuation of a callable bond, we next show the valuation of putable bonds, convertible bonds, and the bond and interest rate options that were examined in Chapter 12. After explaining how the binomial tree can be used to value bonds options, we take up the more technical subject of how the tree can be estimated.

Binomial Interest Rate Model

A binomial model of interest rates assumes a spot rate of a given maturity follows a binomial process where in each period it has either a higher or lower rate. For example, assume that a one-period, riskless spot rate (S) follows a process in which in each period the rate is equal to a proportion u times its beginning-of-the-period value or a proportion d times its initial value, where u is greater than d. After one period, there would be two possible one-period spot rates: $S_u = uS_0$ and $S_d = dS_0$. If the proportions u and d were constant over different periods, then after two periods there would be three possible rates. That is, as shown in Exhibit 13.1, after two periods the one-period spot rate can either equal: $S_{uu} = u^2S_0$, $S_{ud} = udS_0$, or $S_{dd} = d^2S_0$. Similarly, after three periods, the spot rate could take on four possible values: $S_{uuu} = u^3S_0$, $S_{uud} = u^2dS_0$, $S_{udd} = ud^2S_0$, and $S_{ddd} = d^3S_0$.

To illustrate, suppose the current one-period spot rate is 10 percent, the upward parameter u is 1.1 and the downward parameter d is .95. As shown in Exhibit 13.2, the two possible one-period rates after one period are 11 percent and 9.5 percent, the three possible one-period rates after two periods are 12.1 percent, 10.45 percent, and 9.025 percent, and the four possible rates are three periods are 13.31 percent, 11.495 percent, 9.927, and 8.574 percent.

EXHIBIT 13.1 Binomial Tree of One-Period Spot Rates

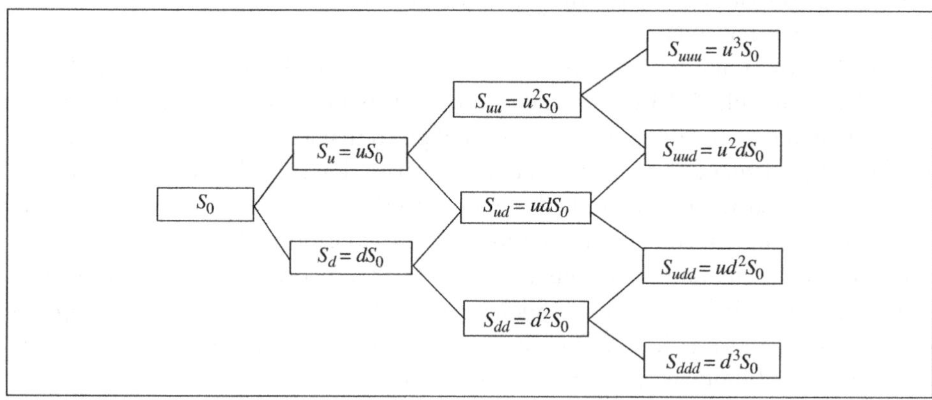

EXHIBIT 13.2 Binomial Tree: $u = 1.1$, $d = 0.95$, $S_0 = 0.10$

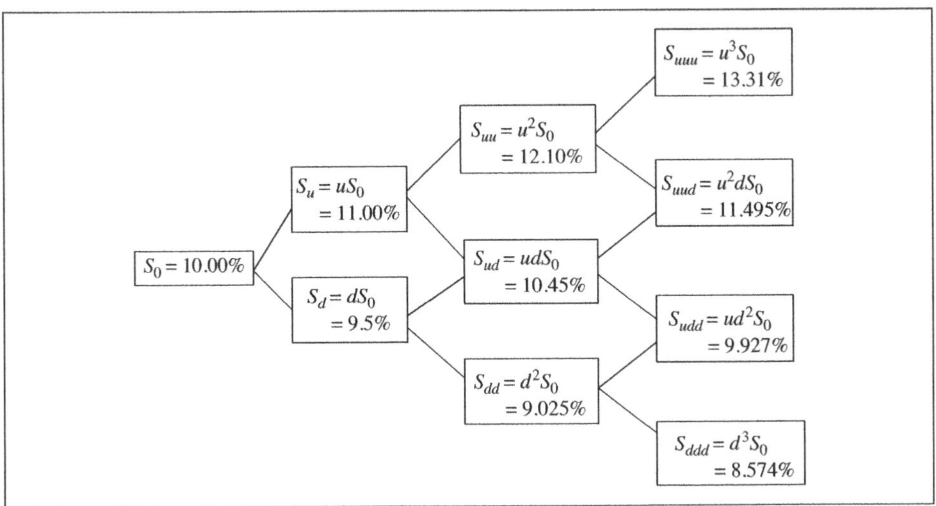

Valuing a Two-Period Bond

Given the possible one-period spot rates, suppose we wanted to value a bond that matures in two periods. Assume that the bond has no default risk or embedded option features and that it pays an 8 percent coupon each period and a \$100 principal at maturity. Since there is no default or call risk, the only risk an investor assumes in buying this bond is market risk. This risk occurs at time period one. At that time, the original two-period bond will have one period to maturity where there is a certain payoff of \$108. We don't know, though, whether the one-period rate will be 11 percent or 9.5 percent. If the rate is 11 percent, then the bond would be worth $B_u = 108/1.11 = 97.297$; if the rate is 9.5 percent, the bond would be worth $B_d = 108/1.095 = 98.630$. Given these two possible values in Period 1, the current value of the two-period bond can be found by calculating the present value of the bond's expected cash flow in Period 1. If we assume that there is an equal probability (q) of the one-period spot rate being higher ($q = .5$) or lower ($1 - q = .5$), then the current value of the two-period bond (B_0) would be 96.330 (see Exhibit 13.3):

$$B_0 = \frac{q\left[B_u + C\right] + (1-q)\left[B_d + C\right]}{1 + S_0}$$

$$B_0 + \frac{.5[97.297 + 8] + .5[98.630 + 8]}{1.10} = 96.330$$

Now suppose that the two-period, 8 percent bond has a call feature that allows the issuer to buy back the bond at a call price (CP) of 98. Using the binomial tree approach, this call option can be incorporated into the valuation of the bond by determining at each node in Period 1 whether or not the issuer would exercise his right to call. The

EXHIBIT 13.3 Value of Two-Period Option-Free Bond

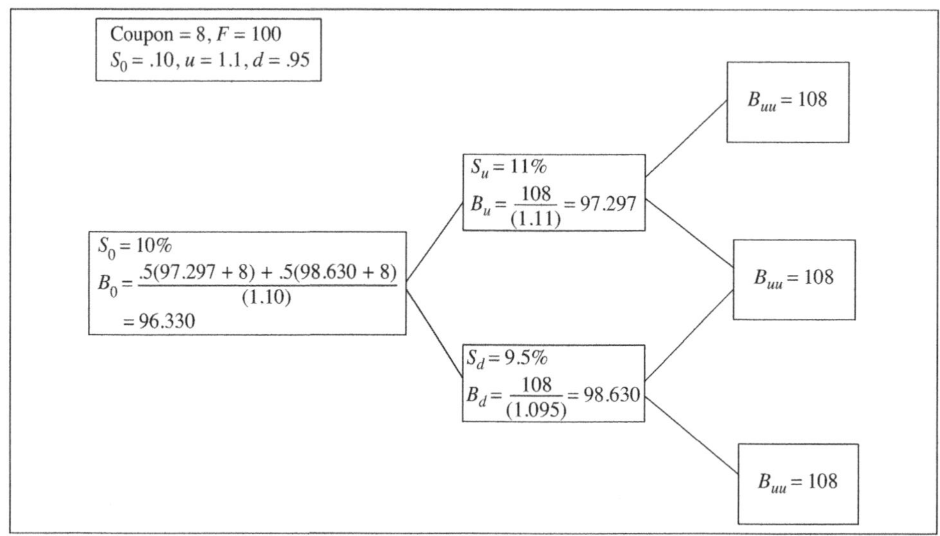

issuer will find it profitable to exercise whenever the bond price is above the call price (assuming no transaction or holding costs). This is the case when the one-period spot rate is 9.5 percent in Period 1 and the bond is priced at 98.630. The price of the bond in this case would be the call price of 98. It is not profitable, however, for the issuer to exercise the call at the spot rate of 11 percent when the bond is worth 97.297; the value of the bond in this case remains at 97.297.[1] In general, since the bond is only exercised when the call price is less than the bond value, the value of the callable bond in Period 1 is therefore the minimum of its call price or its binomial value:

$$B_t^C = \text{Min}[B_t, CP]$$

Rolling the two callable bond values in Period 1 of 97.297 and 98 to the present, we obtain a current price of 96.044:

$$B_t^C = \frac{.5[97.297 + 8] + .5[98 + 8]}{1.10} = 96.044$$

As we should expect, the bond's embedded call option lowers the value of the bond from 96.330 to 96.044. The value of the callable bond in terms of the binomial tree is shown in the top figure of Exhibit 13.4. Note, at each of the nodes in Period 1, the value of the callable bond is determined by selecting the minimum of the binomial bond value or the call price, and then rolling the callable bond values to the current period.

Instead of using a price constraint at each node, the price of the callable bond can alternatively be found by determining the value of call option at each node, V_t^C, and then subtracting that value from the noncallable bond value ($B_t^C = B_t^{NC} - V_t^C$). In this two-period case, the values of the call option are equal to their intrinsic values, IV (or exercise values). The intrinsic value is the maximum of B_t^{NC} – CP or zero:

$$V_t^C = \text{Max}[B_t^{NC} - \text{CP}, 0]$$

As shown in the bottom figure of Exhibit 13.4, the two possible call values in Period 1 are zero and .63 and the corresponding callable bond values are 97.297 and 98—the same values obtained using the minimum price constraint approach. The value of the call option in the current period is equal to the present value of the expected call value in Period 1. In this case, the current value is 0.2864:

$$V_0^C = \frac{.5[0] + .5[.630]}{1.10} = .2864$$

Subtracting the call value of 0.2864 from the noncallable bond value of 96.330, we obtain a callable bond value of 96.044 (see Exhibit 13.4)—the same value obtained using the constraint approach.

EXHIBIT 13.4 Value of Two-Period Callable Bond

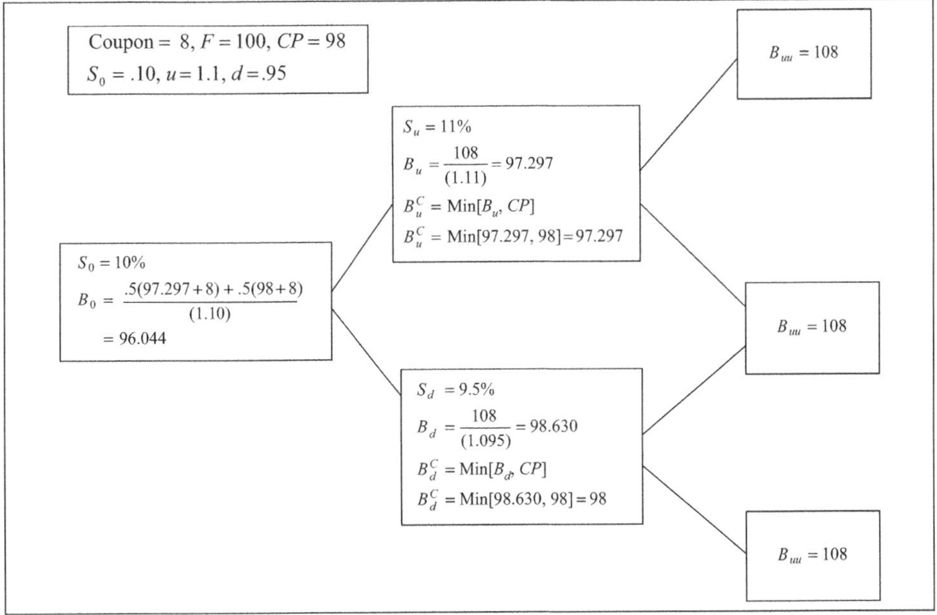

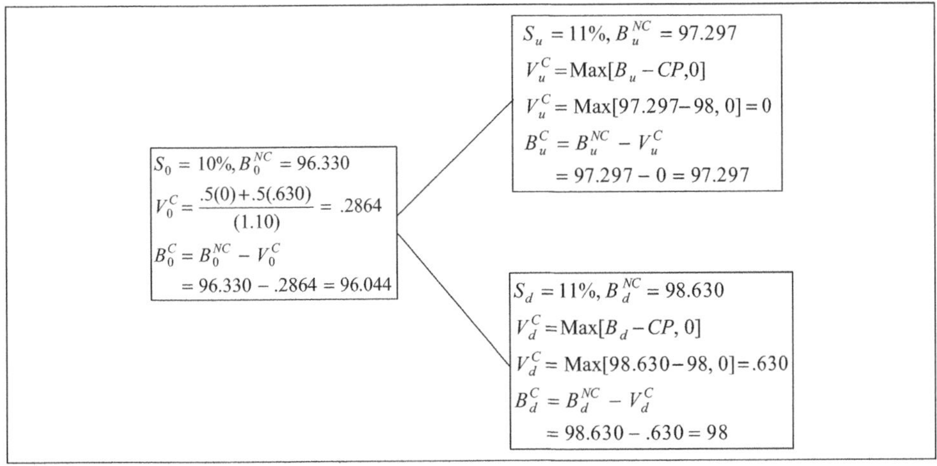

Valuing a Three-Period Bond

The binomial approach to valuing a two-period bond requires only a one-period binomial tree of one-period spot rates. If we want to value a three-period bond, we in turn need a two-period interest rate tree. For example, suppose we wanted to value a three-period, 9 percent coupon bond with no default risk or option features. In this case, market risk exists in two periods: Period 3, where there are three possible spot rates, and Period 2, where there are two possible rates. To value the bond, we first determine the three possible values of the bond in Period 2 given the three possible spot rates and the bond's certain cash flow next period (maturity). As shown in Exhibit 13.5, the three possible values in Period 2 are B_{uu} = 109/1.121 = 97.2346, B_{ud} = 109/1.1045 = 98.6872, and B_{dd} = 99.9771. Given these values, we next roll the tree to the first period and determine the two possible values there. Note, in this period the values are equal to the present values of the expected cash flows in Period 2; that is:

$$B_u = \frac{.5[97.2346+9] + .5[98.6872+9]}{1.11} = 96.3612$$

$$B_d = \frac{.5[98.6872+9] + .5[99.9771+9]}{1.095} = 98.9335$$

EXHIBIT 13.5 Value of Three-Period Option-Free Bond

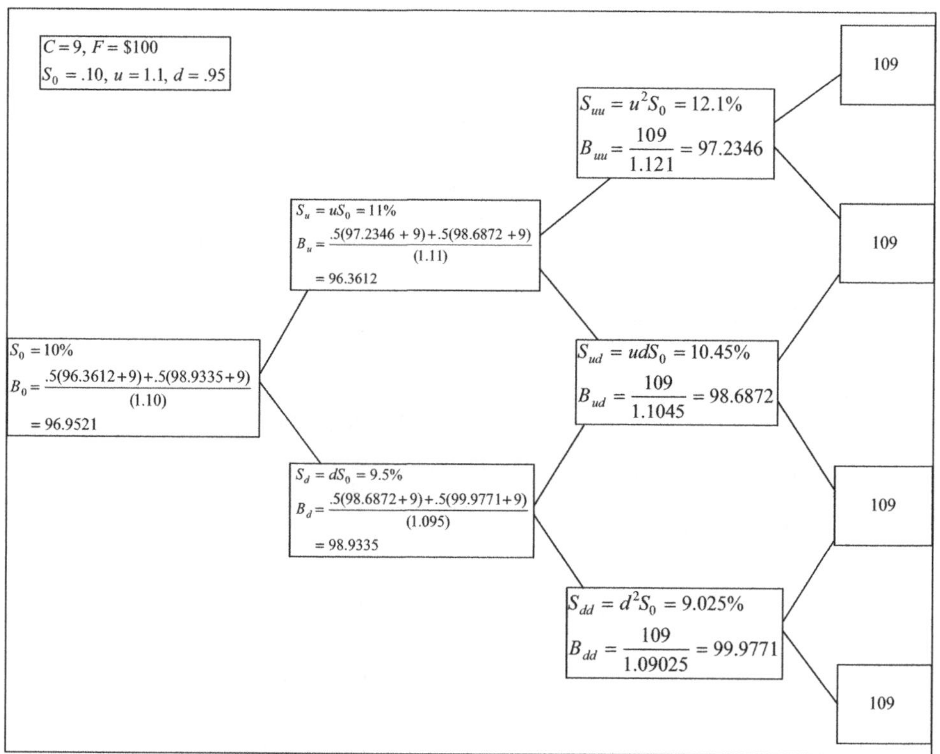

Finally, using the bond values in Period 1, we roll the tree to the current period where we determine the value of the bond to be 96.9521:

$$B_0 = \frac{.5[96.3612 + 9] + .5[98.9335 + 9]]}{1.10} = 96.9521$$

If the bond is callable, we can determine its value by first comparing each of the noncallable bond values with the call price in Period 2 (one period from maturity) and taking the minimum of the two as the callable bond value. We next roll the callable bond values from Period 2 to Period 1 where we determine the two bond values at each node as the present value of the expected cash flow, and then for each case we select the minimum of the value we calculated or the call price. Finally, we roll those two callable bond values to the current period and determine the callable bond's price as the present value of Period 1's expected cash flow.

Exhibit 13.6 shows the binomial tree value of the three-period, 9 percent bond given a call feature with a CP = 98. Note, at the two lower nodes in Period 2, the bond would be called at 98 and therefore the callable bond price would be 98; at the top node, the bond price of 97.2346 would prevail. Rolling these prices to Period

EXHIBIT 13.6 Value of Three-Period Callable Bond

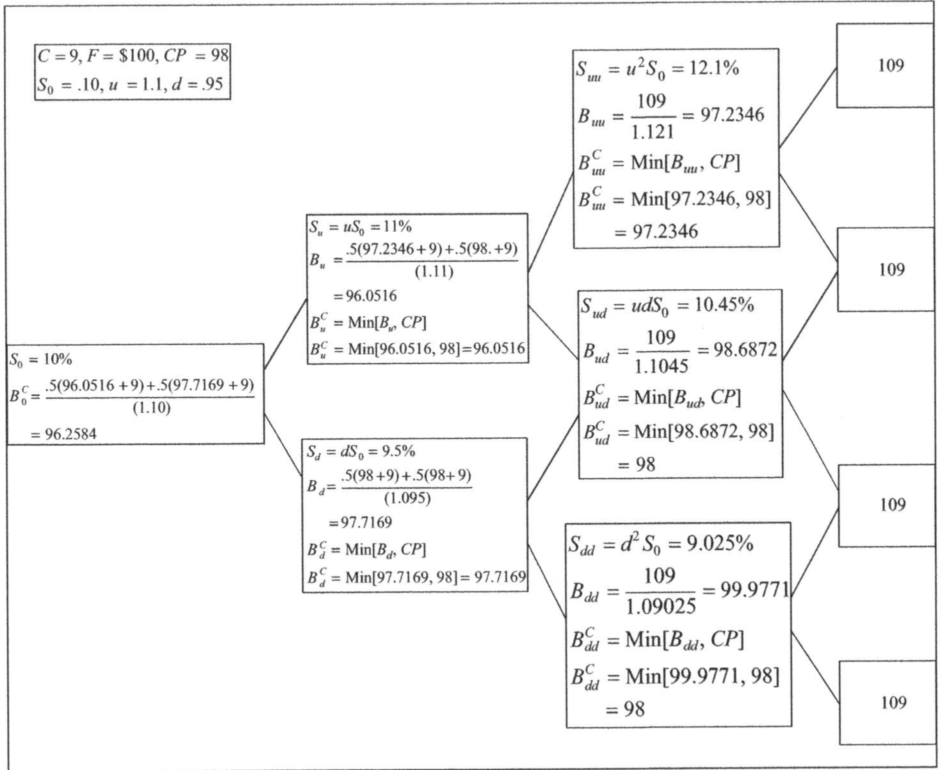

1, the present values of the expected cash flows are 96.0516 at the 11 percent spot rate and 97.7169 at the 9.5 percent rate. Since neither of these values are less than the CP of 98, each represents the callable bond value at that node. Rolling these two values to the current period, we obtain a value of 96.2584 for the three-period callable bond. The alternative approach to valuing the callable bond is to determine the value of the call option at each node and then subtract that value from the noncallable value to obtain the callable bond's price. However, different from the previous two-period case, when there are three periods or more, we need to take into account that prior to maturity the bond issuer has two choices: She can either exercise the option or she can hold it for another period.

Valuing a Three-Period Putable Bond

A putable bond, or put bond, gives the holder the right to sell the bond back to the issuer at a specified exercise price (or put price), PP. In contrast to callable bonds, putable bonds benefit the holder: If the price of the bond decreases below the exercise price, then the bondholder can sell the bond back to the issuer at the exercise price. From the bondholder's perspective, a put option provides a hedge against a decrease in the bond price. If rates decrease in the market, then the bondholder benefits from the resulting higher bond prices, and if rates increase, then the bondholder can exercise, giving her downside protection. Given that the bondholder has the right to exercise, the price of a putable bond will be equal to the price of an otherwise identical nonputable bond plus the value of the put option (V_0^P):

$$B_0^P = B_0^{NP} + V_0^P$$

Since the bondholder will find it profitable to exercise whenever the put price exceeds the bond price, the value of a putable bond can be found using the binomial approach by comparing bond prices at each node with the put price and selecting the maximum of the two: Max[B_t, PP].

To illustrate, suppose the three-period, 9 percent option-free bond in our previous example had a put option giving the bondholder the right to sell the bond back to the issuer at an exercise price of PP = 97 in Periods 1 or 2. Using the two-period tree of one-period spot rates and the corresponding bond values for the option-free bond (Exhibit 13.7), we start, as we did with the callable bond, at Period 2 and investigate each of the nodes to determine if there is an advantage for the holder to exercise. In all three of the cases in Period 2, the bond price exceeds the exercise price; thus, there are no exercise advantages in this period and each of the possible prices of the putable bond are equal to their non-putable values. In Period 1, though, it is profitable for the holder to exercise when the spot rate is 11 percent. At that node, the value of the non-putable bond is 96.3612, compared to PP = 97; thus the value of putable bond is its exercise price of 97:

$$B_u^P = Max[96.3612, 97] = 97$$

EXHIBIT 13.7 Value of Putable Bond

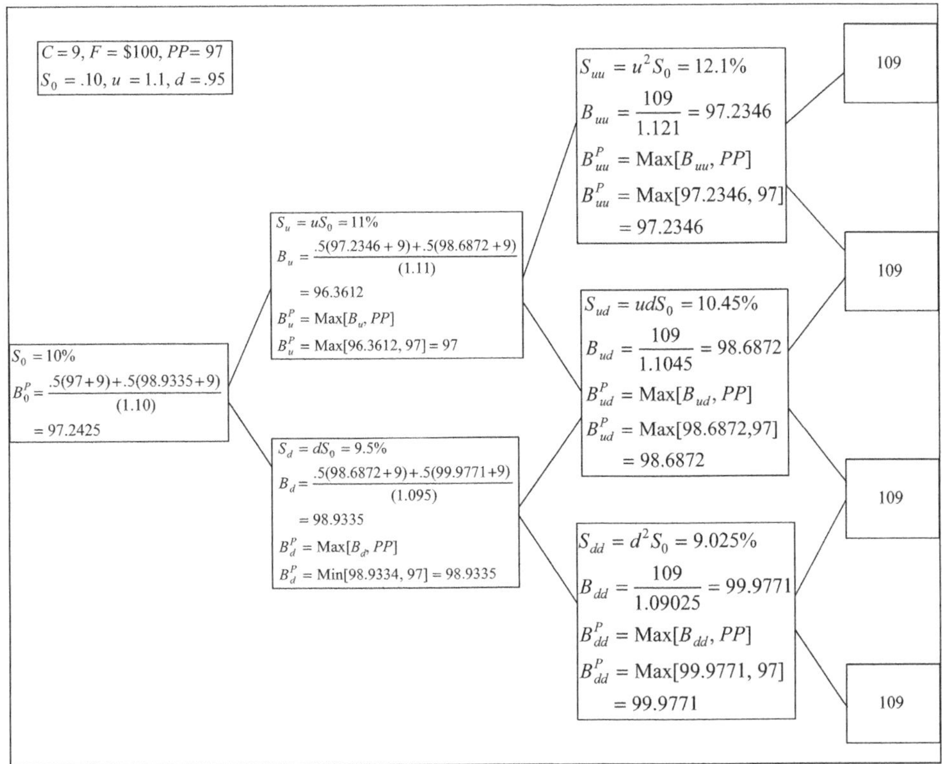

At the lower node in Period 1, it is not profitable to exercise nor is there any holding value of the put option since there is no exercise advantage in Period 2. Thus at the lower node, the nonputable bond price prevails. Rolling the two putable bond values in Period 1 to the present, we obtain a current value of the putable bond of 97.2425:

$$B_0^P = \frac{.5[97+9] \; + .5[98.9335+9]}{1.10} = 97.2425$$

The inclusion of the put option in this example causes the bond price to increase from 96.9521 to 97.2425, reflecting the value the put option has to the bondholder.[2]

Convertible Bonds

A convertible bond gives the holder the right to convert the bond into a specified number of shares of stock. Convertibles are often sold as a subordinate issue, with the conversion feature serving as a bond sweetener. To the investor, convertible bonds offer the potential for a high rate of return if the company does well and its stock price increases, while providing some downside protection as a bond if the stock declines.

Convertibles are usually callable, with the convertible bondholder usually having the right to convert the bond to stock if the issuer does call.

Convertible Bond Terms

Suppose our illustrative three-period, 9 percent bond were convertible into four shares of the underlying company's stock. The conversion features of this bond include its conversion ratio, conversion value, and straight debt value. The *conversion ratio* (*CR*) is the number of shares of stock that can be converted when the bond is tendered for conversion. The conversion ratio for this bond is four. The *conversion value* (*CV*) is the convertible bond's value as a stock. At a given point in time, the conversion value is equal to the conversion ratio times the market price of the stock (P_t^S): $CV_t = (CR)P_t^D$. If the current price of the stock were 92, then the bond's conversion value would be CV = (4)($92) = $368.[3] Finally, the *straight debt value* (*SDV*) is the convertible bond's value as a nonconvertible bond. This value is obtained by discounting the convertible's cash flow by the discount rate on a comparable nonconvertible bond.

Minimum and Maximum Convertible Bond Prices

Arbitrage ensures that the minimum price of a convertible bond is the greater of either its straight debt value or its conversion value:

$$\text{MinB}_t^{CB} = \text{Max}[CV_t, SDV_t]$$

If a convertible bond is priced below its conversion value, arbitrageurs could buy it, convert it to stock, and then sell the stock in the market to earn a riskless profit. Arbitrageurs seeking such opportunities would push the price of the convertible up until it is at least equal to its CV. Similarly, if a convertible is selling below its SDV, then arbitrageurs could profit by buying the convertible and selling it as a regular bond.

In addition to a minimum price, if the convertible is callable, the call price at which the issuer can redeem the bond places a maximum limit on the convertible. That is, the issuer will find it profitable to buy back the convertible bond once its price is equal to the call price. Buying back the bond, in turn, frees the company to sell new stock or bonds at prices higher than the stock or straight debt values associated with the convertible. Thus, the maximum price of a convertible is the call price. The actual price that a convertible will trade for will be at a premium above its minimum value but below its maximum.

Valuation of Convertibles Using Binomial Trees

The valuation of a convertible bond with an embedded call is more difficult than the valuation of a bond with just one option feature. In the case of a callable convertible bond, one has to consider not only the uncertainty of future interest rates, but also the uncertainty of stock prices. A rate decrease, for example, may not only increase the convertible's SDV and the chance the bond could be called, but if the rate decrease is also associated with an increase in the stock price, it may also increase the conversion value of the convertible and the chance of conversion. The valuation of convertibles therefore needs to take into account the random patterns of interest rates, stock prices, and the correlation between them.

To illustrate the valuation of convertibles, consider a three-period, 10 percent convertible bond with a face value $1,000 that can be converted to 10 shares of the underlying company's stock (CR = 10). To simplify the analysis, assume the bond has no call option and no default risk, that the current yield curve is flat at 5 percent, and that the yield curve will stay at 5 percent for the duration of the three periods (i.e., no market risk). In this simplified world, the only uncertainty is the future stock price. Like interest rates, suppose the convertible bond's underlying stock price follows a binomial process where in each period it has an equal chance it can either increase to equal u times its initial value or decrease to equal d times the initial value, where $u = 1.1$, $d = 1/1.1 = .9091$, and the current stock price is $92. The possible stock prices resulting from this binomial process are shown in Exhibit 13.8, along with the convertible bond's conversion values.

Since spot rates are assumed constant, the value of the convertible bond will only depend on the stock price. To value the convertible bond, we start at the maturity date of the bond. At that date, the bondholder will have a coupon worth 100 and will either convert the bond to stock or receive the principal of $1,000. At the top stock price of $122.45, the convertible bondholder would exercise her option, converting

EXHIBIT 13.8 Value of Convertible Bond

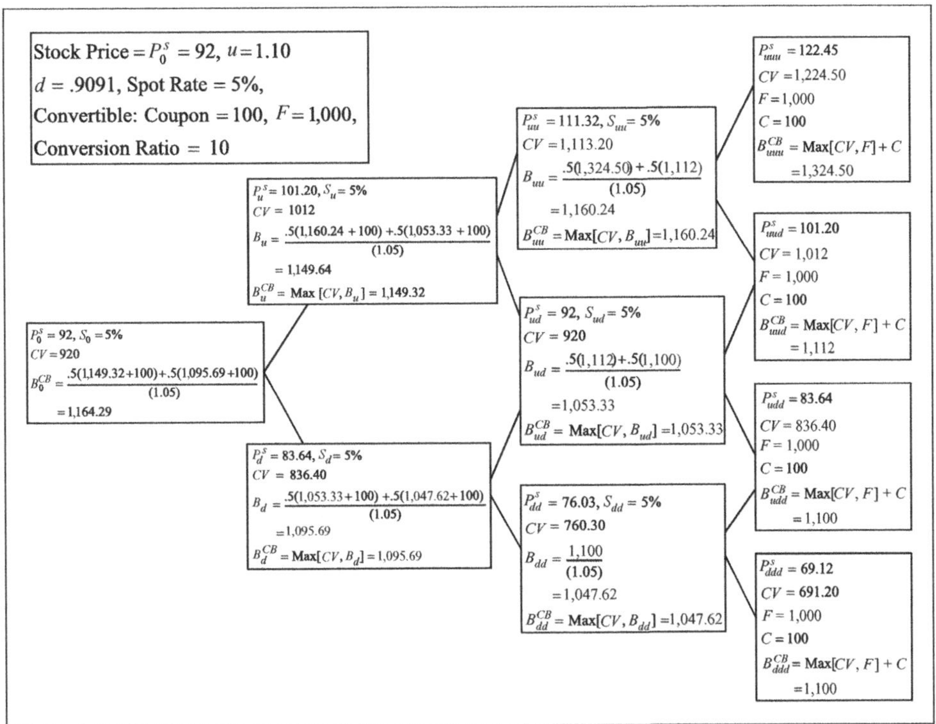

the bond to ten shares of stock. The value of the convertible bond, B^{CB}, at the top node in Period 3 would therefore be equal to its conversion value of $1,224.50 plus the $100 coupon:

$$B^{CB}_{uuu} = \text{Max}[CV_t, F] + C$$

$$B^{CB}_{uuu} = \text{Max}[1{,}224.50, 1{,}000] + 100$$

$$B^{CB}_{uuu} = 1{,}324.50$$

Similarly, at the next stock price of $101.20, the bondholder would also find it profitable to convert; thus, the value of the convertible in this case would be its conversion value of $1,012 plus the $100 coupon. At the lower two stock prices in Period 3 of $83.64 and $69.12, conversion is worthless; thus, the value of the convertible bond is equal to the principal plus the coupon: $1,100.

In Period 2, at each node the value of the convertible bond is equal to the maximum of either the present value of the bond's expected value at maturity or its conversion value. At all three stock prices, the present values of the bond's expected values next period are greater than the bond's conversion values, including at the highest stock price; that is, at $P^S_{uu} = \$111.32$, the CV is $1,113.20 compared to the convertible bond value of $1,160.24; thus the value of the convertible bond is $1,160.24:

$$B_{uu} = \frac{.5[1{,}324.50] + .5[1{,}112]}{1.05} = 1{,}160.24$$

$$B^{CB}_{uu} = \text{Max}[B_{uu}, CV] = [1{,}160.24, 1{,}113.20] = 1{,}160.24$$

Thus, in all three cases, the values of holding the convertible bond are greater than the conversion values. Similarly, the two possible bond values in Period 1 (generated by rolling the three convertible bond values in Period 2 to Period 1) also exceed their conversion values. Rolling the tree to the current period, we obtain a convertible bond value of $1,164.29. As we would expect, this value exceeds both the convertible bond's current conversion value of $920 and its SDV of $1,136.16 (assuming a 5 percent discount rate):

$$SDV = \frac{\$100}{(1.05)} + \frac{\$100}{(1.05)^2} + \frac{\$1{,}100}{(1.05)^3} = \$1{,}136.16$$

As noted, the valuation of a convertible becomes more complex when the bond is callable. With callable convertible bonds, the issuer will find it profitable to call the convertible prior to maturity whenever the price of the convertible is greater than the call price. However, when the convertible bondholder is faced with a call, she usually has the choice of either tendering the bond at the call price or converting it to stock. Since the issuer will call whenever the call price exceeds the convertible bond price, he is in effect forcing the holder to convert. By doing this, the issuer takes away the bondholder's value of holding the convertible, forcing the convertible bond price to equal its conversion value.

To see this, suppose the convertible bond is callable in Periods 1 and 2 at a CP = \$1,100. At the top stock price of \$111.32 in Period 2, the conversion value is \$1,113.20 (see Exhibit 13.9). In this case, the issuer can force the bondholder to convert by calling the bond. The call option therefore reduces the value of the convertible from \$1,160.24 to \$1,113.20. At the other nodes in Period 2, neither conversion by the bondholders or calling by the issuer is economical; thus the bond values prevail. In Period 1, the call price of \$1,100 is below the bond value (\$1,126.92), but above the conversion value (\$1,012). In this case, the issuer would call the bond and the holder would take the call instead of converting. The value of the callable convertible bond in this case would be the call price of \$1,100. At the lower node, calling and converting are not economical and thus the bond value of \$1,095.69 prevails. Rolling Period 1's upper and lower convertible bond values to the current period, we obtain a value for the callable convertible bond of \$1,140.80, which is less than the noncallable convertible bond value of \$1,164.29 and greater than the straight debt value of a noncallable bond of \$1,136.16.

In the above two cases, we assumed for simplicity that the yield curve remained constant at 5 percent for the period. As noted, the complexity of valuing convertibles is taking into account the uncertainty of two variables—stock prices and interest rates. A simple way to model such behavior is to use correlation or regression analysis to first estimate the relationship between a stock's price and the spot rate, and then either

EXHIBIT 13.9 Value of Convertible Bond with Call

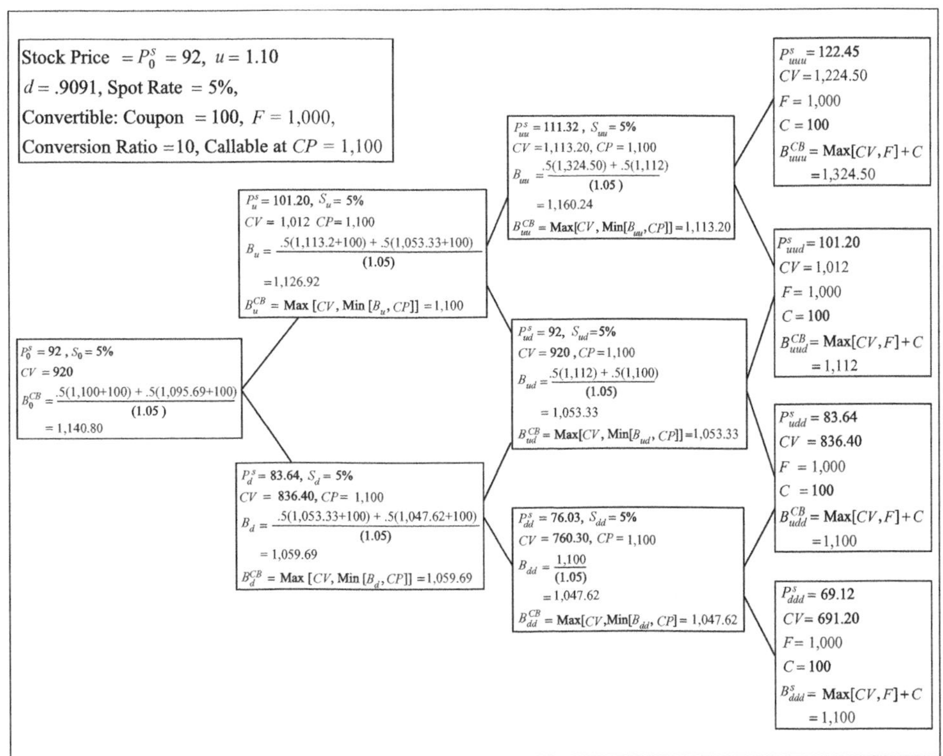

with a binomial model of spot rates identify the corresponding stock prices or with a binomial model of stock prices identify the corresponding spot rates.

It should be noted that modeling a bond with multiple option features and influenced by the random patterns of more than one factor is more complex in practice than the simple model described above. The above model is intended only to provide some insight into the dynamics involved in valuing a bond with embedded convertible and call options given different interest rate and stock price scenarios.

BLOOMBERG CONVERTIBLE BOND SCREENS

- CSCH: Convertible Bond Search
- CUSIP: Convertible Bond screen: CUSIP <Corp>
- OVCV: Convertible Valuation

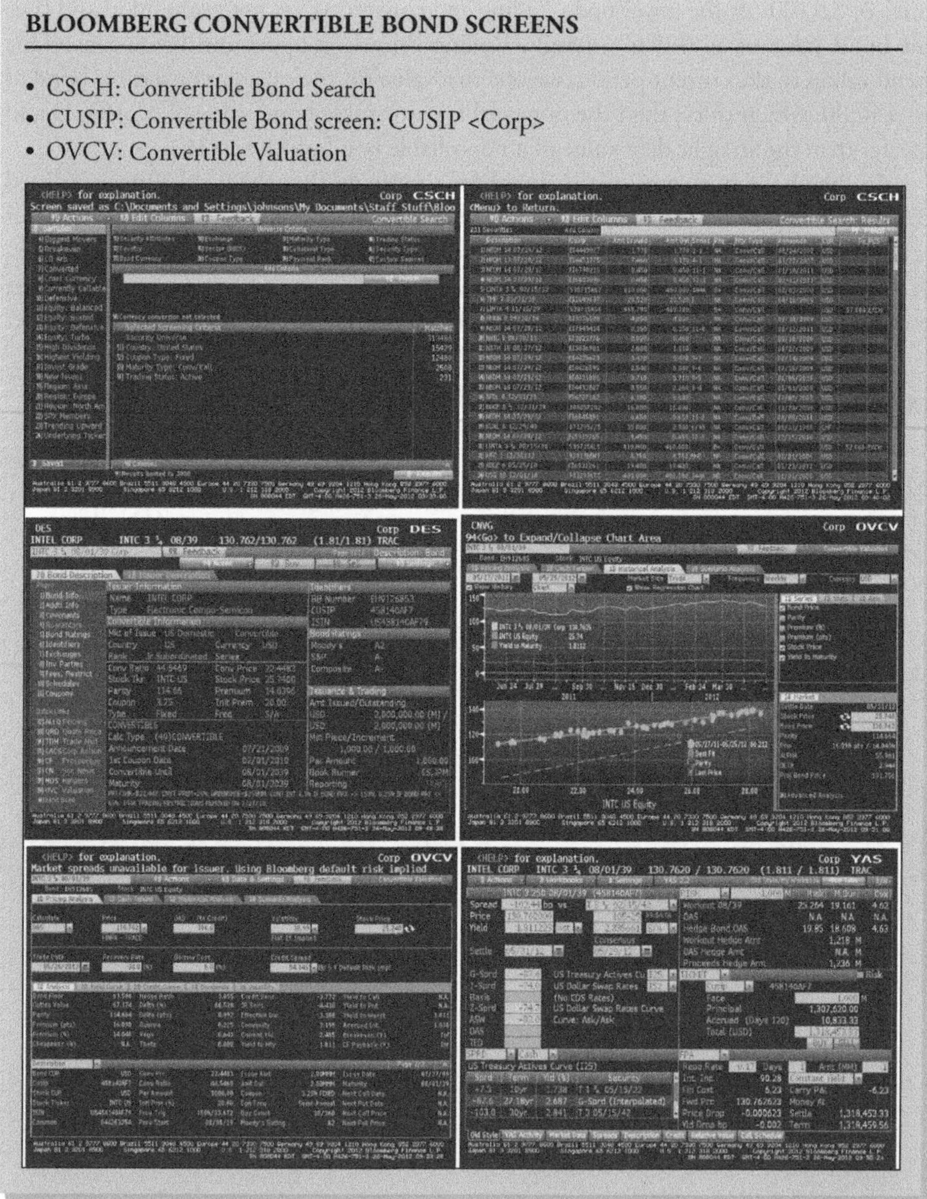

Valuation of Bond and Interest Rate Options

Valuing T-Bill Options with a Binomial Tree

In addition to valuing bonds with embedded options, the binomial interest rate tree can also be used to price bond and interest rate options. Exhibit 13.10 shows a two-period binomial tree for an annualized risk-free spot rate (S) and the corresponding prices on a T-bill (B) with a maturity of 0.25 years and face value of \$100 and also a futures contract (f) on the T-bill, with the futures expiring at the end of Period 2. The length of each period is six months (six-month steps), the upward parameter on the spot rate (u) is 1.1 and the downward parameter (d) is 1/1.1 = 0.9091, the probability of spot rate increasing in each period is .5, and the yield curve is assumed flat. As shown in the exhibit, given an initial spot rate of 5 percent (annual), the two possible spot rates after one period (six months) are 5.5 percent and 4.54545 percent, and the three possible rates after two periods (one year) are 6.05 percent, 5 percent, and 4.13223 percent. At the current spot rate of 5 percent, the price of the T-bill is $B_0 = 98.79$ (= $100/(1.05)^{.25}$); in Period 1, the price is 98.67 when the spot rate is 5.5 percent (= $100/(1.055)^{.25}$) and 98.895 when the rate is 4.54545 percent (= $100/(1.0454545)^{.25}$). In Period 2, the T-bill prices are 98.54, 98.79, and 99 for spot rates of 6.05 percent, 5 percent, and 4.13223 percent, respectively.

EXHIBIT 13.10 Binomial Tree of Spot Rates, T-Bill Prices, and T-Bill Futures Prices

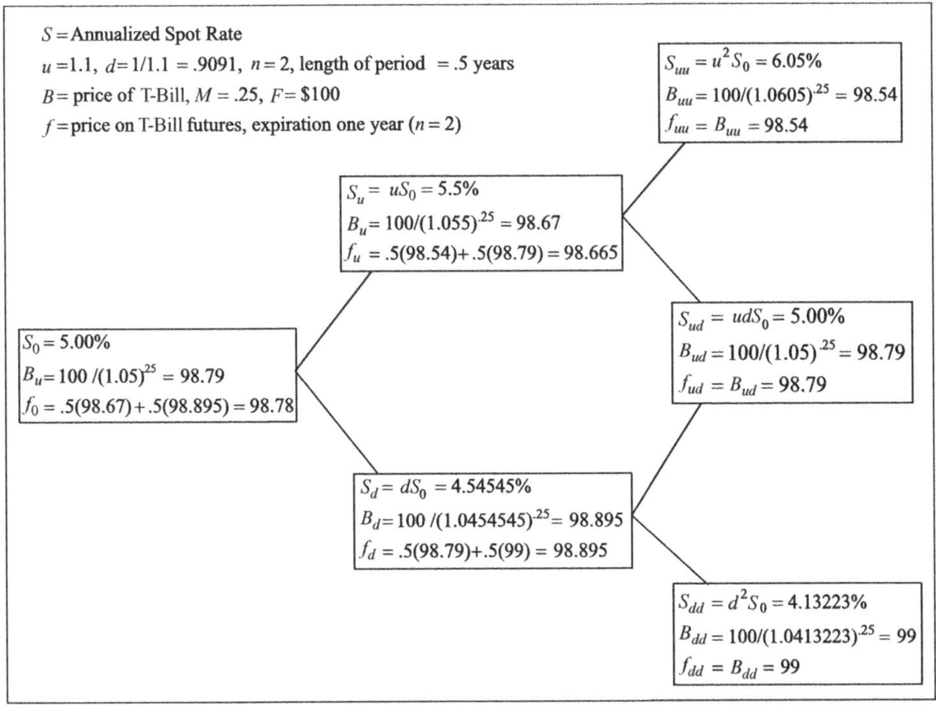

The futures prices shown in Exhibit 13.10 are obtained by assuming a risk neutral market. If the market is risk neutral, then the futures price is an unbiased estimator of the expected spot price: $f_t = E(S_T)$. The futures prices at each node in the exhibit are therefore equal to their expected prices next period. Given the spot T-bill prices in Period 2, the futures prices in Period 1 are 98.665 (= $E(B)$ = .5(98.54) + .5(98.79)) and 98.895 (= $E(B)$ = .5(98.79) + .5(99)). Given these prices, the current futures price is f_0 = 98.78 (= $E(f_1)$ = .5(98.665) + .5(98.895)).

Given the binomial tree of spot rates, prices on the spot T-bill, and prices on the T-bill futures, the values of call and put options on spot and futures T-bills can be determined. For European options, the methodology for determining the price is to start at expiration where we know the possible option values are equal to their intrinsic values, IVs. Given the option's IVs at expiration, we then move to the preceding period and price the option to equal the present value of its expected cash flows for next period. Given these values, we then roll the tree to the next preceding period and again price the option to equal the present value of its expected cash flows. We continue this recursive process to the current period.[4]

Spot T-Bill Call

Suppose we want to value a European call on a spot T-bill with an exercise price of 98.75 per $100 face value and expiration of one year. To value the call option on the T-bill, we start at the option expiration, where we know the possible call values are equal to their intrinsic values, IVs. In this case, at spot rates of 5 percent and 4.13223 percent, the call is in the money with IVs of .04 and .25, respectively, and at the spot rate of 6.05 percent the call is out of the money and thus has an IV of zero (see Exhibit 13.11). Given the three possible option values at expiration, we next move to Period 1 and price the option at the two possible spot rates of 5.5 percent and 4.54545 percent to equal the present values of their expected cash flows next period. Assuming there is an equal probability of the spot rate increasing or decreasing in one period (q = .5), the two possible call values in Period 1 are .01947 and .1418:

$$C_u = \frac{.5(0) + .5(.04)}{(1.055)^{.5}} = .01947 \qquad C_d = \frac{.5(.04) + .5(.25)}{(1.0454545)^{.5}} = .1418$$

Rolling these call values to the current period and again determining option's price as the present value of the expected cash flow, we obtain a price on the European T-bill call of .0787:[5]

$$C_0 = \frac{.5(.01947) + .5(.1418)}{(1.05)^{.5}} = .0787$$

Futures T-Bill Call

If the call option were on a European T-bill futures contract, instead of a spot T-bill, with the futures and option having the same expiration, then the value of the futures

EXHIBIT 13.11 Binomial Tree of Spot Rates and T-Bill Call Prices

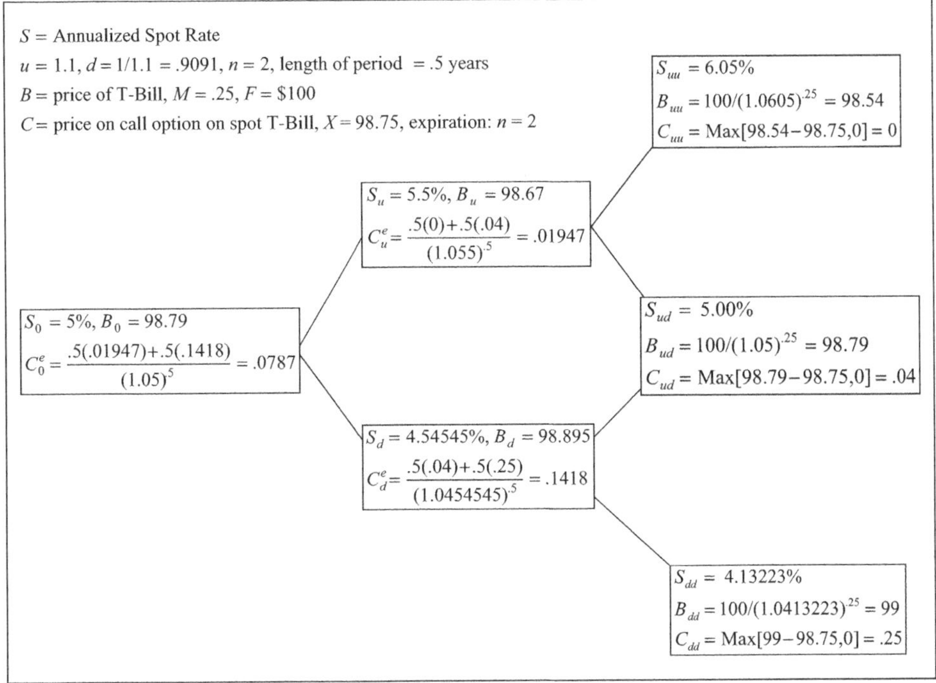

option will be the same as the spot option. That is, at the expiration spot rates of 6.05 percent, 5 percent, and 4.13223 percent, the futures prices on the expiring contract would be equal to the spot prices (98.54, 98.79, and 99), and the corresponding IVs of the European futures call would be 0, .04, and .25—the same as the spot call's IV. Thus, when we roll these call values back to the present period, we end up with the price on the European futures call of .0787—the same as the European spot.

T-Bill Put

In the case of a spot or futures T-bill put, their prices can be determined given a binomial tree of spot rates and their corresponding spot and futures prices. Exhibit 13.12 shows the binomial valuation of a European T-bill futures put contract with an exercise price of 98.75 and expiration of one year (two periods). At the expiration spot rate of 6.05 percent, the put is in the money with an IV of .21, and at the spot rates of 5 percent and 4.13223 percent the put is out of the money. In Period 1, the two possible values for the European put are .1022 and 0. Since these values exceed or equal their IV, they would also be the prices of the put if it were American. Rolling these values to the current period, we obtain the price for the futures put of .05.

EXHIBIT 13.12 Binomial Tree of Spot Rates and T-Bill Futures Put Prices

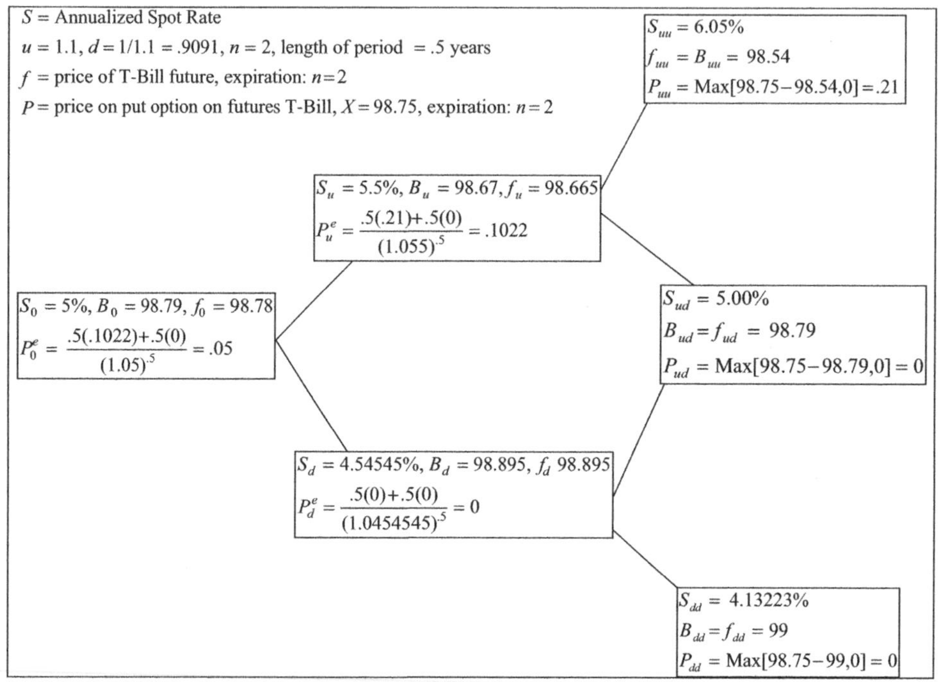

Valuing a Caplet and Floorlet with a Binomial Tree

The price of a caplet or floorlet can also be valued using a binomial tree of the option's reference rate. For example, consider an interest rate call on the spot rate defined by our binomial tree, with an exercise rate of 5 percent, time period applied to the payoff of $\phi = .25$, and notional principal of NP = 100. As shown in Exhibit 13.13, the interest rate call is in the money at expiration only at the spot rate of 6.05 percent. At this rate, the caplet's payoff is .2625 (= (.0605 −.05)(.25)(100)). In Period 1, the value of the caplet is .1278 (= $[.5(.2625)+.5(0)]/(1.055)^{.5}$) at spot rate 5.5 percent and 0 at spot rate 4.54545 percent. Rolling theses values to the current period, in turn, yields a price on the interest rate call of .06236 (= $[.5(.1278) + .5(0)]/(1.05)^{.5}$). In contrast, an interest rate put with similar features would be in the money at expiration at the spot rate of 4.13223 percent, with a payoff of .2169 (= (.05 − .0413223)(.25)(100) and out of the money at spot rates 5 percent and 6.05 percent. In Period 1, the floorlet's values would be .1061 (= $[.5(0) + .5(.2169)]/(1.0454545)^{.5}$) at spot rate 4.454545 percent and 0 at spot rate 6.05 percent. Rolling these values to the present period, we obtain a price on the floorlet of .05177 (= $[.5(0) + .5(.1061)]/(1.05)^{.5}$).

Since a cap is a series of caplets, its price is simply equal to the sum of the values of the individual caplets making up the cap. To price a cap, we can use a binomial tree to price each caplet and then aggregate the caplet values to obtain the value of the

EXHIBIT 13.13 Binomial Tree: Caplet and Floorlet

S = Annualized Spot Rate
$u = 1.1$, $d = 1/1.1 = .9091$, $n = 2$, length of period = .5 years
Caplet and floorlet: Exercise Rate = .05, reference rate = spot rate,
$NP = 100$, $\phi = .25$, and expiration: $n = 2$.

$S_{uu} = 6.05\%$
Caplet = Max[.0605 − .05,0](.25)(100) = .2625
Floorlet = Max[.05 − .0605,0](.25)(100) = 0

$S_u = 5.5\%$
$$\text{Caplet} = \frac{.5(.2625)+.5(0)}{(1.055)^{.5}} = .1278$$
$$\text{Floorlet} = \frac{.5(0)+.5(0)}{(1.055)^{.5}} = 0$$

$S_0 = 5\%$
$$\text{Caplet} = \frac{.5(.1278)+.5(0)}{(1.05)^{.5}} = .06236$$
$$\text{Floorlet} = \frac{.5(0)+.5(.1061)}{(1.05)^{.5}} = .05177$$

$S_{ud} = 5.00\%$
Caplet = Max[.05 − .05,0](.25)(100) = 0
Floorlet = Max[.05 − .05,0](.25)(100) = 0

$S_d = 4.54545\%$
$$\text{Caplet} = \frac{.5(0)+.5(0)}{(1.0454545)^{.5}} = 0$$
$$\text{Floorlet} = \frac{.5(0)+.5(.2169)}{(1.0454545)^{.5}} = .1061$$

$S_{dd} = 4.13223\%$
Caplet = Max[.0413223 − .05,0](.25)(100) = 0
Floorlet = Max[.05 − .0413223,0](.25)(100) = .2169

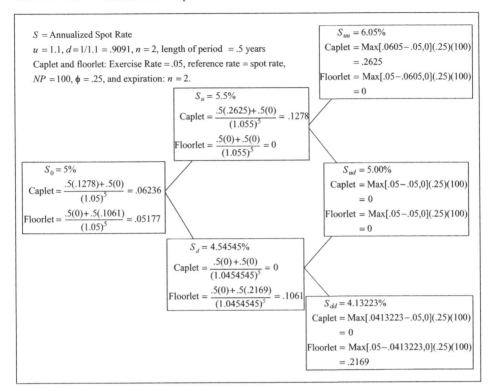

cap. Similarly, the value of a floor can be found by summing the values of the floorlets comprising the floor.

Valuing T-Bond Options with a Binomial Tree

The T-bill underlying the spot or futures T-bill option is a fixed-deliverable bill; that is, the features of the bill (maturity of 91 days and principal of $1 million) do not change during the life of the option. In contrast, the T-bond or T-note underlying a T-bond or T-note option or futures option is a specified T-bond or note or the bond from an eligible group that is most likely to be delivered. Because of the specified bond clause on a T-bond or note option or futures option, the first step in valuing the option is to determine the values of the specified T-bond (or bond most likely to be delivered) at the various nodes on the binomial tree, using the same methodology we used to value a coupon bond.

As an example, consider an OTC spot option on a T-bond with a 6 percent annual coupon, face value of $100, and with three years left to maturity. In valuing the bond, suppose we have a two-period binomial tree of risk-free spot rates, with the length of each period being one year, the estimated upward and downward parameters being u = 1.2 and d = .8333, and the current spot rate being 6 percent (see Exhibit 13.14). To value the T-bond, we start at the bond's maturity (end of Period 3) where the bond's value is equal to the principal plus the coupon, 106. We next determine the three possible values in Period 2 given the three possible spot rates. As shown in Exhibit 13.14, the three possible values of the T-bond in Period 2 are 97.57 (= 106/1.084), 100 (= 106/1.06), and 101.760 (= 106/1.0416667). Given these values, we next roll the tree to the first period and determine the two possible values. The values in that period are equal to the present values of the T-bond's expected cash flows in Period 2; as shown in the exhibit, B_u is equal to 97.747 and B_d is equal to 101.79. Finally, using the bond values in Period 1, we roll the tree to the current period where we determine the value of the T-bond to be 99.78.

Exhibit 13.14 also shows the prices on a two-year futures contract on the three-year, 6 percent T-bond. The prices are generated by assuming a risk-neutral market. As shown, at expiration (period 2) the three possible futures prices are equal to their spot prices: 97.57, 100, 101,76; in Period 1, the two futures prices are equal to their expected spot prices: $f_u = E(B_T) = .5(97.57) + .5(100) = 98.875$ and $f_d = E(B_T) = .5(100) + .5(101.76) = 100.88$; in the current Period, the futures price is $f_0 = E(f_1) = .5(98.785) + .5(100.88) = 99.83$.

EXHIBIT 13.14 Binomial Tree: Spot Rates, T-Bond Prices, and T-Bond Futures Prices

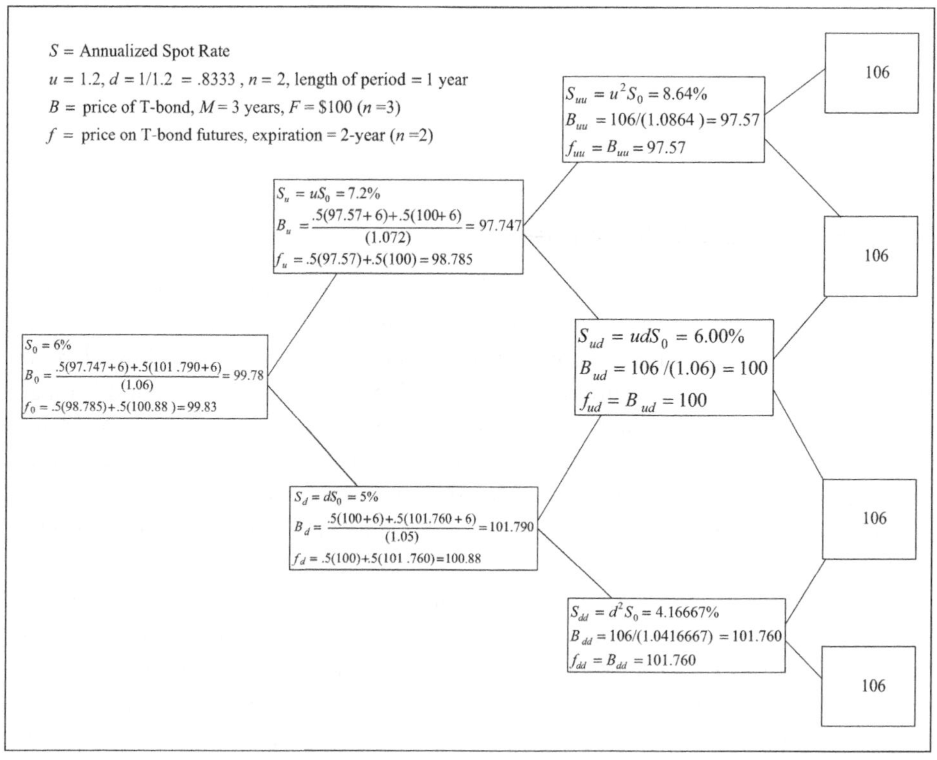

Spot T-Bond Call

Suppose we want to value a European call on the T-bond, with the call having an exercise price of 98 and expiration of two years. At the option expiration, the underlying T-bond has three possible values: 97.57, 100, and 101.76. The 98 T-bond call's respective IVs are therefore 0, 2, and 3.76 (see Exhibit 13.15). Given these values, the call's possible value in Period 1 are .9328 (= (.5(0) + .5(2)) / 1.072) and 2.743 (= (.5(2) + .5(3.76)) / 1.05). Rolling these values to the current period, we obtain the price on the European T-bond call of 1.734 (= (.5(.9328) + .5(2.743)) / 1.06). If the call option were American, then its value at each node is the greater of the value of holding the call or the value from exercising.[6]

Futures T-Bond Call

If the European call were an option on a futures contract on the three-year, 6 percent T-bond (or if that bond were the most likely to-be-delivered bond on the futures contract), with the futures contract expiring at the same time as the option (end of Period 2), then the value of the futures option will be the same as the spot. That is, at expiration the futures prices on the expiring contract would be equal to the spot

EXHIBIT 13.15 Binomial Tree: T-Bond Call Prices

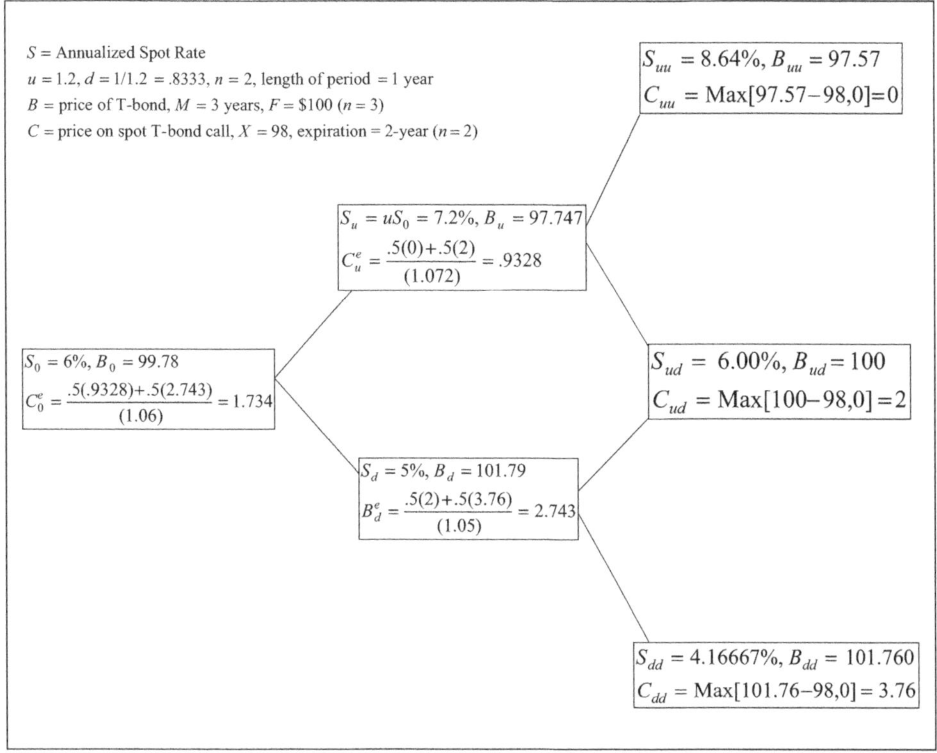

prices, and the corresponding IVs of the European futures call would be the same as the spot call's IV. Thus, when we roll these call values back to the present period, we end up with the price on the European futures call being the same as the European spot: 1.734.[7]

Estimating the Binomial Tree

In practice, determining the value of a bond using a binomial tree requires that we be able to estimate the spot rates defining the tree. There are two general approaches to estimating binomial interest rate movements. The first (models derived by Rendleman and Bartter (1980) and Cox, Ingersoll, and Ross (1985)) is to estimate the u and d parameters based on estimates of the mean and variability of the spot rate's logarithmic return. The second approach (models derived by Black, Derman, and Toy (1990), Ho and Lee (1986), and Heath, Jarrow, and Morton (1992)) is to calibrate the binomial tree to the current spot yield curve and to the interest rate's volatility. This calibration approach solves for the spot rate that satisfies a variability condition and a price condition that ensures that the binomial tree is consistent with the term structure of current spot rates. As background to understanding the u and d formulas, let us first examine subdividing the tree and the probability distribution that characterizes a binomial process.

Subdividing the Binomial Tree

The binomial model is more realistic when we subdivide the periods to maturity or expiration into a number of subperiods. That is, as the number of subperiods increases, the length of each period becomes smaller, making the assumption that the spot rate will either increase or decrease more plausible, and the number of possible rates at maturity increases, which again adds realism to the model. For example, suppose the 3-period bond in our illustrative example were a 3-year bond. Instead of using a 3-period binomial tree, where the length of each period is a year, suppose we evaluate the bond using a 6-period tree with the length of each period being six months. If we do this, we need to divide the 1-year spot rates and the annual coupon by two, adjust the u and d parameters to reflect changes over a six-month period instead of one year (this adjustment will be discussed in the next section), and define the binomial tree of spot rates for five periods, each with a length of 6 months. If we wanted to value the bond every quarter, then we would need an 11-period tree of spot rates with the length of each period being three months and with the annual rates divided by four and u and d adjusted to reflect movements over three months. In general, let h = length of the period in years and n = number of periods of length h defining the maturity of the bond:

$$n = \frac{M}{h} = \frac{\text{Maturity in years}}{\text{Length of period in years}}$$

Thus, a 3-year bond evaluated over quarterly periods (h = .25 of a year), would have a maturity of n = (3 years)/.25 = 12 periods and would require a binomial interest rates tree with $n - 1 = 12 - 1 = 11$ periods. To evaluate the bond over monthly periods (h = 1/12 of a year), the bond's maturity would be n = (3 years)/(1/12 year) = 36 periods and would require a 35-period binomial tree of spot rates; for weekly periods (h = 1/52), the bond's maturity would be 156 periods of length one week, and we would need a 155-period tree of spot rates. Thus, by subdividing we make the length of each period smaller, which makes the assumption of only two possible rates at the end of one period more plausible, and we increase the number of possible rates at maturity.

Binomial Distribution

Assume a simple binomial approach in which in each period the one-period spot rate will either increase to equal a proportion u times its initial value or decrease to equal a proportion d times the initial rate and with the probability of the increase in one period being q = .5. At the end of n periods, this binomial process yields a distribution of $n + 1$ possible spot rates (e.g., for $n = 3$, there are four possible rates: $S_{uuu} = u^3S_0$, $S_{uud} = u^2d\,S_0$, $S_{udd} = ud^2\,S_0$, and $S_{ddd} = d^3S_0$). This distribution, though, is not normally distributed since spot rates cannot be negative (i.e., we normally do not have negative interest rates). However, the distribution of spot rates can be converted into a distribution of logarithmic returns, g_n, where: $g_n = \ln(S_n / S_0)$. This distribution can take on negative values and will be normally distributed if q = .5. Exhibit 13.16 shows the binomial distributions of spot rates for n = 1, 2, 3, and 4 periods and their corresponding logarithmic returns for the case in which u = 1.1, d = .95, S_0 = 10 percent, and q = .5. As shown in the exhibit, when n = 1, there are two possible spot rates of 11 percent and 9.5 percent, with respective logarithmic returns of .0953 and –.0513:

$$g_u = \ln\left(\frac{uS_0}{S_0}\right) = \ln u = \ln 1.1 = .0953$$

$$g_d = \ln\left(\frac{dS_0}{S_0}\right) = \ln d = \ln .95 = -.0513$$

When n = 2, there are three possible spot rates of 12.1 percent, 10.45 percent, and 9.025 percent with corresponding logarithmic returns of

$$g_{uu} = \ln\left(\frac{u^2S_0}{S_0}\right) = \ln u^2 = \ln(1.1^2) = .1906$$

$$g_{ud} = \ln\left(\frac{udS_0}{S_0}\right) = \ln ud = \ln[(1.1)(.95)] = .044$$

$$g_{dd} = \ln\left(\frac{d^2S_0}{S_0}\right) = \ln(d^2) = \ln(.95^2) = -.1026$$

When n = 3, there are four possible spot rates of 13.31 percent, 11.495 percent, 9.9275 percent, and 8.574 percent, with logarithmic returns of 0.2859, 0.1393, -0.0073, and -0.1539, respectively. The probability of attaining any one of these rates is equal to the probability of the spot rate increasing j times in n periods, p_{nj}. That is, the probability of attaining spot rate 10.45 percent in Period 2 is equal to the probability of the spot rate increasing one time (j = 1) in two periods (n = 2), p_{21}. In a binomial process this probability can be found using the following formula:[8]

$$p_{nj} = \frac{n!}{(n-j)!\,j!} q^j (1-q)^{n-j}$$

Thus after two periods, the probability of the spot rate equaling 19.06 percent is p_{22} = .25, 10.45 percent is p_{21} = .5, and 9.025 percent is p_{20} =.25. Using these probabilities, the expected value and the variance of the distribution of logarithmic returns after two periods would be equal to $E(g_2)$ = 4.4 percent and $V(g_2)$ = .0108:

$$E(g_n) = .25(.1906) + .5(.0440) + .25(-.1026) = .044$$

$$V(g_n) = .25[.1906+.044]^2 - .5[.044+.044]^2 - .25[-.1026-.044]^2 = .0108$$

The mean and variance for each of the four distributions are shown at the bottom of Exhibit 13.16. In examining each distribution's mean and variance, note that as the number of periods increases, the expected value and variance increase by a

EXHIBIT 13.16 Binomial Distribution of Logarithmic Returns

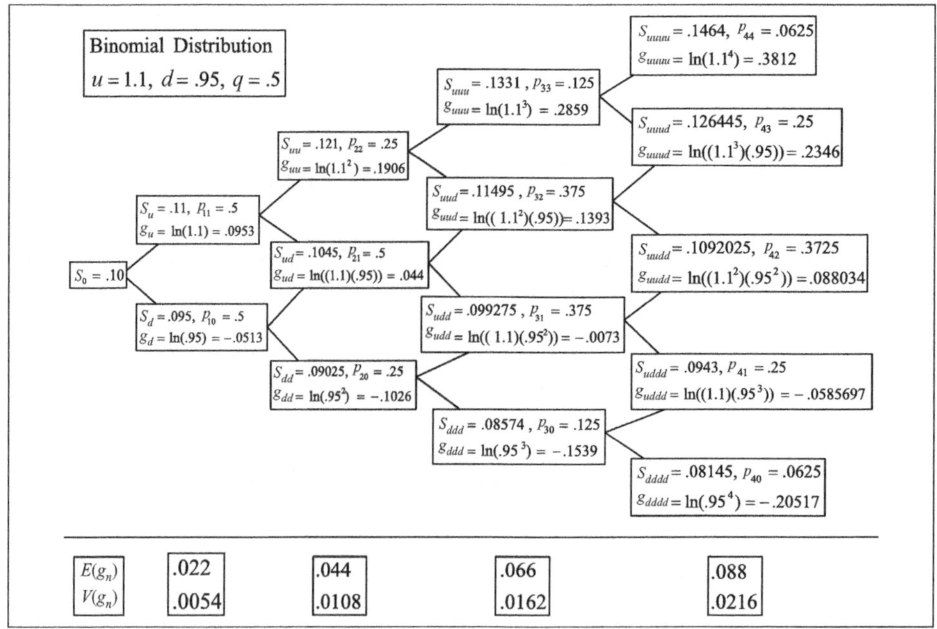

multiplicative factor such that $E(g_n) = nE(g_1)$ and $V(g_n) = nV(g_1)$. Also, note that the expected value and the variance are also equal to

$$E(g_n) = nE(g_1) = n[q \ln u + (1-q)\ln d]$$
$$V(g_n) = nV(g_1) = nq(1-q)[\ln(u/d)]^2$$

u and *d* Estimating Approach

Given the features of a binomial distribution, the formulas for estimating u and d are found by solving for the u and d values that make the expected value and the variance of the binomial distribution of the logarithmic return of spot rates equal to their respective estimated parameter values under the assumption that $q = .5$ (or equivalently that the distribution is normal). If we let μ_e and V_e be the estimated mean and variance of the logarithmic return of spot rates for a period equal in length to n periods, then our objective is to solve for the u and d values that simultaneously satisfy the following equations:

$$nE(g_1) = n[q \ln u + (1-q)\ln d] = \mu_e$$
$$nV(g_1) = nq(1-q)[\ln(u/d)]^2 = V_e$$

If $q = .5$, then the formula values for u and d that satisfy the two equations are

$$u = e^{\sqrt{V_e/n} + \mu_e/n}$$
$$d = e^{-\sqrt{V_e/n} + \mu_e/n}$$

In terms of our example, if the estimated expected value and variance of the logarithmic return were $\mu_e = .044$ and $V_e = .0108$ for a period equal in length to $n = 2$, then using the above equations, u would be 1.1 and d would be .95:

$$u = e^{\sqrt{.0108/2} + .044/2} = 1.1$$
$$d = e^{-\sqrt{.0108/2} + .044/2} = .95$$

Annualized Mean and Variance

In order to facilitate the estimation of u and d for a number of bonds with different maturities, the annualized mean and variance ($\mu^A{}_e$ and $V^A{}_e$) are often used instead of periodic values. Annualized parameters are obtained by simply multiplying the estimated parameters of a given length by the number of periods of that length that make up a year. For example, if quarterly data is used to estimate the mean and variance (μ^q_e and V^q_e), then we simply multiply those estimates by four to obtain the annualized parameters ($\mu^A_e = 4\mu^q_e$ and $V^A_e = 4V^q_e$). Thus, if the estimated quarterly mean and variance were .022 and .0054, then the annualized mean and variance would be .088 and .0216, respectively.[9] Note, when the annualized mean and variance are used, then these parameters must by multiplied by the proportion h, defined earlier as the time of the period being analyzed expressed as a proportion of a year, and n is not needed since h defines the length of tree's period:

$$u = e^{\sqrt{hV_e^A} = h\,\mu_e^A}$$

$$d = e^{-\sqrt{hV_e^A} = h\,\mu_e^A}$$

If the annualized mean and variance of the logarithmic return of one-year spot rates were .044 and .0108, and we wanted to evaluate a three-year bond with six-month periods (h = .5 of a year), then we would use a six-period tree to value the bond (n = (3 years) / .5 = 6 periods) and u and d would be 1.1 and .95: [10]

$$u = e^{\sqrt{(1/2).0108} + (1/2).044} = 1.1$$

$$d = e^{-\sqrt{(1/2).0108} + (1/2).044} = .95$$

Estimating μ^A_e and V^A_e Using Historical Data

To estimate u and d requires estimating the mean and variance: μ^e and V^e. The simplest way to do this is to estimate the parameters using the average mean and variance from an historical sample of spot rates. As an example, historical quarterly one-year spot rates over 13 quarters are shown in Exhibit 13.17. The 12 logarithmic returns are calculated by taking the natural log of the ratio of spot rates in one period to the rate in the previous period (S_t / S_{t-1}). From this data, the historical quarterly logarithmic mean return and variance are

$$\mu_e = \frac{\sum_{t=1}^{12} g_t}{12} = \frac{0}{12} = 0$$

$$V_e = \frac{\sum_{t=1}^{12} [g_t - \mu_e]^2}{11} = \frac{.046297}{11} = .004209$$

Multiplying the historical quarterly mean and variance by four, we obtain an annualized mean and variance, respectively, of 0 and .016836. Given the estimated annualized mean and variance, u and d can be estimated once we determine the number of periods to subdivide (see bottom of Exhibit 13.17).

EXHIBIT 13.17 Estimating Mean and Variance with Historical Data

Quarter	Spot Rate S_t	S_t/S_{t-1}	$g\text{t} = \ln(S_t/\text{St-1})$	$(gt - \mu e)2$
Y1.1	10.6%	–	–	–
Y1.2	10.0%	.9434	–.0583	.003395
Y1.3	9.4%	.9400	–.0619	.003829
Y1.4	8.8%	.9362	–.0659	.004350
Y2.1	9.4%	1.0682	.0660	.004350
Y2.2	10.0%	1.0638	.0619	.003829
Y2.3	10.6%	1.0600	.0583	.003395
Y2.4	10.0%	.9434	–.0583	.003395
Y3.1	9.4%	.9400	–.0619	.003829
Y3.2	8.8%	.9362	–.0660	.004350
Y3.3	9.4%	1.0682	.0660	.004350
Y3.4	10.0%	1.0638	.0619	.003829
Y4.1	10.6%	1.0600	.0583 0	.003395 .046297
			$\mu_e = 0$	$V_e^q = \frac{.046297}{11} = .004209$
$\mu^A{}_e = 4\mu^q{}_e = 4(0) = 0;\ V^A{}_e = 4V^q{}_e = 4(.004209) = .016836$				

Length	h	u	d
Year Quarter Month	1 1/4 1/12	1.1385 1.0670 1.0382	.8783 .9372 .9632

Calibration Model

A binomial interest rates tree generated using the u and d estimation approach is constrained to have an end-of-the-period distribution with a mean and variance that matches the analyst's estimated mean and variance. The tree is not constrained, however, to yield a bond price that matches its equilibrium value—the price obtained by discounting the bond's cash flows by spot rates. As a result, analysts using such models need to make additional assumptions about the risk premium in order to explain the bond's equilibrium price. In contrast, calibration models are constrained to match the current term structure of spot rates and therefore yield bond prices that are equal to their equilibrium values.[11]

The calibration model generates a binomial tree by first finding spot rates that satisfy a variability condition between the upper and lower rates. Given the variability relation, the model then solves for the lower spot rate that satisfies a price condition in which the bond value obtained from the tree is consistent with the equilibrium bond price given the current spot yield curve.

Variability Condition

In our derivation of the formulas for *u* and *d,* we assumed that the distribution of the logarithmic return of spot rates was normal. This assumption also implies the following relationship between the upper and lower spot rate:

$$S_u = S_d\, e^{2\sqrt{V_e/n}}$$

That is, from the binomial process we know

$$S_u = uS_0$$
$$S_d = dS_0$$

Therefore:

$$\frac{S_u}{u} = S_0 = \frac{S_d}{d}$$
$$S_u = S_d \frac{u}{d}$$

Substituting the equations for *u* and *d,* we obtain:

$$S_u = S_d \frac{e^{\sqrt{V_e/n} + \mu_e/n}}{e^{-\sqrt{V_e/n} + \mu_e/n}} = S_d e^{2\sqrt{V_e/n}}$$

or in terms of the annualized variance:

$$S_u = S_d e^{2\sqrt{hV_e^A}}$$

Thus, given a lower rate of 9.5 percent and an annualized variance of .0054, the upper rate for a one-period binomial tree of length one year (h = 1) would be 11 percent: $S_u = 9.5\% e^{2\sqrt{.0054}} = 11\%$. If the current one-year spot rate were 10 percent, then these upper and lower rates would be consistent with the upward and downward parameters of u = 1.1 and d = .95. This variability condition would therefore result in a binomial tree identical to the one shown in Exhibit 13.16.

Price Condition

The calibration model generates a binomial tree that is consistent with the current yield curve for spot rates. For a one-period tree, this is done by solving for a lower spot rate that satisfies the variability relation and also yields a bond price that is equal to the equilibrium bond price. To see this, suppose the current yield curve has one-, two-, and three-year spot rates of y_1 = 10 percent, y_2 = 10.12238 percent, and y_3 = 10.24488 percent, respectively. Furthermore, suppose the estimated annualized logarithmic mean and variance are .048167 and .0054, respectively. Using the u and d approach, a one-period tree of length one year would have up and down parameters of u = 1.12936 and d = .975. Given the current one-period spot rate of $y_1 = S_0$ = 10 percent, the tree's possible spot rate would be S_u = 11.2936 percent and S_d = 9.75 percent. These rates, though, are not consistent with the existing term structure. That is, if we value a two-year zero-coupon with a face value of $1 using this tree, we obtain a value of 0.82258 that, given the two-year spot rate of 10.12238 percent, differs from the equilibrium price on the two-year zero discount bond of B_0^M = .8246:

$$B_0 = \frac{.5B_u + .5B_d}{1+S_0} = \frac{.5[1/1.112936] + .5[1/1.0975]}{1.10} = .82258$$

$$B_0^M = \frac{1}{(1+y_2)^2} = \frac{1}{(1.1012238)^2} = .8246$$

Thus, the tree generated from our estimates of u and d is not consistent with the current interest rate structure, nor is it consistent with the market's expectation of future rates given that expectations are incorporated into the term structure. To make our tree consistent with the term structure, we need to find the S_d value such that when $S_u = S_d e^{2\sqrt{hV_e^A}} = S_d e^{2\sqrt{.0054}}$, the value of the two-year bond obtained from the tree is equal to the current equilibrium price of a two-year zero discount bond. This can be done for a one-period tree algebraically (see bottom of Exhibit 13.18) or iteratively: trying different S_d values until we find that value that equates the binomial price to the equilibrium price. In this case, solving iteratively for S_d yields a rate of 9.5 percent; that is, at S_d = 9.5 percent, we have a binomial tree of one-year spot rates of S_u = 11 percent and S_d = 9.5 percent that simultaneously satisfies our variability condition and price condition; that is, the rate is consistent with the estimated volatility of .0054 and the current yield curve with one-year and two-year spot rates of 10 percent and 10.12238 percent (see Exhibit 13.18).[12]

EXHIBIT 13.18 Calibration of Binomial Tree to a Two-Period Zero-Coupon Bond with Face Value = $1

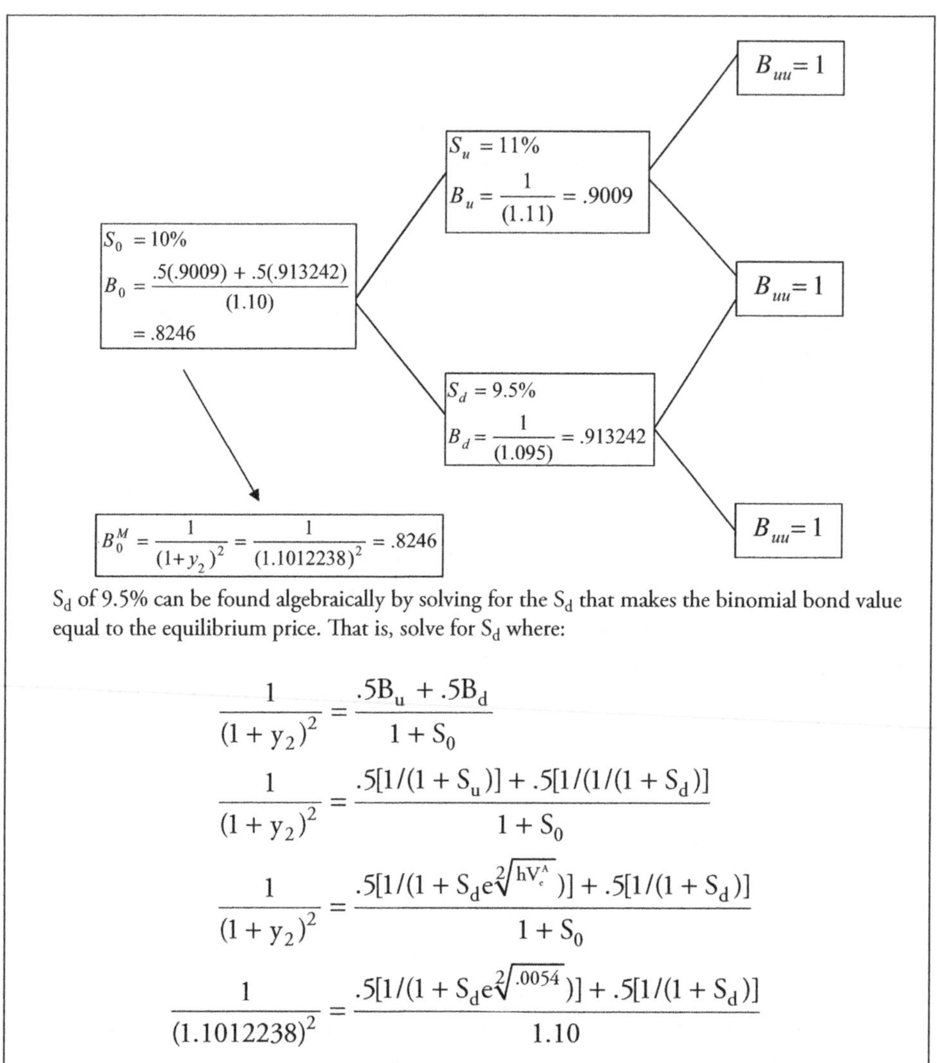
B_{uu}= 1
S_u = 11%
$B_u = \frac{1}{(1.11)} = .9009$
S_0 = 10%
$B_0 = \frac{.5(.9009) + .5(.913242)}{(1.10)}$
= .8246
B_{uu}= 1
S_d = 9.5%
$B_d = \frac{1}{(1.095)} = .913242$
$B_0^M = \frac{1}{(1+y_2)^2} = \frac{1}{(1.1012238)^2} = .8246$
B_{uu}= 1
S_d of 9.5% can be found algebraically by solving for the S_d that makes the binomial bond value equal to the equilibrium price. That is, solve for S_d where:
$\frac{1}{(1+y_2)^2} = \frac{.5B_u + .5B_d}{1+S_0}$
$\frac{1}{(1+y_2)^2} = \frac{.5[1/(1+S_u)] + .5[1/(1/(1+S_d)]}{1+S_0}$
$\frac{1}{(1+y_2)^2} = \frac{.5[1/(1+S_d e^{2\sqrt{hV_e^A}})] + .5[1/(1+S_d)]}{1+S_0}$
$\frac{1}{(1.1012238)^2} = \frac{.5[1/(1+S_d e^{2\sqrt{.0054}})] + .5[1/(1+S_d)]}{1.10}$

Two-Period Binomial Tree

Given our estimated one-year spot rates after one period of 9.5 percent and 11 percent, we can now move to the second period and determine the tree's three possible spot rates using a similar methodology. The variability condition follows the same form as the one period; that is:

$$S_{ud} = S_{dd}\, e^{2\sqrt{hV_e^A}}$$

$$S_{uu} = S_{ud}\, e^{2\sqrt{hV_e^A}} = S_{dd}\, e^{4\sqrt{hV_e^A}}$$

EXHIBIT 13.19 Calibration of Binomial Tree to a Three-Period Zero-Coupon Bond with Face Value = $1

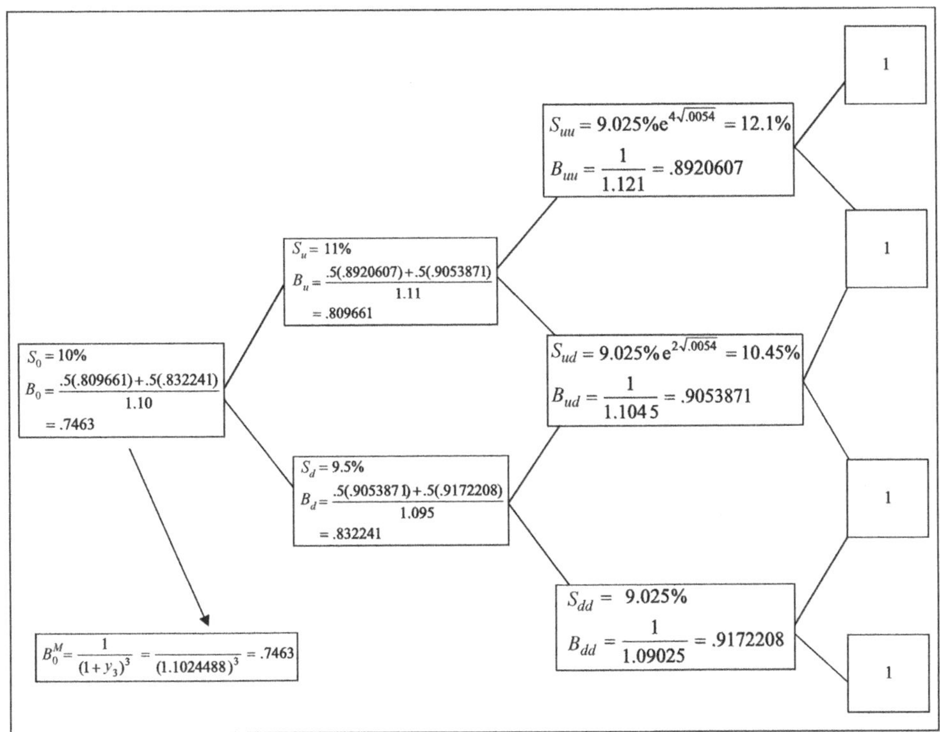

Similarly, the price condition requires that the binomial value of a three-year zero coupon bond be equal to the equilibrium price. Analogous to the one-period case, this condition is found by solving for the lower rate S_{dd} that, along with the above variability conditions and the rates for S_u and S_d obtained previously, yields a value for a three-year zero-coupon bond that is equal to the price on a three-year zero coupon bond yielding 10.24488 percent. Using an iterative approach, we find that a lower rate of S_{dd} = 9.025 percent yields a binomial value that is equal to the equilibrium price of the three-year bond of .7463 (see Exhibit 13.19).

The two-period binomial tree is obtained by combining the upper and lower rates found for the first period with the three rates found for the second period (see Exhibit 13.20). This yields a tree that is consistent with the estimated variability condition and with the current term structure of spot rates. To grow the tree, we continue with this same process. For example, to obtain the four rates in Period 3, we solve for the S_{ddd} that along with the spot rates found previously for periods one and two and the variability relations, yields a value for a four-year zero-coupon bond that is equal to the equilibrium price.

Valuation of Coupon Bonds

One of the features of using a calibrated tree to determine bond values is that the tree will yield prices that are equal to the bond's equilibrium price; that is, the price obtained by discounting cash flows by spot rates. For example, the value of a three-year,

EXHIBIT 13.20 Calibrated Binomial Tree

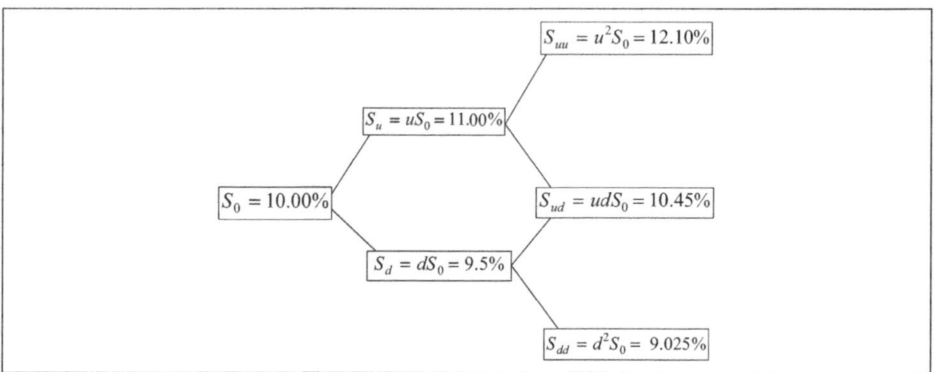

9 percent option-free bond using the tree we just derived is 96.9521 (this is the illustrative example shown in Exhibit 13.5). This value is also equal to the equilibrium bond price obtained by discounting the bond's periodic cash flows at the spot rates of 10 percent, 10.12238 percent and 10.24488 percent:

$$B_3^M = \frac{9}{1.10} + \frac{9}{(1.1012238)^2} + \frac{109}{(1.1024488)^3} = 96.9521$$

This feature should not be too surprising since we derived the tree by calibrating it to current spot rates. Nevertheless, one of the features of the calibrated tree is that it yields values on option-free bonds that are equal to the bond's equilibrium price. The primary purpose of generating the tree, though, is to value bonds with embedded options. In this example, if the three-year bond were callable at 98, then its value would be 96.2584 (see Exhibit 13.6).

Option-Free Features

One of the features of the calibration model is that it prices a bond equal to its equilibrium price. Recall, a bond's equilibrium price is an arbitrage-free price. That is, if the market does not price the bond at its equilibrium value, then arbitrageurs would be able to realize a riskless return either by buying the bond, stripping it into a number of zero discount bonds, and selling them, or by buying a portfolio of zero discount bonds, bundling them into a coupon bond, and selling it. In general, a security can be valued by arbitrage by pricing it to equal the value of its replicating portfolio: a portfolio constructed so that it has the same cash flows. The replicating portfolio of a coupon bond, in turn, is the portfolio of zero discount bonds. Thus, one of the important features of the calibration model is that it yields prices on option-free bonds that are arbitrage free. In addition to satisfying an arbitrage-free condition on option-free bonds, the calibration model also values a bond's embedded options as arbitrage-free prices. Because of the feature of pricing option-free bonds equal to their equilibrium prices, the calibration model is referred to as an *arbitrage-free model.*[13]

The calibration model presented here is the *Black-Derman-Toy model.* In addition to being arbitrage free, its major attribute is that it captures the volatility and drift in rates that are dependent on the current level of interest rates. Other calibration models have been developed that differ in terms of the assumptions they make about the evolution of interest rates. The Ho-Lee model, for example, assumes interest rates each period are determined by the previous rate plus or minus an additive rather than multiplicative random shock. The Black-Karasinski model, in turn, is characterized by a mean reversion process in which short-term rates revert to a central tendency. Each of these models, though, is characterized by the property that if their assumption about the evolution of rates is correct, the model's bond and embedded option prices are supported by arbitrage. This arbitrage-free feature of the calibration model is one of the main reasons that many practitioners favor this model over the equilibrium model based on estimating u and d.

Option-Adjusted Spread, Duration, and Convexity

Option-Adjusted Spread

In addition to the valuation of bonds with embedded options and bond and interest rate options, the binomial tree also can be used to estimate the option spread (the difference in yields between a bond with option features and an otherwise identical option-free bond), as well as the duration and convexity of bonds with embedded option features.

The simplest way to estimate the option spread is to estimate the YTM for a bond with an option given the bond's values as determined by the binomial model, then subtract that rate from the YTM of an otherwise identical option-free bond. For example, in the previous example the value of the three-year, 9 percent callable was 96.2584, whereas the equilibrium price of the noncallable was 96.9521. Using these prices, the YTM on the callable is 10.51832 percent and the YTM on the noncallable is 10.2306, yielding an option spread of .28772 percent:

$$\text{Option-Free Bond: } 96.9521 = \frac{9}{1+YTM} + \frac{9}{(1+YTM)^2} + \frac{109}{(1+YTM)^3} \Rightarrow YTM^{NC} = 10.2306\%$$

$$\text{Callable Bond: } 96.2584 = \frac{9}{1+YTM} + \frac{9}{(1+YTM)^2} + \frac{109}{(1+YTM)^3} \Rightarrow YTM^{C} = 10.51832\%$$

$$\text{Option Spread} = YTM^{C} - YTM^{NC} = 10.51832\% - 10.2306\% = .28772\%$$

One of the problems with using this approach to estimate the spread is that not all of the possible cash flows of the callable bond are considered. In three of the four interest rate scenarios, for example, the bond could be called, changing the cash flow pattern from three periods of 9, 9, and 109 to two periods of 9 and 107. An alternative approach that addresses this problem is the *option-adjusted spread (OAS) analysis.*

OAS analysis solves for the option spread (k) that makes the average of the present values of the bond's cash flows from all of the possible interest rate paths equal to the bond's market price. The first step in this approach is to specify the cash flows and spot rates for each path. In the case of the three-period bond valued with a two-period binomial interest rate tree, there are four possible paths:

	Path 1		Path 2		Path 3		Path 4	
Time	S_t	CF	S_t	CF	S_t	CF	S_t	CF
0	.10	—	.10	—	.10	—	.10	—
1	.0950	–9	.095	–9	.11	–9	.11	–9
2	.09025	107	.1045	107	.1045	107	.121	9
3	—		—		—		—	109

Given the four paths, we next determine the appropriate two-year spot rates (y_2) and three-year rates (y_3) to discount the cash flows. These rates can be found using the geometric mean and the one-year spot rates from the tree; that is:

Path 1

$$y_1 = .10$$

$$y_2 = [(1.10)(1.095)]^{1/2} - 1 = .097497$$

$$y_3 = [(1.10)(1.095)(1.09025)]^{1/3} - 1 = .095076$$

Path 2

$$y_1 = .10$$

$$y_2 = [(1.10)(1.095)]^{1/2} - 1 = .097497$$

$$y_3 = [(1.10)(1.095)(1.1045]^{1/3} - 1 = .099826$$

Path 3

$$y_1 = .10$$

$$y_2 = [(1.10)(1.11)]^{1/2} - 1 = .104989$$

$$y_3 = [(1.10)(1.11)(1.1045]^{1/3} - 1 = .104826$$

Path 4

$$y_1 = .10$$

$$y_2 = [(1.10)(1.11)]^{1/2} - 1 = .104989$$

$$y_3 = [(1.10)(1.11)(1.121]^{1/3} - 1 = .110300$$

Given a discount rate equal to the spot rate plus the spread, *k*, the final step is to solve for the k that makes the average present values of the paths equal to the callable bond's market price, B^M_0; that is:

$$B_0^M = (1/4)\left\{ \begin{array}{l} \left[\dfrac{9}{(1+.10+k)} + \dfrac{9+98}{(1+.097497+k)^2}\right] + \left[\dfrac{9}{(1+.10+k)} + \dfrac{109}{(1+.097497+k)^2}\right] + \\ \left[\dfrac{9}{(1+.10+k)} + \dfrac{109}{(1+.104989+k)^2}\right] + \left[\begin{array}{l}\dfrac{9}{(1+.10+k)} + \dfrac{9}{(1+.104989+k)^2} \\ + \dfrac{109}{(1+.110300+k)^3}\end{array}\right] \end{array} \right\}$$

Note, if the market price is equal to the binomial value we obtained using the calibration model, then the option spread, *k*, is equal to zero. This reflects the fact that we have calibrated the tree to the yield curve and have considered all of the possibilities. In practice, though, we do not expect the market price to equal the binomial value. If the market price is below the binomial value, then k will be positive. For example,

BLOOMBERG OPTION-ADJUSTED SPREAD ANALYSIS SCREEN: OAS1 SCREEN

For a bond with embedded options the OAS1 screen can be used to calculate values for the early redemption features of the selected security. The OAS calculation takes into account all embedded options. A yield does not appear because OAS considers all possible redemptions simultaneously, making it impossible to define a single yield. The spread appears in the OAS (bp) field.

An option-free yield is calculated that shows the yield if all options are removed. This yield can be subtracted from the current YTM to determine the spread due to credit and liquidity risk.

The OAS can be estimated from several models.

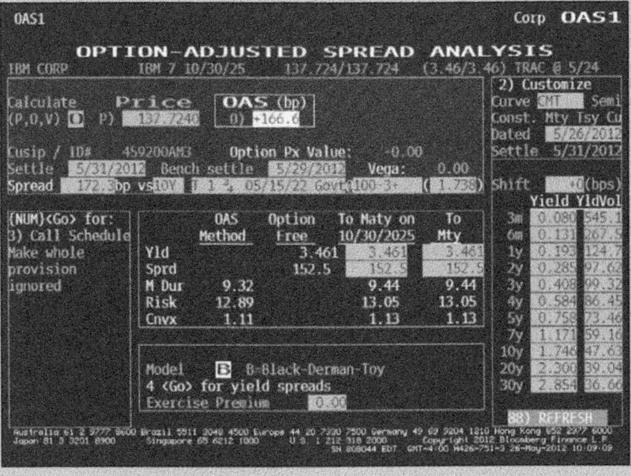

if the market priced the three-period bond at 94.6097, then the OAS (k) would be 2 percent. Many analysts in trying to identify mispriced bonds use the OAS approach to estimate k instead of comparing the market price with the binomial value.

Duration and Convexity

Our earlier measures of bond's duration (Modified and Macauley durations) and convexity did not factor in the bond's embedded option features. As discussed earlier in this text, when a bond has a call option, a rate decrease can lead to an early call, which shortens the life of the bond and lowers its duration, whereas an interest rate increase tends to lengthen the expected life of the bond causing its duration to increase. Thus, the option features of a bond can have a significant impact on the bond's duration, as well as its convexity.

The duration and convexity of bonds with embedded option features can be estimated using a binomial tree and the effective duration and convexity measures defined in Chapter 5:

$$\text{Effective Duration} = \frac{B_- - B_+}{2(B_0)(\Delta y)}$$

$$\text{Effective Convexity} = \frac{B_+ + B_- - 2B_0}{(B_0)(\Delta y)^2}$$

where:

B_- = price associated with a small decrease in rates
B_+ = price associated with small increase in rates

BLOOMBERG OAD, EFFECTIVE DURATION

Effective durations (OAD) and convexity (OAC) that take into account the embedded options on a bond or portfolio are estimated on the Bloomberg PORT screen (Characteristics tab).

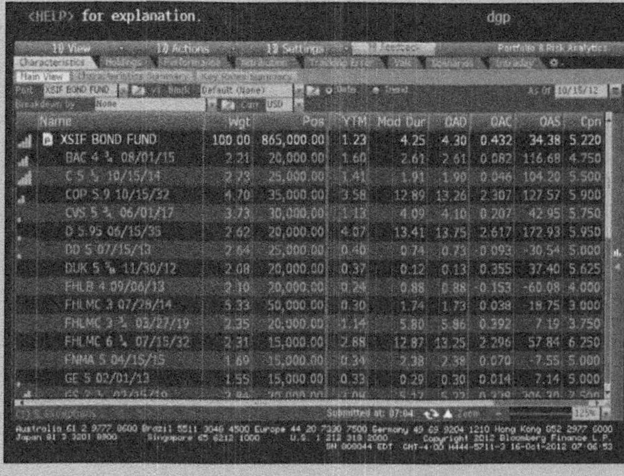

<HELP> for explanation. dgp

Name	Wgt	Pos	YTM	Mod Dur	OAD	OAC	OAS	Cpn
XSIF BOND FUND	100.00	865,000.00	1.23	4.25	4.30	0.432	34.38	5.220
BAC 4 ¾ 08/01/15	2.21	20,000.00	1.60	2.61	2.61	0.082	116.68	4.750
C 5 ½ 10/15/14	2.73	25,000.00	1.41	1.91	1.90	0.046	104.20	5.500
COP 5.9 10/15/32	4.70	35,000.00	3.58	12.89	13.26	2.307	127.57	5.900
CVS 5 ¾ 06/01/17	3.73	30,000.00	1.13	4.09	4.10	0.207	42.95	5.750
D 5.95 06/15/35	2.62	20,000.00	4.07	13.41	13.75	2.617	172.93	5.950
DD 5 07/15/13	2.64	25,000.00	0.40	0.74	0.73	-0.093	-30.54	5.000
DUK 5 ⅝ 11/30/12	2.08	20,000.00	0.37	0.12	0.13	0.355	37.40	5.625
FHLB 4 09/06/13	2.10	20,000.00	0.24	0.88	0.88	-0.153	-60.08	4.000
FHLMC 3 07/28/14	5.33	50,000.00	0.30	1.74	1.73	0.038	-18.75	3.000
FHLMC 3 ¾ 03/27/19	2.35	20,000.00	1.14	5.80	5.86	0.392	7.19	3.750
FHLMC 6 ¼ 07/15/32	2.31	15,000.00	2.88	12.87	13.25	2.296	57.84	6.250
FNMA 5 04/15/15	1.69	15,000.00	0.34	2.38	2.38	0.070	-7.55	5.000
GE 5 02/01/13	1.55	15,000.00	0.33	0.29	0.30	0.014	7.14	5.000

Australia 61 2 9777 8600 Brazil 5511 3048 4500 Europe 44 20 7330 7500 Germany 49 69 9204 1210 Hong Kong 852 2977 6000
Japan 81 3 3201 8900 Singapore 65 6212 1000 U.S. 1 212 318 2000 Copyright 2012 Bloomberg Finance L.P.
SN 000044 EDT GMT-4:00 H444-5711-3 16-Oct-2012 07:06:53

The binomial tree calibrated to the yield curve can be used to estimate B_0, B_-, and B_+. First, the current yield curve and calibrated tree can be used to determine B_0; next, B_- can be estimated by allowing for a small equal decrease in each of the spot yield curve rates (e.g., 10 basis points) and then using the tree calibrated to the new rates to find the price; finally, B_+ can be estimated in a similar way by allowing for a small equal increase in the yield curve's rates and then estimating the bond price using the tree calibrated to these higher rates.

The Black-Scholes and Black Option Pricing Model

Black-Scholes Option Pricing Model for Pricing Embedded Option

Before finishing our analysis of binomial interest rate models and their use in valuing bond and interest rate options and bonds with embedded options, it should be noted that an approximate value of the embedded option features of a bond can also be estimated using the well-known *Black-Scholes Option Pricing Model (B-S OPM)*—a model commonly used in pricing options. The B-S formula for determining the equilibrium price of an embedded call or put option is:

$$V_0^C = B_0 N(d_1) - X\,N(d_2)e^{-R_f T}$$

$$V_0^P = X(1-N(d_2))\,e^{-R_f T} - B_0(1-N(d_1))$$

$$d_1 = \frac{\ln(B_0 / X) + (R_f + .5\sigma^2)T}{\sigma\sqrt{T}}$$

$$d_2 = d_1 - \sigma\sqrt{T}$$

where:

X = call price (CP) or put price (PP)
σ^2 = variance of the logarithmic return of bond prices = $V(\ln(B_n / B_0)$
T = time to expiration expressed as a proportion of a year
R_f = continuously compounded annual risk-free rate (if simple annual rate is R, the continuously compounded rate is $\ln(1 + R)$)
$N(d)$ = cumulative normal probability; this probability can be looked up in a standard normal probability table or by using the following formula:

$$N(d) = 1 - n(d), \text{ for } d < 0$$

$$N(d) = n(d), \text{ for } d > 0$$

where:

$$n(d) = 1 - .5[1 + .196854\,(|d|) + .115194\,(|d|)^2 + .0003444\,(|d|)^3 + .019527(|d|)^4\,]^{-4}$$

$|d|$ = absolute value of d

For example, suppose a three-year, noncallable bond with a 10 percent annual coupon is selling at par (F = 100). A callable bond that is identical in all respects except for its call feature should sell at 100 minus the call price. In this case, suppose the call feature gives the issuer the right to buy the bond back at any time during the bond's life at an exercise price of 115. Assuming a risk-free rate of 6 percent and a variability of σ = .10 on the noncallable bond's logarithmic return, the call price using the Black-Scholes model would be 8.95:

$$V_0^C = B_0 N(d_1) - X\, N(d_2) e^{-R_f T}$$

$$V_0^C = 100(.62519) - 115(.55772)e^{-(.06)(3)} = 8.95$$

$$d_1 = \frac{\ln(100/115) + (.06 + .5(.10^2)3}{.10\sqrt{3}} = .31892$$

$$d_2 = .31892 = .10\sqrt{3} = .14571$$

$$N(d_1) = N(.31892) = .62519$$

$$N(d_2) = N(.14571) = .55772$$

Thus, the price of the callable bond is 91.05:

Price of Callable Bond = Price of Noncallable Bond – Call Premium
Price of Callable Bond = 100 – 8.95 = 91.05

BLOOMBERG OPTION PRICING SCREEN—OV OR OVME

The Bloomberg OV screen calculates the price of an option using the Black-Scholes OPM or the Binomial (Trinomial). The user can input the variability or use the historical volatility or the implied volatility. The OV or OVME screen can be used to value existing options or an option created from an existing security. Below are the B-S OPM values for call and put options on a 30-year T-bond (912810QT8 <Govt>). To access the OV screen: Enter 912810QT8 <Govt> to bring up the menu screen for the T-bond and then enter: OV <Enter> or OVME <Enter>.

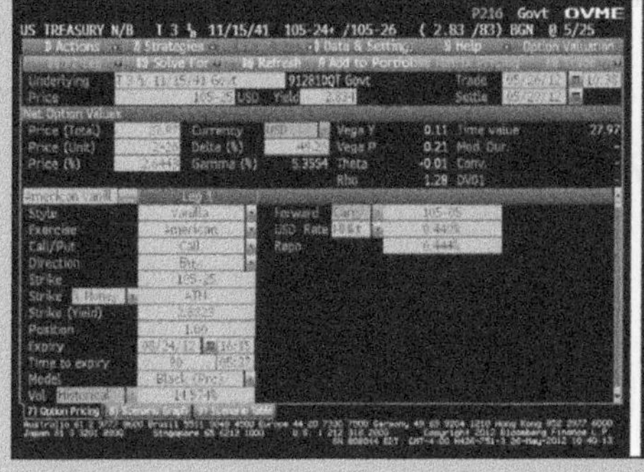

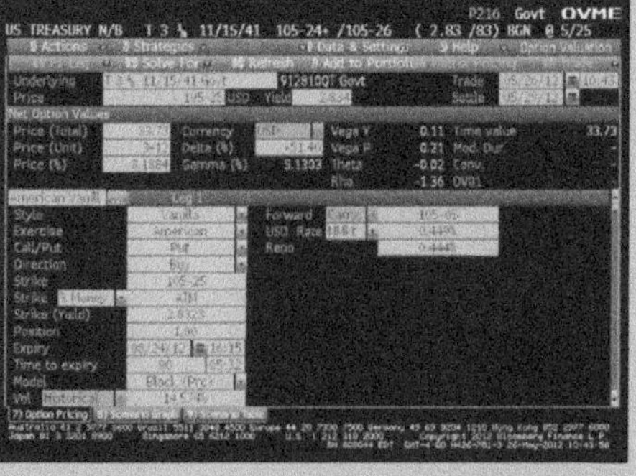

Black Futures Model

An extension of the B-S OPM that is sometimes used to price interest rate options is the Black's futures option model. The model is defined as follows:

$$C_0^* = [f_0 N(d_1) - X\,N(d_2)]e^{-R_f T}$$

$$P_0^* = [X(1-N(d_2)) - f_0(1-N(d_1))]e^{-R_f T}$$

$$d_1 = \frac{\ln(f_0 / X) + (\sigma_f^2 / 2)T}{\sigma_f \sqrt{T}}$$

$$d_2 = d_1 - \sigma_f \sqrt{T}$$

where:

σ_f^2 = variance of the logarithmic return of futures prices = $V(\ln(f_n / f_0)$
T = time to expiration expressed as a proportion of a year
R_f = continuously compounded annual risk-free rate (if simple annual rate is R, the continuously compounded rate is $\ln(1 + R)$
$N(d)$ = cumulative normal probability; this probability can be looked up in a standard normal probability table or by using the following formula:

$$N(d) = 1 - n(d), \text{ for } d < 0$$

$$N(d) = n(d), \text{ for } d > 0,$$

where:

$$n(d) = 1 - .5[1 + .196854\,(|d|) + .115194\,(|d|)^2 + .0003444\,(|d|)^3 + .019527(|d|)^4\,]^{-4}$$

$|d|$ = absolute value of d

Example: T-Bill futures

Consider the European futures T-bill call options we priced earlier in which the futures option had an exercise price of 98.75 and expiration of one year and the current futures price was f_0 = 98.7876. If the simple risk-free rate is 5 percent, implying a continuously compound rate of 4.879 percent (= $\ln(1.05)$, and the annualized standard deviation of the futures logarithmic return, $\sigma(\ln(f_n / f_0)$, is .00158, then using the Black futures model the price of the T-bill futures call would be .07912.

$$C_0^* = [98.7876(.595462) - 98.75(.594847)]e^{-(.04879)(1)} = .07912$$

where:

$$d_1 = \frac{\ln(98.7876/98.75) + (.00158)^2/2)(1)}{.00158\sqrt{1}} = .24175$$

$$d_2 = .24175 - .00158\sqrt{1} = .24017$$

$$N(.24175) = .595462$$

$$N(.24017) = .594847$$

Example: T-Bond Futures

As a second example, consider one-year put and call options on a T-bond futures contract, with each option having an exercise price of \$100,000. Suppose the current futures price is \$96,115, the futures volatility is $\sigma(ln(f_n / f_0) = .10$, and the continuously compound risk-free rate is .065. Using the Black futures option model, the price of the call option would be \$2,137 and the price of the put would be \$5,777:[14]

$$C_0^* = [\$96{,}115(.36447) - \$100{,}000(.327485)]e^{-(.065)(1)} = \$2{,}137$$

$$P_0^* = [\$100{,}000(1-.327485) - \$96{,}115(1-.36447)]e^{-(.065)(1)} = \$5{,}777$$

where:

$$d_1 = \frac{\ln(96115/100{,}000) + (.01/2)(1)}{.10\sqrt{1}} = .-.34625$$

$$d_2 = -.34625 - .10\sqrt{1} = -.44625$$

$$N(-.34625) = .36447$$

$$N(-.44625) = .327485$$

BLOOMBERG OPTION PRICING SCREEN FOR FUTURES OPTIONS—OV OR OVME

The Bloomberg OV or OVME screen calculates the price of a futures option using the Black futures OPM. The user can input the variability or use the historical or the implied volatility. Below are the Black OPM values for call and put options on a futures contract for a December 2012 U.S. Long T-bond - (T-Bond futures: USZ2 <Comdty>; December futures call: USZ2C; December futures put: USZ2P) and the price graphs showing the different model values for different futures prices. To access the OV or OVME screen: Enter USZ2C <Comdty> to bring up the menu screen for the T-bond futures, select exercise price, and then enter: OV <Enter> or OVME <Enter>.

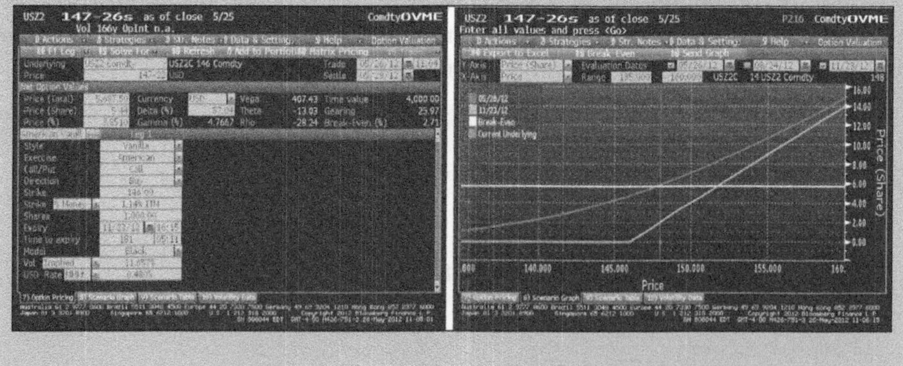

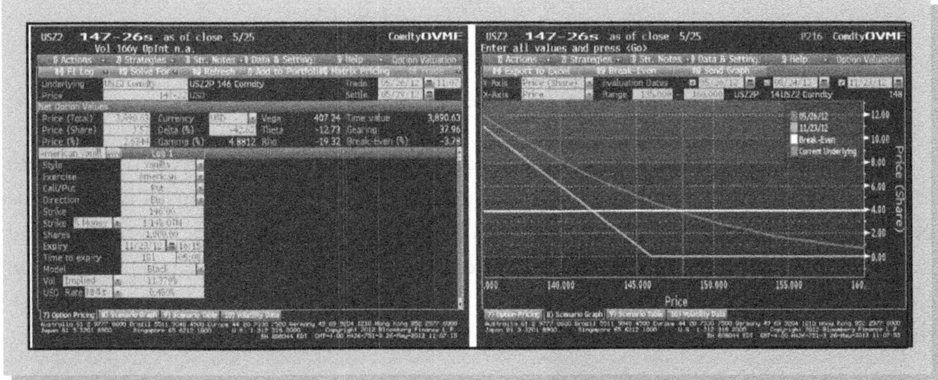

Pricing Caplets and Floorlet with the Black Futures Option Model

The Black futures option model also can be extended to pricing caplets and floorlets by (1) substituting T^* for T in the equation for C^* (for a caplet) or P^* (for a floorlet), where T^* is the time to expiration on the option plus the time period applied to the interest rate payoff time period, ϕ: $T^* = T + \phi$; (2) using an annual continuous compounded risk-free rate for period T^* instead of T; (3) multiplying the Black adjusted-futures option model by the notional principal times the time period: (NP) ϕ.

$$C_0^* = \phi(NP)[RN(d_1) - R_X N(d_2)]e^{-R_f T^*}$$

$$P_0^* = \phi(NP)[R_X(1 - N(d_2)) - R(1 - N(d_1))]e^{-R_f T^*}$$

$$d_1 = \frac{\ln(R/R_X) + (\sigma^2/2)T}{\sigma \ - \sigma \ \sqrt{T}}$$

$$d_2 = d_1 - \sigma \sqrt{T}$$

Example: Pricing a Caplet and a Cap

Consider a caplet with an exercise rate of $X = 7$ percent, NP = \$100,000, $\phi = .25$, expiration = T = .25 year, and reference rate = LIBOR. If the current LIBOR were R = 6 percent, the estimated annualized standard deviation of the LIBOR's logarithmic return were .2, and the continuously compounded risk-free rate were 5.8629 percent, then using the Black model, the price of the caplet would be 4.34.

$$C_0^* = .25(\$100{,}000)[.06(.067845) - .07(.055596)]e^{-(.058629)(.5)} = 4.34$$

where:

$$d_1 = \frac{\ln(.06/.07) + (.04/2)(.25)}{.2\sqrt{.25}} = -1.49151$$

$$d_2 = d_1 - .2\sqrt{.25} \;=\; -1.59151$$
$$N(-1.49151) = .067845$$
$$N(-1.59151) = .055596$$

Suppose the caplet represented part of a contract that caps a two-year floating-rate loan of $100,000 at 7 percent for a three-month period. The cap consist of seven caplets, with expirations of $T = .25$ years, .5, .75, 1, 1.25, 1.5, and 1.75. The value of the cap is equal to the sum of the values of the caplets comprising the cap. If we assume a flat yield curve such that the continuous rate of 5.8629 percent applies, and we use the same volatility of .2 for each caplet, then the value of the cap would be $254.53:

Expiration	Price of Caplet
0.25	4.34
0.50	15.29
0.75	26.74
1.00	37.63
1.25	47.73
1.50	57.04
1.75	65.61
	254.38

In practice, different volatilities for each caplet are used in valuing a cap or floor. The different volatilities are referred to as spot volatilities. They are often estimated by calculating the implied volatility on a comparable Eurodollar futures options.

BLOOMBERG SWAP AND INTEREST RATE DERIVATIVE SCREEN FOR VALUING CAPS AND FLOORS—SWPM

SWPM analyzes, creates, and values swaps and interest rate derivative contracts. The Caps/Floors screen in SWPM can be used to set up caps, floors, and collars and to value them. The Black futures model is used to value a caplet or floorlet and the value of the cap is equal to the sum of each caplet or floorlet value.

For a description of the program, go to IRDD, click "Cap/Floor/Collar/Straddle," and then click "More Info."

To analyze a cap or floor on the SWPM screen, go to the "Products" tab, click "Cap" or "Floor" under the "Options" dropdown. This will bring up the main screen that can be used to create the cap or floor. The cap or floor is valued by using a forward rate curve and the Black OPM; each caplet is valued in the cash flow table. The total market value is shown at the bottom of the main screen.

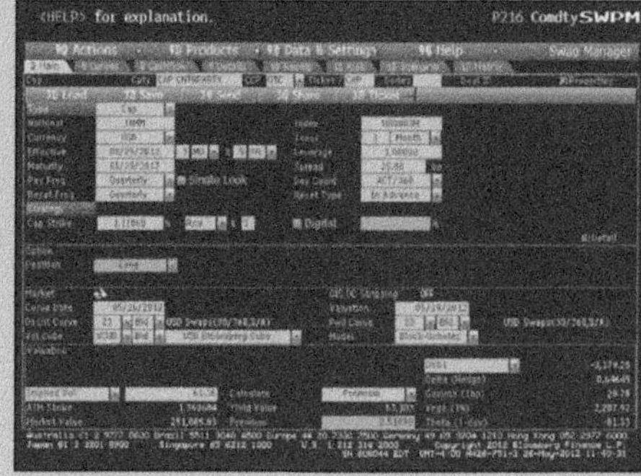

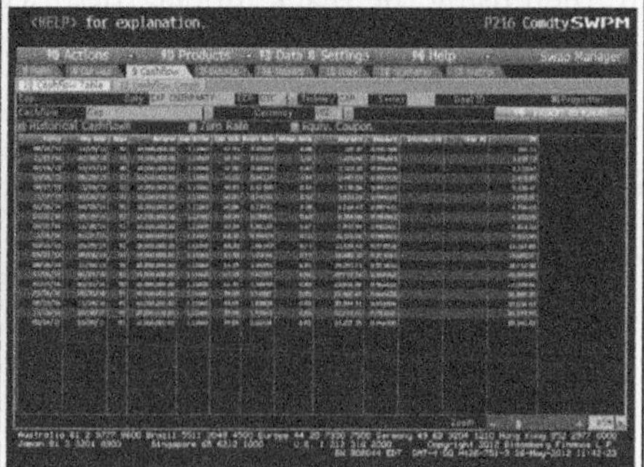

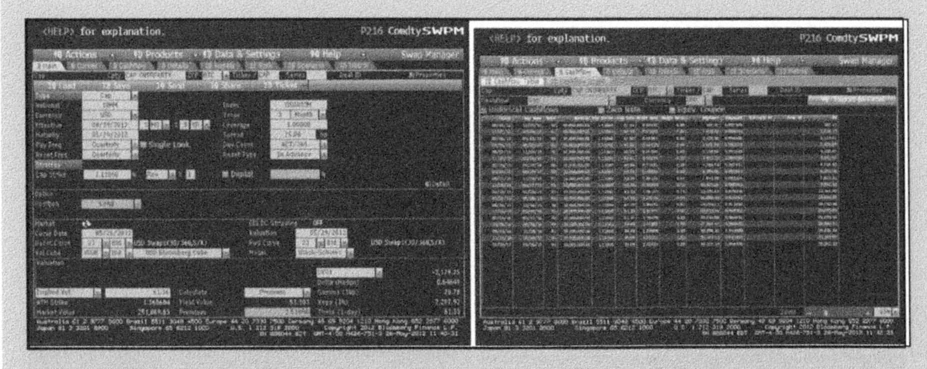

Implied Volatility

The volatility of the underlying security is the only input that needs to be estimated in the B-S OPM, the Black futures model, and the binomial interest rate tree model. Two methods often are used to estimate the variance of the logarithmic return: calculating the historical variance or solving for the security's implied variance. A historical volatility of a security, futures, or spot rate is computed using a sample of historical data (see Exhibit 13.17).

The implied variance is that variance that equates the OPM's value to the market price. Unfortunately, one merely cannot set the option model's price equal to the option's market price, then solve algebraically to find a unique solution for the variance. The implied variance can be found, though, by trial and error: substituting different variance values into the B-S or Black futures model until that variance is found that yields an OPM value equal to the market price. Theoretically, we should expect the implied variance for different options on the same security to be the same. In practice, this does not occur. One way to select an implied variance is to use the arithmetic average for the different implied variances on the stock. A common approach among option traders is to select the volatility based on the option's *volatility smile* and its *volatility term structure.* A volatility smile is a plot of the implied volatilities given different exercise prices. The volatility term structure, in turn, refers to the relation between an option's implied volatility and its time to expiration.

BLOOMBERG IMPLIED VARIANCE CALCULATIONS AND VOLATILITY SMILE

OV or OVME: The Bloomberg option value screens allow for the calculation of the option price using either an historical volatility or an implied variance (Bloomberg). On the OV screen, select Historical or Bloomberg (implied volatility) from the "Vol" box.
Volatility Smile can be accessed from the OV or OVME screen by clicking the "Volatility Data" tab at the bottom.
CV: The CV Screen shows the historical and implied volatility for a security.

(*Continued*)

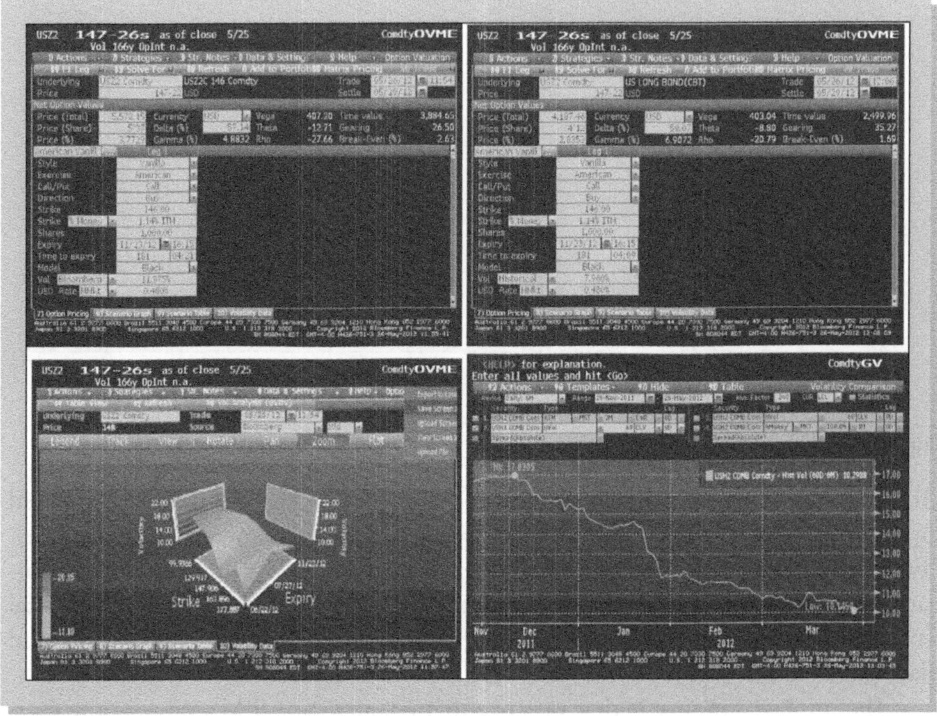

Note on Variability and Use of Black-Scholes Model

Even though the B-S OPM and the Black Model can be used to estimate the equilibrium price of interest rate options, futures options, and bonds with embedded options, there are at least two problems. First, the OPM is based on the assumption that the variance of the underlying asset is constant. In the case of a bond, though, its variability tends to decrease as its maturity becomes shorter. Second, the OPM assumes the interest rate is constant. This assumption does not hold for options on interest-sensitive securities. In spite of these problems, the B-S OPM and the Black futures model are still extensively used to value interest rate options.

Conclusion

Fixed-income securities with embedded options are difficult to value. In this chapter, we have examined how a binomial model that identifies the possible random paths that interest rates follow over time can be used to value bonds with embedded options, as well bond and interest rate options. The model can also be used to value sinking funds in which the issuer has a call option and MBS where there is a prepayment options.[15]

Website Information

FINRA

- Go to www.finra.org/index.htm, Sitemap, Market Data, and Bonds.
- To find bonds with embedded option use the bond search: click the "Corporate" tab, "Advanced Bond Search," and then select call, put, and/or convertible.

Yahoo.com

- To find convertible bond funds, go to http://finance.yahoo.com/funds, click "Fund Screener," and search for convertibles.

Selected References

Bhattacharya, M. 2009. Convertible securities and their valuation. In F. Fabozzi, ed., *The Handbook of Fixed Income Securities,* 7th ed. New York: McGraw-Hill, 1393–1442.

Black, F. 1976. The pricing of commodity contracts. *Journal of Financial Economics* 3:167–179.

Black, F., E. Derman, and W. Toy. 1990. A one-factor model of interest rates and its application to Treasury bond options. *Financial Analysts Journal* 46:33–39.

Black, F., and J. Cox. 1976. Valuing corporate securities: Some effects of bond indenture provisions. *Journal of Finance* 31:351–367.

Black, F., and M. Scholes. 1972. The valuation of option contracts and a test of market efficiency. *Journal of Finance* 27:399–418.

Black, F., and M. Scholes. 1973. The pricing of options and corporate liabilities. *Journal of Political Economy* 81:637–659.

Boyle, P. P. 1977. Options: A Monte Carlo approach. *Journal of Financial Economics* 4:323–338.

Boyle, P. 1988. A lattice framework for option pricing with two state variables. *Journal of Financial and Qualitative Analysis* 23:1–12.

Courtadon, G. 1982. The pricing of options on default-free bonds. *Journal of Financial and Quantitative Analysis* 17:75–100.

Cox, J. C., and S. A. Ross. 1976. The valuation of options for alternative stochastic processes. *Journal of Financial Economics* 3:145–166.

Cox, J. C., J. Ingersoll, and S. Ross. 1985. "The Theory of the Term Structure of Interest Rates." Econometrica 53:385–407.

Cox, J. C., S. A. Ross, and M. Rubinstein. 1979. Option pricing: A simplified approach. *Journal of Financial Economics* 7:229–263.

Cox, J. C., and M. Rubinstein. 1985. *Options Markets.* Englewood Cliffs, NJ: Prentice-Hall.

Dialynas, C. P., S. Durn, and J. C. Ritchie, Jr. 2001. Convertible securities and their investment characteristics. In F. Fabozzi, ed., *The Handbook of Fixed Income Securities,* 6th ed. New York: McGraw-Hill.

Dunn, K., and K. Eades. 1989. Voluntary conversion of convertible securities and the optimal call strategy. *Journal of Financial Economics* 23:273.

Heath, D., R. Jarrow, and A. Morton. 1992. Bond pricing and the term structure of interest rates: A new methodology for contingent claims valuation. *Econometrics* 60:77–105.

Ho, T., and S.-B. Lee. 1986. Term structure movements and pricing interest rate contingent claims. *Journal of Finance* 41:1011–1029.

Hull, J., and A. White. 1990. Pricing interest rate derivative securities. *Review of Financial Studies* 3:573–592.

Jamshidian, P. 1987. *Pricing of Contingent Claims in the One-Factor Term Structure Model.* Trading Analysis Group, Merrill Lynch Capital Markets.

Johnson, R. S. 2009. *Introduction to derivatives: Options, futures, and swaps.* New York: Oxford University Press.

Johnson, R. S., J. E. Pawlukiewicz, and J. M. Mehta. 1997. Binomial option pricing with skewed asset returns. *Review of Quantitative Finance and Accounting* 9:89–101.

Longstaff, F., and E. Schwartz. 1992. Interest rate volatility and the term structure: A two-factor general equilibrium model. *Journal of Finance* 47:1259–1282.

Rendleman, R. J., Jr., and B. J. Bartter. 1980. The pricing of options on debt securities. *Journal of Financial and Quantitative Analysis* 15:11–24.

Stein, J. 1992. Convertible bonds as backdoor financing. *Journal of Financial Economics* 32:1–21.

Sundaresan, S. 1997. *Fixed Income Markets and Their Derivatives.* Cincinnati, OH: Southwestern.

Tsiveriotis, K., and C. Fernandes. 1998. Valuing convertible bonds with credit risk. *Journal of Fixed Income* 8:95–102.

Taggart, R. A. 1996. *Quantitative Analysis for Investment Management.* Upper Saddle River, NJ: Prentice Hall, 118–160.

Tuckman, B. 1995. *Fixed Income Securities.* New York: John Wiley & Sons.

Bloomberg Exercises

1. Evaluate several bonds with call and/or put options. You may want to use Bloomberg's bond search screen, SRCH.
2. Evaluate several convertible bonds. You may want to use the Bloomberg's convertible bond search screen, CSCH. Include the Bloomberg OVCV screen in your evaluation.
3. Select a callable investment-grade corporate bond of interest. You may want to use the Bloomberg search/screen function, SRCH, to find your bonds. Evaluate the bond in terms of its YTM, yield to first call, and yield to worst. Use the OAS1 screen to determine the option-free spread on the bond and the YA screen to determine its total spread. What is the bond's credit and liquidity spread? What is its callable spread?
4. Use Bloomberg's OV or OVME screen to determine the Black Futures call and put option values for several exchange-traded futures options contracts. Type CTM to bring up "Contract Table" menu, click "Bond" on the CTM screen, find the contract of interest, and bring up the contract's menu screen: Ticker <Comdty>. After selecting an option bring up the option's menu screen (Ticker <Comdty>) and then type OV or OVME.
5. Using the OV or OVME screen for the futures option you selected in Question 4, bring up the option's volatility smile (click "Volatility Data" tab). From the volatility smile, determine the implied volatility that matches the option expiration and exercise price. Using that volatility, determine the value of the futures option. How does the value compare to the value obtained using the historical volatility?

Notes

1. In this case, the issuer could buy the bond back at 98, financed by issuing a one-year bond at 9.5 percent interest. One period later the issuer would owe 98(1.095) = 107.31; this

represents a savings of 108 – 107.31 = 0.69. Note, the value of that savings in Period 1 is .69 / 1.095 = 0.63, which is equal to the difference between the bond price and the call price: 98.630 - 98 = .63.

2. The same binomial value can also be found by determining the value of the put option at each node and then pricing the putable bond as the value of an otherwise identical non-putable bond plus the value of the put option. In using the second approach, the value of the put option will be the maximum of either its intrinsic value (or exercising value), IV = Max[$PP - B_p$, 0], or its holding value (the present value of the expected put value next period). In most cases, though, the put's intrinsic value will be greater than its holding value.
3. Another convertible bond term is its conversion price. The *conversion price* is the bond's par value divided by the conversion ratio: F/CR.
4. If the option is American, then its early exercise advantage needs to be taken into account by determining at each node whether or not it is more valuable to hold the option or exercise. This is done by starting one period prior to the expiration of the option and constraining the price of the American option to be the maximum of its binomial value (present value of next period's expected cash flows) or the intrinsic value (i.e., the value from exercising). Those values are then rolled to the next preceding period, and the American option values for that period are obtained by again constraining the option prices to be the maximum of the binomial value or the IV; this process continues to the current period.
5. If the call option is American, its two possible prices in Period 1 are constrained to be the maximum of the binomial value (present value of next period's expected cash flows) or the intrinsic value (i.e., the value from exercising): $C_t^A = Max[C_t, IV]$. In Period 1, the IV slightly exceeds the binomial value when the spot rate is 4.54545 percent. As a result, the American call price is equal to its IV of .145 (see Exhibit 13.11). Rolling this price and the upper rate's price of .01947 to the current period yields a price for the American T-bill call of .08. This price slightly exceeds the European value of .0787, reflecting the early exercise advantage of the American option.
6. Valuing an American T-bond option requires constraining the American price to be the maximum of the binomial value or the IV. In this example, if the T-bond option were American, then in Period 1 the option's price would be equal to its IV of 3.79 at the lower rate. Rolling this price and the upper rate's price of .9328 to the current period yields a price of 2.228.
7. If the futures call were American, then at the spot rate of 5 percent in Period 1, its IV would be 2.88 (= Max[100.88 – 98,0]), exceeding the binomial value of 2.743. Rolling the 2.88 value to the current period yields a price on the American futures option of 1.798 (= .5(.9328) + .5(2.88)) – this price differs from the American spot option price of 2.228. In the case of a European put on a spot or futures T-bond, to value we start at expiration where bond's possible prices are 97.57, 100, and 101.76 and the corresponding IVs of the put are .43, 0, and 0. In Period 1, the put's two possible values would be .2006 (= (.5(.43) + .5(0)) / 1.072) and 0. Rolling these value to the current period yields a price on the European put of .0946 (= (.5(.2006) + .5(0)) / 1.06). Note, that if the spot put were American, then its possible prices in Period 1 would be .253 and 0, and it current price would be .119 (= (.5(.253) + .5(0)) / 1.06); if the futures put were American, there would be no exercise advantage in period 1 and thus the price would be equal to its European value of .0946.
8. *n!* (read as *n factorial*) is the product of all numbers from 1 to *n;* also 0! = 1.

9. Note that the annualized standard deviation cannot be obtained simply by multiplying the quarterly standard deviation by four. Rather, one must first multiply the quarterly variance by four and then take the square root of the resulting annualized variance.
10. Note, in the equations for u and d, as n increases the mean term in the exponent goes to zero quicker than the square root term. As a result, for large n (e.g., n = 30), the mean term's impact on u and d is negligible and u and d can be estimated as:

$$u = e^{\sqrt{V_e / n}} \text{ and } d = e^{-\sqrt{V_e / n}} = 1/u$$

11. The u and d formulas derived here assume an interest rate process in which the variance and mean are stable and where the end-of-the-period distribution is symmetrical. Other models can be used to address cases in which these assumptions do not hold. Merton's mixed diffusion-jump model, for example, accounts for the possibilities of infrequent jumps in the underlying price or interest rate, and Cox and Ross's constant elasticity of variance model is applicable for cases in which the variance is inversely related to the underlying price or rate.
12. It should be noted that the lower rate of 9.5 percent represents a decline from the current rate of 10 percent, which is what we tend to expect in a binomial process. This is because we have calibrated the binomial tree to a relatively flat yield curve. If we had calibrated the tree to a positively sloped yield curve, then it is possible that both rates next period could be greater than the current rate; although the upper rate will be greater than the lower. For example, if the current two-year spot rate were 10.5 percent instead of 10.1022385, then the equilibrium price of a two-year bond would be .8189 and the S_d and S_u values that calibrate the tree to this price and variability of .0054 would be 10.20066 percent and 11.8156 percent. By contrast, if we had calibrated the tree to a negatively sloped curve, then it is possible that both rates next period could be lower than the current one.
13. Students of option pricing may recall that arbitrage-free models can alternatively be priced using a risk-neutral pricing approach. When applied to bond pricing, this approach requires finding the pseudo probabilities that make a binomial tree of bond prices equal to the equilibrium price. The risk-neutral pricing approach is equivalent to the calibration approach.
14. It should be noted that the call and future prices are also consistent with put-call futures parity.
15. For an analysis of valuing MBS and sinking fund call options, see Johnson (2009), Chapters 7 and 22.

CHAPTER 14

Interest Rate and Credit Default Swaps

Introduction

A swap, by definition, is a legal arrangement between two parties to exchange specific payments. There are four types of financial swaps:

1. *Interest rate swaps:* The exchange of fixed-rate payments for floating-rate payments.
2. *Currency swaps:* The exchange of liabilities in different currencies.
3. *Cross-currency swaps:* The combination of an interest rate and currency swap.
4. *Credit default swaps:* Exchange of premium payments for default protection.

In this chapter, we examine the features, markets, and uses of standard interest rate swaps, two interest rate swap derivatives, and the markets, uses and pricing of credit default swaps.

Generic Interest Rate Swaps

Features

The simplest type of interest rate swap is called the *plain vanilla swap* or *generic swap.* In this agreement, one party provides fixed-rate interest payments to another party who provides floating-rate payments. The parties to the agreement are referred to as *counterparties:* The party who pays fixed interest and receives floating is called the *fixed-rate payer;* the other party (who pays floating and receives fixed) is the *floating-rate payer.* The fixed-rate payer is also called the floating-rate receiver and is often referred to as having bought the swap or having a long position; the floating-rate payer is also called the fixed-rate receiver and is referred to as having sold the swap and being short.

On a generic swap, principal payments are not exchanged. As a result, the interest payments are based on a notional principal (NP). The interest rate paid by the fixed payer often is specified in terms of the yield to maturity (YTM) on a T-note plus basis points; the rate paid by the floating payer on a generic swap is the London Interbank Offered Rate (LIBOR). Swap payments on a generic swap are made semiannually and the maturities typically range from 3 to 10 years. In the swap contract, a trade date, effective date, settlement date, and maturity date are specified. The *trade date* is the day the parties agree to commit to the swap; the *effective date* is the date when interest begins to accrue; the *settlement* or *payment date* is when interest payments are made (interest is paid in arrears six months after the effective date); and the *maturity date* is the last payment date. On the payment date, only the interest differential between the counterparties is paid. That is, generic swap payments are based on a *net settlement basis:* The counterparty owing the greater amount pays the difference between what is owed and what is received. Thus, if a fixed-rate payer owes $2 million and a floating-rate payer owes $1.5 million, then only a $0.5 million payment by the fixed payer to the floating payer is made. All of the terms of the swap are specified in a legal agreement signed by both parties called the *confirmation.* The drafting of the confirmation often follows document forms suggested by the *International Swap and Derivative Association* (*ISDA*) in New York. This organization provides a number of master agreements delineating the terminology used in many swap agreements (e.g., what happens in the case of default, the business day convention, and the like).

Interest Rate Swap: Example

Consider an interest rate swap with a maturity of three years, first effective date of 3/23/Y1 and a maturity date of 3/23/Y4. In this swap agreement, assume the fixed-rate payer agrees to pay the current YTM on a three-year T-note of 5 percent plus 50 basis points (bp) and the floating-rate payer agrees to pay the six-month LIBOR as determined on the effective dates with no basis points. Also assume the semiannual interest rates are determined by dividing the annual rates (LIBOR and 5.5 percent) by two. Finally, assume the notional principal on the swap is $10 million. (The calculations will be slightly off because they fail to include the actual day count convention.)

Exhibit 14.1 shows the interest payments on each settlement date based on assumed LIBORs on the effective dates. In examining the table, several points should be noted. First, the payments are determined by the LIBOR prevailing six months prior to the payment date; thus payers on swaps would know their obligations in advance of the payment date. Second, when the LIBOR is below the fixed 5.5 percent

EXHIBIT 14.1 Interest Rate Swap: 5.5 percent/LIBOR Swap with NP = $10 Million

1	2	3	4	5	6
Effective Dates	LIBOR	Floating-Rate Payer's Payment*	Fixed-Rate Payer's Payment**	Net Interest Received by Fixed-Rate Payer Column 3 – Column 4	Net Interest Received by Floating-Rate Payer Column 4 – Column 3
3/23/Y1	0.045				
9/23/Y1	0.050	$225,000	$275,000	-$50,000	$50,000
3/23/Y2	0.055	$250,000	$275,000	-$25,000	$25,000
9/23/Y2	0.060	$275,000	$275,000	$0	$0
3/23/Y3	0.065	$300,000	$275,000	$25,000	-$25,000
9/23/Y3	0.070	$325,000	$275,000	$50,000	-$50,000
3/23/Y4		$350,000	$275,000	$75,000	-$75,000

* (LIBOR/2)($10,000,000)
** (.055/2)*($10,000,000)

rate, the fixed-rate payer pays the interest differential to the floating-rate payer; when it is above 5.5 percent, the fixed-rate payer receives the interest differential from the floating-rate payer. The net interest received by the fixed-rate payer is shown in Column 5 of the table, and the net interest received by the floating-rate payer is shown in Column 6. As we will discuss later, the fixed-rate payer's position is very similar to a short position in a series of Eurodollar futures contracts, with the futures price determined by the fixed rate. The fixed payer's cash flows also can be replicated by the fixed payer buying a $10 million, three-year, floating-rate note (FRN) paying the LIBOR and shorting (issuing) a $10 million, 5.5 percent fixed-rate bond at par. The floating-rate payer's position, in contrast, is similar to a long position in a Eurodollar strip, and it can be replicated by shorting (issuing) a three-year, $10 million FRN paying the LIBOR and purchasing a three-year, $10 million, 5.5 percent fixed-rate bond at par.

BLOOMBERG SWPM SCREEN FOR ANALYZING GENERIC FIXED-/FLOATING-RATE SWAPS:

SWPM <ENTER>
The SWPM screen can be used to create, value, and analyze swaps and interest rate derivatives.
Fixed-/Floating-Rate Swap: To create a fixed-/floating-rate swap on SWPM, go to the "Products" tab and click "Fixed–Floating" under the "Swaps" dropdown. This will bring up the main screen for a generic swap. The swap shown defaults to a five-year swap. You can then change the settings on the main screen.

1. Options on swaps: On the dropdown "Pay Fixed" or "Receive Fixed" (this will automatically adjust for the other leg (counterparty), Notional Principal, Currency, Payment Frequency, Coupon (this is the fixed rate), Spread (the number of basis points to add or subtract from the floating rate, LIBOR).

(*Continued*)

2. Shortcut: Instead of changing the setting on the main tab, you can enter:
   SWPM NP Currency yrs. to maturity fixed rate
   SWPM 100MM USD 5.2
3. Forward graph options: SWPM determines future cash flows at each reset date based on the forward rate at that date. The user can select which yield curve the forward rates are to be determined. On the "Curve" screen ("Curve" tab), one can view the forward graph and make shift adjustment.
4. Discount Rate Option: SWPM also discounts cash flows to determine the market value (shown at the bottom of main screen; the user can also select which yield curve to be used for discounting).

TAB SCREENS

1. "Details" tab shows the details of the swap.
2. "Resets" tab shows the reset rate at each effective date (forward LIBOR plus basis points you added to the spread (one can change the rates from this tab)).
3. "Chart" tab shows graphically the payments, receipts, and net payments. This tab screen can be adjusted to show each counterparty (pay fix or receive fix), cash flow, and market values.
4. "Scenario" tab allows one to make scenario changes for different times and determine the change in value.

Example: Fixed/Floating swap (Leg 1 is fixed-rate payer); NP = $5.75 million; fixed rate (coupon) = 1.5 percent; floating rate = six-month LIBOR + 25 bp; frequency = semi-annual; maturity = five years; forward curve = U.S. swaps (#23); discount curve = U.S. swaps (#23).

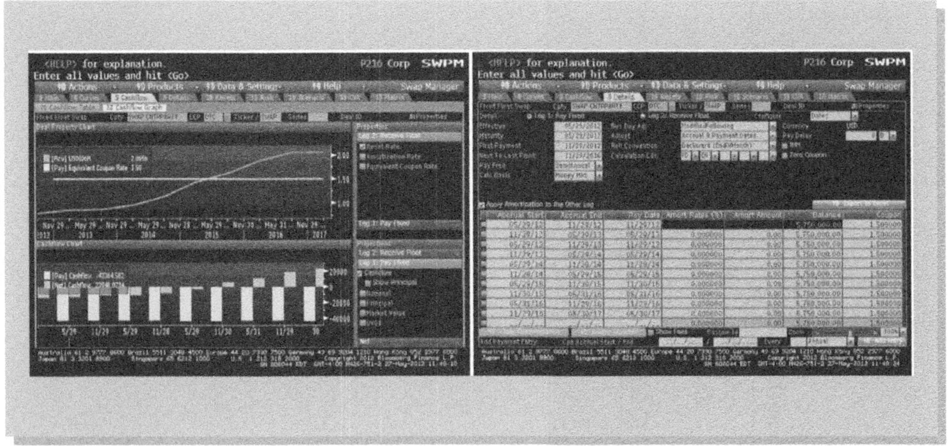

Synthetic Loans

One of the important uses of swaps is in creating a synthetic fixed-rate or floating-rate liability or changing a conventional fixed-rate loan (or floating) to a floating-rate (fixed-rate) one. To illustrate, suppose a corporation with an AAA credit rating wants a three-year, $10 million fixed-rate loan starting on March 23, Y1. Suppose one possibility available to the company is to borrow $10 million from a bank at a fixed rate of 6 percent (assume semiannual payments) with a loan maturity of three years. Suppose, though, that the bank also is willing to provide the company with a three-year floating-rate loan, with the rate set equal to the LIBOR on March 23 and September 23 each year for three years. If a swap agreement identical to the one described above were available, then instead of a direct fixed-rate loan, the company alternatively could attain a fixed-rate loan by borrowing $10 million on the floating-rate loan, then fix the interest rate by taking a fixed-rate payer's position on the swap:

Conventional Floating-Rate Loan	Pay Floating Rate
Swap: Fixed-Rate Payer Position	Pay Fixed Rate
Swap: Fixed-Rate Payer Position	Receive Floating Rate
Synthetic Fixed Rate	Pay Fixed Rate

As shown in Exhibit 14.2, if the floating-rate loan is hedged with a swap, any change in the LIBOR would be offset by an opposite change in the net receipts on the swap position. In this example, the company (as shown in the exhibit) would end up paying a constant $275,000 every sixth month, which equates to an annualized borrowing rate of 5.5 percent: R = 2($275,000) / $10 million = .055. Thus, the corporation would be better off combining the swap position as a fixed-rate payer with the floating-rate loan to create a synthetic fixed-rate loan than simply taking the straight fixed-rate loan.

EXHIBIT 14.2 Synthetic Fixed-Rate Loan: Floating-Rate Loan Set at LIBOR and Fixed-Payer Position on 5.5 Percent/LIBOR Swap

Effective Dates	LIBOR	Swap Floating-Rate Payer's Payment*	Swap Fixed-Rate Payer's Payment**	Swap Net Interest Received by Fixed-Rate Payer Column 3 – Column 4	Loan Interest Paid on Floating-Rate Loan*	Synthetic Loan Payment on Swap and Loan Column 6 – Column 5	Synthetic Loan Effective Annualized Rate***
3/23/Y1	0.0450						
9/23/Y1	0.0500	$225,000	$275,000	–$50,000	$225,000	$275,000	0.06
3/23/Y2	0.0550	$250,000	$275,000	–$25,000	$250,000	$275,000	0.06
9/23/Y2	0.0600	$275,000	$275,000	$0	$275,000	$275,000	0.06
3/23/Y3	0.0650	$300,000	$275,000	$25,000	$300,000	$275,000	0.06
9/23/Y3	0.0700	$325,000	$275,000	$50,000	$325,000	$275,000	0.06
3/23/Y4		$350,000	$275,000	$75,000	$350,000	$275,000	0.06

* (LIBOR/2)($10,000,000)
** (.055/2)($10,000,000)
*** 2 (Payment on Swap and Loan)/$10,000,000

In contrast, a synthetic floating-rate loan is formed by combining a floating-rate payer's position with a fixed-rate loan. This loan then can be used as an alternative to a floating-rate loan:

Conventional Fixed-Rate Loan	Pay Fixed Rate
Swap: Floating-Rate Payer Position	Pay Floating Rate
Swap: Floating-Rate Payer Position	Receive Fixed Rate
Synthetic Floating Rate	Pay Floating Rate

An example of a synthetic floating-rate loan is shown in Exhibit 14.3. The synthetic loan is formed with a 5 percent fixed-rate loan (semiannual payments) and the floating-rate payer's position on our illustrate swap. As shown in the exhibit, the synthetic floating-rate loan yields a 0.5 percent lower interest rate each period (annualized rate) than a floating-rate loan tied to the LIBOR.

Note that in both of the above examples, the borrower is able to attain a better borrowing rate with a synthetic loan using swaps than with a direct loan. When differences between the rates on actual and synthetic loans do exist, then swaps provide an apparent arbitrage use in which borrowers and investors can obtain better rates with synthetic positions formed with swap positions than they can from conventional loans.

Similarities between Swaps and Bond Positions and Eurodollar Futures Strips

Bond Positions

Swaps can be viewed as a combination of a fixed-rate bond and floating-rate note (FRN). As noted, a fixed-rate payer position is equivalent to buying an FRN paying the LIBOR and shorting (issuing) a fixed-rate bond at the swap's fixed rate. From the previous example, the purchase of $10 million worth of three-year FRNs with the rate reset every six months at the LIBOR and the sale of $10 million worth of three-year, 5.5 percent fixed-rate bonds at par would yield the same cash flow as the fixed-rate payer's swap. On the other hand, a floating-rate payer's position is equivalent to shorting (or issuing) an FRN at the LIBOR and buying a fixed-rate bond at the swap's fixed rate. Thus, the purchase of $10 million worth of three-year 5.5 percent fixed-rate bonds at par and the sale of $10 million worth of FRNs paying the LIBOR would yield the same cash flow as the floating-rate payer's swap in the preceding example.

Eurodollar Futures Strip

A plain vanilla swap can also be viewed as a series of Eurodollar futures contracts. To see the similarities, consider a short position in a Eurodollar strip in which the short holder agrees to sell 10 Eurodollar deposits, each with face values of $1 million and maturities of six months, at the IMM-index price of 94.5 (or discount yield of R_D = 5.5 percent), with the expirations on the strip being March 23 and September 23 for a period of two and a half years. Exhibit 14.4 shows the cash flows at the expiration

EXHIBIT 14.3 Synthetic Floating-Rate Loan 5 Percent Fixed-Rate Loan and Floating-Payer Position on 5.5 Percent/LIBOR Swap

Effective Dates	LIBOR	Swap Floating-Rate Payer's Payment*	Swap Fixed-Rate Payer's Payment**	Swap Net Interest Received by Floating-Rate Payer Column 4 – Column 3	Loan Interest Paid on 5% Fixed-Rate Loan	Synthetic Loan Payment on Swap and Loan Column 6 – Column 5	Synthetic Loan Effective Annualized Rate***
3/23/Y1	0.0450						
9/23/Y1	0.0500	$225,000	$275,000	$50,000	$250,000	$200,000	0.040
3/23/Y2	0.0550	$250,000	$275,000	$25,000	$250,000	$225,000	0.045
9/23/Y2	0.0600	$275,000	$275,000	$0	$250,000	$250,000	0.050
3/23/Y3	0.0650	$300,000	$275,000	–$25,000	$250,000	$275,000	0.055
9/23/Y3	0.0700	$325,000	$275,000	–$50,000	$250,000	$300,000	0.060
3/23/Y4		$350,000	$275,000	–$75,000	$250,000	$325,000	0.065

* (LIBOR/2)($10,000,000)
** (.055/2)($10,000,000)
*** 2 (Payment on Swap and Loan)/$10,000,000

EXHIBIT 14.4 Short Positions in Eurodollar Futures

1	2	3	4	5
Closing Dates	LIBOR	f_T	Cash Flow from Short Position $10[f_0 - f_T]$	Cash Flow from Long Position $10[f_T - f_0]$
3/23/Y1	0.050	$975,000	-$25,000	$25,000
9/23/Y1	0.055	$972,500	$0	$0
3/23/Y2	0.060	$970,000	$25,000	-$25,000
9/23/Y2	0.065	$967,500	$50,000	-$50,000
3/23/Y3	0.070	$965,000	$75,000	-$75,000
9/23/Y3	0.075	$962,500	$100,000	-$100,000

$f_0 = 972{,}500$

$$f_T = \left[\frac{100 - (\text{LIBOR})(180/360)}{100}\right](\$1{,}000{,}000)$$

dates from closing the 10 short Eurodollar contracts at the same assumed LIBOR used in the above swap example, with the Eurodollar settlement Index being 100 – LIBOR. Comparing the fixed-rate payer's net receipts shown in Column 5 of Exhibit 14.1 with the cash flows from the short positions on the Eurodollar strip shown in Exhibit 14.4, one can see that the two positions yield the same numbers. However, one difference to note between the Eurodollar strip and the swap is the six-month differential between the swap payment and the futures payments. This time differential is a result of the interest payments on the swap being determined by the LIBOR at the beginning of the period, whereas the futures position's profit is based on the LIBOR at the end of its period.

BLOOMBERG ASW SCREEN:

The Bloomberg ASW screen allows one to calculate the relative value of a selected bond through the interest rate swap market. For example, one can use ASW to determine if it is better to enter into an asset swap versus purchasing a floating-rate instrument. You can also use ASW to determine how much money can be saved in interest costs by issuing a fixed-rate bond and swapping the fixed payments for floating payments.

For example, for a loaded 10-year, 2 percent T-note (to load: go to security's menu page (10-year Treasury: 912828RR3 <Govt>) and type ASW), ASW will create a comparable swap with the same fixed rate of 2 percent and 10-year maturity. One can then select the index for determining the floating rate (e.g., LIBOR) and the forward rate and discount rate curves. ASW shows the swap pricing details (Pricing tab), cash flow details (Cashflow tab) and deal details (Deal Summary tab).

(*Continued*)

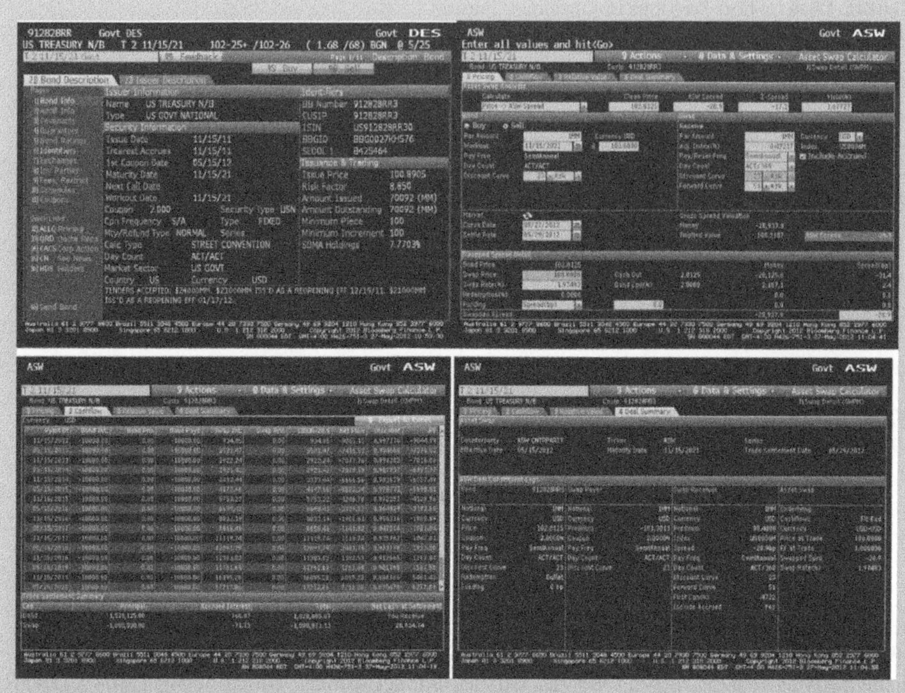

EXAMPLE: FLOATING-RATE NOTE: BAC FLOATER

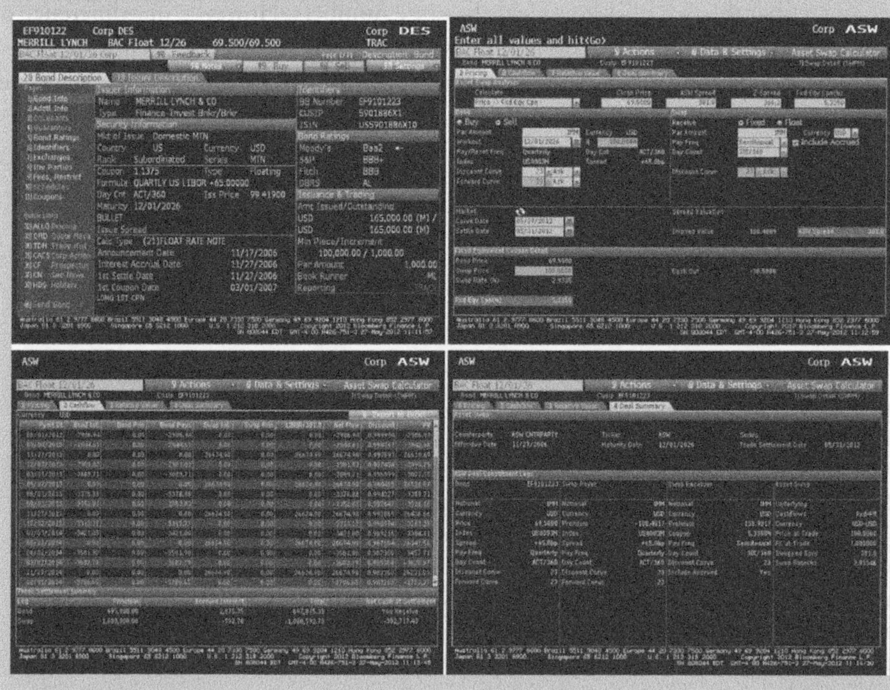

Swap Market

Structure

Corporations, financial institutions, and others who use swaps are linked by a group of brokers and dealers who collectively are referred to as *swap banks*. These swap banks consist primarily of commercial banks and investment bankers. As brokers, swap banks try to match parties with opposite needs (see Exhibit 14.5). Many of the first interest rate swaps were customized brokered deals between counterparties, with the parties often negotiating and transacting directly between themselves. As brokers, the swap bank's role in the contract is to bring the parties together and provide information; swap banks often maintains lists of companies and financial institutions that are potential parties to a swap. Once the swap agreement is closed, the swap broker usually has only a minor continuing role. With some *brokered swaps,* the swap bank guarantees one or both sides of the transaction. With many, though, the counterparties assume the credit risk and make their own assessment of the other party's default potential.

One of the problems with a brokered swap is that it requires each party to have knowledge of the other party's risk profile. Historically, this problem led to more swap banks taking positions as dealers instead of as brokers. With *dealer swaps,* the swap dealer often makes commitments to enter a swap as a counterparty before the other end party has been located. Each of the counterparties (or in this context, the end parties) contracts separately with the swap bank, who acts as a counterparty to each. The end parties, in turn, assume the credit risk of the financial institution instead of that of the other end party, whereas the swap dealer assumes the credit risk of both of the end parties.

EXHIBIT 14.5 Swap Market Structure

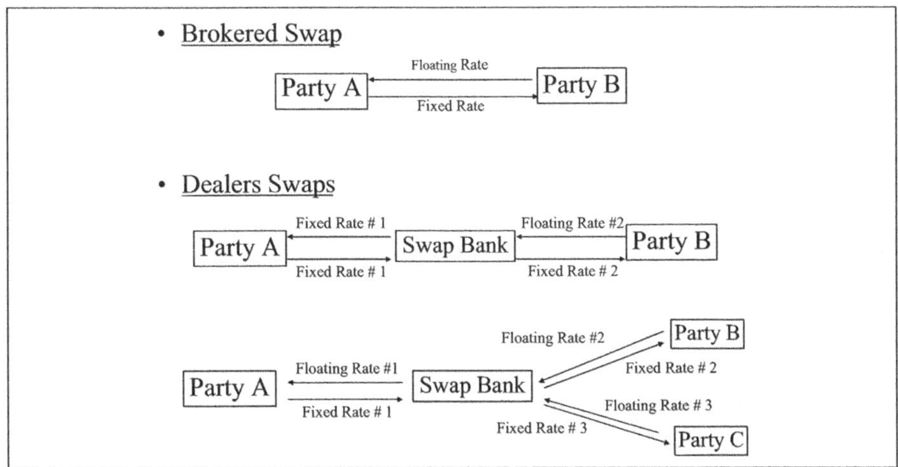

In acting as dealers, swap banks often match a swap agreement with multiple end parties. For example, as illustrated in Exhibit 14.5, a $30 million fixed-for-floating swap between a swap dealer and Party A might be matched with two $15 million floating-for-fixed swaps. Ideally, a swap bank tries to maintain a perfect hedge. In practice, though, swap banks are prepared to enter a swap agreement without an opposite counterparty. This practice is sometimes referred to as *warehousing*. In warehousing, swap banks will try to hedge their swap positions with opposite positions in T-notes and FRNs or using Eurodollar futures contracts. For example, a swap bank might hedge a $10 million, two-year floating-rate position by shorting $10 million worth of two-year T-notes, and then use the proceeds to buy FRNs tied to the LIBOR. In general, most of the commitments a swap bank assumes are hedged through a portfolio of alternative positions—opposite swap positions, spot positions in T-notes and FRNs, or futures positions. This type of portfolio management by swap banks is referred to as *running a dynamic book*.

Swap Market Price Quotes

By convention, the floating rate on a swap is quoted flat without basis point adjustments. The fixed rate on a generic swap, in turn, is quoted in terms of the yield to maturity (YTM) on an on-the-run T-bond or T-note. In a dealer swap, the swap dealer's compensation comes from a markup or bid-ask spread extended to the end parties. The spread is reflected on the fixed-rate side. The swap dealer will provide a bid-ask quote to a potential party, and will in some cases post the bid-and-ask quotes. The quotes are stated in terms of the bid rate the dealer will pay as a fixed payer in return for the LIBOR, and the ask rate the dealer will receive as a floating-rate payer in return for paying the LIBOR. For example, a 70/75 swap spread implies the dealer will buy (take fixed-payer position) at 70 bp over the T-note yield and sell (take floating-payer position) at 75 bp over the T-note yield. The average of the bid and ask rates is known as the *swap rate*.

It should be noted that the fixed and floating rates quoted on a swap are not directly comparable. That is, the T-note assumes a 365-day basis, whereas the LIBOR assumes 360 days. To simplify the exposition, we will ignore the day count conventions in our other examples of generic swaps and simply divide annual rates by two (i.e., we will use a 180/360 day count convention).

Opening Swap Positions

Suppose a corporate treasurer wants to fix the rate on a five-year, $50 million floating-rate debt of the company by taking a fixed-rate payer's position on a five-year swap with a NP of $50 million. To obtain the swap position, suppose the treasurer calls a swap banker for a quote on a fixed-rate payer's position. After assessing the corporation's credit risk, suppose the swap dealer gives the treasurer a swap quote of 100 bp over the current five-year T-note yield, and the corporate treasurer, in turn, accepts. Thus, the treasurer would agree to take the fixed payer's position on the swap at 100 bp above the current five-year T-note. Except for the rate, both parties would mutually agree to the terms of the swap. After agreeing to the terms, the actual rate paid by the fixed payer would typically be set once the swap banker hedges her swap position by taking, for example, a position on an on-the-run T-note. After confirming a quote on a five-year T-note from her bond trader, the swap banker would then instructs the trader to sell (or short) $50 million of 5-year T-notes with the proceeds invested in a five-year FRN paying LIBOR. The yield on the T-note purchased plus the 100 bp would determine the actual rate on the swap. At a later date, the swap banker would most likely close the bond positions used to hedge the swap whenever she finds a floating-rate swap position to take on one or more swaps with similar terms.

Note: Since swap banks can hedge an opening swap positions with positions in an on-the-run T-note and FRN, the rates they, in turn, set on a swap contract are determined by the current T-note yields (with basis points added to reflect credit risk). Thus, opening swap contracts are tied to T-note yields. This relation is also reinforced by an arbitrage strategy consisting of positions in a swap, T-note, and FRN.

Closing Swap Positions

Prior to maturity, swap positions can be closed by selling the swap to a swap dealer or another party. If the swap is closed in this way, the new counterparty either pays or receives an up-front fee to or from the existing counterparty in exchange for receiving the original counterparty's position. Alternatively, the swap holder could also hedge his position by taking an opposite position in a current swap or possibly by hedging the position for the remainder of the maturity period with a futures position. Thus, a fixed-rate payer who unexpectedly sees interest rates decreasing and, as a result, wants to change his position, could do so by selling the swap to a dealer, taking a floating-rate payer's position in a new swap contract, or by going long in an appropriate futures contract; this latter strategy might be advantages if there is only a short period of time left on the swap.

If the fixed-payer swap holder decides to hedge his position by taking an opposite position on a new swap, the new swap position would require a payment of the LIBOR that would cancel out the receipt of the LIBOR on the first swap. The difference in the positions would therefore be equal to the difference in the higher fixed interest that is paid on the first swap and the lower fixed interest rate received on the offsetting swap. For example, suppose in our first illustrative swap example (Exhibit 14.1), a decline in interest rates occurs one year after the initiation of the swap, causing the fixed-rate payer to want to close his position. To this end, suppose the fixed-rate payer offsets his position by entering a new two-year swap as a floating-rate payer in which he agrees to pay the LIBOR for a 5 percent fixed rate. The two positions would result in a fixed payment of $25,000 semiannually for two years ((.005 / 2) NP). If interest rates decline over the next year, this offsetting position would turn out to be the correct strategy.

Offsetting Swap Positions		
Original Swap: Fixed Payer's Position	Pay 5.5%	-5.5%
Original Swap: Fixed Payer's Position	Receive LIBOR	+LIBOR
Offsetting Swap: Floating Payer's Position	Pay LIBOR	-LIBOR
Offsetting Swap: Floating Payer's Position	Receive 5.0%	+5%
	Pay 0.5% (annual)	-0.5% (annual)

Instead of hedging the position, the fixed-rate payer is more likely to close his position by simply selling it to a swap dealer. In acquiring a fixed position at 5.5 percent, the swap dealer would have to take a floating-payer's position to hedge the acquired fixed position. If the fixed rate on a new two-year swap were at 5 percent, the dealer would likewise lose $25,000 semiannually for two year on the two swap positions given a NP of $10 million. Thus, the price the swap bank would charge the fixed payer for buying his swap would be at least equal to the present value a flow of $25,000 for the next four semiannual periods. Given a discount rate of 5 percent, the swap bank would charge the fixed payer a minimum of $94,049 for buying his swap.

$$SV_0^{Fix} = \sum_{t=1}^{4} \frac{-\$25{,}000}{(1+(.05/2))^t} = -\$94{,}049$$

In contrast, if rates had increased, the fixed payer would be able to sell the swap to a dealer at a premium. For example, if the fixed rate on a new swap were 6 percent, a swap dealer would realized a semiannual return of $25,000 for the next two years by buying the 5.5 percent/LIBOR swap and hedging it with a floating position on a two-year, 6 percent/LIBOR swap. Given a 6 percent discount rate, the dealer would pay the fixed payer a maximum of $92,927 for his 5.5 percent/LIBOR swap.

$$SV_0^{Fix} = \sum_{t=1}^{4} \frac{\$25{,}000}{(1+(.06/2))^t} = \$92{,}927$$

Note that the above case illustrates that the value of an existing swap depends on the rates on current swaps. Moreover, the fixed rate on current swaps depends on the yields on T-notes.

Swap Valuation

At origination, most plain vanilla swaps have an economic value of zero. This means that the counterparties are not required to pay each other in the agreement. An economic value of zero requires that the swap's underlying bond positions trade at par—*par value swap.* If this were not the case, then one of the counterparties would need to compensate the other. In this case, the economic value of the swap is not zero. Such a swap is referred to as an *off-market swap.*

Although most plain vanilla swaps are originally par value swaps with economic values of zero, as the above example illustrated, the economic values of existing swaps change over time as rates change; that is, existing swaps become off-market swaps as rates change. In our above example, the fixed-payer's position on the 5.5 percent/LIBOR swap had a value of -\$94,049 one year later when the fixed-rate on new two-year par value swaps was 5 percent; that is, the holder of the fixed position would have to pay the swap bank at least \$94,049 to assume the swap. On the other hand, the fixed-payer's position on the 5.5 percent/LIBOR swap had a value of \$92,927 when the fixed-rate on new two-year par value swaps was 6 percent; that is, the holder of the fixed position would receive \$92,927 from the swap bank.

Just the opposite values apply to the floating position. Continuing with our illustrative example, if the fixed rate on new two-year par value swaps were at 5 percent, then a swap bank who assumed a floating position on a 5.5 percent/LIBOR swap and then hedged it with a fixed position on a current two-year 5 percent/LIBOR swap would gain \$25,000 semiannually over the next two year. As a result, the swap bank would be willing to pay \$94,049 for the floating position. Thus, the floating position on the 5.5 percent swap would have a value of \$94,049:

Offsetting Swap Positions		
Original Swap: Floating Payer's Position	Pay LIBOR	-LIBOR
Original Swap: Floating Payer's Position	Receive 5.5%	+5.5%
Offsetting Swap: Fixed Payer's Position	Pay 5%	-5%
Offsetting Swap: Fixed Payer's Position	Receive LIBOR	+LIBOR
	Receive 0.5% (annual)	0.5% (annual)

$$SV_0^{FL} = \sum_{t=1}^{4} \frac{\$25{,}000}{(1+(.05/2))^t} = \$94{,}049$$

If the fixed rate on new two-year par value swaps were at 6 percent, then a swap bank assuming the floating position on a 5.5 percent/LIBOR swap and hedging it with a fixed position on a current two-year 6 percent/LIBOR swap would lose \$25,000 semiannually over the next year. As a result, the swap bank would charge \$92,927 for assuming the floating position. Thus, the floating position on the 5.5 percent swap would have a negative value of \$92,927:

Offsetting Swap Positions		
Original Swap: Floating Payer's Position	Pay LIBOR	-LIBOR
Original Swap: Floating Payer's Position	Receive 5.5%	+5.5%
Offsetting Swap: Fixed Payer's Position	Pay 6%	-5%
Offsetting Swap: Fixed Payer's Position	Receive LIBOR	+LIBOR
	Pay 0.5% (annual)	-0.5% (annual)

$$SV_0^{FL} = \sum_{t=1}^{4} \frac{-\$25{,}000}{(1+(.06/2))^t} = -\$92{,}927$$

In general, the value of an existing swap is equal to the value of replacing the swap—replacement swap, which depends on current T-note rates. Formally, the values of the fixed and floating swap positions are:

$$SV^{fix} = \left[\sum_{t=1}^{M} \frac{K^P - K^S}{(1+K^P)^t} \right] NP$$

$$SV^{FL} = \left[\sum_{t=1}^{M} \frac{K^S - K^P}{(1+K^P)^t} \right] NP$$

where:

K^S = Fixed rate on the existing swap
K^P = Fixed rate on current par-value swap
SV^{fix} = Swap value of the fixed position on the existing swap
SV^{FL} = Swap value of the floating position on the existing swap

Note that these values are obtained by discounting the net cash flows at the current YTM (K^P). As a result, this approach to valuing off-market swaps is often referred to as the *YTM approach.* However, recall from our discussion of bonds that the equilibrium price of a bond is obtained not by discounting all of the bond's cash flows by a common discount rate, but rather by discounting each of the bond's cash flows by their appropriate spot rates—the rate on a zero-coupon bond. As we have discussed, valuing bonds by using spot rates instead of a common YTM ensures that there are no arbitrage opportunities from buying bonds and stripping them or buying zero discount bonds and bundling them. The argument for pricing bonds in terms of spot rates also applies to the valuation of off-market swaps. Similar to bond valuation, the equilibrium value of a swap is obtained by discounting each of the swap's cash flows by their appropriate spot rates. The valuation of swaps using spot rates is referred to as the *zero-coupon approach.* The approach, in turn, requires generating a spot yield curve for swaps.[1]

Comparative Advantage and the Hidden Option

Comparative Advantage

Swaps are often used by financial and nonfinancial corporations to take advantage of apparent arbitrage opportunities resulting from capital-market inefficiencies. To see this, consider the case of the Star Chemical Company who wants to raise $300 million with a five-year loan to finance an expansion of one of its production plants. Based on its moderate credit ratings, suppose Star can borrow five-year funds at a 10.5 percent fixed rate or at a floating rate equal to LIBOR + 75 bp. Given the choice of financing, Star prefers the fixed-rate loan. Suppose the treasurer of the Star Company contacts his investment banker for suggestions on how to finance the acquisition. The investment banker knows that the Moon Development Company is also looking for five-year funding to finance its proposed $300 million office park development. Given its high credit rating, suppose Moon can borrow the funds for five years at a fixed rate of 9.5 percent or at a floating rate equal to the LIBOR + 25. Given the choice, Moon prefers a floating-rate loan. In summary, Star and Moon have the following fixed and floating-rate loan opportunities:

Company	Fixed Rate	Floating Rate	Preference	Comparative Advantage
Star Company	10.5%	LIBOR + 75 bp	Fixed	Floating
Moon Company	9.5%	LIBOR + 25 bp	Floating	Fixed
Credit Spread	100 bp	50 bp		

In this case, the Moon Company has an absolute advantage in both the fixed and floating markets because of its higher quality rating. However, after looking at the credit spreads of the borrowers in each market, the investment banker realizes that there is a *comparative advantage* for Moon in the fixed market and a comparative advantage for Star in the floating market. That is, Moon has a relative advantage in the fixed market where it gets 100 bp less than Star; Star, in turn, has a relative advantage (or relatively less disadvantage) in the floating-rate market where it only pays 50 bp more than Moon. Thus, lenders in the fixed-rate market supposedly assess the difference between the two creditors to be worth 100 bp, whereas lenders in the floating-rate market assess the difference to be only 50 bp. Whenever a comparative advantage exist, arbitrage opportunities can be realized by each firm borrowing in the market where it has a comparative advantage and then swapping loans or having an swap bank set up a swap.

For the swap to work, the two companies cannot just pass on their respective costs: Star swaps a floating rate at LIBOR + 75 bp for a 10.5 percent fixed; Moon swaps a 9.5 percent fixed for a floating at LIBOR + 25 bp. Typically, the companies divide the differences in credit spreads, with the most creditworthy company taking the most savings. In this case, suppose the investment banker arranges a five-year, 9.5 percent/LIBOR generic swap with a NP of $300 million in which Star takes the fixed-rate payer position and Moon takes the floating-rate payer position.

The Star Company would then issue a $300 million FRN paying LIBOR + 75 bp. This loan, combined with the fixed-rate position on the 9.5 percent/LIBOR swap would give Star a synthetic fixed-rate loan paying 10.25 percent—25 bp less than its direct fixed-rate loan:

Star Company's Synthetic Fixed-Rate Loan		
Issue FRN	Pay LIBOR + 75 bp	-LIBOR - .75%
Swap: Fixed-Rate Payer's Position	Pay 9.5%	-9.5%
Swap: Fixed-Rate Payer's Position	Receive LIBOR	+LIBOR
Synthetic Fixed Rate	Pay 9.5% + .75%	-10.25%
Direct Fixed Rate	Pay 10.5%	-10.5%

The Moon Company, on the other hand, would issue a $300 million, 9.5 percent fixed-rate bond that, when combined with its floating-rate position on the 9.5 percent/LIBOR swap, would give Moon a synthetic floating-rate loan paying LIBOR, which is 25 bp less than the rates paid on the direct floating-rate loan of LIBOR plus 25 bp:

Moon Company's Synthetic Floating-Rate Loan		
Issue 9.5% fixed-rate bond	Pay 9.5%	-9.5%
Swap: Floating-Rate Payer's Position	Pay LIBOR	-LIBOR
Swap: Floating-Rate Payer's Position	Receive 9.5%	+9.5%
Synthetic Fixed Rate	Pay LIBOR	-LIBOR
Direct Fixed Rate	Pay LIBOR + 25bp	-LIBOR - .25%

Thus, the swap makes it possible for both companies to create synthetic loans with better rates than direct ones.

As a rule, for a swap to provide arbitrage opportunities, at least one of the counterparties must have a comparative advantage in one market. The total arbitrage gain available to each party depends on whether one party has an absolute advantage in both markets or each has an absolute advantage in one market. If one party has an absolute advantage in both markets (as in this case), then the arbitrage gain is the difference in the comparative advantages in each market: 50 bp = 100 bp – 50 bp. In this case, Star and Moon split the difference in the 50 bp gain. In contrast, if each party has an absolute advantage in one market, then the arbitrage gain is equal to the sum of the comparative advantages.

Hidden Option

The comparative advantage argument has often been cited as the explanation for the dramatic growth in the swap market. This argument, though, is often questioned on the grounds that the mere use of swaps should over time reduce the credit interest rate differentials in the fixed and flexible markets, taking away the advantages from forming synthetic positions. With observed credit spreads and continuing use of swaps to create synthetic positions, some scholars (Smith, Smithson, and Wakeman, 1986) argue that the comparative advantage that is apparently extant is actually a hidden option embedded in the floating-rate debt position that proponents of the comparative advantage argument fail to include. They argue that the credit spreads that exit are due to the nature of the contracts available to firms in fixed and floating markets. In the floating market, the lender usually has the opportunity to review the floating rate each period and increase the spread over the LIBOR if the borrower's creditworthiness has deteriorated. This option, though, does not usually exist in the fixed market.

In the preceding example, the lower quality Star Company is able to get a synthetic fixed rate at 10.25 percent (.25 percent less than the direct loan). However, using the hidden option argument, this 10.25 percent rate is only realized if Star can maintain its creditworthiness and continue to borrow at a floating rate that is 75 bp above LIBOR. If its credit ratings were to subsequently decline and it had to pay 150 bp above the LIBOR, then its synthetic fixed rate would increase. Moreover, studies have shown that the likelihood of default increases faster over time for lower quality companies than it does for higher quality. In our example, this would mean that the Star Company's credit spread is more likely to rise than the Moon Company's spread and that its expected borrowing rate is greater than the 10.25 percent synthetic rate. As for the higher quality Moon Company, its lower synthetic floating rate of LIBOR does not take into account the additional return necessary to compensate the company for bearing the risk of a default by the Star Company. If it borrowed floating funds directly, the Moon Company would not be bearing this risk.

Swaps Applications

Arbitrage Applications—Synthetic Positions

In the above case, the differences in credit spreads in the fixed-rate and floating-rate debt made it possible for both corporations to obtain different rates with synthetic positions than they could with direct loans. The example represents what is commonly referred to as an arbitrage use of swaps. In general, the presence of comparative advantage or a hidden option makes it possible to create not only synthetic loans with lower rates than direct, but also synthetic investments with rates exceeding those from direct investments. To illustrate this, four cases showing how swaps can be used to create synthetic fixed-rate and floating-rate loans and investments are presented below.

Synthetic Fixed-Rate Loan

Suppose a company is planning on borrowing \$50 million for five years at a fixed-rate. Given a swap market, suppose its alternatives are to issue a five-year, 10 percent, fixed-rate bond paying coupons on a semiannual basis or create a synthetic fixed-rate bond by issuing a five-year floating-rate medium-term note (MTN) paying LIBOR plus 100 bp and taking a fixed-rate payer's position on a swap with a NP of \$50 million. The synthetic fixed-rate MTN will be equivalent to the direct fixed-rate loan if it is formed with a swap that has a fixed rate equal to 9 percent:

Synthetic Fixed-Rate Loan		
Issue FRN	Pay LIBOR + 1%	-LIBOR – 1%
Swap: Fixed-Rate Payer's Position	Pay 9% Fixed Rate	-9%
Swap: Fixed-Rate Payer's Position	Receive LIBOR	+LIBOR
Synthetic Rate	Pay 9% + 1%	-10%
Direct Loan Rate	Pay 10%	-10%

If the company can obtain a fixed rate on a swap that is less than 9 percent, then the company would find it cheaper to finance with the synthetic fixed-rate MTN than the direct. For example, if the company could obtain an 8 percent/LIBOR swap, then the company would be able to create a synthetic 9 percent fixed-rate loan by issuing a floating-rate MTN at LIBOR plus 100 bp and taking the fixed payer's position on the swap:

Synthetic Fixed-Rate Loan		
Issue Floating-Rate MTN (FRN)	Pay LIBOR + 1%	-LIBOR – 1%
Swap: Fixed-Rate Payer's Position	Pay 8% Fixed Rate	-8%
Swap: Fixed-Rate Payer's Position	Receive LIBOR	+LIBOR
Synthetic Rate	Pay 8% + 1%	-9%
Direct Loan Rate	Pay 10%	-10%

Synthetic Floating-Rate Loan

Suppose a bank has just made a five-year, $30 million floating-rate loan that is reset every six months at the LIBOR plus 100 bp. The bank could finance this floating-rate asset by either selling CDs every six month at the LIBOR or by creating a synthetic floating-rate loan by selling a five-year fixed-rate note at 9 percent and taking a floating-rate payer's position on a five-year swap with a NP of $30 million. The synthetic floating-rate loan will be equivalent to the direct floating-rate loan paying LIBOR if the swap has a fixed rate that is equal to the 9 percent fixed rate on the note:

Synthetic Floating-Rate Loan		
Issue 9% Fixed-Rate Note	Pay 9% Fixed Rate	-9%
Swap: Floating-Rate Payer's Position	Pay LIBOR	-LIBOR
Swap: Floating-Rate Payer's Position	Receive 9% Fixed Rate	+9%
Synthetic Rate	Pay LIBOR	-LIBOR
Direct Loan Rate	Pay LIBOR	-LIBOR

Thus, if the bank can obtain a fixed rate on the swap that is greater than 9 percent, say 9.5 percent, then it would find it cheaper to finance its floating-rate loan asset by issuing fixed-rate notes at 9 percent and taking the floating-rate payer's position on the swap. By doing this, the bank's effective interest payments are 50 bp less than LIBOR with a synthetic floating-rate loan formed by selling the 9 percent fixed-rate note and taking a floating-rate payer's position on a five-year, 9.5 percent/LIBOR swap with NP of $30 million:

Synthetic Floating-Rate Loan		
Issue 9% Fixed-Rate Note	Pay 9% Fixed Rate	-9%
Swap: Floating-Rate Payer's Position	Pay LIBOR	-LIBOR
Swap: Floating-Rate Payer's Position	Receive 9.5% Fixed Rate	+9.5%
Synthetic Rate	Pay LIBOR - .5%	-(LIBOR - .5%)
Direct Loan Rate	Pay LIBOR	-LIBOR

Synthetic Fixed-Rate Investment

In the early days of the swap market, swaps were primarily used as a liability management tool. In the late 1980s, investors began to use swaps to try to increase the yield on their investments. A swap used with an asset is sometimes referred to as an *asset-based interest rate swap* or simply an asset swap. In terms of synthetic positions, asset-based swaps can be used to create either fixed-rate or floating-rate investment positions.

Consider the case of an investment fund that is setting up a $100 million collateralized debt obligation (CDO) consisting of five-year, AAA quality, option-free, fixed-rate bonds. If the YTM on such bonds is 6 percent, then the investment company could form the CDO by simply buying $100 million worth of 6 percent coupon bonds at par. Alternatively, it could try to earn a higher return by creating a synthetic fixed-rate bond by buying five-year, high-quality FRNs currently paying the LIBOR plus 100 bp and taking a floating-rate payer's position on a five-year swap with a NP of $100 million. If the fixed rate on the swap is equal to 5 percent (the 6 percent rate on the bonds minus the 100 bp on the FRN), then the synthetic fixed-rate investment will yield the same return as the 6 percent fixed-rate bonds:

Synthetic Fixed-Rate Investment		
Purchase FRN	Receive LIBOR + 1%	+LIBOR + 1%
Swap: Floating-Rate Payer's Position	Pay LIBOR	-LIBOR
Swap: Floating-Rate Payer's Position	Receive 5% Fixed Rate	+5%
Synthetic Rate	Receive 5% + 1%	+6%
Direct Investment Rate	Receive 6%	+6%

If the fixed rate on the swap is greater than 5 percent, then the synthetic fixed-rate loan will yield a higher return than the 6 percent bonds. For example, if the investment company in forming the CDO could take a floating-payer's position on a 5.75 percent/LIBOR swap with maturity of five years, NP of 100 million, and effective dates coinciding with the FRNs' dates, then the investment company would earn a fixed rate of 6.75 percent:

Synthetic Fixed-Rate Investment		
Purchase FRN	Receive LIBOR + 1%	+LIBOR + 1%
Swap: Floating-Rate Payer's Position	Pay LIBOR	-LIBOR
Swap: Floating-Rate Payer's Position	Receive 5.75% Fixed Rate	+5.75%
Synthetic Rate	Receive 6.75%	+6.75%
Direct Investment Rate	Receive 6%	+6%

Synthetic Floating-Rate Investment

This time consider an investment fund that is looking to invest $10 million for three years in a FRN. Suppose the fund can either invest directly in a high-quality, five-year FRN paying LIBOR plus 50 bp, or it can create a synthetic floating-rate investment by investing in a 5-year, 7 percent fixed-rate note selling at par and taking a fixed-rate payer's position. If the fixed rate on the swap is equal to 6.5 percent (the rate on the fixed-rate note minus the BP on the direct FRN investment), then the synthetic floating-rate investment will yield the same return as the FRN:

Synthetic Floating-Rate Investment		
Purchase Fixed-Rate Note	Receive 7%	+7%
Swap: Fixed-Rate Payer's Position	Pay 6.5% Fixed Rate	−6.5%
Swap: Fixed-Rate Payer's Position	Receive LIBOR	+LIBOR
Synthetic Rate	Receive LIBOR + .5%	+LIBOR + .5%
Floating Investment Rate	Receive LIBOR + .5%	+LIBOR + .5%

If the fixed rate on the swap is less than 6.5 percent, then the synthetic floating-rate investment will yield a higher return than the FRN. For example, the fund could obtain a yield of LIBOR plus 100 bp from a synthetic floating-rate investment formed with an investment in the 5-year, 7 percent fixed-rate note and fixed-rate payer's position on a 6 percent/LIBOR swap:

Synthetic Floating-Rate Investment		
Purchase Fixed-Rate Note	Receive 7%	+7%
Swap: Fixed-Rate Payer's Position	Pay 6% Fixed Rate	−6.0%
Swap: Fixed-Rate Payer's Position	Receive LIBOR	+LIBOR
Synthetic Rate	Receive LIBOR + 1%	+LIBOR + 1%
Direct Floating Investment Rate	Receive LIBOR + .5%	+LIBOR + .5%

Hedging

Initially interest rate swaps were used primarily in arbitrage strategies. Today, there is an increased use of swaps for hedging. Hedging with swaps is done primarily to minimize the market risk of positions currently exposed to interest rate changes. For example, suppose a company had previously financed its capital projects with intermediate-term FRNs tied to the LIBOR. Furthermore, suppose the company was expecting a higher interest rate and wanted to fix the rate on its floating-rate debt. To this end, one alternative would be for the company to re-fund its floating-rate debt with fixed-rate obligations. This, though, would require the cost of issuing new debt (underwriting, registration, etc.), as well as the cost of calling the current FRNs or buying the notes in the market if they were not callable. Thus, re-funding would be a relatively costly alternative. Another possibility would be for the company to hedge its floating-rate debt with a strip of short Eurodollar futures contracts. This alternative is relatively inexpensive, but there may be hedging risk. The third alternative would be to combine the company's

FRNs with a fixed-rate payer's position on a swap, thereby creating a synthetic fixed-rate debt position. This alternative of hedging FRNs with swaps, in turn, is less expensive and more efficient than the first alternative of refinancing; plus, it can also effectively minimize hedging risk.

An opposite scenario to the above case would be a company that has intermediate to long-term fixed-rate debt that it wants to make floating either because of a change in its economic structure or because it expects rates will be decreasing. Given the costs of refunding fixed-rate debt with floating-rate debt and the hedging risk problems with futures, the most efficient way for the company to meet this objective would be to create synthetic floating-rate debt by combining its fixed-rate debt with a floating-rate payer's position on a swap.

Speculation

Since swaps are similar to Eurodollar futures contracts, they can be used like them to speculate on short-term interest rate movements. Specifically, as an alternative to a Eurodollar futures strip, speculators who expect short-term rates to increase in the future can take a fixed-rate payer's position; in contrast, speculators who expect short-term rates to decrease can take a floating-rate payer's position. Note, though, that there are differences in maturity, size, and marketability between futures and swaps that need to be taken into account when considering which one to use.

For financial and nonfinancial corporations, speculative positions often take the form of the company changing the exposure of its balance sheet to interest rate changes. For example, suppose a fixed income bond fund with a portfolio measured against a bond index wanted to increase the duration of its portfolio relative to the index's duration based on an expectation of lower interest rate across all maturities. The fund could do this by selling its short-term Treasuries and buying longer-term ones or by taking long positions in Treasury futures. With swaps, the fund could also change its portfolio's duration by taking a floating-rate payer's position on a swap. If they did this and rates were to decrease as expected, then not only would the value of the company's bond portfolio increase but the company would also profit from the swap; however, if rates were to increase, then the company would see decreases in the value of its bond portfolio, as well as losses from its swap positions. By adding swaps, though, the fund has effectively increased its interest rate exposure by increasing its duration.

Instead of increasing its portfolio's duration, the fund may want to reduce or minimized the bond portfolio's interest rate exposure based on an expectation of higher interest rates. In this case, the fund could effectively shorten the duration of its bond fund by taking a fixed-rate payer's position on a swap. If rates were to later increase, then the decline in the value of the company's bond portfolio would be offset by the cash inflow realized from the fixed-payer's position on the swap.

ANALYZING A FIXED-INCOME BOND PORTFOLIO WITH AN ADDED SWAP POSITION USING MARS

SAVING AND LOADING A SWAP TO A PORTFOLIO

To save and load a swap position created in SWPM, go to the "Action" tab and click "Save." This will bring up an input box. In the box, name the swap position (Custom ID), click "Add to Portfolio" in the lower part of the input box, and click "Save." This will take you back to the SWPM main tab. On that screen, type 2 and hit enter (2 <Enter>). This will bring up MARS (Multiasset Risk System) where you can combine a portfolio you have already created in PRTU (select on MARS) with the swap position or import another swap or interest rate derivative position you have already created and saved (select "Swap Position" from "Positions" tab).

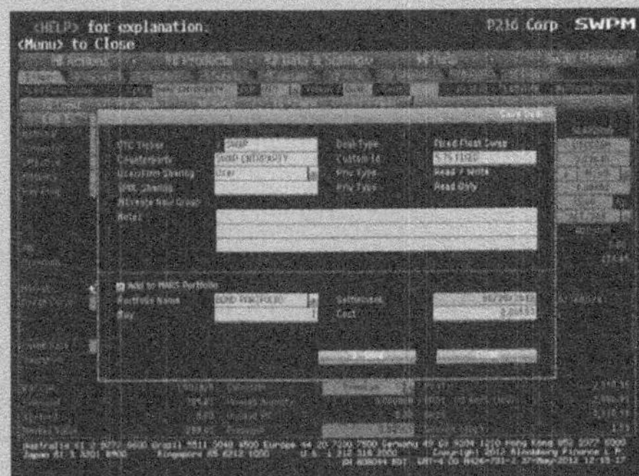

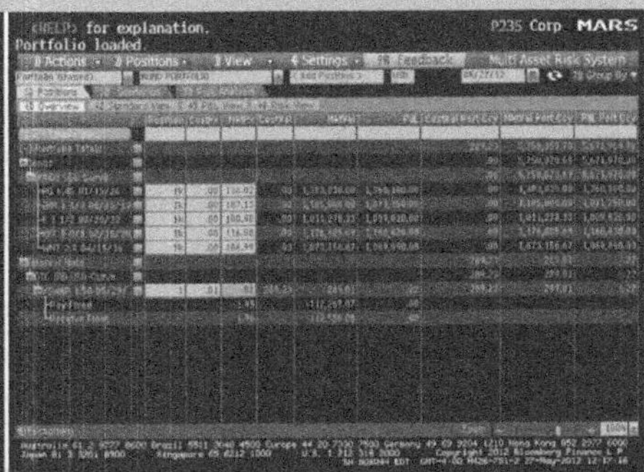

On the MARS (position tab), one can select the entire portfolio, select individual securities, the swap contract, or all positions Using the "Scenario Chart" tab, the selected position can be evaluated in terms of changes in market value, profit and loss, and other parameter values for different interest rates scenarios.

Example:

- Portfolio of five corporate bonds with market value of $5.75 million on 5/27/2012 and generic five-year fixed payer swap with 1.5 percent fixed rate/LIBOR + 25 bp, NP = $5.75 million (swap presented in earlier Bloomberg box).
- Scenario: yield curve shifts: −100 bp to + 100 bp.
- Market value evaluated currently and one year later.
- Analysis: Combined portfolio and fixed payer swap.

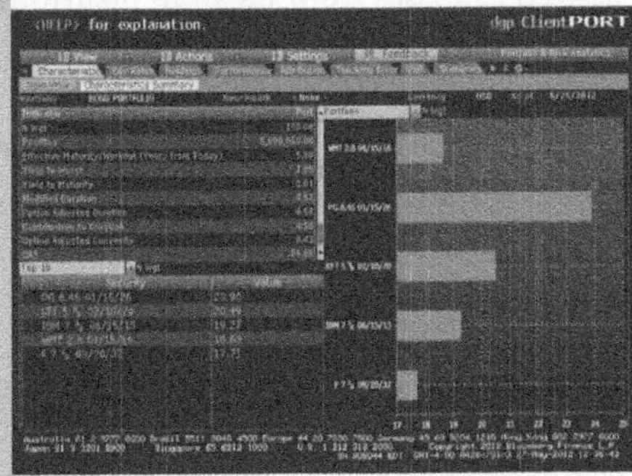

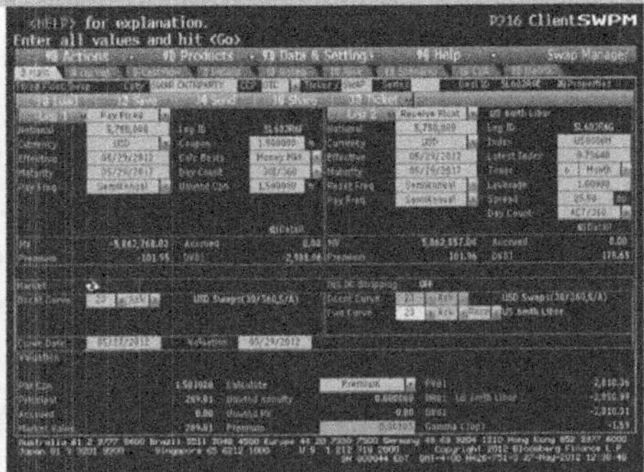

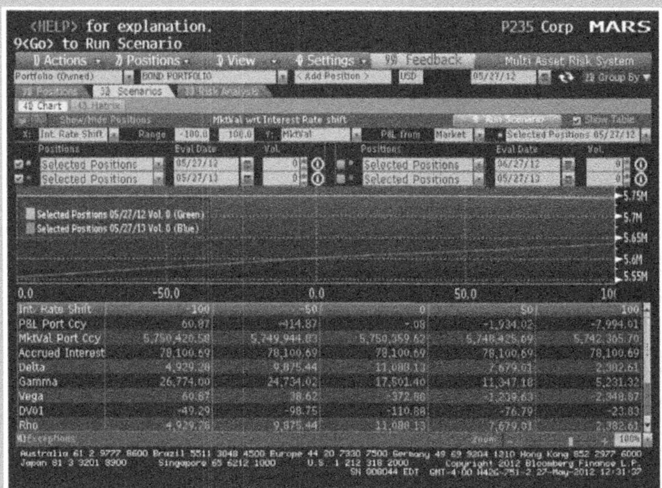

MARS (MULTIASSET RISK SYSTEM): MARS <ENTER>
Using the MARS screen, you can upload any portfolio that you have created and then add futures options, derivatives, ETFs and other security to your portfolio ("Add Position" tab) or add swap positions ("Positions" tab), FRAs, Caps, Floors, and other interest rate products created and saved in SWPM.

IRSB: Generic Interest Rate Swaps Menu

IRDL: Interest Rate Derivative List Created by User

IRDD: Interest Rate Derivatives Menu

Credit Risk

When compared to their equivalent fixed and floating bond positions, swaps have less credit risk. To see this, suppose one party to a swap defaults. Typically, the swap contract allows the nondefaulting party the right to give up to a 20-day notice that a particular date will be the termination date.[2] This notice gives the parties time to determine a settlement amount. The settlement amount depends on the value of an existing swap or equivalently on the terms of a replacement swap. For example, suppose the fixed payer on a 9.5 percent/LIBOR swap with NP of $10 million runs into severe financial problems and defaults on the swap agreement when there are three years and six payments remaining. Suppose the current three-year swap calls for an exchange of 9 percent fixed for LIBOR. To replace the defaulted swap, the nondefaulting floating payer would have to take a new floating position on the 9 percent/LIBOR swap or sell it to a swap bank who would hedge the assumed swap with the floating position. As a result, she (or the swap bank) would be receiving only $450,000 each period instead of the $475,000 on the defaulted swap. Thus, the default represents a semiannual loss of $25,000 for three years. Using 9 percent as the discount rate, the present value of this loss would be $128,947:

$$PV = \sum_{t=1}^{6} \frac{-\$25{,}000}{(1+(.09/2))^t} = -\$128{,}947$$

Thus, given a replacement fixed swap rate of 9 percent, the actual credit risk exposure is $128,947. The replacement value of $128,947 is also the economic value of the original 9.5 percent/LIBOR swap. *Note:* If the replacement fixed swap rate had been 10 percent instead of 9 percent, then the floating payer would have had a positive economic value of $126,892:

$$PV = \sum_{t=1}^{6} \frac{\$25{,}000}{(1+(.10/2))^t} = \$126{,}892$$

Under a higher interest rate scenario, the fixed payer experiencing the financial distress would not have defaulted on the swap, although he may be defaulting on other obligations. The increase in rates in this case has made the swap an asset to the fixed payer instead of a liability.

The example illustrates that two events are necessary for default loss on a swap: an actual default on the agreement and an adverse change in rates. Credit risk on a swap is therefore a function of the joint probability of financial distress and adverse interest rate movements.

In practice, credit risk is often managed by adjusting the negotiated fixed rate on a swap to include a credit risk spread between the parties: a less risky firm (which could be the swap bank acting as dealer) will pay a lower fixed rate or receive a higher fixed rate the riskier the counterparty. The credit rate adjustment also takes into account the probability of rates increasing and decreasing and its impact on the future economic value of the counterparty's swap position. In addition to rate adjustments, swap dealers can also manage credit risk by requiring collateral and maintenance margins.

Forward Swaps

A forward swap is an agreement to enter into a swap that starts at a future date at an interest rate agreed upon today. Like futures contracts on debt securities, forward swaps provide borrowers and investors with a tool for locking in a future interest rate. As such, they can be used to manage interest rate risk for debt and fixed-income positions.

Hedging a Future Loan with a Forward Swap

Financial and nonfinancial institutions that have future borrowing obligations can lock in a future rate by obtaining forward contracts on fixed-payer swap positions.

For example, a company wishing to lock in a rate on a five-year, fixed-rate $100 million loan to start two year from today, could enter a two-year forward swap agreement to pay the fixed rate on a five-year 9 percent/LIBOR swap. At the expiration date on the forward swap, the company could issue floating-rate debt at LIBOR that, when combined with the fixed position on the swap, would provide the company with a synthetic fixed-rate loan paying 9 percent on the floating debt:

At the expiration date on the forward swap:

Instrument	**Action**	
Issue Flexible Rate Note	Pay	-LIBOR
Swap: Fixed-Rate Payer's Position	Pay Fixed Rate	-9%
Swap: Fixed-Rate Payer's Position	Receive LIBOR	+LIBOR
Synthetic Fixed Rate	Net Payment	9%

Alternatively, at the forward swap's expiration date, the company is more likely to sell the five-year 9 percent/LIBOR swap underlying the forward swap contract and issue five-year fixed-rate debt. If the rate on five-year fixed-rate bonds were higher than 9 percent, for example at 10 percent, then the company would be able offset the higher interest by selling its fixed position on the 9 percent/LIBOR swap to a swap dealer for an amount equal to the present value of a five-year annuity equal to 1 percent (difference in rates: 10 percent - 9 percent) times the NP. For example, at 10 percent the value of the underlying 9 percent/LIBOR swap would be $3,860,867 using the YTM swap valuation approach:

$$SV^{fix} = \left[\sum_{t=1}^{10} \frac{(.10/2)-(.09/2)}{(1+(.10/2))^t}\right]\$100{,}000{,}000 = \$3{,}860{,}867$$

With the proceeds of $3,860,867 from closing its swap, the company would only need to raise $96,139,133 (= $100 million - $3,860,867). The company, though, would have to issue $96,139,133 worth of five-year fixed-rate bonds at the higher 10 percent rate. This would result in semiannual interest payments of $4,860,957 (= (.10 / 2)($96,139,133), and the interest rate based on the $100 million funds needed would be approximately 9 percent.

In contrast, if the rate on five-year fixed-rate loans were lower than 9 percent, say 8 percent, then the company would benefit from the lower fixed-rate loan, but would lose an amount equal to the present value of a five-year annuity equal to 1 percent (difference in rates: 8 percent - 9 percent) times the NP when it closed the fixed position. Specifically, at 8 percent, the value of the underlying 9 percent/LIBOR swap is -$4,055,488 using the YTM approach:

$$SV^{fix} = \left[\sum_{t=1}^{10} \frac{(.08/2)-(.09/2)}{(1+(.08/2))^t}\right]\$100{,}000{,}000 = -\$4{,}055{,}448$$

The company would therefore have to pay the swap bank $4,055,488 for assuming its fixed-payers position. With a payment of $4,055,488, the company would need to raise a total of $104,055,488 from it bond issue. The company, though, would be able to issue $104,055,488 worth of five-year fixed-rate bonds at the lower rate of 8 percent rate. Its semiannual interest payments would be $4,162,220 (= .08/2) ($104,055,488), and its rate based on the $100 million funds needed would be approximately 9 percent.

Hedging a Future Investment

Instead of locking in the rate on a future liability, forward swaps can also be used on the asset side to fix the rate on a future investment. Consider the case of an institutional investor planning to invest an expected $10 million cash inflow one year from now in a three-year, high-quality fixed-rate bond. The investor could lock in the future rate by entering a one-year forward swap agreement to receive the fixed rate and pay the floating rate on a three-year, 9 percent/LIBOR swap with a NP of $10 million. At the expiration date on the forward swap, the investor could invest the $10 million cash inflow in a three-year FRN at LIBOR which, when combined with the floating position on the swap, would provide the investor with a synthetic fixed-rate investment paying 9 percent:

At the expiration date on the forward swap:

Instrument	Action	
Buy Flexible Rate Note	Receive	LIBOR
Swap: Floating-Rate Payer's Position	Pay LIBOR	–LIBOR
Swap: Floating-Rate Payer's Position	Receive Fixed Rate	+9%
Synthetic Fixed-Rate Investment	Net Receipt	9%

Instead of a synthetic fixed investment position, the investor is more likely to sell the three-year 9 percent/LIBOR swap underlying the forward swap contract and invest in a five-year fixed-rate note. If the rate on the three-year fixed-rate note were lower than the 9 percent swap rate, then the investor would be able to sell his floating position at a value equal to the present value of an annuity equal to the $10 million NP times the difference between 9 percent and the rate on three-year fixed-rate bonds; this gain would offset the lower return on the fixed-rate bond. For example, if at the forward swaps' expiration date, the rate on three-year, fixed-rate bonds were at 8 percent, and the fixed rate on a three-year par value swap were at 8 percent, then the investment firm would be able to sell its floating-payer's position on the three-year 9 percent/LIBOR swap underlying the forward swap contract to a swap bank for $262,107 (using the YTM approach with a discount rate of 8 percent):

$$SV^{fl} = \left[\sum_{t=1}^{6} \frac{(.09/2)-(.08/2)}{(1+(.08/2))^t}\right]\$10{,}000{,}000 = \$262{,}107$$

The investment firm would therefore invest \$10 million plus the \$262,107 proceeds from closing its swap in 3-year, fixed-rate bonds yielding 8 percent. The yield on an investment of \$10 million, though, would be approximately equal to 9 percent.

On the other hand, if the rate on three-year fixed-rate securities were higher than 9 percent, the investment company would benefit from the higher investment rate, but would lose when it closed its swap position. For example, if at the forward swaps' expiration date, the rate on three-year, fixed-rate bonds were at 10 percent, and the fixed rate on a three-year par value swap were at 10 percent, then the investment firm would have to pay the swap bank \$253,785 for assuming its floating-payers position on the three-year 9 percent/LIBOR swap underlying the forward swap contract:

$$SV^{fl} = \left[\sum_{t=1}^{6} \frac{(.09/2)-(.10/2)}{(1+(.10/2))^t}\right]\$10{,}000{,}000 = -\$253{,}785$$

The investment firm would therefore invest \$9,746,215 (\$10 million minus the \$253,785 costs incurred in closing its swap) in three-year, fixed-rate bonds yielding 10 percent. The yield on an investment of \$10 million, though, would be approximately equal to 9 percent.

Other Uses of Forward Swaps

The examples illustrate that forward swaps are like futures on debt securities. As such, they are used in many of the same ways as futures: locking in future interest rates, speculating on future interest rate changes, and altering a balance sheet's exposure to interest rate changes. Different from futures, though, forward swaps can be customized to fit a particular investment or borrowing need and with the starting dates on forward swaps ranging anywhere from one month to several years, they can be applied to not only short-run but also long-run positions.

Valuation of Forward Swaps

As with many nongeneric swaps, there can be an up-front fee for a forward swap. The value of a forward swap depends on whether the rate on the forward contract's underlying swap is different than its breakeven forward swap rate. The breakeven rate on a generic swap is that rate that equates the present values of the fixed and floating cash flows, with the floating cash flows estimated as implied forward rates generated from the zero-coupon rates on swaps. The breakeven rate on a forward swap is that rate that equates the present value of the fixed-rate flows to the present value of floating-rate flows corresponding to the period of the underlying swap.[3]

Swaptions

As the name suggests, a *swaption* is an option on a swap. The purchaser of a swaption buys the right to start an interest rate swap with a specific fixed rate (exercise rate) and with a maturity at or during a specific time period in the future. If the holder exercises, she takes the swap position, with the swap seller obligated to take the opposite counterparty position. For swaptions, the underlying instrument is a forward swap and the option premium is the up-front fee. The swaption can be either a right to be a payer or the right to be receiver of the fixed rate. A *payer swaption* gives the holder the right to enter a particular swap as the fixed-rate payer (and floating-rate receiver), whereas a *receiver swaption* gives the holder the right to enter a particular swap agreement as the fixed-rate receiver (and floating-rate payer). Swaptions are similar to interest rate options or options on debt securities. They are, however, more varied: They can range from options to begin a one-year swap in three months to a 10-year option on an 8-year swap (sometimes referred to as a 10 × 8 swaption); the exercise periods can vary for American swaptions; swaptions can be written on generic swaps or nongeneric. Like interest rate and debt options, swaptions can be used for speculating on interest rates, hedging debt and asset positions against market risk, and managing a balance sheet's exposure to interest rate changes. In addition, like swaps they also can be used in combination with other securities to create synthetic positions.

Speculation

Suppose a speculator expects the rates on high-quality, five-year fixed-rate bonds to increase from their current 8 percent level. As an alternative to a short T-note futures or an interest rate call position, the speculator could buy a payer swaption. Suppose she elects to buy a one-year European payer swaption on a five-year, 8 percent/LIBOR swap with a NP of $10 million for 50 bp times the NP; that is:

- 1 × 5 payer swaption
- Exercise date = one year
- Exercise rate = 8 percent
- Underlying swap = 5-year, 8 percent/LIBOR with NP = $10 million
- Swap position = fixed payer
- Option premium = 50 bp × NP

On the exercise date, if the fixed rate on a five-year swap were greater than the exercise rate of 8 percent, then the speculator would exercise her swaption at 8 percent. To profit, she could take her 8 percent fixed-rate payer's swap position obtained from exercising and sell it to a swap bank. For example, if current five-year par value swaps were trading at 9 percent and swaps were valued by the YTM approach, then she would be able to sell her 8 percent swap for $395,636:

$$\text{Value of Swap} = \left[\sum_{t=1}^{10} \frac{(.09/2)-(.08/2)}{(1+(.09/2))^t}\right](\$10{,}000{,}000) = \$395{,}636$$

Alternatively, she could exercise and then enter into a reverse swap; for example, at the current swap rate of 8 percent, she could take the floating payer's position on a five-year, 8 percent/LIBOR swap. By doing this she would receive an annuity equal to 1 percent of the NP for five years (or .5 percent semiannually for 10 periods), which has a current value of $395,636:

From Payer Swaption:		
Swap: Fixed-Rate Payer's Position	Pay	8% per year for 5 years
Swap: Fixed-Rate Payer's Position	Receive	LIBOR
From Replacement Swap:		
Swap: Floating-Rate Payer's Position	Receive	9% per year for 5 years
Swap: Floating-Rate Payer's Position	Pay	LIBOR
Net Position	Receive	1% per year for 5 years

If the swap rate at the expiration date were less than 8 percent, then the payer swaption would have no value and the speculator would simply let it expire, losing the premium she paid.

More formally, the intrinsic value or expiation value of the payer swaption is

$$\text{Value of Payer Swaption} = \left[\sum_{t=1}^{10} \frac{Max[(R/2)-(.08/2),0]}{(1+(R/2))^t}\right](\$10{,}000{,}000)$$

For rates, R, on par value five-year swaps exceeding the exercise rate of 8 percent, the value of the payer swaption will be equal to the present value of the interest differential times the notional principal on the swap and for rates less that 8 percent, the swap is worthless. Exhibit 14.6 shows graphically and in a table the values and profits at expiration obtained from closing the payer swaption on the five-year 8 percent/LIBOR swap given different rates at expiration.

Instead of higher rates, suppose the speculator expects rates on five-year high-quality bonds to be lower one year from now. In this case, her strategy would be to buy a receiver swaption. If she bought a receiver swaption similar in terms to the above payer swaption (a one-year option on a five-year, 8 percent/LIBOR swap for $50,000), and the swap rate on a five-year swap were less than 8 percent on the exercise date, then she would realize a gain from exercising and then either selling the floating-payer position or combining it with a fixed payer's position on a replacement swap. For example, if the fixed rate on a five-year par value swap were 7 percent, the investor would exercise her receiver swaption by taking the 8 percent floating-rate payer's swap and then sell the position to swap bank or another party. With the current swap rate at 7 percent, she would be able to sell the 8 percent floating-payer's position for $415,830:

$$\text{Value of Swap} = \left[\sum_{t=1}^{10} \frac{(.08/2)-(.07/2)}{(1+(.07/2))^t}\right](\$10{,}000{,}000) = \$415{,}830$$

EXHIBIT 14.6 Value and Profit at Expiration from 8 percent/LIBOR Payer Swaption

Rates on 5-year Par Value Swaps at Expiration R	Payer Swaption's Interest Differential Max((R-.08)/2, 0)	Value of 8%/LIBOR Payer Swaption at Expiration PV(Max[(R-.08)/2, 0]($10m))	Payer Swaption Cost	Profit from Payer Swaption
0.060	0.0000	$0	$50,000	-$50,000
0.065	0.0000	$0	$50,000	-$50,000
0.070	0.0000	$0	$50,000	-$50,000
0.075	0.0000	$0	$50,000	-$50,000
0.080	0.0000	$0	$50,000	-$50,000
0.085	0.0025	$200,272	$50,000	$150,272
0.090	0.0050	$395,636	$50,000	$345,636
0.095	0.0075	$586,226	$50,000	$536,226
0.100	0.0100	$772,173	$50,000	$722,173

$$\text{Value of Swap} = \left[\sum_{t=1}^{10} \frac{\text{Max}[(R/2)-(.08/2),0]}{(1+(R/2))^t}\right](\$10{,}000{,}000)$$

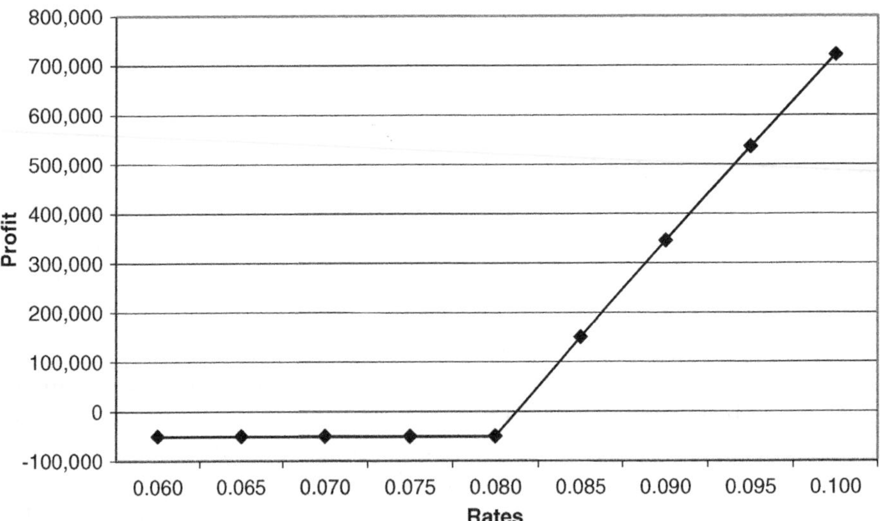

Alternatively, the swaption investor could exercise and then enter into a reverse swap. Thus, if rates were at 7 percent, then the investor would realize a profit of $365,830 (= $415,830 – $50,000) from the receiver swaption. If the swap rate were 8 percent or higher on the exercise date, then the investor would allow the receiver swaption to expire, losing, in turn, her premium of $50,000.

Formally, the value of the 8 percent/LIBOR receiver swaption at expiration is

$$\text{Value of Receiver Swaption} = \left[\sum_{t=1}^{10} \frac{Max[(.08/2)-(R/2),0]}{(1+(R/2))^t}\right](\$10{,}000{,}000)$$

EXHIBIT 14.7 Value and Profit at Expiration from 8 Percent/LIBOR Receiver Swaption

Rates on 5-year Par Value Swaps at Expiration *R*	Receiver Swaption's Interest Differential Max((.08–*R*)/2,0)	Value of 8%/LIBOR Receiver Swaption at Expiration PV(Max[(.08–*R*)/2, 0]($10m))	Receiver Swaption Cost	Profit from Receiver Swaption
0.060	0.0100	$853,020	$50,000	$803,020
0.065	0.0075	$631,680	$50,000	$581,680
0.070	0.0050	$415,830	$50,000	$365,830
0.075	0.0025	$205,320	$50,000	$155,320
0.080	0.0000	$0	$50,000	-$50,000
0.085	0.0000	$0	$50,000	-$50,000
0.090	0.0000	$0	$50,000	-$50,000
0.095	0.0000	$0	$50,000	-$50,000
0.100	0.0000	$0	$50,000	-$50,000

$$\text{Value of Swap} = \left[\sum_{t=1}^{10} \frac{\text{Max}[(.08/2)-(R/2),0]}{(1+(R/2))^t}\right](\$10,000,000)$$

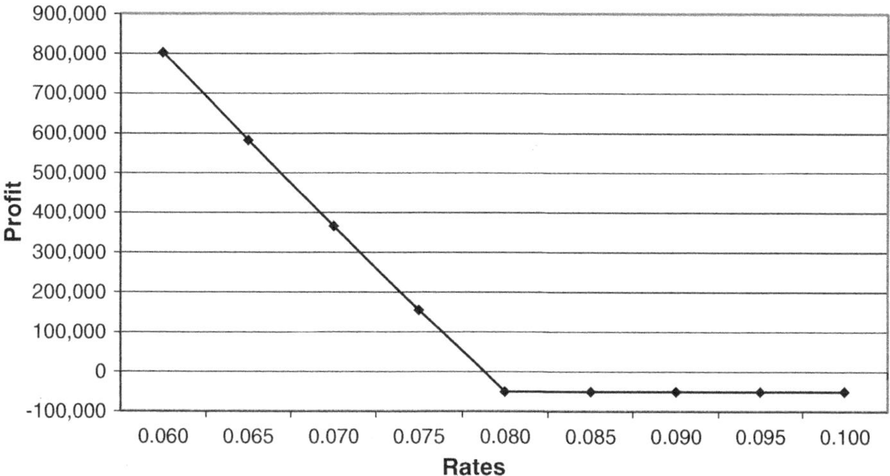

For rates, *R,* on par value five-year swaps less than the exercise rate of 8 percent, the value of the receiver swaption will be equal to the present value of the interest differential times the notional principal on the swap and for rates equal or greater that 8 percent, the swap is worthless. Exhibit 14.7 shows graphically and in a table the values and profits at expiration obtained from closing the receiver swaption on the five-year 8 percent/LIBOR swap given different rates at expiration.

Hedging

Caps and Floors on Future Debt and Investment Positions

Like other option hedging tools, swaptions give investors and borrowers protection against adverse price or interest rate movements, while allowing them to benefit if prices or rates move in their favor. Since receiver swaptions increase in value as rates decrease below the exercise rate, they can be used to establish floors on the rates of return obtained from future fixed-income investments. In contrast, since payer swaptions increase in value as rates increase above the exercise rate, they can be used for capping the rates paid on debt positions.

To illustrate how receiver swaptions are used for establishing a floor, consider the case of an investment fund that has an investment-grade fixed-rate portfolio worth \$30 million in par value that is scheduled to mature in two years. Suppose the fund plans to reinvest the \$30 million in principal for another three years in investment-grade bonds that are currently trading to yield 6 percent, but is worried that interest rate could be lower in two years. To establish a floor on its investment, suppose the fund purchases a two-year receiver swaption on a three-year 6 percent/LIBOR generic swap with a notional principal of \$30 million from First Bank for \$100,000. Two years later, the swaption's value will be greater if interest rates are lower (provided rates are less than 6 percent); this in turn, would offset the lower yields the fund would obtain from investing in lower yielding securities. However, for rates higher than 6 percent, the swaption is worthless, but the fund is able to invest in higher yield securities. Thus, for the cost of \$100,000, the receiver swaption provides the fund a floor.

In contrast to the use of swaptions to establish a floor on a future investment, suppose a firm had a future debt obligation and it wanted to cap the rate. In this case, the firm could purchase a payer swaption. For example, suppose a company has a \$60 million, 9 percent fixed-rate bond obligation maturing in three years that it plans to refinance at that time by issuing new five-year fixed-rate bonds. Suppose the company is worried that interest rate could increase in three years and as a result wants to establish a cap on the rate it would pay on its future five-year bond issue. To cap the rate, suppose the company purchases a three-year payer swaption on a five-year 9 percent/LIBOR generic swap with notional principal of \$60 million from First Bank for \$200,000. Two years later, the swaption's value will be greater if interest rates are higher (provided rates exceed 9 percent); this, in turn, would offset the higher borrowing rates the firm would have when it issues its new fixed-rate bonds. For rates less than 9 percent, however, the swaption is worthless, but the firm benefits with lower rate on new debt issues. Thus, for the cost of \$200,000, the payer swaption provides the fund a cap on it future debt.

Investor Hedging the Risk of an Embedded Call Option

The cap and floor hedging examples illustrate that swaptions are a particularly useful tool in hedging future investment and debt position against adverse interest rate changes. Swaptions can also be used to hedge against the impacts that unfavorable interest rate changes have on investment and debt positions with embedded options. Consider the case of a fixed-income manager holding \$10 million worth of 10-year, high-quality, 8 percent fixed-rate bonds that are callable in two years at a call price equal to par. Suppose the manager expects a decrease in rates over the next two years, increasing the likelihood that his bonds will be called and he will be forced to reinvest in a market with lower rates. To minimize his exposure to this call risk, suppose the manager buys a 2-year receiver swaption on an 8-year, 8 percent/LIBOR swap with a NP of $10 million. If two years later, rates were to increase, then the bonds would not be called and the swaption would have no value. In this case, the fixed income manager would lose the premium he paid for the receiver swaption. However, if two years later, rates on 8-year bonds were lower at say 6 percent, and the bonds were called at a call price equal to par, then the manager would be able to offset the loss from reinvesting the call proceed at lower interest rate by the profits from exercising the receiver swaption.

BLOOMBERG SWPM SCREEN FOR ANALYZING SWAPTIONS: SWPM <ENTER>

The SWPM screen can be used to create, value, and analyze swaptions. To create a swaption on SWPM, go to the "Products" tab and click "Swaption" under the "Options" dropdown. This will bring up the main screen for a swaption. The default on swaption shown is for a one-year, five-year swaption (1 × 5). You can then change the settings on the main screen.

- Options on swaps: On the dropdown "Pay Fixed" or "Receive Fixed," Notional Principal, Currency, Payment Frequency, Coupon (this is the fixed rate), Spread (the number of basis points to add or subtract from the floating rate, LIBOR), Forward Graph, and Discount Rate Option.
- Tab screens: "Details" tab shows the detail of the swap; "Resets" tab shows the reset rate at each effective date; "Cashflow" tab shows cash flows for each counterparty (leg); "Curves" tab; "Scenario" tab.
- Swaption valuation: The Black-Scholes model is used to price the swaption. The user can change the model and the volatility.
- *Note:* Swaption positions such as straddles can be evaluated on SWPM. From the "Products" tab, click "Swaption Strategies" under the "Options" dropdown.
- Note: Using the MARS screen, you can upload any portfolio that you have created and then add a swaption position you have created and saved in SWPM.

Example: 2 × 5 Payer Swaption; NP = $5.25 million; fixed rate (coupon) = 2 percent; floating rate = six-month LIBOR + 50 bp; frequency = semiannual; swap maturity = five years; swaption expiration = three years; forward curve = U.S. swaps (#23); discount curve = U.S. swaps (#23).

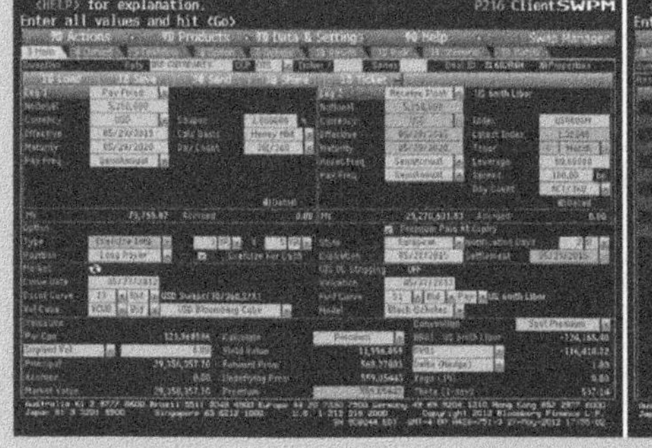

(*Continued*)

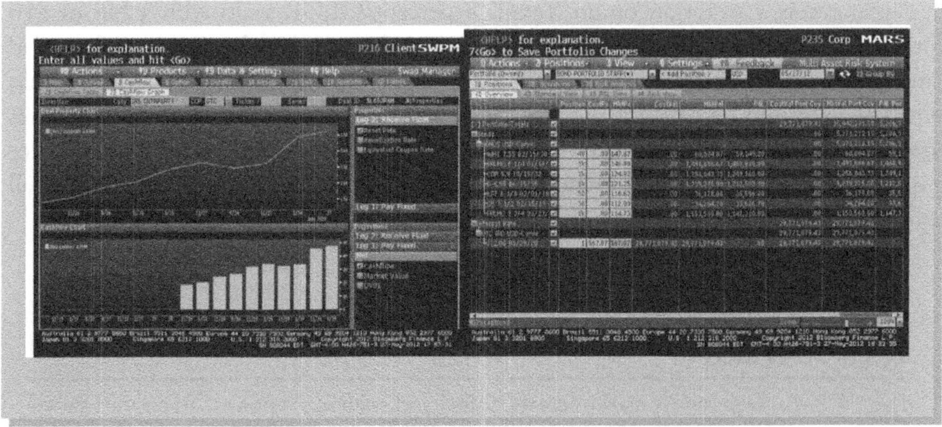

Nongeneric Swaps

Concomitant with this growth of swaps has been the number of innovations introduced in swaps contracts over the years. Today, there are a number of nonstandard or non-generic swaps used by financial and non-financial corporations to manage their varied cash flow and return-risk positions. Non-generic swaps usually differ in terms of their rates, principal, or effective dates. For example, instead of defining swaps in terms of the LIBOR, some swaps use the T-bill rate, prime lending rate, or the Federal Reserve's Commercial Paper Rate Index with different maturities. Similarly, the principals defining a swap can vary. An *amortizing swap,* for example, is a swap in which the NP is reduced over time based on a schedule, whereas a *set-up swap* (sometimes called an *accreting swap*) has its NP increasing over time. A variation of the amortizing swap is the *index-amortizing swap* (also called *index-principal swap*). In this swap, the NP is dependent on interest rates; for example, the lower the interest rate the greater the reduction in principal. There are also *zero-coupon swaps* in which one or both parties do not exchange payments until the maturity on the swap. There are also a number of *non–U.S. dollar interest rate swaps.* These swaps often differ in term of their floating rate: London rate, Frankfort (FIBOR), Copenhagen (CIBOR), Madrid (MIBOR), or Vienna (VIBOR). Finally, there are cancelable and extendable swaps. A *cancelable swap* is a swap in which one of the counterparties has the option to terminate one or more payments. Cancelable swaps can be callable or putable. A *callable cancelable swap* is one in which the fixed payer has the right to early termination. Thus, if rates decrease, the fixed-rate payer on the swap with this embedded call option to early termination can exercise her right to cancel the swap. A *putable cancelable swap,* however, is one in which the floating payer has the right to early cancellation. A floating-rate payer with this option may find it advantageous to exercise his early-termination right when rates increase. An *extendable swap* is just the opposite of a cancelable swap: it is a swap that has an option to lengthen the terms of the original swap. The swap allows the holder to take advantage of current rates and extend the maturity of the swap. Exhibit 14.8 summarizes some of the common nongeneric swaps.

EXHIBIT 14.8 Nongeneric Swaps

- ***Non-LIBOR Swap***: Swaps with floating rates different than LIBOR. Example: T-bill rate, CP rate, or Prime Lending Rate.
- ***Delayed-Rate Set Swap*** allows the fixed payer to wait before locking in a fixed swap rate—the opposite of a forward swap.
- ***Zero Coupon Swap***: Swap in which one or both parties do not exchange payments until maturity on the swap.
- ***Prepaid Swap***: Swap in which the future payments due are discounted to the present and paid at the start.
- ***Delayed-Reset Swap***: The effective date and payment date are the same. The cash flows at time t are determined by the floating rate at time t rather than the rate at time t-1.
- ***Amortizing Swaps:*** Swaps in which the NP decreases over time based on a set schedule.
- ***Set-Up Swap or Accreting Swap***: Swaps in which the NP increases over time based on a set schedule.
- ***Index Amortizing Swap***: Swap in which the NP is dependent on interest rates.
- ***Equity Swap***: Swap in which one party pays the return on a stock index and the other pays a fixed or floating rate.
- ***Basis Swap***: Swaps in which both rates are floating; each party exchanges different floating payments: One party might exchange payments based on LIBOR and the other based on the Federal Reserve Commercial Paper Index.
- ***Total Return Swap***: Returns from one asset are swapped for the returns on another asset.
- ***Non-U.S. Dollar Interest Rate Swap***: Interest-rate swap in a currency different that U.S. dollar with a floating rate often different that the LIBOR: Frankfort rate (FIBOR), Vienna (VIBOR), and the like.

Bloomberg IRDD Screen:

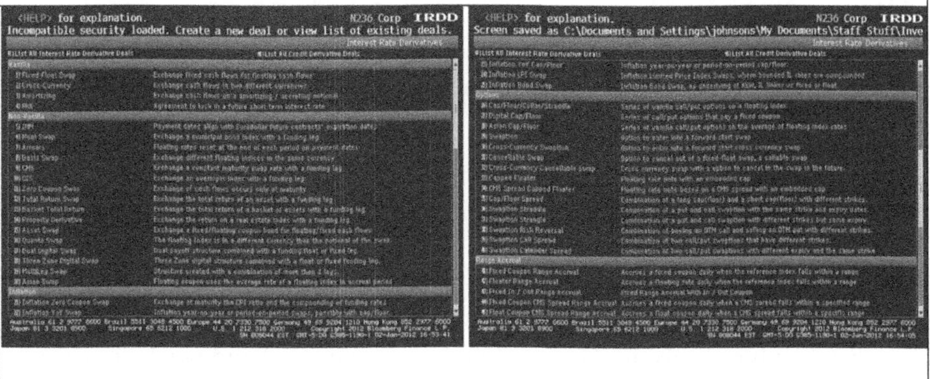

BLOOMBERG SWPM SCREENS:

SWPM <Enter>: Many different swap and interest rate derivative positions can be created, evaluated, and valued in SWPM. Example: Currency, cross currency, cancelable, total return, Asian, and emerging markets.

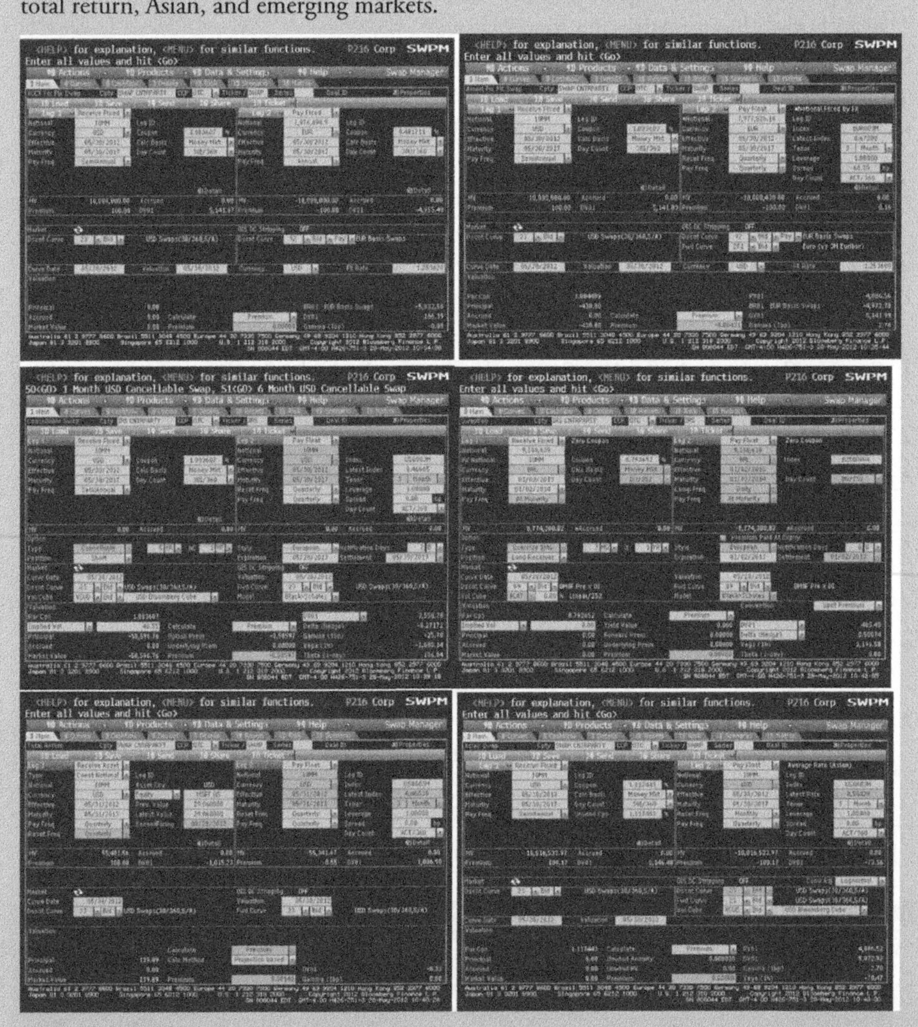

Credit Default Swaps

Traditionally, a bond portfolio manager or a financial institution with a portfolio of loans managed their portfolio's exposure to credit risk by the selection and allocation of credits (bonds or loans) in their portfolio. For example, a bond portfolio manager expecting recession and wanting to reduce her portfolio's exposure to credit risk would sell her lower-quality bonds and buy higher-quality ones. With the development of the credit default swap market, though, a bond manager or lender could change her credit risk by simply buying or selling swaps to change the credit risk profile on either an individual bond or loan or on a bond or loan portfolio.

Generic Credit Default Swap

Credit default swaps and other related credit swap derivatives are contracts in which the payoffs depend on the credit quality of a company. As discussed in Chapter 5, in a standard *credit default swap* (*CDS*), a counterparty buys protection against default by a particular company from another counterparty (seller). The company is known as the reference entity and a default by that company is known as a credit event. The buyer of the CDS makes periodic payments or a premium to the seller until the end of the life of the CDS or until the credit event occurs. If the credit event occurs, the buyer, depending on the contract, has either the right to sell a particular bond (or loan) issued by the company for its par value (physical delivery) or receive a cash settlement based on the difference between the par value and the defaulted bond's market price. In the standard CDS, payments are usually made in arrears either on a quarter, semiannual, or annual basis. The par value of the bond or debt is the notional principal used for determining the payments of the buyer. In many CDS contracts, a number of bonds or credits can be delivered in the case of a default. In the event of a default, the payoff from the CDS is equal to the face value of the bond (or NP) minus the value of the bond just after the default. The value of the bond just after the default expressed as a percentage of the bond's face value is known as the *recovery rate* (*RR*). Thus, the payoff from the CDS is

$$\text{CDS Payoff} = (1 - RR)NP - \text{Accrued Payment}$$

If the recovery value on a $100 million CDS were $30 per $100 face value, then the recovery rate would be 30 percent and the payoff to the CDS buyer would be $70 million (= (1 − .30)$100 million) minus any accrued payment. The payments on a CDS are quoted as an annual percentage of the NP. The payment is referred to as the *CDS spread.*

CDS Spread and Bond Credit Spread—Z-Spread

As noted in Chapter 5, the CDS spread should be approximately equal to the credit spread on the CDS's underlying bond or credit. For example, if the only risk on a five-year BBB corporate bond yielding 8 percent were credit risk (i.e., there is no option risk associated with embedded call options and the like and no liquidity and interest rate risk), and the risk-free rate on five-year investments were 5 percent, then the BBB bond would be trading in the market with a 3 percent credit spread. If the spread on a five-year CDS on a BBB quality bond were 3 percent, then an investor could obtain a five-year risk-free investment yielding 5 percent by either buying a five-year Treasury or by buying the five-year BBB corporate yielding 8 percent and purchasing the CDS on the underlying credit at a 3 percent spread.

If the spread on a CDS were not equal to the credit spread on the underlying bond, then an arbitrage opportunity would exist by taking positions in the bond, risk-free security, and the CDS. For example, if a swap bank were offering the CDS at a 4 percent spread, then an investor looking to invest in the higher yielding five-year BBB bonds could earn 1 percent more than the 8 percent on the BBB bond by creating a synthetic 5-year BBB bond by purchasing the five-year Treasury at 5 percent and selling the CDS at 4 percent. Similarly, a bond portfolio manager holding five-year BBB bonds yielding 8 percent could pick up an additional 1 percent yield with the same credit risk exposure by selling the bonds along with the CDS at 4 percent and then using the proceeds from the bond sale to buy the five-year Treasuries yielding 5 percent. Finally, an arbitrager could realized a free lunch equivalent to a five-year cash flow of 1 percent of the par value on the bond by shorting the BBB bond, selling the CDS, and then using proceeds to purchase five-year Treasuries. With these positions, the arbitrageur for each of the next five years would receive 5 percent from her Treasury investment and 4 percent from her CDS, while paying only 8 percent on her short BBB bond position. Furthermore, her holdings of Treasury securities would enable her to cover her obligation on the CDS if there was a default. That is, in the event of a default she would be able to pay the CDS holder from the net proceed from selling her Treasuries and closing her short BBB bond by buying back the corporate bonds at their defaulted recovery price.[4]

The strategy of selling a lower quality bond (e.g., BBB bond), buying higher-quality bonds (e.g., Treasuries), and selling CDS was the basis of many synthetic collateral debt obligations (CDO) structures. That is, the manager or sponsor of the CDO would issue a CDO (similar to shorting the BBB bond), sell CDS, and purchase investment-grade bonds. Collectively, the actions of the investors, bond portfolio managers, CDO managers, and arbitrageur would have the effect of pushing the spread on CDS toward the spread on the underlying bond. This equilibrium spread is referred to as the *arbitrage-free spread* or *Z-spread.*

Z-Spread and the Probability of the Loss of Principal

The Z-spread can also be thought of as the bond investor's or CDS buyer's probability of loss from the principal from default. That is, the 3 percent premium on the CDS on the five-year BBB bonds should not only be equal to the 3 percent credit spread on the bond, but also a probability of loss principal of 3 percent from a default. Thus, in an efficient market, the credit spread on bonds and the equilibrium spreads on CDS represent the market's implied expectation of the expected loss per year from the principal from default. To see this, consider a portfolio of five-year BBB bonds trading at a 3 percent credit spread. The 3 percent premium that investors receive from the bond portfolio represents their compensation for an implied expected loss of 3 percent per year of the principal from the defaulted bonds. If the spread were 3 percent and bond investors believed that the expected loss from default on such bonds would be only 2 percent per year of the principal, then the bond investors would want more BBB bonds, driving the price up and the yield down until the premium reflected a

2 percent spread. Similarly, if the spread were 3 percent and bond investors believed the default loss on a portfolio of BBB bonds would be 4 percent per year, then the demand and price for such bonds would decrease, increasing the yield to reflect a credit spread of 4 percent. Thus, in an efficient market, the credit spread on bonds and the equilibrium spreads on CDSs represent the market's implied expectation of the expected loss per year from the principal from default. In the case of a CDS, the equilibrium spread can therefore be defined as the implied probability of default loss of the principal on the contract.

BLOOMBERG WCDS

The WCDS screen monitors current values and changes to credit default swap spreads. WCDS uses either regional CDS end-of-day prices or composite regional intraday prices as the basis for its analysis.

<HELP> for explanation. Corp **WCDS**
Enter # <Go> to view curve in CDSD. 99 <Go> to save user selections

WORLD CDS PRICING Page 1/44

Source CMAN CMA NY EOD Mid/Last Spreads (New York)
Select Single Name CDS Fitch Rating 20) Edit All Sector All
Search Corporate Ticker GO Country All Currency USD

Reference Name	5 Year	Fitch	Spread Abs	Chg	Time	3 Mon
1) 3M Co	CMMM1U5	N.A.	29.000	+.000	05/25	1.500
2) ACE Ltd	CACE1U5	A+	76.500	+1.000	05/25	17.330
3) AES Corp/The	CAES1U5	BB-	407.175	-1.090	05/25	114.385
4) AK Steel Corp	CAKS1U5	N.A.	*1004.895	-13.480	05/25	202.810
5) AMP Group Holdings L..	CAMH1U5	N.A.	187.500	-.840	05/25	37.680
6) ARAMARK Corp	CT371596	B	361.440	-5.130	05/25	11.440
7) AT&T Corp	CATT1U5	A	40.715	-6.505	05/25	1.805
8) AT&T Inc	CSBC1U5	A	97.500	-.840	05/25	14.320
9) AT&T Mobility LLC	CCNG1U5	A	24.765	+.215	05/25	8.265
10) Abbott Laboratories	CABT1U5	A+	50.160	+.980	05/25	-8.320
11) Abu Dhabi Commercial..	CT423011	A+	208.715	-2.815	05/25	3.665
12) Abu Dhabi National E..	CX407153	N.A.	175.975	-2.425	05/25	-14.630
13) Advanced Micro Devic..	CT355268	B	*505.965	-3.035	05/25	136.365
14) Aetna Inc	CAET1U5	A	72.800	-.060	05/25	17.070
15) Agile Property Holdi..	CT409638	N.A.	*980.415	+2.145	05/25	-43.700
16) Agrium Inc	CAGU1U5	N.A.	111.030	+3.940	05/25	15.700
17) Air Products & Chemi..	CAPD1U5	N.A.	70.790	+.560	05/25	5.790
18) Alcatel-Lucent USA I..	CLU1U5	NR	*1145.320	-8.695	05/25	279.670

Australia 61 2 9777 8600 Brazil 5511 3048 4500 Europe 44 20 7330 7500 Germany 49 69 9204 1210 Hong Kong 852 2977 6000
Japan 81 3 3201 8900 Singapore 65 6212 1000 U.S. 1 212 318 2000
SN 808044 EDT GMT-4:00 H426-751-3 28-May-2012 10:56:19

BLOOMBERG CDS SCREENS—CORPORATIONS

- To access the CDS list on a specified company: Ticker CDS <Corp>.
- To access the menu for a specific CDS: BB ID <Equity>.
- Example: Kraft: Kft CDS <Corp>; Example: Kraft 10-year CDS: CKFT1US <Equity>.
- Screens to access on the menu: DES, ALLQ (Composite Quotes), GP, and CDSW (Valuation).
- **DRSK:** The DRSK screen provides estimates for the default probability, credit rating, and the five-year CDS spread for a selected company and its peers.

(Continued)

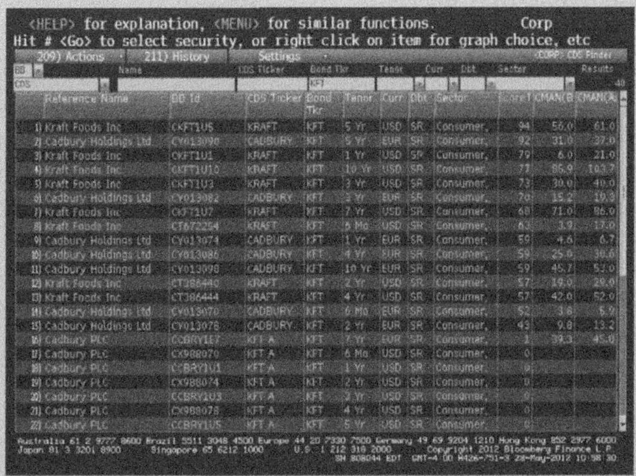

<HELP> for explanation, <MENU> for similar functions. Corp
Hit # <Go> to select security, or right click on item for graph choice, etc

209) Actions · 211) History · Settings · <CORP> CDS Finder

	Reference Name	BB Id	CDS Ticker	Bond Tkr	Tenor	Curr	Dbt	Sector	Score	CMAN(B	CMAN(A
1)	Kraft Foods Inc	CKFT1U5	KRAFT	KFT	5 Yr	USD	SR	Consumer,	94	56.0	61.0
2)	Cadbury Holdings Ltd	CY013090	CADBURY	KFT	5 Yr	EUR	SR	Consumer,	92	31.0	37.0
3)	Kraft Foods Inc	CKFT1U1	KRAFT	KFT	1 Yr	USD	SR	Consumer,	79	6.0	21.0
4)	Kraft Foods Inc	CKFT1U10	KRAFT	KFT	10 Yr	USD	SR	Consumer,	77	85.9	103.7
5)	Kraft Foods Inc	CKFT1U3	KRAFT	KFT	3 Yr	USD	SR	Consumer,	73	30.0	40.0
6)	Cadbury Holdings Ltd	CY013082	CADBURY	KFT	3 Yr	EUR	SR	Consumer,	70	15.2	19.3
7)	Kraft Foods Inc	CKFT1U7	KRAFT	KFT	7 Yr	USD	SR	Consumer,	68	71.0	86.0
8)	Kraft Foods Inc	CT672254	KRAFT	KFT	6 Mo	USD	SR	Consumer,	63	3.9	17.0
9)	Cadbury Holdings Ltd	CY013074	CADBURY	KFT	1 Yr	EUR	SR	Consumer,	59	4.6	6.7
10)	Cadbury Holdings Ltd	CY013086	CADBURY	KFT	4 Yr	EUR	SR	Consumer,	59	25.6	30.6
11)	Cadbury Holdings Ltd	CY013098	CADBURY	KFT	10 Yr	EUR	SR	Consumer,	59	45.7	53.0
12)	Kraft Foods Inc	CT386440	KRAFT	KFT	2 Yr	USD	SR	Consumer,	57	19.0	29.0
13)	Kraft Foods Inc	CT386444	KRAFT	KFT	4 Yr	USD	SR	Consumer,	57	42.0	52.0
14)	Cadbury Holdings Ltd	CY013070	CADBURY	KFT	6 Mo	EUR	SR	Consumer,	52	3.8	6.9
15)	Cadbury Holdings Ltd	CY013078	CADBURY	KFT	2 Yr	EUR	SR	Consumer,	43	9.8	13.2
16)	Cadbury PLC	CCBRY1E7	KFT A	KFT	7 Yr	EUR	SR	Consumer,	1	39.3	45.0
17)	Cadbury PLC	CX988070	KFT A	KFT	6 Mo	USD	SR	Consumer,	0		
18)	Cadbury PLC	CCBRY1U1	KFT A	KFT	1 Yr	USD	SR	Consumer,	0		
19)	Cadbury PLC	CX988074	KFT A	KFT	2 Yr	USD	SR	Consumer,	0		
20)	Cadbury PLC	CCBRY1U3	KFT A	KFT	3 Yr	USD	SR	Consumer,	0		
21)	Cadbury PLC	CX988078	KFT A	KFT	4 Yr	USD	SR	Consumer,	0		
22)	Cadbury PLC	CCBRY1U5	KFT A	KFT	5 Yr	USD	SR	Consumer,	0		

Australia 61 2 9777 8600 Brazil 5511 3048 4500 Europe 44 20 7330 7500 Germany 49 69 9204 1210 Hong Kong 852 2977 6000
Japan 81 3 3201 8900 Singapore 65 6212 1000 U.S. 1 212 318 2000 Copyright 2012 Bloomberg Finance L.P.
SN 808044 EDT GMT-4:00 H426-751-3 28-May-2012 10:58:30

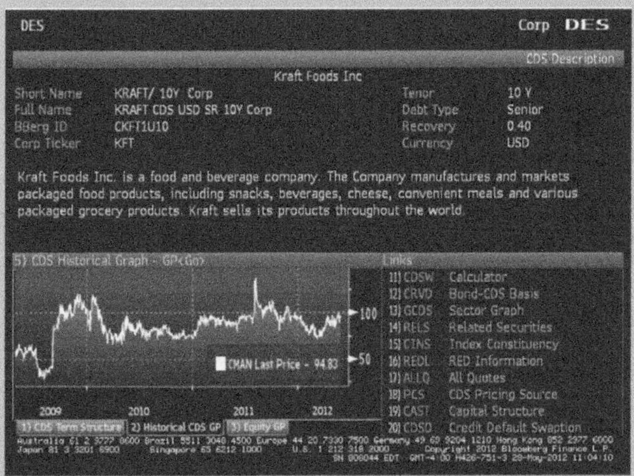

ALLQ Corp ALLQ

KRAFT CDS USD SR 10Y · 93) Launchpad · All Quotes
11:04:53 · 94) Suspend Sorting · 97) Settings

PCS	Firm Name	Bid Spd / Ask Spd	Cpn	BSz(MM) / ASz(MM)	Time
CMAN	CMA New York	85.930 / 103.730		x	05/25
CBIT	BBG CDS Intra TK	87.832 / 98.575		x	11:02
CBIL	BBG CDS Intra LN	87.832 / 98.575		x	11:02
CBIN	BBG CDS Intra NY	87.832 / 98.575		x	11:02
CMAI	CMA Intraday	84.530 / 102.770		x	10:30
CBGN	BBG CDS 5:15PM NY	88.295 / 98.893		x	05/25
CBGL	BBG CDS 5:15PM LN	88.295 / 98.892		x	05/25
CBED	BBG CDS EOD	88.294 / 98.892		x	05/25
CMAN	CMA New York	85.930 / 103.730		x	05/25
CMAL	CMA London	85.930 / 103.730		x	05/25
CBGT	BBG CDS 5:15PM TK	87.931 / 98.677		x	04:15
CMAT	CMA Tokyo	84.830 / 103.080		x	03:30

98) Filter and PCS Defaults
PCS Defaults 1st 2nd 3rd 4th 5th CMAN
Filter By ◦ Show All Sources • Executable Quotes Only • Enabled Dealers Only • Firm Pricing Only
Legend Firm Pricing / Enabled Dealers / Executable Quotes / Best Bid/Ask / Last Mid Quote

Australia 61 2 9777 8600 Brazil 5511 3048 4500 Europe 44 20 7330 7500 Germany 49 69 9204 1210 Hong Kong 852 2977 6000
Japan 81 3 3201 8900 Singapore 65 6212 1000 U.S. 1 212 318 2000 Copyright 2012 Bloomberg Finance L.P.
SN 808044 EDT GMT-4:00 H426-751-3 28-May-2012 11:04:53

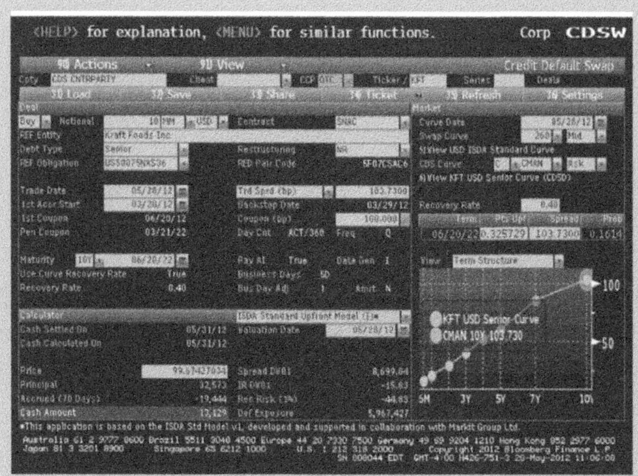
<HELP> for explanation, <MENU> for similar functions.
Corp CDSW
Credit Default Swap
KFT USD Senior Curve
CMAN 10Y 103.730
100
50
5M 3Y 5Y 7Y 10Y

KRAFT CDS SR 10Y 94.8Y as of close 5/25 CMAN
Bid 85.9 Ask 103.7
Corp GP
Last Price 94.830
High on 08/08/11 137.270
Average 93.773
Low on 03/05/12 72.505
140
130
120
110
100
94.830
90
80
70
Jun
Sep
2011
Dec
Mar
2012

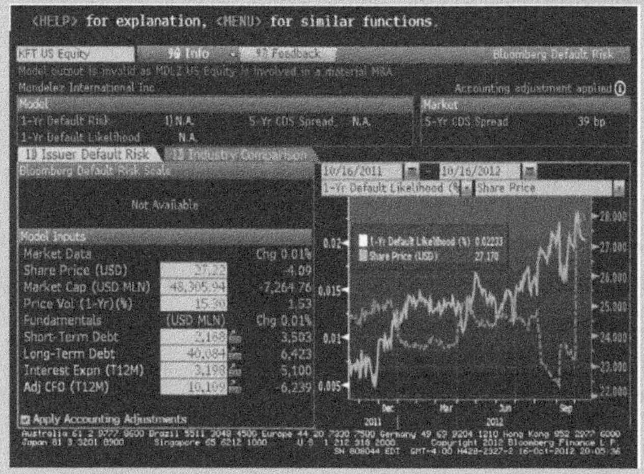
<HELP> for explanation, <MENU> for similar functions.
KFT US Equity
Bloomberg Default Risk
Mondelez International Inc
Model
Market
5-Yr CDS Spread 39 bp
1) Issuer Default Risk
Not Available
Model Inputs
Market Data
Share Price (USD) 27.22
Market Cap (USD MLN) 48,305.94
Price Vol (1-Yr)(%) 15.30
Fundamentals
Short-Term Debt
Long-Term Debt
Interest Expn (T12M)
Adj CFO (T12M)
Apply Accounting Adjustments

(*Continued*)

CDS Valuation

The total value of a CDS's payments is equal to the sum of the present values of the periodic CDS spread (Z) times the NP over the life of the CD discounted at the risk-free rate (R):

$$PV(\text{CDS Payments}) = \sum_{t=1}^{M} \frac{Z\,NP}{(1+R)^t}$$

The present value of the payment on a 5-year CDS with an equilibrium spread of 2 percent and a NP of $100 would be $84.25 given R of 6 percent and annual compounding:

$$PV(\text{CDS Payments}) = \sum_{t=1}^{5} \frac{(.02)(\$100)}{(1.06)^t} = \$84.25$$

The buyer (seller) of this five-year CDS would therefore be willing to make (receive) payments over five years that have a present value of $84.25 per $100 of NP. Since the spread can also be viewed as an expected loss of principal, the present value of the payments is also equal to the expected default protection the buyer (seller) receives (pays). The value of the CDS protection, in turn, is equal to the present value of the expected payout in the case of default:

$$PV(\text{Expected Payout}) = \sum_{t=1}^{M} \frac{p_t\,NP(1-RR)}{(1+R)^t}$$

where:

p_t = probability of default in period t conditional on no earlier default

RR = recovery rate (as a proportion of the face value) on the bond at the time of default

NP = notional principal equal to the par value of the bond

Note that the probability of default, p_t, is the conditional probability of no prior defaults that was defined in Chapter 5. Thus the conditional probability of default in year 3 is based on the probability that the bond will survive until year 3. Conditional default probabilities are referred to as *default intensities.*

Instead of defining a CDS's expected payout in terms periodic probability density, p_t, the CDS's expected payout can alternatively be defined by the average conditional default loss probability, $\bar{p}$:

$$PV(\text{Expected Payout}) = \sum_{t=1}^{M} \frac{\bar{p}\,NP(1-RR)}{(1+R)^t} = \bar{p}NP(1-RR)\sum_{t=1}^{M} \frac{1}{(1+R)^t}$$

Given an equilibrium spread of .02 and a recovery rate of 30 percent, the implied probability density for our illustrative CDS would be .02857. This implied probability is obtained by solving for $\bar{p}$ that makes the present value of the expected payout equal to present value of the payments:

$$PV(\text{Expected Payout}) = PV(\text{Payments})$$

$$\sum_{t=1}^{M} \frac{\bar{p}\,NP(1-RR)}{(1+R)^t} = \sum_{t=1}^{M} \frac{Z\,NP}{(1+R)^t}$$

$$\bar{p} = \frac{Z}{(1-RR)}$$

$$\bar{p} = \frac{.02}{(1-.30)} = .02857$$

Note that if there were no recovery (RR = 0), then the implied probability would be equal to the spread Z, which as we noted earlier can be thought of as the probability of default of principal. The probability density implied by the market is referred to as the risk-neutral probability since it is based on an equilibrium spread that is arbitrage free.[5]

Alternative CDS Valuation Approach

Suppose in our illustrative example, the estimated default intensity, sometimes referred to as the *real-world probability,* on the five-year BBB bond were .02 and not the implied probability of .02857. In this case, the present value of the CDS expected payout would be \$58.97 instead of \$84.25:

$$PV(\text{Expected Payout}) = \sum_{t=1}^{5} \frac{(.02)(\$100)(1-.30)}{(1.06)^t} = \$58.97$$

Given the spread on the CDS is at 2 percent and the present value of the payments are \$84.25, buyers of the CDS would have to pay more on the CDS than the value they receive on the expected payoff (\$58.97). If the real-world probability density of .02 is accurate, then buyers of the CDS would eventually push the spread down until it is equal to the value of the protection. For the payment on the CDS to match the expected protection, the spread would have to equal .014. This implied spread is found by solving for the Z that equates the present value of the payments to the present value of the expected payout given the real world probability of $\bar{p}$ = .02 and the estimated recovery rate of RR = .30. That is:

$$PV(\text{Payments}) = PV(\text{Expected Payout})$$

$$\sum_{t=1}^{M} \frac{Z\,NP}{(1+R)^t} = \sum_{t=1}^{M} \frac{\bar{p}\,NP(1-RR)}{(1+R)^t}$$

$$Z = \bar{p}(1-RR)$$

$$Z = (.02)(1-.30) = .014$$

We now have two alternative methods for pricing a CDS. On the one hand, we can value the CDS swap given the credit spread in the market and then determine the present value of the payments; thus, in terms of our example, we would use the market spread of 2 percent and value the swap at $84.25 with the implied probability density (or risk-neutral probability) being .02857. On the other hand, we can value the swap given estimated probabilities of default and then determine the present value of the expected payout; in terms of our example, we would use the estimated real world probability of .02 and value the CDS at $58.97 with the implied credit spread being .014.

The argument for pricing CDS using real world probabilities ultimately depends on the ability of practitioners to estimated default probabilities. There are several approaches for estimating conditional probabilities. The simplest and most direct one is to estimate the probabilities based on historical default rates. Exhibit 14.9 shows the cumulative default rates, unconditional probability rates, and conditional probability rates (probability intensities) for corporate bonds with quality ratings of Aaa, Baa, B, and Caa. The probabilities shown in the table are the average historical cumulative default rates from 1970 to 2006 as compiled by Moody's. As explained in Chapter 5, the unconditional probabilities are the probabilities of default in a given year as viewed from time zero. The unconditional probability of a bond defaulting during year t is equal to the difference in the cumulative probability in year t minus the cumulative probability of default in year $t-1$. As shown in the table, the probability of a Caa bond default during year 4 is equal to 7.18 percent (= 46.9 percent - 39.72 percent). Finally, the conditional probability is the probability of default in a given year conditional on no prior defaults. This probability is equal to unconditional probability of default in time t as a proportion of the bond's probability of survival at the beginning of the period. The probability of survival is equal to 100 minus the cumulative probability. For example, the probability that a Caa bond will survive until the end of year 3 is 60.28 percent (100 minus its cumulative probability 39.72 percent), and the probability that the Caa bond will default during year 4 conditional on no prior defaults is 11.91 percent (= 7.18 percent/60.28 percent). As noted earlier, conditional probabilities of default are known as default intensities. These probabilities, in turn, can be used to determine the expected payoff on a swap.

Using the conditional probabilities generated from the historical cumulative default rates, the values and spreads for four CDS with quality ratings of Aaa, Baa, B, and Caa are shown in Exhibit 14.9. Each swap is assumed to have a maturity of five years, annual payments, NP of $100, and recovery rate of 30 percent. The values are obtained by determining the present values of the expected payoff, with the discount rate assumed to be 6 percent and with the possible defaults assumed to occur at the end each year (implying there are no accrued payments). The spreads on the CDS are the spreads that equate the present value of the payments to the present value of the expected payoff. For example, the present value of the expected payoff for the CDS with a B quality rating is 17.78:

$$PV(\text{Expected Payoff}) = \sum_{t=1}^{M} \frac{p_t \, NP(1-RR)}{(1+R)^t}$$

$$PV(\text{Expected Payoff}) =$$

$$\$100)(1-.3)\left[\frac{.0524}{(1.06)}+\frac{.06395}{(1.06)^2}+\frac{.0647125}{(1.06)^3}+\frac{.0603905}{(1.06)^4}+\frac{.00608082}{(1.06)^5}\right]$$

$$PV(\text{Expected Payoff}) = 17.78$$

EXHIBIT 14.9 Cumulative Default Rates, Probability Intensities, and CDS Values and Spreads

Average Cumulative Default Rates 1970-2006 (Moody's) in %

Year	1	2	3	4	5	PV(Expected Payoff) NP=\$100 and RR = .3	CDS Spread Z
Aaa							
Cumulative Probability (%)	0.00000	0.00000	0.00000	0.03000	0.10000		
Unconditional Probability (%)	0.00000	0.00000	0.00000	0.03000	0.07000		
Conditional Probability p (%)	0.00000	0.00000	0.00000	0.03000	0.07002		
Present Value of p at 6%	0	0	0	0.0237628	0.052324	0.053260605	0.00013
Baa							
Cumulative Probability (%)	0.18000	0.51000	0.93000	1.43000	1.94000		
Unconditional Probability (%)	0.18000	0.33000	0.42000	0.50000	0.51000		
Conditional Probability p (%)	0.18000	0.33060	0.42215	0.50469	0.51740		
Present Value of p at 6%	0.169811321	0.294228	0.354448	0.3997646	0.38663	1.123417867	0.002666953
B							
Cumulative Probability (%)	5.24000	11.30000	17.04000	22.05000	26.79000		
Unconditional Probability (%)	5.24000	6.06000	5.74000	5.01000	4.74000		
Conditional Probability p (%)	5.24000	6.39510	6.47125	6.03905	6.08082		
Present Value of p at 6%	4.943396226	5.691619	5.433387	4.7834972	4.543943	17.77709035	0.04220217
Caa							
Cumulative Probability (%)	19.48000	30.49000	39.72000	46.90000	52.62000		
Unconditional Probability (%)	19.48000	11.01000	9.23000	7.18000	5.72000		
Conditional Probability p (%)	19.48000	13.67362	13.27866	11.91108	10.77213		
Present Value of p at 6%	18.37735849	12.16947	11.14902	9.4346923	8.049561	41.42607634	0.098344009

$$\text{PV(Expected Payoff)} = \sum_{t=1}^{M} \frac{p_t\, NP(1-RR)}{(1+R)^t} \qquad Z = \frac{\sum_{t=1}^{M} \frac{P_t(1-RR)}{(1+R)^t}}{\sum_{t=1}^{M} \frac{1}{(1+R)^t}}$$

The spread on the B quality CDS that equates the present value of its payments to the expected payoff of \$17.78 is .0422:

$$\sum_{t=1}^{M} \frac{Z\,NP}{(1+R)^t} = \sum_{t=1}^{M} \frac{p_t\,NP(1-RR)}{(1+R)^t}$$

$$Z \sum_{t=1}^{5} \frac{\$100}{(1.06)^t} = \$17.78$$

$$Z = \frac{\$17.78}{\sum_{t=1}^{5} \frac{\$100}{(1.06)^t}} = \frac{\$17.78}{\$421.2364} = .0422$$

As shown in the exhibit, the present values of the expected payoffs on the Caa quality CDS is \$41.43 and its spread is 0.0983. As expected, the CDS values and spreads are greater, the greater the default risk.

The above default rates are based on historical frequencies. Past frequencies are often not the best predictors of futures probabilities. There are a number of other more advanced estimating techniques that practitioners can use to determine default probabilities. Several of these estimating approaches are referenced at the end of this chapter. Of particular note is Gaussian Copula Model.

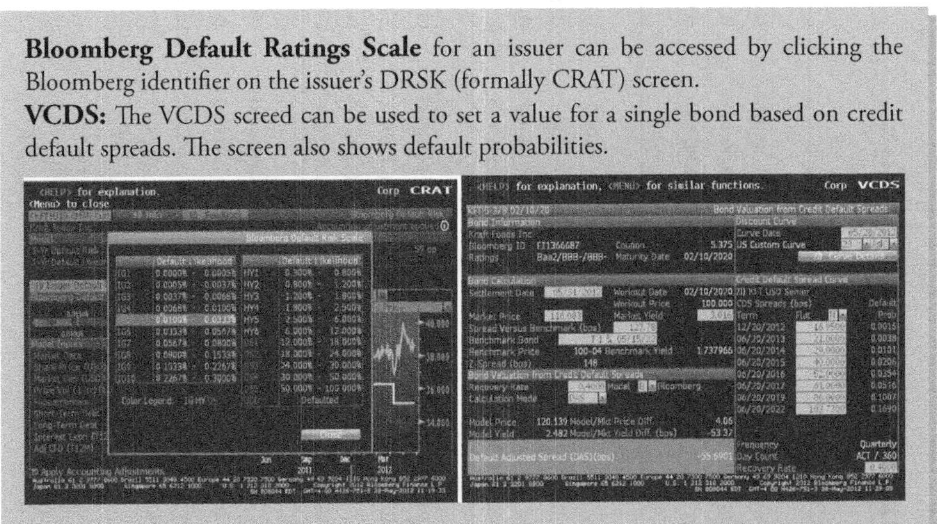

Bloomberg Default Ratings Scale for an issuer can be accessed by clicking the Bloomberg identifier on the issuer's DRSK (formally CRAT) screen.
VCDS: The VCDS screed can be used to set a value for a single bond based on credit default spreads. The screen also shows default probabilities.

The Value of an Off-Market CDS Swap

Similar to a generic par value interest rate swap, a swap rate on a new CDS is generally set so that there is not an initial exchange of money. Over time and as economic conditions change the credit spreads on new CDSs, the value of an existing CDS will change. For example, suppose one year after a bond fund manager bought our illustrative five-year CDS on BBB bond at the 2 percent spread, the economy became weaker and credit spreads on four-year BBB bonds and new CDSs on such bonds were 50 bp greater at 2.5 percent (assume for this discussion that CDS spreads are determine by bond credit spreads in the market). Suppose the bond fund manager sold her 2 percent CDS to a swap bank who hedged the CDS by selling a new 2.5 percent CDS on the four-year BBB bond. With a buyer's position on the assumed 2 percent CDS and seller's position on the 2.5 percent CDS, the swap bank, in turn, would gain 0.5 percent of the NP for the next four years. Given a discount rate of 6 percent, the present value of this gain would be \$1.73 per \$100 NP. The swap banks would therefore pay the bond manager a maximum of \$1.73 for assuming the swap.

Offsetting Swap Positions		
Buyer of 2% CDS Swap	Pay 2% of NP	Receive Default Protection
Seller of 2.5% CDS Swap	Receive 2.5%	Pay Default Protection
	Receive .5% per year	

$$SV = \sum_{t=1}^{4} \frac{(\text{Current Spread} - \text{Existing Spread})(NP)}{(1+R)^t} = \sum_{t=1}^{4} \frac{0.005(\$100)}{(1.06)^t} = \$1.73$$

With four years left on the current swap, the increase in credit spreads in the market has increased the value of the buyer's position on the CDS swap by \$1.73 from \$6.93 to 8.66:

$$\text{Existing CDS: PV(CDS Payments)} = \sum_{t=1}^{4} \frac{(.02)(\$100)}{(1.06)^t} = \$6.93$$

$$\text{Current PV(CDS Payments)} = \sum_{t=1}^{4} \frac{(.025)(\$100)}{(1.06)^t} = \$8.66$$

$$\text{Change in Value} = \$1.73$$

The increase in value on the buyer's position of the exiting swap reflects the fact that with poorer economic conditions the 2 percent swap payments now provide greater default protection (i.e., the present value of the expect payout is greater).

For the seller of the CDS, the increase in credit spreads causes a decrease in the value on seller's positions. For example, suppose that an insurance company was the one who sold the five-year CDS on the BBB bond at the 2 percent spread

EXHIBIT 14.10 Other CDSs and Credit Derivatives

Binary CDS: A binary CDS is identical to the generic CDS except that the payoff in the case of a default is a specified dollar amount. Often the fixed payoff is the principal on the underlying credit. When this is the case, then the only difference between the generic and binary swap is that the generic CDS adjusts the payoff by subtracting the recovery value, whereas the binary CDS does not. Without the recovery value, the value of a binary CDS is more sensitive to changes in credit spreads or default probabilities.

Basket CDS: In a basket credit default swap, there is a group of reference entities or credits instead of one and there is usually a specified payoff whenever one of the reference entities defaults. Basket CDS can vary by the type of agreement governing the payout. For example, an ***add-up basket CDS*** provides a payout when any reference credit in the basket defaults; a ***first-to-default CDS*** provides a payout only when the first entry defaults; a ***second-to-default CDS*** provides a payout when the second default occurs; an ***nth-to-default CDS*** provides a payout when the nth credit entry defaults. Typically, after the relevant entry defaults, the swap is terminated.

CDS Forward Contracts: A CDS forward contract is a contract to take a buyer's position or a seller's position on a particular CDS at a specified spread at some future date. CDS forward contracts provide a tool for locking in the credit spread on future credit positions.

CDS Option Contracts: A CDS option is an option to buy or sell a particular CDS at a specified swap rate at a specified future time. For example, a one-year option to buy a 5-year CDS on GE for 300 basis points. At expiration, the holder of this option would exercise her right to take the buyer's position at 300 basis points if current 5-year CDSs on GE were greater than 300 basis points; in contrast, she would allow the option to expire and take the current CDS on GE if it is offered at 300 basis points or less.

Contingent CDS: A contingent CDS provides a payout that is contingent on two or more events occurring. For example, the payoff might require both a credit default of the reference entity and an additional event such as a credit event with another entity or a change in a market variable.

Total Return Swaps: In a total return swap, there is an agreement to exchange the return on an asset (such a bond, bond portfolio, stock, or stock portfolio) for some benchmark rate such as LIBOR plus basis points. In the case of an exchange of the return on a bond or bond portfolio for LIBOR and basis points, the return on the bond includes coupons and gains and losses on the bond. Such a swap allows parties to trade different risk, including credit risk.

Equity Swap: In an equity swap, one party agrees to pay the return on an equity index, such as the S&P 500, and the other party agrees to pay a floating rate (LIBOR) or fixed rate. For example, on an S&P 500/LIBOR swap, the equity-payer would agree to pay the six-month rate of change on the S&P 500 (e.g., proportional change in the index between effective dates) times a NP in return for LIBOR times NP, and the debt payer would agree to pay the LIBOR in return for the S&P 500 return. Equity swaps are useful to fund managers who want to increase or decrease the equity or bond exposure of their portfolios as part of their overall asset allocation strategy.

CAT Bond: A CAT bond pays the buyer a higher-than-normal interest rate. In return for the additional interest, the CAT bondholder agrees to provide protection for losses from a specified event up to a specified amount or when the losses exceed a specified amount. For example, an insurance company could issue a CAT bond with a principal of $200 million against a hurricane cost exceeding $300 million. The CAT bondholders would then lose some or possibly all principal if the event occurs and the cost exceeds $300 million.

to the bond portfolio manager (via a swap bank) and that one year later the credit spread on new four-year CDS on BBB bonds was again at 2.5 percent. If the insurance company were to sell its seller's position to a swap bank, the swap bank could hedge the assumed position by taking a buyer's position on a new 4-year, 2.5 percent CDS on the BBB bond. With the offsetting positions, the swap bank would lose 0.5 percent of the NP for the next four years. Given a discount rate of 6 percent, the present value of this loss would be $1.73 per $100 NP. The swap banks would therefore charge the insurance company at least $1.73 for assuming the seller's position on the swap.

To summarize, an increase in the credit spread will increase the value of the buyer's position on an existing CDS and decrease the seller's position. Just the opposite occurs if economic conditions improve and credit spreads decrease.

Other Credit Derivatives

The market for CDS has grown dramatically over the last decade, although it has slowed in the aftermath of 2008 financial crisis. With that growth there has been an increase in the creation of other credit derivatives. The most noteworthy of these other credit derivative are the binary swap, credit swap basket, CDS forward contracts, CDS option contracts, contingent swaps, and total return swaps (see Exhibit 14.10)

Conclusion

In this chapter, we have examined the markets, uses, and valuation of generic interest rate swaps, swap derivatives, and CDS. Like interest rate options and futures, swaps provide investors and borrowers with a tool for hedging asset and liability positions against interest rate and credit risk, speculating on interest rate and credit movements, and improving the returns received on fixed income investments or paid on debt positions. Swaps, in turn, have become a basic financial engineering tool to apply to a variety of financial problems.

We, of course, have not exhausted all derivative securities, just as we have not covered all the strategies, uses, markets, and pricing of debt securities. What we hope we have done here and in this last part of the book, though, is develop a foundation for the understanding of derivative products and their important applications in debt management. To this extent, we also hope our odyssey into the world of bonds and their derivative has established a foundation and methodology for understanding the markets and uses of fixed-income securities.

Website Information

For information on the International Swap and Derivative Association and size of the markets, go to www.isda.org.

Selected References

Bhattacharya, A. K., and F. J. Fabozzi. 2001. Interest-rate swaps. In F. Fabozzi, ed., *The Handbook of Fixed Income Securities*, 6th ed. New York: McGraw-Hill.

Bicksler, J., and A. H. Chen. 1986. An economic analysis of interest rate swaps. *Journal of Finance* 41:645–655.

Brown, K. C., and D. J. Smith. 1991. Plain vanilla swaps: Market structures, applications, and credit risk. In C. R. Beidleman, ed., *Interest Rate Swaps*. Homewood, IL: Business One Irwin.

Cooper, I., and A. S. Mello. 1991. The default risk of swaps. *Journal of Finance* 48:597–620.

Cucchissi, P. G., and R. M. Tuffli. 1991. Swaptions applications. In C. R. Beidleman, ed., *Interest Rate Swaps*. Homewood, IL: Business One Irwin.

Darby, M. R. 1994. Over-the-counter derivatives and systemic risk to the global financial system. National Bureau of Economic Research Working Paper Series, No. 4801.

Froot, K. A. 2001. The market for catastrophe risk: A clinical examination. *Journal of Financial Economics* 60:529–571.

Goodman, L. S. 1991. Capital market applications of interest rate swaps. In C. R. Beidleman, ed., *Interest Rate Swaps*. Homewood, IL: Business One Irwin.

Haubrich, J. G. 2001. Swaps and the swaps yield curve. *Economic commentary*, Federal Reserve Bank of Cleveland (December):1–4.

Hull, J. C. 2005. *Option, Futures, and Other Derivatives*, 6th ed. Upper Saddle River, NJ: Prentice Hall, Chapters 20–21.

Hull, J., M. Predescu, and A. White. 2004. Relationship between credit default swap spreads, bond yields, and credit rating announcements. *Journal of Banking and Finance* 28:2789–2811.

Hull, J. C., and A. White. 2004. Valuation of a CDO and *n*th-to-default swap without Monte Carlo simulation. *Journal of Derivatives* 12:8–23.

Hull, J. C., and A. White. 2000. Valuing credit default swaps I: No counterparty default risk. *Journal of Derivatives* 8:29–40.

Hull, J. C., and A. White. 2001. Valuing credit default swaps II: Modeling default correlations. *Journal of Derivatives* 8:12–22.

Iben, B. 1991. Interest rate swap evaluation. In C. R. Beidleman, ed., *Interest Rate Swaps*. Homewood, IL: Business One Irwin, Chapter 12.

Johnson, R. S. 2009. *Introduction to Derivatives: Options, Futures, and Swaps*. New York: Oxford University Press, Chapters 17–19.

Kawaller, I. B. 1991. A swap alternative: Eurodollar strips. In C. R. Beidleman, ed., *Interest rate swaps*. Homewood, IL: Business One Irwin.

Litzenberger, R. H. 1992. Swaps: Plain and fanciful. *Journal of Finance* 47:831–850.

Marshall, J. F., and K. R. Kapner. 1993. *Understanding Swaps*. New York: John Wiley & Sons.

Pergam, A. S. 1994. Swaps: A legal perspective. In J. C. Francis and A. S. Wolf, ed., *The Handbook of Interest Rate Risk Management*. New York: Irwin Professional.

Smith, D. J. 1997. Aggressive corporate finance: A close look at the Procter and Gamble–Bankers Trust leveraged swap. *Journal of Derivatives* 4:67–79.

Smith, C. W., C. W. Smithson, and L. M. Wakeman. 1986. The evolving market for swaps. *Midland Corporate Finance Journal* 3:20–32.

Smith, C. W., C. W. Smithson, and L. M. Wakeman. 1988. The market for interest rate swaps. *Financial Management* 17:34–44.

Sun, T., S. Sundaresan, and C. Wang. 1993. Interest rate swaps: An empirical investigation. *Journal of Financial Economics* 36:77–99.

Titman, S. 1992. Interest rate swaps and corporate financing choices. *Journal of Finance* 47: 1503–1516.

Turnbull, S. M. 1987. Swaps: A zero sum game. *Financial Management* 16:15–21.

Wall, L. D., and J. J. Pringle. 1989. Alternative explanations of interest rate swaps: A theoretical and empirical analysis. *Financial Management* 18:59–73.

Bloomberg Exercises

1. Use the Bloomberg SWPM screen to create and analyze a fixed-/floating-rate swap. Tabs screen to include in your analysis: Details, Resets, Cashflow (Cashflow Table and Cashflow Graph), and Curves. Save the swap position you created in SWPM: go to the "Actions" tab and click "Save," in the box, name the swap position (Custom ID), and click "Save." Go to IRDL to identify your swap.
2. Construct a portfolio using PRTU consisting of Treasury notes and bonds with a portfolio market value close to the notional principal and an average maturity close to the maturity of the swap you created in Exercise 1.
   a. Analyze the interest rate risk of the portfolio using the Bloomberg MARS screen: MARS <Enter>; upload portfolio. On the MARS Scenario tab, set scenario periods, interest rate shifts (e.g., -50 bp to 50 bp) and y-axis (e.g., profit/loss or market value). Comment on the relation between the market value or profit/loss and interest rate relation.
   b. On your MARS screen, add the fixed/floating swap you created and saved in Exercise 1. From the "Positions" tab, click "Exiting SWPM Deals," and identify and select the swap you created. Analyze the interest rate risk of the swap using the MARS screen: On the MARS "Scenario" tab, set scenario periods, interest rate shifts (e.g., -50 bp to 50 bp) and y-axis (e.g., profit/loss or market value). Comment on the relation between the market value or profit/loss and interest rate relation.
   c. Analyze the interest rate risk of the bond portfolio with a long position in the swap using the MARS screen. You may have to adjust the size of the swap to reflect the size of the portfolio. Comment on the relation between the market value or profit/loss and interest rate relation.
   d. Analyze the interest rate risk of the bond portfolio with a short position in the swap using the MARS screen. You may have to adjust the size of the swap to reflect the size of the portfolio. Comment on the relation between the market value or profit/loss and interest rate relation.
3. Use the Bloomberg SWPM screen to create and analyze a swaption on a fixed-/floating-rate swap similar to the one you created in Exercise 1. To create a swaption on SWPM, go to the "Products" tab and click "Swaption" from the "Options" dropdown. Tabs to include in your analysis: Details, Resets, Cashflows, and Curves. Save the swaption position you created in SWPM: go to the "Actions" tab and click "Save," in the box, name the swap position (Custom ID), click "click "Save." Go to IRDL to identify your swap.
4. The Bloomberg ASW screen allows one to calculate the relative value of a selected bond through the interest rate swap market. Select a dollar-denominated, fixed-income, intermediate-term Treasury or investment-grade bond and use ASW to determine how much money can be saved in interest costs by issuing the bond and swapping the fixed payments for floating payments on the swap created in ASW. To access: load bond: Bond Ticker <Govt> or <Corp>; type ASW. ASW tabs to consider: Pricing, Cashflow, and Deal Summary.

5. Select a CDS on a company of interest with investment-grade bonds (Ticker CDS <Corp>) and analyze it using the following screens: DES, ALLQ (Composite Quotes), GP, and CDSW (Valuation). Use the Bloomberg DRSK screen (type DRSK on CDS menu) to determine the history of the implied probability of default loss (on DRSK chart the probability can be found on the dropdown).
6. Select a CDS on a company of interest with non-investment-grade bonds (Ticker CDS <Corp>) and analyze it using the following screens: DES, ALLQ (Composite Quotes), GP, and CDSW (Valuation). Use the Bloomberg DRSK screen to determine the history of implied probability of default loss for company.

Notes

1. For an analysis of the zero-coupon approach to valuing swaps, see Johnson, *Introduction to Derivatives,* Chapter 19.
2. Swaps fall under contract law and not security law. The mechanism for default is governed by the swap contract, with many patterned after International Swap and Derivatives Association (ISDA) documents.
3. For an analysis of break-even forward rates and the pricing of forward swaps and swaptions, see Johnson (2009), Chapter 19.
4. However, suppose a bank were offering the above CDS for 2 percent instead of 3 percent. In this case, an investor looking for a five-year risk-free investment would find it advantageous to create the synthetic risk-free investment with the BBB bond and the CDS. That is, the investor could earn 1 percent more than the yield on the Treasury by buying the five-year BBB corporate yielding 8 percent and purchasing the CDS on the underlying credit at 2 percent. In addition to the investor gaining, an arbitrager could also realized a free lunch equivalent to a five-year cash flow of 1 percent of the par value of the bond by shorting the Treasury at 5 percent and then using the proceeds to buy the BBB corporate and the CDS. These actions by investors and arbitrageurs, in turn, would have the impact of pushing the spread on the CDS towards 3 percent—the underlying bond's credit risk spread.
5. The estimated recover rate, RR, is generally treated as a given. For generic CDS the value of the CDS is not as sensitive to RR as it is to Z. Default studies by Moody's found that from 1982 to 2003, recovery rates on corporate bonds as a percentage of face value have ranged from 51.6 percent for senior secured debt to 24.5 percent for junior subordinated debt.

Appendix A
Primer on Return, Present Value, and Future Value

Holding Period Yield

The rate of return an investor earns from holding a security is equal to the total dollar return received from the security per period of time (e.g., year) expressed as a proportion of the price paid for the security. The total dollar return includes income payments (coupon interest or dividends), interest earned from reinvesting the income during the period, and capital gains or losses realized when the security is sold or matures. For example, an investor who purchased XYZ stock for S_0 = \$100, then received \$10 in dividends (D) two years later when he sold the stock for S_T = \$120, would realized a rate of return for this two-year period of 20 percent:

$$\text{Rate of return} = \frac{D + S_T - S_0}{S_0} = \frac{\$10 + \$110 - \$100}{\$100} = 0.20$$

Similarly, a bond investor who bought a Treasury bond on April 20th for P_0^B = \$95,000 and then sold it for P_N^B = \$96,000 on October 20th just after receiving a coupon of C = \$4,000, would earn a rate of return for this six-month period of 5.263 percent:

$$\text{Rate of return} - \frac{C + P_T^B - P_0^B}{P_0^B} = \frac{\$4{,}000 + \$96{,}000 - \$95{,}000}{\$95{,}000} = 0.05263$$

Both the bond and stock rates of return are measured as *holding period yields,* HPY. The HPY is the rate earned from holding the security for one period (e.g., one year or six months). The HPY can alternatively be expressed in terms of the security's *holding period return,* HPR, minus one, where the HPR is the ratio of the ending-period value (e.g, $D + S_T$) to the beginning period value (S_0). That is:

$$HPY = \frac{\text{Ending value}}{\text{Beginning value}} - 1$$

$$HPY = HPR - 1$$

$$HPY = \frac{D + S_T}{S_0} - 1; \; HPY = \frac{C + P_T^B}{P_0^B} - 1$$

Annualized HPY

In order to evaluate alternative investments with different holding periods, investment analysts often annualize the rate of return. The simplest way to annualize a return is to multiply the periodic rate of return by the number of periods of that length in a year. Thus, to annualize the HPY on the bond investment, we would multiply the six-month HPY of .05263 by 2 to obtain .10526; to annualize the stock's rate of return, we would multiple the two-year HPY of 0.20 by HF to get .10. This method for annualizing rates of return, though, does not take into account the interest that could be earned from reinvesting the cash flows. That is, a \$1 investment in the bond would yield \$1.0526 after six months, which could be reinvested. If it is reinvested for six months at the same six-month rate of 5.26 percent, then the dollar investment would be worth \$1.108 after one year. Thus, the *effective annual rate* (i.e., the rate that takes into account the reinvestment of interest or the compounding of interest) is 10.8 percent. The *effective annualized HPY* (HPY^A) can be calculated using the following formula:

$$HPY^A = HPR^{1/M} - 1$$

where M = number of years the investment is held.

Thus, the effective annualized HPY for the bond investment would be 10.8 percent, and the effective HPY^A for the stock investment would be 9.544 percent:

$$HPY^A = HPR^{1/M} - 1$$

$$HPY^A = \left[\frac{\$4{,}000 + \$96{,}000}{\$95{,}000}\right]^{1/0.5} - 1 = .108$$

$$HPY^A = \left[\frac{\$10 + \$110}{\$100}\right]^{1/2} - 1 = .0954$$

The two-year HPY on the stock of 20 percent reflects annual compounding. That is, \$1 after one year would be worth \$1.0954, which reinvested for the next year would equal \$1.20:

$$\$1.00(1.0954)(1.0954) = (1.0954)^2 = \$1.20$$

Required Rates of Return and Value for a Single-Period Cash Flow

The price of a security and its rate of return are related. When an investor knows the price of a security and its cash flow, she can determine the rate of return. Alternatively, when the investor knows her *required rate of return* and the security's cash flow, she can determine the value of the security or the price she is willing to pay. For example, an investor who requires an annual 10 percent rate of return in order to invest in a one-year, AAA bond paying a single cash flow of coupon interest of \$10 and a principal of \$100 at maturity would value the bond at \$100. This price can be found by expressing the equation for the HPY in terms of its price. That is:

$$\text{Rate of return} = R = \frac{C + P_T^B}{P_0^B} - 1$$

$$P_0^B(1+R) = C + P_T^B$$

$$P_0^B = \frac{C + P_0^B}{(1+R)}$$

$$P_0^B = \frac{\$10 + \$100}{1.10} = \$100$$

If the bond were priced in the market below \$100, the investor would consider it underpriced, yielding a rate of return that exceeds her required rate of 10 percent; if the bond were priced above \$100, she would consider the bond to be overpriced, yielding a rate of return less than 10 percent.

Future and Present Values

Future Value

The above value and return relations can be described in terms of the present values and future values of investments and future receipts. More formally, the future value of any amount invested today is

$$P_N = P_0(1+R)^N$$

where:

N = number of periods of the investment
P_N = future value of investment N periods from present (future value, FV)
P_0 = Initial investment value (present value, PV)
R = rate per period (periodic rate)
$(1 + R)^N$ = future value of \$1 invested today for N periods at a compound rate of R

In terms of the preceding bond example, the future value (FV) of the bond investment of \$100 at 10 percent is \$110 (coupon and principal):

$$P_1 = P_0(1+R)^1$$

$$P_1 = \$100(1.10) = \$110$$

An investment fund that invested \$1,000,000 in a security that paid 10 percent per year for three years would, in turn, have \$1,331,000 at the end of three years:

$$P_N = P_0\,(1+R)^N$$

$$P_3 = \$1{,}000{,}000\;(1.10)^3 = \$1{,}331{,}000$$

If the interest is paid more than once a year, then the rate of return and the number of periods must be adjusted. Specifically, let

n = the number of times interest in paid per year

M = number of years of the investment

$$\text{Period rate } = R = \frac{\text{Annual rate}}{n}$$

N = number of periods of the investment = (n) (M)

If an investment fund invested \$1,000,000 in a three-year security that paid annual interest at 10 percent for three years with the interest paid semiannually, then the investment would be worth \$1,340,095.64 after three years:

$n = 2$

$M = 3$ years

$$\text{Period rate } = R = \frac{\text{Annual rate}}{n} = \frac{.10}{2} = .05$$

N = number of periods of the investment = (n) (M) = (2)(3) = 6

$$P_N = P_0\,(1+R)^N$$

$$P_6 = \$1{,}000{,}000\;(1.05)^6 = \$1{,}340{,}095.64$$

Note that with semiannual interest payments, there are more opportunities for reinvesting the interest received. As a result, the future value of the investment is greater with interest paid semiannually than annually.

Future Value of an Annuity

An annuity is a periodic investment or receipt. For example, an investment of \$1 million each year for three years would be an example of an investment annuity and a security paying \$50 every six months for 10 years would be an example of a receipt annuity. The future value of an annuity (A) is equal to the sum of the future values of each investment at the investment horizon:

$$P_N = A(1+R)^{N-1} + A(1+R)^{N-2} + A(1+R)^{N-3} + \ldots + A(1+R)^{N-N}$$

$$P_N = \sum_{t=1}^{N} A(1+R)^{N-t}$$

As an example, suppose an investment fund owned $50,000,000 of bonds maturing in three years that promised to pay 10 percent per year and $50,000,000 at the end of three years. If the fund reinvested the annual interest of $5,000,000 at a rate of 10 percent, then at the end of three years the sum of the annual interest payments would be worth $16,550,000:

Year	0	1	2	3	3	Values
A		$5,000,000.00			$5,000,000(1.10)^2	$6,050,000.00
A			$5,000,000.00		$5,000,000(1.10)^1	$5,500,000.00
A				$5,000,000.00	$5,000,000(1.10)^0	$5,000,000.00
					Horizon Value = P_N	$16,550,000.00

$$P_N = \sum_{t=1}^{N} A(1+R)^{N-t}$$

$$P_3 = \sum_{t=1}^{3} \$5{,}000{,}000(1+R)^{3-t}$$

$$P_N = \$5{,}000{,}000(1.10)^{3-1} + \$5{,}000{,}000(1.10)^{3-2} + \$5{,}000{,}000(1.10)^{3-3}$$

$$P_N = \$16{,}550{,}000$$

At the end of three years, the fund would have $50 million in principal, $15 million in interest, and $1,550,000 (= $16,550,000 – $15,000,000) in interest earned from reinvesting the interest.

The equation for the future value of an annuity is equal to the annuity times the future value of $1 invested each period for *N* periods:

$$P_N = \sum_{t=1}^{N} A(1+R)^{N-t}$$

$$P_N = A\sum_{t=1}^{N} (1+R)^{N-t}$$

The future value of $1 invested each period for *N* periods is defined as the future value interest factor of an annuity, $FVIF_a$. The formula for determining $FVIF_a$ is

$$FVIF_a = \sum_{t=1}^{N} (1+R)^{N-t} = \left[\frac{(1+R)^N - 1}{R}\right]$$

Substituting the formula for the $FVIF_a$ into the equation for P_N, the future value of annuity can alternatively be expressed as:

$$P_N = A\sum_{t=1}^{N}(1+R)^{N-t}$$

$$P_N = A\left[\frac{(1+R)^N - 1}{R}\right]$$

In terms of our example:

$$P_3 = \$5,000,000\sum_{t=1}^{3}(1.10)^{3-t}$$

$$P_3 = \$5,000,000\left[\frac{(1.10)^3 - 1}{.10}\right]$$

$$P_3 = \$16,550,000$$

Note: If the bond investment fund received interest semiannually, then the fund would receive $2,500,000 every six months. If the semiannual reinvestment rate were 5 percent, then the sum of the future values of the interest payments would be $17,004,782:

Year	0.0	0.5	1.0	1.5	2.0	2.5	3.0	3	Values
N		1	2	3	4	5	6	6	
A		$2,500,000						$2,500,000(1.05)^5$	$3,190,704
A			$2,500,000					$2,500,000(1.05)^4$	$3,038,766
A				$2,500,000				$2,500,000(1.05)^3$	$2,894,063
A					$2,500,000			$2,500,000(1.05)^2$	$2,756,250
A						$2,500,000		$2,500,000(1.05)^1$	$2,625,000
A							$2,500,000	$2,500,000(1.05)^0$	$2,500,000
								Horizon Value = P_N	$17,004,782

$$P_N = A\sum_{t=1}^{N}(1+R)^{N-t}$$

$$P_6 = \$2,500,000\sum_{t=1}^{6}(1.05)^{6-t}$$

$$P_6 = \$2,500,000\left[\frac{(1.05)^6 - 1}{.05}\right]$$

$$P_6 = \$17,004,782$$

Present Value

The present value is the amount that must be invested today to realize a specific future value. The present value of one future receipt is:

$$P_0 = \frac{P_N}{(1+R)^N}$$

Thus, \$1,331,000 received three years from now would be worth \$1 million given a rate of return of 10 percent and annual compounding:

$$P_0 = \frac{P_N}{(1+R)^N}$$

$$P_0 = \frac{\$1{,}331{,}000}{(1.10)^3} = \$1{,}000{,}000$$

\$1,340,095.64 received three years from now ($M = 3$), would be worth \$1 million given a 5 percent semiannual rate, and two compoundings per year ($n = 2$ and $N = nM = (2)(3) = 6$):

$$P_0 = \frac{P_N}{(1+R)^N}$$

$$P_0 = \frac{\$1{,}340{,}095.64}{(1.05)^6} = \$1{,}000{,}000$$

The method of computing the present value is referred to as *discounting,* and the interest rate used to discount is referred to as the *discount rate.*

Present Value of an Annuity

When a fixed dollar annuity is received each period, the series is also called an annuity. If the first payment is received one period from the present, the annuity is referred to as an *ordinary annuity;* if the first payment is immediate, then the annuity is called an *annuity due.* The present value of an ordinary annuity is the sum of the present values of each annuity received:

$$P_0 = \frac{A}{(1+R)^1} + \frac{A}{(1+R)^2} + \frac{A}{(1+R)^3} + \ldots + \frac{A}{(1+R)^N}$$

$$P_0 = \sum_{t=1}^{N} \frac{A}{(1+R)^t}$$

$$P_0 = A\sum_{t=1}^{N} \frac{1}{(1+R)^t}$$

$\sum_{t=1}^{N} \frac{1}{(1+R)^t}$ is the present value of $1 received each period for N periods. It is referred to as the present value interest factor of an annuity, $PVIF_a$. $PVIF_a$ is equal to

$$PVIF_a = \sum_{t=1}^{N} \frac{1}{(1+R)^t} = \left[\frac{1-(1/(1+R)^N}{R}\right]$$

Thus, an investor who received $100 at the end of each year for three years would have an investment currently worth $248.69 given a discount rate of 10 percent:

Year	0	0	1	2	3
A	$90.91	$\$100/(1.10)^1$	$100.00		
A	$82.64	$\$100/(1.10)^2$		$100.00	
A	$75.13	$\$100/(1.10)^3$			$100.00
	$248.69	Present Value = P_0			

$$P_0 = \sum_{t=1}^{3} \frac{\$100}{(1.10)^t} = \frac{\$100}{(1.10)^1} + \frac{\$100}{(1.10)^2} + \frac{\$100}{(1.10)^3}$$

$$P_0 = \$100 \sum_{t=1}^{3} \frac{1}{(1.10)^t}$$

$$P_0 = \$100\left[\frac{1-(1/(1.10)^3}{.10}\right]$$

$$P_0 = \$248.69$$

If the investment paid $50 every six months and the appropriate six-month rate were 5 percent, then the present value of the $50 annuity would be $253.78:

Year	0	0	0.5	1.0	1.5	2.0	2.5	3.0
Number of semiannual periods from present	0	0	1	2	3	4	5	6
A	$47.62	$\$50/(1.05)^1$	$50					
A	$45.35	$\$50/(1.05)^2$		$50				
A	$43.19	$\$50/(1.05)^3$			$50			
A	$41.14	$\$50/(1.05)^4$				$50		
A	$39.18	$\$50/(1.05)^5$					$50	
A	$37.31	$\$50/(1.05)^6$						$50
	$253.78	Present Value = P_0						

$$P_0 = \$50\sum_{t=1}^{6}\frac{1}{(1.05)^t}$$

$$P_0 = \$50\left[\frac{1-(1/(1.05)^6}{.05}\right]$$

$$P_0 = \$253.78$$

Valuing a Bond

The price of any security is equal to the present value of its expected cash flows. For many bonds, the cash flow consists of fixed coupon payments paid over a specified number of periods and a principal payment at maturity. The fixed coupon payments are an annuity and their value can be found by computing the present value of annuity. The value of the principal payment, in turn, can be found by simply computing the present value of the principal.

For example, suppose an investor planned to buy a three-year bond, paying a coupon (C) of \$100 at the end of each year plus a \$1,000 principal (F) at end of year three. If she required an annual rate of return 10 percent, then using the present value approach she would value the bond at \$1,000:

$$P_0^B = \sum_{t=1}^{N}\frac{C}{(1+R)^t} + \frac{F}{(1+R)^N}$$

$$P_0^B = \sum_{t=1}^{3}\frac{\$100}{(1.10)^t} = \frac{\$1,000}{(1.10)^3}$$

$$P_0^B = \frac{\$100}{(1.10)} + \frac{\$100}{(1.10)^2} + \frac{\$100}{(1.10)^3} + \frac{\$1,000}{(1.10)^3} = \$1,000$$

or

$$P_0^B = C\sum_{t=1}^{N}\frac{1}{(1+R)^t} + \frac{F}{(1+R)^N}$$

$$P_0^B = C\left[\frac{1-1/(1+R)^N}{R}\right] + \frac{F}{(1+R)^N}$$

$$P_0^B = \$100\left[\frac{1-1/(1.10)^3}{.10}\right] + \frac{\$1,000}{(1.10)^3}$$

$$P_0^B = \$248.69 + 751.31 = \$1,000$$

If the investor required a higher rate of return on the bond of 12 percent, then she would value the bond at $951.96, less than $1,000:

$$P_0^B = \sum_{t=1}^{N} \frac{C}{(1+R)^t} + \frac{F}{(1+R)^N}$$

$$P_0^B = \sum_{t=1}^{3} \frac{\$100}{(1.12)^t} + \frac{\$1{,}000}{(1.12)^3}$$

$$P_0^B = \$100 \sum_{t=1}^{3} \frac{1}{(1.12)^t} + \frac{\$1{,}000}{(1.12)^3}$$

$$P_0^B = \$100 \left[\frac{1 - 1/(1.12)^3}{.12} \right] + \frac{\$1{,}000}{(1.12)^3}$$

$$P_0^B = \$240.18 + \$711.78 = \$951.96$$

If we reverse the case and assume that our investor actually paid $951.96 for the three-year bond, then her annualized rate of return from the investment would be the discount rate of 12 percent: the rate that equates the present value of the security's cash flows to the current price of the security:

$$\$951.96 = \frac{\$100}{(1+R)^1} + \frac{\$100}{(1+R)^2} + \frac{\$100 + \$1{,}000}{(1+R)^3} \Rightarrow R = .12$$

As we discuss in Chapter 3, for multiple-period investments, the discount rate is the most acceptable way of determining the rate of return or yield on an investment. It is analogous to the internal rate of return used in capital budgeting. As a rate of return measure, it includes the return from the income (coupons or dividends), the interest earned from reinvesting the income, and any capital gains or losses. Unfortunately, unless the cash flows are equal, solving for R requires an iterative (trial and error) procedure: substituting different R values, until an R is found that equates the present value of the cash flows to the security's price.

Finally, note that if the three-year bond paying $100 annual coupons paid the coupons semiannually and the investor required a semiannual rate of return of 5 percent, then the value of the bond would be $1,000:

$$P_0^B = \sum_{t=1}^{N} \frac{C}{(1+R)^t} + \frac{F}{(1+R)^N}$$

$$P_0^B = \sum_{t=1}^{6} \frac{\$50}{(1.05)^t} + \frac{\$1{,}000}{(1.05)^6}$$

$$P_0^B = \$50\left[\frac{1 - 1/(1.05)^6}{.05}\right] + \frac{\$1{,}000}{(1.05)^6}$$

$$P_0^B = \$253.78 + \$746.22 = \$1{,}000$$

If we reverse this case and assume that our investor actually paid \$1,000 for the three-year bond, then her semiannual rate of return from the investment would be the discount rate of 5 percent, her simple annualized rate would be 10 percent (= (2)(5 percent)), and her effective annualized rate (the rate that accounts for reinvesting the 5 percent earned) would be 10.25 percent:

$$\$1{,}000 = \sum_{t=1}^{6} \frac{\$50}{(1+R)^t} + \frac{\$1{,}000}{(1+R)^6} \Rightarrow R = 5\%$$

$$\text{Simple annual rate} = (n)(R) = (2)(.05) = .10$$

$$\text{Effective annual rate} = (1+R)^n - 1 = (1.05)^2 - 1 = .1025$$

Appendix B Uses of Exponents and Logarithms

Exponential Functions

An exponential function is one whose independent variable is an exponent. For example:

$$y = b^t$$

where:

y = dependent variable
t = independent variable
b = base ($b > 1$)

In calculus, many exponential functions use as their base the irrational number 2.71828, denoted by the symbol *e:*

$$e = 2.71828$$

An exponential function that uses *e* as its base is defined as a natural exponential function. For example:

$$y = e^2$$

$$y = Ae^{Rt}$$

These functions also can be expressed as:

$$y = exp(t)$$

$$y = A\ exp\ (Rt)$$

In calculus, natural exponential functions have the useful property of being their own derivative. In addition to this mathematical property, *e* also has a finance meaning. Specifically, *e* is equal to the future value (FV) of \$1 compounded continuously for one period at a nominal interest rate (R) of 100 percent.

To see e as a future value, consider the future value of an investment of A dollars invested at an annual nominal rate of R for t years, and compounded m times per year. That is:

$$FV = A\left(1 + \frac{R}{m}\right)^{mt} \tag{B.1}$$

If we let A = \$1, t = one year, and R = 100 percent, then the FV would be:

$$FV = \$1\left(1 + \frac{1}{m}\right)^{m} \tag{B.2}$$

If the investment is compounded one time (m = 1), then the value of the \$1 at end of the year will be \$2; if it is compounded twice (m = 2), the end-of-year value will be \$2.25; if it is compounded 100 times (m = 100), then the value will be 2.7048138.

$$m = 1: \qquad FV = \$1\left(1 + \frac{1}{1}\right)^{1} = \$2.00$$

$$m = 2: \qquad FV = \$1\left(1 + \frac{1}{2}\right)^{2} = \$2.25$$

$$m = 100: \qquad FV = \$1\left(1 + \frac{1}{100}\right)^{100} = \$2.7048138$$

$$m = 1{,}000: \qquad FV = \$1\left(1 + \frac{1}{1{,}000}\right)^{1{,}000} = \$2.716924$$

As m becomes large, the FV approaches the value of \$2.71828. Thus, in the limit:

$$FV = \lim_{m \to \infty}\left(1 + \frac{1}{m}\right)^{m} = 2.71828 \tag{B.3}$$

If A dollars are invested instead of \$1, and the investment is made for t years instead of one year, then given a 100 percent interest rate the future value after t years would be:

$$FV = Ae^{t} \tag{B.4}$$

Finally, if the nominal interest rate is different than 100 percent, then the FV is:

$$FV = Ae^{Rt} \tag{B.5}$$

To prove Equation (B.5), rewrite Equation (B.1) as follows:

$$FV = A\left(1 + \frac{R}{m}\right)^{mt}$$

$$FV = A\left[\left(1 + \frac{R}{m}\right)^{m/R}\right]^{Rt} \tag{B.6}$$

If we invert R / m in the inner term, we get:

$$FV = A\left[\left(1 + \frac{1}{m/R}\right)^{m/R}\right]^{Rt} \tag{B.7}$$

The inner term takes the same form as Equation (B.2). As shown earlier, this term, in turn, approaches e as m approaches infinity. Thus, for continuous compounding the FV is:

$$FV = Ae^{Rt}$$

Thus, a two-year investment of $100 at a 10 percent annual nominal rate with continuous compounding would be worth $122.14 at the end of year 2:

$$FV = \$100e^{(.10)(2)} = \$122.14$$

Logarithms

A logarithm (or log) is the power to which a base must be raised to equal a particular number. For example, given:

$$5^2 = 25,$$

the power (or log) to which the base 5 must be raised to equal 25 is 2. Thus, the log of 25 to the base 5 is 2:

$$\log_5 25 = 2$$

In general:

$$y = b^t \iff \log_b y = t$$

Two numbers that are frequently used as the base are 10 and the number *e.* If 10 is used as the base, the logarithm is known as the common log. Some of the familiar common logs are:

$$\log_{10} 1{,}000 = 3 \qquad (10^3 = 1{,}000)$$
$$\log_{10} 100 = 2 \qquad (10^2 = 100)$$
$$\log_{10} 10 = 1 \qquad (10^1 = 10)$$
$$\log_{10} 1 = 0 \qquad (10^0 = 1)$$
$$\log_{10} 0.1 = -1 \qquad (10^{-1} = \frac{1}{10^1} = .10)$$
$$\log_{10} 0.01 = -2 \qquad (10^{-2} = \frac{1}{10^2} = \frac{1}{100} = .01)$$

When *e* is the base, the log is defined as the natural logarithm (denoted log_e or *ln*).
For the natural log we have:

$$y = e^t \Leftrightarrow \log_e y = \ln y = t$$
$$\ln e^t = t$$

Thus given an expression such as $y = e^t$, the exponent t is automatically the natural log.

Rules of Logarithms

Like exponents, logarithms have a number of useful algebraic properties. The properties are stated below in terms of natural logs; the properties, though, do apply to any log regardless of its base.

Equality:	If $X = Y$, then $\ln X = \ln Y$
Product Rule:	$\ln(XY) = \ln X + \ln Y$
Quotient Rule:	$\ln(X/Y) = \ln X - \ln Y$
Power Rule:	$\ln(X^a) = a \ln X$

Uses of Logarithms

The above properties of logarithms make logarithms useful in solving a number of algebraic problems.

Solving for R

In finance, logs can be used to solve for R when there is continuous compounding. That is, from Equation (B.5):

$$FV = Ae^{Rt}$$

Using the above log properties R can be found as follows:

$$Ae^{Rt} = FV$$

$$e^{Rt} = \frac{FV}{A}$$

$$\ln\left(e^{Rt}\right) = \ln\left(\frac{FV}{A}\right)$$

$$Rt = \ln\left(\frac{FV}{A}\right)$$

$$R = \frac{\ln(FV / A)}{t}$$

Thus, a \$100 investment that pays \$120 at the end of two years would yield a nominal annual rate of 9.12 percent given continuous compounding: R = *ln*(\$120/\$100)/2 = .0912. Similarly, a pure discount bond selling for \$980 and paying \$1,000 at the end of 91 days would yield a nominal annual rate of 8.10 percent given continuous compounding:

$$R = \frac{\ln(\$1{,}000 / \$980)}{91/365} = .0810$$

Logarithmic Return

The expression for the rate of return on a security currently priced at S_0 and expected to be S_T at the end of one period ($t = 1$) can be found using Equation (B.5). That is:

$$S_T = S_0 e^{Rt}$$

$$R = \ln\left(\frac{S_T}{S_0}\right)$$

When the rate of return on a security is expressed as the natural log of S_T/S_0, it is referred to as the security's logarithmic return. Thus, a security currently priced at

$100 and expected to be $110 at the end of the period would have an expected logarithmic return of 9.53 percent: $R = ln(\$110/100) = .0953$.

Time

Using logarithms one can solve for t in either the discrete or continuous compounding cases. That is:

$$FV = A(1+R)^t$$
$$A(1+R)^t = FV$$
$$\ln\left[(1+R)^t\right] = \ln\left(\frac{FV}{A}\right)$$
$$t\ln[1+R] = \ln\left(\frac{FV}{A}\right)$$
$$t = \frac{\ln(FV/A)}{\ln(1+R)}$$

$$Ae^{Rt} = FV$$
$$e^{Rt} = \frac{FV}{A}$$
$$\ln\left(e^{Rt}\right) = \ln\left(\frac{FV}{A}\right)$$
$$Rt = \ln\left(\frac{FV}{A}\right)$$
$$t = \frac{\ln(FV/A)}{R}$$

The equations can be used in problems in which one knows the interest or growth rate and wants to know how long it will take for an investment to grow to equal a certain terminal value. For example, given an annual interest rate of 10 percent (no annual compounding) an investment of $800 would take 2.34 years to grow to $1,000:

$$t = \frac{\ln(\$1{,}000/\$800)}{\ln(1.10)} = 2.34 \text{ Years}$$

Selected Reference

Chiang, A. C. 1976. *Fundamental Methods of Mathematical Economics*. New York: McGraw-Hill, 267–302.

Appendix C Directory Listing of Bloomberg Screens by Menu and Function

Functions to Get Started

BU	Bloomberg training resources
EASY	Display of tips
NEXT	Fact sheets, brochures, and videos about Bloomberg screens and enhancements
BBXL	Overview of how to import Bloomberg data to Excel
BLP	Bloomberg Launchpad for setting up interactive workstation

News

NI	News search by category
TOP	Top news stories
TOP NW	Top news stories worldwide
TOPD	Top stock news
TOP BON	Top bond information
NI FED	Federal Reserve information

Searches and Screeners

SECF	Security finder screen searches
EQS	Equity screeners stock searches
SRCH	Custom bond search
FSRC	Fund search
MSRC	Municipal bond search
SMUN	Municipal bond search
MUNI	Municipal search
CSCH	Convertible bond search
NI	News search
TNI	Advance news search
MA	Merger and acquisition searches
RATC	Search for credit rating changes

PSCH	Preferred stock search
MSCH	Money market search
CTM	Search commodities exchanges
RES	Research search
AV	Bloomberg's media links
LIVE	Bloomberg's live links
BBLS	Search for legal documents
ETF	Exchange-traded products
CRVF	Curve finder
PGM	Money market securities by programs
MBSS	Mortgage-backed security search and screener

Monitors

FIT	Bond monitor screen
WB	Global bonds
RATT	Show trends in bond quality ratings
RATC	Displays and searches for bond credit rating changes
CSDR	Sovereign debt ratings
IM	Directory of country monitors
BTMM	Bond monitor
WEI	Monitors world equity indexes
IMAP	Monitors equity prices across regions, sectors, and stocks
MMAP	Displays global markets segments and stocks in that segment
MOST	Displays most active stocks
NIM	Monitors news and security information for new security issues
IPO	Monitors new stock issues
EVTS	Monitors corporate events
MNSA	Today's announced merger and acquisition deals
PREL	Pipeline of announced bonds
DIS	Distressed bonds
BNKF	Bankruptcy filings
TACT	Trade activity
BRIEF	Daily economic newsletter
EIU	Economist Intelligence Unit
IECO	Global comparison of economic statistics
FXIP	Foreign exchange information portal
CENB	Central bank menu: Use to access platforms of central banks
FED	Federal Reserve Bank portal
ECB	European Central Bank portal
IECO	Global comparison of economic statistics
PE	Private equity
RATD	Links to Moody's, Standard and Poor's, Fitch, and other agency service information

DRAM	Analysis of a group of securities or portfolios in terms of their default risk, CDS spread, and Bloomberg credit risk score
COMB	List of the selected bond's comparable bonds and their features, including spreads to benchmark, z-spread, and CDS spread
GOVI	Matrix of yield spread information for sovereign debt of a selected tenor
IYC	Menu for yield curves screens
CDSW	Terms of the selected bond's issuer's CDS and the implied probability of default
SOVR	CDS for countries, presented in tables and graphs
FICM	Fixed-Income Monitor
FDCP	CP outstanding
CPPR	Direct CP issuers
HOIN	Housing and construction
LEAG	Underwriter rankings
LMX	Underwriter/legal advisors ranking
DMMV	Developed markets monitor
MOSB	Most active exchange traded bonds
PGM	Money market lookup
EPR	Exchange information
EIS	Exchange products and menus
MMTK	List of market makers and their corresponding codes
REIT	Real estate investment trust (REIT) menu
RMEN	Real estate indices of the world

Economic and Financial Market Information

ECOF	Macroeconomic information (employment, economic indicators, housing prices) by country and region
ECO	Calendar of economic releases
COUN	Country information
WECO	World economic calendar and economic indicators
FOMC	Information on policy changes of the FOMC
FED	Calendar of Federal Reserve releases
YCRV	Yield curves
ECST	Key economic statistics by country
EIU	Economist Intelligence Unit
IECO	Global comparison of economic statistics
BRIEF	Daily economic newsletter
AV	Bloomberg's media links

Bank Security Information

MMR	Money market rates monitor
PGM	Money market lookup program
MSCH	Money market search

LSRC	Search for loans, including leveraged loans
PREL	Loan pipeline
LONZ	Loan homepage
BBAM	Information on LIBOR and other rates
BTMM	Money market rates

Investment Fund Screens

FMAP	Fund map
FUND	Funds and holding menu
FL	Fund look-up
NI FND	Fund news
FSRC	Fund searches
WMF	Best mutual fund players snapshot
HFND	Hedged funds menu page
HFR	Hedge fund research
HEDN	Hedge fund news
FLNG	Aggregated 13F filings
WHF	Best hedge fund player snapshot
REIT	REIT menu screen
NI REIT	REIT news

Bloomberg Credit Crisis Screens

SBPR	Subprime news
STNI	Rumors and speculation
LEAD	Economic activity trends
HSST	U.S. housing and construction statistics
DQRP	Ranks deals by collateral performance
DQSP	Delinquent loan data by servicer
DELQ	Credit card delinquency rate
BBMD	Mortgage delinquency monitor
REDQ	Commercial real estate delinquencies
DQLO	Delinquency rates by loan originators
TARP	TARP recipients
TALF	TALF program
STRS	Stress test overviews
GGRP	Government relief programs
NI TARP	TARP news

Industrial Sectors

BI	Industry research portal

Sample of Law Functions on BLAW: <Law>

BLAW	Law and cases menu
LLRT	Law alerts
DCKS	U.S. court filings

EUCF EU court filings
BBLS Search for legal documents

Sample of Functions and Information on the Equity Menu Screen: <Equity> <Enter>

SECF Security finder
TK Ticker lookup
MMAP Market heat map
EA Earnings analysis
QRM Bid/ask quotes
IMOV Equity index movers
MOST Most active stocks
HILO Stocks, mutual funds, ABSs, and REITs that have 52-week high or low
HALT List of suspended or halted stocks by exchange
TOP STK Top Bloomberg news headline related to stocks
CACT Displays calendar of corporate actions
FMAP Fund heat map
FLNG Filings
FSRC Fund search
IPO New issues
LTOP Top underwriters
WPE World equity index ratios
CORR Correlation matrix
MRA Multiple regression

Sample of Functions for a Stock on the Equity Menu Screen: Ticker <Equity> <Enter>

GP Price and volume graph
GIP Intraday graph
COMP Compares the returns of security with benchmark index
BETA Beta calculations
HRA Historical regression
HS Historical spreads
HVG Volatility graph
ECCG Credit company graph
SPLC Supply chain
OMON Options
WMON Warrants
FA Financials
RV Relative value of company's fundamentals with peer group
GF Fundamentals graphs
ANR Analyst recommendation
RSI Relative strength index

MACD	Moving averages
GOC	Overview chart
BOLL	Bollinger bands
GM	Money flow
CNDL	Bullish and bearish trends
OWN	Stock ownership
DDIS	Debt distribution
ISSD	Issuer description
HDS	Equity holders
AGGD	Debt holders
CACS	Corporate action calendar
LITI	Litigation
RELS	Related securities
BRC	Company research
ISSD	Issuer description
EE	Earnings and estimates

Sample of Functions on Index Menu Screen: <Index> <Enter>

WEI	Global indexes
IMOV	Index movers
LEHM	Barclays indexes
SPG	S&P global indexes
EMEQ	Emerging markets
RMEN	Real estate indexes
HOIN	Housing/construction indexes

Sample of Functions on Index Menu for an Index: Index Ticker <Index> <Enter>

DES	Description
MEMB	Index weightings
GWGT	Group sub-indexes and weighting
MRR	Member returns
RV	Relative value
IMAP	Intraday market map
GP	Price graph
GIP	Intraday graph
FA	Financial analysis
GF	Fundamentals graphs
HRA	Regression
COMP	Total returns
HGV	Volatility graphs
OMON	Index options
RSI	Relative strength index
MACD	Moving averages

GOC	Overview chart
BOLL	Bollinger bands

Sample of Functions for a Corporate Bond on the Bond's Corp Menu: Bond Identifier (CUSIP) <Corp> <Enter> or <Corp> <Enter>

ISSD	Quick overview of a company's key ratios
DDIS	Company's outstanding debt
NIM	Monitoring of new bonds
SRCH	Finds corporate bonds using Bloomberg's search function
SECF	Security finder
DES	Information on the bond's coupons, day-count convention, maturity, and other features
BFV	Menu screen to analyze where the bond should trade given comparable bonds
YA	Bonds price, YTM, and yield to worst
RATC	Evaluation of credit ratings
CRPR	Evaluation of a corporation's current credit ratings
RVM	Evaluation of a bond's spread
COMB	Comparative bond analysis
TRA	Total return analysis
OAS1	OAS analysis
SP	Strip valuation
FISA	Fixed income scenario analysis
DRSK	Analysis of a company's credit risk
RATT	Current and historical numbers of upgrades and downgrades
RATD	Links to Moody's, Standard and Poor's, Fitch, and other agency service information
DRAM	Analysis of a group of securities or portfolios in terms of their default risk, CDS spread, and a Bloomberg credit risk score
CDSW	Terms of the selected bond's issuer's CDS and the implied probability of default
SOVR	CDS for countries, displayed in tables and graphs
FIHZ	Total return on a selected bond for a selected horizon period, discount yield at the HD, and the reinvestment rate
FDCP	CP outstanding
CPPR	Direct CP issuer

Sample of Functions on Treasury Securities from Govt Menu: Country Ticker <Govt> or Treasury Tk <Govt> <Enter>

DES	Information on the bond's coupon, day-count convention, maturity, and other features
BFV	Bloomberg fair value
YA	Yield analysis
OAS1	OAS analysis

SP	Strip valuation
SRCH	Bond search
SECF	Security finder
BTMM	Major rates and security information
GGR	Global summary of government bill and bond rates for countries
FMC	Yields across maturities of multiple corporate and government bonds
TRA	Total return
FIHZ	Total return analysis
FISA	Fixed income scenario analysis
FIT	Monitors and compares prices of government security dealers
YCRV	Yield curves
AUCR	Auction results
ECO20	Select government auction/purchase results

Agency Securities

FHLMC <Corp>	Federal Home Loan Mortgage Corporation
FNMA <Corp>	Federal National Mortgage Association
FHLB <Corp>	Federal Home Loan Bank System
FAMCA <Corp>	Federal Agriculture Mortgage Association
FFCB <Corp>	Federal Farm Credit Bank
TVA <Corp>	Tennessee Valley Authority
IBRD <Corp>	International Bank for Reconstruction and Development
SLMA <Corp>	Student Loan Marketing Association:
EXI	Bonds with export-import bank guarantee
PXAM	Active agencies
ADN	Agency offerings

Sample of Functions for Municipal Bonds on Muni Menu Screen:
Ticker <Muni> <Enter> or <Muni> <Enter>

PICK	Finds the latest municipal offering
MSRC	Finds municipals using Bloomberg's customized search
SMUN	Issuer search
MIFA	Municipal screen
DES	Description
RCHG	Ratings history
TDH	Trade history
YA	Yield analysis
TRA	Total return analysis
HP	Historical analysis
CF	Municipal filings
ISSD	Issuer description
IMGR	Recently issued

Sample of Functions for Currency on Currency Menu Screen: Ticker <Crncy> <Enter> or <Crncy> <Enter>

WCR	World currency rates
FRD	Forward rates
ALLQ	Currency quotes
FXIP	Currency market overview
FXC	Currency rate matrix
FXFR	Forward and spot exchange rates
GP	Price graph
GIP	Intraday graph

Sample of Functions on Mortgage and Asset-Backed Securities Menu: Security Ticker <Mtge> Or <Mtge> <Enter>

ABS	Asset-backed security tickers
CMBS	Commercial MBS monitor
MBSS	Pool search
MCAL	New issue calendar
MP	Mortgage payments
DES	Description
BBMD	Mortgage delinquency
MBAI	Mortgage Bankers Association
HSST	Housing and construction
HOIN	Global housing
SECF	Security finder screen; searches for mortgage pools by types of mortgages
CFT	Cash flow table; can be used to analyze the mortgage collateral
VAC	All classes of MBS created from the collateral
SPA	Structural pay down of all classes of a MBS
YA	Yield analysis
TRA	Total return analysis
MTCL	Collateral analysis
CLP	Collateral performance
CLC	Collateral composition
MTST	Structure analysis
CLASS	Listings, descriptions, and terms for different MBS and ABS securities
DV	Vector analysis screen
VBPM	Prepayment vector graph
LLKU	Commercial MBS Screener
AUTO	List of auto loan issuers
HEQ	List of home equity loans by issuer
CARD	List of credit card receivables by issuer

Yield Curve Information

YCRV	Current and historical yield curves for government and corporate bond
IYC	Yield curves menu
FWCV	Projection of implied forward rates
CRVF	Curve finder

Investment Funds

ETF	Exchange-traded funds
FSRC	Investment fund search
FMAP	Fund heat map
SECF	Search screen

Sample of Portfolio Functions—PRTU and PMEN

Portfolio Maintenance

PRTU	Create portfolio
PMEN	Portfolio menu
RPT	Reports menu
PCPY	Copy portfolios
PFST	Portfolio defaults
BBU	Portfolio uploads from Excel
PDIS	Share portfolios
PMAC	Macro setup for comparing portfolios

Portfolio Reporting and Analytics

PORT	Portfolio risk analytics
BPRA	Portfolio risk overview
PDSP	Portfolio display
NPH	Portfolio news
PREP	Distribution report
FSTA	Fund style
BRSK	Risk overview
LRSK	Liquidity risk
PDVD	Dividend
PCF	Cash flows
RVP	Relative valuation
EVTS	Events calendar
CACT	Corporate actions
PSH	Proposed trade and impact analysis on current portfolio
PSA	Shock analysis on current portfolio given multiple yield curve shifts
BSA	Bond scenario analysis
DRAM	Default risk monitor

Portfolio Basket

CIXB	Calculation of historical returns of inputted stocks, bonds, commodities or portfolio, and allows the security or portfolio to be treated as an index to be analyzed on the Index menu.

Futures, Options, and Swaps

CTM	Contract table menu for deriviatives Commodity Ticker <Comdty> <Enter>
IRDD	Interest rate derivatives list
SWPM	Bloomberg swaps and interest rate derivatives screen
FIHR	Bloomberg hedging screen (use for loaded bond)
EDA	Eurodollar futures contracts screen; EDA <Comdty>
EDS	Eurodollar futures analysis
OMON	Option monitor
OMST	Finds the most actively traded options on a particular stock
OSA	Option strategy functions: generates profit tables and graphs
OVME (OV)	Values of options using the Black-Scholes, binomial, and other option pricing models
SKEW	Volatility smiles and surfaces
HVG	Historical volatility function
HIVG	Historical implied volatilities
OV	Option Greek: delta, theta, gamma, vega and rho
FRAZ	Forward rate agreements
MARS	Multi-Asset Risk System—Analyzes portfolio and derivative positions
WCDS	Credit default rate monitor
FVD	Finds the fair value and carrying cost value—Menu
DLV	Cheapest-to-deliver bond
CALL	A security's call values, implied volatilities, and Greeks
PUT	A security's put values, implied volatilities, and Greeks
COAT	Call option value sensitivity analysis
OVX	Evaluation of exotic options
CDSW	Credit default swap valuation calculator
FXFR	Forward and spot quotes
FXDV	Foreign exchange derivative menu
EXS	Futures expirations schedule
OTD	Description of futures option
OSL	Option strike list
OVCV	Convertible bond valuation
ASW	Calculation of the relative value of a selected bond with the interest rate swap market
IRSB	Generic interest rate swaps menu
CSCH	Convertible search

IRDL	Interest rate derivative list created by user
WCDS	World credit default spread monitor
Ticker CDS <Corp>	Credit default swap menu list for a specified issuer
VCDS	Value of a single bond based on its credit default spread

Index

D

S

T

Printed and bound by CPI Group (UK) Ltd, Croydon, CR0 4YY

23/04/2025

14661013-0005